FLORIDA RULES OF JUDICIAL ADMINISTRATION

2018 EDITION

Rules reflect all changes through 43 FLW S15. Subsequent amendments, if any, can be found at www.floridasupremecourt.org/decisions/rules.shtml. The Florida Bar also updates the rules on its website at www.FloridaBar.org (on the home page, click "Rules Updates").

THE FLORIDA BAR

CONTINUING LEGAL EDUCATION

Distributed by LexisNexis®
1275 Broadway, Albany, NY 12204-2694
800/833-9844 • Fax: 800/643-1280
www.lexisnexis.com

THE FLORIDA BAR

The Florida Bar and LexisNexis

working together for Florida's Lawyers

Through a joint publishing relationship, The Florida Bar and LexisNexis have combined their expertise to best serve the information needs of those practicing law in Florida. The Legal Publications staff writes and edits the publications; LexisNexis provides printing, distribution, and customer service support.

If you have any questions:

Contact The Florida Bar
For questions regarding content, authors, CLE schedules, member benefits, and other Bar matters.

The Florida Bar
651 East Jefferson Street
Tallahassee, FL 32399-2300
Phone: 850/561-5600
Fax: 850/561-5826
www.floridabar.org

Contact LexisNexis
For questions regarding billing, subscriptions, purchases, or other Florida Bar products.

LexisNexis
1275 Broadway
Albany, NY 12204-2694
Phone: 800/833-9844
Fax: 800/643-1280
www.lexisnexis.com/flabar
customer.support@lexisnexis.com

International Standard Book Number: 978-1-5221-5028-2

(Pub No. 22763)

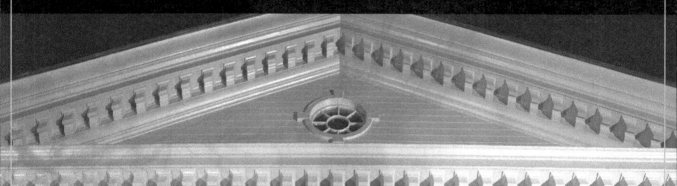

CONTINUING LEGAL EDUCATION COMMITTEE
2017-2018

Jenifer S McCaffrey Lehner, Chair
Rosanna Manuela Catalano, Vice Chair
Elaine Laverne Thompson, Vice Chair
Sandra Fascell Diamond, Board Liaison

Albert Louis Alguadich, Jr.
Vivian Arenas-Battles
Christopher Michael Bentley
Sam Wood Boone Jr.
Carolyn Beth Brombacher
Paul Henry Chipok
Patricia Dawson
Ava K Doppelt
James A Edwards
Bogdan Enica
Shereaann Ferrer
Francine Marie Ffolkes
William Paul Galione
Kathy Newman Grunewald

David H Harris
Fritznie Abigail Jarbath
Martin D Kahn
John Elliott Leighton
Marsha Gerre Madorsky
Eric Lynn Meeks
Kimberly Clark Menchion
Manuel Menendez, Jr
Rinky S. Parwani
Jose Antonio Raposo Jr.
Aloyma M Sanchez
Evett Louise Simmons
Phyllis Carole Taite
T Rankin Terry, Jr.

Representative Members

Radha Vinod Bachman
Timothy Patrick Chinaris
Micah Graham Fogarty
Leopoldo Garcia Jr.
Margaret Rowell Good
Douglas Avery Greenbaum
Susan Odzer Hugentugler
Jan Leslie Jacobowitz
Kimberly Dawn Kolback
Patrick W Krechowski
Bruce Douglas Lamb
Michele L Lieberman
Jennifer Lucas-Ross
Jani E Maurer

Kimberly Clark Menchion
Anthony Bernard Miller
Anthony Charles Musto
Jerry Ray Poole Jr.
Mercy Roberg
Raul Ruiz
Katherine Alena Sanoja
Aleksandra Joanna Sikorska
Vicki Lynn Sproat
Robert S. Swaine
Kim Watson Torres
Lee Ford Tritt
Peter Francis Valori
Carol Lynne Zeiner

Mission

The mission of the Continuing Legal Education Committee is to assist the members of The Florida Bar in their continuing legal education and to facilitate the development, production, and delivery of quality CLE opportunities for the benefit of Bar members in coordination with the sections, committees, and staff of The Florida Bar and others who participate in the CLE process.

PREFACE

This manual is another in a continuing series of publications designed to aid Florida lawyers to practice more efficiently and effectively.

This manual will be updated annually to reflect statutory revisions.

Krys Godwin, Director
Legal Publications
February 2018

USE OF LEXIS®

The Florida Bar acknowledges the use of LEXIS® computerized legal research service to assist in the legal editing of its manuals and supplements. Members of The Florida Bar can obtain membership group subscription information for LEXIS® services by calling the LEXIS® Membership Group at 800/356-6548.

CITATIONS TO OPINIONS ADOPTING OR AMENDING RULES

ORIGINAL ADOPTION, effective 7-1-78: 360 So.2d 1076.

OTHER OPINIONS:

Effective 1-1-79:	364 So.2d 466.	Amended 2.070(f).
Effective 7-1-79:	372 So.2d 449.	Amended 2.010–2.130.
Effective 2-21-80:	380 So.2d 1027.	Amended 2.060(b).
Effective 1-1-81:	389 So.2d 202.	Four-year-cycle revision. Amended 2.050(e), 2.130.
Effective 1-1-81:	391 So.2d 214.	Amended 2.040(b)(3), 2.050(c).
Effective 1-1-82:	403 So.2d 926.	Added 2.075.
Effective 12-1-83:	442 So.2d 198.	Added 2.035.
Effective 2-23-84:	446 So.2d 87.	Amended 2.035.
Effective 1-1-85:	458 So.2d 1110.	Four-year-cycle revision. Amended 2.140(b)(2); added 2.130(b)(5); renumbered 2.130(b)(6).
Effective 1-1-85:	462 So.2d 444.	Added 2.071.
Effective 3-1-85:	465 So.2d 1217.	Added 2.125.
Effective 7-1-86:	493 So.2d 423.	Added 2.085.
Effective 2-1-87:	500 So.2d 524.	Amended 2.040(a)(2), 2.050(c).
Effective 7-1-87:	507 So.2d 1390.	Amended 2.050(d), 2.070(e).
Effective 7-1-87:	509 So.2d 276.	Amended 2.130(f).
Effective 1-1-88:	518 So.2d 258.	Added 2.150.
Effective 1-1-89:	532 So.2d 667.	See revised opinion at 536 So.2d 195.
Effective 1-1-89:	536 So.2d 195.	Four-year-cycle revision. Amended 2.050(c), 2.060(d), (h)–(j), 2.070(h), 2.085(a), (c).
Effective 6-1-89:	543 So.2d 1244.	Added 2.125(b)(1)(I), (b)(1)(J).
Effective 11-9-89:	552 So.2d 194.	Added 2.125(b)(1)(K).
Effective 1-11-90:	555 So.2d 848.	Added 2.125(b)(1)(L).
Effective 1-18-90:	550 So.2d 457.	Added 2.055.
Effective 6-15-90:	560 So.2d 786.	Added 2.030(a)(3)(D).
Effective 10-22-92:	607 So.2d 39.	Amended 2.130(b)(3).
Effective 10-29-92:	608 So.2d 472.	Added 2.051.
Effective 1-1-93:	609 So.2d 465.	Four-year-cycle revision. Substantively amended 2.040(b)(5), 2.055, 2.060, 2.071, 2.085, 2.130; added 2.160, 2.170.
Effective 12-23-93:	634 So.2d 604.	Amended 2.110(b).
Effective 2-9-95:	650 So.2d 30.	Amended 2.170.
Effective 2-23-95:	650 So.2d 38.	Amended 2.070.
Effective 3-23-95:	651 So.2d 1185.	Amended 2.051.
Effective 3-30-95:	652 So.2d 811.	Amended 2.125.
Effective 5-9-95:	654 So.2d 917.	Amended 2.070(d)(2).
Effective 6-15-95:	656 So.2d 926.	Amended 2.125.
Effective 1-1-96:	661 So.2d 806.	Amended 2.070(b).
Effective 1-1-96:	665 So.2d 218.	Amended 2.035.
Effective 4-11-96:	672 So.2d 523.	Amended 2.050(b)(4), 2.050(b)(7); added 2.050(h).
Effective 6-27-96:	675 So.2d 1376.	Added 2.072.
Effective 8-29-96:	678 So.2d 1285.	Added court commentary to 2.050.
Effective 1-1-97:	681 So.2d 698.	Added 2.060(f), renumbered 2.060(f)–(l); amended 2.075, 2.090.
Effective 1-1-97:	682 So.2d 89.	Four-year-cycle revision. Added 2.030(a)(2)(B)(iv), 2.052, 2.065, 2.135, 2.180; amended 2.050(c), (e)(1)(F), (e)(3), (h), 2.055(c), 2.125 (for style); deleted 2.055(e).
Effective 2-7-97:	688 So.2d 320.	Added 2.050(b)(10).

Effective 7-17-97:	697 So.2d 144.	Partially suspended application of 2.055(c) until January 1, 1999.
Effective 1-1-98:	701 So.2d 1164.	Amended 2.060(f), 2.090(c).
Effective 11-20-97:	701 So.2d 864.	Amended 2.050(b)(10).
Effective 1-1-99:	711 So.2d 29.	Amended 2.055(c), added a new (d), and redesignated former (d) as (e).
Effective 2-1-99:	746 So.2d 1073.	Amended 2.051(c)(7).
Effective 5-25-00:	766 So.2d 999.	Added 2.071(f).
Effective 7-14-00:	772 So.2d 532.	Added 2.070(i).
Effective 12-1-00:	774 So.2d 625.	Added 2.053.
Effective 1-1-01:	780 So.2d 819.	Four-year-cycle revision. Amended 2.020, 2.053(b)(1)(A), 2.060, 2.070, 2.071(d), 2.130(a), (c), (e)–(g); added 2.061, 2.140(c).
Effective 7-1-01:	796 So.2d 477.	Added 2.054.
Effective 10-1-01:	797 So.2d 1213.	Amended 2.050(b).
Effective 1-1-02:	812 So.2d 401.	Amended 2.054(e).
Effective 3-7-02:	825 So.2d 889.	Amended 2.030, 2.040, 2.051, 2.075; added 2.076 and Judicial Branch Retention Schedule for Administrative Records.
Effective 10-1-02:	826 So.2d 233.	Amended 2.050, 2.052, 2.085.
Effective 9-19-02:	828 So.2d 994.	Amended 2.130.
Effective 7-10-03:	851 So.2d 698.	Amended 2.050, 2.053, 2.130.
Effective 1-1-04:	851 So.2d 698.	Two-year-cycle revision. Amended 2.060, 2.070, 2.085, 2.160, 2.170.
Effective 1-1-04:	860 So.2d 394.	Amended 2.060.
Effective 10-14-04:	888 So.2d 614.	Amended 2.035.
Effective 1-1-05:	885 So.2d 870.	Amended 2.160.
Effective 1-1-05:	889 So.2d 68.	Amended 2.085.
Effective 5-12-05:	907 So.2d 1138.	Amended 2.061.
Effective 11-3-05:	915 So.2d 157.	Two-year-cycle revision. Amended 2.130.
Effective 1-1-06:	915 So.2d 157.	Two-year-cycle revision. Amended 2.050, 2.051, 2.060, 2.071, 2.085.
Effective 1-1-06:	915 So.2d 145.	Amended 2.030.
Effective 2-16-06:	921 So.2d 615.	Adopted 2.036.
Effective 3-2-06:	923 So.2d 1160.	Amended 2.050.
Effective 7-1-06:	933 So.2d 504.	Adopted 2.073(a)–(d), (f).
Effective 7-6-06:	933 So.2d 1136.	Amended 2.035.
Effective 9-21-06:	939 So.2d 966.	Reorganization of rules. Adopted 2.140(g).
Effective 9-28-06:	939 So.2d 1051.	Amended 2.235.
Effective 4-5-07:	954 So.2d 16.	Amended 2.420.
Effective 5-17-07:	957 So.2d 1168.	Adopted 2.244.
Effective 11-3-07:	915 So.2d 145.	Amended 2.150(b)(3) [2.320(b)(3)].
Effective 1-1-08:	967 So.2d 178.	Adopted 2.256, 2.430(l)
Effective 1-17-08:	973 So.2d 437.	Amended 2.430.
Effective 1-31-08:	974 So.2d 1066.	Amended 2.240.
Effective 4-1-08:	978 So.2d 805.	Amended 2.215.
Effective 7-1-08:	933 So.2d 504.	Adopted 2.073(e) [2.560(e)].
Effective 10-1-08:	992 So.2d 237.	Amended 2.215.
Effective 1-1-09:	986 So.2d 560.	Three-year-cycle revision. Amended 2.130, 2.140, 2.215, 2.330.
Effective 1-1-09:	991 So.2d 842.	Amended 2.510.
Effective 7-16-09:	13 So.3d 1044.	Amended 2.535.
Effective 3-18-10:	31 So.3d 756.	Amended 2.420.
Effective 5-20-10:	41 So.3d 881.	Amended 2.540.

Effective 7-1-10:	41 So.3d 128.	Adopted 2.236.
Effective 10-1-10:	31 So.3d 756.	Amended 2.420(d).
Effective 12-9-10:	51 So.3d 1151.	Amended 2.320(a)(2).
Effective 2-24-11:	75 So.3d 1241.	Amended 2.215(b)(10)(C).
Effective 7-7-11:	68 So.3d 228.	Amended 2.420(d)(1)(B)(xx).
Effective 10-1-11:	80 So.3d 317.	Adopted 2.425.
Effective 10-6-11:	75 So.3d 203.	Amended 2.545(d)(2).
Effective 1-1-12:	73 So.3d 210.	Three-year-cycle revision. Amended 2.505(f)(1), 2.510(a), (b)(2), 2.525(g), 2.530(d)(1); adopted 2.526.
Effective 2-9-12:	121 So.3d 1.	Amended 2.205, 2.210, 2.215, 2.220, 2.225, 2.230, 2.235, 2.244.
Effective 7-12-12:	95 So.3d 115.	Amended 2.425.
Effective 9-1-12	102 So.3d 505.	Amended 2.515, Adopted 2.516.
Effective 10-01-12:	95 So.3d 96.	Adopted 2.514.
Effective 6-21-12:	102 So.3d 451.	Amended 2.430, 2.510, 2.516, 2.520, 2.525, 2.535.
Effective 12-20-12:	119 So3d 1211.	Amended 2.205, 2.220.
Effective 2-7-13:	124 So.3d 807.	Amended 2.140.
Effective 4-4-13	112 So.3d 1173.	Amended 2.516.
Effective 5-1-13:	124 So.3d 819.	Amended 2.420.
Effective 10-1-13:	118 So.3d 193.	Adopted 2.451.
Effective 10-31-13:	125 So.3d 754.	Amended 2.220.
Effective 11-14-13:	126 So.3d 222.	Amended 2.515, 2.516, 2.525.
Effective 11-14-13:	129 So.3d 358.	Amended 2.240, 2.241.
Effective 1-1-14:	125 So.3d 743.	Amended 2.205, 2.210.
Effective 4-1-14:	132 So.3d 1114.	Amended 2.545.
Effective 1-15-15:	148 So.3d 1171.	Amended 2.215, 2.535.
Effective 1-15-15:	150 So.3d 787.	Amended 2.430, 2.510.
Effective 1-1-15:	39 FLW S718.	Amended 2.520. (Opinion withdrawn; see below.)
Effective 1-22-15:	156 So.3d 499.	Amended 2.420.
Effective 4-2-15:	161 So.3d 1254.	Amended 2.520.
Effective 9-10-15:	174 So.3d 991.	Adopted 2.340.
Effective 10-1-15:	176 So.3d 267.	Amended 2.560, Adopted 2.565.
Effective 2-4-16:	198 So.3d 592.	Amended 2.425.
Effective 3-24-16:	190 So.3d 1053.	Amended 2.535.
Effective 4-16-16:	189 So.3d 141.	Amended 2.516 and 2.525.
Effective 4-21-16:	190 So.3d 1080.	Amended 2.240.
Effective 12-8-16:	206 So.3d 1.	Amended 2.560 and 2.565.
Effective 4-6-17:	214 So.3d 623.	Amended 2.205.
Effective 1-1-18:	226 So.3d 223.	Amended 2.140, 2.510, 2.516.
Effective 1-18-18:	43 FLW S15.	Amended 2.420.

NOTE TO USERS: Rules reflect all changes through 43 FLW S15. Subsequent amendments, if any, can be found at www.floridasupremecourt.org/decisions/rules.shtml. The Florida Bar also updates the rules on its website at www.FloridaBar.org (on the homepage click "Rules Updates").

TRACING TABLE

Former Florida Rules of Judicial Administration — Current Florida Rules of Judicial Administration

Former	Current	Former	Current	Current	Former	Current	Former
2.010	2.110	2.130(a)	2.140(d)	2.110	2.010	2.520	2.055
2.020	2.120		2.140(a)	2.120	2.020	2.525	2.090
2.030	2.205		2.140(b)	2.130	2.135	2.530	2.071
2.035	2.240		2.140(c)	2.140(a)	2.130(b)	2.535	2.070
2.036	2.241		2.140(e)	(b)	2.130(c)	2.540	2.065
2.040	2.210		2.140(f)	(c)	2.130(d)	2.545(a)	2.085(a)
2.050	2.215		2.140(g)	(d)	2.130(a)		2.085(b)
2.051	2.420		2.140(h)	(e)	2.130(e)		2.085(c)
2.052	2.550	2.135	2.130	(f)	2.130(f)		2.085(d)
2.053	2.230	2.140	2.310	(g)	---		2.085(e)
2.054	2.235	2.150	2.320	(h)	2.130(g)	2.550	2.052
2.055	2.520	2.160	2.330	2.205	2.030	2.555(a)	2.080(c)
2.060(a)	2.505(a)	2.170	2.450	2.210	2.040	(b)	2.080(d)
(b)	2.505(b)	2.180	2.260	2.215	2.050	(c)	2.080(e)
(c)	2.515(a)			2.220(c)	2.120	2.560	2.073
(d)	2.515(b)			2.225	2.125		
(e)	2.515(c)			2.230	2.053		
(f)	2.505(c)			2.235	2.054		
(g)	2.505(d)			2.240	2.035		
(h)	2.505(e)			2.241	2.036		
(i)	2.505(f)			2.244	---		
(j)	2.505(g)			2.245(a)	2.080(a)		
(k)	2.505(h)			(b)	2.080(b)		
2.061	2.510			2.250(a)	2.085(f)		
2.065	2.540			(b)	2.085(g)		
2.070	2.535			2.255	2.100		
2.071	2.530			2.256	---		
2.072	2.410			2.260	2.180		
2.073	2.560			2.265	2.110		
2.075	2.430			2.310	2.140		
2.076	2.440			2.320	2.150		
2.080(a)	2.245(a)			2.330	2.160		
(b)	2.245(b)			2.410	2.072		
(c)	2.555(a)			2.420	2.051		
(d)	2.555(b)			2.430	2.075		
(e)	2.555(c)			2.440	2.076		
2.085(a)	2.545(a)			2.450	2.170		
(b)	2.545(b)			2.505(a)	2.060(a)		
(c)	2.545(c)			(b)	2.060(b)		
(d)	2.545(d)			(c)	2.060(f)		
(e)	2.545(e)			(d)	2.060(g)		
(f)	2.250(a)			(e)	2.060(h)		
(g)	2.250(b)			(f)	2.060(i)		
2.090	2.525			(g)	2.060(j)		
2.100	2.255			(h)	2.060(k)		
2.110	2.265			2.510	2.061		
2.120	2.220			2.515(a)	2.060(c)		
2.125	2.225			(b)	2.060(d)		
				(c)	2.060(e)		

[NOTE: The Florida Rules of Judicial Administration were reorganized and renumbered in *In Re: Amendments to the Florida Rules of Judicial Administration — Reorganization of the Rules*, 939 So.2d 966 (Fla. 2006).]

TABLE OF CONTENTS

FLORIDA RULES OF JUDICIAL ADMINISTRATION

PART I. GENERAL PROVISIONS

RULE 2.110. SCOPE AND PURPOSE

These rules, cited as "Florida Rules of Judicial Administration" and abbreviated as "Fla. R. Jud. Admin.," shall take effect at 12:01 a.m. on July 1, 1979. They shall apply to administrative matters in all courts to which the rules are applicable by their terms. The rules shall be construed to secure the speedy and inexpensive determination of every proceeding to which they are applicable. These rules shall supersede all conflicting rules and statutes.

RULE 2.120. DEFINITIONS

The following terms have the meanings shown as used in these rules:

(a) Court Rule: A rule of practice or procedure adopted to facilitate the uniform conduct of litigation applicable to all proceedings, all parties, and all attorneys.

(b) Local Court Rule:

(1) A rule of practice or procedure for circuit or county application only that, because of local conditions, supplies an omission in or facilitates application of a rule of statewide application and does not conflict therewith.

(2) A rule that addresses other matters that are required by the Florida Constitution, general law, rules of court, or a supreme court opinion to be adopted by or in a local rule.

(c) Administrative Order: A directive necessary to administer properly the court's affairs but not inconsistent with the constitution or with court rules and administrative orders entered by the supreme court.

RULE 2.130. PRIORITY OF FLORIDA RULES OF APPELLATE PROCEDURE

The Florida Rules of Appellate Procedure shall control all proceedings in the supreme court and the district courts, and all proceedings in which the circuit courts exercise their appellate jurisdiction, notwithstanding any conflicting rules of procedure.

RULE 2.140. AMENDING RULES OF COURT

(a) Amendments Generally. The following procedure shall be followed for consideration of rule amendments generally other than those adopted under subdivisions (d), (e), (f), and (g):

(1) Proposals for court rules, amendments to them, or abrogation of them may be made by any person.

(2) Proposals shall be submitted to the clerk of the supreme court, the committee chair(s) of a Florida Bar committee listed in subdivision (a)(3), or the Bar staff liaison of The Florida Bar in writing and shall include a general description of the proposed rule change or a specified proposed change in content. The clerk of the supreme court shall refer proposals to the appropriate committee under subdivision (a)(3).

(3) The Florida Bar shall appoint the following committees to consider rule proposals: Civil Procedure Rules Committee, Criminal Procedure Rules Committee, Small Claims Rules Committee, Traffic Court Rules Committee, Appellate Court Rules Committee, Juvenile Court Rules Committee, Code and Rules of Evidence Committee, Rules of Judicial Administration Committee, Probate Rules Committee, and Family Law Rules Committee.

(4) Each committee shall be composed of attorneys and judges with extensive experience and training in the committee's area of concentration. Members of the Rules of Judicial Administration Committee shall also have previous rules committee experience or substantial experience in the administration of the Florida court system. The chair of each rules committee shall appoint one of its members to the Rules of Judicial Administration Committee to serve as a regular member of the Rules of Judicial Administration Committee to facilitate and implement routine periodic reporting by and to the Rules of Judicial Administration Committee on the development and progress of rule proposals under consideration and their potential impact on other existing or proposed rules. The members of each rules committee shall

serve for 3-year staggered terms, except members appointed by a rules committee chair to the Rules of Judicial Administration Committee who shall serve at the pleasure of the respective rules committee chairs. The president-elect of The Florida Bar shall appoint sitting members of each rules committee to serve as chair(s) and vice chair(s) for each successive year.

(5) The rules committees may originate proposals and shall regularly review and reevaluate the rules to advance orderly and inexpensive procedures for the administration of justice. The committees shall consider and vote on each proposal. The rules committees may accept or reject proposed amendments or may amend proposals. The rules committees shall prepare meeting agendas and minutes reflecting the status of rules proposals under consideration and actions taken. Copies of the minutes shall be furnished to the clerk of the supreme court, to the board of governors of The Florida Bar, and to the proponent of any proposal considered at the meeting. Each rules committee shall furnish promptly and timely to every other rules committee all meeting agendas and all minutes or other record of action taken.

(6) The Rules of Judicial Administration Committee shall serve as the central rules coordinating committee. All committees shall provide a copy of any proposed rules changes to the Rules of Judicial Administration Committee within 30 days of a committee's affirmative vote to recommend the proposed change to the supreme court. The Rules of Judicial Administration Committee shall then refer all proposed rules changes to those rules committees that might be affected by the proposed change.

(7) Whenever the Rules of Judicial Administration Committee receives a request to coordinate the submission of a single comprehensive report of proposed rule amendments on behalf of multiple rules committees, the general procedure shall be as follows:

(A) The subcommittee chairs handling the matter for each committee will constitute an ad hoc committee to discuss the various committees' recommendations and to formulate time frames for the joint response. The chair of the ad hoc committee will be the assigned Rules of Judicial Administration Committee subcommittee chair.

(B) At the conclusion of the work of the ad hoc committee, a proposed joint response will be prepared by the ad hoc committee and distributed to the committee chairs for each committee's review and final comments.

(C) The Rules of Judicial Administration Committee shall be responsible for filing the comprehensive final report.

(b) Schedule for Regular-Cycle Rules Proposals.

(1) Each committee shall report all proposed rule changes on a staggered basis (with the first cycle starting in 2006). Reports shall be made by the Criminal Procedure Rules Committee, the Traffic Court Rules Committee, and the Juvenile Court Rules Committee in 2006; by the Civil Procedure Rules Committee, the Probate Rules Committee, the Small Claims Rules Committee, and the Code and Rules of Evidence Committee in 2007; and by the Family Law Rules Committee, the Appellate Court Rules Committee, and the Rules of Judicial Administration Committee in 2008. Thereafter, the cycle shall repeat.

(2) No later than June 15 of the year prior to each reporting year or such other date as the board of governors of The Florida Bar may set, each reporting committee shall submit all proposed rule changes to the board of governors with the committee's final numerical voting record on each proposal. Contemporaneously with reporting proposed rule changes to the board of governors, each committee report shall be furnished to the Speaker of the Florida House of Representatives, the President of the Florida Senate, and the chairs of the House and Senate committees as designated by the Speaker and the President, and published on the website of The Florida Bar and in The Florida Bar *News.* Any person desiring to comment upon proposed rule changes shall submit written comments to the appropriate committee chair(s) no later than August 1 of the year prior to each reporting year. Each committee shall consider any comments submitted and thereafter report to the board of governors, no later than October 31 of the year prior to each reporting year, any revisions to the proposed rule changes. Contemporaneously with reporting any revi-

sions to the board of governors, each committee's revised proposed rule changes shall be furnished to the Speaker of the Florida House of Representatives, the President of the Florida Senate, and the chairs of the House and Senate committees as designated by the Speaker and the President, and published on the website of The Florida Bar and in The Florida Bar *News*. Any person desiring to comment thereafter shall submit written comments to the supreme court in accordance with subdivision (b)(6).

(3) No later than December 15 of the year prior to each reporting year, the board of governors shall consider the proposals and shall vote on each proposal to recommend acceptance, rejection, or amendment.

(4) No later than February 1 of each reporting year, each committee and the executive director of The Florida Bar shall file a report of its proposed rule changes with the supreme court. Each committee may amend its recommendations to coincide with the recommendations of the board of governors or may decline to do so or may amend its recommendations in another manner. Any such amendments shall also be reported to the supreme court. The report and proposed rule changes must conform to the Guidelines for Rules Submissions approved by administrative order and posted on the websites of the supreme court and The Florida Bar. Consistent with the requirements that are fully set forth in the Guidelines, the report shall include:

(A) a list of the proposed changes, together with a detailed explanation of each proposal that includes a narrative description of how each amendment changes the language of the rule and a thorough discussion of the reason for each change;

(B) the final numerical voting record of the proposals in the committee;

(C) the name and address of the proponent of each change, if other than a member of the rules committee;

(D) a report of the action taken by the committee on comments submitted in accordance with subdivision (b)(2);

(E) a report of the action and voting record of the board of governors;

(F) any dissenting views of the committee and, if available, of the board; and

(G) an appendix containing all comments submitted to the committee, all relevant background documents, the proposed amendments in legislative format, and a two-column chart setting forth the proposed changes in legislative format in the left column and a brief summary of the explanation of each change given in the report in the right column.

The report and the proposed rule changes shall be filed with the supreme court in an electronic format approved by the supreme court.

(5) If oral argument is deemed necessary, the supreme court shall establish a date in the month of June of each reporting year for oral argument on the proposals. Notice of the oral argument on the proposals and a copy of the proposals shall be furnished to the affected committee chair(s) and vice chair(s), the executive director and staff liaison of The Florida Bar, all members of the Judicial Management Council, the clerk and chief judge of each district court of appeal, the clerk and chief judge of each judicial circuit, the Speaker of the Florida House of Representatives, the President of the Florida Senate, the chairs of the House and Senate committees as designated by the Speaker and the President, and any person who has asked in writing filed with the clerk of the supreme court for a copy of the notice. The clerk may provide the notice electronically. The recommendations or a resume of them shall be published on the websites of the supreme court and The Florida Bar and in The Florida Bar *News* before the oral argument or consideration of the proposals without oral argument. Notice of the oral argument, if scheduled, shall also be published on the website of the supreme court.

(6) Within the time allowed for comments set by the supreme court, any person may file comments concerning the proposals. All comments and other submissions by interested persons shall be filed with the clerk of the supreme court and served on the chair(s) of the appropriate rules committee, the Bar

staff liaison, and on the proponent of the rule change if other than a member of the rules committee. The chair(s) of the rules committee and the executive director of The Florida Bar shall file a response to all comments within the time period set by the court. All comments and other submissions regarding the rule change proposals shall be filed in an approved electronic format with the supreme court. As soon as practicable after the date of filing, the clerk of the supreme court shall publish on the website of the supreme court all comments and the responses of the chair(s) of the rules committee that have been filed concerning the rule change proposals. All requests or submissions by a rules committee made in connection with a pending rule change proposal shall be filed with the clerk of the supreme court and thereafter published by the clerk of the supreme court on the websites of the supreme court and The Florida Bar.

(7) Opinions adopting the proposals should be issued in sufficient time for the rule changes to take effect on January 1 of the year following the reporting year. The supreme court may permit motions for rehearing to be filed on behalf of any person who filed a comment, The Florida Bar, any bar association, and the affected committee.

(c) **Rejected Proposals.** If a committee rejects a proposal, the proponent may submit the proposed rule to the board of governors and shall notify the chair(s) and vice chair(s) of the affected committee of the submission of the proposed rule to the board of governors. Minority reports of committees are allowed and may be submitted to both the board of governors and the supreme court.

(d) **Emergency Amendments by Court.** The supreme court, with or without notice, may change court rules at any time if an emergency exists that does not permit reference to the appropriate committee of The Florida Bar for recommendations. The rule changes must conform to the Guidelines for Rules Submissions approved by administrative order and posted on the websites of the supreme court and The Florida Bar. The change may become effective immediately or at a future time. In either event, the court shall give notice of and fix a date for further consideration of the change. Any person may file comments concerning the change, seeking its abrogation or a delay in the effective date, in accordance with the procedures set forth in subdivision (b)(6). The court may allow oral argument in support of such comments by The Florida Bar, by its sections and committees, and by other bar associations. Notice of the oral argument, if scheduled, on the change and a copy of the change shall be furnished to the affected committee chair(s) and vice chair(s), the executive director and staff liaison of The Florida Bar, all members of the Judicial Management Council, the clerk and chief judge of each district court of appeal, the clerk and chief judge of each judicial circuit, the Speaker of the Florida House of Representatives, the President of the Florida Senate, the chairs of the House and Senate committees as designated by the Speaker and the President, and any person who has asked in writing filed with the clerk of the supreme court for a copy of the notice. The clerk may provide the notice electronically. Notice of the change shall be published on the websites of the supreme court and The Florida Bar, and in The Florida Bar *News* either before or after the change is adopted. Notice of the oral argument, if scheduled, shall also be published on the website of the supreme court.

(e) **Out-of-Cycle Committee Proposals.**

(1) **Emergency Proposals and Proposals in Response to Legislative Changes.** If, in the opinion of a committee, a proposal is of an emergency nature or a rule amendment is necessary due to changes in legislation, and the board of governors concurs, proposals may be made at any time to the supreme court. The report and proposed rule changes may be filed without prior publication for comment and must conform to the Guidelines for Rules Submissions approved by administrative order and posted on the websites of the supreme court and The Florida Bar. The rules committees' fast-track procedures shall be used to address legislative changes to ensure that any resulting proposed rule amendments are filed with and can be adopted by the court before or soon after the effective date of the legislation. If the court agrees that an emergency exists or a rule change is necessary due to a legislative change, the court may publish the rule amendment for comment after adopting it or may set a time for oral argument or for consideration of the proposal without oral argument. Notice of the oral

argument on the proposals, if scheduled before or after adoption, and a copy of the proposals shall be furnished to the affected committee chair(s) and vice chair(s), the executive director and the staff liaison of The Florida Bar, all members of the Judicial Management Council, the clerk and chief judge of each district court of appeal, the clerk and chief judge of each judicial circuit, the Speaker of the Florida House of Representatives, the President of the Florida Senate, the chairs of the House and Senate committees as designated by the Speaker and the President, and any person who has asked in writing filed with the clerk of the supreme court for a copy of the notice. The clerk may provide the notice electronically. Prior to or after their adoption, the recommendations or a resume of them shall be published on the websites of the supreme court and The Florida Bar, and in The Florida Bar *News*. Any person may file comments concerning the changes, in accordance with the procedures set forth in subdivision (b)(6). Notice of the oral argument, if scheduled, shall also be published on the website of the supreme court.

(2) Non-Emergency Out-of-Cycle Proposals. If, in the opinion of a committee, a proposal is not of an emergency nature, but is sufficiently necessary to the administration of justice that it should not wait until the next regular-cycle submission, and the board of governors concurs, proposals may be made out-of-cycle at any time to the supreme court. The report and proposed rule changes must conform to the Guidelines for Rules Submissions approved by administrative order and posted on the websites of the supreme court and The Florida Bar. Such out-of-cycle submissions must be published in The Florida Bar *News* and posted on the website of The Florida Bar for comment, and such comment must be reviewed and addressed by the committee prior to the out-of-cycle rule submission to the board of governors to recommend acceptance, rejection, or amendment. If the supreme court agrees that a proposal should be addressed before the next regular-cycle report, the supreme court may set a time for oral argument or for consideration of the proposal without oral argument. Notice of the oral argument on the proposals, if scheduled, and a copy of the proposals shall be furnished to the affected committee chair(s) and vice chair(s), the executive director and the staff liaison of

The Florida Bar, all members of the Judicial Management Council, the clerk and chief judge of each district court of appeal, the clerk and chief judge of each judicial circuit, the Speaker of the Florida House of Representatives, the President of the Florida Senate, the chairs of the House and Senate committees as designated by the Speaker and the President, the person who initially proposed the matter to the committee, and any person who has asked in writing filed with the clerk of the supreme court for a copy of the notice. The clerk may provide the notice electronically. The recommendations or a resume of them shall be published on the websites of the supreme court and The Florida Bar, and in The Florida Bar *News* for comment before the oral argument or consideration of the proposals without oral argument. Any person may file comments concerning the proposals, in accordance with the procedures set forth in subdivision (b)(6). Notice of the oral argument, if scheduled, shall also be published on the website of the supreme court.

(f) Request by Court. The supreme court may direct special consideration of a proposal at times other than those specified in this rule and may require a committee to report its recommendation with the recommendations of the board of governors. All requests or submissions by a rules committee made in connection with a request under this subdivision shall be filed with or submitted to the clerk of the supreme court as provided in this subdivision.

(1) Recommended Rule Changes. A rule change recommended in response to a request under this subdivision shall be included in the rules committee's next regular-cycle report filed under subdivision (b), unless the court directs or the committee determines and the board of governors agrees that the rule change should be submitted out of cycle. If the committee submits a recommended change out of cycle, the procedures for out-of-cycle rule proposals under subdivision (e) shall apply, except the report shall state that it is filed in response to a request by the court under this subdivision.

(2) No Action Recommendations. If the court refers a matter to a rules committee for consideration only and does not direct the committee to propose a rule change, and after considering the matter referred the committee determines that no rule change is warranted, the committee shall submit a "no action report" to the court explaining its recommendation that no rule change is needed. A no action recommendation should not be included in a report proposing rule changes filed under any other subdivision of this rule. After the court considers the recommendation, the clerk shall notify the rules committee chair(s) and the executive director and the staff liaison of The Florida Bar whether any further action is required of the committee.

(g) Amendments to the Rules of Judicial Administration.

(1) Amendments Without Referral to Rules Committee. Changes to the Rules of Judicial Administration contained in Part II, State Court Administration, of these rules, and rules 2.310, and 2.320, contained in Part III, Judicial Officers, generally will be considered and adopted by the supreme court without reference to or proposal from the Rules of Judicial Administration Committee. The supreme court may amend rules under this subdivision at any time, with or without notice. If a change is made without notice, the court shall fix a date for future consideration of the change and the change shall be published on the websites of the supreme court and The Florida Bar, and in The Florida Bar *News*. Any person may file comments concerning the change, in accordance with the procedures set forth in subdivision (b)(6). The court may hear oral argument on the change. Notice of the oral argument on the change, if scheduled, and a copy of the change shall be provided in accordance with subdivision (d).

(2) Other Amendments. Amendments to all other Rules of Judicial Administration shall be referred to or proposed by the Rules of Judicial Administration Committee and adopted by the supreme court as provided in subdivisions (a), (b), (c), (d), (e), and (f).

(h) Local Rules Proposed by Trial Courts. The foregoing procedure shall not apply to local rules proposed by a majority of circuit and county judges in the circuit. The chief justice of the supreme court may appoint a Local Rule Advisory Committee to consider and make recommendations to the court concerning

local rules and administrative orders submitted pursuant to rule 2.215(e).

Committee Notes

1980 Amendment. Rule 2.130 [renumbered as 2.140 in 2006] is entirely rewritten to codify the procedures for changes to all Florida rules of procedure as set forth by this court in *In re Rules of Court: Procedure for Consideration of Proposals Concerning Practice and Procedure*, 276 So.2d 467 (Fla.1972), and to update those procedures based on current practice. The Supreme Court Rules Advisory Committee has been abolished, and the Local Rules Advisory Committee has been established.

PART II. STATE COURT ADMINISTRATION

RULE 2.205. THE SUPREME COURT

(a) Internal Government.

(1) Exercise of Powers and Jurisdiction.

(A) The supreme court shall exercise its powers, including establishing policy for the judicial branch, and jurisdiction en banc. Five justices shall constitute a quorum and the concurrence of 4 shall be necessary to a decision. In cases requiring only a panel of 5, if 4 of the 5 justices who consider the case do not concur, it shall be submitted to the other 2 justices.

(B) Consistent with the authority of the supreme court to establish policy, including recommending state budget and compensation priorities for the judicial branch, no judge, supreme court created committee, commission, task force, or similar group, and no conference (Conference of District Court of Appeal Judges, Conference of Circuit Court Judges, Conference of County Court Judges) is permitted to recommend state budget priorities, including compensation and benefits, to the legislative or executive branch that have not been approved by the supreme court. This subdivision is not intended to apply to judges expressing their personal views who affirmatively make it explicitly clear that they are not speaking on behalf of the judicial branch.

(C) Newly created judicial branch commissions, committees, task forces, work groups, and similar study or advisory groups must be established by the supreme court, not solely by the chief justice. Such study or advisory groups may be created and charged by rule adopted by the court, or by administrative order issued by the chief justice in accordance with court action. Members of such groups shall be appointed by administrative order of the chief justice, after consultation with the court. When practicable, ad hoc committees and other ad hoc study or advisory groups, which should be used to address specific problems, shall be established under the umbrella of an existing committee or commission, which should be used to address long-term problems.

(2) Chief Justice.

(A) The chief justice shall be chosen by majority vote of the justices for a term of 2 years commencing on July 1, 2012. The selection of the chief justice should be based on managerial, administrative, and leadership abilities, without regard to seniority only. A chief justice may serve successive terms limited to a total of 8 years. The chief justice may be removed by a vote of 4 justices. If a vacancy occurs, a successor shall be chosen promptly to serve the balance of the unexpired term.

(B) The chief justice shall be the administrative officer of the judicial branch and of the supreme court and shall be responsible for the dispatch of the business of the branch and of the court and direct the implementation of policies and priorities as determined by the supreme court for the operation of the branch and of the court. The administrative powers and duties of the chief justice shall include, but not be limited to:

(i) the responsibility to serve as the primary spokesperson for the judicial branch regarding policies and practices that have statewide impact including, but not limited to, the judicial branch's management, operation, strategic plan, legislative agenda and budget priorities;

(ii) the power to act on requests for stays during the pendency of proceedings, to order the consolidation of cases, to determine all procedural motions and petitions relating to the time for filing and size of briefs and other papers provided for under the rules of this court, to advance or continue cases, and to rule on

other procedural matters relating to any proceeding or process in the court;

(iii) the power to assign active or retired county, circuit, or appellate judges or justices to judicial service in this state, in accordance with subdivisions (a)(3) and (a)(4) of this rule;

(iv) the power, upon request of the chief judge of any circuit or district, or sua sponte, in the event of natural disaster, civil disobedience, or other emergency situation requiring the closure of courts or other circumstances inhibiting the ability of litigants to comply with deadlines imposed by rules of procedure applicable in the courts of this state, to enter such order or orders as may be appropriate to suspend, toll, or otherwise grant relief from time deadlines imposed by otherwise applicable statutes and rules of procedure for such period as may be appropriate, including, without limitation, those affecting speedy trial procedures in criminal and juvenile proceedings, all civil process and proceedings, and all appellate time limitations;

(v) the authority to directly inform all judges on a regular basis by any means, including, but not limited to, email on the state of the judiciary, the state of the budget, issues of importance, priorities and other matters of statewide interest; furthermore, the chief justice shall routinely communicate with the chief judges and leaders of the district courts, circuit and county court conferences by the appropriate means;

(vi) the responsibility to exercise reasonable efforts to promote and encourage diversity in the administration of justice; and

(vii) the power to perform such other administrative duties as may be required and which are not otherwise provided for by law or rule.

(C) The chief justice shall be notified by all justices of any contemplated absences from the court and the reasons therefor. When the chief justice is to be temporarily absent, the chief justice shall select the justice longest in continuous service as acting chief justice.

(D) If the chief justice dies, retires, or is unable to perform the duties of the office, the justice longest in continuous service shall perform the duties during the period of incapacity or until a successor chief justice is elected.

(E) The chief justice shall meet on a regular basis with the chief judges of the district courts and the chief judges of the circuit courts to discuss and provide feedback for implementation of policies and practices that have statewide impact including, but not limited to, the judicial branch's management, operation, strategic plan, legislative agenda and budget priorities. Such meetings shall, if practicable, occur at least quarterly and be conducted in-person. At the discretion of the chief justice, any of these meetings may be combined with other judicial branch and leadership meetings and, where practicable include the justices of the supreme court.

(3) Administration.

(A) The chief justice may, either upon request or when otherwise necessary for the prompt dispatch of business in the courts of this state, temporarily assign justices of the supreme court, judges of district courts of appeal, circuit judges, and judges of county courts to any court for which they are qualified to serve. Any consenting retired justice or judge may be assigned to judicial service and receive compensation as provided by law.

(B) For the purpose of judicial administration, a "retired judge" is defined as a judge not engaged in the practice of law who has been a judicial officer of this state. A retired judge shall comply with all requirements that the supreme court deems necessary relating to the recall of retired judges.

(C) When a judge who is eligible to draw retirement compensation has entered the private practice of law, the judge may be eligible for recall to judicial service upon cessation of the private practice of law and approval of the judge's application to the court. The application shall state the period of time the judge has not engaged in the practice of law, and must be approved by the court before the judge shall be eligible for recall to judicial service.

(D) A "senior judge" is a retired judge who is eligible to serve on assignment to temporary judicial duty.

(4) Assignments of Justices and Judges.

(A) When a justice of the supreme court is unable to perform the duties of office, or when necessary for the prompt dispatch of the business of the court, the chief justice may assign to the court any judge who is qualified to serve, for such time as the chief justice may direct. However, no retired justice who is eligible to serve on assignment to temporary judicial duty or other judge who is qualified to serve may be assigned to the supreme court, or continue in such assignment, after 7 sitting duly sworn justices are available and able to perform the duties of office.

(B) When a judge of any district court of appeal is unable to perform the duties of office, or when necessary for the prompt dispatch of the business of the court, the chief judge shall advise the chief justice and the chief justice may assign to the court any judge who is qualified to serve, for such time or such proceedings as the chief justice may direct.

(C) When any circuit or county judge is unable to perform the duties of office, or when necessary for the prompt dispatch of the business of the court, the chief judge of the circuit may assign any judge in the circuit to temporary service for which the judge is qualified, in accordance with rule 2.215. If the chief judge deems it necessary, the chief judge may request the chief justice to assign a judge to the court for such time or such proceedings as the chief justice may direct.

(b) Clerk.

(1) Appointment. The supreme court shall appoint a clerk who shall hold office at the pleasure of the court and perform such duties as the court directs. The clerk's compensation shall be fixed by law. The clerk's office shall be in the supreme court building. The clerk shall devote full time to the duties of the office and shall not engage in the practice of law while in office.

(2) Custody of Records, Files, and Seal. All court records and the seal of the court shall be kept in the office and the custody of the clerk. The clerk shall not allow any court record to be taken from the clerk's office or the courtroom, except by a justice of the court or upon the order of the court.

(3) Records of Proceedings. The clerk shall keep such records as the court may from time to time order or direct. The clerk shall keep a docket or equivalent electronic record of all cases that are brought for review to, or that originate in, the court. Each case shall be numbered in the order in which the notice, petition, or other initial pleading originating the cause is filed in the court.

(4) Filing Fee. In all cases filed in the court, the clerk shall require the payment of a fee as provided by law when the notice, petition, or other initial pleading is filed. The payment shall not be exacted in advance in appeals in which a party has been adjudicated insolvent for the purpose of an appeal or in appeals in which the state is the real party in interest as the moving party. The payment of the fee shall not be required in habeas corpus proceedings, or appeals therefrom, arising out of or in connection with criminal actions.

(5) Issuance and Recall of Mandate; Recordation and Notification. The clerk shall issue such mandates or process as may be directed by the court. If, within 120 days after a mandate has been issued, the court directs that a mandate be recalled, then the clerk shall recall the mandate. Upon the issuance or recall of any mandate, the clerk shall record the issuance or recall in a book or equivalent electronic record kept for that purpose, in which the date of issuance or date of recall and the manner of transmittal of the process shall be noted. In proceedings in which no mandate is issued, upon final adjudication of the pending cause the clerk shall transmit to the party affected thereby a copy of the court's order or judgment. The clerk shall notify the attorneys of record of the issuance of any mandate, the recall of any mandate, or the rendition of any final judgment. The clerk shall furnish without charge to all attorneys of record in any cause a copy of any order or written opinion rendered in such action.

(6) Return of Original Papers. Upon the conclusion of any proceeding in the supreme court, the clerk shall return to the clerk of the lower court the original papers or files transmitted to the court for use in the cause.

(c) Librarian.

(1) Appointment. The supreme court shall appoint a librarian of the supreme court and such assistants as may be necessary. The supreme court library shall be in the custody of the librarian, but under the exclusive control of the court. The library shall be open to members of the bar of the supreme court, to members of the legislature, to law officers of the executive or other departments of the state, and to such other persons as may be allowed to use the library by special permission of the court.

(2) Library Hours. The library shall be open during such times as the reasonable needs of the bar require and shall be governed by regulations made by the librarian with the approval of the court.

(3) Books. Books shall not be removed from the library except for use by, or upon order of, any justice.

(d) Marshal.

(1) Appointment. The supreme court shall appoint a marshal who shall hold office at the pleasure of the court and perform such duties as the court directs. The marshal's compensation shall be fixed by law.

(2) Duties. The marshal shall have power to execute process of the court throughout the state and such other powers as may be conferred by law. The marshal may deputize the sheriff or a deputy sheriff in any county to execute process of the court and shall perform such clerical or ministerial duties as the court may direct or as required by law. Subject to the direction of the court, the marshal shall be custodian of the supreme court building and grounds.

(e) State Courts Administrator.

(1) Appointment. The supreme court shall appoint a state courts administrator who shall serve at the pleasure of the court and perform such duties as the court directs. The state courts administrator's compensation shall be fixed by law.

(2) Duties. The state courts administrator shall supervise the administrative office of the Florida courts, which shall be maintained at such place as directed by the supreme court; shall employ such other personnel as the court deems necessary to aid in the administration of the state courts system; shall represent the state courts system before the legislature and other bodies with respect to matters affecting the state courts system and functions related to and serving the system; shall supervise the preparation and submission to the supreme court, for review and approval, of a tentative budget request for the state courts system and shall appear before the legislature in accordance with the court's directions in support of the final budget request on behalf of the system; shall inform the judiciary of the state courts system's final budget request and any proposed substantive law changes approved by the supreme court; shall assist in the preparation of educational and training materials for the state courts system and related personnel, and shall coordinate or assist in the conduct of educational and training sessions for such personnel; shall assist all courts in the development of improvements in the system, and submit to the chief justice and the court appropriate recommendations to improve the state courts system; and shall collect and compile uniform financial and other statistical data or information reflective of the cost, workloads, business, and other functions related to the state courts system. The state courts administrator is the custodian of all records in the administrator's office.

(f) Open Sessions. All sessions of the court shall be open to the public, except proceedings designated as confidential by the court and conference sessions held for the discussion and consideration of pending cases, for the formulation of opinions by the court, and for the discussion or resolution of other matters related to the administration of the state courts system.

(g) Designation of Assigned Judges. When any judge of another court is assigned for temporary service on the supreme court, that judge shall be designated, as author or participant, by name and initials followed by the words "Associate Justice."

RULE 2.210. DISTRICT COURTS OF APPEAL

(a) Internal Government.

(1) Exercise of Powers and Jurisdiction. Three judges shall constitute a panel for and shall consider each case, and the concurrence of a majority of the panel shall be necessary to a decision.

(2) Chief Judge.

(A) The selection of a chief judge should be based on managerial, administrative, and leadership abilities, without regard to seniority only.

(B) The chief judge shall be the administrative officer of the court, and shall, consistent with branch-wide policies, direct the formation and implementation of policies and priorities for the operation of the court. The chief judge shall exercise administrative supervision over all judges and court personnel. The chief judge shall be responsible to the chief justice of the supreme court. The chief judge may enter and sign administrative orders. The administrative powers and duties of the chief judge include, but are not limited to, the power to order consolidation of cases, and to assign cases to the judges for the preparation of opinions, orders, or judgments. The chief judge shall have the authority to require all judges of the court, court officers and court personnel, to comply with all court and judicial branch policies, administrative orders, procedures, and administrative plans.

(C) The chief judge shall maintain liaison in all judicial administrative matters with the chief justice of the supreme court, and shall, considering available resources, ensure the efficient and proper administration of the court. The chief judge shall develop an administrative plan that shall include an administrative organization capable of effecting the prompt disposition of cases, the assignment of judges, other court officers, and court personnel, and the control of dockets. The administrative plan shall include a consideration of the statistical data developed by the case reporting system.

(D) All judges shall inform the chief judge of any contemplated absences that will affect the progress of the court's business. If a judge is temporarily absent, is disqualified in an action, or is unable to perform the duties of the office, the chief judge or the chief judge's designee may assign a matter pending before the judge to any other judge or any additional assigned judge of the same court. If it appears to the chief judge that the speedy, efficient, and proper administration of justice so requires, the chief judge shall request the chief justice of the supreme court to assign temporarily an additional judge or judges from outside the court to duty in the court requiring assistance, and shall advise the chief justice whether or not the approval of the chief judge of the court from which the assignment is to be made has been obtained. The assigned judges shall be subject to administrative supervision of the chief judge for all purposes of this rule. Nothing in this rule shall restrict the constitutional powers of the chief justice of the supreme court to make such assignments as the chief justice shall deem appropriate.

(E) The chief judge shall regulate the use of all court facilities, regularly examine the dockets of the courts under the chief judge's administrative supervision, and require a report on the status of the matters on the docket. The chief judge may take such action as may be necessary to cause the docket to be made current.

(F) The chief judge shall be chosen by a majority of the active judges of the court for a term commencing on July 1 of each odd-numbered year, and shall serve for a term of 2 years. A chief judge may serve for successive terms but in no event shall the total term as chief judge exceed 8 years. In the event of a vacancy, a successor shall be chosen promptly to serve the balance of the unexpired term. If the chief judge is unable to discharge these duties, the judge longest in continuous service or, as between judges with equal continuous service, the one having the longest unexpired term and able to do so, shall perform the duties of chief judge pending the chief judge's return to duty. Judges shall notify the chief judge of any contemplated absence from the court and the reasons therefor. A chief judge may be removed as chief judge by the supreme court, acting as the administrative supervisory body of all courts, or by a two-thirds vote of the active judges.

(G) The failure of any judge to comply with an order or directive of the chief judge shall be considered neglect of duty and may be reported by the chief judge to the chief justice of the supreme court who shall have the authority to take such corrective action as may be appropriate. The chief judge may report the neglect of duty by a judge to the Judicial Qualifications Commission or other appropriate person or body, or take such other corrective action as may be appropriate.

(H) At the call of the chief justice, the chief judges of the circuit court and district courts of appeal shall meet on a regular basis and with each other and with the chief justice to discuss and provide feedback for implementation of policies and practices that have statewide impact including, but not limited to, the judicial branch's management, operation, strategic plan, legislative agenda and budget priorities. Such meetings shall, if practicable, occur at least quarterly and be conducted in person. At the discretion of the chief justice, any of these meetings may be combined with other judicial branch and leadership meetings.

(I) The chief judge shall have the responsibility to exercise reasonable efforts to promote and encourage diversity in the administration of justice.

(b) Clerk.

(1) Appointment. The court shall appoint a clerk who shall hold office at the pleasure of the court and perform such duties as the court directs. The clerk's compensation shall be fixed by law. The clerk's office shall be in the headquarters of the court. The clerk's time shall be devoted to the duties of the office and the clerk shall not engage in the private practice of law while serving as clerk. All court records and the seal of the court shall be kept in the office and the custody of the clerk. The clerk shall not allow any court record to be taken from the clerk's office or the courtroom, except by a judge of the court or upon order of the court.

(2) Records of Proceedings. The clerk shall keep such records as the court may from time to time order or direct. The clerk shall keep a docket or equivalent electronic record of all cases that are brought for review to, or that originate in, the court. Each case shall be numbered in the order that the notice, petition, other initial pleading originating the proceeding is filed in the court.

(3) Filing Fee. In all cases filed in the court, the clerk shall require the payment of a fee as provided by law at the time the notice, petition, or other initial pleading is filed. The payment shall not be exacted in advance in appeals in which a party has been adjudicated insolvent for the purpose of an appeal or in appeals in which the state is the real party in interest as the moving party. The payment of the fee shall not be required in habeas corpus proceedings or appeals therefrom.

(4) Issuance and Recall of Mandate; Recordation and Notification. The clerk shall issue such mandates or process as may be directed by the court. If, within 120 days after a mandate has been issued, the court directs that a mandate be recalled, then the clerk shall recall the mandate. If the court directs that a mandate record shall be maintained, then upon the issuance or recall of any mandate the clerk shall record the issuance or recall in a book or equivalent electronic record kept for that purpose, in which shall be noted the date of issuance or the date of recall and the manner of transmittal of the process. In proceedings in which no mandate is issued, upon final adjudication of the pending cause the clerk shall transmit to the party affected thereby a copy of the court's order or judgment. The clerk shall notify the attorneys of record of the issuance of any mandate, the recall of any mandate, or the rendition of any final judgment. The clerk shall furnish without charge to all attorneys of record in any cause a copy of any order or written opinion rendered in such action.

(5) Return of Original Papers. The clerk shall retain all original papers, files, and exhibits transmitted to the court for a period of not less than 30 days after rendition of the opinion or order denying any motion pursuant to Florida Rule of Appellate Procedure 9.330, whichever is later. If no discretionary review proceeding or appeal has been timely commenced in the supreme court to review the court's

decision within 30 days, the clerk shall transmit to the clerk of the trial court the original papers, files, and exhibits. If a discretionary review proceeding or appeal has been timely commenced in the supreme court to review the court's decision, the original papers, files, and exhibits shall be retained by the clerk until transmitted to the supreme court or, if not so transmitted, until final disposition by the supreme court and final disposition by the court pursuant to the mandate issued by the supreme court.

(c) Marshal.

(1) Appointment. The court shall appoint a marshal who shall hold office at the pleasure of the court and perform such duties as the court directs. The marshal's compensation shall be fixed by law.

(2) Duties. The marshal shall have power to execute process of the court throughout the district, and in any county therein may deputize the sheriff or a deputy sheriff for such purpose. The marshal shall perform such clerical or ministerial duties as the court may direct or as are required by law. The marshal shall be custodian of the headquarters occupied by the court, whether the headquarters is an entire building or a part of a building.

(d) Open Sessions. All sessions of the court shall be open to the public, except conference sessions held for the discussion and consideration of pending cases, for the formulation of opinions by the court, and for the discussion or resolution of other matters related to the administration of the court.

(e) Designation of Assigned Judges. When any justice or judge of another court is assigned for temporary service on a district court of appeal, that justice or judge shall be designated, as author or participant, by name and initials followed by the words "Associate Judge."

RULE 2.215. TRIAL COURT ADMINISTRATION

(a) Purpose. The purpose of this rule is to fix administrative responsibility in the chief judges of the circuit courts and the other judges that the chief judges may designate. When these rules refer to the court, they shall be construed to apply to a judge of the court when the context requires or permits.

(b) Chief Judge.

(1) The chief judge shall be a circuit judge who possesses managerial, administrative, and leadership abilities, and shall be selected without regard to seniority only.

(2) The chief judge shall be the administrative officer of the courts within the circuit and shall, consistent with branch-wide policies, direct the formation and implementation of policies and priorities for the operation of all courts and officers within the circuit. The chief judge shall exercise administrative supervision over all judges and court personnel within the judicial circuit. The chief judge shall be responsible to the chief justice of the supreme court. The chief judge may enter and sign administrative orders, except as otherwise provided by this rule. The chief judge shall have the authority to require that all judges of the court, other court officers, and court personnel comply with all court and judicial branch policies, administrative orders, procedures and administrative plans.

(3) The chief judge shall maintain liaison in all judicial administrative matters with the chief justice of the supreme court, and shall, considering available resources, ensure the efficient and proper administration of all courts within that circuit. The chief judge shall develop an administrative plan that shall be filed with the supreme court and shall include an administrative organization capable of effecting the prompt disposition of cases; assignment of judges, other court officers, and all other court personnel; control of dockets; regulation and use of courtrooms; and mandatory periodic review of the status of the inmates of the county jail. The plan shall be compatible with the development of the capabilities of the judges in such a manner that each judge will be qualified to serve in any division, thereby creating a judicial pool from which judges may be assigned to various courts throughout the state. The administrative plan shall include a consideration of the statistical data developed by the case reporting system. Questions concerning the administration or management of the courts of the circuit shall be directed to the chief justice of the supreme court through the state courts administrator.

(4) The chief judge shall assign judges to the courts and divisions, and shall determine the length of each assignment. The chief judge is authorized to order consolidation of cases, and to assign cases to a judge or judges for the preparation of opinions, orders, or judgments. All judges shall inform the chief judge of any contemplated absences that will affect the progress of the court's business. If a judge is temporarily absent, is disqualified in an action, or is unable to perform the duties of the office, the chief judge or the chief judge's designee may assign a proceeding pending before the judge to any other judge or any additional assigned judge of the same court. The chief judge may assign any judge to temporary service for which the judge is qualified in any court in the same circuit. If it appears to the chief judge that the speedy, efficient, and proper administration of justice so requires, the chief judge shall request the chief justice of the supreme court to assign temporarily an additional judge or judges from outside the circuit to duty in the court requiring assistance, and shall advise the chief justice whether or not the approval of the chief judge of the circuit from which the assignment is to be made has been obtained. The assigned judges shall be subject to administrative supervision of the chief judge for all purposes of this rule. When assigning a judge to hear any type of postconviction or collateral relief proceeding brought by a defendant who has been sentenced to death, the chief judge shall assign to such cases a judge qualified to conduct such proceedings under subdivision (b)(10) of this rule. Nothing in this rule shall restrict the constitutional powers of the chief justice of the supreme court to make such assignments as the chief justice shall deem appropriate.

(5) The chief judge may designate a judge in any court or court division of circuit or county courts as "administrative judge" of any court or division to assist with the administrative supervision of the court or division. To the extent practical, the chief judge shall assign only one administrative judge to supervise the family court. The designee shall be responsible to the chief judge, shall have the power and duty

to carry out the responsibilities assigned by the chief judge, and shall serve at the pleasure of the chief judge.

(6) The chief judge may require the attendance of prosecutors, public defenders, clerks, bailiffs, and other officers of the courts, and may require from the clerks of the courts, sheriffs, or other officers of the courts periodic reports that the chief judge deems necessary.

(7) The chief judge shall regulate the use of all court facilities, regularly examine the dockets of the courts under the chief judge's administrative supervision, and require a report on the status of the matters on the dockets. The chief judge may take such action as may be necessary to cause the dockets to be made current. The chief judge shall monitor the status of all postconviction or collateral relief proceedings for defendants who have been sentenced to death from the time that the mandate affirming the death sentence has been issued by the supreme court and shall take the necessary actions to assure that such cases proceed without undue delay. On the first day of every January, April, July, and October, the chief judge shall inform the chief justice of the supreme court of the status of all such cases.

(8) The chief judge or the chief judge's designee shall regularly examine the status of every inmate of the county jail.

(9) The chief judge may authorize the clerks of the courts to maintain branch county court facilities. When so authorized, clerks of court shall be permitted to retain in such branch court facilities all county court permanent records of pending cases, and may retain and destroy these records in the manner provided by law.

(10)(A) The chief judge shall not assign a judge to preside over a capital case in which the state is seeking the death penalty, or collateral proceedings brought by a death row inmate, until that judge has become qualified to do so by:

(i) presiding a minimum of 6 months in a felony criminal division or in a division that includes felony criminal cases, and

(ii) successfully attending the "Handling Capital Cases" course offered through the Florida Court Education Council. A judge whose caseload includes felony criminal cases must attend the "Handling Capital Cases" course as soon as practicable, or upon the direction of the chief judge.

(B) The chief justice may waive these requirements in exceptional circumstances at the request of the chief judge.

(C) Following attendance at the "Handling Capital Cases" course, a judge shall remain qualified to preside over a capital case by attending a "Capital Case Refresher" course once during each of the subsequent continuing judicial education (CJE) reporting periods. A judge who has attended the "Handling Capital Cases" course and who has not taken the "Capital Case Refresher" course within any subsequent continuing judicial education reporting period must requalify to preside over a capital case by attending the refresher course.

(D) The refresher course shall be at least a 6-hour course and must be approved by the Florida Court Education Council. The course must contain instruction on the following topics: penalty phase, jury selection, and proceedings brought pursuant to Florida Rule of Criminal Procedure 3.851.

(11) The failure of any judge to comply with an order or directive of the chief judge shall be considered neglect of duty and may be reported by the chief judge to the chief justice of the supreme court who shall have the authority to take any corrective action as may be appropriate. The chief judge may report the neglect of duty by a judge to the Judicial Qualifications Commission or other appropriate person or body, or take such other corrective action as may be appropriate.

(12) At the call of the chief justice, the chief judges of the circuit court and district courts of appeal shall meet on a regular basis and with each other and with the chief justice to discuss and provide feedback for implementation of policies and practices that have statewide impact including, but not limited to, the judicial branch's management, operation, strategic

plan, legislative agenda and budget priorities. Such meetings shall, if practicable, occur at least quarterly and be conducted in person. At the discretion of the chief justice, any of these meetings may be combined with other judicial branch and leadership meetings.

(13) The chief judge shall have the responsibility to exercise reasonable efforts to promote and encourage diversity in the administration of justice.

(c) Selection. The chief judge shall be chosen by a majority of the active circuit and county court judges within the circuit for a term of 2 years commencing on July 1 of each odd-numbered year, or if there is no majority, by the chief justice, for a term of 2 years. The election for chief judge shall be held no sooner than February 1 of the year during which the chief judge's term commences beginning July 1. All elections for chief judge shall be conducted as follows:

(1) All ballots shall be secret.

(2) Any circuit or county judge may nominate a candidate for chief judge.

(3) Proxy voting shall not be permitted.

(4) Any judge who will be absent from the election may vote by secret absentee ballot obtained from and returned to the Trial Court Administrator.

A chief judge may be removed as chief judge by the supreme court, acting as the administrative supervisory body of all courts, or may be removed by a two-thirds vote of the active judges. The purpose of this rule is to fix a 2-year cycle for the selection of the chief judge in each circuit. A chief judge may serve for successive terms but in no event shall the total term as chief judge exceed 8 years. A chief judge who is to be temporarily absent shall select an acting chief judge from among the circuit judges. If a chief judge dies, retires, fails to appoint an acting chief judge during an absence, or is unable to perform the duties of the office, the chief justice of the supreme court shall appoint a circuit judge to act as chief judge during the absence or disability, or until a successor chief judge is elected to serve the unexpired term. When the office of chief judge is temporarily vacant

pending action within the scope of this paragraph, the duties of court administration shall be performed by the circuit judge having the longest continuous service as a judge or by another circuit judge designated by that judge.

(d) Circuit Court Administrator. Each circuit court administrator shall be selected or terminated by the chief judge subject to concurrence by a majority vote of the circuit and county judges of the respective circuits.

(e) Local Rules and Administrative Orders.

(1) Local court rules as defined in rule 2.120 may be proposed by a majority of the circuit and county judges in the circuit. The judges shall notify the local bar within the circuit of the proposal, after which they shall permit a representative of the local bar, and may permit any other interested person, to be heard orally or in writing on the proposal before submitting it to the supreme court for approval. When a proposed local rule is submitted to the supreme court for approval, the following procedure shall apply:

(A) Local court rule proposals shall be submitted to the supreme court in January of each year. The supreme court may accept emergency proposals submitted at other times.

(B) Not later than February 15 of each year, the clerk of the supreme court shall submit all local court rule proposals to the Supreme Court Local Rules Advisory Committee created by rule 2.140. At the same time, the clerk of the supreme court shall send copies of the proposed rules to the appropriate committees of The Florida Bar. The Florida Bar committees, any interested local bar associations, and any other interested person shall submit any comments or responses that they wish to make to the Supreme Court Local Rules Advisory Committee on or before March 15 of the year.

(C) The Supreme Court Local Rules Advisory Committee shall meet on or before April 15 to consider the proposals and any comments submitted by interested parties. The committee shall transmit its recommendations to the supreme court concerning each proposal, with the reasons for its recommendations, within 15 days after its meeting.

(D) The supreme court shall consider the recommendations of the committee and may resubmit the proposals with modifications to the committee for editorial comment only. The supreme court may set a hearing on any proposals, or consider them on the recommendations and comments as submitted. If a hearing is set, notice shall be given to the chief judge of the circuit from which the proposals originated, the executive director of The Florida Bar, the chair of the Rules of Judicial Administration Committee of The Florida Bar, any local bar associations, and any interested persons who made comments on the specific proposals to be considered. The supreme court shall act on the proposals promptly after the recommendations are received or heard.

(E) If a local court rule is approved by the supreme court, it shall become effective on the date set by that court.

(F) A copy of all local court rules approved by the supreme court shall be indexed and recorded by the clerk of the circuit court in each county of the circuit where the rules are effective. A set of the recorded copies shall be readily available for inspection as a public record, and copies shall be provided to any requesting party for the cost of duplication. The chief judge of the circuit may provide for the publication of the rules. The clerk of the supreme court shall furnish copies of each approved local court rule to the executive director of The Florida Bar.

(2) Any judge or member of The Florida Bar who believes that an administrative order promulgated under subdivision (b)(2) of this rule is a court rule or a local rule as defined in rule 2.120, rather than an administrative order, may apply to the Supreme Court Local Rules Advisory Committee for a decision on the question. The decisions of the committee concerning the determination of the question shall be reported to the supreme court, and the court shall follow the procedure set forth in subdivision (D) above in considering the recommendation of the committee.

(3) All administrative orders of a general and continuing nature, and all others designated by the chief judge, shall be indexed and recorded by the clerk of the circuit court in each county where the orders are effective. A set of the recorded copies shall be readily available for inspection as a public record, and copies shall be provided to any requesting party for the cost of duplication. The chief judge shall, on an annual basis, direct a review of all local administrative orders to ensure that the set of copies maintained by the clerk remains current and does not conflict with supreme court or local rules.

(4) All local court rules entered pursuant to this section shall be numbered sequentially for each respective judicial circuit.

(f) Duty to Rule within a Reasonable Time. Every judge has a duty to rule upon and announce an order or judgment on every matter submitted to that judge within a reasonable time. Each judge shall maintain a log of cases under advisement and inform the chief judge of the circuit at the end of each calendar month of each case that has been held under advisement for more than 60 days.

(g) Duty to Expedite Priority Cases. Every judge has a duty to expedite priority cases to the extent reasonably possible. Priority cases are those cases that have been assigned a priority status or assigned an expedited disposition schedule by statute, rule of procedure, case law, or otherwise. Particular attention shall be given to all juvenile dependency and termination of parental rights cases, cases involving families and children in need of services, challenges involving elections and proposed constitutional amendments, and capital postconviction cases. As part of an effort to make capital postconviction cases a priority, the chief judge shall have the discretion to create a postconviction division to handle capital postconviction, as well as non-capital postconviction cases, and may assign one or more judges to that division.

(h) Neglect of Duty. The failure of any judge, clerk, prosecutor, public defender, attorney, court reporter, or other officer of the court to comply with an order or directive of the chief judge shall be considered neglect of duty and shall be reported by the chief judge to the chief justice of the supreme court. The chief justice may report the neglect of duty by a judge to the Judicial Qualifications Commission, and neglect of duty by other officials to the governor of Florida or other appropriate person or body.

(i) Status Conference After Compilation of Record in Death Case. In any proceeding in which a defendant has been sentenced to death, the circuit judge assigned to the case shall take such action as may be necessary to ensure that a complete record on appeal has been properly prepared. To that end, the judge shall convene a status conference with all counsel of record as soon as possible after the record has been prepared pursuant to rule of appellate procedure 9.200(d) but before the record has been transmitted. The purpose of the status conference shall be to ensure that the record is complete.

Committee Notes

2008 Amendment. The provisions in subdivision (g) of this rule should be read in conjunction with the provisions of rule 2.545(c) governing priority cases.

Court Commentary

1996 Court Commentary. Rule 2.050(h) [renumbered as 2.215(h) in 2006] should be read in conjunction with Florida Rule of Appellate Procedure 9.140(b)(4)(A).

1997 Court Commentary. [Rule 2.050(b)(10), renumbered as 2.215(b)(10) in 2006]. The refresher course may be a six-hour block during any Florida Court Education Council approved course offering sponsored by any approved Florida judicial education provider, including the Florida College of Advanced Judicial Studies or the Florida Conference of Circuit Judges. The block must contain instruction on the following topics: penalty phase, jury selection, and rule 3.850 proceedings.

Failure to complete the refresher course during the three-year judicial education reporting period will necessitate completion of the original "Handling Capital Cases" course.

2002 Court Commentary. Recognizing the inherent differences in trial and appellate court dockets, the last sentence of subdivision (g) is intended to conform to the extent practicable with appellate rule 9.146(g), which requires appellate courts to give priority to appeals in juvenile dependency and termination of parental rights cases, and in cases involving families and children in need of services.

Criminal Court Steering Committee Notes

2014 Amendment. Capital postconviction cases were added to the list of priority cases.

RULE 2.220. CONFERENCES OF JUDGES

(a) Conference of County Court Judges.

(1) Creation. There shall be a "Conference of County Court Judges of Florida," consisting of the active and senior county court judges of the State of Florida.

(2) Purpose. The purpose of the conference shall be:

(A) the betterment of the judicial system of the state;

(B) the improvement of procedure and practice in the several courts;

(C) to conduct conferences and institutes for continuing judicial education and to provide forums in which the county court judges of Florida may meet and discuss mutual problems and solutions; and

(D) to provide input to the Unified Committee on Judicial Compensation on judicial compensation and benefit issues, and to assist the judicial branch in soliciting support and resources on these issues.

(3) Officers. Management of the conference shall be vested in the officers of the conference, an executive committee, and a board of directors.

(A) The officers of the conference shall be:

(i) the president, president-elect, immediate past president, secretary, and treasurer, who shall be elected at large; and

(ii) one vice-president elected from each appellate court district.

(B) The executive committee shall consist of the officers of the conference and an executive secretary.

(C) The board of directors shall consist of the executive committee and a member elected from each judicial circuit.

(D) There shall be an annual meeting of the conference.

(E) Between annual meetings of the conference, the affairs of the conference shall be managed by the executive committee.

(4) Authority. The conference may adopt governance documents, the provisions of which shall not be inconsistent with this rule.

(b) Conference of Circuit Court Judges.

(1) Organization. There shall be a "Conference of Circuit Court Judges of Florida," consisting of the active and retired circuit judges of the several judicial circuits of the state, excluding retired judges practicing law.

(2) Purpose. The purpose of the conference shall be:

(A) the betterment of the judicial system of the state;

(B) the improvement of procedure and practice in the several courts;

(C) to conduct conferences and institutes for continuing judicial education and to provide forums in which the circuit court judges of Florida may meet and discuss mutual problems and solutions;

(D) to provide input to the Unified Committee on Judicial Compensation on judicial compensation and benefit issues, and to assist the judicial branch in soliciting support and resources on these issues;

(E) to report to the Florida Supreme Court recommendations as the conference may have concerning the improvement of procedure and practice in the several courts;

(F) to confer with the Florida Supreme Court regarding concerns the conference may have concerning the laws of this state affecting the administration of justice; and

(G) to provide to the Florida Legislature recommendations as the conference may have concerning laws of this state affecting the administration of justice.

(3) Officers. Management of the conference shall be vested in the officers of the conference, an executive committee, and a board of directors.

(A) The officers of the conference shall be the chair, chair-elect, secretary, and treasurer.

(B) The executive committee shall consist of the officers of the conference and such other members as the conference shall determine.

(C) The board of directors shall consist of the executive committee and membership in one shall be identical to membership of the other.

(D) There shall be an annual meeting of the conference.

(E) Between annual meetings of the conference, the affairs of the conference shall be managed by the executive committee.

(4) Authority. The conference may adopt governance documents, the provisions of which shall not be inconsistent with this rule.

(c) Conference of District Court of Appeal Judges.

(1) Creation. There shall be a "Florida Conference of District Court of Appeal Judges," consisting of the active and senior district court of appeal judges of the State of Florida.

(2) Purpose. The purpose of the conference shall be:

(A) the betterment of the judicial system of the state;

(B) the improvement of procedure and practice in the several courts;

(C) to conduct conferences and institutes for continuing judicial education and to provide forums in which the district court of appeal judges of Florida may meet and discuss mutual problems and solutions; and

(D) to provide input to the Unified Committee on Judicial Compensation on judicial compensation and benefit issues, and to assist the judicial branch in soliciting support and resources on these issues.

(3) Officers. Management of the conference shall be vested in the officers of the conference and an executive committee.

(A) The officers of the conference shall be the president, president-elect, and secretary-treasurer.

(B) The executive committee shall consist of the president and president-elect of the conference and the chief judge of each district court of appeal.

(C) There shall be an annual meeting of the conference.

(D) Between annual meetings of the conference, the affairs of the conference shall be managed by the executive committee.

(4) Authority. The conference may adopt governance documents, the provisions of which shall not be inconsistent with this rule.

Editor's Notes: As adopted, subdivision (c)(3) includes subdivisions (D) and (E), which the editors have redesignated as current (C) and (D), respectively.

RULE 2.225. JUDICIAL MANAGEMENT COUNCIL

(a) Creation and Responsibilities. There is hereby created the Judicial Management Council of Florida, which shall meet at least quarterly, and be charged with the following responsibilities:

(1) identifying potential crisis situations affecting the judicial branch and developing strategy to timely and effectively address them;

(2) identifying and evaluating information that would assist in improving the performance and effectiveness of the judicial branch (for example, information including, but not limited to, internal operations for cash flow and budget performance, and statistical information by court and type of cases for (i) number of cases filed, (ii) aged inventory of cases — the number and age of cases pending, (iii) time to disposition — the percentage of cases disposed or otherwise resolved within established time frames, and (iv) clearance rates — the number of outgoing cases as a percentage of the number of incoming cases);

(3) developing and monitoring progress relating to long-range planning for the judicial branch;

(4) reviewing the charges of the various court and Florida Bar commissions and committees, recommending consolidation or revision of the commissions and committees, and recommending a method for the coordination of the work of those bodies based on the proposed revisions; and

(5) addressing issues brought to the council by the supreme court.

(b) Referrals. The chief justice and the supreme court shall consider referring significant new issues or problems with implications for judicial branch policy to the Judicial Management Council prior to the creation of any new committees.

(c) Supreme Court Action on Recommendations by the Judicial Management Council. The supreme court may take any or all of the following actions on recommendations made by the Judicial Management Council:

(1) adopt the recommendation of the council in whole or in part, with or without conditions, including but not limited to:

(A) directing that action be taken to influence or change administrative policy, management practices, rules, or programs that are the subject of the recommendations;

(B) including the recommendation in the judicial branch's legislative agenda or budget requests;

(2) refer specific issues or questions back to the council for further study or alternative recommendations;

(3) reject the recommendation or decision in whole or in part;

(4) refer the recommendation to other entities, such as the Florida Legislature, the governor, the cabinet, executive branch agencies, or The Florida Bar, as the supreme court deems appropriate; or

(5) take alternative action.

(d) Membership.

(1) The council shall consist of 15 voting members, including the chief justice, who shall chair the council, an additional justice of the supreme court, representatives from each level of court, and public members.

(2) All voting members shall be appointed by the supreme court. Each member, other than the chief justice, will initially be appointed for a 2- or 4- year term, with the terms staggered to ensure continuity and experience on the council and for 4-year terms thereafter.

(3) The state courts administrator shall be a nonvoting member. The council may request other nonvoting persons to participate on an as-needed temporary basis to gain expertise and experience in certain issues on review.

(e) Staff Support and Funding. The Office of the State Courts Administrator shall provide primary staff support to the Judicial Management Council. Adequate staffing and other resources shall be made available to the Office of the State Courts Administrator to ensure the effective and efficient completion of tasks assigned to the Judicial Management Council. Sufficient resources shall also be provided for meetings of the Judicial Management Council and its committees or subcommittees, and other expenses necessary to the satisfactory completion of its work.

RULE 2.230. TRIAL COURT BUDGET COMMISSION

(a) Purpose. The purpose of this rule is to establish a Trial Court Budget Commission that will have the responsibility for developing and overseeing the administration of trial court budgets in a manner which ensures equity and fairness in state funding among the 20 judicial circuits.

(b) Responsibilities. The Trial Court Budget Commission is charged with specific responsibility to:

(1) establish budgeting and funding policies and procedures consistent with judicial branch plans and policies, directions from the supreme court, and in consideration of input from the Commission on Trial Court Performance and Accountability and other supreme court committees and from the Florida Conference of Circuit Court Judges and the Florida Conference of County Court Judges;

(2) make recommendations to the supreme court on the trial court component of the annual judicial branch budget request;

(3) advocate for the trial court component of the annual judicial branch budget request and associated statutory changes;

(4) make recommendations to the supreme court on funding allocation formulas and budget implementation and criteria as well as associated accountability mechanisms based on actual legislative appropriations;

(5) monitor trial court expenditure trends and revenue collections to identify unanticipated budget problems and to ensure the efficient use of resources;

(6) recommend statutory and rule changes related to trial court budgets;

(7) develop recommended responses to findings on financial audits and reports from the Supreme Court Inspector General, Auditor General, Office of Program Policy Analysis and Government Accountability, and other governmental entities charged with auditing responsibilities regarding trial court budgeting when appropriate;

(8) recommend to the supreme court trial court budget reductions required by the legislature;

(9) identify potential additional sources of revenue for the trial courts;

(10) recommend to the supreme court legislative pay plan issues for trial court personnel, except the

commission shall not make recommendations as to pay or benefits for judges; and

(11) request input from the Commission on Trial Court Performance and Accountability on recommendations from that commission that may impact the trial court budget or require funding.

(c) Operational Procedures. The Trial Court Budget Commission will establish operating procedures necessary to carry out its responsibilities as outlined in subdivision (b), subject to final approval by the supreme court. These procedures shall include:

(1) a method for ensuring input from interested constituencies, including the chief judges and trial court administrators of the trial courts, other members of the trial court judiciary, the Judicial Management Council, the Commission on Trial Court Performance and Accountability, and other judicial branch committees and commissions; and

(2) a method for appeal of the decisions of the Trial Court Budget Commission. Appeals may be made only by a chief judge on behalf of a circuit. Appeals may be heard only by the Trial Court Budget Commission unless the appeal is based on the failure of the commission to adhere to its operating procedures, in which case the appeal may be made to the supreme court.

(d) Action by Supreme Court or Chief Justice on Recommendations of Trial Court Budget Commission. The supreme court or chief justice, as appropriate, may take any or all of the following actions on recommendations made by the Trial Court Budget Commission:

(1) The adoption of the recommendations of the commission made in accordance with the discharge of its responsibilities listed in subdivision (b) in whole.

(2) The adoption of the recommendations in part and referral of specific issues or questions back to the commission for further study or alternative recommendations.

(e) Membership and Organization. The Trial Court Budget Commission will be composed of 21

voting members appointed by the chief justice who will represent the interests of the trial courts generally rather than the individual interests of a particular circuit or division. The respective presidents of the Conference of Circuit Court Judges, and the Conference of County Court Judges, and the chair of the Commission on Trial Court Performance and Accountability shall serve as ex officio nonvoting members of the Commission. The chief justice will make appointments to ensure that the broad interests of the trial courts are represented by including members who have experience in different divisions, who have expertise in court operations or administrative matters, and who offer geographic, racial, ethnic, and gender diversity.

(1) The membership must include 14 trial court judges and 7 trial court administrators.

(2) The chief justice will appoint 1 member to serve as chair and 1 member to serve as vice chair, each for a 2-year term.

(3) A supreme court justice will be appointed by the chief justice to serve as supreme court liaison.

(4) No circuit will have more than 2 members on the commission.

(5) The original members of the commission will be appointed as follows:

(A) 7 members shall be appointed for a 2-year term;

(B) 7 members shall be appointed for a 4-year term; and

(C) 7 members shall be appointed for one 6-year term.

All subsequent members will each be appointed for one 6-year term. In the event of a vacancy, the chief justice will appoint a new member to serve for the remainder of the departing member's term.

(6) The commission may establish subcommittees as necessary to satisfactorily carry out its responsi-

bilities. Subcommittees may make recommendations only to the commission as a whole. The chair of the commission may appoint a non-commission member to serve on a subcommittee.

(f) Staff Support and Funding. The Office of the State Courts Administrator will provide primary staff support to the commission. Adequate staffing and resources will be made available to the Office of the State Courts Administrator to ensure the commission is able to fulfill its responsibilities as outlined in the rule. Sufficient resources will also be provided for the commission and its subcommittees to meet and otherwise complete its work.

RULE 2.235. DISTRICT COURT OF APPEAL BUDGET COMMISSION

(a) Purpose. The purpose of this rule is to establish a District Court of Appeal Budget Commission with responsibility for developing and overseeing the administration of district court budgets in a manner which ensures equity and fairness in state funding among the 5 districts.

(b) Responsibilities. The District Court of Appeal Budget Commission is charged with specific responsibility to:

(1) establish budgeting and funding policies and procedures consistent with judicial branch plans and policies, directions from the supreme court, and in consideration of input from the Commission on District Court of Appeal Performance and Accountability, and other supreme court committees;

(2) make recommendations to the supreme court on a unitary district court component of the annual judicial branch budget request;

(3) advocate for the district court component of the annual judicial branch budget request;

(4) make recommendations to the supreme court on funding allocation formulas and/or criteria as well as associated accountability mechanisms based on actual legislative appropriations;

(5) monitor district court expenditure trends and revenue collections to identify unanticipated budget problems and to ensure the efficient use of resources;

(6) recommend statutory and rule changes related to district court budgets;

(7) develop recommended responses to findings on financial audits and reports from the Supreme Court Inspector General, Auditor General, Office of Program Policy Analysis and Government Accountability, and other governmental entities charged with auditing responsibilities regarding district court budgeting when appropriate;

(8) recommend to the supreme court district court budget reductions required by the legislature;

(9) identify potential additional sources of revenue for the district courts;

(10) recommend to the supreme court legislative pay plan issues for district court personnel, except the commission shall not make recommendations as to pay or benefits for judges; and

(11) request input from the Commission on District Court of Appeal Performance and Accountability on recommendations from that commission that may impact the district court budget or require funding.

(c) Operational Procedures. The District Court of Appeal Budget Commission will establish operating procedures necessary to carry out its responsibilities as outlined in subdivision (b), subject to final approval by the supreme court. These procedures shall include:

(1) a method for ensuring input from interested constituencies, including the chief judges, marshals, and clerks of the district courts, other members of the district court judiciary, the Judicial Management Council, the Commission on District Court of Appeal Performance and Accountability, and other judicial branch committees and commissions; and

(2) a method for appeal of the decisions of the District Court of Appeal Budget Commission. Appeals may be made only by a chief judge on behalf of the district. Appeals may be heard only by the District Court of Appeal Budget Commission unless the appeal is based on the failure of the commission to adhere to its operating procedures, in which case the appeal may be made to the supreme court.

(d) Action by Supreme Court or Chief Justice on Recommendations of the District Court of Appeal Budget Commission. The supreme court or chief justice, as appropriate, may take any or all of the following actions on recommendations made by the District Court of Appeal Budget Commission:

(1) The adoption of the recommendations of the commission made in accordance with the discharge of its responsibilities listed in subdivision (b) in whole.

(2) The adoption of the recommendations in part and referral of specific issues or questions back to the commission for further study or alternative recommendations.

(e) Membership and Organization. The District Court of Appeal Budget Commission will be composed of 10 voting members appointed by the chief justice who will represent the interests of the district courts generally rather than the individual interests of a particular district.

(1) The membership shall include the chief judge of each district court of appeal, who shall serve for his or her term as chief judge. The membership shall also include one additional judge from each district court of appeal, appointed by the chief justice, with advice from each chief judge. The marshal of each district court of appeal shall serve as a nonvoting member. Ex officio nonvoting members shall also include the chairs of the District Court of Appeal Performance and Accountability Commission and the Appellate Court Technology Committee, and the president of the District Court of Appeal Judges Conference.

(2) The chief justice will appoint 1 member to serve as chair and 1 member to serve as vice chair, each for a four-year term, or until the member's term on the commission expires.

(3) The commission may establish subcommittees as necessary to satisfactorily carry out its responsibilities. Subcommittees may make recommendations only to the commission as a whole. The chair of the commission may appoint a non-commission member to serve on a subcommittee.

(4) Effective July 1, 2013, the commission shall be reconstituted with staggered terms for voting mem-

bers, as follows: (A) The chief judge of each district will be appointed for his or her term as chief judge. (B) The additional judge from each odd-numbered district will be appointed for a four-year term. (C) The additional judge from each even-numbered district will be appointed for a two-year term, and thereafter to four-year terms. (D) Each nonvoting member will serve so long as he or she continues to hold the office which entitles him or her to membership on the commission.

(f) Staff Support and Funding. The Office of the State Courts Administrator will provide primary staff support to the commission. Adequate staffing and resources will be made available to the Office of the State Courts Administrator to ensure the commission is able to fulfill its responsibilities as outlined in this rule. Sufficient resources will also be provided for the commission and its subcommittees to meet and otherwise complete its work.

RULE 2.236. FLORIDA COURTS TECHNOLOGY COMMISSION

(a) Purpose. The purpose of this rule is to establish a Florida Courts Technology Commission with responsibility for overseeing, managing, and directing the development and use of technology within the judicial branch under the direction of the supreme court as specified in this rule. For the purpose of this rule, the term "judicial branch" does not include The Florida Bar, the Florida Board of Bar Examiners, or the Judicial Qualifications Commission.

(b) Responsibilities. The Florida Courts Technology Commission is charged with specific responsibility to:

(1) make recommendations to the supreme court on all matters of technology policy impacting the judicial branch to allow the supreme court to establish technology policy in the branch;

(2) make recommendations to the supreme court regarding policies for public access to electronic court records;

(3) make recommendations to the supreme court about the relative priorities of various technology

projects within the judicial branch so that the supreme court can establish priorities. The commission should coordinate with the Trial Court Budget Commission and District Court of Appeal Budget Commission to secure funds for allocation of those priorities;

(4) direct and establish priorities for the work of all technology committees in the judicial branch, including the Appellate Court Technology Committee, and review and approve recommendations made by any court committee concerning technology matters or otherwise implicating court technology policy;

(5) establish, periodically review, and update technical standards for technology used and to be used in the judicial branch to receive, manage, maintain, use, secure, and distribute court records by electronic means, consistent with the technology policies established by the supreme court. These standards shall be coordinated with the strategic plans of the judicial branch, rules of procedure, applicable law, and directions from the supreme court, and shall incorporate input from the public, clerks of court, supreme court committees and commissions, and other groups involved in the application of current technology to the judicial branch;

(6) create procedures whereby courts and clerks and other applicable entities can apply for approval of new systems, or modifications to existing systems, that involve the application of technology to the receipt, management, maintenance, use, securing, and distribution of court records within the judicial branch, and between the public and the judicial branch;

(7) evaluate all such applications to determine whether they comply with the technology policies established by the supreme court and the procedures and standards created pursuant to this rule, and approve those applications deemed to be effective and found to be in compliance;

(8) develop and maintain security policies that must be utilized to ensure the integrity and availability of court technology systems and related data;

(9) ensure principles of accessibility are met for all court technology projects, with consideration and application of the requirements of the Americans with Disabilities Act of 1990 and any other applicable state or federal disability laws;

(10) ensure that the technology utilized in the judicial branch is capable of required integration;

(11) periodically review and evaluate all approved technology in the judicial branch to determine its adherence to current supreme court technology policies and standards;

(12) review annual and periodic reports on the status of court technology systems and proposals for technology improvements and innovation throughout the judicial branch;

(13) recommend statutory and rule changes or additions relating to court technology and the receipt, maintenance, management, use, securing, and distribution of court records by electronic means;

(14) identify technology issues that require attention in the judicial branch upon:

(A) referral from the chief justice;

(B) referral from the supreme court; or

(C) identification by the Florida Courts Technology Commission on its own initiative based on recommendations of the public, commission members, judges, justice system partners, The Florida Bar, clerks of court, the Florida Legislature (either informally or through the passage of legislation), the Governor, the cabinet, or executive branch agencies; and

(15) coordinate proposed amendments to rules of court procedure and judicial administration necessary to effectuate the commission's charge with appropriate Florida Bar rules committees.

If a program, system, or application is found not to comply with the policies established by the supreme court or the standards and procedures established by the commission, the commission may require that it be terminated or modified or subject to such conditions as the commission deems appropriate.

(c) Operational Procedures. The Florida Courts Technology Commission shall establish operating procedures necessary to carry out its responsibilities as outlined in subdivision (b), subject to final approval by the supreme court. These procedures shall include:

(1) a method for ensuring input from all interested constituencies in the state of Florida;

(2) a method for monitoring the development of new court technology projects, reviewing reports on new technology projects, and reviewing the annual reports;

(3) a method whereby courts and clerks and other applicable entities can apply for approval of new technology systems or applications, or modifications to existing systems or applications, that affect the receipt, management, maintenance, use, securing, and distribution of court records;

(4) a system to evaluate all applications for new or modified technology systems to determine whether they comply with the policies and technical standards established by the supreme court and the procedures created pursuant to this rule, and are otherwise appropriate to implement in the judicial branch;

(5) a process for making decisions on all applications for new or modified technology systems and communicating those decisions to interested parties. If an application is found to comply with technology policies and standards, the commission may approve the application and its written approval shall authorize the applicant to proceed. For all applications that are not approved, the commission shall assist the applicant in remedying any deficiencies that the commission identifies;

(6) a method to monitor all technology programs, systems, and applications used in the judicial branch to ensure that such programs, systems, and applications are operating in accordance with the technology policies established by the supreme court and technical standards established by the commission. The commission may ask any operator of a program, system, or application to appear before it for examination into whether the program, system, or application complies with technology policies and standards;

(7) a process to conduct the limited, short-term work of the commission through work groups that it may constitute from time to time. Work groups may make recommendations to the commission as a whole. The chair of the commission may appoint non-commission members to serve on any work group; and

(8) a process to conduct substantial work of the commission requiring long-term commitment through subcommittees. Subcommittees may make recommendations to the commission as a whole. The chair of the commission may appoint non-commission members to serve on any subcommittee.

(d) Action by Supreme Court or Chief Justice on Recommendations of or Decisions by Florida Courts Technology Commission. The supreme court or chief justice, as appropriate, may take any of the following actions on recommendations or decisions made by the Florida Courts Technology Commission:

(1) Adopt the recommendation or decision of the commission in whole or in part, with or without conditions.

(2) Refer specific issues or questions back to the commission for further study or alternative recommendations.

(3) Reject the recommendation or decision in whole or in part.

(4) Take alternative action.

(e) Membership and Organization.

(1) The Florida Courts Technology Commission shall be composed of 25 voting members appointed by the chief justice after consultation with the court. All members shall represent the interests of the public and of Florida courts generally rather than the separate interests of any particular district, circuit, county, division, or other organization. The membership shall include members who have experience in different divisions of courts, in court operations, and in using technology in court for case processing, management, and administrative purposes, and shall provide geographic, racial, ethnic, gender, and other diversity.

(2) The membership shall include 2 district court judges, 5 circuit court judges (1 of whom must be a chief judge), 2 county court judges, 3 court administrators, 3 court technology officers, 4 clerks of court (1 of whom must be a clerk of an appellate court), 4 members of The Florida Bar (1 of whom must be a member of the Board of Governors of The Florida Bar), and 2 members of the public at large.

(3) The members of the commission who are judicial officers, court technology officers, and court administrators must constitute a majority of the commission and must constitute a majority of any quorum at all meetings of the commission.

(4) A supreme court justice shall be appointed by the chief justice to serve as supreme court liaison to the commission.

(5) Each member will be initially appointed for a 1-, 2-, or 3-year term, with the terms staggered to ensure continuity and experience on the commission and for three year terms thereafter. Retention and reappointment of each member will be at the discretion of the chief justice.

(6) The chief justice shall appoint 1 member to serve as chair for a two-year term.

(f) Schedule of Reports. The Florida Courts Technology Commission shall prepare an annual report of its activities, which shall include its recommendations for changes or additions to the technology policies or standards of Florida courts, its recommendations for setting or changing priorities among the programs within the responsibility of the commission to assist with budget resources available, its recommendations for changes to rules, statutes, or regulations that affect technology in Florida courts and the work of the commission. The report also shall include recommendations of the Appellate Court Technology Committee that implicate court technology policy and the action taken on those recommendations by the commission. This report shall be submitted to the supreme court on April 1 of each year.

(g) Appellate Court Technology Committee.

(1) Purpose. The purpose of this subdivision is to establish the Appellate Court Technology Committee

as a standing committee of the Florida Courts Technology Commission responsible for providing technical guidance and consultation to the commission regarding information systems development and operational policies and procedures relating to automation in the district courts of appeal.

(2) Responsibilities. The Appellate Court Technology Committee is charged with specific responsibility to:

(A) coordinate with and provide advice to the Florida Courts Technology Commission regarding the development of standards and policies for implementing new technologies, system security, public access to district court information, and system support;

(B) develop, recommend, and implement policy and procedures consistent with the overall policy of the supreme court relating to technology issues affecting the district courts of appeal;

(C) recommend and coordinate the purchase and upgrade of hardware and software in relation to the district courts' office automation systems and networks;

(D) oversee and direct expenditures of designated state court system trust funds for technology needs in the district courts;

(E) promote orientation and education programs on technology and its effective utilization in the district court environment;

(F) ensure principles of accessibility are met for all court technology projects, with consideration and application of the requirements of the Americans with Disabilities Act of 1990 and any other applicable state or federal disability laws;

(G) propose amendments to rules of court procedure and judicial administration necessary to effectuate the committee's charge, after coordination with appropriate Florida Bar rules committees; and

(H) identify budget issues and funding sources and coordinate with the District Court of Appeal Budget

Commission on recommendations requiring additional funding or resources for implementation in the district courts of appeal.

(3) Membership and Terms.

(A) The chief justice will select the chair of the committee from among the judges of the district courts, with input from the chief judges.

(B) The chief judges of the remaining district courts will designate a representative from each of their courts to serve as member of the committee.

(C) The chair and members will serve 3-year terms. Retention and reappointment of the chair will be at the discretion of the chief justice. Retention and reappointment of the representative from each district court will be at the discretion of the district court chief judge.

(4) **Commission Approval and Reporting of Policy Recommendations.** Committee recommendations that implicate court technology policy must be reviewed and approved by the commission. The commission will report the committee's policy recommendations and the action taken on them by the commission to the supreme court. The committee may submit to the court a companion report on its recommendations, supporting or opposing the action taken by the commission.

(h) **Staff Support and Funding.** The Office of the State Courts Administrator shall provide primary staff support to the Florida Courts Technology Commission and the Appellate Court Technology Committee. Adequate staffing and resources shall be made available by the Office of the State Courts Administrator to ensure that the commission and committee are able to fulfill their responsibilities under this rule.

RULE 2.240. DETERMINATION OF NEED FOR ADDITIONAL JUDGES

(a) **Purpose.** The purpose of this rule is to set forth uniform criteria used by the supreme court in determining the need for additional judges, except supreme court justices, and the necessity for decreasing the number of judges, pursuant to article V, section 9, Florida Constitution. These criteria form the primary basis for the supreme court's determination of need for additional judges. Unforeseen developments, however, may have an impact upon the judiciary resulting in needs which cannot be foreseen or predicted by statistical projections. The supreme court, therefore, may also consider any additional information found by it to be relevant to the process. In establishing criteria for the need for additional appellate court judges, substantial reliance has been placed on the findings and recommendations of the Commission on District Court of Appeal Performance and Accountability. *See In re Report of the Comm'n on Dist. Court of Appeal Performance and Accountability—Rule of Judicial Admin. 2.035*, 933 So.2d 1136 (Fla. 2006).

(b) **Criteria.**

(1) **Trial Courts.**

(A) Assessment of judicial need at the trial court level is based primarily upon the application of case weights to circuit and county court caseload statistics supplied to the Office of the State Courts Administrator by the clerks of the circuit courts, pursuant to rule 2.245, Florida Rules of Judicial Administration. Such case weights provide a quantified measure of judicial time spent on case-related activity, translating judicial caseloads into judicial workload by factoring in the relative complexity by case type in the following manner:

(i) The circuit court case weights are applied to forecasted case filings, which include circuit criminal (includes felony, drug court, and worthless check cases), circuit civil (includes matters involving claims of $15,000.01 and above), family (includes domestic relations, juvenile dependency, and juvenile delinquency cases), and probate (includes guardianship, mental health, and trust cases).

(ii) The county court case weights are applied to forecasted filings, which include county criminal (includes misdemeanor, violations of county and municipal ordinance, worthless check, driving under the influence, and other criminal traffic cases), and county civil (includes small claims, matters involving claims ranging from $5,000.01 to $15,000, landlord-tenant, and civil traffic infraction cases).

(B) Other factors may be utilized in the determination of the need for one or more additional judges. These factors include, but are not limited to, the following:

(i) The availability and use of county court judges in circuit court.

(ii) The availability and use of senior judges to serve on a particular court.

(iii) The availability and use of magistrates and hearing officers.

(iv) The extent of use of alternative dispute resolution.

(v) The number of jury trials.

(vi) Foreign language interpretations.

(vii) The geographic size of a circuit, including travel times between courthouses in a particular jurisdiction.

(viii) Law enforcement activities in the court's jurisdiction, including any substantial commitment of additional resources for state attorneys, public defenders, and local law enforcement.

(ix) The availability and use of case-related support staff and case management policies and practices.

(x) Caseload trends.

(C) The Commission on Trial Court Performance and Accountability shall review the trial court workload trends and case weights and consider adjustments no less than every five years.

(2) District Courts of Appeal.

(A) The criteria for determining the need to certify the need for increasing or decreasing the number of judges on a district court of appeal shall include the following factors:

(i) workload factors to be considered include: trends in case filings; trends in changes in case mix;

trends in the backlog of cases ready for assignment and disposition; trends in the relative weight of cases disposed on the merits per judge; and changes in statutes, rules of court, and case law that directly or indirectly impact judicial workload.

(ii) efficiency factors to be considered include: a court's ability to stay current with its caseload, as indicated by measurements such as trend in clearance rate; trends in a court's percentage of cases disposed within the time standards set forth in the Rules of Judicial Administration and explanation/justification for cases not resolved within the time standards; and a court's utilization of resources, case management techniques and technologies to maximize the efficient adjudication of cases, research of legal issues, and preparation and distribution of decisions.

(iii) effectiveness factors to be considered include the extent to which each judge has adequate time to: thoroughly research legal issues, review briefs and memoranda of law, participate in court conferences on pending cases, hear and dispose of motions, and prepare correspondence, orders, judgments and opinions; expedite appropriate cases; prepare written opinions when warranted; develop, clarify, and maintain consistency in the law within that district; review all decisions rendered by the court; perform administrative duties relating to the court; and participate in the administration of the justice system through work in statewide committees.

(iv) professionalism factors to be considered include: the extent to which judges report that they have time to participate, including teaching, in education programs designed to increase the competency and efficiency of the judiciary and justice system as well as the competency of lawyers; provide guidance and instruction for the professional development of court support staff; and participate in appropriate activities of the legal profession at both the state and local levels to improve the relationship between the bench and bar, to enhance lawyer professionalism, and to improve the administration of justice.

(B) The court will presume that there is a need for an additional appellate court judgeship in any district for which a request is made and where the relative weight of cases disposed on the merits per judge would have exceeded the weighted case disposition threshold after application of the proposed additional judge(s).

(i) The relative weight of cases disposed on the merits shall be determined based upon case disposition statistics supplied to the state courts administrator by the clerks of the district courts of appeal, multiplied by the relative case weights established pursuant to subdivision (b)(2)(B)(ii), and divided by 100.

(ii) The Commission on District Court of Appeal Performance and Accountability shall review the workload trends of the district courts of appeal and consider adjustments in the relative case weights and the weighted case disposition threshold every four years. Any such recommended adjustment shall be subject to the approval of the supreme court.

(c) Additional Trial Court Workload Factors. Because summary statistics reflective of the above criteria do not fully measure judicial workload, the supreme court will receive and consider, among other things, information about the time to perform and volume of the following activities, which also comprise the judicial workload of a particular jurisdiction:

(1) review appellate court decisions;

(2) research legal issues;

(3) review briefs and memoranda of law;

(4) participate in court conferences on pending cases;

(5) hear and dispose of motions;

(6) prepare correspondence, orders, judgments, and decisional opinions;

(7) review presentence investigative reports and predispositional reports in delinquency and dependency cases;

(8) review petitions and motions for post-conviction relief;

(9) perform administrative duties relating to the court;

(10) participate in meetings with those involved in the justice system; and

(11) participate in educational programs designed to increase the competency and efficiency of the judiciary.

(d) Certification Process. The process by which certification of the need to increase or decrease the number of judges shall include:

(1) The state courts administrator will distribute a compilation of summary statistics and projections to each chief judge at a time designated by the chief justice.

(2) Each chief judge shall submit to the chief justice a request for any increase or decrease in the number of judges in accordance with the following:

(A) Trial Courts. Each chief judge will then consider these criteria, additional workload factors, and summary statistics, and submit to the chief justice a request for any increases or decreases under article V, section 9, of the Florida Constitution that the chief judge feels are required.

(B) District Courts. Each chief judge will then consider the criteria of this rule and the summary statistics; if a new judge is requested, the chief judge shall prepare a report showing the need for a new judge based upon the application of the criteria in this rule.

(i) Any request for a new district court judge shall be submitted to the District Court of Appeal Budget Commission for review and approval.

(ii) The chief judge of a district court of appeal shall submit the report showing the need together with the approval of the District Court of Appeal Budget Commission to the chief justice.

(3) The chief justice and the state courts administrator may then confer with the chief judge and other

representatives of the court submitting the request as well as representatives of The Florida Bar and the public to gather additional information and clarification about the need in the particular jurisdiction.

(4) The chief justice will submit recommendations to the supreme court, which will thereafter certify to the legislature its findings and recommendations concerning such need.

(5) The supreme court, in conjunction with the certification process under this rule, shall also consider the necessity for increasing, decreasing, or redefining appellate districts and judicial circuits as required by article V, section 9, of the Florida Constitution and as set forth in Florida Rule of Judicial Administration 2.241.

Court Commentary

1983 Adoption. Article V, section 9, of the Florida Constitution authorizes the establishment, by rule, of uniform criteria for the determination of the need for additional judges, except supreme court justices, the necessity for decreasing the number of judges and for increasing, decreasing, or redefining appellate districts and judicial circuits. Each year since the adoption of article V in 1972, this court, pursuant to section 9, has certified its determination of need to the legislature based upon factors and criteria set forth in our certification decisions. This rule is intended to set forth criteria and workload factors previously developed, adopted, and used in this certification process, as summarized and specifically set forth in *In re Certificate of Judicial Manpower*, 428 So. 2d 229 (Fla. 1983); *In re Certificate of Judicial Manpower*, 396 So. 2d 172 (Fla. 1981); and *In re Certification*, 370 So. 2d 365 (Fla. 1979).

2004 Amendment. Subdivision (b)(2) was amended to provide more specific criteria and workload factors to be used in determining the need for increasing or decreasing the number of judges on the District Courts of Appeal. In addition, the caseload level at which the court will presume that there is a need for an additional appellate judge has been increased from 250 to 350 filings per judge.

2006 Amendment. Subdivision (a) is amended to be consistent with the 2006 adoption of rule 2.036 relating to the criteria for determining the necessity and for increasing, decreasing, or redefining appellate districts and judicial circuits, pursuant to article V, section 9, Florida Constitution. The Court adopts the Commission on District Court of Appeal Performance and Accountability's conclusion that a single case filing threshold is insufficient to capture the intricacies that make up judicial workload in the district courts. The Commission's alternative to the 350-filings-per-judge threshold is a weighted case dispositions per judge, which the Commission determined to be a meaningful measure of judicial workload.

The relative weighted caseload is determined by surveying a representative sample of judges on the relative degree of judicial effort put into each category of cases based upon an agreed typical case having a value of 100. Each category was assigned a relative weight number based upon the statewide average of the weight calculated through the survey. These weights were then applied to each court's dispositions on the merits to determine the weighted caseload value and divided by 100.

This approach accommodates the important distinction between the number of cases filed and the judicial effort required to dispose of those cases. While the number of cases continues to increase, trends in the types of cases filed have dramatically changed the nature of the work that the district court judges handle. The weighted caseload approach not only accommodates the differences in types of cases by measuring their relative workload demands for judges, but it also accommodates the work performed by legal support staff.

Subdivision (b)(2)(B) establishes a presumption that the relative weight of cases disposed on the merits should fall below 280 per judge. Chief judges must consider the impact that the addition of a judge would have on this measure when applied to their courts' dispositions on the merits for the previous year.

Every four years the Commission will measure the relative judicial effort associated with the cases disposed on the merits for the year immediately preceding. This will be accomplished by asking a representative sample of judges to approximate the relative weight of cases in relation to a mid-ranked case. The resulting weights will then be applied to each court's dispositions on the merits to determine the weighted caseload value per judge.

2013 Amendment. Subdivision (d)(5) was added to ensure the certification process under rule 2.240(d) is conducted in conjunction with the related process for determinations regarding increases, decreases, or redefinition of appellate districts and judicial circuits under Florida Rule of Judicial Administration 2.241.

RULE 2.241. DETERMINATION OF THE NECESSITY TO INCREASE, DECREASE, OR REDEFINE JUDICIAL CIRCUITS AND APPELLATE DISTRICTS

(a) **Purpose.** The purpose of this rule is to establish uniform criteria for the supreme court's determination of the necessity for increasing, decreasing, or redefining judicial circuits and appellate districts as required by article V, section 9, of the Florida Constitution. This rule also provides for an assessment committee and a certification process to assist the court in certifying to the legislature its findings and recommendations concerning such need.

(b) **Certification Process.** A certification process shall be completed in conjunction with the supreme court's annual determination regarding the need for judges under Florida Rule of Judicial Administration 2.240(d) and in accordance with the following:

(1) The supreme court shall certify a necessity to increase, decrease, or redefine judicial circuits and appellate districts when it determines that the judicial process is adversely affected by circumstances that present a compelling need for the certified change.

(2) The supreme court may certify a necessity to increase, decrease, or redefine judicial circuits and appellate districts when it determines that the judicial process would be improved significantly by the certified change.

(3) The state courts administrator will distribute a compilation of summary statistics and projections to each chief judge at a time designated by the chief justice.

(4) Each chief judge shall consider criteria as may apply under rules 2.241(c) and 2.241(d), as well as any other relevant factors, and shall inform the chief justice of any perceived need to increase, decrease, or redefine the state's judicial circuits or appellate districts.

(5) Having been advised in these matters by the chief justice and taking into consideration other relevant factors, the supreme court, finding cause for further inquiry, may appoint an assessment committee to consider the capacity of the courts to effectively fulfill their constitutional and statutory responsibilities as well as any attendant need to increase, decrease, or redefine appellate districts and judicial circuits.

(6) If an assessment committee is appointed, the committee shall confer with the chief judges and other representatives of appellate districts and judicial circuits, district court of appeal and/or trial court budget commissions, The Florida Bar, and the public for purposes of gathering additional information regarding matters within its charge and shall submit written recommendations to the supreme court.

(7) The supreme court shall consider the assessment committee's recommendations within a time frame it deems appropriate.

(8) Whether or not an assessment committee is appointed, the supreme court shall balance the potential impact and disruption caused by changes in judicial circuits and appellate districts against the need to address circumstances that limit the quality and efficiency of, and public confidence in, the judicial process. Given the impact and disruption that can arise from any alteration in judicial structure, prior to recommending a change in judicial circuits or appellate districts, the supreme court shall consider less disruptive adjustments including, but not limited to, the addition of judges, the creation of branch locations, geographic or subject-matter divisions within judicial circuits or appellate districts, deployment of new technologies, and increased ratios of support staff per judge.

(c) **Criteria for Judicial Circuits.** The following criteria shall be considered when determining the necessity for increasing, decreasing, or redefining judicial circuits as required by article V, section 9, of the Florida Constitution:

(1) **Effectiveness.** Factors to be considered for this criterion include the extent to which each court:

(A) expedites appropriate cases;

(B) handles its workload in a manner permitting its judges to prepare written decisions when warranted;

(C) is capable of accommodating changes in statutes or case law impacting workload or court operations; and

(D) handles its workload in a manner permitting its judges to serve on committees for the judicial system.

(2) **Efficiency.** Factors to be considered for this criterion are the extent to which each court:

(A) stays current with its caseload, as indicated by measurements such as the clearance rate;

(B) adjudicates a high percentage of its cases within the time standards set forth in the Rules of Judicial Administration and has adequate procedures to ensure efficient, timely disposition of its cases; and

(C) uses its resources, case management techniques, and technologies to improve the efficient adjudication of cases, research of legal issues, and issuance of decisions.

(3) Access to Courts. Factors to be considered for this criterion are the extent to which:

(A) litigants, including self-represented litigants, have meaningful access consistent with due process; and

(B) decisions of a court are available in a timely and efficient manner.

(4) Professionalism. Factors to be considered for this criterion are the extent to which each court:

(A) handles workload issues in a manner permitting its judges adequate time and resources to participate in continuing judicial education and to stay abreast of the law in order to maintain a qualified judiciary;

(B) is capable of recruiting and retaining qualified staff; and

(C) affords staff adequate time to participate in continuing education and specialized training.

(5) Public Trust and Confidence. Factors to be considered for this criterion are the extent to which each court:

(A) handles workload in a manner permitting its judges adequate time for community involvement;

(B) affords access to open court and other public proceedings for the general public;

(C) fosters public trust and confidence given its geography and demographic composition; and

(D) attracts a diverse group of well-qualified applicants for judicial vacancies, including applicants from all counties within the circuit.

(6) Additional criteria. Such other factors as are regularly considered when making a determination

with respect to the need for additional judges under Florida Rule of Judicial Administration 2.240(b)(1) and (c).

(d) Criteria for District Courts. The following criteria shall be considered when determining the necessity for increasing, decreasing, or redefining appellate districts as required by article V, section 9, of the Florida Constitution:

(1) Effectiveness. Factors to be considered for this criterion are the extent to which each court:

(A) expedites appropriate cases;

(B) handles workload in a manner permitting its judges to prepare written opinions when warranted;

(C) functions in a collegial manner;

(D) handles workload in a manner permitting its judges to develop, clarify, and maintain consistency in the law within that district, including consistency between written opinions and per curiam affirmances without written opinions;

(E) handles its workload in a manner permitting its judges to harmonize decisions of their court with those of other district courts or to certify conflict when appropriate;

(F) handles its workload in a manner permitting its judges to have adequate time to review all decisions rendered by the court;

(G) is capable of accommodating changes in statutes or case law impacting workload or court operations; and

(H) handles its workload in a manner permitting its judges to serve on committees for the judicial system.

(2) Efficiency. Factors to be considered for this criterion are the extent to which each court:

(A) stays current with its caseload, as indicated by measurements such as the clearance rate;

(B) adjudicates a high percentage of its cases within the time standards set forth in the Rules of

Judicial Administration and has adequate procedures to ensure efficient, timely disposition of its cases; and

(C) uses its resources, case management techniques, and other technologies to improve the efficient adjudication of cases, research of legal issues, and preparation and distribution of decisions.

(3) Access to Appellate Review. Factors to be considered for this criterion are the extent to which:

(A) litigants, including self-represented litigants, have meaningful access to a district court for mandatory and discretionary review of cases, consistent with due process;

(B) litigants are afforded efficient access to the court for the filing of pleadings and for oral argument when appropriate; and

(C) orders and opinions of a court are available in a timely and efficient manner.

(4) Professionalism. Factors to be considered for this criterion are the extent to which each court:

(A) handles its workload in a manner permitting its judges adequate time and resources to participate in continuing judicial education opportunities and to stay abreast of the law in order to maintain a qualified judiciary;

(B) is capable of recruiting and retaining qualified staff; and

(C) affords staff adequate time to participate in continuing education and specialized training

(5) Public Trust and Confidence. Factors to be considered for this criterion are the extent to which each court:

(A) handles its workload in a manner permitting its judges adequate time for community involvement;

(B) provides adequate access to oral arguments and other public proceedings for the general public within its district;

(C) fosters public trust and confidence given its geography and demographic composition and;

(D) attracts diverse group of well-qualified applicants for judicial vacancies, including applicants from all circuits within the district.

(e) Results of determination. Only upon the supreme court's finding that a need exists for increasing, decreasing, or redefining appellate districts and judicial circuits, shall the court, acting prior to the next regular session of the legislature, certify to the legislature its findings and recommendations concerning such need.

Committee Notes

District Court of Appeal Workload and Jurisdiction Committee Notes 2006 Adoption. Article V, section 9 of the Florida constitution states that:

"The supreme court shall establish by rule uniform criteria for the determination of the need for additional judges except supreme court justices, the *necessity* for decreasing the number of judges and for increasing, decreasing or redefining appellate districts. If the supreme court finds that a *need* exists for . . . increasing, decreasing or redefining appellate districts . . . , it shall, prior to the next regular session of the legislature, certify to the legislature its findings and recommen dations concerning such need."

(Emphasis added.) Thus, the constitution uses only "need" when describing the uniform criteria for certifying additional judges, but uses both "necessity" and "need" when describing the uniform criteria for increasing, decreasing, or redefining appellate districts. The supreme court has never determined whether this language compels differing tests for the two certifications. Subdivision (c) of this rule uses the phrase "certify a necessity." The Committee on District Court of Appeal Workload and Jurisdiction determined that the two standards set forth in that subdivision recognize the supreme court's obligation to recommend a change to the structure of the district courts when circumstances reach the level of necessity that compels a change, but also recognize the court's discretion to recommend a change to the structure of the district courts when improvements are needed.

The criteria set forth in this rule are based on studies of the workload, jurisdiction, and performance of the appellate courts, and the work of the Committee on District Court of Appeal Workload and Jurisdiction in 2005. In establishing these criteria, substantial reliance was placed on empirical research conducted by judicial branch committees and on other statistical data concerning cases, caseloads, timeliness of case processing, and manner for disposition of cases, collected by the Office of the State Courts Administrator Office as required by section 25.075, Florida Statutes (2004), and Florida Rule of Judicial Administration 2.030(e)(2).

The workload and jurisdiction committee considered the impact of computer technology on appellate districts. It is clear that, at this time or in the future, technology can be deployed to allow litigants efficient access to a court for filing of pleadings and for participation in oral argument, and that it can expand the general public's access to the courts. It is possible that technology will substantially alter the appellate review process in the future and that appellate courts may find that technology permits or even requires different districting techniques. This rule was designed to allow these issues to be addressed by the assessment committee and the supreme court without mandating any specific approach.

The five basic criteria in subdivision (d) are not listed in any order of priority. Thus, for example, the workload and jurisdiction committee did not intend efficiency to be a more important criterion than engendering public trust and confidence.

Subdivision (d)(2)(A) recognizes that the court currently provides the legislature with an annual measurement of the appellate courts' "clearance rate," which is the ratio between the number of cases that are resolved during a fiscal year and the new cases that are filed during the same period. Thus, a clearance rate of one hundred percent reflects a court that is disposing of pending cases at approximately the same rate that new cases arrive. Given that other measurements may be selected in the future, the rule does not mandate sole reliance on this measurement.

Subdivision (d)(5)(E) recognizes that a district court's geographic territory may be so large that it limits or discourages applicants for judicial vacancies from throughout the district and creates the perception that a court's judges do not reflect the makeup of the territory.

Court Commentary

2013 Amendment. The rule has been amended so the supreme court's annual certification process will include an analysis of the need to increase, decrease, or redefine judicial circuits. The requirement for an assessment committee to analyze, once every eight years, the capacity of the district courts to fulfill their duties has been deleted. Instead, the chief judges of the trial and appellate courts will review annual statistics provided by the state courts administrator, along with the criteria set forth in the rule and any other relevant factors, and inform the chief justice of any perceived need. Taking these and other concerns into consideration, the supreme court may appoint an assessment committee to make further inquiry. If an assessment committee is appointed, the supreme court will consider the committee's recommendations and will certify to the legislature its own findings and recommendations concerning such need.

RULE 2.244. JUDICIAL COMPENSATION

(a) **Statement of Purpose.** The purpose of this rule is to set forth the official policy of the judicial branch of state government concerning the appropriate salary relationships between justices and judges at the various levels of the state courts system and the mechanism for advancing judicial compensation and benefits issues. Although ultimate discretion in establishing judicial compensation is vested in the Florida Legislature, the salary relationships referenced in this rule reflect the policy of the judicial branch when requesting adjustments to judicial salaries.

(b) **Annual Salaries.** The annual salary of a district court of appeal judge should be equal to 95 percent of the annual salary of a supreme court justice. The annual salary of a circuit court judge should be equal to 90 percent of the annual salary of a supreme court justice. The annual salary of a county court judge should be equal to 85 percent of the annual salary of a supreme court justice.

(c) **Unified Committee on Judicial Compensation.**

(1) **Creation.** There shall be created a Unified Committee on Judicial Compensation to address judicial pay and benefits issues.

(2) **Purpose.** The purpose of the Unified Committee on Judicial Compensation shall be to:

(A) develop and recommend to the supreme court judicial pay and benefits priorities; and

(B) advocate for judicial pay and benefits issues approved by the supreme court for inclusion in the annual judicial branch budget request.

(3) **Membership.** The membership shall include the chief justice of the supreme court, the presidents and presidents-elect of the Conference of District Court of Appeal Judges, the Conference of Circuit Court Judges, and the Conference of County Court Judges, and the chairs and vice-chairs of the District Court Budget Commission and the Trial Court Budget Commission.

(4) **Staffing.** The Office of the State Courts Administrator will provide primary staff support to the committee.

RULE 2.245. CASE REPORTING SYSTEM FOR TRIAL COURTS

(a) **Reporting.** The clerk of the circuit court shall report the activity of all cases before all courts within the clerk's jurisdiction to the supreme court in the manner and on the forms established by the office of the state courts administrator and approved by order of the court. In those jurisdictions where separate offices of the clerk of the circuit court and clerk of the county court have been established by law, the clerk of the circuit court shall report the activity of all cases before the circuit court, and the clerk of the county court shall report the activity of all cases before the county court.

(b) Uniform Case Numbering System.

(1) The clerk of the circuit court and the clerk of the county court, where that separate office exists, shall use the Uniform Case Numbering System. The uniform case number shall appear upon the case file, the docket and minute books (or their electronic equivalent), and the complaint.

(2) The office of the state courts administrator shall distribute to the respective clerks of the circuit and county courts appropriate instructions regarding the nature and use of the Uniform Case Numbering System.

RULE 2.250. TIME STANDARDS FOR TRIAL AND APPELLATE COURTS AND REPORTING REQUIREMENTS

(a) Time Standards. The following time standards are hereby established as a presumptively reasonable time period for the completion of cases in the trial and appellate courts of this state. It is recognized that there are cases that, because of their complexity, present problems that cause reasonable delays. However, most cases should be completed within the following time periods:

(1) Trial Court Time Standards.

(A) Criminal.

Felony—180 days (arrest to final disposition)

Misdemeanor—90 days (arrest to final disposition)

(B) Civil.

Jury cases—18 months (filing to final disposition)

Non-jury cases—12 months (filing to final disposition)

Small Claims—95 days (filing to final disposition)

(C) Domestic Relations.

Uncontested—90 days (filing to final disposition)

Contested—180 days filing to final disposition)

(D) Probate.

Uncontested, no federal estate tax return—12 months (from issuance of letters of administration to final discharge)

Uncontested, with federal estate tax return—12 months (from the return's due date to final discharge)

Contested—24 months (from filing to final discharge)

(E) Juvenile Delinquency.

Disposition hearing—120 days (filing of petition or child being taken into custody to hearing)

Disposition hearing (child detained)—36 days (date of detention to hearing)

(F) Juvenile Dependency.

Disposition hearing (child sheltered)—88 days (shelter hearing to disposition)

Disposition hearing (child not sheltered)—120 days (filing of petition for dependency to hearing)

(G) Permanency Proceedings.

Permanency hearing—12 months (date child is sheltered to hearing)

(2) Supreme Court and District Courts of Appeal Time Standards. Rendering a decision — within 180 days of either oral argument or the submission of the case to the court panel for a decision without oral argument, except in juvenile dependency or termination of parental rights cases, in which a decision should be rendered within 60 days of either oral argument or submission of the case to the court panel for a decision without oral argument.

(3) Florida Bar Referee Time Standards: Report of referee—within 180 days of being assigned to hear the case

(4) Circuit Court Acting as Appellate Court:

Ninety days from submission of the case to the judge for review

(b) Reporting of Cases. The time standards require that the following monitoring procedures be implemented:

All pending cases in circuit and district courts of appeal exceeding the time standards shall be listed separately on a report submitted quarterly to the chief justice. The report shall include for each case listed the case number, type of case, case status (active or inactive for civil cases and contested or uncontested for domestic relations and probate cases), the date of arrest in criminal cases, and the original filing date in civil cases. The Office of the State Courts Administrator will provide the necessary forms for submission of this data. The report will be due on the 15th day of the month following the last day of the quarter.

RULE 2.255. STATEWIDE GRAND JURY

(a) Procedure. The chief judge of each judicial circuit shall cause a list of those persons whose names have been drawn and certified for jury duty in each of the counties within that circuit to be compiled. The lists shall be taken from the male and female population over the age of 18 years and having the other constitutional and statutory qualifications for jury duty in this state not later than the last day of the first week of December of each year. From the lists so compiled, the chief judge shall cause to be selected, by lot and at random, and by any authorized method including mechanical, electronic, or electrical device, a list of prospective grand jurors from each county whose number shall be determined on the basis of 3 jurors for each 3,000 residents or a fraction thereof in

each county. The lists from which the names are drawn may be, but are not required to be, the same lists from which petit and grand juries are drawn in each county and circuit. After compilation, the statewide grand jury lists shall be submitted to the state courts administrator not later than February 15 of each year.

(b) Population. For the purposes of this rule, the population of each county shall be in accordance with the latest United States Decennial Census as set forth in the Florida Statutes.

(c) Excuses.

(1) The judge appointed to preside over the statewide grand jury may issue an order appointing the chief judge of the judicial circuit where a prospective grand juror resides to determine whether service on the statewide grand jury will result in an unreasonable personal or financial hardship because of the location or projected length of the grand jury investigation.

(2) The chief judge of the circuit shall determine whether a prospective grand juror fails to meet the qualifications of a juror in the county where the person resides. The determination shall be made only for those prospective grand jurors who contact the chief judge and request disqualification.

(3) The chief judge of the circuit shall excuse any prospective grand juror who requests and is qualified for exemption from grand jury service pursuant to general law, or from service as a juror in the county where the person resides. The chief judge shall inform the judge appointed to preside over the statewide grand jury without delay of any determination.

RULE 2.256. JUROR TIME MANAGEMENT

(a) Optimum Use. The services of prospective jurors should be employed so as to achieve optimum use with a minimum of inconvenience to jurors.

(b) Minimum Number. A minimally sufficient number of jurors needed to accommodate trial activity should be determined. This information and appropriate management techniques should be used to adjust both the number of individuals summoned for jury duty and the number assigned to jury panels, consistent with any administrative orders issued by the Chief Justice.

(c) Courtroom Assignment. Each prospective juror who has reported to the courthouse should be assigned a courtroom for voir dire before any prospective juror is assigned a second time.

(d) Calendar Coordination. Jury management and calendar management should be coordinated to make effective use of jurors.

RULE 2.260. CHANGE OF VENUE

(a) Preliminary Procedures. Prior to entering an order to change venue to a particular circuit in a criminal case or in any other case in which change of venue will likely create an unusual burden for the transferee circuit, the chief judge in the circuit in which the case originated shall contact the chief judge in the circuit to which the case is intended to be moved to determine the receiving county's ability to accommodate the change of venue. It is the intent of this rule that the county identified to receive the case shall do so unless the physical facilities or other resources in that county are such that moving the case to that county would either create an unsafe situation or adversely affect the operations of that court. Any conflict between the circuits regarding a potential change of venue shall be referred to the chief justice of the Florida Supreme Court for resolution.

(b) Presiding Judge. The presiding judge from the originating court shall accompany the change of venue case, unless the originating and receiving courts agree otherwise.

(c) Reimbursement of Costs. As a general policy the county in which an action originated shall reimburse the county receiving the change of venue case for any ordinary expenditure and any extraordinary but reasonable and necessary expenditure that would not otherwise have been incurred by the receiving county. For purposes of this section, ordinary expenditure, extraordinary expenditure, and nonreimbursable expenditure are defined as follows:

(1) Ordinary expenditures include:

(A) juror expenses not reimbursed by the State of Florida;

(B) court reporter expenses, including appearances by either official or freelance reporters, transcripts, and other expenses associated with the creation of a court record;

(C) court interpreters;

(D) maintenance of evidence, including the cost of handling, storing, or maintaining the evidence beyond the expenses normally incurred by the receiving county;

(E) services and supplies purchased as a result of the change of venue;

(F) overtime expenditures for regular court and clerk staff attributable to the change of venue; and

(G) trial-related expenses, including conflict attorney fees; all expert, law enforcement, or ordinary witness costs and expenses; and investigator expenses.

(2) Extraordinary but reasonable and necessary expenses include:

(A) security-related expenditures, including overtime for security personnel;

(B) facility remodeling or renovation; and

(C) leasing or renting of space or equipment.

Except in emergencies or unless it is impracticable to do so, a receiving county should give notice to the chief judge and clerk of the county in which the action originated before incurring any extraordinary expenditures.

(3) Nonreimbursable expenses include:

(A) normal operating expenses, including the overhead of the receiving county; and

(B) equipment that is purchased and kept by the receiving county that can be used for other purposes or cases.

(d) Documentation of Costs. No expenses shall be submitted for reimbursement without supporting documentation, such as a claim, invoice, bill, statement, or time sheet. Any required court order or approval of costs shall also be sent to the originating court.

(e) Timing of Reimbursement. Unless both counties agree to other terms, reimbursement of all expenses by the originating county shall be paid or disputed in writing on or before the sixtieth day after the receipt of the claim for reimbursement. Payment of a disputed amount shall be made on or before the sixtieth day after the resolution of this dispute. Any amount subject to dispute shall be expeditiously resolved by authorized representatives of the court administrator's office of the originating and receiving counties.

(f) Media Relations. Procedures to accommodate the media shall be developed by the receiving county immediately upon notice of the change of venue when the change of venue is reasonably expected to generate an unusual amount of publicity. These procedures must be approved by the chief judge of the receiving circuit and implemented pursuant to administrative order by the presiding judge. The presiding judge shall obtain the concurrence of the chief judge before entering any orders that vary from or conflict with existing administrative orders of the receiving circuit.

(g) Case File. The clerk of the circuit court in the originating county shall forward the original case file to the clerk in the receiving county. The receiving clerk shall maintain the file and keep it secure until the trial has been concluded. During the trial, any documents or exhibits that have been added shall be properly marked and added to the file in a manner consistent with the policy and procedures of the receiving county. After the conclusion of the trial, the file shall be returned to the clerk in the county of origin.

RULE 2.265. MUNICIPAL ORDINANCE VIOLATIONS

(a) References to Abolished Municipal Courts. All references to a municipal court or municipal judge in rules promulgated by the supreme court, in the Florida Statutes, and in any municipal ordinance shall be deemed to refer, respectively, to the county court or county court judge.

(b) Costs in County Courts. The chief judge of a circuit shall by administrative order establish a schedule of costs, in conformity with any provisions of law, to be assessed against a defendant in the county court and paid to the county for violations of municipal ordinances which are prosecuted in county court. The costs shall be assessed as a set dollar amount per conviction, not to exceed $50 excluding any other statutory costs.

(c) Collection of Outstanding Fines. All cases for which outstanding fines, civil penalties, and costs are being collected by a municipality shall be retained by the municipality until collected or until the offender defaults on payment. If a default occurs, the municipality may institute summary claims proceedings to collect the outstanding fines.

(d) Judicial Notice of Municipal Ordinances. The judges of the county courts may take judicial notice of any municipal ordinance if a certified copy of the ordinance has been filed in the office of the clerk of circuit court or, in those counties having a clerk of the county court, filed in that office, and if a certified copy of the ordinance is presented to the court.

(e) Style of Municipal Ordinance Cases. All prosecutions for violations of municipal ordinances in county court shall have the following style: City of
.... v. ....

PART III. JUDICIAL OFFICERS

RULE 2.310. JUDICIAL DISCIPLINE, REMOVAL, RETIREMENT, AND SUSPENSION

(a) Filing. Any recommendations to the supreme court from the Judicial Qualifications Commission pursuant to article V, section 12, of the Florida Constitution shall be in writing. The original and 7 copies shall be filed with the clerk of the court, and a copy shall be served expeditiously on the justice or judge against whom action is sought.

(b) Procedure.

(1) Promptly upon the filing of a recommendation from the commission, the court shall determine whether the commission's recommendation complies with all requirements of the constitution and the commission's rules. Upon determining that the recommendation so complies, and unless the court otherwise directs, an order shall issue directing the justice or judge to show cause in writing why the recommended action should not be taken.

(2) The justice or judge may file a response in writing within the time set by the court in its order to show cause, and the commission may serve a reply within 20 days from service of the response.

(3) If requested by the commission, or by a justice or judge at the time of filing a response, the court may allow oral argument on the commission's recommendation.

(c) Costs. The supreme court may award reasonable and necessary costs, including costs of investigation and prosecution, to the prevailing party. Neither attorneys' fees nor travel expenses of commission personnel shall be included in an award of costs. Taxable costs may include:

(1) court reporters' fees, including per diem fees, deposition costs, and costs associated with the preparation of the transcript and record; and

(2) witness expenses, including travel and out-of-pocket expenses.

RULE 2.320. CONTINUING JUDICIAL EDUCATION

(a) Purpose. This rule sets forth the continuing education requirement for all judges in the state judicial system.

(b) Education Requirements.

(1) Applicability. All Florida county, circuit, and appellate judges and Florida supreme court justices shall comply with these judicial education requirements. Retired judges who have been approved by the supreme court to be assigned to temporary active duty as authorized by section 25.073, Florida Statutes (1991), shall also comply with the judicial education requirements.

(2) Minimum Requirements. Each judge and justice shall complete a minimum of 30 credit hours of approved judicial education programs every 3 years. Beginning January 1, 2012, 4 hours must be in the area of judicial ethics; prior to that date, 2 hours in the area of judicial ethics are required. Approved courses in fairness and diversity also can be used to fulfill the judicial ethics requirement. In addition to the 30-hour requirement, every judge new to a level of trial court must complete the Florida Judicial College program in that judge's first year of judicial service following selection to that level of court; every new appellate court judge or justice must, within 2 years following selection to that level of court, complete an approved appellate-judge program. Every new appellate judge who has never been a trial judge or who has never attended Phase I of the Florida Judicial College as a magistrate must also attend Phase I of the Florida Judicial College in that judge's first year of judicial service following the judge's appointment. Credit for teaching a course for which mandatory judicial education credit is available will be allowed on the basis of 2 1/2 hours' credit for each instructional hour taught, up to a maximum of 5 hours per year.

(3) Mediation Training. Prior to conducting any mediation, a senior judge shall have completed a minimum of one judicial education course offered by the Florida Court Education Council. The course shall specifically focus on the areas where the Code of Judicial Conduct or the Florida Rules for Certified and Court-Appointed Mediators could be violated.

(c) Course Approval. The Florida Court Education Council, in consultation with the judicial conferences, shall develop approved courses for each state court jurisdiction. Courses offered by other judicial and legal education entities must be approved by the council before they may be submitted for credit.

(d) Waiver. The Florida Court Education Council is responsible for establishing a procedure for considering and acting upon waiver and extension requests on an individual basis.

(e) Reporting Requirements and Sanctions. The Florida Court Education Council shall establish a procedure for reporting annually to the chief justice on compliance with this rule. Each judge shall submit to the Court Education Division of the Office of the State Courts Administrator an annual report showing the judge's attendance at approved courses. Failure to comply with the requirements of this rule will be reported to the chief justice of the Florida supreme court for such administrative action as deemed necessary. The chief justice may consider a judge's or justice's failure to comply as neglect of duty and report the matter to the Judicial Qualifications Commission.

RULE 2.330. DISQUALIFICATION OF TRIAL JUDGES

(a) Application. This rule applies only to county and circuit judges in all matters in all divisions of court.

(b) Parties. Any party, including the state, may move to disqualify the trial judge assigned to the case on grounds provided by rule, by statute, or by the Code of Judicial Conduct.

(c) Motion. A motion to disqualify shall:

(1) be in writing;

(2) allege specifically the facts and reasons upon which the movant relies as the grounds for disqualification;

(3) be sworn to by the party by signing the motion under oath or by a separate affidavit; and

(4) include the dates of all previously granted motions to disqualify filed under this rule in the case and the dates of the orders granting those motions.

The attorney for the party shall also separately certify that the motion and the client's statements are made in good faith. In addition to filing with the clerk, the movant shall immediately serve a copy of the motion on the subject judge as set forth in Florida Rule of Civil Procedure 1.080.

(d) Grounds. A motion to disqualify shall show:

(1) that the party fears that he or she will not receive a fair trial or hearing because of specifically described prejudice or bias of the judge; or

(2) that the judge before whom the case is pending, or some person related to said judge by consanguinity or affinity within the third degree, is a party thereto or is interested in the result thereof, or that said judge is related to an attorney or counselor of record in the cause by consanguinity or affinity within the third degree, or that said judge is a material witness for or against one of the parties to the cause.

(e) Time. A motion to disqualify shall be filed within a reasonable time not to exceed 10 days after discovery of the facts constituting the grounds for the motion and shall be promptly presented to the court for an immediate ruling. Any motion for disqualification made during a hearing or trial must be based on facts discovered during the hearing or trial and may be stated on the record, provided that it is also promptly reduced to writing in compliance with subdivision (c) and promptly filed. A motion made during hearing or trial shall be ruled on immediately.

(f) Determination—Initial Motion. The judge against whom an initial motion to disqualify under subdivision (d)(1) is directed shall determine only the legal sufficiency of the motion and shall not pass on the truth of the facts alleged. If the motion is legally sufficient, the judge shall immediately enter an order granting disqualification and proceed no further in the action. If any motion is legally insufficient, an order denying the motion shall immediately be entered. No other reason for denial shall be stated, and an order of denial shall not take issue with the motion.

(g) Determination—Successive Motions. If a judge has been previously disqualified on motion for alleged prejudice or partiality under subdivision (d)(1), a successor judge shall not be disqualified based on a successive motion by the same party unless the successor judge rules that he or she is in fact not fair or impartial in the case. Such a successor judge may rule on the truth of the facts alleged in support of the motion.

(h) Prior Rulings. Prior factual or legal rulings by a disqualified judge may be reconsidered and vacated or amended by a successor judge based upon a motion for reconsideration, which must be filed within 20 days of the order of disqualification, unless good cause is shown for a delay in moving for reconsideration or other grounds for reconsideration exist.

(i) Judge's Initiative. Nothing in this rule limits the judge's authority to enter an order of disqualification on the judge's own initiative.

(j) Time for Determination. The judge shall rule on a motion to disqualify immediately, but no later than 30 days after the service of the motion as set forth in subdivision (c). If not ruled on within 30 days of service, the motion shall be deemed granted and the moving party may seek an order from the court directing the clerk to reassign the case.

RULE 2.340. JUDICIAL ATTIRE

During any judicial proceeding, robes worn by a judge must be solid black with no embellishment.

PART IV. JUDICIAL PROCEEDINGS AND RECORDS

RULE 2.410. POSSESSION OF COURT RECORDS

No person other than judges and authorized court employees shall remove court records as defined in rule 2.430 from the clerk's office except by order of the chief judge or chief justice upon a showing of good cause.

Court Commentary

1996 Adoption. This rule was written as a result of the problems being encountered in the removal of files from clerks' offices. While the purpose of the rule is to discourage the removal of court files, it is not intended to prohibit chief judges or the chief justice from issuing for good cause a general order providing that attorneys or authorized individuals may be allowed to check out files on a routine basis to assist in the administrative efficiency of a court. We note that section 28.13, Florida Statutes (1995), similarly prohibits the removal of files from clerks' offices.

RULE 2.420. PUBLIC ACCESS TO AND PROTECTION OF JUDICIAL BRANCH RECORDS

(a) Scope and Purpose. Subject to the rulemaking power of the Florida Supreme Court provided by article V, section 2, Florida Constitution, the following rule shall govern public access to and the protection of the records of the judicial branch of government. The public shall have access to all records of the judicial branch of government, except as provided below. Access to all electronic and other court records shall be governed by the Standards for Access to Electronic Court Records and Access Security Matrix, as adopted by the supreme court in Administrative Order AOSC14-19 or the then-current Standards for Access. Remote access to electronic court records shall be permitted in counties where the supreme court's conditions for release of such records are met.

(b) Definitions.

(1) "Records of the judicial branch" are all records, regardless of physical form, characteristics, or means of transmission, made or received in connection with the transaction of official business by any judicial branch entity and consist of:

(A) "court records," which are the contents of the court file, including the progress docket and other similar records generated to document activity in a case, transcripts filed with the clerk, documentary exhibits in the custody of the clerk, and electronic records, videotapes, or stenographic tapes of depositions or other proceedings filed with the clerk, and electronic records, videotapes, or stenographic tapes of court proceedings; and

(B) "administrative records," which are all other records made or received pursuant to court rule, law, or ordinance, or in connection with the transaction of official business by any judicial branch entity.

(2) "Judicial branch" means the judicial branch of government, which includes the state courts system, the clerk of court when acting as an arm of the court, The Florida Bar, the Florida Board of Bar Examiners, the Judicial Qualifications Commission, and all other entities established by or operating under the authority of the supreme court or the chief justice.

(3) "Custodian." The custodian of all administrative records of any court is the chief justice or chief judge of that court, except that each judge is the

custodian of all records that are solely within the possession and control of that judge. As to all other records, the custodian is the official charged with the responsibility for the care, safekeeping, and supervision of such records. All references to "custodian" mean the custodian or the custodian's designee.

(4) "Confidential," as applied to information contained within a record of the judicial branch, means that such information is exempt from the public right of access under article I, section 24(a) of the Florida Constitution and may be released only to the persons or organizations designated by law, statute, or court order. As applied to information contained within a court record, the term "exempt" means that such information is confidential. Confidential information includes information that is confidential under this rule or under a court order entered pursuant to this rule. To the extent reasonably practicable, restriction of access to confidential information shall be implemented in a manner that does not restrict access to any portion of the record that is not confidential.

(5) "Affected non-party" means any non-party identified by name in a court record that contains confidential information pertaining to that non-party.

(6) "Filer" means any person who files a document in court records, except "filer" does not include the clerk of court or designee of the clerk, a judge, magistrate, hearing officer, or designee of a judge, magistrate, or hearing officer.

(c) Confidential and Exempt Records. The following records of the judicial branch shall be confidential:

(1) Trial and appellate court memoranda, drafts of opinions and orders, court conference records, notes, and other written materials of a similar nature prepared by judges or court staff acting on behalf of or at the direction of the court as part of the court's judicial decision-making process utilized in disposing of cases and controversies before Florida courts unless filed as a part of the court record;

(2) Memoranda or advisory opinions that relate to the administration of the court and that require con-

fidentiality to protect a compelling governmental interest, including, but not limited to, maintaining court security, facilitating a criminal investigation, or protecting public safety, which cannot be adequately protected by less restrictive measures. The degree, duration, and manner of confidentiality imposed shall be no broader than necessary to protect the compelling governmental interest involved, and a finding shall be made that no less restrictive measures are available to protect this interest. The decision that confidentiality is required with respect to such administrative memorandum or written advisory opinion shall be made by the chief judge;

(3)(A) Complaints alleging misconduct against judges until probable cause is established;

(B) Complaints alleging misconduct against other entities or individuals licensed or regulated by the courts, until a finding of probable cause or no probable cause is established, unless otherwise provided. Such finding should be made within the time limit set by law or rule. If no time limit is set, the finding should be made within a reasonable period of time;

(4) Periodic evaluations implemented solely to assist judges in improving their performance, all information gathered to form the bases for the evaluations, and the results generated therefrom;

(5) Only the names and qualifications of persons applying to serve or serving as unpaid volunteers to assist the court, at the court's request and direction, shall be accessible to the public. All other information contained in the applications by and evaluations of persons applying to serve or serving as unpaid volunteers shall be confidential unless made public by court order based upon a showing of materiality in a pending court proceeding or upon a showing of good cause;

(6) Copies of arrest and search warrants and supporting affidavits retained by judges, clerks, or other court personnel until execution of said warrants or until a determination is made by law enforcement authorities that execution cannot be made;

(7) All records made confidential under the Florida and United States Constitutions and Florida and federal law;

(8) All records presently deemed to be confidential by court rule, including the Rules for Admission to the Bar, by Florida Statutes, by prior case law of the State of Florida, and by the rules of the Judicial Qualifications Commission;

(9) Any court record determined to be confidential in case decision or court rule on the grounds that:

(A) confidentiality is required to:

(i) prevent a serious and imminent threat to the fair, impartial, and orderly administration of justice;

(ii) protect trade secrets;

(iii) protect a compelling governmental interest;

(iv) obtain evidence to determine legal issues in a case;

(v) avoid substantial injury to innocent third parties;

(vi) avoid substantial injury to a party by disclosure of matters protected by a common law or privacy right not generally inherent in the specific type of proceeding sought to be closed;

(vii) comply with established public policy set forth in the Florida or United States Constitution or statutes or Florida rules or case law;

(B) the degree, duration, and manner of confidentiality ordered by the court shall be no broader than necessary to protect the interests set forth in subdivision (c)(9)(A); and

(C) no less restrictive measures are available to protect the interests set forth in subdivision (c)(9)(A).

(10) The names and any identifying information of judges mentioned in an advisory opinion of the Judicial Ethics Advisory Committee.

(d) Procedures for Determining Confidentiality of Court Records.

(1) The clerk of the court shall designate and maintain the confidentiality of any information contained within a court record that is described in subdivision (d)(1)(A) or (d)(1)(B) of this rule. The following information shall be maintained as confidential:

(A) information described by any of subdivisions (c)(1) through (c)(6) of this rule; and

(B) except as provided by court order, information subject to subdivision (c)(7) or (c)(8) of this rule that is currently confidential or exempt from section 119.07, Florida Statutes, and article I, section 24(a) of the Florida Constitution as specifically stated in any of the following statutes or court rules as they may be amended or renumbered:

(i) Chapter 39 records relating to dependency matters, termination of parental rights, guardians ad litem, child abuse, neglect, and abandonment. §§ 39.0132(3), 39.0132(4)(a), Fla. Stat.

(ii) Adoption records. § 63.162, Fla. Stat.

(iii) Social Security, bank account, charge, debit, and credit card numbers. § 119.0714(1)(i)-(j), (2)(a)-(e), Fla. Stat. (Unless redaction is requested pursuant to § 119.0714(2), Fla. Stat., this information is exempt only as of January 1, 2012.)

(iv) HIV test results and the identity of any person upon whom an HIV test has been performed. § 381.004(2)(e), Fla. Stat.

(v) Records, including test results, held by the Department of Health or its authorized representatives relating to sexually transmissible diseases. § 384.29, Fla. Stat.

(vi) Birth records and portions of death and fetal death records. §§ 382.008(6), 382.025(1), Fla. Stat.

(vii) Information that can be used to identify a minor petitioning for a waiver of parental notice when seeking to terminate pregnancy. § 390.01116, Fla. Stat.

(viii) Clinical records under the Baker Act. § 394.4615(7), Fla. Stat.

(ix) Records of substance abuse service providers which pertain to the identity, diagnosis, and prognosis of and service provision to individuals, § 397.501(7), Fla. Stat., and all petitions, court orders, and related records for involuntary assessment and stabilization of an individual, § 397.6760, Fla. Stat.

(x) Clinical records of criminal defendants found incompetent to proceed or acquitted by reason of insanity. § 916.107(8), Fla. Stat.

(xi) Estate inventories and accountings. § 733.604(1), Fla. Stat.

(xii) The victim's address in a domestic violence action on petitioner's request. § 741.30(3)(b), Fla. Stat.

(xiii) Protected information regarding victims of child abuse or sexual offenses. §§ 119.071(2)(h), 119.0714(1)(h), Fla. Stat.

(xiv) Gestational surrogacy records. § 742.16(9), Fla. Stat.

(xv) Guardianship reports, orders appointing court monitors, and orders relating to findings of no probable cause in guardianship cases. §§ 744.1076, 744.3701, Fla. Stat.

(xvi) Grand jury records. §§ 905.17, 905.28(1), Fla. Stat.

(xvii) Records acquired by courts and law enforcement regarding family services for children. § 984.06(3)-(4), Fla. Stat.

(xviii) Juvenile delinquency records. §§ 985.04(1), 985.045(2), Fla. Stat.

(xix) Records disclosing the identity of persons subject to tuberculosis proceedings and records held by the Department of Health or its authorized representatives relating to known or suspected cases of tuberculosis or exposure to tuberculosis. §§ 392.545, 392.65, Fla. Stat.

(xx) Complete presentence investigation reports. Fla. R. Crim. P. 3.712.

(xxi) Forensic behavioral health evaluations under Chapter 916. § 916.1065, Fla. Stat.

(xxii) Eligibility screening, substance abuse screening, behavioral health evaluations, and treatment status reports for defendants referred to or considered for referral to a drug court program. § 397.334(10)(a), Fla. Stat.

(2) The filer of any document containing confidential information described in subdivision (d)(1)(B) shall, at the time of filing, file with the clerk a "Notice of Confidential Information within Court Filing" in order to indicate that confidential information described in subdivision (d)(1)(B) of this rule is included within the document being filed and also indicate that either the entire document is confidential or identify the precise location of the confidential information within the document being filed. If an entire court file is maintained as confidential, the filer of a document in such a file is not required to file the notice form. A form Notice of Confidential Information within Court Filing accompanies this rule.

(A) If any document in a court file contains confidential information as described in subdivision (d)(1)(B), the filer, a party, or any affected non-party may file the Notice of Confidential Information within Court Filing if the document was not initially filed with a Notice of Confidential Information within Court Filing and the confidential information is not maintained as confidential by the clerk. The Notice of Confidential Information within Court Filing filed pursuant to this subdivision must also state the title and type of document, date of filing (if known), date of document, docket entry number, indicate that either the entire document is confidential or identify the precise location of the confidential information within the document, and provide any other information the clerk may require to locate the confidential information.

(B) The clerk of court shall review filings identified as containing confidential information to determine whether the purported confidential information is facially subject to confidentiality under subdivision (d)(1)(B). If the clerk determines that filed information is not subject to confidentiality under subdivision (d)(1)(B), the clerk shall notify the filer of the Notice of Confidential Information within Court Filing in writing within 5 days of filing the notice and thereafter shall maintain the information as confidential for 10 days from the date such notification by the clerk is served. The information shall not be held as confidential for more than that 10-day period, unless a motion has been filed pursuant to subdivision (d)(3).

(3) The filer of a document with the court shall ascertain whether any information contained within the document may be confidential under subdivision (c) of this rule notwithstanding that such information is not itemized at subdivision (d)(1) of this rule. If the filer believes in good faith that information is confidential but is not described in subdivision (d)(1) of this rule, the filer shall request that the information be maintained as confidential by filing a "Motion to Determine Confidentiality of Court Records" under the procedures set forth in subdivision (e), (f), or (g), unless:

(A) the filer is the only individual whose confidential information is included in the document to be filed or is the attorney representing all such individuals; and

(B) a knowing waiver of the confidential status of that information is intended by the filer. Any interested person may request that information within a court file be maintained as confidential by filing a motion as provided in subdivision (e), (f), or (g).

(4) If a notice of confidential information is filed pursuant to subdivision (d)(2), or a motion is filed pursuant to subdivision (e)(1) or (g)(1) seeking to determine that information contained in court records is confidential, or pursuant to subdivision (e)(5) or (g)(5) seeking to vacate an order that has determined that information in a court record is confidential or seeking to unseal information designated as confidential by the clerk of court, then the person filing the notice or motion shall give notice of such filing to any affected non-party. Notice pursuant to this provision must:

(A) be filed with the court;

(B) identify the case by docket number;

(C) describe the confidential information with as much specificity as possible without revealing the confidential information, including specifying the precise location of the information within the court record; and

(D) include:

(i) in the case of a motion to determine confidentiality of court records, a statement that if the motion is denied then the subject material will not be treated as confidential by the clerk; and

(ii) in the case of a motion to unseal confidential records or a motion to vacate an order deeming records confidential, a statement that if the motion is granted, the subject material will no longer be treated as confidential by the clerk.

Any notice described herein must be served pursuant to subdivision (k), if applicable, together with the motion that gave rise to the notice in accordance with subdivision (e)(5) or (g)(5).

(5) Except when the entire court file is maintained as confidential, if a judge, magistrate, or hearing officer files any document containing confidential information, the confidential information within the document must be identified as "confidential" and the title of the document must include the word "confidential." The clerk must maintain the confidentiality of the identified confidential information. A copy of the document edited to omit the confidential information shall be provided to the clerk for filing and recording purposes.

(e) Request to Determine Confidentiality of Trial Court Records in Noncriminal Cases.

(1) A request to determine the confidentiality of trial court records in noncriminal cases under subdivision (c) must be made in the form of a written motion captioned "Motion to Determine Confidentiality of Court Records." A motion made under this subdivision must:

(A) identify the particular court records or a portion of a record that the movant seeks to have determined as confidential with as much specificity as possible without revealing the information subject to the confidentiality determination;

(B) specify the bases for determining that such court records are confidential without revealing confidential information; and

(C) set forth the specific legal authority and any applicable legal standards for determining such court records to be confidential without revealing confidential information.

Any written motion made under this subdivision must include a signed certification by the party or the attorney for the party making the request that the motion is made in good faith and is supported by a sound factual and legal basis. Information that is subject to such a motion must be treated as confidential by the clerk pending the court's ruling on the motion. A response to a written motion filed under this subdivision may be served within 10 days of service of the motion. Notwithstanding any of the foregoing, the court may not determine that the case number, docket number, or other number used by the clerk's office to identify the case file is confidential.

(2) Except when a motion filed under subdivision (e)(1) represents that all parties agree to all of the relief requested, the court must, as soon as practicable but no later than 30 days after the filing of a motion under this subdivision, hold a hearing before ruling on the motion. Whether or not any motion filed under subdivision (e)(1) is agreed to by the parties, the court may in its discretion hold a hearing on such motion. Any hearing held under this subdivision must be an open proceeding, except that any person may request that the court conduct all or part of the hearing in camera to protect the interests set forth in subdivision (c). Any person may request expedited consideration of and ruling on the motion. The movant shall be responsible for ensuring that a complete record of any hearing held pursuant to this subdivision is created, either by use of a court reporter or by any recording device that is provided as a matter of right by the court. The court may in its discretion require prior public notice of the hearing on such a motion in accordance with the procedure for providing public

notice of court orders set forth in subdivision (e)(4) or by providing such other public notice as the court deems appropriate. The court must issue a ruling on the motion within 30 days of the hearing.

(3) Any order granting in whole or in part a motion filed under subdivision (e) must state the following with as much specificity as possible without revealing the confidential information:

(A) the type of case in which the order is being entered;

(B) the particular grounds under subdivision (c) for determining the information is confidential;

(C) whether any party's name is determined to be confidential and, if so, the particular pseudonym or other term to be substituted for the party's name;

(D) whether the progress docket or similar records generated to document activity in the case are determined to be confidential;

(E) the particular information that is determined to be confidential;

(F) identification of persons who are permitted to view the confidential information;

(G) that the court finds that: (i) the degree, duration, and manner of confidentiality ordered by the court are no broader than necessary to protect the interests set forth in subdivision (c); and (ii) no less restrictive measures are available to protect the interests set forth in subdivision (c); and

(H) that the clerk of the court is directed to publish the order in accordance with subdivision (e)(4).

(4) Except as provided by law or court rule, notice must be given of any written order granting in whole or in part a motion made under subdivision (e)(1) as follows:

(A) within 10 days following the entry of the order, the clerk of court must post a copy of the order on the clerk's website and in a prominent public location in the courthouse; and

(B) the order must remain posted in both locations for no less than 30 days. This subdivision shall not apply to orders determining that court records are confidential under subdivision (c)(7) or (c)(8).

(5) If a nonparty requests that the court vacate all or part of an order issued under subdivision (e) or requests that the court order the unsealing of records designated as confidential under subdivision (d), the request must be made by a written motion, filed in that court, that states with as much specificity as possible the bases for the motion. The motion must set forth the specific legal authority and any applicable legal standards supporting the motion. The movant must serve all parties and all affected non-parties with a copy of the motion. Except when a motion filed under this subdivision represents that all parties and affected non-parties agree to all of the relief requested, the court must, as soon as practicable but no later than 30 days after the filing of a motion under this subdivision, hold a hearing on the motion. Regardless of whether any motion filed under this subdivision is agreed to by the parties and affected non-parties, the court may in its discretion hold a hearing on such motion. Any person may request expedited consideration of and ruling on the motion. Any hearing held under this subdivision must be an open proceeding, except that any person may request that the court conduct all or part of the hearing in camera to protect the interests set forth in subdivision (c). The court must issue a ruling on the motion within 30 days of the hearing. The movant shall be responsible for ensuring that a complete record of any hearing held under this subdivision be created, either by use of a court reporter or by any recording device that is provided as a matter of right by the court. This subdivision shall not apply to orders determining that court records are confidential under subdivision (c)(7) or (c)(8).

(f) Request to Determine Confidentiality of Court Records in Criminal Cases.

(1) Subdivisions (e) and (h) shall apply to any motion by the state, a defendant, or an affected non-party to determine the confidentiality of trial court records in criminal cases under subdivision (c), except as provided in subdivision (f)(3). As to any motion filed in the trial court under subdivision (f)(3), the following procedure shall apply:

(A) Unless the motion represents that the state, defendant(s), and all affected non-parties subject to the motion agree to all of the relief requested, the court must hold a hearing on the motion filed under this subdivision within 15 days of the filing of the motion. Any hearing held under this subdivision must be an open proceeding, except that any person may request that the court conduct all or part of the hearing in camera to protect the interests set forth in subdivision (c)(9)(A).

(B) The court shall issue a written ruling on a motion filed under this subdivision within 10 days of the hearing on a contested motion or within 10 days of the filing of an agreed motion.

(2) Subdivision (g) shall apply to any motion to determine the confidentiality of appellate court records under subdivision (c), except as provided in subdivision (f)(3). As to any motion filed in the appellate court under subdivision (f)(3), the following procedure shall apply:

(A) The motion may be made with respect to a record that was presented or presentable to a lower tribunal, but no determination concerning confidentiality was made by the lower tribunal, or a record presented to an appellate court in an original proceeding.

(B) A response to a motion filed under this subdivision may be served within 10 days of service of the motion.

(C) The court shall issue a written ruling on a motion filed under this subdivision within 10 days of the filing of a response on a contested motion or within 10 days of the filing of an uncontested motion.

(3) Any motion to determine whether a court record that pertains to a plea agreement, substantial assistance agreement, or other court record that reveals the identity of a confidential informant or active criminal investigative information is confidential under subdivision (c)(9)(A)(i), (c)(9)(A)(iii),

(c)(9)(A)(v), or (c)(9)(A)(vii) of this rule may be made in the form of a written motion captioned "Motion to Determine Confidentiality of Court Records." Any motion made pursuant to this subdivision must be treated as confidential and indicated on the docket by generic title only, pending a ruling on the motion or further order of the court. As to any motion made under this subdivision, the following procedure shall apply:

(A) Information that is the subject of such motion must be treated as confidential by the clerk pending the court's ruling on the motion. Filings containing the information must be indicated on the docket in a manner that does not reveal the confidential nature of the information.

(B) The provisions of subdivisions (e)(3)(A)-(G), (g)(7), (h), and (j), shall apply to motions made under this subdivision. The provisions of subdivisions (e)(1), (e)(2), (e)(3)(H), (e)(4), and (e)(5) shall not apply to motions made under this subdivision.

(C) No order entered under this subdivision may authorize or approve the sealing of court records for any period longer than is necessary to achieve the objective of the motion, and in no event longer than 120 days. Extensions of an order issued hereunder may be granted for 60-day periods, but each such extension may be ordered only upon the filing of another motion in accordance with the procedures set forth under this subdivision. In the event of an appeal or review of a matter in which an order is entered under this subdivision, the lower tribunal shall retain jurisdiction to consider motions to extend orders issued hereunder during the course of the appeal or review proceeding.

(D) The clerk of the court shall not publish any order of the court issued hereunder in accordance with subdivision (e)(4) or (g)(4) unless directed by the court. The docket shall indicate only the entry of the order.

(4) This subdivision does not authorize the falsification of court records or progress dockets.

(g) Request to Determine Confidentiality of Appellate Court Records in Noncriminal Cases.

(1) Subdivision (e)(1) shall apply to any motion filed in the appellate court to determine the confidentiality of appellate court records in noncriminal cases under subdivision (c). Such a motion may be made with respect to a record that was presented or presentable to a lower tribunal, but no determination concerning confidentiality was made by the lower tribunal, or a record presented to an appellate court in an original proceeding.

(2) A response to a motion filed under subdivision (g)(1) may be served within 10 days of service of the motion. The court shall issue a written ruling on a written motion filed under this subdivision within 30 days of the filing of a response on a contested motion or within 30 days of the filing of an uncontested written motion.

(3) Any order granting in whole or in part a motion filed under subdivision (g)(1) must be in compliance with the guidelines set forth in subdivisions (e)(3)(A)-(e)(3)(H). Any order requiring the sealing of an appellate court record operates to also make those same records confidential in the lower tribunal during the pendency of the appellate proceeding.

(4) Except as provided by law, within 10 days following the entry of an order granting a motion under subdivision (g)(1), the clerk of the appellate court must post a copy of the order on the clerk's website and must provide a copy of the order to the clerk of the lower tribunal, with directions that the clerk is of the lower tribunal shall seal the records identified in the order. The order must remain posted by the clerk of the appellate court for no less than 30 days.

(5) If a nonparty requests that the court vacate all or part of an order issued under subdivision (g)(3), or requests that the court order the unsealing of records designated as confidential under subdivision (d), the request must be made by a written motion, filed in that

court, that states with as much specificity as possible the bases for the request. The motion must set forth the specific legal authority and any applicable legal standards supporting the motion. The movant must serve all parties and all affected non-parties with a copy of the motion. A response to a motion may be served within 10 days of service of the motion.

(6) The party seeking to have an appellate record sealed under this subdivision has the responsibility to ensure that the clerk of the lower tribunal is alerted to the issuance of the order sealing the records and to ensure that the clerk takes appropriate steps to seal the records in the lower tribunal.

(7) Upon conclusion of the appellate proceeding, the lower tribunal may, upon appropriate motion showing changed circumstances, revisit the appellate court's order directing that the records be sealed.

(8) Records of a lower tribunal determined to be confidential by that tribunal must be treated as confidential during any review proceedings. In any case where information has been determined to be confidential under this rule, the clerk of the lower tribunal shall so indicate in the index transmitted to the appellate court. If the information was determined to be confidential in an order, the clerk's index must identify such order by date or docket number. This subdivision does not preclude review by an appellate court, under Florida Rule of Appellate Procedure 9.100(d), or affect the standard of review by an appellate court, of an order by a lower tribunal determining that a court record is confidential.

(h) Oral Motions to Determine Confidentiality of Trial Court Records.

(1) Notwithstanding the written notice requirements of subdivision (d)(2) and written motion requirements of subdivisions (d)(3), (e)(1), and (f), the movant may make an oral motion to determine the confidentiality of trial court records under subdivision (c), provided:

(A) except for oral motions under subdivision (f)(3), the oral motion otherwise complies with subdivision (e)(1);

(B) all parties and affected non-parties are present or properly noticed or the movant otherwise demonstrates reasonable efforts made to obtain the attendance of any absent party or affected non-party;

(C) the movant shows good cause why the movant was unable to timely comply with the written notice requirements as set forth in subdivision (d)(2) or the written motion requirement as set forth in subdivision (d)(3), (e)(1), or (f), as applicable;

(D) the oral motion is reduced to written form in compliance with subdivision (d), (e)(1), or (f), as applicable, and is filed within 5 days following the date of making the oral motion;

(E) except for oral motions under subdivision (f)(3), the provisions of subdivision (e)(2) shall apply to the oral motion, procedure and hearing;

(F) the provisions of subdivisions (f)(1)(A) and (f)(1)(B) and (f)(3) shall apply to any oral motion under subdivision (f)(3); and

(G) oral motions are not applicable to subdivision (f)(2) or (g) or extensions of orders under subdivision (f)(3)(C).

(2) The court may deny any oral motion made pursuant to subdivision (h)(1) if the court finds that the movant had the ability to timely comply with the written notice requirements in subdivision (d) or the written motion requirements of subdivision (d)(3), (e)(1), or (f), as applicable, or the movant failed to provide adequate notice to the parties and affected non-parties of the confidentiality issues to be presented to the court.

(3) Until the court renders a decision regarding the confidentiality issues raised in any oral motion, all references to purported confidential information as set forth in the oral motion shall occur in a manner that does not allow public access to such information.

(4) If the court grants in whole or in part any oral motion to determine confidentiality, the court shall issue a written order that does not reveal the confidential information and complies with the applicable subdivision of this rule as follows:

(A) For any oral motion under subdivision (e) or (f)(1), except subdivisions (f)(1)(A) and (f)(1)(B), the written order must be issued within 30 days of the hearing and must comply with subdivision (e)(3).

(B) For any oral motion under subdivision (f)(3), the written order must be issued within 10 days of the hearing on a contested motion or filing of an agreed motion and must comply with subdivision (f)(3).

(i) Sanctions. After notice and an opportunity to respond, and upon determining that a motion, filing, or other activity described below was not made in good faith and was not supported by a sound legal or factual basis, the court may impose sanctions against any party or non-party and/or their attorney, if that party or non-party and/or their attorney, in violation of the applicable provisions of this rule:

(1) seeks confidential status for non-confidential information by filing a notice under subdivision (d)(2);

(2) seeks confidential status for non-confidential information by making any oral or written motion under subdivision (d)(3), (e), (f), (g), or (h);

(3) seeks access to confidential information under subdivision (j) or otherwise;

(4) fails to file a Notice of Confidential Information within Court Filing in compliance with subdivision (d)(2);

(5) makes public or attempts to make public by motion or otherwise information that should be maintained as confidential under subdivision (c), (d), (e), (f), (g), or (h); or

(6) otherwise makes or attempts to make confidential information part of a non-confidential court record.

Nothing in this subdivision is intended to limit the authority of a court to enforce any court order entered pursuant to this rule.

(j) Procedure for Obtaining Access to Confidential Court Records.

(1) The clerk of the court must allow access to confidential court records to persons authorized by law, or any person authorized by court order.

(2) A court order allowing access to confidential court records may be obtained by filing a written motion which must:

(A) identify the particular court record(s) or a portion of the court record(s) to which the movant seeks to obtain access with as much specificity as possible without revealing the confidential information;

(B) specify the bases for obtaining access to such court records;

(C) set forth the specific legal authority for obtaining access to such court records; and

(D) contain a certification that the motion is made in good faith and is supported by a sound factual and legal basis.

(3) The movant must serve a copy of the written motion to obtain access to confidential court records on all parties and reasonably ascertainable affected non-parties and the court must hold a hearing on the written motion within a reasonable period of time.

(4) Any order granting access to confidential court records must:

(A) describe the confidential information with as much specificity as possible without revealing the confidential information, including specifying the precise location of the information within the court records;

(B) identify the persons who are permitted to view the confidential information in the court records;

(C) identify any person who is permitted to obtain copies of the confidential court records; and

(D) state the time limits imposed on such access, if any, and any other applicable terms or limitations to such access.

(5) The filer of confidential court records, that filer's attorney of record, or that filer's agent as authorized by that filer in writing may obtain access to such confidential records pursuant to this subdivision.

(6) Unless otherwise provided, an order granting access to confidential court records under this subdivision shall not alter the confidential status of the record.

(k) Procedure for Service on Victims and Affected Non-parties and When Addresses Are Confidential.

(1) In criminal cases, when the defendant is required to serve any notice or motion described in this rule on an alleged victim of a crime, service shall be on the state attorney, who shall send or forward the notice or motion to the alleged victim.

(2) Except as set forth in subdivision (k)(1), when serving any notice or motion described in this rule on any affected non-party whose name or address is not confidential, the filer or movant shall use reasonable efforts to locate the affected non-party and may serve such affected non-party by any method set forth in Florida Rule of Judicial Administration 2.516.

(3) Except as set forth in subdivision (k)(1), when serving any notice or motion described in this rule and the name or address of any party or affected non-party is confidential, the filer or movant must state prominently in the caption of the notice or motion "Confidential Party or Confidential Affected Non-Party - Court Service Requested." When a notice or motion so designated is filed, the court shall be responsible for providing a copy of the notice or motion to the party or affected non-party, by any method permitted in Florida Rule of Judicial Administration 2.516, in such a way as to not reveal the confidential information.

(*l*) Denial of Access Request for Administrative Records. Expedited review of denials of access to administrative records of the judicial branch shall be provided through an action for mandamus or other appropriate relief, in the following manner:

(1) When a judge who has denied a request for access to records is the custodian, the action shall be filed in the court having appellate jurisdiction to review the decisions of the judge denying access. Upon order issued by the appellate court, the judge denying access to records shall file a sealed copy of the requested records with the appellate court.

(2) All other actions under this rule shall be filed in the circuit court of the circuit in which such denial of access occurs.

(m) Procedure for Public Access to Judicial Branch Records. Requests and responses to requests for access to records under this rule shall be made in a reasonable manner.

(1) Requests for access to judicial branch records shall be in writing and shall be directed to the custodian. The request shall provide sufficient specificity to enable the custodian to identify the requested records. The reason for the request is not required to be disclosed.

(2) The custodian shall be solely responsible for providing access to the records of the custodian's entity. The custodian shall determine whether the requested record is subject to this rule and, if so, whether the record or portions of the record are exempt from disclosure. The custodian shall determine the form in which the record is provided. If the request is denied, the custodian shall state in writing the basis for the denial.

(3) Fees for copies of records in all entities in the judicial branch of government, except for copies of court records, shall be the same as those provided in section 119.07, Florida Statutes.

Committee Notes

1995 Amendment. This rule was adopted to conform to the 1992 addition of article I, section 24, to the Florida Constitution. Amendments to this rule were adopted in response to the 1994 recommendations of the Study Committee on Confidentiality of Records of the Judicial Branch.

Subdivision (b) has been added by amendment and provides a definition of "judicial records" that is consistent with the definition of "court records" contained in rule 2.075(a)(1) [renumbered as 2.430(a)(1) in 2006] and the definition of "public records" contained in chapter 119, Florida Statutes. The word "exhibits" used in this definition of judicial records is intended to refer only to documentary evidence and does not refer to tangible items of evidence such as firearms, narcotics, etc. Judicial records within this definition include all judicial records and data regardless of the form in which they are kept. Reformatting of information may be necessary to protect copyrighted material. *Seigle v. Barry*, 422 So. 2d 63 (Fla. 4th DCA 1982), *review denied*, 431 So. 2d 988 (Fla. 1983).

The definition of "judicial records" also includes official business information transmitted via an electronic mail (e-mail) system. The judicial branch is presently experimenting with this new technology. For example, e-mail is currently being used by the judicial branch to transmit between judges and staff multiple matters in the courts including direct communications between judges and staff and other judges, proposed drafts of opinions and orders, memoranda concerning pending cases, proposed jury instructions, and even votes on proposed opinions. All of this type of information is exempt from public disclosure under rules 2.051(c)(1) and (c)(2) [renumbered as 2.420(c)(1) and (c)(2) in 2006]. With few exceptions, these examples of e-mail transmissions are sent and received between judicial officials and employees within a particular court's jurisdiction. This type of e-mail is by its very nature almost always exempt from public record disclosure pursuant to rule 2.051(c). In addition, official business e-mail transmissions sent to or received by judicial officials or employees using dial-in equipment, as well as the use of on-line outside research facilities such as Westlaw, would also be exempt email under rule 2.051(c). On the other hand, we recognize that not all e-mail sent and received within a particular court's jurisdiction will fall into an exception under rule 2.051(c). The fact that a non-exempt e-mail message made or received in connection with official court business is transmitted intra-court does not relieve judicial officials or employees from the obligation of properly having a record made of such messages so they will be available to the public similar to any other written communications. It appears that official business e-mail that is sent or received by persons outside a particular court's jurisdiction is largely non-exempt and is subject to recording in some form as a public record. Each court should develop a means to properly make a record of non-exempt official business e-mail by either electronically storing the mail or by making a hard copy. It is important to note that, although official business communicated by e-mail transmissions is a matter of public record under the rule, the exemptions provided in rule 2.051(c) exempt many of these judge/staff transmissions from the public record. E-mail may also include transmissions that are clearly not official business and are, consequently, not required to be recorded as a public record. Each court should also publish an e-mail address for public access. The individual e-mail addresses of judicial officials and staff are exempt under rule 2.051(c)(2) to protect the compelling interests of maintaining the uninterrupted use of the computer for research, word-processing, preparation of opinions, and communication during trials, and to ensure computer security.

Subdivision (c)(3) was amended by creating subparts (a) and (b) to distinguish between the provisions governing the confidentiality of complaints against judges and complaints against other individuals or entities licensed or regulated by the Supreme Court.

Subdivision (c)(5) was amended to make public the qualifications of persons applying to serve or serving the court as unpaid volunteers such as guardians ad litem, mediators, and arbitrators and to make public the applications and evaluations of such persons upon a showing of materiality in a pending court proceeding or upon a showing of good cause.

Subdivision (c)(9) has also been amended. Subdivision (c)(9) was adopted to incorporate the holdings of judicial decisions establishing that confidentiality may be required to protect the rights of defendants, litigants, or third parties; to further the administration of justice; or to otherwise promote a compelling governmental interest. *Barron v. Florida Freedom Newspapers, Inc.*, 531 So.2d 113 (Fla.1988); *Miami Herald Publishing Co. v. Lewis*, 426 So.2d 1 (Fla.1982). Such confidentiality may be implemented by court rule, as well as by judicial decision, where necessary for the effective administration of justice. *See, e.g.*, Fla.R.Crim.P. 3.470, (Sealed Verdict); Fla.R.Crim.P. 3.712, (Presentence Investigation Reports); Fla.R.Civ.P. 1.280(c), (Protective Orders).

Subdivision (c)(9)(D) requires that, except where otherwise provided by law or rule of court, reasonable notice shall be given to the public of any order closing a court record. This subdivision is not applicable to court proceedings. Unlike the closure of court proceedings, which has been held to require notice and hearing prior to closure, *see Miami Herald Publishing Co. v. Lewis*, 426 So. 2d 1 (Fla.1982), the closure of court records has not required prior notice. Requiring prior notice of closure of a court record may be impractical and burdensome in emergency circumstances or when closure of a court record requiring confidentiality is requested during a judicial proceeding. Providing reasonable notice to the public of the entry of a closure order and an opportunity to be heard on the closure issue adequately protects the competing interests of confidentiality and public access to judicial records. *See Florida Freedom Newspapers, Inc. v. Sirmons*, 508 So.2d 462 (Fla. 1st DCA 1987), *approved, Barron v. Florida Freedom Newspapers, Inc.*, 531 So.2d 113 (Fla.1988); *State ex rel. Tallahassee Democrat v. Cooksey*, 371 So.2d 207 (Fla. 1st DCA 1979). Subdivision (c)(9)(D), however, does not preclude the giving of prior notice of closure of a court record, and the court may elect to give prior notice in appropriate cases.

Court Commentary

2002 Court Commentary. The custodian is required to provide access to or copies of records but is not required either to provide information from records or to create new records in response to a request. Op. Atty. Gen. Fla. 80-57 (1980); *Wootton v. Cook*, 590 So.2d 1039 (Fla. 1st DCA 1991); *Seigle v. Barry*, 422 So.2d 63 (Fla. 4th DCA 1982).

The writing requirement is not intended to disadvantage any person who may have difficulty writing a request; if any difficulty exists, the custodian should aid the requestor in reducing the request to writing.

It is anticipated that each judicial branch entity will have policies and procedures for responding to public records requests.

The 1995 commentary notes that the definition of "judicial records" added at that time is consistent with the definition of "court records" contained in rule 2.075(a)(1) [renumbered as 2.430(a)(1) in 2006] and the definition of "public records" contained in chapter 119, Florida Statutes. Despite the commentary, these definitions are not the same. The definitions added in 2002 are intended to clarify that records of the judicial branch include court records as defined in rule 2.075(a)(1) and administrative records. The definition of records of the judicial branch is consistent with the definition of "public records" in chapter 119, Florida Statutes.

2005 Court Commentary. Under courts' inherent authority, appellate courts may appoint a special magistrate to serve as commissioner for the court to make findings of fact and oversee discovery in review proceedings under subdivision (d) of this rule. Cf. *State ex rel. Davis v. City of Avon Park*, 158 So. 159 (Fla. 1934) (recognizing appellate courts' inherent authority to do all things reasonably necessary for administration of justice within the scope of courts' jurisdiction, including the appointment of a commissioner to make findings of fact); *Wessells v. State*, 737 So. 2d 1103 (Fla. 1st DCA 1998) (relinquishing jurisdiction to circuit court for appointment of a special master to serve as commissioner for court to make findings of fact).

2007 Court Commentary. New subdivision (d) applies only to motions that seek to make court records in noncriminal cases confidential in accordance with subdivision (c)(9).

2007 Committee Commentary. Subdivision (d)(2) is intended to permit a party to make use of any court-provided recording device or system that is available generally for litigants' use, but is not intended to require the court system to make such devices available where they are not already in use and is not intended to eliminate any cost for use of such system that is generally borne by a party requesting use of such system.

IN THE _____ ......(NAME OF
COURT)....., FLORIDA

CASE NO.: _____

_____
Plaintiff/Petitioner,

v.

_____
Defendant/Respondent.
_____/

NOTICE OF CONFIDENTIAL INFORMATION WITHIN COURT FILING

Pursuant to Florida Rule of Judicial Administration 2.420(d)(2), I hereby certify:

( ) (1) I am filing herewith a document containing confidential information as described in Rule 2.420(d)(1)(B) and that:

(a) The title/type of document is: _____, and:

(b)( ) the entire document is confidential, or
(   ) the confidential information within the document is precisely located at:
_____.

OR

( ) (2) A document was previously filed in this case that contains confidential information as described in Rule 2.420(d)(1)(B), but a Notice of Confidential Information within Court Filing was not filed with the document and the confidential information was not maintained as confidential by the clerk of the court. I hereby notify the clerk that this confidential information is located as follows:

(a) Title/type of document: _____;
(b) Date of filing (if known): _____;
(c) Date of document: _____;
(d) Docket entry number: _____;
(e) ( ) Entire document is confidential, or
    ( ) Precise location of confidential information in document: _____
_____.

_____
Filer's Signature

CERTIFICATE OF SERVICE

I HEREBY CERTIFY that a copy of the foregoing was furnished by (e-mail) (delivery) (mail) (fax) on: (All Parties and Affected Non-Parties. Note: If the name or address of a Party or Affected Non-Party is confidential

DO NOT include such information in this Certificate of Service. Instead, serve the State Attorney or request Court Service. See Rule 2.420(k)) _____, on _____, 20 ____.

Name ....

Address ....

Phone ....

Florida Bar No. (if applicable) ......

E-mail address ....

Note: The clerk of court shall review filings identified as containing confidential information to determine whether the information is facially subject to confidentiality under subdivision (d)(1)(B). The clerk shall notify the filer in writing within 5 days if the clerk determines that the information is NOT subject to confidentiality, and the records shall not be held as confidential for more than 10 days, unless a motion is filed pursuant to subdivision (d)(3) of the Rule. Fla. R. Jud. Admin. 2.420(d)(2).

RULE 2.425. MINIMIZATION OF THE FILING OF SENSITIVE INFORMATION

(a) Limitation for Court Filings. Unless authorized by subdivision (b), statute, another rule of court, or the court orders otherwise, designated sensitive information filed with the court must be limited to the following format:

(1) The initials of a person known to be a minor;

(2) The year of birth of a person's birth date;

(3) No portion of any

(A) social security number,

(B) bank account number,

(C) credit card account number,

(D) charge account number, or

(E) debit account number,

(4) The last four digits of any

(A) taxpayer identification number (TIN),

(B) employee identification number,

(C) driver's license number,

(D) passport number,

(E) telephone number,

(F) financial account number, except as set forth in subdivision (a)(3),

(G) brokerage account number,

(H) insurance policy account number,

(I) loan account number,

(J) customer account number, or

(K) patient or health care number;

(5) A truncated version of any

(A) email address,

(B) computer user name,

(C) password, or

(D) personal identification number (PIN); and

(6) A truncated version of any other sensitive information as provided by court order.

(b) Exceptions. Subdivision (a) does not apply to the following:

(1) An account number which identifies the property alleged to be the subject of a proceeding;

(2) The record of an administrative or agency proceeding;

(3) The record in appellate or review proceedings;

(4) The birth date of a minor whenever the birth date is necessary for the court to establish or maintain subject matter jurisdiction;

(5) The name of a minor in any order relating to parental responsibility, time-sharing, or child support;

(6) The name of a minor in any document or order affecting the minor's ownership of real property;

(7) The birth date of a party in a writ of attachment or notice to payor;

(8) In traffic and criminal proceedings

(A) a pro se filing;

(B) a court filing that is related to a criminal matter or investigation and that is prepared before the filing of a criminal charge or is not filed as part of any docketed criminal case;

(C) an arrest or search warrant or any information in support thereof;

(D) a charging document and an affidavit or other documents filed in support of any charging document, including any driving records;

(E) a statement of particulars;

(F) discovery material introduced into evidence or otherwise filed with the court;

(G) all information necessary for the proper issuance and execution of a subpoena duces tecum;

(H) information needed to contact witnesses who will support the defendant's claim of newly discovered evidence under Florida Rule of Criminal Procedure 3.851; and

(I) information needed to complete a sentencing scoresheet;

(9) Information used by the clerk for case maintenance purposes or the courts for case management purposes; and

(10) Information which is relevant and material to an issue before the court.

(c) **Remedies.** Upon motion by a party or interested person or sua sponte by the court, the court may order remedies, sanctions or both for a violation of subdivision (a). Following notice and an opportunity to respond, the court may impose sanctions if such filing was not made in good faith.

(d) **Motions Not Restricted.** This rule does not restrict a party's right to move for protective order, to move to file documents under seal, or to request a determination of the confidentiality of records.

(e) **Application.** This rule does not affect the application of constitutional provisions, statutes, or rules of court regarding confidential information or access to public information.

RULE 2.430. RETENTION OF COURT RECORDS

(a) **Definitions.** The following definitions apply to this rule:

(1) "Court records" mean the contents of the court file, including the progress docket and other similar records generated to document activity in a case, transcripts filed with the clerk, documentary exhibits in the custody of the clerk, and electronic records, video tapes, or stenographic tapes of depositions or other proceedings filed with the clerk, and electronic records, videotapes or stenographic tapes of court proceedings.

(2) "After a judgment has become final" means:

(A) when a final order, final judgment, final docket entry, final dismissal, or nolle prosequi has been entered as to all parties, no appeal has been taken, and the time for appeal has expired; or

(B) when a final order, final judgment, or final docket entry has been entered, an appeal has been taken, the appeal has been disposed of, and the time for any further appellate proceedings has expired.

(3) "Permanently recorded" means that a document has been microfilmed, optically imaged, or recorded onto an electronic record keeping system in accordance with standards adopted by the Supreme Court of Florida.

(b) **Permanently Recorded Records.**

(1) Court records, except exhibits, that have been permanently recorded may be destroyed or otherwise disposed of by the clerk at any time after a judgment has become final.

(2) Any physical media submitted to the clerk for the purpose of filing information contained in the media may be destroyed, retained, or otherwise disposed of by the clerk once the contents of the media have been made a part of the court record.

(c) **Records Not Permanently Recorded.** No court records under this subdivision shall be destroyed or disposed of until the final order, final docket entry, or final judgment is permanently recorded for, or recorded in, the public records. The time periods shall not apply to any action in which the court orders the court records to be kept until the court orders otherwise. When an order is entered to that effect, the progress docket and the court file shall be marked by the clerk with a legend showing that the court records are not to be destroyed or disposed of without a further order of court. Any person may apply for an order suspending or prohibiting destruction or disposition of court records in any proceeding. Court records, except exhibits, that are not permanently recorded may be destroyed or disposed of by the clerk after a judgment has become final in accordance with the following schedule:

(1) For trial courts

(A) 60 days — Parking tickets and noncriminal traffic infractions after required audits have been completed.

(B) 2 years — Proceedings under the Small Claims Rules, Medical Mediation Proceedings.

(C) 5 years — Noncriminal ordinance violations, civil litigation proceedings in county court other than those under the Small Claims Rules, and civil proceedings in circuit court except marriage dissolutions and adoptions.

(D) 10 years — Probate, guardianship, and mental health proceedings.

(E) 10 years — Felony and misdemeanor cases in which no information or indictment was filed or in which all charges were dismissed, or in which the state announced a nolle prosequi, or in which the defendant was adjudicated not guilty.

(F) 75 years — Juvenile proceedings containing an order permanently depriving a parent of custody of a child, and adoptions, and all felony and misdemeanor cases not previously destroyed.

(G) Juvenile proceedings not otherwise provided for in this subdivision shall be kept for 5 years after the last entry or until the child reaches the age of majority, whichever is later.

(H) Marriage dissolutions — 10 years from the last record activity. The court may authorize destruction of court records not involving alimony, support, or custody of children 5 years from the last record activity.

(2) For district courts of appeal

(A) 2 years — noncriminal court records.

(B) 5 years — Criminal court records.

(3) For the Supreme Court

(A) 5 years — All cases disposed of by order not otherwise provided for in this rule.

(B) 10 years — Cases disposed of by order involving individuals licensed or regulated by the court and noncriminal court records involving the unauthorized practice of law.

(d) Records to Be Retained Permanently. The following court records shall be permanently recorded or permanently retained:

(1) progress dockets, and other similar records generated to document activity in a case, and

(2) court records of the supreme court in which the case was disposed of by opinion.

(e) Court Reporters' Notes. Court reporters or persons acting as court reporters for judicial or discovery proceedings shall retain the original notes or electronic records of the proceedings or depositions until the times specified below:

(1) 2 years from the date of preparing the transcript — Judicial proceedings, arbitration hearings, and discovery proceedings when an original transcript has been prepared.

(2) 10 years — Judicial proceedings in felony cases when a transcript has not been prepared.

(3) 5 years — All other judicial proceedings, arbitration hearings, and discovery proceedings when a transcript has not been prepared.

When an agreement has been made between the reporter and any other person and the person has paid the reasonable charges for storage and retention of the notes, the notes or records shall be kept for any longer time agreed on. All reporters' notes shall be retained in a secure place in Florida.

(f) Exhibits.

(1) Exhibits in criminal proceedings shall be disposed of as provided by law.

(2) All other exhibits shall be retained by the clerk until 90 days after a judgment has become final. If an exhibit is not withdrawn pursuant to subdivision (i) within 90 days, the clerk may destroy or dispose of the exhibits after giving the parties or their attorneys of record 30 days' notice of the clerk's intention to do so. Exhibits shall be delivered to any party or attorney of record calling for them during the 30-day time period.

(g) Disposition Other Than Destruction. Before destruction or disposition of court records under this rule, any person may apply to the court for an order requiring the clerk to deliver to the applicant the court records that are to be destroyed or disposed of. All parties shall be given notice of the application. The court shall dispose of that court record as appropriate.

(h) Release of Court Records. This rule does not limit the power of the court to release exhibits or other parts of court records that are the property of the person or party initially placing the items in the court records. The court may require copies to be substituted as a condition to releasing the court records under this subdivision.

(i) Right to Expunge Records. Nothing in this rule shall affect the power of the court to order records expunged.

(j) Sealed Records. No record which has been sealed from public examination by order of court shall be destroyed without hearing after such notice as the court shall require.

(k) Destruction of Jury Notes. At the conclusion of the trial and promptly following discharge of the jury, the court shall collect all juror notes and immediately destroy the juror notes.

RULE 2.440. RETENTION OF JUDICIAL BRANCH ADMINISTRATIVE RECORDS

(a) Definitions.

(1) "Judicial branch" means the judicial branch of government, which includes the state courts system, the clerk of court when acting as an arm of the court, The Florida Bar, the Florida Board of Bar Examiners, the Judicial Qualifications Commission, and all other entities established by or operating under the authority of the supreme court or the chief justice.

(2) "Records of the judicial branch" means all records, regardless of physical form, characteristics, or means of transmission, made or received in connection with the transaction of official business by any judicial branch entity and consists of:

(A) "court records," which means the contents of the court file, including the progress docket and other similar records generated to document activity in a case, transcripts filed with the clerk, documentary exhibits in the custody of the clerk, and electronic records, videotapes, or stenographic tapes of depositions or other proceedings filed with the clerk, and electronic records, videotapes, or stenographic tapes of court proceedings; and

(B) "administrative records," which means all other records made or received pursuant to court rule, law, or ordinance, or in connection with the transaction of official business by any judicial branch entity.

(b) Retention requirements. Administrative records in the judicial branch shall be retained in accordance with the Judicial Branch Records Retention Schedule approved by the supreme court.

Court Commentary

2002 Commentary. This rule does not apply to court records and files that are governed by rule 2.075 [renumbered as 2.430 in 2006]. This rule applies to administrative records.

To provide a consistent schedule for retention of administrative records in the judicial branch, the Supreme Court Workgroup on Public Records recommended that the Court adopt the Judicial Branch Records Retention Schedule. This schedule uses the legislatively authorized Department of State retention schedules, as appropriate, and includes a schedule for other records that are unique to the judicial branch. *[This schedule is set forth at the end of these rules.]*

RULE 2.450. TECHNOLOGICAL COVERAGE OF JUDICIAL PROCEEDINGS

(a) Electronic and Still Photography Allowed. Subject at all times to the authority of the presiding judge to: (i) control the conduct of proceedings before the court; (ii) ensure decorum and prevent distractions; and (iii) ensure the fair administration of justice in the pending cause, electronic media and still photography coverage of public judicial proceedings in the appellate and trial courts of this state shall be allowed in accordance with the following standards of conduct and technology promulgated by the Supreme Court of Florida.

(b) Equipment and Personnel.

(1) At least 1 portable television camera, operated by not more than 1 camera person, shall be permitted in any trial or appellate court proceeding. The number of permitted cameras shall be within the sound discretion and authority of the presiding judge.

(2) Not more than 1 still photographer, using not more than 2 still cameras, shall be permitted in any proceeding in a trial or appellate court.

(3) Not more than 1 audio system for radio broadcast purposes shall be permitted in any proceeding in a trial or appellate court. Audio pickup for all media purposes shall be accomplished from existing audio systems present in the court facility. If no technically suitable audio system exists in the court facility, microphones and related wiring essential for media purposes shall be unobtrusive and shall be located in places designated in advance of any proceeding by the chief judge of the judicial circuit or district in which the court facility is located.

(4) Any "pooling" arrangements among the media required by these limitations on equipment and personnel shall be the sole responsibility of the media without calling upon the presiding judge to mediate any dispute as to the appropriate media representative or equipment authorized to cover a particular proceeding. In the absence of advance media agreement on

disputed equipment or personnel issues, the presiding judge shall exclude all contesting media personnel from a proceeding.

(c) Sound and Light Criteria.

(1) Only television photographic and audio equipment that does not produce distracting sound or light shall be used to cover judicial proceedings. No artificial lighting device of any kind shall be used in connection with the television camera.

(2) Only still camera equipment that does not produce distracting sound or light shall be used to cover judicial proceedings. No artificial lighting device of any kind shall be used in connection with a still camera.

(3) It shall be the affirmative duty of media personnel to demonstrate to the presiding judge adequately in advance of any proceeding that the equipment sought to be used meets the sound and light criteria enunciated in this rule. A failure to obtain advance judicial approval for equipment shall preclude its use in any proceeding.

(d) Location of Equipment Personnel.

(1) Television camera equipment shall be positioned in such location in the court facility as shall be designated by the chief judge of the judicial circuit or district in which such facility is situated. The area designated shall provide reasonable access to coverage. If and when areas remote from the court facility that permit reasonable access to coverage are provided, all television camera and audio equipment shall be positioned only in such area. Videotape recording equipment that is not a component part of a television camera shall be located in an area remove from the court facility.

(2) A still camera photographer shall position himself or herself in such location in the court facility as shall be designated by the chief judge of the judicial circuit or district in which such facility is situated. The area designated shall provide reasonable access to coverage. Still camera photographers shall assume a fixed position within the designated area and, once

established in a shooting position, shall act so as not to call attention to themselves through further movement. Still camera photographers shall not be permitted to move about in order to obtain photographs of court proceedings.

(3) Broadcast media representatives shall not move about the court facility while proceedings are in session, and microphones or taping equipment once positioned as required by subdivision (b)(3) shall not be moved during the pendency of the proceeding.

(e) Movement During Proceedings. News media photographic or audio equipment shall not be placed in or removed from the court facility except before commencement or after adjournment of proceedings each day, or during a recess. Neither television film magazines nor still camera film or lenses shall be changed within a court facility except during a recess in the proceeding.

(f) Courtroom Light Sources. With the concurrence of the chief judge of a judicial circuit or district in which a court facility is situated, modifications and additions may be made in light sources existing in the facility, provided such modifications or additions are installed and maintained without public expense.

(g) Conferences of Counsel. To protect the attorney-client privilege and the effective right to counsel, there shall be no audio pickup or broadcast of conferences that occur in a court facility between attorneys and their clients, between co-counsel of a client, or between counsel and the presiding judge held at the bench.

(h) Impermissible Use of Media Material. None of the film, videotape, still photographs, or audio reproductions developed during or by virtue of coverage of a judicial proceeding shall be admissible as evidence in the proceeding out of which it arose, in any proceeding subsequent or collateral thereto, or upon retrial or appeal of such proceedings.

(i) Appellate Review. Review of an order excluding the electronic media from access to any proceeding, excluding coverage of a particular participant, or upon any other matters arising under these standards

shall be pursuant to Florida Rule of Appellate Procedure 9.100(d).

Court Commentary

1994 Amendment. This rule was copied from Canon 3A(7) of the Code of Judicial Conduct. Canon 3A(7) represented a departure from former Canon 3A(7) [ABA Canon 35]. The former canon generally proscribed electronic media and still photography coverage of judicial proceedings from within and in areas immediately adjacent to the courtroom, with three categories of exceptions - (a) use for judicial administration, (b) coverage of investitive, ceremonial, and naturalization proceedings, and (c) use for instructional purposes in educational institutions. Subject to the limitations and promulgation of standards as mentioned therein, the revised canon constituted a general authorization for electronic media and still photography coverage for all purposes, including the purposes expressed as exceptions in the former canon. Limited only by the authority of the presiding judge in the exercise of sound discretion to prohibit filming or photographing of particular participants, consent of participants to coverage is not required. The text of the rule refers to public judicial proceedings. This is in recognition of the authority reposing in the presiding judge, upon the exercise of sound discretion, to hold certain judicial proceedings or portions thereof in camera, and in recognition of the fact that certain proceedings or portions thereof are made confidential by statute. The term "presiding judge" includes the chief judge of an appellate tribunal.

RULE 2.451. USE OF ELECTRONIC DEVICES

(a) Electronic Devices Defined. An electronic device is any device capable of making or transmitting still or moving photographs, video recordings, or images of any kind; any device capable of creating, transmitting, or receiving text or data; and any device capable of receiving, transmitting, or recording sound. Electronic devices include, without limitation, film cameras, digital cameras, video cameras, any other type of camera, cellular telephones, tape recorders, digital voice recorders, any other type of audio recorders, laptop computers, personal digital assistants, or other similar technological devices with the ability to make or transmit video recordings, audio recordings, images, text, or data.

(b) Use of Electronic Devices by Jurors.

(1) Electronic devices, as that term is defined in subdivision (a), may be removed as directed by the presiding judge from all members of a jury panel at any time before deliberations, but such electronic devices must be removed from all members of a jury panel before jury deliberations begin. The electronic

devices will be removed and appropriately secured by the bailiff or other person designated by the chief judge.

(2) Any electronic devices removed from members of a jury panel may be returned to the members of the jury panel during recesses in the trial. When jurors are sequestered, the presiding judge may determine whether the electronic devices will be removed from jurors during the entire period of sequestration.

(3) From the time a person reports for jury service until the person is discharged from jury service, that person is prohibited from using electronic devices for any of the following purposes:

(A) making or transmitting still or moving photographs, audio recordings, video recordings, or images of any kind of the court proceedings;

(B) transmitting or accessing text or data during the court proceedings;

(C) transmitting or accessing text or data about the case on which the juror is serving;

(D) researching, transmitting, or accessing information about the case on which the juror is serving;

(E) otherwise communicating about the case on which the juror is serving; or

(F) otherwise communicating about the jury deliberations.

(4) Nothing in this rule is to be construed to limit or impair the authority of a chief judge or presiding judge to grant permission to a juror to retain his or her electronic device during trial proceedings.

(5) The jury summons mailed to prospective jurors should contain a notice that electronic devices will be removed from all members of a jury panel before jury deliberations begin and as directed by the presiding judge, may be removed at other stages of a trial. At the beginning of the trial, the presiding judge should advise the jury panel about the removal of electronic devices.

(c) Use of Electronic Devices by Others.

(1) The use of electronic devices in a courtroom is subject at all times to the authority of the presiding judge or quasi-judicial officer to

(A) control the conduct of proceedings before the court;

(B) ensure decorum and prevent distractions; and

(C) ensure the fair administration of justice in the pending cause.

(2) The use of electronic devices in a courthouse or court facility is subject at all times to the authority of the chief judge to

(A) ensure decorum and prevent distractions;

(B) ensure the fair administration of justice; and

(C) preserve court security.

Court Commentary

2013 Adoption. Subdivision (c), Use of Electronic Devices by Others, parallels Florida Rule of Judicial Administration 2.450(a) regarding the use of electronic devices by the media.

PART V. PRACTICE OF LAW

A. ATTORNEYS

RULE 2.505. ATTORNEYS

(a) Scope and Purpose. All persons in good standing as members of The Florida Bar shall be permitted to practice in Florida. Attorneys of other states who are not members of the Florida Bar in good standing shall not engage in the practice of law in Florida except to the extent permitted by rule 2.510.

(b) Persons Employed by the Court. Except as provided in this subdivision, no full-time employee of the court shall practice as an attorney in any court or before any agency of government while continuing in that position. Any attorney designated by the chief justice or chief judge may represent the court, any court employee in the employee's official capacity, or any judge in the judge's official capacity, in any proceeding in which the court, employee, or judge is an interested party. An attorney formerly employed by a court shall not represent anyone in connection with a matter in which the attorney participated personally and substantially while employed by the court, unless all parties to the proceeding consent after disclosure.

(c) Attorney Not to Be Surety. No attorneys or other officers of court shall enter themselves or be taken as bail or surety in any proceeding in court.

(d) Stipulations. No private agreement or consent between parties or their attorneys concerning the practice or procedure in an action shall be of any force unless the evidence of it is in writing, subscribed by the party or the party's attorney against whom it is alleged. Parol agreements may be made before the court if promptly made a part of the record or incorporated in the stenographic notes of the proceedings, and agreements made at depositions that are incorporated in the transcript need not be signed when signing of the deposition is waived. This rule shall not apply to settlements or other substantive agreements.

(e) Appearance of Attorney. An attorney may appear in a proceeding in any of the following ways:

(1) By serving and filing, on behalf of a party, the party's first pleading or paper in the proceeding.

(2) By substitution of counsel, but only by order of court and with written consent of the client, filed with the court. The court may condition substitution upon payment of, or security for, the substituted attorney's fees and expenses, or upon such other terms as may be just.

(3) By filing with the court and serving upon all parties a notice of appearance as counsel for a party that has already appeared in a proceeding pro se or as co-counsel for a party that has already appeared in a proceeding by non-withdrawing counsel.

(f) Termination of Appearance of Attorney. The appearance of an attorney for a party in a proceeding shall terminate only in one of the following ways:

(1) Withdrawal of Attorney. By order of court, where the proceeding is continuing, upon motion and

hearing, on notice to all parties and the client, such motion setting forth the reasons for withdrawal and the client's last known address, telephone number, including area code, and email address.

(2) Substitution of Attorney. By order of court, under the procedure set forth in subdivision (e)(2) of this rule.

(3) Termination of Proceeding. Automatically, without order of court, upon the termination of a proceeding, whether by final order of dismissal, by final adjudication, or otherwise, and following the expiration of any applicable time for appeal, where no appeal is taken.

(4) Filing of Notice of Completion. For limited representation proceedings under Florida Family Law Rule of Procedure 12.040, automatically, by the filing of a notice of completion titled "Termination of Limited Appearance" pursuant to rule 12.040(c).

(g) Law Student Participation. Eligible law students shall be permitted to participate as provided under the conditions of chapter 11 of the Rules Regulating The Florida Bar as amended from time to time.

(h) Attorney as Agent of Client. In all matters concerning the prosecution or defense of any proceeding in the court, the attorney of record shall be the agent of the client, and any notice by or to the attorney or act by the attorney in the proceeding shall be accepted as the act of or notice to the client.

Court Commentary

1997 Amendment. Originally, the rule provided that the followup filing had to occur within ten days. In the 1997 amendment to the rule, that requirement was modified to provide that the follow-up filing must occur "immediately" after a document is electronically filed. The "immediately thereafter" language is consistent with language used in the rules of procedure where, in a somewhat analogous situation, the filing of a document may occur after service. See, e.g., Florida Rule of Civil Procedure 1.080(d) ("All original papers shall be filed with the court either before service or *immediately thereafter.*") (emphasis added). "Immediately thereafter" has been interpreted to mean "filed with reasonable promptness." *Miami Transit Co. v. Ford*, 155 So. 2d 360 (Fla. 1963).

The use of the words "other person" in this rule is not meant to allow a nonlawyer to sign and file pleadings or other papers on behalf of another. Such conduct would constitute the unauthorized practice of law.

2003 Amendment. Rule Regulating the Florida Bar 4-1.12(c), which addresses the imputed disqualification of a law firm, should be looked to in conjunction with the rule 2.060(b) [renumbered as 2.505(b) in 2006] restriction on representation by a former judicial staff attorney or law clerk.

RULE 2.510. FOREIGN ATTORNEYS

(a) **Eligibility.** Upon filing a verified motion with the court, an attorney who is an active member in good standing of the bar of another state and currently eligible to practice law in a state other than Florida may be permitted to appear in particular cases in a Florida court upon such conditions as the court may deem appropriate, provided that a member of The Florida Bar in good standing is associated as an attorney of record. The foreign attorney must make application in each court in which a case is filed even if a lower tribunal granted a motion to appear in the same case. In determining whether to permit a foreign attorney to appear pursuant to this rule, the court may consider, among other things, information provided under subdivision (b)(3) concerning discipline in other jurisdictions. No attorney is authorized to appear pursuant to this rule if the attorney (1) is a Florida resident, unless the attorney has an application pending for admission to The Florida Bar and has not previously been denied admission to The Florida Bar; (2) is a member of The Florida Bar but is ineligible to practice law; (3) has previously been disciplined or held in contempt by reason of misconduct committed while engaged in representation permitted pursuant to this rule provided, however, the contempt is final and has not been reversed or abated; (4) has failed to provide notice to The Florida Bar or pay the filing fee as required in subdivision (b)(7); or (5) is engaged in a "general practice" before Florida courts. For purposes of this rule, more than 3 appearances within a 365-day period in separate cases shall be presumed to be a "general practice." Appearances at different levels of the court system in the same case shall be deemed 1 appearance for the purposes of determining whether a foreign attorney has made more than 3 appearances within a 365-day period. In cases involving indigent or pro bono clients, the court may waive the filing fee for good cause shown. This rule shall not affect the eligibility of a foreign attorney to appear in a Florida court when authorized by federal law.

(b) **Contents of Verified Motion.** A form verified motion accompanies this rule and shall be utilized by the foreign attorney. The verified motion required by subdivision (a) shall include:

(1) a statement identifying all jurisdictions in which the attorney is an active member in good standing and currently eligible to practice law, including all assigned bar numbers and attorney numbers, for which a certificate of good standing is not required;

(2) a statement identifying by date, case name, and case number all other matters in Florida state courts in which pro hac vice admission has been sought in the preceding 5 years, including any lower tribunals for the case in which the motion is filed, and whether such admission was granted or denied;

(3) a statement identifying all jurisdictions in which disciplinary, suspension, disbarment, or contempt proceedings have been initiated against the attorney in the preceding 5 years including the date on which the proceeding was initiated, the nature of the alleged violation, and the result of the proceeding including the sanction, if any, imposed;

(4) a statement identifying the date on which the legal representation at issue commenced, and the party or parties represented;

(5) a statement that all applicable provisions of these rules and the rules regulating the Florida bar have been read, and that the verified motion complies with those rules;

(6) the name, record bar address, and membership status of the Florida bar member or members associated for purposes of the representation;

(7) a certificate indicating service of the verified motion upon all counsel of record in the matter in which leave to appear pro hac vice is sought and upon The Florida Bar at its Tallahassee office accompanied by a nonrefundable $250.00 filing fee made payable to The Florida Bar or notice that the movant has requested a judicial waiver of said fee; and

(8) a verification by the attorney seeking to appear pursuant to this rule and the signature of the Florida bar member or members associated for purposes of the representation.

IN THE _____ COURT OF THE _____ JUDICIAL CIRCUIT,
_____ IN AND FOR _____, COUNTY, FLORIDA

Case No. _____

_____
    Plaintiff

Division _____

vs.

_____
    Defendant

VERIFIED MOTION FOR ADMISSION TO APPEAR *PRO HAC VICE*

PURSUANT TO FLORIDA RULE OF JUDICIAL ADMINISTRATION 2.510

Comes now _____, Movant herein, and respectfully represents the following:

1. [ ] Movant resides in _____, _____.
                       (City)   (State)
Movant is not a resident of the State of Florida.

    [ ] Movant is a resident of the State of Florida and has an application pending for admission to The Florida Bar and has not previously been denied admission to The Florida Bar.

2. Movant is an attorney and a member of the law firm of (or practices law under the name of) _____ with offices at _____(Street Address)_____, _____(City)_____, _____(County)_____ _____(State)_____ _____(Zip Code)_____ _____(Telephone)_____ .

3. Movant has been retained personally or as a member of the above-named law firm on __(Date Representation Commenced)__ by ____(Name of Party or Parties)____ to provide legal representation in connection with the above-styled matter now pending before the above-named court of the State of Florida.

4. Movant is an active member in good standing and currently eligible to practice law in the following jurisdiction(s): Include attorney or bar number(s). (Attach an additional sheet if necessary.)

    JURISDICTION   ATTORNEY/BAR NUMBER

_____

_____

_____

_____

_____

5. There have been no disciplinary, suspension, disbarment, or contempt proceedings initiated against Movant in the preceding 5 years, except as provided below (give jurisdiction of proceeding, date upon which proceeding was initiated, nature of alleged violation, statement of whether the proceeding has concluded or is still pending,

and sanction, if any, imposed):
(Attach an additional sheet if necessary.)

_____
_____
_____
_____
_____

6. Movant, either by resignation, withdrawal, or otherwise, never has terminated or attempted to terminate Movant's office as an attorney in order to avoid administrative, disciplinary, disbarment, or suspension proceedings.

7. Movant is not an inactive member of The Florida Bar.

8. Movant is not now a member of The Florida Bar.

9. Movant is not a suspended member of The Florida Bar.

10. Movant is not a disbarred member of The Florida Bar nor has Movant received a disciplinary resignation or disciplinary revocation from The Florida Bar.

11. Movant has not previously been disciplined or held in contempt by reason of misconduct committed while engaged in representation pursuant to Florida Rule of Judicial Administration 2.510, except as provided below (give date of disciplinary action or contempt, reasons therefor, and court imposing contempt):
(Attach an additional sheet if necessary.)

_____
_____
_____
_____
_____

12. Movant has filed motion(s) to appear as counsel in Florida state courts during the past five (5) years in the following matters: (Attach an additional sheet if necessary)

Date of Motion	Case Name	Case Number	Court	Date Motion	Granted/Denied

13. Local counsel of record associated with Movant in this matter is _____ (Name and Florida Bar Number)   who is an active member in good standing of The Florida Bar and has offices at _____(Street   Address)_____ , _____(City)_____ , _____(County)_____ , Florida, ___(Zip Code)_____ (Telephone with area code)_____ .

(If local counsel is not an active member of The Florida Bar in good standing, please provide information as to local counsel's membership status _____)

14. Movant has read the applicable provisions of Florida Rule of Judicial Administration 2.510 and Rule 1-3.10 of the Rules Regulating The Florida Bar and certifies that this verified motion complies with those rules.

15. Movant agrees to comply with the provisions of the Florida Rules of Professional Conduct and consents to the jurisdiction of the courts and the Bar of the State of Florida.

WHEREFORE, Movant respectfully requests permission to appear in this court for this cause only.

Dated this _____ day of _____, 20____.

_____

Movant

_____

Address

_____

Address

_____

City, State, Zip Code

_____

Telephone Number

_____

E-mail Address

STATE OF _____

COUNTY OF _____

I, _____, do hereby swear or affirm under penalty of perjury that I am the Movant in the above-styled matter; that I have read the foregoing Motion and know the contents thereof, and the contents are true of my own knowledge and belief.

_____

Movant

I hereby consent to be associated as local counsel of record in this cause pursuant to Florida Rule of Judicial Administration 2.510.

Dated this _____ day of _____, 20____.

_____

Local Counsel of Record

_____

Address

_____

Address

_____

City, State, Zip Code

_____
Telephone Number

_____
Florida Bar Number

_____
E-mail Address

CERTIFICATE OF SERVICE

I HEREBY CERTIFY that a true and correct copy of the foregoing motion was served by mail to PHV Admissions, The Florida Bar, 651 East Jefferson Street, Tallahassee, Florida 32399–2333 accompanied by payment of the $250.00 filing fee made payable to The Florida Bar, or notice that the movant has requested a judicial waiver of said fee; and by (e-mail) (delivery) (mail) (fax) to (name of attorney or party if not represented)

_____
_____
_____

this _____ day of _____, 20 ____.

_____
Movant

B. PRACTICE AND LITIGATION PROCEDURES

RULE 2.514. COMPUTING AND EXTENDING TIME

(a) Computing Time. The following rules apply in computing time periods specified in any rule of procedure, local rule, court order, or statute that does not specify a method of computing time.

(1) Period Stated in Days or a Longer Unit. When the period is stated in days or a longer unit of time

(A) exclude the day of the event that triggers the period;

(B) count every day, including intermediate Saturdays, Sundays, and legal holidays; and

(C) include the last day of the period, but if the last day is a Saturday, Sunday, or legal holiday, or falls within any period of time extended through an order of the chief justice under Florida Rule of Judicial Administration 2.205(a)(2)(B)(iv), the period continues to run until the end of the next day that is not a Saturday, Sunday, or legal holiday and does not fall within any period of time extended through an order of the chief justice.

(2) Period Stated in Hours. When the period is stated in hours

(A) begin counting immediately on the occurrence of the event that triggers the period;

(B) count every hour, including hours during intermediate Saturdays, Sundays, and legal holidays; and

(C) if the period would end on a Saturday, Sunday, or legal holiday, or during any period of time extended through an order of the chief justice under Florida Rule of Judicial Administration 2.205(a)(2)(B)(iv), the period continues to run until the same time on the next day that is not a Saturday, Sunday, or legal holiday and does not fall within any period of time extended through an order of the chief justice.

(3) Period Stated in Days Less Than Seven Days. When the period stated in days is less than 7 days, intermediate Saturdays, Sundays, and legal holidays shall be excluded in the computation.

(4) "Last Day" Defined. Unless a different time is set by a statute, local rule, or court order, the last day ends

(A) for electronic filing or for service by any means, at midnight; and

(B) for filing by other means, when the clerk's office is scheduled to close.

(5) "Next Day" Defined. The "next day" is determined by continuing to count forward when the period is measured after an event and backward when measured before an event.

(6) "Legal Holiday" Defined. "Legal holiday" means

(A) the day set aside by section 110.117, Florida Statutes, for observing New Year's Day, Martin Luther King, Jr.'s Birthday, Memorial Day, Independence Day, Labor Day, Veterans' Day, Thanksgiving Day, the Friday after Thanksgiving Day, or Christmas Day, and

(B) any day observed as a holiday by the clerk's office or as designated by the chief judge.

(b) Additional Time after Service by Mail or E-mail. When a party may or must act within a specified time after service and service is made by mail or e-mail, 5 days are added after the period that would otherwise expire under subdivision (a).

RULE 2.515. SIGNATURE AND CERTIFICATES OF ATTORNEYS AND PARTIES

(a) Attorney's Signature and Certificates. Every document of a party represented by an attorney shall be signed by at least 1 attorney of record in that attorney's individual name whose current record Florida Bar address, telephone number, including area code, primary e-mail address and secondary e-mail addresses, if any, and Florida Bar number shall be stated, and who shall be duly licensed to practice law in Florida or who shall have received permission to appear in the particular case as provided in rule 2.510. The attorney may be required by the court to give the address of, and to vouch for the attorney's authority to represent, the party. Except when otherwise specifically provided by an applicable rule or statute, documents need not be verified or accompanied by affidavit. The signature of an attorney shall constitute a certificate by the attorney that:

(1) the attorney has read the document;

(2) to the best of the attorney's knowledge, information, and belief there is good ground to support the document;

(3) the document is not interposed for delay; and

(4) the document contains no confidential or sensitive information, or that any such confidential or sensitive information has been properly protected by complying with the provisions of rules 2.420 and 2.425. If a document is not signed or is signed with intent to defeat the purpose of this rule, it may be stricken and the action may proceed as though the document had not been served.

(b) Pro Se Litigant Signature. A party who is not represented by an attorney shall sign any document and state the party's address and telephone number, including area code.

(c) Form of Signature.

(1) The signatures required on documents by subdivisions (a) and (b) of this rule may be:

(A) original signatures;

(B) original signatures that have been reproduced by electronic means, such as on electronically transmitted documents or photocopied documents;

(C) an electronic signature indicator using the "/s/," "s/," or "/s" [name] formats authorized by the person signing a document electronically served or filed; or

(D) any other signature format authorized by general law, so long as the clerk where the proceeding is pending has the capability of receiving and has obtained approval from the Supreme Court of Florida to accept pleadings and documents with that signature format.

(2) By serving a document, or by filing a document by electronic transmission using an attorney's assigned electronic filing credentials:

(A) that attorney certifies compliance with subdivision (a)(1) through (a)(4) and accepts responsibility for the document for all purposes under this rule;

(B) that attorney certifies compliance with all rules of procedure regarding service of the document on attorneys and parties;

(C) that attorney certifies that every person identified as a signer in the document as described in subdivision (c)(1)(C) has authorized such signature; and

(D) every signing attorney is as responsible for the document as if that document had been served by such signing attorney or filed using the assigned electronic filing credentials of such signing attorney.

RULE 2.516. SERVICE OF PLEADINGS AND DOCUMENTS

(a) Service; When Required. Unless the court otherwise orders, or a statute or supreme court administrative order specifies a different means of service, every pleading subsequent to the initial pleading and every other document filed in any court proceeding, except applications for witness subpoenas and documents served by formal notice or required to be served in the manner provided for service of formal notice, must be served in accordance with this rule on each party. No service need be made on parties against whom a default has been entered, except that pleadings asserting new or additional claims against them must be served in the manner provided for service of summons.

(b) Service; How Made. When service is required or permitted to be made upon a party represented by an attorney, service must be made upon the attorney unless service upon the party is ordered by the court.

(1) Service by Electronic Mail ("e-mail"). All documents required or permitted to be served on another party must be served by e-mail, unless the parties otherwise stipulate or this rule otherwise provides. A filer of an electronic document has complied with this subdivision if the Florida Courts e-filing Portal ("Portal") or other authorized electronic filing system with a supreme court approved electronic service system ("e-Service system") served the document by e-mail or provided a link by e-mail to the document on a website maintained by a clerk ("e-Service"). The filer of an electronic document must verify that the Portal or other e-Service system uses the names and e-mail addresses provided by the parties pursuant to subdivision (b)(1)(A).

(A) Service on Attorneys. Upon appearing in a proceeding, an attorney must designate a primary e-mail address and may designate no more than two secondary e-mail addresses and is responsible for the accuracy of and changes to that attorney's own e-mail addresses maintained by the Portal or other e-Service system. Thereafter, service must be directed to all designated e-mail addresses in that proceeding. Every document filed or served by an attorney thereafter must include the primary e-mail address of that attorney and any secondary e-mail addresses. If an attorney does not designate any e-mail address for service, documents may be served on that attorney at the e-mail address on record with The Florida Bar.

(B) Exception to E-mail Service on Attorneys. Upon motion by an attorney demonstrating that the attorney has no e-mail account and lacks access to the Internet at the attorney's office, the court may excuse the attorney from the requirements of e-mail service. Service on and by an attorney excused by the court from e-mail service must be by the means provided in subdivision (b)(2).

(C) Service on and by Parties Not Represented by an Attorney. Any party not represented by an attorney may serve a designation of a primary e-mail address and also may designate no more than two secondary e-mail addresses to which service must be

directed in that proceeding by the means provided in subdivision (b)(1) of this rule. If a party not represented by an attorney does not designate an e-mail address for service in a proceeding, service on and by that party must be by the means provided in subdivision (b)(2).

(D) Time of Service. Service by e-mail is complete on the date it is sent.

(i) If, however, the e-mail is sent by the Portal or other e-Service system, service is complete on the date the served document is electronically filed.

(ii) If the person required to serve a document learns that the e-mail was not received by an intended recipient, the person must immediately resend the document to that intended recipient by e-mail, or by a means authorized by subdivision (b)(2) of this rule.

(iii) E-mail service, including e-Service, is treated as service by mail for the computation of time.

(E) Format of E-mail for Service. Service of a document by e-mail is made by an e-mail sent to all addresses designated by the attorney or party with either (a) a copy of the document in PDF format attached or (b) a link to the document on a website maintained by a clerk.

(i) All documents served by e-mail must be sent by an e-mail message containing a subject line beginning with the words "SERVICE OF COURT DOCUMENT" in all capital letters, followed by the case number and case style of the proceeding in which the documents are being served.

(ii) The body of the e-mail must identify the court in which the proceeding is pending, the case number, the name of the initial party on each side, the title of each document served with that e-mail, and the name and telephone number of the person required to serve the document.

(iii) Any document served by e-mail may be signed by any of the "/s/", "/s", or "s/" formats.

(iv) Any e-mail which, together with its attached documents, exceeds the appropriate size limitations specified in the Florida Supreme Court Standards for Electronic Access to the Court, must be divided and sent as separate e-mails, no one of which may exceed the appropriate size limitations specified in the Florida Supreme Court Standards for Electronic Access to the Court and each of which must be sequentially numbered in the subject line.

(2) Service by Other Means. In addition to, and not in lieu of, service by e-mail, service may also be made upon attorneys by any of the means specified in this subdivision. If a document is served by more than one method of service, the computation of time for any response to the served document shall be based on the method of service that provides the shortest response time. Service on and by all parties who are not represented by an attorney and who do not designate an e-mail address, and on and by all attorneys excused from e-mail service, must be made by delivering a copy of the document or by mailing it to the party or attorney at their last known address or, if no address is known, by noting the non-service in the certificate of service, and stating in the certificate of service that a copy of the served document may be obtained, on request, from the clerk of the court or from the party serving the document. Service by mail is complete upon mailing. Delivery of a copy within this rule is complete upon:

(A) handing it to the attorney or to the party,

(B) leaving it at the attorney's or party's office with a clerk or other person in charge thereof,

(C) if there is no one in charge, leaving it in a conspicuous place therein,

(D) if the office is closed or the person to be served has no office, leaving it at the person's usual place of abode with some person of his or her family above 15 years of age and informing such person of the contents, or

(E) transmitting it by facsimile to the attorney's or party's office with a cover sheet containing the sender's name, firm, address, telephone number, and facsimile number, and the number of pages transmitted. When service is made by facsimile, a copy must also be served by any other method permitted by this rule. Facsimile service occurs when transmission is complete.

(F) Service by delivery shall be deemed complete on the date of the delivery.

(c) Service; Numerous Defendants. In actions when the parties are unusually numerous, the court may regulate the service contemplated by these rules on motion or on its own initiative in such manner as may be found to be just and reasonable.

(d) Filing. All documents must be filed with the court either before service or immediately thereafter, unless otherwise provided for by general law or other rules. If the original of any bond or other document required to be an original is not placed in the court file or deposited with the clerk, a certified copy must be so placed by the clerk.

(e) Filing Defined. The filing of documents with the court as required by these rules must be made by filing them with the clerk in accordance with Rule 2.525, except that the judge may permit documents to be filed with the judge, in which event the judge must note the filing date before him or her on the documents and transmit them to the clerk. The date of filing is that shown on the face of the document by the judge's notation or the clerk's time stamp, whichever is earlier.

(f) Certificate of Service. When any attorney certifies in substance:

"I certify that the foregoing document has been furnished to (here insert name or names, addresses used for service, and mailing addresses) by (e-mail) (delivery) (mail) (fax) on .....(date).....

_____

Attorney"

the certificate is taken as prima facie proof of such service in compliance with this rule.

(g) Service by Clerk. When the clerk is required to serve notices and other documents, the clerk may do so by e-mail as provided in subdivision (b)(1) or by any other method permitted under subdivision (b)(2). Service by a clerk is not required to be by e-mail.

(h) Service of Orders.

(1) A copy of all orders or judgments must be transmitted by the court or under its direction to all parties at the time of entry of the order or judgment. No service need be made on parties against whom a default has been entered except orders setting an action for trial and final judgments that must be prepared and served as provided in subdivision (h)(2). The court may require that orders or judgments be prepared by a party, may require the party to furnish the court with stamped, addressed envelopes for service of the order or judgment, and may require that proposed orders and judgments be furnished to all parties before entry by the court of the order or judgment. The court may serve any order or judgment by e-mail to all attorneys who have not been excused from e-mail service and to all parties not represented by an attorney who have designated an e-mail address for service.

(2) When a final judgment is entered against a party in default, the court must mail a conformed copy of it to the party. The party in whose favor the judgment is entered must furnish the court with a copy of the judgment, unless it is prepared by the court, with the address of the party to be served. If the address is unknown, the copy need not be furnished.

(3) This subdivision is directory and a failure to comply with it does not affect the order or judgment, its finality, or any proceedings arising in the action.

RULE 2.520. DOCUMENTS

(a) Electronic Filing Mandatory. All documents filed in any court shall be filed by electronic transmission in accordance with rule 2.525. "Documents" means pleadings, motions, petitions, memoranda, briefs, notices, exhibits, declarations, affidavits, orders, judgments, decrees, writs, opinions, and any paper or writing submitted to a court.

(b) Type and Size. Documents subject to the exceptions set forth in rule 2.525(d) shall be legibly typewritten or printed, on only one side of letter sized (8 1/2 by 11 inch) white recycled paper with one inch margins and consecutively numbered pages. For purposes of this rule, paper is recycled if it contains a minimum content of 50 percent waste paper. Reduction of legal-size (8 1/2 by 14 inches) documents to letter size (8 1/2 by 11 inches) is prohibited. All documents filed by electronic transmission shall comply with rule 2.526 and be filed in a format capable of being electronically searched and printed in a format consistent with the provisions of this rule.

(c) Exhibits. Any exhibit or attachment to any document may be filed in its original size.

(d) Recording Space and Space for Date and Time Stamps.

(1) On all documents prepared and filed by the court or by any party to a proceeding which are to be recorded in the public records of any county, including but not limited to final money judgments and notices of lis pendens, a 3-inch by 3-inch space at the top right-hand corner on the first page and a 1-inch by 3-inch space at the top right-hand corner on each subsequent page shall be left blank and reserved for use by the clerk of court.

(2) On all documents filed with the court, a 1-inch margin on all sides must be left blank for date and time stamps.

(A) Format. Date and time stamp formats must include a single line detailing the name of the court or Portal and shall not include clerk seals. Date stamps must be 8 numerical digits separated by slashes with 2 digits for the month, 2 digits for the day, and 4 digits for the year. Time stamps must be formatted in 12 hour time frames with a.m. or p.m. included. The font size and type must meet the Americans with Disabilities Act requirements.

(B) Location. The Portal stamp shall be on the top left of the document. The Florida Supreme Court and district courts of appeal stamps shall be on the left margin horizontally. Any administrative agency stamp shall be on the right margin horizontally. The clerk's stamp for circuit and county courts shall be on the bottom of the document.

(C) Paper Filings. When a document is filed in paper as authorized by rule, the clerk may stamp the paper document in ink with the date and time of filing instead of, or in addition to, placing the electronic stamp as described in subdivision (B). The ink stamp on a paper document must be legible on the electronic version of the document, and must neither obscure the content or other date stamp, nor occupy space otherwise reserved by subdivision (B).

(e) Exceptions to Recording Space. Any documents created by persons or entities over which the filing party has no control, including but not limited to wills, codicils, trusts, or other testamentary documents; documents prepared or executed by any public officer; documents prepared, executed, acknowledged, or proved outside of the State of Florida; or documents created by State or Federal government agencies, may be filed without the space required by this rule.

(f) Noncompliance. No clerk of court shall refuse to file any document because of noncompliance with this rule. However, upon request of the clerk of court, noncomplying documents shall be resubmitted in accordance with this rule.

Court Commentary

1989 Adoption. Rule 2.055 [renumbered as 2.520 in 2006] is new. This rule aligns Florida's court system with the federal court system and the court systems of the majority of our sister states by requiring in subdivision (a) that all pleadings, motions, petitions, briefs, notices, orders, judgments, decrees, opinions, or other papers filed with any Florida court be submitted on paper measuring 8 1/2 by 11 inches. Subdivision (e) provides a 1-year transition period from the effective date of January 1, 1990, to January 1, 1991, during which time filings that traditionally have been accepted on legal-size paper will be accepted on either legal- or letter-size paper. The 1-year transition period was provided to allow for the depletion of inventories of legal-size paper and forms. The 1-year transition period was not intended to affect compliance with Florida Rule of Appellate Procedure 9.210(a)(1), which requires that typewritten appellate briefs be filed on paper measuring 8 1/2 by 11 inches. Nor was it intended that the requirement of Florida Rule of Appellate Procedure 9.210(a)(1) that printed briefs measure 6 by 9 inches be affected by the requirements of subdivision (a).

Subdivision (b), which recognizes an exception for exhibits or attachments, is intended to apply to documents such as wills and traffic citations which traditionally have not been generated on lettersize paper.

Subdivision (c) was adopted to ensure that a 1 1/2 inch square at the top right-hand corner of all filings is reserved for use by the clerk of court. Subdivision (d) was adopted to ensure that all papers and documents submitted for filing will be considered filed on the date of submission regardless of paper size. Subdivision (d) also ensures that after the 1-year transition period of subdivision (e), filings that are not in compliance with the rule are resubmitted on paper measuring 8 1/2 by 11 inches.

This rule is not intended to apply to those instruments and documents presented to the clerk of the circuit court for recording in the Official Records under section 28.222, Florida Statutes (1987). It is also not intended to apply to matters submitted to the clerk of the circuit court in the capacity as ex officio clerk of the board of county commissioners pursuant to article VIII, section (1)(d), Florida Constitution.

1996 Amendment. Subdivision (c) was amended to make the blank space requirements for use by the clerk of the court consistent with section 695.26, Florida Statutes (1995). Subdivision (e) was eliminated because the transition period for letter-size and recycled paper was no longer necessary.

RULE 2.525. ELECTRONIC FILING

(a) Definition. "Electronic transmission of documents" means the sending of information by electronic signals to, by or from a court or clerk which when received can be transformed and stored or transmitted on paper, microfilm, magnetic storage device, optical imaging system, CD-ROM, flash drive, other electronic data storage system, server, case maintenance system ("CM"), electronic court filing ("ECF") system, statewide or local electronic portal ("e-portal"), or other electronic record keeping system authorized by the supreme court in a format sufficient to communicate the information on the original document in a readable format. Electronic transmission of documents includes electronic mail ("e-mail") and any internet-based transmission procedure, and may include procedures allowing for documents to be signed or verified by electronic means.

(b) Application. Only the electronic filing credentials of an attorney who has signed a document may be used to file that document by electronic transmission. Any court or clerk may accept the electronic transmission of documents for filing and may send documents by electronic transmission after the clerk, together with input from the chief judge of the circuit, has obtained approval of the procedures, programs, and standards for electronic filing from the supreme court ("ECF Procedures"). All ECF Procedures must comply with the then-current e-filing standards, as promulgated by the supreme court in Administrative Order No. AOSC09-30, or subsequent administrative order.

(c) Documents Affected.

(1) All documents that are court records, as defined in rule 2.430(a)(1), must be filed by electronic transmission provided that:

(A) the clerk has the ability to accept and retain such documents;

(B) the clerk or the chief judge of the circuit has requested permission to accept documents filed by electronic transmission; and

(C) the supreme court has entered an order granting permission to the clerk to accept documents filed by electronic transmission.

(2) The official court file is a set of electronic documents stored in a computer system maintained by the clerk, together with any supplemental non-electronic documents and materials authorized by this rule. It consists of:

(A) documents filed by electronic transmission under this rule;

(B) documents filed in paper form under subdivision (d) that have been converted to electronic form by the clerk;

(C) documents filed in paper form before the effective date of this rule that have been converted to electronic form by the clerk;

(D) documents filed in paper form before the effective date of this rule or under subdivision (d), unless such documents are converted into electronic form by the clerk;

(E) electronic documents filed pursuant to subdivision (d)(5); and

(F) materials and documents filed pursuant to any rule, statute or court order that either cannot be converted into electronic form or are required to be maintained in paper form.

(3) The documents in the official court file are deemed originals for all purposes except as otherwise provided by statute or rule.

(4) Any document in paper form submitted under subdivision (d) is filed when it is received by the clerk or court and the clerk shall immediately thereafter convert any filed paper document to an electronic document. "Convert to an electronic document" means optically capturing an image of a paper document and using character recognition software to recover as much of the document's text as practicable and then indexing and storing the document in the official court file.

(5) Any storage medium submitted under subdivision (d)(5) is filed when received by the clerk or court and the clerk shall immediately thereafter transfer the electronic documents from the storage device to the official court file.

(6) If the filer of any paper document authorized under subdivision (d) provides a self-addressed, postage-paid envelope for return of the paper document after it is converted to electronic form by the clerk, the clerk shall place the paper document in the envelope and deposit it in the mail. Except when a paper document is required to be maintained, the clerk may recycle any filed paper document that is not to be returned to the filer.

(7) The clerk may convert any paper document filed before the effective date of this rule to an electronic document. Unless the clerk is required to maintain the paper document, if the paper document has been converted to an electronic document by the clerk, the paper document is no longer part of the official court file and may be removed and recycled.

(d) Exceptions. Paper documents and other submissions may be manually submitted to the clerk or court:

(1) when the clerk does not have the ability to accept and retain documents by electronic filing or has not had ECF Procedures approved by the supreme court;

(2) for filing by any self-represented party or any self-represented nonparty unless specific ECF Procedures provide a means to file documents electronically. However, any self-represented nonparty that is a

governmental or public agency and any other agency, partnership, corporation, or business entity acting on behalf of any governmental or public agency may file documents by electronic transmission if such entity has the capability of filing documents electronically;

(3) for filing by attorneys excused from e-mail service in accordance with rule 2.516(b);

(4) when submitting evidentiary exhibits or filing non-documentary materials;

(5) when the filing involves documents in excess of the appropriate size limitations specified in the Florida Supreme Court Standards for Electronic Access to the Court. For such filings, documents may be transmitted using an electronic storage medium that the clerk has the ability to accept, which may include a CD-ROM, flash drive, or similar storage medium;

(6) when filed in open court, as permitted by the court;

(7) when paper filing is permitted by any approved statewide or local ECF procedures; and

(8) if any court determines that justice so requires.

(e) Service.

(1) Electronic transmission may be used by a court or clerk for the service of all orders of whatever nature, pursuant to rule 2.516(h), and for the service of any documents pursuant to any ECF Procedures, provided the clerk, together with input from the chief judge of the circuit, has obtained approval from the supreme court of ECF Procedures containing the specific procedures and program to be used in transmitting the orders and documents. All other requirements for the service of such orders must be met.

(2) Any document electronically transmitted to a court or clerk must also be served on all parties and interested persons in accordance with the applicable rules of court.

(f) Administration.

(1) Any clerk who, after obtaining supreme court approval, accepts for filing documents that have been electronically transmitted must:

(A) provide electronic or telephonic access to its equipment, whether through an e-portal or otherwise, during regular business hours, and all other times as practically feasible;

(B) accept electronic transmission of the appropriate size limitations specified in the Florida Supreme Court Standards for Electronic Access to the Court; and

(C) accept filings in excess of the appropriate size limitations specified in the Florida Supreme Court Standards for Electronic Access to the Court by electronic storage device or system, which may include a CD-ROM, flash drive, or similar storage system.

(2) All attorneys, parties, or other persons using this rule to file documents are required to make arrangements with the court or clerk for the payment of any charges authorized by general law or the supreme court before filing any document by electronic transmission.

(3) The filing date for an electronically transmitted document is the date and time that such filing is acknowledged by an electronic stamp or otherwise, pursuant to any procedure set forth in any ECF Procedures approved by the supreme court, or the date the last page of such filing is received by the court or clerk.

(4) Any court or clerk may extend the hours of access or increase the page or size limitations set forth in this subdivision.

(g) Accessibility. All documents transmitted in any electronic form under this rule must comply with the accessibility requirements of Florida Rule of Judicial Administration 2.526.

Court Commentary

1997 Amendment. Originally, the rule provided that the follow-up filing had to occur within ten days. In the 1997 amendment to the rule, that requirement was modified to provide that the follow-up filing must occur "immediately" after a document is electronically filed. The "immediately thereafter" language is consistent with language used in the rules of procedure where, in a somewhat analogous situation, the filing of a document may occur after service. *See, e.g.*, Florida Rule of Civil Procedure 1.080(d) ("All original papers shall be filed with the court either before service or *immediately thereafter.*") (emphasis added). "Immediately thereafter" has been interpreted to mean "filed with reasonable promptness." *Miami Transit Co. v. Ford*, 155 So.2d 360 (Fla.1963).

The use of the words "other person" in this rule is not meant to allow a nonlawyer to sign and file pleadings or other papers on behalf of another. Such conduct would constitute the unauthorized practice of law.

RULE 2.526. ACCESSIBILITY OF INFORMATION AND TECHNOLOGY

Any document that is or will become a judicial branch record, as defined in rule 2.420(b)(1), and that is transmitted in an electronic form, as defined in rule 2.525, must be formatted in a manner that complies with all state and federal laws requiring that electronic judicial records be accessible to persons with disabilities, including without limitation the Americans with Disabilities Act and Section 508 of the federal Rehabilitation Act of 1973 as incorporated into Florida law by section 282.603(1), Florida Statutes (2010), and any related federal or state regulations or administrative rules.

RULE 2.530. COMMUNICATION EQUIPMENT

(a) **Definition.** Communication equipment means a conference telephone or other electronic device that permits all those appearing or participating to hear and speak to each other, provided that all conversation of all parties is audible to all persons present.

(b) **Use by all Parties.** A county or circuit court judge may, upon the court's own motion or upon the written request of a party, direct that communication equipment be used for a motion hearing, pretrial conference, or a status conference. A judge must give notice to the parties and consider any objections they may have to the use of communication equipment before directing that communication equipment be used. The decision to use communication equipment over the objection of parties will be in the sound discretion of the trial court, except as noted below.

(c) **Use Only by Requesting Party.** A county or circuit court judge may, upon the written request of a

party upon reasonable notice to all other parties, permit a requesting party to participate through communication equipment in a scheduled motion hearing; however, any such request (except in criminal, juvenile, and appellate proceedings) must be granted, absent a showing of good cause to deny the same, where the hearing is set for not longer than 15 minutes.

(d) **Testimony.**

(1) **Generally.** A county or circuit court judge, general magistrate, special magistrate, or hearing officer may allow testimony to be taken through communication equipment if all parties consent or if permitted by another applicable rule of procedure.

(2) **Procedure.** Any party desiring to present testimony through communication equipment shall, prior to the hearing or trial at which the testimony is to be presented, contact all parties to determine whether each party consents to this form of testimony. The party seeking to present the testimony shall move for permission to present testimony through communication equipment, which motion shall set forth good cause as to why the testimony should be allowed in this form.

(3) **Oath.** Testimony may be taken through communication equipment only if a notary public or other person authorized to administer oaths in the witness's jurisdiction is present with the witness and administers the oath consistent with the laws of the jurisdiction.

(4) **Confrontation Rights.** In juvenile and criminal proceedings the defendant must make an informed waiver of any confrontation rights that may be abridged by the use of communication equipment.

(5) **Video Testimony.** If the testimony to be presented utilizes video conferencing or comparable two-way visual capabilities, the court in its discretion may modify the procedures set forth in this rule to accommodate the technology utilized.

(e) **Burden of Expense.** The cost for the use of the communication equipment is the responsibility of the requesting party unless otherwise directed by the court.

(f) Override of Family Violence Indicator. Communications equipment may be used for a hearing on a petition to override a family violence indicator under Florida Family Law Rule of Procedure 12.650.

RULE 2.535. COURT REPORTING

(a) Definitions.

(1) "Approved court reporter" means a court employee or contractor who performs court reporting services, including transcription, at public expense and who meets the court's certification, training, and other qualifications for court reporting.

(2) "Approved transcriptionist" means a court employee, contractor, or other individual who performs transcription services at public expense and who meets the court's certification, training, and other qualifications for transcribing proceedings.

(3) "Civil court reporter" means a court reporter who performs court reporting services in civil proceedings not required to be reported at public expense, and who meets the court's certification, training, and other qualifications for court reporting.

(4) "Court reporting" means the act of making a verbatim record of the spoken word, whether by the use of written symbols, stenomask equipment, stenographic equipment, or electronic devices, in any proceedings pending in any of the courts of this state, including all discovery proceedings conducted in connection therewith, any proceedings reported for the court's own use, and all proceedings required by statute to be reported by a certified or officialan approved court reporter or civil court reporter. It does not mean the act of taking witness statements not intended for use in court as substantive evidence.

(5) "Electronic record" means the audio, analog, digital, or video record of a court proceeding.

(6) "Official record" means the transcript, which is the written or electronically stored record of court proceedings and depositions prepared in accordance with the requirements of subdivision (f).

(b) When Court Reporting Required. Any proceeding shall be reported on the request of any party. The party so requesting shall pay the reporting fees, but this requirement shall not preclude the taxation of costs as authorized by law.

(c) Record. When trial proceedings are being reported, no part of the proceedings shall be omitted unless all of the parties agree to do so and the court approves the agreement. When a deposition is being reported, no part of the proceedings shall be omitted unless all of the parties and the witness so agree. When a party or a witness seeks to terminate or suspend the taking of a deposition for the time necessary to seek a court order, the court reporter shall discontinue reporting the testimony of the witness.

(d) Ownership of Records. The chief judge of the circuit in which a proceeding is pending, in his or her official capacity, is the owner of all records and electronic records made by an official court reporter or quasi-judicial officer in proceedings required to be reported at public expense and proceedings reported for the court's own use.

(e) Fees. The chief judge shall have the discretion to adopt an administrative order establishing maximum fees for court reporting services. Any such order must make a specific factual finding that the setting of such maximum fees is necessary to ensure access to the courts. Such finding shall include consideration of the number of court reporters in the county or circuit, any past history of fee schedules, and any other relevant factors.

(f) Transcripts. Transcripts of all judicial proceedings, including depositions, shall be uniform in and for all courts throughout the state and shall be stored in an electronic format sufficient to communicate the information contained in proceedings in a readable format, and capable of being transmitted electronically as set forth in rule 2.525. Any transcripts stored in electronic form must be capable of being printed in accordance with this rule. The form, size, spacing, and method of printing transcripts are as follows:

(1) All proceedings shall be printed on paper 8 1/2 inches by 11 inches in size and bound on the left.

(2) There shall be no fewer than 25 printed lines per page with all lines numbered 1 through 25, respectively, and with no more than a double space between lines.

(3) Font size or print shall be 9 or 10 pica, 12-point courier, or 12-point Times New Roman print with no less than 56 characters per line on questions and answers unless the text of the speaker ends short of marginal requirements.

(4) Colloquy material shall begin on the same line following the identification of the speaker, with no more than 2 spaces between the identification of the speaker and the commencement of the colloquy. The identification of the speaker in colloquy shall begin no more than 10 spaces from the left margin, and carry-over colloquy shall be indented no more than 5 spaces from the left margin.

(5) Each question and answer shall begin on a separate line no more than 5 spaces from the left margin with no more than 5 spaces from the "Q" or "A" to the text. Carry-over question and answer lines shall be brought to the left margin.

(6) Quoted material shall begin no more than 10 spaces from the left margin with carry-over lines beginning no more than 10 spaces from the left margin.

(7) Indentations of no more than 10 spaces may be used for paragraphs, and all spaces on a line as herein provided shall be used unless the text of the speaker ends short of marginal requirements.

(8) One-line parentheticals may begin at any indentation. Parentheticals exceeding 1 line shall begin no more than 10 spaces from the left margin, with carry-over lines being returned to the left margin.

(9) Individual volumes of a transcript, including depositions, shall be no more than 200 pages in length, inclusive of the index.

(10) Deviation from these standards shall not constitute grounds for limiting use of transcripts in the trial or appellate courts.

(g) Officers of the Court. Approved court reporters, civil court reporters, and approved transcriptionists are officers of the court for all purposes while acting as court reporters in judicial proceedings or discovery proceedings or as transcriptionists. Approved court reporters, civil court reporters, and approved transcriptionists shall comply with all rules and statutes governing the proceeding that are applicable to court reporters and approved transcriptionists.

(h) Court Reporting Services at Public Expense.

(1) When Reporting Is Required. All proceedings required by law, court rule, or administrative order to be reported shall be reported at public expense.

(2) When Reporting May Be Required. Proceedings reported for the court's own use may be reported at public expense.

(3) Circuit Plan. The chief judge, after consultation with the circuit court and county court judges in the circuit, shall enter an administrative order developing and implementing a circuit-wide plan for the court reporting of all proceedings required to be reported at public expense using either full or part time court employees or independent contractors. The plan shall ensure that all court reporting services are provided by approved court reporters or approved transcriptionists. This plan may provide for multiple service delivery strategies if they are necessary to ensure the efficient provision of court reporting services. Each circuit's plan for court reporting services shall be developed after consideration of guidelines issued by the Office of the State Courts Administrator.

(4) Electronic Recording and Transcription of Proceedings without Court Reporters. A chief judge may enter a circuit-wide administrative order, which shall be recorded, authorizing the electronic recording and subsequent transcription by approved court reporters or approved transcriptionists, of any judicial proceedings, including depositions, that are otherwise required to be reported by a court reporter. Appropriate procedures shall be prescribed in the order which shall:

(A) set forth responsibilities for the court's support personnel to ensure a reliable record of the proceedings;

(B) provide a means to have the recording transcribed by approved court reporters or approved transcriptionists, either in whole or in part, when necessary for an appeal or for further use in the trial court; and

(C) provide for the safekeeping of such recordings.

(5) Safeguarding Confidential Communications When Electronic Recording Equipment Is Used in the Courtroom.

(A) Court personnel shall provide notice to participants in a courtroom proceeding that electronic recording equipment is in use and that they should safeguard information they do not want recorded.

(B) Attorneys shall take all reasonable and available precautions to protect disclosure of confidential communications in the courtroom. Such precautions may include muting microphones or going to a designated location that is inaccessible to the recording equipment.

(C) Participants have a duty to protect confidential information.

(6) Grand Jury Proceedings. Testimony in grand jury proceedings shall be reported by an approved court reporter, but shall not be transcribed unless required by order of court. Other parts of grand jury proceedings, including deliberations and voting, shall not be reported. The approved court reporter's work product, including stenographic notes, electronic recordings, and transcripts, shall be filed with the clerk of the court under seal.

(i) Court Reporting Services in Capital Cases. The chief judge, after consultation with the circuit court judges in the circuit, shall enter an administrative order developing and implementing a circuit-wide plan for court reporting in all trials in which the state seeks the death penalty and in capital postconviction proceedings. The plan shall prohibit the use of digital court reporting as the court reporting system and shall require the use of all measures necessary to expedite the preparation of the transcript, including but not limited to:

(1) where available, the use of an approved court reporter who has the capacity to provide real-time transcription of the proceedings;

(2) if real-time transcription services are not available, the use of a computer-aided transcription qualified court reporter;

(3) the use of scopists, text editors, alternating court reporters, or other means to expedite the finalization of the certified transcript; and

(4) the imposition of reasonable restrictions on work assignments by employee or contract approved court reporters to ensure that transcript production in capital cases is given a priority.

(j) Juvenile Dependency and Termination of Parental Rights Cases. Transcription of hearings for appeals of orders in juvenile dependency and termination of parental rights cases shall be given priority, consistent with rule 2.215(g), over transcription of all other proceedings, unless otherwise ordered by the court based upon a demonstrated exigency.

Committee Notes

The definitions of "electronic record" in subdivision (a)(5) and of "official record" in subdivision (a)(6) are intended to clarify that when a court proceeding is electronically recorded by means of audio, analog, digital, or video equipment, and is also recorded via a written transcript prepared by a court reporter, the written transcript shall be the "official record" of the proceeding to the exclusion of all electronic records. While the term "record" is used within Rule 2.535 and within Fla. R. App. P. 9.200, it has a different meaning within the unique context of each rule. Accordingly, the meaning of the term "record" as defined for purposes of this rule does not in any way alter, amend, change, or conflict with the meaning of the term "record" as defined for appellate purposes in Fla. R. App. P. 9.200(a).

RULE 2.540. REQUESTS FOR ACCOMMODATIONS BY PERSONS WITH DISABILITIES

(a) Duties of Court. Qualified individuals with a disability will be provided, at the court's expense, with accommodations, reasonable modifications to rules, policies, or practices, or the provision of auxiliary aids and services, in order to participate in programs or activities provided by the courts of this state. The court may deny a request only in accordance with subdivision (e).

(b) Definitions. The definitions encompassed in the Americans with Disabilities Act of 1990, 42 U.S.C. § 12101, et seq., are incorporated into this rule.

(c) Notice Requirement.

(1) All notices of court proceedings to be held in a public facility, and all process compelling appearance at such proceedings, shall include the following statement in bold face, 14-point Times New Roman or Courier font:

"If you are a person with a disability who needs any accommodation in order to participate in this proceeding, you are entitled, at no cost to you, to the provision of certain assistance. Please contact [identify applicable court personnel by name, address, and telephone number] at least 7 days before your scheduled court appearance, or immediately upon receiving this notification if the time before the scheduled appearance is less than 7 days; if you are hearing or voice impaired, call 771."

(2) Each trial and appellate court shall post on its respective website and in each court facility the procedures for obtaining an accommodation as well as the grievance procedure adopted by that court.

(d) Process for Requesting Accommodations. The process for requesting accommodations is as follows:

(1) Requests for accommodations under this rule may be presented on a form approved or substantially similar to one approved by the Office of the State Courts Administrator, in another written format, or orally. Requests must be forwarded to the ADA coordinator, or designee, within the time frame provided in subdivision (d)(3).

(2) Requests for accommodations must include a description of the accommodation sought, along with a statement of the impairment that necessitates the accommodation and the duration that the accommodation is to be provided. The court, in its discretion, may require the individual with a disability to provide additional information about the impairment. Requests for accommodation shall not include any information regarding the merits of the case.

(3) Requests for accommodations must be made at least 7 days before the scheduled court appearance, or immediately upon receiving notification if the time before the scheduled court appearance is less than 7 days. The court may, in its discretion, waive this requirement.

(e) Response to Accommodation Request. The court must respond to a request for accommodation as follows:

(1) The court must consider, but is not limited by, the provisions of the Americans with Disabilities Act of 1990 in determining whether to provide an accommodation or an appropriate alternative accommodation.

(2) The court must inform the individual with a disability of the following:

(A) That the request for accommodation is granted or denied, in whole or in part, and if the request for accommodation is denied, the reason therefor; or that an alternative accommodation is granted;

(B) The nature of the accommodation to be provided, if any; and

(C) The duration of the accommodation to be provided.

If the request for accommodation is granted in its entirety, the court shall respond to the individual with a disability by any appropriate method. If the request is denied or granted only in part, or if an alternative accommodation is granted, the court must respond to the individual with a disability in writing, as may be appropriate, and if applicable, in an alternative format.

(3) If the court determines that a person is a qualified person with a disability and an accommoda-

tion is needed, a request for accommodation may be denied only when the court determines that the requested accommodation would create an undue financial or administrative burden on the court or would fundamentally alter the nature of the service, program, or activity.

(f) Grievance Procedure.

(1) Each judicial circuit and appellate court shall establish and publish grievance procedures that allow for the resolution of complaints. Those procedures may be used by anyone who wishes to file a complaint alleging discrimination on the basis of disability in the provision of services, activities, programs, or benefits by the Florida State Courts System.

(2) If such grievance involves a matter that may affect the orderly administration of justice, it is within the discretion of the presiding judge to stay the proceeding and seek expedited resolution of the grievance.

RULE 2.545. CASE MANAGEMENT

(a) Purpose. Judges and lawyers have a professional obligation to conclude litigation as soon as it is reasonably and justly possible to do so. However parties and counsel shall be afforded a reasonable time to prepare and present their case.

(b) Case Control. The trial judge shall take charge of all cases at an early stage in the litigation and shall control the progress of the case thereafter until the case is determined. The trial judge shall take specific steps to monitor and control the pace of litigation, including the following:

(1) assuming early and continuous control of the court calendar;

(2) identifying priority cases as assigned by statute, rule of procedure, case law, or otherwise;

(3) implementing such docket control policies as may be necessary to advance priority cases to ensure prompt resolution;

(4) identifying cases subject to alternative dispute resolution processes;

(5) developing rational and effective trial setting policies; and

(6) advancing the trial setting of priority cases, older cases, and cases of greater urgency.

(c) Priority Cases.

(1) In all noncriminal cases assigned a priority status by statute, rule of procedure, case law, or otherwise, any party may file a notice of priority status explaining the nature of the case, the source of the priority status, any deadlines imposed by law on any aspect of the case, and any unusual factors that may bear on meeting the imposed deadlines.

(2) If, in any noncriminal case assigned a priority status by statute, rule of procedure, case law, or otherwise, a party is of the good faith opinion that the case has not been appropriately advanced on the docket or has not received priority in scheduling consistent with its priority case status, that party may seek review of such action by motion for review to the chief judge or to the chief judge's designee. The filing of such a motion for review will not toll the time for seeking such other relief as may be afforded by the Florida Rules of Appellate Procedure.

(d) Related Cases.

(1) The petitioner in a family case as defined in this rule shall file with the court a notice of related cases in conformity with family law form 12.900(h), if related cases are known or reasonably ascertainable. A case is related when:

(A) it involves any of the same parties, children, or issues and it is pending at the time the party files a family case; or

(B) it affects the court's jurisdiction to proceed; or

(C) an order in the related case may conflict with an order on the same issues in the new case; or

(D) an order in the new case may conflict with an order in the earlier litigation.

(2) "Family cases" include dissolution of marriage, annulment, support unconnected with dissolu-

tion of marriage, paternity, child support, UIFSA, custodial care of and access to children, proceedings for temporary or concurrent custody of minor children by extended family, adoption, name change, declaratory judgment actions related to premarital, martial, or postmarital agreements, civil domestic, repeat violence, dating violence, stalking, and sexual violence injunctions, juvenile dependency, termination of parental rights, juvenile delinquency, emancipation of a minor, CINS/FINS, truancy, and modification and enforcement of orders entered in these cases.

(3) The notice of related cases shall identify the caption and case number of the related case, contain a brief statement of the relationship of the actions, and contain a statement addressing whether assignment to one judge or another method of coordination will conserve judicial resources and promote an efficient determination of the actions.

(4) The notice of related cases shall be filed with the initial pleading by the filing attorney or self-represented petitioner. The notice shall be filed in each of the related cases that are currently open and pending with the court and served on all other parties in each of the related cases, and as may be directed by the chief judge or designee. Parties may file joint notices. A notice of related cases filed pursuant to this rule is not an appearance. If any related case is confidential and exempt from public access by law, then a Notice of Confidential Information Within Court Filing as required by Florida Rule of Judicial Administration 2.420 shall accompany the notice. Parties shall file supplemental notices as related cases become known or reasonably ascertainable.

(5) Each party has a continuing duty to inform the court of any proceedings in this or any other state that could affect the current proceeding.

(6) Whenever it appears to a party that two or more pending cases present common issues of fact and that assignment to one judge or another method of coordination will significantly promote the efficient administration of justice, conserve judicial resources, avoid inconsistent results, or prevent multiple court appearances by the same parties on the same issues, the party may file a notice of related cases requesting coordination of the litigation.

(e) **Continuances.** All judges shall apply a firm continuance policy. Continuances should be few, good cause should be required, and all requests should be heard and resolved by a judge. All motions for continuance shall be in writing unless made at a trial and, except for good cause shown, shall be signed by the party requesting the continuance. All motions for continuance in priority cases shall clearly identify such priority status and explain what effect the motion will have on the progress of the case.

Committee Notes

The provisions in subdivision (c) of this rule governing priority cases should be read in conjunction with the provisions of rule 2.215(g), governing the duty to expedite priority cases.

RULE 2.550. CALENDAR CONFLICTS

(a) **Guidelines.** In resolving calendar conflicts between the state courts of Florida or between a state court and a federal court in Florida, the following guidelines must be considered:

(1) Any case priority status established by statute, rule of procedure, case law, or otherwise shall be evaluated to determine the effect that resolving a calendar conflict might have on the priority case or cases.

(2) Juvenile dependency and termination of parental rights cases are generally to be given preference over other cases, except for speedy trial and capital cases.

(3) Criminal cases are generally to be given preference over civil cases.

(4) Jury trials are generally to be given preference over non-jury trials.

(5) Appellate arguments, hearings, and conferences are generally to be given preference over trial court proceedings.

(6) The case in which the trial date has been first set should generally take precedence.

(b) **Additional Circumstances.** Factors such as cost, numbers of witnesses and attorneys involved, travel, length of trial, age of case, and other relevant matters may warrant deviation from these case guidelines.

(c) Notice and Agreement; Resolution by Judges. When an attorney is scheduled to appear in 2 courts at the same time and cannot arrange for other counsel to represent the clients' interests, the attorney shall give prompt written notice of the conflict to opposing counsel, the clerk of each court, and the presiding judge of each case, if known. If the presiding judge of the case cannot be identified, written notice of the conflict shall be given to the chief judge of the court having jurisdiction over the case, or to the chief judge's designee. The judges or their designees shall confer and undertake to avoid the conflict by agreement among themselves. Absent agreement, conflicts should be promptly resolved by the judges or their designees in accordance with the above case guidelines.

Committee Notes

1996 Adoption. The adoption of this rule was prompted by the Resolution of the Florida State-Federal Judicial Council Regarding Calendar Conflicts Between State and Federal Courts, which states as follows:

WHEREAS, the great volume of cases filed in the state and federal courts of Florida creates calendar conflicts between the state and federal courts of Florida which should be resolved in a fair, efficient and orderly manner to allow for judicial efficiency and economy; and

WHEREAS, the Florida State-Federal Judicial Council which represents the Bench and Bar of the State of Florida believes that it would be beneficial to formally agree upon and publish recommended procedures and priorities for resolving calendar conflicts between the state and federal courts of Florida;

NOW, THEREFORE, BE IT RESOLVED

In resolving calendar conflicts between the state and federal courts of Florida, the following case priorities should be considered:

1. Criminal cases should prevail over civil cases.

2. Jury trials should prevail over non-jury trials.

3. Appellate arguments, hearings, and conferences should prevail over trials.

4. The case in which the trial date has been first set should take precedence.

5. Circumstances such as cost, numbers of witnesses and attorneys involved, travel, length of trial, age of case and other relevant matters may warrant deviation from this policy. Such matters are encouraged to be resolved through communication between the courts involved.

Where an attorney is scheduled to appear in two courts - trial or appellate, state or federal - at the same time and cannot arrange for other counsel in his or her firm or in the case to represent his or her client's interest, the attorney shall give prompt written notice to opposing counsel, the clerk of each court, and the presiding judge of each case, if known, of the conflict. If the presiding judge of a case cannot be identified, written notice of the conflict shall be given to the chief judge of the court having jurisdiction over the case, or to his or her designee. The judges or their designees shall confer and undertake to avoid the conflict by agreement among themselves. Absent agreement, conflicts should be promptly resolved by the judges or their designees in accordance with the above case priorities.

In jurisdictions where calendar conflicts arise with frequency, it is recommended that each court involved consider appointing a calendar conflict coordinator to assist the judges in resolving calendar conflicts by obtaining information regarding the conflicts and performing such other ministerial duties as directed by the judges.

REVISED AND READOPTED at Miami, Florida, this 13th day of January, 1995.

Court Commentary

2002 Court Commentary. As provided in subdivision (c), when a scheduling conflict involves different courts, the presiding judges should confer and undertake to agree on a resolution, using the guidelines provided in this rule.

RULE 2.555. INITIATION OF CRIMINAL PROCEEDINGS

(a) Major Statutory Offense. Law enforcement officers, at the time of the filing of a complaint with the clerk of court, shall designate whether the most serious charge on the complaint is a felony or a misdemeanor. The state attorney or the state attorney's designee, at the time of the filing of an original information or an original indictment with the clerk of court, shall designate whether the most serious offense on the information or the indictment is a felony or misdemeanor. Complaints, original informations, and original indictments on which the most serious charge is a felony shall be filed with the clerk of the circuit court.

(b) Ordinance Violations. In cases when the state attorney has the responsibility for the prosecution of county or municipal ordinance violations, where such ordinances have state statutory equivalents, the state attorney or the state attorney's designee shall set forth at the top of the face of the accusatory instrument the exact statute number of the single most serious offense charged.

(c) Information or Indictment after County Court Proceedings Begun. When action in a criminal case has been initiated in county court, and subsequently the state attorney files a direct information or the grand jury indicts the defendant, the state attorney or the state attorney's designee shall notify the clerk without delay.

RULE 2.560. APPOINTMENT OF SPOKEN LANGUAGE COURT INTERPRETERS FOR NON-ENGLISH-SPEAKING AND LIMITED-ENGLISH-PROFICIENT PERSONS

(a) Criminal or Juvenile Delinquency Proceedings. In any criminal or juvenile delinquency proceeding in which a non-English-speaking or limited-English-proficient person is the accused, an interpreter for the non-English-speaking or limited-English-proficient person shall be appointed. In any criminal or juvenile delinquency proceeding in which a non-English-speaking or limited-English-proficient person is a victim, an interpreter shall be appointed unless the court finds that the victim does not require the services of a court-appointed interpreter.

(b) Other Proceedings. In all other proceedings in which a non-English-speaking or limited-English-proficient person is a litigant, an interpreter for the non-English-speaking or limited-English-proficient litigant shall be appointed if the court determines that the litigant's inability to comprehend English deprives the litigant of an understanding of the court proceedings, that a fundamental interest is at stake (such as in a civil commitment, termination of parental rights, paternity, or dependency proceeding), and that no alternative to the appointment of an interpreter exists.

(c) Witnesses. In any proceeding in which a non-English-speaking or limited-English-proficient person is a witness, the appointment of an interpreter shall be governed by the applicable provisions of the Florida Evidence Code.

(d) Compliance with Title VI of the Civil Rights Act of 1964. In making determinations regarding the appointment of an interpreter, the court should ensure compliance with the requirements of Title VI of the Civil Rights Act of 1964.

(e) Qualifications of Interpreter.

(1) Appointment of Interpreters when Certified or Other Duly Qualified Interpreters Are Available. Whenever possible, a certified or other duly qualified interpreter, as defined in the Rules for Certification and Regulation of Spoken Language Court Interpreters, shall be appointed. Preference shall be given to appointment of certified and language skilled interpreters, then to persons holding a provisionally approved designation.

(2) Appointment of Interpreters when Certified or Other Duly Qualified Interpreters Are Unavailable. If, after diligent search, a certified, language skilled, or provisionally approved interpreter is not available, the presiding judge, magistrate, or hearing officer, finding good cause, may appoint an interpreter who is otherwise registered with the Office of the State Courts Administrator in accordance with the Rules for Certification and Regulation of Spoken Language Court Interpreters. No appointment shall be made under this subdivision unless the presiding judge, magistrate, or hearing officer makes a determination, on the record, the proposed interpreter is competent to interpret in the proceedings.

(3) Appointment in Exceptional Circumstances. If after diligent search no interpreter qualifying under subdivision (e)(1) or (e)(2) of this rule is available at the time interpreter services are needed, the presiding judge, magistrate, or hearing officer, finding good cause exists for the appointment of an interpreter not qualifying under subdivision (e)(1) or (e)(2), such as the prevention of burdensome delay, the request or consent of the non-English-speaking or limited-English-proficient person, or other unusual circumstance, may appoint an interpreter who is not certified, language skilled, provisionally approved, or otherwise registered with the Office of the State Courts Administrator. No appointment, including appointment of interpreters available via remote technology, shall be made under this subdivision unless the presiding judge, magistrate, or hearing officer finds the proposed interpreter is competent to interpret in the proceedings. This finding must be made on the record based, not only on the unavailability of an interpreter otherwise qualified in a particular language, but also on specific exigent circumstances given the demands of the case and the interpreter's sworn assertion he or she is able, either in direct or relay/intermediary interpretation, to communicate effectively in the languages in which interpreter services are required. An appointment under this subdivision shall excuse an interpreter so appointed from the registration requirements under the Rules for Certification and Regulation of Spoken Language Court Interpreters, but only for the delivery of the specific services for which the interpreter is appointed.

(4) On-the-Record Objections or Waivers in Criminal and Juvenile Delinquency Proceedings. In any criminal or juvenile delinquency proceeding in which the interpreter is not appointed under subdivision (e)(1) of this rule, the court shall advise the accused, on the record, that the proposed interpreter is not certified, language skilled, or provisionally approved pursuant to the Rules for Certification and Regulation of Spoken Language Court Interpreters. The accused's objection to the appointment of a proposed interpreter, or the accused's waiver of the appointment of a certified, language skilled, or provisionally approved interpreter, shall also be on the record.

(5) Additional on-the-Record Findings, Objections, and Waivers Required at Subsequent Proceedings. The appointment of an interpreter who is not certified, language skilled, or provisionally approved in accordance with the Rules for Certification and Regulation of Spoken Language Court Interpreters shall be limited to a specific proceeding and shall not be extended to subsequent proceedings in a case without additional findings of good cause and qualification as required by subdivisions (e)(2) and (e)(3) of this rule, and additional compliance with the procedures for on-the-record objections or waivers provided for in subdivision (e)(4) of this rule.

(f) Privileged Communications. Whenever a person communicates through an interpreter to any person under circumstances that would render the communication privileged and such person could not be compelled to testify as to the communication, the privilege shall also apply to the interpreter.

(g) Definitions. When used in this rule, the following terms shall have the meanings set forth below:

(1) Limited-English-Proficient Person. A person who is unable to communicate effectively in English because the individual's primary language is not English and he or she has not developed fluency in the English language. A person with limited English proficiency may have difficulty speaking, reading, writing, or understanding English.

(2) Proceeding. Any hearing or trial, excluding an administrative hearing or trial, presided over by a judge, general magistrate, special magistrate, or hearing officer within the state courts.

RULE 2.565. RETENTION OF SPOKEN LANGUAGE COURT INTERPRETERS FOR NON-ENGLISH-SPEAKING AND LIMITED-ENGLISH-PROFICIENT PERSONS BY ATTORNEYS OR SELF-REPRESENTED LITIGANTS

(a) Retention of Interpreters when Certified or Other Duly Qualified Interpreters Are Available. In the absence of a requirement that a spoken language interpreter be appointed by the Court under rule 2.560, when the services of an interpreter are required to assist a non-English-speaking or limited-English-proficient litigant or witness in a court proceeding or court-related proceeding as defined in the Rules for Certification and Regulation of Spoken Language Court Interpreters, an attorney or self-represented litigant shall, whenever possible, retain a certified, language skilled or provisionally approved interpreter, as defined in the Rules for Certification and Regulation of Spoken Language Court Interpreters. Preference shall be given to retention of certified and language skilled interpreters, then to persons holding a provisionally approved designation.

(b) Retention of Interpreters when Certified or Other Duly Qualified Interpreters Are Unavailable. If, after diligent search, a certified, language skilled, or provisionally approved interpreter is not available, an attorney or self-represented litigant may retain an interpreter who is otherwise registered with the Office of the State Courts Administrator in accordance with the Rules for Certification and Regulation of Spoken Language Court Interpreters.

(c) Retention in Exceptional Circumstances. If, after diligent search, no interpreter qualifying under subdivision (a) or (b) of this rule is available, an attorney or self-represented litigant, for good cause, may retain an interpreter who is not certified, language skilled, provisionally approved, or otherwise registered with the Office of the State Courts Administrator.

(d) Written Declaration Substantiating Good Cause. No interpreter shall be retained under subdivision (c) unless the attorney or a self-represented litigant states under oath or affirms in a verified writing that:

(1) a diligent search has been conducted;

(2) neither a certified, language skilled, provisionally approved interpreter nor an interpreter otherwise registered with the Office of the State Courts Administrator is available to interpret in person or via remote technology; and

(3) to the best of the attorney or self-represented litigant's information and belief, the proposed interpreter is competent to interpret. In addition, the written declaration shall include the full name, mailing address, and telephone number of the proposed interpreter; the non-English language interpreted; the date of the interpreted event; and nature of the interpreted event.

(e) Filing and Retention of Written Declaration. An attorney or self-represented litigant substantiating good cause under subdivision (d) shall submit via e-mail, a copy of the verified written declaration with the Court Interpreter Program Office in the Office of the State Courts Administrator. A prescribed form and dedicated e-mail address appear on the Court's website. The filer shall thereafter furnish a copy to the proposed interpreter, and shall:

(1) file the original declaration in any pending court action or administrative action and serve a copy thereof on all other parties; or

(2) if no action is pending at the time interpreter services are provided, retain the original declaration and serve a copy thereof on the non-English-speaking or limited-English-proficient person at the time interpreter services are provided. The declaration shall be made available to all other parties and to any state court or administrative judge, magistrate, or hearing officer upon request in any action later filed to which the interpreted event is relevant. The filing with the Office of the State Courts Administrator of a written declaration in substantial conformity with this subdivision shall excuse the proposed interpreter from the registration requirements under the Rules for Certification and Regulation of Spoken Language Interpreters for the delivery of the specific interpreter services for which certification is made.

(f) Time for Preparation, Submission, Filing, and Service. Verified written declarations required by this rule shall be prepared, submitted to the Office of State Courts Administrator, filed with the Clerk of Court, when required, and served on all parties in advance of the proceedings to which they are relevant. When compliance with this subdivision is impossible or impracticable due to the existence of emergency or other extraordinary circumstances, the attorney or self-represented litigant shall:

(1) comply with the preparation, submission, filing, and service requirements of this rule as soon as is practicable following the conclusion of the proceeding; and

(2) include in the verified written declaration a brief statement describing the emergency or other extraordinary circumstances justifying post-proceeding compliance.

Appendix
State of Florida
Judicial Branch
Records Retention Schedule
for Administrative Records.

GENERAL APPLICATION.

This record retention schedule does not impose a duty to create records contained in the schedule. The purpose of the schedule is to authorize destruction of records after the retention period has elapsed. The records custodian may retain records longer than required by the schedule. This schedule authorizes destruction of records unless otherwise provided by court rule.

The retention period should be calculated from the time that the record is completed. For purposes of calculating the retention period, fiscal records should be considered completed at the end of a fiscal year. All retention periods are subject to the caveat "provided that applicable audits have been released."

The records custodian of the judicial branch entity that creates a record creates the "record copy" and is responsible for its retention in accordance with this schedule. The records custodian of the judicial branch entity that properly receives a record from outside the judicial branch has the "record copy" and is responsible for its retention in accordance with this schedule. Duplicates are only required to be retained until obsolete, superseded or administrative value is lost.

"Record Series" means a group of related documents arranged under a single filing arrangement or kept together as a unit because they consist of the same form, relate to the same subject, result from the same activity, or have certain common characteristics.

ACQUISITION RECORDS: LIBRARY. This record series consists of information on the acquisition of library materials including: books, periodicals, filmstrips, software, compact discs, video/audio tapes, and other non-print media. This information may include the accession date and method, the publisher and cost, the date entered into the collection, dates removed from collection, and method of final disposal.
RETENTION: Retain for life of material.

ADMINISTRATIVE CONVENIENCE RECORDS. This record series consists of a subject file, generally filed alphabetically, which is located away from the official files, such as in the Director's and other supervisory offices. The file contains DUPLICATES of correspondence, reports, publications, memoranda, etc., and is used as a working file or reference file on subjects which are currently significant or which may become significant in the near future. The material filed in this series is NOT the official file or record copy but is maintained for the convenience of the officials in carrying out their elected or appointed duties.
RETENTION: Retain until obsolete, superseded or administrative value is lost.

ADMINISTRATIVE RECORDS: PUBLIC OFFICIALS/COURT ADMINISTRATORS. This record series consists of office files documenting the substantive actions of elected or appointed officials and the court administrator. These records constitute the official record of a judicial branch entity's performance of its functions and formulation of policy and program initiative. This series will include various types of records such as correspondence; memoranda; statements prepared for delivery at meetings, conventions or other public functions that are designed to advertise and promote programs, activities and policies of the judicial branch entity; interviews; and reports concerning development and implementation of activities of the judicial branch entity. **"These records may have archival value."**
RETENTION: 10 years.

ADMINISTRATIVE SUPPORT RECORDS. This record series consists of records accumulated relative to internal administrative activities rather than the functions for which the office exists. Normally, these records document procedures; the expenditure of funds, including budget material; day-to-day management of office personnel including training and travel; supplies, office services and equipment requests and receipts and other recorded experiences that do not serve as official documentation of the programs of the office. However, because the content of these records vary so greatly in content and value (containing some duplicates and record copies), a relatively large proportion of them are of continuing value and may be subject to the audit process. Note: Reference a more applicable records series first if one exists. **"These records may have archival value."**
RETENTION: 2 years.

ADVERTISEMENTS: LEGAL. This record series consists of advertisements which have appeared in newspapers or in the "Administrative Weekly" on matters pertaining to the judicial branch entity and other legal ads which may or may not indirectly affect the judicial branch entity; i.e., bid invitations for construction jobs, public hearings or notices, public sales. See also "BID RECORDS: CAPITAL IMPROVEMENT SUCCESS-FUL BID", "BID RECORDS: CAPITAL IMPROVEMENT UNSUCCESSFUL BIDS" and "BID RECORDS: NON-CAPITAL IMPROVEMENT."
RETENTION: 5 years.

AFFIRMATIVE ACTION RECORDS. This record series consists of copies of reports submitted to the Equal Employment Opportunity Commission (EEOC) per their requirements for the judicial branch entity's affirmative action plan. It may also include discrimination complaints, correspondence and investigative papers pertaining to the judicial branch entity's affirmative action plan. See also "EQUAL EMPLOYMENT OPPORTUNITY COMPLIANCE RECORDS."
RETENTION: 2 years.

APPLICATIONS: GUARDIAN AD LITEM, MEDIATION, OTHERS. This record series consists of applications, supporting documents, correspondence and reports relating to the application of a person to be certified as a mediator, a program to be approved to offer training for mediators, a volunteer to be approved by the Guardian ad Litem Program, or other persons or programs regulated in the judicial branch.
RETENTION: 5 years after the person or program is no longer regulated by the judicial branch.

APPLICATIONS: LIBRARY CARDS. This record series consists of library card applications which must be renewed on an annual, bi-annual, or other basis. The application may include the patron's name, address, telephone number, date of birth, as well as a statement of liability for the care and timely return of all materials checked out or utilized by the patron.
RETENTION: Retain for 30 days after expiration.

APPRAISALS: LAND PURCHASES (NOT PURCHASED). This record series consists of documents pertaining to land not purchased by a judicial branch entity and all supporting documents. See also "APPRAISALS: LAND PURCHASES (PURCHASED)."
RETENTION: 3 years.

APPRAISALS: LAND PURCHASES (PURCHASED). This record series consists of documents pertaining to land purchased by a judicial branch entity and all supporting documents. See also "APPRAISALS: LAND PURCHASES (NOT PURCHASED)."
RETENTION: Retain as long as judicial branch entity retains property.

ARCHITECTURAL PLANS/SPECIFICATIONS: PRELIMINARY DRAWINGS. This record series consists of those graphic and engineering preliminary drawing records that depict conceptual as well as precise measured information essential for the planning and construction of facilities.
RETENTION: Retain until completion and acceptance.

ATTENDANCE AND LEAVE RECORDS. This record series consists of requests or applications for vacation, sick, family medical leave (FMLA) and other types of leave including leave of absences, timesheets or timecards

along with any required documentation (medical statements or excuses from a physician, jury duty summons, or military orders, etc.) submitted by an employee to document authorized absences.
RETENTION: 3 years.

AUDITS: INDEPENDENT. This record series consists of a report issued by an independent auditor to establish the position of the judicial branch entity being audited against its standard of performance. See also, "AUDITS: INTERNAL," "AUDITS: STATE/FEDERAL" and "AUDITS: SUPPORTING DOCUMENTS."
RETENTION: 10 years.

AUDITS: INTERNAL. This record series consists of a report issued by an internal auditor to establish the position of a judicial branch entity being audited against its standard of performance. See also, "AUDITS: INDEPENDENT," "AUDITS: STATE/FEDERAL" and "AUDITS: SUPPORTING DOCUMENTS."
RETENTION: 3 years.

AUDITS: STATE/FEDERAL. This record series consists of a report issued by a federal or state auditor to establish the position of a judicial branch entity being audited against its standard of performance. See also, "AUDITS: INDEPENDENT," "AUDITS: INTERNAL" and "AUDITS: SUPPORTING DOCUMENTS."
"These records may have archival value."
RETENTION: 10 years.

AUDITS: SUPPORTING DOCUMENTS. This record series consists of the documentation and supporting documents used to develop the audit report with all bills, accounts, records and transactions. See also "AUDITS: INDEPENDENT," "AUDITS: INTERNAL" and "AUDITS: STATE/FEDERAL."
RETENTION: 3 years.

BACKGROUND/Security Checks. This record series consists of background/security checks for potential new hires and promotions. These checks may include a background and driver's license screening, reference check, and verification of academic standing. The files might include notices of not being hired based on the outcome of a security check and a opportunity for rebuttal. Supporting documentation consists of fingerprint cards, copy of the driver's license, copy of the transcript release form, returned form reference letters, and other necessary information.
RETENTION: 4 anniversary years.

BANK ACCOUNT AUTHORIZATION RECORDS. This record series consists of an authorization to maintain a bank account and who is authorized to sign off on the account.
RETENTION: 1 year after superseded by new authorization.

BAR APPLICANTS: ADMITTED. This record series consists of bar applications, supporting documents, all investigative materials, of administrative value, correspondence, reports, and similar materials accumulated during the bar admissions process regarding bar applicants who were subsequently admitted to The Florida Bar.
RETENTION: Bar application and fingerprint card, 5 years; all other materials, 1 year.

BAR APPLICANTS: NOT ADMITTED (WITH NO RECOMMENDATION). This record series consists of bar applications, supporting documents, all investigative materials of administrative value, correspondence, reports, and similar materials accumulated during the bar admissions process regarding bar applicants who have not been admitted to The Florida Bar and who have not received an unfavorable recommendation by the Florida Board of Bar Examiners.
RETENTION: 20 years or the death of the applicant, whichever is earlier.

BAR APPLICANTS: NOT ADMITTED (WITH UNFAVORABLE RECOMMENDATION). This record series consists of bar applications, supporting documents, all investigative materials of administrative value, correspondence, reports, and similar materials accumulated during the bar admissions process regarding bar applicants who have not been admitted to The Florida Bar and who have received an unfavorable

recommendation by the Florida Board of Bar Examiners by either a negotiated consent judgment or the issuance of findings of fact and conclusions of law.
RETENTION: 40 years or the death of the applicant, whichever is earlier.

BAR EXAMINATION/ANSWERS. This record series consists of answers to essay questions and answer sheets to machine-scored questions submitted by bar applicants during the bar examination administered by the Florida Board of Bar Examiners.
RETENTION: Until the conclusion of the administration of the next successive general bar examination.

BAR EXAMINATION/FLORIDA PREPARED PORTION. This record series consists of the portion of the bar examination prepared by the Florida Board of Bar Examiners.
RETENTION: 10 years from the date of the administration of the examination.

BID RECORDS: CAPITAL IMPROVEMENT SUCCESSFUL BIDS. This record series consists of information relative to the processing and letting of capital improvement successful bids including legal advertisements, "Requests for Proposal," technical specifications, correspondence, "Invitations to Bid," bid tabulations and bid responses. "Capital Improvements" shall mean enhancement to buildings, fixtures and all other improvements to land. See also "BID RECORDS: CAPITAL IMPROVEMENT UNSUCCESSFUL BIDS" and "BID RECORDS: NON-CAPITAL IMPROVEMENT."
RETENTION: 10 years.

BID RECORDS: CAPITAL IMPROVEMENT UNSUCCESSFUL BIDS. This record series consists of information relative to the processing and letting of capital improvement unsuccessful bids including legal advertisements, "Requests for Proposal," technical specifications, correspondence, "Invitations to Bid," bid tabulations and bid responses. "Capital Improvements" shall mean enhancement to buildings, fixtures and all other improvements to land. See also "BID RECORDS: CAPITAL IMPROVEMENT SUCCESSFUL BIDS" and "BID RECORDS: NON-CAPITAL IMPROVEMENT."
RETENTION: 5 years.

BID RECORDS: NON-CAPITAL IMPROVEMENT. This record series consists of information relative to the processing and letting of successful and unsuccessful noncapital improvement bids including legal advertisements, "Requests for Proposal," technical specifications, correspondence, "Invitations to Bid," bid tabulations and bid responses. See also "BID RECORDS: CAPITAL IMPROVEMENT SUCCESSFUL BIDS" and "BID RECORDS: CAPITAL IMPROVEMENT UNSUCCESSFUL BIDS."
RETENTION: 5 years.

BIOGRAPHICAL FILES. This record series consists of vitas, biographies, photographs and newspaper clippings of employees.
RETENTION: Retain until obsolete, superseded or administrative value is lost.

BUDGET RECORDS: APPROVED ANNUAL BUDGET. This record series consists of the approved annual budget and its amendments. See also "BUDGET RECORDS: SUPPORTING DOCUMENTS" **"These records may have archival value."**
RETENTION: Permanent.

BUDGET RECORDS: SUPPORTING DOCUMENTS. This record series consists of any supporting documentation supporting budget matters and is filed chronologically. See also "BUDGET RECORDS: APPROVED ANNUAL BUDGET."
RETENTION: 3 years.

BUILDING PLANS. This record series consists of graphic and engineering records that depict conceptual as well as precise measured information essential for the planning and construction of buildings. See also "ARCHITECTURAL PLANS/SPECIFICATIONS: PRELIMINARY DRAWINGS."
RETENTION: Retain for life of structure.

CALENDARS. This record series consists of a calendar showing official daily appointments and meetings. **RETENTION:** 1 year.

CASE RELATED RECORDS NOT IN THE CUSTODY OF THE CLERK AND /OR NOT IN CASE FILE. This record series includes records that are related to a trial court records as defined in Rule 2.420, Florida Rules of Judicial Administration, because they are not filed with the clerk of court and are not included in the court file. These records include, but are not limited to, drug court evaluation and progress reports, mediation reports, deferred prosecution and diversion records, and arbitration reports. Case-related trial court documents may be destroyed or disposed of after a judgment has become final in record accordance with the following schedule:
RETENTION:

(A) 60 days- Parking tickets and noncriminal traffic infractions after required audits have been completed.

(B) 2 years- Proceedings under the Small Claims Rules, Medical Mediation Proceedings.

(C) 5 years- Misdemeanor actions, criminal traffic violations, ordinance violations, civil litigation proceedings in county court other than those under the Small Claims Rules, and civil proceedings in circuit court except marriage dissolutions and adoptions.

(D) 10 years- Probate, guardianship, and mental health proceedings.

(E) 10 years- Felony cases in which no information or indictment was filed or in which all charges were dismissed, or in which the state announced a nolle prosequi, or in which the defendant was adjudicated not guilty.

(F) 75 years- juvenile proceedings containing an order permanently depriving a parent of custody of a child, and adoptions and all felony cases not previously destroyed.

(G) Juvenile proceedings not otherwise provided for in this subdivision shall be kept for 5 years after the last entry or until the child reaches the age of majority, whichever is later.

(H) Marriage dissolutions- 10 years from the last record activity. The court may authorize destruction of court records not involving alimony, support, or custody of children 5 years from the last record activity.

CERTIFICATION FORWARD DOCUMENTS. This record series consists of lists of encumbrances to be applied against certified forward money which is money brought forward from the previous fiscal year for goods and services which were not received until the current fiscal year. See also "ENCUMBRANCE RECORDS."
RETENTION: 3 years.

CHILD SUPPORT/ALIMONY DISBURSEMENT RECORDS: DETAIL. This series consists of records documenting disbursement of child support or alimony. The series includes, but is not limited to, check registers, check stubs, cancelled checks, cancelled warrants, disbursement ledgers, transaction journals, vendor invoice, refund records and other accounts payable related documentation.
RETENTION: 5 fiscal years.

CHILD SUPPORT/ALIMONY DISBURSEMENT RECORDS: SUMMARY. This series consists of records providing summary or aggregate documentation of expenditures or transfers moneys for child support or alimony. The series may include, but is not limited to, trail balance reports, check logs and registers, summary reports, summary journal transactions and other accounts payable summary related documentation.
RETENTION: 10 fiscal years.

CHILD SUPPORT/ALIMONY RECEIPT/REVENUE RECORDS: DETAIL. This series consists of records documenting specific receipts/revenues collected for child support or alimony. The series may include, but is not limited to, cash receipts, receipt books, deposit receipts, bank validated deposit slips, depository ledger reports filed with Clerk of Court, transaction journals, refund records, bad check records and other accounts receivable related documentation.
RETENTION: 5 fiscal years.

CHILD SUPPORT/ALIMONY RECEIPT/REVENUE RECORDS: SUMMARY. This series consists of records providing summary or aggregate documentation of receipts/revenues collected for child support or alimony. The series may include, but is not limited to, monthly statements of bank accounts, trial balance reports, bank statements, credit and debit card reports, collection balance sheets and other receivable summary related documentation.
RETENTION: 10 fiscal years.

COMPLAINTS: CITIZENS/CONSUMERS/EMPLOYEES. This record series consists of individual complaints received from citizens, consumers or employees. This file may include the name, address, date of complaint, telephone number, the complaint to whom referred and date, action taken and signature of person taking the action.
RETENTION: 1 year.

CONTINUING EDUCATION RECORDS. This record series consists of continuing education records, including records of judicial education.
RETENTION: 2 years.

CONTRACTS/LEASES/AGREEMENTS: CAPITAL IMPROVEMENT/REAL PROPERTY. This record series consists of legal documents, correspondence, reports, etc., relating to the negotiation, fulfillment and termination of capital improvement or real property contracts, leases or agreements to which the agency is a party, including contracts, leases or agreements with architects, engineers, builders, and construction companies. "Capital Improvements" shall mean improvements to real property (land, buildings, including appurtenances, fixtures and fixed equipment, structures, etc.), that add to the value and extend the useful life of the property, including construction of new structures, replacement or rehabilitation of existing structures (e.g., major repairs such as roof replacement), or removal of closed structures. 'Real Property' means land, buildings, and fixtures. The terms "land," "real estate," "realty" and "real property" may be used interchangeably. See also "CONTRACTS/LEASES/AGREEMENTS: NON-CAPITAL IMPROVEMENT."
RETENTION: 10 fiscal years after completion or termination of contract/lease/agreement.

CONTRACTS/LEASES/AGREEMENTS: NON-CAPITAL IMPROVEMENT. This record series consists of legal documents, correspondence, reports, etc., relating to the negotiation, fulfillment and termination of non-capital improvement contracts, leases or agreements to which the agency is a party. In addition, it includes the various contracts, leases or agreements entered into for the purchase of goods and services such as the purchase of gas, fuel oil and annual purchases of inventory-maintained items. See also "CONTRACTS/LEASES/AGREEMENTS: CAPITAL IMPROVEMENT/REAL PROPERTY."
RETENTION: 5 fiscal years after completion or termination of contract/lease/agreement.

CORRESPONDENCE & MEMORANDA: ADMINISTRATIVE. This record series consists of routine correspondence and memoranda of a general nature that is associated with administrative practices but that does not create policy or procedure, document the business of a particular program, or act as a receipt. See also "INFORMATION REQUEST RECORDS." **"These records may have archival value."**
RETENTION: 3 years.

CORRESPONDENCE & MEMORANDA: PROGRAM AND POLICY DEVELOPMENT. This record series consists of correspondence and memoranda of any nature that is associated with a specific program or the

development of policy and procedure. **"These records may have archival value."**
RETENTION: 5 years.

COURT REGISTRY. This record series consists of records, ledgers and journals showing amounts paid into the Court Registry, held by the Court, and paid out by the Court.
RETENTION: Permanent.

COURT REPORTS. This record series consists of court reports, including SRS, jury management, witness management, uniform case reporting system records, and other statistical court reports.
RETENTION: 3 years.

DEEDS: PROPERTY. This record series consists of property deeds. Series may include appraisals, surveys, and other supporting documents.
RETENTION: Retain as long as property is retained.

DELAYED BIRTH (APPLICATION/CERTIFICATE/AFFIDAVITS, ETC.) This record series consists of an application signed by a judge for a birth (other than in a hospital usually). This record is filed with the County Court pursuant to Section 382.0195(4)(a), Florida Statutes. Once signed, the application becomes an order. The record copy is sent to Vital Statistics.
RETENTION: Permanent.

DIRECTIVES/POLICIES/PROCEDURES. This record series consists of the official management statements of policy for the organization, supporting documents, and the operating procedures which outline the methods for accomplishing the functions and activities assigned to the judicial branch entity. It includes all memoranda and correspondence generated relating to the policies and procedures which are to be followed by employees. See also "CORRESPONDENCE & MEMORANDA: PROGRAM AND POLICY DEVELOPMENT." **"These records may have archival value."**
RETENTION: 2 years.

DISASTER PREPAREDNESS DRILLS. This record series consists of the results of disaster preparedness exercises and the supporting documents including scenarios, location of safety related drills, time tables, response times, probable outcomes, areas of difficulties, descriptions of how difficulties were resolved, and areas for improvement. Types of drills include: fire, tornado, safety, hurricane and SARA chemical spills. See also "DIRECTIVES/POLICIES/PROCEDURES" and "DISASTER PREPAREDNESS PLANS."
RETENTION: 3 years.

DISASTER PREPAREDNESS PLANS. This record series consists of disaster preparedness and recovery plans adopted by a judicial branch entity. See also "DIRECTIVE/POLICIES/PROCEDURES."
RETENTION: Retain until obsolete, superseded or administrative value is lost.

DISBURSEMENT RECORDS: DETAIL. This series consists of records documenting specific expenditures or transfers of agency moneys for the procurement of commodities and services and other purposes. The series may include, but is not limited to, procurement records such as requisitions, requisition logs, purchase orders, contracts, purchasing card (p-card) receipts, vendor invoices, receiving reports, acceptances of contract deliverables, approvals, and related documentation; and expenditure records for disbursements made through checks, warrants, electronic fund transfers (EFT), purchasing cards, or other methods, such as payment vouchers, approvals, check registers, cancelled checks, check stubs, cancelled warrants, disbursement ledgers, journal transactions, expenditure detail reports, refund records and other accounts payable and related documentation. Retention is based on s. 95.11(2), F.S., Statute of Limitations on contracts, obligations, or liabilities. See also "DISBURSEMENT RECORDS: SUMMARY," "PURCHASING RECORDS," and "TRAVEL RECORDS."
RETENTION: 5 fiscal years.

DISBURSEMENT RECORDS: SUMMARY. This series consists of records providing summary or aggregate documentation of expenditures or transfers of agency moneys for the procurement of commodities and services

and other purposes. The series may include, but is not limited to, summary records such as trial balance reports, check logs and registers, summary expenditure reports, federal grant final closeout reports, summary journal transactions, and other accounts payable summary and related documentation. See also "DISBURSEMENT RECORDS: DETAIL."
RETENTION: 10 fiscal years.

DISCIPLINARY CASE FILES. This record series consists of both sustained formal or informal disciplinary cases investigated that allege employee misconduct or violations of department regulations and orders, and state/federal statutes. It includes statements by the employee, witnesses, and the person filing the complaint. "Formal discipline" is defined as disciplinary action involving demotion, removal from office, suspension, or other similar action. "Informal discipline" is defined as any disciplinary action involving written and verbal reprimands, memoranda, or other similar action. This record series also can consist of formal and informal disciplinary cases that were determined as not sustained, unfounded, or exonerated charges. See also "PERSONNEL RECORDS".
RETENTION: 5 years.

DRAFTS AND WORKING PAPERS. This record series consists of documents, correspondence, reports, memos, and other materials in preliminary or developmental form before their iteration as a final product. Drafts may include copies of materials circulated for review for grammar, spelling, and content. Working papers may include notes and miscellaneous documents and materials used in compiling and assembling the final product. Note that some draft documents and working papers may have long-term value; such documents may even have archival or historical value. Such records might be better placed under the record series "Administrator Records: Public Officials/Court Administrators."
RETENTION: Retain until obsolete, superseded or administrative value is lost.

DRUG TEST RECORDS. This record series consists of the positive or negative results of a drug test under the Drug Free Workplace Act or as required for CDL or other drivers under US DOT regulations as well as records related to canceled tests. This series might include documents generated in decisions to administer reasonable suspicion or post-accident testing, or in verifying the existence of a medical explanation of the inability of the driver to provide adequate breath or to provide a urine specimen for testing. In addition, the case file could include: the employer's copy of an alcohol test form, including the results of the test; a copy of the controlled substances test chain of custody control form; documents sent by the Medical Review Officer (MRO) to the employer; notice to report for testing; affidavit signed by the employee stating any prescription drugs or over the counter medication currently taken; and final clearance to resume working. This record series can also consist of documentation, including memorandum and correspondence, related to an employee's refusal to take or submit samples for an alcohol and/or controlled substances test(s).
RETENTION: 5 years.

ELECTRONIC FUNDS TRANSFER RECORDS. This record series consists of documentation necessary to establish and maintain the electronic transfer of funds from one financial institution to another. The documentation may include, but is not limited to: an agreement between the two parties; a form which lists both institutions' names, their routing numbers, the name of the account holder, and the account's authorizing signature; a canceled deposit slip or check; and the paperwork for the termination of service or transfer of service to a new institution. This series does not include the paperwork on a specific individual deposit or payment.
RETENTION: 5 fiscal years.

ELECTRONIC RECORDS SOFTWARE. This record series consists of proprietary and non-proprietary software as well as related documentation that provides information about the content, structure and technical specifications of computer systems necessary for retrieving information retained in machine-readable format. These records may be necessary to an audit process.
RETENTION: Retain as long as there are software dependent records.

EMPLOYEE PRE-COUNSELING RECORDS. This record series consists of material and supporting documentation which provide documentation of initial contact with an employee regarding incidents which may or may not lead to disciplinary action. This series is not considered in and of itself a part of the employee discipline record.
RETENTION: 1 year.

EMPLOYMENT EXAMINATION RECORDS. This record series consists of test plans, announcements, grades, grading scales, keyed exams, test monitor's list of candidates, any research toward the development of the tests, and any other selection or screening criteria. See "PERSONNEL RECORDS" and "RECRUITMENT & SELECTION PACKAGES."
RETENTION: 4 anniversary years.

ENCUMBRANCE RECORDS. This record series consists of documents and reports which document funds that have been encumbered. See also "CERTIFICATION FORWARD DOCUMENTS."
RETENTION: 3 years.

ENDOWMENTS, BEQUESTS AND TRUST FUND RECORDS. This record series consists of creating, establishing or contributing to endowments, bequests and trust fund records. **"These records may have archival value."**
RETENTION: Permanent.

ENVIRONMENTAL REGULATION RECORDS. This record series consists of permits, reviews, supporting documents and correspondence resulting from environmental regulation requirements.
RETENTION: 5 years.

EQUAL EMPLOYMENT OPPORTUNITY COMPLIANCE RECORDS. This record series consists of EEO-5 and supporting documents, reviews, background papers and correspondence relating to employment papers and correspondence relating to employment statistics (race, sex, age, etc.). See also "AFFIRMATIVE ACTION RECORDS."
RETENTION: 4 anniversary years after final action.

EQUIPMENT/VEHICLE MAINTENANCE RECORDS. This record series documents service, maintenance, and repairs to agency equipment and vehicles, including program changes to electronic equipment. The series may include, but is not limited to, work orders and documentation of dates/history of repairs, locations, cost of parts, hours worked, etc. Records for all agency vehicles, including ground, air, and water vehicles, are covered by this series. See also "VEHICLE RECORDS."
RETENTION: 1 fiscal year after disposition of equipment.

EQUIPMENT/VEHICLE USAGE RECORDS. This record series documents use of agency equipment and vehicles, including, but not limited to, vehicle logs indicating driver, destination, fuel/service stops, and odometer readings and/or total trip mileage; equipment usage logs and/or reports; and other usage documentation. See also "VEHICLE RECORDS."
RETENTION:

a) Record copy. 1 calendar year.

b) Duplicates. Retain until obsolete, superseded, or administrative value is lost.

EXPENDITURE PLANS: CAPITAL. This record series consists of capital improvement expenditure plans.
RETENTION: Permanent.

FACILITY RESERVATION/Rental records. This record series consists of forms generated in the process of renting or scheduling a public meeting hall or room, conference site, to a citizen or family, private organization,

or other public agency. These forms include, but are not limited to, name of renter, renter's address and telephone number, method of payment, acknowledgment of rules, liability, damage waivers, and the date and time of the rental as well as what facility or portion of a facility is to be reserved. These forms may contain a check number, corresponding receipt number, an amount as well as deposit information. There may also be a floor plan denoting the desired arrangement of tables or chairs as requested by the renter.
RETENTION: 5 fiscal years.

FEASIBILITY STUDY RECORDS. This record series consists of working papers, correspondence, consulting firm reports and management committee reports investigating various projects of the judicial branch entity.
RETENTION: 3 years.

FEDERAL AND STATE TAX FORMS/REPORTS. This record series consists of W-2 Forms, W-4 Forms, W-9 Forms, 940 Forms, 941-E Forms, 1099 Forms, 1099 Reports and UTC-6 Forms. The retention period mentioned below for the record (master) copy was established pursuant to Section 26 CFR 31.6001-1(2).
RETENTION: 4 calendar years.

GENERAL LEDGERS: ANNUAL SUMMARY. This record series consists of ledgers containing accounts to which debits and credits are posted from supporting documents of original entry. It includes all permanent ledger entries.
RETENTION: Permanent.

GRAND JURY NOTES. This record series consists of stenographic records, notes, and transcriptions made by the court reporter or stenographer during the grand jury session. These records are normally kept in a sealed container and are not subject to public inspection pursuant to Section 905.17(1), Florida Statutes. A Court order must be obtained for disposition.
RETENTION: 10 years from closing of session.

GRAND JURY RECORDS. This record series consists of jury summons, requests for recusal, juror payments, information to jurors' employers, lists of jurors, juror questionnaires, and other records related to a grand jury. This record series includes records related to a grand jury and the statewide grand jury.
RETENTION: 2 years.

GRANT FILES. This record series consists of financial, management and any other related material which is generated subsequent to application for or expenditure of grant funds. These files include all applications, supporting documentation, contracts, agreements, and routine reports. Check with applicable grant agency for any additional requirements. Project completion has not occurred until all reporting requirements are satisfied and final payments have been received. See also "PROJECT FILES: FEDERAL", and "PROJECT FILES: NONCAPITAL IMPROVEMENT". **"These records may have archival value."**
RETENTION: 5 fiscal years after completion of project.

GRIEVANCE FILES (EMPLOYMENT). This record series consists of records of all proceedings in the settlement of disputes between employer and employee. See also "PERSONNEL RECORDS."
RETENTION: 3 years.

HEALTH RECORDS: BLOOD BORNE PATHOGEN/ASBESTOS/EXPOSURE. This record series consists of medical records of employees who may have or did come into contact with blood or other potentially hazardous materials. These confidential records include the employee's name, social security number, hepatitis B vaccination status including the dates of testing, results of examinations, medical testing, and follow up procedures, a copy of the healthcare professional's written opinion, a list of complaints which may be related to the exposure, and a copy of information provided to the healthcare professional. This record series can also consist of documents which record the exposure or possible exposure of an employee to a blood borne pathogen, contagion, radiation and chemicals above the acceptable limits or dosage. These documents may include

statistical analyses, incident reports, material safety data sheets, copies of medical records or reports, risk management assessments, and other necessary data to support the possibility of exposure. *Please refer to 20 CFR 1910.1030.*
RETENTION: 30 years after termination, retirement, or separation from employment.

INCIDENT REPORTS. This record series consists of reports of incidents which occur at a public facility or on publicly owned property. It may include alarm malfunctions, suspicious persons, maintenance problems, or any other circumstance that should be noted for future reference or follow up.
RETENTION: 4 years.

INFORMATION REQUEST RECORDS. This record series consists of correspondence accumulated in answering inquiries from the public. See also "CORRESPONDENCE & MEMORANDA: ADMINISTRA-TIVE."
RETENTION: 1 year.

INSPECTION RECORDS: FIRE/SECURITY/SAFETY. This record series consists of inspection reports for fire, security, and safety.
RETENTION: 4 years.

INSPECTION REPORTS: FIRE EXTINGUISHER (ANNUAL). This records series consists of annual fire extinguisher inspection reports.
RETENTION: 1 anniversary year or life of equipment, whichever is sooner.

INSURANCE RECORDS. This record series consists of all policies, claim filing information, correspondence and claims applications made by an agency, premium payment records which includes fire, theft, liability, medical, life, etc. on agency's property or employees. The record series also consists of a list of any insurance carriers and the premium payment amounts paid to them.
RETENTION: 5 years after final disposition of claim or expiration of policy.

INVENTORY RECORDS: PHYSICAL. This record series consists of all information regarding the physical inventory of all Operating Capital Outlay (O.C.O.) items which require an identification number and tag. Included in these reports are items sold through the auctions process as well as the Fixed Inventory Report showing all property owned by the judicial branch entity. See also "SUPPLY RECORDS."
RETENTION: 3 years.

JQC — JUDICIAL FINANCIAL DISCLOSURE FORMS. This record consists of all financial disclosure forms filed by the judiciary with the Judicial Qualifications Commission.
RETENTION: 10 years.

JQC — JUDICIAL COMPLAINTS. This record consists of individual complaints received from citizens, judges, or lawyers against members of the judiciary.
RETENTION: 3 years if complaint summarily dismissed. For the lifetime of the judge against whom the complaint has been filed in all other cases.

JUROR NOTES. Juror notes shall consist of any written notes taken by jurors during civil or criminal trials.
RETENTION: Immediate destruction upon issuance of a verdict or if the trial ends prematurely as a result of a mistrial, plea, or settlement.

JURY RECORDS. This record series consists of jury summons, requests for recusal, juror payments, information to jurors' employers, lists of jurors, juror questionnaires, and other records related to the jury pool. This record series includes records related to petit juries.
RETENTION: 2 years.

KEY AND BADGE ISSUANCE RECORDS. This record series consists of the key control system which includes receipts for keys and security or identification badges issued by employees. See also "VISITOR

LOGS".
RETENTION: Retain as long as employee is employed.

LAW OFFICE MANAGEMENT ASSISTANCE SERVICE RECORDS. This record series consists of all materials in connection with consultations or advice given in the course of office management assistance services provided to an attorney, legal office, or law firm.
RETENTION: Retain until obsolete, superseded or administrative value is lost.

LEAVE TRANSACTION REPORTS. This record series consists of the printed record generated through COPES of the total hours used and the accrual earned during a pay period. It also consists of the leave balances of vacation, sick and compensatory leave for all employees in the agency.
RETENTION: 3 years.

LEGISLATION RECORDS. This record series consists of proposed legislation for the Florida Legislature and all supporting documentation, analysis or tracking information. **"These records may have archival value."**
RETENTION: Retain until obsolete, superseded or administrative value is lost.

LIBRARY CIRCULATION RECORDS. This record series consists of the transactions devised to make library materials and equipment available to the entire library clientele. Also, includes delinquent records and charges, copies of incoming and outgoing interlibrary loan requests for books, magazine articles, microfilms, renewals and subject searches.
RETENTION: 3 years.

LITIGATION CASE FILES. This record series consists of legal documents, notes, reports, background material, etc. created in the preparation of handling legal disputes involving a judicial branch entity. See also, "OPINIONS: LEGAL (ATTORNEY)," and "OPINIONS: LEGAL (SUPPORTING DOCUMENTS)."
RETENTION: 5 years after case closed or appeal process expired.

MAIL: UNDELIVERABLE FIRST CLASS. This record series consists of mail from any judicial branch entity, returned due to an incorrect address or postage. See also "MAILING LISTS" and "POSTAGE RECORDS."
RETENTION: 1 year.

MAILING LISTS. This record series consists of mailing lists. See also "MAIL: UNDELIVERABLE FIRST CLASS" and "POSTAGE RECORDS."
RETENTION: Retain until obsolete, superseded or administrative value is lost.

MANAGEMENT SURVEYS/STUDIES: INTERNAL. This record series consists of the raw data and work papers for any survey conducted to study management issues such as client/patron/employee satisfaction and service improvement. This data may include survey response cards, the results of telephone polls, tally sheets, opinion cards for suggestion boxes, and other records related to the study of internal operations. This does not include a consultant report. The final computation of the data is produced as a survey report and may be scheduled either as part of a feasibility study, project case file, or an operational/statistical report - depending on the nature and depth of the survey/study.
RETENTION: 1 year after final data or report released.

MATERIALS SAFETY RECORDS. This record series consists of a list of toxic substances to which an employee is, has been or may be exposed to during the course of their employment with an employer who manufacturers, produces, uses, applies or stores toxic substances in the work place.
RETENTION: 30 years.

MEMORANDA - LEGAL: Court's decision-making. This record series consists of memoranda, drafts or other documents involved in a court's judicial decision-making process.
RETENTION: Retain until obsolete, superseded or administrative value is lost.

MINUTES: OFFICIAL MEETINGS. This record series consists of the minutes of meetings convened to establish policy or precedent and includes meetings of the Board of Governors of The Florida Bar and The Florida Board of Bar Examiners, and court administrative conferences. See also "MINUTES: OTHER MEETINGS" and "MINUTES: OFFICIAL MEETINGS (AUDIO/VISUAL RECORDINGS)." **"These records may have archival value."**
RETENTION: Permanent.

MINUTES: OFFICIAL MEETINGS (AUDIO/VISUAL RECORDINGS). This record series consists of official audio and video recordings of meetings. See also, "MINUTES: OTHER MEETINGS."
RETENTION: Until minutes are prepared.

MINUTES: OFFICIAL MEETINGS (SUPPORTING DOCUMENTS). This record series consists of the agenda and supporting documents for official meetings. See also "MINUTES: OTHER MEETINGS" and "MINUTES: OFFICIAL MEETINGS (AUDIO/VISUAL RECORDINGS)."
RETENTION: 3 years.

MINUTES: OTHER MEETINGS. This record series consists of minutes from all meetings which are not included in "MINUTES: OFFICIAL MEETINGS."
RETENTION: 1 year.

MONTHLY DISTRIBUTION OF FINES. This record series consists of monthly reports, prepared by the clerk, of all fines imposed under the penal laws of the state and the proceeds of all forfeited bail bonds or recognizance which are paid into the fine and forfeiture fund. The report contains the amount of fines imposed by the court and of bonds forfeited and judgments rendered on said forfeited bonds, and into whose hands they had been paid or placed for collection, the date of conviction in each case, the term of imprisonment, and the name of the officer to whom commitment was delivered.
RETENTION: 3 fiscal years.

NEWS RELEASES. This record series consists of news releases distributed by the judicial branch entity and news releases received from other offices for informational purposes. See also "PUBLIC INFORMATION CASE FILES," and "PRE-PUBLICATIONS AND MEDIA ITEM RECORDS." **"These records may have archival value."**
RETENTION: 90 days.

OPERATIONAL AND STATISTICAL REPORT RECORDS: OFFICE. This record series consists of daily, weekly, monthly, biannual, and annual narrative and statistical reports of office operations made within and between judicial branch entities. Also included in this series are activity reports demonstrating the productivity of an employee or the work tasks completed for a period of time (hourly/daily/weekly).
RETENTION: Retain until obsolete, superseded or administrative value is lost.

OPINIONS: ETHICS. This record series consists of advisory ethical opinions issued by the appropriate committee in response to an inquiry from a regulated person or entity. **"These records may have archival value."**
RETENTION: Permanent.

OPINIONS: ETHICS (SUPPORTING DOCUMENTS). This record series consists of supporting documents relating to advisory ethical opinions.
RETENTION: 3 years.

OPINIONS: LEGAL (ATTORNEY). This record series consists of written opinions of lasting significance establishing policy or precedent answering legal questions involving questions of interpretation of Florida or federal law. This does not include memoranda, drafts or other documents involved in a court's judicial decision-making process. See also "CORRESPONDENCE & MEMORANDA: PROGRAM AND POLICY

DEVELOPMENT", "LITIGATION CASE FILES," "MEMORANDA — LEGAL" and "OPINIONS: LEGAL (SUPPORTING DOCUMENTS)." **"These records may have archival value."**
RETENTION: Permanent.

OPINIONS: LEGAL (SUPPORTING DOCUMENTS). This record series consists of the supporting documentation to the opinions that answer legal questions involving questions of interpretation of Florida or Federal law. See also "LITIGATION CASE FILES" and "OPINIONS: LEGAL (ATTORNEY)."
RETENTION: 3 years.

ORDERS: ADMINISTRATIVE. This record series consists of administrative orders as defined in Rule of Judicial Administration 2.020(c).
RETENTION: Permanent.

ORGANIZATION CHARTS. This record series consists of organizational charts that show lines of authority and responsibility within and between judicial branch entities. See also "DIRECTIVES/POLICIES/PROCE-DURES."
RETENTION: Retain until obsolete, superseded or administrative value is lost.

OTHERWISE UNCATEGORIZED RECORDS. This record series consists of all records which are not otherwise specified in this schedule.
RETENTION: Retain until obsolete, superseded or administrative value is lost.

PARKING DECAL/PERMIT RECORDS. This record series consists of parking applications for automobile and motor bike decals for employees. See also "VEHICLE RECORDS."
RETENTION: 2 years.

PAYROLL RECORDS. This record series consists of the following: a form used by staff to rectify errors in payroll processing including: wrong name, incorrect deductions or salary, inaccurate tax information, or other problems; forms authorizing direct deductions for insurance, union dues, credit unions, savings bonds, charitable contributions, deferred compensation, day care, etc.; any payroll record posted to the employee's applicable retirement plan, in any format (plus indices, if applicable), which are used to document payment for retirement or other purposes during an employee's duration of employment and also lists each rate(s) of pay changes.
RETENTION: 4 years.

PAYROLL RECORDS: REGISTERS (POSTED). This record series consists of records posted to the employee's retirement plan, in any format (plus indexes, if applicable), which are used to document payment for retirement or other purposes during an employee's duration of employment and also lists each rate of pay. Please note that the information in this record series should be posted to an applicable retirement plan. See also other "PAYROLL RECORDS" and "SOCIAL SECURITY CONTROLLED SUMMARY RECORDS."
RETENTION: 4 years.

PERSONNEL RECORDS. This record series consists of an application for employment, resume, personnel action reports, directly related correspondence, oath of loyalty, fingerprints, medical examination reports, performance evaluation reports, worker's compensation reports, and other related materials. See also "EM-PLOYMENT EXAMINATION RECORDS," "DISCIPLINARY CASE FILES," and other "PERSONNEL RECORDS."
RETENTION: 25 years after separation or termination of employment.

PERSONNEL RECORDS: LOCATOR. This record series consists of a log or card of where to locate personnel including name of individual, location to be found, date, address, emergency contact and other general information.
RETENTION: Retain until obsolete, superseded or administrative value is lost.

PERSONNEL RECORDS: OPS/TEMPORARY EMPLOYMENT. This record series consists of all information relating to each O.P.S. or temporary employee within each judicial branch entity. Also, records may

include an employment application, resume, personnel action forms and any correspondence relating to that individual. Temporary employment may include personnel from a local employment agency. See also "EMPLOYMENT EXAMINATION RECORDS," "DISCIPLINARY CASE FILES," and other "PERSONNEL RECORDS."
RETENTION: 3 years.

PETTY CASH DOCUMENTATION RECORDS. This record series consists of receipts, bills and monthly balances indicating amount needed for replenishing this revolving account.
RETENTION: 3 years.

POSITION DESCRIPTION RECORDS. This record series consists of specifically assigned duties and responsibilities for a particular position, including percentage breakdown of duties.
RETENTION: 2 years after superseded.

POSTAGE RECORDS. This record series consists of a detailed listing showing the amount of postage used, date, unused balance and purpose. See also "MAILING LISTS" and "MAIL: UNDELIVERABLE FIRST CLASS."
RETENTION: 3 years.

PRE-PUBLICATIONS AND MEDIA ITEM RECORDS. This record series consists of records used to generate publications such as catalogs, pamphlets and leaflets and other media items including rough, blue lined, and final copies. See also "NEWS RELEASES" and "PUBLIC INFORMATION CASE FILES".
RETENTION: Retain until receipt of final copy.

PROCLAMATIONS/RESOLUTIONS. This record series consists of an expression of a governing body or public official concerning administrative matters, an expression of a temporary character or a provision for the disposition of a particular item of the administrative business of a governing body or judicial branch entity. See also, "DIRECTIVES/POLICIES/PROCEDURES." **"These records may have archival value."**
RETENTION: Permanent.

PROCLAMATIONS/RESOLUTIONS: SUPPORTING DOCUMENTS. This record series consists of documents that were used to prepare a proclamation or resolution. See also "PROCLAMATIONS/RESOLUTIONS" and "DIRECTIVES/POLICIES/PROCEDURES."
RETENTION: 3 years.

PROGRAM/SUBJECT/REFERENCE FILES. This record series may contain correspondence, reports, memoranda, studies, articles, etc. regarding topics of interest to or addressed by a judicial branch entity. See also, "ADMINISTRATIVE RECORDS: PUBLIC OFFICIALS/COURT ADMINISTRATORS".
RETENTION: Retain until obsolete, superseded, or administrative value is lost.

PROJECT FILES: CAPITAL IMPROVEMENT. This record series consists of correspondence or memoranda, drawings, resolutions, narratives, budget revisions, survey information, change orders, computer runs and reports all pertaining to capital improvement projects, construction and contract specifications for various proposed projects sent out for bid. See also "PROJECT FILES: FEDERAL," and "PROJECT FILES: NON-CAPITAL IMPROVEMENT."
RETENTION: 10 years.

PROJECT FILES: FEDERAL. This record series consists of original approved project contracts, agreements, awards, and line-item budgets, budget amendments, cash requests, correspondence and audit reports. See also "GRANT FILES" and "PROJECT FILES: CAPITAL IMPROVEMENT."
RETENTION: 5 years.

PROJECT FILES: NON-CAPITAL IMPROVEMENT. This record series consists of correspondence or memoranda, drawings, resolutions, narratives, budget revisions, survey information, change orders, computer

runs and reports all pertaining to projects in progress, construction and contract specifications for various proposed projects sent out for bid. See also "GRANT FILES," "PROJECT FILES: CAPITAL IMPROVEMENT," and "PROJECT FILES: FEDERAL."
RETENTION: 5 years.

PROPERTY TRANSFER FORMS. This record series consists of all capital and non-capital property transfer forms to declare surplus or transfer to another unit of local or state government. This series does not include real property transfers.
RETENTION: 1 year.

PUBLIC INFORMATION CASE FILES. This record series consists of speeches and drafts, contact prints, negatives, enlargements from negatives and transparencies created as illustrations in publications or as visual displays of activities of the judicial branch entity. See also "NEWS RELEASES," and "PRE-PUBLICATIONS AND MEDIA ITEM RECORDS." **These records may have archival value.**
RETENTION: 90 days.

PUBLIC PROGRAM/EVENT RECORDS: CONTRACTED. This record series consists of case files of events or programs which are available to the public or segments of the public. Files may include copies of contracts or agreements, participant or performer information, program details and arrangements, photo or video tapes. See also "PUBLIC PROGRAM/EVENT RECORDS: NON-CONTRACTED."
RETENTION: 5 years.

PUBLIC PROGRAM/EVENT RECORDS: NON-CONTRACTED. This record series consists of case files of events or programs which are available to the public or segments of the public. Files may include, copies of contracts or agreements, participant or performer information, program details and arrangements, photo or video tapes. See also "PUBLIC PROGRAM/EVENT RECORDS: CONTRACTED."
RETENTION: 3 years.

PURCHASING RECORDS. This record series consists of a copy of the purchase order which is retained by the originating office while another is sent by the purchasing office to the appropriate vendor for action. The series may include, but is not limited to, copies of requisitions sent by the originating office to supply, purchasing, graphics, duplicating, or other sections for action; copies of receiving reports; and a log of outstanding and paid requisitions and purchase orders used for cross-referencing purposes. See also "DISBURSEMENT RECORDS: DETAIL."
RETENTION: 5 fiscal years.

RECEIPT/REVENUE RECORDS: DETAIL. This series consists of records documenting specific receipts/revenues collected by an agency through cash, checks, electronic fund transfers (EFT), credit and debit cards, or other methods. The series may include, but is not limited to, records such as cash collection records and reports, cash receipt books, cash register tapes, deposit/transfer slips, EFT notices, credit and debit card records, receipt ledgers, receipt journal transactions and vouchers, refund records, bad check records, and other accounts receivable and related documentation. Retention is based on s. 95.11(2), F.S., Statute of Limitations on contracts, obligations, or liabilities. See also "RECEIPT/REVENUE RECORDS: SUMMARY."
RETENTION: 5 fiscal years provided applicable audits have been released.

RECEIPT/REVENUE RECORDS: SUMMARY. This series consists of records providing summary or aggregate documentation of receipts/revenues collected by an agency. The series may include, but is not limited to, records such as trial balance reports, bank statements, credit and debit card reports, revenue reconciliations, collection balance sheets, and other accounts receivable summary and related documentation. See also "RECEIPT/REVENUE RECORDS: DETAIL."
RETENTION: 10 fiscal years provided applicable audits have been released.

RECEIPTS: REGISTERED AND CERTIFIED MAIL. This record series consists of receipts for registered and certified mail sent out or received by a particular judicial branch entity. See also "MAIL: UNDELIVER-

ABLE FIRST CLASS," and "POSTAGE RECORDS."
RETENTION: 1 year.

RECRUITMENT & SELECTION PACKAGES. This record series consists of all records which document the selection process and justify the selection process and justify the selection decision including: details of the job analysis and identification of the knowledge, skills and abilities necessary to perform the job; application forms and/or resumes for employment including demographic data of applicants including but not limited to race, sex, age and veteran status; list of all applicants' name and ratings or rankings (if applicable) for each selection technique; description of the selection process; selection techniques used, including samples, supplemental applications, etc.; the current position description; the names and titles of all persons administering the selection process or participating in making selection decisions; the job opportunity announcement and any other recruitment efforts; and other information that affects the selection decisions. See also "EMPLOYMENT EXAMINATION RECORDS".
RETENTION: 4 anniversary years after personnel action and any litigation is resolved.

SALARY COMPARISON REPORTS. This record series consists of a report which is distributed and provided for reference purposes only. This data is compiled from records located in the Personnel Office.
RETENTION: 1 year.

SALARY SCHEDULES. This record series consists of a pay grade comparison chart or log indicating the salary classification for each position.
RETENTION: 10 years.

SEARCH COMMITTEE RECORDS. This record series consists of minutes, reports, vitas, resumes, interview score sheets, interview results, list of priority hires, a personnel requisition, references of applicants and the affirmative action compliance report.
RETENTION: 180 days.

SEARCH WARRANTS SERVED: NO ARREST/NO CASE FILED. This record series consists of the original affidavit for search warrant, search warrant and return of the search warrant. Series may also include property inventory and receipt, if any property was obtained. After execution of the warrant it is filed with the Clerk of Court as served with no arrest having been made. Since no court case is generated, these are kept as a separate record series.
RETENTION: 1 year after date of return.

SOCIAL SECURITY CONTROLLED SUMMARY RECORDS. This record series consists of a judicial branch entity's copy of the State's FICA report mailed to the Division of Retirement. Report lists the total taxable wages plus the amount withheld from employee wages plus employer's contribution. See also "PAYROLL RECORDS."
RETENTION: 4 calendar years after due date of tax.

STATE AUTOMATED MANAGEMENT ACCOUNTING SYSTEM (SAMAS) REPORTS. This record series consists of reports of all updated transactions entered into the system and a financial statement for each month for all divisions of judicial branch entities.
RETENTION: 3 years.

STATE AWARDS AND RECOGNITION FILES. This record series consists of data relating to the State Meritorious Service Awards Program. File contains employee suggestion forms (Form DMS/EPE.AWP01), evaluations, adoption forms and payment records. It also contains Superior Accomplishment nomination forms and payment records. Summary information submitted to the Department of Management Services for Annual Workforce Report (Form DMS/EPE.AWP02) is also contained in this record series.
RETENTION: 3 years.

SUPPLY RECORDS. This record series consists of documentation of a perpetual inventory of expendable supplies located in a central supply office for use by judicial branch entity employees. Included in this series is a listing of all available supplies which is distributed periodically or upon request. See also "INVENTORY RECORDS: PHYSICAL."
RETENTION: 3 years.

SURVEILLANCE VIDEO TAPES. This record series consists of surveillance video tapes created to monitor activities occurring both within and outside of public buildings. This tape may play an integral part in prosecution or disciplinary actions.
RETENTION: 30 days, then erase and reuse provided any necessary images are saved.

TELEPHONE CALL RECORDS: LONG DISTANCE. This record series consists of documentation and logs of separately billed long distance telephone service.
RETENTION: 1 year.

TRAINING MATERIAL RECORDS. This record series consists of materials used in training, such as films, slides, commentaries, manuals, workbooks and other related items. This records series does not include individual training records.
RETENTION: Retain until obsolete, superseded or administrative value is lost.

TRAINING RECORDS: EMPLOYEE. This record series consists of a record for each employee which may include all educational and training records of the employee. See also "PERSONNEL RECORDS."
RETENTION: 3 years.

TRANSITORY MESSAGES. This record series consists of those records that are created primarily for the communication of information, as opposed to communications designed for the perpetuation of knowledge. Transitory messages do not set policy, establish guidelines or procedures, certify a transaction, or become a receipt. The informal tone of transitory messages might be compared to the communication that might take place during a telephone conversation or a conversation in an office hallway. Transitory messages would include, but would not be limited to: E-mail messages with short-lived, or no administrative value, voice mail, self-sticking notes, and telephone messages.
RETENTION: Retain until obsolete, superseded or administrative value is lost.

TRAVEL RECORDS. This record series consists of records required to support reimbursement of expenses incurred during official travel.
RETENTION: 5 fiscal years.

UNCLAIMED PROPERTY RECORDS. This record series consists of forms required by the State Comptroller's Office for the registration of abandoned tangible or intangible property. These forms are required under Chapter 717 of the Florida Statutes. The judicial branch entity holding the unclaimed property is to maintain a list of the specific type of property, amount, name, and last known address of the owner.
RETENTION: 5 years after the property becomes reportable.

UNEMPLOYMENT COMPENSATION RECORDS. This record series consists of reports submitted to the State on a quarterly basis stating the name of each employee, employee number, amount of wages paid during quarter subject to unemployment benefits, social security number, number of weeks covered and other pertinent information which is retained by the State for determination of unemployment benefits due to applicants for same. Also includes, receipts and statements of charges.
RETENTION: 5 fiscal years.

VEHICLE ACCIDENT REPORTS. This record series consists of reports of employees that are involved in accidents in a judicial branch entity vehicle or in their own vehicle during the course of official business. See also "VEHICLE RECORDS."
RETENTION: 4 anniversary years.

VEHICLE RECORDS. This record series consists of all pertinent records pertaining to each vehicle owned by the judicial branch entity. The records usually consist of the vehicle registration papers, copy of the title, inspection information, maintenance agreements, credit card information, confidential tag issuance information and any other information relating to the vehicle. See also "VEHICLE ACCIDENT REPORTS."
RETENTION: 1 year after disposition of vehicle.

VENDOR FILES. This record series consists of vendor invoices for items purchased or leased, received and paid for.
RETENTION: 3 years.

VISITOR LOGS. This record series consists of records documenting employees' and visitors' entrance into a judicial branch entity's building during and after office hours. See also "KEY AND BADGE ISSUANCE RECORDS."
RETENTION: 30 days.

WIRE AND ORAL COMMUNICATIONS: APPLICATIONS, ORDERS AND AUDIO RECORDINGS. This record series consists of applications for an order authorizing the interception of a wire or oral communications and orders granted pursuant to Chapter 934, Florida Statutes. Also included are original recordings of the contents of any wire or oral communication made pursuant to Section 934.09, Florida Statutes. They shall not be destroyed except upon an order of the issuing or denying judge, or that judge's successor in office, and in any event shall be kept for ten (10) years.
RETENTION: 10 years (upon permission of the Court).

WITNESS SUBPOENAS/LISTS. This record series consists of subpoena lists that may be used to establish witness payments.
RETENTION: 3 years.

WORK ORDERS. This record series consists of information reflecting the individual history of major or minor maintenance or services requiring a work order request. Work order includes dates, locations, cost of labor, hours worked, equipment cost per hour, material used and cost, and other pertinent details. This item does not include equipment maintenance records. See also "EQUIPMENT/VEHICLE MAINTENANCE RECORDS."
RETENTION: 3 years.

WORK SCHEDULES. This record series consists of any scheduling documentation for shift or part time employees. These records may include hours scheduled to work, the switching of hours with another employee, the location or route of work assignment, and anticipated starting and ending times.
RETENTION: 1 year.

WORKERS' COMPENSATION RECORDS. This record series consists of the first report of injury and the employer's supplemental reports including, if used, OSHA Form No. 200 as well as its predecessor forms No. 100 and 102 and OSHA Form No. 101. These records are created pursuant to Florida Statutes Section 440.09 and OSHA standards 1904.2, 1904.4, and 1904.5.
RETENTION: 5 years.

INDEX TO FLORIDA RULES OF JUDICIAL ADMINISTRATION

———

FLORIDA RULES OF JUVENILE PROCEDURE

2018 Edition

(Includes rules and Chapters 39, 984, and 985, Florida Statutes)

Rules reflect all changes through 2018 WL 654523, 2018 Fla. Lexis 280. Subsequent amendments, if any, can be found at www.floridasupremecourt.org/decisions/rules.shtml. The Florida Bar also updates the rules on its website at www.FloridaBar.org (on the homepage click "Rules Updates").

CONTINUING LEGAL EDUCATION PUBLICATIONS

THE FLORIDA BAR
TALLAHASSEE, FLORIDA 32399-2300

CITATIONS TO OPINIONS ADOPTING OR AMENDING RULES

ORIGINAL ADOPTION, effective 7-1-77: 345 So.2d 655.

OTHER OPINIONS:

Effective 7-1-79:	372 So.2d 449.	Deleted 8.020.
Effective 1-1-81:	393 So.2d 1077.	Amended 8.010-8.050, 8.070, 8.100-8.150, 8.170-8.260, 8.280- 8.300, 8.320-8.340; deleted 8.160, 8.310; replaced 8.923-8.924; added 8.925-8.931.
Effective 9-1-82:	418 So.2d 1004.	Amended 8.170, 8.300.
Effective 1-1-85:	462 So.2d 399.	Four-year-cycle revision; divided rules into two parts. Amended 8.030-8.050, 8.070, 8.110-8.130, 8.150, 8.180-8.240, 8.280-8.300; deleted 8.060, 8.340; added 8.160, 8.500-8.870; replaced 8.250, 8.260.
Effective 9-19-85:	475 So.2d 1240.	Amended 8.040.
Effective 1-1-89:	530 So.2d 920.	Four-year-cycle revision; all committee notes before 1984 deleted. Amended 8.050-8.190, 8.260, 8.320, 8.530, 8.710, 8.720; deleted 8.160, 8.310, 8.909, 8.914; replaced 8.923-8.924.
Effective 1-1-89:	532 So.2d 1272.	Amended 8.180.
Effective 10-1-89:	549 So.2d 663.	Added Part III, 8.880-8.887.
Effective 3-1-90:	557 So.2d 1360.	Amended 8.610, 8.630, 8.710, 8.800.
Effective 7-1-91:	589 So.2d 818.	Reorganized and renumbered rules. Amended 8.000-8.013, 8.025-8.040, 8.060-8.065, 8.075, 8.085-8.130, 8.140, 8.150-8.180, 8.200-8.275, 8.285, 8.300-8.320, 8.330-8.400, 8.415, 8.700-8.710, 8.720-8.725, 8.735, 8.904-8.909, 8.931-8.932, 8.948, 8.965, 8.980; deleted 8.915-8.931; added 8.015, 8.045, 8.070, 8.080, 8.325, 8.405-8.410, 8.500-8.530, 8.600-8.695, 8.902-8.903, 8.911-8.913, 8.930, 8.937-8.947, 8.960-8.964, 8.966-8.967, 8.981-8.984.
Effective 1-1-93:	608 So.2d 478.	Amended 8.045, 8.060, 8.085, 8.160, 8.205-8.210, 8.225, 8.235, 8.325, 8.340, 8.515, 8.640, 8.982; added 8.104, 8.185; deleted 8.175, 8.200, 8.280, 8.600, 8.700.
Effective 12-22-94:	648 So.2d 115.	Amended 8.090, 8.415; added 8.227.
Effective 1-26-95:	649 So.2d 1370.	Amended 8.090-8.104, 8.120, 8.245, 8.947, 8.961; added 8.949-8.950.
Effective 9-28-95:	661 So.2d 800.	Amended 8.210, 8.400-8.410, 8.500-8.505, 8.520, 8.530.
Effective 10-1-96:	681 So.2d 666.	Amended 8.060.
Effective 10-31-96:	684 So.2d 756.	Amended 8.095.
Effective 1-1-97:	684 So.2d 756.	Four-year-cycle revision. Amended 8.013, 8.035, 8.075, 8.085, 8.105, 8.115-8.120, 8.215, 8.225, 8.265, 8.305, 8.315, 8.405-8.410, 8.510, 8.525, 8.610, 8.617, 8.625, 8.635, 8.909, 8.940-8.942, 8.946-8.947, 8.950, 8.961, 8.964-8.967, 8.982; added 8.535, 8.951, 8.968-8.969.
Effective 7-10-97:	696 So.2d 763.	Added 8.290.
Effective 10-1-98:	725 So.2d 296.	Amended 8.000, 8.201, 8.210-8.215, 8.225, 8.240-8.255, 8.290, 8.305-8.330, 8.340-8.345, 8.400-8.415, 8.500-8.525, 8.535, 8.960-8.964, 8.966-8.967, 8.969, 8.980-8.981, 8.983-8.984; added 8.959, 8.965, 8.970-8.972, 8.979, 8.985-8.986; deleted 8.405, 8.530, 8.967, 8.982.
Effective 12-3-98:	724 So.2d 1153.	Amended 8.060.
Effective 4-29-99:	753 So.2d 541.	Amended 8.100.
Effective 7-1-99:	753 So.2d 1214.	Amended 8.210, 8.225, 8.235, 8.275, 8.305-8.310, 8.320-8.330, 8.345, 8.400-8.415, 8.500-8.510, 8.525.

Effective 1-1-01:	783 So.2d 138.	Four-year-cycle revision. Amended 8.013-8.015, 8.030, 8.040, 8.060, 8.070, 8.085, 8.095, 8.115-8.120, 8.185, 8.205-8.215, 8.225-8.260, 8.290-8.320, 8.330, 8.340-8.510, 8.520, 8.610, 8.625, 8.635, 8.655, 8.690-8.695, 8.710, 8.902-8.903, 8.905-8.909, 8.913-8.930, 8.932-8.936, 8.938, 8.940-8.942, 8.947-8.951, 8.959-8.961, 8.964-8.966; added 8.031, 8.041, 8.224; deleted 8.227, committee note to Part III, 8.946.
Effective 1-1-01:	789 So.2d 951.	Amended 8.330, 8.525.
Effective 3-1-01:	796 So.2d 468.	Amended 8.305, 8.400, 8.505; added 8.217.
Effective 1-15-02:	816 So.2d 536.	Amended 8.135, 8.510.
Effective 1-1-03:	827 So.2d 219.	Two-year cycle revision. Amended 8.030-8.031, 8.085, 8.110, 8.185, 8.201, 8.210, 8.225, 8.245, 8.255, 8.265, 8.345, 8.525, 8.635, 8.959-8.960, 8.967, 8.979; added 8.929; deleted 8.275.
Effective 3-6-03:	842 So.2d 763.	Added 8.350.
Effective 10-1-04:	887 So.2d 1090.	Amended 8.060, 8.625.
Effective 1-27-05:	894 So.2d 875.	Two-year cycle revision. Amended 8.165, 8.203, 8.240-8.245, 8.255, 8.290-8.305, 8.315, 8.325, 8.400-8.415, 8.500-8.515, 8.525, 8.535, 8.603, 8.908, 8.911, 8.959-8.960, 8.979; added 8.257.
Effective 3-3-05:	898 So.2d 47.	Amended 8.041, 8.225, 8.415, 8.929, 8.947.
Effective 6-30-05:	907 So.2d 1161.	Added 8.800-8.835, 8.987-8.991.
Effective 11-17-05:	915 So.2d 592.	Amended 8.010, 8.013, 8.415, 8.929, 8.947, 8.970; added 8.355, 8.973, 8.974.
Effective 1-1-06:	915 So.2d 145.	Amended 8.290.
Effective 7-6-06:	934 So.2d 438.	Amended 8.805, 8.820, 8.987, 8.991; added 8.992.
Effective 1-1-07:	939 So.2d 74.	Three-year cycle revision. Amended 8.045, 8.090, 8.135, 8.210, 8.257, 8.350, 8.515, 8.535, 8.911, 8.930, 8.964, 8.966, 8.980-8.983; added 8.975.
Effective 2-8-07:	951 So.2d 804.	Amended 8.240, 8.250, 8.257, 8.305, 8.330, 8.400-8.415, 8.929, 8.947, 8.950-8.951, 8.961, 8.966, 8.970; added 8.420-8.430, 8.976-8.977.
Effective 6-21-07:	959 So.2d 250.	Amended 8.075, 8.115.
Effective 7-12-07:	960 So.2d 764.	Added 8.978.
Effective 6-26-08	985 So.2d 534.	Amended 8.100.
Effective 7-1-08:	981 So.2d 463.	Amended 8.165.
Effective 9-25-08:	992 So.2d 242.	Amended 8.225, 8.962-8.963, 8.968, 8.977.
Effective 3-19-09:	5 So.3d 665.	Amended 8.225.
Effective 10-1-09:	22 So.3d 9.	Amended 8.305, 8.961; added 8.292, 8.958, 8.961(a).
Effective 11-12-09:	24 So.3d 47.	Amended 8.330, 8.525, 8.983-8.984; added 8.275, 8.332.
Effective 1-1-10:	26 So.3d 552.	Amended 8.010, 8.070, 8.080, 8.100, 8.115, 8.130, 8.235, 8.257, 8.265, 8.310, 8.400-8.410, 8.505; added 8.978(a), 8.982.
Effective 6-24-10:	41 So.3d 888.	Added 8.003.
Effective 1-1-11:	48 So.3d 809.	Amended 8.010.
Effective 10-20-11:	75 So.3d 216.	Amended 8.820, 8.825, 8.947, 8.987, 8.990, 8.992; added 8.840.
Effective 6-1-12:	88 So.3d 142.	Amended 8.255
Effective 9-1-12:	102 So.3d 505.	Amended 8.085, 8.225, 8.635, and 8.903.
Effective 10-1-12:	95 So.3d 96.	Amended 8.085, 8.180, 8.240, 8.630.
Effective 10-1-12:	101 So.3d 368.	Amended 8.201, 8.425, 8.500, 8.510, 8.980.
Effective 10-1-12:	102 So.3d 451.	Amended 8.000, 8.205, 8.217, 8.230, 8.415, 8.690, adopted 8.004, re-numbered parts within rules.

Effective 5-23-13:	115 So.3d 286.	Amended 8.035, 8.070, 8.075, 8.080, 8.115, 8.201, 8.225, 8.260, 8.285, 8.340, 8.345, 8.350, 8.908, 8.929, 8.947, 8.959, 8.960, 8.961, 8.963, 8.964, 8.965, 8.966, 8.967, 8.970, 8.973, 8.975, 8.979, 8.982, adopted 8.226, 8.286, 8.347, 8.517, 8.952.
Effective 10-3-13:	123 So.3d 1139.	Amended 8.085, 8.225, 8.635.
Effective 10-3-13:	123 So.3d 1128.	Amended 8.060, 8.095, 8.135, 8.255, 8.345, 8.425, 8.947.
Effective 3-20-14:	136 So.3d 508.	Adopted 8.401, 8.435, amended 8.415, 8.973, deleted 8.971, 8.972.
Effective 10-1-14:	141 So.3d 1172.	Amended 8.290.
Effective 2-19-15:	158 So.3d 523.	Amended 8.305, 8.310, 8.350, 8.355, 8.415, 8.960, 8.961, 8.970, 8.973A, 8.973B, 8.973C; adopted 8.231.
Effective 1-1-16:	175 So.3d 263.	Amended 8.075, 8.165, 8.315, 8.332, 8.345; adopted 8.850-8.870, deleted 8.962, 8.963.
Effective 1-21-16:	191 So.3d 257.	Amended 8.305, 8.310, 8.350, 8.355, 8.415, 8.960, 8.961, 8.970, 8.973A, 8.973B, 8.973C; adopted 8.231.
Effective 2-11-16:	184 So.3d 1116.	Amended 8.150.
Effective 3-23-17:	213 So.3d 803.	Amended 8.510, 8.517, 8.525, 8.983, 8.984; adopted 8.530, 8.9831, 8.9832.
Effective 2-1-18:	2018 WL 654523, 2018 Fla. Lexis 280	Amended 8.305, 8.325, 8.335, 8.340, 8.345, 8.347, 8.400, 8.401, 8.415, 8.435, 8.505, 8.967, 8.973A, 8.973B, 8.973C.

NOTE TO USERS: Rules in this pamphlet are effective through 2018 WL 654523, 2018 Fla. Lexis 280. Subsequent amendments, if any, can be found at www.floridasupremecourt.org/decisions/rules.shtml. The Florida Bar also updates the rules on its website at www.FloridaBar.org (on the home page click "Rules Updates").

TABLE OF CONTENTS

PART V. OTHER PROCEEDINGS

A. GUARDIAN ADVOCATES FOR DRUG-DEPENDENT NEWBORNS

B. JUDICIAL WAIVER OF PARENTAL NOTICE OF TERMINATION OF PREGNANCY

C. TRUANCY PROCEEDINGS

8.992.   MINOR'S PETITION TO CHIEF JUDGE TO REQUIRE A HEARING ON HER
          PETITION FOR JUDICIAL WAIVER OF NOTICE

FLORIDA STATUTES
CHAPTER 39
CHAPTER 984
CHAPTER 985

SUBJECT INDEX

FLORIDA RULES OF JUVENILE PROCEDURE

PART I. RULES OF GENERAL APPLICATION

RULE 8.000. SCOPE AND PURPOSE

These rules shall govern the procedures in the juvenile division of the circuit court in the exercise of its jurisdiction under Florida law.

Part II of these rules governs the procedures for delinquency cases in the juvenile court. Part IV governs the procedures for families and children in need of services cases in the juvenile court. The Department of Juvenile Justice shall be referred to as the "department" in these parts.

Part III of these rules governs the procedures for dependency cases in the juvenile court. The Department of Children and Family Services shall be referred to as the "department" in that part.

These rules are intended to provide a just, speedy, and efficient determination of the procedures covered by them and shall be construed to secure simplicity in procedure and fairness in administration.

They shall be known as the Florida Rules of Juvenile Procedure and may be cited as Fla. R. Juv. P.

When appropriate the use of singular nouns and pronouns shall be construed to include the plural and the use of plural nouns and pronouns shall be construed to include the singular.

Committee Notes

1991 Amendment. All rules have been edited for style and to remove gender bias. The rules have been reorganized and renumbered to correspond to the types and stages of juvenile proceedings. Cross-references have been changed accordingly.

1992 Amendment. Scope and purpose, previously found in rules 8.000, 8.200, 8.600, and 8.700, has been consolidated into one rule. Designations of subparts within the delinquency part of the rules have been changed accordingly. Reference to the civil rules, previously found in rule 8.200, has been removed because the rules governing dependency and termination of parental rights proceedings are self-contained and no longer need to reference the Florida Rules of Civil Procedure.

RULE 8.003. FAMILY LAW COVER SHEET

The party opening or reopening a case under Parts II, III, IV, or V of these rules shall file with the clerk of the circuit court Florida Family Law Rules of Procedure Form 12.928, Cover Sheet for Family Law Cases.

RULE 8.004. ELECTRONIC FILING

(a) All documents that are court records, as defined in Florida Rule of Judicial Administration 2.430(a)(1), are to be filed by electronic transmission, consistent with the requirements of Florida Rule of Judicial Administration 2.525, provided that:

(1) the clerk has the ability to accept and retain such documents;

(2) the clerk or the chief judge of the circuit has requested permission to accept documents filed by electronic transmission; and

(3) the supreme court has entered an order granting permission to the clerk to accept documents filed by electronic transmission.

(b) All documents filed by electronic transmission under this rule satisfy any requirement for the filing of an original, except where the court, law, or these rules otherwise provide for the submittal of an original.

(c) The following paper documents or other submissions may be manually submitted to the clerk for filing under the following circumstances:

(1) when the clerk does not have the ability to accept and retain documents by electronic filing or has not had electronic court filing procedures (ECF Procedures) approved by the supreme court;

(2) by any self-represented party or any self-represented nonparty unless specific ECF Procedures provide a means to file documents electronically. However, any self-represented nonparty that is a governmental or public agency and any other agency, partnership, corporation, or business entity acting on behalf of any governmental or public agency may file documents by electronic transmission if such entity has the capability of filing documents electronically;

(3) by attorneys excused from e-mail service pursuant to these rules or Florida Rule of Judicial Administration 2.516;

(4) when submitting evidentiary exhibits or filing non-documentary materials;

(5) when the filing involves documents in excess of 25 megabytes (25 MB) in size. For such filings, documents may be transmitted using an electronic storage medium that the clerk has the ability to accept, which may include a CD-ROM, flash drive, or similar storage medium;

(6) when filed in open court, as permitted by the court;

(7) when paper filing is permitted by any approved statewide or local ECF procedures; and

(8) if any court determines that justice so requires.

(d) The filing date for an electronically transmitted document is the date and time that such filing is acknowledged by an electronic stamp, or otherwise, pursuant to any procedure set forth in any electronic court filing procedures (ECF Procedures) approved by the supreme court, or the date the last page of such filing is received by the court or clerk.

(e) Where these rules are silent, Florida Rule of Judicial Administration 2.525 controls.

(f) Electronic transmission may be used by a court for the service of all orders, pursuant to Florida Rule of Judicial Administration 2.516, and for the service of filings pursuant to any ECF Procedures, provided the clerk, together with input from the chief judge of the circuit, has obtained approval from the supreme court of ECF Procedures containing the specific procedures and program to be used in transmitting the orders and filings.

PART II. DELINQUENCY PROCEEDINGS

A. PRELIMINARY PROCEEDINGS

RULE 8.005. ORDERING CHILDREN INTO CUSTODY

If a verified petition has been filed, or if, prior to the filing of a petition, an affidavit or sworn testimony is presented to the court, either of which alleges facts which under existing law are sufficient to authorize that a child be taken into custody, the court may issue an order to a person, authorized to do so, directing that the child be taken into custody. The order shall:

(a) be in writing;

(b) specify the name and address of the child or, if unknown, designate the child by any name or description by which the child can be identified with reasonable certainty;

(c) specify the age and sex of the child or, if the child's age is unknown, that he or she is believed to be of an age subject to the jurisdiction of the circuit court as a juvenile case;

(d) state the reasons why the child is being taken into custody;

(e) order that the child be brought immediately before the court or be taken to a place of detention designated by the court to be detained pending a detention hearing;

(f) state the date when issued and the county and court where issued; and

(g) be signed by the court with the title of office.

RULE 8.010. DETENTION HEARING

(a) **When Required.** No detention order provided for in rule 8.013 shall be entered without a hearing at which all parties shall have an opportunity to be heard on the necessity for the child's being held in detention, unless the court finds that the parent or custodian cannot be located or that the child's mental or physical condition is such that a court appearance is not in the child's best interest.

(b) **Time.** The detention hearing shall be held within the time limits as provided by law. A child who is detained shall be given a hearing within 24 hours after being taken into custody.

(c) **Place.** The detention hearing may be held in the county where the incident occurred, where the child is taken into custody, or where the child is detained.

(d) Notice. The intake officer shall make a diligent effort to notify the parent or custodian of the child of the time and place of the hearing. The notice may be by the most expeditious method available. Failure of notice to parents or custodians or their nonattendance at the hearing shall not invalidate the proceeding or the order of detention.

(e) Appointment of Counsel. At the detention hearing, the child shall be advised of the right to be represented by counsel. Counsel shall be appointed if the child qualifies, unless the child waives counsel in writing subject to the requirements of rule 8.165.

(f) Advice of Rights. At the detention hearing the persons present shall be advised of the purpose of the hearing and the child shall be advised of:

(1) the nature of the charge for which he or she was taken into custody;

(2) that the child is not required to say anything and that anything said may be used against him or her;

(3) if the child's parent, custodian, or counsel is not present, that he or she has a right to communicate with them and that, if necessary, reasonable means will be provided to do so; and

(4) the reason continued detention is requested.

(g) Issues. At this hearing the court shall determine the following:

(1) The existence of probable cause to believe the child has committed a delinquent act. This issue shall be determined in a nonadversary proceeding. The court shall apply the standard of proof necessary for an arrest warrant and its finding may be based upon a sworn complaint, affidavit, deposition under oath, or, if necessary, upon testimony under oath properly recorded.

(2) The need for detention according to the criteria provided by law. In making this determination in addition to the sworn testimony of available witnesses all relevant and material evidence helpful in determining the specific issue, including oral and written reports, may be relied on to the extent of its probative value, even though it would not be competent at an adjudicatory hearing.

(3) The need to release the juvenile from detention and return the child to the child's nonresidential commitment program.

(h) Probable Cause. If the court finds that such probable cause exists, it shall enter an order making such a finding and may, if other statutory needs of detention exist, retain the child in detention. If the court finds that such probable cause does not exist, it shall forthwith release the child from detention. If the court finds that one or more of the statutory needs of detention exists, but is unable to make a finding on the existence of probable cause, it may retain the child in detention and continue the hearing for the purpose of determining the existence of probable cause to a time within 72 hours of the time the child was taken into custody. The court may, on a showing of good cause, continue the hearing a second time for not more than 24 hours beyond the 72-hour period. Release of the child based on no probable cause existing shall not prohibit the filing of a petition and further proceedings thereunder, but shall prohibit holding the child in detention prior to an adjudicatory hearing.

(i) Presence of Counsel. The state attorney or assistant state attorney and public defender or assistant public defender shall attend the detention hearing. Detention hearings shall be held with adequate notice to the public defender and state attorney. An official record of the proceedings shall be maintained. If the child has retained counsel or expresses a desire to retain counsel and is financially able, the attendance of the public defender or assistant public defender is not required at the detention hearing.

RULE 8.013. DETENTION PETITION AND ORDER

(a) Time Limitation. No child taken into custody shall be detained, as a result of the incident for which taken into custody, longer than as provided by law unless a detention order so directing is made by the court following a detention hearing.

(b) Petition. The detention petition shall:

(1) be in writing and be filed with the court;

(2) state the name and address of the child or, if unknown, designate the child by any name or description by which he or she can be identified with reasonable certainty;

(3) state the age and sex of the child or, if the age is unknown, that the child is believed to be of an age which will make him or her subject to the procedures covered by these rules;

(4) state the reasons why the child is in custody and needs to be detained;

(5) recommend the place where the child is to be detained or the agency to be responsible for the detention; and

(6) be signed by an authorized agent of the Department of Juvenile Justice or by the state attorney or assistant state attorney.

(c) Order. The detention order shall:

(1) be in writing;

(2) state the name and address of the child or, if unknown, designate the child by any name or description by which he or she can be identified with reasonable certainty;

(3) state the age and sex of the child or, if the age is unknown, that the child is believed to be of an age which will make him or her subject to the procedures covered by these rules;

(4) order that the child shall be held in detention and state the reasons therefor, or, if appropriate, order that the child be released from detention and returned to his or her nonresidential commitment program;

(5) make a finding that probable cause exists that the child is delinquent or that such a finding cannot be made at this time and that the case is continued for such a determination to a time certain within 72 hours from the time the child is taken into custody unless this time is extended by the court for good cause shown for not longer than an additional 24 hours;

(6) designate the place where the child is to be detained or the person or agency that will be responsible for the detention and state any special conditions found to be necessary;

(7) state the date and time when issued and the county and court where issued, together with the date and time the child was taken into custody;

(8) direct that the child be released no later than 5:00 p.m. on the last day of the specified statutory detention period, unless a continuance has been granted to the state or the child for cause; and

(9) be signed by the court with the title of office.

RULE 8.015. ARRAIGNMENT OF DETAINED CHILD

(a) When Required. If a petition for delinquency is filed and the child is being detained, whether in secure, nonsecure, or home detention, the child shall be given a copy of the petition and shall be arraigned within 48 hours of the filing of the petition, excluding Saturdays, Sundays, or legal holidays.

(b) Notice.

(1) Personal appearance of any person in a hearing before the court shall obviate the necessity of serving process on that person.

(2) The clerk of the court shall give notice of the time and place of the arraignment to the parent or guardian of the child and the superintendent of the detention center by:

(A) summons;

(B) written notice; or

(C) telephone notice.

(3) The superintendent of the detention center, or designee, also shall verify that a diligent effort has been made to notify the parent or guardian of the child of the time and place of the arraignment.

(4) Failure of notice to the parent or guardian, or nonattendance of the parent or guardian at the hearing, shall not invalidate the proceeding.

This rule corresponds to section 985.215(7), Florida Statutes, which requires detained children to be arraigned within 48 hours of the filing of the delinquency petition. This statutory requirement does not allow the normal summons process to take place. The rule, therefore, creates an option for the clerk of the court to notice the parent by phone or in writing.

B. PLEADINGS, PROCESS, AND ORDERS

RULE 8.025. STYLE OF PLEADINGS AND ORDERS

All pleadings and orders shall be styled: "In the interest of ...., a child," or: "In the interest of ...., children."

RULE 8.030. COMMENCEMENT OF FORMAL PROCEEDINGS

(a) **Allegations as to Child.** All proceedings shall be initiated by the filing of a petition by a person authorized by law to do so. A uniform traffic complaint may be considered a petition, but shall not be subject to the requirements of rule 8.035.

(b) **Allegations as to Parents or Legal Guardians.** In any delinquency proceeding in which the state is seeking payment of restitution or the performance of community service work by the child's parents or legal guardians, a separate petition alleging the parents' or legal guardians' responsibility shall be filed and served on the parents or legal guardians of the child.

RULE 8.031. PETITION FOR PARENTAL SANCTIONS

(a) **Contents.** Each petition directed to the child's parents or legal guardians shall be entitled a petition for parental sanctions and shall allege all facts showing the appropriateness of the requested sanction against the child's parents or legal guardians.

(b) **Verification.** The petition shall be signed by the state attorney or assistant state attorney, stating under oath the petitioner's good faith in filing the petition.

(c) **Amendments.** At any time before the hearing, an amended petition for parental sanctions may be filed or the petition may be amended on motion. Amendments shall be freely permitted in the interest of justice and the welfare of the child. A continuance may be granted on motion and a showing that the amendment prejudices or materially affects any party.

RULE 8.035. PETITIONS FOR DELINQUENCY

(a) **Contents of Petition.**

(1) Each petition shall be entitled a petition for delinquency and shall allege facts showing the child to have committed a delinquent act. The petition must be a plain, concise, and definite written statement of the essential facts constituting the offense charged.

(2) The petition shall contain allegations as to the identity and residence of the parents or custodians, if known.

(3) In petitions alleging delinquency, each count shall recite the official or customary citations of the statute, ordinance, rule, regulation, or other provision of the law which the child is alleged to have violated, including the degree of each offense.

(4) Two or more allegations of the commission of delinquent acts may appear in the same petition, in separate counts.

(5) Two or more children may be the subject of the same petition if they are alleged to have participated in the same act or transaction or in the same series of acts or transactions constituting an offense or offenses. The children may be named in one or more counts together or separately and all of them need not be named in each count.

(6) Allegations made in one count shall not be incorporated by reference in another count.

(b) **Verification.** The petition shall be signed by the state attorney or assistant state attorney, stating under oath the petitioner's good faith in filing the petition. No objection to a petition on the grounds that it was not signed or verified, as herein provided, shall be entertained after a plea to the merits.

(c) **Child's Right to Copy of Petition.** Upon application to the clerk, a child must be furnished a copy of the petition and the endorsements on it at least 24 hours before being required to plead to the petition.

(d) Amendments. At any time prior to the adjudicatory hearing an amended petition may be filed or the petition may be amended on motion. Amendments shall be freely permitted in the interest of justice and the welfare of the child. A continuance may be granted upon motion and a showing that the amendment prejudices or materially affects any party.

(e) Statement of Particulars. The court, on motion, must order the prosecuting attorney to furnish a statement of particulars when the petition on which the child is to be tried fails to inform the child of the particulars of the offense sufficiently to enable the child to prepare a defense. The statement of particulars must specify as definitely as possible the place, date, and all other material facts of the crime charged that are specifically requested and are known to the prosecuting attorney. Reasonable doubts concerning the construction of this rule shall be resolved in favor of the child.

(f) Defects and Variances. No petition or any count thereof shall be dismissed, or any judgment vacated, on account of any defect in the form of the petition or of misjoinder of offenses or for any cause whatsoever.

RULE 8.040. PROCESS

(a) Summons.

(1) Upon the filing of a petition upon a child who is not detained by order of the court, the clerk shall issue a summons. The summons shall require the person on whom it is served to appear for a hearing at a time and place specified. The time of the hearing shall not be less than 24 hours after service of the summons. The summons shall require the custodian to produce the child at the said time and place. A copy of the delinquency petition shall be attached to the summons.

(2) If the child is being detained by order of the court, process shall be in accordance with the rule pertaining to the arraignment of a detained child.

(b) Service.

(1) Generally. The summons and other process shall be served upon such persons and in such manner

as required by law. If the parents or custodian are out of the state and their address is known the clerk shall give them notice of the proceedings by mail. Service of process may be waived.

(2) Petition for Parental Sanctions. A petition for parental sanctions may be served on the child's parents or legal guardians in open court at any hearing concerning the child, but must be served at least 72 hours before the hearing at which parental sanctions are being sought. The petition for parental sanctions also may be served in accordance with chapter 48, Florida Statutes.

Committee Notes

1991 Amendment. This rule clearly defines the difference in procedures for summons for detained and nondetained children.

2000 Amendment. Subsection (b)(2) was added to provide requisite notice to the parents or legal guardians of a child when the state is seeking restitution or wishes to impose other sanctions against the parent or legal guardian. See *S.B.L., Natural Mother of J.J. v. State*, 737 So. 2d 1131 (Fla. 1st DCA 1999); *A.G., Natural Mother of S.B. v. State*, 736 So. 2d 151 (Fla. 1st DCA 1999).

RULE 8.041. WITNESS ATTENDANCE AND SUBPOENAS

(a) Attendance. A witness summoned by a subpoena in an adjudicatory hearing shall remain in attendance at the adjudicatory hearing until excused by the court or by both parties. A witness who departs without being excused properly may be held in criminal contempt of court.

(b) Subpoenas Generally.

(1) Subpoenas for testimony before the court and subpoenas for production of tangible evidence before the court may be issued by the clerk of the court, by any attorney of record in an action, or by the court on its own motion.

(2) Except as otherwise required by this rule, the procedure for issuance of a subpoena (except for a subpoena duces tecum) by an attorney of record in a proceeding shall be as provided in the Florida Rules of Civil Procedure.

(c) Subpoenas for Testimony or Production of Tangible Evidence.

(1) Every subpoena for testimony or production of tangible evidence before the court shall be issued by

an attorney of record in an action or by the clerk under the seal of the court. The subpoena shall state the name of the court and the title of the action and shall command each person to whom it is directed to attend and give testimony or produce evidence at a time and place specified.

(2) On oral request of an attorney of record, and without a witness praecipe, the clerk shall issue a subpoena for testimony before the court or a subpoena for tangible evidence before the court. The subpoena shall be signed and sealed but otherwise blank, both as to the title of the action and the name of the person to whom it is directed. The subpoena shall be filled in before service by the attorney.

(d) Subpoenas for Production of Tangible Evidence. If a subpoena commands the person to whom it is directed to produce the books, papers, documents, or tangible things designated in it, the court, on motion made promptly and in any event at or before the time specified in the subpoena for compliance with it, may

(1) quash or modify the subpoena if it is unreasonable and oppressive, or

(2) condition denial of the motion on the advancement by the person in whose behalf the subpoena is issued of the reasonable cost of producing the books, papers, documents, or tangible things.

RULE 8.045. NOTICE TO APPEAR

(a) Definition. A notice to appear, unless indicated otherwise, means a written order issued by a law enforcement officer or authorized agent of the department, in lieu of taking a child into custody or detaining a child, which requires a child accused of violating the law to appear in a designated court or governmental office at a specified date and time.

(b) By Arresting Officer. If a child is taken into custody for a violation of law and the officer elects to release the child as provided by law to a parent, responsible adult relative, or legal guardian, a notice to appear may be issued to the child by the officer unless:

(1) the child fails or refuses to sufficiently identify himself or herself or supply the required information;

(2) the child refuses to sign the notice to appear;

(3) the officer has reason to believe that the continued liberty of the child constitutes an unreasonable risk of bodily injury to the child or others;

(4) the child has no ties with the jurisdiction reasonably sufficient to ensure an appearance or there is substantial risk that the child will refuse to respond to the notice;

(5) the officer has any suspicion that the child may be wanted in any jurisdiction; or

(6) it appears that the child has previously failed to respond to a notice or a summons or has violated the conditions of any pretrial release program.

(c) By Departmental Agent. If a child is taken into custody by an authorized agent of the department as provided by law, or if an authorized agent of the department takes custody of a child from a law enforcement officer and the child is not detained, the agent shall issue a notice to appear to the child upon the child's release to a parent, responsible adult relative, or legal guardian.

(d) How and When Served. If a notice to appear is issued, 6 copies shall be prepared. One copy of the notice shall be delivered to the child and 1 copy shall be delivered to the person to whom the child is released. In order to secure the child's release, the child and the person to whom the child is released shall give their written promise that the child will appear as directed in the notice by signing the remaining copies. One copy is to be retained by the issuer and 3 copies are to be filed with the clerk of the court.

(e) Distribution of Copies. The clerk shall deliver 1 copy of the notice to appear to the state attorney and 1 copy to the department and shall retain 1 copy in the court's file.

(f) Contents. A notice to appear shall contain the following information:

(1) The name and address of the child and the person to whom the child was released.

(2) The date of the offense(s).

(3) The offense(s) charged by statute and municipal ordinance, if applicable.

(4) The counts of each offense.

(5) The time and place where the child is to appear.

(6) The name and address of the trial court having jurisdiction to try the offense(s) charged.

(7) The name of the arresting officer or authorized agent of the department.

(8) The signatures of the child and the person to whom the child was released.

(g) Failure to Appear. When a child signs a written notice to appear and fails to respond to the notice, an order to take into custody shall be issued.

(h) Form of Notice. The notice to appear shall be substantially as found in form 8.930.

Committee Notes

1991 Adoption. This rule allows juveniles to be released with definite notice as to when they must return to court. This should help decrease the number of juveniles held in detention centers awaiting a court date. It also should provide a mechanism to divert juveniles to programs more efficiently. The change also should decrease the number of summons issued by the clerk.

1992 Amendment. A summons is not sworn but the arrest affidavit that is filed with the notice to appear is sworn. The notice to appear, which is more like a summons, does not need to be sworn.

RULE 8.055. ORDERS

All orders of the court shall be reduced to writing as soon after they are entered as is consistent with orderly procedure and shall contain findings of fact as required by law.

C. DISCOVERY

RULE 8.060. DISCOVERY

(a) Notice of Discovery.

(1) After the filing of the petition, a child may elect to utilize the discovery process provided by these rules, including the taking of discovery depositions, by filing with the court and serving upon the petitioner a "notice of discovery" which shall bind both the petitioner and the child to all discovery procedures contained in these rules. Participation by a child in the discovery process, including the taking of any deposition by a child, shall be an election to participate in discovery. If any child knowingly or purposely shares in discovery obtained by a codefendant, the child shall be deemed to have elected to participate in discovery.

(2) Within 5 days of service of the child's notice of discovery, the petitioner shall serve a written discovery exhibit which shall disclose to the child or the child's counsel and permit the child or the child's counsel to inspect, copy, test, and photograph the following information and material within the petitioner's possession or control:

(A) A list of the names and addresses of all persons known to the petitioner to have information which may be relevant to the allegations, to any defense with respect thereto, or to any similar fact evidence to be presented at trial under section 90.402(2), Florida Statutes. The names and addresses of persons listed shall be clearly designated in the following categories:

(i) Category A. These witnesses shall include

(a) eye witnesses;

(b) alibi witnesses and rebuttal to alibi witnesses;

(c) witnesses who were present when a recorded or unrecorded statement was taken from or made by the child or codefendant, which shall be separately identified within this category;

(d) investigating officers;

(e) witnesses known by the petitioner to have any material information that tends to negate the guilt of the child as to the petition's allegations;

(f) child hearsay witnesses; and

(g) expert witnesses who have not provided a written report and a curriculum vitae or who are going to testify.

(ii) Category B. All witnesses not listed in either Category A or Category C.

(iii) Category C. All witnesses who performed only ministerial functions or whom the petitioner does not intend to call at the hearing and whose involvement with and knowledge of the case is fully set out in a police report or other statement furnished to the defense.

(B) The statement of any person whose name is furnished in compliance with the preceding paragraph. The term "statement" as used herein means a written statement made by said person and signed or otherwise adopted by him or her and also includes any statement of any kind or manner made by such person and written or recorded or summarized in any writing or recording. The term "statement" is specifically intended to include all police and investigative reports of any kind prepared for or in connection with the case, but shall not include the notes from which such reports are compiled.

(C) Any written or recorded statements and the substance of any oral statements made by the child and known to the petitioner, including a copy of any statements contained in police reports or summaries, together with the name and address of each witness to the statements.

(D) Any written or recorded statements, and the substance of any oral statements, made by a codefendant if the hearing is to be a joint one.

(E) Those portions of recorded grand jury minutes that contain testimony of the child.

(F) Any tangible papers or objects which were obtained from or belonged to the child.

(G) Whether the petitioner has any material or information which has been provided by a confidential informant.

(H) Whether there has been any electronic surveillance, including wiretapping, of the premises of the child, or of conversations to which the child was a party, and any documents relating thereto.

(I) Whether there has been any search or seizure and any document relating thereto.

(J) Reports or statements of experts made in connection with the particular case, including results of physical or mental examinations and of scientific tests, experiments, or comparisons.

(K) Any tangible papers or objects which the petitioner intends to use in the hearing and which were not obtained from or belonged to the child.

(3) As soon as practicable after the filing of the petition, the petitioner shall disclose to the child any material information within the state's possession or control which tends to negate the guilt of the child as to the petition's allegations.

(4) The petitioner shall perform the foregoing obligations in any manner mutually agreeable to the petitioner and the child or as ordered by the court.

(5) Upon a showing of materiality to the preparation of the defense, the court may require such other discovery to the child as justice may require.

(b) Required Disclosure to Petitioner.

(1) If a child elects to participate in discovery, within 5 days after receipt by the child of the discovery exhibit furnished by the petitioner under this rule, the following disclosures shall be made:

(A) The child shall furnish to the petitioner a written list of all persons whom the child expects to call as witnesses at the hearing. When the petitioner subpoenas a witness whose name has been furnished by the child, except for hearing subpoenas, reasonable notice shall be given to the child as to the time and location of examination pursuant to the subpoena. At such examination, the child through counsel shall have the right to be present and to examine the witness. The physical presence of the child shall be governed by rule 8.060(d)(6).

(B) The child shall serve a written discovery exhibit which shall disclose to the petitioner and permit the petitioner to inspect, copy, test, and photograph the following information and material which is in the child's possession or control:

(i) The statement of any person whom the child expects to call as a trial witness other than that of the child.

(ii) Reports or statements of experts made in connection with the particular case, including results of physical or mental examinations and of scientific tests, experiments, or comparisons.

(iii) Any tangible papers or objects which the child intends to use in the hearing.

(2) The child shall perform the foregoing obligations in any manner mutually agreeable to the child and the petitioner or as ordered by the court.

(3) The filing of a motion for protective order by the petitioner will automatically stay the times provided for in this subdivision. If a protective order is granted, the child may, within 2 days thereafter, or at any time before the petitioner furnishes the information or material which is the subject of the motion for protective order, withdraw the demand and not be required to furnish reciprocal discovery.

(c) Limitations on Disclosure.

(1) Upon application, the court may deny or partially restrict disclosure authorized by this rule if it finds there is a substantial risk to any person of physical harm, intimidation, bribery, economic reprisals, or unnecessary annoyance or embarrassment resulting from such disclosure, which outweighs any usefulness of the disclosure to the party requesting it.

(2) The following matters shall not be subject to disclosure:

(A) Disclosure shall not be required of legal research or of records, correspondence, or memoranda, to the extent that they contain the opinion, theories, or conclusions of the prosecuting or defense attorney or members of their legal staff.

(B) Disclosure of a confidential informant shall not be required unless the confidential informant is to be produced at a hearing or a failure to disclose the informant's identity will infringe upon the constitutional rights of the child.

(d) Depositions.

(1) Time and Location.

(A) At any time after the filing of the petition alleging a child to be delinquent, any party may take the deposition upon oral examination of any person authorized by this rule.

(B) Depositions of witnesses residing in the county in which the adjudicatory hearing is to take place shall be taken in the building in which the adjudicatory hearing is to be held, another location agreed on by the parties, or a location designated by the court. Depositions of witnesses residing outside the county in which the adjudicatory hearing is to take place shall take place in a court reporter's office in the county and state in which the witness resides, another location agreed to by the parties, or a location designated by the court.

(2) Procedure.

(A) The party taking the deposition shall give reasonable written notice to each other party and shall make a good faith effort to coordinate the date, time, and location of the deposition to accommodate the schedules of other parties and the witness to be deposed. The notice shall state the time and the location of the deposition and the name of each person to be examined, and include a certificate of counsel that a good faith effort was made to coordinate the deposition schedule.

(B) Upon application, the court or the clerk of the court may issue subpoenas for the persons whose depositions are to be taken.

(C) After notice to the parties the court, for good cause shown, may change the time or location of the deposition.

(D) In any case, no person shall be deposed more than once except by consent of the parties or by order of the court issued on good cause shown.

(E) Except as otherwise provided by this rule, the procedure for taking the deposition, including the scope of the examination and the issuance of a subpoena (except for a subpoena duces tecum) for deposition by an attorney of record in the action shall be the same as that provided in the Florida Rules of Civil Procedure.

(F) The child, without leave of court, may take the deposition of any witness listed by the petitioner as a Category A witness or listed by a codefendant as a witness to be called at a joint hearing. After receipt by the child of the discovery exhibit, the child, without leave of court, may take the deposition of any unlisted witness who may have information relevant to the petition's allegations. The petitioner, without leave of court, may take the deposition of any witness listed by the child to be called at a hearing.

(G) No party may take the deposition of a witness listed by the petitioner as a Category B witness except upon leave of court with good cause shown. In determining whether to allow a deposition, the court should consider the consequences to the child, the complexities of the issues involved, the complexity of the testimony of the witness (e.g., experts), and the other opportunities available to the child to discover the information sought by deposition.

(H) A witness listed by the petitioner as a Category C witness shall not be subject to deposition unless the court determines that the witness should be listed in another category.

(I) No deposition shall be taken in a case in which a petition has been filed alleging that the child committed only a misdemeanor or a criminal traffic offense when all other discovery provided by this rule has been complied with unless good cause can be shown to the trial court. In determining whether to allow a deposition, the court should consider the consequences to the child, the complexity of the issues involved, the complexity of the witness's testimony (e.g., experts), and the other opportunities available to the child to discover the information sought by deposition. However, this prohibition against the taking of depositions shall not be applicable if following the furnishing of discovery by the

child the petitioner then takes the statement of a listed defense witness pursuant to section 27.04, Florida Statutes.

(3) Use of Deposition. Any deposition taken pursuant to this rule may be used at any hearing covered by these rules by any party for the purpose of impeaching the testimony of the deponent as a witness.

(4) Introduction of Part of Deposition. If only part of a deposition is offered in evidence by a party, an adverse party may require the introduction of any other part that in fairness ought to be considered with the part introduced, and any party may introduce any other parts.

(5) Sanctions. A witness who refuses to obey a duly served subpoena for the taking of a deposition may be adjudged in contempt of the court from which the subpoena issued.

(6) Physical Presence of Child. The child shall not be physically present at a deposition except upon stipulation of the parties or as provided by this rule.

The court may order the physical presence of the child upon a showing of good cause. In ruling, the court may consider

(A) the need for the physical presence of the child to obtain effective discovery;

(B) the intimidating effect of the child's presence on the witness, if any;

(C) any cost or inconvenience which may result; and

(D) any alternative electronic or audio-visual means available to protect the child's ability to participate in discovery without the child's physical presence.

(7) Statements of Law Enforcement Officers. Upon stipulation of the parties and the consent of the witness, the statement of a law enforcement officer may be taken by telephone in lieu of deposition of the officer. In such case, the officer need not be under oath. The statement, however, shall be recorded and may be used for impeachment at trial as a prior inconsistent statement pursuant to the Florida Evidence Code.

(8) Depositions of Law Enforcement Officers. Subject to the general provisions of this rule, law enforcement officers shall appear for deposition, without subpoena, upon written notice of taking deposition delivered at the address designated by the law enforcement agency or department or, if no address has been designated, to the address of the law enforcement agency or department, 5 days prior to the date of the deposition. Law enforcement officers who fail to appear for deposition after being served notice are subject to contempt proceedings.

(9) Videotaped Depositions. Depositions of children under the age of 16 shall be videotaped upon demand of any party unless otherwise ordered by the court. The court may order videotaping of a deposition or taking of a deposition of a witness with fragile emotional strength to be in the presence of the trial judge or a special magistrate.

(e) Perpetuating Testimony.

(1) After the filing of the petition and upon reasonable notice, any party may apply for an order to perpetuate testimony of a witness. The application shall be verified or supported by the affidavits of credible persons, and shall state that the prospective witness resides beyond the territorial jurisdiction of the court or may be unable to attend or be prevented from attending the subsequent court proceedings, or that grounds exist to believe that the witness will absent himself or herself from the jurisdiction of the court, that the testimony is material, and that it is necessary to take the deposition to prevent a failure of justice.

(2) If the application is well founded and timely made, the court shall order a commission to be issued to take the deposition of the witness to be used in subsequent court proceedings and that any designated books, papers, documents, or tangible objects, not privileged, be produced at the same time and place.

The commission may be issued to any official court reporter, whether the witness be within or without the state, transcribed by the reporter, and filed in the court. The commission shall state the time and place of the deposition and be served on all parties.

(3) No deposition shall be used or read in evidence when the attendance of the witness can be procured. If it shall appear to the court that any person whose deposition has been taken has absented himself or herself by procurement, inducements, or threats by or on behalf of any party, the deposition shall not be read in evidence on behalf of that party.

(f) Nontestimonial Discovery. After the filing of the petition, upon application, and subject to constitutional limitations, the court may with directions as to time, place, and method, and upon conditions which are just, require:

(1) the child in all proceedings to:

(A) appear in a lineup;

(B) speak for identification by a witness to an offense;

(C) be fingerprinted;

(D) pose for photographs not involving reenactment of a scene;

(E) try on articles of clothing;

(F) permit the taking of specimens of material under the fingernails;

(G) permit the taking of samples of blood, hair, and other materials of the body which involve no unreasonable intrusion thereof;

(H) provide specimens of handwriting; or

(I) submit to a reasonable physical or medical inspection of his or her body; and

(2) such other discovery as justice may require upon a showing that such would be relevant or material.

(g) Court May Alter Times. The court may alter the times for compliance with any discovery under these rules on good cause shown.

(h) Supplemental Discovery. If, subsequent to compliance with these rules, a party discovers additional witnesses, evidence, or material which the party would have been under a duty to disclose or produce at the time of such previous compliance, the party shall promptly disclose or produce such witnesses, evidence, or material in the same manner as required under these rules for initial discovery.

(i) Investigations Not to Be Impeded. Except as otherwise provided for matters not subject to disclosure or restricted by protective orders, neither the counsel for the parties nor other prosecution or defense personnel shall advise persons having relevant material or information, except for the child, to refrain from discussing the case with opposing counsel or showing opposing counsel any relevant material, nor shall they otherwise impede opposing counsel's investigation of the case.

(j) Protective Orders. Upon a showing of good cause, the court shall at any time order that specified disclosures be restricted, deferred, or exempted from discovery, that certain matters are not to be inquired into or that the scope of the deposition be limited to certain matters, that a deposition be sealed and after being sealed be opened only by order of the court, or make such other order as is appropriate to protect a witness from harassment, unnecessary inconvenience, or invasion of privacy, including prohibiting the taking of a deposition. All material and information to which a party is entitled, however, must be disclosed in time to permit such party to make beneficial use of it.

(k) Motion to Terminate or Limit Examination. At any time during the taking of a deposition, on motion of a party or of the deponent, and upon a showing that the examination is being conducted in bad faith or in such manner as to unreasonably annoy, embarrass, or oppress the deponent or party, the court in which the action is pending or the circuit court where the deposition is being taken may (1) terminate the deposition, (2) limit the scope and manner of the taking of the deposition, (3) limit the time of the deposition, (4) continue the deposition to a later time, (5) order the deposition to be taken in open court and, in addition, (6) may impose any sanction authorized by this rule. If the order terminates the deposition, it shall be resumed thereafter only upon the order of the court in which the action is pending. Upon demand of any party or deponent, the taking of the deposition shall be suspended for the time necessary to make a motion for an order.

(*l*) In Camera and Ex Parte Proceedings.

(1) Any person may move for an order denying or regulating disclosure of sensitive matters. The court may consider the matters contained in the motion in camera.

(2) Upon request, the court shall allow the child to make an ex parte showing of good cause for taking the deposition of a Category B witness.

(3) A record shall be made of proceedings authorized under this subdivision. If the court enters an order granting relief after an in camera inspection or ex parte showing, the entire record of the proceeding shall be sealed and preserved in the records of the court, to be made available to the appellate court in the event of an appeal.

(m) Sanctions.

(1) If at any time during the course of the proceedings it is brought to the attention of the court that a party has failed to comply with an applicable discovery rule or with an order issued pursuant to an applicable discovery rule, the court may:

(A) order such party to comply with the discovery or inspection of materials not previously disclosed or produced;

(B) grant a continuance;

(C) grant a mistrial;

(D) prohibit the party from calling a witness not disclosed or introducing in evidence the material not disclosed; or

(E) enter such order as it deems just under the circumstances.

(2) Willful violation by counsel or a party not represented by counsel of an applicable discovery rule or an order issued pursuant thereto may subject counsel or a party not represented by counsel to appropriate sanction by the court. The sanctions may include, but are not limited to, contempt proceedings against the attorney or party not represented by counsel, as well as the assessment of costs incurred by the opposing party, when appropriate.

Court Commentary

1996 Amendment. This amendment generally conforms the rule to the 1996 amendment to Florida Rule of Criminal Procedure 3.220.

RULE 8.065. NOTICE OF DEFENSE OF ALIBI

(a) Notice to State Attorney. After a petition has been served the state attorney may demand in writing that the child, who intends to offer an alibi defense, shall provide the state attorney with the details of the alibi as to the time and place where the child claims to have been at the time of the alleged offense and the names and addresses of such witnesses as may appear to testify thereon. The child shall comply as above not less than 10 days before the trial date.

(b) Rebuttal Witness List. The state attorney shall, within 5 days of the receipt thereof, provide the child with a list of such witnesses to be called to rebut the alibi testimony.

(c) Sanctions. Should the child fail or refuse to comply with the provisions hereof, the court may in its discretion exclude testimony of alibi witnesses other than the child or, should the state attorney fail to comply herewith, the court may in its discretion exclude rebuttal testimony offered by the state.

(d) Waiver of Rule. For good cause shown, the court may waive the requirements of this rule.

D. ARRAIGNMENTS AND PLEAS

RULE 8.070. ARRAIGNMENTS

(a) Appointment of Counsel. Prior to the adjudicatory hearing the court may conduct a hearing to determine whether a guilty, nolo contendere, or not guilty plea to the petition shall be entered and whether the child is represented by counsel or entitled to appointed counsel as provided by law. Counsel shall be appointed if the child qualifies for such appointment and does not waive counsel in writing subject to the requirements of rule 8.165.

(b) Plea. The reading or statement as to the charge or charges may be waived by the child. No child, whether represented by counsel or otherwise, shall be called on to plead unless and until he or she has had a reasonable time within which to deliberate thereon. If the child is represented by counsel, counsel may file a written plea of not guilty at or before arraignment and arraignment shall then be deemed waived. If a plea of guilty or nolo contendere is entered, the court shall proceed as set forth under rule 8.115, disposition hearings. If a plea of not guilty is entered, the court shall set an adjudicatory hearing within the period of time provided by law. The child is entitled to a reasonable time in which to prepare for trial.

Committee Notes

1991 Adoption. This rule creates an arraignment proceeding that is referred to in section 985.215(7), Florida Statutes.

RULE 8.075. PLEAS

No written answer to the petition nor any other pleading need be filed. No child, whether represented by counsel or otherwise, shall be called upon to plead until he or she has had a reasonable time within which to deliberate thereon.

(a) Acceptance of Plea. In delinquency cases the child may plead guilty, nolo contendere, or not guilty. The court may refuse to accept a plea of guilty or nolo contendere, and shall not accept either plea without first determining that the plea is made voluntarily and with a full understanding of the nature of the allegations and the possible consequences of such plea and that there is a factual basis for such plea.

(b) Plan of Proposed Treatment, Training, or Conduct. After the filing of a petition and prior to the adjudicatory hearing, a plan of proposed treatment, training, or conduct may be submitted on behalf of the child in lieu of a plea. The appropriate agencies of the

Department of Juvenile Justice or other agency as designated by the court shall be the supervising agencies for said plan and the terms and conditions of all such plans shall be formulated in conjunction with the supervising agency involved. The submission of a plan is not an admission of the allegations of the petition of delinquency.

If such a plan is submitted the procedure shall be as follows:

(1) The plan must be in writing, agreed to and signed in all cases by the state attorney, the child, and, when represented, by the child's counsel, and, unless excused by the court, by the parents or custodian. An authorized agent of the supervising agency involved shall indicate whether the agency recommends the acceptance of the plan.

(2) The plan shall contain a stipulation that the speedy trial rule is waived and shall include the state attorney's consent to defer the prosecution of the petition.

(3) After hearing, which may be waived by stipulation of the parties and the supervising agency, the court may accept the plan and order compliance therewith, or may reject it. If the plan is rejected by the court, the court shall state on the record the reasons for rejection.

(4) Violations of the conditions of the plan shall be presented to the court by motion by the supervising agency or by any party. If the court, after hearing, finds a violation has occurred, it may take such action as is appropriate to enforce the plan, modify the plan by supplemental agreement, or set the case for hearing on the original petition.

(5) The plan shall be effective for an indeterminate period, for such period as is stated therein, or until the petition is dismissed.

(6) Unless otherwise dismissed, the petition may be dismissed on the motion of the person submitting the plan or the supervising agency, after notice of hearing and a finding of substantial compliance with the provisions and intent of the plan.

(c) Written Answer. A written answer admitting or denying the allegations of the petition may be filed by the child joined by a parent, custodian, or the child's counsel. If the answer admits the allegations of the petition it must acknowledge that the child has been advised of the right to counsel, the right to remain silent, and the possible dispositions available to the court and shall include a consent to a predispositional study. Upon the filing of such an answer a hearing for adjudication or adjudication and disposition shall be set at the earliest practicable time.

(d) Entry of Plea by Court. If a child stands mute or pleads evasively, a plea of not guilty shall be entered by the court.

(e) Withdrawal of Plea Before Disposition. The court may in its discretion for good cause shown at any time prior to the beginning of a disposition hearing permit a plea of guilty or nolo contendere to be withdrawn, and if a finding that the child committed a delinquent act has been entered thereon, set aside such finding and allow another plea to be substituted for the plea of guilty or nolo contendere. In the subsequent adjudicatory hearing the court shall not consider the plea which was withdrawn as an admission.

(f) Withdrawal of Plea After Disposition. A child who pleads guilty or nolo contendere without expressly reserving the right to appeal a legally dispositive issue may file a motion to withdraw the plea within 30 days after rendition of the disposition, but only on the grounds that

(1) the lower tribunal lacked subject matter jurisdiction;

(2) there has been a violation of the plea agreement;

(3) the plea was involuntary;

(4) there has been a sentencing error; or

(5) as otherwise provided by law.

(g) Withdrawal of Plea After Drug Court Transfer. A child who pleads guilty or nolo contendere to a charge for the purpose of transferring the case, as provided by law, may file a motion to withdraw the plea upon successful completion of the juvenile drug court treatment program.

RULE 8.080. ACCEPTANCE OF GUILTY OR NOLO CONTENDERE PLEA

(a) Voluntariness. Before accepting a plea of guilty or nolo contendere, the court shall determine that the plea is knowingly and voluntarily entered and that there is a factual basis for it. Counsel for the prosecution and the defense shall assist the court in this determination.

(b) Open Court. All pleas shall be taken in open court, except the hearing may be closed as provided by law.

(c) Determination by Court. The court, when making this determination, should place the child under oath and shall address the child personally. The court shall determine that the child understands each of the following rights and consequences of entering a guilty or nolo contendere plea:

(1) The nature of the charge to which the plea is offered and the possible dispositions available to the court.

(2) If the child is not represented by an attorney, that the child has the right to be represented by an attorney at every stage of the proceedings and, if necessary, one will be appointed. Counsel shall be appointed if the child qualifies for such appointment and does not waive counsel in writing subject to the requirements of rule 8.165.

(3) That the child has the right to plead not guilty, or to persist in that plea if it had already been made, and that the child has the right to an adjudicatory hearing and at that hearing has the right to the assistance of counsel, the right to compel the attendance of witnesses on his or her behalf, the right to confront and cross-examine witnesses against him or her, and the right not to be compelled to incriminate himself or herself.

(4) That, if the child pleads guilty or nolo contendere, without express reservation of the right to appeal, the right to appeal all matters relating to the judgment, including the issue of guilt or innocence, is relinquished, but the right to review by appropriate collateral attack is not impaired.

(5) That, if the child pleads guilty or nolo contendere, there will not be a further adjudicatory hearing of any kind, so that by pleading so the right to an adjudicatory hearing is waived.

(6) That, if the child pleads guilty or nolo contendere, the court may ask the child questions about the offense to which the child has pleaded, and, if those questions are answered under oath, on the record, the answers may later be used against the child in a prosecution for perjury.

(7) The complete terms of any plea agreement including specifically all obligations the child will incur as a result.

(8) That, if the child pleads guilty or nolo contendere to certain sexual offenses, the child may be required to register as a sexual offender.

(9) That, if the child pleads guilty or nolo contendre, and the offense to which the child is pleading is a sexually violent offense or a sexually motivated offense, or if the child has been previously adjudicated for such an offense, the plea may subject the child to involuntary civil commitment as a sexually violent predator on completion of his or her sentence. It shall not be necessary for the trial judge to determine whether the present or prior offenses were sexually motivated, as this admonition shall be given to all children in all cases.

(10) That, if the child pleads guilty or nolo contendere, and the child is not a United States citizen, the facts underlying the plea may subject the child to deportation pursuant to the laws and regulations governing the United States Citizenship and Immigration Services. It shall not be necessary for the trial judge to inquire as to whether the child is a United States citizen, as this admonition shall be given to all children in all cases.

(d) Acknowledgment by Child. Before the court accepts a guilty or nolo contendere plea, the court must determine that the child either:

(1) acknowledges guilt; or

(2) acknowledges that the plea is in the child's best interest, while maintaining innocence.

(e) Of Record. These proceedings shall be of record.

(f) When Binding. Prior to the court's acceptance of a plea, the parties must notify the court of any plea agreement and may notify the court of the reasons for the plea agreement. Thereafter, the court must advise the parties whether the court accepts or rejects the plea agreement and may state its reasons for a rejection of the plea agreement. No plea offer or negotiation is binding until it is accepted by the court after making all the inquiries, advisements, and determinations required by this rule. Until that time, it may be withdrawn by either party without any necessary justification.

(g) Withdrawal of Plea When Judge Does Not Concur. If the trial judge does not concur in a tendered plea of guilty or nolo contendere arising from negotiations, the plea may be withdrawn.

(h) Failure to Follow Procedures. Failure to follow any of the procedures in this rule shall not render a plea void, absent a showing of prejudice.

E. MOTIONS AND SERVICE OF PLEADINGS

RULE 8.085. PREHEARING MOTIONS AND SERVICE

(a) Prehearing Motions.

(1) Motions in General. Every motion made before a hearing and any pleading in response to the motion shall be in writing and shall be signed by the party making the motion and the party's attorney. This requirement may be waived by the court for good cause shown.

(2) Motion to Dismiss. All defenses not raised by a plea of not guilty or denial of the allegations of the petition shall be made by a motion to dismiss the petition. If a motion to dismiss is granted, the child who is detained under an order entered under rule 8.013 may be continued in detention under the said order upon the representation that a new or amended petition will be filed.

(3) Motion to Suppress. Any confession or admission obtained illegally or any evidence obtained by an unlawful search and seizure may be suppressed on motion by the child.

(A) Every motion to suppress shall clearly state the particular evidence sought to be suppressed, the reason for the suppression, and a general statement of the facts on which the motion is based.

(B) Before hearing evidence, the court shall determine if the motion is legally sufficient. If it is not, the motion shall be denied. If the court hears the motion on its merits, the moving party shall present evidence in support thereof and the state may offer rebuttal evidence.

(4) Motion to Sever. A motion may be made for the severance of 2 or more counts in a multi-count petition, or for the severance of the cases of 2 or more children to be adjudicated in the same hearing. The court may grant motions for severance of counts and severance of jointly brought cases for good cause shown.

(5) Time for Filing. Any motion to suppress, sever, or dismiss shall be made prior to the date of the adjudicatory hearing unless an opportunity to make such motion previously did not exist or the party making the motion was not aware of the grounds for the motion.

(6) Sworn Motions to Dismiss. Before the adjudicatory hearing the court may entertain a motion to dismiss on the ground that there are no material disputed facts and the undisputed facts do not establish a prima facie case of guilt against the child. The facts on which such motion is based shall be specifically alleged and the motion sworn to by the child. The motion shall be filed a reasonable time before the date of the adjudicatory hearing. The state may traverse or demur to this motion. Factual matters alleged in it shall be deemed admitted unless specifically denied by the state in a traverse. The court, in its discretion, may receive evidence on any issue of fact necessary to decide the motion. The motion shall be dismissed if the state files a written traverse that with specificity denies under oath the material fact or facts alleged in the motion to dismiss. Any demurrer or traverse shall be filed a reasonable time before the hearing on the motion to dismiss.

(b) Service of Pleadings and Papers.

(1) When Required. Unless the court orders otherwise, every pleading subsequent to the initial petition, every order, every written motion, unless it is one as to which hearing ex parte is authorized, and every written notice filed in the case shall be served on each party; however, nothing herein shall be construed to require that a plea be in writing or that an application for witness subpoena be served.

(2) How Made. When service is required or permitted to be made upon a party represented by an attorney, service shall be made upon the attorney unless service upon the party is ordered by the court. Service upon the attorney or party shall be made by electronic mail (e-mail) consistent with the requirements of Florida Rule of Judicial Administration 2.516, unless the parties stipulate otherwise. Service on and by all parties who are not represented by an attorney and who do not designate an e-mail address, and on and by all attorneys excused from e-mail service, must be made by delivering a copy or by mailing it to the attorney or party's last known address or, if no address is known, by leaving it with the clerk of the court. Service by mail shall be complete upon mailing. Delivery of a copy within this rule shall mean:

(A) handing it to the attorney or the party;

(B) leaving it at the attorney's office, with the person in charge thereof;

(C) if there is no one in charge of the office, leaving it in a conspicuous place therein;

(D) if the office is closed or the person to serve has no office, leaving it at his or her usual place of abode with some person of the family above 15 years of age and informing such person of the contents thereof; or

(E) transmitting it by facsimile to the attorney's or party's office with a cover sheet containing the sender's name, firm, address, telephone number, and facsimile number, the number of pages transmitted, and the recipient's facsimile number. When service is made by facsimile, a copy shall also be served by any other method permitted by this rule. Facsimile service occurs when the transmission is complete.

(3) Filing. All documents must be filed with the court either before service or immediately thereafter. If the document required to be filed is to be an original and is not placed in the court file or deposited with the clerk, a certified copy must be so placed by the clerk.

(4) Filing with Court Defined. The filing of documents with the court as required by these rules shall be made by filing them with the clerk of the court in accordance with rule 8.004, except that the judge may permit documents to be filed with the judge, in which event the judge must note the filing date before him or her on the documents and transmit them to the clerk. The date of filing is that shown on the face of the document by the notation of the judge or the time stamp of the clerk, whichever is earlier.

(5) Certificate of Service. When any authorized person shall in substance certify:

"I certify that a copy/copies has/have been furnished to (insert name or names) by (e-mail) (delivery) (mail) (fax) on (date).

_____
                      Title"

the certificate shall be taken as prima facie proof of such service in compliance with all rules of court and law.

(6) People Who May Certify Service. Service of pleadings and orders required to be served as provided by subdivision (2) may be certified by an attorney of record, clerk or deputy clerk, court, or authorized agent of the Department of Juvenile Justice in the form provided in subdivision (b)(5).

(c) Format for E-mail Service. All documents served by e-mail must be attached to an e-mail message containing a subject line beginning with the words "SERVICE OF COURT DOCUMENT" in all capital letters, followed by the case number of the proceeding in which the documents are being served. The body of the e-mail must identify the court in which the proceeding is pending, the case number, the name of the parties on each side, the style of the proceeding, the title of each document served with that e-mail, and the sender's name and telephone number. Any e-mail which, together with its attachments, exceeds five megabytes (5MB) in size, must be divided and sent as separate e-mails, numbered in the subject line, no one of which may exceed 5 MB in size.

(d) Time for Service of Motions and Notice of Hearing. Service by e-mail is complete on the date it is sent and must be treated as service by mail for the computation of time. If the sender learns that the e-mail did not reach the address of the person to be served, the sender must immediately send another copy by e-mail, or by means authorized by subdivision (b)(2). If e-mail service is excused, a copy of any written motion which may not be heard ex parte and a copy of the notice of the hearing thereof shall be served a reasonable time before the time specified for the hearing. If a document is served by more than one method of service, the computation of time for any response to the served document shall be based on the method of service that provides the shortest response time.

(e) Pleading to Be Signed by Attorney. Every written paper or pleading of a party represented by an attorney shall be signed in the attorney's individual name by such attorney, whose mailing address, primary e-mail address and telephone number, including area code, and Florida Bar number shall be stated, and who shall be duly licensed to practice law in Florida. Any document served by e-mail may be signed by any of the "/s/," "/s," or "s/" formats. The attorney may be required by an order of court to vouch for the authority to represent such party and to give the address of such party. Except when otherwise specifically provided by these rules or applicable statute, pleadings as such need not be verified or accompanied by affidavit.

(f) Pleading to Be Signed by Unrepresented Party. A party who has no attorney but represents

himself or herself shall sign the written pleading or other paper to be filed and state his or her primary e-mail address, mailing address, and telephone number, including area code.

(g) Effect of Signing Pleading. The signature of a person shall constitute a certificate that the paper or pleading has been read; that to the best of the person's knowledge, information, and belief there is good ground to support it; and that it is not interposed for delay. If a pleading or paper is not signed, or is signed with intent to defeat the purpose of this rule, it may be stricken and the action may proceed as though the pleading or paper had not been served.

(h) Service of Orders. A copy of all orders must be transmitted by the court or under its direction to all parties at the time of the entry of the order. The court may require that orders be prepared by a party, may require the party to furnish the court with stamped addressed envelopes for service of the order or judgment, and may require that proposed orders be furnished to all parties before entry by the court of the order. The court may serve any order by e-mail to all attorneys who were not excused from e-mail service and to all parties not represented by an attorney who have designated an e-mail address for service. This subdivision is directory, and a failure to comply with it does not affect the order or its finality or any proceedings arising in the matter.

Committee Notes

1991 Amendment. (a)(6) This creates a procedure for dismissal similar to Florida Rule of Criminal Procedure 3.190(c)(4).

1992 Amendments. (d) Rules 8.240(c)(2) and 8.630(c)(2) allow 5 days for service by mail. This change conforms this rule.

(f) The current rule implies that a written pleading must be filed. No written pleadings are required.

(e) and (g) The language from (e) was moved to create this new subdivision. The current rule applies only to attorneys. These requirements also should apply to nonattorneys who sign and file papers. This rule conforms with proposed revisions to rules 8.230 and 8.640.

RULE 8.090. SPEEDY TRIAL

(a) Time. If a petition has been filed alleging a child to have committed a delinquent act, the child shall be brought to an adjudicatory hearing without demand within 90 days of the earlier of the following:

(1) The date the child was taken into custody.

(2) The date of service of the summons that is issued when the petition is filed.

(b) Dismissal. If an adjudicatory hearing has not commenced within 90 days, upon motion timely filed with the court and served upon the prosecuting attorney, the respondent shall be entitled to the appropriate remedy as set forth in subdivision (m). The court before granting such motion shall make the required inquiry under subdivision (d).

(c) Commencement. A child shall be deemed to have been brought to trial if the adjudicatory hearing begins before the court within the time provided.

(d) Motion to Dismiss. If the adjudicatory hearing is not commenced within the periods of time established, the respondent shall be entitled to the appropriate remedy as set forth in subdivision (m) unless any of the following situations exist:

(1) The child has voluntarily waived the right to speedy trial.

(2) An extension of time has been ordered under subdivision (f).

(3) The failure to hold an adjudicatory hearing is attributable to the child, a co-respondent in the same adjudicatory hearing, or their counsel.

(4) The child was unavailable for the adjudicatory hearing. A child is unavailable if:

(A) the child or the child's counsel fails to attend a proceeding when their presence is required; or

(B) the child or the child's counsel is not ready for the adjudicatory hearing on the date it is scheduled.

No presumption of nonavailability attaches, but if the state objects to dismissal and presents any evidence tending to show nonavailability, the child must, by competent proof, establish availability during the term.

(5) The demand referred to in subdivision (g) is invalid.

(6) If the court finds dismissal is not appropriate, the pending motion to dismiss shall be denied, and an adjudicatory hearing shall commence within 90 days of a written or recorded order of denial.

(e) Incompetency of child. Upon the filing of a motion to declare the child incompetent, the speedy trial period shall be tolled until a subsequent finding of the court that the child is competent to proceed.

(f) Extension of Time. The period of time established by subdivision (a) may be extended as follows:

(1) Upon stipulation, announced to the court or signed by the child or the child's counsel and the state.

(2) By written or recorded order of the court on the court's own motion or motion by either party in exceptional circumstances. The order extending the period shall recite the reasons for the extension and the length of the extension. Exceptional circumstances are those which require an extension as a matter of substantial justice to the child or the state or both. Such circumstances include:

(A) unexpected illness or unexpected incapacity or unforeseeable and unavoidable absence of a person whose presence or testimony is uniquely necessary for a full and adequate trial;

(B) a showing by the state that the case is so unusual and so complex, due to the number of respondents or the nature of the prosecution or otherwise, that it is unreasonable to expect adequate investigation or preparation within the periods of time established by this rule;

(C) a showing by the state that specific evidence or testimony is not available, despite diligent efforts to secure it, but will become available at a later time;

(D) a showing by the child or the state of necessity for delay grounded on developments which could not have been anticipated and which will materially affect the trial;

(E) a showing that a delay is necessary to accommodate a co-respondent, where there is a reason not to sever the cases in order to proceed promptly with trial of the respondent; or

(F) a showing by the state that the child has caused major delay or disruption of preparation or proceedings, such as by preventing the attendance of witnesses or otherwise.

Exceptional circumstances shall not include general congestion of the court's docket, lack of diligent preparation or failure to obtain available witnesses, or other avoidable or foreseeable delays.

(3) By written or recorded order of the court for a period of reasonable and necessary delay resulting from proceedings including, but not limited to, an examination and hearing to determine the mental competency or physical ability of the respondent to stand trial for hearings or pretrial motions, for appeals by the state, and for adjudicatory hearings of other pending charges against the child.

(g) Speedy Trial upon Demand. Except as otherwise provided by this rule and subject to the limitations imposed by subdivision (h), the child shall have the right to demand a trial within 60 days, by filing a written pleading entitled "Demand for Speedy Trial" with the court and serving it upon the prosecuting attorney.

(1) No later than 5 days from the filing of a demand for speedy trial, the court shall set the matter for report, with notice to all parties, for the express purpose of announcing in open court receipt of the demand and of setting the case for trial.

(2) At the report the court shall set the case for trial to commence at a date no less than 5 days nor more than 45 days from the date of the report.

(3) The failure of the court to hold such a report date on a demand which has been properly filed shall not interrupt the running of any time periods under this subdivision (g).

(4) In the event that the child shall not have been brought to trial within 50 days of the filing of the demand, the child shall have the right to the appropriate remedy as set forth in subdivision (m).

(h) Demand for Speedy Trial; Effect. A demand for speedy trial shall be deemed a pleading by the respondent that he or she is available for the adjudicatory hearing, has diligently investigated the case, and is prepared or will be prepared for the adjudicatory hearing within 5 days. A demand may not be withdrawn by the child, except on order of the court, with consent of the state, or on good cause shown. Good cause for continuance or delay on behalf of the accused shall not thereafter include nonreadiness for the adjudicatory hearing, except as to matters which may arise after the demand for the adjudicatory hearing is filed and which could not reasonably have been anticipated by the accused or defense counsel.

(i) Dismissal after Demand. If an adjudicatory hearing has not commenced within 50 days after a demand for speedy trial, upon motion timely filed with the court having jurisdiction and served upon the prosecuting attorney, the child shall have the right to the appropriate remedy as set forth in subdivision (m), provided the court has made the required inquiry under subdivision (d).

(j) Effect of Mistrial, Appeal, or Order of New Trial. A child who is to be tried again or whose adjudicatory hearing has been delayed by an appeal by the state or the respondent shall be brought to trial within 90 days from the date of declaration of a mistrial by the trial court, the date of an order by the trial court granting a new trial, or the date of receipt by the trial court of a mandate, order, or notice of whatever form from an appellate or other reviewing court which makes possible a new trial for the respondent, whichever is last. If the child is not brought to trial within the prescribed time periods, the child shall be entitled to the appropriate remedy as set forth in subdivision (m).

(k) Discharge from Delinquent Act or Violation of Law; Effect. Discharge from a delinquent act or violation of law under this rule shall operate to bar prosecution of the delinquent act or violation of law charged and all other offenses on which an adjudicatory hearing has not begun or adjudication obtained or withheld and that were, or might have been, charged as a lesser degree or lesser included offense.

(*l*) Nolle Prosequi; Effect. The intent and effect of this rule shall not be avoided by the state entering a nolle prosequi to a delinquent act or violation of law charged and by prosecuting a new delinquent act or violation of law grounded on the same conduct or episode or otherwise by prosecuting new and different charges based on the same delinquent conduct or episode, whether or not the pending charge is suspended, continued, or the subject of the entry of a nolle prosequi.

(m) Remedy for Failure to Try Respondent Within the Specified Time.

(1) No remedy shall be granted to any respondent under this rule until the court shall have made the required inquiry under subdivision (d).

(2) The respondent may, at any time after the expiration of the prescribed time period, file a motion for discharge. Upon filing the motion the respondent shall simultaneously file a notice of hearing. The motion for discharge and its notice of hearing shall be served upon the prosecuting attorney.

(3) No later than 5 days from the date of the filing of a motion for discharge, the court shall hold a hearing on the motion and, unless the court finds that one of the reasons set forth in subdivision (d) exists, shall order that the respondent be brought to trial within 10 days. If the respondent is not brought to trial within the 10-day period through no fault of the respondent, the respondent shall be forever discharged from the crime.

Committee Notes

1991 Amendment. (m)(2) This rule requires a notice of hearing at the time of filing the motion for discharge to ensure that the child's motion is heard in a timely manner. A dissenting opinion in the committee was that this change does not protect the child's rights but merely ensures that the case is not dismissed because of clerical error.

RULE 8.095. PROCEDURE WHEN CHILD BELIEVED TO BE INCOMPETENT OR INSANE

(a) Incompetency at Time of Adjudicatory Hearing or Hearing on Petition Alleging Violation of Juvenile Probation in Delinquency Cases.

(1) Motion.

(A) A written motion for examination of the child made by counsel for the child shall contain a certifi-

cate of counsel that the motion is made in good faith and on reasonable grounds to believe that the child is incompetent to proceed. To the extent that it does not invade the lawyer-client privilege, the motion shall contain a recital of the specific observations of and conversations with the child that have formed the basis for the motion.

(B) A written motion for examination of the child made by counsel for the state shall contain a certificate of counsel that the motion is made in good faith and on reasonable grounds to believe the child is incompetent to proceed and shall include a recital of the specific facts that have formed the basis for the motion, including a recitation of the observations of and statements of the child that have caused the state to file the motion.

(2) Setting Hearing. If at any time prior to or during the adjudicatory hearing or hearing on a violation of juvenile probation, the court has reasonable grounds to believe the child named in the petition may be incompetent to proceed with an adjudicatory hearing, the court on its own motion or motion of counsel for the child or the state shall immediately stay the proceedings and fix a time for a hearing for the determination of the child's mental condition.

(3) Child Found Competent to Proceed. If at the hearing provided for in subdivision (a)(2) the child is found to be competent to proceed with an adjudicatory hearing, the court shall enter an order so finding and proceed accordingly.

(4) Child Found Incompetent to Proceed. If at the hearing provided for in subdivision (a)(2) the child is found to be incompetent to proceed, the child must be adjudicated incompetent to proceed and may be involuntarily committed as provided by law to the Department of Children and Families for treatment upon a finding of clear and convincing evidence that:

(A) The child is mentally ill or intellectually disabled and because of the mental illness or intellectual disability of the child:

(i) the child is manifestly incapable of surviving with the help of willing and responsible family or friends, including available alternative services, and without treatment the child is likely to either suffer from neglect or refuse to care for himself or herself, and such neglect or refusal poses a real and present threat of substantial harm to the child's well-being; or

(ii) there is a substantial likelihood that in the near future the child will inflict serious bodily harm on himself or herself or others, as evidenced by recent behavior causing, attempting, or threatening such harm; and

(B) All available less restrictive treatment alternatives, including treatment in community residential facilities or community inpatient settings which would offer an opportunity for improvement of the child's condition are inappropriate.

(5) Hearing on Competency. Not later than 6 months after the date of commitment, or at the end of any period of extended treatment or training, or at any time the service provider determines the child has attained competency or no longer meets the criteria for commitment, the service provider must file a report with the court and all parties. Upon receipt of this report, the court shall set a hearing to determine the child's competency.

(A) If the court determines that the child continues to remain incompetent, the court shall order appropriate nondelinquent hospitalization or treatment in conformity with this rule and the applicable provisions of chapter 985, Florida Statutes.

(B) If the court determines the child to be competent, it shall enter an order so finding and proceed accordingly.

(6) Commitment. Each child who has been adjudicated incompetent to proceed and who meets the criteria for commitment in Subdivision (a)(4) must be committed to the Department of Children and Families. The department must train or treat the child in the least restrictive alternative consistent with public safety. Any commitment of a child to a secure residential program must be to a program separate from adult forensic programs. If the child attains competency, case management and supervision of the

child will be transferred to the Department of Juvenile Justice to continue delinquency proceedings. The court retains authority, however, to order the Department of Children and Families to provide continued treatment to maintain competency.

(A) A child adjudicated incompetent because of intellectual disablity may be ordered into a program designated by the Department of Children and Families for intellectually disabled children.

(B) A child adjudicated incompetent because of mental illness may be ordered into a program designated by the Department of Children and Families for mentally ill children.

(7) Continuing Jurisdiction and Dismissal of Jurisdiction.

(A) If a child is determined to be incompetent to proceed, the court shall retain jurisdiction of the child for up to 2 years after the date of the order of incompetency, with reviews at least every 6 months to determine competency. If the court determines at any time that the child will never become competent to proceed, the court may dismiss the delinquency petition or petition alleging violation of juvenile probation.

(B) If, at the end of the 2-year period following the date of the order of incompetency, the child has not attained competency and there is no evidence that the child will attain competency within a year, the court must dismiss the delinquency petition.

(C) If necessary, the court may order that proceedings under chapter 393 or 394, Florida Statutes, be instituted. Such proceedings must be instituted no less than 60 days before the dismissal of the delinquency petition. The juvenile court may conduct all proceedings and make all determinations under chapter 393 or 394, Florida Statutes.

(8) Treatment Alternatives to Commitment. If a child who is found to be incompetent does not meet the commitment criteria of subdivision (a)(4), the court shall order the Department of Children and Families to provide appropriate treatment and training in the community. All court-ordered treatment must be in the least restrictive setting consistent with public safety. Any residential program must be separate from an adult forensic program. If a child is ordered to receive such services, the services shall be provided by the Department of Children and Families. The competency determination must be reviewed at least every 6 months, or at the end of any extended period of treatment or training, and any time the child appears to have attained competency or will never attain competency, by the service provider. A copy of a written report evaluating the child's competency must be filed by the provider with the court, the Department of Children and Families, the Department of Juvenile Justice, the state, and counsel for the child.

(9) Speedy Trial Tolled. Upon the filing of a motion by the child's counsel alleging the child to be incompetent to proceed or upon an order of the court finding a child incompetent to proceed, speedy trial shall be tolled until a subsequent finding of the court that the child is competent to proceed. Proceedings under this subdivision initiated by the court on its own motion or the state's motion may toll the speedy trial period pursuant to rule 8.090(e).

(b) Insanity at Time of Delinquent Act or Violation of Juvenile Probation.

(1) If the child named in the petition intends to plead insanity as a defense, the child shall advise the court in writing not less than 10 days before the adjudicatory hearing and shall provide the court with a statement of particulars showing as nearly as possible the nature of the insanity expected to be proved and the names and addresses of witnesses expected to prove it. Upon the filing of this statement, on motion of the state, or on its own motion, the court may cause the child to be examined in accordance with the procedures in this rule.

(2) The court, upon good cause shown and in its discretion, may waive these requirements and permit the introduction of the defense, or may continue the hearing for the purpose of an examination in accordance with the procedures in this rule. A continuance granted for this purpose will toll the speedy trial rule and the limitation on detention pending adjudication.

(c) Appointment of Expert Witnesses; Detention of Child for Examination.

(1) When a question has been raised concerning the sanity or competency of the child named in the petition and the court has set the matter for an adjudicatory hearing, hearing on violation of juvenile probation, or a hearing to determine the mental condition of the child, the court may on its own motion, and shall on motion of the state or the child, appoint no more than 3, nor fewer than 2, disinterested qualified experts to examine the child as to competency or sanity of the child at the time of the commission of the alleged delinquent act or violation of juvenile probation. Attorneys for the state and the child may be present at the examination. An examination regarding sanity should take place at the same time as the examination into the competence of the child to proceed, if the issue of competency has been raised. Other competent evidence may be introduced at the hearing. The appointment of experts by the court shall not preclude the state or the child from calling other expert witnesses to testify at the adjudicatory hearing, hearing on violation of juvenile probation, or at the hearing to determine the mental condition of the child.

(2) The court only as provided by general law may order the child held in detention pending examination. This rule shall in no way be construed to add any detention powers not provided by statute or case law.

(3) When counsel for a child adjudged to be indigent or partially indigent, whether public defender or court appointed, shall have reason to believe that the child may be incompetent to proceed or may have been insane at the time of the alleged delinquent act or juvenile probation violation, counsel may so inform the court. The court shall appoint 1 expert to examine the child to assist in the preparation of the defense. The expert shall report only to counsel for the child, and all matters related to the expert shall be deemed to fall under the lawyer-client privilege.

(4) For competency evaluations related to intellectual disability, the court shall order the Developmental Services Program Office of the Department of Children and Families to examine the child to determine if

the child meets the definition of intellectual disability in section 393.063, Florida Statutes, and, if so, whether the child is competent to proceed or amenable to treatment through the Department of Children and Families' intellectual disability services or programs.

(d) Competence to Proceed; Scope of Examination and Report.

(1) Examination by Experts. On appointment by the court, the experts shall examine the child with respect to the issue of competence to proceed as specified by the court in its order appointing the experts.

(A) The experts first shall consider factors related to whether the child meets the criteria for competence to proceed; that is, whether the child has sufficient present ability to consult with counsel with a reasonable degree of rational understanding and whether the child has a rational and factual understanding of the present proceedings.

(B) In considering the competence of the child to proceed, the examining experts shall consider and include in their reports the child's capacity to:

(i) appreciate the charges or allegations against the child;

(ii) appreciate the range and nature of possible penalties that may be imposed in the proceedings against the child, if applicable;

(iii) understand the adversary nature of the legal process;

(iv) disclose to counsel facts pertinent to the proceedings at issue;

(v) display appropriate courtroom behavior; and

(vi) testify relevantly.

The experts also may consider any other factors they deem to be relevant.

(C) Any report concluding that a child is not competent must include the basis for the competency determination.

(2) Treatment Recommendations. If the experts find that the child is incompetent to proceed, they shall report on any recommended treatment for the child to attain competence to proceed. A recommendation as to whether residential or nonresidential treatment or training is required must be included. In considering issues related to treatment, the experts shall report on the following:

(A) The mental illness, intellectual disability, or mental age causing incompetence.

(B) The treatment or education appropriate for the mental illness or intellectual disability of the child and an explanation of each of the possible treatment or education alternatives, in order of recommendation.

(C) The availability of acceptable treatment or education. If treatment or education is available in the community, the experts shall so state in the report.

(D) The likelihood of the child attaining competence under the treatment or education recommended, an assessment of the probable duration of the treatment required to restore competence, and the probability that the child will attain competence to proceed in the foreseeable future.

(E) Whether the child meets the criteria for involuntary hospitalization or involuntary admissions to residential services under chapter 985, Florida Statutes.

(3) Insanity. If a notice of intent to rely on an insanity defense has been filed before an adjudicatory hearing or a hearing on an alleged violation of juvenile probation, when ordered by the court the experts shall report on the issue of the child's sanity at the time of the delinquent act or violation of juvenile probation.

(4) Written Findings of Experts. Any written report submitted by the experts shall:

(A) identify the specific matters referred for evaluation;

(B) describe the procedures, techniques, and tests used in the examination and the purposes of each;

(C) state the expert's clinical observations, findings, and opinions on each issue referred for evaluation by the court and indicate specifically those issues, if any, on which the expert could not give an opinion; and

(D) identify the sources of information used by the expert and present the factual basis for the expert's clinical findings and opinions.

(5) Limited Use of Competency Evidence.

(A) The information contained in any motion by the child for determination of competency to proceed or in any report filed under this rule as it relates solely to the issues of competency to proceed and commitment, and any information elicited during a hearing on competency to proceed or commitment held under this rule, shall be used only in determining the mental competency to proceed, the commitment of the child, or other treatment of the child.

(B) The child waives this provision by using the report, or any parts of it, in any proceeding for any other purpose. If so waived, the disclosure or use of the report, or any portion of it, shall be governed by the applicable rules of evidence and juvenile procedure. If a part of a report is used by the child, the state may request the production of any other portion that, in fairness, ought to be considered.

(e) Procedures after Judgment of Not Guilty by Reason of Insanity.

(1) When the child is found not guilty of the delinquent act or violation of juvenile probation because of insanity, the court shall enter such a finding and judgment.

(2) After finding the child not guilty by reason of insanity, the court shall conduct a hearing to determine if the child presently meets the statutory criteria for involuntary commitment to a residential psychiatric facility.

(A) If the court determines that the required criteria have been met, the child shall be committed by the juvenile court to the Department of Children and Families for immediate placement in a residential psychiatric facility.

(B) If the court determines that such commitment criteria have not been established, the court, after hearing, shall order that the child receive recommended and appropriate treatment at an outpatient facility or service.

(C) If the court determines that treatment is not needed, it shall discharge the child.

(D) Commitment to a residential psychiatric facility of a child adjudged not guilty by reason of insanity shall be governed by the provisions of chapters 985 or 394, Florida Statutes, except that requests for discharge or continued involuntary hospitalization of the child shall be directed to the court that committed the child.

(E) If a child is not committed to a residential psychiatric facility and has been ordered to receive appropriate treatment at an outpatient facility or service and it appears during the course of the ordered treatment

(i) that treatment is not being provided or that the child now meets the criteria for hospitalization, the court shall conduct a hearing pursuant to subdivision (e)(2) of this rule.

(ii) that the child no longer requires treatment at an outpatient facility or service, the court shall enter an order discharging the child.

(F) During the time the child is receiving treatment, either by hospitalization or through an outpatient facility or service, any party may request the court to conduct a hearing to determine the nature, quality, and need for continued treatment. The hearing shall be conducted in conformity with subdivision (e)(2) of this rule.

(G) No later than 30 days before reaching age 19, a child still under supervision of the court under this rule shall be afforded a hearing. At the hearing, a determination shall be made as to the need for continued hospitalization or treatment. If the court determines that continued care is appropriate, proceedings shall be initiated under chapter 394, Florida Statutes. If the court determines further care to be unnecessary, the court shall discharge the child.

F. HEARINGS

RULE 8.100. GENERAL PROVISIONS FOR HEARINGS

Unless otherwise provided, the following provisions apply to all hearings:

(a) Presence of the Child. The child shall be present unless the court finds that the child's mental or physical condition is such that a court appearance is not in the child's best interests.

(b) Use of Restraints on the Child. Instruments of restraint, such as handcuffs, chains, irons, or straitjackets, may not be used on a child during a court proceeding and must be removed prior to the child's appearance before the court unless the court finds both that:

(1) The use of restraints is necessary due to one of the following factors:

(A) Instruments of restraint are necessary to prevent physical harm to the child or another person;

(B) The child has a history of disruptive courtroom behavior that has placed others in potentially harmful situations or presents a substantial risk of inflicting physical harm on himself or herself or others as evidenced by recent behavior; or

(C) There is a founded belief that the child presents a substantial risk of flight from the courtroom; and

(2) There are no less restrictive alternatives to restraints that will prevent flight or physical harm to the child or another person, including, but not limited to, the presence of court personnel, law enforcement officers, or bailiffs.

(c) Absence of the Child. If the child is present at the beginning of a hearing and during the progress of the hearing voluntarily absents himself or herself from the presence of the court without leave of the court, or

is removed from the presence of the court because of disruptive conduct during the hearing, the hearing shall not be postponed or delayed, but shall proceed in all respects as if the child were present in court at all times.

(d) Invoking the Rule. Prior to the examination of any witness the court may, and on the request of any party in an adjudicatory hearing shall, exclude all other witnesses. The court may cause witnesses to be kept separate and to be prevented from communicating with each other until all are examined.

(e) Continuances. The court may grant a continuance before or during a hearing for good cause shown by any party.

(f) Record of Testimony. A record of the testimony in all hearings shall be made by an official court reporter, a court approved stenographer, or a recording device. The records shall be preserved for 5 years from the date of the hearing. Official records of testimony shall be provided only on request of a party or a party's attorney or on a court order.

(g) Notice. When these rules do not require a specific notice, all parties will be given reasonable notice of any hearing.

RULE 8.104. TESTIMONY BY CLOSED-CIRCUIT TELEVISION

(a) Requirements for Use. In any case the trial court may order the testimony of a victim or witness under the age of 16 to be taken outside the courtroom and shown by means of closed-circuit television if on motion and hearing in camera, the trial court determines that the victim or witness would suffer at least moderate emotional or mental harm due to the presence of the defendant child if the witness is required to testify in open court.

(b) Persons Who May File Motion. The motion may be filed by:

(1) the victim or witness or his or her attorney, parent, legal guardian, or guardian ad litem;

(2) the trial judge on his or her own motion;

(3) the prosecuting attorney; or

(4) the defendant child or his or her counsel.

(c) Persons Who May Be Present During Testimony. Only the judge, prosecutor, witness or victim, attorney for the witness or victim, defendant child's attorney, operator of the equipment, an interpreter, and some other person who in the opinion of the court contributes to the well-being of the victim or witness and who will not be a witness in the case may be in the room during the recording of the testimony.

(d) Presence of Defendant Child. During the testimony of the victim or witness by closed-circuit television, the court may require the defendant child to view the testimony from the courtroom. In such case, the court shall permit the defendant child to observe and hear the testimony, but shall ensure that the victim or witness cannot hear or see the defendant child. The defendant child's right to assistance of counsel, which includes the right to immediate and direct communication with counsel conducting cross examination, shall be protected and, on the defendant child's request, such communication shall be provided by any appropriate electronic method.

(e) Findings of Fact. The court shall make specific findings of fact on the record as to the basis for its ruling under this rule.

(f) Time for Motion. The motion referred to in subdivision (a) may be made at anytime with reasonable notice to each party.

Committee Notes

1992 Adoption. Addition of this rule is mandated by section 92.55, Florida Statutes (1989).

RULE 8.105. WAIVER OF JURISDICTION

(a) On Demand. On demand for waiver of jurisdiction, the court shall enter a written order setting forth the demand, waiving jurisdiction, and certifying the case for trial as if the child were an adult. The demand shall be made in the form provided by law prior to the commencement of an adjudicatory hearing. A certified copy of the order shall be furnished to the clerk of the court having jurisdiction to try the child as an adult and to the prosecuting officer of the said child within 5 days of the demand being made. The court may order that the child be delivered to the sheriff of the county in which the court that is to try the child is located.

(b) Involuntary Waiver; Hearing.

(1) As provided by law, the state attorney may, or if required, shall, file a motion requesting the court to waive its jurisdiction and certify the case to the appropriate court for trial as if the child were an adult.

(2) Following the filing of the motion of the state attorney, summons shall be issued and served in conformity with the provision of rule 8.040. A copy of the motion and a copy of the delinquency petition, if not already served, shall be attached to each summons.

(3) No plea to a petition shall be accepted by the court prior to the disposition of the motion to waive jurisdiction.

(4) After the filing of the report required by law, the court shall conduct a hearing on the motion to determine the existence of the criteria established by law for waiver of jurisdiction.

(5) After hearing as provided in this rule:

(A) The court may enter an order waiving jurisdiction and certifying the case for trial as if the child were an adult as provided by law. The order shall set forth the basis for waiver of jurisdiction and certification to the appropriate court, with copies provided to all parties and the department. A certified copy of the order shall be furnished to the clerk of the court having jurisdiction to try the child as an adult and to the prosecuting officer of the said court within 5 days of the date of the order. The child shall be delivered immediately to the sheriff of the county in which the court that is to try the child as an adult is located.

(B) The court may enter an order denying waiver of jurisdiction, and give reasons for this denial, as provided by law. If the waiver is denied, the same judge, with the consent of the child and the state, may proceed immediately with the adjudicatory hearing.

(c) Bail. If the child is delivered to the sheriff under subdivision (a) or (b) the court shall fix bail. A certified copy of the order shall be furnished to the sheriff.

RULE 8.110. ADJUDICATORY HEARINGS

(a) Appearances; Pleas. The child shall appear before the court at the times set and, unless a written plea has been filed, enter a plea of guilty, not guilty, or, with the consent of the court, nolo contendere.

(b) Preparation of Case. If the child pleads not guilty the court may proceed at once to an adjudicatory hearing, or may continue the case to allow sufficient time on the court calendar for a hearing or to give the state or the child a reasonable time for the preparation of the case.

(c) Trial by Court. The adjudicatory hearing shall be conducted by the judge without a jury. At this hearing the court determines whether the allegations of the petition have been sustained.

(d) Testimony. The child may be sworn and testify in his or her own behalf. The child may be cross-examined as other witnesses. No child shall be compelled to give testimony against himself or herself, nor shall any prosecuting attorney be permitted to comment on the failure of the child to testify in his or her own behalf. A child offering no testimony in his or her own behalf except his or her own shall be entitled to the concluding argument.

(e) Joint and Separate Trials. When 2 or more children are alleged to have committed a delinquent act or violation of law, they shall be tried jointly unless the court in its discretion orders separate trials.

(f) Dismissal. If the court finds that the allegations in the petition have not been sustained, it shall enter an order so finding and dismissing the case.

(g) Dispositional Alternatives. If the court finds that the evidence supports the allegations of the petition, it may enter an order of adjudication or withhold adjudication as provided by law. If the pre-disposition report required by law is available, the court may proceed immediately to disposition or continue the case for a disposition hearing. If the report is not available, the court will continue the case for a disposition hearing and refer it to the appropriate agency or agencies for a study and recommendation. If the case is continued the court may order the child detained.

(h) Degree of Offense. If in a petition there is alleged an offense which is divided into degrees, the court may find the child committed an offense of the degree alleged or of any lesser degree.

(i) Specifying Offense Committed. If in a petition more than one offense is alleged the court shall state in its order which offense or offenses it finds the child committed.

(j) Lesser Included Offenses. On a petition on which the child is to be tried for any offense, the court may find the child committed:

(1) an attempt to commit the offense, if the attempt is an offense and is supported by the evidence; or

(2) any offense that as a matter of law is a necessarily included offense or a lesser included offense of the offense charged in the petition and is supported by the evidence.

(k) Motion for Judgment of Dismissal. If at the close of the evidence for the petitioner, the court is of the opinion that the evidence is insufficient to establish a prima facie case of guilt against the child, it may, or on the motion of the state attorney or the child shall, enter an order dismissing the petition for insufficiency of the evidence.

RULE 8.115. DISPOSITION HEARING

(a) Information Available to Court. At the disposition hearing the court, after establishing compliance with the dispositional considerations, determinations, and discussions required by law, may receive any relevant and material evidence helpful in determining the proper disposition to be made. It shall include written reports required by law, and may include, but shall not be limited to, the child's need for substance abuse evaluation and/or treatment, and any psychiatric or psychological evaluations of the child that may be obtained and that are relevant and material. Such evidence may be received by the court and may be relied upon to the extent of its probative value, even though not competent in an adjudicatory hearing. In any case in which it is necessary or consented to by the parties that disposition be pronounced by a judge other than the judge who presided at the adjudicatory hearing or accepted a plea of guilty or nolo contendere, the sentencing judge shall not pronounce disposition until the judge becomes acquainted with what transpired at the adjudicatory hearing, or the facts concerning the plea and the offense, including any plea discussions if a plea of guilty or nolo contendere was entered.

(b) Appointment of Counsel. Counsel shall be appointed at all disposition hearings, including cases transferred from other counties and restitution hearings, if the child qualifies for such appointment and does not waive counsel in writing as required by rule 8.165.

(c) Disclosure. The child, the child's attorney, the child's parent or custodian, and the state attorney shall be entitled to disclosure of all information in the predisposition report and all reports and evaluations used by the department in the preparation of the report.

(d) Disposition Order. The disposition order shall be prepared and distributed by the clerk of the court. Copies shall be provided to the child, defense attorney, state attorney, and department representative. Each case requires a separate disposition order. The order shall:

(1) state the name and age of the child;

(2) state the disposition of each count, specifying the charge title, degree of offense, and maximum penalty defined by statute and specifying the amount of time served in secure detention before disposition;

(3) state general and specific conditions or sanctions;

(4) make all findings of fact required by law;

(5) state the date and time when issued and the county and court where issued; and

(6) be signed by the court with the title of office.

(e) Fingerprints. The child's fingerprints shall be affixed to the order of disposition.

Committee Notes

1991 Amendment. (c) Section 985.23(3)(e), Florida Statutes, requires the court to fingerprint any child who is adjudicated or has adjudication withheld for a felony. This rule extends this requirement to all dispositions. Sentencing guidelines include scorable points for misdemeanor offenses as well as for felonies. This procedure also should assist in identifying juveniles who use false names and birthdates, which can result in the arrest of an innocent child whose name was used by the offender.

RULE 8.120. POST-DISPOSITION HEARING

(a) Revocation of Juvenile Probation.

(1) A child who has been placed on juvenile probation may be brought before the court upon allegations of violation(s).

(2) Any proceeding alleging a violation shall be initiated by the filing of a sworn affidavit of the material facts supporting the allegation(s). The affidavit shall be executed by the child's juvenile probation officer or other person having actual knowledge of the facts. Copies of the affidavit shall be provided to the court, the state attorney, and the Department of Juvenile Justice.

(3) When revocation proceedings are sought by the state attorney or the Department of Juvenile Justice, the proceedings shall be initiated by the filing of a petition alleging violation of juvenile probation. The petition shall incorporate and reference the affidavit described in subdivision (a)(2). All such petitions must be signed and filed by legal counsel.

(4) The court may initiate revocation proceedings by the entry of an order initiating revocation proceedings. The order must incorporate and reference the affidavit described in subdivision (a)(2).

(5) All interested persons, including the child, shall have an opportunity to be heard. After such hearing, the court shall enter an order revoking, modifying, terminating, or continuing juvenile probation. Upon the revocation of juvenile probation, the court shall,

when the child has been placed on juvenile probation and adjudication has been withheld, adjudicate the child delinquent. In all cases after a revocation of juvenile probation, the court shall enter a new disposition order.

(b) Retention of Authority over Discharge. When the court has retained authority over discharge of a delinquent child from placement or commitment as provided by law, prior to any discharge from placement or commitment, the Department of Juvenile Justice shall notify the court, the state attorney, the victim of the offense or offenses for which the child was placed under supervision of the department, and the child of its intention to discharge the child. Thereafter, any interested party may request a hearing, within the time prescribed by law, to address the discharge.

G. RELIEF FROM ORDERS AND JUDGMENTS

RULE 8.130. MOTION FOR REHEARING

(a) Basis. After the court has entered an order ruling on a pretrial motion, an order of adjudication, or an order withholding adjudication, any party may move for rehearing upon one or more of the following grounds:

(1) That the court erred in the decision of any matter of law arising during the hearing.

(2) That a party did not receive a fair and impartial hearing.

(3) That any party required to be present at the hearing was not present.

(4) That there exists new and material evidence which, if introduced at the hearing, would probably have changed the court's decision and could not with reasonable diligence have been discovered before and produced at the hearing.

(5) That the court is without jurisdiction of the proceeding.

(6) That the judgment is contrary to the law and evidence.

(b) Time and Method.

(1) A motion for rehearing may be made and ruled upon immediately after the court announces its judgment but must be made within 10 days of the entry of the order being challenged.

(2) If the motion is made in writing, it shall be served as provided in these rules for service of other pleadings.

(3) A motion for rehearing shall toll the time for the taking of an appeal.

(c) Court Action.

(1) If the motion for rehearing is granted, the court may vacate or modify the order or any part thereof and allow additional proceedings as it deems just. It may enter a new judgment, and may order or continue the child in detention pending further proceedings.

(2) The court on its own initiative may vacate or modify any order within the time limitation provided in subdivision (b).

RULE 8.135. CORRECTION OF DISPOSITION OR COMMITMENT ORDERS

(a) Correction. A court at any time may correct an illegal disposition or commitment order imposed by it. However, a party may not file a motion to correct under this subdivision during the time allowed for the filing of a motion under subdivision (b)(1) or during the pendency of a direct appeal.

(b) Motion to Correct Disposition or Commitment Error. A motion to correct any disposition or commitment order error, including an illegal disposition or commitment, may be filed as allowed by this subdivision. The motion must identify the error with specificity and provide a proposed correction. A response to the motion may be filed within 15 days either admitting or contesting the alleged error. Motions may be filed by the state under this subdivision only if the correction of the error would benefit the child or to correct a scrivener's error.

(1) Motion Before Appeal. During the time allowed for the filing of a notice of appeal, a child, the state, or the department may file a motion to correct a disposition or commitment order error.

(A) This motion stays rendition under Florida Rule of Appellate Procedure 9.020(i).

(B) Unless the trial court determines that the motion can be resolved as a matter of law without a hearing, it shall hold an initial hearing no later than 10 days from the filing of the motion, with notice to all parties, for the express purpose of either ruling on the motion or determining the need for an evidentiary hearing. If an evidentiary hearing is needed, it shall be set no more than 10 days from the date of the initial hearing. Within 30 days from the filing of the motion, the trial court shall file an order ruling on the motion. If no order is filed within 30 days, the motion shall be deemed denied.

(2) Motion Pending Appeal. If an appeal is pending, a child or the state may file in the trial court a motion to correct a disposition or commitment order error. The motion may be filed by appellate counsel and must be served before the party's first brief is served. A notice of pending motion to correct disposition or commitment error shall be filed in the appellate court, which notice shall automatically extend the time for the filing of the brief, until 10 days after the clerk of the circuit court transmits the supplemental record under Florida Rule of Appellate Procedure 9.140(f)(6).

(A) The motion shall be served on the trial court and on all trial and appellate counsel of record. Unless the motion expressly states that appellate counsel will represent the movant in the trial court, trial counsel will represent the movant on the motion under Florida Rule of Appellate Procedure 9.140(d). If the state is the movant, trial counsel will represent the child unless appellate counsel for the child notifies trial counsel and the trial court that appellate counsel will represent the child on the state's motion.

(B) The trial court shall resolve this motion in accordance with subdivision (b)(1)(B) of this rule.

(C) Under Florida Rule of Appellate Procedure 9.140(f)(6), the clerk of the circuit court shall supple-ment the appellate record with the motion, the order, any amended disposition, and, if designated, a transcript of any additional portion of the proceedings.

RULE 8.140. EXTRAORDINARY RELIEF

(a) Basis. On motion and upon such terms as are just, the court may relieve a party or the party's legal representative from an order, judgment, or proceeding for the following reasons:

(1) Mistake, inadvertence, surprise, or excusable neglect.

(2) Newly discovered evidence which by due diligence could not have been discovered in time to move for rehearing.

(3) Fraud (intrinsic or extrinsic), misrepresentation, or other misconduct of any other party.

(4) That the order or judgment is void.

(b) Time. The motion shall be made within a reasonable time and, for reasons (1), (2), and (3), not more than 1 year after the judgment, order, or proceeding was taken.

RULE 8.145. SUPERSEDEAS ON APPEAL

(a) Granting of Supersedeas. The court in considering the welfare and best interest of the child and the interest of the public may grant a supersedeas in its discretion on such conditions as it may determine are appropriate.

(b) Preeminence of Rule. This rule shall be to the exclusion of any other court rule providing for supersedeas on appeal.

H. CONTEMPT

RULE 8.150. CONTEMPT

(a) Contempt of Court. The court may punish any child for contempt under this rule for interfering with the court or court administration, or for violating any order of the court. A child under the jurisdiction of the juvenile court may be subject to contempt under this rule even upon reaching the age of majority. If the child is found in contempt and sentenced to secure detention, on motion by any party the court must review the placement of the child to determine whether it is appropriate for the child to remain detained.

(b) Direct Contempt. After a hearing, a contempt may be punished immediately if the court saw or heard the conduct constituting the contempt that was committed in the actual presence of the court. The child has a right to legal counsel and the right to have legal counsel appointed by the court if the child is indigent. The court must inform the child as to the basis for the contempt by reciting the facts on which the contempt is based. Before the adjudication of guilt the court must inquire as to whether there is any cause to show why the child should not be adjudged guilty of contempt by the court and sentenced therefor. The child must be given the opportunity to present evidence of excusing or mitigating circumstances. The judgment must be signed by the court and entered of record. Sentence must be pronounced in open court.

(c) Indirect Contempt. An indirect contempt may be prosecuted in the following manner:

(1) Legal Counsel. Counsel must be appointed for all contempt hearings if the child qualifies for such appointment, or the child has the right to retain counsel, unless the child waives counsel in writing as required by rule 8.165.

(2) Order to Show Cause. On affidavit of any person having personal knowledge of the facts, the court may issue and sign an order to show cause. The order must state the essential facts constituting the contempt charged and require the child to appear before the court to show cause why the child should not be held in contempt of court. If the contempt charged involves disrespect to or criticism of a judge, on motion by the child, the judge must be disqualified by the chief judge of the circuit. The order must specify the time and place of the hearing, with a reasonable time allowed for the preparation of a defense after service of the order on the child. It must be served in the same manner as a summons. Nothing herein shall be construed to prevent the child from waiving the service of process.

(3) Motions; Answer. The child may move to dismiss the order to show cause, move for a statement

of particulars, admit to the offense, or enter a denial and request a hearing.

(4) Detention Before the Hearing. The court may only detain the child before the contempt hearing solely on the contempt proceeding if the court provides clear and convincing reasons in writing demonstrating the court's belief that the child will fail to appear in response to the order to show cause.

(5) Hearing. The judge may conduct a hearing without assistance of counsel or may be assisted in the prosecution of the contempt by the state attorney or by an attorney appointed for that purpose. At the hearing, the child has the following rights:

(A) The right to be represented by legal counsel.

(B) The right to testify in the child's own defense.

(C) The right to confront witnesses.

(D) The right to subpoena and present witnesses.

(E) The right to have the hearing recorded and a copy of such recording.

(F) The right to have a transcript of the proceeding.

(G) The right to appeal.

(6) Verdict; Judgment. At the conclusion of the hearing the court must sign a judgment of guilty or not guilty. If the court finds the child guilty, the judgment should include a recital of the facts that constituted the contempt.

(7) Sentence. Before the pronouncement of sentence the court must inform the child of the accusation and judgment against him or her and inquire as to whether there is any cause to show why sentence should not be pronounced. The child must be afforded the opportunity to present evidence of mitigating circumstances. The court must consider all available and appropriate sentences, including alternative sanctions. The court must pronounce the sentence in open court and in the presence of the child.

I. GENERAL PROVISIONS

RULE 8.160. TRANSFER OF CASES

The court may transfer any case, after adjudication or when adjudication is withheld, to the circuit court for the county of the circuit in which is located the domicile or usual residence of the child or such other circuit court as the court may determine to be for the best interest of the child. No case shall be transferred to another county under this rule unless a plea of nolo contendere or guilty has been entered by the child on the charge being transferred, or until the transferring court has found the child committed the offense in question after an adjudicatory hearing in the county where the offense occurred. Any action challenging the entry of a plea or the adjudicatory hearing result must be brought in the transferring court's county. The transferring court shall enter an order transferring its jurisdiction and certifying the case to the proper court. The transferring court shall furnish the following to the state attorney, the public defender, if counsel was previously appointed, and the clerk of the receiving court within 5 days:

(a) A certified copy of the order of transfer, which shall include, but not be limited to:

(1) specific offense that the child was found to have committed;

(2) degree of the offense;

(3) name of parent/custodian to be summoned;

(4) address at which the child should be summoned for disposition;

(5) name and address of victim;

(6) whether the child was represented by counsel; and

(7) findings of fact, after hearing or stipulation, regarding the amount of damages or loss caused directly or indirectly by the child's offense, for purposes of restitution.

(b) A certified copy of the delinquency petition.

(c) A copy of the juvenile referral or complaint.

(d) Any reports and all previous orders including orders appointing counsel entered by the court in the interest of that child.

Committee Notes

1992 Amendment. The purpose of this amendment is to require the court hearing the substantive charge to determine the value of the victim's damage or loss caused by the child's offense. The victim and witnesses necessary to testify as to damage and loss are more often residents of the transferring court's county, rather than the receiving court's.

1991 Amendment. This rule requires the transferring court to provide sufficient information to the receiving court when transferring the case to another jurisdiction to comply with the requirements of chapter 39, Florida Statutes.

RULE 8.165. PROVIDING COUNSEL TO PARTIES

(a) Duty of the Court. The court shall advise the child of the child's right to counsel. The court shall appoint counsel as provided by law unless waived by the child at each stage of the proceeding. Waiver of counsel can occur only after the child has had a meaningful opportunity to confer with counsel regarding the child's right to counsel, the consequences of waiving counsel, and any other factors that would assist the child in making the decision to waive counsel. This waiver shall be in writing.

(b) Waiver of Counsel.

(1) The failure of a child to request appointment of counsel at a particular stage in the proceedings or the child's announced intention to plead guilty shall not, in itself, constitute a waiver of counsel at any subsequent stage of the proceedings.

(2) A child shall not be deemed to have waived the assistance of counsel until the entire process of offering counsel has been completed and a thorough inquiry into the child's comprehension of that offer and the capacity to make that choice intelligently and understandingly has been made.

(3) If the child is entering a plea to or being tried on an allegation of committing a delinquent act, the written waiver shall also be submitted to the court in the presence of a parent, legal custodian, responsible adult relative, or attorney assigned by the court to assist the child. The assigned attorney shall verify on the written waiver and on the record that the child's decision to waive counsel has been discussed with the child and appears to be knowing and voluntary.

(4) No waiver shall be accepted if it appears that the party is unable to make an intelligent and understanding choice because of mental condition, age, education, experience, the nature or complexity of the case, or other factors.

(5) If a waiver is accepted at any stage of the proceedings, the offer of assistance of counsel shall be renewed by the court at each subsequent stage of the proceedings at which the party appears without counsel.

RULE 8.170. GUARDIAN AD LITEM

At any stage of the proceedings, the court may appoint a guardian ad litem for the child.

A guardian ad litem shall not be required to post bond but shall file an acceptance of the office.

RULE 8.180. COMPUTATION AND ENLARGEMENT OF TIME

(a) **Computation.** Computation of time shall be governed by Florida Rule of Judicial Administration 2.514, except for rules 8.013 and 8.010, to which rule 2.514(a)(2)(C) shall not apply and the statutory time period shall govern.

(b) **Enlargement of Time.** When by these rules or by notice given thereunder or by order of court an act is required or allowed to be done at or within a specified time, the court for good cause shown may, at any time, in its discretion:

(1) with or without notice, order the period enlarged if request therefor is made before the expiration of the period originally prescribed or as extended by a previous order; or

(2) Upon motion made and notice after the expiration of the specified period permit the act to be done where the failure to act was the result of excusable neglect.

But it may not, except as provided by law or elsewhere in these rules, extend the time for making a motion for a new trial, a motion for rehearing, judgment of acquittal, vacation of judgment, or for

taking an appeal. This rule shall not be construed to apply to detention hearings.

RULE 8.185. COMMUNITY ARBITRATION

(a) **Referral.** A case may be referred to community arbitration as provided by law. The chief judge of each judicial circuit shall maintain a list of qualified persons who have agreed to serve as community arbitrators for the purpose of carrying out the provisions of chapter 985, Florida Statutes.

(b) **Arbitrator Qualifications.** Each community arbitrator or member of a community arbitration panel shall be selected pursuant to law and shall meet the following minimum qualification and training requirements:

(1) Be at least 18 years of age.

(2) Be a person of the temperament necessary to deal properly with cases involving children and with the family crises likely to be presented.

(3) Pass a law enforcement records check and a Department of Children and Family Services abuse registry background check, as determined by the written guidelines developed by the chief judge of the circuit, the senior circuit court judge assigned to juvenile cases in the circuit, and the state attorney.

(4) Observe a minimum of 3 community arbitration hearings conducted by an approved arbitrator in a juvenile case.

(5) Conduct at least 1 juvenile community arbitration hearing under the personal observation of an approved community arbitrator.

(6) Successfully complete a training program consisting of not less than 8 hours of instruction including, but not limited to, instruction in:

(A) conflict resolution;

(B) juvenile delinquency law;

(C) child psychology; and

(D) availability of community resources.

The chief judge of the circuit, the senior circuit judge assigned to juvenile cases in the circuit, and the state attorney shall develop specific written guidelines for the training program and may specify additional qualifications as necessary.

Committee Notes

1992 Adoption. This rule provides qualification and training requirements for arbitrators as required by section 985.304(3), Florida Statutes. It was the committee's intention to set minimal qualifications and to allow local programs to determine additional requirements.

PART III. DEPENDENCY AND TERMINATION OF PARENTAL RIGHTS PROCEEDINGS

A. GENERAL PROVISIONS

RULE 8.201. COMMENCEMENT OF PROCEEDINGS

(a) Commencement of Proceedings. Proceedings are commenced when:

(1) an initial shelter petition is filed;

(2) a petition alleging dependency is filed;

(3) a petition for termination of parental rights is filed;

(4) a petition for an injunction to prevent child abuse under chapter 39, Florida Statutes, is filed;

(5) a petition or affidavit for an order to take into custody is filed; or

(6) any other petition authorized by chapter 39, Florida Statutes, is filed.

(b) File to Be Opened. Upon commencement of any proceeding, the clerk shall open a file and assign a case number.

RULE 8.203. APPLICATION OF UNIFORM CHILD CUSTODY JURISDICTION AND ENFORCEMENT ACT

Any pleading filed commencing proceedings as set forth in rule 8.201 shall be accompanied by an affidavit, to the extent of affiant's personal knowledge, under the Uniform Child Custody Jurisdiction and Enforcement Act. Each party has a continuing duty to inform the court of any custody proceeding in this or any other state of which information is obtained during the proceeding.

RULE 8.205. TRANSFER OF CASES

(a) Transfer of Cases Within Circuit Court. If it should appear at any time in a proceeding initiated in a division other than the division of the circuit court assigned to handle dependency matters that facts are alleged that essentially constitute a dependency or the termination of parental rights, the court may upon consultation with the administrative judge assigned to dependency cases order the transfer of action and the transmittal of all relevant documents to the division assigned to handle dependency matters. The division assigned to handle dependency matters shall then assume jurisdiction only over matters pertaining to dependency, custody, visitation, and child support.

(b) Transfer of Cases Within the State of Florida. The court may transfer any case after adjudication, when adjudication is withheld, or before adjudication where witnesses are available in another jurisdiction, to the circuit court for the county in which is located the domicile or usual residence of the child or such other circuit as the court may determine to be for the best interest of the child and to promote the efficient administration of justice. The transferring court shall enter an order transferring its jurisdiction and certifying the case to the proper court, furnishing all parties, the clerk, and the attorney's office handling dependency matters for the state in the receiving court a copy of the order of transfer within 5 days. The clerk shall also transmit a certified copy of the file to the receiving court within 5 days.

(c) Transfer of Cases Among States. If it should appear at any time that an action is pending in another state, the court may transfer jurisdiction over the action to a more convenient forum state, may stay the proceedings, or may dismiss the action.

Committee Notes

1992 Amendment. Plans under rule 8.327 were deleted in the 1991 revision to the rules, but are being reinstated as "stipulations" in the 1992 revisions. This change corrects the cross-reference.

RULE 8.210. PARTIES AND PARTICIPANTS

(a) Parties. For the purpose of these rules the terms "party" and "parties" shall include the petitioner, the child, the parent(s) of the child, the department, and the guardian ad litem or the representative of the guardian ad litem program, when the program has been appointed.

(b) Participants. "Participant" means any person who is not a party but who should receive notice of hearings involving the child. Participants include foster parents or the legal custodian of the child, identified prospective parents, actual custodians of the child, grandparents entitled to notice of an adoption proceeding as provided by law, the state attorney, and any other person whose participation may be in the best interest of the child. The court may add additional participants. Participants may be granted leave by the court to be heard without the necessity of filing a motion to intervene and shall have no other rights of a party except as provided by law.

(c) Parent or Legal Custodian. For the purposes of these rules, when the phrase "parent(s) or legal custodian(s)" is used, it refers to the rights or responsibilities of the parent and, only if there is no living parent with intact parental rights, to the rights or responsibilities of the legal custodian who has assumed the role of the parent.

RULE 8.215. GUARDIAN AD LITEM

(a) Request. At any stage of the proceedings, any party may request or the court may appoint a guardian ad litem to represent any child alleged to be dependent.

(b) Appointment. The court shall appoint a guardian ad litem to represent the child in any proceeding as required by law and shall ascertain at each stage of the proceeding whether a guardian ad litem should be appointed if one has not yet been appointed.

(c) Duties and Responsibilities. The guardian ad litem shall be a responsible adult, who may or may not be an attorney, or a certified guardian ad litem program, and shall have the following responsibilities:

(1) To gather information concerning the allegations of the petition and any subsequent matters arising in the case and, unless excused by the court, to file a written report. This report shall include a summary of the guardian ad litem's findings, a statement of the wishes of the child, and the recommendations of the guardian ad litem and shall be provided to all parties and the court at least 72 hours before the hearing for which the report is prepared.

(2) To be present at all court hearings unless excused by the court.

(3) To represent the interests of the child until the jurisdiction of the court over the child terminates, or until excused by the court.

(4) To perform such other duties as are consistent with the scope of the appointment.

(d) Bond. A guardian ad litem shall not be required to post bond but shall file an acceptance of the office.

(e) Service. A guardian ad litem shall be entitled to receive service of pleadings and papers as provided by rule 8.225.

(f) Practice of Law by Lay Guardians. The duties of lay guardians shall not include the practice of law.

(g) Substitution or Discharge. The court, on its own motion or that of any party, including the child, may substitute or discharge the guardian ad litem for reasonable cause.

Committee Notes

1991 Amendment. (c)(1) This section allows a report to be submitted before any hearing, not only the disposition hearing.

RULE 8.217. ATTORNEY AD LITEM

(a) Request. At any stage of the proceedings, any party may request or the court may consider whether an attorney ad litem is necessary to represent any child alleged, or found, to be dependent, if one has not already been appointed.

(b) Appointment. The court may appoint an attorney ad litem to represent the child in any proceeding as allowed by law.

(c) Duties and Responsibilities. The attorney ad litem shall be an attorney who has completed any additional requirements as provided by law. The attorney ad litem shall have the responsibilities provided by law.

(d) Service. An attorney ad litem shall be entitled to receive and must provide service of pleadings and documents as provided by rule 8.225.

RULE 8.220. STYLE OF PLEADING AND ORDERS

All pleadings and orders shall be styled: "In the interest of ...., a child," or: "In the interest of ...., children."

RULE 8.224. PERMANENT MAILING ADDRESS

(a) Designation. On the first appearance before the court, each party shall provide a permanent mailing address to the court. The court shall advise each party that this address will be used by the court, the petitioner, and other parties for notice unless and until the party notifies the court and the petitioner, in writing, of a new address.

(b) Effect of Filing. On the filing of a permanent address designation with the court, the party then has an affirmative duty to keep the court and the petitioner informed of any address change. Any address change must be filed with the court as an amendment to the permanent address designation.

(c) Service to Permanent Mailing Address. Service of any summons, notice, pleadings, subpoenas, or other papers to the permanent mailing address on file with the court will be presumed to be appropriate service.

RULE 8.225. PROCESS, DILIGENT SEARCHES, AND SERVICE OF PLEADINGS AND PAPERS

(a) Summons and Subpoenas.

(1) Summons. Upon the filing of a dependency petition, the clerk shall issue a summons. The summons shall require the person on whom it is served to appear for a hearing at a time and place specified not less than 72 hours after service of the summons. A copy of the petition shall be attached to the summons.

(2) Subpoenas. Subpoenas for testimony before the court, for production of tangible evidence, and for taking depositions shall be issued by the clerk of the court, the court on its own motion, or any attorney of record for a party. Subpoenas may be served within the state by any person over 18 years of age who is not a party to the proceeding. In dependency and termination of parental rights proceedings, subpoenas may also be served by authorized agents of the department or the guardian ad litem. Except as otherwise required by this rule, the procedure for issuance of a subpoena by an attorney of record in a proceeding shall be as provided in the Florida Rules of Civil Procedure.

(3) Service of Summons and Other Process to Persons Residing in the State. The summons and other process shall be served upon all parties other than the petitioner as required by law. The summons and other process may be served by authorized agents of the department or the guardian ad litem.

(A) Service by publication shall not be required for dependency hearings and shall be required only for service of summons in a termination of parental rights proceeding for parents whose identities are known but whose whereabouts cannot be determined despite a diligent search. Service by publication in these circumstances shall be considered valid service.

(B) The failure to serve a party or give notice to a participant in a dependency hearing shall not affect the validity of an order of adjudication or disposition if the court finds that the petitioner has completed a diligent search that failed to ascertain the identity or location of that party.

(C) Personal appearance of any person in a hearing before the court eliminates the requirement for serving process upon that person.

(4) Service of Summons and Other Process to Persons Residing Outside of the State in Dependency Proceedings.

(A) Service of the summons and other process on parents, parties, participants, petitioners, or persons outside this state shall be in a manner reasonably calculated to give actual notice, and may be made:

(i) by personal delivery outside this state in a manner prescribed for service of process within this state;

(ii) in a manner prescribed by the law of the place in which service is made for service of process in that place in an action in any of its courts of general jurisdiction;

(iii) by any form of mail addressed to the person to be served and requesting a receipt; or

(iv) as directed by the court. Service by publication shall not be required for dependency hearings.

(B) Notice under this rule shall be served, mailed, delivered, or last published at least 20 days before any hearing in this state.

(C) Proof of service outside this state may be made by affidavit of the person who made the service or in the manner prescribed by the law of this state, the order pursuant to which the service is made, or the law of the place in which the service is made. If service is made by mail, proof may be in a receipt signed by the addressee or other evidence of delivery to the addressee.

(D) Personal appearance of any person in a hearing before the court eliminates the requirement for serving process upon that person.

(b) Diligent Search.

(1) Location Unknown. If the location of a parent is unknown and that parent has not filed a permanent address designation with the court, the petitioner shall complete a diligent search as required by law.

(2) Affidavit of Diligent Search. If the location of a parent is unknown after the diligent search has been completed, the petitioner shall file with the court an affidavit of diligent search executed by the person who made the search and inquiry.

(3) Court Review of Affidavit. The court must review the affidavit of diligent search and enter an order determining whether the petitioner has completed a diligent search as required by law. In termination of parental rights proceedings, the clerk must not certify a notice of action until the court enters an order finding that the petitioner has conducted a diligent search as required by law. In a dependency proceeding, if the court finds that the petitioner has conducted a diligent search, the court may proceed to grant the requested relief of the petitioner as to the parent whose location is unknown without further notice.

(4) Continuing Duty. After filing an affidavit of diligent search in a dependency or termination of parental rights proceeding, the petitioner, and, if the court requires, the department, are under a continuing duty to search for and attempt to serve the parent whose location is unknown until excused from further diligent search by the court. The department shall report on the results of the continuing search at each court hearing until the person is located or until further search is excused by the court.

(c) Identity of Parent Unknown.

(1) If the identity of a parent is unknown, and a petition for dependency, shelter care, or termination of parental rights is filed, the court shall conduct the inquiry required by law. The information required by law may be submitted to the court in the form of a sworn affidavit executed by a person having personal knowledge of the facts.

(2) If the court inquiry fails to identify any person as a parent or prospective parent, the court shall so find and may proceed to grant the requested relief of the petitioner as to the unknown parent without further notice.

(d) Identity and Location Determined. If an inquiry or diligent search identifies and locates any person who may be a parent or prospective parent, the court must require that notice of the hearing be provided to that person.

(e) Effect of Failure to Serve. Failure to serve parents whose identity or residence is unknown shall not affect the validity of an order of adjudication or disposition if the court finds the petitioner has completed a diligent search.

(f) Notice and Service of Pleadings and Papers.

(1) Notice of Arraignment Hearings in Dependency Cases. Notice of the arraignment hearing must be served on all parties with the summons and petition. The document containing the notice to appear in a dependency arraignment hearing must contain, in type at least as large as the balance of the document, the following or substantially similar language: "FAILURE TO PERSONALLY APPEAR AT THE ARRAIGNMENT HEARING CONSTITUTES CONSENT TO THE ADJUDICATION OF THIS CHILD (OR THESE CHILDREN) AS A DEPENDENT CHILD (OR CHILDREN) AND MAY ULTIMATELY RESULT IN LOSS OF CUSTODY OF THIS CHILD (OR THESE CHILDREN)." Any preadoptive parents of the children and all participants, including the child's foster parents and relative caregivers, must be notified of the arraignment hearing.

(2) Notice of Assessment of Child Support. Other than as part of a disposition order, if the court, on its own motion or at the request of any party, seeks to impose or enforce a child support obligation on any parent, all parties and participants are entitled to reasonable notice that child support will be addressed at a future hearing.

(3) Notice of Hearings to Participants and Parties Whose Identity or Address are Known. Any preadoptive parents, all participants, including foster parents and relative caregivers, and parties whose identity and address are known must be notified of all proceedings and hearings, unless otherwise provided by law. Notice involving emergency hearings must be that which is most likely to result in actual notice. It is the duty of the petitioner or moving party to notify any preadoptive parents, all participants, including foster parents and relative caregivers, and parties known to the petitioner or moving party of all hearings, except hearings which must be noticed by the court. Additional notice is not required if notice was provided to the parties in writing by the court or is contained in prior court orders and those orders

were provided to the participant or party. All foster or preadoptive parents must be provided at least 72 hours notice, verbally or in writing, of all proceedings or hearings relating to children in their care or children they are seeking to adopt to ensure the ability to provide input to the court. This subdivision shall not be construed to require that any foster parent, preadoptive parent, or relative caregiver be made a party to the proceedings solely on the basis of notice and a right to be heard.

(4) Service of Pleadings, Orders, and Papers. Unless the court orders otherwise, every pleading, order, and paper filed in the action after the initial petition, shall be served on each party or the party's attorney. Nothing herein shall be construed to require that a plea be in writing or that an application for witness subpoena be served.

(5) Method of Service. When service is required or permitted to be made upon a party or participant represented by an attorney, service shall be made upon the attorney unless service upon the party or participant is ordered by the court.

(A) Excusing of Service. Service is excused if the identity or residence of the party or participant is unknown and a diligent search for that person has been completed in accordance with law.

(B) Service by Electronic Mail ("e-mail"). Service of a document by e-mail is made by an e-mail sent to all addresses designated by the attorney or party with either (a) a copy of the document in PDF format attached or (b) a link to the document on a website maintained by a clerk.

(i) Service on Attorneys. Upon appearing in a proceeding, an attorney must designate a primary e-mail address and may designate no more than two secondary e-mail addresses to which service must be directed in that proceeding. Every document filed by an attorney thereafter must include the primary e-mail address of that attorney and any secondary e-mail addresses. If an attorney does not designate any e-mail address for service, documents may be served on that attorney at the e-mail address on record with The Florida Bar.

(ii) Exception to E-mail Service on Attorneys. Service by an attorney on another attorney must be made by e-mail unless the parties stipulate otherwise. Upon motion by an attorney demonstrating that the attorney has no e-mail account and lacks access to the Internet at the attorney's office, the court may excuse the attorney from the requirements of e-mail service. Service on and by an attorney excused by the court from e-mail service must be by the means provided in subdivision (c)(6) of this rule.

(iii) Service on and by Parties Not Represented by an Attorney. Any party not represented by an attorney may serve a designation of a primary e-mail address and also may designate no more than two secondary e-mail addresses to which service must be directed in that proceeding. If a party not represented by an attorney does not designate an e-mail address for service in a proceeding, service on and by that party must be by the means provided in subdivision (c)(6) of this rule.

(iv) Format of E-mail for Service. All documents served by e-mail must be attached to an e-mail message containing a subject line beginning with the words "SERVICE OF COURT DOCUMENT" in all capital letters, followed by the case number of the proceeding in which the documents are being served. The body of the e-mail must identify the court in which the proceeding is pending, the case number, the name of the initial party on each side, the title of each document served with that e-mail, and the sender's name and telephone number. Any e-mail which, together with its attachments, exceeds five megabytes (5MB) in size, must be divided and sent as separate e-mails, numbered in the subject line, no one of which may exceed 5MB in size.

(v) Time of Service. Service by e-mail is complete on the date sent and must be treated as service by mail for the computation of time. If the sender learns that the e-mail did not reach the address of the person to be served, the sender must immediately send another copy by e-mail or by a means authorized by subdivision (f)(6).

(6) Service by Other Means. In addition to, and not in lieu of, service by e-mail, service may also be made upon attorneys by any of the means specified in this subdivision. If a document is served by more than one method of service, the computation of time for any response to the served document shall be based on the method of service that provides the shortest response time. Service on and by all parties and participants who are not represented by an attorney and who do not designate an e-mail address, and on and by all attorneys excused from e-mail service, must be made by delivering a copy of the document or by mailing it to the party or participant at their permanent mailing address if one has been provided to the court or to the party, participant, or attorney at their last known address or, if no address is known, by leaving it with the clerk of the court. Service by mail is complete upon mailing. Delivery of a copy within this rule is complete upon:

(A) handing it to the attorney or to the party or participant,

(B) leaving it at the attorney's, party's or participant's office with a clerk or other person in charge thereof,

(C) if there is no one in charge, leaving it in a conspicuous place therein,

(D) if the office is closed or the person to be served has no office, leaving it at the person's usual place of abode with some person of his or her family above 15 years of age and informing such person of the contents, or

(E) transmitting it by facsimile to the attorney's, party's, or participant's office with a cover sheet containing the sender's name, firm, address, telephone number, and facsimile number, and the number of pages transmitted. When service is made by facsimile, a copy must also be served by any other method permitted by this rule. Facsimile service occurs when transmission is complete.

(F) Service by delivery shall be deemed complete on the date of delivery.

(7) Filing. All documents must be filed with the court either before service or immediately thereafter.

If the original of any bond or other document is required to be an original and is not placed in the court file or deposited with the clerk, a certified copy must be so placed by the clerk.

(8) Filing Defined. The filing of documents with the court as required by these rules must be made by filing them with the clerk, except that the judge may permit documents to be filed with the judge, in which event the judge must note the filing date before him or her on the documents and transmit them to the clerk. The date of filing is that shown on the face of the document by the judge's notation or the clerk's time stamp, whichever is earlier.

(9) Certificate of Service. When any attorney certifies in substance:

"I certify that a copy hereof has been furnished to (here insert name or names and addresses used for service) by (e-mail) (delivery) (mail) (fax) on .... (date) ....

Attorney"

the certificate must be taken as prima facie proof of such service in compliance with this rule.

(10) Service by Clerk. When the clerk is required to serve notices and other documents, the clerk may do so by e-mail or by another method permitted under subdivision (c). Service by a clerk is not required to be by e-mail.

(11) Service of Orders.

(A) A copy of all orders or judgments must be transmitted by the court or under its direction to all parties at the time of entry of the order or judgment. No service need be made on parties against whom a default has been entered except orders setting an action for trial and final judgments that must be prepared and served as provided in subdivision (c)(11)(B). The court may require that orders or judgments be prepared by a party, may require the party to furnish the court with stamped addressed envelopes for service of the order or judgment, and

may require that proposed orders and judgments be furnished to all parties before entry by the court of the order or judgment. The court may serve any order or judgment by e-mail to all attorneys who have not been excused from e-mail service and to all parties not represented by an attorney who have designated an e-mail address for service.

(B) When a final judgment is entered against a party in default, the court must mail a conformed copy of it to the party. The party in whose favor the judgment is entered must furnish the court with a copy of the judgment, unless it is prepared by the court and with the address of the party to be served. If the address is unknown, the copy need not be furnished.

(C) This subdivision is directory and a failure to comply with it does not affect the order or judgment or its finality or any proceedings arising in the action.

RULE 8.226. DETERMINATION OF PARENTHOOD

(a) In General. The court must determine the identity of all parents and prospective parents at the initial hearing in proceedings under chapter 39, Florida Statutes, as provided by law. Nothing in this rule prevents a parent or prospective parent from pursuing remedies under chapter 742, Florida Statutes. The court having jurisdiction over the dependency matter may conduct proceedings under chapter 742, Florida Statutes, either as part of the chapter 39, Florida Statutes, proceeding or in a separate action under chapter 742, Florida Statutes.

(b) Appearance of Prospective Parent.

(1) If a prospective parent appears in the chapter 39, Florida Statutes, proceeding, the court shall advise the prospective parent of the right to become a parent in the proceeding by completing a sworn affidavit of parenthood and filing the affidavit with the court or the department. This subdivision shall not apply if the court has identified both parents of the child as defined by law.

(2) If the prospective parent seeks to become a parent in the chapter 39, Florida Statutes, proceeding, the prospective parent shall complete a sworn affidavit

of parenthood and file the affidavit with the court or the department. If a party objects to the entry of the finding that the prospective parent is a parent in the proceeding, or if the court on its own motion requires further proceedings to determine parenthood, the court shall not enter an order finding parenthood until proceedings under chapter 742, Florida Statutes, have been concluded. The prospective parent shall continue to receive notice of hearings as a participant pending the proceedings under chapter 742, Florida Statutes. If no other party objects and the court does not require further proceedings to determine parenthood, the court shall enter an order finding that the prospective parent is a parent in the proceeding.

(3) If the prospective parent is uncertain about parenthood and requests further proof of parenthood, or if there is more than one prospective parent for the same child, the juvenile court may conduct proceedings under chapter 742, Florida Statutes, to determine parenthood. At the conclusion of the chapter 742, Florida Statutes, proceedings, the court shall enter an order determining parenthood.

(4) Provided that paternity has not otherwise been established by operation of law or court order, at any time prior to the court entering a finding that the prospective parent is the parent in the proceeding, the prospective parent may complete and file with the court or the department a sworn affidavit of nonpaternity declaring that the prospective parent is not the parent of the child and waiving all potential rights to the child and rights to further notices of hearing and court filings in the proceeding.

(5) If the court has identified both parents of a child as defined by law, the court shall not recognize an alleged biological parent as a parent in the proceeding until a court enters an order pursuant to law establishing the alleged biological parent as a parent in the proceeding.

RULE 8.230. PLEADINGS TO BE SIGNED

(a) **Pleading to Be Signed by Attorney.** Every written document or pleading of a party represented by an attorney shall be signed in the attorney's individual name by such attorney, whose Florida Bar number, address, and telephone number, including area code, shall be stated and who shall be duly licensed to practice law in Florida. The attorney may be required by an order of court to vouch for the authority to represent such party and to give the address of such party. Except when otherwise specifically provided by these rules or applicable statute, pleadings as such need not be verified or accompanied by affidavit.

(b) **Pleading to Be Signed by Unrepresented Party.** A party who has no attorney but who represents himself or herself shall sign a written pleading or other document to be filed and state his or her address and telephone number, including area code.

(c) **Effect of Signing Pleading.** The signature of a person shall constitute a certificate that the document or pleading has been read; that to the best of the person's knowledge, information, and belief there is good ground to support it; and that it is not interposed for delay. If a pleading or document is not signed, or is signed with intent to defeat the purpose of this rule, it may be stricken and the action may proceed as though the pleading or document had not been filed.

Committee Notes

1991 Amendment. The current rule implies that a written pleading must be filed. No written pleadings are required.

1992 Amendments. (a) and (c) The language from (a) was moved to create this new subdivision. The current rule only applies to attorneys. These requirements also should apply to nonattorneys who sign and file documents. This change conforms to proposed changes for rules 8.085 and 8.640.

RULE 8.231. PROVIDING COUNSEL TO DEPENDENT CHILDREN WITH SPECIAL NEEDS WHO HAVE A STATUTORY RIGHT TO COUNSEL

(a) **Applicability.** This rule applies to children for whom the court must appoint counsel under section 39.01305, Florida Statutes. This rule does not affect the court's authority to appoint counsel for any other child.

(b) **Duty of Court.** The court shall appoint an attorney to represent any child who has special needs as defined in section 39.01305, Florida Statutes, and who is subject to any proceeding under Chapter 39, Florida Statutes.

(c) Duties of Attorney. The attorney shall provide the child the complete range of legal services, from the removal from the home or from the initial appointment through all available appellate proceedings. With permission of the court, the attorney may arrange for supplemental or separate counsel to represent the child in appellate proceedings.

RULE 8.235. MOTIONS

(a) Motions in General. An application to the court for an order shall be made by motion which shall be in writing unless made during a hearing; shall be signed by the party making the motion or by the party's attorney; shall state with particularity the grounds therefor; and shall set forth the relief or order sought. The requirement of writing is fulfilled if the motion is stated in a written notice of the hearing of the motion or in a written report to the court for a scheduled hearing provided the notice or report are served on the parties as required by law.

(b) Motion to Dismiss. Any party may file a motion to dismiss any petition, allegations in the petition, or other pleading, setting forth the grounds on which the motion is based. If a motion to dismiss the petition is granted when a child is being sheltered under an order, the child may be continued in shelter under previous order of the court upon the representation that a new or amended petition will be filed.

(c) Sworn Motion to Dismiss. Before the adjudicatory hearing the court may entertain a motion to dismiss the petition or allegations in the petition on the ground that there are no material disputed facts and the undisputed facts do not establish a prima facie case of dependency. The facts on which such motion is based shall be specifically alleged and the motion sworn to by the party. The motion shall be filed a reasonable time before the date of the adjudicatory hearing. The opposing parties may traverse or demur to this motion. Factual matters alleged in it shall be deemed admitted unless specifically denied by the party. The motion shall be denied if the party files a written traverse that with specificity denies under oath the material fact or facts alleged in the motion to dismiss.

(d) Motion to Sever. A motion may be made for a severance of 2 or more counts of a multi-count petition, or for the severance of the cases of 2 or more children alleged to be dependent in the same petition. The court may grant motions for severance of jointly-brought cases for good cause shown.

Committee Notes

1992 Amendment. This rule allows any party to move for dismissal based on the grounds that there are no material facts in dispute and that these facts are not legally sufficient to prove dependency.

RULE 8.240. COMPUTATION, CONTINUANCE, EXTENSION, AND ENLARGEMENT OF TIME

(a) Computation. Computation of time shall be governed by Florida Rule of Judicial Administration 2.514, except for rules 8.300 and 8.305, to which rule 2.514(a)(2)(C) shall not apply and the statutory time period shall govern.

(b) Enlargement of Time. When by these rules, by a notice given under them, or by order of court an act is required or allowed to be done at or within a specified time, the court for good cause shown, within the limits established by law, and subject to the provisions of subdivision (d) of this rule, may, at any time, in its discretion (1) with or without notice, order the period enlarged if a request is made before the expiration of the period originally prescribed or as extended by a previous order, or (2) on motion made and notice after the expiration of the specified period permit the act to be done when the failure to act was the result of excusable neglect. The court may not, except as provided by law or elsewhere in these rules, extend the time for making a motion for new trial, for rehearing, or vacation of judgment, or for taking an appeal. This rule shall not be construed to apply to shelter hearings.

(c) Time for Service of Motions and Notice of Hearing. A copy of any written motion that may not be heard ex parte and a copy of the notice of hearing shall be served a reasonable time before the time specified for the hearing.

(d) Continuances and Extensions of Time.

(1) A motion for continuance, extension, or waiver of the time standards provided by law and found in this rule shall be in writing and signed by the requesting

party. On a showing of good cause, the court shall allow a motion for continuance or extension to be made ore tenus at any time during the proceedings.

(2) A motion for continuance, extension, or waiver of the time standards provided by law shall not be made in advance of the particular circumstance or need that would warrant delay of the proceedings.

(3) A motion for continuance, extension, or waiver of the time standards provided by law shall state all of the facts that the movant contends entitle the movant to a continuance, extension, or waiver of time including:

(A) the task that must be completed by the movant to preserve the rights of a party or the best interest of the child who is the subject of the proceedings;

(B) the minimum number of days absolutely necessary to complete this task; and

(C) the total number of days the proceedings have been continued at the request of any party within any 12-month period.

(4) These time limitations do not include the following:

(A) Periods of delay resulting from a continuance granted at the request of the child's counsel or the child's guardian ad litem or, if the child is of sufficient capacity to express reasonable consent, at the request of or with the consent of the child.

(B) Periods of delay because of unavailability of evidence that is material to the case if the requesting party has exercised due diligence to obtain the evidence and there are substantial grounds to believe that the evidence will be available within 30 days. However, if the requesting party is not prepared to proceed within 30 days, any other party may move for issuance of an order to show cause or the court on its own motion may impose appropriate sanctions, which may include dismissal of the petition.

(C) Periods of delay to allow the requesting party additional time to prepare the case and additional time is justified because of an exceptional circumstance.

(D) Reasonable periods of delay necessary to accomplish notice of the hearing to the parent or legal custodian.

(5) Notwithstanding subdivision (4), proceedings may not be continued or extended for more than a total of 60 days for all parties within any 12-month period. A continuance or extension of time standards beyond 60 days in any 12-month period may be granted only on a finding by the court of extraordinary circumstances and that the continuance or extension of time standards is necessary to preserve the constitutional rights of a party or that there is substantial evidence demonstrating that the child's best interests will be affirmatively harmed without the granting of a continuance or extension of time.

RULE 8.245. DISCOVERY

(a) **Scope of Discovery.** Unless otherwise limited by the court in accordance with these rules, the scope of discovery is as follows:

(1) **In General.** Parties may obtain discovery regarding any matter, not privileged, that is relevant to the subject matter of the pending action, whether it relates to the claim or defense of the party seeking discovery or the claim or defense of any other party, including the existence, description, nature, custody, condition, and location of any books, documents, or other tangible things and the identity and location of persons having knowledge of any discoverable matter. It is not ground for objection that the information sought will be inadmissible at the hearing if the information sought appears reasonably calculated to lead to the discovery of admissible evidence.

(2) **Claims of Privilege or Protection of Trial Preparation Materials.** When a party withholds information otherwise discoverable under these rules by claiming that it is privileged or subject to protection as trial preparation material, the party shall make the claim expressly and describe the nature of the document, communications, or things not produced or disclosed in a manner that, without revealing information itself privileged or protected, will allow other parties to assess the applicability of the privilege or protection.

(b) **Required Disclosure.**

(1) At any time after the filing of a shelter petition, a petition alleging a child to be a dependent child, or

a petition for termination of parental rights, on written demand of any party, the party to whom the demand is directed shall disclose and permit inspecting, copying, testing, or photographing matters material to the cause. If the child had no living parent with intact parental rights at the time the dependency allegations arose, then the person who was serving as the legal custodian of the child at that time is entitled to obtain discovery during the pendency of a shelter or dependency petition.

(2) The following information shall be disclosed by any party on demand:

(A) The names and addresses of all persons known to have information relevant to the proof or defense of the petition's allegations.

(B) The statement of any person furnished in compliance with the preceding paragraph. The term "statement" means a written statement made by this person and signed or otherwise adopted or approved by the person, or a stenographic, mechanical, electronic, or other recording, or a transcript of it, or that is a substantially verbatim recital of an oral statement made by this person to an officer or agent of the state and recorded contemporaneously with the making of the oral statement. The court may prohibit any party from introducing in evidence the material not disclosed, to secure and maintain fairness in the just determination of the cause.

(C) Any written or recorded statement and the substance of any oral statement made by the demanding party or a person alleged to be involved in the same transaction. If the number of oral statements made to any person are so numerous that, as a practical matter, it would be impossible to list the substance of all the oral statements, then the party to whom the demand is directed will disclose that person's identity and the fact that this person has knowledge of numerous statements. This disclosure will allow the demanding party to depose that person.

(D) Tangible papers or objects belonging to the demanding party that are to be used at the adjudicatory hearing.

(E) Reports or statements of experts, including results of physical or mental examinations and of scientific tests, experiments, or comparisons.

(3) The disclosures required by subdivision (a) of this rule shall be made within 10 days from the receipt of the demand for them. Disclosure may be made by allowing the requesting party to review the files of the party from whom discovery is requested after redaction of nondiscoverable information.

(c) Limitations on Disclosure.

(1) On application, the court may deny or partially restrict disclosure authorized by this rule if it finds there is a substantial risk to any person of physical harm, intimidation, bribery, economic reprisals, or unnecessary annoyance or embarrassment resulting from the disclosure, that outweighs any usefulness of the disclosure to the party requesting it.

(2) Disclosure shall not be required of legal research or of records, correspondence, or memoranda, to the extent that they contain the opinion, theories, or conclusions of the parties' attorneys or members of their legal staff.

(d) Production of Documents and Things for Inspection and Other Purposes.

(1) Request; Scope. Any party may request any other party

(A) to produce and permit the party making the request, or someone acting on the requesting party's behalf, to inspect and copy any designated documents, including writings, drawings, graphs, charts, photographs, phono-records, and other data compilations from which information can be obtained, translated, if necessary, by the party to whom the request is directed through detection devices into reasonably usable form, that constitute or contain matters within the scope of subdivision (a) and that are in the possession, custody, or control of the party to whom the request is directed; and

(B) to inspect and copy, test, or sample any tangible things that constitute or contain matters within the scope of subdivision (a) and that are in the possession, custody, or control of the party to whom the request is directed.

(2) Procedure. Without leave of court the request may be served on the petitioner after commencement of proceedings and on any other party with or after service of the summons and initial petition on that party. The request shall set forth the items to be inspected, either by individual item or category, and describe each item and category with reasonable particularity. The request shall specify a reasonable time, place, and manner of making the inspection or performing the related acts. The party to whom the request is directed shall serve a written response within 15 days after service of the request, except that a respondent may serve a response within 30 days after service of the process and initial pleading on that respondent. The court may allow a shorter or longer time. For each item or category the response shall state that inspection and related activities will be permitted as requested unless the request is objected to, in which event the reasons for the objection shall be stated. If an objection is made to part of an item or category, the part shall be specified. When producing documents, the producing party shall either produce them as they are kept in the usual course of business or shall identify them to correspond with the categories in the request. The party submitting the request may move for an order under subdivision (k) concerning any objection, failure to respond to the request, or any part of it, or failure to permit inspection as requested.

(3) Persons Not Parties. This rule does not preclude an independent action against a person not a party for production of documents and things.

(4) Filing of Documents. Unless required by the court, a party shall not file any of the documents or things produced with the response. Documents or things may be filed when they should be considered by the court in determining a matter pending before the court.

(e) Production of Documents and Things Without Deposition.

(1) Request; Scope. A party may seek inspection and copying of any documents or things within the scope of subdivision (d)(1) from a person who is not a party by issuance of a subpoena directing the production of the documents or things when the requesting party does not seek to depose the custodian or other person in possession of the documents or things.

(2) Procedure. A party desiring production under this rule shall serve notice on every other party of the intent to serve a subpoena under this rule at least 5 days before the subpoena is issued if service is by delivery and 10 days before the subpoena is issued if service is by mail. The proposed subpoena shall be attached to the notice and shall state the time, place, and method for production of the documents or things, and the name and address of the person who is to produce the documents or things, if known, and if not known, a general description sufficient to identify the person or the particular class or group to which the person belongs; shall include a designation of the items to be produced; and shall state that the person who will be asked to produce the documents or things has the right to object to the production under this rule and that the person will not be required to surrender the documents or things. A copy of the notice and proposed subpoena shall not be furnished to the person on whom the subpoena is to be served. If any party serves an objection to production under this rule within 10 days of service of the notice, the documents or things shall not be produced under this rule and relief may be obtained under subdivision (g).

(3) Subpoena. If no objection is made by a party under subdivision (e)(2), an attorney of record in the action may issue a subpoena or the party desiring production shall deliver to the clerk for issuance a subpoena and a certificate of counsel or pro se party that no timely objection has been received from any party. The clerk shall issue the subpoena and deliver it to the party desiring production. The subpoena shall be identical to the copy attached to the notice, shall specify that no testimony may be taken, and shall require only production of the documents or things specified in it. The subpoena may give the recipient an option to deliver or mail legible copies of the documents or things to the party serving the subpoena. The person on whom the subpoena is served may condition the preparation of copies on the payment in advance of the reasonable costs of preparing the copies. The subpoena shall require production only in the county of the residence of the custodian or other person in possession of the documents or things or in the county where the documents or things are located or where the custodian or person in possession usually conducts business. If the person on whom the subpoena is served objects at any time before the production of the documents or things, the documents or things shall not be produced under this rule, and relief may be obtained under subdivision (g).

(4) Copies Furnished. If the subpoena is complied with by delivery or mailing of copies as provided in subdivision (e)(3), the party receiving the copies shall furnish a legible copy of each item furnished to any other party who requests it on the payment of the reasonable cost of preparing the copies.

(5) Independent Action. This rule does not affect the right of any party to bring an independent action for production of documents and things.

(f) Protective Orders. On motion by a party or by the person from whom discovery is sought, and for good cause shown, the court in which the action is pending may make any order to protect a party or person from annoyance, embarrassment, oppression, or undue burden or expense that justice requires, including one or more of the following:

(1) that the discovery not be had;

(2) that the discovery may be had only on specified terms and conditions, including a designation of the time or place;

(3) that the discovery may be had only by a method of discovery other than that selected by the party seeking discovery;

(4) that certain matters not be inquired into, or that the scope of the discovery be limited to certain matters;

(5) that discovery be conducted with no one present except persons designated by the court;

(6) that a deposition after being sealed be opened only by order of the court;

(7) that confidential research or information not be disclosed or be disclosed only in a designated way; and

(8) that the parties simultaneously file specified documents or information enclosed in sealed envelopes to be opened as directed by the court.

If the motion for a protective order is denied in whole or in part, the court may, on such terms and conditions as are just, order that any party or person provide or permit discovery.

(g) Depositions.

(1) Time and Place.

(A) At any time after the filing of the petition alleging a child to be dependent or a petition for termination of parental rights, any party may take the deposition on oral examination of any person who may have information relevant to the allegations of the petition.

(B) The deposition shall be taken in a building in which the adjudicatory hearing may be held, in another place agreed on by the parties, or where the trial court may designate by special or general order. A resident of the state may be required to attend an examination only in the county in which he or she resides, is employed, or regularly transacts business in person.

(2) Procedure.

(A) The party taking the deposition shall give written notice to each other party. The notice shall state the time and place the deposition is to be taken and the name of each person to be examined.

(B) Subpoenas for taking depositions shall be issued by the clerk of the court, the court, or any attorney of record for a party.

(C) After notice to the parties the court, for good cause shown, may extend or shorten the time and may change the place of taking.

(D) Except as otherwise provided by this rule, the procedure for taking the deposition, including the scope of the examination and obtaining protective orders, shall be the same as that provided by the Florida Rules of Civil Procedure.

(3) Use of Deposition. Any deposition taken under this rule may be used at any hearing covered by these rules by any party for the following purposes:

(A) For the purpose of impeaching the testimony of the deponent as a witness.

(B) For testimonial evidence, when the deponent, whether or not a party, is unavailable to testify because of one or more of the following reasons:

(i) He or she is dead.

(ii) He or she is at a greater distance than 100 miles from the place of hearing or is out of the state, unless it appears that the absence of the witness was procured by the party offering the deposition.

(iii) The party offering the deposition has been unable to procure the attendance of the witness by subpoena.

(iv) He or she is unable to attend or testify because of age, illness, infirmity, or imprisonment.

(v) It has been shown on application and notice that such exceptional circumstances exist as to make it desirable, in the interest of justice and with due regard to the importance of presenting the testimony of witnesses orally in open court, to allow the deposition to be used.

(vi) The witness is an expert or skilled witness.

(4) Use of Part of Deposition. If only part of a deposition is offered in evidence by a party, an adverse party may require the party to introduce any other part that in fairness ought to be considered with the part introduced, and any party may introduce any other parts.

(5) Refusal to Obey Subpoena. A person who refuses to obey a subpoena served on the person for the taking of a deposition may be adjudged in contempt of the court from which the subpoena issued.

(6) Limitations on Use. Except as provided in subdivision (3), no deposition shall be used or read in evidence when the attendance of the witness can be procured. If it appears to the court that any person whose deposition has been taken has absented himself or herself by procurement, inducements, or threats by or on behalf of any party, the deposition shall not be read in evidence on behalf of that party.

(h) Perpetuating Testimony Before Action or Pending Appeal.

(1) Before Action.

(A) Petition. A person who desires to perpetuate the person's own testimony or that of another person regarding any matter that may be cognizable in any court of this state may file a verified petition in the circuit court in the county of the residence of any expected adverse party. The petition shall be titled in the name of the petitioner and shall show:

(i) that the petitioner expects to be a party to an action cognizable in a court of Florida, but is presently unable to bring it or cause it to be brought;

(ii) the subject matter of the expected action and the person's interest in it;

(iii) the facts that the person desires to establish by the proposed testimony and the reasons for desiring to perpetuate it;

(iv) the names or a description of the persons expected to be adverse parties and their names and addresses so far as known; and

(v) the names and addresses of the persons to be examined and the substance of the testimony expected to be elicited from each and asking for an order authorizing the petitioner to take the deposition of the persons to be examined named in the petition for the purpose of perpetuating their testimony.

(B) Notice and Service. The petitioner shall serve a notice on each person named in the petition as an expected adverse party, with a copy of the petition, stating that the petitioner will apply to the court at a time and place in the notice for an order described in the petition. At least 20 days before the date of the hearing, the notice shall be served either within or without the county in the manner provided by law for serving of summons. However, if service cannot with due diligence be made on any expected adverse party named in the petition, the court may order service by publication or otherwise and shall appoint an attorney for persons not served in the manner provided by law for service of summons. The attorney shall represent the adverse party and, if he or she is not otherwise represented, shall cross-examine the deponent.

(C) Order and Examination. If the court is satisfied that the perpetuation of the testimony may prevent a failure or delay of justice, it shall make an order designating or describing the persons whose depositions may be taken and specifying the subject matter of the examination and whether the deposition shall be taken on oral examination or written interrogatories. The deposition may then be taken in accordance with these rules and the court may make orders in accordance with the requirements of these rules. For the purpose of applying these rules to depositions for perpetuating testimony, each reference in them to the court in which the action is pending shall be deemed to refer to the court in which the petition for the deposition was filed.

(D) Use of Deposition. If a deposition to perpetuate testimony is taken under these rules, it may be used in any action involving the same subject matter subsequently brought in any court of Florida in accordance with the provisions of subdivision (g)(3).

(2) Pending Appeal. If an appeal has been taken from a judgment of any court or before the taking of an appeal if the time for it has not expired, the court in which the judgment was rendered may allow the taking of the depositions of witnesses to perpetuate their testimony for use in further proceedings in the court. In such case, the party who desires to perpetuate the testimony may move for leave to take the deposition on the same notice and service as if the action were pending in the court. The motion shall show the names and addresses of persons to be examined, the substance of the testimony expected to be elicited from each, and the reasons for perpetuating the testimony. If the court finds that the perpetuation is proper to avoid a failure or delay in justice, it may

make orders as provided for by this rule and the deposition may then be taken and used in the same manner and under the same conditions as are prescribed in these rules for depositions taken in actions pending in the court.

(3) Perpetuation Action. This rule does not limit the power of a court to entertain an action to perpetuate testimony.

(i) Rules Governing Depositions of Children Under 16.

(1) The taking of a deposition of a child witness or victim under the age of 16 may be limited or precluded by the court for good cause shown.

(2) The court after proper notice to all parties and an evidentiary hearing, based on good cause shown, may set conditions for the deposition of a child under the age of 16 including:

(A) designating the place of the deposition;

(B) designating the length of time of the deposition;

(C) permitting or prohibiting the attendance of any person at the deposition;

(D) requiring the submission of questions before the examination;

(E) choosing a skilled interviewer to pose the questions;

(F) limiting the number or scope of the questions to be asked; or

(G) imposing any other conditions the court feels are necessary for the protection of the child.

(3) Good cause is shown based on, but not limited to, one or more of the following considerations:

(A) The age of the child.

(B) The nature of the allegations.

(C) The relationship between the child victim and the alleged abuser.

(D) The child has undergone previous interviews for the purposes of criminal or civil proceedings that were recorded either by videotape or some other manner of recording and the requesting party has access to the recording.

(E) The examination would adversely affect the child.

(F) The manifest best interests of the child require the limitations or restrictions.

(4) The court, in its discretion, may order the consolidation of the taking of depositions of a child under the age of 16 when the child is the victim or witness in a pending proceeding arising from similar facts or circumstances.

(j) Supplemental Discovery. If, subsequent to compliance with these rules, a party discovers additional witnesses, evidence, or material that the party would have been under a duty to disclose or produce at the time of the previous compliance, the party shall promptly disclose or produce such witnesses, evidence, or material in the same manner as required under these rules for initial discovery.

(k) Sanctions.

(1) If at any time during the course of the proceedings, it is brought to the attention of the court that a party has failed to comply with an applicable discovery rule or with an order issued under an applicable discovery rule, the court may:

(A) order the party to comply with the discovery or inspection of materials not previously disclosed or produced;

(B) grant a continuance;

(C) order a new hearing;

(D) prohibit the party from calling a witness not disclosed or introducing in evidence the material not disclosed; or

(E) enter an order that it deems just under the circumstances.

(2) Willful violation by counsel of an applicable discovery rule or an order issued under it may subject counsel to appropriate sanction by the court.

Committee Notes

1991 Amendment. (a)(1) Termination of parental rights proceedings have been added to discovery procedures.

RULE 8.250. EXAMINATIONS, EVALUATION, AND TREATMENT

(a) Child. Mental or physical examination of a child may be obtained as provided by law.

(b) Parent, Legal Custodian, or Other Person who has Custody or is Requesting Custody. At any time after the filing of a shelter, dependency, or termination of parental rights petition, or after an adjudication of dependency or a finding of dependency when adjudication is withheld, when the mental or physical condition, including the blood group, of a parent, legal custodian, or other person who has custody or is requesting custody of a child is in controversy, any party may request the court to order the person to submit to a physical or mental examination or a substance abuse evaluation or assessment by a qualified professional. The order may be made only on good cause shown and after notice to the person to be examined and to all parties and shall specify the time, place, manner, conditions, and scope of the examination and the person or persons by whom it is to be made. The person whose examination is sought may, after receiving notice of the request for an examination, request a hearing seeking to quash the request. The court may, on its own motion, order a parent, legal custodian, or other person who has custody or is requesting custody to undergo such evaluation, treatment, or counseling activities as authorized by law.

Committee Notes

1991 Amendment. This rule allows any party to request an evaluation but provides a mechanism for a hearing to quash the request.

RULE 8.255. GENERAL PROVISIONS FOR HEARINGS

(a) Presence of Counsel. The department must be represented by an attorney at every stage of these proceedings.

(b) Presence of Child.

(1) The child has a right to be present at all hearings.

(2) If the child is present at the hearing, the court may excuse the child from any portion of the hearing when the court determines that it would not be in the child's best interest to remain.

(3) If a child is not present at a hearing, the court shall inquire and determine the reason for the absence of the child. The court shall determine whether it is in the best interest of the child to conduct the hearing without the presence of the child or to continue the hearing to provide the child an opportunity to be present at the hearing.

(4) Any party may file a motion to require or excuse the presence of the child.

(c) Separate Examinations. The child and the parents, caregivers, or legal custodians of the child may be examined separately and apart from each other.

(d) Examination of Child; Special Protections.

(1) Testimony by Child. A child may be called to testify in open court by any party to the proceeding or the court, and may be examined or cross-examined.

(2) In-Camera Examination.

(A) On motion and hearing, the child may be examined by the court outside the presence of other parties as provided by law. The court shall assure that proceedings are recorded, unless otherwise stipulated by the parties.

(B) The motion may be filed by any party or the trial court on its own motion.

(C) The court shall make specific written findings of fact, on the record, as to the basis for its ruling. These findings may include but are not limited to:

(i) the age of the child;

(ii) the nature of the allegation;

(iii) the relationship between the child and the alleged abuser;

(iv) the likelihood that the child would suffer emotional or mental harm if required to testify in open court;

(v) whether the child's testimony is more likely to be truthful if given outside the presence of other parties;

(vi) whether cross-examination would adversely affect the child; and

(vii) the manifest best interest of the child.

(D) The child may be called to testify by means of closed-circuit television or by videotaping as provided by law.

(e) Invoking the Rule. Before the examination of any witness the court may, and on the request of any party shall, exclude all other witnesses. The court may cause witnesses to be kept separate and to be prevented from communicating with each other until all are examined.

(f) Continuances. As permitted by law, the court may grant a continuance before or during a hearing for good cause shown by any party.

(g) Record. A record of the testimony in all hearings shall be made by an official court reporter, a court-approved stenographer, or a recording device.

The records of testimony shall be preserved as required by law. Official records of testimony shall be transcribed only on order of the court.

(h) Notice. When these rules do not require a specific notice, all parties will be given reasonable notice of any hearing.

(i) Advising Parents. At any hearing when it has been determined that reunification is not a viable alternative, and prior to the filing of the petition for termination of parental rights, the court shall advise the parent of the availability of private placement of the child with an adoption entity as defined in Chapter 63, Florida Statutes.

Committee Notes

1991 Amendment. (b) This change allows a child to be present instead of mandating the child's presence when the child's presence would not be in his or her best interest. The court is given the discretion to determine the need for the child to be present.

1992 Amendment. This change was made to reflect a moderated standard for in camera examination of a child less rigid than the criminal law standard adopted by the committee in the 1991 rule revisions.

2005 Amendment. Subdivision (i) was deleted because provisions for general masters were transferred to rule 8.257.

RULE 8.257. GENERAL MAGISTRATES

(a) Appointment. Judges of the circuit court may appoint as many general magistrates from among the members of The Florida Bar in the circuit as the judges find necessary, and the general magistrates shall continue in office until removed by the court. The order of appointment shall be recorded. Every person appointed as a general magistrate shall take the oath required of officers by the Constitution and the oath shall be recorded before the magistrate discharges any duties of that office.

(b) Referral.

(1) Consent. No matter shall be heard by a general magistrate without an appropriate order of referral and the consent to the referral of all parties. Consent, as defined in this rule, to a specific referral, once given, cannot be withdrawn without good cause shown before the hearing on the merits of the matter referred. Consent may be express or implied in accordance with the requirements of this rule.

(2) Objection. Objection. A written objection to the referral to a general magistrate must be filed within 10 days of the service of the order of referral. If the time set for the hearing is less than 10 days after service of the order of referral, the objection must be filed before commencement of the hearing. Failure to file a written objection within the applicable time period is deemed to be consent to the order of referral.

(3) Order.

(A) The order of referral shall contain the following language in bold type:

A REFERRAL TO A GENERAL MAGISTRATE REQUIRES THE CONSENT OF ALL PARTIES. YOU ARE ENTITLED TO HAVE THIS MATTER HEARD BEFORE A JUDGE. IF YOU DO NOT WANT TO HAVE THIS MATTER HEARD BEFORE THE GENERAL MAGISTRATE, YOU MUST FILE A WRITTEN OBJECTION TO THE REFERRAL WITHIN 10 DAYS OF THE TIME OF SERVICE OF THIS ORDER. IF THE TIME SET FOR THE HEARING IS LESS THAN 10 DAYS AFTER THE SERVICE OF THIS ORDER, THE OBJECTION MUST BE MADE BEFORE THE HEARING. FAILURE TO FILE A WRITTEN OBJECTION WITHIN THE APPLICABLE TIME PERIOD IS DEEMED TO BE A CONSENT TO THE REFERRAL.

REVIEW OF THE REPORT AND RECOMMENDATIONS MADE BY THE GENERAL MAGISTRATE SHALL BE BY EXCEPTIONS AS PROVIDED IN FLORIDA RULE OF JUVENILE PROCEDURE 8.257(f). A RECORD, WHICH INCLUDES A TRANSCRIPT OF PROCEEDINGS, ELECTRONIC RECORDING OF PROCEEDINGS, OR STIPULATION BY THE PARTIES OF THE EVIDENCE CONSIDERED BY THE GENERAL MAGISTRATE AT THE PROCEEDINGS, WILL BE REQUIRED TO SUPPORT THE EXCEPTIONS.

(B) The order of referral shall state with specificity the matter or matters being referred. The order of referral shall also state whether electronic recording or a court reporter is provided by the court.

(4) Setting Hearing. When a referral is made to a general magistrate, any party or the general magistrate may set the action for hearing.

(c) General Powers and Duties. Every general magistrate shall perform all of the duties that pertain to the office according to the practice in chancery and rules of court and under the direction of the court. A general magistrate shall be empowered to administer oaths and conduct hearings, which may include the taking of evidence. All grounds for disqualification of a judge shall apply to general magistrates.

(d) Hearings.

(1) The general magistrate shall assign a time and place for proceedings as soon as reasonably possible after the referral is made and give notice to each of the parties either directly or by directing counsel to file and serve a notice of hearing. If any party fails to appear, the general magistrate may proceed ex parte or may adjourn the proceeding to a future day, giving notice of the adjournment to the absent party. The general magistrate shall proceed with reasonable diligence in every referral and with the least delay practicable. Any party may apply to the court for an order to the general magistrate to speed the proceedings and to make the report and to certify to the court the reason for any delay.

(2) The general magistrate shall take testimony and establish a record which may be by electronic means as provided by Florida Rule of Judicial Administration 2.535(g)(3) or by a court reporter. The parties may not waive this requirement.

(3) The general magistrate shall have authority to examine under oath the parties and all witnesses on all matters contained in the referral, to require production of all books, papers, writings, vouchers, and other documents applicable to it, and to examine on oath orally all witnesses produced by the parties. The general magistrate may take all actions concerning evidence that can be taken by the circuit court and in the same manner. The general magistrate shall have the same powers as a circuit judge to use communications equipment as defined and regulated by Florida Rule of Judicial Administration 2.530.

(4) The notice or order setting a matter for hearing shall state whether electronic recording or a court reporter is provided by the court. If the court provides electronic recording, the notice shall also state that any party may provide a court reporter at that party's expense, subject to the court's approval.

(e) Report.

(1) The general magistrate shall file a report that includes findings of fact, conclusions of law, and recommendations and serve copies on all parties. If a court reporter was present, the report shall contain the name and address of the reporter.

(2) The report and recommendations shall contain the following language in bold type:

SHOULD YOU WISH TO SEEK REVIEW OF THE REPORT AND RECOMMENDATIONS MADE BY THE GENERAL MAGISTRATE, YOU MUST FILE EXCEPTIONS WITHIN 10 DAYS OF SERVICE OF THE REPORT AND RECOMMENDATIONS IN ACCORDANCE WITH FLORIDA RULE OF JUVENILE PROCEDURE 8.257(f). YOU WILL BE REQUIRED TO PROVIDE THE COURT WITH A RECORD SUFFICIENT TO SUPPORT YOUR EXCEPTIONS WITHIN 10 DAYS OF SERVICE OF THE REPORT AND RECOMMENDATIONS OR YOUR EXCEPTIONS WILL BE DENIED. A RECORD ORDINARILY INCLUDES A TRANSCRIPT OF PROCEEDINGS, ELECTRONIC RECORDING OF PROCEEDINGS, OR STIPULATION BY THE PARTIES OF THE EVIDENCE CONSIDERED BY THE GENERAL MAGISTRATE AT THE PROCEEDINGS. THE PERSON SEEKING REVIEW MUST HAVE THE TRANSCRIPT PREPARED FOR THE COURT'S REVIEW.

(f) Exceptions. The parties may file exceptions to the report within 10 days from the time it is served on them. Any party may file cross-exceptions within 5 days from the service of the exceptions. However, the filing of cross-exceptions shall not delay the hearing on the exceptions unless good cause is shown. If no exceptions are filed within that period, the court shall take appropriate action on the report. If exceptions are filed, they shall be heard on reasonable notice by either party or the court.

(g) Record.

(1) For the purpose of the hearing on exceptions, a record, substantially in conformity with this rule, shall be provided to the court by the party seeking review. The record shall consist of:

(A) the court file;

(B) all depositions and evidence presented to the general magistrate; and

(C) the transcript of the proceedings, electronic recording of the proceedings, or stipulation by the parties of the evidence considered by the general magistrate at the proceedings.

(2) The transcript of the proceedings, electronic recording of the proceedings, or stipulation by the parties of the evidence considered by the general magistrate at the proceedings, if any, shall be delivered to the judge and provided to all other parties not less than 48 hours before the hearing on exceptions.

(3) If less than a full transcript or electronic recording of the proceedings taken before the general magistrate is ordered prepared by the excepting party, that party shall promptly file a notice setting forth the portions of the transcript or electronic recording that have been ordered. The responding party shall be permitted to designate any additional portions of the transcript or electronic recording necessary to the adjudication of the issues raised in the exceptions or cross-exceptions.

(4) The cost of the original and all copies of the transcript or electronic recording of the proceedings shall be borne initially by the party seeking review. Should any portion of the transcript or electronic recording be required as a result of a designation filed by the responding party, the party making the designation shall bear the initial cost of the additional transcript or electronic recording.

(h) Prohibition on Magistrate Presiding over Certain Hearings. Notwithstanding the provisions of this rule, a general magistrate shall not preside over a shelter hearing under section 39.402, Florida Statutes, an adjudicatory hearing under section 39.507, Florida Statutes, or an adjudicatory hearing under section 39.809, Florida Statutes.

RULE 8.260. ORDERS

(a) General Requirements. All orders of the court must be reduced to writing as soon after they are entered as is consistent with orderly procedure, and must contain specific findings of fact and conclusions of law, and must be signed by the judge as provided by law.

(b) Transmittal to Parties. A copy of all orders must be transmitted by the court or under its direction to all parties at the time of entry of the order.

(c) Other Options. The court may require

(1) that orders be prepared by a party;

(2) that the party serve the order; and

(3) on a case-by-case basis, that proposed orders be furnished to all parties before entry of the order by the court.

(d) Precedence of Orders. Orders of the circuit court hearing dependency matters must be filed in any dissolution or other custody action or proceeding involving the same child. These orders must take precedence over other orders affecting the placement of, access to, parental time with, adoption of, or parental rights and responsibilities for the same minor child, unless jurisdiction has been terminated. These orders may be filed under seal and need not be open to inspection by the public.

RULE 8.265. MOTION FOR REHEARING

(a) Basis. After the court has entered an order, any party may move for rehearing upon one or more of the following grounds:

(1) That the court erred in the decision of any matter of law arising during the hearing.

(2) That a party did not receive a fair and impartial hearing.

(3) That any party required to be present at the hearing was not present.

(4) That there exists new and material evidence, which, if introduced at the hearing would probably have changed the court's decision and could not with reasonable diligence have been discovered before and produced at the hearing.

(5) That the court is without jurisdiction of the proceeding.

(6) That the judgment is contrary to the law and evidence.

(b) Time and Method.

(1) A motion for rehearing may be made and ruled upon immediately after the court announces its judgment but must be made within 10 days of the entry of the order.

(2) If the motion is made in writing, it shall be served as provided in these rules for service of other pleadings.

(3) A motion for rehearing shall not toll the time for the taking of an appeal. The court shall rule on the motion for rehearing within 10 days of filing or it is deemed denied.

(c) Court Action.

(1) A rehearing may be granted to all or any of the parties on all or any part of the issues. All orders granting a rehearing shall state the specific issues to be reheard.

(2) If the motion for rehearing is granted the court may vacate or modify the order or any part of it and allow additional proceedings as it deems just. It may enter a new judgment, and may order or continue the child in a shelter or out-of-home placement pending further proceedings.

(3) The court on its own initiative may vacate or modify any order within the time limitation provided in subdivision (b).

RULE 8.270. RELIEF FROM JUDGMENTS OR ORDERS

(a) Clerical Mistakes. Clerical mistakes in judgments, orders, or other parts of the record and errors therein arising from oversight or omission may be corrected by the court at any time on its own initiative or on motion of any party, after such notice, if any, as the court orders. During the pendency of an appeal such mistakes may be so corrected before the record on appeal is docketed in the appellate court and thereafter while the appeal is pending may be so corrected with leave of the appellate court.

(b) Extraordinary Relief. On motion and upon such terms as are just, the court may relieve a party or the party's legal representative from an order, judgment, or proceeding for the following reasons:

(1) Mistake, inadvertence, surprise, or excusable neglect.

(2) Newly discovered evidence which by due diligence could not have been discovered in time to move for rehearing.

(3) Fraud (intrinsic or extrinsic), misrepresentation, or other misconduct of any other party.

(4) That the order or judgment or any part thereof is void.

The motion shall be made within a reasonable time, and for reasons (1), (2), and (3) not more than 1 year after the judgment, order, or proceeding was taken.

(c) Limitation. After the court loses jurisdiction of the cause, as provided by law, a motion for relief of judgment or order under subdivision (b) shall not be heard.

RULE 8.276. APPEAL PROCEDURES

Florida Rule of Appellate Procedure 9.146 generally governs appeals in juvenile dependency and termination of parental rights cases.

RULE 8.285. CRIMINAL CONTEMPT

(a) Direct Contempt. A contempt may be punished summarily if the court saw or heard the conduct constituting the contempt committed in the actual presence of the court. The judgment of guilt of contempt shall include a recital of those facts upon which the adjudication of guilt is based. Prior to the adjudication of guilt the court shall inform the person accused of the accusation and inquire as to whether there is any cause to show why he or she should not be adjudged guilty of contempt by the court and sentenced. The accused shall be given the opportunity to present evidence of excusing or mitigating circumstances. The judgment shall be signed by the court and entered of record. Sentence shall be pronounced in open court.

(b) Indirect Contempt. An indirect contempt shall be prosecuted in the following manner:

(1) Order to Show Cause. The court on its own motion or upon affidavit of any person having knowledge of the facts may issue and sign an order directed to the one accused of contempt, stating the essential facts constituting the contempt charged and requiring the accused to appear before the court to show cause why he or she should not be held in contempt of court. The order shall specify the time and place of the hearing, with a reasonable time allowed for the preparation of a defense after service of the order on the one accused. It shall be served in the same manner as a summons. Nothing herein shall be construed to prevent the one accused of contempt from waiving the service of process.

(2) Motions; Answer. The accused, personally or by counsel, may move to dismiss the order to show cause, move for a statement of particulars, or answer such order by way of explanation or defense. All motions and the answer shall be in writing unless specified otherwise by the court. The accused's omission to file a motion or answer shall not be deemed an admission of guilt of the contempt charged.

(3) Order of Arrest; Bail. The court may issue an order of arrest of the one accused of contempt if the court has reason to believe the accused will not appear in response to the order to show cause. The accused shall be entitled to bail in the manner provided by law in criminal cases.

(4) Arraignment; Hearing. The accused may be arraigned at the hearing, or prior thereto upon request.

A hearing to determine the guilt or innocence of the accused shall follow a plea of not guilty. The court may conduct a hearing without assistance of counsel or may be assisted by the state attorney or by an attorney appointed for the purpose. The accused is entitled to be represented by counsel, have compulsory process for the attendance of witnesses, and may testify in his or her own defense. All issues of law and fact shall be determined by the court.

(5) Disqualification of the Judge. If the contempt charged involves disrespect to or criticism of a judge, the judge shall be disqualified by the chief judge of the circuit.

(6) Verdict; Judgment. At the conclusion of the hearing the court shall sign and enter of record a judgment of guilty or not guilty. There should be included in a judgment of guilty a recital of the facts constituting the contempt of which the accused has been found and adjudicated guilty.

(7) Sentence. Prior to the pronouncement of sentence the court shall inform the accused of the accusation and judgment against him or her and inquire as to whether there is any cause to show why sentence should not be pronounced. The accused shall be afforded the opportunity to present evidence of mitigating circumstances. The sentence shall be pronounced in open court and in the presence of the one found guilty of contempt.

RULE 8.286. CIVIL CONTEMPT

(a) Applicability. This rule governs indirect civil contempt proceedings in matters related to juvenile dependency. The use of civil contempt sanctions under this rule must be limited to those used to compel compliance with a court order or to compensate a movant for losses sustained as a result of a contemnor's willful failure to comply with a court order. Contempt sanctions intended to punish an offender or to vindicate the authority of the court are criminal in nature and are governed by rule 8.285.

(b) Motion and Notice. Civil contempt may be initiated by motion. The motion must recite the essential facts constituting the acts alleged to be contemptuous. No civil contempt may be imposed without notice to the alleged contemnor and without providing the alleged contemnor with an opportunity to be heard. The civil contempt motion and notice of hearing may be served by mail provided notice by mail is reasonably calculated to apprise the alleged contemnor of the pendency of the proceedings. The notice must specify the time and place of the hearing and must contain the following language: "FAILURE TO APPEAR AT THE HEARING MAY RESULT IN THE COURT ISSUING A WRIT OF BODILY ATTACHMENT FOR YOUR ARREST. IF YOU ARE ARRESTED, YOU MAY BE HELD IN JAIL UP TO 48 HOURS BEFORE A HEARING IS HELD."

(c) Hearing. In any civil contempt hearing, after the court makes an express finding that the alleged contemnor had notice of the motion and hearing:

(1) The court shall determine whether the movant has established that a prior order was entered and that the alleged contemnor has failed to comply with all or part of the prior order.

(2) If the court finds the movant has established all of the requirements in subdivision (c)(1) of this rule, the court must,

(A) if the alleged contemnor is present, determine whether the alleged contemnor had the present ability to comply with the prior court order; or

(B) if the alleged contemnor fails to appear, set a reasonable purge based on the circumstances of the parties.

The court may issue a writ of bodily attachment and direct that, upon execution of the writ of bodily attachment, the alleged contemnor be brought before the court within 48 hours for a hearing on whether the alleged contemnor has the present ability to comply with the prior court order and, if so, whether the failure to comply is willful.

(d) Order and Sanctions. After hearing the testimony and evidence presented, the court must enter a written order granting or denying the motion for contempt.

(1) An order finding the alleged contemnor to be in contempt must contain a finding that a prior order was entered, that the alleged contemnor has failed to comply with the prior court order, that the alleged contemnor had the present ability to comply, and that the alleged contemnor willfully failed to comply with the prior court order. The order must contain a recital of the facts on which these findings are based.

(2) If the court grants the motion for contempt, the court may impose appropriate sanctions to obtain compliance with the order including incarceration, attorneys' fees and costs, compensatory or coercive fines, and any other coercive sanction or relief permitted by law provided the order includes a purge provision as set forth in subdivision (e) of this rule.

(e) Purge. If the court orders incarceration, a coercive fine, or any other coercive sanction for failure to comply with a prior order, the court must set conditions for purge of the contempt, based on the contemnor's present ability to comply. The court must include in its order a separate affirmative finding that the contemnor has the present ability to comply with the purge and the factual basis for that finding. The court may grant the contemnor a reasonable time to comply with the purge conditions. If the court orders incarceration but defers incarceration for more than 48 hours to allow the contemnor a reasonable time to comply with the purge conditions, and the contemnor fails to comply within the time provided, the movant must file an affidavit of noncompliance with the court. The court then may issue a writ of bodily attachment. Upon incarceration, the contemnor must be brought before the court within 48 hours for a determination of whether the contemnor continues to have the present ability to comply with the purge.

(f) Review after Incarceration. Notwithstanding the provisions of this rule, at any time after a contemnor is incarcerated, the court on its own motion or motion of any party may review the contemnor's present ability to comply with the purge and the duration of incarceration and modify any prior orders.

(g) Other Relief. When there is a failure to comply with a court order but the failure is not willful, nothing in this rule shall be construed as precluding the court from granting such relief as may be appropriate under the circumstances.

RULE 8.290. DEPENDENCY MEDIATION

(a) Definitions. The following definitions apply to this rule:

(1) "Dependency matters" means proceedings arising under Chapter 39, Florida Statutes.

(2) "Dependency mediation" means mediation of dependency matters.

(3) "Mediation" means a process whereby a neutral third person called a mediator acts to encourage and facilitate the resolution of a dispute between two or more parties. It is an informal and nonadversarial process with the objective of helping the disputing parties reach a mutually acceptable and voluntary agreement. In mediation, decision-making authority rests with the parties. The role of the mediator includes, but is not limited to, assisting the parties in identifying issues, fostering joint problem-solving, and exploring settlement alternatives.

(b) Applicability. This rule applies only to mediation of dependency matters.

(c) Compliance with Statutory Time Requirements. Dependency mediation shall be conducted in compliance with the statutory time requirements for dependency matters.

(d) Referral. Except as provided by this rule, all matters and issues described in subdivision (a)(1) may be referred to mediation. All referrals to mediation shall be in written form, shall advise the parties of their right to counsel, and shall set a date for hearing before the court to review the progress of the mediation. The mediator or mediation program shall be appointed by the court or stipulated to by the parties. If the court refers the matter to mediation, the mediation order shall address all applicable provisions of this rule. The mediation order shall be served on all parties and on counsel under the provisions of the Florida Rules of Juvenile Procedure.

(e) Appointment of the Mediator.

(1) Court Appointment. The court, in the order of referral to mediation, shall appoint a certified dependency mediator selected by rotation or by such other procedures as may be adopted by administrative order of the chief judge in the circuit in which the action is pending.

(2) Party Stipulation. Within 10 days of the filing of the order of referral to mediation, the parties may agree upon a stipulation with the court designating:

(A) another certified dependency mediator, other than a senior judge presiding as a judge in that circuit, to replace the one selected by the judge; or

(B) a mediator, other than a senior judge, who is not certified as a mediator but who, in the opinion of the parties and upon review by the presiding judge, is otherwise qualified by training or experience to mediate all or some of the issues in the particular case.

(f) Fees. Dependency mediation referrals may be made to a mediator or mediation program that charges a fee. Any order of referral to a mediator or mediation program charging a fee shall advise the parties that they may timely object to mediation on grounds of financial hardship. On the objection of a party or the court's own motion, the court may, after considering the objecting party's ability to pay and any other pertinent information, reduce or eliminate the fee.

(g) Objection to Mediation. Within 10 days of the filing of the order of referral to mediation, any party or participant ordered to mediation may make a written objection to the court about the order of referral if good cause for such objection exists. If a party objects, mediation shall not be conducted until the court rules on the objection.

(h) Scheduling. The mediation conference may be held at any stage of the proceedings. Unless otherwise scheduled by the court, the mediator or the mediation program shall schedule the mediation conference.

(i) Disqualification of the Mediator. Any party may move to enter an order disqualifying a mediator for good cause. If the court rules that a mediator is disqualified from mediating a case, an order shall be entered with the name of a qualified replacement. Nothing in this provision shall preclude mediators from disqualifying themselves or refusing any assignment.

(j) Substitute Mediator. If a mediator agreed upon by the parties or appointed by a court cannot serve, a substitute mediator can be agreed upon or appointed in the same manner as the original mediator. A mediator shall not mediate a case assigned to another mediator without the agreement of the parties or approval of the court. A substitute mediator shall have the same qualifications as the original mediator.

(k) Discovery. Unless stipulated by the parties or ordered by the court, the mediation process shall not suspend discovery.

(*l*) Appearances.

(1) Order Naming or Prohibiting Attendance of Parties. The court shall enter an order naming the parties and the participants who must appear at the mediation and any parties or participants who are prohibited from attending the mediation. Additional participants may be included by court order or by mutual agreement of all parties.

(2) Physical Presence of Adult Parties and Participants. Unless otherwise agreed to by the parties or ordered by the court, any party or participant ordered to mediation shall be physically present at the mediation conference. Persons representing an agency, department, or program must have full authority to enter into an agreement that shall be binding on that agency, department, or program. In the discretion of the mediator, and with the agreement of the attending parties, dependency mediation may proceed in the absence of any party or participant ordered to mediation.

(3) Appearance of Counsel. In the discretion of the mediator, and with the agreement of the attending parties, dependency mediation may proceed in the absence of counsel unless otherwise ordered by the court.

(4) Appearance of Child. The court may prohibit the child from appearing at mediation upon determining that such appearance is not in the best interest of the child. No minor child shall be required to appear at mediation unless the court has previously determined by written order that it is in the child's best interest to be physically present. The court shall specify in the written order of referral to mediation any special protections necessary for the child's appearance.

(5) Sanctions for Failure to Appear. If a party or participant ordered to mediation fails to appear at a duly-noticed mediation conference without good cause, the court, on motion of any party or on its own motion, may impose sanctions. Sanctions against the party or participant failing to appear may include one or more of the following: contempt of court, an award of mediator fees, an award of attorney fees, an award of costs, or other remedies as deemed appropriate by the court.

(m) Caucus with Parties and Participants. During the mediation session, the mediator may meet and consult privately with any party, participant, or counsel.

(n) Continuances. The mediator may end the mediation session at any time and may set new times for reconvening the mediation. No further notification shall be required for parties or participants present at the mediation session.

(o) Report on Mediation.

(1) If agreement is reached on all or part of any matter or issue, including legal or factual issues to be determined by the court, the agreement shall be immediately reduced to writing, signed by the attending parties, and promptly submitted to the court by the mediator with copies to all parties and counsel.

(2) If the parties do not reach an agreement as to any matter as a result of mediation, the mediator shall report the lack of an agreement to the court without comment or recommendation.

(p) Court Hearing and Order On Mediated Agreement. On receipt of a full or partial mediation agreement, the court shall hold a hearing and enter an order accepting or rejecting the agreement consistent with the best interest of the child. The court may modify the terms of the agreement with the consent of all parties to the agreement.

(q) Imposition of Sanctions On Breach of Agreement. In the event of any breach or failure to perform under the court-approved agreement, the court, on a motion of any party or on its own motion, may impose sanctions. The sanctions may include contempt of court, vacating the agreement, imposition of costs and attorney fees, or any other remedy deemed appropriate by the court.

Committee Notes

1997 Adoption. In considering the provision regarding the appearance of the child found in subdivision (*l*)(4), the Committee considered issues concerning the child's right to participate and be heard in mediation and the need to protect the child from participating in proceedings when such participation would not be in the best interest of the child. The Committee has addressed only the issue of mandating participation of the child in mediation. In circumstances where the court has not mandated that the child appear in mediation, the Committee believes that, in the absence of an order prohibiting the child from mediation, the participation of the child in mediation will be determined by the parties.

Whenever the court, pursuant to subdivision (p) determines whether to accept, reject, or modify the mediation agreement, the Committee believes that the court shall act in accordance with the confidentiality requirements of chapter 44, Florida Statutes.

RULE 8.292. APPOINTMENT AND DISCHARGE OF SURROGATE PARENT

(a) Appointment. Unless appointed by the district school superintendent, the court must appoint a surrogate parent for a child known to the department who has or is suspected of having a disability when

(1) after reasonable efforts, no parent can be located; or

(2) a court of competent jurisdiction over a child under Chapter 39, Florida Statutes, has determined that no person has the authority under the Individuals with Disabilities Education Act, including the parent or parents subject to the dependency action, or no person has the authority, willingness, or ability to serve as the educational decision maker for the child without judicial action.

(b) Who May Be Appointed. The surrogate parent must meet the minimum criteria established by law.

(c) Recognition of Surrogate Parent. The dependency court and school district must recognize the initial individual appointed as surrogate parent.

(d) Duties and Responsibilities. The surrogate parent must be acquainted with the child and become knowledgeable about the child's disability and education needs and

(1) must represent the child in all matters relating to identification, evaluation, and educational placement and the provision of a free and appropriate education to the child;

(2) must represent the interests and safeguard the rights of the child in educational decisions that affect the child, and enjoy all the procedural safeguards afforded a parent regarding the identification, evaluation, and educational placement of a student with a disability or a student who is suspected of having a disability; and

(3) does not have the authority to represent the interests of the child regarding the child's care, maintenance, custody, residential placement, or any other area not specifically related to the education of the child, unless the same person is appointed by the court for those purposes.

(e) Notice of Appointment. When the court appoints a surrogate parent, notice must be provided as soon as practicable to the child's school.

(f) Substitution or Discharge. The court may, through a determination of the best interest of the child or as otherwise established by law, find that it is appropriate to substitute or discharge the surrogate parent. The surrogate parent must continue in the appointed role until discharged.

B. TAKING CHILDREN INTO CUSTODY AND SHELTER HEARINGS

RULE 8.300. TAKING INTO CUSTODY

(a) Affidavit. An affidavit or verified petition may be filed alleging facts under existing law sufficient to establish grounds to take a child into custody. The affidavit or verified petition shall:

(1) be in writing and signed;

(2) specify the name, address, date of birth, and sex of the child, or, if unknown, designate the child by any name or description by which he or she can be identified with reasonable certainty;

(3) specify that the child is of an age subject to the jurisdiction of the court; and

(4) state the reasons the child should be taken into custody.

(b) Criteria for Order. The Court may issue an order to take a child into custody based on sworn testimony meeting the criteria in subdivision (a).

(c) Order. The order to take into custody shall:

(1) be in writing and signed;

(2) specify the name, address, and sex of the child or, if unknown, designate the child by any name or description by which he or she can be identified with reasonable certainty;

(3) specify that the child is of an age subject to the jurisdiction of the court;

(4) state the reasons the child should be taken into custody;

(5) order that the child be held in a suitable place pending transfer of physical custody to an authorized agent of the department; and

(6) state the date when issued, and the county and court where issued.

RULE 8.305. SHELTER PETITION, HEARING, AND ORDER

(a) Shelter Petition. If a child has been or is to be removed from the home and maintained in an out-of-home placement for more than 24 hours, the person requesting placement shall file a written petition that shall:

(1) specify the name, address, date of birth, and sex of the child or, if unknown, designate the child by any name or description by which he or she can be

identified with reasonable certainty and shall indicate whether the child has a special need requiring appointment of counsel as defined in section 39.01305, Florida Statutes;

(2) specify the name and address, if known, of the child's parents or legal custodian and how each was notified of the shelter hearing;

(3) if the child has been removed from the home, state the date and time of the removal;

(4) specify that the child is of an age subject to the jurisdiction of the court;

(5) state the reasons the child needs to be placed in a shelter;

(6) list the reasonable efforts, if any, that were made by the department to prevent or eliminate the need for the removal or continued removal of the child from the home or, if no such efforts were made, a description of the emergency that prevented these efforts;

(7) recommend where the child is to be placed or the agency to be responsible for placement;

(8) if the children are currently not placed together, specify the reasonable efforts of the department to keep the siblings together after the removal from the home, why a foster home is not available to place the siblings, or why it is not in the best interest of the child that all the siblings be placed together in out-of-home care;

(9) specify ongoing visitation or interaction between the siblings or if sibling visitation or interaction is not recommended, specify why visitation or interaction would be contrary to the safety or well-being of the child; and

(10) be signed by the petitioner and, if represented by counsel, by the petitioner's attorney.

(b) Shelter Hearing.

(1) The parents or legal custodians of the child shall be given actual notice of the date, time, and

location of the shelter hearing. If the parents are outside the jurisdiction of the court, are not known, cannot be located, or refuse or evade service, they shall be given such notice as best ensures their actual knowledge of the date, time, and location of the shelter hearing. If the parents or legal custodians are not present at the hearing, the person providing, or attempting to provide, notice to the parents or legal custodians shall advise the court in person or by sworn affidavit of the attempts made to provide notice and the results of those attempts.

(2) The court shall conduct an informal hearing on the petition within the time limits provided by law. The court shall determine at the hearing the existence of probable cause to believe the child is dependent and whether the other criteria provided by law for placement in a shelter have been met. The shelter hearing may be continued for up to 72 hours with the child remaining in shelter care if either:

(A) the parents or legal custodians appear for the shelter hearing without legal counsel and request a continuance to consult with legal counsel; or

(B) the court determines that additional time is necessary to obtain and review documents pertaining to the family to appropriately determine the risk to the child.

(3) The issue of probable cause shall be determined in a nonadversarial manner, applying the standard of proof necessary for an arrest warrant.

(4) At the hearing, all interested persons present shall have an opportunity to be heard and present evidence on the criteria for placement provided by law.

(5) The court may base its determination on a sworn complaint, testimony, or an affidavit and may hear all relevant and material evidence, including oral and written reports, to the extent of its probative value even though it would not be competent at an adjudicatory hearing.

(6) The court shall advise the parent or legal custodian of:

(A) the right to be represented by counsel as provided by law;

(B) the reason the child is in custody and why continued placement is requested;

(C) the right to present placement alternatives; and

(D) the time, date, and location of the next hearing and of the importance of the parents' or legal custodians' active participation in subsequent proceedings and hearings.

(7) The court shall appoint:

(A) a guardian ad litem to represent the child unless the court finds representation unnecessary;

(B) an attorney to represent the child if the court finds the appointment necessary or required by law; and

(C) an attorney for indigent parents unless waived by the parent.

(8) The court shall determine visitation rights absent a clear and convincing showing that visitation is not in the best interest of the child.

(9) If the identity of a parent is unknown, the court must conduct the inquiry required by law.

(10) The court shall inquire of the parents whether the parents have relatives who might be considered for placement of the child. The parents shall provide to the court and all parties identification and location information regarding the relatives. The court shall advise the parents that the parents have a continuing duty to inform the department of any relative who should be considered for placement of the child.

(11) The court shall advise the parents that if the parents fail to substantially comply with the case plan their parental rights may be terminated and the child's out-of-home placement may become permanent.

(12) The court must request that the parents consent to provide access to the child's medical and

educational records and provide information to the court, the department, or its contract agencies, and any guardian ad litem or attorney for the child. If a parent is unavailable, is unable to consent, or withholds consent and the court determines access to the records and information is necessary to provide services for the child, the court shall issue an order granting access.

(13) The court may order the parents to provide all known medical information to the department and to any others granted access.

(14) If the child has or is suspected of having a disability and the parent is unavailable pursuant to law, the court must appoint a surrogate parent or refer the child to' the district school superintendent for appointment of a surrogate parent.

(15) If the shelter hearing is conducted by a judge other than a judge assigned to hear dependency cases, a judge assigned to hear dependency cases shall hold a shelter review on the status of the child within 2 working days after the shelter hearing.

(c) Shelter Order. An order granting shelter care must identify the parties present at the hearing and contain written findings that:

(1) placement in shelter care is necessary based on the criteria provided by law;

(2) placement in shelter care is in the best interest of the child;

(3) the department made reasonable efforts to keep the siblings together after the removal from the home and specifies if the children are currently not placed together, why a foster home is not available or why it is not in the best interest of the child that all the siblings be placed together in out-of-home care;

(4) specifies on-going visitation or interaction between the siblings or if sibling visitation or interaction is not recommended, specifies why visitation or interaction would be contrary to the safety or well-being of the child;

(5) continuation of the child in the home is contrary to the welfare of the child because the home

situation presents a substantial and immediate danger to the child's physical, mental, or emotional health or safety that cannot be mitigated by the provision of preventative services;

(6) there is probable cause to believe the child is dependent;

(7) the department has made reasonable efforts to prevent or eliminate the need for removal of the child from the home, including a description of which specific services, if available, could prevent or eliminate the need for removal or continued removal from the home, the date by which the services are expected to become available, and, if services are not available to prevent or eliminate the need for removal or continued removal of the child from the home, an explanation of why the services are not available for the child;

(8) the court notified the parents or legal custodians of the time, date, and location of the next dependency hearing, and of the importance of their active participation in all subsequent proceedings and hearings; and

(9) the court notified the parents or legal custodians of their right to counsel as provided by law.

(d) Release from Shelter Care. No child shall be released from shelter care after a shelter order has been entered except on order of the court unless the shelter order authorized release by the department.

C. PETITION, ARRAIGNMENT, ADJUDICATION, AND DISPOSITION

RULE 8.310. DEPENDENCY PETITIONS

(a) Contents.

(1) A dependency petition may be filed as provided by law. Each petition shall be entitled a petition for dependency and shall allege sufficient facts showing the child to be dependent based upon applicable law.

(2) The petition shall contain allegations as to the identity and residence of the parents or legal custodians, if known.

(3) The petition shall identify the age, sex, and name of the child. Two or more children may be the subject of the same petition.

(4) Two or more allegations of dependency may appear in the same petition, in separate counts. The petition need not contain allegations of acts or omissions by both parents.

(5) The petition must describe what voluntary services, safety planning and/or dependency mediation the parents or legal custodians were offered and the outcome of each.

(6) The petition shall identify each child who has a special need requiring appointment of counsel as defined in section 39.01305, Florida Statutes.

(b) Verification. The petition shall be signed stating under oath the signer's good faith in filing the petition. No objection to a petition on the grounds that it was not signed or verified, as herein provided, shall be entertained after a plea to the merits.

(c) Amendments. At any time prior to the conclusion of an adjudicatory hearing, an amended petition may be filed or the petition may be amended by motion; however, after a written answer or plan has been filed, amendments shall be permitted only with the permission of the court, unless all parties consent. Amendments shall be freely permitted in the interest of justice and the welfare of the child. A continuance may be granted on motion and a showing that the amendment prejudices or materially affects any party.

(d) Defects and Variances. No petition or any count thereof shall be dismissed, or any judgment vacated, on account of any defect in the form of the petition or of misjoinder of counts. If the court is of the opinion that the petition is so vague, indistinct, and indefinite as to mislead the child, parent, or legal custodian and prejudice any of them in the preparation of a defense, the petitioner may be required to furnish a more definite statement.

(e) Voluntary Dismissal. The petitioner without leave of the court, at any time prior to entry of an order of adjudication, may request a voluntary dismissal of the petition or any allegations of the petition by serving a notice requesting dismissal on all parties, or, if during a hearing, by so stating on the record. The petition or any allegations in the petition shall be dismissed. If the petition is dismissed, the court loses jurisdiction unless another party adopts the petition within 72 hours.

Committee Notes

1991 Amendment. (c) The time limit for amending a petition has been extended to be consistent with civil pleading procedures. The best interest of the child requires liberal amendments. The procedures for determining if a party has been prejudiced have not been changed.

(e) This section has been reworded to provide a procedure for notice to all parties before dismissal and to allow adoption of a petition by another party.

RULE 8.315. ARRAIGNMENTS AND PREHEARING CONFERENCES

(a) Arraignment.

(1) Before the adjudicatory hearing, the court must conduct a hearing to determine whether an admission, consent, or denial to the petition shall be entered, and whether the parties are represented by counsel or are entitled to appointed counsel as provided by law.

(2) If an admission or consent is entered and no denial is entered by any other parent or legal custodian, the court must enter a written order finding dependency based on the allegations of the dependency petition by a preponderance of the evidence. The court shall schedule a disposition hearing to be conducted within 15 days. If a denial is entered, the court shall set an adjudicatory hearing within the period of time provided by law and appoint counsel when required.

(3) If one parent enters an admission or consent and the other parent who is present enters a denial to the allegations of the dependency petition, the court must enter a written order finding dependency based on the allegations of the dependency petition that pertain to the parent who enters an admission or consent by a preponderance of the evidence. The court must then reserve ruling on whether the parent who entered the denial contributed to the dependency status of the child pursuant to the statutory definition

of a dependent child until the parent enters an admission or consent to the dependency petition, the court conducts an adjudicatory hearing, or the issue is otherwise resolved.

(4) If one parent enters an admission or consent and the identity or location of the other parent is unknown, the court must enter a written order finding dependency based on the allegations of the dependency petition by a preponderance of the evidence. The court must then reserve ruling on whether the parent whose identity or location is unknown contributed to the dependency status of the child pursuant to the statutory definition of a dependent child until the parent enters an admission or consent to the dependency petition, the court conducts an adjudicatory hearing, or the court proceeds as provided by law regarding a parent whose identity or location is unknown.

(5) If the court enters a written order finding dependency, the court must schedule a disposition hearing to be conducted within 15 days. If a denial is entered, the court must set an adjudicatory hearing within the period of time provided by law and appoint counsel when required.

(b) Withdrawal of Plea. The court may for good cause, at any time before the beginning of a disposition hearing, permit an admission of the allegations of the petition or a consent to dependency to be withdrawn and, if an adjudication has been entered, set aside the adjudication. In a subsequent adjudicatory hearing the court shall disregard an admission or consent that has been withdrawn.

(c) Prehearing Conference. Before any adjudicatory hearing, the court may set or the parties may request that a prehearing conference be held to determine the order in which each party may present witnesses or evidence, the order in which cross-examination and argument shall occur, and any other matters that may aid in the conduct of the adjudicatory hearing to prevent any undue delay in the adjudicatory hearing. The court may also enter findings on the record of any stipulations entered into by the parties and consider any other matters that may aid in the conduct of the adjudicatory hearing.

(d) Status Hearing. Within 60 days of the filing of the petition, a status hearing must be held with all parties present unless an adjudicatory or disposition hearing has begun. Subsequent status hearings must be held every 30 days unless an adjudicatory or disposition hearing has begun.

Committee Notes

1991 Amendment. (d) This section requires a status hearing every 30 days to ensure prompt resolution of the case while preserving the rights of all parties.

RULE 8.320. PROVIDING COUNSEL TO PARTIES

(a) Duty of the Court.

(1) At each stage of the dependency proceeding the court shall advise the parent of the right to have counsel present.

(2) The court shall appoint counsel to indigent parents or others who are so entitled to as provided by law, unless appointment of counsel is waived by that person.

(3) The court shall ascertain whether the right to counsel is understood.

(b) Waiver of Counsel.

(1) No waiver of counsel shall be accepted where it appears that the parent is unable to make an intelligent and understanding choice because of age, education, experience, the nature or complexity of the case, or other factors.

(2) A waiver of counsel made in court shall be of record. The court shall question the party in sufficient detail to ascertain that the waiver is made knowingly, intelligently, and voluntarily.

(3) If a waiver is accepted at any stage of the proceedings, the offer of assistance of counsel shall be renewed by the court at each subsequent stage of the proceedings at which the party appears without counsel.

RULE 8.325. ANSWERS AND PLEADINGS

(a) No Answer Required. No written answer to the petition need be filed by the parent or legal custodian. The parent or legal custodian of the child may enter an oral or written answer to the petition or remain silent.

(b) Denial of Allegations. If the parent or legal custodian denies the allegations of the petition, remains silent, or pleads evasively, the court shall enter a denial of dependency and set the case for an adjudicatory hearing.

(c) Admission of or Consent to Dependency. The parent or legal custodian may admit or consent to a finding of dependency. The court shall determine that any admission or consent to a finding of dependency is made voluntarily and with a full understanding of the nature of the allegations and the possible consequences of the admission or consent, and that the parent has been advised of the right to be represented by counsel. The court shall incorporate these findings into its order in addition to findings of fact specifying the act or acts causing dependency, by whom committed, and facts on which the findings are based.

RULE 8.330. ADJUDICATORY HEARINGS

(a) Hearing by Judge. The adjudicatory hearing shall be conducted by the judge, without a jury, utilizing the rules of evidence in use in civil cases. At this hearing the court shall determine whether the allegations of the dependency petition have been sustained by a preponderance of the evidence. If the court is of the opinion that the allegations are sustained by clear and convincing evidence, it may enter an order so stating.

(b) Examination of Witnesses. A party may call any person as a witness. A party shall have the right to examine or cross-examine all witnesses. However, the child and the parents, caregivers, or legal custodians of the child may be examined separately and apart from each other.

(c) Presence of Parties. All parties have the right to be present at all hearings. A party may appear in person or, at the discretion of the court for good cause shown, by an audio or audiovisual device. No party shall be excluded from any hearing unless so ordered by the court for disruptive behavior or as provided by law. If a person appears for the arraignment hearing

and the court orders that person to personally appear at the adjudicatory hearing for dependency, stating the date, time, and place of the adjudicatory hearing, then that person's failure to appear for the scheduled adjudicatory hearing constitutes consent to a dependency adjudication.

(d) Joint and Separate Hearings. When 2 or more children are alleged to be dependent children, the hearing may be held simultaneously when the several children involved are related to each other or involved in the same case, unless the court orders separate hearings.

(e) Motion for Judgment of Dismissal. In all proceedings, if at the close of the evidence for the petitioner the court is of the opinion that the evidence is insufficient to warrant a finding of dependency, it may, and on the motion of any party shall, enter an order dismissing the petition for insufficiency of the evidence or find that allegations in the petition have not been sustained. If the court finds that allegations in the petition have not been sustained but does not dismiss the petition, the parties, including all parents, shall continue to receive pleadings, notices, and documents and to have the right to be heard.

(f) Dismissal. If the court shall find that the allegations in the petition have not been sustained, it shall enter an order dismissing the case for insufficiency of the evidence or find that allegations in the petition have not been sustained. If the court finds that allegations in the petition have not been sustained but does not dismiss the petition, the parties, including all parents, shall continue to receive pleadings, notices, and documents and to have the right to be heard.

Committee Notes

1991 Amendment. (a) This change gives the court the option of making a finding based on a higher burden of proof to eliminate the need for a repetitive hearing on the same evidence if a termination of parental rights petition is filed.

RULE 8.332. ORDER FINDING DEPENDENCY

(a) Finding of Dependency. In all cases in which dependency is established, the court must enter a written order stating the legal basis for a finding of dependency, specifying the facts upon which the finding of dependency is based, and stating whether the court made the finding by a preponderance of the evidence or by clear and convincing evidence. The court must include the dates of the adjudicatory hearing, if any, in the order.

(b) Adjudication of Dependency.

(1) If the court finds that the child named in the petition is dependent, the court must enter an order adjudicating the child dependent if the child is placed or will continue to be placed in an out-of-home placement. Following a finding of dependency, the court must schedule a disposition hearing within 30 days after the last day of the adjudicatory hearing pursuant to these rules.

(2) If the court enters findings that only one parent contributed to the dependency status of the child but allegations of dependency remain unresolved as to the other parent, the court must enter a written order finding dependency based on the allegations of the dependency petition concerning the one parent. The court must then reserve ruling on findings regarding the other parent based on the unresolved allegations until the parent enters an admission or consent to the dependency petition, the court conducts an evidentiary hearing on the findings, the court proceeds as provided by law regarding a parent whose identity or location is unknown, or the issue is otherwise resolved.

(3) The court may enter an order adjudicating the child dependent if the child remains in or is returned to the home.

(4) For as long as a court maintains jurisdiction over a dependency case, only one order adjudicating each child in the case dependent shall be entered. This order establishes the legal status of the child for purposes of proceedings under Chapter 39, Florida Statutes, and may be based on the conduct of one parent, both parents, or a legal custodian. With the exception of proceedings pursuant to a termination of parental rights, the child's dependency status may not be retried or readjudicated. All subsequent orders finding that a parent contributed to the dependency

status of the child shall supplement the initial order of adjudication.

(c) Withhold of Adjudication of Dependency.

(1) If the court finds that the child named in the petition is dependent, but finds that no action other than supervision in the child's home is required, it may enter an order briefly stating the facts on which its finding is based, but withholding an order of adjudication and placing the child in the child's home under the supervision of the department. The department must file a case plan and the court must review the case plan pursuant to these rules.

(2) If the court later finds that the parents of the child have not complied with the conditions of supervision imposed, including the case plan, the court may, after a hearing to establish the noncompliance, but without further evidence of the state of dependency, enter an order of adjudication and shall thereafter have full authority under this chapter to provide for the child as adjudicated. If the child is to remain in an out-of-home placement by order of the court, the court must adjudicate the child dependent. If the court adjudicates the child dependent, the court must then conduct a disposition hearing.

(d) Failure to Substantially Comply. The court must advise the parents that, if the parents fail to substantially comply with the case plan, their parental rights may be terminated and the child's out-of-home placement may become permanent.

(e) Inquiry Regarding Relatives for Placement. If the child is in out-of-home care, the court must inquire of the parent or parents whether the parent or parents have relatives who might be considered as placement for the child. The parent or parents must provide to the court and all parties identification and location information for the relatives.

RULE 8.335. ALTERNATIVES PENDING DISPOSITION

If the court finds that the evidence supports the allegations of the petition, it may make a finding of dependency as provided by law. If the reports required by law are available, the court may proceed to disposition or continue the case for a disposition hearing. If the case is continued, the court may refer the case to appropriate agencies for additional study and recommendation. The court may order the child continued in placement, designate the placement or the agency that will be responsible for the child's placement, and enter such other orders deemed necessary to protect the health, safety, and well-being of the child, including diagnosis, evaluation, treatment, and visitation.

RULE 8.340. DISPOSITION HEARINGS

(a) Information Available to Court. At the disposition hearing the court, after establishing compliance with the dispositional considerations, determinations, and discussions required by law, may receive any relevant and material evidence helpful in determining the proper disposition to be made. It must include written reports required by law, and may include, but is not limited to, any psychiatric or psychological evaluations of the child or his or her parent, caregiver, or legal custodian that may be obtained and that are relevant and material. Such evidence may be received by the court and may be relied upon to the extent of its probative value, even though not competent in an adjudicatory hearing.

(b) Disclosure to Parties. All parties are entitled to disclosure of all information in all reports submitted to the court.

(c) Orders of Disposition. The court shall in its written order of disposition include:

(1) the placement or custody of the child;

(2) special conditions of placement and visitation;

(3) evaluation, counseling, treatment activities, and other actions to be taken by the parties, if ordered;

(4) persons or entities responsible for supervising or monitoring services to the child and parent;

(5) continuation or discharge of the guardian ad litem, as appropriate;

(6) date, time, and location of next scheduled review hearing, as required by law;

(7) child support payments, if the child is in an out-of-home placement;

(8) if the child is placed in foster care, the reasons why the child was not placed in the legal custody of an adult relative, legal custodian, or other adult approved by the court and a further determination as to whether diligent efforts were made by the department to locate an adult relative, legal custodian, or other adult willing to care for the child instead of placement with the department;

(9) such other requirements to protect the health, safety, and well- being of the child, to preserve the stability of the child's educational placement, and to promote family preservation or reunification whenever possible; and

(10) approval of the case plan and any reports required by law as filed with the court. If the court does not approve the case plan at the disposition hearing, the court must set a hearing within 30 days after the disposition hearing to review and approve the case plan.

Committee Notes

1992 Amendment. Dismissal of a petition is not appropriate after adjudication.

RULE 8.345. POST-DISPOSITION RELIEF

(a) Motion for Modification of Placement. A child who has been placed in his or her own home, in the home of a relative, or in some other place, under the supervision or legal custody of the department, may be brought before the court by the department or any interested person on a motion for modification of placement. If neither the department, the child, the parents, the legal custodian, nor any appointed guardian ad litem or attorney ad litem object to the change, then the court may enter an order making the change in placement without a hearing. If the department, the child, the parents, the legal custodian, or any appointed guardian ad litem or attorney ad litem object to the change of placement, the court shall conduct a hearing and thereafter enter an order changing the placement, modifying the conditions of placement, continuing placement as previously ordered, or placing the child with the department or a licensed child-caring agency.

(1) In cases in which the issue before the court is whether a child should be reunited with a parent, and the child is currently placed with someone other than a parent, the court must review the conditions for return and determine whether the circumstances that caused the out-of-home placement and issues subsequently identified have been remedied to the extent that the return of the child to the home with an in-home safety plan prepared or approved by the department will not be detrimental to the child's safety, well-being, and physical, mental, and emotional health.

(2) In cases in which the issue before the court is whether a child who is placed in the custody of a parent should be reunited with the other parent upon a finding that the circumstances that caused the out-of-home placement and issues subsequently identified have been remedied to the extent that the return of the child to the home of the other parent with an in-home safety plan prepared or approved by the department will not be detrimental to the child, the court must determine that the safety, well-being, and physical, mental, and emotional health of the child would not be endangered by reunification and that reunification would be in the best interest of the child.

(b) Motion for Termination of Supervision or Jurisdiction. Any party requesting termination of agency supervision or the jurisdiction of the court or both shall do so by written motion or in a written report to the court. The court must hear all parties present and enter an order terminating supervision or terminating jurisdiction and supervision or continuing them as previously ordered. The court shall not terminate jurisdiction unless the child is returned to the parent and has been in the placement for at least 6 months, the child is adopted, or the child attains the age of 18, unless the court has extended jurisdiction.

RULE 8.347. MOTION TO SUPPLEMENT ORDER OF ADJUDICATION, DISPOSITION ORDER, AND CASE PLAN

(a) Motion. After the court has entered an order of adjudication of dependency, any party may file a motion for the court to supplement the order of adjudication with findings that a parent or legal custodian contributed to the dependency status of the child pursuant to the statutory definition of a dependent child. The motion may also request that the court supplement the disposition order and the case plan.

(b) Contents.

(1) The motion must identify the age, sex, and name of the children whose parent or legal custodian is the subject of the motion.

(2) The motion must specifically identify the parent or legal custodian who is the subject of the motion.

(3) The motion must allege sufficient facts showing that a parent or legal custodian contributed to the dependency status of the child pursuant to the statutory definition of a dependent child.

(c) Verification. The motion must be signed under oath, stating that the signer is filing the motion in good faith.

(d) Amendments. At any time prior to the conclusion of an evidentiary hearing on the motion, an amended motion may be filed or the motion may be amended by oral motion. A continuance may be granted on motion and a showing that the amendment prejudices or materially affects any party.

(e) Notice.

(1) In General. Parents or legal custodians who have previously been properly served with the dependency petition or who have previously appeared in the dependency proceeding shall be served with a notice of hearing and copies of the motion and the initial order of adjudication of dependency in the same manner as the service of documents that are filed after the service of the initial dependency petition as provided in these rules. The notice shall require the person on whom it is served to appear for the preliminary hearing on the motion at a time and place specified, not less than 72 hours after service of the motion. The document containing the notice to respond or appear must contain, in type at least as large as the balance of the document, the following or substantially similar language: "FAILURE TO PER-SONALLY APPEAR AT THE PRELIMINARY HEARING ON THE MOTION CONSTITUTES YOUR CONSENT TO THE COURT'S FINDING THAT YOU CONTRIBUTED TO THE DEPEN-DENCY STATUS OF THE CHILD PURSUANT TO THE STATUTORY DEFINITION OF A DEPEN-DENT CHILD AND MAY ULTIMATELY RESULT IN LOSS OF CUSTODY OF THIS CHILD (OR CHILDREN)."

(2) Summons.

(A) Parents or legal custodians who have not been properly served with the dependency petition or who have not previously appeared in the dependency proceeding must be properly served with a summons and copies of the motion and the initial order of adjudication of dependency. The summons must require the person on whom it is served to appear for a preliminary hearing on the motion at a time and place specified, not less than 72 hours after service of the summons. The summons must contain, in type at least as large as the balance of the document, the following or substantially similar language: "FAILURE TO PERSONALLY APPEAR AT THE PRELIMINARY HEARING ON THE MOTION CONSTITUTES YOUR CONSENT TO THE COURT'S FINDING THAT YOU CONTRIBUTED TO THE DEPEN-DENCY STATUS OF THE CHILD PURSUANT TO THE STATUTORY DEFINITION OF A DEPEN-DENT CHILD AND MAY ULTIMATELY RESULT IN LOSS OF CUSTODY OF THIS CHILD (OR CHILDREN)."

(B) Upon the filing of the motion and upon request, the clerk shall issue a summons.

(C) The movant shall not be required to serve a summons on a parent or legal custodian who has previously been properly served with the dependency petition or who has appeared in the dependency proceeding.

(D) The summons shall be served in the same manner as service of a dependency petition as required by law.

(E) Service by publication of the motion shall not be required.

(F) If the location of the party to be served is unknown, the court may enter an order granting the motion only if the movant has properly served the person subject to the motion, the person subject to the motion has appeared in the proceeding, or the movant has conducted a diligent search and filed with the court an affidavit of diligent search.

(G) Personal appearance of any person in a hearing before the court on the motion eliminates the requirement for serving process upon that person.

(f) Preliminary Hearing on Motion.

(1) The court must conduct a preliminary hearing and determine whether the parent or legal custodian who is the subject of the motion:

(A) has been properly served with the summons or notice, and with copies of the motion and initial order of adjudication of dependency;

(B) is represented by counsel or is entitled to appointed counsel as provided by law; and

(C) wishes to challenge the motion or consent to the court granting the motion.

(2) If the parent or legal custodian who is the subject of the motion wishes to challenge the motion, the court must schedule an evidentiary hearing on the motion within 30 days.

(3) If the parent or legal custodian who is the subject of the motion wishes to consent to the motion without admitting or denying the allegations of the motion, the court shall enter an order supplementing the initial order of adjudication of dependency based on the sworn allegations of the motion. Failure of the person properly served with notice to personally appear at the preliminary hearing on the motion constitutes the person's consent to the court's finding that the person contributed to the dependency status of the child pursuant to the statutory definition of a dependent child.

(g) Evidentiary Hearing.

(1) Hearing Procedures. The hearing shall be conducted in the same manner and with the same procedures as the adjudicatory hearing on the dependency petition as provided in these rules.

(2) Motion for Judgment Denying Motion. In all proceedings, if at the close of the evidence for the movant, the court is of the opinion that the evidence is insufficient to warrant findings that a parent or legal custodian contributed to the dependency status of the child pursuant to the statutory definition of a dependent child, it may, and on the motion of any party must, enter an order denying the motion for insufficiency of the evidence.

(3) Denial of Motion. If the court, at the conclusion of the evidence, finds that the allegations in the motion have not been sustained, the court shall enter an order denying the motion.

(4) Granting of the Motion. If the court finds that the movant has proven the allegations of the motion, the court shall enter an order granting the motion as provided in these rules.

(5) Failure to Appear. If a person appears for the preliminary hearing on the motion and the court orders that person to personally appear at the evidentiary hearing on the motion, stating the date, time, and place of the evidentiary hearing, then that person's failure to appear for the scheduled evidentiary hearing constitutes consent to the court's finding that the person contributed to the dependency status of the child pursuant to the statutory definition of a dependent child.

(h) Supplemental Order of Adjudication.

(1) If the parent or legal custodian consents to the motion and its allegations or if the court finds that the movant has proven the allegations of the motion at an evidentiary hearing, the court shall enter a written order granting the motion and specifying facts that support findings that a parent or legal custodian contributed to the dependency status of the child pursuant to the statutory definition of a dependent child and stating whether the court made the finding by a preponderance of the evidence or by clear and convincing evidence.

(2) If necessary, the court shall schedule a supplemental disposition hearing within 15 days.

(3) The court shall advise the parent who is the subject of the motion that if the parent fails to substantially comply with the case plan, parental rights may be terminated.

(4) If the child is in out-of-home placement, the court shall inquire of the parents whether the parents have relatives who might be considered as placement for the child. The parents shall provide to the court and to all parties the identity and location of the relatives.

(i) Supplemental Disposition Hearing.

(1) Hearing. If necessary, the court shall conduct a supplemental disposition hearing pursuant to the same procedures for a disposition hearing and case plan review hearing as provided by law.

(2) Supplemental Reports and Case Plan.

(A) A written case plan and any reports required by law prepared by an authorized agent of the department must be filed with the court, served upon the parents of the child, provided to the representative of the guardian ad litem program, if the program has been appointed, and provided to all other parties not less than 72 hours before the supplemental disposition hearing.

(B) The court may grant an exception to the requirement for any reports required by law by separate order or within the judge's order of disposition upon a finding that all the family and child information required by law is available in other documents filed with the court.

(3) Supplemental Order of Disposition. The court shall in its written supplemental order of disposition include:

(A) the placement or custody of the child;

(B) special conditions of placement and visitation;

(C) evaluation, counseling, treatment activities, and other actions to be taken by the parties, when ordered;

(D) the names of the supervising or monitoring agencies, and the continuation or discharge of the guardian ad litem, when appropriate;

(E) the date, time, and location for the next case review as required by law;

(F) child support payments, if the child is in an out-of-home placement;

(G) if the child is placed in foster care, the reasons why the child was not placed in the legal custody of an adult relative, legal custodian, or other adult approved by the court;

(H) approval of the case plan and any reports required by law or direction to amend the case plan within 30 days; and

(I) such other requirements as are deemed necessary to protect the health, safety, and well-being of the child.

RULE 8.350. PLACEMENT OF CHILD INTO RESIDENTIAL TREATMENT CENTER AFTER ADJUDICATION OF DEPENDENCY

(a) **Placement.**

(1) **Treatment Center Defined.** Any reference in this rule to a residential treatment center is to a residential treatment center or facility licensed under section 394.875, Florida Statutes, for residential mental health treatment. Any reference to hospital is to a hospital licensed under chapter 395, Florida Statutes, for residential mental health treatment. This rule does not apply to placement under sections 394.463 or 394.467, Florida Statutes.

(2) **Basis for Placement.** The placement of any child who has been adjudicated dependent for residential mental health treatment shall be as provided by law.

(3) **Assessment by Qualified Evaluator.** Whenever the department believes that a child in its legal custody may require placement in a residential treatment center or hospital, the department shall arrange to have the child assessed by a qualified evaluator as provided by law and shall file notice of this with the court and all parties. Upon the filing of this notice by the department, the court shall appoint a guardian ad litem for the child, if one has not already been appointed, and shall also appoint an attorney for the child. All appointments pursuant to this rule shall conform to the provisions of rule 8.231. Both the guardian ad litem and attorney shall meet the child and shall have the opportunity to discuss the child's suitability for residential treatment with the qualified evaluator conducting the assessment. Upon the completion of the evaluator's written assessment, the department shall provide a copy to the court and to all parties. The guardian ad litem shall also provide a written report to the court and to all parties indicating the guardian ad litem's recommendation as to the child's placement in residential treatment and the child's wishes.

(4) **Motion for Placement.** If the department seeks to place the child in a residential treatment center or hospital, the department shall immediately file a motion for placement of the child with the court. This motion shall include a statement as to why the child is suitable for this placement and why less restrictive alternatives are not appropriate and also shall include the written findings of the qualified evaluator. The motion shall state whether all parties, including the child, are in agreement. Copies of the motion must be served on the child's attorney and all parties and participants.

(5) **Immediate Placement.** If the evaluator's written assessment indicates that the child requires immediate placement in a residential treatment center or hospital and that such placement cannot wait for a hearing, then the department may place the child pending a hearing, unless the court orders otherwise.

(6) **Guardian ad Litem.** The guardian ad litem must be represented by an attorney at all proceedings under this rule, unless the guardian ad litem is acting as an attorney.

(7) **Status Hearing.** Upon the filing of a motion for placement, the court shall set the matter for a status hearing within 48 hours, excluding weekends and holidays. The department shall timely provide

notice of the date, time, and place of the hearing to all parties and participants.

(8) Notice of Hearing. The child's attorney or guardian ad litem shall notify the child of the date, time, and place of the hearing. No hearing shall proceed without the presence of the child's attorney. The guardian ad litem may be excused by the court for good cause shown.

(9) Disagreement with Placement. If no party disagrees with the department's motion at the status hearing, then the motion for placement may be approved by the court. However, if any party, including the child, disagrees, then the court shall set the matter for hearing within 10 working days.

(10) Presence of Child. The child shall be present at the hearing unless the court determines pursuant to subdivision (c) that a court appearance is not in the child's best interest. In such circumstances, the child shall be provided the opportunity to express his or her views to the court by a method deemed appropriate by the court.

(11) Hearing on Placement.

(A) At the hearing, the court shall consider, at a minimum, all of the following:

(i) based on an independent assessment of the child, the recommendation of a department representative or authorized agent that the residential treatment or hospitalization is in the child's best interest and a showing that the placement is the least restrictive available alternative;

(ii) the recommendation of the guardian ad litem;

(iii) the written findings of the evaluation and suitability assessment prepared by a qualified evaluator; and

(iv) the views regarding placement in residential treatment that the child expresses to the court.

(B) All parties shall be permitted to present evidence and witnesses concerning the suitability of the placement.

(C) If the court determines that the child is not suitable for residential treatment, the court shall order the department to place the child in the least restrictive setting that is best suited to meet the child's needs.

(b) Continuing Residential Placement Reviews.

(1) The court shall conduct a hearing to review the status of the child's residential treatment plan no later than 3 months after the child's admission to the residential treatment program. An independent review of the child's progress toward achieving the goals and objectives of the treatment plan must be completed by a qualified evaluator and submitted to the court, the child's attorney, and all parties in writing at least 72 hours before the 3-month review hearing.

(2) Review hearings shall be conducted every 3 months thereafter, until the child is placed in a less restrictive setting. At each 3-month review hearing, if the child is not represented by an attorney, the court shall appoint counsel. At the 3-month review hearing the court shall determine whether the child disagrees with continued placement.

(3) If the court determines at any hearing that the child is not suitable for continued residential treatment, the court shall order the department to place the child in the least restrictive setting that is best suited to meet the child's needs.

(c) Presence of Child. The child shall be present at all court hearings unless the court finds that the child's mental or physical condition is such that a court appearance is not in the child's best interest. In such circumstances, the child shall be provided the opportunity to express his or her views to the court by a method deemed appropriate by the court.

(d) Standard of Proof. At the hearing, the court shall determine whether the evidence supporting involuntary commitment of a dependent child to a residential mental health treatment facility is clear and convincing.

RULE 8.355. ADMINISTRATION OF PSYCHOTROPIC MEDICATION TO A CHILD IN SHELTER CARE OR IN FOSTER CARE WHEN PARENTAL CONSENT HAS NOT BEEN OBTAINED

(a) Motion for Court Authorization for Administration of Psychotropic Medications.

(1) Whenever the department believes that a child in its physical or legal custody requires the administration of a psychotropic medication, and the child's parents or legal guardians have not provided express and informed consent as provided by law, the department or its agent shall file a motion with the court to authorize the administration of the psychotropic medication before the administration of the medication, except as provided in subdivision (c) of this rule. In all cases in which a motion is required, the motion shall include the following information:

(A) The written report of the department describing the efforts made to enable the prescribing physician to obtain express and informed consent for providing the medication to the child and describing other treatments considered or recommended for the child;

(B) The prescribing physician's signed medical report, as required by law; and

(C) Whether the prescribing physician has obtained the child's assent to take the medication.

(2) If the child declines to assent to the proposed administration of psychotropic medication the court shall appoint an attorney to represent the child and a hearing shall be held on the department's motion. The appointment shall conform to the provisions of rule 8.231.

(3) The department must serve a copy of the motion, and notify all parties and the child's attorney, if appointed, of its proposed administration of psychotropic medication to the child in writing, or by whatever other method best ensures that all parties receive notification of the proposed action, within 48 hours after filing the motion for court authorization.

(4) If any party other than the child objects to the proposed administration of the psychotropic medication to the child, that party must file its objection within 2 working days after being notified of the department's motion.

(b) Court Action on Department's Motion for Administration of Psychotropic Medication.

(1) If the child assents and no party timely files an objection to the department's motion, the court may enter its order authorizing the proposed administration of the psychotropic medication without a hearing. Based on its determination of the best interests of the child, the court may order additional medical consultation or require the department to obtain a second opinion within a reasonable time, not more than 21 calendar days. When the court orders an additional medical consultation or second medical opinion, the department shall file a written report including the results of this additional consultation or a copy of the second medical opinion with the court within the time required by the court, and shall serve a copy of the report as required by subdivision (a)(2) of this rule.

(2) If the child does not assent to the medication or any party timely files its objection to the proposed administration of the psychotropic medication to the child, the court shall hold a hearing as soon as possible on the department's motion.

(A) At such hearing, the medical report of the prescribing physician is admissible in evidence.

(B) At such hearing, the court shall ask the department whether additional medical, mental health, behavioral, counseling, or other services are being provided to the child that the prescribing physician considers to be necessary or beneficial in treating the child's medical condition, and which the physician recommends or expects to be provided to the child with the medication.

(C) The court may order additional medical consultation or a second medical opinion, as provided in subdivision (b)(1) of this rule.

(D) After considering the department's motion and any testimony received, the court may order that the department provide or continue to provide the proposed psychotropic medication to the child, on a determination that it is in the child's best interest to do so.

(c) Emergency Situations.

(1) Shelter Care. When a child is initially removed from the home and taken into custody under section 39.401, Florida Statutes, and the department continues to administer a current prescription of psychotropic medication to the child, the department shall request court authorization for the continued administration of the medication at the shelter hearing. This request shall be included in the shelter petition.

(A) The department shall provide all information in its possession to the court in support of its request at the shelter hearing. The court may authorize the continued administration of the psychotropic medication only until the arraignment hearing on the petition for adjudication, or for 28 days following the date of the child's removal, whichever occurs first.

(B) When the department believes, based on the required physician's evaluation, that it is appropriate to continue the psychotropic medication beyond the time authorized by the court at the shelter hearing, the department shall file a motion seeking continued court authorization at the same time as it files the dependency petition, within 21 days after the shelter hearing.

(2) When Delay Would Cause Significant Harm. Whenever the department believes, based on the certification of the prescribing physician, that delay in providing the prescribed psychotropic medication to the child would, more likely than not, cause significant harm to the child, the department must submit a motion to the court seeking continuation of the medication within 3 working days after the department begins providing the medication to the child.

(A) The motion seeking authorization for the continued administration of the psychotropic medication to the child shall include all information required in subdivision (a)(1) of this rule. The required medical report must also include the specific reasons why the child may experience significant harm, and the nature and the extent of the potential harm, resulting from a delay in authorizing the prescribed medication.

(B) The department shall serve the motion on all parties within 3 working days after the department begins providing the medication to the child.

(C) The court shall hear the department's motion at the next regularly scheduled court hearing required by law, or within 30 days after the date of the prescription, whichever occurs sooner. However, if any party files an objection to the motion, the court shall hold a hearing within 7 days.

(3) In Emergency Psychiatric Placements. The department may authorize the administration of psychotropic medications to a child in its custody in advance of a court order in hospitals, crisis stabilization units, and in statewide inpatient psychiatric programs. Should the department do so, it must seek court authorization for the continued administration of the medication as required in subdivision (a) of this rule.

D. CASE PLANS

RULE 8.400. CASE PLAN DEVELOPMENT

(a) Case Planning Conference. The case plan must be developed in a face-to-face conference with the parents, the guardian ad litem, attorney ad litem and, if appropriate, the child and the temporary custodian of the child.

(b) Contents. The case plan must be written simply and clearly in English and the principal language of the parents, if possible. Each case plan must contain

(1) a description of the problem being addressed, including the parent's behavior or acts resulting in risk to the child and the reason for the intervention by the department;

(2) a permanency goal;

(3) if it is a concurrent plan, a description of the permanency goal of reunification with the parent or

legal custodian and one of the remaining permanency goals;

(4) the date the compliance period expires; and

(5) a written notice to the parent that failure of the parent to substantially comply with the case plan may result in the termination of parental rights, and that a material breach of the case plan may result in the filing of a petition for termination of parental rights sooner than the expiration of the compliance period.

(c) Expiration of Case Plan. The case plan compliance period expires no later than 12 months after the date the child was initially removed from the home or the date the case plan was accepted by the court, whichever occurs first.

(d) Department Responsibility.

(1) The department shall prepare a draft of a case plan for each child receiving services under Chapter 39, Florida Statutes.

(2) The department shall document, in writing, a parent's unwillingness or inability to participate in the development of the case plan, provide the written documentation to the parent when available for the court record, and prepare a case plan.

(3) After the case plan has been developed, and before acceptance by the court, the department shall make the appropriate referrals for services that will allow the parents to begin the agreed-upon tasks and services immediately if the parents agree to begin compliance.

(4) The department must immediately give the parties, including the child if appropriate, a signed copy of the agreed-upon case plan.

(5) The department must prepare, but need not submit to the court, a case plan for a child who will be in care no longer than 30 days unless that child is placed in out of home care a second time within a 12-month period.

(6) The department must prepare a case plan for a child in out of home care within 60 days after the department removes the child from the home and shall submit the plan to the court before the disposition hearing for the court to review and approve.

(7) Not less than 3 business days before the disposition or case plan review hearing, the department must file a case plan with the court.

(8) After jurisdiction attaches, the department shall file with the court all case plans, including all case plans prepared before jurisdiction of the court attached. The department shall provide a copy of the case plans filed to all the parties whose whereabouts are known, not less than 3 business days before the disposition or case plan review hearing.

(9) The department must attach a copy of the child's transition plan, if applicable, to the case plan.

(e) Signature. The case plan must be signed by all parties except the child, if the child is not of an age or capacity to participate in the case planning process.

(f) Service. Each party, including the child, if appropriate, must be provided with a copy of the case plan not less than 3 business days before the disposition or case plan review hearing. If the location of a parent is unknown, this fact must be documented in writing and included in the plan.

RULE 8.401. CASE PLAN DEVELOPMENT FOR YOUNG ADULTS

(a) Case Planning Conference. The case plan must be developed in a face-to-face conference with the young adult, the guardian ad litem, attorney ad litem and, when appropriate, the legal guardian of the young adult, if the young adult is not of the capacity to participate in the case planning process.

(b) Contents. The case plan must be written simply and clearly in English and the principal language of the young adult. Each case plan must contain

(1) a description of the services, including independent living services, to be provided to the young adult;

(2) a copy of the young adult's transition plan;

(3) the permanency goal of transition from licensed care to independent living; and

(4) the date the compliance period expires.

(c) Department Responsibility.

(1) After the case plan has been developed, the department must prepare the written case plan for each young adult receiving services under Chapter 39, Florida Statutes.

(2) After the case plan has been developed, and before acceptance by the court, the department must make the appropriate referrals for services that will allow the young adult to begin receiving the agreed-upon services immediately.

(3) The department must immediately provide the young adult a signed copy of the agreed-upon case plan.

(4) Not less than 3 business days before a judicial review or permanency hearing, the department must file the case plan with the court.

(5) The department must attach a copy of the young adult's transition plan to the case plan.

(d) Signature. The case plan must be signed by the young adult, all parties and, when appropriate, the legal guardian if the young adult is not of the capacity to participate in the case planning process.

(e) Service. Each party must be served with a copy of the case plan not less than 3 business days before the judicial review hearing. If the location of the young adult is unknown, this fact must be documented in writing and filed with the court.

(f) Re-admitted to Care. If the department petitions the court for reinstatement of jurisdiction after a young adult has been re-admitted to care under Chapter 39, Florida Statutes, the department must file an updated case plan.

RULE 8.410. APPROVAL OF CASE PLANS

(a) Hearing. The court shall review the contents of the case plan at the disposition or case plan review hearing unless a continuance for the filing of the case plan has been granted by the court.

(b) Determinations by Court. At the hearing, the court shall determine if:

(1) The plan is consistent with the previous orders of the court placing the child in care.

(2) The plan is consistent with the requirements for the content of a case plan as provided by law.

(3) The parents were advised of their right to have counsel present at all prior hearings and the parents were advised of their right to participate in the preparation of the case plan and to have counsel or any other person assist in the preparation of the case plan.

(4) The case plan is meaningful and designed to address the facts, circumstances, and problems on which the court based its order of dependency for the child.

(5) The plan adequately addresses the goals and needs of the child.

(c) Amendment of Initial Case Plan. During the hearing, if the court determines that the case plan does not meet statutory requirements and include previous court orders, it shall order the parties to make amendments to the plan. The amended plan must be submitted to the court within 30 days for another hearing and approval. A copy of the amended plan must be provided to each party, if the location of the party is known, at least 3 business days before filing with the court. If the parties do not agree on the final terms, the court shall order those conditions and tasks it believes must be accomplished to obtain permanency for the child. In addition, the court may order the department to provide those services necessary to assist in achieving the goal of the case plan.

(d) Entry of Findings. The court shall enter its findings with respect to the review of the case plan in writing and make specific findings on each element required by law to be included in a case plan.

(e) Review Hearing. The court will set a hearing to review the performance of the parties to the case plan no later than 90 days after the disposition hearing or the hearing at which the case plan was approved, 6 months from the date on which the child was removed from the home, or 6 months from the date of the last judicial review, whichever comes first.

RULE 8.415. JUDICIAL REVIEW OF DEPENDENCY CASES

(a) Required Review. All dependent children must have their status reviewed as provided by law. Any party may petition the court for a judicial review as provided by law.

(b) Scheduling Hearings.

(1) Initial Review Hearing. The court must determine when the first review hearing must be held and the clerk of the court must immediately schedule the review hearing. In no case may the hearing be scheduled for later than 6 months from the date of removal from the home or 90 days from the disposition or case plan approval hearing, whichever comes first. In every case, the court must conduct a judicial review at least every 6 months.

(2) Subsequent Review Hearings. At each judicial review hearing, the court must schedule the next judicial review hearing which must be conducted within 6 months. The clerk of the court, at the judicial review hearing, must provide the parties, the social service agency charged with the supervision of care, custody, or guardianship of the child, the foster parent or legal custodian in whose home the child resides, any preadoptive parent, and such other persons as the court may direct with written notice of the date, time, and location of the next judicial review hearing.

(3) Review Hearings for Children 17 Years of Age. The court must hold a judicial review hearing within 90 days after a child's 17th birthday. The court must also issue an order, separate from the order on judicial review, that the specific disabilities of nonage of the child have been removed pursuant to sections 743.044, 743.045, 743.046, and 743.047, Florida Statutes, as well as any other disabilities of nonage that the court finds to be in the child's best interest to remove. The court must continue to hold timely judicial review hearings. The department must update the child's transition plan before each judicial review hearing as required by law. If necessary, the court may review the status of the child more frequently during the year before the child's 18th birthday. At the last review hearing before the child reaches 18 years of age, the court must also address whether the child plans to remain in foster care, and, if so, ensure that the child's transition plan complies with the law. The court must approve the child's transition plan before the child's 18th birthday.

(4) Review Hearings for Young Adults in Foster Care. The court must review the status of a young adult at least every six months and must hold a permanency review hearing at least annually while the young adult remains in foster care. The young adult or any other party to the dependency case may request an additional hearing or judicial review.

(c) Report. In all cases, the department or its agent must prepare a report to the court. The report must contain facts showing the court to have jurisdiction of the cause as a dependency case. It must contain information as to the identity and residence of the parent, if known, and the legal custodian, the dates of the original dependency adjudication and any subsequent judicial review proceedings, the results of any safe-harbor placement assessment including the status of the child's placement, and a request for one or more of the following forms of relief:

(1) that the child's placement be changed;

(2) that the case plan be continued to permit the parents or social service agency to complete the tasks assigned to them in the agreement;

(3) that proceedings be instituted to terminate parental rights and legally free the child for adoption; or

(4) that the child has a special need as defined in section 39.01305, Florida Statutes, who is not represented by an attorney, and who requires appointment of an attorney.

(d) Service. A copy of the report containing recommendations and, if not previously provided by the court, a notice of review hearing must be served on all persons who are required by law to be served at least 72 hours before the judicial review hearing.

(e) Information Available to Court. At the judicial review hearing the court may receive any relevant and material evidence pertinent to the cause. This must include written reports required by law and may include, but must not be limited to, any psychiatric or psychological evaluations of the child or parent, caregiver, or legal custodian that may be obtained and that are material and relevant. This evidence may be received by the court and relied on to the extent of its probative value, even though it may not be competent in an adjudicatory hearing.

(f) Court Action.

(1) The court must hold a hearing to review the compliance of the parties with the case plan and to determine what assigned tasks were and were not accomplished and the reasons for any noncompliance. The court must also determine the frequency, kind, and duration of contacts among siblings who have been separated during placement, as well as any efforts undertaken to reunite separated siblings, if doing so is in the best interest of each child.

(2) If the court finds that the parents have substantially complied with the case plan, the court must return the child to the custody of the parents if the court is satisfied that reunification will not be detrimental to the child's safety, well-being, or physical, mental, or emotional health.

(3) If the court finds that the social service agency has not complied with its obligations, the court may find the social service agency to be in contempt, must order the social service agency to submit its plan for compliance with the case plan, and must require the social service agency to show why the child could not be safely returned to the home of the parents. If the court finds that the child could not be safely returned to the parents, it must extend the case plan for a period of not more than 6 months to allow the social service agency to comply with its obligations under the case plan.

(4) At any judicial review held under section 39.701(3), Florida Statutes, if, in the opinion of the court, the department has not met its obligations to the child as stated in the written case plan or in the provision of independent living services, the court may issue an order directing the department to show cause as to why it has not done so. If the department cannot justify its noncompliance, the court may give the department 30 days within which to comply and, on failure to comply, the court may hold the department in contempt.

(5) The court shall appoint an attorney to represent a child with special needs as required by rule 8.231, and who is not already represented by an attorney.

(6) The court must enter a written order on the conclusion of the review hearing including a statement of the facts, those findings it was directed to determine by law, a determination of the future course of the proceedings, and the date, time, and place of the next hearing.

(g) Jurisdiction.

(1) When a child is returned to the parents, the court must not terminate its jurisdiction over the child until 6 months after the return. Based on a report of the department and any other relevant factors, the court must then determine whether jurisdiction should be continued or terminated. If its jurisdiction is to be terminated, it must enter an order to that effect.

(2) When a child has not been returned to the parent, but has been permanently committed to the department for subsequent adoption, the court must continue to hold judicial review hearings on the status of the child at least every 6 months until the adoption is finalized. These hearings must be held in accordance with these rules.

(3) If a young adult petitions the court at any time before his or her 19th birthday requesting the court's continued jurisdiction, the court may retain or reinstate jurisdiction for a period of time not to continue beyond the date of the young adult's 19th birthday for the purpose of determining whether appropriate services that were required to be provided to the young adult before reaching 18 years of age have been provided.

(4) If a young adult has chosen to remain in extended foster care after he or she has reached 18 years of age, the department may not close a case and the court may not terminate jurisdiction until the court finds, following a hearing, that the appropriate statutory criteria have been met.

(5) If a petition for special immigrant juvenile status and an application for adjustment of status have been filed on behalf of a foster child and the petition and application have not been granted by the time the child reaches 18 years of age, the court may retain jurisdiction solely for the purpose of allowing the continued consideration of the petition and application by federal authorities. Review hearings must be set solely for the purpose of determining the status of the petition and application. The court's jurisdiction must terminate on the final decision of the federal authorities, or on the immigrant child's 22nd birthday, whichever occurs first.

(h) Administrative Review. The department, under a formal agreement with the court in particular cases, may conduct administrative reviews instead of judicial reviews for children in out-of-home placement. Notice must be provided to all parties. An administrative review may not be substituted for the first judicial review or any subsequent 6-month review. Any party may petition the court for a judicial review as provided by law.

(i) Concurrent Planning.

(1) At the initial judicial review hearing, the court must make findings regarding the likelihood of the child's reunification with the parent or legal custodian within 12 months after the removal of the child from the home.

(2) If the court makes a written finding that it is not likely that the child will be reunified with the parent or legal custodian within 12 months after the child was removed from the home, the department must file a motion to amend the case plan and declare that it will use concurrent planning for the case plan.

(3) The department must file the motion to amend the case plan no later than 10 business days after receiving the written finding of the court and attach the proposed amended case plan to the motion.

(4) If concurrent planning is already being used, the case plan must document the efforts the department is making to complete the concurrent goal.

Committee Notes

1991 Adoption. The rule allows for certain forms of relief pertinent to foster care review. It allows the court to order commencement of a termination of parental rights proceeding if the parents are not in compliance. The court is also permitted to extend or modify the plan.

RULE 8.420. CASE PLAN AMENDMENTS

(a) Modifications. After the case plan has been developed, the tasks and services agreed upon in the plan may not be changed or altered except as follows.

(1) The case plan may be amended at any time to change the goal of the plan, employ the use of concurrent planning, add or remove tasks the parent must complete to substantially comply with the plan, provide appropriate services for the child, and update the child's health, mental health, and education records.

(2) The case plan may be amended on approval of the court if all parties are in agreement regarding the amendments to the plan and the amended plan is signed by all parties and submitted to the court with a memorandum of explanation.

(3) The case plan may be amended by the court or on motion of any party at any hearing to change the goal of the plan, employ the use of concurrent planning, or add or remove the tasks the parent must complete in order to substantially comply with the plan, if there is a preponderance of evidence demonstrating the need for the amendment.

(4) The case plan may be amended by the court or on motion of any party at any hearing to provide appropriate services to the child if there is competent evidence demonstrating the need for the amendment.

(5) The case plan is deemed amended as to the child's health, mental health, and education records when the child's updated health and education records are filed by the department.

(b) Basis to Amend the Case Plan. The need to amend the case plan may be based on information discovered or circumstances arising after the approval of the case plan for:

(1) a previously unaddressed condition that, without services, may prevent the child from safely returning to or remaining in the home;

(2) the child's need for permanency;

(3) the failure of a party to substantially comply with a task in the original case plan, including the ineffectiveness of a previously offered service;

(4) an error or oversight in the case plan; or

(5) information discovered or circumstances arising after the approval of the plan regarding the provision of safe and proper care for the child.

(c) Service. A copy of the amended plan must be immediately given to all parties.

RULE 8.425. PERMANENCY HEARINGS

(a) Required Review. A permanency hearing must be held no later than 12 months after the date the child was removed from the home or within 30 days after a court determines that reasonable efforts to return a child to either parent are not required, whichever occurs first. A permanency hearing must be held at least every 12 months for any child who continues to be supervised by the department or awaits adoption.

(b) Determinations at Hearing.

(1) The court shall determine

(A) whether the current permanency goal for the child is appropriate or should be changed;

(B) when the child will achieve one of the permanency goals; and

(C) whether the department has made reasonable efforts to finalize the permanency plan currently in effect.

(2) The court shall approve a permanency goal for the child as provided by law choosing from the following options, listed in order of preference:

(A) reunification;

(B) adoption, if a petition for termination of parental rights has been or will be filed;

(C) permanent guardianship of a dependent child under section 39.6221, Florida Statutes;

(D) permanent placement with a fit and willing relative under section 39.6231, Florida Statutes; or

(E) placement in another planned permanent living arrangement under section 39.6241, Florida Statutes.

(3) The best interest of the child is the primary consideration in determining the permanency goal. The court must also consider the reasonable preference of the child if the court has found the child to be of sufficient intelligence, understanding, and experience to express a preference and any recommendation of the guardian ad litem.

(4) If the court approves a permanency goal of adoption, the court shall advise the parents of the availability of private placement of the child with an adoption entity, as defined in chapter 63, Florida Statutes.

(c) Case Plan. The case plan must list the tasks necessary to finalize the permanency placement and shall be amended at the permanency hearing if necessary. If a concurrent case plan is in place, the court shall approve a single goal that is in the child's best interest.

(d) Permanency Order.

(1) The findings of the court regarding reasonable efforts to finalize the permanency plan must be explicitly documented, made on a case-by-case basis, and stated in the court order.

(2) The court shall enter an order approving the permanency goal for the child.

(3) If the court approves a permanency goal of adoption, the order approving this goal shall include a provision stating that the court advised the parents of

the availability of private placement of the child with an adoption entity as defined in chapter 63, Florida Statutes, during the permanency hearing.

(4) If the court approves a permanency goal of permanent guardianship of a dependent child, placement with a fit and willing relative, or another planned permanent living arrangement, the court shall make findings as to why this permanent placement is established without adoption of the child to follow. The department and the guardian ad litem must provide the court with a recommended list and description of services needed by the child, such as independent living services and medical, dental, educational, or psychological referrals, and a recommended list and description of services needed by his or her caregiver.

(5) If the court establishes a permanent guardianship for the child, the court's written order shall

(A) transfer parental rights with respect to the child relating to protection, education, care and control of the person, custody of the person, and decision-making on behalf of the child to the permanent guardian;

(B) list the circumstances or reasons why the child's parents are not fit to care for the child and why reunification is not possible by referring to specific findings of fact made in its order adjudicating the child dependent or by making separate findings of fact;

(C) state the reasons why a permanent guardianship is being established instead of adoption;

(D) specify the frequency and nature of visitation or contact between the child and his or her parents, siblings, and grandparents; and

(E) require that the permanent guardian not return the child to the physical care and custody of the person from whom the child was removed without the approval of the court.

(6) The court shall retain jurisdiction over the case and the child shall remain in the custody of the permanent guardian unless the order creating the permanent guardianship is modified by the court. The court shall discontinue regular review hearings and relieve the department of the responsibility for supervising the placement of the child. Notwithstanding the retention of jurisdiction, the placement shall be considered permanency for the child.

(7) If the court permanently places a child with a fit and willing relative, the court's written order shall

(A) list the circumstances or reasons why reunification is not possible by referring to specific findings of fact made in its order adjudicating the child dependent or by making separate findings of fact;

(B) state the reasons why permanent placement with a fit and willing relative is being established instead of adoption;

(C) specify the frequency and nature of visitation or contact between the child and his or her parents, siblings, and grandparents; and

(D) require that the relative not return the child to the physical care and custody of the person from whom the child was removed without the approval of the court.

(8) If the court establishes another planned permanent living arrangement as the child's permanency option:

(A) The court must find that a more permanent placement, such as adoption, permanent guardianship, or placement with a fit and willing relative, is not in the best interests of the child.

(B) The department shall document reasons why the placement will endure and how the proposed arrangement will be more stable and secure than ordinary foster care.

(C) The court must find that the health, safety, and well-being of the child will not be jeopardized by such an arrangement.

(D) The court must find that compelling reasons exist to show that placement in another planned permanent living arrangement is the most appropriate permanency goal.

(e) Entry of Separate Order Establishing Permanency. If the court permanently places a child in a permanent guardianship or with a fit and willing relative, the court shall enter a separate order establishing the authority of the permanent guardian or relative to care for the child, reciting that individual's powers and authority with respect to the child and providing any other information the court deems proper which can be provided to persons who are not parties to the proceeding as necessary, notwithstanding the confidentiality provisions of Chapter 39, Florida Statutes.

(f) Recommendations for Sustaining Permanency. If the court approves a goal of placement with a fit and willing relative or another planned permanent living arrangement, the department and the guardian ad litem must provide the court with a recommended list and description of services needed by the child, and a recommended list and description of services needed by his or her caregiver.

RULE 8.430. MODIFICATION OF PERMANENCY ORDER

(a) Best Interests of Child. The permanency placement is intended to continue until the child reaches the age of majority and may not be disturbed absent a finding by the court that the circumstances of the permanency placement are no longer in the best interest of the child.

(b) Request for Modification by a Parent.

(1) If a parent who has not had his or her parental rights terminated makes a motion for reunification or increased contact with the child, the court shall first hold a hearing to determine whether the dependency case should be reopened and whether there should be a modification of the order. At the hearing, the parent must demonstrate that the safety, well-being, and physical, mental, and emotional health of the child is not endangered by the modification.

(2) The court shall base its decision concerning any motion by a parent for reunification or increased contact with a child on the effect of the decision on the safety, well-being, and physical and emotional health of the child. Factors that must be considered and addressed in the findings of fact of the order on the motion must include

(A) the compliance or noncompliance of the parent with the case plan;

(B) the circumstances which caused the child's dependency and whether those circumstances have been resolved;

(C) the stability and length of the child's placement;

(D) the preference of the child, if the child is of sufficient age and understanding to express a preference;

(E) the recommendation of the current custodian; and

(F) the recommendation of the guardian ad litem, if one has been appointed.

RULE 8.435. REINSTATEMENT OF JURISDICTION FOR YOUNG ADULT

(a) Petition for Reinstatement of Jurisdiction.

(1) If a young adult who is between the ages of 18 and 21, or 22 if the young adult has a disability, is re-admitted to foster care, the department shall petition the court to reinstate jurisdiction over the young adult.

(2) The petition for reinstatement of jurisdiction must be in writing and specify that the young adult meets the eligibility requirements for readmission to foster care as provided by law. The petition is not required to be sworn and notarized.

(3) The department shall serve the young adult and any party a copy of the petition for reinstatement of jurisdiction.

(b) Hearing on Petition for Reinstatement of Jurisdiction.

(1) Upon filing of the petition for reinstatement of jurisdiction, the court shall schedule and conduct a

hearing on the petition for reinstatement of jurisdiction.

(2) The department shall serve the young adult and any party a notice of the hearing on the petition for reinstatement of jurisdiction.

(c) Order on Petition for Reinstatement of Jurisdiction.

(1) If the department establishes that the young adult meets the eligibility requirements for readmission to foster care as provided by law, the court shall enter an order reinstating jurisdiction over the young adult.

(2) In the order reinstating jurisdiction, the court shall schedule a judicial review hearing to take place within 6 months.

E. TERMINATION OF PARENTAL RIGHTS

RULE 8.500. PETITION

(a) Initiation of Proceedings.

(1) All proceedings seeking the termination of parental rights to a child shall be initiated by the filing of an original petition in the pending dependency action, if any.

(2) A petition for termination of parental rights may be filed at any time by the department, the guardian ad litem, or any person having knowledge of the facts. Each petition shall be titled a petition for termination of parental rights.

(3) When provided by law, a separate petition for dependency need not be filed.

(b) Contents.

(1) The petition shall contain allegations as to the identity and residence of the parents, if known.

(2) The petition shall identify the age, sex, and name of the child. Two or more children may be the subject of the same petition.

(3) The petition shall include facts supporting allegations that each of the applicable statutory elements for termination of parental rights has been met.

(4) When required by law, the petition shall contain a showing that the parents were offered a case plan and did not substantially comply with it.

(5) The petition shall contain an allegation that the parents will be informed of the availability of private placement of the child with an adoption entity, as defined in chapter 63, Florida Statutes.

(6) The petition shall have a certified copy of the birth certificate of each child named in it attached unless the petitioner, after diligent search and inquiry, is unable to produce it, in which case the petition shall state the date and place of birth of each child, unless these matters cannot be ascertained after diligent search and inquiry or for other good cause.

(c) **Verification.** The petition shall be signed under oath stating the good faith of the petitioner in filing it. No objection to a petition on the grounds that it was not signed or verified as required shall be entertained after a plea to the merits.

(d) **Amendments.** At any time before the conclusion of an adjudicatory hearing, an amended petition may be filed or the petition may be amended by motion. However, after a written answer has been filed or the adjudicatory hearing has commenced, amendments shall be permitted only with the permission of the court unless all parties consent. Amendments shall be freely permitted in the interest of justice and the welfare of the child. A continuance shall be granted on motion and a showing that the amendment prejudices or materially affects any party.

(e) **Defects and Variances.** No petition or any count of it shall be dismissed, or any judgment vacated, because of any defect in the form of the petition or of misjoinder of counts. If the court is of the opinion that the petition is so vague, indistinct, and indefinite as to mislead the parent and prejudice him or her in the preparation of a defense, the petitioner will be required to furnish a more definite statement.

(f) **Voluntary Dismissal.** The petitioner, without leave of the court, at any time before entry of an order of adjudication, may request a voluntary dismissal of the petition by serving a notice of request of dismissal on all parties or, if during a hearing, by so stating on the record. The petition shall be dismissed and the court loses jurisdiction unless another party adopts the petition within 72 hours. Unless otherwise stated, the dismissal shall be without prejudice.

(g) Parental Consent.

(1) The parents of the child may consent to the petition for termination of parental rights at any time, in writing or orally, on the record.

(2) If, before the filing of the petition for termination of parental rights, the parents have consented to the termination of parental rights and executed surrenders and waivers of notice of hearing as provided by law, this shall be alleged in the petition and copies shall be attached to the petition and presented to the court.

(3) If the parents appear and enter an oral consent on the record to the termination of parental rights, the court shall determine the basis on which a factual finding may be made and shall incorporate these findings into its order of disposition.

RULE 8.505. PROCESS AND SERVICE

(a) Personal Service. On the filing of a petition requesting the termination of parental rights, a copy of the petition and notice of the date, time, and place of the advisory hearing must be personally served on

(1) the parents;

(2) the legal custodians or caregivers of the child;

(3) if the natural parents are dead or unknown, a living relative of the child, unless on diligent search and inquiry no relative can be found;

(4) any person who has physical custody of the child;

(5) any grandparents entitled by law to notice of the adoption proceeding;

(6) any prospective parent identified by law, unless a court order has been entered which indicates no

further notice is required, or if the prospective father executes an affidavit of nonpaternity or a consent to termination of his parental rights which is accepted by the court after notice and opportunity to be heard by all parties to address the best interests of the child in accepting such affidavit;

(7) the guardian ad litem for the child or the representative of the guardian ad litem program, if the program has been appointed;

(8) the attorney ad litem for the child if one has been appointed; and

(9) any other person as provided by law.

(b) Contents. The document containing the notice to appear shall notify the required persons of the filing of the petition and must contain in type at least as large as the balance of the document the following or substantially similar language:

> "FAILURE TO PERSONALLY APPEAR AT THE ADVISORY HEARING CONSTITUTES CONSENT TO THE TERMINATION OF PARENTAL RIGHTS OF THIS CHILD (THESE CHILDREN). IF YOU FAIL TO APPEAR ON THE DATE AND TIME SPECIFIED, YOU MAY LOSE ALL LEGAL RIGHTS AS A PARENT TO THE CHILD OR CHILDREN NAMED IN THE PETITION ATTACHED TO THIS NOTICE."

(c) Constructive Service. Parties whose identities are known and on whom personal service of process cannot be effected shall be served by publication as provided by law. The notice of action shall contain the initials of the child and the child's date of birth. There shall be no other identifying information of the child in the notice of action. The notice of action shall include the full name and last known address of the person subject to the notice. The notice of action shall not contain the name or any other identifying information of the other parents or prospective parents who are not subject to the notice.

(d) Waiver of Service. Service of process may be waived, as provided by law, for persons who have executed a written surrender of the child to the department.

RULE 8.510. ADVISORY HEARING AND PRETRIAL STATUS CONFERENCES

(a) Advisory Hearing.

(1) An advisory hearing on the petition to terminate parental rights must be held as soon as possible after service of process can be effected, but no less than 72 hours following service of process. Personal appearance of any person at the advisory hearing eliminates the time requirement for serving process on that person.

(2) The court must:

(A) advise the parents of their right to counsel including the right to an effective attorney and appoint an attorney in accordance with legal requirements;

(B) advise the parents of the availability of private placement of the child with an adoption entity, as defined in chapter 63, Florida Statutes;

(C) determine whether an admission, consent, or denial to the petition shall be entered; and

(D) appoint a guardian ad litem if one has not already been appointed.

(3) If a parent served with notice fails to personally appear at the advisory hearing, the court shall enter a consent to the termination of parental rights petition for the parent who failed to personally appear.

(4) If an admission or consent is entered by all parents for a named child included in the petition for termination of parental rights and the court finds that termination of parental rights is in the best interest of the child, the court shall proceed to disposition alternatives as provided by law.

(5) If a denial is entered, the court shall set an adjudicatory hearing within the period of time provided by law or grant a continuance until the parties have sufficient time to proceed to an adjudicatory hearing.

(b) Pretrial Status Conference. Not less than 10 days before the adjudicatory hearing on a petition for involuntary termination of parental rights, the court shall conduct a pretrial status conference to determine the order in which each party may present witnesses or evidence, the order in which cross-examination and argument shall occur, and any other matters that may aid in the conduct of the adjudicatory hearing.

(c) Voluntary Terminations. An advisory hearing may not be held if a petition is filed seeking an adjudication to voluntarily terminate parental rights. Adjudicatory hearings for petitions for voluntary termination must be set within 21 days of the filing of the petition. Notice of intent to rely on this subdivision must be filed with the court as required by law.

RULE 8.515. PROVIDING COUNSEL TO PARTIES

(a) Duty of the Court.

(1) At each hearing, the court shall advise unrepresented parents of their right to have counsel present, unless the parents have voluntarily executed a written surrender of the child and consent to the entry of a court order terminating parental rights.

(2) The court shall appoint counsel for indigent parents as provided by law. The court may appoint counsel for other parties as provided by law.

(3) The court shall ascertain whether the right to counsel is understood. If the right to counsel is waived by any parent the court shall ascertain if the right to counsel is knowingly and intelligently waived.

(4) The court shall enter its findings with respect to the appointment or waiver of counsel of indigent parents or the waiver of the right to have counsel present.

(5) Once counsel has been retained or appointed to represent a parent, the attorney shall continue to represent the parent throughout the proceedings or until the court has approved discontinuing the attorney-client relationship. If the attorney-client relationship is discontinued, the court shall advise the parent of the right to have new counsel retained or appointed for the remainder of the proceedings.

(b) Waiver of Counsel.

(1) No waiver shall be accepted if it appears that the parent is unable to make an intelligent and understanding choice because of mental condition, age, education, experience, the nature or complexity of the case, or other factors.

(2) A waiver of counsel shall be made in court and be of record. The court shall question the parent in sufficient detail to ascertain that the waiver is made knowingly and intelligently.

(3) If a waiver is accepted at any hearing, the offer of assistance of counsel shall be renewed by the court at each subsequent hearing at which the parent appears without counsel.

RULE 8.517. WITHDRAWAL AND APPOINTMENT OF ATTORNEY

(a) Withdrawal of Attorney after Order Adjudicating Child Dependent. After an order of adjudication of dependency or an order of dependency disposition has been entered, the attorney of record for a parent or legal custodian in a dependency proceeding shall not be permitted to withdraw as the attorney until the following have occurred:

(1) The attorney certifies that after discussing appellate remedies with the parent or legal custodian, the parent or legal custodian elects not to appeal the order; or

(2) The attorney certifies that after discussing appellate remedies with the parent or legal custodian, the parent or legal custodian elects to appeal the order, and

(A) a notice of appeal containing the signatures of the attorney and the parent or legal custodian has been filed or a notice of appeal containing the signature only of the attorney has been filed if the parent or legal custodian elects to appeal but is unable to personally timely sign the notice and that an amended notice of appeal containing the parent's or legal custodian's signature will be filed;

(B) directions to clerk, if necessary, have been filed;

(C) a motion to transcribe the requisite proceedings has been filed;

(D) a designation to the court reporter specifying the proceedings that must be transcribed in order to obtain review of the issues on appeal and designating the parties to receive a copy of the transcripts has been filed; and

(E) an order appointing appellate counsel, if any, has been entered.

Conformed copies of each of these documents shall be attached to the motion to withdraw.

(3) If the attorney is unable to contact the parent or legal custodian regarding appellate remedies, the attorney certifies and describes the efforts made to contact the parent or legal custodian.

(b) Withdrawal of Attorney after Order Terminating Parental Rights. After an order terminating parental rights has been entered, the attorney of record for a parent in a termination of parental rights proceeding shall not be permitted to withdraw as attorney until the following have occurred:

(1) Discussion of Appeal.

(A) The attorney certifies that after discussing appellate remedies with the parent, the parent elects not to appeal the order terminating parental rights; or

(B) The attorney certifies that after discussing appellate remedies with the parent, the parent elects to appeal the order terminating parental rights; and

(i) a notice of appeal containing the signatures of the attorney and the parent has been filed or a notice of appeal containing the signature only of the attorney has been filed if the parent elects to appeal but is unable to personally timely sign the notice and that an amended notice of appeal containing the parent's signature will be filed;

(ii) directions to clerk, if necessary, have been filed;

(iii) a motion to transcribe the requisite proceedings has been filed;

(iv) a designation to the court reporter specifying the proceedings that must be transcribed in order to obtain review of the issues on appeal and designating the parties to receive a copy of the transcripts has been filed; and

(v) an order appointing appellate counsel, if any, has been entered.

Conformed copies of each of these documents shall be attached to the motion to withdraw.

(2) Discussion of Ineffective Assistance of Counsel Claim.

(A) The attorney certifies that after discussing the right of a parent to file a motion claiming ineffective assistance of counsel, the parent elects not to file the motion, or

(B) The attorney certifies that after discussing the right of the parent to file a motion claiming ineffective assistance of counsel, the parent elects to file a motion. Consequently, the attorney must immediately seek to withdraw from representation of the parent.

(3) Inability to Discuss Remedies. If the attorney is unable to contact the parent regarding appellate remedies and the right to file a motion claiming ineffective assistance of counsel, the attorney certifies and describes the efforts made to contact the parent.

(c) Appointment of Appellate Counsel. If the court permits the attorney to withdraw, the court must expeditiously appoint appellate counsel for indigent parents pursuant to law. The indigent parent is not entitled to a court-appointed attorney in any trial court proceeding regarding a motion claiming ineffective assistance of counsel. However, a parent may independently retain an attorney to assist in any trial court proceeding regarding a motion claiming ineffective assistance of counsel.

Conformed copies of each of these documents shall be attached to the motion to withdraw.

(d) Service of Order Appointing Attorney. Following rendition of an order appointing appellate counsel, the court must serve the order on the appointed appellate counsel and the clerk of the appellate court.

Committee Notes

Amendment 2017. Significant amendments were made to create a process for claiming ineffective assistance of counsel in termination of parental rights proceedings. *J.B., etc. v. Florida Department of Children and Families,* 170 So. 3d 780 (Fla. 2015). A parent's right to appointed counsel is governed by sections 39.013(9)a. and 27.511, Florida Statutes.

RULE 8.520. ANSWERS AND RESPONSIVE PLEADINGS

(a) No Written Answer Required. No answer to the petition need be filed by the parent. The parent of the child may enter an oral or written answer to the petition or appear and remain silent.

(b) Plea of Denial. If the parent denies the allegations of the petition, appears and remains silent, or pleads evasively, the court shall enter a denial and shall set the case for an adjudicatory hearing.

(c) Plea of Admission or Consent. If the parent appears and enters a plea of admission or consent to the termination of parental rights, the court shall determine that the admission or consent is made voluntarily and with a full understanding of the nature of the allegations and the possible consequences of the plea and that the parent has been advised of the right to be represented by counsel. The court shall incorporate these findings into its order of disposition, in addition to findings of fact specifying the act or acts causing the termination of parental rights.

RULE 8.525. ADJUDICATORY HEARINGS

(a) Hearing by Judge. The adjudicatory hearing shall be conducted by the judge without a jury using the rules of evidence for civil cases. At this hearing the court shall determine whether the elements required by law for termination of parental rights have been established by clear and convincing evidence.

(b) Time of Hearing. The adjudicatory hearing shall be held within 45 days after the advisory hearing, unless all necessary parties stipulate to some other hearing date. Reasonable continuances may be granted for purposes of investigation, discovery, procuring counsel or witnesses, or for other good cause shown.

(c) Examination of Witnesses. A party may call any person, including a child, as a witness. A party shall have the right to examine or cross-examine all witnesses.

(d) Presence of Parties. All parties have the right to be present at all termination hearings. A party may appear in person or, at the discretion of the court for good cause shown, by an audio or audiovisual device. No party shall be excluded from any hearing unless so ordered by the court for disruptive behavior or as provided by law. If a parent appears for the advisory hearing and the court orders that parent to personally appear at the adjudicatory hearing for the petition for termination of parental rights, stating the date, time, and location of this hearing, then failure of that parent to personally appear at the adjudicatory hearing shall constitute consent for termination of parental rights.

(e) Examination of Child. The court may hear the testimony of the child outside the physical presence of the parties as provided by rule 8.255. Counsel for the parties shall be present during all examinations. The court may limit the manner in which counsel examine the child.

(f) Previous Testimony Admissible. To avoid unnecessary duplication of expenses, in-court testimony previously given at any properly noticed hearing may be admitted, without regard to the availability of the witnesses, if the recorded testimony itself is made available. Consideration of previous testimony does not preclude the parties from calling the witness to answer supplemental questions.

(g) Joint and Separate Hearings. When 2 or more children are the subject of a petition for termination of parental rights, the hearings may be held simultaneously if the children are related to each other or involved in the same case, unless the court orders separate hearings.

(h) Motion for Judgment of Dismissal. In all termination of parental rights proceedings, if at the close of the evidence for the petitioner the parents move for a judgment of dismissal and the court is of the opinion that the evidence is insufficient to sustain the grounds for termination alleged in the petition, it shall enter an order denying the termination and proceed with dispositional alternatives as provided by law.

(i) Advisement of Right to Appeal and File Ineffective Assistance of Counsel Motion. At the conclusion of the adjudicatory hearing, the court must orally inform the parents of the right to appeal any order terminating parental rights to the district court of appeal and the right to file a motion in the circuit court claiming that counsel provided ineffective assistance.

(j) Order.

(1) Terminating Parental Rights.

(A) If the court finds after all of the evidence has been presented that the elements and one of the grounds for termination of parental rights have been established by clear and convincing evidence, the court shall enter a written order terminating parental rights and proceed with dispositional alternatives as provided by law.

(B) The order must contain the findings of fact and conclusions of law on which the decision was based. The court shall include the dates of the adjudicatory hearing in the order.

(C) The order must include a brief statement informing the parents of the right to appeal the order to the district court of appeal and the right to file a motion in the circuit court alleging that counsel provided ineffective assistance and a brief explanation of the procedure for filing such a claim.

(D) The parties may stipulate, or the court may order, that parents or relatives of the parent whose rights are terminated be allowed to maintain some contact with the child. If the court orders continued contact, the nature and frequency of this contact must be stated in a written order. The visitation order may be reviewed on motion of any party, including a prospective adoptive parent, and must be reviewed by the court at the time the child is placed for adoption.

(2) Denying Termination of Parental Rights. If the court finds after all of the evidence has been presented that the grounds for termination of parental rights have not been established by clear and convincing evidence, but that the grounds for dependency have been established by a preponderance of the evidence, the court shall adjudicate or readjudicate the child dependent and proceed with dispositional alternatives as provided by law.

(3) Dismissing Petition. If the court finds after all of the evidence has been presented that the allegations in the petition do not establish grounds for dependency or termination of parental rights, it shall enter an order dismissing the petition.

RULE 8.530. PARENT'S MOTION CLAIMING INEFFECTIVE ASSISTANCE OF COUNSEL FOLLOWING ORDER TERMINATING PARENTAL RIGHTS

(a) Duty of the Court to Advise. At the conclusion of the termination of parental rights adjudicatory hearing, the court must orally inform the parents who are represented by an attorney of the right to appeal an order terminating parental rights to the district court of appeal and the right to file a motion in the circuit court claiming that an attorney provided ineffective assistance if the court enters an order terminating parental rights. In addition, the written order terminating parental rights must include a brief statement informing the parents of the right to file a motion claiming ineffective assistance of counsel and a brief explanation of the procedure for filing the motion.

(b) Duty of Attorney to Advise. After entry of an order terminating parental rights, an attorney must discuss appellate remedies with the parent and determine whether the parent elects to appeal the order terminating parental rights. The attorney must also inquire whether the parent intends to file a motion claiming ineffective assistance of counsel. If the parent states an intention to file a motion claiming ineffective assistance of counsel, then the attorney must immediately seek withdrawal pursuant to these rules.

(c) Motion and Jurisdiction. After the court has entered a written order terminating parental rights, a parent may file a motion in the circuit court claiming that the parent's attorney provided ineffective assistance. If a notice of appeal of the order terminating parental rights is filed, the trial court continues to have jurisdiction to consider a motion claiming ineffective assistance of counsel.

(d) Court-Appointed Attorney.

(1) An indigent parent is not entitled to a court-appointed attorney to assist the parent in preparing, filing, or litigating a motion claiming ineffective assistance of counsel. However, the parent may independently obtain an attorney to represent the parent in pursuing the motion.

(2) An indigent parent is otherwise entitled to a court-appointed attorney as provided by law in both the trial and appellate court in a termination of parental rights proceeding, and is entitled to a court-appointed attorney concerning appellate review of the trial court's order on the motion for ineffective assistance of counsel.

(e) Time Limitations. A motion claiming ineffective assistance of counsel must be filed within 20 days of the date the court entered the written order terminating parental rights.

(f) Toll of Time for Appeal. The timely filing of a motion claiming ineffective assistance of counsel tolls rendition of the order terminating parental rights for purposes of appeal until the circuit court enters an order on the motion or for 50 days from the date the court entered the written order terminating parental rights, whichever occurs first.

(g) Contents of Motion.

(1) The motion must be in writing and under oath stating that all of the facts stated are true and correct.

(2) The motion must contain the case name and number and identify the date the written order terminating parental rights was entered.

(3) The motion must contain the current mailing address and e-mail address, if any, and the phone

number(s) of the parent filing the motion for the purpose of receiving notices and orders.

(4) The motion must identify specific acts or omissions in the attorney's representation of the parent during the termination of parental rights proceedings that constituted a failure to provide reasonable, professional assistance and explain how the acts or omissions prejudiced the parent's case to such an extent that but for counsel's deficient performance the parent's rights would not have been terminated.

(h) Amendments to Motion. If the motion claiming ineffective assistance of counsel is timely filed, the parent may file amended motions without permission of the court within 20 days from the date the court entered the written order terminating parental rights. The court may order the moving parent to file an amended motion as provided in this rule.

(i) Delivery of Motion to Judge. On filing of the motion, the clerk of court must immediately provide the motion and court file to the judge who entered the order terminating parental rights.

(j) Response to Motion. No answer or responsive pleading is required from any other party to the termination of parental rights proceeding.

(k) Service of the Motion. The parent claiming ineffective assistance of counsel must serve the motion on all parties to the termination of parental rights proceeding and to the attorney the parent claims provided ineffective assistance.

(*l*) Summary Denial of Motion.

(1) Untimely Motion. The court must enter an order within 5 days from the date the motion or amended motion was filed summarily denying with prejudice any motion filed after the 20-day limitation for filing. The order shall be considered the final order for purposes of appeal.

(2) Insufficient Motion. If the motion or amended motion is legally insufficient as alleged, the court may enter an order summarily denying the motion within 5 days from the date the motion or amended motion was

filed. A motion is legally insufficient when the allegations of ineffective assistance of counsel during the termination of parental rights proceedings, if taken as true, did not prejudice the parent's case to such an extent that but for counsel's deficient performance the parent's rights would not have been terminated. The order denying a motion as legally insufficient must set forth the basis for the conclusion the motion is legally insufficient. The court must not summarily deny a motion as insufficient for reasons other than legally insufficient allegations claiming ineffective assistance of counsel. If the court denies the motion as legally insufficient and does not direct the filing of an amended motion, then the order shall be considered the final order for purposes of appeal.

(m) Order for Amended Motion. If the motion or amended motion is legally insufficient as alleged, the court may enter an order within 5 days from the date the motion, or amended motion, was filed authorizing the moving parent to file an amended motion within 10 days of the date of the written order permitting amendment.

(n) Evidentiary Hearing on Motion.

(1) Scheduling of Hearing. If the motion is timely and, in the court's opinion, contains sufficient allegations, the court must conduct an evidentiary hearing as expeditiously as possible in light of the other time limitations in this rule.

(2) Notice of Hearing. The court must issue a notice of the hearing on the motion to the parties and participants of the termination of parental rights proceeding and to the attorney who the parent claimed provided ineffective assistance. The notice must state the issues to be determined and that the moving parent is required to present evidence at the hearing on the motion.

(3) Record of Termination of Parental Rights Adjudicatory Hearing. If necessary, the court may order an expedited record for review, which may include an electronic recording in lieu of a transcript, of the termination of parental rights adjudicatory hearing. If the judge conducting the motion hearing is different from the judge who presided at the termination of parental rights adjudicatory hearing, the court must order an expedited record for review, which may include an electronic recording in lieu of a transcript, of the termination of parental rights adjudicatory hearing.

(4) Burden to Present Evidence and Proof. At the evidentiary hearing, the moving parent has the burden of presenting evidence and the burden of proving specific acts or omissions of an attorney's representation of the parent during the termination of parental rights proceedings that constituted a failure to provide reasonable, professional assistance, and how the errors or omissions prejudiced the parent's case to such an extent that but for counsel's deficient performance the parent's rights would not have been terminated. All other parties may present evidence regarding the claims raised.

(5) Order from Evidentiary Hearing. At the conclusion of the hearing on the motion, the court must enter an order granting or denying the motion within 5 days from the evidentiary hearing.

(A) Grant of Motion. If the court determines that the attorney during the termination of parental rights proceedings failed to provide reasonable, professional assistance and that the errors or omissions prejudiced the parent's case to such an extent that but for counsel's deficient performance the parent's rights would not have been terminated, the court must enter an order granting the motion stating the reasons for granting the motion and vacating the order terminating parental rights without prejudice. In the order, the court must schedule an adjudicatory hearing on the petition for termination of parental rights to take place no later than 45 days from the order granting the motion. The court must then appoint an attorney to represent the parent in further proceedings, as provided by law.

(B) Denial of Motion. If the court determines that the attorney during the termination of parental rights proceedings provided reasonable, professional assistance or determines that no errors or omissions prejudiced the parent's case in the termination proceedings to such an extent that but for counsel's deficient performance the parent's rights would not

have been terminated, the court must enter an order denying the motion, stating the reasons for denial. The order resolves all the claims raised in the motion and shall be considered the final order for purposes of appeal.

(o) Failure to Enter Order. If the court does not enter an order granting or denying the motion within 50 days from the date the court entered the written order terminating parental rights, the motion shall be deemed denied with prejudice.

(p) Service of Order. The clerk of the court must serve any order entered under this rule on the parties, including to the moving parent at the parent's address on file with the clerk, within 48 hours from the rendition of the order indicating the date of service by an appropriate certificate of service.

(q) Successive Motions. No second or successive motion claiming ineffective assistance of counsel shall be allowed except as provided in this rule. No motion for rehearing shall be allowed in response to the court's ruling on the motion claiming ineffective assistance of counsel.

(r) Appeals. Florida Rule of Appellate Procedure 9.146 applies to the appeal of an order on a motion claiming ineffective assistance of counsel in termination of parental rights proceedings.

RULE 8.535. POSTDISPOSITION HEARINGS

(a) Initial Hearing. If the court terminates parental rights, a postdisposition hearing must be set within 30 days after the date of disposition. At the hearing, the department or licensed child-placing agency shall provide to the court a plan for permanency for the child.

(b) Subsequent Hearings. Following the initial postdisposition hearing, the court shall hold hearings every 6 months to review progress being made toward permanency for the child until the child is adopted or reaches the age of 18, whichever occurs first. Review hearings for alternative forms of permanent placement shall be held as provided by law.

(c) Continuing Jurisdiction. The court that terminates the parental rights to a child under chapter 39,

Florida Statutes, shall retain exclusive jurisdiction in all matters pertaining to the child's adoption under chapter 63, Florida Statutes. The petition for adoption must be filed in the division of the circuit court that entered the judgment terminating parental rights, unless a motion for change of venue is granted as provided by law.

(d) Withholding Consent to Adopt.

(1) When a petition for adoption and a favorable home study under section 39.812(5), Florida Statutes, have been filed and the department's consent has not been filed, the court shall conduct a hearing to determine if the department has unreasonably withheld consent.

(2) In reviewing whether the department unreasonably withheld its consent to adopt, the court shall determine whether the department abused its discretion by withholding consent to the adoption by the petitioner. In making this determination, the court shall consider all relevant information, including information obtained or otherwise used by the department in selecting the adoptive family, pursuant to Florida Administrative Code Chapter 65C.

(3) If the court determines that the department unreasonably withheld consent to adopt, and the petitioner has filed with the court a favorable home study as required by law, the court shall incorporate its findings into a written order with specific findings of fact as to how the department abused its discretion in withholding its consent to adopt, and the consent of the department shall be waived.

PART IV. PROCEEDINGS FOR FAMILIES AND CHILDREN IN NEED OF SERVICES

RULE 8.601. COMMENCEMENT OF PROCEEDINGS

(a) Pleadings. All proceedings shall be initiated by the filing of:

(1) a request to take into custody;

(2) a petition for children in need of services; or

(3) a shelter petition.

(b) File to Be Opened. Upon commencement of any proceeding, the clerk shall open a file and assign a case number.

RULE 8.603. APPLICATION OF UNIFORM CHILD CUSTODY JURISDICTION AND ENFORCEMENT ACT

Any pleading filed commencing proceedings as set forth in rule 8.601 shall be accompanied by an affidavit, to the extent of affiant's personal knowledge, under the Uniform Child Custody Jurisdiction and Enforcement Act. Each party has a continuing duty to inform the court of any custody, dependency, or children in need of services proceeding in this or any other state of which the party obtains information during the proceeding.

RULE 8.605. TRANSFER OF CASES

(a) Transfer of Cases Within the State of Florida. After the commencement of a proceeding pursuant to rule 8.601, the court may transfer any case after adjudication, when adjudication is withheld, or before adjudication where witnesses are available in another jurisdiction, to the circuit court for the county in which is located the domicile or usual residence of the child or such other circuit as the court may determine to be for the best interest of the child and to promote the efficient administration of justice. The transferring court shall enter an order transferring its jurisdiction and certifying the case to the proper court, furnishing all parties, the clerk, and the state attorney of the receiving court a copy of the order of transfer within 5 days. The clerk shall also transmit a certified copy of the file to the receiving court within 5 days.

(b) Transfer of Cases Among States. If it should appear at any time that an action involving the child is pending in another state, the court may transfer jurisdiction, stay the proceedings, or dismiss the action as provided by law.

RULE 8.610. PARTIES

(a) Definitions. For the purposes of these rules the terms "party" and "parties" shall include the petitioner, the child, the parent, the guardian ad litem where appointed, the custodian, and every person upon whom service of summons is required by law.

(b) Other Parties. The state attorney's office, the Department of Children and Family Services, or the Department of Juvenile Justice may become a party upon notice to all other parties and the court. The court may add additional parties.

RULE 8.615. PROVIDING COUNSEL TO PARTIES

(a) Duty of the Court.

(1) At each stage of the proceeding the court shall advise all parties of their right to have counsel present. The court shall appoint counsel to insolvent persons who are so entitled as provided by law. The court shall ascertain whether the right to counsel is understood and, where appropriate, knowingly and intelligently waived. The court shall enter its findings in writing with respect to the appointment or waiver of counsel for insolvent parties.

(2) The court may appoint an attorney for the child or parent, guardian, or custodian of the child as provided by law.

(b) Waiver of Counsel.

(1) No waiver shall be accepted where it appears that the party is unable to make an intelligent and understanding choice because of mental condition, age, education, experience, the nature or complexity of the case, or other factors.

(2) A waiver of counsel shall be made in court and be of record.

(3) If a waiver is accepted at any stage of the proceedings, the offer of assistance of counsel shall be renewed by the court at each subsequent stage of the proceedings at which the party appears without counsel.

RULE 8.617. GUARDIAN AD LITEM

(a) Appointment. At any stage of the proceedings any party may request, or the court may appoint, a guardian ad litem to represent any child alleged to be in need of services or from a family in need of services.

(b) Qualifications; Responsibilities. The guardian ad litem shall be an attorney or other responsible adult and shall have the following responsibilities:

(1) To investigate the allegations of the petition and any subsequent matters arising in the case and, unless excused by the court, to file a written report. This report shall include a statement of the wishes of the child and the recommendations of the guardian ad litem and shall be provided to all parties and the court at least 48 hours before the disposition hearing.

(2) To be present at all court hearings unless excused by the court.

(3) To represent the interest of the child until the jurisdiction of the court over the child terminates or until excused by the court.

(4) To perform such other duties and undertake such other responsibilities as the court may direct.

(c) Bond Not Required. A guardian ad litem shall not be required to post bond but shall file an acceptance of the office.

(d) Receiving Service. A guardian ad litem shall be entitled to receive service of pleadings and papers as provided by rule 8.635.

(e) Lay Guardians' Duties. The duties of lay guardians shall not include the practice of law.

(f) Substitution or Discharge. The court, on its own motion or that of any party, including the child, may substitute or discharge the guardian ad litem for reasonable cause.

RULE 8.620. STYLE OF PLEADINGS AND ORDERS

All pleadings and orders shall be styled: "In the interest of ...., a child", or "In the interest of ...., children."

RULE 8.625. GENERAL PROVISIONS FOR HEARINGS

(a) Presence of Counsel. The Department of Children and Family Services or the Department of Juvenile Justice must be represented by an attorney at every stage of these proceedings when such department is a party.

(b) Presence of Child. The child shall be present unless the child's presence is waived. If the child is present at the beginning of a hearing and during the progress of the hearing voluntarily absents himself or herself from the presence of the court without leave of the court, or is removed from the presence of the court because of disruptive conduct during the hearing, the hearing shall not be postponed or delayed, but shall proceed in all respects as if the child were present in court at all times.

(c) In Camera Proceedings. The child may be examined by the court outside the presence of other parties under circumstances as provided by law. The court shall assure that the proceedings are recorded unless otherwise stipulated by the parties.

(d) Invoking the Rule. Before the examination of any witness the court may, and on the request of any party shall, exclude all other witnesses. The court may cause witnesses to be kept separate and to be prevented from communicating with each other until all are examined.

(e) Continuances. The court may grant a continuance before or during a hearing for good cause shown by any party.

(f) Record. A record of the testimony in all hearings shall be made by an official court reporter, a court-approved stenographer, or a recording device. The records of testimony shall be preserved as required by law. Official records of testimony shall be transcribed only on order of the court.

(g) Notice. Where these rules do not require a specific notice, all parties will be given reasonable notice of any hearing.

(h) Magistrates. Pursuant to the Florida Rules of Civil Procedure, both general and special magistrates may be appointed to hear issues involved in proceedings under this part.

RULE 8.630. COMPUTATION AND ENLARGEMENT OF TIME

(a) Computation. Computation of time shall be governed by Florida Rule of Judicial Administration, except for rule 8.655, to which rule 2.514(a)(2)(C) shall not apply and the statutory time period shall govern.

(b) Enlargement of Time. When by these rules, by a notice given thereunder, or by order of court an act is required or allowed to be done at or within a specified time, the court for good cause shown may, at any time in its discretion, (1) with or without notice order the period enlarged if the request is made before the expiration of the period originally prescribed or as extended by a previous order, or (2) upon motion made and notice after the expiration of the specified period permit the act to be done where the failure to act was the result of excusable neglect; but it may not, except as provided by law or elsewhere in these rules, extend the time for making motion for new trial, for rehearing, or for vacation of judgment or for taking an appeal. This rule shall not be construed to apply to detention or shelter hearings.

(c) Time for Service of Motions and Notice of Hearing. A copy of any written motion which may not be heard ex parte and a copy of the notice of the hearing thereof shall be served a reasonable time before the time specified for the hearing.

RULE 8.635. PROCESS

(a) Summons and Subpoenas.

(1) Summons. Upon the filing of a petition, the clerk shall issue a summons. The summons shall require the person on whom it is served to appear for a hearing at a time and place specified. Except in cases of medical emergency, the time of hearing shall not be less than 24 hours after service of the summons. If the child is not detained by an order of the court, the summons shall require the custodian to produce the child at the said time and place. A copy of the petition shall be attached to the summons.

(2) Subpoenas. Upon the application of a party, the clerk shall issue, and the court on its own motion may issue, subpoenas requiring attendance and testimony of witnesses and production of records, documents, or other tangible objects at any hearing. This subdivision shall not in any way limit the state attorney's power to issue subpoenas.

(3) Service. The summons and other process shall be served upon such persons and in such manner as required by law. If the parents or custodian are out of the state and their address is known, the clerk shall give them notice of the proceedings by mail. Service of process may be waived. Authorized agents of the Department of Juvenile Justice may also serve summons and other process upon such persons and in such manner as required by law.

(b) Service of Pleadings and Papers.

(1) When Required. Unless the court orders otherwise, or a statute or supreme court administrative order specifies a different means of service, every pleading subsequent to the initial petition, every order, every written motion, unless it is one as to which hearing ex parte is authorized, and every written notice filed in the case shall be served on each party; however, nothing herein shall be construed to require that a plea be in writing or that an application for witness subpoenas be served.

(2) How Made. When service is required or permitted to be made upon a party represented by an attorney, service shall be made upon the attorney unless service upon the party is ordered by the court. All documents required or permitted to be served on another party must be served by e-mail, unless the parties otherwise stipulate or this rule otherwise provides.

(A) Service by Electronic Mail ("e-mail"). Service of a document by e-mail is made by an e-mail sent to all addresses designated by the attorney or party with either (a) a copy of the document in PDF format attached or (b) a link to the document on a website maintained by a clerk. Any document served by e-mail may be signed by any of the "/s/," "/s," or "s/" formats, so long as the filed document is signed in accordance with the applicable rules of court.

(i) Service on Attorneys. Upon appearing in any proceeding, an attorney must designate a principal e-mail address and may designate no more than two secondary e-mail addresses to which service must be directed in that proceeding. Every document filed by an attorney thereafter must include in the signature block the principal e-mail address of that attorney and any secondary e-mail addresses. If an attorney does not designate any e-mail address for service, documents may be served on that attorney at the e-mail address on record with The Florida Bar.

(ii) Exception to E-mail Service on Attorneys. Upon motion by an attorney demonstrating that the attorney has no e-mail account and lacks access to the Internet at the attorney's office, the court may excuse the attorney from the requirements of e-mail service. Service on and by an attorney excused by the court from e-mail service must be by the means provided in subdivision (b)(2)(B) of this rule.

(iii) Service on and by Parties not Represented by an Attorney. Any party not represented by an attorney may serve a designation of a principal e-mail address and also may designate no more than two secondary e-mail addresses to which service must be directed in that proceeding by the means provided in subdivision (b)(2)(A) of this rule. If a party not represented by an attorney does not designate an e-mail address for service in a proceeding, service on and by that party must be by the means provided in subdivision (b)(2)(B) of this rule.

(iv) Format of E-mail for Service. All documents served by e-mail must be sent by an e-mail message containing a subject line beginning with the words "SERVICE OF COURT DOCUMENT" in all capital letters, followed by the case number of the proceeding in which the documents are being served. The body of the e-mail must identify the court in which the proceeding is pending, the case number, the name of the initial party on each side, the title of each document served with that e-mail, and the sender's name and telephone number. Any e-mail which, together with its attachments, exceeds five megabytes (5MB) in size, must be divided and sent as separate e-mails, numbered in the subject line, no one of which may exceed 5MB in size.

(v) Time of Service. Service by e-mail is complete on the day it is sent and must be treated as service by mail for the computation of time. If the sender learns that the e-mail did not reach the address of the person to be served, the sender must immediately serve another copy by e-mail, or by a means authorized by subdivision (b)(2)(B) of this rule.

(B) Service by Other Means. In addition to, and not in lieu of, service by e-mail, service may also be made upon attorneys by the means specified in this subdivision. Service on and by all parties who are not represented by an attorney and who do not designate an e-mail address, and on and by all attorneys excused from e-mail service, must be made by delivering a copy of the document or by mailing it to the party or attorney at their last known address or, if no address is known, by leaving it with the clerk of the court. Service by mail is complete upon mailing. Delivery of a copy within this rule is complete upon:

(i) handing it to the attorney or to the party;

(ii) leaving it at the attorney's or party's office with a clerk or other person in charge thereof;

(iii) if there is no one in charge, leaving it in a conspicuous place therein;

(iv) if the office is closed or the person to be served has no office, leaving it at the person's usual place of abode with some person of his or her family above 15 years of age and informing such person of the contents; or

(v) transmitting it by facsimile to the attorney's or party's office with a cover sheet containing the sender's name, firm, address, telephone number, and facsimile number, and the number of pages transmitted. When service is made by facsimile, a copy must also be served by any other method permitted by this rule. Facsimile service occurs when transmission is complete.

(vi) Service shall be deemed complete on the date of delivery.

(C) Numerous Parties. In an action where the parties are unusually numerous, the court may regu-late the service contemplated by these rules on motion or on its own initiative in such manner as may be found to be just and reasonable.

(3) Filing. All documents must be filed with the court either before service or immediately thereafter, unless otherwise provided for by general law or other rules. If the original of any bond or document required to be an original is not placed in the court file or deposited with the clerk, a certified copy may be so placed by the clerk.

(4) Filing with Court Defined. The filing of documents with the court as required by these rules shall be made by filing them with the clerk in accordance with rule 8.004 except that the judge may permit documents to be filed with the judge, in which event the judge must note the filing date before him or her on the documents and transmit them to the clerk. The date of filing is the date shown on the face of the document by the judge's notation or the clerk's time stamp, whichever is earlier.

(5) Certificate of Service. When any attorney shall in substance certify:

"I certify that a copy/copies has/have been furnished to (insert name or names) by (e-mail) (delivery) (mail) (fax) on (date).

_____

                     Title"

this certificate shall be taken as prima facie proof of such service in compliance with this rule.

(6) Service by Clerk. When the clerk is required to serve notices and other documents, the clerk may do so by e-mail or by any other method permitted in subdivision (b)(2). Service by a clerk is not required to be by e-mail.

(c) Service of Orders. A copy of all orders or judgments must be transmitted by the court or under its direction to all parties at the time of entry of the order or judgment. The court may require that orders or judgments be prepared by a party, may require the party to furnish the court with stamped addressed envelopes for service of the order or judgment, and may require that proposed orders and judgments be furnished to all parties before entry by the court of the order or judgment. The court may serve any order or judgment by e-mail to all attorneys who have designated an e-mail address for service and to all parties not represented by an attorney who have designated an e-mail address for service. This subdivision is directory and a failure to comply with it does not affect the order or its finality or any proceedings arising in the action.

RULE 8.640. PLEADINGS TO BE SIGNED

(a) Pleadings to be Signed by Attorney. Every written paper or pleading of a party represented by an attorney shall be signed in the attorney's individual name by the attorney, whose Florida Bar number, address, and telephone number, including area code, shall be stated, and who shall be duly licensed to practice law in Florida. The attorney may be required by an order of court to vouch for the authority to represent such party and to give the address of such party. Except when otherwise specifically provided by these rules or applicable statute, pleadings need not be verified or accompanied by affidavit.

(b) Pleadings to be Signed by Unrepresented Party. A party who is unrepresented shall sign a written pleading or other paper to be filed and state the party's address and telephone number, including area code.

(c) Effect of Signing Pleading. The signature of a person shall constitute a certificate that the paper or pleading has been read; that to the best of the person's knowledge, information, and belief there is good ground to support it; and that it is not interposed for delay. If a pleading or paper is not signed, or is signed with intent to defeat the purpose of this rule, it may be stricken and the action may proceed as though the pleading or paper had not been served.

Committee Notes

1992 Amendment. (a) and (c) The language from (a) was moved to create this new subdivision. The current rule applies only to attorneys. These requirements also should apply to nonattorneys who sign and file papers. This rule conforms to proposed revisions to rules 8.085 and 8.230.

(b) The current rule implies that a written pleading must be filed. No written pleadings are required.

RULE 8.645. ORDERS

Upon the conclusion of all hearings, the court shall enter its decisions in a written order. All orders of the court shall be reduced to writing as soon after they are entered as is consistent with orderly procedure and shall contain findings of fact and conclusions of law.

RULE 8.650. TAKING INTO CUSTODY

(a) Affidavit. An affidavit may be filed by any person alleging facts under existing law sufficient to establish grounds to take a child into custody. The affidavit shall:

(1) be in writing and signed;

(2) specify the name, address, and sex of the child or, if unknown, designate the child by any name or description by which the child can be identified with reasonable certainty;

(3) specify that the child is of an age subject to the jurisdiction of the court; and

(4) state the reasons why the child is being taken into custody.

(b) Criteria for Order. The court may issue an order to take a child into custody based on sworn testimony meeting the criteria set forth in subdivision (a).

(c) Order. The order to take into custody shall:

(1) be in writing and signed;

(2) specify the name, address, and sex of the child or, if unknown, designate the child by any name or description by which the child can be identified with reasonable certainty;

(3) specify that the child is of an age subject to the jurisdiction of the court;

(4) state the reasons why the child is being taken into custody;

(5) order that the child be placed in a suitable place pending a shelter hearing as provided by law; and

(6) state the date when issued and the county and court where issued.

RULE 8.655. SHELTER PETITION, HEARING, AND ORDER

(a) Shelter Petition. If child is to be placed in a shelter after being taken into custody for a period longer than 24 hours, the person requesting placement shall file a written petition which shall:

(1) specify the name, address, and sex of the child, or, if unknown, designate the child by any name or description by which the child can be identified with reasonable certainty;

(2) specify that the child is of an age subject to the jurisdiction of the court;

(3) state the reasons why the child needs to be placed in a shelter;

(4) recommend where the child is to be placed or the agency to be responsible for placement;

(5) be signed by the attorney for the petitioner; and

(6) include a certificate of service to all parties and their attorneys of record.

(b) Shelter Hearing.

(1) The petitioner shall make a diligent effort to notify the parent or custodian of the child and shall notify his or her attorney of record of the date, time, and place of the hearing. The petitioner shall list all parties notified of the hearing on the certificate of service on the shelter petition.

(2) The court shall conduct an informal hearing on the petition within the time period provided by law. The court shall determine at the hearing whether the criteria provided by law for placement in a shelter have been met.

(3) At the hearing all interested persons present shall have an opportunity to be heard on the criteria for placement as provided by law.

(4) The court may base its determination on a sworn complaint, testimony, or affidavit and may hear all relevant and material evidence, including oral and written reports, to the extent of its probative value even though it would not be competent at an adjudicatory hearing.

(5) The court shall advise the parties of:

(A) their right to be represented by counsel as provided by law;

(B) the reason for the child being in custody and why continued placement is requested; and

(C) their right to present placement alternatives.

(c) Shelter Order.

The order shall be in writing and shall:

(1) state the name, age, and sex of the child and, if the child's age is unknown, that the child is believed to be of an age which makes him or her subject to the jurisdiction of the court;

(2) include findings as provided by law;

(3) designate the place where the child is to be placed or the person or agency that will be responsible for this placement along with any special conditions found to be necessary;

(4) state the date and time where issued;

(5) indicate when the child shall be released from the shelter or set a review of shelter hearing within the time limits provided by law; and

(6) include a certificate of service to all parties and their attorneys of record.

(d) Release From Shelter Care. No child shall be released from shelter after a shelter order has been entered except on order of the court unless the shelter order authorizes release by the department.

RULE 8.660. PETITIONS

(a) Contents of Petition.

(1) Only those authorized by law may file a petition alleging that a child is in need of services. Each

petition shall be entitled a petition for child(ren) in need of services and shall allege sufficient facts showing the child to be in need of services based upon applicable law.

(2) The petition shall contain allegations as to the identity and residence of the parents or custodians, if known.

(3) The petition shall identify the age, sex, and name of the child. Two or more children may be the subject of the same petition.

(4) More than one allegation of children in need of services may appear in the same petition, in separate counts.

(b) Verification. The petition shall be signed by the petitioner, stating under oath the petitioner's good faith. No objection to the petition on the grounds that it was not signed or verified, as herein provided, shall be entertained after a plea to the merits.

(c) Amendments. At any time before or during an adjudicatory hearing, an amended petition may be filed or the petition may be amended by motion. Amendments shall be freely permitted in the interest of justice and the welfare of the child. A continuance may be granted upon motion and a showing that the amendment prejudices or materially affects any party.

(d) Defects and Variances. No petition or any count thereof shall be dismissed, or any judgment vacated, on account of any defect in the form of the petition or of misjoinder of counts. If the court is of the opinion that the petition is so vague, indistinct, and indefinite as to mislead the child, parent, or custodian and prejudice any of them in the preparation of a defense, the petitioner may be required to furnish a more definite statement.

(e) Voluntary Dismissal. At any time before entry of an order of adjudication, the child(ren) in need of services petition may be voluntarily dismissed by petitioner without leave of the court by serving a notice of dismissal on all parties or, if during a hearing, by so stating on the record. Unless otherwise stated, the dismissal shall be without prejudice.

RULE 8.665. ANSWERS, ARRAIGNMENTS, AND PREHEARING CONFERENCES

(a) Answers. The child, parent, or custodian of the child may enter an oral or written answer to the petition or remain silent. If the child remains silent or pleads evasively, or the parent, guardian, or legal custodian denies it, the court shall enter a denial of the petition. The court shall determine that any admission or consent to the petition is made voluntarily and with a full understanding of the nature of the allegations and the possible consequences of such admission or consent and that the parties have been advised of the right to be represented by counsel. The court shall incorporate these findings into its order in addition to findings of fact specifying the act or acts, by whom committed, and facts upon which the findings are based. If the answer admits the allegations of the petition it shall constitute consent to a predisposition study.

(b) Arraignment. If a written answer has not been filed by the child, parent, guardian, or legal custodian before the adjudicatory hearing, the court shall conduct a hearing to determine whether an admission, consent, or denial of the petition shall be entered and whether the parties are represented by counsel or are entitled to appointed counsel as pro-vided by law. If an admission or consent is entered, the court shall proceed as set forth in rule 8.690. If a denial is entered the court shall set an adjudicatory hearing within the period of time provided by law and appoint counsel when required.

(c) Withdrawal of Plea. The court may at any time before the beginning of a disposition hearing permit an admission of the allegations of the petition to be withdrawn and, if an adjudication has been entered thereon, set aside such adjudication. In the subsequent adjudicatory hearing the court shall disregard an admission that has been withdrawn.

(d) Prehearing Conference. Before the conduct of any adjudicatory hearing the court may set or the parties may request that a prehearing conference be held to determine the order in which each party may present witnesses or evidence and the order in which cross-examination and argument shall occur. The court also may enter findings on the record of any stipulations entered into by the parties and consider any other matters which may aid in the conduct of the adjudicatory hearing.

RULE 8.670. MOTIONS

(a) Motions in General. An application to the court for an order shall be made by a motion which shall be in writing, unless made during a hearing; be signed by the party making the motion or by the party's attorney; state with particularity the grounds therefor; and set forth the relief or order sought. The requirement of writing is fulfilled if the motion is stated in the written notice of the hearing of the motion.

(b) Motion to Dismiss. Any party may file a motion to dismiss any petition or other pleading, setting forth the grounds on which the motion is based. If a motion to dismiss is granted where a child is being detained under an order, the child may be continued in shelter under previous order of the court upon the representation that a new or amended petition will be filed.

(c) Motion to Sever. A motion may be made to sever 2 or more counts of a multicount petition or to sever the cases of 2 or more children alleged to be in need of services in the same petition. The court may grant motions for severance of jointly brought cases for good cause shown.

RULE 8.675. EXAMINATIONS, EVALUATION, AND TREATMENT

(a) Child. Mental or physical examination of a child may be obtained as provided by law.

(b) Parent, Guardian, or Other Person Requesting Custody. At any time after the filing of a petition, when the mental or physical condition, including the blood group, of a parent, guardian, or other person requesting custody of a child is in controversy, the court may order the person to submit to a physical or mental examination by a qualified professional. The order may be made only on good cause shown and on notice to the person as to the time, place, manner, conditions, and scope of the examination and the

person or persons by whom it is to be made. The court may, on its own motion or the motion of any party, order a parent, guardian, or other person requesting custody of the child to undergo such evaluation, treatment, or counseling activities as authorized by law.

RULE 8.680. DISCOVERY

Discovery will be allowed only upon order of the court and then as provided by rule 8.245.

Committee Notes

1992 Amendment. The present wording is somewhat ambiguous in the use of the word "and." The change clarifies the committee's intent.

RULE 8.685. ADJUDICATORY HEARINGS

(a) Hearing by Judge. The adjudicatory hearing shall be conducted by the judge without a jury utilizing the rules of evidence. At this hearing the court shall determine whether the allegations of the petition have been sustained.

(b) Examination of Witnesses. Any party shall have the right to examine or cross-examine the witnesses.

(c) Presence of Parties. All parties have the right to be present at all adjudicatory hearings. No party shall be excluded from the hearing unless so ordered by the court for disruptive behavior.

(d) Joint and Separate Hearings. When 2 or more children are alleged to be children in need of services, the hearing may be held simultaneously when the several children involved are related to each other or involved in the same case, unless the court orders separate hearings.

(e) Motion for Judgment of Dismissal. In all proceedings if at the close of the evidence for the petitioner the court is of the opinion that the evidence is insufficient as a matter of law to warrant a finding of child(ren) in need of services, it may, and on the motion of any party shall, enter an order dismissing the petition for insufficiency of evidence.

(f) Findings and Orders. If the court finds that the evidence supports the allegations of the petition, it may make a finding that the child is in need of services as provided by law. In all cases the court shall enter a written order specifying the facts upon which the findings are based. If the predisposition and other reports required by law are unavailable, or by order of the court, any portion of the disposition hearing may be reset within a reasonable time. If the case is continued the court may refer the case to appropriate agencies for additional study and recommendation. The court may order the child into a suitable placement under such reasonable conditions as the court may direct.

RULE 8.690. DISPOSITION HEARINGS

(a) **Information Available to Court.** At the disposition hearing the court, after establishing compliance with the dispositional considerations, determinations, and discussions required by law, may receive any relevant and material evidence helpful in determining the proper disposition to be made. It shall include written reports required by law and may include evaluations of the child or the parent or custodian that may be obtained and that are relevant and material. Such evidence may be received by the court and may be relied upon to the extent of its probative value even though not competent in an adjudicatory hearing.

(b) **Disclosure to Parties.** All parties shall be entitled to disclosure of all information in all reports submitted to the court.

(c) **Orders of Disposition.** The court shall in its written order of disposition include:

(1) the placement or custody of the child;

(2) special conditions of placement and visitation;

(3) evaluation, counseling, treatment activities, and other actions to be taken by the parties where ordered;

(4) supervising or monitoring agencies and continuation or discharge of the guardian ad litem, when appropriate;

(5) the period of time or date for subsequent case review when required by law; and

(6) such other requirements deemed necessary to protect the health, safety, and well-being of the child.

(d) **Out-of-Home Placement.** If the court places the child in out-of-home placement, subsequent proceedings shall be governed by part IIID of these rules.

RULE 8.695. POSTDISPOSITION RELIEF

(a) **Modification of Placement.** A child who has been placed in the child's own home, in the home of a relative, or in some other place under the supervision of the department may be brought before the court by the parent, guardian, or any interested person on a motion for modification of placement. Upon notice to all parties, the court shall conduct a hearing and enter an order changing the placement, modifying the conditions of placement, continuing placement as previously ordered, or placing the child with the department or a licensed child-caring agency.

(b) **Motion for Termination of Supervision or Jurisdiction.** Any party requesting termination of agency supervision or the jurisdiction of the court, or both, shall do so by motion. The court shall hear all parties present and enter an order terminating supervision or terminating jurisdiction and supervision or continuing them as previously ordered. The court shall not terminate jurisdiction unless the child is returned to the parent or placed with a legal guardian.

PART V. OTHER PROCEEDINGS

A. GUARDIAN ADVOCATES FOR DRUG-DEPENDENT NEWBORNS

RULE 8.705. COMMENCEMENT OF PROCEEDINGS

(a) **Petition to Be Filed.** All proceedings under this part shall be initiated by the filing of a petition for the appointment of a guardian advocate.

(b) **File to Be Opened.** Upon commencement of any proceeding, the clerk shall open a file and assign a case number.

RULE 8.710. PARTIES

(a) **Definitions.** For the purpose of these rules the terms "party" and "parties" shall include the petitioner, the child, the parent, the guardian ad litem where appointed, the custodian, and every person upon whom service of summons is required by law.

(b) Other Parties. The state attorney's office or the Department of Children and Family Services may become a party upon notice to all other parties and notice to the court. The court may add additional parties.

RULE 8.715. GUARDIAN AD LITEM

The court may appoint a guardian ad litem to represent the interests of the child.

RULE 8.720. PROCESS AND SERVICE

(a) Summons.

(1) Personal appearance of a person in a hearing before the court shall obviate the necessity of serving process upon that person.

(2) Upon the filing of the petition, and upon request of the petitioner, the clerk or deputy clerk shall issue a summons.

(3) The summons shall require the person on whom it is served to appear for a hearing at a time and place specified. Except in cases of medical emergency, the time of hearing shall not be less than 24 hours after service of the summons. The summons shall be directed to and shall be served upon the parents. It shall not be necessary to the validity of the proceedings that the parents be present if their identity or presence is unknown after a diligent search and inquiry have been made; if they have become residents of a state other than this state; or if they evade service or ignore summons, but in this event the person who made the search and inquiry shall file a certificate of those facts.

(b) Subpoenas. Upon the application of a party, the clerk or deputy clerk shall issue, and the court on its own motion may issue, subpoenas requiring attendance and testimony of witnesses and production of records, documents, or other tangible objects at any hearing.

RULE 8.725. PETITION

(a) Contents of Petition.

(1) The petition shall allege sufficient facts showing grounds for appointment of a guardian advocate based upon applicable law.

(2) The petition shall contain allegations as to the identity and residence of the parents or custodians, if known.

(3) The petition shall identify the age, sex, and name of the child. Two or more children may be the subject of the same petition.

(b) Voluntary Dismissal. The petitioner without leave of the court, at any time prior to the entry of the order, may request a voluntary dismissal of the petition by serving a notice of request for dismissal on all parties or, if during a hearing, by so stating on the record. The petition shall be dismissed and the court loses jurisdiction unless another party adopts the petition within 48 hours. Unless otherwise stated, the dismissal shall be without prejudice.

RULE 8.730. HEARING

(a) Time Limit. All hearings shall be carried out as provided by law within the time limits proscribed therein.

(b) Orders.

(1) In all cases at the conclusion of the hearing the court shall enter a written order granting or denying the petition.

(2) An order granting the appointment of a guardian advocate shall specify the term of appointment and not exceed that provided by law.

RULE 8.735. REVIEW AND REMOVAL

(a) Review by Court. The court may review the appointment of a guardian advocate at any time but shall review the appointment within the time limits as provided by law.

(b) Reauthorization or Removal. The reauthorization or removal of the guardian advocate shall be governed as provided by law.

B. JUDICIAL WAIVER OF PARENTAL NOTICE OF TERMINATION OF PREGNANCY

RULE 8.800. APPLICABILITY

These rules apply to proceedings instituted pursuant to section 390.01114, Florida Statutes.

RULE 8.805. COMMENCEMENT OF PROCEEDINGS

(a) Petition to Be Filed. Proceedings for a judicial waiver of parental notice of termination of pregnancy shall be commenced by the filing of a petition in circuit court.

(b) Pseudonymous Petitions. Petitions filed under a pseudonym or initials shall be filed simultaneously with a sworn statement containing the minor's true name, date of birth, address and the case number. A certified copy of this Sworn Statement of True Name and Pseudonym shall be given to the minor at the time it is filed. The original sworn statement shall be kept under seal at all times and may only be opened at the minor's request or by court order.

(c) Notice Under Pseudonymous Petitions. So that the minor may receive notice in a safe and secure manner, the minor shall elect to receive notice through the address and phone number of a trusted third person or by personally contacting the clerk's office. If the minor elects to personally contact the clerk's office, she must still provide an address and phone number of a third person through which to receive notice in the event that the court needs to provide notice at a time other than when the minor personally contacts the clerk's office.

(d) Procedures Upon Filing Petition. Upon the filing of a petition, the clerk of the circuit court shall immediately:

(1) open a new file and assign a new case number;

(2) provide the minor with a certified copy of Form 8.988[,] Sworn Statement of True Name and Pseudonym;

(3) provide the minor with Form 8.989[,] Advisory Notice to Minor;

(4) present the petition to the court for scheduling of the hearing and appointment of counsel, if requested; and

(5) provide notice of the hearing to the minor. If it is not possible for the clerk to immediately provide notice at the time the minor files the petition, the clerk shall provide notice through the method elected by the minor in the petition.

(e) Fees and Costs. No filing fees or court costs shall be assessed against any pregnant minor who petitions a court for a waiver of parental notice.

RULE 8.810. PETITION

The petition shall include:

(a) the pseudonym or initials of the minor;

(b) the age of the minor;

(c) a statement that the minor is pregnant and notice has not been waived;

(d) a statement that the minor desires to terminate her pregnancy without notice to a parent or legal guardian; and

(e) a short and plain statement of facts to establish any of the following:

(1) The minor is sufficiently mature to decide whether to terminate her pregnancy.

(2) The minor is a victim of child abuse or sexual abuse by one or both of her parents or a guardian.

(3) Notification of a parent or guardian is not in the best interest of the minor.

RULE 8.815. COUNSEL

As provided by section 390.01114(4)(a), Florida Statutes, the circuit court shall advise the minor that she has a right to court-appointed counsel and shall provide her with counsel upon her request at no cost.

RULE 8.820. HEARING

(a) Hearing by Judge. A judge shall conduct an informal hearing on the petition within the time limits provided by law and these rules. General magistrates and special magistrates shall not hear a petition for a judicial waiver of parental notice of termination of pregnancy.

(b) Evidence. The judge shall hear evidence relating to the emotional development, maturity, intellect, and understanding of the minor, and all other relevant evidence.

(c) Burdens of Proof.

(1) A finding that the minor is sufficiently mature to decide whether to terminate her pregnancy requires proof by clear and convincing evidence.

(2) A finding that the minor is a victim of child abuse or sexual abuse inflicted by one or both of her parents or a guardian requires proof by a preponderance of the evidence.

(3) A finding that notification of a parent or guardian is not in the best interest of the minor requires proof by clear and convincing evidence.

(d) Time Limits. As provided by section 390.01114(4)(b), Florida Statutes:

(1) Cases commenced under this rule take precedence over other pending matters as necessary to ensure that the court can make its ruling and issue written findings of fact and conclusions of law within 3 business days of the filing of the petition.

(2) The 3-business-day time limit may be extended at the request of the minor; however, the court remains under an obligation to rule on the petition as soon as practically possible.

(3) If the court fails to rule within the 3-business day period and an extension has not been requested by the minor, the minor may immediately thereafter petition the chief judge of the circuit for a hearing. The chief judge must ensure that a hearing is held within 48 hours after receipt of the minor's petition, and an order is entered within 24 hours after the hearing.

(e) Confidentiality of Hearings. Hearings under this part shall be closed to the public and all records thereof shall remain confidential as provided by sections 390.01114(4)(e) and 390.01116, Florida Statutes. Persons other than the petitioner may be permit-

ted to attend the hearing at the request of the petitioner. The court shall advise all persons in attendance that the hearing is confidential.

RULE 8.825. ORDER AND JUDGMENT

At the conclusion of the hearing, the court shall issue written and specific findings of fact and conclusions of law in support of its decision, including findings of fact and conclusions of law relating to the maturity of the minor, and order that a confidential record be maintained.

RULE 8.830. TRANSCRIPTS

A court that conducts proceedings pursuant to these rules shall provide for a written transcript of all testimony and proceedings as provided by section 390.01114(4)(e), Florida Statutes.

RULE 8.835. CONFIDENTIALITY OF RECORDS

(a) As provided by section 390.01116, Florida Statutes, any information including the petition, documents, transcripts, recordings of cases, and any other information that could be used to identify a minor who has petitioned the court for a judicial waiver of parental notice of termination of pregnancy is confidential and exempt from section 119.07(1), Florida Statutes, and section 24(a), Article I of the State Constitution.

(b) So that the minor shall remain anonymous, the court file shall be sealed unless otherwise ordered by the court.

RULE 8.840. REMAND OF PROCEEDINGS

In the event the minor appeals a determination by the circuit court under these rules and the appellate court remands the matter to the trial court, the trial court must enter its ruling within 3 business days after the remand.

C. TRUANCY PROCEEDINGS

RULE 8.850. APPLICABILITY

These rules apply to proceedings instituted under section 984.151, Florida Statutes.

RULE 8.855. COMMENCEMENT OF PROCEEDINGS

(a) Petition to Be Filed. Proceedings to determine or enforce truancy actions under this section must be commenced by filing a petition in the circuit court in the circuit in which the student is enrolled.

(b) Jurisdiction. While original jurisdiction to hear a truancy petition shall be in the circuit court, a general or special magistrate may be used in these proceedings, pursuant to Supreme Court rules.

(c) Summons. Upon the filing of a petition, the clerk shall issue a summons to the parent, guardian, or legal custodian of the student, or if the student is in foster care, the case manager, directing that person and the student to appear for a hearing at a time and place specified in the summons.

RULE 8.860. PETITION

(a) Contents. The petition shall include:

(1) The name, age, and address of the student;

(2) The name and address of the student's parent, guardian, or legal custodian and, if the student is in foster care, the case manager;

(3) The name and address of the school in which the student is enrolled;

(4) A statement that outlines the efforts the school has made to get the student to attend school;

(5) The number of out of school contacts between the school system and the student's parent, guardian, or legal custodian; and

(6) The number of days, by date, the student has missed school.

(b) Sworn by Superintendent. The petition shall be sworn to by the superintendent of the school system involved or his or her designee.

RULE 8.865. HEARINGS

(a) Time Requirements. Once the petition is filed, the court shall hear the petition within 30 days.

(b) Attendance Required. The student and the student's parent, guardian, or legal custodian or, if the student is in foster care, the case manager, shall attend the hearing.

RULE 8.870. ORDER

(a) Requirement to Attend School. If the court determines that a student did miss any of the alleged days, the court shall order the student to attend school and the parent, guardian, legal custodian, or, if the student is in foster care, the case manager, to ensure that the student attends school.

(b) Other Sanctions. If the court determines that a student did miss any of the alleged days, the court may order any of the following:

(1) The student to participate in alternative sanctions to include mandatory attendance at alternative classes to be followed by mandatory community service hours for up to six months;

(2) The student or the student's parent, guardian, or legal custodian, to participate in homemaker or parent aide services;

(3) The student or the student's parent, guardian, or legal custodian to participate in and complete intensive crisis counseling and/or community mental health services;

(4) The student and the student's parent, guardian, or legal custodian to participate in services provided by voluntary or community agencies as available;

(5) The student or the student's parent, guardian, or legal custodian to participate in vocational, job training, or employment services.

(c) Referral to Case Staffing Committee. If the student does not successfully complete the sanctions ordered, the case shall be referred to the case staffing committee, with a recommendation to file a child in need of services petition under Chapter 984, Florida Statutes.

(d) Participation by Parent, Guardian, Legal Custodian, or Student. The parent, guardian, or legal custodian and the student shall participate as ordered or required by the court, in any sanction or services ordered pursuant to this rule.

(e) Enforcement by Contempt. The court shall enforce such requirements through its contempt power, pursuant to Chapter 984, Florida Statutes.

PART VI. FORMS FOR USE WITH RULES OF JUVENILE PROCEDURE

Editor's Notes: — The following forms are sufficient for the matters that are covered by them. As long as the substance is expressed without prolixity, the forms may be varied to meet the facts of a particular case. Captions, verifications, and certificates of service, except for the designation of the paper, are omitted from most forms. General forms for these are provided at the beginning of the forms.

The Florida Supreme Court per curiam opinion of December 24, 1980 (393 So. 2d 1077), in which the forms appear, provides: "Nothing in the Forms shall be deemed to be a part of these Rules."

Committee Notes

1991 Amendment. These forms have been updated to conform to revisions to Chapter 39, Florida Statutes, and the Florida Rules of Juvenile Procedure. As the court has stated before, the forms are not intended to be part of the rules and are provided for convenience only.

A. GENERAL FORMS

FORM 8.901. CAPTION OF PLEADINGS AND ORDERS

NAME OF COURT

In the Interest of
................., ...a child/children.....

.....(Designation of Pleading or Order).....

FORM 8.902. VERIFICATION

STATE OF FLORIDA

COUNTY OF ....

Before me, the undersigned authority, personally appeared .....(name)....., who, being sworn, says the .....(document)..... is filed in good faith and on information, knowledge, and belief is true.

Sworn to and subscribed before me on .....(date)......

————————————————

(Title)

Committee Notes

1991 Adoption. The above verification should be added to petitions and motions as required by law.

FORM 8.903. CERTIFICATE OF SERVICE

I certify that a copy of .....(document)..... has been furnished to .....(name(s))..... by .....e-mail/U.S. mail/hand delivery/fax..... on .....(date)......

————————————————

(Title)

Committee Notes

1991 Adoption. The above may be added to petitions, orders, and other forms as required.

FORM 8.904. AFFIDAVIT FOR ORDER TO TAKE INTO CUSTODY

AFFIDAVIT

STATE OF FLORIDA

COUNTY OF ....

Before me, the undersigned authority, personally appeared affiant, who, being sworn, made the following allegations of facts: .... and requested that the court issue an order to take into custody the below-.....named/described..... child/children.

Name(s) ....

Age(s) .... Sex ....

Date(s) of birth ....

Race ....

Address ....

Identifying description ....

Parent/Custodian ....

Address ....

Affiant

..... Address .....

FORM 8.905. ORDER TO TAKE INTO CUSTODY

ORDER TO TAKE INTO CUSTODY

TO: ....

A .....verified petition/affidavit..... having been filed in this case, alleging facts which under existing law are determined to be sufficient to authorize taking into custody the below-.....named/identified..... .....child/children....., believed to be of an age subject to the juvenile jurisdiction of the circuit court; therefore

You are commanded to take the following .....child/children..... into custody:

Name(s) ....

Age(s) .... Sex ....

Date(s) of birth ....

Race ....

Address ....

Identifying description ....

Parent/Custodian ....

Address ....

For the following reasons: ....

Upon taking the .....child/children..... into custody, you will deliver .....him/her/them..... to: .... to be held pending a .....detention/shelter..... hearing or upon further order of this court.

ORDERED in the circuit court in and for .... County, Florida, on .....(date)......

Circuit Judge

RETURN

This order to take into custody was executed at .....m., on .....(date)....., by the undersigned.

(Title)

RETURN TO ISSUING COURT UPON THE CHILD'S 19TH BIRTHDAY.

FORM 8.906. RELEASE ORDER

RELEASE ORDER

The court now finding that the above-named .....child/children....., previously .....placed in shelter care/detained....., should be released.

It is ADJUDGED:

1. That .... shall be released immediately to ....

2. It is FURTHER ADJUDGED that ....

ORDERED in the circuit court in and for .... County, Florida, on .....(date)......

Circuit Judge

FORM 8.907. TRANSFER ORDER

TRANSFER ORDER

This case being before this court for consideration of transfer to a court having juvenile jurisdiction in another county, the court finds:

1. That on .....(date)....., following a hearing on the petition of ...., the court .....entered an order of adjudication/withheld adjudication/accepted a plan of proposed treatment, training, or conduct......

2. That it would be in the best interest of the above-named .....child/children..... that this case be transferred to the circuit court of another county because: ....

3. That a dispositional order .....was/was not..... made in this case.

It is recommended to the receiving court that: ....

It is ADJUDGED:

1. That the jurisdiction of this court in this case and of the .....child/children..... involved is transferred to the circuit court in and for .... County, Florida, of the ..... Judicial Circuit, for any and all proceedings deemed necessary.

2. That within 5 days from the date of this order the clerk of this court shall forward a certified copy of:

(a) The order of transfer, which shall include but not be limited to:

(i) Specific offense that the child was found to have committed;

(ii) Degree of offense;

(iii) Name of parent/custodian to be summoned;

(iv) Address at which the child should be summoned for disposition;

(v) Name and address of the victim; and

(vi) Whether the child was represented by counsel.

(b) A certified copy of the delinquency petition;

(c) A copy of the juvenile referral or complaint; and

(d) Any reports and all previous orders including orders appointing counsel entered by the court in the interest of that child.

These documents shall be forwarded to the clerk of the receiving court; state attorney of the receiving court; public defender of the receiving court, if counsel previously has been appointed; and ....

ORDERED in the circuit court in and for .... County, Florida, on .....(date)......

_____
Circuit Judge

FORM 8.908. SUMMONS

SUMMONS

STATE OF FLORIDA
TO ...., ...a child/children..... and ...., ...parent(s)/custodian.....:

A petition under oath has been filed in this court alleging the above-named .....child/children..... to be .... under the laws of the State of Florida, a copy of which was attached hereto;

You are to appear before the Honorable ...., Circuit Judge, at .....m., on .....(date)....., at the county courthouse of .... County, at ...., Florida, for the hearing of this petition. The .....parent(s)/custodian..... is/are required to produce the .....child/children..... at that time and place unless the .....child/children..... .....is/are..... in detention or shelter care at that time.

COMMENT: The following paragraph must be in bold, 14 pt. Times New Roman or Courier font.

If you are a person with a disability who needs any accommodation to participate in this proceeding, you are entitled, at no cost to you, to the provision of certain assistance. Please contact .....(name, address, telephone number)..... at least 7 days before your scheduled court appearance, or immediately upon receiving this notification if the time before the scheduled appearance is less than 7 days. If you are hearing or voice impaired, call 711.

You may be held in contempt of court if you fail to appear.

WITNESS my hand and seal of this court at .... County, Florida, on .....(date)......

..................., Clerk of Circuit Court

.... County, Florida

By: _____D.C.

FORM 8.909. PLAN FOR TREATMENT, TRAINING, OR CONDUCT

PLAN FOR TREATMENT, TRAINING, OR CONDUCT

TO: ...., Circuit Judge

Instead of a plea to the petition filed on .....(date)....., alleging the above-named .....child/ children..... to be ...., the following proposed plan for treatment, training, or conduct, formulated in conjunction with the supervising agency, is now submitted, with the request that it be accepted by the court and that prosecution of the said petition be deferred.

This agreement is entered into with full knowledge and disclosure of all the facts and circumstances of this case, and in consideration thereof, and the promise of fulfillment of its terms and conditions, each of the undersigned agrees as follows: ....

It is further agreed:

1. That the speedy trial rule is waived,

2. That a hearing for the acceptance of this plan .....is/is not..... waived,

3. That this plan, as agreed to here, shall be in effect until ....

In witness whereof the undersigned have affixed their hands on .....(date)......

_____
Child

_____
.....Parent(s) or Custodian(s).....

_____
Attorney for
.....Child/Parent(s)/Custodian(s).....

..................., Department of Juvenile Justice, Supervising Agency, Recommends: .....Acceptance/ Rejection......

_____
Authorized Agent

CONSENT IN DELINQUENCY CASES

The undersigned, being familiar with contents of this plan for treatment, training, or conduct and the delinquency petition on which it is based, consents to defer prosecution of the petition.

Dated: ....

....
State Attorney

By: _____
Assistant State Attorney

ORDER

The foregoing plan for treatment, training, or conduct having been properly submitted and having been given consideration by the court,

It is ADJUDGED:

____ 1. That the plan is approved and the parties thereto shall comply with its terms and conditions.

____ 2. That the plan is disapproved and an adjudicatory hearing on the petition shall be scheduled.

ORDERED at ...., ... County, Florida, on .....(date)......

_____
Circuit Judge

FORM 8.911. UNIFORM CHILD CUSTODY JURISDICTION AND ENFORCEMENT ACT AFFIDAVIT

See Fla. Sup. Ct. App. Fam. L. Form 12.902(d).

FORM 8.912. PETITION TO SHOW CAUSE

PETITION BY AFFIDAVIT FOR ORDER TO SHOW CAUSE

1. This is a proceeding for an order to show why the below-named witness, ..., should not be held in contempt of court.

2. Petitioner is .....(title)......

3. A subpoena was duly served on .....(name)....., at .....(time)..... by .....(name)..... who was then and there authorized to serve said subpoena. A copy of the receipt evidencing service is attached and incorporated by reference. Said .....(name)..... did not appear on .....(date)....., at .....(time)..... in response to that subpoena and to this date has not appeared.

WHEREFORE, the undersigned does respectfully request the court to issue an order to direct .....(name)..... to appear before the court to show cause why .....(name)..... should not be held in contempt of court.

_____
Petitioner

FORM 8.913. ORDER TO SHOW CAUSE

ORDER TO SHOW CAUSE

This cause came on to be heard on the petition for order to show cause directed to .....(name)..... for failure .....(specify)..... on .....(date)...... (See attached affidavit.)

NOW, THEREFORE, you, ...(name)....., are hereby ORDERED to appear before this court located at ...., on .....(date)....., at .....(time)....., to show cause why you should not be held in contempt of this court, for your failure to .....(specify)......

DONE AND ORDERED on .....(date)....., at ...., ... County, Florida.

_____
Circuit Judge

B. DELINQUENCY FORMS

FORM 8.929. DETENTION ORDER

DETENTION HEARING ORDER

Pick up order for absconding from:
..... home detention
..... probation
..... commitment
..... other: ....

Present before the court:
..... the child;
....(name)....., Assistant State Attorney;
....(name)....., Assistant Public Defender/ defense attorney;
....(name)....., parent/legal guardian;
....(name)....., DJJ juvenile probation officer;
....(name)....., Department of Children and Family Services
....(name)....., guardian ad litem

DJJ Supervision status:
..... None
..... Home detention
..... Probation
..... Committed to ..... level
..... CINS/FINS
..... Conditional release

Other court involvement:
Dependency: ..... Yes ..... No ..... Unknown
Domestic relations:..... Yes ..... No ..... Unknown
Domestic violence:..... Yes ..... No ..... Unknown

The court finds that the child was taken into custody at ..... a.m./p.m., on .....(date)......

Probable cause that the child committed delinquent acts was:
..... found.
..... not found.
..... reset within 48 hours of custody.
Risk assessment instrument (RAI) score: ....
Score amended to: ....
..... Meets detention criteria.

IT IS ORDERED that the above-named child be:

..... released to the custody of .....(name).....
..... held in secure detention for domestic violence

charge under section 985.245, Florida Statutes. The court finds:

..... respite care is not available for the child; and

..... it is necessary to place the child in secure detention to protect the victim from injury.

..... detained by the Department of Juvenile Justice in

..... home detention.

..... home detention with electronic monitoring.

..... secure detention.

with the following special conditions:

    ..... attend school regularly.

    ..... attend evaluation as follows:

        ..... physical.

        ..... psychological.

        ..... ADM.

        ..... other ....

    ..... no (..... harmful) contact with .....(name).....

    ..... drug testing.

    ..... no drug and alcohol use.

    ..... other: ....

    ..... released from detention and returned to the child's nonresidential commitment program.

Reasons for court ordering more restrictive placement than RAI score: ....

It is FURTHER ORDERED that unless an adjudicatory hearing has begun or a subsequent modification order is entered, the child shall be released no later than 5:00 p.m. on .....(date)..... to .....(name(s))....., who is/are

..... the parent(s)

..... a relative

..... foster care

.... program

....him/her..... self

..... other ....

IT IS FURTHER ORDERED under section 985.039, Florida Statutes

..... The parent/guardian of the child, ...(name)....., shall pay to the Department of Juvenile Justice, 2737 Centerview Drive, Tallahassee, FL 32399-3100, $5 per day for each day the juvenile is in secure detention.

..... The parent/guardian of the child, ...(name)....., shall pay to the Department of Juvenile Justice, 2737 Centerview Drive, Tallahassee, FL 32399-3100, $1 per day for each day the child is in home detention.

..... The parent/guardian of the child, ...(name)....., shall pay to the Department of Juvenile Justice, 2737 Centerview Drive, Tallahassee, FL 32399-3100, a REDUCED rate of $..... per day for each day the child is in detention status. This reduced fee is based on the court's finding

    ..... that the parent/guardian was the victim of the delinquent act or violation of law for which the child is currently detained and is cooperating in the investigation of the offense; or

    ..... of indigency or significant financial hardship. The facts supporting this finding are: ....

..... The parent/guardian of the child, ...(name)....., ...(address)....., shall be liable for .....% of the payment.

..... The .....supervision fee/cost of care..... is WAIVED based on the court's finding

    ..... that the parent/guardian was the victim of the delinquent act or violation of law for which the child is currently detained and is cooperating in the investigation of the offense; or

    ..... of indigency or significant financial hardship. The facts supporting this finding are: ....

If the child's case is dismissed or if the child is found not guilty of the charges or court order, then the parent/guardian shall not be liable for fees under this order.

Unless modified by subsequent notice, the NEXT COURT APPEARANCE:

    ..... will be at .....(time)..... on .....(date)..... at .....(location)......

..... is to be set.

COMMENT: The following paragraph must be in bold, 14 pt. Times New Roman or Courier font.

If you are a person with a disability who needs any accommodation in order to participate in this proceeding, you are entitled, at no cost to you, to the provision of certain assistance. Please contact .....(name, address, telephone number)..... at least 7 days before your scheduled court appearance, or immediately upon receiving this notification if the time before the scheduled appearance is less than 7 days. If you are hearing or voice impaired, call 711.

Note: The child's parent/legal guardian shall advise Clerk's Office and DJJ of any address change.

..... Department of Juvenile Justice shall transfer the child to .... Detention Center.

..... Other: ....

DONE AND ORDERED in .... County, Florida at ..... a.m./p.m. on .....(date)......

Circuit Judge

Copies to: ....

FORM 8.930. JUVENILE NOTICE TO APPEAR

JUVENILE NOTICE TO APPEAR

DATE .... AGENCY ....
CASE NO. ....
PARENT, ADULT RELATIVE, LEGAL GUARDIAN .....(name).....

I am the .....(relationship to child)..... of .....(child's name)..... and promise to ensure that the child appears on .....(date)..... at .....(time)..... at .....(location)...... I also promise immediately to notify the office of the state attorney at .....(telephone number)..... and the clerk of the court at .....(telephone number)..... of any change in the child's address.

Signature of Parent/Adult

Relative/Legal Guardian
.....(address).....
.....(telephone number).....
.....(date).....
.....(address and telephone number of child, if different).....

- - - - - - - - - - - - - -

I, ...(child's name)....., understand that I have been charged with a law violation, ...(offense(s))....., and that I am being released at this time to the custody of .....(parent, adult relative, or legal guardian's name)......

I promise to appear on .....(date)..... at .....(time)..... at .....(location)...., and to appear as required for any additional conferences or appearances scheduled by DJJ or the court. I understand that my failure to appear shall result in a custody order being issued and that I will be picked up and taken to detention.

Child's Signature

Date ....
Arresting Officer ....

Releasing officer or DJJ counselor authorizing release

DJJ Intake Telephone Number ....

ATTACH TO ARREST AFFIDAVIT

FORM 8.931. DELINQUENCY PETITION

PETITION

Your petitioner respectfully represents that .... whose date(s) of birth .....is/are..... and who reside(s) at ....is/are..... delinquent and that this court has jurisdiction of this cause because of the following allegations of facts: ....

That the parents or custodians are:

....
Mother   Residence

....

Father   Residence

....

Custodian   Residence

WHEREFORE, your petitioner requests process may issue to bring the above-named parties before the court on a day and time designated to be dealt with according to law.

Dated: ....

_____

Petitioner

FORM 8.932. APPLICATION FOR COUNSEL AND ORDER

APPLICATION FOR COUNSEL AND ORDER

STATE OF FLORIDA
COUNTY OF ....

Before me, the undersigned authority, personally appeared affiant, who, being duly sworn, says:

1. That I understand a delinquency complaint has been made against me and, being advised of my right to an attorney, now request appointment of counsel.

2. Being without sufficient funds, property or assets of any kind, I will be deprived of my right to representation unless I am adjudged insolvent and counsel appointed to represent me.

3. That I have been informed that a lien for the value of the legal services rendered to me by the public defender may be imposed by law on any property I now or may hereafter have in this state.

Dated: ....

_____

Affiant Child

STATEMENT OF PARENT(S)

The undersigned are informed and understand that liability for cost of representation of this child by the public defender can be assessed against the parent(s) by court order in an amount not to exceed the amount provided by law.

_____

Parent

_____

Parent

ORDER

The court finds that this child is indigent, as defined by law, and is desirous of counsel; it is, therefore,

ORDERED

1. That this child is declared to be insolvent.

2. That ...., Public Defender for the ..... Judicial Circuit, State of Florida, is hereby appointed as counsel to represent this child in all matters in defense of the delinquency complaint herein made.

DONE AND ORDERED in the circuit court in and for .... County, Florida, on .....(date)......

_____

Circuit Judge

FORM 8.933. WAIVER OF COUNSEL

WAIVER OF COUNSEL

I, the undersigned child, ... years of age, understand:

(1) That a complaint of delinquency alleging that I did: .... has been made against me;

(2) That I have a right to a lawyer and that if I am unable to pay a lawyer and wish to have one appointed, a lawyer will be provided immediately.

I understand this right to and offer of a lawyer and, being aware of the effect of this waiver, I knowingly, intelligently, understandingly and of my own free will now choose to and, by the signing of this waiver, do hereby waive my right to a lawyer and elect to proceed in this case without benefit of a lawyer.

Date: ....

Child

This waiver of counsel was signed in the presence of the undersigned witnesses who, by their signature, attest to its voluntary execution by this child.

Witness: _____

Witness: _____

STATEMENT OF PARENT OR RESPONSIBLE ADULT

This waiver of counsel was read by me and explained fully to this child in my presence. I understand the right of this child to an attorney and as the .... of this child I consent to a waiver of this right.

Date: ....

- - - - - - - - - - - - - - - -

ORDER ASSESSING ATTORNEY'S FEE

The child herein, having been represented by the Public Defender in this cause pursuant to section 27.52, Florida Statutes, it is

ORDERED AND ADJUDGED that a reasonable attorney's fee for services rendered by the Public Defender to the child in this cause is $.......... and that said fee is hereby assessed against ...., the father, and ...., the mother, in favor of the State of Florida.

DONE AND ORDERED at ...., Florida, on .....(date)......

Circuit Judge

FORM 8.934. ORDER TO DETERMINE MENTAL CONDITION

ORDER TO DETERMINE
MENTAL CONDITION

It having been made known to the court and the court finding that reasonable grounds exist to believe that this child may be incompetent to proceed with an adjudicatory hearing, and that a hearing should be scheduled to examine this child and determine .....his/her..... mental condition, it is

ADJUDGED:

1. That all proceedings in this case are now stayed, pending further order of this court.

2. That a hearing to determine the mental condition of this child is scheduled before me at ..... m., on .....date......

3. That the following named persons are hereby appointed as disinterested qualified experts to examine this child as to competency and to testify as to the child's mental condition at the hearing above scheduled:

(1) ....
　　　　Name　　　　　　　　　　　Address

(2) ....
　　　　Name　　　　　　　　　　　Address

(3) ....
　　　　Name　　　　　　　　　　　Address

4. That this child shall be held temporarily in the custody of ...., who shall produce the child for examination by the above-named at a time and place to be arranged.

ORDERED at ...., ...
County, Florida, ...date......

Circuit Judge

FORM 8.935. ORDER OF INCOMPETENCY

ORDER OF INCOMPETENCY

The above-named child being before the court for inquiry into .....his/her..... mental condition and a determination of .....his/her..... competency to proceed with an adjudicatory hearing, from the evidence the court finds:

That the said child is mentally incompetent to proceed with the adjudicatory hearing.

It is, therefore, ADJUDGED that proceedings shall be commenced immediately for the involuntary hospitalization of this child by ...., as provided by law, and the said child shall .... pending disposition of those proceedings.

All proceedings in this case are stayed pending such action.

ORDERED AT ...., Florida, on .....(date)......

_____
Circuit Judge

FORM 8.936. ORDER OF COMPETENCY

ORDER OF COMPETENCY

The above-named child being before the court for inquiry into .....his/her..... mental condition and a determination of .....his/her..... competency to proceed with an adjudicatory hearing, from the evidence the court finds:

That the child is mentally competent to proceed with the adjudicatory hearing.

It is, therefore, ADJUDGED that the adjudicatory hearing in this case shall .....commence/resume..... at ..... m., on .....(date)......

ORDERED at ...., Florida, on .....(date)......

_____
Circuit Judge

FORM 8.937. DEMAND FOR VOLUNTARY WAIVER

DEMAND FOR VOLUNTARY WAIVER OF JURISDICTION

The child files this demand for voluntary waiver of jurisdiction pursuant to rule 8.105, Florida Rules of Juvenile Procedure, and shows that the child desires the court to waive jurisdiction and certify the case for trial in adult court as if the child were an adult to face adult punishments or penalties.

Date: ....

_____
Child

_____
Parent/Legal Guardian

FORM 8.938. ORDER OF VOLUNTARY WAIVER

VOLUNTARY WAIVER ORDER

Upon the demand for voluntary waiver filed by the child, it is hereby ORDERED AND ADJUDGED as follows:

1. A demand for voluntary waiver of jurisdiction was filed by the child and parent/legal guardian on .....(date)......

2. The court waives jurisdiction to try the child pursuant to chapter 985, Florida Statutes.

3. The above cause is certified for trial as if the child were an adult.

4. A certified copy of this order shall be furnished to the clerk of the court having jurisdiction to try the child as an adult and to the prosecuting officer of said child.

5. The child shall be forthwith delivered to the sheriff of the county in which the court that is to try the child is located. Bond is set at $ ....

DONE AND ORDERED in chambers at ...., ...(date)......

_____
Circuit Judge

FORM 8.939. MOTION FOR INVOLUNTARY WAIVER

MOTION FOR INVOLUNTARY WAIVER

The State of Florida, having considered the recommendation of the intake officer, petitions the court to waive jurisdiction pursuant to rule 8.105, Florida Rules of Juvenile Procedure, and shows:

The child was 14 or more years of age at the alleged time of commission of the violation of law for which the child is charged.

[Add the following paragraph, if applicable]

The child has been previously adjudicated delinquent for a violent crime against a person, to wit .....(offense)....., and is currently charged with a second or subsequent such offense.

Wherefore, the State of Florida requests the court to conduct a hearing on this motion for the purpose of determining whether the court should waive its jurisdiction and certify the case to the appropriate court for trial as if the child were an adult.

_____

Petitioner

FORM 8.940. MOTION TO COMPILE REPORT

MOTION TO COMPILE REPORT

The State of Florida, having filed a petition for involuntary waiver, moves the court for an order requiring the department to prepare a study and report to the court, in writing, considering the following relevant factors:

1. The seriousness of the alleged offense to the community and whether the protection of the community is best served by transferring the child for adult sanctions.

2. Whether the alleged offense was committed in an aggressive, violent, premeditated, or willful manner.

3. Whether the alleged offense was against persons or against property.

4. The probable cause as found in the report, affidavit, or complaint.

5. The desirability of trial and disposition of the entire offense in one court when the child's associates in the alleged crime are adults or children who are to be tried as adults who will be or have been charged with a crime.

6. The sophistication and maturity of the child.

7. The record and previous history of the child including:

    a. Previous contact with the department, other law enforcement agencies, and the courts;

    b. Prior periods of juvenile probation;

    c. Prior adjudications that the child committed a delinquent act or violation of law, greater weight being given if the child previously had been found by a court to have committed a delinquent act involving an offense classified as a felony or had twice previously been found to have committed a delinquent act involving an offense classified as a misdemeanor; and

    d. Prior commitments to institutions.

8. The prospects for adequate protection of the public and the likelihood of reasonable rehabilitation of the child, if found to have committed the alleged offense, by the use of procedures, services, and facilities currently available to the court.

WHEREFORE, the State of Florida requests an order directing the department to prepare a study and report in writing prior to the waiver hearing.

_____

Petitioner

FORM 8.941. ORDER TO COMPILE REPORT

ORDER TO COMPILE REPORT

Upon the motion of the State of Florida, the department shall prepare a study and report to the court, in writing, considering the following relevant factors:

1. The seriousness of the alleged offense to the community and whether the protection of the community is best served by transferring the child for adult sanctions.

2. Whether the alleged offense was committed in an aggressive, violent, premeditated, or willful manner.

3. Whether the alleged offense was against persons or against property.

4. The probable cause as found in the report, affidavit, or complaint.

5. The desirability of trial and disposition of the entire offense in one court when the child's associates in the alleged crime are adults or children who are to be tried as adults who will be or have been charged with a crime.

6. The sophistication and maturity of the child.

7. The record and previous history of the child including:

    a. Previous contact with the department, other law enforcement agencies, and the courts;

    b. Prior periods of juvenile probation;

    c. Prior adjudications that the child committed a delinquent act or violation of law, greater weight being given if the child had previously been found by a court to have committed a delinquent act involving an offense classified as a felony or had twice previously been found to have committed a delinquent act involving an offense classified as a misdemeanor; and

    d. Prior commitments to institutions.

8. The prospects for adequate protection of the public and the likelihood of reasonable rehabilitation of the child, if found to have committed the alleged offense, by the use of procedures, services, and facilities currently available to the court.

DONE AND ORDERED in chambers at ...., Florida, ...(date)......

Circuit Judge

FORM 8.942. ORDER OF INVOLUNTARY WAIVER

ORDER OF INVOLUNTARY WAIVER

A petition was filed in this cause on .....(date)...... Prior to the adjudicatory hearing on the petition, the State of Florida filed a motion requesting that the court waive its jurisdiction and certify the case to the appropriate court for trial as if the child were an adult. This cause came before the court on the motion.

The following were present .....(names)..... with .....(name)....., representing the State of Florida and .....(name)....., representing the Department of Juvenile Justice.

The court heard the evidence presented by the State of Florida and the child to determine whether the jurisdiction of this court should be waived and the case certified to the appropriate court for trial as if the child were an adult. The court finds that it is in the public interest that the jurisdiction of this court be waived and that the case be certified to the appropriate court having jurisdiction to try an adult who is charged with a like offense based on the following findings of fact:

1. Age of child .....

2. Seriousness of alleged offense ....

3. Manner of commission of offense ....

4. Nature of offense (person or property) ....

5. Probable cause as found in the report, affidavit, or complaint ....

6. Desirability of trial and disposition of entire offense in one court ....

7. Sophistication and maturity of the child ....

8. Record and previous history of the child ....

9. Prospects for adequate protection of the public and rehabilitation of child ....

IT IS ADJUDGED that the jurisdiction of this court is waived and that this case is transferred to the .....(court)..... for trial as if the child were an adult.

The child shall be held by the sheriff of this county unless a bond in the amount of $.......... is posted. The child shall appear before .....(court)..... on .....(date)..... to answer the State of Florida on the foregoing charges.

DONE AND ORDERED in chambers at ...., Florida, on .....(date)......

_____

Circuit Judge

FORM 8.947. DISPOSITION ORDER—DELINQUENCY.

DISPOSITION ORDER

A petition was filed on .....(date)....., alleging .....(name)....., ... age, to be a delinquent child. The court finds that it has jurisdiction of the proceedings.

Present before the court were:

..... the child;
....(name)....., Assistant State Attorney;
....(name)....., Assistant Public Defender/defense attorney;
....(name)....., guardian;
....(name)....., DJJ juvenile probation officer.

At the hearing on .....(date)....., after .....entry of a plea/an adjudicatory hearing....., the child was found to have committed the delinquent acts listed below:

	Count	Count	Count	Count
Charge	....	....	....	....
Lesser	....	....	....	....
Maximum	....	....	....	....
Degree	....	....	....	....
Guilty	....	....	....	....
Nolo contendere	....	....	....	....
Nolle prosse	....	....	....	....
Adjudicated	....	....	....	....
Adj. withheld	....	....	....	....

The predisposition report was .....received and considered/waived by the child......

The court, having considered the evidence and comments offered by those present, having inquired, and being otherwise fully advised in the premises ORDERS THAT:

..... Adjudication of delinquency is withheld.

..... The child is adjudicated delinquent.

..... The child is committed to ..... a licensed child caring agency ..... the Department of Juvenile Justice for placement in:

..... a minimum-risk nonresidential commitment program, for an indeterminate period, but no longer than the child's 21st birthday or the maximum term of imprisonment an adult may serve for each count listed above, whichever comes first.

..... a ..... low- or ..... moderate-risk commitment program, for an indeterminate period, but no longer than the child's 21st birthday or the maximum term of imprisonment an adult may serve for each count listed above, whichever comes first, because:

..... the child is before the court for the disposition of a felony;

..... the child has previously been adjudicated for a felony offense;

..... the child previously has been adjudicated or had adjudication withheld for three or more misdemeanor offenses;

..... the child is before the court for disposition for a violation of sections 800.03, 806.031, or 828.12, Florida Statutes; or

..... the court finds by a preponderance of the evidence that the protection of the public requires such placement or that the particular needs of the child would be best served by such placement. The facts supporting this finding are: ....

..... a high-risk commitment program, for an indeterminate period, but no longer than the child's 21st birthday or the maximum terms of imprisonment an adult may serve for each count listed above, whichever comes first, because the child is before the court for the disposition of a felony.

..... a maximum-risk commitment program, for an indeterminate period, but no longer than the child's 21st birthday or the maximum term of imprisonment an adult may serve for each count listed above, whichever comes first, because the child meets the criteria in section 985.465 or 985.494, Florida Statutes.

..... The child is allowed ..... days credit for time spent in secure detention or incarceration before this date.

..... The child shall be placed on

..... home detention .....with/without..... electronic monitoring until placement.

..... secure detention until placement.

..... The court has orally pronounced its reasons for adjudicating and committing this child.

..... The court retains jurisdiction to accept or reject the discharge of this child from commitment, as provided by law.

..... The child is placed on post-commitment juvenile probation for an indefinite period not to exceed the child's 19th birthday or the maximum term of imprisonment an adult could receive for each count listed above, whichever comes first.

..... JUVENILE PROBATION: The child is .....placed on/continued in ..... juvenile probation under supervision of .....the Department of Juvenile Justice/.....(name)..... and

..... the court having withheld adjudication of delinquency, for an indefinite period not to exceed the child's 19th birthday.

..... the court having adjudicated the child delinquent, for an indefinite period not to exceed the child's 19th birthday or the maximum term of imprisonment an adult could receive for each count listed above, except for a second degree misdemeanor, six months, whichever comes first.

..... DISMISS: The case is dismissed.

..... Disposition on each count is .....concurrent/ consecutive......

..... This case disposition is .....concurrent/consecutive..... with case number ....

GENERAL CONDITIONS OF JUVENILE PROBATION. The child shall abide by all of the following conditions:

1. The child shall obey all laws.

2. The child shall be employed full-time or attend school with no unexcused absences, suspensions, or disciplinary referrals.

3. The child shall not change or leave .....his/ her..... residence, school, or place of employment without the consent of .....his/her..... parents and juvenile probation officer.

4. The child shall answer truthfully all questions of .....his/her..... juvenile probation officer and carry out all instructions of the court and juvenile probation officer.

5. The child shall keep in contact with the juvenile probation officer in the manner prescribed by the juvenile probation officer.

6. The child shall not use or possess alcoholic beverages or controlled substances.

SPECIAL CONDITIONS OF JUVENILE PROBATION. The child shall abide by all of the conditions marked below:

..... Restitution is ordered. Parent and child are responsible, ... jointly and severally.

..... Amount is reserved.

..... $.......... to be paid to .....(name)..... Payments shall begin .....(date)..... and continue at the rate of $.......... each month.

..... The court retains jurisdiction under Chapter 985, Florida Statutes, to enforce its restitution order, regardless of the age of the child.

..... Community Service ..... hours are to be performed by the child at the rate of ..... hours per month. Written proof is to be provided to the juvenile probation officer.

..... A letter of apology to be written by the child to .....(name)..... within ..... days. The letter must be a minimum of ..... words.

..... A ..... word essay to be written by the child on .....(subject)..... and provided to the juvenile probation officer within 30 days.

..... The child may have no .... contact with victim(s), ...(name(s))......

..... A .....mental health/substance abuse..... evaluation to be completed by the child within ..... days. The child will attend and participate in every scheduled appointment and successfully attend and complete any and all recommended evaluations and treatment.

..... The parent(s) .....is/are..... to complete counseling in ......

..... A curfew is set for the child at .... p.m. Sunday through Thursday and .... p.m. Friday and Saturday.

..... The child's driver's license is .....suspended/revoked/withheld..... for .....(time period)......

..... The child is to complete a .....detention/jail/prison..... tour within ..... days.

..... The child will be subject to random urinalysis.

..... The child will be electronically monitored.

..... The child will successfully complete all sanctions of the original juvenile probation order.

..... Other: ....

..... The child must pay court costs of $....., as specified below.

GUN CHARGES

..... The court finds that one of the above charges involves the use or possession of a firearm and further ORDERS the following:

..... The child's driver's license is .....suspended/revoked..... for .....½..... years.

..... The child is to serve .....15/21..... days in the Juvenile Detention Center, and shall not receive credit for time served prior to adjudication.

THE COURT FURTHER FINDS AND ORDERS:

..... The child must:

..... pay $.......... (no less than $50 per case when a misdemeanor offense is charged) or $.......... (no less than $100 per case when a felony offense is charged), the costs of prosecution and investigation, under sections 938.27 and 985.032, Florida Statutes.

..... pay $.........., the Crime Compensation Trust Fund fee, under section 938.03, Florida Statutes;

..... pay $.........., the Teen Court cost, under section 938.19, Florida Statutes (if authorized by county ordinance);

..... pay $.........., the Public Defender application fee, under section 27.52, Florida Statutes;

..... pay $.........., the Public Defender attorney fee, under section 938.29, Florida Statutes;

..... pay $.........., other costs, under section(s) ...., Florida Statutes.

..... The child has been adjudicated delinquent and the child is required to pay $.......... an additional cost, under section 939.185, Florida Statutes, if authorized by county ordinance.

..... The child has been adjudicated delinquent and assessed a fine and the child is required to pay $.......... to the Crime Prevention Trust Fund, under section 775.083(2), Florida Statutes.

..... The child has committed an enumerated crime against a minor and the child is required to pay $.........., under section 938.10, Florida Statutes.

..... The child has violated chapter 794, Florida Statutes (sexual battery) or chapter 800 (lewdness; indecent exposure) and is ordered to make restitution to the Crimes Compensation Trust

Fund under section 960.28(5), Florida Statutes, for the cost of the forensic physical examination.

..... The child has the inability to pay all court costs, including costs of prosecution, public defender application fees and costs of representation, and shall perform ..... hours of community service in lieu of these costs and fees.

..... The child .....has been adjudicated delinquent/ has entered a plea of no contest/has entered a plea of guilty..... to a felony or an enumerated misdemeanor, and the child is required to submit specimens under section 943.325, Florida Statutes.

..... Under section 985.039, Florida Statutes:

..... the parent/legal guardian, ...(name)....., shall pay to the Department of Juvenile Justice, 2737 Centerview Drive, Tallahassee, FL 32399-3100, $5 per day for each day the child is in residential commitment.

..... the parent/legal guardian, ...(name)....., shall pay to the Department of Juvenile Justice, 2737 Centerview Drive, Tallahassee, FL 32399-3100, $1 per day for each day the child is on probation, nonresidential commitment, or conditional release.

..... the parent/legal guardian, ...(name)....., shall pay to the Department of Juvenile Justice, 2737 Centerview Drive, Tallahassee, FL 32399-3100, a REDUCED fee of $..... per day for each day the child is in the custody of or supervised by the department. This reduced fee is based on the court's finding:

..... that the parent/legal guardian was the victim of the delinquent act or violation of law for which the child is currently before the court and is cooperating in the investigation of the offense.

..... of indigency or significant financial hardship. The facts supporting this finding are: ....

..... The cost of care/supervision fee is WAIVED based on the court's finding:

..... that the parent/legal guardian was the victim of the delinquent act or violation of law for which the child is currently before the court and is cooperating in the investigation of the offense.

..... of indigency or significant financial hardship. The facts supporting this finding are: ....

..... The parent/guardian, ...(name)....., ...(address)....., shall be liable for .....% of the payment. The parent/guardian, ...(name)....., ...(address)....., shall be liable for .....% of the payment.

The child is placed on notice that the court may modify the conditions of .....his/her..... juvenile probation at any time and may revoke the juvenile probation if there is a violation of the conditions imposed.

The parties are advised that an appeal is allowed within 30 days of the date of this order.

DONE AND ORDERED in .....(city)....., ... County, Florida on .....(date)....., at ..... a.m./p.m.

                  Circuit Judge

Copies to:

FORM 8.948. PETITION FOR REVOCATION OF JUVENILE PROBATION

PETITION FOR REVOCATION OF JUVENILE PROBATION

The petitioner represents to the court that ...., whose residence and address is .... was adjudicated a .... child and placed on juvenile probation by order of this court dated ...., and that the child has violated the conditions of juvenile probation in a material respect by: ....

The petitioner represents further that the parent(s) or custodian(s) .....is/are.....:

....
Mother   Residence

....
Father   Residence

....
Custodian   Residence

WHEREFORE, your petitioner requests that process may issue to bring the above-named child before this court to be dealt with according to law.

Date: ....

_____
Petitioner

FORM 8.949. ORDER FOR HIV TESTING

ORDER FOR HUMAN IMMUNODEFICIENCY VIRUS (HIV) TESTING

The court having been requested by the .....victim/ victim's legal guardian/minor victim's parent..... for disclosure of the child's HIV test results FINDS that:

The child, ...(name)....., ...is alleged by petition for delinquency to have committed/has been adjudicated delinquent for..... a sexual offense proscribed in chapter 794 or section 800.004, Florida Statutes, involving the transmission of body fluids from one person to another.

It is ORDERED AND ADJUDGED that:

1. The child, ...(name)....., shall immediately undergo Human Immunodeficiency Virus testing.

2. The testing shall be performed under the direction of the Department of Health in accordance with section 381.004, Florida Statutes.

3. The results of the test performed on the child pursuant to this order shall not be admissible in any juvenile proceeding arising out of the .....alleged sexual offense/sexual offense......

4. The results of the test shall be disclosed, under the direction of the department, to the child and to the ..... victim/victim's legal guardian/minor victim's parent...... The department shall ensure that the provisions of section 381.004, Florida Statutes, for

personal counseling are available to the party requesting the test results.

DONE AND ORDERED at ...., Florida, ...(date)......

_____
Circuit Judge

FORM 8.950. RESTITUTION ORDER

JUDGMENT AND RESTITUTION ORDER

THIS CAUSE was heard on .....(date)....., on the state's motion for an order requiring the child, born .....(date)....., or .....his/her..... parent(s), to pay restitution costs for the benefit of the victim pursuant to sections 985.0301(5)(i), 985.437, and 775.089, Florida Statutes.

Name of victim: ....

Attorney or Advocate: ....

Address: ....

The court being fully advised in the premises, it is ORDERED AND ADJUDGED:

The state's motion is granted and the .....child/ child's parent(s), ...(name(s))....., shall pay restitution for the benefit of the victim named above as follows:

..... $..... for medical and related services and devices relating to physical, psychiatric, and psychological care, including nonmedical care rendered in accordance with a recognized method of healing.

..... $..... for necessary physical and occupational therapy and rehabilitation.

..... $..... to reimburse the victim for income lost as a result of the offense.

..... $..... for necessary funeral and related services, if the offense caused bodily injury resulting in the death of the victim.

..... $..... for damages resulting from the offense.

..... $..... for ....

The total amount of restitution due is $......

Payment shall be made to the clerk of the circuit court.

Payment schedule:

..... Installment payments of $..... payable on a .....weekly/monthly..... basis.

..... Payment is due in full.

..... The court finds that the .....child/child's parent(s)..........is/are..... unable to pay and orders the child to perform ..... hours of community service in lieu of .....partial/total..... restitution.

The court retains jurisdiction over this child beyond .....his/her..... nineteenth birthday in order to enforce the provisions of this order and retains jurisdiction to modify the restitution in this case.

Other, specified conditions: ....

IT IS FURTHER ORDERED AND ADJUDGED that the clerk of the court shall provide the victim named above a certified copy of this order for the victim to record this judgment as a lien, pursuant to section 55.10, Florida Statutes.

IT IS FURTHER ORDERED AND ADJUDGED that this judgment may be enforced by the state or the victim in order to receive restitution in the same manner as a judgment in a civil action. Execution shall issue for all payments required under this order.

DONE AND ORDERED AT .....(city)....., ...(county)....., Florida, on .....(date)......

_____
Circuit Judge

Copies to:
State Attorney
Counsel for Child
Victim
Department of Juvenile Justice
Parent(s)

FORM 8.951. MOTION FOR JUVENILE SEXUAL OFFENDER PLACEMENT

MOTION FOR JUVENILE SEXUAL OFFENDER PLACEMENT

Comes now the .....State of Florida, by and through the undersigned assistant state attorney/Department of Juvenile Justice, by and through its undersigned counsel....., and moves the court for Juvenile Sexual Offender placement. In support thereof, movant would show:

..... that the juvenile has been found by the court, under section 985.35, Florida Statutes, to have committed a violation of chapter 794, chapter 796, chapter 800, section 827.071, or section 847.0133, Florida Statutes; or

..... that the juvenile has been found to have committed any violation of law or delinquent act involving juvenile sexual abuse as defined in section 985.475(1), Florida Statutes.

Placement in a juvenile sexual offender program is required for the protection of the public and would best serve the needs of this juvenile.

WHEREFORE, as this child meets the juvenile sexual offender placement criteria, the .....state/department..... respectfully requests this court to enter an order placing the child as a juvenile sexual offender under section 985.48, Florida Statutes.

Date: ....

_____
Assistant State Attorney/DJJ Attorney
.....(address & phone no.).....
Florida Bar No.: ....

FORM 8.952. FINDINGS FOR JUVENILE SEXUAL OFFENDER REGISTRATION

REQUIRED FINDINGS FOR JUVENILE SEXUAL OFFENDER REGISTRATION

The following findings are to be made for adjudications of delinquency made on or after July 1, 2007, for committing, or attempting, soliciting, or conspiring to commit any of the following offenses, when the offender is 14 years of age or older at the time of the offense.

Check the appropriate charge and make the corresponding findings:

Date of the offense: ....
Offender's age at date of offense: ....
Victim's age at date of offense: ....

..... **F.S. 794.011: Sexual Battery:** Oral, anal, or vaginal penetration by, or union with, the sexual organ of another, or the anal or vaginal penetration of another by any other object.

(Sexual offender registration is required if the offender is 14 years of age or older at the time of the offense.)

..... **F.S. 800.40(4)(b): Lewd or Lascivious Battery:** Encouraging, forcing, or enticing any person less than 16 years of age to engage in sadomasochistic abuse, sexual bestiality, prostitution, or any other act involving sexual activity.

(Sexual offender registration is required if the offender is 14 years of age or older at the time of the offense and at least one of the lines below is checked "Yes.")

Was the victim under the age of 12 at the time of the offense? Yes ..... No .....

Did the sexual activity involve force or coercion? Yes ..... No .....

..... **F.S. 800.04(5)(d): Lewd or Lascivious Molestation — Victim 12-15:** Intentionally touching the breasts, genitals, genital area, buttocks, or the clothing covering them, of a person 12 years of age or older but less than 16 years of age, or forcing or enticing a person less than 16 years of age to so touch the perpetrator.

(Sexual offender registration is required if the offender is 14 years of age or older at the time of the offense and **both** boxes below are checked "Yes.")

Did the sexual activity involve unclothed genitals? Yes ..... No .....

Did the sexual activity involve force or coercion? Yes ..... No .....

..... **F.S. 800.04(5)(c): Lewd or Lascivious Molestation — Victim 12:** Intentionally touching the breasts, genitals, genital area, buttocks, or the clothing covering them, of a person less than 12 years of age, or forcing or enticing a person less than 12 years of age to so touch the perpetrator.

(Sexual offender registration is required if the offender is 14 years of age or older at the time of the offense and the box below is checked "Yes.")

Did the sexual activity involve unclothed genitals? Yes ..... No .....

(Check one only)

SEXUAL OFFENDER REGISTRATION IS REQUIRED .....

SEXUAL OFFENDER REGISTRATION IS NOT REQUIRED .....

DONE AND ORDERED ON .....(date)......

_____

Circuit Judge

C. DEPENDENCY FORMS

FORM 8.958. ORDER APPOINTING SURROGATE PARENT

ORDER APPOINTING SURROGATE PARENT FOR DEPENDENT CHILD WHO HAS OR IS SUSPECTED OF HAVING A DISABILITY

The court finds that:

1. The child has, or is suspected of having, a disability as defined in the Individuals with Disabilities in Education Act ("IDEA") and F.S. 1003.01(3).

2. A surrogate parent is needed to act in the place of a parent in educational decision-making and in safeguarding the child's rights under the IDEA.

3. The child is entitled, under the Individuals with Disabilities in Education Act ("IDEA"), 20 U.S.C. § 1415(b)(2); 34 C.F.R. §§ 300.515 and 303.406; F.S. 39.0016(3)-(4), 39.4085(17); and Fla. Admin. Code 6A-6.0333, to the assistance of a surrogate parent because (check all that apply):

..... Parental rights have been terminated
..... Parents cannot be located

..... No parent is available to make education decisions related to the child's disability

..... Foster parent is unwilling or unable to make educational decisions related to the child's disability

..... Relative or non-relative caregiver is unwilling or unable to make educational decisions related to the child's disability

..... Child resides in a group home or therapeutic foster home

..... Other: ....

ACCORDINGLY, it is ORDERED that:

1. .....(Name)..... is appointed as a surrogate parent for .....(child's name)......

2. The surrogate parent named above has the following rights, duties, and responsibilities:

    a. to request or respond to requests for evaluations of the child;

    b. to review and keep confidential the child's educational records;

    c. to request and participate in school meetings including Individual Education Plan (IEP) meetings;

    d. to express approval or disapproval of a child's educational placement or IEP;

    [e.] to monitor the child's educational development;

    [f.] to help the child access available and needed educational services;

    [g.] to aid the child in securing all rights provided the child under the IDEA;

    [h.] to meet the child face-to-face

    [i.] to be afforded all of the due process rights parents hold under the IDEA

3. The surrogate parent may also do the following: (check all that apply)

..... attend appropriate court hearings to address the educational needs of the child. The surrogate parent will be provided notice of all dependency court hearings.

..... attend dependency staffings. The community-based care provider will invite the surrogate parent to all permanency staffings and any other staffings when the child's educational needs will be addressed. See F.A.C. 65C-28.006.

....

....

4. As to issues affecting the provision of a Free Appropriate Public Education, principals, teachers, administrators, and other employees of the .... County Public Schools shall communicate with the surrogate parent and accept the requests or decisions of the surrogate parent in the same manner as if he or she were the child's parent.

5. Unless the court explicitly orders otherwise, the surrogate parent does not have the right and responsibility to register the child in school, and grant or withhold consent for ordinary school decisions not related to IDEA (such as field trips, sports and club activities, medical care, etc.).

6. The surrogate parent must have access to and keep confidential the child's records including, but not limited to, records from the school system, community-based care provider or agency, and any mental health or medical evaluations or assessments.

7. By law, the surrogate parent has no liability for actions taken in good faith on behalf of the child in protecting the special education rights of the child.

ORDERED on .....(date)....., in ...., ... County, Florida.

_____
                    Circuit Judge

Copies to:

County Public Schools c/o Director, Exceptional Student Education,

Surrogate parent named above
(Check all that apply)
..... Attorney for DCF: .....(name).....
..... DCF caseworker: .....(name).....
..... Guardian ad Litem: .....(name).....
..... Attorney for mother: .....(name).....
..... Attorney for father: .....(name).....
..... Attorney for child: .....(name).....
..... Child named above .....(name).....
..... Foster parent: .....(name).....
..... Relative caregiver: .....(name).....
..... Child's principal: .....(name)..... at
.... School
..... Other: ....
..... Other: ....

FORM 8.959. SUMMONS FOR DEPENDENCY ARRAIGNMENT

SUMMONS AND NOTICE OF HEARING

STATE OF FLORIDA

TO: .....(name and address of person being summoned).....

.....(Petitioner's name)..... has filed in this court a petition, alleging under oath that the above-named child(ren) is/are dependent under the laws of the State of Florida and requesting that a summons issue in due course requiring that you appear before this court to be dealt with according to law. A copy of the petition is attached to this summons.

You are to appear before this Court at .....(location of hearing)....., at .....(time and date of hearing)......

FAILURE TO PERSONALLY APPEAR AT THE ARRAIGNMENT HEARING CONSTITUTES CONSENT TO THE ADJUDICATION OF THIS CHILD (OR CHILDREN) AS A DEPENDENT CHILD (OR CHILDREN) AND MAY ULTIMATELY RESULT IN LOSS OF CUSTODY OF THIS CHILD (OR CHILDREN).

IF YOU FAIL TO APPEAR YOU MAY BE HELD IN CONTEMPT OF COURT.

COMMENT: The following paragraph must be in bold, 14 pt. Times New Roman or Courier font.

If you are a person with a disability who needs any accommodation to participate in this proceeding, you are entitled, at no cost to you, to the provision of certain assistance. Please contact .....(name, address, telephone number)..... at least 7 days before your scheduled court appearance, or immediately upon receiving this notification if the time before the scheduled appearance is less than 7 days. If you are hearing or voice impaired, call 711.

Witness my hand and seal of this court at .....(city, county, and state)....., on .....(date)......

CLERK OF COURT

BY: _____

DEPUTY CLERK

NOTIFICACIÓN y CITACIÓN
PARA LA AUDIENCIA

ESTADO DE LA FLORIDA

PARA: _____
(Nombre y direccion de la persona a ser citada)

CONSIDERANDO, que _____
(Nombre del(a) demandante)

ha interpuesto en este Juzgado una petición en la cual alega bajo juramente la dependencia del(los) niño(s) según las leyes del Estado de la Florida, adjuntándose copia de la misma, y está solicitando la emisión oportuna de una citación para exigir su comparecencia ante este juzgado para tratar el asunto conforme a la ley.

POR LO TANTO, se le ordena comparecer ante este Juzgado en _____ a las
(lugar de la audiencia)

_____
(hora y fecha de la audiencia)

SI USTED NO COMPARECE PERSONALMENTE A LA AUDIENCIA INCOATORIA, ESTO SIGNIFICARÁ QUE USTED ACCEDE A LA ADJUDICACIÓN DE DEPENDENCIA DE ESTE(OS) NIÑO(S) Y FINALMENTE, PODRÁ RESULTAR EN LA PERDIDA DE LA TUTELA DEL(OS) NIÑO(S).

SI USTED NO COMPARECE, SE LO PODRÁ JUZGAR EN DESACATO DEL TRIBUNAL.

Si usted es una persona con una discapacidad que necesita cualquier tipo de trato especial para participar en este procedimiento, usted tiene derecho, sin costa alguno para usted, para la presetación de asistencia determinadas. Póngase en contacto con .....(nombre, dirección, número de teléfono)..... por lo menos 7 dias antes la aparición en la corte programado, o immediatamente después de reciber esta notification, si el tiempo antes de la comparecencia prevista es inferiof a 7 dias. Si usted está oyendo o voz alterada, llame al 711.

Firmado y sigilado en este Juzgado en _____ el _____

(ciudad, condado y estado)   (fecha)

ESCRIBANO DEL TRIBUNAL

POR: _____

ESCRIBANO DELEGADO

MANDA AK AVÈTISMAN POU YON CHITA TANDE.

LETA FLORID

POU: .....(non ak adrès pou moun yo voye manda-a).....

KÒM, tantiske, ...(non pati ki fé demann-nan)..... fé yon demann devan tribinal-la, epi li sèmante timoun-nan(yo), swa dizan bezwen pwoteksyon leta dapre règ lalwa nan Leta Florid, yon kopi enfòmasyon sou akizasyon-an kwoke nan lèt sa-a. Yo mande pou yo sèvi-w ak yon manda touswit, ki pou fose-w prezante devan tribinal la pou yo ka koresponn avèk ou, dapre lalwa.

ALÒ, pou sa yo kòmande-w pou prezante devan tribinal sa-a, ki nan ....., (adrès tribinal-la)....., a .....(nan dat ak lè, chita tande-a).....

SI OU PA PREZANTE PESONÈLMAN NAN CHITA TANDE-A, POU YO KA AVÈTI-W AK AKIZASYON OFISYÈL-LA, SA KA LAKÒZ YO DESIDE OU KONSANTI TIMOUN-NAN(YO), BEZWEN PWOTEKSYON LETA, EPI LI KA LAKÒZ OU PÈDI DWA-OU KÒM PARAN TIMOUN SA-A(YO).

SI OU PA PREZANTE, YO GEN DWA CHAJE-W, KMKWA OU MANKE TRIBINAL LA DEGA.

Si ou se yon moun infirm, ki beswen èd ou ki bewsen ke o akomode w pou ou patispe nan pwosedi sa yo, ou genyen dwa, san ke ou pa peye, a setin èd. Silvouple kontake .....(non, address, telephone)...... o moin 7 jou avan dat ou genyen rendevou pou ale nan tribunal, ou si le ou resevwa avi a, genyen mouins ke 7 jou avan date endevou tribunal la. Ou si ou pa tande pale, rele nan nimerro sa 711.

Mwen siyen non mwen, epi mete so mwen, nan dokiman tribinal-la sa-a, kòm temwen, nan .....(vil, distrik, eta)....., nan .....(dat)......

GREFYE TRIBINAL-LA

PA: _____

ASISTAN GREFYE TRIBINAL-LA

FORM 8.960. SHELTER PETITION

AFFIDAVIT AND PETITION FOR PLACEMENT IN SHELTER

COMES NOW, the undersigned, who being first duly sworn says:

1. On .....(date)..... at ..... a.m./p.m. the above named minor child(ren) was/were found within the jurisdiction of this court.

..... The child(ren) was/were taken into custody by ....

..... The child(ren) need(s) to be taken into protective custody.

2. The name, age, special needs, and residence of this/these child(ren) is/are:

Name	Birth date	Sex	Special Needs	Address
....	....	....	....	....
....	....	....	....	....
....	....	....	....	....

3. The name, relationship to the child(ren) and address of the child(ren)'s parents or other legal custodian(s) is/are:

Name	Relationship	Address
....	....	....
....	....	....
....	....	....

4. The following individuals who were listed in #3 above have been notified in the following manner of the date, time, and location of this hearing:

Name	Manner Notified
....	....
....	....
....	....

5. There is probable cause that the child(ren)

..... a. has/have been abused, abandoned, or neglected or is/are in imminent danger of illness or injury as a result of abuse, abandonment, or neglect;

..... b. was/were with a parent or legal custodian who has materially violated a condition of placement imposed by the court;

..... c. has/have no parent, legal custodian, or responsible adult relative immediately known and available to provide supervision and care; because ....

6. The provision of appropriate and available services will not eliminate the need for placement of the child(ren) in shelter care because:

..... a. an emergency existed in which the child(ren) could not safely remain in the home;

..... b. the home situation presents a substantial and immediate danger to the child(ren) which cannot be mitigated by the provision of preventive services;

..... c. the child(ren) could not be protected in the home despite the provision of the following services and efforts made by the Department of Children and Families to prevent or eliminate the need for placement in shelter care;

..... d. the child(ren) cannot safely remain at home because there are no preventive services that can ensure the safety of the child(ren).

7. The department has made reasonable efforts to keep the siblings together after the removal from the home. The reasonable efforts of the department were ....

..... a. The children are currently placed together ....

..... b. A foster home is not available to place the siblings together because ....

..... c. It is not in the best interest of each child that all the siblings be placed together in out-of-home care because ....

8. On-going visitation or interaction between the siblings .....(list)..... is

..... a. recommended as follows ....

..... b. not recommended because visitation or interaction would be contrary to the safety or well-being of .....name(s))..... because ....

9. The child(ren) is/are in need of and the petitioner requests the appointment of a guardian ad litem.

10. The petitioner requests that the parents, if able, be ordered to pay fees for the care, support, and maintenance of the child(ren) as established by the department under chapter 39, Florida Statutes.

11. The petitioner requests that the parents be ordered to provide to the Department of Children and Families and the Department of Revenue financial information necessary to accurately calculate child support under section 61.30, Florida Statutes, within 28 days of this order.

12. This affidavit and petition is filed in good faith and under oath.

WHEREFORE, the affiant requests that this court order that this/these child(ren) be placed in the custody of the department until further order of this court and that the place of such custody shall be:

..... at the discretion of the Department of Children and Families;

..... at the home of a responsible adult relative, ...(name)....., whose address is ....;

..... other.

Moving Party

.....(attorney's name).....
.....(address and telephone number).....
E-mail address: ....
Florida Bar number: ....

Verification

NOTICE TO PARENTS/GUARDIANS/ LEGAL CUSTODIANS

A date and time for an arraignment hearing is normally set at this shelter hearing. If one is not set or if there are questions, you should contact the Juvenile Court Clerk's office at .... A copy of the Petition for Dependency will be given to you or to your attorney, if you have one. A copy will also be available in the clerk's office. You have a right to have an attorney represent you at this hearing and during the dependency proceedings and an attorney will be appointed for you if you request an attorney and the court finds that you are unable to afford an attorney.

COMMENT: The following paragraph must be in bold, 14 pt. Times New Roman or Courier font.

If you are a person with a disability who needs any accommodation to participate in this proceeding, you are entitled, at no cost to you, to the provision of certain assistance. Please contact .....(name, address, telephone number)..... at least 7 days before your scheduled court appearance, or immediately upon receiving this notification if the time before the scheduled appearance is less than 7 days. If you are hearing or voice impaired, call 711.

FORM 8.961. SHELTER ORDER

ORDER FOR PLACEMENT IN SHELTER

THIS CAUSE came on to be heard under chapter 39, Florida Statutes, on the sworn AFFIDAVIT AND PETITION FOR PLACEMENT IN SHELTER CARE filed by .....(petitioner's name)....., on .....(date)...... The following persons appeared before the court:

..... Petitioner ....
..... Petitioner's attorney ....
..... Mother ....
..... Father(s) ....
..... Legal custodian(s) ....
..... Guardian ad litem ....
..... GAL attorney ....
..... Attorney for the Child ....
..... Other: ....

and the Court having reviewed its file and having been otherwise duly advised in the premises finds as follows:

1. The minor child(ren), ..., was/were found within the jurisdiction of this court and is/are of an age subject to the jurisdiction of this court.

2. PLACEMENT IN SHELTER.

..... The minor child(ren) was/were placed in shelter on .....(date)..... at ..... a.m./p.m. by .....(name)....., a duly authorized agent of the department.

..... The minor child(ren) need(s) to be placed in shelter at the request of the petitioner for the reasons stated in this order.

3. **PARENTS/CUSTODIANS.** The parents/custodians of the minor child(ren) are:

	Name	Address
Mother:	....	....
Father of	.....(child's name).....:	
	....	....
Other:	.....(relationship and to which child).....	
	....	....

4. **INABILITY TO NOTIFY AND/OR LOCATE PARENTS/CUSTODIANS.** The petitioner has made a good faith effort to notify and/or locate, but was unable to notify and/or locate .....(name(s))....., a parent or legal custodian of the minor child(ren).

5. **NOTIFICATION.** Each parent/legal custodian not listed in #4 above was:

..... duly notified that the child(ren) was/were taken into custody;

..... duly notified to be present at this hearing;

..... served with a statement setting forth a summary of procedures involved in dependency cases;

..... advised of their right to counsel; and

     ..... was represented by counsel, ...(name).....

     ..... knowingly, voluntarily, and intelligently waived the right; or

     ..... the court declined to accept the waiver because ....

     ..... requested appointment of counsel, but the court declined appointment because he/she did not qualify as indigent.

     ..... requested appointment of counsel and counsel was appointed.

6. PROBABLE CAUSE.

..... Based on the allegations in the Affidavit and Petition for Placement in Shelter, there is probable cause to believe that the child(ren) is/are dependent based on allegations of abuse, abandonment, or neglect or substantial risk of same.

..... A finding of probable cause cannot be made at this time and the court requires additional information to determine the risk to the child(ren). The following information must be provided to the court during the continuation of this hearing: .....(information to be provided)...... This hearing is continued for 72 hours, until .....(date and time)...... The children will remain in shelter care.

7. NEED FOR PLACEMENT.
Placement of the child(ren) in shelter care is in the best interest of the child(ren). Continuation in the home is contrary to the welfare of the child(ren) because the home situation presents a substantial and immediate danger which cannot be mitigated by the provision of preventive services and placement is necessary to protect the child(ren) as shown by the following facts:

..... the child(ren) was/were abused, abandoned, or neglected, or is/are suffering from or in imminent danger of injury or illness as a result of abuse, abandonment, or neglect, specifically: ....

..... the custodian has materially violated a condition of placement imposed by the court, specifically: ....

..... the child(ren) has/have no parent, legal custodian, or responsible adult relative immediately known and available to provide supervision and care, specifically: ....

8. REASONABLE EFFORTS.

..... Reasonable efforts to prevent or eliminate the need for removing the child(ren) from the home have been made by the department, which provided the following services to the family: ....

..... The following specific services, if available, could prevent or eliminate the need for removal or continued removal of the child from the home ....

..... The date these services are expected to be available is ....

..... The department is deemed to have made reasonable efforts to prevent or eliminate the need for removal from the home because:

     ..... The first contact with the department occurred during an emergency.

     ..... The appraisal of the home situation by the department indicates a substantial and immediate danger to the child(ren) which cannot be mitigated by the provision of preventive services.

     ..... The child(ren) cannot safely remain at home because no services exist that can ensure the safety of the child(ren). Services are not available because ....

..... Even with appropriate services, the child(ren)'s safety cannot be ensured.

..... The department has made reasonable efforts to keep siblings together after the removal from the home. The reasonable efforts of the department were ....

..... It is not in the best interest of each child that all the siblings be placed together in out-of-home care because ....

9. **RELATIVE PLACEMENT.**

..... The court asked any parents present whether the parents have relatives that might be considered as a placement for the child(ren)

..... The court advised any parents present that the parents have a continuing duty to inform the department of any relative who should be considered for placement of the child.

..... By this order, the court notifies the relatives who are providing out-of-home care for the child(ren) of the right to attend all subsequent hearings, to submit reports to the court, and to speak to the court regarding the child(ren), if they so desire.

It is, therefore, ORDERED AND ADJUDGED, as follows:

..... 1. The child(ren) shall remain/be placed in the shelter custody of:

..... the department, with the department having the discretion to shelter the child(ren) with a relative or other responsible adult on completion of a positive homestudy, abuse registry, and criminal background checks.

..... all the children shall be placed together in a foster home if available.

..... a foster home is not available for all the children because ....

..... placement of all the children in the same foster home is not in the best interest of the child(ren) .....(identify the child(ren))..... because ....

..... Other: ....

2. The child(ren) ..... may ..... may not be returned to the parent/custodian without further order of this court.

3. a. The Guardian Ad Litem Program is appointed.

b. An attorney shall be appointed for ....,

..... the child/children has/have special needs as defined in section 39.01305, Florida Statutes.

..... it is necessary.

4. The parents, within 28 days of the date of this order, shall provide to the department the information necessary to accurately calculate child support under section 61.30, Florida Statutes. The parents shall pay child support in accordance with Florida Statutes.

5. The legal custodian, or in the absence of the legal custodian, the department and its agents, are hereby authorized to provide consent for and to obtain ordinary and necessary medical and dental treatment and examination for the above child(ren) including blood testing deemed medically appropriate, and necessary preventive care, including ordinary immunizations and tuberculin testing.

6. Visitation with the child(ren) shall be as follows:

By the parents ....

Between the sibling children ....

Visitation or interaction between the children .....(identify child(ren))..... is not ordered as it will be contrary to the safety or well-being of .....(identify child(ren))..... because ....

7. The parents shall provide to the court and all parties identification and location information regarding potential relative placements.

8. The relatives who are providing out-of-home care for the child(ren) have the right to attend all subsequent hearings, to submit reports to the court, and to speak to the court regarding the child(ren), if they so desire.

9. **IF THE PARENTS FAIL TO SUBSTANTIALLY COMPLY WITH THE CASE PLAN, THEIR PARENTAL RIGHTS MAY BE TERMINATED AND THE CHILD(REN)'S OUT-OF-HOME PLACEMENT MAY BECOME PERMANENT.**

10. Special conditions: ....

11. This court retains jurisdiction over this matter to enter any other and further orders as may be deemed to be in the best interest and welfare of this/these child(ren).

12. If a Petition for Dependency is subsequently filed in this cause, the **Arraignment Hearing is scheduled for .....(date)....., at ..... a.m./p.m. at .....(location of arraignment)...... The parents have a right to be represented by an attorney at the arraignment hearing and during the dependency proceedings.**

COMMENT: The following paragraph must be in bold, 14 pt. Times New Roman or Courier font.

If you are a person with a disability who needs any accommodation in order to participate in this proceeding, you are entitled, at no cost to you, to the provision of certain assistance. Please contact .....(name, address, telephone number)..... at least 7 days before your scheduled court appearance, or immediately upon receiving this notification if the time before the scheduled appearance is less than 7 days. If you are hearing or voice impaired, call 711.

ORDERED in .... County, Florida on .....(date)....., at ..... a.m./p.m.

Circuit Judge

FORM 8.961(A). ORDER AUTHORIZING ACCESS TO CHILD'S MEDICAL AND EDUCATIONAL RECORDS

ORDER AUTHORIZING ACCESS TO CHILD'S MEDICAL AND EDUCATIONAL RECORDS

THIS CAUSE came on to be heard under sec. 39.402, Florida Statutes, concerning access to the medical and educational records of ...., a child.

The Court finds:

A. As to medical records and information:

...., mother/father of ...., the child, consents to the entry of this order, and to the court's providing access to the child's medical records to the department, its contract agencies, and any guardian ad litem and attorney for the child, and to provide the child's medical information to the court.

..... No parent or legal guardian of the child is available or able to consent to the entry of this order, or the parents withhold consent to providing access to the child's medical records and/or to providing the requested medical information.

..... Access to the child's medical records and information is necessary to provide services to the child.

B. As to educational records and information:

...., mother/father of ...., the child, consents to the entry of this order, and to the court's providing access to the child's educational records to the department, its contract agencies, and any guardian ad litem and attorney for the child, and to provide the child's educational information to the court.

..... No parent or legal guardian of the child is available or able to consent to the entry of this order, or the parents withhold consent to providing access to the child's educational records and/or to providing the requested educational information.

..... Access to the child's educational records and information is necessary to provide services to the child.

Therefore, it is ORDERED:

The department, ...(name of CBC)....., its contract agencies, ...(name)....., guardian ad litem, and .....(name)....., attorney for child, are authorized to access .....(child's name)..... 's medical and educational records and information, until further order of this court.

..... This order does not address the child's privacy rights to any of these records or information that may exist under Florida law. The child may assert to this court any objection under privacy rights to the release of this information.

ORDERED on .....(date)....., in ...., ... County, Florida.

Circuit Judge

Copies to:

(Check all that apply)
..... Attorney for DCF: .....(name).....
..... Caseworker: .....(name).....
..... Guardian ad Litem: .....(name).....
..... Attorney for mother: .....(name).....
..... Attorney for father: .....(name).....
..... Attorney ad litem for child: .....(name).....
..... Child named above .....(name).....
..... Other: ....
..... Other: ....

FORM 8.964. DEPENDENCY PETITION

PETITION FOR DEPENDENCY

COMES NOW, Petitioner, ...(name)....., by and through undersigned counsel, and petitions this court to adjudicate the above-named minor child(ren) to be dependent within the meaning and intent of chapter 39, Florida Statutes. As grounds, petitioner alleges the following:

1. This court has jurisdiction over the minor child(ren), ...(name(s))....., a .....(gender)..... child, whose date(s) of birth is/are ...., and who, at the time the dependency arose, was/were in the custody of .....(name(s))......

2. The natural mother of the minor child(ren) is .....(name(s))....., a resident of .....(state)....., whose address is ....

3. The father of the minor child(ren), ...(name(s))..... is .....(name)....., whose address is .... The father .....is..... is not married to the mother, and .....is..... is not listed on the child(ren)'s birth certificate(s). The mother filed a Sworn Statement About Identity or Location of Father with this court on .....(date)....., which named .... as the father.

4. The UCCJEA Affidavit ..... is attached ..... was filed with the Court on .....(date)..... and is incorporated by reference.

5. The child(ren) is/are dependent within the meaning and intent of chapter 39, Florida Statutes, in that the mother/father/parents/legal custodian/caregiver(s) abused, abandoned, or neglected the minor child(ren) on or about .....(date)....., by: .... and that these activities and environments cause the child(ren)'s physical, mental, or emotional health to be in danger of being significantly impaired.

OR

5. The above named child(ren) is/are presently under substantial risk or imminent threat of harm or abuse or neglect, within the meaning and intent of chapter 39, Florida Statutes, which is likely to cause the child(ren)'s physical health to be significantly impaired because ....

6. The department is unable to ensure the protection of the minor child(ren) without judicial intervention.

7. The mother/father/parents has/have received the following services: ....

8. A shelter hearing was held on .....(date)....., and the child(ren) was/were placed in the custody of ....

9. An arraignment hearing

..... needs to be scheduled.

..... is scheduled for .....(date and time)......

10. A guardian ad litem

..... needs to be appointed.

..... was appointed at the shelter hearing to represent the child(ren).

11. Under chapter 39, Florida Statutes, the clerk of the court is required to issue a summons to the following parents or custodians:

The natural mother, ...(name)....., whose address is ....

The natural father, ...(name)....., whose address is ....

.....(Additional fathers and their addresses)......

WHEREFORE, the petitioner asks that process may issue in due course to bring the above-named parties before the court to be dealt with according to the law, to adjudicate the named minor child(ren) named to be dependent.

.....(Petitioner's name).....

.....(Attorney's name).....
.....(address and telephone number).....
.....Florida Bar number.....

Verification
Certificate of service

NOTICE OF RIGHTS

PLEASE READ THIS PETITION BEFORE ENTERING THE COURTROOM.

YOU HAVE A RIGHT TO HAVE COUNSEL PRESENT AT THIS HEARING.

BY COPY OF THIS PETITION, THE PARENTS, CAREGIVERS, AND/OR LEGAL CUS- **TODIANS ARE NOTIFIED OF THEIR RIGHT TO HAVE LEGAL COUNSEL PRESENT FOR ANY PROCEEDING RESULTING FROM THIS PETITION OR TO REQUEST THE COURT TO HAVE COUNSEL APPOINTED, IF INDIGENT.**

Further, these persons are informed of the following:

An arraignment is set on this matter for .....(date)....., at ..... a.m./p.m., at .....(location)...... The purpose of the arraignment is to advise as to the allegations contained in the Petition For Dependency. When your case is called, the Judge will ask you to enter a plea to this petition. The plea entered may be one of the following:

1. Admit: This means you admit that the petition states the truth and you do not want a trial.

2. Consent: This means you neither admit nor deny the petition, but do not want a trial.

(If you enter either of the above two pleas, the court will set a disposition date for the matter. At disposition, the court will decide where the child will stay and under what conditions).

3. Deny: This means you deny the allegations of the petition and wish the state to attempt to prove them at a trial.

4. Continue: This means you wish time to confer with an attorney, before entering a plea. If you enter this plea, the court will schedule another hearing in approximately 2 weeks. At that time, another arraignment hearing will be held, and you (or your attorney) must enter one of the above three pleas.

COMMENT: The following paragraph must be in bold, 14 pt. Times New Roman or Courier font.

If you are a person with a disability who needs any accommodation in order to participate in this proceeding, you are entitled, at no cost to you, to the provision of certain assistance. Please contact .....(name, address, and telephone number)..... at

least 7 days before your scheduled court appearance, or immediately upon receiving this notification if the time before the scheduled appearance is less than 7 days. If you are hearing or voice impaired, call 711.

FORM 8.965. ARRAIGNMENT ORDER

ORDER ON ARRAIGNMENT AND NOTICE OF NEXT HEARING

THIS CAUSE came to be heard on .....(date)....., under chapter 39, Florida Statutes on the Petition For Dependency filed by .....(name)....., for arraignment of .....(name(s)).... The following persons appeared before the Court:

....(Name)....., Petitioner
....(Name)....., Attorney for the petitioner
....(Name)....., Attorney for the department
....(Name)....., Department caseworker
....(Name)....., Mother
....(Name)....., Attorney for mother
....(Name)....., Father of .....(child).....
....(Name)....., Attorney for father
....(Name)....., Guardian ad litem
....(Name)....., Attorney for guardian ad
         litem
....(Name)....., Legal custodian
....(Name)....., Attorney for legal custodian
....(Name)....., Other ....

The court having considered the Petition for Dependency and having heard testimony and argument, and having been otherwise duly advised in the premises finds:

1. This court has jurisdiction over the subject matter of this action; and

2. The mother, ...(name)..... :

..... was ..... was not noticed of this hearing;

..... did not appear, and the court:
..... entered a consent by default
..... did not enter a consent by default;

..... appeared with counsel ..... appeared without counsel and:

..... was ..... was not advised of her right to legal counsel;

..... knowingly, intelligently, and voluntarily, ... waived ..... did not waive her right to legal counsel; and

..... was ..... was not determined to qualify as indigent and ..... was ..... was not appointed an attorney.

..... was served with a petition for dependency, and entered a plea of: ..... Admit, ... Deny, ... Consent, ... No Plea, ... Continuance

..... The Petitioner

..... will continue a diligent search and will attempt service.

..... has conducted an adequate diligent search and is excused from further diligent search and further attempts at service.

3. The father, ...(name)..... :

..... was ..... was not noticed of this hearing;

..... did not appear, and the court:
..... entered a consent by default
..... did not enter a consent by default;

..... appeared with counsel ..... appeared without counsel and:

..... was ..... was not advised of his right to legal counsel;

..... knowingly, intelligently, and voluntarily ..... waived ..... did not waive his right to legal counsel; and

..... was ..... was not determined to qualify as indigent and ..... was ..... was not appointed an attorney.

..... was served with a petition for dependency, and entered a plea of: ..... Admit, ...

Deny, ... Consent, ... No Plea, ... Continuance

..... The Petitioner

     ..... will continue a diligent search and will attempt service.

     ..... has conducted an adequate diligent search and is excused from further diligent search and further attempts at service.

4. That the child(ren)'s current placement in shelter care:

     ..... is no longer appropriate, and the child(ren) shall be returned to ....

     ..... is appropriate, in that the child(ren) is/are in a setting which is as family-like as possible, consistent with the child(ren)'s best interest and special needs; and, that returning the child(ren) to the home would be contrary to the best interest of the minor child(ren); and, that every reasonable effort has been made to eliminate the need for placement of the child(ren) in shelter care, but present circumstances of the child(ren) and the family are such that shelter care is the only way to ensure the child(ren)'s health, safety, and well-being.

5. Additional findings: ....

THEREFORE, based on the foregoing findings of fact, it is hereby ORDERED and ADJUDGED that:

1. The minor child(ren) shall

     ..... be ..... returned to ..... remain in the care and custody of .....(name).....

     ..... remain in the care and custody of the department in shelter care pending adjudication and disposition or until further order of this court.

2. The child(ren): ..... is/are ..... is/are not adjudicated dependent at this hearing.

3. ..... Mediation ..... A case planning conference is/are ordered at this time and shall be conducted on .....(date)..... at ..... a.m./p.m., at .....(location)...... All parties, unless otherwise specified, shall attend.

4. As to the mother, ...(name)....., the court:

     Accepts the plea of: ..... Admit, ... Deny, ... Consent, ... Continuance.

     ..... Appoints ..... Does not appoint an attorney.

     Sets a hearing for ..... re-arraignment ..... adjudicatory trial ..... disposition and case plan hearing ..... trial status on .....(date)..... at ..... a.m./p.m.

5. As to the father, ...(name)....., the court:

     Accepts the plea of: ..... Admit, ... Deny, ... Consent, ... Continuance.

     ..... Appoints ..... Does not appoint an attorney.

     Sets a hearing for ..... re-arraignment ..... adjudicatory trial ..... disposition and case plan hearing ..... trial status on .....(date)..... at ..... a.m./p.m.

6. All prior orders not inconsistent with the present order shall remain in full force and effect.

DONE AND ORDERED on .....(date).....

_____
Circuit Judge

NOTICE OF HEARING

The Juvenile Court hereby gives notice of hearing in the above-styled cause on .....(date)..... at ..... a.m./p.m., before .....(judge)....., at .....(location)..... or as soon thereafter as counsel can be heard.

COMMENT: The following paragraph must be in bold, 14 pt. Times New Roman or Courier font.

If you are a person with a disability who needs any accommodation in order to participate in this proceeding, you are entitled, at no cost to you, to the provision of certain assistance. Please contact .....(name, address, and telephone number)..... at least 7 days before your scheduled court appearance, or immediately upon receiving this notification if the time before the scheduled appearance is less than 7 days. If you are hearing or voice impaired, call 711.

PLEASE BE GOVERNED ACCORDINGLY.

Copies furnished to:

FORM 8.966. ADJUDICATION ORDER—DEPENDENCY

ORDER OF ADJUDICATION

THIS CAUSE came before this court on .....(date)....., under chapter 39, Florida Statutes, for adjudication of the Petition for Dependency filed by .....(petitioner's name)...... Present before the court were

....(name)....., Petitioner
....(name)....., Attorney for the petitioner
....(name)....., Attorney for the department
....(name)....., Department caseworker
....(name)....., Mother
....(name)....., Attorney for mother
....(name)....., Father of .....(child).....
....(name)....., Attorney for father
....(name)....., Guardian ad litem
....(name)....., Attorney for guardian ad litem
....(name)....., Legal custodian
....(name)....., Attorney for legal custodian
....(Name(s))....., Minor child(ren)
....(name)....., Attorney ad litem for minor child(ren)
....(name)....., Other ....

The court having heard testimony and argument and being otherwise fully advised in the premises finds:

1. That the minor child(ren) who is/are the subject matter of these proceedings, is/are dependent within the meaning and intent of chapter 39, Florida Statutes, and is/are (a) resident(s) of the State of Florida.

2. The mother, ...(name)..... :

..... was ..... was not noticed of this hearing;

..... did not appear, and the court:

     ..... entered a Consent for failure to appear after proper notice.

     ..... did not enter a Consent for failure to appear after proper notice.

..... appeared with counsel;

..... appeared without counsel and:

     ..... was ..... was not advised of her right to legal counsel,

     ..... knowingly, intelligently, and voluntarily ..... waived ..... did not waive her right to legal counsel and

     ..... was ..... was not determined to qualify as indigent and

     ..... was ..... was not appointed an attorney.

3. The father, ...(name)..... :

..... was ..... was not noticed of this hearing;

..... did not appear, and the court:

     ..... entered a Consent for failure to appear after proper notice.

     ..... did not enter a Consent for failure to appear after proper notice.

..... appeared with counsel;

..... appeared without counsel and:

     ..... was ..... was not advised of his right to legal counsel,

..... knowingly, intelligently, and voluntarily ..... waived ..... did not waive his right to legal counsel and

..... was ..... was not determined to qualify as indigent and

..... was ..... was not appointed an attorney.

..... 4. That the child(ren) is/are dependent within the meaning and intent of chapter 39, Florida Statutes, in that the mother, ...(name)....., abused, neglected, or abandoned the minor child(ren) by .... These facts were proven by ..... preponderance of the evidence ..... clear and convincing evidence.

..... 5. That the child(ren) is/are dependent within the meaning and intent of chapter 39, Florida Statutes, in that the father, ...(name)....., abused, neglected, or abandoned the minor child(ren) by .... These facts were proven by ..... preponderance of the evidence ..... clear and convincing evidence.

COMMENT: Use 6, 7, and 8 only if the child is in out-of-home placement.

6. That the Court finds that it is in the best interest of the child(ren) to remain in out-of-home care.

7. That every reasonable effort was made to eliminate the need for placement of the child(ren) in out-of-home care but the present circumstances of the child(ren) and the ..... mother ..... father are such that out-of-home care is the only way to ensure the health, safety, and well being of the child(ren), in that ....

8. That the child(ren)'s placement in .....(type of placement)..... is in a setting which is as family like and as close to the home as possible, consistent with the child(ren)'s best interests and special needs.

9. That returning the minor child(ren) to the custody of .....(person who had previous legal custody)..... would be contrary to the best interest and welfare of the minor child(ren).

10. The Court inquired of any parents present whether they have relatives who might be considered for placement of the child(ren).

THEREFORE, based upon the foregoing findings, it is ORDERED AND ADJUDGED that:

1. The minor child(ren), ...(name(s))....., is/are adjudicated dependent.

2. The child(ren) shall remain in the care and custody of

..... the department in shelter care

..... other .....(name).....

pending disposition.

3. The parents shall provide to the Court and all parties identification and location information regarding potential relative placements.

4. **THE COURT ADVISED THE PARENTS THAT IF THE PARENTS FAIL TO SUBSTANTIALLY COMPLY WITH THE CASE PLAN THEIR PARENTAL RIGHTS MAY BE TERMINATED AND THE CHILD(REN)'S OUT-OF-HOME PLACEMENT MAY BECOME PERMANENT.**

5. This court shall retain jurisdiction over this cause to enter any such further orders that may be deemed necessary for the best interest and welfare of the minor child(ren).

6. All prior orders not inconsistent with the present order shall remain in full force and effect.

7. Disposition is scheduled for .....(date)....., at ..... a.m./p.m.

DONE AND ORDERED on .....date..... at .....(city)....., Florida.

Circuit Judge

NOTICE OF HEARING

The Juvenile Court hereby gives notice of hearing in the above styled cause on .....(date)..... at ..... a.m./p.m., before .....(judge)....., at .....(location)....., or as soon thereafter as counsel can be heard.

COMMENT: The following paragraph must be in bold, 14 pt. Times New Roman or Courier font.

If you are a person with a disability who needs any accommodation in order to participate in this proceeding, you are entitled, at no cost to you, to the provision of certain assistance. Please contact .....(name, address, and telephone number)..... at least 7 days before your scheduled court appearance, or immediately upon receiving this notification if the time before the scheduled appearance is less than 7 days. If you are hearing or voice impaired, call 711.

PLEASE BE GOVERNED ACCORDINGLY.

Copies furnished to:

FORM 8.967. ORDER OF DISPOSITION, ACCEPTANCE OF CASE PLAN, AND NOTICE OF HEARING

ORDER OF DISPOSITION,
ACCEPTANCE OF CASE PLAN,
AND NOTICE OF HEARING

THIS CAUSE came before this court on .....(date)....., under chapter 39, Florida Statutes, for disposition of the Petition for Dependency and acceptance of the Case Plan filed by the Department of Children and Family Services.

The following persons appeared before the court:

....(name)....., Petitioner
....(name)....., Attorney for the petitioner
....(name)....., Attorney for the department
....(name)....., Department caseworker
....(name)....., Mother
....(name)....., Attorney for mother
....(name)....., Father of .....(child).....
....(name)....., Attorney for father
....(name)....., Guardian ad litem
....(name)....., Attorney for guardian ad litem
....(name)....., Legal custodian
....(name)....., Attorney for legal custodian
....(name)....., Other: ....

The court having considered the family functioning assessment and Case Plan filed by the department and having heard testimony and argument and being otherwise fully advised in the premises finds that:

1. The minor child(ren) who is/are the subject matter of these proceedings, was/were adjudicated dependent within the meaning and intent of chapter 39, Florida Statutes, continue to be dependent, and is/are residents of the State of Florida.

2. The minor child(ren) is/are of an age subject to the jurisdiction of this Court.

3. The following parties were notified of this hearing and provided a copy of the Case Plan and family functioning assessment filed in this cause:

....(name)....., Petitioner
....(name)....., Attorney for the petitioner
....(name)....., Attorney for the department
....(name)....., Department caseworker
....(name)....., Mother
....(name)....., Attorney for mother
....(name)....., Father of .....(child).....
....(name)....., Attorney for father
....(name)....., Guardian ad litem
....(name)....., Attorney for guardian ad litem
....(name)....., Other: ....

4. The mother, ...(name)..... :

..... did not appear and ..... was ..... was not represented by legal counsel;

..... appeared ..... with ..... without legal counsel and ..... was ..... was not advised of her right to legal counsel;

..... knowingly, intelligently, and voluntarily ..... waived ..... did not waive her right to legal counsel; and

..... was ..... was not determined to qualify as indigent and ..... was ..... was not appointed an attorney.

5. The father, ...(name)..... :

..... did not appear and ..... was ..... was not represented by legal counsel;

..... appeared ..... with ..... without legal counsel and ..... was ..... was not advised of his right to legal counsel;

..... knowingly, intelligently, and voluntarily ..... waived ..... did not waive his right to legal counsel; and

..... was ..... was not determined to qualify as indigent and ..... was ..... was not appointed an attorney.

6. The following parents/legal custodians were notified of their right to participate in the preparation of the case plan and to receive assistance from any other person in the preparation of the case plan: .....(names of persons notified)......

7. The department filed a family functioning assessment with the court on .....(date)..... This family functioning assessment ..... is ..... is not in compliance with the statutory requirements.

8. The department filed a case plan with the court on .....(date)......

    a. The terms of the case plan ..... are ..... are not consistent with the requirements of the law and previous orders of this court.

    b. The case plan ..... is ..... is not meaningful and designed to address the facts and circumstances on which the court based the finding of dependency.

    c. The case plan ..... is ..... is not in the best interest of the minor child(ren).

    d. The case plan's stated goal of .... is ..... is not a reasonable goal.

    e. The parents ..... have ..... do not have the ability to comply with the terms of the case plan.

9. There is a need for temporary child support from .....(noncustodial parent(s)).... and that he/she/they ..... has/have ..... do/does not have the ability to pay child support.

COMMENT: Use 10, 11 & 12 if child(ren) is/are not placed in the home of a parent.

10. It is in the best interest of the minor child(ren) to be placed in the care and custody of .....(placement ordered)......

11. Placement of the minor child(ren) in the care and custody of .....(placement ordered)..... is in a setting which is as family like and as close to the home as possible, consistent with the child(ren)'s best interests and special needs.

12. Return of the minor child(ren) to the custody of .....(person from whom child(ren) was/were originally removed)..... would be contrary to the best interest and welfare of the minor child(ren). The child(ren) cannot safely ..... remain ..... return home with services and removal of the child(ren) is necessary to protect the child(ren), in that ....

13. Prevention or reunification services ..... were not ..... were indicated and are as listed: .....(services indicated)...... Further efforts could not have shortened separation of this family because: ....

COMMENT: Use 14 if the goal of the case plan is reunification.

14. Reasonable efforts to prevent or eliminate the need for removal of the child(ren) have been made by the department, which provided the following services: ....

COMMENT: Use 15 if child(ren) remain(s) or is/are returned to the parent(s).

15. The child(ren) can safely ..... remain with ..... be returned to .....(parent(s)'s name(s))..... as long as he/she/they comply(ies) with the following: ....

THEREFORE, based upon the foregoing findings, it is hereby ORDERED AND ADJUDGED that:

..... 1. The minor child(ren), ...(name(s))..... be placed in the custody of .....(name)....., under supervision of the department.

2. The family functioning assessment filed by the department is:

    ..... not accepted and a continuance was requested.

..... accepted by the court.

..... accepted by the court with the following amendments: ....

3. The case plan filed by the department is:

..... not accepted and a continuance is granted for 30 days or less.

..... accepted by the court.

..... accepted by the court with the following amendments: ....

4. All parties are ordered to comply with the provisions of the case plan and any amendments made to it.

COMMENT: Use 5, 6 & 7 if child(ren) is/are placed outside the home.

..... 5. The mother, ...(name)....., shall pay child support in the amount of $......... by the .....(day)..... of each month to .....(where money is to be paid)...., beginning on .....(date)..... and continuing until such time as payments begin to be deducted by income deduction order. All child support payments shall be paid to the Clerk of the Circuit Court designated to receive child support payments.

..... 6. The father, ...(name)....., shall pay child support in the amount of $......... by the .....(day)..... of each month to .....(where money is to be paid)...., beginning on .....(date)..... and continuing until such time as payments begin to be deducted by income deduction order. All child support payments shall be paid to the Clerk of the Circuit Court designated to receive child support payments.

..... 7. The legal custodian shall have the right to authorize for the child(ren) any emergency medical treatment and any ordinary and necessary medical and dental examinations and treatment, including blood testing, preventive care including ordinary immunizations, tuberculin testing, and well- child care, but not including nonemergency surgery, general anesthesia, provision of psychotropic medications, or other extraordinary procedures for which a separate order or informed consent as provided by law is required.

8. Other: ....

9. All prior orders not inconsistent with the present order shall remain in full force and effect.

10. This court shall retain jurisdiction over this cause to enter any such further orders that may be deemed necessary for the best interest and welfare of the minor child(ren).

11. This matter is scheduled for Judicial Review on .....(date)..... at .....(time)......

DONE AND ORDERED in ...., Florida, on .....(date)......

_____
Circuit Judge

NOTICE OF HEARING

The Juvenile Court hereby gives notice of hearing in the above-styled cause on .....(date)..... at ..... a.m./p.m., before .....(judge)....., at .....(location)....., or as soon thereafter as counsel can be heard.

COMMENT: The following paragraph must be in bold, 14 pt. Times New Roman or Courier font.

If you are a person with a disability who needs any accommodation in order to participate in this proceeding, you are entitled, at no cost to you, to the provision of certain assistance. Please contact .....(name, address, and telephone number)..... at least 7 days before your scheduled court appearance, or immediately upon receiving this notification if the time before the scheduled appearance is less than 7 days. If you are hearing or voice impaired, call 711.

PLEASE BE GOVERNED ACCORDINGLY.

Copies furnished to:

FORM 8.968. AFFIDAVIT OF DILIGENT SEARCH

AFFIDAVIT OF DILIGENT SEARCH

STATE OF FLORIDA
COUNTY OF ....

BEFORE ME, the undersigned authority, personally appeared .....(name)....., affiant, who, being first duly sworn, deposes and says that .....he/she..... made a diligent search and inquiry to determine the residence of .....(name)....., the .....parent/prospective parent..... of .....(name(s) of child(ren))...., and the results are as follows:

1. Affiant has received the name of the .....(parent/prospective parent)..... from .....(name)......

2. Affiant has had no face-to-face contact with the .....(name of parent/prospective parent)......

3. On .....(date)..... affiant telephoned information at .....(name)..... and was informed that there was no listing for .....(name of parent/prospective parent)......

4. On .....(date)..... affiant searched the .....(city)..... telephone directory and was unable to locate a listing for .....(name of parent/prospective parent)......

5. On .....(date)..... affiant sent a certified letter, return receipt requested, to .....(address)...., a last known address of .....(name of parent/prospective parent)...... On .....(date)..... affiant received the unclaimed receipt by return mail.

6. On .....(date)..... affiant visited .....(address)...., the last known address of .....(name of parent/prospective parent)...., and was informed by .....(name)..... that .....(name of parent/prospective parent)..... no longer resides there.

7. Affiant has made inquiries of all relatives of .....(name of parent/prospective parent)..... of the child, including the other parent, made known to me by the petitioner and .....(name)...... The names, addresses, and telephone numbers of those relatives contacted are: ...... None of the relatives contacted know the current residence or whereabouts of .....(name of parent/prospective parent)......

8. Affiant has made inquiries of all offices of program areas, including but not limited to mental health, of the Department of Children and Family Services likely to have information about .....(name of parent/prospective parent)...... The names, addresses, and/or telephone numbers of those offices are: .... No one in any of these offices knows the current residence or address of .....(name of parent/prospective parent)......

9. Affiant has made inquiries of other state and federal agencies likely to have information about .....(name of parent/prospective parent)...... The names, addresses, and/or telephone numbers of those agencies: .... No one in any of these agencies knows the current residence or whereabouts of .....(name of parent/prospective parent)......

10. Affiant has made inquiries of appropriate utility and postal providers. The names, addresses, and/or telephone numbers of those providers are: .... None of those providers know the current residence or whereabouts of .....(name of parent/prospective parent)......

11. Affiant has made inquiries of appropriate law enforcement agencies. The names, addresses, and/or telephone numbers of those agencies are: ....(Name of parent/prospective parent)..... is not known to any of these agencies.

12. Affiant has made inquiries of the federal armed services, including the United States Army, Navy, Air Force, Marine Corps., and National Guard. .....(name of parent/prospective parent)..... is not currently a member of these services.

13. Affiant has made inquiries of all hospitals in the .... area. The names, addresses, and/or telephone numbers of those hospitals are: ....(Name of parent/prospective parent)..... is not currently a patient at, nor has .....he/she..... recently been admitted to, these hospitals.

14. Affiant has conducted a thorough search of at least one electronic database specifically designed for

locating persons including .....(name of database)...... No information regarding .....(name of parent/prospective parent)..... was found in this electronic database.

15. .....(Name of parent/prospective parent)..... .....is/is not..... over 18 years of age.

16. Affiant is unable to determine the residence or whereabouts of .....(name of parent/prospective parent)..... and thus cannot personally serve process upon .....him/her......

_____
Affiant

Before me, the undersigned authority, personally appeared .....(name)....., the petitioner in this action, who is personally known to me/produced .....(document)..... as identification....., and who affirms that the allegations are filed in good faith and are true and correct to the best of petitioner's knowledge.

SWORN TO AND SUBSCRIBED before me .....(date)......

_____
NOTARY PUBLIC
Name: ....
Commission No.: ....
My commission expires: ....

OR

Verification (see Form 8.902).

FORM 8.969. SWORN STATEMENT REGARDING IDENTITY OR LOCATION OF FATHER

SWORN STATEMENT REGARDING IDENTITY OR LOCATION OF FATHER

1. My name is: ....
   My address is: ....

2. I am related to .....(child's name)..... because I am his/her ....

3. I understand that I am answering these questions under oath and from my own personal knowledge and I swear to tell the truth. I understand that this sworn statement will be filed with the court.

4. The mother of the child WAS married to .....(name)..... at the probable time of conception of the child.

OR

The mother of the child WAS NOT married at the probable time of conception of the child.

OR

I do not know whether or not the mother was married at the probable time of conception of the child.

5. The mother of this child WAS married to .....(name)..... at the time of this child's birth.

OR

The mother of this child WAS NOT married at the time of this child's birth.

OR

I do not know whether the mother of this child was married at the time of this child's birth.

6. The mother of this child WAS living with/cohabiting with .....(name)..... at the time of the probable conception of this child.

OR

The mother of this child WAS NOT living with/cohabiting with any man at the probable time of conception of this child.

OR

I do not know whether the mother of this child was living with/cohabiting with any man at the probable time of conception of this child.

7. The mother of this child HAS received payments or promises of child support with respect to this child or because of her pregnancy from .....(name)......

OR

The mother of this child HAS NOT received payments or promises of child support with respect to this child or because of her pregnancy from anyone.

OR

I do not know whether the mother has received any payments.

8. The mother named .... as the father on the child's birth certificate.

OR

The mother DID NOT name a father on the child's birth certificate.

OR

I do not know whether the mother named a father on the child's birth certificate.

9. The mother named .... as the father of this child in connection with applying for public assistance.

OR

The mother HAS NOT named anyone as the father of this child in connection with applying for public assistance.

OR

I do not know whether the mother has named anyone as the father of this child in connection with applying for public assistance benefits.

10. .....(name)..... has been named in a paternity case or acknowledged paternity in a jurisdiction where the mother lived at the time of or since the conception of this child or where this child resides or has resided.

OR

No man has been named in a paternity case or acknowledged paternity of this child in a jurisdiction

where the mother lived at the time of or since the conception of this child or where this child resides or has resided.

OR

I do not know if any man has been named in a paternity suit regarding this child.

11. List the name, date of birth, social security number, and last-known address of any man listed in this sworn statement:

Name: ....
Date of birth: ....
Social Security No.: ....
Last-known address: ....

12. Do you know any other information about the identity or location of any man listed in this sworn statement? ..... Yes ..... No. If so, please give that information: ....

I UNDERSTAND THAT THIS DOCUMENT WILL BE FILED WITH THE COURT. UNDER PENALTY OF PERJURY, I DECLARE THAT I HAVE READ IT AND THAT THE FACTS STATED ARE TRUE.

Date: ....

_____
Signature

Witnessed by .....(name)....., who is an authorized agent of the Department of Children and Family Services and who attests that the person who signed this statement provided proof of identity as indicated:

..... Driver's license, number: ....
..... Passport, number and country: ....
..... Resident Alien (Green Card), number: ....
..... Armed Forces Identification, number: ....
..... Other: ....

FORM 8.970. ORDER ON JUDICIAL REVIEW

ORDER ON JUDICIAL REVIEW AND NOTICE OF NEXT HEARING

THIS CAUSE came on to be heard on .....(date)..... for Judicial Review on the report filed by the Department of Children and Families in this cause under chapter 39, Florida Statutes.

The following persons appeared before the court:

....(name)....., Child
....(name)....., Attorney for the child
....(name)....., Petitioner
....(name)....., Attorney for the petitioner
....(name)....., Attorney for the department
....(name)....., Department caseworker
....(name)....., Mother
....(name)....., Attorney for mother
....(name)....., Father of .....(child).....
....(name)....., Attorney for father
....(name)....., Guardian ad litem
....(name)....., Attorney for guardian ad litem
....(name)....., Legal custodian
....(name)....., Attorney for legal custodian
....(name)....., Other: ....

and the court having considered

..... Judicial Review and Social Study Report filed by the Department
..... Statement/homestudy filed by the Department
..... Report of the Guardian Ad Litem
..... Case plan filed by the Department
..... Statement by the Child's Caretaker
..... Whether or not the child is a citizen and, if the child is not a citizen, the steps that have been taken to address the citizenship or residency status of the child
..... Other: ....

AND THE COURT having heard testimony and argument, and having been otherwise duly advised in the premises finds:

1. That the minor child(ren) who is/are the subject matter of these proceedings, was/were adjudicated dependent, continue to be dependent, is/are of an age subject to the jurisdiction of the court, and is/are resident(s) of the state of Florida.

2. The following parties were notified of this hearing and provided a copy of the documents filed for this hearing:

....(name)....., Petitioner
....(name)....., Attorney for the petitioner
....(name)....., Attorney for the department
....(name)....., Department caseworker
....(name)....., Mother
....(name)....., Attorney for mother
....(name)....., Father of .....(child).....
....(name)....., Attorney for father
....(name)....., Guardian ad litem
....(name)....., Attorney for guardian ad litem
....(name)....., Legal custodian
....(name)....., Attorney for legal custodian
....(name)....., Attorney for the child
....(name)....., Other: ....

3. The mother, ...(name)..... :

..... did not appear and ..... was ..... was not represented by legal counsel;

..... appeared ..... with ..... without legal counsel and ..... was ..... was not advised of her right to legal counsel;

knowingly, intelligently, and voluntarily ..... waived ..... did not waive her right to legal counsel; and

..... was ..... was not determined to qualify as indigent and

..... was ..... was not appointed an attorney.

4. The father, ...(name)..... :

..... did not appear and ..... was ..... was not represented by legal counsel;

..... appeared ..... with ..... without legal counsel and ..... was ..... was not advised of his right to legal counsel;

knowingly, intelligently, and voluntarily ..... waived ..... did not waive his right to legal counsel; and

..... was ..... was not determined to qualify as indigent and

..... was ..... was not appointed an attorney.

COMMENT: Repeat above for each father.

5. The department filed a judicial review report with the court on .....(date)...... This judicial review report ..... is ..... is not in compliance with the statutory requirements.

6. The following parents/legal custodians were notified of their right to participate in the preparation of the case plan and to receive assistance from any other person in the preparation of the case plan: .....(names of those notified)......

7. The mother has complied with the following tasks in the case plan: .....(list tasks complied with)......

8. The mother has not complied with the following tasks in the case plan: .....(list tasks not complied with)......

9. The father, ...(father's name)....., has complied with the following tasks in the case plan: .....(list tasks complied with)......

10. The father, ...(father's name)....., has not complied with the following tasks in the case plan: .....(list tasks not complied with)......

11. The mother ..... has ..... has not complied with court ordered visitation as follows: .....(explanation of visitation compliance)......

12. The father, ...(father's name)....., ... has ..... has not complied with court ordered visitation as follows: .....(explanation of visitation compliance)......

13. The department ..... has ..... has not complied with court ordered visitation as follows: .....(explanation of visitation compliance)......

14. The mother ..... has ..... has not complied with court ordered financial support for the child as follows: .....(explanation of financial compliance)......

15. The father, ...(father's name)....., ... has ..... has not complied with court ordered financial support for the child as follows: .....(explanation of financial compliance)......

16. The mother ..... has ..... has not complied with court ordered meetings with the department as follows: .....(explanation of meeting compliance)......

17. The father, ...(father's name)....., ... has ..... has not complied with court ordered meetings with the department as follows: .....(explanation of meetings compliance)......

18. The department ..... has ..... has not complied with court ordered meetings with the parents as follows: .....(explanation of meetings compliance)......

COMMENT: Use 19, 20, 21, 22, 23, & 24 if child(ren) is/are not placed in the home of a parent.

..... 19. It is in the best interest of the minor child(ren) to be placed in the care and custody of .....(placement ordered)......

..... 20. Placement of the minor child(ren) in the care and custody of .....(placement ordered)..... is in a setting which is as family like and as close to the home as possible, consistent with the child(ren)'s best interests and special needs.

..... 21. The children ..... are ..... are not separated in their placements. The following efforts have been made to reunite separated siblings: ....
..... It is not in the best interest of each sibling to be reunited in their placement because: ....
..... Each sibling has the following frequency, kind and duration of contacts: ....

..... 22. Return of the minor child(ren) to the custody of .....(person(s) from whom child(ren) was/were originally removed)..... would be contrary to the best interest and welfare of the minor child(ren). The child(ren) cannot safely ..... remain ..... return home with services and removal of the child(ren) is necessary to protect the child(ren).

..... 23. Prevention or reunification services .....were not .....were indicated and are as follows: .....(services indicated)...... Further efforts could not have shortened separation of this family because ....

..... 24. The likelihood of the children's reunification with the parent or legal custodian within 12 months is ....

COMMENT: Use 25 if child(ren) remain(s) or is/are returned to the parent(s).

..... 25. The child(ren) can safely ..... remain with ..... be returned to .....(parent('s)(s') name(s)).... as long as he/she/they comply(ies) with the following: ....

The safety, well-being, and physical, mental, and emotional health of the child(ren) are not endangered by allowing the child(ren) to ..... remain ..... return home.

THEREFORE, based upon the foregoing findings, it is hereby ORDERED AND ADJUDGED that:

1. The minor child(ren), ...(name(s)).... be placed in the custody of .....(name)...., under supervision of the department.

2. The judicial review report filed by the department is:

..... not accepted and a continuance was requested.

..... accepted by the court.

..... 3. The court finds that it is not likely that the child(ren) will be reunified with the parent or legal custodian within 12 months after the child was removed from the home. The department shall file a motion within 10 days of receipt of this written order to amend the case plan to incorporate concurrent planning into the case plan.

4. The court inquired of any parents present whether they have relatives who might be considered for placement of the children.

5. Other: ....

6. All prior orders not inconsistent with the present order shall remain in full force and effect.

7. This court shall retain jurisdiction over this cause to enter any such further orders as may be deemed necessary for the best interest and welfare of the minor child(ren).

8. This matter is scheduled for Judicial Review on .....(date)..... at .....(time)......

DONE AND ORDERED in ...., Florida, on .....(date)..... at .....(time)......

_____
Circuit Judge

NOTICE OF HEARING

The Juvenile Court hereby gives notice of hearing in the above-styled cause on .....(date)..... at ..... a.m./p.m., before .....(judge)....., at .....(location)....., or as soon thereafter as counsel can be heard.

COMMENT: The following paragraph must be in bold, 14 pt. Times New Roman or Courier font.

If you are a person with a disability who needs any accommodation in order to participate in this proceeding, you are entitled, at no cost to you, to the provision of certain assistance. Please contact .....(name, address, and telephone number)..... at least 7 days before your scheduled court appearance, or immediately upon receiving this notification if the time before the scheduled appearance is less than 7 days. If you are hearing or voice impaired, call 711.

PLEASE BE GOVERNED ACCORDINGLY.

Copies furnished to:

FORM 8.973A. ORDER ON JUDICIAL REVIEW FOR CHILD AGE 17 OR OLDER.

ORDER ON JUDICIAL REVIEW FOR CHILD OVER AGE 17 AND NOTICE OF NEXT HEARING

THIS CAUSE came on to be heard on .....(date)..... for Judicial Review on the report filed by the Department of Children and Families in this cause under chapter 39, Florida Statutes.

The following persons appeared before the court:
....(Name)....., Child
....(Name)....., Attorney for the Child
....(Name)....., Petitioner
....(Name)....., Attorney for the petitioner
....(Name)....., Attorney for the department
....(Name)....., Department caseworker
....(Name)....., Mother
....(Name)....., Attorney for mother
....(Name)....., Father of .....(child).....
....(Name)....., Attorney for father
....(Name)....., Guardian ad litem
....(Name)....., Attorney for guardian ad litem
....(Name)....., Legal custodian
....(Name)....., Attorney for legal custodian
....(Name)....., Other: ....

and the court having considered:

..... Judicial Review Social Study Report filed by the Department;

..... Because the child reached the age of 17 within the past 90 days, written verification that the child:

     ..... Has been provided with a current Medicaid card and has been provided all necessary information concerning the Medicaid program;

     ..... Has been provided with a certified copy of his or her birth certificate and has a valid Florida driver's license or has been provided with a Florida identification card;

     ..... Has a social security card and has been provided information relating to Social Security Insurance benefits, if the child is believed to be eligible;

     ..... Has received a full accounting if there is a Master Trust for the child and has been informed as to how to access those funds;

..... Has been provided with information related to the Road-to-Independence Program, including eligibility requirements, information on participation, and assistance in gaining admission to the program; If the child is eligible for the Road-to-Independence Program, has been informed that he or she may reside with the licensed foster family or group care provider with whom the child was residing at the time of attaining his or her 18th birthday or may reside in another licensed foster home or with a group care provider arranged by the department;

..... Has an open bank account or the identification necessary to open a bank account and the information necessary to acquire essential banking and budgeting skills;

..... Has been provided with information on public assistance and how to apply;

..... Has been provided a clear understanding of where he or she will be living on his or her 18th birthday, how living expenses will be paid, and what educational program the child will be enrolled in;

..... Has been provided with information as to the child's ability to remain in care until he/she reaches 21 years of age or 22 years of age if he/she has a disability;

..... Has been provided with a letter stating the dates that the child is under the jurisdiction of the court;

..... Has been provided with a letter stating that the child is in compliance with financial aid documentation requirements;

..... Has been provided his or her educational records;

..... Has been provided his or her entire health and mental health records;

..... Has been provided with information concerning the process for accessing his or her case file;

..... Has been provided with a statement encouraging the child to attend all judicial review hearings occurring after his or her 17th birthday; and

..... Has been provided with information on how to obtain a driver license or learner's driver license.

..... Statement/homestudy filed by the Department;

..... Report of the Guardian Ad Litem;

..... A case plan, dated ...., filed by the Department that includes information related to independent living services that have been provided since the child's 13th birthday or since the date the child came into foster care, whichever came later;

..... Statement by the child's caretaker on the progress the child has made in acquiring independent living skills;

..... Whether or not the child is a citizen and, if the child is not a citizen, the steps that have been taken to address the citizenship or residency status of the child;

..... Other: ....

AND THE COURT having heard testimony and argument, and having been otherwise duly advised in the premises finds:

1. That the minor child(ren) who is/are the subject matter of these proceedings was/were adjudicated dependent, continue to be dependent, is/are of an age subject to the jurisdiction of the court, and is/are resident(s) of the state of Florida.

2. The following parties were notified of this hearing and provided a copy of the documents filed for this hearing:

....(Name)....., Child
....(Name)....., Attorney for the Child
....(Name)....., Petitioner
....(Name)....., Attorney for the petitioner
....(Name)....., Attorney for the department
....(Name)....., Department caseworker
....(Name)....., Mother
....(Name)....., Attorney for mother
....(Name)....., Father of .....(child).....
....(Name)....., Attorney for father
....(Name)....., Guardian ad litem
....(Name)....., Attorney for guardian ad litem
....(Name)....., Legal custodian
....(Name)....., Attorney for legal custodian
....(Name)....., Other: ....

3. The child has been given the opportunity to address the court with any information relevant to the child's best interests.

4. The mother, ...(name).....:

..... did not appear and ..... was ..... was not represented by legal counsel;

..... appeared ..... with ..... without legal counsel and ..... was ..... was not advised of her right to legal counsel;

knowingly, intelligently, and voluntarily ..... waived ..... did not waive her right to legal counsel; and

..... was ..... was not determined to qualify as indigent and

..... was ..... was not appointed an attorney.

5. The father, ...(name).....:

..... did not appear and ..... was ..... was not represented by legal counsel;

..... appeared ..... with ..... without legal counsel and ..... was ..... was not advised of his right to legal counsel;

knowingly, intelligently, and voluntarily ..... waived ..... did not waive his right to legal counsel; and

..... was ..... was not determined to qualify as indigent and

..... was ..... was not appointed an attorney.

COMMENT: Repeat above for each father.

6. The department filed a judicial review report with the court on .....(date)...... This judicial review report ..... is ..... is not in compliance with the statutory requirements.

7. The following parents/legal custodians were notified of their right to participate in the preparation of the case plan and to receive assistance from any other person in the preparation of the case plan: .....(names of those notified)......

8. The mother has complied with the following tasks in the case plan: .....(list tasks complied with)......

9. The mother has not complied with the following tasks in the case plan: .....(list tasks not complied with)......

10. The father, ...(father's name)....., has complied with the following tasks in the case plan: .....(list tasks complied with)......

11. The father, ...(father's name)....., has not complied with the following tasks in the case plan: .....(list tasks not complied with)......

12. The mother ..... has ..... has not complied with court ordered visitation as follows: .....(explanation of visitation compliance)......

13. The father, ...(father's name)....., ... has ..... has not complied with court ordered visitation as follows: .....(explanation of visitation compliance)......

14. The department ..... has ..... has not complied with court ordered visitation as follows: .....(explanation of visitation compliance)......

15. The mother ..... has ..... has not complied with court ordered financial support for the child as follows: .....(explanation of financial compliance)......

16. The father, ...(father's name)....., ... has ..... has not complied with court ordered financial support for the child as follows: .....(explanation of financial compliance)......

17. The mother ..... has ..... has not complied with court ordered meetings with the department as follows: .....(explanation of meetings compliance)......

18. The father, ...(father's name)....., ... has ..... has not complied with court ordered meetings with the department as follows: .....(explanation of meetings compliance)......

19. The department ..... has ..... has not complied with court ordered meetings with the parents as follows: .....(explanation of meetings compliance)......

COMMENT: Use 20, 21, 22, 23, & 24 if child(ren) is/are not placed in the home of a parent.

..... 20. It is in the best interest of the minor child(ren) to be placed in the care and custody of .....(placement ordered)......

..... 21. Placement of the minor child(ren) in the care and custody of .....(placement ordered)..... is in a setting which is as family like and as close to the home as possible, consistent with the child(ren)'s best interests and special needs.

..... 22. The children ..... are ..... are not separated in their placements. The following efforts have been made to reunite the siblings: ....
..... It is not in the siblings' best interest to be reunited in their placement because: ....
..... The separate siblings have the following frequency, kind and duration of contacts: ....

..... 23. Return of the minor child(ren) to the custody of .....(person(s) from whom child(ren) was/were originally removed)..... would be contrary to the best interest and welfare of the minor child(ren). The child(ren) cannot safely ..... remain ..... return home with services and removal of the child(ren) is necessary to protect the child(ren).

..... 24. Prevention or reunification services .....

were not ..... were indicated and are as follows: .....(services indicated)...... Further efforts could not have shortened separation of this family because ....

COMMENT: Use 25 if child(ren) remain(s) or is/are returned to the parent(s).

..... 25. The child(ren) can safely ..... remain with ..... be returned to .....(parent('s)(s') name(s)).... as long as he/she/they comply(ies) with the following: .... The safety, well-being, and physical, mental, and emotional health of the child(ren) are not endangered by allowing the child(ren) to ..... remain ..... return home.

..... 26. The child's petition and application for special immigrant juvenile status or other immigration decision remains pending.

..... 27. The department ..... has ..... has not complied with its obligation as specified in the written case plan or in the provision of independent living services as required by Florida Statutes.

THEREFORE, based upon the foregoing findings, it is hereby ORDERED AND ADJUDGED that:

1. The minor child(ren), ...(name(s))....., be placed in the custody of .....(name)....., under supervision of the department.

2. The judicial review report filed by the department is:

..... not accepted and a continuance was requested.

..... accepted by the court.

3. Other: ....

4. All prior orders not inconsistent with the present order shall remain in full force and effect.

5. This court shall retain jurisdiction over this cause to enter any such further orders as may be deemed necessary for the best interest and welfare of the minor child(ren).

6. This court shall retain jurisdiction until the final decision is rendered by the federal immigration authorities, or upon the immigrant child's 22nd birthday, whichever shall occur first.

7. This court shall retain jurisdiction until the child's 19th birthday for the purpose of determining whether appropriate services that were required to be provided to the young adult before reaching 18 years of age have been provided to the youth.

8. This court shall retain jurisdiction until the child's 21st birthday, or 22nd birthday if the child has a disability, unless the young adult chooses to leave foster care upon reaching 18 years of age, or if the young adult does not meet the eligibility requirements to remain in foster care or chooses to leave care at any time prior to the 21st birthday, or 22nd birthday if the child has a disability.

9. This matter is scheduled for Judicial Review on .....(date)..... at .....(time)......

DONE AND ORDERED in ...., Florida, on .....(date)......

_____
Circuit Judge

NOTICE OF HEARING

The Juvenile Court hereby gives notice of hearing in the above-styled cause on .....(date)..... at ..... a.m./p.m., before .....(judge)....., at .....(location)....., or as soon thereafter as counsel can be heard.

COMMENT: The following paragraph must be in bold, 14 pt. Times New Roman or Courier font.

If you are a person with a disability who needs any accommodation in order to participate in this proceeding, you are entitled, at no cost to you, to the provision of certain assistance. Please contact .....(name, address, and telephone number)..... at least 7 days before your scheduled court appearance, or immediately upon receiving this notification if the time before the scheduled appearance is less than 7 days. If you are hearing or voice impaired, call 711.

PLEASE BE GOVERNED ACCORDINGLY.

Copies furnished to: ....

FORM 8.973B. ORDER ON JUDICIAL REVIEW.

ORDER ON LAST JUDICIAL REVIEW BEFORE CHILD REACHES AGE 18 AND NOTICE OF NEXT HEARING

THIS CAUSE came on to be heard on .....(date)..... for Judicial Review on the report filed by the Department of Children and Families in this cause under chapter 39, Florida Statutes.

The following persons appeared before the court:
....(Name)....., Child
....(Name)....., Attorney for the Child
....(Name)....., Petitioner
....(Name)....., Attorney for the petitioner
....(Name)....., Attorney for the department
....(Name)....., Department caseworker
....(Name)....., Mother
....(Name)....., Attorney for mother
....(Name)....., Father of .....(child).....
....(Name)....., Attorney for father
....(Name)....., Guardian ad litem
....(Name)....., Attorney for guardian ad litem
....(Name)....., Legal custodian
....(Name)....., Attorney for legal custodian
....(Name)....., Other: ....

and the court having considered:

..... Judicial Review Social Study Report filed by the Department;

..... Statement/homestudy filed by the Department;

..... Report of the Guardian Ad Litem;

..... A case plan, dated ...., filed by the Department that includes information related to independent living services that have been provided since the child's 13th birthday or since the date the child came into foster care, whichever came later;

..... Statement by the child's caretaker on the progress the child has made in acquiring independent living skills;

..... Whether or not the child is a citizen and, if the child is not a citizen, the steps that have been taken to address the citizenship or residency status of the child;

..... A copy of the child's transition plan;

..... Other: ....

AND THE COURT having heard testimony and argument, and having been otherwise duly advised in the premises finds:

1. That the minor child(ren) who .....is/are..... the subject matter of these proceedings .....was/were..... adjudicated dependent, continue to be dependent, is/are of an age subject to the jurisdiction of the court, and .....is/are..... resident(s) of the state of Florida.

2. The following parties were notified of this hearing and provided a copy of the documents filed for this hearing:
....(Name)....., Child
....(Name)....., Attorney for the Child
....(Name)....., Petitioner
....(Name)....., Attorney for the petitioner
....(Name)....., Attorney for the department
....(Name)....., Department caseworker
....(Name)....., Mother
....(Name)....., Attorney for mother
....(Name)....., Father of .....(child).....
....(Name)....., Attorney for father
....(Name)....., Guardian ad litem
....(Name)....., Attorney for guardian ad litem
....(Name)....., Legal custodian
....(Name)....., Attorney for legal custodian
....(Name)....., Other: ....

3. The child has been given the opportunity to address the court with any information relevant to the child's best interests.

4. The mother, ...(name).....:

..... did not appear and ..... was ..... was not represented by legal counsel;

..... appeared ..... with ..... without legal counsel and ..... was ..... was not advised of her right to legal counsel;

knowingly, intelligently, and voluntarily

..... waived ..... did not waive her right to legal counsel; and

..... was ..... was not determined to qualify as indigent and

..... was ..... was not appointed an attorney.

5. The father, ...(name).....:

..... did not appear and ..... was ..... was not represented by legal counsel;

..... appeared ..... with ..... without legal counsel and ..... was ..... was not advised of his right to legal counsel;

knowingly, intelligently, and voluntarily ..... waived ..... did not waive his right to legal counsel; and

..... was ..... was not determined to qualify as indigent and

..... was ..... was not appointed an attorney.

COMMENT: Repeat above for each father.

6. The department filed a judicial review report with the court on .....(date)...... This judicial review report ..... is ..... is not in compliance with the statutory requirements.

7. The following parents/legal custodians were notified of their right to participate in the preparation of the case plan and to receive assistance from any other person in the preparation of the case plan: .....(names of those notified)......

8. The mother has complied with the following tasks in the case plan: .....(list tasks complied with)......

9. The mother has not complied with the following tasks in the case plan: .....(list tasks not complied with)......

10. The father, ...(father's name)....., has complied with the following tasks in the case plan: .....(list tasks complied with)......

11. The father, ...(father's name)....., has not complied with the following tasks in the case plan: .....(list tasks not complied with)......

12. The mother ..... has ..... has not complied with court ordered visitation as follows: .....(explanation of visitation compliance)......

13. The father, ...(father's name)....., ... has ..... has not complied with court ordered visitation as follows: .....(explanation of visitation compliance)......

14. The department ..... has ..... has not complied with court ordered visitation as follows .....(explanation of visitation compliance)......

15. The mother ..... has ..... has not complied with court ordered financial support for the child as follows: .....(explanation of financial compliance)......

16. The father, ...(father's name)....., ... has ..... has not complied with court ordered financial support for the child as follows: .....(explanation of financial compliance)......

17. The mother ..... has ..... has not complied with court ordered meetings with the department as follows: .....(explanation of meetings compliance)......

18. The father, ...(father's name)....., ... has ..... has not complied with court ordered meetings with the department as follows: .....(explanation of meetings compliance)......

19. The department ..... has ..... has not complied with court ordered meetings with the parents as follows: .....(explanation of meetings compliance)......

COMMENT: Use 20, 21, 22, 23, & 24 if child(ren) is/are not placed in the home of a parent.

20. It is in the best interest of the minor child(ren) to be placed in the care and custody of .....(placement ordered)......

21. Placement of the minor child(ren) in the care and custody of .....(placement ordered)..... is in a setting which is as family like and as close to the home as possible, consistent with the child(ren)'s best interests and special needs.

..... 22. The children ..... are ..... are not separated in their placements. The following efforts have been made to reunite separated siblings: ....

..... It is not in the best interest of each sibling to be reunited in their placement because: ....

..... Each sibling has the following frequency, kind, and duration of contacts: ....

23. Return of the minor child(ren) to the custody of .....(person(s) from whom child(ren) was/were originally removed)..... would be contrary to the best interest and welfare of the minor child(ren). The child(ren) cannot safely ..... remain ..... return home with services and removal of the child(ren) is necessary to protect the child(ren).

24. Prevention or reunification services ..... were not ..... were indicated and are as follows: .....(services indicated)...... Further efforts could not have shortened separation of this family because ....

COMMENT: Use 25 if child(ren) remain(s) or is/are returned to the parent(s).

25. The child(ren) can safely ..... remain with ..... be returned to ..... (parent('s)(s') name(s))..... as long as he/she/they comply(ies) with the following: .... The safety, well-being, and physical, mental, and emotional health of the child(ren) are not endangered by allowing the child(ren) to ..... remain ..... return home.

26. The child's petition and application for special immigrant juvenile status or other immigration decision remains pending.

27. The department ..... has ..... has not complied with its obligation as specified in the written case plan or in the provision of independent living services as required by Florida Statutes.

..... 28. The child does plan on remaining in foster care.

a. the child will meet the requirements by ....

b. the supervised living arrangement will be ....

c. the child has been informed of ....

..... (1) the right to continued support and services;

..... (2) the right to request termination of this court's jurisdiction and to be discharged from foster care;

..... (3) the opportunity to reenter foster care pursuant to Florida law.

..... 29. The child does not plan on remaining in foster care. The child has been informed of:

..... a. services or benefits for which the child may be eligible based upon the child's placement and length of time spent in licensed foster care;

..... b. services or benefits that may be lost through a termination of the court's jurisdiction; and

..... c. other federal, state, local, or community-based services or supports available to the child.

THEREFORE, based upon the foregoing findings, it is hereby ORDERED AND ADJUDGED that:

1. The minor child(ren), ...(name(s))....., be placed in the custody of .....(name)....., under supervision of the department.

2. The judicial review report filed by the department is: ..... not accepted and a continuance was requested ..... accepted by the court.

3. The child's transition plan is: ..... not approved and a continuance was requested ..... approved by the court.

4. Other: ....

5. All prior orders not inconsistent with the present order shall remain in full force and effect.

6. This court shall retain jurisdiction over this cause to enter any such further orders as may be deemed necessary for the best interest and welfare of the minor child(ren).

7. This court shall retain jurisdiction until the final decision is rendered by the federal immigration authorities, or upon the immigrant child's 22nd birthday, whichever shall occur first.

8. This court shall retain jurisdiction until the child's 19th birthday for the purpose of determining

whether appropriate services that were required to be provided to the young adult before reaching 18 years of age have been provided to the youth.

9. This court shall retain jurisdiction until the child's 21st birthday, or 22nd birthday if the child has a disability, unless the young adult chooses to leave foster care upon reaching 18 years of age, or if the young adult does not meet the eligibility requirements to remain in foster care or chooses to leave care at any time prior to the 21st birthday, or the 22nd birthday if the young adult has a disability.

10. This matter is scheduled for Judicial Review on .....(date)..... at .....(time)......

DONE AND ORDERED in ...., Florida, on .....(date)......

_____
Circuit Judge

NOTICE OF HEARING

The Juvenile Court hereby gives notice of hearing in the above-styled cause on .....(date)..... at ..... a.m./p.m., before .....(judge)....., at .....(location)....., or as soon thereafter as counsel can be heard.

COMMENT: The following paragraph must be in bold, 14 pt. Times New Roman or Courier font.

If you are a person with a disability who needs any accommodation in order to participate in this proceeding, you are entitled, at no cost to you, to the provision of certain assistance. Please contact .....(name, address, and telephone number)..... at least 7 days before your scheduled court appearance, or immediately upon receiving this notification if the time before the scheduled appearance is less than 7 days. If you are hearing or voice impaired, call 711.

PLEASE BE GOVERNED ACCORDINGLY.

Copies furnished to: ....

FORM 8.973C. ORDER ON JUDICIAL REVIEW FOR YOUNG ADULTS IN EXTENDED FOSTER CARE.

ORDER ON JUDICIAL REVIEW FOR YOUNG ADULTS IN EXTENDED FOSTER CARE AND NOTICE OF NEXT HEARING

THIS CAUSE came on to be heard on .....(date)..... for Judicial Review on the report filed by the Department of Children and Families in this cause under chapter 39, Florida Statutes.

The following persons appeared before the court:
....(Name)....., Young Adult
....(Name)....., Attorney for the Young Adult
....(Name)....., Petitioner
....(Name)....., Attorney for the petitioner
....(Name)....., Attorney for the department
....(Name)....., Department caseworker
....(Name)....., Guardian ad litem
....(Name)....., Attorney for guardian ad litem
....(Name)....., Other: ....

and the court having considered:

.....   Judicial Review Social Study Report filed by the Department;

.....   Case Plan filed by the Department;

.....   Report of the Guardian Ad Litem;

.....   A copy of the young adult's transition plan;

.....   Other: ....

AND THE COURT having heard testimony and argument, and having been otherwise duly advised in the premises finds:

1. The young adult ..... is ..... is not making progress in meeting the case plan goals, as follows: ....

2. The case plan and/or the young adult's transition plan shall be amended as follows: ....

3. The Department and all services providers ..... have ..... have not provided the appropriate services listed in the case plan. ..... The Department must take the following action to ensure the young adult receives identified services that have not been provided: ....

..... 4. The young adult ..... is ..... is not separated from siblings in out-of-home care.
The following efforts have been made to reunite separated siblings:

....
....
....
..... It is not in the best interest of each sibling to be reunited in their placement because:

....
....
..... Each sibling has the following frequency, kind and duration of contacts:

....
....
....

..... 5. Jurisdiction in this case should be terminated based on the following facts:

..... a. The young adult has requested termination of jurisdiction; or

..... b. The young adult has been informed by the department of his or her right to attend this hearing and has provided written consent to waive this right, and

..... c. The young adult has been informed of the potential negative effects of early termination of care, the option to reenter care before reaching 21 years of age, or 22 years of age if the young adult has a disability, the procedure for and the limitations on reentering care, and the availability of alternative services, and has signed a document attesting that he or she has been so informed and understands these provisions; or

..... d. The young adult has voluntarily left the program, has not signed the document indicated above, and is unwilling to participate in any further court proceeding; or

..... e. The young adult has been involuntarily discharged from the program by written notification dated ...., and the young adult has not appealed the discharge decision.

THEREFORE, based upon the foregoing findings, it is hereby ORDERED AND ADJUDGED that:

1. The judicial review report filed by the department is:

..... not accepted and a continuance was requested.

..... accepted by the court.

2. All prior orders not inconsistent with the present order shall remain in full force and effect.

..... 3. This court shall retain jurisdiction until the young adult's 19th birthday for the purpose of determining whether appropriate services that were required to be provided to the young adult before reaching 18 years of age have been provided to the youth; or

..... 4. This court shall retain jurisdiction until the young adult's 21st birthday, or 22 years of age if the young adult has a disability, unless the young adult chooses to leave foster care upon reaching 18 years of age, or if the young adult does not meet the eligibility requirements to remain in foster care or chooses to leave care at any time prior to the 21st birthday; or

..... 5. Jurisdiction over this cause is hereby terminated.

..... 6. Other: ....

..... 7. This matter is scheduled for Judicial Review on .....(date)..... at .....(time)......

DONE AND ORDERED in ...., Florida, on .....(date)......

Circuit Judge

NOTICE OF HEARING

The Juvenile Court hereby gives notice of hearing in the above-styled cause on .....(date)..... at ..... a.m./p.m., before .....(judge)....., at ..... (location)....., or as soon thereafter as counsel can be heard.

COMMENT: The following paragraph must be in bold, 14 pt. Times New Roman or Courier font.

If you are a person with a disability who needs any accommodation in order to participate in this proceeding, you are entitled, at no cost to you, to the provision of certain assistance. Please contact .....(name, address, and telephone number)..... at least 7 days before your scheduled court appearance, or immediately upon receiving this notification if the time before the scheduled appearance is less than 7 days. If you are hearing or voice impaired, call 711.

PLEASE BE GOVERNED ACCORDINGLY.

Copies furnished to: ....

FORM 8.974. PETITION TO EXTEND OR REINSTATE COURT'S JURISDICTION

PETITION TO EXTEND JURISDICTION OR TO REINSTATE JURISDICTION AND TO SCHEDULE HEARING

I, ...(name, address, and date of birth)..... request the court, under section 39.013(2), Florida Statutes to

..... extend jurisdiction, or

..... reinstate jurisdiction,

and to schedule a hearing in this matter.

1. I am currently or was on my 18th birthday in the legal custody of the Department of Children and Family Services.

2. ..... a. I am requesting that the court review the aftercare support, Road-to-Independence scholarship, transitional support, mental health services, and/or developmental disability services to the extent authorized by law.

..... b. A petition for special immigrant juvenile status has been filed on my behalf and the application will not be granted by the time I reach 18 years of age.

WHEREFORE, I request this court extend or reinstate jurisdiction in this case and schedule a hearing as soon as possible.

.....(name).....
.....(address).....
.....(phone number).....

FORM 8.975. DEPENDENCY ORDER WITHHOLDING ADJUDICATION

ORDER OF ADJUDICATION

THIS CAUSE came before this court on .....(date)....., under chapter 39, Florida Statutes, for adjudication of the Petition for Dependency filed by ..... (petitioner's name) ...... Present before the court were

....(name)....., Petitioner
....(name)....., Attorney for the petitioner
....(name)....., Attorney for the department
....(name)....., Department caseworker
....(name)....., Mother
....(name)....., Attorney for mother
....(name)....., Father of .....(child) .....
....(name)....., Attorney for father
....(name)....., Guardian ad litem
....(name)....., Attorney for guardian ad litem
....(name)....., Legal custodian
....(name)....., Attorney for legal custodian
....(name)....., Other ....

The court having heard testimony and argument and being otherwise fully advised in the premises finds:

1. That the minor child(ren) who is/are the subject matter of these proceedings, is/are dependent within

the meaning and intent of chapter 39, Florida Statutes, and is/are (a) resident(s) of the State of Florida.

2. The mother, ...(name)..... :

..... was ..... was not noticed of this hearing;

..... did not appear, and the court:

..... entered a Consent for failure to appear after proper notice.

..... did not enter a Consent for failure to appear after proper notice.

..... appeared with counsel;

..... appeared without counsel and:

..... was ..... was not advised of her right to legal counsel,

..... knowingly, intelligently, and voluntarily ..... waived ..... did not waive her right to legal counsel and

..... was ..... was not determined to qualify as indigent and

..... was ..... was not appointed an attorney.

3. The father, ...(name)..... :

..... was ..... was not noticed of this hearing;

..... did not appear, and the court:

..... entered a Consent for failure to appear after proper notice.

..... did not enter a Consent for failure to appear after proper notice.

..... appeared with counsel;

..... appeared without counsel and:

..... was ..... was not advised of his right to legal counsel,

..... knowingly, intelligently, and voluntarily ..... waived ..... did not waive his right to legal counsel and

..... was ..... was not determined to qualify as indigent and

..... was ..... was not appointed an attorney.

..... 4. That the child(ren) is/are dependent within the meaning and intent of chapter 39, Florida Statutes, in that the mother, ...(name)....., abused, neglected or abandoned the minor child(ren) by ...... These facts were proven by ..... preponderance of the evidence ..... clear and convincing evidence.

..... 5. That the child(ren) is/are dependent within the meaning and intent of chapter 39, Florida Statutes, in that the father, ...(name)....., abused, neglected or abandoned the minor child(ren) by ...... These facts were proven by ..... preponderance of the evidence ..... clear and convincing evidence.

..... 6. That the parties have filed a mediation agreement in which the parent(s) consent(s) to the adjudication of dependency of the child(ren) in conjunction with a withhold of adjudication, which the court accepts.

7. Under section 39.507(5), Florida Statutes, the Court finds that the child(ren) named in the petition are dependent, but finds that no action other than supervision in the child(ren)'s home is required.

THEREFORE, based upon the foregoing findings, it is ORDERED AND ADJUDGED that:

1. Under section 39.507(5), Florida Statutes, the Court hereby withholds adjudication of dependency of the minor child(ren). The child(ren) shall be .....returned/continued..... in (child(ren)'s home) under the supervision of the department. If this court later finds that the parents have not complied with the conditions of supervision imposed, the court may, after a hearing to establish the noncompliance, but without further evidence of the state of dependency, enter an order of adjudication.

2. This court shall retain jurisdiction over this cause to enter any such further orders that may be deemed

necessary for the best interest and welfare of the minor child(ren).

3. All prior orders not inconsistent with the present order shall remain in full force and effect.

4. Disposition is scheduled for …..(date)…., at ….. a.m./p.m.

DONE AND ORDERED on ….. date ……

_____
Circuit Judge

NOTICE OF HEARING

The Juvenile Court hereby gives notice of hearing in the above styled cause on …..(date)….. at …..a.m./p.m., before …..(judge)….., at …..(location)….., or as soon thereafter as counsel can be heard.

COMMENT: The following paragraph must be in bold, 14 pt. Times New Roman or Courier font.

If you are a person with a disability who needs any accommodation in order to participate in this proceeding, you are entitled, at no cost to you, to the provision of certain assistance. Please contact …..(name, address, and telephone number)….. at least 7 days before your scheduled court appearance, or immediately upon receiving this notification if the time before the scheduled appearance is less than 7 days. If you are hearing or voice impaired, call 711.

PLEASE BE GOVERNED ACCORDINGLY.

Copies furnished to:

FORM 8.976. PROPOSED RELATIVE PLACEMENT

PROPOSED RELATIVES FOR PLACEMENT

Pursuant to Chapter 39, Florida Statutes, the …..mother/father….. hereby provides the court and the parties with the names and location of relatives who might be considered for placement of the child(ren). The …..mother/father….. will continue to inform the court and the parties of any relative who should be considered for placement of the child(ren) with the filing of subsequent forms.

MATERNAL

Name: ……………………………………….
Address: …………………………………….
Phone number: …………………………….
Relationship to child: ……………………..

Name: ……………………………………….
Address: …………………………………….
Phone number: …………………………….
Relationship to child: ……………………..

Name: ……………………………………….
Address: …………………………………….
Phone number: …………………………….
Relationship to child: ……………………..

Name: ……………………………………….
Address: …………………………………….
Phone number: …………………………….
Relationship to child: ……………………..

PATERNAL

Name: ……………………………………….
Address: …………………………………….
Phone number: …………………………….
Relationship to child: ……………………..

Name: ……………………………………….
Address: …………………………………….
Phone number: …………………………….
Relationship to child: ……………………..

Name: ……………………………………….
Address: …………………………………….
Phone number: …………………………….
Relationship to child: ……………………..

Name: ……………………………………….
Address: …………………………………….
Phone number: …………………………….
Relationship to child: ……………………..

Name: ……………………………………….
Address: …………………………………….
Phone number: …………………………….
Relationship to child: ……………………..

The above information is true and correct to the best of my knowledge.

Dated ....

(Mother's Signature)
Printed name: ....

(Father's Signature)
Printed name: ....

FORM 8.977. ORDER AUTHORIZING CHILD TO ENTER INTO RESIDENTIAL LEASEHOLD AND SECURE UTILITY SERVICES BEFORE THE CHILD'S 18TH BIRTHDAY

ORDER AUTHORIZING CHILD TO ENTER INTO RESIDENTIAL LEASEHOLD AND TO SECURE RESIDENTIAL UTILITY SERVICES BEFORE THE CHILD'S 18TH BIRTHDAY

THIS CAUSE came before the court to remove the disabilities of nonage of .....(name)....., for the purposes of entering into a residential leasehold and to secure residential utility services. The court being fully advised in the premises FINDS as follows:

.....(Name)..... is 17 years of age, meets the requirements of sections 743.045 and 743.046, Florida Statutes, and is entitled to the benefits of those statutes.

THEREFORE, based on these findings of fact, it is ORDERED AND ADJUDGED that the disabilities of nonage of .....(name)..... are hereby removed for the purposes of entering a residential leasehold and securing residential utility services. .....(Name)..... is hereby authorized to make and execute contracts, releases, and all other instruments necessary for the purposes of entering into a residential leasehold and securing residential utility services. The contracts or other instruments made by .....(name)..... for the purposes of entering into a residential leasehold and securing residential utility services shall have the same effect as though they were the obligations of a person who is not a minor.

ORDERED at ...., Florida, on .....(date)......

Circuit Judge

Copies to:

FORM 8.978. ORDER AUTHORIZING CHILD TO SECURE DEPOSITORY FINANCIAL SERVICES BEFORE THE CHILD'S 18TH BIRTHDAY

ORDER AUTHORIZING CHILD TO SECURE DEPOSITORY FINANCIAL SERVICES BEFORE THE CHILD'S 18TH BIRTHDAY

THIS CAUSE came before the court to remove the disabilities of nonage of .....(name)....., for the purpose of securing depository financial services, and the court being fully advised in the premises FINDS as follows:

.....(name)..... is at least 16 years of age, meets the requirements of section 743.044, Florida Statutes, and is entitled to the benefits of that statute.

THEREFORE, based on these findings of fact, it is ORDERED AND ADJUDGED that the disabilities of nonage of .....(name)..... are hereby removed for the purpose of securing depository financial services.

.....(name)..... is hereby authorized to make and execute contracts, releases, and all other instruments necessary for the purpose of securing depository financial services. The contracts or other instruments made by .....(name)..... for the purpose of securing depository financial services have the same effect as though they were the obligations of a person who is not a minor.

ORDERED at ...., Florida, on .....(date)......

Circuit Judge

Copies to:

FORM 8.978(a). ORDER CONCERNING YOUTH'S ELIGIBILITY FOR FLORIDA'S TUITION AND FEE EXEMPTION

ORDER CONCERNING ELIGIBILITY FOR FLORIDA'S TUITION AND FEE EXEMPTION

THIS CAUSE comes before the court to determine .....(name)..... 's eligibility for the tuition and fee exemption under Chapter 1009, Florida Statutes, and the court being fully advised in the premises, it is

ORDERED AND ADJUDGED that .....(name)...... is eligible, under Chapter 1009, Florida Statutes, and therefore exempt from the payment of tuition and fees, including lab fees, at a school district that provides postsecondary career programs, community college, or state university.

ORDERED at ...., Florida, on .....(date)......

_____
Circuit Judge

Copies to:

D. TERMINATION OF PARENTAL RIGHTS FORMS

FORM 8.979. SUMMONS FOR ADVISORY HEARING

SUMMONS AND NOTICE OF ADVISORY HEARING FOR TERMINATION OF PARENTAL RIGHTS AND GUARDIANSHIP

STATE OF FLORIDA

TO: .....(name and address of person being summoned).....

A Petition for Termination of Parental Rights under oath has been filed in this court regarding the above-referenced child(ren), a copy of which is attached. You are to appear before .....(judge)....., at .....(time and location of hearing)....., for a TERMINATION OF PARENTAL RIGHTS ADVISORY HEARING. You must appear on the date and at the time specified.

FAILURE TO PERSONALLY APPEAR AT THIS ADVISORY HEARING CONSTITUTES CON- **SENT TO THE TERMINATION OF PARENTAL RIGHTS TO THIS CHILD (THESE CHILDREN). IF YOU FAIL TO APPEAR ON THE DATE AND TIME SPECIFIED YOU MAY LOSE ALL LEGAL RIGHTS TO THE CHILD (OR CHILDREN) NAMED IN THE PETITION ATTACHED TO THIS NOTICE.**

COMMENT: The following paragraph must be in bold, 14 pt. Times New Roman or Courier font.

If you are a person with a disability who needs any accommodation to participate in this proceeding, you are entitled, at no cost to you, to the provision of certain assistance. Please contact .....(name, address, telephone number)..... at least 7 days before your scheduled court appearance, or immediately upon receiving this notification if the time before the scheduled appearance is less than 7 days. If you are hearing or voice impaired, call 711.

Witness my hand and seal of this court at .....(city, county, state)..... on .....(date)......

CLERK OF COURT
BY: _____
DEPUTY CLERK

AVISO Y CITACIÓN PARA LA AUDIENCIA INFORMATIVA SOBRE LA TERMINACIÓN DE LOS DERECHOS PATERNALES Y DE LA TUTELA

ESTADO DE LA FLORIDA

PARA: _____
(Nombre y dirección de la persona a ser citada)

CONSIDERANDO que se ha interpuesto en este Juzgado una solicitud bajo juramento para la terminación de los derechos paternales con respecto al(os) niño(s) en referencia, adjuntándose copia de la misma. Mediante la presente se le ordena comparecer ante el _____ a las _____
(Juez)　　　(hora y lugar de la audiencia)
para una AUDIENCIA INFORMATIVA SOBRE LA TERMINACIÓN DE LOS DERECHOS PATERNALES. Usted deberá comparecer en le fecha y hora indicadas.

SI USTED NO COMPARECE PERSONALMENTE A LA AUDIENCIA

INFORMATIVA, ESTO SIGNIFICARÁ QUE USTED ACCEDE A LA TERMINACIÓN DE SUS DERECHOS PATERNALES CON RESPECTO A ESTE(OS) NIÑO(S). SI USTED NO COMPARECE EN LA FECHA Y HORA INDICADAS, USTED PODRÁ PERDER TODOS SUS DERECHOS LEGALES CON RESPECTO AL/LOS NIÑO(S) MENCIONADO(S) EN LA PETICIÓN ADJUNTA A ESTE AVISO.

Si usted es una persona con una discapacidad que necesita cualquier tipo de trato especial para participar en este procedimiento, usted tiene derecho, sin costa alguno para usted, para la presetación de asistencia determinadas. Póngase en contacto con .....(nombre, dirección, número de teléfono)..... por lo menos 7 dias antes la aparición en la corte programado, o immediatamente después de recibir esta notification, si el tiempo antes de la comparecencia prevista es inferiof a 7 dias. Si usted está oyendo o voz alterada, llame al 711.

Firmado y sigilado en este Juzgado
———————————————— el —————
(ciudad, condado, estado)   (fecha)

ESCRIBANO DEL TRIBUNAL
POR: —————————————
ESCRIBANO DELEGADO

MANDA AK AVÈTISMAN POU ENFOME-W SOU YON CHITA TANDE, POU YO ANILE DWA-W KÒM PARAN AK KÒM GADYEN.

Leta Florid

POU: .....(non ak adrès moun yo voye manda-a) .....

KÒM, tandiske, gen yon demann sèmante pou anile dwa paran-yo, ki prezante devan tribinal-la, konsènan timoun ki nonmen nan lèt sa-a, piwo-a, yon kopi dokiman-an kwoke nan dosye-a., yo bay lòd pou prezante devan .....(Jij-la)....., a .....(nan.lè ak adrès chita tande-a)....., NAN YON CHITA TANDE POU YO ENFÒME-W, YO GEN LENTANSYON POU ANILE DWA-OU KÒM PARAN. Ou fèt pou prezante nan dat ak lè ki endike-a.

SI OU PA PREZANTE PÈSONÈLMAN NAN CHITA TANDE-A, POU YO ENFÒME-W, YO

GEN LENTANSYON POU ANILE DWA-OU KÒM PARAN, SA KA LAKÒZ YO DESIDE OU KONSANTI TIMOUN SA-A (YO), BEZWEN PWOTEKSYON LETA EPI SA KA LAKÒZ OU PÈDI DWA-OU KÒM PARAN TIMOUN SA-A(YO), KI GEN NON YO MAKE NAN KOPI DEMANN-NAN, KI KWOKE NAN AÈVTISMAN-AN

Si ou se yon moun infirm, ki beswen èd ou ki bewsen ke o akomode w pou ou patispe nan pwosedi sa yo, ou genyen dwa, san ke ou pa peye, a setin èd. Silvouple kontake .....(non, address, telephone)...... o moin 7 jou avan dat ou genyen rendevou pou ale nan tribunal, ou si le ou resevwa avi a, genyen mouins ke 7 jou avan date endevou tribunal la. Ou si ou pa tande pale, rele nan nimerro sa 711.

Mwen siyen non mwen e mete so mwen nan dokiman tribinal-la kòm temwen nan .....(vil, distrik, eta)....., nan .....(dat)......

GREFYE TRIBINAL-LA
PA: —————————————
ASISTAN GREFYE TRIBINAL-LA

FORM 8.980. PETITION FOR TERMINATION OF PARENTAL RIGHTS BASED ON VOLUNTARY RELINQUISHMENT

PETITION FOR TERMINATION OF PARENTAL RIGHTS

Petitioner, ...(name)....., respectfully petitions this court for termination of parental rights and permanent commitment of the minor child(ren), ...(name(s))....., to .....(agency name)..... for the purpose of subsequent adoption, and as grounds states the following:

A. PARTIES

1. The child, ...(name)....., is a male/female child born on .....(date)....., at .....(city, county, state)...... At the time of the filing of this petition, the child is .....(age)...... A copy of the child's birth certificate is attached to this Petition and incorporated as Petitioner's Exhibit ......

COMMENT: Repeat above for each child on petition.

2. The child(ren) is/are presently in the care and custody of .....(name)....., and is/are residing in .... County, Florida.

3. An affidavit under the Uniform Child Custody Jurisdiction and Enforcement Act is attached to this as Petitioner's Exhibit ......

4. The natural mother of the child(ren) is .....(name)....., who resides at ....

5. The natural/alleged/putative father of the child(ren) .....(name(s))..... is .....(name)....., who resides at ....

COMMENT: Repeat #5 as necessary.

6. A guardian ad litem ..... has ..... has not been appointed to represent the interests of the child(ren) in this cause.

B. GROUNDS FOR TERMINATION

1. The parent(s) have been advised of their right to legal counsel at all hearings that they attended.

2. The parents will be informed of the availability of private placement of the child with an adoption entity as defined in chapter 63, Florida Statutes.

3. The mother, ...(name)....., freely, knowingly, voluntarily, and ..... with ..... without advice of legal counsel executed an Affidavit and Acknowledgment of Surrender, Consent, and Waiver of Notice on .....(date)....., for termination of her parental rights to the minor child, ...(name)....., under section 39.806(1)(a), Florida Statutes.

COMMENT: Repeat above as necessary.

4. The father, ...(name)....., freely, knowingly, and voluntarily, and ..... with ..... without advice of legal counsel executed an Affidavit and Acknowledgment of Surrender, Consent, and Waiver of Notice on .....(date)....., for termination of his parental rights to the minor child, ...(name)....., under section 39.806(1)(a), Florida Statutes.

COMMENT: Repeat above as necessary.

5. Under the provisions of chapter 39, Florida Statutes, it is in the manifest best interest of the child(ren) for parental rights to be terminated for the following reasons:

    ..... allegations which correspond to sections 39.810(1)-(11), Florida Statutes.

6. A copy of this petition shall be served on the natural mother, ...(name).....; the father(s), ...(name(s)).....; the custodian, ...(name).....; and the guardian ad litem, ...(name).....

7. This petition is filed in good faith and under oath.

WHEREFORE, the petitioner respectfully requests that this court grant this petition; find that the parents have voluntarily surrendered their parental rights to the minor child(ren); find that termination of parental rights is in the manifest best interests of this/these child(ren); and that this court enter an order permanently committing this/these child(ren) to the .....(name)..... for subsequent adoption.

_____
    .....(petitioner's name and
    identifying information).....

Verification

_____
    .....(attorney's name).....
    .....(address and telephone
    number).....
    .....(email address(es).....
    .....Florida Bar number.....

Certificate of Service

FORM 8.981. PETITION FOR INVOLUNTARY TERMINATION OF PARENTAL RIGHTS

PETITION FOR TERMINATION OF PARENTAL RIGHTS

Petitioner, ...(petitioner's name)....., respectfully petitions this court for termination of parental rights and permanent commitment of the minor child(ren), ...(name(s))....., to .....(agency name)..... for the purpose of subsequent adoption, and as grounds states the following:

A. PARTIES

1. The child, …..(name)….., is a male/female child born on …..(date)….., at …..(city, county, state)…… At the time of the filing of this petition, the child is …..(age) …… A copy of the child's birth certificate is attached to this Petition and incorporated as Petitioner's Exhibit ……

COMMENT: Repeat above for each child on petition.

2. The child(ren) is/are presently in the care and custody of …..(name)….., and is/are residing in ………………… County, Florida.

3. An affidavit under the Uniform Child Custody Jurisdiction and Enforcement Act is attached to this as Petitioner's Exhibit ……

4. The natural mother of the child(ren) is …..(name)….., who resides at ……

5. The natural/alleged/putative father of the child(ren) …..(name(s))….. is …..(name)….., who resides at ……………………………………………..

COMMENT: Repeat #5 as necessary.

6. A guardian ad litem ….. has ….. has not been appointed to represent the interests of the child(ren) in this cause.

B. GROUNDS FOR TERMINATION

1. The parents have been advised of their right to legal counsel at all hearings that they attended.

2. On or about …..(date(s))….., the following occurred: …..(acts which were basis for dependency or TPR, if filed directly)……

3. The mother has …..(grounds for TPR)….. the minor child(ren) within the meaning and intent of section 39.806, Florida Statutes, in that: …..(allegations which form the statutory basis for grounds)……

4. The father has …..(grounds for TPR)….. the minor child(ren) within the meaning and intent of section 39.806, Florida Statutes, in that: …..(allegations which form the statutory basis for grounds)……

5. Under the provisions of sections 39.810(1)-(11), Florida Statutes, it is in the manifest best interests of the child(ren) for parental rights of …..(name(s))….. to be terminated for the following reasons: …..(allegations for each statutory factor in the manifest best interest test)……

6. A copy of this petition shall be served on the natural mother, …..(name)….., father(s), …..(name(s))….., the custodian, …..(name)…..; and the guardian ad litem, …..(name)……

7. This petition is filed by the petitioner in good faith and under oath.

WHEREFORE, the petitioner respectfully requests that this court grant this petition; find that the parents have abused, neglected, or abandoned the minor child(ren); find that termination of parental rights is in the manifest best interests of this/these child(ren); and that this court enter an order permanently committing this/these child(ren) to …..(agency)….. for subsequent adoption.

…..(petitioner's name and identifying information)…..

Verification

…..(attorney's name)…..
…..(address and telephone number)…..
…..(Florida Bar number)…..

Certificate of Service

FORM 8.982. NOTICE OF ACTION FOR ADVISORY HEARING

…..(Child(ren)'s initials and date(s) of birth)…..

NOTICE OF ACTION AND OF ADVISORY HEARING FOR TERMINATION OF PARENTAL RIGHTS AND GUARDIANSHIP

STATE OF FLORIDA

TO: …..(name and address of person being summoned)…..

A Petition for Termination of Parental Rights under oath has been filed in this court regarding the above-referenced child(ren). You are to appear before

.....(judge)....., at .....(time and address of hearing)....., for a TERMINATION OF PARENTAL RIGHTS ADVISORY HEARING. You must appear on the date and at the time specified.

FAILURE TO PERSONALLY APPEAR AT THIS ADVISORY HEARING CONSTITUTES CONSENT TO THE TERMINATION OF PARENTAL RIGHTS TO THIS CHILD (THESE CHILDREN). IF YOU FAIL TO APPEAR ON THE DATE AND TIME SPECIFIED YOU MAY LOSE ALL LEGAL RIGHTS TO THE CHILD (OR CHILDREN) WHOSE INITIALS APPEAR ABOVE.

COMMENT: The following paragraph must be in bold, 14 pt. Times New Roman or Courier font.

If you are a person with a disability who needs any accommodation to participate in this proceeding, you are entitled, at no cost to you, to the provision of certain assistance. Please contact .....(name, address, telephone number)..... at least 7 days before your scheduled court appearance, or immediately upon receiving this notification if the time before the scheduled appearance is less than 7 days. If you are hearing or voice impaired, call 711.

Witness my hand and seal of this court at .....(city, county, state)..... on .....(date)......

CLERK OF COURT
BY: _____
DEPUTY CLERK

AVISO Y CITACION PARA LA AUDIENCIA INFORMATIVA SOBRE LA TERMINACION DE LOS DERECHOS PATERNALES Y DE LA TUTELA

ESTADO DE LA FLORIDA

PARA: _____.

(Nombre y direccion de la persona a ser citada)

CONSIDERANDO que se ha interpuesto en este Juzgado una solicitud bajo juramento para la terminacion de los derechos paternales con respecto al(os) nino(s) en referencia, adjuntandose copia de la misma. Mediante la presente se le ordena comparecer ante el

(Juez)

a las para una AUDIENCIA INFORMATIVA SOBRE LA

(hora y lugar de la audiencia)

TERMINACION DE LOS DERECHOS PATERNALES. Usted debera comparecer en le fecha y hora indicadas.

SI USTED NO COMPARECE PERSONALMENTE A LA AUDIENCIA INFORMATIVA, ESTO SIGNIFICARA QUE USTED ACCEDE A LA TERMINACION DE SUS DERECHOS PATERNALES CON RESPECTO A ESTE(OS) NINO(S). SI USTED NO COMPARECE EN LA FECHA Y HORA INDICADAS, USTED PODRA PERDER TODOS SUS DERECHOS LEGALES CON RESPECTO AL/LOS NINO(S) MENCIONADO(S) EN LA PETICION ADJUNTA A ESTE AVISO.

Si usted es una persona con una discapacidad que necesita cualquier tipo de trato especial para participar en este procedimiento, usted tiene derecho, sin costa alguno para usted, para la presetación de asistencia determinadas. Póngase en contacto con .....(nombre, dirección, número de teléfono)..... por lo menos 7 dias antes la aparición en la corte programado, o immediatamente después de recibir esta notification, si el tiempo antes de la comparecencia prevista es inferiof a 7 dias. Si usted está oyendo o voz alterada, llame al 711.

Firmado y sigilado en este Juzgado el

(ciudad, condado, estado) (fecha)

ESCRIBANO DEL TRIBUNAL
POR: _____
ESCRIBANO DELEGADO

MANDA AK AVTISMAN POU ENFOME-W SOU YON CHITA TANDE, POU YO ANILE DWA-W KM PARAN AK KM GADYEN.

LETA FLORID

POU: .....(non ak adrs moun yo voye manda-a).....

KOM, tandiske, gen yon demann smante pou anile dwa paran-yo, ki prezante devan tribinal-la, konsnan timoun ki nonmen nan lt sa-a, piwo-a, yon kopi dokiman-an kwoke nan dosye-a., yo bay ld pou prezante devan .....(Jij-la)....., a .....(nan.l ak adrs chita tande-a)....., NAN YON CHITA TANDE POU YO ENFME-W, YO GEN LENTANSYON POU ANILE DWA-OU KM PARAN. Ou ft pou prezante nan dat ak l ki endike-a.

SI OU PA PREZANTE PSONLMAN NAN CHITA TANDE-A, POU YO ENFME-W, YO GEN LENTANSYON POU ANILE DWA-OU KM PARAN, SA KA LAKZ YO DESIDE OU KONSANTI TIMOUN SA-A (YO), BEZWEN PWOTEKSYON LETA EPI SA KA LAKZ OU PDI DWA-OU KM PARAN TIMOUN SA-A(YO), KI GEN NON YO MAKE NAN KOPI DEMANN-NAN, KI KWOKE NAN AVTISMAN-AN

Si ou se yon moun infirm, ki beswen èd ou ki bewsen ke o akomode w pou ou patispe nan pwosedi sa yo, ou genyen dwa, san ke ou pa peye, a setin èd. Silvouple kontake .....(non, address, telephone)...... o moin 7 jou avan dat ou genyen rendevou pou ale nan tribunal, ou si le ou resevwa avi a, genyen mouins ke 7 jou avan date endevou tribunal la. Ou si ou pa tande pale, rele nan nimerro sa 711.

Mwen siyen non mwen e mete so mwen nan dokiman tribinal-la km temwen nan .....(vil, distrik, eta)....., nan .....(dat)......

GREFYE TRIBINAL-LA
PA: _____
ASISTAN GREFYE TRIBINAL-LA

FORM 8.983. ORDER INVOLUNTARILY TERMINATING PARENTAL RIGHTS

ORDER INVOLUNTARILY TERMINATING PARENTAL RIGHTS

THIS CAUSE came before this court on .....(all dates of the adjudicatory hearing)..... for an adjudi-catory hearing on the Petition for Termination of Parental Rights filed by .....(name)...... Present before the court were:

....(name)....., Petitioner
....(name)....., Attorney for the petitioner
....(name)....., Attorney for the department
....(name)....., Department caseworker
....(name)....., Child
....(name)....., Attorney for Child
....(name)....., Mother
....(name)....., Attorney for mother
....(name)....., Father of .....(child).....
....(name)....., Attorney for father
....(name)....., Guardian ad litem
....(name)....., Attorney for guardian ad litem
....(name)....., Legal custodian
....(name)....., Attorney for legal custodian
....(name)....., Other: ....

The court has carefully considered and weighed the testimony of all witnesses. The court has received and reviewed all exhibits.

COMMENT: Add the following only if necessary.

The petitioner has sought termination of the parental rights of .....(parent(s)) who is/are subject of petition)......

The court finds that the parent(s), ...(name(s))....., has/have .....(list grounds proved)....., under chapter 39, Florida Statutes. The grounds were proved by clear and convincing evidence. Further, the court finds that termination of parental rights of the parent(s), ...name(s)....., is clearly in the manifest best interests of the child(ren). The findings of fact and conclusions of law supporting this decision are as follows:

1. At all stages of these proceedings the parent(s) was/were advised of his/her/their right to legal counsel, or was/were in fact represented by counsel.

2. On or about .....(date(s))....., the following occurred: .....(acts which were basis for dependency or TPR, if filed directly)......

3. The mother has .....(grounds for TPR)..... the minor child(ren) within the meaning and intent of

section 39.806, Florida Statutes, in that: .....(findings that form the statutory basis for grounds)......

4. The father has .....(grounds for TPR)..... the minor child(ren) within the meaning and intent of section 39.806, Florida Statutes, in that: .....(findings that form the statutory basis for grounds)......

5. The minor child(ren) to whom .....(parent's(s') name(s))..... parental rights are being terminated are at substantial risk of significant harm. Termination of parental rights is the least restrictive means to protect the child(ren) from harm.

6. Under the provisions of sections 39.810(1)—(11), Florida Statutes, it is in the manifest best interests of the child(ren) for parental rights of .....(name(s))..... to be terminated for the reasons below. The court has considered all relevant factors and finds as follows:

(a) Regarding any suitable permanent custody arrangement with a relative of the child(ren), the court finds ....

(b) Regarding the ability and disposition of the parent or parents to provide the child(ren) with food, clothing, medical care, or other remedial care recognized and permitted under state law instead of medical care, and other material needs of the child(ren), the court finds ....

(c) Regarding the capacity of the parent or parents to care for the child(ren) to the extent that the child(ren)'s safety, well-being, and physical, mental, and emotional health will not be endangered upon the child(ren)'s return home, the court finds ....

(d) Regarding the present mental and physical health needs of the child(ren) and such future needs of the child(ren) to the extent that such future needs can be ascertained based on the present condition of the child(ren), the court finds ....

(e) Regarding the love, affection, and other emotional ties existing between the child(ren) and the child(ren)'s parent or parents, siblings, and other relatives, and the degree of harm to the child(ren) that

would arise from the termination of parental rights and duties, the court finds ....

(f) Regarding the likelihood of an older child remaining in long-term foster care upon termination of parental rights, due to emotional or behavioral problems or any special needs of the child(ren), the court finds ....

(g) Regarding the child(ren)'s ability to form a significant relationship with a parental substitute and the likelihood that the child(ren) will enter into a more stable and permanent family relationship as a result of permanent termination of parental rights and duties, the court finds ....

(h) Regarding the length of time that the child(ren) has lived in a stable, satisfactory environment and the desirability of maintaining continuity, the court finds ....

(i) Regarding the depth of the relationship existing between the child(ren) and present custodian, the court finds ....

(j) Regarding the reasonable preferences and wishes of the child(ren), if the court deems the child(ren) to be of sufficient intelligence, understanding, and experience to express a preference, the court finds ....

(k) Regarding the recommendations for the child(ren) provided by the child(ren)'s guardian ad litem or the legal representative, the court finds ....

(*l*) Regarding other relevant factors including ...., the court finds ....

COMMENT: Add items 7, 8, and 9 as applicable.

7. Under section 39.811(6)(.....), Florida Statutes, the court terminates the parental rights of only .....(parent whose rights are being terminated)..... as to the minor child(ren), ...(child(ren)'s name(s))...... Specifically, the court finds that .....(specific findings of fact under section 39.811(6), Florida Statutes)......

8. Under sections 39.509(5) and 39.811(7)(a), Florida Statutes, the court finds that continued

grandparental visitation is not in the best interests of the child(ren) or that such visitation would interfere with the permanency goals for the child(ren) for the following reasons ....

9. Under section 39.811(7)(b), Florida Statutes, the court finds that although parental rights are being terminated, the best interests of .....(names of child(ren) to which this provision applies)..... support continued communication or contact by .....(names of parents, siblings, or relatives of the parent whose rights are terminated and to which this provision applies)..... except as provided above. The nature and frequency of the communication or contact shall be as follows .... It may be reviewed on motion of any party or an identified prospective adoptive parent.

THEREFORE, after weighing the credibility of the witnesses, weighing all statutory factors, and based on the findings of fact and conclusions of law above, the court hereby ORDERS AND ADJUDGES THAT:

1. The petition filed by .....(name)..... is granted as to the parent(s), ...(name(s))......

2. The parental rights of the father, ...(name)....., and of the mother, ...(name)....., to the child, ...(name)....., are hereby terminated under section 39.806(.....), Florida Statutes.

COMMENT: Repeat the above for each child and parent, as necessary.

3. Under sections 39.811(2) and (5), Florida Statutes, the child(ren), ...(name(s))....., are placed in the custody of .....(agency)..... for the purpose of subsequent adoption.

4. The 30-day permanency plan required by section 39.811(8), Florida Statutes, shall be filed and heard at .....(time)..... on .....(date)..... in .....(location)......

DONE AND ORDERED on .....(date)....., in .....(city and county)....., Florida.

_____

Circuit Judge

NOTICE

Under section 39.815, Florida Statutes, any child, any parent, guardian ad litem, or legal custodian of any child, any other party to the proceeding who is affected by an order of the court, or the department may appeal to the appropriate District Court of Appeal within the time and in the manner prescribed by the Florida Rules of Appellate Procedure, which is 30 days from the date this order is rendered (signed and filed). A parent may have the right to a court-appointed attorney as provided by law.

Under Florida Rule of Juvenile Procedure 8.530, a parent, who had an attorney in the termination of parental rights proceeding, shall have 20 days after this order terminating parental rights is entered to file a motion in the trial court claiming ineffective assistance of counsel. A parent does not have the right to a court-appointed attorney to assist the parent with a motion claiming ineffective assistance of counsel, but the parent may independently obtain an attorney to represent the parent in the motion. The motion must contain the case name, case number, and identify the date the written order terminating parental rights was entered. The motion must also contain the current mailing address and e-mail address, if any, and the phone number(s) of the parent filing the motion for the purpose of receiving notices and orders. In the motion, the parent must identify specific acts or omissions in the attorney's representation of the parent during the termination proceedings that the parent claims constituted a failure to provide reasonable, professional assistance, and the parent must explain how the errors or omissions prejudiced the parent's case to such an extent that but for counsel's deficient performance the rights of the parent would not have been terminated.

Copies to:

FORM 8.9831. MOTION CLAIMING INEFFECTIVE ASSISTANCE OF COUNSEL AFTER ORDER TERMINATING PARENTAL RIGHTS

MOTION CLAIMING INEFFECTIVE ASSISTANCE OF COUNSEL AFTER ORDER TERMINATING PARENTAL RIGHTS

Moving parent, ...(name)....., ...(address)....., ...(e-mail address)....., ...(phone number)....., requests this court to vacate the order terminating parental rights pursuant to Florida Rule of Juvenile Procedure 8.530.

1. I was the parent of .....(name(s) of child(ren)).... at the time the court entered an order terminating my parental rights on .....(date)..... in .....(case number and case name)......

2. My attorney failed to provide me with reasonable, professional assistance by doing or not doing the following actions during the termination of parental rights proceedings: (use whatever space is necessary to explain your claims)

_____
_____
_____
_____
_____
_____

Comment: The phrase "termination of parental rights proceedings" is not limited to the termination of parental rights trial.

3. My attorney's actions or inactions prejudiced my case to such an extent that my parental rights would not have been terminated because: (use whatever space is necessary to explain your claims)

_____
_____
_____
_____
_____

WHEREFORE, I request that the court enter an order granting this motion, vacating the order terminating parental rights, and providing any other relief the court deems proper.

I understand that I am swearing or affirming under oath to the truthfulness of the claims made in this verified motion and that punishment for knowingly making a false statement includes fines and/or imprisonment.

_____
(Your signature)

I certify that a copy of this document was .....(mailed, faxed and mailed, hand delivered, or e-mailed)..... to the person(s) listed below on .....(date)..... or was not delivered to the person(s) listed below because ....

List each party or the party's attorney who you served:
Name: ....
Address: ....
Telephone Number: ....
Fax Number: ....
E-mail Address: ....

_____
(Your signature)

FORM 8.9832. ORDER ON MOTION CLAIMING INEFFECTIVE ASSISTANCE OF COUNSEL AFTER ORDER TERMINATING PARENTAL RIGHTS

ORDER ON MOTION CLAIMING INEFFECTIVE ASSISTANCE OF COUNSEL AFTER ORDER TERMINATING PARENTAL RIGHTS

THIS CAUSE came before this court on .....(date)..... on the Motion Claiming Ineffective Assistance of Counsel after Order Terminating Parental Rights filed by .....(name)...... Present before the court were:

....(name)....., Moving Parent
....(name)....., Attorney for Moving Parent
....(name)....., Trial Attorney for Moving

Parent

....(name)....., Attorney for the department

....(name)....., Department caseworker'

....(name)....., Child

....(name)....., Attorney for Child

....(name)....., Mother

....(name)....., Attorney for mother

....(name)....., Father of .....(child).....

....(name)....., Attorney for father

....(name)....., Guardian ad litem

....(name)....., Attorney for guardian ad litem

....(name)....., Legal custodian'

....(name)....., Attorney for legal custodian

....(name)....., Other ....

Comment: Complete the following section if the court denies the motion without a hearing.

The court has carefully considered the motion and reviewed all necessary documents. The court finds that the motion should be denied without a hearing because:

..... The motion is untimely.

1. The order terminating parental rights was entered on .....(date)......

2. The moving parent filed the motion claiming ineffective assistance of counsel on .....(date)......

3. Therefore, the moving parent filed the motion past the 20-day time limitation.

..... The motion is insufficient as alleged. The court finds that the moving parent failed to allege specific facts that, if taken as true, would support a finding that the attorney during the termination of parental rights proceedings failed to provide reasonable, professional assistance, and that any errors or omissions prejudiced the parent's case to such an extent that but for counsel's deficient performance the rights of the parent would not have been terminated. Specifically the court finds: .....(findings)......

Comment: Complete the following section if the court finds that the motion is insufficient and directs the moving parent to file an amended motion.

The court has carefully considered the motion and reviewed all necessary documents.

..... The motion is insufficient as alleged. The court finds that the moving parent failed to allege specific facts that would support a finding that the attorney during the termination of parental rights proceedings failed to provide reasonable, professional assistance, and that any errors or omissions prejudiced the parent's case to such an extent that but for counsel's deficient performance the rights of the parent would not have been terminated. Specifically the court finds: .....(findings)...... However, the court finds that the moving parent should be provided the opportunity to file an amended motion.

Comment: Complete the following section if the court previously found that the motion was insufficient, directed the moving parent to file an amended motion, and the parent failed to file an amended motion within the time permitted.

The court previously carefully considered the motion and reviewed all necessary documents.

..... On .....(date)....., the court found the motion is insufficient as alleged. The court found that the moving parent failed to allege specific facts that would support a finding that the attorney during the termination of parental rights proceedings failed to provide reasonable, professional assistance, and that any errors or omissions prejudiced the parent's case to such an extent that but for counsel's deficient performance the rights of the parent would not have been terminated. Specifically the court found: .....(findings)......

..... On .....(date)....., the court entered a written order providing the parent an opportunity to file an amended motion. The parent did not file an amended motion within 10 days of the date of the written order permitting amendment.

Comment: Complete the following section if the court hearing was conducted:

The court has carefully considered the motion, reviewed all necessary documents, and having heard argument of counsel and testimony, the court finds:

..... The motion is granted because the attorney during the termination of parental rights proceedings failed to provide reasonable, professional assistance, and the errors or omissions prejudiced the parent's case to such an extent that but for counsel's deficient performance the rights of the parent would not have been terminated. Specifically the court finds: .....(findings)......

..... The motion is denied because the attorney during the termination of parental rights proceedings did not fail to provide reasonable, professional assistance, or any errors or omissions that were made did not prejudice the moving parent's case to such an extent that but for counsel's deficient performance the rights of the parent would not have been terminated. Specifically, the court finds: .....(findings)......

THEREFORE, the court hereby ORDERS AND ADJUDGES THAT:

..... The motion claiming ineffective assistance of counsel is denied with prejudice.

..... The motion claiming ineffective assistance of counsel is insufficient as alleged. The moving parent may file an amended motion. Any amended motion shall be filed within 10 days of the date of this order or the court may summarily deny the motion.

..... The motion claiming ineffective assistance of counsel is granted. The order terminating parental rights entered on .....(date)..... is hereby vacated and set aside as to .....(name of moving parent)...... An adjudicatory hearing is hereby scheduled for .....(date (no later than 45 days from this order))....., and, as the court finds the parent is indigent, ...(name of counsel)..... is hereby appointed to represent .....(name of moving parent)..... in the termination of parental rights proceedings.

DONE AND ORDERED on .....(date)....., in .....(city and county)....., Florida.

Circuit Judge

Copies to:

FORM 8.984. ORDER TERMINATING PARENTAL RIGHTS (VOLUNTARY)

ORDER TERMINATING PARENTAL RIGHTS (VOLUNTARY)

THIS CAUSE came before this court on .....(all dates of the adjudicatory hearing)..... for an adjudicatory hearing on the petition for termination of parental rights filed by .....(name)...... Present before the court were:

....(name)....., Petitioner
....(name)....., Attorney for the petitioner
....(name)....., Attorney for the department
....(name)....., Department/agency caseworker
....(name)....., Child
....(name)....., Attorney/Attorney ad litem for Child
....(name)....., Mother
....(name)....., Attorney for mother
....(name)....., Father of .....(child).....
....(name)....., Attorney for father
....(name)....., Guardian ad litem
....(name)....., Attorney for guardian ad litem
....(name)....., Legal custodian
....(name)....., Attorney for legal custodian
....(name)....., Other: ....

..... The mother, ...(name)....., executed a voluntary surrender of her parental rights for the minor child(ren), ...(name(s))....., which is accepted by the court without objection.

COMMENT: Repeat the following as necessary.

..... The father, ...(name)....., executed a voluntary surrender of his parental rights for the minor child(ren), ...(name(s))....., which is accepted by the court without objection.

The court has carefully considered the testimony of witnesses, reviewed the exhibits, reviewed the file, heard argument of counsel, and considered recommendations and arguments of all parties. The court finds by clear and convincing evidence that the parents, ...(names)....., have surrendered their parental rights to the minor child(ren) under section 39.806(1)(a), Florida Statutes, and that termination of parental rights is in the manifest best interests of the child(ren). The specific facts and findings supporting this decision are as follows:

1. That the mother, ...(name)....., ... was ..... was not personally served with the summons and the petition.

COMMENT: Service is not required if surrender was signed before filing of petition.

2. That the father, ...(name)....., ... was ..... was not personally served with the summons and the petition.

COMMENT: Service is not required if surrender was signed before filing of petition.

3. That the parents were advised of their right to counsel in all prior dependency court proceedings which they attended. The mother has been represented by legal counsel, ...(name)....., starting on or about .....(date)...... The father has been represented by legal counsel, ...(name)....., starting on or about .....(date)......

4. The mother, ...(name)....., freely, knowingly, voluntarily, and ..... with ..... without advice of legal counsel executed an affidavit and acknowledgment of surrender, consent, and waiver of notice on .....(date)....., for termination of her parental rights to the minor child(ren), under section 39.806(1)(a), Florida Statutes.

5. The father, ...(name)....., freely, knowingly, voluntarily, and ..... with ..... without advice of legal counsel executed an affidavit and acknowledgment of surrender, consent, and waiver of notice on .....(date)....., for termination of his parental rights to the minor child(ren), under section 39.806(1)(a), Florida Statutes.

6. That at all times relevant to this action the interests of this/these child(ren) has/have been represented by a guardian ad litem. The guardian ad litem, ...(name)....., ... agrees ..... does not agree that it is in the best interests of the child(ren) for parental rights to be terminated in this cause.

COMMENT: Guardian ad litem not required in voluntary surrender.

7. Under the provisions of sections 39.810(1)-(11), Florida Statutes, it is in the manifest best interests of the child(ren) for parental rights to be terminated for the following reasons:

(a) Regarding any suitable permanency custody arrangement with a relative of the child(ren), the court finds ....

(b) Regarding the ability and disposition of the parent or parents to provide the child(ren) with food, clothing, medical care or other remedial care recognized and permitted under state law instead of medical care, and other materials needs of the child(ren), the court finds ....

(c) Regarding the capacity of the parent or parents to care for the child(ren) to the extent that the child(ren)'s safety, well-being, and physical, mental, and emotional health will not be endangered upon the child(ren)'s return home, the court finds ....

(d) Regarding the present mental and physical health needs of the child(ren) and such future needs of the child(ren) to the extent that such future needs can be ascertained based on the present condition of the child(ren), the court finds ....

(e) Regarding the love, affection, and other emotional ties existing between the child(ren) and the child(ren)'s parent or parents, siblings, and other relatives, and the degree of harm to the child(ren) that would arise from the termination of parental rights and duties, the court finds ....

(f) Regarding the likelihood of an older child remaining in long-term foster care upon termination of parental rights, due to emotional or behavioral problems or any special needs of the child(ren), the court finds ....

(g) Regarding the child(ren)'s ability to form a significant relationship with a parental substitute and the likelihood that the child(ren) will enter into a more stable and permanent family relationship as a result of permanent termination of parental rights and duties, the court finds ....

(h) Regarding the length of time that the child(ren) has lived in a stable, satisfactory environment and the desirability of maintaining continuity, the court finds ....

(i) Regarding the depth of the relationship existing between the child(ren) and present custodian, the court finds ....

(j) Regarding the reasonable preferences and wishes of the child(ren), if the court deems the child(ren) to be of sufficient intelligence, understanding, and experience to express a preference, the court finds ....

(k) Regarding the recommendations for the child(ren) provided by the child(ren)'s guardian ad litem or the legal representative, the court finds ....

(*l*) Regarding other relevant factors including ...., the court finds ....

THEREFORE, it is ORDERED AND ADJUDGED that:

1. The petition for termination of parental rights is GRANTED.

2. The parental rights of the father, ...(name)....., and of the mother, ...(name)..... to the child(ren), ...(name(s))....., are hereby terminated under section 39.806(.....), Florida Statutes.

COMMENT: Repeat the above for each child and parent on petition.

3. The child(ren), ...(name(s))....., is/are hereby placed in the permanent care and custody of .....(agency name)..... for subsequent adoption.

4. A hearing for the department to provide a plan for permanency for the child(ren) shall be held on .....(date)....., within 30 days of rendering of order, at .....(time)......

DONE AND ORDERED on .....(date)....., in .... County, Florida.

_____
Circuit Judge

Copies to:

NOTICE

Under section 39.815, Florida Statutes, any child, any parent, guardian ad litem, or legal custodian of any child, any other party to the proceeding who is affected by an order of the court, or the department may appeal to the appropriate District Court of Appeal within the time and in the manner prescribed by the Florida Rule of Appellate Procedure, which is 30 days from the date this order is rendered (signed and filed). A parent may have the right to a court-appointed attorney as provided by law.

Under Florida Rule of Juvenile Procedure 8.530, a parent, who had an attorney in the termination of parental rights proceeding, shall have 20 days after this order terminating parental rights is entered to file a motion in the trial court claiming ineffective assistance of counsel. A parent does not have the right to a court-appointed attorney to assist the parent with a motion claiming ineffective assistance of counsel, but the parent may independently obtain an attorney to represent the parent in the motion. The motion must contain the case name, case number, and identify the date the written order terminating parental rights was entered. The motion must also contain the current mailing address and e-mail address, if any, and the phone number(s) of the parent filing the motion for the purpose of receiving notices and orders. In the motion, the parent must identify specific acts or omissions in the attorney's representation of the parent during the termination proceedings that the parent claims constituted a failure to provide reasonable, professional assistance, and the parent must explain how the errors or omissions preju-

diced the parent's case to such an extent that but for counsel's deficient performance the rights of the parent would not have been terminated.

FORM 8.985. MOTION TO TERMINATE SUPERVISION AND JURISDICTION

MOTION TO TERMINATE SUPERVISION AND JURISDICTION

The Department of Children and Family Services, by and through its undersigned counsel, moves this court for an order terminating the department's supervision and the court's jurisdiction and closing the file in the above-styled cause, and as grounds states:

1. The parental rights previously were terminated and the child(ren) was/were permanently committed to the care and custody of the department for adoption by order of this court.

2. The adoption was finalized on .....(date)......

WHEREFORE, the Department of Children and Family Services requests that this court terminate jurisdiction and the department's supervision and that the file be closed.

_____

.....(attorney's name).....
.....(address and telephone number).....
.....(Florida Bar number).....

Certificate of Service

FORM 8.986. ORDER TERMINATING SUPERVISION AND JURISDICTION

ORDER TERMINATING SUPERVISION AND JURISDICTION

THIS CAUSE having come before the court on motion to terminate supervision and jurisdiction filed by the Department of Children and Family Services, and the court being otherwise advised in the premises, find the following:

1. The parental rights previously were terminated and the child(ren) was/were permanently committed

to the care and custody of the department for subsequent adoption by order of this court.

2. The adoption was finalized on .....(date)......

THEREFORE, based on these findings of fact, it is ORDERED AND ADJUDGED:

That the supervision of the Department of Children and Family Services and this court's jurisdiction are terminated.

DONE AND ORDERED on .....(date)......

_____
Circuit Judge

Copies furnished to:

E. JUDICIAL WAIVER OF PARENTAL NOTICE OF TERMINATION OF PREGNANCY FORMS

FORM 8.987. PETITION FOR JUDICIAL WAIVER OF PARENTAL NOTICE OF TERMINATION OF PREGNANCY

IN THE CIRCUIT COURT OF THE ....
JUDICIAL CIRCUIT

IN AND FOR .... COUNTY, FLORIDA

In the Interest of .... (pseudonym or initials of minor)

Case No.: ....
Division: ....

PETITION FOR JUDICIAL WAIVER OF PARENTAL NOTICE OF TERMINATION OF PREGNANCY

I certify that the following information is true and correct:

(1) The pseudonym or initials of the minor (is/are) ...., and the minor has filed a Sworn Statement of True Name and Pseudonym with the clerk.

(2) The minor is ..... years old.

(3) The minor is pregnant and notice has not been waived.

(4) The minor desires to terminate her pregnancy without notice to a parent or legal guardian for one or more of the following reasons:
[check all that apply]

..... a. The minor is sufficiently mature to decide whether to terminate her pregnancy, for the following reason(s):
....
....
....

.... b. The minor is a victim of child abuse or sexual abuse inflicted by one or both of her parents or a guardian.

..... c. Notification of a parent or guardian is not in the best interest of the minor, for the following reason(s):
....
....
....

(5) The minor requests that the court enter an order authorizing her to consent to the performance or inducement of a termination of pregnancy without notification of a parent or guardian.

(6) The minor requests the appointment of an attorney to represent her in this matter: [check one]:

..... yes

..... no

(7) The minor elects the following method or methods for receiving notices of hearings or other court actions in this case:

.... Through a third party whose name is .... and whose address and phone number for purposes of notice are ....
....

.... The minor will contact the office of the clerk of court at the following phone number ....

I understand that by signing this form I am swearing to or affirming the truthfulness of the claims made in this petition and that the punishment for knowingly making a false statement includes fines, imprisonment, or both.

Signature: _____

Date: ....

(You may sign a name other than your true name, such as Jane Doe or other pseudonym under which your petition is being filed.)

FORM 8.988. SWORN STATEMENT OF TRUE NAME AND PSEUDONYM

SWORN STATEMENT OF TRUE NAME AND PSEUDONYM

NOTICE TO THE CLERK OF COURT: A CERTIFIED COPY OF THIS DECLARATION WITH THE CASE NUMBER NOTED ON IT SHALL BE GIVEN TO THE MINOR AFTER SHE SIGNS IT.

THE ORIGINAL SHALL IMMEDIATELY BE PLACED IN A SEALED ENVELOPE WHICH SHALL BE FILED UNDER SEAL AND KEPT UNDER SEAL AT ALL TIMES.

(1) My true name is ...., and my address is
(print your name)

....
(print your address)

(2) My date of birth is ....

(3) I have filed a Petition for Judicial Waiver of Parental Notice of Termination of Pregnancy under the name or initials .... on .....(date)......

I understand that by signing this form I am swearing to or affirming the truthfulness of the information herein and that the punishment for knowingly making a false statement includes fines, imprisonment or both.

Dated: .... Signature: _____
(You must sign your true name.)

FORM 8.989. ADVISORY NOTICE TO MINOR

ADVISORY NOTICE TO MINOR

[CASE NO.: ....]

YOU ARE NOTIFIED as follows:

YOUR CASE NUMBER APPEARS AT THE TOP OF THIS FORM. KEEP IT IN A SAFE PLACE. YOU CANNOT GET INFORMATION FROM THE CLERK WITHOUT YOUR CASE NUMBER.

YOU HAVE BEEN GIVEN A COPY OF THE SWORN STATEMENT YOU SIGNED WITH YOUR TRUE NAME. KEEP IT IN A SAFE PLACE. YOU MAY NEED TO SHOW IT AND THE FINAL JUDGMENT IN YOUR CASE TO YOUR DOCTOR BEFORE TERMINATING YOUR PREGNANCY.

All information in your case is confidential. No papers will be sent to your home, and you will be contacted by this court only through the method you elected in the petition. Your name will not be on your court papers.

If you would like an attorney to help you with your case, the court will appoint one for you at no cost to you. Your attorney will receive notices about your case so he or she can prepare for and attend hearings with you. You may also name someone else you trust to receive notices for you. You can also contact the clerk of court yourself to check on your case.

You have a right to a hearing and a decision on your case within 48 hours of filing your petition unless you or your attorney waives this right or asks for an extension of time. If this time limit is not met you have the right to ask the clerk for a form that will allow your doctor to perform a termination of pregnancy without notifying a parent.

If the court dismisses your petition, you have the right to appeal. You will be given information regarding how to proceed with an appeal, and if you would like an attorney to help you with an appeal, you may request that the court appoint one.

I certify that I have given a copy of this advisory form to the minor.

Dated: ....

_____
Clerk of the Court
.... County Courthouse
.............., Florida

FORM 8.990. FINAL ORDER GRANTING PETITION FOR JUDICIAL WAIVER OF PARENTAL NOTICE OF TERMINATION OF PREGNANCY

FINAL ORDER GRANTING PETITION FOR JUDICIAL WAIVER OF PARENTAL NOTICE OF TERMINATION OF PREGNANCY

THIS CAUSE having come before the court on a petition for judicial waiver of parental notice of termination of pregnancy and the court being otherwise advised in the premises, finds the following:

..... The minor has proven by clear and convincing evidence that she is sufficiently mature to decide whether to terminate her pregnancy, for the following reason(s): ....
....
....
....

The court has considered the following factors in reaching this decision that the minor is sufficiently mature to decide whether to terminate her pregnancy and makes the following findings:

The minor's age is .....

The minor's overall intelligence indicates ....

The minor's emotional development and stability indicates ....

The minor's credibility and demeanor as a witness indicates ....

The minor's ability to accept responsibility is demonstrated by ....

The minor's ability to assess both the immediate and long-range consequences of the minor's choices is demonstrated by ....

The minor's ability to understand and explain the medical risks of terminating her pregnancy and to apply that understanding to her decision is indicated by ....

Whether there may be any undue influence by another on the minor's decision to have an abortion. ....

..... The minor has proven by a preponderance of the evidence that she is a victim of child abuse or sexual abuse inflicted by one or both of her parents or a guardian, for the following reason(s): ....
....
....
....

The court, having made a finding under this section, will report the abuse as is required by section 39.201, Florida Statutes.

..... The minor has proven by clear and convincing evidence that notification of a parent or guardian is not in the best interest of the minor, for the following reason(s): ....
....
....
....

THEREFORE, it is ORDERED AND ADJUDGED that:

1. The petition for judicial waiver of parental notice of termination of pregnancy is GRANTED.

2. The minor may consent to the performance or inducement of a termination of pregnancy without notice to a parent or guardian.

3. The clerk shall keep and maintain a confidential record of these proceedings as provided by section 390.01116, Florida Statutes, and shall seal the record.

DONE AND ORDERED in the ..... court in and for ..... County, Florida, on .....(date)......

_____
Judge

FORM 8.991. FINAL ORDER DISMISSING PETITION FOR JUDICIAL WAIVER OF PARENTAL NOTICE OF TERMINATION OF PREGNANCY

FINAL ORDER DISMISSING PETITION FOR JUDICIAL WAIVER OF PARENTAL NOTICE OF TERMINATION OF PREGNANCY

THIS CAUSE having come before the court on a petition for judicial waiver of parental notice of termination of pregnancy and the court being otherwise advised in the premises, finds the following:

The minor has not proven by sufficient evidence any of the criteria that would permit a judicial waiver of the parental notification requirements of section 390.01114(3), Florida Statutes, for the following reasons: ....
....
....
....
....

THEREFORE, it is ORDERED AND ADJUDGED that:

1. The petition for judicial waiver of parental notice of termination of pregnancy is DISMISSED.

2. The clerk shall keep and maintain a confidential record of these proceedings as provided by section 390.01116, Florida Statutes, and shall seal the record.

3. The clerk shall immediately provide Form 9.900(f) Notice of Appeal of an Order Dismissing a Petition for Judicial Waiver of Parental Notice of Termination of Pregnancy and Advisory Notice to Minor to the minor or petitioner if other than the minor.

DONE AND ORDERED in the ..... court in and for .... County, Florida, on .....(date)......

_____
Judge

FORM 8.992. MINOR'S PETITION TO CHIEF JUDGE TO REQUIRE A HEARING ON HER PETITION FOR JUDICIAL WAIVER OF NOTICE

MINOR'S PETITION TO CHIEF JUDGE TO REQUIRE A HEARING ON HER PETITION FOR JUDICIAL WAIVER OF NOTICE

I, ...(name)....., hereby petition the chief judge of this judicial circuit for an order directing the judge to whom this case is assigned to hold a hearing within 48 hours after receipt of this petition by the chief judge, and requiring the court to enter an order on my petition for judicial waiver of notice within 24 hours after the hearing.

In support of this petition, I say:

My petition for judicial waiver of notice was filed with the Clerk on .....(date).....

The third business day from the date of filing my petition was .....(date).....

I have not requested an extension of time for the hearing required to be conducted.

No hearing has been conducted by the court within the time required by statute.

WHEREFORE, I ask the chief judge to enter an order requiring the hearing on the petition for judicial waiver to be conducted within the next 48 hours, and requiring the court to enter its order within 24 hours after that hearing.

Signature: _____

Date: _____

Time: _____

[to be stamped by Clerk]

TITLE V.

JUDICIAL BRANCH.

CHAPTER 39.
PROCEEDINGS RELATING TO CHILDREN.

PART I.
GENERAL PROVISIONS.

§ 39.001. Purposes and intent; personnel standards and screening.

(1) PURPOSES OF CHAPTER. — The purposes of this chapter are:

(a) To provide for the care, safety, and protection of children in an environment that fosters healthy social, emotional, intellectual, and physical development; to ensure secure and safe custody; to promote the health and well-being of all children under the state's care; and to prevent the occurrence of child abuse, neglect, and abandonment.

(b) To recognize that most families desire to be competent caregivers and providers for their children and that children achieve their greatest potential when families are able to support and nurture the growth and development of their children. Therefore, the Legislature finds that policies and procedures that provide for prevention and intervention through the department's child protection system should be based on the following principles:

1. The health and safety of the children served shall be of paramount concern.

2. The prevention and intervention should engage families in constructive, supportive, and non-adversarial relationships.

3. The prevention and intervention should intrude as little as possible into the life of the family, be focused on clearly defined objectives, and keep the safety of the child or children as the paramount concern.

4. The prevention and intervention should be based upon outcome evaluation results that demonstrate success in protecting children and supporting families.

(c) To provide a child protection system that reflects a partnership between the department, other agencies, the courts, law enforcement agencies, service providers, and local communities.

(d) To provide a child protection system that is sensitive to the social and cultural diversity of the state.

(e) To provide procedures which allow the department to respond to reports of child abuse, abandonment, or neglect in the most efficient and effective manner that ensures the health and safety of children and the integrity of families.

(f) To preserve and strengthen the child's family ties whenever possible, removing the child from parental custody only when his or her welfare cannot be adequately safeguarded without such removal.

(g) To ensure that the parent or legal custodian from whose custody the child has been taken assists the department to the fullest extent possible in locating relatives suitable to serve as caregivers for the child and provides all medical and educational information, or consent for access thereto, needed to help the child.

(h) To ensure that permanent placement with the biological or adoptive family is achieved as soon as possible for every child in foster care and that no child remains in foster care longer than 1 year.

(i) To secure for the child, when removal of the child from his or her own family is necessary, custody, care, and discipline as nearly as possible equivalent to that which should have been given by the parents; and to ensure, in all cases in which a child must be removed from parental custody, that the child is placed in an approved relative home, licensed foster home, adoptive home, or independent living program that provides the most stable and potentially permanent living arrangement for the child, as determined by the court. All placements shall be in a safe environment where drugs and alcohol are not abused.

(j) To ensure that, when reunification or adoption is not possible, the child will be prepared for alternative permanency goals or placements, to include, but not be limited to, long-term foster care, independent living, custody to a relative on a permanent basis with or without legal guardianship, or custody to a foster parent or legal custodian on a permanent basis with or without legal guardianship.

(k)   To make every possible effort, if two or more children who are in the care or under the supervision of the department are siblings, to place the siblings in the same home; and in the event of permanent placement of the siblings, to place them in the same adoptive home or, if the siblings are separated while under the care or supervision of the department or in a permanent placement, to keep them in contact with each other.

(*l*)   To provide judicial and other procedures to assure due process through which children, parents, and guardians and other interested parties are assured fair hearings by a respectful and respected court or other tribunal and the recognition, protection, and enforcement of their constitutional and other legal rights, while ensuring that public safety interests and the authority and dignity of the courts are adequately protected.

(m)   To ensure that children under the jurisdiction of the courts are provided equal treatment with respect to goals, objectives, services, and case plans, without regard to the location of their placement. It is the further intent of the Legislature that, when children are removed from their homes, disruption to their education be minimized to the extent possible.

(n)   To create and maintain an integrated prevention framework that enables local communities, state agencies, and organizations to collaborate to implement efficient and properly applied evidence-based child abuse prevention practices.

(o)   To preserve and strengthen families who are caring for medically complex children.

(p)   To provide protective investigations that are conducted by trained persons in a complete and fair manner, that are promptly concluded, and that consider the purposes of this subsection and the general protections provided by law relating to child welfare.

(2)   DEPARTMENT CONTRACTS. — The department may contract with the Federal Government, other state departments and agencies, county and municipal governments and agencies, public and private agencies, and private individuals and corporations in carrying out the purposes of, and the responsibilities established in, this chapter.

(a)   If the department contracts with a provider for any program for children, all personnel, including owners, operators, employees, and volunteers, in the facility must be of good moral character. A volunteer who assists on an intermittent basis for less than 10 hours per month need not be screened if a person who meets the screening requirement of this section is always present and has the volunteer within his or her line of sight.

(b)   The department shall require employment screening, and rescreening no less frequently than once every 5 years, pursuant to chapter 435, using the level 2 standards set forth in that chapter for personnel in programs for children or youths.

(c)   The department may grant exemptions from disqualification from working with children as provided in s. 435.07.

(d)   The department shall require all job applicants, current employees, volunteers, and contract personnel who currently perform or are seeking to perform child protective investigations to be drug tested pursuant to the procedures and requirements of s. 112.0455, the Drug-Free Workplace Act. The department is authorized to adopt rules, policies, and procedures necessary to implement this paragraph.

(e)   The department shall develop and implement a written and performance-based testing and evaluation program to ensure measurable competencies of all employees assigned to manage or supervise cases of child abuse, abandonment, and neglect.

(3)   GENERAL PROTECTIONS FOR CHILDREN. — It is a purpose of the Legislature that the children of this state be provided with the following protections:

(a)   Protection from abuse, abandonment, neglect, and exploitation.

(b)   A permanent and stable home.

(c)   A safe and nurturing environment which will preserve a sense of personal dignity and integrity.

(d)   Adequate nutrition, shelter, and clothing.

(e)   Effective treatment to address physical, social, and emotional needs, regardless of geographical location.

(f)   Access to sufficient supports and services for medically complex children to allow them to remain in the least restrictive and most nurturing environment, which includes services in an amount and scope comparable to those services the child would receive in out-of-home care placement.

(g)   Equal opportunity and access to quality and effective education, which will meet the individual needs of each child, and to recreation and other community resources to develop individual abilities.

(h)   Access to preventive services.

(i)   An independent, trained advocate, when intervention is necessary and a skilled guardian or caregiver in a safe environment when alternative placement is necessary.

(4)   SERVICES FOR MEDICALLY COMPLEX CHILDREN. — The department shall maintain a program of family-centered services and supports for medically complex children. The purpose of the program is to prevent abuse and neglect of medically complex children while enhancing the capacity of families to provide for their children's needs. Program services must include outreach, early intervention, and the provision of other supports and services to meet the child's needs. The department shall collaborate with all relevant state and local agencies to provide needed services.

(5) SEXUAL EXPLOITATION SERVICES.

(a)　The Legislature recognizes that child sexual exploitation is a serious problem nationwide and in this state. The children at greatest risk of being sexually exploited are runaways and throwaways. Many of these children have a history of abuse and neglect. The vulnerability of these children starts with isolation from family and friends. Traffickers maintain control of child victims through psychological manipulation, force, drug addiction, or the exploitation of economic, physical, or emotional vulnerability. Children exploited through the sex trade often find it difficult to trust adults because of their abusive experiences. These children make up a population that is difficult to serve and even more difficult to rehabilitate.

(b)　The Legislature establishes the following goals for the state related to the status and treatment of sexually exploited children in the dependency process:

1.　To ensure the safety of children.

2.　To provide for the treatment of such children as dependent children rather than as delinquents.

3.　To sever the bond between exploited children and traffickers and to reunite these children with their families or provide them with appropriate guardians.

4.　To enable such children to be willing and reliable witnesses in the prosecution of traffickers.

(c)　The Legislature finds that sexually exploited children need special care and services in the dependency process, including counseling, health care, substance abuse treatment, educational opportunities, and a safe environment secure from traffickers.

(d)　The Legislature further finds that sexually exploited children need the special care and services described in paragraph (c) independent of their citizenship, residency, alien, or immigrant status. It is the intent of the Legislature that this state provide such care and services to all sexually exploited children in this state who are not otherwise receiving comparable services, such as those under the federal Trafficking Victims Protection Act, 22 U.S.C. ss. 7101 et seq.

(6) MENTAL HEALTH AND SUBSTANCE ABUSE SERVICES.

(a)　The Legislature recognizes that early referral and comprehensive treatment can help combat mental illnesses and substance abuse disorders in families and that treatment is cost-effective.

(b)　The Legislature establishes the following goals for the state related to mental illness and substance abuse treatment services in the dependency process:

1.　To ensure the safety of children.

2.　To prevent and remediate the consequences of mental illnesses and substance abuse disorders on families involved in protective supervision or foster care and reduce the occurrences of mental illnesses and substance abuse disorders, including alcohol abuse or related disorders, for families who are at risk of being involved in protective supervision or foster care.

3.　To expedite permanency for children and reunify healthy, intact families, when appropriate.

4.　To support families in recovery.

(c)　The Legislature finds that children in the care of the state's dependency system need appropriate health care services, that the impact of mental illnesses and substance abuse disorders on health indicates the need for health care services to include treatment for mental health and substance abuse disorders for children and parents, where appropriate, and that it is in the state's best interest that such children be provided the services they need to enable them to become and remain independent of state care. In order to provide these services, the state's dependency system must have the ability to identify and provide appropriate intervention and treatment for children with personal or family-related mental illness and substance abuse problems.

(d)　It is the intent of the Legislature to encourage the use of the mental health court program model established under chapter 394 and the drug court program model established under s. 397.334 and authorize courts to assess children and persons who have custody or are requesting custody of children where good cause is shown to identify and address mental illnesses and substance abuse disorders as the court deems appropriate at every stage of the dependency process. Participation in treatment, including a mental health court program or a treatment-based drug court program, may be required by the court following adjudication. Participation in assessment and treatment before adjudication is voluntary, except as provided in s. 39.407(16).

(e)　It is therefore the purpose of the Legislature to provide authority for the state to contract with mental health service providers and community substance abuse treatment providers for the development and operation of specialized support and overlay services for the dependency system, which will be fully implemented and used as resources permit.

(f)　Participation in a mental health court program or a treatment-based drug court program does not divest any public or private agency of its responsibility for a child or adult, but is intended to enable these agencies to better meet their needs through shared responsibility and resources.

(7) PARENTAL, CUSTODIAL, AND GUARDIAN RESPONSIBILITIES. — Parents, custodians, and guardians are deemed by the state to be responsible for providing their children with sufficient support, guidance, and supervision. The state further recognizes that the ability of parents, custodians, and guardians to

fulfill those responsibilities can be greatly impaired by economic, social, behavioral, emotional, and related problems. It is therefore the policy of the Legislature that it is the state's responsibility to ensure that factors impeding the ability of caregivers to fulfill their responsibilities are identified through the dependency process and that appropriate recommendations and services to address those problems are considered in any judicial or nonjudicial proceeding.

(8) LEGISLATIVE INTENT FOR THE PREVENTION OF ABUSE, ABANDONMENT, AND NEGLECT OF CHILDREN. — The incidence of known child abuse, abandonment, and neglect has increased rapidly over the past 5 years. The impact that abuse, abandonment, or neglect has on the victimized child, siblings, family structure, and inevitably on all citizens of the state has caused the Legislature to determine that the prevention of child abuse, abandonment, and neglect shall be a priority of this state. To further this end, it is the intent of the Legislature that an Office of Adoption and Child Protection be established.

(9) OFFICE OF ADOPTION AND CHILD PROTECTION.

(a) For purposes of establishing a comprehensive statewide approach for the promotion of adoption, support of adoptive families, and prevention of child abuse, abandonment, and neglect, the Office of Adoption and Child Protection is created within the Executive Office of the Governor. The Governor shall appoint a Chief Child Advocate for the office.

(b) The Chief Child Advocate shall:

1. Assist in developing rules pertaining to the promotion of adoption, support of adoptive families, and implementation of child abuse prevention efforts.

2. Act as the Governor's liaison with state agencies, other state governments, and the public and private sectors on matters that relate to the promotion of adoption, support of adoptive families, and child abuse prevention.

3. Work to secure funding and other support for the state's promotion of adoption, support of adoptive families, and child abuse prevention efforts, including, but not limited to, establishing cooperative relationships among state and private agencies.

4. Develop a strategic program and funding initiative that links the separate jurisdictional activities of state agencies with respect to promotion of adoption, support of adoptive families, and child abuse prevention. The office may designate lead and contributing agencies to develop such initiatives.

5. Advise the Governor and the Legislature on statistics related to the promotion of adoption, support of adoptive families, and child abuse prevention trends in this state; the status of current adoption programs and services, current child abuse prevention programs and services, the funding of adoption, support of adoptive families, and child abuse prevention programs and services; and the status of the office with regard to the development and implementation of the state strategy for the promotion of adoption, support of adoptive families, and child abuse prevention.

6. Develop public awareness campaigns to be implemented throughout the state for the promotion of adoption, support of adoptive families, and child abuse prevention.

(c) The office is authorized and directed to:

1. Oversee the preparation and implementation of the state plan established under subsection (10) and revise and update the state plan as necessary.

2. Provide for or make available continuing professional education and training in the prevention of child abuse and neglect.

3. Work to secure funding in the form of appropriations, gifts, and grants from the state, the Federal Government, and other public and private sources in order to ensure that sufficient funds are available for the promotion of adoption, support of adoptive families, and child abuse prevention efforts.

4. Make recommendations pertaining to agreements or contracts for the establishment and development of:

a. Programs and services for the promotion of adoption, support of adoptive families, and prevention of child abuse and neglect.

b. Training programs for the prevention of child abuse and neglect.

c. Multidisciplinary and discipline-specific training programs for professionals with responsibilities affecting children, young adults, and families.

d. Efforts to promote adoption.

e. Postadoptive services to support adoptive families.

5. Monitor, evaluate, and review the development and quality of local and statewide services and programs for the promotion of adoption, support of adoptive families, and prevention of child abuse and neglect and shall publish and distribute an annual report of its findings on or before January 1 of each year to the Governor, the Speaker of the House of Representatives, the President of the Senate, the head of each state agency affected by the report, and the appropriate substantive committees of the Legislature. The report shall include:

a. A summary of the activities of the office.

b. A summary of the adoption data collected and reported to the federal Adoption and Foster Care Analysis and Reporting System (AFCARS) and the federal Administration for Children and Families.

c. A summary of the child abuse prevention data collected and reported to the National Child Abuse and Neglect Data System (NCANDS) and the federal Administration for Children and Families.

d. A summary detailing the timeliness of the adoption process for children adopted from within the child welfare system.

e. Recommendations, by state agency, for the further development and improvement of services and programs for the promotion of adoption, support of adoptive families, and prevention of child abuse and neglect.

f. Budget requests, adoption promotion and support needs, and child abuse prevention program needs by state agency.

6. Work with the direct-support organization established under s. 39.0011 to receive financial assistance.

(10) PLAN FOR COMPREHENSIVE APPROACH.

(a) The office shall develop a state plan for the promotion of adoption, support of adoptive families, and prevention of abuse, abandonment, and neglect of children and shall submit the state plan to the Speaker of the House of Representatives, the President of the Senate, and the Governor no later than December 31, 2008. The Department of Children and Families, the Department of Corrections, the Department of Education, the Department of Health, the Department of Juvenile Justice, the Department of Law Enforcement, and the Agency for Persons with Disabilities shall participate and fully cooperate in the development of the state plan at both the state and local levels. Furthermore, appropriate local agencies and organizations shall be provided an opportunity to participate in the development of the state plan at the local level. Appropriate local groups and organizations shall include, but not be limited to, community mental health centers; guardian ad litem programs for children under the circuit court; the school boards of the local school districts; the Florida local advocacy councils; community-based care lead agencies; private or public organizations or programs with recognized expertise in working with child abuse prevention programs for children and families; private or public organizations or programs with recognized expertise in working with children who are sexually abused, physically abused, emotionally abused, abandoned, or neglected and with expertise in working with the families of such children; private or public programs or organizations with expertise in maternal and infant health care; multidisciplinary child protection teams; child day care centers; law enforcement agencies; and the circuit courts, when guardian ad litem programs are not available in the local area. The state plan to be provided to the Legislature and the Governor shall include, as a minimum, the information required of the various groups in paragraph (b).

(b) The development of the state plan shall be accomplished in the following manner:

1. The office shall establish a Child Abuse Prevention and Permanency Advisory Council composed of an adoptive parent who has adopted a child from within the child welfare system and representatives from each state agency and appropriate local agencies and organizations specified in paragraph (a). The advisory council shall serve as the research arm of the office and shall be responsible for:

a. Assisting in developing a plan of action for better coordination and integration of the goals, activities, and funding pertaining to the promotion and support of adoption and the prevention of child abuse, abandonment, and neglect conducted by the office in order to maximize staff and resources at the state level. The plan of action shall be included in the state plan.

b. Assisting in providing a basic format to be utilized by the districts in the preparation of local plans of action in order to provide for uniformity in the district plans and to provide for greater ease in compiling information for the state plan.

c. Providing the districts with technical assistance in the development of local plans of action, if requested.

d. Assisting in examining the local plans to determine if all the requirements of the local plans have been met and, if they have not, informing the districts of the deficiencies and requesting the additional information needed.

e. Assisting in preparing the state plan for submission to the Legislature and the Governor. Such preparation shall include the incorporation into the state plan of information obtained from the local plans, the cooperative plans with the members of the advisory council, and the plan of action for coordination and integration of state departmental activities. The state plan shall include a section reflecting general conditions and needs, an analysis of variations based on population or geographic areas, identified problems, and recommendations for change. In essence, the state plan shall provide an analysis and summary of each element of the local plans to provide a statewide perspective. The state plan shall also include each separate local plan of action.

f. Conducting a feasibility study on the establishment of a Children's Cabinet.

g. Working with the specified state agency in fulfilling the requirements of subparagraphs 2., 3., 4., and 5.

2. The office, the department, the Department of Education, and the Department of Health shall work together in developing ways to inform and instruct parents of school children and appropriate

district school personnel in all school districts in the detection of child abuse, abandonment, and neglect and in the proper action that should be taken in a suspected case of child abuse, abandonment, or neglect, and in caring for a child's needs after a report is made. The plan for accomplishing this end shall be included in the state plan.

3. The office, the department, the Department of Law Enforcement, and the Department of Health shall work together in developing ways to inform and instruct appropriate local law enforcement personnel in the detection of child abuse, abandonment, and neglect and in the proper action that should be taken in a suspected case of child abuse, abandonment, or neglect.

4. Within existing appropriations, the office shall work with other appropriate public and private agencies to emphasize efforts to educate the general public about the problem of and ways to detect child abuse, abandonment, and neglect and in the proper action that should be taken in a suspected case of child abuse, abandonment, or neglect. The plan for accomplishing this end shall be included in the state plan.

5. The office, the department, the Department of Education, and the Department of Health shall work together on the enhancement or adaptation of curriculum materials to assist instructional personnel in providing instruction through a multidisciplinary approach on the identification, intervention, and prevention of child abuse, abandonment, and neglect. The curriculum materials shall be geared toward a sequential program of instruction at the four progressional levels, K-3, 4-6, 7-9, and 10-12. Strategies for encouraging all school districts to utilize the curriculum are to be included in the state plan for the prevention of child abuse, abandonment, and neglect.

6. Each district of the department shall develop a plan for its specific geographical area. The plan developed at the district level shall be submitted to the advisory council for utilization in preparing the state plan. The district local plan of action shall be prepared with the involvement and assistance of the local agencies and organizations listed in this paragraph, as well as representatives from those departmental district offices participating in the promotion of adoption, support of adoptive families, and treatment and prevention of child abuse, abandonment, and neglect. In order to accomplish this, the office shall establish a task force on the promotion of adoption, support of adoptive families, and prevention of child abuse, abandonment, and neglect. The office shall appoint the members of the task force in accordance with the membership requirements of this section. The office shall ensure that individuals from both urban and rural areas and an adoptive parent who has adopted a child from within the child welfare system are represented on the task force. The task force shall develop a written statement clearly identifying its operating procedures, purpose, overall responsibilities, and method of meeting responsibilities. The district plan of action to be prepared by the task force shall include, but shall not be limited to:

a. Documentation of the magnitude of the problems of child abuse, including sexual abuse, physical abuse, and emotional abuse, and child abandonment and neglect in its geographical area.

b. A description of programs currently serving abused, abandoned, and neglected children and their families and a description of programs for the prevention of child abuse, abandonment, and neglect, including information on the impact, cost-effectiveness, and sources of funding of such programs.

c. Information concerning the number of children within the child welfare system available for adoption who need child-specific adoption promotion efforts.

d. A description of programs currently promoting and supporting adoptive families, including information on the impact, cost-effectiveness, and sources of funding of such programs.

e. A description of a comprehensive approach for providing postadoption services. The continuum of services shall include, but not be limited to, sufficient and accessible parent and teen support groups; case management, information, and referral services; and educational advocacy.

f. A continuum of programs and services necessary for a comprehensive approach to the promotion of adoption and the prevention of all types of child abuse, abandonment, and neglect as well as a brief description of such programs and services.

g. A description, documentation, and priority ranking of local needs related to the promotion of adoption, support of adoptive families, and prevention of child abuse, abandonment, and neglect based upon the continuum of programs and services.

h. A plan for steps to be taken in meeting identified needs, including the coordination and integration of services to avoid unnecessary duplication and cost, and for alternative funding strategies for meeting needs through the reallocation of existing resources, utilization of volunteers, contracting with local universities for services, and local government or private agency funding.

i. A description of barriers to the accomplishment of a comprehensive approach to the promotion of adoption, support of adoptive families, and prevention of child abuse, abandonment, and neglect.

j. Recommendations for changes that can be accomplished only at the state program level or by legislative action.

(11) FUNDING AND SUBSEQUENT PLANS.

(a) All budget requests submitted by the office, the department, the Department of Health, the Department of Education, the Department of Juvenile Justice, the Department of Corrections, the Agency for Persons with Disabilities, or any other agency to the Legislature for funding of efforts for the promotion of adoption, support of adoptive families, and prevention of child abuse, abandonment, and neglect shall be based on the state plan developed pursuant to this section.

(b) The office and the other agencies and organizations listed in paragraph (10)(a) shall readdress the state plan and make necessary revisions every 5 years, at a minimum. Such revisions shall be submitted to the Speaker of the House of Representatives and the President of the Senate no later than June 30 of each year divisible by 5. At least biennially, the office shall review the state plan and make any necessary revisions based on changing needs and program evaluation results. An annual progress report shall be submitted to update the state plan in the years between the 5-year intervals. In order to avoid duplication of effort, these required plans may be made a part of or merged with other plans required by either the state or Federal Government, so long as the portions of the other state or Federal Government plan that constitute the state plan for the promotion of adoption, support of adoptive families, and prevention of child abuse, abandonment, and neglect are clearly identified as such and are provided to the Speaker of the House of Representatives and the President of the Senate as required under this section.

(12) LIBERAL CONSTRUCTION. — It is the intent of the Legislature that this chapter be liberally interpreted and construed in conformity with its declared purposes.

HISTORY:

S. 1, ch. 26880, 1951; s. 1, ch. 73-231; s. 1, ch. 78-414; s. 1, ch. 82-62; s. 62, ch. 85-81; s. 1, ch. 85-206; s. 10, ch. 85-248; s. 19, ch. 86-220; s. 1, ch. 90-53; ss. 1, 2, ch. 90-208; s. 2, ch. 90-306; s. 2, ch. 91-33; s. 68, ch. 91-45; s. 13, ch. 91-57; s. 5, ch. 93-156; s. 23, ch. 93-200; s. 19, ch. 93-230; s. 14, ch. 94-134; s. 14, ch. 94-135; ss. 9, 10, ch. 94-209; s. 1332, ch. 95-147; s. 7, ch. 95-152; s. 8, ch. 95-158; ss. 15, 30, ch. 95-228; s. 116, ch. 95-418; s. 1, ch. 96-268; ss. 128, 156, ch. 97-101; s. 69, ch. 97-103; s. 3, ch. 97-237; s. 119, ch. 97-238; s. 8, ch. 98-137; s. 18, ch. 98-403; s. 1, ch. 99-193; s. 13, ch. 2000-139; s. 5, ch. 2000-151; s. 5, ch. 2000-263; s. 34, ch. 2004-267; s. 2, ch. 2006-97, eff. June 7, 2006; s. 1, ch. 2006-194, eff. July 1, 2006; s. 2, ch. 2006-227, eff. July 1, 2006; s. 1, ch. 2007-124, eff. July 1, 2007; s. 3, ch. 2008-6, eff. July 1, 2008; s. 1, ch. 2010-114, eff. Aug. 1, 2010; s. 42, ch. 2011-142, eff. July 1, 2011; s. 19, ch. 2012-116, eff. July 1, 2012; s. 2, ch. 2012-105, eff. Jan. 1, 2013; s. 4, ch. 2013-15, eff. July 2, 2013; s. 9, ch. 2014-19, eff. July 1, 2014; s. 2, ch. 2014-224, eff. July 1, 2014; s. 1, ch. 2016-127, eff. July 1, 2016; s. 82, ch. 2016-241, eff. July 1, 2016.

Editor's notes.

Section 34, ch. 2004-267, reenacted paragraph (b) of subsection (2) without change, effective July 1, 2004, to incorporate amendments to statutory sections referenced therein.

Former s. 39.20; subsections (3)-(5) former s. 39.002, s. 409.70, subsections (6)-(8) former s. 415.501.

Section 58, ch. 2010-114 provides: "The changes made by this act are intended to be prospective in nature. It is not intended that persons who are employed or licensed on the effective date of this act be rescreened until such time as they are otherwise required to be rescreened pursuant to law, at which time they must meet the requirements for screening as set forth in this act."

Section 1, ch. 2012-105, provides: "This act may be cited as the 'Florida Safe Harbor Act.' "

§ 39.0011. Direct-support organization. [Repealed October 1, 2017]

(1) The Office of Adoption and Child Protection may establish a direct-support organization to assist the state in carrying out its purposes and responsibilities regarding the promotion of adoption, support of adoptive families, and prevention of child abuse, abandonment, and neglect by raising money; submitting requests for and receiving grants from the Federal Government, the state or its political subdivisions, private foundations, and individuals; and making expenditures to or for the benefit of the office. The sole purpose for the direct-support organization is to support the office. Such a direct-support organization is an organization that is:

(a) Incorporated under chapter 617 and approved by the Department of State as a Florida corporation not for profit;

(b) Organized and operated to make expenditures to or for the benefit of the office; and

(c) Approved by the office to be operating for the benefit of and in a manner consistent with the goals of the office and in the best interest of the state.

(2) The number of members on the board of directors of the direct-support organization shall be determined by the Chief Child Advocate. Membership on the board of directors of the direct-support organization shall include, but not be limited to, a guardian ad litem; a member of a local advocacy council; a representative from a community-based care lead agency; a representative from a private or public organization or program with recognized expertise in working with child abuse prevention programs for children and families; a representative of a private or public organization or program with recognized expertise in working with children who are sexually abused, physically abused, emotionally abused, abandoned, or neglected and with expertise in working with the families of such children; an individual working at a state adoption agency; and the parent of a child adopted from within the child welfare system.

(3) The direct-support organization shall operate under written contract with the office.

(4) All moneys received by the direct-support organization shall be deposited into an account of the

direct-support organization and shall be used by the organization in a manner consistent with the goals of the office.

(5) This section is repealed October 1, 2017, unless reviewed and saved from repeal by the Legislature.

HISTORY:
S. 2, ch. 2007-124, eff. July 1, 2007; s. 5, ch. 2014-96, eff. June 13, 2014.

§ 39.0014. Responsibilities of public agencies.

All state, county, and local agencies shall cooperate, assist, and provide information to the Office of Adoption and Child Protection and the department as will enable them to fulfill their responsibilities under this chapter.

HISTORY:
S. 2, ch. 99-193; s. 2, ch. 2006-194, eff. July 1, 2006; s. 3, ch. 2007-124, eff. July 1, 2007.

§ 39.00145. Records concerning children.

(1) The case record of every child under the supervision of or in the custody of the department, the department's authorized agents, or providers contracting with the department, including community-based care lead agencies and their subcontracted providers, must be maintained in a complete and accurate manner. The case record must contain, at a minimum, the child's case plan required under part VII of this chapter and the full name and street address of all shelters, foster parents, group homes, treatment facilities, or locations where the child has been placed.

(2) Notwithstanding any other provision of this chapter, all records in a child's case record must be made available for inspection, upon request, to the child who is the subject of the case record and to the child's caregiver, guardian ad litem, or attorney.

(a) A complete and accurate copy of any record in a child's case record must be provided, upon request and at no cost, to the child who is the subject of the case record and to the child's caregiver, guardian ad litem, or attorney.

(b) The department shall release the information in a manner and setting that are appropriate to the age and maturity of the child and the nature of the information being released, which may include the release of information in a therapeutic setting, if appropriate. This paragraph does not deny the child access to his or her records.

(c) If a child or the child's caregiver, guardian ad litem, or attorney requests access to the child's case record, any person or entity that fails to provide any record in the case record under assertion of a claim of exemption from the public records requirements of chapter 119, or fails to provide access within a reasonable time, is subject to sanctions and penalties under s. 119.10.

(d) For the purposes of this subsection, the term "caregiver" is limited to parents, legal custodians, permanent guardians, or foster parents; employees of a residential home, institution, facility, or agency at which the child resides; and other individuals legally responsible for a child's welfare in a residential setting.

(3) If a court determines that sharing information in the child's case record is necessary to ensure access to appropriate services for the child or for the safety of the child, the court may approve the release of confidential records or information contained in them.

(4) Notwithstanding any other provision of law, all state and local agencies and programs that provide services to children or that are responsible for a child's safety, including the Department of Juvenile Justice, the Department of Health, the Agency for Health Care Administration, the Agency for Persons with Disabilities, the Department of Education, the Department of Revenue, the school districts, the Statewide Guardian Ad Litem Office, and any provider contracting with such agencies, may share with each other confidential records or information that are confidential or exempt from disclosure under chapter 119 if the records or information are reasonably necessary to ensure access to appropriate services for the child, including child support enforcement services, or for the safety of the child. However:

(a) Records or information made confidential by federal law may not be shared.

(b) This subsection does not apply to information concerning clients and records of certified domestic violence centers, which are confidential under s. 39.908 and privileged under s. 90.5036.

HISTORY:
S. 1, ch. 2009-34, eff. July 1, 2009; s. 2, ch. 2009-43, eff. July 1, 2009; s. 40, ch. 2011-213, eff. July 1, 2011.

§ 39.0015. Child abuse prevention training in the district school system [Repealed.]

Repealed by s. 38, ch. 2011-213, effective July 1, 2011.

HISTORY:
SS. 1, 2, 3, 4, 5, 6, ch. 85-248; s. 49, ch. 86-220; s. 129, ch. 97-101; s. 67, ch. 97-190; s. 42, ch. 98-280; s. 19, ch. 98-403; s. 3, ch. 99-193; s. 3, ch. 2000-135; s. 14, ch. 2000-139; s. 11, ch. 2001-60; s. 884, ch. 2002-387; s. 28, ch. 2006-86, eff. July 1, 2006; s. 3, ch. 2006-194, eff. July 1, 2006; s. 24, ch. 2008-245, eff. June 30, 2008.

§ 39.0016. Education of abused, neglected, and abandoned children; agency agreements; children having or suspected of having a disability.

(1) DEFINITIONS. — As used in this section, the term:

(a) "Children known to the department" means children who are found to be dependent or children in shelter care.

(b) "Department" means the Department of Children and Families or a community-based care lead agency acting on behalf of the Department of Children and Families, as appropriate.

(c) "Surrogate parent" means an individual appointed to act in the place of a parent in educational decisionmaking and in safeguarding a child's rights under the Individuals with Disabilities Education Act and this section.

(2) AGENCY AGREEMENTS.

(a) The department shall enter into an agreement with the Department of Education regarding the education and related care of children known to the department. Such agreement shall be designed to provide educational access to children known to the department for the purpose of facilitating the delivery of services or programs to children known to the department. The agreement shall avoid duplication of services or programs and shall provide for combining resources to maximize the availability or delivery of services or programs. The agreement must require the Department of Education to access the department's Florida Safe Families Network to obtain information about children known to the department, consistent with the Family Educational Rights and Privacy Act (FERPA), 20 U.S.C. s. 1232g.

(b) The department shall enter into agreements with district school boards or other local educational entities regarding education and related services for children known to the department who are of school age and children known to the department who are younger than school age but who would otherwise qualify for services from the district school board. Such agreements shall include, but are not limited to:

1. A requirement that the department shall:

a. Ensure that children known to the department are enrolled in school or in the best educational setting that meets the needs of the child. The agreement shall provide for continuing the enrollment of a child known to the department at the school of origin when possible if it is in the best interest of the child, with the goal of minimal disruption of education.

b. Notify the school and school district in which a child known to the department is enrolled of the name and phone number of the child known to the department caregiver and caseworker for child safety purposes.

c. Establish a protocol for the department to share information about a child known to the department with the school district, consistent with the Family Educational Rights and Privacy Act, since the sharing of information will assist each agency in obtaining education and related services for the benefit of the child. The protocol must require the district school boards or other local educational entities to access the department's Florida Safe Families Network to obtain information about children known to the depart-

ment, consistent with the Family Educational Rights and Privacy Act (FERPA), 20 U.S.C. s. 1232g.

d. Notify the school district of the department's case planning for a child known to the department, both at the time of plan development and plan review. Within the plan development or review process, the school district may provide information regarding the child known to the department if the school district deems it desirable and appropriate.

e. Show no prejudice against a caregiver who desires to educate at home a child placed in his or her home through the child welfare system.

2. A requirement that the district school board shall:

a. Provide the department with a general listing of the services and information available from the district school board to facilitate educational access for a child known to the department.

b. Identify all educational and other services provided by the school and school district which the school district believes are reasonably necessary to meet the educational needs of a child known to the department.

c. Determine whether transportation is available for a child known to the department when such transportation will avoid a change in school assignment due to a change in residential placement. Recognizing that continued enrollment in the same school throughout the time the child known to the department is in out-of-home care is preferable unless enrollment in the same school would be unsafe or otherwise impractical, the department, the district school board, and the Department of Education shall assess the availability of federal, charitable, or grant funding for such transportation.

d. Provide individualized student intervention or an individual educational plan when a determination has been made through legally appropriate criteria that intervention services are required. The intervention or individual educational plan must include strategies to enable the child known to the department to maximize the attainment of educational goals.

3. A requirement that the department and the district school board shall cooperate in accessing the services and supports needed for a child known to the department who has or is suspected of having a disability to receive an appropriate education consistent with the Individuals with Disabilities Education Act and state implementing laws, rules, and assurances. Coordination of services for a child known to the department who has or is suspected of having a disability may include:

a. Referral for screening.

b. Sharing of evaluations between the school district and the department where appropriate.

c. Provision of education and related services appropriate for the needs and abilities of the child known to the department.

d. Coordination of services and plans between the school and the residential setting to avoid duplication or conflicting service plans.

e. Appointment of a surrogate parent, consistent with the Individuals with Disabilities Education Act and pursuant to subsection (3), for educational purposes for a child known to the department who qualifies.

f. For each child known to the department 14 years of age and older, transition planning by the department and all providers, including the department's independent living program staff, to meet the requirements of the local school district for educational purposes.

(c) This subsection establishes standards and not rights. This subsection does not require the delivery of any particular service or level of service in excess of existing appropriations. A person may not maintain a cause of action against the state or any of its subdivisions, agencies, contractors, subcontractors, or agents based upon this subsection becoming law or failure by the Legislature to provide adequate funding for the achievement of these standards. This subsection does not require the expenditure of funds to meet the standards established in this subsection except funds specifically appropriated for such purpose.

(3) CHILDREN HAVING OR SUSPECTED OF HAVING A DISABILITY.

(a)1. The Legislature finds that disability is a natural part of the human experience and in no way diminishes the right of individuals to participate in or contribute to society. Improving educational results for children with disabilities is an essential element of our public policy of ensuring equality of opportunity, full participation, independent living, and economic self-sufficiency for individuals with disabilities.

2. The Legislature also finds that research and experience have shown that the education of children with disabilities can be made more effective by:

a. Having high expectations for these children and ensuring their access to the general education curriculum in the regular classroom, to the maximum extent possible.

b. Providing appropriate exceptional student education, related services, and aids and supports in the least restrictive environment appropriate for these children.

c. Having a trained, interested, and consistent educational decisionmaker for the child

when the parent is determined to be legally unavailable or when the foster parent is unwilling, has no significant relationship with the child, or is not trained in the exceptional student education process.

3. It is, therefore, the intent of the Legislature that all children with disabilities known to the department, consistent with the Individuals with Disabilities Education Act, have available to them a free, appropriate public education that emphasizes exceptional student education and related services designed to meet their unique needs and prepare them for further education, employment, and independent living and that the rights of children with disabilities are protected.

(b)1. Each district school superintendent or dependency court must appoint a surrogate parent for a child known to the department who has or is suspected of having a disability, as defined in s. 1003.01(3), when:

a. After reasonable efforts, no parent can be located; or

b. A court of competent jurisdiction over a child under this chapter has determined that no person has the authority under the Individuals with Disabilities Education Act, including the parent or parents subject to the dependency action, or that no person has the authority, willingness, or ability to serve as the educational decisionmaker for the child without judicial action.

2. A surrogate parent appointed by the district school superintendent or the court must be at least 18 years old and have no personal or professional interest that conflicts with the interests of the student to be represented. Neither the district school superintendent nor the court may appoint an employee of the Department of Education, the local school district, a community-based care provider, the Department of Children and Families, or any other public or private agency involved in the education or care of the child as appointment of those persons is prohibited by federal law. This prohibition includes group home staff and therapeutic foster parents. However, a person who acts in a parental role to a child, such as a foster parent or relative caregiver, is not prohibited from serving as a surrogate parent if he or she is employed by such agency, willing to serve, and knowledgeable about the child and the exceptional student education process. The surrogate parent may be a court-appointed guardian ad litem or a relative or nonrelative adult who is involved in the child's life regardless of whether that person has physical custody of the child. Each person appointed as a surrogate parent must have the knowledge and skills acquired by successfully completing training using materials developed and approved by the

Department of Education to ensure adequate representation of the child.

3. If a guardian ad litem has been appointed for a child, the district school superintendent must first consider the child's guardian ad litem when appointing a surrogate parent. The district school superintendent must accept the appointment of the court if he or she has not previously appointed a surrogate parent. Similarly, the court must accept a surrogate parent duly appointed by a district school superintendent.

4. A surrogate parent appointed by the district school superintendent or the court must be accepted by any subsequent school or school district without regard to where the child is receiving residential care so that a single surrogate parent can follow the education of the child during his or her entire time in state custody. Nothing in this paragraph or in rule shall limit or prohibit the continuance of a surrogate parent appointment when the responsibility for the student's educational placement moves among and between public and private agencies.

5. For a child known to the department, the responsibility to appoint a surrogate parent resides with both the district school superintendent and the court with jurisdiction over the child. If the court elects to appoint a surrogate parent, notice shall be provided as soon as practicable to the child's school. At any time the court determines that it is in the best interests of a child to remove a surrogate parent, the court may appoint a new surrogate parent for educational decisionmaking purposes for that child.

6. The surrogate parent shall continue in the appointed role until one of the following occurs:

a. The child is determined to no longer be eligible or in need of special programs, except when termination of special programs is being contested.

b. The child achieves permanency through adoption or legal guardianship and is no longer in the custody of the department.

c. The parent who was previously unknown becomes known, whose whereabouts were unknown is located, or who was unavailable is determined by the court to be available.

d. The appointed surrogate no longer wishes to represent the child or is unable to represent the child.

e. The superintendent of the school district in which the child is attending school, the Department of Education contract designee, or the court that appointed the surrogate determines that the appointed surrogate parent no longer adequately represents the child.

f. The child moves to a geographic location that is not reasonably accessible to the appointed surrogate.

7. The appointment and termination of appointment of a surrogate under this paragraph shall be entered as an order of the court with a copy of the order provided to the child's school as soon as practicable.

8. The person appointed as a surrogate parent under this paragraph must:

a. Be acquainted with the child and become knowledgeable about his or her disability and educational needs.

b. Represent the child in all matters relating to identification, evaluation, and educational placement and the provision of a free and appropriate education to the child.

c. Represent the interests and safeguard the rights of the child in educational decisions that affect the child.

9. The responsibilities of the person appointed as a surrogate parent shall not extend to the care, maintenance, custody, residential placement, or any other area not specifically related to the education of the child, unless the same person is appointed by the court for such other purposes.

10. A person appointed as a surrogate parent shall enjoy all of the procedural safeguards afforded a parent with respect to the identification, evaluation, and educational placement of a student with a disability or a student who is suspected of having a disability.

11. A person appointed as a surrogate parent shall not be held liable for actions taken in good faith on behalf of the student in protecting the special education rights of the child.

(4) TRAINING. — The department shall incorporate an education component into all training programs of the department regarding children known to the department. Such training shall be coordinated with the Department of Education and the local school districts. The department shall offer opportunities for education personnel to participate in such training. Such coordination shall include, but not be limited to, notice of training sessions, opportunities to purchase training materials, proposals to avoid duplication of services by offering joint training, and incorporation of materials available from the Department of Education and local school districts into the department training when appropriate. The department training components shall include:

(a) Training for surrogate parents to include how an ability to learn of a child known to the department is affected by abuse, abandonment, neglect, and removal from the home.

(b) Training for parents in cases in which reunification is the goal, or for preadoptive parents when adoption is the goal, so that such parents learn how to access the services the child known to the department needs and the importance of their involvement in the education of the child known to the department.

(c) Training for caseworkers and foster parents to include information on the right of the child known to the department to an education, the role of an education in the development and adjustment of a child known to the department, the proper ways to access education and related services for the child known to the department, and the importance and strategies for parental involvement in education for the success of the child known to the department.

(d) Training of caseworkers regarding the services and information available through the Department of Education and local school districts, including, but not limited to, the current Sunshine State Standards, the Surrogate Parent Training Manual, and other resources accessible through the Department of Education or local school districts to facilitate educational access for a child known to the department.

HISTORY:
S. 3, ch. 2004-356; s. 1, ch. 2009-35, eff. July 1, 2009; s. 10, ch. 2014-19, eff. July 1, 2014; s. 1, ch. 2015-130, eff. July 1, 2015.

Editor's notes.
The Individuals with Disabilities Education Act, referred to in this section, is codified as 20 U.S.C.S. § 1400 et seq.
Section 44, ch. 2013-27, provides: "The Division of Law Revision and Information is requested to prepare a reviser's bill for the 2014 Regular Session of the Legislature to change the term 'Sunshine State Standards' to 'Next Generation Sunshine State Standards' wherever the term appears in the Florida Statutes."

§ 39.01. Definitions.

When used in this chapter, unless the context otherwise requires:

(1) "Abandoned" or "abandonment" means a situation in which the parent or legal custodian of a child or, in the absence of a parent or legal custodian, the caregiver, while being able, has made no significant contribution to the child's care and maintenance or has failed to establish or maintain a substantial and positive relationship with the child, or both. For purposes of this subsection, "establish or maintain a substantial and positive relationship" includes, but is not limited to, frequent and regular contact with the child through frequent and regular visitation or frequent and regular communication to or with the child, and the exercise of parental rights and responsibilities. Marginal efforts and incidental or token visits or communications are not sufficient to establish or maintain a substantial and positive relationship with a child. A man's acknowledgement of paternity of the child does not limit the period of time considered in determining whether the child was abandoned. The term does not include a surrendered newborn infant as described in s. 383.50, a "child in need of services" as defined in chapter 984, or a "family in need of services" as defined in chapter 984. The incarceration, repeated incarceration, or extended incarceration of a parent, legal custodian, or caregiver responsible for a child's welfare may support a finding of abandonment.

(2) "Abuse" means any willful act or threatened act that results in any physical, mental, or sexual abuse, injury, or harm that causes or is likely to cause the child's physical, mental, or emotional health to be significantly impaired. Abuse of a child includes acts or omissions. Corporal discipline of a child by a parent or legal custodian for disciplinary purposes does not in itself constitute abuse when it does not result in harm to the child.

(3) "Addictions receiving facility" means a substance abuse service provider as defined in chapter 397.

(4) "Adjudicatory hearing" means a hearing for the court to determine whether or not the facts support the allegations stated in the petition in dependency cases or in termination of parental rights cases.

(5) "Adult" means any natural person other than a child.

(6) "Adoption" means the act of creating the legal relationship between parent and child where it did not exist, thereby declaring the child to be legally the child of the adoptive parents and their heir at law, and entitled to all the rights and privileges and subject to all the obligations of a child born to the adoptive parents in lawful wedlock.

(7)
"Juvenile sexual abuse" means any sexual behavior by a child which occurs without consent, without equality, or as a result of coercion. For purposes of this subsection, the following definitions apply:

(a) "Coercion" means the exploitation of authority or the use of bribes, threats of force, or intimidation to gain cooperation or compliance.

(b) "Equality" means two participants operating with the same level of power in a relationship, neither being controlled nor coerced by the other.

(c) "Consent" means an agreement, including all of the following:

1. Understanding what is proposed based on age, maturity, developmental level, functioning, and experience.

2. Knowledge of societal standards for what is being proposed.

3. Awareness of potential consequences and alternatives.

4. Assumption that agreement or disagreement will be accepted equally.

5. Voluntary decision.

6. Mental competence.

Juvenile sexual behavior ranges from noncontact sexual behavior such as making obscene phone calls, exhibitionism, voyeurism, and the showing or taking of lewd photographs to varying degrees of direct sexual contact, such as frottage, fondling, digital penetration, rape, fellatio, sodomy, and various other sexually aggressive acts.

(8) "Arbitration" means a process whereby a neutral third person or panel, called an arbitrator or an arbitra-

tion panel, considers the facts and arguments presented by the parties and renders a decision which may be binding or nonbinding.

(9) "Authorized agent" or "designee" of the department means an employee, volunteer, or other person or agency determined by the state to be eligible for state-funded risk management coverage, which is assigned or designated by the department to perform duties or exercise powers under this chapter.

(10) "Caregiver" means the parent, legal custodian, permanent guardian, adult household member, or other person responsible for a child's welfare as defined in subsection (48).

(11) "Case plan" means a document, as described in s. 39.6011, prepared by the department with input from all parties. The case plan follows the child from the provision of voluntary services through any dependency, foster care, or termination of parental rights proceeding or related activity or process.

(12) "Child" or "youth" means any unmarried person under the age of 18 years who has not been emancipated by order of the court.

(13) "Child protection team" means a team of professionals established by the Department of Health to receive referrals from the protective investigators and protective supervision staff of the department and to provide specialized and supportive services to the program in processing child abuse, abandonment, or neglect cases. A child protection team shall provide consultation to other programs of the department and other persons regarding child abuse, abandonment, or neglect cases.

(14) "Child who has exhibited inappropriate sexual behavior" means a child who has been found by the department or the court to have committed an inappropriate sexual act.

(15) "Child who is found to be dependent" means a child who, pursuant to this chapter, is found by the court:

(a) To have been abandoned, abused, or neglected by the child's parent or parents or legal custodians;

(b) To have been surrendered to the department, the former Department of Health and Rehabilitative Services, or a licensed child-placing agency for purpose of adoption;

(c) To have been voluntarily placed with a licensed child-caring agency, a licensed child-placing agency, an adult relative, the department, or the former Department of Health and Rehabilitative Services, after which placement, under the requirements of this chapter, a case plan has expired and the parent or parents or legal custodians have failed to substantially comply with the requirements of the plan;

(d) To have been voluntarily placed with a licensed child-placing agency for the purposes of subsequent adoption, and a parent or parents have

signed a consent pursuant to the Florida Rules of Juvenile Procedure;

(e) To have no parent or legal custodians capable of providing supervision and care;

(f) To be at substantial risk of imminent abuse, abandonment, or neglect by the parent or parents or legal custodians; or

(g) To have been sexually exploited and to have no parent, legal custodian, or responsible adult relative currently known and capable of providing the necessary and appropriate supervision and care.

(16) "Child support" means a court-ordered obligation, enforced under chapter 61 and ss. 409.2551 - 409.2597, for monetary support for the care, maintenance, training, and education of a child.

(17) "Circuit" means any of the 20 judicial circuits as set forth in s. 26.021.

(18) "Comprehensive assessment" or "assessment" means the gathering of information for the evaluation of a child's and caregiver's physical, psychiatric, psychological, or mental health; developmental delays or challenges; and educational, vocational, and social condition and family environment as they relate to the child's and caregiver's need for rehabilitative and treatment services, including substance abuse treatment services, mental health services, developmental services, literacy services, medical services, family services, and other specialized services, as appropriate.

(19) "Concurrent planning" means establishing a permanency goal in a case plan that uses reasonable efforts to reunify the child with the parent, while at the same time establishing another goal that must be one of the following options:

(a) Adoption when a petition for termination of parental rights has been filed or will be filed;

(b) Permanent guardianship of a dependent child under s. 39.6221;

(c) Permanent placement with a fit and willing relative under s. 39.6231; or

(d) Placement in another planned permanent living arrangement under s. 39.6241.

(20) "Court," unless otherwise expressly stated, means the circuit court assigned to exercise jurisdiction under this chapter.

(21) "Department" means the Department of Children and Families.

(22) "Diligent efforts by a parent" means a course of conduct which results in a meaningful change in the behavior of a parent that reduces risk to the child in the child's home to the extent that the child may be safely placed permanently back in the home as set forth in the case plan.

(23) "Diligent efforts of social service agency" means reasonable efforts to provide social services or reunification services made by any social service agency that is a party to a case plan.

(24) "Diligent search" means the efforts of a social service agency to locate a parent or prospective parent

whose identity or location is unknown, initiated as soon as the social service agency is made aware of the existence of such parent, with the search progress reported at each court hearing until the parent is either identified and located or the court excuses further search.

(25) "Disposition hearing" means a hearing in which the court determines the most appropriate protections, services, and placement for the child in dependency cases.

(26) "Expedited termination of parental rights" means proceedings wherein a case plan with the goal of reunification is not being offered.

(27) "False report" means a report of abuse, neglect, or abandonment of a child to the central abuse hotline, which report is maliciously made for the purpose of:

(a) Harassing, embarrassing, or harming another person;

(b) Personal financial gain for the reporting person;

(c) Acquiring custody of a child; or

(d) Personal benefit for the reporting person in any other private dispute involving a child.

The term "false report" does not include a report of abuse, neglect, or abandonment of a child made in good faith to the central abuse hotline.

(28) "Family" means a collective body of persons, consisting of a child and a parent, legal custodian, or adult relative, in which:

(a) The persons reside in the same house or living unit; or

(b) The parent, legal custodian, or adult relative has a legal responsibility by blood, marriage, or court order to support or care for the child.

(29) "Foster care" means care provided a child in a foster family or boarding home, group home, agency boarding home, child care institution, or any combination thereof.

(30) "Harm" to a child's health or welfare can occur when any person:

(a) Inflicts or allows to be inflicted upon the child physical, mental, or emotional injury. In determining whether harm has occurred, the following factors must be considered in evaluating any physical, mental, or emotional injury to a child: the age of the child; any prior history of injuries to the child; the location of the injury on the body of the child; the multiplicity of the injury; and the type of trauma inflicted. Such injury includes, but is not limited to:

1. Willful acts that produce the following specific injuries:

a. Sprains, dislocations, or cartilage damage.

b. Bone or skull fractures.

c. Brain or spinal cord damage.

d. Intracranial hemorrhage or injury to other internal organs.

e. Asphyxiation, suffocation, or drowning.

f. Injury resulting from the use of a deadly weapon.

g. Burns or scalding.

h. Cuts, lacerations, punctures, or bites.

i. Permanent or temporary disfigurement.

j. Permanent or temporary loss or impairment of a body part or function.

As used in this subparagraph, the term "willful" refers to the intent to perform an action, not to the intent to achieve a result or to cause an injury.

2. Purposely giving a child poison, alcohol, drugs, or other substances that substantially affect the child's behavior, motor coordination, or judgment or that result in sickness or internal injury. For the purposes of this subparagraph, the term "drugs" means prescription drugs not prescribed for the child or not administered as prescribed, and controlled substances as outlined in Schedule I or Schedule II of s. 893.03.

3. Leaving a child without adult supervision or arrangement appropriate for the child's age or mental or physical condition, so that the child is unable to care for the child's own needs or another's basic needs or is unable to exercise good judgment in responding to any kind of physical or emotional crisis.

4. Inappropriate or excessively harsh disciplinary action that is likely to result in physical injury, mental injury as defined in this section, or emotional injury. The significance of any injury must be evaluated in light of the following factors: the age of the child; any prior history of injuries to the child; the location of the injury on the body of the child; the multiplicity of the injury; and the type of trauma inflicted. Corporal discipline may be considered excessive or abusive when it results in any of the following or other similar injuries:

a. Sprains, dislocations, or cartilage damage.

b. Bone or skull fractures.

c. Brain or spinal cord damage.

d. Intracranial hemorrhage or injury to other internal organs.

e. Asphyxiation, suffocation, or drowning.

f. Injury resulting from the use of a deadly weapon.

g. Burns or scalding.

h. Cuts, lacerations, punctures, or bites.

i. Permanent or temporary disfigurement.

j. Permanent or temporary loss or impairment of a body part or function.

k. Significant bruises or welts.

(b) Commits, or allows to be committed, sexual battery, as defined in chapter 794, or lewd or lascivious acts, as defined in chapter 800, against the child.

(c) Allows, encourages, or forces the sexual exploitation of a child, which includes allowing, encouraging, or forcing a child to:

1. Solicit for or engage in prostitution; or

2. Engage in a sexual performance, as defined by chapter 827.

(d) Exploits a child, or allows a child to be exploited, as provided in s. 450.151.

(e) Abandons the child. Within the context of the definition of "harm," the term "abandoned the child" or "abandonment of the child" means a situation in which the parent or legal custodian of a child or, in the absence of a parent or legal custodian, the caregiver, while being able, has made no significant contribution to the child's care and maintenance or has failed to establish or maintain a substantial and positive relationship with the child, or both. For purposes of this paragraph, "establish or maintain a substantial and positive relationship" includes, but is not limited to, frequent and regular contact with the child through frequent and regular visitation or frequent and regular communication to or with the child, and the exercise of parental rights and responsibilities. Marginal efforts and incidental or token visits or communications are not sufficient to establish or maintain a substantial and positive relationship with a child. The term "abandoned" does not include a surrendered newborn infant as described in s. 383.50, a child in need of services as defined in chapter 984, or a family in need of services as defined in chapter 984. The incarceration, repeated incarceration, or extended incarceration of a parent, legal custodian, or caregiver responsible for a child's welfare may support a finding of abandonment.

(f) Neglects the child. Within the context of the definition of "harm," the term "neglects the child" means that the parent or other person responsible for the child's welfare fails to supply the child with adequate food, clothing, shelter, or health care, although financially able to do so or although offered financial or other means to do so. However, a parent or legal custodian who, by reason of the legitimate practice of religious beliefs, does not provide specified medical treatment for a child may not be considered abusive or neglectful for that reason alone, but such an exception does not:

1. Eliminate the requirement that such a case be reported to the department;

2. Prevent the department from investigating such a case; or

3. Preclude a court from ordering, when the health of the child requires it, the provision of medical services by a physician, as defined in this section, or treatment by a duly accredited practitioner who relies solely on spiritual means for healing in accordance with the tenets and practices of a well-recognized church or religious organization.

(g) Exposes a child to a controlled substance or alcohol. Exposure to a controlled substance or alcohol is established by:

1. A test, administered at birth, which indicated that the child's blood, urine, or meconium contained any amount of alcohol or a controlled substance or metabolites of such substances, the presence of which was not the result of medical treatment administered to the mother or the newborn infant; or

2. Evidence of extensive, abusive, and chronic use of a controlled substance or alcohol by a parent when the child is demonstrably adversely affected by such usage.

As used in this paragraph, the term "controlled substance" means prescription drugs not prescribed for the parent or not administered as prescribed and controlled substances as outlined in Schedule I or Schedule II of s. 893.03.

(h) Uses mechanical devices, unreasonable restraints, or extended periods of isolation to control a child.

(i) Engages in violent behavior that demonstrates a wanton disregard for the presence of a child and could reasonably result in serious injury to the child.

(j) Negligently fails to protect a child in his or her care from inflicted physical, mental, or sexual injury caused by the acts of another.

(k) Has allowed a child's sibling to die as a result of abuse, abandonment, or neglect.

(l) Makes the child unavailable for the purpose of impeding or avoiding a protective investigation unless the court determines that the parent, legal custodian, or caregiver was fleeing from a situation involving domestic violence.

(31) "Impending danger" means a situation in which family behaviors, attitudes, motives, emotions, or situations pose a threat that may not be currently active but that can be anticipated to become active and to have severe effects on a child at any time.

(32) "Institutional child abuse or neglect" means situations of known or suspected child abuse or neglect in which the person allegedly perpetrating the child abuse or neglect is an employee of a private school, public or private day care center, residential home, institution, facility, or agency or any other person at such institution responsible for the child's care as defined in subsection (48).

(33) "Judge" means the circuit judge exercising jurisdiction pursuant to this chapter.

(34) "Legal custody" means a legal status created by a court which vests in a custodian of the person or guardian, whether an agency or an individual, the right to have physical custody of the child and the right and duty to protect, nurture, guide, and discipline the child and to provide him or her with food, shelter, education, and ordinary medical, dental, psychiatric, and psychological care.

(35) "Legal father" means a man married to the mother at the time of conception or birth of their child, unless paternity has been otherwise determined by a

court of competent jurisdiction. If the mother was not married to a man at the time of birth or conception of the child, the term means a man named on the birth certificate of the child pursuant to s. 382.013(2), a man determined by a court order to be the father of the child, or a man determined to be the father of the child by the Department of Revenue as provided in s. 409.256.

(36) "Licensed child-caring agency" means a person, society, association, or agency licensed by the department to care for, receive, and board children.

(37) "Licensed child-placing agency" means a person, society, association, or institution licensed by the department to care for, receive, or board children and to place children in a licensed child-caring institution or a foster or adoptive home.

(38) "Licensed health care professional" means a physician licensed under chapter 458, an osteopathic physician licensed under chapter 459, a nurse licensed under part I of chapter 464, a physician assistant licensed under chapter 458 or chapter 459, or a dentist licensed under chapter 466.

(39) "Likely to injure oneself" means that, as evidenced by violent or other actively self-destructive behavior, it is more likely than not that within a 24-hour period the child will attempt to commit suicide or inflict serious bodily harm on himself or herself.

(40) "Likely to injure others" means that it is more likely than not that within a 24-hour period the child will inflict serious and unjustified bodily harm on another person.

(41) "Mediation" means a process whereby a neutral third person called a mediator acts to encourage and facilitate the resolution of a dispute between two or more parties. It is an informal and nonadversarial process with the objective of helping the disputing parties reach a mutually acceptable and voluntary agreement. The role of the mediator includes, but is not limited to, assisting the parties in identifying issues, fostering joint problem solving, and exploring settlement alternatives.

(42) "Medical neglect" means the failure to provide or the failure to allow needed care as recommended by a health care practitioner for a physical injury, illness, medical condition, or impairment, or the failure to seek timely and appropriate medical care for a serious health problem that a reasonable person would have recognized as requiring professional medical attention. Medical neglect does not occur if the parent or legal guardian of the child has made reasonable attempts to obtain necessary health care services or the immediate health condition giving rise to the allegation of neglect is a known and expected complication of the child's diagnosis or treatment and:

(a) The recommended care offers limited net benefit to the child and the morbidity or other side effects of the treatment may be considered to be greater than the anticipated benefit; or

(b) The parent or legal guardian received conflicting medical recommendations for treatment from multiple practitioners and did not follow all recommendations.

(43) "Mental injury" means an injury to the intellectual or psychological capacity of a child as evidenced by a discernible and substantial impairment in the ability to function within the normal range of performance and behavior.

(44) "Necessary medical treatment" means care which is necessary within a reasonable degree of medical certainty to prevent the deterioration of a child's condition or to alleviate immediate pain of a child.

(45) "Neglect" occurs when a child is deprived of, or is allowed to be deprived of, necessary food, clothing, shelter, or medical treatment or a child is permitted to live in an environment when such deprivation or environment causes the child's physical, mental, or emotional health to be significantly impaired or to be in danger of being significantly impaired. The foregoing circumstances shall not be considered neglect if caused primarily by financial inability unless actual services for relief have been offered to and rejected by such person. A parent or legal custodian legitimately practicing religious beliefs in accordance with a recognized church or religious organization who thereby does not provide specific medical treatment for a child may not, for that reason alone, be considered a negligent parent or legal custodian; however, such an exception does not preclude a court from ordering the following services to be provided, when the health of the child so requires:

(a) Medical services from a licensed physician, dentist, optometrist, podiatric physician, or other qualified health care provider; or

(b) Treatment by a duly accredited practitioner who relies solely on spiritual means for healing in accordance with the tenets and practices of a well-recognized church or religious organization.
Neglect of a child includes acts or omissions.

(46) "Next of kin" means an adult relative of a child who is the child's brother, sister, grandparent, aunt, uncle, or first cousin.

(47) "Office" means the Office of Adoption and Child Protection within the Executive Office of the Governor.

(48) "Other person responsible for a child's welfare" includes the child's legal guardian or foster parent; an employee of any school, public or private child day care center, residential home, institution, facility, or agency; a law enforcement officer employed in any facility, service, or program for children that is operated or contracted by the Department of Juvenile Justice; or any other person legally responsible for the child's welfare in a residential setting; and also includes an adult sitter or relative entrusted with a child's care. For the purpose of departmental investigative jurisdiction, this definition does not include the following persons

when they are acting in an official capacity: law enforcement officers, except as otherwise provided in this subsection; employees of municipal or county detention facilities; or employees of the Department of Corrections.

(49) "Out-of-home" means a placement outside of the home of the parents or a parent.

(50) "Parent" means a woman who gives birth to a child and a man whose consent to the adoption of the child would be required under s. 63.062(1). The term "parent" also means legal father as defined in this section. If a child has been legally adopted, the term "parent" means the adoptive mother or father of the child. For purposes of this chapter only, when the phrase "parent or legal custodian" is used, it refers to rights or responsibilities of the parent and, only if there is no living parent with intact parental rights, to the rights or responsibilities of the legal custodian who has assumed the role of the parent. The term does not include an individual whose parental relationship to the child has been legally terminated, or an alleged or prospective parent, unless:

(a) The parental status falls within the terms of s. 39.503(1) or s. 63.062(1); or

(b) Parental status is applied for the purpose of determining whether the child has been abandoned.

(51) "Participant," for purposes of a shelter proceeding, dependency proceeding, or termination of parental rights proceeding, means any person who is not a party but who should receive notice of hearings involving the child, including the actual custodian of the child, the foster parents or the legal custodian of the child, identified prospective parents, and any other person whose participation may be in the best interest of the child. A community-based agency under contract with the department to provide protective services may be designated as a participant at the discretion of the court. Participants may be granted leave by the court to be heard without the necessity of filing a motion to intervene.

(52) "Party" means the parent or parents of the child, the petitioner, the department, the guardian ad litem or the representative of the guardian ad litem program when the program has been appointed, and the child. The presence of the child may be excused by order of the court when presence would not be in the child's best interest. Notice to the child may be excused by order of the court when the age, capacity, or other condition of the child is such that the notice would be meaningless or detrimental to the child.

(53) "Permanency goal" means the living arrangement identified for the child to return to or identified as the permanent living arrangement of the child. The permanency goal is also the case plan goal. If concurrent case planning is being used, reunification may be pursued at the same time that another permanency goal is pursued.

(54) "Permanency plan" means the plan that establishes the placement intended to serve as the child's permanent home.

(55) "Permanent guardian" means the relative or other adult in a permanent guardianship of a dependent child under s. 39.6221.

(56) "Permanent guardianship of a dependent child" means a legal relationship that a court creates under s. 39.6221 between a child and a relative or other adult approved by the court which is intended to be permanent and self-sustaining through the transfer of parental rights with respect to the child relating to protection, education, care and control of the person, custody of the person, and decisionmaking on behalf of the child.

(57) "Physical injury" means death, permanent or temporary disfigurement, or impairment of any bodily part.

(58) "Physician" means any licensed physician, dentist, podiatric physician, or optometrist and includes any intern or resident.

(59) "Preliminary screening" means the gathering of preliminary information to be used in determining a child's need for further evaluation or assessment or for referral for other substance abuse services through means such as psychosocial interviews; urine and breathalyzer screenings; and reviews of available educational, delinquency, and dependency records of the child.

(60) "Present danger" means a significant and clearly observable family condition that is occurring at the current moment and is already endangering or threatening to endanger the child. Present danger threats are conspicuous and require that an immediate protective action be taken to ensure the child's safety.

(61) "Preventive services" means social services and other supportive and rehabilitative services provided to the parent or legal custodian of the child and to the child for the purpose of averting the removal of the child from the home or disruption of a family which will or could result in the placement of a child in foster care. Social services and other supportive and rehabilitative services shall promote the child's developmental needs and need for physical, mental, and emotional health and a safe, stable, living environment, shall promote family autonomy, and shall strengthen family life, whenever possible.

(62) "Prospective parent" means a person who claims to be, or has been identified as, a person who may be a mother or a father of a child.

(63) "Protective investigation" means the acceptance of a report alleging child abuse, abandonment, or neglect, as defined in this chapter, by the central abuse hotline or the acceptance of a report of other dependency by the department; the investigation of each report; the determination of whether action by the court is warranted; the determination of the disposition of each report without court or public agency action when appropriate; and the referral of a child to another public or private agency when appropriate.

(64) "Protective investigator" means an authorized agent of the department who receives and investigates

reports of child abuse, abandonment, or neglect; who, as a result of the investigation, may recommend that a dependency petition be filed for the child; and who performs other duties necessary to carry out the required actions of the protective investigation function.

(65) "Protective supervision" means a legal status in dependency cases which permits the child to remain safely in his or her own home or other nonlicensed placement under the supervision of an agent of the department and which must be reviewed by the court during the period of supervision.

(66) "Qualified professional" means a physician or a physician assistant licensed under chapter 458 or chapter 459; a psychiatrist licensed under chapter 458 or chapter 459; a psychologist as defined in s. 490.003(7) or a professional licensed under chapter 491; or a psychiatric nurse as defined in s. 394.455.

(67) "Relative" means a grandparent, great-grandparent, sibling, first cousin, aunt, uncle, great-aunt, great-uncle, niece, or nephew, whether related by the whole or half blood, by affinity, or by adoption. The term does not include a stepparent.

(68) "Reunification services" means social services and other supportive and rehabilitative services provided to the parent of the child, to the child, and, where appropriate, to the relative placement, nonrelative placement, or foster parents of the child, for the purpose of enabling a child who has been placed in out-of-home care to safely return to his or her parent at the earliest possible time. The health and safety of the child shall be the paramount goal of social services and other supportive and rehabilitative services. The services shall promote the child's need for physical, developmental, mental, and emotional health and a safe, stable, living environment; shall promote family autonomy; and shall strengthen family life, whenever possible.

(69) "Safety plan" means a plan created to control present or impending danger using the least intrusive means appropriate to protect a child when a parent, caregiver, or legal custodian is unavailable, unwilling, or unable to do so.

(70) "Secretary" means the Secretary of Children and Families.

(71) "Sexual abuse of a child" for purposes of finding a child to be dependent means one or more of the following acts:

(a) Any penetration, however slight, of the vagina or anal opening of one person by the penis of another person, whether or not there is the emission of semen.

(b) Any sexual contact between the genitals or anal opening of one person and the mouth or tongue of another person.

(c) Any intrusion by one person into the genitals or anal opening of another person, including the use of any object for this purpose, except that this does not include any act intended for a valid medical purpose.

(d) The intentional touching of the genitals or intimate parts, including the breasts, genital area, groin, inner thighs, and buttocks, or the clothing covering them, of either the child or the perpetrator, except that this does not include:

1. Any act which may reasonably be construed to be a normal caregiver responsibility, any interaction with, or affection for a child; or

2. Any act intended for a valid medical purpose.

(e) The intentional masturbation of the perpetrator's genitals in the presence of a child.

(f) The intentional exposure of the perpetrator's genitals in the presence of a child, or any other sexual act intentionally perpetrated in the presence of a child, if such exposure or sexual act is for the purpose of sexual arousal or gratification, aggression, degradation, or other similar purpose.

(g) The sexual exploitation of a child, which includes the act of a child offering to engage in or engaging in prostitution, or the act of allowing, encouraging, or forcing a child to:

1. Solicit for or engage in prostitution;

2. Engage in a sexual performance, as defined by chapter 827; or

3. Participate in the trade of human trafficking as provided in s. 787.06(3)(g).

(72) "Shelter" means a placement with a relative or a nonrelative, or in a licensed home or facility, for the temporary care of a child who is alleged to be or who has been found to be dependent, pending court disposition before or after adjudication.

(73) "Shelter hearing" means a hearing in which the court determines whether probable cause exists to keep a child in shelter status pending further investigation of the case.

(74) "Sibling" means:

(a) A child who shares a birth parent or legal parent with one or more other children; or

(b) A child who has lived together in a family with one or more other children whom he or she identifies as siblings.

(75) "Social service agency" means the department, a licensed child-caring agency, or a licensed child-placing agency.

(76) "Social worker" means any person who has a bachelor's, master's, or doctoral degree in social work.

(77) "Substance abuse" means using, without medical reason, any psychoactive or mood-altering drug, including alcohol, in such a manner as to induce impairment resulting in dysfunctional social behavior.

(78) "Substantial compliance" means that the circumstances which caused the creation of the case plan have been significantly remedied to the extent that the well-being and safety of the child will not be endangered upon the child's remaining with or being returned to the child's parent.

(79) "Taken into custody" means the status of a child immediately when temporary physical control

over the child is attained by a person authorized by law, pending the child's release or placement.

(80) "Temporary legal custody" means the relationship that a court creates between a child and an adult relative of the child, legal custodian, agency, or other person approved by the court until a more permanent arrangement is ordered. Temporary legal custody confers upon the custodian the right to have temporary physical custody of the child and the right and duty to protect, nurture, guide, and discipline the child and to provide the child with food, shelter, and education, and ordinary medical, dental, psychiatric, and psychological care, unless these rights and duties are otherwise enlarged or limited by the court order establishing the temporary legal custody relationship.

(81) "Victim" means any child who has sustained or is threatened with physical, mental, or emotional injury identified in a report involving child abuse, neglect, or abandonment, or child-on-child sexual abuse.

HISTORY:
S. 1, ch. 26880, 1951; ss. 1, 2, ch. 67-585; s. 3, ch. 69-353; s. 4, ch. 69-365; ss. 19, 35, ch. 69-106; s. 1, ch. 71-117; s. 1, ch. 71-130; s. 10, ch. 71-355; ss. 4, 5, ch. 72-179; ss. 19, 30, ch. 72-404; ss. 2, 23, ch. 73-231; s. 1, ch. 74-368; ss. 15, 27, 28, ch. 75-48; s. 4, ch. 77-147; s. 2, ch. 78-414; s. 9, ch. 79-164; s. 2, ch. 79-203; s. 1, ch. 80-290; ss. 1, 17, ch. 81-218; ss. 4, 15, ch. 84-311; s. 4, ch. 85-80; s. 2, ch. 85-206; ss. 73, 78, ch. 86-220; s. 1, ch. 87-133; s. 1, ch. 87-289; s. 12, ch. 87-397; s. 1, ch. 88-319; s. 10, ch. 88-337; s. 2, ch. 90-53; s. 3, ch. 90-208; s. 3, ch. 90-306; s. 2, ch. 90-309; s. 69, ch. 91-45; s. 1, ch. 91-183; s. 1, ch. 92-158; s. 1, ch. 92-170; ss. 1, 4(1st), 14, ch. 92-287; s. 13, ch. 93-39; s. 6, ch. 93-230; s. 1, ch. 94-164; s. 11, ch. 94-209; s. 50, ch. 94-232; s. 1333, ch. 95-147; s. 8, ch. 95-152; s. 1, ch. 95-212; s. 4, ch. 95-228; s. 1, ch. 95-266; ss. 3, 43, ch. 95-267; s. 3, ch. 96-369; s. 2, ch. 96-398; s. 20, ch. 96-402; s. 23, ch. 97-96; s. 158, ch. 97-101; s. 44, ch. 97-190; s. 4, ch. 97-234; s. 111, ch. 97-238; s. 1, ch. 97-276; s. 1, ch. 98-49; s. 176, ch. 98-166; s. 7, ch. 98-280; s. 20, ch. 98-403; s. 15, ch. 99-2; s. 3, ch. 99-168; s. 2, ch. 99-186; s. 4, ch. 99-193; s. 15, ch. 2000-139; s. 2, ch. 2000-188; s. 82, ch. 2000-318; s. 9, ch. 2000-320; s. 14, ch. 2002-1; s. 2, ch. 2006-62, eff. July 1, 2006; s. 1, ch. 2006-86, eff. July 1, 2006; s. 4, ch. 2006-194, eff. July 1, 2006; s. 4, ch. 2007-124, eff. July 1, 2007; s. 1, ch. 2008-90, eff. July 1, 2008; s. 1, ch. 2008-154, eff. July 1, 2008; s. 1, ch. 2008-245, eff. June 30, 2008; s. 1, ch. 2009-21, eff. July 7, 2009; s. 3, ch. 2012-105, eff. Jan. 1, 2013; s. 1, ch. 2012-178, eff. July 1, 2012; ss. 11, 11, ch. 2014-19, eff. July 1, 2014; s. 14, ch. 2014-160, eff. Oct. 1, 2014; s. 3, ch. 2014-224, eff. July 1, 2014; s. 2, ch. 2015-34, eff. May 14, 2015; s. 1, ch. 2016-24, eff. Oct. 1, 2016; s. 1, ch. 2016-71, eff. July 1, 2016; s. 11, ch. 2016-105, eff. July 1, 2016; s. 1, ch. 2016-241, eff. July 1, 2016; s. 2, ch. 2017-151, eff. July 1, 2017.

Editor's notes.
Section 1, ch. 2012-105, provides: "This act may be cited as the 'Florida Safe Harbor Act.'"

§ 39.011. Immunity from liability.

(1) In no case shall employees or agents of the department or a social service agency acting in good faith be liable for damages as a result of failing to provide services agreed to under the case plan unless the failure to provide such services occurs as a result of bad faith or malicious purpose or occurs in a manner exhibiting wanton and willful disregard of human rights, safety, or property.

(2) The inability or failure of the department or of a social service agency or the employees or agents of the social service agency to provide the services agreed to under the case plan shall not render the state or the social service agency liable for damages unless such failure to provide services occurs in a manner exhibiting wanton or willful disregard of human rights, safety, or property.

(3) A member or agent of a citizen review panel acting in good faith is not liable for damages as a result of any review or recommendation with regard to a dependency matter unless such member or agent exhibits wanton and willful disregard of human rights or safety, or property.

HISTORY:
S. 9, ch. 87-289; s. 13, ch. 90-306; s. 7, ch. 97-95; s. 21, ch. 98-403; s. 5, ch. 99-193.

Editor's notes.
Former s. 39.455.

§ 39.012. Rules for implementation.

The department shall adopt rules for the efficient and effective management of all programs, services, facilities, and functions necessary for implementing this chapter. Such rules may not conflict with the Florida Rules of Juvenile Procedure. All rules and policies must conform to accepted standards of care and treatment.

HISTORY:
S. 2, ch. 87-289; s. 4, ch. 90-208; s. 12, ch. 94-209; s. 1, ch. 97-101; s. 120, ch. 97-238; s. 22, ch. 98-403.

§ 39.0121. Specific rulemaking authority.

Pursuant to the requirements of s. 120.536, the department is specifically authorized to adopt, amend, and repeal administrative rules which implement or interpret law or policy, or describe the procedure and practice requirements necessary to implement this chapter, including, but not limited to, the following:

(1) Background screening of department employees and applicants; criminal records checks of prospective foster and adoptive parents; and drug testing of protective investigators.

(2) Reporting of child abuse, neglect, and abandonment; reporting of child-on-child sexual abuse; false reporting; child protective investigations; taking a child into protective custody; and shelter procedures.

(3) Confidentiality and retention of department records; access to records; and record requests.

(4) Department and client trust funds.

(5) Requesting of services from child protection teams.

(6) Consent to and provision of medical care and treatment for children in the care of the department.

(7) Federal funding requirements and procedures; foster care and adoption subsidies; and subsidized independent living.

(8) Agreements with law enforcement and other state agencies; access to the National Crime Information Center (NCIC); and access to the parent locator service.

(9) Licensing, registration, and certification of child day care providers, shelter and foster homes, and residential child-caring and child-placing agencies.

(10) The Intensive Crisis Counseling Program and any other early intervention programs and kinship care assistance programs.

(11) Department contracts, pilot programs, and demonstration projects.

(12) Legal and casework procedures, including, but not limited to, mediation, diligent search, stipulations, consents, surrenders, and default, with respect to dependency, termination of parental rights, adoption, guardianship, and kinship care proceedings.

(13) Legal and casework management of cases involving in-home supervision and out-of-home care, including judicial reviews, administrative reviews, case plans, and any other documentation or procedures required by federal or state law.

(14) Injunctions and other protective orders, domestic-violence-related cases, and certification of domestic violence centers.

(15) Provision for making available to all physical custodians and family services counselors the information required by s. 39.6012(2) and for ensuring that this information follows the child until permanency has been achieved.

(16) Provisions for reporting, locating, recovering, and stabilizing children whose whereabouts become unknown while they are involved with the department and for preventing recurrences of such incidents. At a minimum, the rules must:

(a) Provide comprehensive, explicit, and consistent guidelines to be followed by the department's employees and contracted providers when the whereabouts of a child involved with the department are unknown.

(b) Include criteria to determine when a child is missing for purposes of making a report to a law enforcement agency, and require that in all cases in which a law enforcement agency has accepted a case for criminal investigation pursuant to s. 39.301(2)(c) and the child's whereabouts are unknown, the child shall be considered missing and a report made.

(c) Include steps to be taken by employees and contracted providers to ensure and provide evidence that parents and guardians have been advised of the requirements of s. 787.04(3) and that violations are reported.

HISTORY:
S. 23, ch. 98-403; s. 6, ch. 99-193; s. 2, ch. 2006-86, eff. July 1, 2006; s. 2, ch. 2008-245, eff. June 30, 2008; s. 1, ch. 2010-210, eff. July 1, 2010; s. 41, ch. 2011-213, eff. July 1, 2011.

§ 39.013. Procedures and jurisdiction; right to counsel.

(1) All procedures, including petitions, pleadings, subpoenas, summonses, and hearings, in this chapter shall be conducted according to the Florida Rules of Juvenile Procedure unless otherwise provided by law. Parents must be informed by the court of their right to counsel in dependency proceedings at each stage of the dependency proceedings. Parents who are unable to afford counsel must be appointed counsel.

(2) The circuit court has exclusive original jurisdiction of all proceedings under this chapter, of a child voluntarily placed with a licensed child-caring agency, a licensed child-placing agency, or the department, and of the adoption of children whose parental rights have been terminated under this chapter. Jurisdiction attaches when the initial shelter petition, dependency petition, or termination of parental rights petition, or a petition for an injunction to prevent child abuse issued pursuant to s. 39.504, is filed or when a child is taken into the custody of the department. The circuit court may assume jurisdiction over any such proceeding regardless of whether the child was in the physical custody of both parents, was in the sole legal or physical custody of only one parent, caregiver, or some other person, or was not in the physical or legal custody of any person when the event or condition occurred that brought the child to the attention of the court. When the court obtains jurisdiction of any child who has been found to be dependent, the court shall retain jurisdiction, unless relinquished by its order, until the child reaches 21 years of age, or 22 years of age if the child has a disability, with the following exceptions:

(a) If a young adult chooses to leave foster care upon reaching 18 years of age.

(b) If a young adult does not meet the eligibility requirements to remain in foster care under s. 39.6251 or chooses to leave care under that section.

(c) If a young adult petitions the court at any time before his or her 19th birthday requesting the court's continued jurisdiction, the juvenile court may retain jurisdiction under this chapter for a period not to exceed 1 year following the young adult's 18th birthday for the purpose of determining whether appropriate services that were required to be provided to the young adult before reaching 18 years of age have been provided.

(d) If a petition for special immigrant juvenile status and an application for adjustment of status have been filed on behalf of a foster child and the petition and application have not been granted by the time the child reaches 18 years of age, the court may retain jurisdiction over the dependency case solely for the purpose of allowing the continued consideration of the petition and application by federal authorities. Review hearings for the child shall be set solely for the purpose of determining the status of the petition and application. The court's jurisdiction terminates upon the final decision of the federal authorities. Retention of jurisdiction in this instance does not affect the services available to a young adult under s. 409.1451. The court may not retain jurisdiction of the case after the immigrant child's 22nd birthday.

(3) When a child is under the jurisdiction of the circuit court pursuant to this chapter, the circuit court assigned to handle dependency matters may exercise the general and equitable jurisdiction over guardianship proceedings under chapter 744 and proceedings for temporary custody of minor children by extended family under chapter 751.

(4) Orders entered pursuant to this chapter which affect the placement of, access to, parental time with, adoption of, or parental rights and responsibilities for a minor child shall take precedence over other orders entered in civil actions or proceedings. However, if the court has terminated jurisdiction, the order may be subsequently modified by a court of competent jurisdiction in any other civil action or proceeding affecting placement of, access to, parental time with, adoption of, or parental rights and responsibilities for the same minor child.

(5) The court shall expedite the resolution of the placement issue in cases involving a child who has been removed from the parent and placed in an out-of-home placement.

(6) The court shall expedite the judicial handling of all cases when the child has been removed from the parent and placed in an out-of-home placement.

(7) Children removed from their homes shall be provided equal treatment with respect to goals, objectives, services, and case plans, without regard to the location of their placement.

(8) For any child who remains in the custody of the department, the court shall, within the month which constitutes the beginning of the 6-month period before the child's 18th birthday, hold a hearing to review the progress of the child while in the custody of the department.

(9)(a) At each stage of the proceedings under this chapter, the court shall advise the parents of the right to counsel. The court shall appoint counsel for indigent parents. The court shall ascertain whether the right to counsel is understood. When right to counsel is waived, the court shall determine whether the waiver is knowing and intelligent. The court shall enter its findings in writing with respect to the appointment or waiver of counsel for indigent parents or the waiver of counsel by nonindigent parents.

(b) Once counsel has entered an appearance or been appointed by the court to represent the parent of the child, the attorney shall continue to represent the parent throughout the proceedings. If the attor-

ney-client relationship is discontinued, the court shall advise the parent of the right to have new counsel retained or appointed for the remainder of the proceedings.

(c)1. A waiver of counsel may not be accepted if it appears that the parent is unable to make an intelligent and understanding choice because of mental condition, age, education, experience, the nature or complexity of the case, or other factors.

2. A waiver of counsel made in court must be of record.

3. If a waiver of counsel is accepted at any hearing or proceeding, the offer of assistance of counsel must be renewed by the court at each subsequent stage of the proceedings at which the parent appears without counsel.

(d) This subsection does not apply to any parent who has voluntarily executed a written surrender of the child and consents to the entry of a court order terminating parental rights.

(10) Court-appointed counsel representing indigent parents at shelter hearings shall be paid from state funds appropriated by general law.

(11) The court shall encourage the Statewide Guardian Ad Litem Office to provide greater representation to those children who are within 1 year of transferring out of foster care.

(12) The department shall be represented by counsel in each dependency proceeding. Through its attorneys, the department shall make recommendations to the court on issues before the court and may support its recommendations through testimony and other evidence by its own employees, employees of sheriff's offices providing child protection services, employees of its contractors, employees of its contractor's subcontractors, or from any other relevant source.

HISTORY:
  S. 20, ch. 78-414; s. 5, ch. 84-311; s. 4, ch. 87-289; s. 4, ch. 90-306; s. 2, ch. 92-158; s. 3, ch. 94-164; s. 5, ch. 95-228; s. 8, ch. 98-280; s. 24, ch. 98-403; s. 7, ch. 99-193; s. 16, ch. 2000-139; s. 1, ch. 2002-216; s. 1, ch. 2005-179; s. 3, ch. 2005-239; s. 3, ch. 2006-86, eff. July 1, 2006; s. 5, ch. 2006-194, eff. July 1, 2006; s. 2, ch. 2012-178, eff. July 1, 2012; s. 2, ch. 2013-178, eff. Jan. 1, 2014; s. 4, ch. 2014-224, eff. July 1, 2014; s. 3, ch. 2017-151, eff. July 1, 2017.

Editor's notes.
  Former s. 39.40.

§ 39.01305. Appointment of an attorney for a dependent child with certain special needs.

(1)(a) The Legislature finds that:

1. All children in proceedings under this chapter have important interests at stake, such as health, safety, and well-being and the need to obtain permanency.

2. A dependent child who has certain special needs has a particular need for an attorney to represent the dependent child in proceedings under this chapter, as well as in fair hearings and

appellate proceedings, so that the attorney may address the child's medical and related needs and the services and supports necessary for the child to live successfully in the community.

(b) The Legislature recognizes the existence of organizations that provide attorney representation to children in certain jurisdictions throughout the state. Further, the statewide Guardian Ad Litem Program provides best interest representation for dependent children in every jurisdiction in accordance with state and federal law. The Legislature, therefore, does not intend that funding provided for representation under this section supplant proven and existing organizations representing children. Instead, the Legislature intends that funding provided for representation under this section be an additional resource for the representation of more children in these jurisdictions, to the extent necessary to meet the requirements of this chapter, with the cooperation of existing local organizations or through the expansion of those organizations. The Legislature encourages the expansion of pro bono representation for children. This section is not intended to limit the ability of a pro bono attorney to appear on behalf of a child.

(2) As used in this section, the term "dependent child" means a child who is subject to any proceeding under this chapter. The term does not require that a child be adjudicated dependent for purposes of this section.

(3) An attorney shall be appointed for a dependent child who:

(a) Resides in a skilled nursing facility or is being considered for placement in a skilled nursing home;

(b) Is prescribed a psychotropic medication but declines assent to the psychotropic medication;

(c) Has a diagnosis of a developmental disability as defined in s. 393.063;

(d) Is being placed in a residential treatment center or being considered for placement in a residential treatment center; or

(e) Is a victim of human trafficking as defined in s. 787.06(2)(d).

(4)(a) Before a court may appoint an attorney, who may be compensated pursuant to this section, the court must request a recommendation from the Statewide Guardian Ad Litem Office for an attorney who is willing to represent a child without additional compensation. If such an attorney is available within 15 days after the court's request, the court must appoint that attorney. However, the court may appoint a compensated attorney within the 15-day period if the Statewide Guardian Ad Litem Office informs the court that it will not be able to recommend an attorney within that time period.

(b) After an attorney is appointed, the appointment continues in effect until the attorney is allowed to withdraw or is discharged by the court or until the case is dismissed. An attorney who is appointed under this section to represent the child shall provide the complete range of legal services, from the removal from home or from the initial appointment through all available appellate proceedings. With the permission of the court, the attorney for the dependent child may arrange for supplemental or separate counsel to represent the child in appellate proceedings. A court order appointing an attorney under this section must be in writing.

(5) Except if the attorney has agreed to provide pro bono services, an appointed attorney or organization must be adequately compensated and provided with access to funding for expert witnesses, depositions, and other costs of litigation. Payment to an attorney is subject to appropriations and subject to review by the Justice Administrative Commission for reasonableness. The Justice Administrative Commission shall contract with attorneys appointed by the court. Attorney fees may not exceed $1,000 per child per year.

(6) The department shall develop procedures to identify a dependent child who has a special need specified under subsection (3) and to request that a court appoint an attorney for the child.

(7) The department may adopt rules to administer this section.

(8) This section does not limit the authority of the court to appoint an attorney for a dependent child in a proceeding under this chapter.

(9) Implementation of this section is subject to appropriations expressly made for that purpose.

HISTORY:
S. 1, ch. 2014-227, eff. July 1, 2014.

§ 39.0131. Permanent mailing address designation.

Upon the first appearance before the court, each party shall provide to the court a permanent mailing address. The court shall advise each party that this address will be used by the court and the petitioner for notice purposes unless and until the party notifies the court and the petitioner in writing of a new mailing address.

HISTORY:
S. 11, ch. 94-164; s. 25, ch. 98-403.

Editor's notes.
Former s. 39.4057.

§ 39.0132. Oaths, records, and confidential information.

(1) The judge, clerks or deputy clerks, or authorized agents of the department shall each have the power to administer oaths and affirmations.

(2) The court shall make and keep records of all cases brought before it pursuant to this chapter and shall preserve the records pertaining to a dependent child until 7 years after the last entry was made, or until the child is 18 years of age, whichever date is first

reached, and may then destroy them, except that records of cases where orders were entered permanently depriving a parent of the custody of a juvenile shall be preserved permanently. The court shall make official records, consisting of all petitions and orders filed in a case arising pursuant to this chapter and any other pleadings, certificates, proofs of publication, summonses, warrants, and other writs which may be filed therein.

(3) The clerk shall keep all court records required by this chapter separate from other records of the circuit court. All court records required by this chapter shall not be open to inspection by the public. All records shall be inspected only upon order of the court by persons deemed by the court to have a proper interest therein, except that, subject to the provisions of s. 63.162, a child and the parents of the child and their attorneys, guardian ad litem, law enforcement agencies, and the department and its designees shall always have the right to inspect and copy any official record pertaining to the child. The Justice Administrative Commission may inspect court dockets required by this chapter as necessary to audit compensation of court-appointed attorneys. If the docket is insufficient for purposes of the audit, the commission may petition the court for additional documentation as necessary and appropriate. The court may permit authorized representatives of recognized organizations compiling statistics for proper purposes to inspect and make abstracts from official records, under whatever conditions upon their use and disposition the court may deem proper, and may punish by contempt proceedings any violation of those conditions.

(4)(a)1. All information obtained pursuant to this part in the discharge of official duty by any judge, employee of the court, authorized agent of the department, correctional probation officer, or law enforcement agent is confidential and exempt from s. 119.07(1) and may not be disclosed to anyone other than the authorized personnel of the court, the department and its designees, correctional probation officers, law enforcement agents, guardian ad litem, and others entitled under this chapter to receive that information, except upon order of the court.

2.a. The following information held by a guardian ad litem is confidential and exempt from s. 119.07(1) and s. 24(a), Art. I of the State Constitution:

(I) Medical, mental health, substance abuse, child care, education, law enforcement, court, social services, and financial records.

(II) Any other information maintained by a guardian ad litem which is identified as confidential information under this chapter.

b. Such confidential and exempt information may not be disclosed to anyone other than the authorized personnel of the court, the department and its designees, correctional probation officers, law enforcement agents, guardians ad litem, and others entitled under this chapter to receive that information, except upon order of the court.

(b) The department shall disclose to the school superintendent the presence of any child in the care and custody or under the jurisdiction or supervision of the department who has a known history of criminal sexual behavior with other juveniles; is an alleged juvenile sex offender, as defined in s. 39.01; or has pled guilty or nolo contendere to, or has been found to have committed, a violation of chapter 794, chapter 796, chapter 800, s. 827.071, or s. 847.0133, regardless of adjudication. Any employee of a district school board who knowingly and willfully discloses such information to an unauthorized person commits a misdemeanor of the second degree, punishable as provided in s. 775.082 or s. 775.083.

(5) All orders of the court entered pursuant to this chapter shall be in writing and signed by the judge, except that the clerk or deputy clerk may sign a summons or notice to appear.

(6) No court record of proceedings under this chapter shall be admissible in evidence in any other civil or criminal proceeding, except that:

(a) Records of proceedings under this chapter forming a part of the record on appeal shall be used in the appellate court in the manner hereinafter provided.

(b) Records necessary therefor shall be admissible in evidence in any case in which a person is being tried upon a charge of having committed perjury.

(c) Records of proceedings under this chapter may be used to prove disqualification pursuant to s. 435.06 and for proof regarding such disqualification in a chapter 120 proceeding.

(d) A final order entered pursuant to an adjudicatory hearing is admissible in evidence in any subsequent civil proceeding relating to placement of, access to, parental time with, adoption of, or parental rights and responsibilities for the same child or a sibling of that child.

(e) Evidence admitted in any proceeding under this chapter may be admissible in evidence when offered by any party in a subsequent civil proceeding relating to placement of, access to, parental time with, adoption of, or parental rights and responsibilities for the same child or a sibling of that child if:

1. Notice is given to the opposing party or opposing party's counsel of the intent to offer the evidence and a copy of such evidence is delivered to the opposing party or the opposing party's counsel; and

2. The evidence is otherwise admissible in the subsequent civil proceeding.

(7) Final orders, records, and evidence in any proceeding under this chapter which are subsequently admitted in evidence pursuant to subsection (6) remain subject to subsections (3) and (4).

HISTORY:
S. 20, ch. 78-414; s. 15, ch. 79-164; s. 3, ch. 87-238; s. 40, ch. 89-526; s. 7, ch. 90-208; s. 13, ch. 90-360; s. 16, ch. 91-57; s. 18, ch. 93-39; s. 32, ch. 95-228; s. 119, ch. 95-418; s. 3, ch. 96-268; s. 16, ch. 96-406; s. 1, ch. 98-158; s. 26, ch. 98-403; s. 16, ch. 99-2; s. 8, ch. 99-193; s. 10, ch. 99-284; s. 17, ch. 2000-139; s. 2, ch. 2005-213; s. 24, ch. 2005-236; s. 4, ch. 2005-239; s. 12, ch. 2008-4, eff. July 1, 2008; s. 1, ch. 2010-75, eff. Oct. 1, 2010.

Editor's notes.
Former s. 39.411.

§ 39.0133. Court and witness fees.

In all proceedings under this chapter, no court fees shall be charged against, and no witness fees shall be allowed to, any party to a petition or any parent or legal custodian or child named in a summons. Other witnesses shall be paid the witness fees fixed by law.

HISTORY:
S. 20, ch. 78-414; s. 27, ch. 98-403.

Editor's notes.
Former s. 39.414.

§ 39.0134. Appointed counsel; compensation.

(1) If counsel is entitled to receive compensation for representation pursuant to a court appointment in a dependency proceeding or a termination of parental rights proceeding pursuant to this chapter, compensation shall be paid in accordance with s. 27.5304. The state may acquire and enforce a lien upon court-ordered payment of attorney's fees and costs in the same manner prescribed in s. 938.29.

(2)(a) A parent whose child is dependent, regardless of whether adjudication was withheld, or whose parental rights are terminated and who has received the assistance of the office of criminal conflict and civil regional counsel, or any other court-appointed attorney, or who has received due process services after being found indigent for costs, shall be liable for payment of the assessed application fee under s. 57.082, together with reasonable attorney's fees and costs as determined by the court.

(b) If reasonable attorney's fees or costs are assessed, the court, at its discretion, may make payment of the fees or costs part of any case plan in dependency proceedings. However, a case plan may not remain open for the sole issue of payment of attorney's fees or costs. At the court's discretion, a lien upon court-ordered payment of attorney's fees and costs may be ordered by the court and enforced in the same manner prescribed in s. 938.29.

(c) The clerk of the court shall transfer monthly all attorney's fees and costs collected under this subsection to the Department of Revenue for deposit into the Indigent Civil Defense Trust Fund, to be used as appropriated by the Legislature and consistent with s. 27.5111.

HISTORY:
S. 12, ch. 84-311; s. 9, ch. 87-289; s. 28, ch. 98-403; s. 9, ch. 99-193; s. 57, ch. 2003-402; s. 36, ch. 2004-265; s. 19, ch. 2010-162, eff. July 1, 2010; s. 2, ch. 2016-10, eff. May 10, 2016.

Editor's notes.
Former ss. 39.415, 39.474.

§ 39.0135. Operations and Maintenance Trust Fund.

The department shall deposit all child support payments made to the department pursuant to this chapter into the Operations and Maintenance Trust Fund. The purpose of this funding is to care for children who are committed to the temporary legal custody of the department.

HISTORY:
S. 87, ch. 86-220; s. 10, ch. 90-306; s. 16, ch. 96-418; s. 167, ch. 97-101; s. 29, ch. 98-403.

Editor's notes.
Former s. 39.418.

§ 39.0136. Time limitations; continuances.

(1) The Legislature finds that time is of the essence for establishing permanency for a child in the dependency system. Time limitations are a right of the child which may not be waived, extended, or continued at the request of any party except as provided in this section.

(2) The time limitations in this chapter do not include:

(a) Periods of delay resulting from a continuance granted at the request of the child's counsel or the child's guardian ad litem or, if the child is of sufficient capacity to express reasonable consent, at the request or with the consent of the child. The court must consider the best interests of the child when determining periods of delay under this section.

(b) Periods of delay resulting from a continuance granted at the request of any party if the continuance is granted:

1. Because of an unavailability of evidence that is material to the case if the requesting party has exercised due diligence to obtain evidence and there are substantial grounds to believe that the evidence will be available within 30 days. However, if the requesting party is not prepared to proceed within 30 days, any other party may move for issuance of an order to show cause or the court on its own motion may impose appropriate sanctions, which may include dismissal of the petition.

2. To allow the requesting party additional time to prepare the case and additional time is justified because of an exceptional circumstance.

(c) Reasonable periods of delay necessary to accomplish notice of the hearing to the child's parent or legal custodian; however, the petitioner shall continue regular efforts to provide notice to the parents during the periods of delay.

(3) Notwithstanding subsection (2), in order to expedite permanency for a child, the total time allowed for continuances or extensions of time may not exceed 60 days within any 12-month period for proceedings conducted under this chapter. A continuance or extension of time may be granted only for extraordinary circumstances in which it is necessary to preserve the constitutional rights of a party or if substantial evidence exists to demonstrate that without granting a continuance or extension of time the child's best interests will be harmed.

(4) Notwithstanding subsection (2), a continuance or an extension of time is limited to the number of days absolutely necessary to complete a necessary task in order to preserve the rights of a party or the best interests of a child.

HISTORY:
S. 4, ch. 2006-86, eff. July 1, 2006.

§ 39.0137. Federal law; rulemaking authority.

(1) This chapter does not supersede the requirements of the Indian Child Welfare Act, 25 U.S.C. ss. 1901 et seq., or the Multi-Ethnic Placement Act of 1994, Pub. L. No. 103-382, as amended, or the implementing regulations.

(2) The department is encouraged to enter into agreements with recognized American Indian tribes in order to facilitate the implementation of the Indian Child Welfare Act.

HISTORY:
S. 5, ch. 2006-86, eff. July 1, 2006; s. 20, ch. 2012-116, eff. July 1, 2012.

§ 39.0138. Criminal history and other records checks; limit on placement of a child.

(1) The department shall conduct a records check through the State Automated Child Welfare Information System (SACWIS) and a local and statewide criminal history records check on all persons, including parents, being considered by the department for placement of a child under this chapter, including all nonrelative placement decisions, and all members of the household, 12 years of age and older, of the person being considered. For purposes of this section, a criminal history records check may include, but is not limited to, submission of fingerprints to the Department of Law Enforcement for processing and forwarding to the Federal Bureau of Investigation for state and national criminal history information, and local criminal records checks through local law enforcement agencies of all household members 18 years of age and older and other visitors to the home. An out-of-state criminal history records check must be initiated for any person 18 years of age or older who resided in another state if that state allows the release of such records. The department shall establish by rule standards for evaluating any information contained in the automated system relating to a person who must be screened for purposes of making a placement decision.

(2) The department may not place a child with a person other than a parent if the criminal history records check reveals that the person has been convicted of any felony that falls within any of the following categories:

(a) Child abuse, abandonment, or neglect;

(b) Domestic violence;

(c) Child pornography or other felony in which a child was a victim of the offense; or

(d) Homicide, sexual battery, or other felony involving violence, other than felony assault or felony battery when an adult was the victim of the assault or battery.

(3) The department may not place a child with a person other than a parent if the criminal history records check reveals that the person has, within the previous 5 years, been convicted of a felony that falls within any of the following categories:

(a) Assault;

(b) Battery; or

(c) A drug-related offense.

(4) The department may place a child in a home that otherwise meets placement requirements if a name check of state and local criminal history records systems does not disqualify the applicant and if the department submits fingerprints to the Department of Law Enforcement for forwarding to the Federal Bureau of Investigation and is awaiting the results of the state and national criminal history records check.

(5) Persons with whom placement of a child is being considered or approved must disclose to the department any prior or pending local, state, or national criminal proceedings in which they are or have been involved.

(6) The department may examine the results of any criminal history records check of any person, including a parent, with whom placement of a child is being considered under this section. The complete criminal history records check must be considered when determining whether placement with the person will jeopardize the safety of the child being placed.

(7)(a) The court may review a decision of the department to grant or deny the placement of a child based upon information from the criminal history records check. The review may be upon the motion of any party, the request of any person who has been denied a placement by the department, or on the court's own motion. The court shall prepare written findings to support its decision in this matter.

(b) A person who is seeking placement of a child but is denied the placement because of the results of a criminal history records check has the burden of setting forth sufficient evidence of rehabilitation to show that the person will not present a danger to the child if the placement of the child is allowed. Evidence of rehabilitation may include, but is not limited to, the circumstances surrounding the incident providing the basis for denying the application, the time period that has elapsed since the incident, the nature of the harm caused to the victim, whether the victim was a child, the history of the person since the incident, whether the person has complied with any requirement to pay restitution, and any other evidence or circumstances indicating that the person will not present a danger to the child if the placement of the child is allowed.

HISTORY:

S. 6, ch. 2006-86, eff. July 1, 2006; s. 3, ch. 2008-245, eff. June 30, 2008; s. 3, ch. 2012-178, eff. July 1, 2012.

§ 39.0139. Visitation or other contact; restrictions.

(1) SHORT TITLE. — This section may be cited as the "Keeping Children Safe Act."

(2) LEGISLATIVE FINDINGS AND INTENT.

(a) The Legislature finds that:

1. For some children who are abused, abandoned, or neglected by a parent or other caregiver, abuse may include sexual abuse.

2. These same children are at risk of suffering from further harm during visitation or other contact.

3. Visitation or other contact with the child may be used to influence the child's testimony.

(b) It is the intent of the Legislature to protect children and reduce the risk of further harm to children who have been sexually abused or exploited by a parent or other caregiver by placing additional requirements on judicial determinations related to contact between a parent or caregiver who meets the criteria under paragraph (3)(a) and a child victim in any proceeding pursuant to this chapter.

(3) PRESUMPTION OF DETRIMENT.

(a) A rebuttable presumption of detriment to a child is created when:

1. A court of competent jurisdiction has found probable cause exists that a parent or caregiver has sexually abused a child as defined in s. 39.01;

2. A parent or caregiver has been found guilty of, regardless of adjudication, or has entered a plea of guilty or nolo contendere to, charges under the following statutes or substantially similar statutes of other jurisdictions:

a. Section 787.04, relating to removing minors from the state or concealing minors contrary to court order;

b. Section 794.011, relating to sexual battery;

c. Section 798.02, relating to lewd and lascivious behavior;

d. Chapter 800, relating to lewdness and indecent exposure;

e. Section 826.04, relating to incest; or

f. Chapter 827, relating to the abuse of children; or

3. A court of competent jurisdiction has determined a parent or caregiver to be a sexual predator as defined in s. 775.21 or a parent or caregiver has received a substantially similar designation under laws of another jurisdiction.

(b) For purposes of this subsection, "substantially similar" has the same meaning as in s. 39.806(1)(d) 2.

(c) A person who meets any of the criteria set forth in paragraph (a) may not visit or have contact with a child without a hearing and order by the court.

(4) HEARINGS. — A person who meets any of the criteria set forth in paragraph (3)(a) who seeks to begin or resume contact with the child victim shall have the right to an evidentiary hearing to determine whether contact is appropriate.

(a) Prior to the hearing, the court shall appoint an attorney ad litem or a guardian ad litem for the child if one has not already been appointed. Any attorney ad litem or guardian ad litem appointed shall have special training in the dynamics of child sexual abuse.

(b) At the hearing, the court may receive and rely upon any relevant and material evidence submitted to the extent of its probative value, including written and oral reports or recommendations from the child protection team, the child's therapist, the child's guardian ad litem, or the child's attorney ad litem, even if these reports, recommendations, and evidence may not be admissible under the rules of evidence.

(c) If the court finds the person proves by clear and convincing evidence that the safety, well-being, and physical, mental, and emotional health of the child is not endangered by such visitation or other contact, the presumption in subsection (3) is rebutted and the court may allow visitation or other contact. The court shall enter a written order setting forth findings of fact and specifying any conditions it finds necessary to protect the child.

(d) If the court finds the person did not rebut the presumption established in subsection (3), the court shall enter a written order setting forth findings of fact and prohibiting or restricting visitation or other contact with the child.

(5) CONDITIONS. — Any visitation or other contact ordered under paragraph (4)(d) shall be:

(a) Supervised by a person who has previously received special training in the dynamics of child sexual abuse; or

(b) Conducted in a supervised visitation program, provided that the program has an agreement with the court and a current affidavit of compliance on file with the chief judge of the circuit in which the program is located affirming that the program has agreed to comply with the minimum standards contained in the administrative order issued by the Chief Justice of the Supreme Court on November 17, 1999, and provided the program has a written agreement with the court and with the department as described in s. 753.05 containing policies and guidelines specifically related to referrals involving child sexual abuse.

(6) ADDITIONAL CONSIDERATIONS.

(a) Once a rebuttable presumption of detriment has arisen under subsection (3) or if visitation is ordered under subsection (4) and a party or participant, based on communication with the child or other firsthand knowledge, informs the court that a person is attempting to influence the testimony of the child, the court shall hold a hearing within 7 business days to determine whether it is in the best interests of the child to prohibit or restrict visitation or other contact with the person who is alleged to have influenced the testimony of the child.

(b) If a child is in therapy as a result of any finding or conviction contained in paragraph (3)(a) and the child's therapist reports that the visitation or other contact is impeding the child's therapeutic progress, the court shall convene a hearing within 7 business days to review the terms, conditions, or appropriateness of continued visitation or other contact.

HISTORY:

S. 1, ch. 2007-109, eff. July 1, 2007; s. 1, ch. 2011-209, eff. July 1, 2011; s. 5, ch. 2013-15, eff. July 2, 2013; s. 37, ch. 2016-24, eff. Oct. 1, 2016.

§ 39.0141. Missing children; report required.

Whenever the whereabouts of a child involved with the department become unknown, the department, the community-based care provider, or the sheriff's office providing investigative services for the department shall make reasonable efforts, as defined by rule, to locate the child. If, pursuant to criteria established by rule, the child is determined to be missing, the department, the community-based care provider, or the sheriff's office shall file a report that the child is missing in accordance with s. 937.021.

HISTORY:

S. 4, ch. 2008-245, eff. June 30, 2008.

PART II.
REPORTING CHILD ABUSE.

§ 39.201. Mandatory reports of child abuse, abandonment, or neglect; mandatory reports of death; central abuse hotline.

(1)(a) Any person who knows, or has reasonable cause to suspect, that a child is abused, abandoned, or neglected by a parent, legal custodian, caregiver, or other person responsible for the child's welfare, as defined in this chapter, or that a child is in need of supervision and care and has no parent, legal custodian, or responsible adult relative immediately known and available to provide supervision and care shall report such knowledge or suspicion to the department in the manner prescribed in subsection (2).

(b) Any person who knows, or who has reasonable cause to suspect, that a child is abused by an adult other than a parent, legal custodian, caregiver, or other person responsible for the child's welfare, as defined in this chapter, shall report such knowledge or suspicion to the department in the manner prescribed in subsection (2).

(c) Any person who knows, or has reasonable cause to suspect, that a child is the victim of childhood sexual abuse or the victim of a known or suspected juvenile sexual offender, as defined in this chapter, shall report such knowledge or suspicion to the department in the manner prescribed in subsection (2).

(d) Reporters in the following occupation categories are required to provide their names to the hotline staff:

1. Physician, osteopathic physician, medical examiner, chiropractic physician, nurse, or hospital personnel engaged in the admission, examination, care, or treatment of persons;

2. Health or mental health professional other than one listed in subparagraph 1.;

3. Practitioner who relies solely on spiritual means for healing;

4. School teacher or other school official or personnel;

5. Social worker, day care center worker, or other professional child care, foster care, residential, or institutional worker;

6. Law enforcement officer; or

7. Judge.

The names of reporters shall be entered into the record of the report, but shall be held confidential and exempt as provided in s. 39.202.

(e) A professional who is hired by or enters into a contract with the department for the purpose of treating or counseling any person, as a result of a report of child abuse, abandonment, or neglect, is not required to again report to the central abuse hotline the abuse, abandonment, or neglect that was the subject of the referral for treatment.

(f) An officer or employee of the judicial branch is not required to again provide notice of reasonable cause to suspect child abuse, abandonment, or neglect when that child is currently being investigated by the department, there is an existing dependency case, or the matter has previously been reported to the department, provided there is reasonable cause to believe the information is already known to the department. This paragraph applies only when the information has been provided to the officer or employee in the course of carrying out his or her official duties.

(g) Nothing in this chapter or in the contracting with community-based care providers for foster care and related services as specified in s. 409.987 shall be construed to remove or reduce the duty and responsibility of any person, including any employee of the community-based care provider, to report a suspected or actual case of child abuse, abandonment, or neglect or the sexual abuse of a child to the department's central abuse hotline.

(h) An officer or employee of a law enforcement agency is not required to provide notice to the department of reasonable cause to suspect child abuse by an adult other than a parent, legal custodian, caregiver, or other person responsible for the child's welfare when the incident under investigation by the law enforcement agency was reported to law enforcement by the Central Abuse Hotline through the electronic transfer of the report or call. The department's Central Abuse Hotline is not required to electronically transfer calls and reports received pursuant to paragraph (2)(b) to the county sheriff's office if the matter was initially reported to the department by the county sheriff's office or another law enforcement agency. This paragraph applies only when the information related to the alleged child abuse has been provided to the officer or employee of a law enforcement agency or Central Abuse Hotline employee in the course of carrying out his or her official duties.

(2)(a) Each report of known or suspected child abuse, abandonment, or neglect by a parent, legal custodian, caregiver, or other person responsible for the child's welfare as defined in this chapter, except those solely under s. 827.04(3), and each report that a child is in need of supervision and care and has no parent, legal custodian, or responsible adult relative immediately known and available to provide supervision and care shall be made immediately to the department's central abuse hotline. Such reports may be made on the single statewide toll-free telephone number or via fax, web-based chat, or web-based report. Personnel at the department's central abuse hotline shall determine if the report received meets the statutory definition of child abuse, abandonment, or neglect. Any report meeting one of these definitions shall be accepted for the protective investigation pursuant to part III of this chapter. Any call received from a parent or legal custodian seeking assistance for himself or herself which does not meet the criteria for being a report of child abuse, abandonment, or neglect may be accepted by the hotline for response to ameliorate a potential future risk of harm to a child. If it is determined by a child

welfare professional that a need for community services exists, the department shall refer the parent or legal custodian for appropriate voluntary community services.

(b) Each report of known or suspected child abuse by an adult other than a parent, legal custodian, caregiver, or other person responsible for the child's welfare, as defined in this chapter, shall be made immediately to the department's central abuse hotline. Such reports may be made on the single statewide toll-free telephone number or via fax, web-based chat, or web-based report. Such reports or calls shall be immediately electronically transferred to the appropriate county sheriff's office by the central abuse hotline.

(c) Reports involving juvenile sexual abuse or a child who has exhibited inappropriate sexual behavior shall be made and received by the department. An alleged incident of juvenile sexual abuse involving a child who is in the custody of or protective supervision of the department shall be reported to the department's central abuse hotline.

1. The central abuse hotline shall immediately electronically transfer the report or call to the county sheriff's office. The department shall conduct an assessment and assist the family in receiving appropriate services pursuant to s. 39.307, and send a written report of the allegation to the appropriate county sheriff's office within 48 hours after the initial report is made to the central abuse hotline.

2. The department shall ensure that the facts and results of any investigation of child sexual abuse involving a child in the custody of or under the protective supervision of the department are made known to the court at the next hearing or included in the next report to the court concerning the child.

(d) If the report is of an instance of known or suspected child abuse, abandonment, or neglect that occurred out of state and the alleged perpetrator and the child alleged to be a victim live out of state, the central abuse hotline shall not accept the report or call for investigation, but shall transfer the information on the report to the appropriate state.

(e) If the report is of an instance of known or suspected child abuse involving impregnation of a child under 16 years of age by a person 21 years of age or older solely under s. 827.04(3), the report shall be made immediately to the appropriate county sheriff's office or other appropriate law enforcement agency. If the report is of an instance of known or suspected child abuse solely under s. 827.04(3), the reporting provisions of this subsection do not apply to health care professionals or other persons who provide medical or counseling services to pregnant children when such reporting would interfere with the provision of medical services.

(f)   Reports involving known or suspected institutional child abuse or neglect shall be made and received in the same manner as all other reports made pursuant to this section.

(g)   Reports involving surrendered newborn infants as described in s. 383.50 shall be made and received by the department.

1.   If the report is of a surrendered newborn infant as described in s. 383.50 and there is no indication of abuse, neglect, or abandonment other than that necessarily entailed in the infant having been left at a hospital, emergency medical services station, or fire station, the department shall provide to the caller the name of a licensed child-placing agency on a rotating basis from a list of licensed child-placing agencies eligible and required to accept physical custody of and to place newborn infants left at a hospital, emergency medical services station, or fire station. The report shall not be considered a report of abuse, neglect, or abandonment solely because the infant has been left at a hospital, emergency medical services station, or fire station pursuant to s. 383.50.

2.   If the call, fax, web-based chat, or web-based report includes indications of abuse or neglect beyond that necessarily entailed in the infant having been left at a hospital, emergency medical services station, or fire station, the report shall be considered as a report of abuse, neglect, or abandonment and shall be subject to the requirements of s. 39.395 and all other relevant provisions of this chapter, notwithstanding any provisions of chapter 383.

(h)   Hotline counselors shall receive periodic training in encouraging reporters to provide their names when reporting abuse, abandonment, or neglect. Callers shall be advised of the confidentiality provisions of s. 39.202. The department shall secure and install electronic equipment that automatically provides to the hotline the number from which the call or fax is placed or the Internet protocol (IP) address from which the report is received. This number shall be entered into the report of abuse, abandonment, or neglect and become a part of the record of the report, but shall enjoy the same confidentiality as provided to the identity of the reporter pursuant to s. 39.202.

(i)   The department shall voice-record all incoming or outgoing calls that are received or placed by the central abuse hotline which relate to suspected or known child abuse, neglect, or abandonment. The department shall maintain an electronic copy of each fax and web-based report. The recording or electronic copy of each fax and web-based report shall become a part of the record of the report but, notwithstanding s. 39.202, shall be released in full only to law enforcement agencies and state attorneys for the purpose of investigating and prosecut-

ing criminal charges pursuant to s. 39.205, or to employees of the department for the purpose of investigating and seeking administrative penalties pursuant to s. 39.206. Nothing in this paragraph shall prohibit the use of the recordings, the electronic copies of faxes, and web-based reports by hotline staff for quality assurance and training.

(j)1.   The department shall update the web form used for reporting child abuse, abandonment, or neglect to:

a.   Include qualifying questions in order to obtain necessary information required to assess need and a response.

b.   Indicate which fields are required to submit the report.

c.   Allow a reporter to save his or her report and return to it at a later time.

2.   The report shall be made available to the counselors in its entirety as needed to update the Florida Safe Families Network or other similar systems.

(k)   The department shall conduct a study to determine the feasibility of using text and short message service formats to receive and process reports of child abuse, abandonment, or neglect to the central abuse hotline.

(3)   Any person required to report or investigate cases of suspected child abuse, abandonment, or neglect who has reasonable cause to suspect that a child died as a result of child abuse, abandonment, or neglect shall report his or her suspicion to the appropriate medical examiner. The medical examiner shall accept the report for investigation and shall report his or her findings, in writing, to the local law enforcement agency, the appropriate state attorney, and the department. Autopsy reports maintained by the medical examiner are not subject to the confidentiality requirements provided for in s. 39.202.

(4)   The department shall operate and maintain a central abuse hotline to receive all reports made pursuant to this section in writing, via fax, via web-based reporting, via web-based chat, or through a single statewide toll-free telephone number, which any person may use to report known or suspected child abuse, abandonment, or neglect at any hour of the day or night, any day of the week. The department shall promote public awareness of the central abuse hotline through community-based partner organizations and public service campaigns. The central abuse hotline is the first step in the safety assessment and investigation process. The central abuse hotline shall be operated in such a manner as to enable the department to:

(a)   Immediately identify and locate prior reports or cases of child abuse, abandonment, or neglect through utilization of the department's automated tracking system.

(b)   Monitor and evaluate the effectiveness of the department's program for reporting and investigating suspected abuse, abandonment, or neglect of children through the development and analysis of statistical and other information.

(c) Track critical steps in the investigative process to ensure compliance with all requirements for any report of abuse, abandonment, or neglect.

(d) Maintain and produce aggregate statistical reports monitoring patterns of child abuse, child abandonment, and child neglect. The department shall collect and analyze child-on-child sexual abuse reports and include the information in aggregate statistical reports. The department shall collect and analyze, in separate statistical reports, those reports of child abuse and sexual abuse which are reported from or occurred on the campus of any Florida College System institution, state university, or non-public college, university, or school, as defined in s. 1000.21 or s. 1005.02.

(e) Serve as a resource for the evaluation, management, and planning of preventive and remedial services for children who have been subject to abuse, abandonment, or neglect.

(f) Initiate and enter into agreements with other states for the purpose of gathering and sharing information contained in reports on child maltreatment to further enhance programs for the protection of children.

(5) The department shall be capable of receiving and investigating, 24 hours a day, 7 days a week, reports of known or suspected child abuse, abandonment, or neglect and reports that a child is in need of supervision and care and has no parent, legal custodian, or responsible adult relative immediately known and available to provide supervision and care. If it appears that the immediate safety or well-being of a child is endangered, that the family may flee or the child will be unavailable for purposes of conducting a child protective investigation, or that the facts otherwise so warrant, the department shall commence an investigation immediately, regardless of the time of day or night. In all other child abuse, abandonment, or neglect cases, a child protective investigation shall be commenced within 24 hours after receipt of the report. In an institutional investigation, the alleged perpetrator may be represented by an attorney, at his or her own expense, or accompanied by another person, if the person or the attorney executes an affidavit of understanding with the department and agrees to comply with the confidentiality provisions of s. 39.202. The absence of an attorney or other person does not prevent the department from proceeding with other aspects of the investigation, including interviews with other persons. In institutional child abuse cases when the institution is not operating and the child cannot otherwise be located, the investigation shall commence immediately upon the resumption of operation. If requested by a state attorney or local law enforcement agency, the department shall furnish all investigative reports to that agency.

(6) Information in the central abuse hotline may not be used for employment screening, except as provided in s. 39.202(2)(a) and (h) or s. 402.302(15). Information in the central abuse hotline and the department's automated abuse information system may be used by the department, its authorized agents or contract providers, the Department of Health, or county agencies as part of the licensure or registration process pursuant to ss. 402.301 - 402.319 and ss. 409.175 - 409.176. Pursuant to s. 39.202(2)(q), the information in the central abuse hotline may also be used by the Department of Education for purposes of educator certification discipline and review.

(7) On an ongoing basis, the department's quality assurance program shall review calls, fax reports, and web-based reports to the hotline involving three or more unaccepted reports on a single child, where jurisdiction applies, in order to detect such things as harassment and situations that warrant an investigation because of the frequency or variety of the source of the reports. A component of the quality assurance program shall analyze unaccepted reports to the hotline by identified relatives as a part of the review of screened out calls. The Program Director for Family Safety may refer a case for investigation when it is determined, as a result of this review, that an investigation may be warranted.

HISTORY:
  SS. 1, 2, 3, 4, 5, 6, ch. 63-24; s. 941, ch. 71-136; ss. 1, 1A, ch. 71-97; s. 32, ch. 73-334; s. 65, ch. 74-383; s. 1, ch. 75-101; s. 1, ch. 75-185; s. 4, ch. 76-237; s. 1, ch. 77-77; s. 3, ch. 77-429; ss. 1, 2, ch. 78-322; s. 3, ch. 78-326; s. 22, ch. 78-361; s. 1, ch. 78-379; s. 181, ch. 79-164; s. 1, ch. 79-203; s. 7, ch. 84-226; s. 37, ch. 85-54; s. 68, ch. 86-163; s. 34, ch. 87-238; s. 21, ch. 88-337; s. 33, ch. 89-294; s. 6, ch. 90-50; s. 51, ch. 90-306; s. 7, ch. 91-57; s. 17, ch. 91-71; s. 6, ch. 93-25; s. 59, ch. 94-164; ss. 22, 44, ch. 95-228; s. 9, ch. 95-266; s. 51, ch. 95-267; s. 133, ch. 95-418; s. 1, ch. 96-215; s. 14, ch. 96-268; s. 14, ch. 96-402; s. 271, ch. 96-406; s. 1041, ch. 97-103; s. 43, ch. 97-264; s. 257, ch. 98-166; s. 31, ch. 98-403; s. 4, ch. 99-168; s. 10, ch. 99-193; s. 41, ch. 2000-139; s. 3, ch. 2000-188; s. 1, ch. 2000-217; s. 1, ch. 2001-53; s. 1, ch. 2003-127; s. 7, ch. 2006-86, eff. July 1, 2006; s. 2, ch. 2008-90, eff. July 1, 2008; s. 5, ch. 2008-245, eff. June 30, 2008; s. 3, ch. 2009-43, eff. July 1, 2009; s. 1, ch. 2012-155, eff. Oct. 1, 2012; s. 4, ch. 2012-178, eff. July 1, 2012; s. 6, ch. 2013-15, eff. July 2, 2013; s. 4, ch. 2013-219, eff. July 1, 2013; ss. 5, 50, ch. 2014-224, eff. July 1, 2014; s. 1, ch. 2016-58, eff. July 1, 2016; s. 1, ch. 2016-238, eff. July 1, 2016.

Editor's notes
  Section 1 of ch. 2009-43 provides: "This act may be cited as the 'Zahid Jones, Jr., Give Grandparents and Other Relatives a Voice Act.'"
  Former ss. 828.041, 827.07(3), (4), (9), (13); s. 415.504.

Amendments.
  The 2014 amendment by s. 5, ch. 2014-224, effective July 1, 2014, rewrote (2)(c), which formerly read: "Reports involving a known or suspected juvenile sexual offender or a child who has exhibited inappropriate sexual behavior shall be made and received by the department. 1. The department shall determine the age of the alleged offender, if known. 2. If the alleged offender is 12 years of age or younger, the central abuse hotline shall immediately electronically transfer the report or call to the county sheriff's office. The department shall conduct an assessment and assist the family in receiving appropriate services pursuant to s. 39.307, and send a written report of

the allegation to the appropriate county sheriff's office within 48 hours after the initial report is made to the central abuse hotline. 3. If the alleged offender is 13 years of age or older, the central abuse hotline shall immediately electronically transfer the report or call to the appropriate county sheriff's office and send a written report to the appropriate county sheriff's office within 48 hours after the initial report to the central abuse hotline."

The 2014 amendment by s. 50, ch. 2014-224, effective July 1, 2014, substituted " s. 409.987 " for " s. 409.1671" in (1)(g).

§ 39.2015. Critical incident rapid response team.

(1) As part of the department's quality assurance program, the department shall provide an immediate multiagency investigation of certain child deaths or other serious incidents. The purpose of such investigation is to identify root causes and rapidly determine the need to change policies and practices related to child protection and child welfare.

(2) An immediate onsite investigation conducted by a critical incident rapid response team is required for all child deaths reported to the department if the child or another child in his or her family was the subject of a verified report of suspected abuse or neglect during the previous 12 months. The secretary may direct an immediate investigation for other cases involving death or serious injury to a child, including, but not limited to, a death or serious injury occurring during an open investigation.

(3) Each investigation shall be conducted by a multiagency team of at least five professionals with expertise in child protection, child welfare, and organizational management. The team may consist of employees of the department, community-based care lead agencies, Children's Medical Services, and community-based care provider organizations; faculty from the institute consisting of public and private universities offering degrees in social work established pursuant to s. 1004.615; or any other person with the required expertise. The team shall include, at a minimum, a child protection team medical director. The majority of the team must reside in judicial circuits outside the location of the incident. The secretary shall appoint a team leader for each group assigned to an investigation.

(4) An investigation shall be initiated as soon as possible, but not later than 2 business days after the case is reported to the department. A preliminary report on each case shall be provided to the secretary no later than 30 days after the investigation begins.

(5) Each member of the team is authorized to access all information in the case file.

(6) All employees of the department or other state agencies and all personnel from community-based care lead agencies and community-based care lead agency subcontractors must cooperate with the investigation by participating in interviews and timely responding to any requests for information. The members of the team may only access the records and information of contracted provider organizations which are available to the department by law.

(7) The secretary shall develop cooperative agreements with other entities and organizations as necessary to facilitate the work of the team.

(8) The members of the team may be reimbursed by the department for per diem, mileage, and other reasonable expenses as provided in s. 112.061. The department may also reimburse the team member's employer for the associated salary and benefits during the time the team member is fulfilling the duties required under this section.

(9) Upon completion of the investigation, the department shall make the team's final report, excluding any confidential information, available on its website.

(10) The secretary, in conjunction with the institute established pursuant to s. 1004.615, shall develop guidelines for investigations conducted by critical incident rapid response teams and provide training to team members. Such guidelines must direct the teams in the conduct of a root-cause analysis that identifies, classifies, and attributes responsibility for both direct and latent causes for the death or other incident, including organizational factors, preconditions, and specific acts or omissions resulting from either error or a violation of procedures. The department shall ensure that each team member receives training on the guidelines before conducting an investigation.

(11) The secretary shall appoint an advisory committee made up of experts in child protection and child welfare, including the Statewide Medical Director for Child Protection under the Department of Health, a representative from the institute established pursuant to s. 1004.615, an expert in organizational management, and an attorney with experience in child welfare, to conduct an independent review of investigative reports from the critical incident rapid response teams and to make recommendations to improve policies and practices related to child protection and child welfare services. The advisory committee shall meet at least once each quarter and shall submit quarterly reports to the secretary which include findings and recommendations. The secretary shall submit each report to the Governor, the President of the Senate, and the Speaker of the House of Representatives.

HISTORY:
S. 6, ch. 2014-224, eff. Jan. 1, 2015; s. 1, ch. 2015-79, eff. July 1, 2015; s. 1, ch. 2015-177, eff. July 1, 2015.

§ 39.202. Confidentiality of reports and records in cases of child abuse or neglect.

(1) In order to protect the rights of the child and the child's parents or other persons responsible for the child's welfare, all records held by the department concerning reports of child abandonment, abuse, or neglect, including reports made to the central abuse hotline and all records generated as a result of such reports, shall be confidential and exempt from the provisions of s. 119.07(1) and shall not be disclosed except as specifically authorized by this chapter. Such

exemption from s. 119.07(1) applies to information in the possession of those entities granted access as set forth in this section.

(2) Except as provided in subsection (4), access to such records, excluding the name of the reporter which shall be released only as provided in subsection (5), shall be granted only to the following persons, officials, and agencies:

(a) Employees, authorized agents, or contract providers of the department, the Department of Health, the Agency for Persons with Disabilities, the Office of Early Learning, or county agencies responsible for carrying out:

1. Child or adult protective investigations;

2. Ongoing child or adult protective services;

3. Early intervention and prevention services;

4. Healthy Start services;

5. Licensure or approval of adoptive homes, foster homes, child care facilities, facilities licensed under chapter 393, family day care homes, providers who receive school readiness funding under part VI of chapter 1002, or other homes used to provide for the care and welfare of children;

6. Employment screening for caregivers in residential group homes; or

7. Services for victims of domestic violence when provided by certified domestic violence centers working at the department's request as case consultants or with shared clients.

Also, employees or agents of the Department of Juvenile Justice responsible for the provision of services to children, pursuant to chapters 984 and 985.

(b) Criminal justice agencies of appropriate jurisdiction.

(c) The state attorney of the judicial circuit in which the child resides or in which the alleged abuse or neglect occurred.

(d) The parent or legal custodian of any child who is alleged to have been abused, abandoned, or neglected, and the child, and their attorneys, including any attorney representing a child in civil or criminal proceedings. This access shall be made available no later than 60 days after the department receives the initial report of abuse, neglect, or abandonment. However, any information otherwise made confidential or exempt by law shall not be released pursuant to this paragraph.

(e) Any person alleged in the report as having caused the abuse, abandonment, or neglect of a child. This access shall be made available no later than 60 days after the department receives the initial report of abuse, abandonment, or neglect and, when the alleged perpetrator is not a parent, shall be limited to information involving the protective investigation only and shall not include any information relating to subsequent dependency proceedings. However, any information otherwise made confiden-

tial or exempt by law shall not be released pursuant to this paragraph.

(f) A court upon its finding that access to such records may be necessary for the determination of an issue before the court; however, such access shall be limited to inspection in camera, unless the court determines that public disclosure of the information contained therein is necessary for the resolution of an issue then pending before it.

(g) A grand jury, by subpoena, upon its determination that access to such records is necessary in the conduct of its official business.

(h) Any appropriate official of the department or the Agency for Persons with Disabilities who is responsible for:

1. Administration or supervision of the department's program for the prevention, investigation, or treatment of child abuse, abandonment, or neglect, or abuse, neglect, or exploitation of a vulnerable adult, when carrying out his or her official function;

2. Taking appropriate administrative action concerning an employee of the department or the agency who is alleged to have perpetrated child abuse, abandonment, or neglect, or abuse, neglect, or exploitation of a vulnerable adult; or

3. Employing and continuing employment of personnel of the department or the agency.

(i) Any person authorized by the department who is engaged in the use of such records or information for bona fide research, statistical, or audit purposes. Such individual or entity shall enter into a privacy and security agreement with the department and shall comply with all laws and rules governing the use of such records and information for research and statistical purposes. Information identifying the subjects of such records or information shall be treated as confidential by the researcher and shall not be released in any form.

(j) The Division of Administrative Hearings for purposes of any administrative challenge.

(k) Any appropriate official of a Florida advocacy council investigating a report of known or suspected child abuse, abandonment, or neglect; the Auditor General or the Office of Program Policy Analysis and Government Accountability for the purpose of conducting audits or examinations pursuant to law; or the guardian ad litem for the child.

(l) Employees or agents of an agency of another state that has comparable jurisdiction to the jurisdiction described in paragraph (a).

(m) The Public Employees Relations Commission for the sole purpose of obtaining evidence for appeals filed pursuant to s. 447.207. Records may be released only after deletion of all information which specifically identifies persons other than the employee.

(n) Employees or agents of the Department of Revenue responsible for child support enforcement activities.

(o) Any person in the event of the death of a child determined to be a result of abuse, abandonment, or neglect. Information identifying the person reporting abuse, abandonment, or neglect shall not be released. Any information otherwise made confidential or exempt by law shall not be released pursuant to this paragraph.

(p) An employee of the local school district who is designated as a liaison between the school district and the department pursuant to an interagency agreement required under s. 39.0016 and the principal of a public school, private school, or charter school where the child is a student. Information contained in the records which the liaison or the principal determines are necessary for a school employee to effectively provide a student with educational services may be released to that employee.

(q) An employee or agent of the Department of Education who is responsible for the investigation or prosecution of misconduct by a certified educator.

(r) Staff of a children's advocacy center that is established and operated under s. 39.3035.

(s) A physician licensed under chapter 458 or chapter 459, a psychologist licensed under chapter 490, or a mental health professional licensed under chapter 491 engaged in the care or treatment of the child.

(t) Persons with whom the department is seeking to place the child or to whom placement has been granted, including foster parents for whom an approved home study has been conducted, the designee of a licensed residential group home described in s. 39.523, an approved relative or nonrelative with whom a child is placed pursuant to s. 39.402, preadoptive parents for whom a favorable preliminary adoptive home study has been conducted, adoptive parents, or an adoption entity acting on behalf of preadoptive or adoptive parents.

(3) The department may release to professional persons such information as is necessary for the diagnosis and treatment of the child or the person perpetrating the abuse or neglect.

(4) Notwithstanding any other provision of law, when a child under investigation or supervision of the department or its contracted service providers is determined to be missing, the following shall apply:

(a) The department may release the following information to the public when it believes the release of the information is likely to assist efforts in locating the child or to promote the safety or well-being of the child:

1. The name of the child and the child's date of birth;

2. A physical description of the child, including at a minimum the height, weight, hair color, eye color, gender, and any identifying physical characteristics of the child; and

3. A photograph of the child.

(b) With the concurrence of the law enforcement agency primarily responsible for investigating the incident, the department may release any additional information it believes likely to assist efforts in locating the child or to promote the safety or well-being of the child.

(c) The law enforcement agency primarily responsible for investigating the incident may release any information received from the department regarding the investigation, if it believes the release of the information is likely to assist efforts in locating the child or to promote the safety or well-being of the child.

The good faith publication or release of this information by the department, a law enforcement agency, or any recipient of the information as specifically authorized by this subsection shall not subject the person, agency, or entity releasing the information to any civil or criminal penalty. This subsection does not authorize the release of the name of the reporter, which may be released only as provided in subsection (5).

(5) The name of any person reporting child abuse, abandonment, or neglect may not be released to any person other than employees of the department responsible for child protective services, the central abuse hotline, law enforcement, the child protection team, or the appropriate state attorney, without the written consent of the person reporting. This does not prohibit the subpoenaing of a person reporting child abuse, abandonment, or neglect when deemed necessary by the court, the state attorney, or the department, provided the fact that such person made the report is not disclosed. Any person who reports a case of child abuse or neglect may, at the time he or she makes the report, request that the department notify him or her that a child protective investigation occurred as a result of the report. Any person specifically listed in s. 39.201(1) who makes a report in his or her official capacity may also request a written summary of the outcome of the investigation. The department shall mail such a notice to the reporter within 10 days after completing the child protective investigation.

(6) All records and reports of the child protection team of the Department of Health are confidential and exempt from the provisions of ss. 119.07(1) and 456.057, and shall not be disclosed, except, upon request, to the state attorney, law enforcement, the department, and necessary professionals, in furtherance of the treatment or additional evaluative needs of the child, by order of the court, or to health plan payors, limited to that information used for insurance reimbursement purposes.

(7) The department shall make and keep reports and records of all cases under this chapter and shall preserve the records pertaining to a child and family until the child who is the subject of the record is 30 years of age, and may then destroy the records.

(a) Within 90 days after the child leaves the department's custody, the department shall give a notice to the person having legal custody of the child, or to the young adult who was in the department's custody, which specifies how the records may be obtained.

(b) The department may adopt rules regarding the format, storage, retrieval, and release of such records.

(8) A person who knowingly or willfully makes public or discloses to any unauthorized person any confidential information contained in the central abuse hotline is subject to the penalty provisions of s. 39.205. This notice shall be prominently displayed on the first sheet of any documents released pursuant to this section.

HISTORY:
SS. 1, 2, 3, 4, 5, 6, ch. 63-24; s. 941, ch. 71-136; ss. 1, 1A, ch. 71-97; s. 32, ch. 73-334; s. 65, ch. 74-383; s. 1, ch. 75-101; s. 1, ch. 75-185; s. 4, ch. 76-237; s. 1, ch. 77-77; s. 3, ch. 77-429; ss. 1, 2, ch. 78-322; s. 3, ch. 78-326; s. 22, ch. 78-361; s. 1, ch. 78-379; s. 181, ch. 79-164; s. 1, ch. 79-203; s. 488, ch. 81-259; s. 11, ch. 84-226; s. 39, ch. 85-54; s. 14, ch. 85-224; s. 36, ch. 87-238; s. 2, ch. 88-80; s. 8, ch. 88-219; s. 26, ch. 88-337; s. 5, ch. 89-170; s. 5, ch. 89-278; s. 36, ch. 89-294; s. 2, ch. 89-535; s. 8, ch. 90-50; s. 7, ch. 90-208; s. 54, ch. 90-306; s. 9, ch. 91-57; s. 20, ch. 91-71; ss. 43, 48, ch. 92-58; s. 32, ch. 93-39; s. 16, ch. 93-214; s. 58, ch. 94-218; ss. 25, 46, ch. 95-228; s. 28, ch. 95-267; s. 15, ch. 96-402; s. 275, ch. 96-406; s. 1044, ch. 97-103; s. 15, ch. 97-276; s. 3, ch. 97-299; s. 15, ch. 98-137; s. 32, ch. 98-166; s. 3, ch. 98-255; s. 45, ch. 98-280; s. 32, ch. 98-403; s. 5, ch. 99-168; s. 11, ch. 99-193; s. 1, ch. 99-369; s. 18, ch. 2000-139; s. 2, ch. 2000-217; s. 6, ch. 2000-263; s. 51, ch. 2000-349; s. 12, ch. 2001-60; s. 27, ch. 2001-266; s. 2, ch. 2003-146; s. 1, ch. 2005-173; s. 1, ch. 2005-213; s. 6, ch. 2006-194, eff. July 1, 2006; s. 3, ch. 2006-227, eff. July 1, 2006; s. 2, ch. 2009-34, eff. July 1, 2009; s. 2, ch. 2009-35, eff. July 1, 2009; s. 4, ch. 2009-43, eff. July 1, 2009; s. 2, ch. 2010-210, eff. July 1, 2010; s. 2, ch. 2016-58, eff. July 1, 2016; s. 2, ch. 2016-238, eff. July 1, 2016; s. 4, ch. 2017-151, eff. July 1, 2017.

Editor's notes.
Section 1 of ch. 2009-43 provides: "This act may be cited as the 'Zahid Jones, Jr., Give Grandparents and Other Relatives a Voice Act.'"
Former ss. 828.041, 827.07(15); s. 415.51.
Paragraph (q) was also enacted by s. 1, ch. 2005-213, and that version reads: "(q) The executive director or equivalent, and his or her designee, of a children's advocacy center that is established and operated under s. 39.3035."

§ 39.2021. Release of confidential information.

(1) Any person or organization, including the Department of Children and Families, may petition the court for an order making public the records of the Department of Children and Families which pertain to investigations of alleged abuse, abandonment, or neglect of a child. The court shall determine whether good cause exists for public access to the records sought or a portion thereof. In making this determination, the court shall balance the best interests of the child who is the focus of the investigation and the interest of that child's siblings, together with the privacy rights of other persons identified in the reports, against the public interest. The public interest in access to such records is reflected in s. 119.01(1), and includes the need for citizens to know of and adequately evaluate the actions of the Department of Children and Families

and the court system in providing children of this state with the protections enumerated in s. 39.001. However, this subsection does not contravene s. 39.202, which protects the name of any person reporting the abuse, abandonment, or neglect of a child.

(2) In cases involving serious bodily injury to a child, the Department of Children and Families may petition the court for an order for the immediate public release of records of the department which pertain to the protective investigation. The petition must be personally served upon the child, the child's parent or guardian, and any person named as an alleged perpetrator in the report of abuse, abandonment, or neglect. The court must determine whether good cause exists for the public release of the records sought no later than 24 hours, excluding Saturdays, Sundays, and legal holidays, after the date the department filed the petition with the court. If the court does not grant or deny the petition within the 24-hour time period, the department may release to the public summary information including:

(a) A confirmation that an investigation has been conducted concerning the alleged victim.

(b) The dates and brief description of procedural activities undertaken during the department's investigation.

(c) The date of each judicial proceeding, a summary of each participant's recommendations made at the judicial proceeding, and the ruling of the court.

The summary information shall not include the name of, or other identifying information with respect to, any person identified in any investigation. In making a determination to release confidential information, the court shall balance the best interests of the child who is the focus of the investigation and the interests of that child's siblings, together with the privacy rights of other persons identified in the reports against the public interest for access to public records. However, this subsection does not contravene s. 39.202, which protects the name of any person reporting abuse, abandonment, or neglect of a child.

(3) When the court determines that good cause for public access exists, the court shall direct that the department redact the name of, and other identifying information with respect to, any person identified in any protective investigation report until such time as the court finds that there is probable cause to believe that the person identified committed an act of alleged abuse, abandonment, or neglect.

HISTORY:
S. 1, ch. 2004-335; s. 12, ch. 2014-19, eff. July 1, 2014.

§ 39.2022. Public disclosure of reported child deaths.

(1) It is the intent of the Legislature to provide prompt disclosure of the basic facts of all deaths of children from birth through 18 years of age which occur

in this state and which are reported to the department's central abuse hotline. Disclosure shall be posted on the department's public website. This section does not limit the public access to records under any other provision of law.

(2) Notwithstanding s. 39.202, if a child death is reported to the central abuse hotline, the department shall post on its website all of the following:

(a) The date of the child's death.

(b) Any allegations of the cause of death or the preliminary cause of death, and the verified cause of death, if known.

(c) The county where the child resided.

(d) The name of the community-based care lead agency, case management agency, or out-of-home licensing agency involved with the child, family, or licensed caregiver, if applicable.

(e) Whether the child has been the subject of any prior verified reports to the department's central abuse hotline.

(f) Whether the child was younger than 5 years of age at the time of his or her death.

HISTORY:
S. 7, ch. 2014-224, eff. July 1, 2014.

§ 39.203. Immunity from liability in cases of child abuse, abandonment, or neglect.

(1)(a) Any person, official, or institution participating in good faith in any act authorized or required by this chapter, or reporting in good faith any instance of child abuse, abandonment, or neglect to the department or any law enforcement agency, shall be immune from any civil or criminal liability which might otherwise result by reason of such action.

(b) Except as provided in this chapter, nothing contained in this section shall be deemed to grant immunity, civil or criminal, to any person suspected of having abused, abandoned, or neglected a child, or committed any illegal act upon or against a child.

(2)(a) No resident or employee of a facility serving children may be subjected to reprisal or discharge because of his or her actions in reporting abuse, abandonment, or neglect pursuant to the requirements of this section.

(b) Any person making a report under this section shall have a civil cause of action for appropriate compensatory and punitive damages against any person who causes detrimental changes in the employment status of such reporting party by reason of his or her making such report. Any detrimental change made in the residency or employment status of such person, including, but not limited to, discharge, termination, demotion, transfer, or reduction in pay or benefits or work privileges, or negative evaluations within a prescribed period of time shall establish a rebuttable presumption that such action was retaliatory.

HISTORY:
SS. 1, 2, 3, 4, 5, 6, ch. 63-24; s. 941, ch. 71-136; ss. 1, 1A, ch. 71-97; s. 32, ch. 73-334; s. 65, ch. 74-383; s. 1, ch. 75-101; s. 1, ch. 75-185; s. 4, ch. 76-237; s. 1, ch. 77-77; s. 3, ch. 77-429; ss. 1, 2, ch. 78-322; s. 3, ch. 78-326; s. 22, ch. 78-361; s. 1, ch. 78-379; s. 181, ch. 79-164; s. 1, ch. 79-203; s. 27, ch. 88-337; s. 55, ch. 90-306; s. 63, ch. 94-164; s. 73, ch. 97-103; s. 33, ch. 98-403; s. 12, ch. 99-193.

Editor's notes.
Former ss. 828.041, 827.07(7); s. 415.511.

§ 39.204. Abrogation of privileged communications in cases involving child abuse, abandonment, or neglect.

The privileged quality of communication between husband and wife and between any professional person and his or her patient or client, and any other privileged communication except that between attorney and client or the privilege provided in s. 90.505, as such communication relates both to the competency of the witness and to the exclusion of confidential communications, shall not apply to any communication involving the perpetrator or alleged perpetrator in any situation involving known or suspected child abuse, abandonment, or neglect and shall not constitute grounds for failure to report as required by s. 39.201 regardless of the source of the information requiring the report, failure to cooperate with law enforcement or the department in its activities pursuant to this chapter, or failure to give evidence in any judicial proceeding relating to child abuse, abandonment, or neglect.

HISTORY:
SS. 1, 2, 3, 4, 5, 6, ch. 63-24; s. 941, ch. 71-136; ss. 1, 1A, ch. 71-97; s. 32, ch. 73-334; s. 65, ch. 74-383; s. 1, ch. 75-101; s. 1, ch. 75-185; s. 4, ch. 76-237; s. 1, ch. 77-77; s. 3, ch. 77-429; ss. 1, 2, ch. 78-322; s. 3, ch. 78-326; s. 22, ch. 78-361; s. 1, ch. 78-379; s. 181, ch. 79-164; s. 1, ch. 79-203; s. 2, ch. 85-28; s. 64, ch. 94-164; s. 74, ch. 97-103; s. 34, ch. 98-403; s. 3, ch. 2002-174.

Editor's notes.
Former ss. 828.041, 827.07(8); s. 415.512.

§ 39.205. Penalties relating to reporting of child abuse, abandonment, or neglect.

(1) A person who is required to report known or suspected child abuse, abandonment, or neglect and who knowingly and willfully fails to do so, or who knowingly and willfully prevents another person from doing so, commits a felony of the third degree, punishable as provided in s. 775.082, s. 775.083, or s. 775.084. A judge subject to discipline pursuant to s. 12, Art. V of the Florida Constitution shall not be subject to criminal prosecution when the information was received in the course of official duties.

(2) Unless the court finds that the person is a victim of domestic violence or that other mitigating circumstances exist, a person who is 18 years of age or older and lives in the same house or living unit as a child who is known or suspected to be a victim of child abuse, neglect of a child, or aggravated child abuse, and knowingly and willfully fails to report the child abuse

commits a felony of the third degree, punishable as provided in s. 775.082, s. 775.083, or s. 775.084.

(3) Any Florida College System institution, state university, or nonpublic college, university, or school, as defined in s. 1000.21 or s. 1005.02, whose administrators knowingly and willfully, upon receiving information from faculty, staff, or other institution employees, fail to report known or suspected child abuse, abandonment, or neglect committed on the property of the university, college, or school, or during an event or function sponsored by the university, college, or school, or who knowingly and willfully prevent another person from doing so, shall be subject to fines of $1 million for each such failure.

(a) A Florida College System institution subject to a fine shall be assessed by the State Board of Education.

(b) A state university subject to a fine shall be assessed by the Board of Governors.

(c) A nonpublic college, university, or school subject to a fine shall be assessed by the Commission for Independent Education.

(4) Any Florida College System institution, state university, or nonpublic college, university, or school, as defined in s. 1000.21 or s. 1005.02, whose law enforcement agency fails to report known or suspected child abuse, abandonment, or neglect committed on the property of the university, college, or school, or during an event or function sponsored by the university, college, or school, shall be subject to fines of $1 million for each such failure assessed in the same manner as subsection (3).

(5) Any Florida College System institution, state university, or nonpublic college, university, or school, as defined in s. 1000.21 or s. 1005.02, shall have the right to challenge the determination that the institution acted knowingly and willfully under subsection (3) or subsection (4) in an administrative hearing pursuant to s. 120.57; however, if it is found that actual knowledge and information of known or suspected child abuse was in fact received by the institution's administrators and was not reported, a presumption of a knowing and willful act will be established.

(6) A person who knowingly and willfully makes public or discloses any confidential information contained in the central abuse hotline or in the records of any child abuse, abandonment, or neglect case, except as provided in this chapter, commits a misdemeanor of the second degree, punishable as provided in s. 775.082 or s. 775.083.

(7) The department shall establish procedures for determining whether a false report of child abuse, abandonment, or neglect has been made and for submitting all identifying information relating to such a report to the appropriate law enforcement agency and shall report annually to the Legislature the number of reports referred.

(8) If the department or its authorized agent has determined during the course of its investigation that a report is a false report, the department may discontinue all investigative activities and shall, with the consent of the alleged perpetrator, refer the report to the local law enforcement agency having jurisdiction for an investigation to determine whether sufficient evidence exists to refer the case for prosecution for filing a false report as defined in s. 39.01. During the pendency of the investigation, the department must notify the local law enforcement agency of, and the local law enforcement agency must respond to, all subsequent reports concerning children in that same family in accordance with s. 39.301. If the law enforcement agency believes that there are indicators of abuse, abandonment, or neglect, it must immediately notify the department, which must ensure the safety of the children. If the law enforcement agency finds sufficient evidence for prosecution for filing a false report, it must refer the case to the appropriate state attorney for prosecution.

(9) A person who knowingly and willfully makes a false report of child abuse, abandonment, or neglect, or who advises another to make a false report, is guilty of a felony of the third degree, punishable as provided in s. 775.082 or s. 775.083. Anyone making a report who is acting in good faith is immune from any liability under this subsection.

(10) The State Board of Education shall adopt rules to implement this section as it relates to Florida College System institutions; the Commission for Independent Education shall adopt rules to implement this section as it relates to nonpublic colleges, universities, and schools; and the Board of Governors shall adopt regulations to implement this section as it relates to state universities.

HISTORY:

SS. 1, 2, 3, 4, 5, 6, ch. 63-24; s. 941, ch. 71-136; ss. 1, 1A, ch. 71-97; s. 32, ch. 73-334; s. 65, ch. 74-383; s. 1, ch. 75-101; s. 1, ch. 75-185; s. 4, ch. 76-237; s. 1, ch. 77-77; s. 3, ch. 77-429; ss. 1, 2, ch. 78-322; s. 3, ch. 78-326; s. 22, ch. 78-361; s. 1, ch. 78-379; s. 181, ch. 79-164; s. 1, ch. 79-203; s. 28, ch. 88-337; s. 56, ch. 90-306; s. 10, ch. 91-57; s. 21, ch. 91-71; s. 251, ch. 91-224; s. 10, ch. 93-25; s. 276, ch. 96-406; s. 4, ch. 98-111; s. 35, ch. 98-403; s. 6, ch. 99-168; s. 3, ch. 2000-217; s. 4, ch. 2002-70; s. 29, ch. 2006-86, eff. July 1, 2006; s. 25, ch. 2008-245, eff. June 30, 2008; s. 5, ch. 2012-178, eff. July 1, 2012; s. 2, ch. 2012-155, eff. Oct. 1, 2012; s. 3, ch. 2013-51, eff. July 1, 2013.

Editor's notes.

Former ss. 828.041, 827.07(18); s. 415.513.

§ 39.206. Administrative fines for false report of abuse, abandonment, or neglect of a child; civil damages.

(1) In addition to any other penalty authorized by this section, chapter 120, or other law, the department may impose a fine, not to exceed $10,000 for each violation, upon a person who knowingly and willfully makes a false report of abuse, abandonment, or neglect of a child, or a person who counsels another to make a false report.

(2) If the department alleges that a person has filed a false report with the central abuse hotline, the department must file a Notice of Intent which alleges the name, age, and address of the individual, the facts constituting the allegation that the individual made a false report, and the administrative fine the department proposes to impose on the person. Each time that a false report is made constitutes a separate violation.

(3) The Notice of Intent to impose the administrative fine must be served upon the person alleged to have filed the false report and the person's legal counsel, if any. Such Notice of Intent must be given by certified mail, return receipt requested.

(4) Any person alleged to have filed the false report is entitled to an administrative hearing, pursuant to chapter 120, before the imposition of the fine becomes final. The person must request an administrative hearing within 60 days after receipt of the Notice of Intent by filing a request with the department. Failure to request an administrative hearing within 60 days after receipt of the Notice of Intent constitutes a waiver of the right to a hearing, making the administrative fine final.

(5) At the administrative hearing, the department must prove by a preponderance of the evidence that the person filed a false report with the central abuse hotline. The administrative hearing officer shall advise any person against whom a fine may be imposed of that person's right to be represented by counsel at the administrative hearing.

(6) In determining the amount of fine to be imposed, if any, the following factors shall be considered:

(a) The gravity of the violation, including the probability that serious physical or emotional harm to any person will result or has resulted, the severity of the actual or potential harm, and the nature of the false allegation.

(b) Actions taken by the false reporter to retract the false report as an element of mitigation, or, in contrast, to encourage an investigation on the basis of false information.

(c) Any previous false reports filed by the same individual.

(7) A decision by the department, following the administrative hearing, to impose an administrative fine for filing a false report constitutes final agency action within the meaning of chapter 120. Notice of the imposition of the administrative fine must be served upon the person and the person's legal counsel, by certified mail, return receipt requested, and must state that the person may seek judicial review of the administrative fine pursuant to s. 120.68.

(8) All amounts collected under this section shall be deposited into an appropriate trust fund of the department.

(9) A person who is determined to have filed a false report of abuse, abandonment, or neglect is not entitled to confidentiality. Subsequent to the conclusion of all administrative or other judicial proceedings con-

cerning the filing of a false report, the name of the false reporter and the nature of the false report shall be made public, pursuant to s. 119.01(1). Such information shall be admissible in any civil or criminal proceeding.

(10) A person who knowingly and willfully makes a false report of abuse, abandonment, or neglect of a child, or a person who counsels another to make a false report may be civilly liable for damages suffered, including reasonable attorney fees and costs, as a result of the filing of the false report. If the name of the person who filed the false report or counseled another to do so has not been disclosed under subsection (9), the department as custodian of the records may be named as a party in the suit until the dependency court determines in a written order upon an in camera inspection of the records and report that there is a reasonable basis for believing that the report was false and that the identity of the reporter may be disclosed for the purpose of proceeding with a lawsuit for civil damages resulting from the filing of the false report. The alleged perpetrator may submit witness affidavits to assist the court in making this initial determination.

(11) Any person making a report who is acting in good faith is immune from any liability under this section and shall continue to be entitled to have the confidentiality of their identity maintained.

HISTORY:

S. 65, ch. 94-164; s. 5, ch. 98-111; s. 36, ch. 98-403; s. 13, ch. 99-193.

Editor's notes.

Former s. 415.5131.

PART III.
PROTECTIVE INVESTIGATIONS.

§ 39.301. Initiation of protective investigations.

(1) Upon receiving a report of known or suspected child abuse, abandonment, or neglect, or that a child is in need of supervision and care and has no parent, legal custodian, or responsible adult relative immediately known and available to provide supervision and care, the central abuse hotline shall determine if the report requires an immediate onsite protective investigation. For reports requiring an immediate onsite protective investigation, the central abuse hotline shall immediately notify the department's designated district staff responsible for protective investigations to ensure that an onsite investigation is promptly initiated. For reports not requiring an immediate onsite protective investigation, the central abuse hotline shall notify the department's designated district staff responsible for protective investigations in sufficient time to allow for an investigation. At the time of notification, the central abuse hotline shall also provide information to district staff on any previous report concerning a subject of the

present report or any pertinent information relative to the present report or any noted earlier reports.

(2)(a)　The department shall immediately forward allegations of criminal conduct to the municipal or county law enforcement agency of the municipality or county in which the alleged conduct has occurred.

(b)　As used in this subsection, the term "criminal conduct" means:

1.　A child is known or suspected to be the victim of child abuse, as defined in s. 827.03, or of neglect of a child, as defined in s. 827.03.

2.　A child is known or suspected to have died as a result of abuse or neglect.

3.　A child is known or suspected to be the victim of aggravated child abuse, as defined in s. 827.03.

4.　A child is known or suspected to be the victim of sexual battery, as defined in s. 827.071, or of sexual abuse, as defined in s. 39.01.

5.　A child is known or suspected to be the victim of institutional child abuse or neglect, as defined in s. 39.01, and as provided for in s. 39.302(1).

6.　A child is known or suspected to be a victim of human trafficking, as provided in s. 787.06.

(c)　Upon receiving a written report of an allegation of criminal conduct from the department, the law enforcement agency shall review the information in the written report to determine whether a criminal investigation is warranted. If the law enforcement agency accepts the case for criminal investigation, it shall coordinate its investigative activities with the department, whenever feasible. If the law enforcement agency does not accept the case for criminal investigation, the agency shall notify the department in writing.

(d)　The local law enforcement agreement required in s. 39.306 shall describe the specific local protocols for implementing this section.

(3)　The department shall maintain a single, standard electronic child welfare case file for each child whose report is accepted by the central abuse hotline for investigation. Such file must contain information concerning all reports received by the abuse hotline concerning that child and all services received by that child and family. The file must be made available to any department staff, agent of the department, or contract provider given responsibility for conducting a protective investigation.

(4)　To the extent practical, all protective investigations involving a child shall be conducted or the work supervised by a single individual in order for there to be broad knowledge and understanding of the child's history. When a new investigator is assigned to investigate a second and subsequent report involving a child, a multidisciplinary staffing shall be conducted which includes new and prior investigators, their supervisors, and appropriate private providers in order to

ensure that, to the extent possible, there is coordination among all parties. The department shall establish an internal operating procedure that ensures that all required investigatory activities, including a review of the child's complete investigative and protective services history, are completed by the investigator, reviewed by the supervisor in a timely manner, and signed and dated by both the investigator and the supervisor.

(5)(a)　Upon commencing an investigation under this part, the child protective investigator shall inform any subject of the investigation of the following:

1.　The names of the investigators and identifying credentials from the department.

2.　The purpose of the investigation.

3.　The right to obtain his or her own attorney and ways that the information provided by the subject may be used.

4.　The possible outcomes and services of the department's response.

5.　The right of the parent or legal custodian to be engaged to the fullest extent possible in determining the nature of the allegation and the nature of any identified problem and the remedy.

6.　The duty of the parent or legal custodian to report any change in the residence or location of the child to the investigator and that the duty to report continues until the investigation is closed.

(b)　The investigator shall fully inform parents or legal custodians of their rights and options, including opportunities for audio or video recording of investigators' interviews with parents or legal custodians or children.

(6)　Upon commencing an investigation under this part, if a report was received from a reporter under s. 39.201(1)(b), the protective investigator must provide his or her contact information to the reporter within 24 hours after being assigned to the investigation. The investigator must also advise the reporter that he or she may provide a written summary of the report made to the central abuse hotline to the investigator which shall become a part of the electronic child welfare case file.

(7)　An assessment of safety and the perceived needs for the child and family shall be conducted in a manner that is sensitive to the social, economic, and cultural environment of the family. This assessment must include a face-to-face interview with the child, other siblings, parents, and other adults in the household and an onsite assessment of the child's residence.

(8)　Protective investigations shall be performed by the department or its agent.

(9)(a)　For each report received from the central abuse hotline and accepted for investigation, the department or the sheriff providing child protective investigative services under s. 39.3065, shall perform the following child protective investigation activities to determine child safety:

1. Conduct a review of all relevant, available information specific to the child and family and alleged maltreatment; family child welfare history; local, state, and federal criminal records checks; and requests for law enforcement assistance provided by the abuse hotline. Based on a review of available information, including the allegations in the current report, a determination shall be made as to whether immediate consultation should occur with law enforcement, the child protection team, a domestic violence shelter or advocate, or a substance abuse or mental health professional. Such consultations should include discussion as to whether a joint response is necessary and feasible. A determination shall be made as to whether the person making the report should be contacted before the face-to-face interviews with the child and family members.

2. Conduct face-to-face interviews with the child; other siblings, if any; and the parents, legal custodians, or caregivers.

3. Assess the child's residence, including a determination of the composition of the family and household, including the name, address, date of birth, social security number, sex, and race of each child named in the report; any siblings or other children in the same household or in the care of the same adults; the parents, legal custodians, or caregivers; and any other adults in the same household.

4. Determine whether there is any indication that any child in the family or household has been abused, abandoned, or neglected; the nature and extent of present or prior injuries, abuse, or neglect, and any evidence thereof; and a determination as to the person or persons apparently responsible for the abuse, abandonment, or neglect, including the name, address, date of birth, social security number, sex, and race of each such person.

5. Complete assessment of immediate child safety for each child based on available records, interviews, and observations with all persons named in subparagraph 2. and appropriate collateral contacts, which may include other professionals. The department's child protection investigators are hereby designated a criminal justice agency for the purpose of accessing criminal justice information to be used for enforcing this state's laws concerning the crimes of child abuse, abandonment, and neglect. This information shall be used solely for purposes supporting the detection, apprehension, prosecution, pretrial release, posttrial release, or rehabilitation of criminal offenders or persons accused of the crimes of child abuse, abandonment, or neglect and may not be further disseminated or used for any other purpose.

6. Document the present and impending dangers to each child based on the identification of inadequate protective capacity through utilization of a standardized safety assessment instrument. If present or impending danger is identified, the child protective investigator must implement a safety plan or take the child into custody. If present danger is identified and the child is not removed, the child protective investigator shall create and implement a safety plan before leaving the home or the location where there is present danger. If impending danger is identified, the child protective investigator shall create and implement a safety plan as soon as necessary to protect the safety of the child. The child protective investigator may modify the safety plan if he or she identifies additional impending danger.

a. If the child protective investigator implements a safety plan, the plan must be specific, sufficient, feasible, and sustainable in response to the realities of the present or impending danger. A safety plan may be an in-home plan or an out-of-home plan, or a combination of both. A safety plan may include tasks or responsibilities for a parent, caregiver, or legal custodian. However, a safety plan may not rely on promissory commitments by the parent, caregiver, or legal custodian who is currently not able to protect the child or on services that are not available or will not result in the safety of the child. A safety plan may not be implemented if for any reason the parents, guardian, or legal custodian lacks the capacity or ability to comply with the plan. If the department is not able to develop a plan that is specific, sufficient, feasible, and sustainable, the department shall file a shelter petition. A child protective investigator shall implement separate safety plans for the perpetrator of domestic violence, if the investigator, using reasonable efforts, can locate the perpetrator to implement a safety plan, and for the parent who is a victim of domestic violence as defined in s. 741.28. Reasonable efforts to locate a perpetrator include, but are not limited to, a diligent search pursuant to the same requirements as in s. 39.503. If the perpetrator of domestic violence is not the parent, guardian, or legal custodian of any child in the home and if the department does not intend to file a shelter petition or dependency petition that will assert allegations against the perpetrator as a parent of a child in the home, the child protective investigator shall seek issuance of an injunction authorized by s. 39.504 to implement a safety plan for the perpetrator and impose any other conditions to protect the child. The safety plan for the parent who is a victim of domestic violence may not be shared with the perpetrator. If any party to a safety plan fails to comply with the safety plan resulting in the child being unsafe, the department shall file a shelter petition.

b. The child protective investigator shall collaborate with the community-based care lead agency in the development of the safety plan as necessary to ensure that the safety plan is specific, sufficient, feasible, and sustainable. The child protective investigator shall identify services necessary for the successful implementation of the safety plan. The child protective investigator and the community-based care lead agency shall mobilize service resources to assist all parties in complying with the safety plan. The community-based care lead agency shall prioritize safety plan services to families who have multiple risk factors, including, but not limited to, two or more of the following:

(I) The parent or legal custodian is of young age;

(II) The parent or legal custodian, or an adult currently living in or frequently visiting the home, has a history of substance abuse, mental illness, or domestic violence;

(III) The parent or legal custodian, or an adult currently living in or frequently visiting the home, has been previously found to have physically or sexually abused a child;

(IV) The parent or legal custodian or an adult currently living in or frequently visiting the home has been the subject of multiple allegations by reputable reports of abuse or neglect;

(V) The child is physically or developmentally disabled; or

(VI) The child is 3 years of age or younger.

c. The child protective investigator shall monitor the implementation of the plan to ensure the child's safety until the case is transferred to the lead agency at which time the lead agency shall monitor the implementation.

(b) For each report received from the central abuse hotline, the department or the sheriff providing child protective investigative services under s. 39.3065, shall determine the protective, treatment, and ameliorative services necessary to safeguard and ensure the child's safety and well-being and development, and cause the delivery of those services through the early intervention of the department or its agent. Whenever a delay or disability of the child is suspected, the parent must be referred to a local child developmental screening program, such as the Child Find program of the Florida Diagnostic and Learning Resource System, for screening of the child. As applicable, child protective investigators must inform parents and caregivers how and when to use the injunction process under s. 741.30 to remove a perpetrator of domestic violence from the home as an intervention to protect the child.

1. If the department or the sheriff providing child protective investigative services determines that the interests of the child and the public will be best served by providing the child care or other treatment voluntarily accepted by the child and the parents or legal custodians, the parent or legal custodian and child may be referred for such care, case management, or other community resources.

2. If the department or the sheriff providing child protective investigative services determines that the child is in need of protection and supervision, the department may file a petition for dependency.

3. If a petition for dependency is not being filed by the department, the person or agency originating the report shall be advised of the right to file a petition pursuant to this part.

4. At the close of an investigation, the department or the sheriff providing child protective services shall provide to the person who is alleged to have caused the abuse, neglect, or abandonment and the parent or legal custodian a summary of findings from the investigation and provide information about their right to access confidential reports in accordance with s. 39.202.

(10)(a) The department's training program for staff responsible for responding to reports accepted by the central abuse hotline must also ensure that child protective responders:

1. Know how to fully inform parents or legal custodians of their rights and options, including opportunities for audio or video recording of child protective responder interviews with parents or legal custodians or children.

2. Know how and when to use the injunction process under s. 39.504 or s. 741.30 to remove a perpetrator of domestic violence from the home as an intervention to protect the child.

3. Know how to explain to the parent, legal custodian, or person who is alleged to have caused the abuse, neglect, or abandonment the results of the investigation and to provide information about his or her right to access confidential reports in accordance with s. 39.202, prior to closing the case.

(b) To enhance the skills of individual staff members and to improve the region's and district's overall child protection system, the department's training program at the regional and district levels must include results of qualitative reviews of child protective investigation cases handled within the region or district in order to identify weaknesses as well as examples of effective interventions which occurred at each point in the case.

(c) For all reports received, detailed documentation is required for the investigative activities.

(11) The department shall incorporate into its quality assurance program the monitoring of reports that

receive a child protective investigation to determine the quality and timeliness of safety assessments, engagements with families, teamwork with other experts and professionals, and appropriate investigative activities that are uniquely tailored to the safety factors associated with each child and family.

(12)   If the department or its agent is denied reasonable access to a child by the parents, legal custodians, or caregivers and the department deems that the best interests of the child so require, it shall seek an appropriate court order or other legal authority before examining and interviewing the child.

(13)   Onsite visits and face-to-face interviews with the child or family shall be unannounced unless it is determined by the department or its agent or contract provider that such unannounced visit would threaten the safety of the child.

(14)(a)   If the department or its agent determines that a child requires immediate or long-term protection through medical or other health care or homemaker care, day care, protective supervision, or other services to stabilize the home environment, including intensive family preservation services through the Intensive Crisis Counseling Program, such services shall first be offered for voluntary acceptance unless:

1.   There are high-risk factors that may impact the ability of the parents or legal custodians to exercise judgment. Such factors may include the parents' or legal custodians' young age or history of substance abuse, mental illness, or domestic violence; or

2.   There is a high likelihood of lack of compliance with voluntary services, and such noncompliance would result in the child being unsafe.

(b)   The parents or legal custodians shall be informed of the right to refuse services, as well as the responsibility of the department to protect the child regardless of the acceptance or refusal of services. If the services are refused, a collateral contact shall include a relative, if the protective investigator has knowledge of and the ability to contact a relative. If the services are refused and the department deems that the child's need for protection requires services, the department shall take the child into protective custody or petition the court as provided in this chapter. At any time after the commencement of a protective investigation, a relative may submit in writing to the protective investigator or case manager a request to receive notification of all proceedings and hearings in accordance with s. 39.502. The request shall include the relative's name, address, and phone number and the relative's relationship to the child. The protective investigator or case manager shall forward such request to the attorney for the department. The failure to provide notice to either a relative who requests it pursuant to this subsection or to a relative who is providing out-of-home care for a child may not result in any previous action of the court at any stage or proceeding in dependency or termination of parental rights under any part of this chapter being set aside, reversed, modified, or in any way changed absent a finding by the court that a change is required in the child's best interests.

(c)   The department, in consultation with the judiciary, shall adopt by rule:

1.   Criteria that are factors requiring that the department take the child into custody, petition the court as provided in this chapter, or, if the child is not taken into custody or a petition is not filed with the court, conduct an administrative review. Such factors must include, but are not limited to, noncompliance with a safety plan or the case plan developed by the department, and the family under this chapter, and prior abuse reports with findings that involve the child, the child's sibling, or the child's caregiver.

2.   Requirements that if after an administrative review the department determines not to take the child into custody or petition the court, the department shall document the reason for its decision in writing and include it in the investigative file. For all cases that were accepted by the local law enforcement agency for criminal investigation pursuant to subsection (2), the department must include in the file written documentation that the administrative review included input from law enforcement. In addition, for all cases that must be referred to child protection teams pursuant to s. 39.303(4) and (5), the file must include written documentation that the administrative review included the results of the team's evaluation.

(15)   When a child is taken into custody pursuant to this section, the authorized agent of the department shall request that the child's parent, caregiver, or legal custodian disclose the names, relationships, and addresses of all parents and prospective parents and all next of kin, so far as are known.

(16)   The department shall complete its protective investigation within 60 days after receiving the initial report, unless:

(a)   There is also an active, concurrent criminal investigation that is continuing beyond the 60-day period and the closure of the protective investigation may compromise successful criminal prosecution of the child abuse or neglect case, in which case the closure date shall coincide with the closure date of the criminal investigation and any resulting legal action.

(b)   In child death cases, the final report of the medical examiner is necessary for the department to close its investigation and the report has not been received within the 60-day period, in which case the report closure date shall be extended to accommodate the report.

(c)   A child who is necessary to an investigation has been declared missing by the department, a law enforcement agency, or a court, in which case the 60-day period shall be extended until the child has been located or until sufficient information exists to close the investigation despite the unknown location of the child.

(17)   Immediately upon learning during the course of an investigation that:

(a)   The immediate safety or well-being of a child is endangered;

(b)   The family is likely to flee;

(c)   A child died as a result of abuse, abandonment, or neglect;

(d)   A child is a victim of aggravated child abuse as defined in s. 827.03; or

(e)   A child is a victim of sexual battery or of sexual abuse,

the department shall notify the jurisdictionally responsible state attorney, and county sheriff's office or local police department, and, within 3 working days, transmit a full written report to those agencies. The law enforcement agency shall review the report and determine whether a criminal investigation needs to be conducted and shall assume lead responsibility for all criminal fact-finding activities. A criminal investigation shall be coordinated, whenever possible, with the child protective investigation of the department. Any interested person who has information regarding an offense described in this subsection may forward a statement to the state attorney as to whether prosecution is warranted and appropriate.

(18)   In a child protective investigation or a criminal investigation, when the initial interview with the child is conducted at school, the department or the law enforcement agency may allow, notwithstanding s. 39.0132(4), a school staff member who is known by the child to be present during the initial interview if:

(a)   The department or law enforcement agency believes that the school staff member could enhance the success of the interview by his or her presence; and

(b)   The child requests or consents to the presence of the school staff member at the interview.

School staff may be present only when authorized by this subsection. Information received during the interview or from any other source regarding the alleged abuse or neglect of the child is confidential and exempt from s. 119.07(1), except as otherwise provided by court order. A separate record of the investigation of the abuse, abandonment, or neglect may not be maintained by the school or school staff member. Violation of this subsection is a misdemeanor of the second degree, punishable as provided in s. 775.082 or s. 775.083.

(19)   When a law enforcement agency conducts a criminal investigation into allegations of child abuse, neglect, or abandonment, photographs documenting the abuse or neglect shall be taken when appropriate.

(20)   Within 15 days after the case is reported to him or her pursuant to this chapter, the state attorney shall report his or her findings to the department and shall include in such report a determination of whether or not prosecution is justified and appropriate in view of the circumstances of the specific case.

(21)   When an investigation is closed and a person is not identified as a caregiver responsible for the abuse, neglect, or abandonment alleged in the report, the fact that the person is named in some capacity in the report may not be used in any way to adversely affect the interests of that person. This prohibition applies to any use of the information in employment screening, licensing, child placement, adoption, or any other decisions by a private adoption agency or a state agency or its contracted providers, except that a previous report may be used to determine whether a child is safe and what the known risk is to the child at any stage of a child protection proceeding.

(22)   If, after having been notified of the requirement to report a change in residence or location of the child to the protective investigator, a parent or legal custodian causes the child to move, or allows the child to be moved, to a different residence or location, or if the child leaves the residence on his or her own accord and the parent or legal custodian does not notify the protective investigator of the move within 2 business days, the child may be considered to be a missing child for the purposes of filing a report with a law enforcement agency under s. 937.021.

(23)   If, at any time during a child protective investigation, a child is born into a family under investigation or a child moves into the home under investigation, the child protective investigator shall add the child to the investigation and assess the child's safety pursuant to subsection (7) and paragraph (9)(a).

HISTORY:

S. 38, ch. 98-403; s. 7, ch. 99-168; s. 14, ch. 99-193; s. 4, ch. 2000-217; s. 2, ch. 2001-50; s. 2, ch. 2003-127; s. 2, ch. 2005-173; s. 8, ch. 2006-86, eff. July 1, 2006; s. 1, ch. 2006-306, eff. July 1, 2006; s. 6, ch. 2008-245, eff. June 30, 2008; s. 5, ch. 2009-43, eff. July 1, 2009; s. 42, ch. 2011-213, eff. July 1, 2011; s. 6, ch. 2012-178, eff. July 1, 2012; s. 8, ch. 2014-224, eff. July 1, 2014; s. 5, ch. 2015-177, eff. July 1, 2015; s. 5, ch. 2017-151, eff. July 1, 2017.

Editor's notes.

Section 1 of ch. 2009-43 provides: "This act may be cited as the 'Zahid Jones, Jr., Give Grandparents and Other Relatives a Voice Act.' "

The phrase "within 3 working days" in subsection (17) is as amended by s. 14, ch. 99-193. The amendment by s. 7, ch. 99-168, used "within 3 days."

The phrase "full written report" in subsection (17) is as amended by s. 14, ch. 99-193. The amendment by s. 7, ch. 99-168, did not include the word "full."

§ 39.302.   Protective investigations of institutional child abuse, abandonment, or neglect.

(1)   The department shall conduct a child protective investigation of each report of institutional child abuse, abandonment, or neglect. Upon receipt of a report that

alleges that an employee or agent of the department, or any other entity or person covered by s. 39.01(32) or (48), acting in an official capacity, has committed an act of child abuse, abandonment, or neglect, the department shall initiate a child protective investigation within the timeframe established under s. 39.201(5) and notify the appropriate state attorney, law enforcement agency, and licensing agency, which shall immediately conduct a joint investigation, unless independent investigations are more feasible. When conducting investigations or having face-to-face interviews with the child, investigation visits shall be unannounced unless it is determined by the department or its agent that unannounced visits threaten the safety of the child. If a facility is exempt from licensing, the department shall inform the owner or operator of the facility of the report. Each agency conducting a joint investigation is entitled to full access to the information gathered by the department in the course of the investigation. A protective investigation must include an interview with the child's parent or legal guardian. The department shall make a full written report to the state attorney within 3 working days after making the oral report. A criminal investigation shall be coordinated, whenever possible, with the child protective investigation of the department. Any interested person who has information regarding the offenses described in this subsection may forward a statement to the state attorney as to whether prosecution is warranted and appropriate. Within 15 days after the completion of the investigation, the state attorney shall report the findings to the department and shall include in the report a determination of whether or not prosecution is justified and appropriate in view of the circumstances of the specific case.

(2)(a) If in the course of the child protective investigation, the department finds that a subject of a report, by continued contact with children in care, constitutes a threatened harm to the physical health, mental health, or welfare of the children, the department may restrict a subject's access to the children pending the outcome of the investigation. The department or its agent shall employ the least restrictive means necessary to safeguard the physical health, mental health, and welfare of the children in care. This authority shall apply only to child protective investigations in which there is some evidence that child abuse, abandonment, or neglect has occurred. A subject of a report whose access to children in care has been restricted is entitled to petition the circuit court for judicial review. The court shall enter written findings of fact based upon the preponderance of evidence that child abuse, abandonment, or neglect did occur and that the department's restrictive action against a subject of the report was justified in order to safeguard the physical health, mental health, and welfare of the children in care. The restrictive action of the department shall be effective for no more than 90 days without a judicial finding supporting the actions of the department.

(b) Upon completion of the department's child protective investigation, the department may make application to the circuit court for continued restrictive action against any person necessary to safeguard the physical health, mental health, and welfare of the children in care.

(3) Pursuant to the restrictive actions described in subsection (2), in cases of institutional abuse, abandonment, or neglect in which the removal of a subject of a report will result in the closure of the facility, and when requested by the owner of the facility, the department may provide appropriate personnel to assist in maintaining the operation of the facility. The department may provide assistance when it can be demonstrated by the owner that there are no reasonable alternatives to such action. The length of the assistance shall be agreed upon by the owner and the department; however, the assistance shall not be for longer than the course of the restrictive action imposed pursuant to subsection (2). The owner shall reimburse the department for the assistance of personnel provided.

(4) The department shall notify the Florida local advocacy council in the appropriate district of the department as to every report of institutional child abuse, abandonment, or neglect in the district in which a client of the department is alleged or shown to have been abused, abandoned, or neglected, which notification shall be made within 48 hours after the department commences its investigation.

(5) The department shall notify the state attorney and the appropriate law enforcement agency of any other child abuse, abandonment, or neglect case in which a criminal investigation is deemed appropriate by the department.

(6) In cases of institutional child abuse, abandonment, or neglect in which the multiplicity of reports of abuse, abandonment, or neglect or the severity of the allegations indicates the need for specialized investigation by the department in order to afford greater safeguards for the physical health, mental health, and welfare of the children in care, the department shall provide a team of persons specially trained in the areas of child abuse, abandonment, and neglect investigations, diagnosis, and treatment to assist the local office of the department in expediting its investigation and in making recommendations for restrictive actions and to assist in other ways deemed necessary by the department in order to carry out the provisions of this section. The specially trained team shall also provide assistance to any investigation of the allegations by local law enforcement and the Department of Law Enforcement.

(7) When an investigation of institutional abuse, neglect, or abandonment is closed and a person is not identified as a caregiver responsible for the abuse, neglect, or abandonment alleged in the report, the fact that the person is named in some capacity in the report

may not be used in any way to adversely affect the interests of that person. This prohibition applies to any use of the information in employment screening, licensing, child placement, adoption, or any other decisions by a private adoption agency or a state agency or its contracted providers.

(a) However, if such a person is a licensee of the department and is named in any capacity in three or more reports within a 5-year period, the department may review those reports and determine whether the information contained in the reports is relevant for purposes of determining whether the person's license should be renewed or revoked. If the information is relevant to the decision to renew or revoke the license, the department may rely on the information contained in the report in making that decision.

(b) Likewise, if a person is employed as a caregiver in a residential group home licensed pursuant to s. 409.175 and is named in any capacity in three or more reports within a 5-year period, the department may review all reports for the purposes of the employment screening required pursuant to s. 409.145(2)(e).

HISTORY:

S. 39, ch. 98-403; s. 8, ch. 99-168; s. 15, ch. 99-193; s. 42, ch. 2000-139; s. 7, ch. 2000-263; s. 3, ch. 2003-127; s. 3, ch. 2005-173; s. 30, ch. 2006-86, eff. July 1, 2006; s. 7, ch. 2006-194, eff, July 1, 2006; s. 26, ch. 2008-245, eff. June 30, 2008; s. 7, ch. 2012-178, eff. July 1, 2012; s. 51, ch. 2014-224, eff. July 1, 2014; s. 6, ch. 2017-151, eff. July 1, 2017.

§ 39.303. Child protection teams and sexual abuse treatment programs; services; eligible cases.

(1) The Children's Medical Services Program in the Department of Health shall develop, maintain, and coordinate the services of one or more multidisciplinary child protection teams in each of the service circuits of the Department of Children and Families. Such teams may be composed of appropriate representatives of school districts and appropriate health, mental health, social service, legal service, and law enforcement agencies. The Department of Health and the Department of Children and Families shall maintain an interagency agreement that establishes protocols for oversight and operations of child protection teams and sexual abuse treatment programs. The State Surgeon General and the Deputy Secretary for Children's Medical Services, in consultation with the Secretary of Children and Families and the Statewide Medical Director for Child Protection, shall maintain the responsibility for the screening, employment, and, if necessary, the termination of child protection team medical directors in the 15 circuits.

(2)(a) The Statewide Medical Director for Child Protection must be a physician licensed under chapter 458 or chapter 459 who is a board-certified pediatrician with a subspecialty certification in child abuse from the American Board of Pediatrics.

(b) Each child protection team medical director must be a physician licensed under chapter 458 or chapter 459 who is a board-certified physician in pediatrics or family medicine and, within 2 years after the date of employment as a child protection team medical director, obtains a subspecialty certification in child abuse from the American Board of Pediatrics or within 2 years meet the minimum requirements established by a third-party credentialing entity recognizing a demonstrated specialized competence in child abuse pediatrics pursuant to paragraph (d). Each child protection team medical director employed on July 1, 2015, must, by July 1, 2019, either obtain a subspecialty certification in child abuse from the American Board of Pediatrics or meet the minimum requirements established by a third-party credentialing entity recognizing a demonstrated specialized competence in child abuse pediatrics pursuant to paragraph (d). Child protection team medical directors shall be responsible for oversight of the teams in the circuits.

(c) All medical personnel participating on a child protection team must successfully complete the required child protection team training curriculum as set forth in protocols determined by the Deputy Secretary for Children's Medical Services and the Statewide Medical Director for Child Protection.

(d) Contingent on appropriations, the Department of Health shall approve one or more third-party credentialing entities for the purpose of developing and administering a professional credentialing program for child protection team medical directors. Within 90 days after receiving documentation from a third-party credentialing entity, the department shall approve a third-party credentialing entity that demonstrates compliance with the following minimum standards:

1. Establishment of child abuse pediatrics core competencies, certification standards, testing instruments, and recertification standards according to national psychometric standards.

2. Establishment of a process to administer the certification application, award, and maintenance processes according to national psychometric standards.

3. Demonstrated ability to administer a professional code of ethics and disciplinary process that applies to all certified persons.

4. Establishment of, and ability to maintain, a publicly accessible Internet-based database that contains information on each person who applies for and is awarded certification, such as the person's first and last name, certification status, and ethical or disciplinary history.

5. Demonstrated ability to administer biennial continuing education and certification renewal requirements.

6. Demonstrated ability to administer an education provider program to approve qualified train-

ing entities and to provide precertification training to applicants and continuing education opportunities to certified professionals.

(3) The Department of Health shall use and convene the child protection teams to supplement the assessment and protective supervision activities of the family safety and preservation program of the Department of Children and Families. This section does not remove or reduce the duty and responsibility of any person to report pursuant to this chapter all suspected or actual cases of child abuse, abandonment, or neglect or sexual abuse of a child. The role of the child protection teams is to support activities of the program and to provide services deemed by the child protection teams to be necessary and appropriate to abused, abandoned, and neglected children upon referral. The specialized diagnostic assessment, evaluation, coordination, consultation, and other supportive services that a child protection team must be capable of providing include, but are not limited to, the following:

(a) Medical diagnosis and evaluation services, including provision or interpretation of X rays and laboratory tests, and related services, as needed, and documentation of related findings.

(b) Telephone consultation services in emergencies and in other situations.

(c) Medical evaluation related to abuse, abandonment, or neglect, as defined by policy or rule of the Department of Health.

(d) Such psychological and psychiatric diagnosis and evaluation services for the child or the child's parent or parents, legal custodian or custodians, or other caregivers, or any other individual involved in a child abuse, abandonment, or neglect case, as the team may determine to be needed.

(e) Expert medical, psychological, and related professional testimony in court cases.

(f) Case staffings to develop treatment plans for children whose cases have been referred to the team. A child protection team may provide consultation with respect to a child who is alleged or is shown to be abused, abandoned, or neglected, which consultation shall be provided at the request of a representative of the family safety and preservation program or at the request of any other professional involved with a child or the child's parent or parents, legal custodian or custodians, or other caregivers. In every such child protection team case staffing, consultation, or staff activity involving a child, a family safety and preservation program representative shall attend and participate.

(g) Case service coordination and assistance, including the location of services available from other public and private agencies in the community.

(h) Such training services for program and other employees of the Department of Children and Families, employees of the Department of Health, and other medical professionals as is deemed appropri-

ate to enable them to develop and maintain their professional skills and abilities in handling child abuse, abandonment, and neglect cases.

(i) Educational and community awareness campaigns on child abuse, abandonment, and neglect in an effort to enable citizens more successfully to prevent, identify, and treat child abuse, abandonment, and neglect in the community.

(j) Child protection team assessments that include, as appropriate, medical evaluations, medical consultations, family psychosocial interviews, specialized clinical interviews, or forensic interviews.

A child protection team that is evaluating a report of medical neglect and assessing the health care needs of a medically complex child shall consult with a physician who has experience in treating children with the same condition.

(4) The child abuse, abandonment, and neglect reports that must be referred by the department to child protection teams of the Department of Health for an assessment and other appropriate available support services as set forth in subsection (3) must include cases involving:

(a) Injuries to the head, bruises to the neck or head, burns, or fractures in a child of any age.

(b) Bruises anywhere on a child 5 years of age or under.

(c) Any report alleging sexual abuse of a child.

(d) Any sexually transmitted disease in a prepubescent child.

(e) Reported malnutrition of a child and failure of a child to thrive.

(f) Reported medical neglect of a child.

(g) Any family in which one or more children have been pronounced dead on arrival at a hospital or other health care facility, or have been injured and later died, as a result of suspected abuse, abandonment, or neglect, when any sibling or other child remains in the home.

(h) Symptoms of serious emotional problems in a child when emotional or other abuse, abandonment, or neglect is suspected.

(5) All abuse and neglect cases transmitted for investigation to a circuit by the hotline must be simultaneously transmitted to the child protection team for review. For the purpose of determining whether a face-to-face medical evaluation by a child protection team is necessary, all cases transmitted to the child protection team which meet the criteria in subsection (4) must be timely reviewed by:

(a) A physician licensed under chapter 458 or chapter 459 who holds board certification in pediatrics and is a member of a child protection team;

(b) A physician licensed under chapter 458 or chapter 459 who holds board certification in a specialty other than pediatrics, who may complete the review only when working under the direction of the child protection team medical director or a physician licensed under chapter 458 or chapter 459 who holds board certification in pediatrics and is a member of a child protection team;

(c) An advanced registered nurse practitioner licensed under chapter 464 who has a specialty in pediatrics or family medicine and is a member of a child protection team;

(d) A physician assistant licensed under chapter 458 or chapter 459, who may complete the review only when working under the supervision of the child protection team medical director or a physician licensed under chapter 458 or chapter 459 who holds board certification in pediatrics and is a member of a child protection team; or

(e) A registered nurse licensed under chapter 464, who may complete the review only when working under the direct supervision of the child protection team medical director or a physician licensed under chapter 458 or chapter 459 who holds board certification in pediatrics and is a member of a child protection team.

(6) A face-to-face medical evaluation by a child protection team is not necessary when:

(a) The child was examined for the alleged abuse or neglect by a physician who is not a member of the child protection team, and a consultation between the child protection team medical director or a child protection team board-certified pediatrician, advanced registered nurse practitioner, physician assistant working under the supervision of a child protection team medical director or a child protection team board-certified pediatrician, or registered nurse working under the direct supervision of a child protection team medical director or a child protection team board-certified pediatrician, and the examining physician concludes that a further medical evaluation is unnecessary;

(b) The child protective investigator, with supervisory approval, has determined, after conducting a child safety assessment, that there are no indications of injuries as described in paragraphs (4)(a)-(h) as reported; or

(c) The child protection team medical director or a child protection team board-certified pediatrician, as authorized in subsection (5), determines that a medical evaluation is not required.

Notwithstanding paragraphs (a), (b), and (c), a child protection team medical director or a child protection team pediatrician, as authorized in subsection (5), may determine that a face-to-face medical evaluation is necessary.

(7) In all instances in which a child protection team is providing certain services to abused, abandoned, or neglected children, other offices and units of the Department of Health, and offices and units of the Department of Children and Families, shall avoid duplicating the provision of those services.

(8) The Department of Health child protection team quality assurance program and the Family Safety Program Office of the Department of Children and Families shall collaborate to ensure referrals and responses to child abuse, abandonment, and neglect reports are appropriate. Each quality assurance program shall include a review of records in which there are no findings of abuse, abandonment, or neglect, and the findings of these reviews shall be included in each department's quality assurance reports.

(9)(a) Children's Medical Services shall convene a task force to develop a standardized protocol for forensic interviewing of children suspected of having been abused. The Department of Health shall provide staff to the task force as necessary. The task force shall include:

1. A representative from the Florida Prosecuting Attorneys Association.

2. A representative from the Florida Psychological Association.

3. The Statewide Medical Director for Child Protection.

4. A representative from the Florida Public Defender Association.

5. The executive director of the Statewide Guardian Ad Litem Office.

6. A representative from a community-based care lead agency.

7. A representative from Children's Medical Services.

8. A representative from the Florida Sheriffs Association.

9. A representative from the Florida Chapter of the American Academy of Pediatrics.

10. A representative from the Florida Network of Children's Advocacy Centers.

11. Other representatives designated by Children's Medical Services.

(b) Children's Medical Services must provide the standardized protocol to the President of the Senate and the Speaker of the House of Representatives by July 1, 2018.

(c) Members of the task force are not entitled to per diem or other payment for service on the task force.

(10) The Children's Medical Services program in the Department of Health shall develop, maintain, and coordinate the services of one or more sexual abuse treatment programs.

(a) A child under the age of 18 who is alleged to be a victim of sexual abuse, his or her siblings, non-offending caregivers, and family members who have been impacted by sexual abuse are eligible for services.

(b) Sexual abuse treatment programs must provide specialized therapeutic treatment to victims of child sexual abuse, their siblings, non-offending caregivers, and family members to assist in recovery from sexual abuse, to prevent developmental impairment, to restore the children's pre-abuse level of developmental functioning, and to promote healthy, non-abusive relationships. Therapeutic intervention services must include crisis intervention, clinical treatment, and individual, family, and group therapy.

(c) The sexual abuse treatment programs and child protection teams must provide referrals for victims of child sexual abuse and their families, as appropriate.

HISTORY:
S. 9, ch. 84-226; s. 63, ch. 85-81; s. 23, ch. 88-337; s. 53, ch. 90-306; s. 24, ch. 95-228; s. 273, ch. 96-406; s. 1043, ch. 97-103; s. 4, ch. 97-237; s. 13, ch. 98-137; s. 31, ch. 98-166; s. 40, ch. 98-403; s. 9, ch. 99-168; s. 42, ch. 99-397; s. 5, ch. 2000-217; s. 2, ch. 2000-367; s. 9, ch. 2006-86, eff. July 1, 2006; s. 4, ch. 2008-6, eff. July 1, 2008; s. 13, ch. 2014-19, eff. July 1, 2014; s. 9, ch. 2014-224, eff. July 1, 2014; s. 2, ch. 2015-177, eff. July 1, 2015; s. 1, ch. 2017-153, eff. July 1, 2017.

Editor's notes.
Former s. 415.5055.

§ 39.3031. Rules for implementation of s. 39.303.

The Department of Health, in consultation with the Department of Children and Families, shall adopt rules governing the child protection teams and sexual abuse treatment programs pursuant to s. 39.303, including definitions, organization, roles and responsibilities, eligibility, services and their availability, qualifications of staff, and a waiver-request process.

HISTORY:
S. 16, ch. 98-137; s. 17, ch. 99-2; s. 43, ch. 2011-213, eff. July 1, 2011; s. 14, ch. 2014-19, eff. July 1, 2014; s. 7, ch. 2015-177, eff. July 1, 2015; s. 2, ch. 2017-153, eff. July 1, 2017.

§ 39.3032. Memorandum of agreement.

A memorandum of agreement shall be developed between the Department of Children and Families and the Department of Health that specifies how the teams will work with child protective investigation and service staff, that requires joint oversight by the two departments of the activities of the teams, and that specifies how that oversight will be implemented.

HISTORY:
S. 17, ch. 98-137; s. 15, ch. 2014-19, eff. July 1, 2014.

§ 39.3035. Child advocacy centers; standards; state funding.

(1) In order to become eligible for a full membership in the Florida Network of Children's Advocacy Centers, Inc., a child advocacy center in this state shall:

(a) Be a private, nonprofit incorporated agency or a governmental entity.

(b) Be a child protection team, or by written agreement incorporate the participation and services of a child protection team, with established community protocols which meet all of the requirements of the National Network of Children's Advocacy Centers, Inc.

(c) Have a neutral, child-focused facility where joint department and law enforcement interviews take place with children in appropriate cases of suspected child sexual abuse or physical abuse. All multidisciplinary agencies shall have a place to interact with the child as investigative or treatment needs require.

(d) Have a minimum designated staff that is supervised and approved by the local board of directors or governmental entity.

(e) Have a multidisciplinary case review team that meets on a regularly scheduled basis or as the caseload of the community requires. The team shall consist of representatives from the Office of the State Attorney, the department, the child protection team, mental health services, law enforcement, and the child advocacy center staff. Medical personnel and a victim's advocate may be part of the team.

(f) Provide case tracking of child abuse cases seen through the center. A center shall also collect data on the number of child abuse cases seen at the center, by sex, race, age, and other relevant data; the number of cases referred for prosecution; and the number of cases referred for mental health therapy. Case records shall be subject to the confidentiality provisions of s. 39.202.

(g) Provide referrals for medical exams and mental health therapy. The center shall provide followup on cases referred for mental health therapy.

(h) Provide training for various disciplines in the community that deal with child abuse.

(i) Have an interagency commitment, in writing, covering those aspects of agency participation in a multidisciplinary approach to the handling of child sexual abuse and serious physical abuse cases.

(2) Provide assurance that child advocacy center employees and volunteers at the center are trained and screened in accordance with s. 39.001(2).

(3) A child advocacy center within this state may not receive the funds generated pursuant to s. 938.10, state or federal funds administered by a state agency, or any other funds appropriated by the Legislature unless all of the standards of subsection (1) are met and the screening requirement of subsection (2) is met. The Florida Network of Children's Advocacy Centers, Inc., shall be responsible for tracking and documenting compliance with subsections (1) and (2) for any of the funds it administers to member child advocacy centers.

(a) Funds for the specific purpose of funding children's advocacy centers shall be appropriated to the Department of Children and Families from funds collected from the additional court cost imposed in cases of certain crimes against minors under s. 938.10. Funds shall be disbursed to the Florida Network of Children's Advocacy Centers, Inc., as established under this section, for the purpose of providing community-based services that augment, but do not duplicate, services provided by state agencies.

(b) The board of directors of the Florida Network of Children's Advocacy Centers, Inc., shall retain 10 percent of all revenues collected to be used to match local contributions, at a rate not to exceed an equal match, in communities establishing children's advocacy centers. The board of directors may use up to 5 percent of the remaining funds to support the activities of the network office and must develop funding criteria and an allocation methodology that ensures an equitable distribution of remaining funds among network participants. The criteria and methodologies must take into account factors that include, but need not be limited to, the center's accreditation status with respect to the National Children's Alliance, the number of clients served, and the population of the area being served by the children's advocacy center.

(c) At the end of each fiscal year, each children's advocacy center receiving revenue as provided in this section must provide a report to the board of directors of the Florida Network of Children's Advocacy Centers, Inc., which reflects center expenditures, all sources of revenue received, and outputs that have been standardized and agreed upon by network members and the board of directors, such as the number of clients served, client demographic information, and number and types of services provided. The Florida Network of Children's Advocacy Centers, Inc., must compile reports from the centers and provide a report to the President of the Senate and the Speaker of the House of Representatives in August of each year beginning in 2005.

HISTORY:
S. 41, ch. 98-403; s. 16, ch. 99-193; s. 37, ch. 2004-265; s. 6, ch. 2006-1, eff. July 4, 2006; s. 5, ch. 2008-16, eff. July 1, 2008; s. 16, ch. 2014-19, eff. July 1, 2014.

§ 39.30351. Child Advocacy Trust Fund [Repealed.]

Repealed by s. 6, ch. 2008-16, effective July 1, 2008.

HISTORY:
S. 1, ch. 2004-302.

§ 39.304. Photographs, medical examinations, X rays, and medical treatment of abused, abandoned, or neglected child.

(1)(a) Any person required to investigate cases of suspected child abuse, abandonment, or neglect may take or cause to be taken photographs of the areas of trauma visible on a child who is the subject of a report. Any child protection team that examines a child who is the subject of a report must take, or cause to be taken, photographs of any areas of trauma visible on the child. Photographs of physical abuse injuries, or duplicates thereof, shall be provided to the department for inclusion in the investigative file and shall become part of that file. Photographs of sexual abuse trauma shall be made part of the child protection team medical record.

(b) If the areas of trauma visible on a child indicate a need for a medical examination, or if the child verbally complains or otherwise exhibits distress as a result of injury through suspected child abuse, abandonment, or neglect, or is alleged to have been sexually abused, the person required to investigate may cause the child to be referred for diagnosis to a licensed physician or an emergency department in a hospital without the consent of the child's parents or legal custodian. Such examination may be performed by any licensed physician or an advanced registered nurse practitioner licensed pursuant to part I of chapter 464. Any licensed physician, or advanced registered nurse practitioner licensed pursuant to part I of chapter 464, who has reasonable cause to suspect that an injury was the result of child abuse, abandonment, or neglect may authorize a radiological examination to be performed on the child without the consent of the child's parent or legal custodian.

(2) Consent for any medical treatment shall be obtained in the following manner.

(a)1. Consent to medical treatment shall be obtained from a parent or legal custodian of the child; or

2. A court order for such treatment shall be obtained.

(b) If a parent or legal custodian of the child is unavailable and his or her whereabouts cannot be reasonably ascertained, and it is after normal working hours so that a court order cannot reasonably be obtained, an authorized agent of the department shall have the authority to consent to necessary medical treatment for the child. The authority of the department to consent to medical treatment in this circumstance shall be limited to the time reasonably necessary to obtain court authorization.

(c) If a parent or legal custodian of the child is available but refuses to consent to the necessary treatment, a court order shall be required unless the situation meets the definition of an emergency in s. 743.064 or the treatment needed is related to suspected abuse, abandonment, or neglect of the child by a parent or legal custodian. In such case, the department shall have the authority to consent to necessary medical treatment. This authority is limited to the time reasonably necessary to obtain court authorization.

In no case shall the department consent to sterilization, abortion, or termination of life support.

(3) Any facility licensed under chapter 395 shall provide to the department, its agent, or a child protection team that contracts with the department any photograph or report on examinations made or X rays taken pursuant to this section, or copies thereof, for the purpose of investigation or assessment of cases of

abuse, abandonment, neglect, or exploitation of children.

(4) Any photograph or report on examinations made or X rays taken pursuant to this section, or copies thereof, shall be sent to the department as soon as possible and shall be preserved in permanent form in records held by the department.

(5) The county in which the child is a resident shall bear the initial costs of the examination of the allegedly abused, abandoned, or neglected child; however, the parents or legal custodian of the child shall be required to reimburse the county for the costs of such examination, other than an initial forensic physical examination as provided in s. 960.28, and to reimburse the department for the cost of the photographs taken pursuant to this section. A medical provider may not bill a child victim, directly or indirectly, for the cost of an initial forensic physical examination.

HISTORY:
SS. 1, 2, 3, 4, 5, 6, ch. 63-24; s. 941, ch. 71-136; ss. 1, 1A, ch. 71-97; s. 32, ch. 73-334; s. 65, ch. 74-383; s. 1, ch. 75-101; s. 1, ch. 75-185; s. 4, ch. 76-237; s. 1, ch. 77-77; s. 3, ch. 77-429; ss. 1, 2, ch. 78-322; s. 3, ch. 78-326; s. 22, ch. 78-361; s. 1, ch. 78-379; s. 181, ch. 79-164; s. 1, ch. 79-203; s. 75, ch. 86-220; s. 24, ch. 88-337; s. 35, ch. 89-294; s. 2, ch. 95-185; s. 133, ch. 97-101; s. 71, ch. 97-103; s. 42, ch. 98-403; s. 10, ch. 99-168; s. 17, ch. 99-193; s. 6, ch. 2000-217; s. 83, ch. 2000-318; s. 6, ch. 2009-43, eff. July 1, 2009.

Editor's notes.
Section 1 of ch. 2009-43 provides: "This act may be cited as the 'Zahid Jones, Jr., Give Grandparents and Other Relatives a Voice Act.' "
Former ss. 828.041, 827.07(5); s. 415.507.

§ 39.305. Intervention and treatment in sexual abuse cases; model plan. [Repealed.]

Repealed by s. 38, ch. 2011-213, effective July 1, 2011.

HISTORY:
S. 38, ch. 85-54; s. 135, ch. 97-101; s. 14, ch. 98-137; s. 43, ch. 98-403.

§ 39.306. Child protective investigations; working agreements with local law enforcement.

The department shall enter into agreements with the jurisdictionally responsible county sheriffs' offices and local police departments that will assume the lead in conducting any potential criminal investigations arising from allegations of child abuse, abandonment, or neglect. The written agreement must specify how the requirements of this chapter will be met. For the purposes of such agreement, the jurisdictionally responsible law enforcement entity is authorized to share Florida criminal history and local criminal history information that is not otherwise exempt from s. 119.07(1) with the district personnel, authorized agent, or contract provider directly responsible for the child protective investigation and emergency child placement. The agencies entering into such agreement must comply with s. 943.0525. Criminal justice information provided

by such law enforcement entity shall be used only for the purposes specified in the agreement and shall be provided at no charge. Notwithstanding any other provision of law, the Department of Law Enforcement shall provide to the department electronic access to Florida criminal justice information which is lawfully available and not exempt from s. 119.07(1), only for the purpose of child protective investigations and emergency child placement. As a condition of access to such information, the department shall be required to execute an appropriate user agreement addressing the access, use, dissemination, and destruction of such information and to comply with all applicable laws and regulations, and rules of the Department of Law Enforcement.

HISTORY:
S. 44, ch. 98-403; s. 11, ch. 99-168.

§ 39.3065. Sheriffs of certain counties to provide child protective investigative services; procedures; funding.

(1) As described in this section, the Department of Children and Families shall, by the end of fiscal year 1999-2000, transfer all responsibility for child protective investigations for Pinellas County, Manatee County, Broward County, and Pasco County to the sheriff of that county in which the child abuse, neglect, or abandonment is alleged to have occurred. Each sheriff is responsible for the provision of all child protective investigations in his or her county. Each individual who provides these services must complete the training provided to and required of protective investigators employed by the Department of Children and Families.

(2) During fiscal year 1998-1999, the Department of Children and Families and each sheriff's office shall enter into a contract for the provision of these services. Funding for the services will be appropriated to the Department of Children and Families, and the department shall transfer to the respective sheriffs for the duration of fiscal year 1998-1999, funding for the investigative responsibilities assumed by the sheriffs, including federal funds that the provider is eligible for and agrees to earn and that portion of general revenue funds which is currently associated with the services that are being furnished under contract, and including, but not limited to, funding for all investigative, supervisory, and clerical positions; training; all associated equipment; furnishings; and other fixed capital items. The contract must specify whether the department will continue to perform part or none of the child protective investigations during the initial year. The sheriffs may either conduct the investigations themselves or may, in turn, subcontract with law enforcement officials or with properly trained employees of private agencies to conduct investigations related to neglect cases only. If such a subcontract is awarded, the sheriff must take full responsibility for any safety decision made by the

subcontractor and must immediately respond with law enforcement staff to any situation that requires removal of a child due to a condition that poses an immediate threat to the child's life. The contract must specify whether the services are to be performed by departmental employees or by persons determined by the sheriff. During this initial year, the department is responsible for quality assurance, and the department retains the responsibility for the performance of all child protective investigations. The department must identify any barriers to transferring the entire responsibility for child protective services to the sheriffs' offices and must pursue avenues for removing any such barriers by means including, but not limited to, applying for federal waivers. By January 15, 1999, the department shall submit to the President of the Senate, the Speaker of the House of Representatives, and the chairs of the Senate and House committees that oversee departmental activities a report that describes any remaining barriers, including any that pertain to funding and related administrative issues. Unless the Legislature, on the basis of that report or other pertinent information, acts to block a transfer of the entire responsibility for child protective investigations to the sheriffs' offices, the sheriffs of Pasco County, Manatee County, Broward County, and Pinellas County, beginning in fiscal year 1999-2000, shall assume the entire responsibility for such services, as provided in subsection (3).

(3)(a) Beginning in fiscal year 1999-2000, the sheriffs of Pasco County, Manatee County, Broward County, and Pinellas County have the responsibility to provide all child protective investigations in their respective counties. Beginning in fiscal year 2000-2001, the Department of Children and Families is authorized to enter into grant agreements with sheriffs of other counties to perform child protective investigations in their respective counties.

(b) The sheriffs shall operate, at a minimum, in accordance with the performance standards and outcome measures established by the Legislature for protective investigations conducted by the Department of Children and Families. Each individual who provides these services must complete, at a minimum, the training provided to and required of protective investigators employed by the Department of Children and Families.

(c) Funds for providing child protective investigations must be identified in the annual appropriation made to the Department of Children and Families, which shall award grants for the full amount identified to the respective sheriffs' offices. Notwithstanding the provisions of ss. 216.181(16)(b) and 216.351, the Department of Children and Families may advance payments to the sheriffs for child protective investigations. Funds for the child protective investigations may not be integrated into the sheriffs' regular budgets. Budgetary data and other data relating to the performance of child protective investigations must be maintained separately from all other records of the sheriffs' offices and reported to the Department of Children and Families as specified in the grant agreement.

(d) Program performance evaluation shall be based on criteria mutually agreed upon by the respective sheriffs and the Department of Children and Families. The program performance evaluation shall be conducted by a team of peer reviewers from the respective sheriffs' offices that perform child protective investigations and representatives from the department. The Department of Children and Families shall submit an annual report regarding quality performance, outcome-measure attainment, and cost efficiency to the President of the Senate, the Speaker of the House of Representatives, and to the Governor no later than January 31 of each year the sheriffs are receiving general appropriations to provide child protective investigations.

HISTORY:
S. 2, ch. 98-180; ss. 12, 53, ch. 99-228; s. 3, ch. 2000-139; ss. 20, 66, ch. 2000-171; s. 13, ch. 2001-60; s. 17, ch. 2014-19, eff. July 1, 2014.

§ 39.3068. Reports of medical neglect.

(1) Upon receiving a report alleging medical neglect, the department or sheriff's office shall assign the case to a child protective investigator who has specialized training in addressing medical neglect or working with medically complex children if such investigator is available. If a child protective investigator with specialized training is not available, the child protective investigator shall consult with department staff with such expertise.

(2) The child protective investigator who has interacted with the child and the child's family shall promptly contact and provide information to the child protection team. The child protection team shall assist the child protective investigator in identifying immediate responses to address the medical needs of the child with the priority of maintaining the child in the home if the parents will be able to meet the needs of the child with additional services. The child protective investigator and the child protection team must use a family-centered approach to assess the capacity of the family to meet those needs. A family-centered approach is intended to increase independence on the part of the family, accessibility to programs and services within the community, and collaboration between families and their service providers. The ethnic, cultural, economic, racial, social, and religious diversity of families must be respected and considered in the development and provision of services.

(3) The child shall be evaluated by the child protection team as soon as practicable. If the child protection team reports that medical neglect is substantiated, the department shall convene a case staffing

which shall be attended, at a minimum, by the child protective investigator; department legal staff; and representatives from the child protection team that evaluated the child, Children's Medical Services, the Agency for Health Care Administration, the community-based care lead agency, and any providers of services to the child. However, the Agency for Health Care Administration is not required to attend the staffing if the child is not Medicaid eligible. The staffing shall consider, at a minimum, available services, given the family's eligibility for services; services that are effective in addressing conditions leading to medical neglect allegations; and services that would enable the child to safely remain at home. Any services that are available and effective shall be provided.

HISTORY:

S. 10, ch. 2014-224, eff. July 1, 2014; s. 2, ch. 2015-79, eff. July 1, 2015.

§ 39.307. Reports of child-on-child sexual abuse.

(1) Upon receiving a report alleging juvenile sexual abuse or inappropriate sexual behavior as defined in s. 39.01, the department shall assist the family, child, and caregiver in receiving appropriate services to address the allegations of the report.

(a) The department shall ensure that information describing the child's history of child sexual abuse is included in the child's electronic record. This record must also include information describing the services the child has received as a result of his or her involvement with child sexual abuse.

(b) Placement decisions for a child who has been involved with child sexual abuse must include consideration of the needs of the child and any other children in the placement.

(c) The department shall monitor the occurrence of child sexual abuse and the provision of services to children involved in child sexual abuse or juvenile sexual abuse, or who have displayed inappropriate sexual behavior.

(2) The department, contracted sheriff's office providing protective investigation services, or contracted case management personnel responsible for providing services, at a minimum, shall adhere to the following procedures:

(a) The purpose of the response to a report alleging juvenile sexual abuse behavior or inappropriate sexual behavior shall be explained to the caregiver.

1. The purpose of the response shall be explained in a manner consistent with legislative purpose and intent provided in this chapter.

2. The name and office telephone number of the person responding shall be provided to the caregiver of the alleged abuser or child who has exhibited inappropriate sexual behavior and the victim's caregiver.

3. The possible consequences of the department's response, including outcomes and services, shall be explained to the caregiver of the alleged abuser or child who has exhibited inappropriate sexual behavior and the victim's caregiver.

(b) The caregiver of the alleged abuser or child who has exhibited inappropriate sexual behavior and the victim's caregiver shall be involved to the fullest extent possible in determining the nature of the sexual behavior concerns and the nature of any problem or risk to other children.

(c) The assessment of risk and the perceived treatment needs of the alleged abuser or child who has exhibited inappropriate sexual behavior, the victim, and respective caregivers shall be conducted by the district staff, the child protection team of the Department of Health, and other providers under contract with the department to provide services to the caregiver of the alleged offender, the victim, and the victim's caregiver.

(d) The assessment shall be conducted in a manner that is sensitive to the social, economic, and cultural environment of the family.

(e) If necessary, the child protection team of the Department of Health shall conduct a physical examination of the victim, which is sufficient to meet forensic requirements.

(f) Based on the information obtained from the alleged abuser or child who has exhibited inappropriate sexual behavior, his or her caregiver, the victim, and the victim's caregiver, an assessment of service and treatment needs must be completed and, if needed, a case plan developed within 30 days.

(g) The department shall classify the outcome of the report as follows:

1. Report closed. Services were not offered because the department determined that there was no basis for intervention.

2. Services accepted by alleged abuser. Services were offered to the alleged abuser or child who has exhibited inappropriate sexual behavior and accepted by the caregiver.

3. Report closed. Services were offered to the alleged abuser or child who has exhibited inappropriate sexual behavior, but were rejected by the caregiver.

4. Notification to law enforcement. The risk to the victim's safety and well-being cannot be reduced by the provision of services or the caregiver rejected services, and notification of the alleged delinquent act or violation of law to the appropriate law enforcement agency was initiated.

5. Services accepted by victim. Services were offered to the victim and accepted by the caregiver.

6. Report closed. Services were offered to the victim but were rejected by the caregiver.

(3) If services have been accepted by the alleged abuser or child who has exhibited inappropriate sexual behavior, the victim, and respective caregivers, the department shall designate a case manager and develop a specific case plan.

(a) Upon receipt of the plan, the caregiver shall indicate its acceptance of the plan in writing.

(b) The case manager shall periodically review the progress toward achieving the objectives of the plan in order to:

1. Make adjustments to the plan or take additional action as provided in this part; or

2. Terminate the case if indicated by successful or substantial achievement of the objectives of the plan.

(4) Services provided to the alleged abuser or child who has exhibited inappropriate sexual behavior, the victim, and respective caregivers or family must be voluntary and of necessary duration.

(5) If the family or caregiver of the alleged abuser or child who has exhibited inappropriate sexual behavior fails to adequately participate or allow for the adequate participation of the child in the services or treatment delineated in the case plan, the case manager may recommend that the department:

(a) Close the case;

(b) Refer the case to mediation or arbitration, if available; or

(c) Notify the appropriate law enforcement agency of failure to comply.

(6) At any time, as a result of additional information, findings of facts, or changing conditions, the department may pursue a child protective investigation as provided in this chapter.

(7) The department may adopt rules to administer this section.

HISTORY:
S. 8, ch. 95-266; s. 50, ch. 95-267; s. 13, ch. 97-98; s. 9, ch. 98-137; s. 45, ch. 98-403; s. 4, ch. 2003-127; s. 7, ch. 2008-245, eff. June 30, 2008; s. 8, ch. 2012-178, eff. July 1, 2012; s. 11, ch. 2014-224, eff. July 1, 2014; s. 6, ch. 2015-2, eff. June 30, 2015.

Editor's notes.
Former s. 415.50171.

§ 39.308. Guidelines for onsite child protective investigation.

The Department of Children and Families, in collaboration with the sheriffs' offices, shall develop guidelines for conducting an onsite child protective investigation that specifically does not require the additional activities required by the department and for conducting an enhanced child protective investigation, including determining whether compelling evidence exists that no maltreatment occurred, conducting collateral contacts, contacting the reporter, updating the risk assessment, and providing for differential levels of documentation between an onsite and an enhanced onsite child protective investigation.

HISTORY:
S. 11, ch. 2003-127; s. 18, ch. 2014-19, eff. July 1, 2014.

PART IV.
FAMILY BUILDERS PROGRAM
[REPEALED].

§ 39.311. Establishment of Family Builders Program [Repealed.]

Repealed by s. 38, ch. 2011-213, effective July 1, 2011.

HISTORY:
S. 3, ch. 90-182; s. 66, ch. 90-306; s. 5, ch. 91-183; s. 66, ch. 94-164; s. 27, ch. 95-267; s. 136, ch. 97-101; s. 47, ch. 98-403; s. 18, ch. 99-193.

§ 39.312. Goals [Repealed.]

Repealed by s. 38, ch. 2011-213, effective July 1, 2011.

HISTORY:
S. 4, ch. 90-182; s. 67, ch. 90-306; s. 6, ch. 91-183; s. 125, ch. 94-209; s. 48, ch. 98-403; s. 19, ch. 99-193.

§ 39.313. Contracting of services [Repealed.]

Repealed by s. 38, ch. 2011-213, effective July 1, 2011.

HISTORY:
S. 5, ch. 90-182; s. 68, ch. 90-306; s. 49, ch. 98-403; s. 20, ch. 99-193.

§ 39.314. Eligibility for Family Builders Program services [Repealed.]

Repealed by s. 38, ch. 2011-213, effective July 1, 2011.

HISTORY:
S. 6, ch. 90-182; s. 69, ch. 90-306; s. 7, ch. 91-183; s. 50, ch. 98-403.

§ 39.315. Delivery of Family Builders Program services [Repealed.]

Repealed by s. 38, ch. 2011-213, effective July 1, 2011.

HISTORY:
S. 7, ch. 90-182; s. 70, ch. 90-306; s. 8, ch. 91-183; s. 51, ch. 98-403.

§ 39.316. Qualifications of Family Builders Program workers [Repealed.]

Repealed by s. 38, ch. 2011-213, effective July 1, 2011.

HISTORY:
S. 8, ch. 90-182; s. 71, ch. 90-306; s. 9, ch. 91-183; s. 52, ch. 98-403.

§ 39.317. Outcome evaluation [Repealed.]

Repealed by s. 38, ch. 2011-213, effective July 1, 2011.

HISTORY:

S. 9, ch. 90-182; s. 72, ch. 90-306; s. 10, ch. 91-183; s. 53, ch. 98-403.

§ 39.318. Funding [Repealed.]

Repealed by s. 38, ch. 2011-213, effective July 1, 2011.

HISTORY:

S. 10, ch. 90-182; s. 73, ch. 90-306; s. 11, ch. 91-183; s. 54, ch. 98-403.

PART IV.
TAKING CHILDREN INTO CUSTODY AND SHELTER HEARINGS.

§ 39.395. Detaining a child; medical or hospital personnel.

Any person in charge of a hospital or similar institution, or any physician or licensed health care professional treating a child may detain that child without the consent of the parents, caregiver, or legal custodian, whether or not additional medical treatment is required, if the circumstances are such, or if the condition of the child is such that returning the child to the care or custody of the parents, caregiver, or legal custodian presents an imminent danger to the child's life or physical or mental health. Any such person detaining a child shall immediately notify the department, whereupon the department shall immediately begin a child protective investigation in accordance with the provisions of this chapter and shall make every reasonable effort to immediately notify the parents or legal custodian that such child has been detained. If the department determines, according to the criteria set forth in this chapter, that the child should be detained longer than 24 hours, it shall petition the court through the attorney representing the Department of Children and Families as quickly as possible and not to exceed 24 hours, for an order authorizing such custody in the same manner as if the child were placed in a shelter. The department shall attempt to avoid the placement of a child in an institution whenever possible.

HISTORY:

S. 56, ch. 98-403; s. 21, ch. 99-193; s. 19, ch. 2014-19, eff. July 1, 2014.

§ 39.401. Taking a child alleged to be dependent into custody; law enforcement officers and authorized agents of the department.

(1) A child may only be taken into custody:

(a) Pursuant to the provisions of this part, based upon sworn testimony, either before or after a petition is filed; or

(b) By a law enforcement officer, or an authorized agent of the department, if the officer or authorized agent has probable cause to support a finding:

1. That the child has been abused, neglected, or abandoned, or is suffering from or is in imminent danger of illness or injury as a result of abuse, neglect, or abandonment;

2. That the parent or legal custodian of the child has materially violated a condition of placement imposed by the court; or

3. That the child has no parent, legal custodian, or responsible adult relative immediately known and available to provide supervision and care.

(2) If the law enforcement officer takes the child into custody, that officer shall:

(a) Release the child to:

1. The parent or legal custodian of the child;

2. A responsible adult approved by the court when limited to temporary emergency situations;

3. A responsible adult relative or the adoptive parent of the child's sibling who shall be given priority consideration over a nonrelative placement when this is in the best interests of the child; or

4. A responsible adult approved by the department; or

(b) Deliver the child to an authorized agent of the department, stating the facts by reason of which the child was taken into custody and sufficient information to establish probable cause that the child is abandoned, abused, or neglected, or otherwise dependent. For such a child for whom there is also probable cause to believe he or she has been sexually exploited, the law enforcement officer shall deliver the child to the department.

For cases involving allegations of abandonment, abuse, or neglect, or other dependency cases, within 3 days after such release or within 3 days after delivering the child to an authorized agent of the department, the law enforcement officer who took the child into custody shall make a full written report to the department.

(3) If the child is taken into custody by, or is delivered to, an authorized agent of the department, the agent shall review the facts supporting the removal with an attorney representing the department. The purpose of the review is to determine whether there is probable cause for the filing of a shelter petition.

(a) If the facts are not sufficient, the child shall immediately be returned to the custody of the parent or legal custodian.

(b) If the facts are sufficient and the child has not been returned to the custody of the parent or legal custodian, the department shall file the petition and schedule a hearing, and the attorney representing the department shall request that a shelter hearing be held within 24 hours after the removal of the child. While awaiting the shelter hearing, the authorized agent of the department may place the child in licensed shelter care or may release the child to a parent or legal custodian or responsible adult relative or the adoptive parent of the child's sibling who shall be given priority consideration over a licensed placement, or a responsible adult approved by the department if this is in the best interests of the child. Placement of a child which is not in a licensed shelter must be preceded by a criminal history records check as required under s. 39.0138. In addition, the department may authorize placement of a housekeeper/homemaker in the home of a child alleged to be dependent until the parent or legal custodian assumes care of the child.

(4) When a child is taken into custody pursuant to this section, the department shall request that the child's parent, caregiver, or legal custodian disclose the names, relationships, and addresses of all parents and prospective parents and all next of kin of the child, so far as are known.

(5) Judicial review and approval is required within 24 hours after placement for all nonrelative placements. A nonrelative placement must be for a specific and predetermined period of time, not to exceed 12 months, and shall be reviewed by the court at least every 6 months. If the nonrelative placement continues for longer than 12 months, the department shall request the court to establish permanent guardianship or require that the nonrelative seek licensure as a foster care provider within 30 days after the court decision. Failure to establish permanent guardianship or obtain licensure does not require the court to change a child's placement unless it is in the best interest of the child to do so.

HISTORY:
    S. 20, ch. 78-414; s. 4, ch. 87-133; s. 11, ch. 88-337; s. 2, ch. 90-204; s. 226, ch. 95-147; s. 6, ch. 95-228; s. 2, ch. 97-276; s. 57, ch. 98-403; s. 22, ch. 99-193; s. 8, ch. 2008-245, eff. June 30, 2008; s. 4, ch. 2012-105, eff. Jan. 1, 2013; s. 4, ch. 2014-161, eff. July 1, 2014.

Editor's notes.
    Section 1, ch. 2012-105, provides: "This act may be cited as the 'Florida Safe Harbor Act.' "

§ 39.402. Placement in a shelter.

(1) Unless ordered by the court under this chapter, a child taken into custody shall not be placed in a shelter prior to a court hearing unless there is probable cause to believe that:

(a) The child has been abused, neglected, or abandoned, or is suffering from or is in imminent danger of illness or injury as a result of abuse, neglect, or abandonment;

(b) The parent or legal custodian of the child has materially violated a condition of placement imposed by the court; or

(c) The child has no parent, legal custodian, or responsible adult relative immediately known and available to provide supervision and care.

(2) A child taken into custody may be placed or continued in a shelter only if one or more of the criteria in subsection (1) applies and the court has made a specific finding of fact regarding the necessity for removal of the child from the home and has made a determination that the provision of appropriate and available services will not eliminate the need for placement.

(3) Whenever a child is taken into custody, the department shall immediately notify the parents or legal custodians, shall provide the parents or legal custodians with a statement setting forth a summary of procedures involved in dependency cases, and shall notify them of their right to obtain their own attorney.

(4) If the department determines that placement in a shelter is necessary under subsections (1) and (2), the authorized agent of the department shall authorize placement of the child in a shelter.

(5)(a) The parents or legal custodians of the child shall be given such notice as best ensures their actual knowledge of the date, time, and location of the shelter hearing. If the parents or legal custodians are outside the jurisdiction of the court, are not known, or cannot be located or refuse or evade service, they shall be given such notice as best ensures their actual knowledge of the date, time, and location of the shelter hearing. The person providing or attempting to provide notice to the parents or legal custodians shall, if the parents or legal custodians are not present at the hearing, advise the court either in person or by sworn affidavit, of the attempts made to provide notice and the results of those attempts.

(b) The parents or legal custodians shall be given written notice that:

1. They will be given an opportunity to be heard and to present evidence at the shelter hearing; and

2. They have the right to be represented by counsel, and, if indigent, the parents have the right to be represented by appointed counsel, at the shelter hearing and at each subsequent hearing or proceeding, pursuant to the procedures set forth in s. 39.013. If the parents or legal custodians appear for the shelter hearing without legal counsel, then, at their request, the shelter hearing may be continued up to 72 hours to enable the parents or legal custodians to consult legal counsel. If a continuance is requested by the parents or legal custodians, the child shall be continued in shelter care for the length of the continuance, if granted by the court.

(6)(a) The circuit court, or the county court if previously designated by the chief judge of the circuit court for such purpose, shall hold the shelter hearing.

(b) The shelter petition filed with the court must address each condition required to be determined by the court in paragraphs (8)(a), (b), (d), and (h).

(7) A child may not be removed from the home or continued out of the home pending disposition if, with the provision of appropriate and available early intervention or preventive services, including services provided in the home, the child could safely remain at home. If the child's safety and well-being are in danger, the child shall be removed from danger and continue to be removed until the danger has passed. If the child has been removed from the home and the reasons for his or her removal have been remedied, the child may be returned to the home. If the court finds that the prevention or reunification efforts of the department will allow the child to remain safely at home, the court shall allow the child to remain in the home.

(8)(a) A child may not be held in a shelter longer than 24 hours unless an order so directing is entered by the court after a shelter hearing. In the interval until the shelter hearing is held, the decision to place the child in a shelter or release the child from a shelter lies with the protective investigator.

(b) The parents or legal custodians of the child shall be given such notice as best ensures their actual knowledge of the time and place of the shelter hearing. The failure to provide notice to a party or participant does not invalidate an order placing a child in a shelter if the court finds that the petitioner has made a good faith effort to provide such notice. The court shall require the parents or legal custodians present at the hearing to provide to the court on the record the names, addresses, and relationships of all parents, prospective parents, and next of kin of the child, so far as are known.

(c) At the shelter hearing, the court shall:

1. Appoint a guardian ad litem to represent the best interest of the child, unless the court finds that such representation is unnecessary;

2. Inform the parents or legal custodians of their right to counsel to represent them at the shelter hearing and at each subsequent hearing or proceeding, and the right of the parents to appointed counsel, pursuant to the procedures set forth in s. 39.013;

3. Give the parents or legal custodians an opportunity to be heard and to present evidence; and

4. Inquire of those present at the shelter hearing as to the identity and location of the legal father. In determining who the legal father of the child may be, the court shall inquire under oath of those present at the shelter hearing whether they have any of the following information:

a. Whether the mother of the child was married at the probable time of conception of the child or at the time of birth of the child.

b. Whether the mother was cohabiting with a male at the probable time of conception of the child.

c. Whether the mother has received payments or promises of support with respect to the child or because of her pregnancy from a man who claims to be the father.

d. Whether the mother has named any man as the father on the birth certificate of the child or in connection with applying for or receiving public assistance.

e. Whether any man has acknowledged or claimed paternity of the child in a jurisdiction in which the mother resided at the time of or since conception of the child or in which the child has resided or resides.

f. Whether a man is named on the birth certificate of the child pursuant to s. 382.013(2).

g. Whether a man has been determined by a court order to be the father of the child.

h. Whether a man has been determined to be the father of the child by the Department of Revenue as provided in s. 409.256.

(d) At the shelter hearing, in order to continue the child in shelter care:

1. The department must establish probable cause that reasonable grounds for removal exist and that the provision of appropriate and available services will not eliminate the need for placement; or

2. The court must determine that additional time is necessary, which may not exceed 72 hours, in which to obtain and review documents pertaining to the family in order to appropriately determine the risk to the child during which time the child shall remain in the department's custody, if so ordered by the court.

(e) At the shelter hearing, the department shall provide the court copies of any available law enforcement, medical, or other professional reports, and shall also provide copies of abuse hotline reports pursuant to state and federal confidentiality requirements.

(f) At the shelter hearing, the department shall inform the court of:

1. Any identified current or previous case plans negotiated in any district with the parents or caregivers under this chapter and problems associated with compliance;

2. Any adjudication of the parents or caregivers of delinquency;

3. Any past or current injunction for protection from domestic violence; and

4. All of the child's places of residence during the prior 12 months.

(g) At the shelter hearing, each party shall provide to the court a permanent mailing address. The court shall advise each party that this address will be used by the court and the petitioner for notice purposes unless and until the party notifies the court and the petitioner in writing of a new mailing address.

(h) The order for placement of a child in shelter care must identify the parties present at the hearing and must contain written findings:

1. That placement in shelter care is necessary based on the criteria in subsections (1) and (2).

2. That placement in shelter care is in the best interest of the child.

3. That continuation of the child in the home is contrary to the welfare of the child because the home situation presents a substantial and immediate danger to the child's physical, mental, or emotional health or safety which cannot be mitigated by the provision of preventive services.

4. That based upon the allegations of the petition for placement in shelter care, there is probable cause to believe that the child is dependent or that the court needs additional time, which may not exceed 72 hours, in which to obtain and review documents pertaining to the family in order to appropriately determine the risk to the child.

5. That the department has made reasonable efforts to prevent or eliminate the need for removal of the child from the home. A finding of reasonable effort by the department to prevent or eliminate the need for removal may be made and the department is deemed to have made reasonable efforts to prevent or eliminate the need for removal if:

a. The first contact of the department with the family occurs during an emergency;

b. The appraisal of the home situation by the department indicates that the home situation presents a substantial and immediate danger to the child's physical, mental, or emotional health or safety which cannot be mitigated by the provision of preventive services;

c. The child cannot safely remain at home, either because there are no preventive services that can ensure the health and safety of the child or because, even with appropriate and available services being provided, the health and safety of the child cannot be ensured; or

d. The parent or legal custodian is alleged to have committed any of the acts listed as grounds for expedited termination of parental rights in s. 39.806(1)(f)-(i).

6. That the department has made reasonable efforts to keep siblings together if they are removed and placed in out-of-home care unless such placement is not in the best interest of each child. It is preferred that siblings be kept together in a foster home, if available. Other reasonable efforts shall include short-term placement in a group home with the ability to accommodate sibling groups if such a placement is available. The department shall report to the court its efforts to place siblings together unless the court finds that such placement is not in the best interest of a child or his or her sibling.

7. That the court notified the parents, relatives that are providing out-of-home care for the child, or legal custodians of the time, date, and location of the next dependency hearing and of the importance of the active participation of the parents, relatives that are providing out-of-home care for the child, or legal custodians in all proceedings and hearings.

8. That the court notified the parents or legal custodians of their right to counsel to represent them at the shelter hearing and at each subsequent hearing or proceeding, and the right of the parents to appointed counsel, pursuant to the procedures set forth in s. 39.013.

9. That the court notified relatives who are providing out-of-home care for a child as a result of the shelter petition being granted that they have the right to attend all subsequent hearings, to submit reports to the court, and to speak to the court regarding the child, if they so desire.

(9)(a) At any shelter hearing, the department shall provide to the court a recommendation for scheduled contact between the child and parents, if appropriate. The court shall determine visitation rights absent a clear and convincing showing that visitation is not in the best interest of the child. Any order for visitation or other contact must conform to s. 39.0139. If visitation is ordered but will not commence within 72 hours of the shelter hearing, the department shall provide justification to the court.

(b) If siblings who are removed from the home cannot be placed together, the department shall provide to the court a recommendation for frequent visitation or other ongoing interaction between the siblings unless this interaction would be contrary to a sibling's safety or well-being. If visitation among siblings is ordered but will not commence within 72 hours after the shelter hearing, the department shall provide justification to the court for the delay.

(10)(a) The shelter hearing order shall contain a written determination as to whether the department has made a reasonable effort to prevent or eliminate the need for removal or continued removal of the child from the home. This determination must include a description of which specific services, if available, could prevent or eliminate the need for removal or continued removal from the home and the date by which the services are expected to become available.

(b) If services are not available to prevent or eliminate the need for removal or continued removal of the child from the home, the written determination must also contain an explanation describing why the services are not available for the child.

(c) If the department has not made an effort to prevent or eliminate the need for removal, the court shall order the department to provide appropriate and available services to ensure the protection of the child in the home when the services are necessary for the child's health and safety.

(11)(a) If a child is placed in a shelter pursuant to a court order following a shelter hearing, the court shall require in the shelter hearing order that the parents of the child, or the guardian of the child's estate, if possessed of assets which under law may be disbursed for the care, support, and maintenance of the child, to pay, to the department or institution having custody of the child, fees as established by the department. When the order affects the guardianship estate, a certified copy of the order shall be delivered to the judge having jurisdiction of the guardianship estate. The shelter order shall also require the parents to provide to the department and any other state agency or party designated by the court, within 28 days after entry of the shelter order, the financial information necessary to accurately calculate child support pursuant to s. 61.30.

(b)   The court shall request that the parents consent to provide access to the child's medical records and provide information to the court, the department or its contract agencies, and any guardian ad litem or attorney for the child. If a parent is unavailable or unable to consent or withholds consent and the court determines access to the records and information is necessary to provide services to the child, the court shall issue an order granting access. The court may also order the parents to provide all known medical information to the department and to any others granted access under this subsection.

(c)   The court shall request that the parents consent to provide access to the child's educational records and provide information to the court, the department or its contract agencies, and any guardian ad litem or attorney for the child. If a parent is unavailable or unable to consent or withholds consent and the court determines access to the records and information is necessary to provide services to the child, the court shall issue an order granting access.

(d)   The court may appoint a surrogate parent or may refer the child to the district school superintendent for appointment of a surrogate parent if the child has or is suspected of having a disability and the parent is unavailable pursuant to s. 39.0016(3)(b).

(12)   In the event the shelter hearing is conducted by a judge other than the juvenile court judge, the juvenile court judge shall hold a shelter review on the status of the child within 2 working days after the shelter hearing.

(13)   A child may not be held in a shelter under an order so directing for more than 60 days without an adjudication of dependency. A child may not be held in a shelter for more than 30 days after the entry of an order of adjudication unless an order of disposition has been entered by the court.

(14)   The time limitations in this section do not include:

(a)   Periods of delay resulting from a continuance granted at the request or with the consent of the child's counsel or the child's guardian ad litem, if one has been appointed by the court, or, if the child is of sufficient capacity to express reasonable consent, at the request or with the consent of the child's attorney or the child's guardian ad litem, if one has been appointed by the court, and the child.

(b)   Periods of delay resulting from a continuance granted at the request of any party, if the continuance is granted:

1.   Because of an unavailability of evidence material to the case when the requesting party has exercised due diligence to obtain such evidence and there are substantial grounds to believe that such evidence will be available within 30 days. However, if the requesting party is not prepared to proceed within 30 days, any other party, inclusive of the parent or legal custodian, may move for issuance of an order to show cause or the court on its own motion may impose appropriate sanctions, which may include dismissal of the petition.

2.   To allow the requesting party additional time to prepare the case and additional time is justified because of an exceptional circumstance.

(c)   Reasonable periods of delay necessary to accomplish notice of the hearing to the child's parents or legal custodians; however, the petitioner shall continue regular efforts to provide notice to the parents or legal custodians during such periods of delay.

(d)   Reasonable periods of delay resulting from a continuance granted at the request of the parent or legal custodian of a subject child.

(e)   Notwithstanding the foregoing, continuances and extensions of time are limited to the number of days absolutely necessary to complete a necessary task in order to preserve the rights of a party or the best interests of a child. Time is of the essence for the best interests of dependent children in conducting dependency proceedings in accordance with the time limitations set forth in this chapter. Time limitations are a right of the child which may not be waived, extended, or continued at the request of any party in advance of the particular circumstances or need arising upon which delay of the proceedings may be warranted.

(f)   Continuances or extensions of time may not total more than 60 days for all parties within any 12-month period during proceedings under this chapter. A continuance or extension beyond the 60 days may be granted only for extraordinary circumstances necessary to preserve the constitutional rights of a party or when substantial evidence demonstrates that the child's best interests will be affirmatively harmed without the granting of a continuance or extension of time.

(15)   The department, at the conclusion of the shelter hearing, shall make available to parents or legal custodians seeking voluntary services, any referral

information necessary for participation in such identified services. The parents' or legal custodians' participation in the services shall not be considered an admission or other acknowledgment of the allegations in the shelter petition.

(16) At the conclusion of a shelter hearing, the court shall notify all parties in writing of the next scheduled hearing to review the shelter placement. The hearing shall be held no later than 30 days after placement of the child in shelter status, in conjunction with the arraignment hearing, and at such times as are otherwise provided by law or determined by the court to be necessary.

(17) At the shelter hearing, the court shall inquire of the parent whether the parent has relatives who might be considered as a placement for the child. The parent shall provide to the court and all parties identification and location information regarding the relatives. The court shall advise the parent that the parent has a continuing duty to inform the department of any relative who should be considered for placement of the child.

(18) The court shall advise the parents that, if the parents fail to substantially comply with the case plan, their parental rights may be terminated and that the child's out-of-home placement may become permanent.

HISTORY:

S. 20, ch. 78-414; s. 13, ch. 80-290; s. 6, ch. 84-311; s. 5, ch. 85-80; s. 82, ch. 86-220; s. 5, ch. 87-133; s. 5, ch. 87-289; s. 12, ch. 88-337; s. 1, ch. 90-167; s. 7, ch. 90-208; s. 5, ch. 90-306; s. 3, ch. 92-158; s. 3, ch. 92-170; s. 7, ch. 92-287; s. 4, ch. 94-164; s. 58, ch. 94-209; s. 7, ch. 95-228; s. 3, ch. 97-96; s. 3, ch. 97-276; s. 58, ch. 98-403; s. 12, ch. 99-168; s. 23, ch. 99-193; s. 19, ch. 2000-139; s. 6, ch. 2000-151; s. 7, ch. 2000-217; s. 2, ch. 2001-68; s. 2, ch. 2002-216; s. 1, ch. 2005-65; s. 10, ch. 2006-86, eff. July 1, 2006; s. 2, ch. 2007-109, eff. July 1, 2007; s. 3, ch. 2009-35, eff. July 1, 2009; s. 7, ch. 2009-43, eff. July 1, 2009; s. 12, ch. 2014-224, eff. July 1, 2014; s. 7, ch. 2017-151, eff. July 1, 2017.

Editor's notes.

Section 1 of ch. 2009-43 provides: "This act may be cited as the 'Zahid Jones, Jr., Give Grandparents and Other Relatives a Voice Act.'"

§ 39.407. Medical, psychiatric, and psychological examination and treatment of child; physical, mental, or substance abuse examination of person with or requesting child custody.

(1) When any child is removed from the home and maintained in an out-of-home placement, the department is authorized to have a medical screening performed on the child without authorization from the court and without consent from a parent or legal custodian. Such medical screening shall be performed by a licensed health care professional and shall be to examine the child for injury, illness, and communicable diseases and to determine the need for immunization. The department shall by rule establish the invasiveness of the medical procedures authorized to be performed under this subsection. In no case does this subsection authorize the department to consent to medical treatment for such children.

(2) When the department has performed the medical screening authorized by subsection (1), or when it is otherwise determined by a licensed health care professional that a child who is in an out-of-home placement, but who has not been committed to the department, is in need of medical treatment, including the need for immunization, consent for medical treatment shall be obtained in the following manner:

(a)1. Consent to medical treatment shall be obtained from a parent or legal custodian of the child; or

2. A court order for such treatment shall be obtained.

(b) If a parent or legal custodian of the child is unavailable and his or her whereabouts cannot be reasonably ascertained, and it is after normal working hours so that a court order cannot reasonably be obtained, an authorized agent of the department shall have the authority to consent to necessary medical treatment, including immunization, for the child. The authority of the department to consent to medical treatment in this circumstance shall be limited to the time reasonably necessary to obtain court authorization.

(c) If a parent or legal custodian of the child is available but refuses to consent to the necessary treatment, including immunization, a court order shall be required unless the situation meets the definition of an emergency in s. 743.064 or the treatment needed is related to suspected abuse, abandonment, or neglect of the child by a parent, caregiver, or legal custodian. In such case, the department shall have the authority to consent to necessary medical treatment. This authority is limited to the time reasonably necessary to obtain court authorization.

In no case shall the department consent to sterilization, abortion, or termination of life support.

(3)(a)1. Except as otherwise provided in subparagraph (b)1. or paragraph (e), before the department provides psychotropic medications to a child in its custody, the prescribing physician shall attempt to obtain express and informed consent, as defined in s. 394.455(15) and as described in s. 394.459(3)(a), from the child's parent or legal guardian. The department must take steps necessary to facilitate the inclusion of the parent in the child's consultation with the physician. However, if the parental rights of the parent have been terminated, the parent's location or identity is unknown or cannot reasonably be ascertained, or the parent declines to give express and informed consent, the department may, after consultation with the prescribing physician, seek court authorization to provide the psychotropic medications to the child. Unless parental rights have been terminated and if it is possible to do so, the department shall continue to involve the parent in the decisionmaking process regarding the provision of psychotropic medications. If, at any time, a parent whose parental rights have not been terminated provides express and informed consent to the provision of a psychotropic medication, the requirements of this section that the department seek court authorization do not apply to that medication until such time as the parent no longer consents.

2. Any time the department seeks a medical evaluation to determine the need to initiate or continue a psychotropic medication for a child, the department must provide to the evaluating physician all pertinent medical information known to the department concerning that child.

(b)1. If a child who is removed from the home under s. 39.401 is receiving prescribed psychotropic medication at the time of removal and parental authorization to continue providing the medication cannot be obtained, the department may take possession of the remaining medication and may continue to provide the medication as prescribed until the shelter hearing, if it is determined that the medication is a current prescription for that child and the medication is in its original container.

2. If the department continues to provide the psychotropic medication to a child when parental authorization cannot be obtained, the department shall notify the parent or legal guardian as soon as possible that the medication is being provided to the child as provided in subparagraph 1. The child's official departmental record must include the reason parental authorization was not initially obtained and an explanation of why the medication is necessary for the child's well-being.

3. If the department is advised by a physician licensed under chapter 458 or chapter 459 that the child should continue the psychotropic medication and parental authorization has not been obtained, the department shall request court authorization at the shelter hearing to continue to provide the psychotropic medication and shall provide to the court any information in its possession in support of the request. Any authorization granted at the shelter hearing may extend only until the arraignment hearing on the petition for adjudication of dependency or 28 days following the date of removal, whichever occurs sooner.

4. Before filing the dependency petition, the department shall ensure that the child is evaluated by a physician licensed under chapter 458 or chapter 459 to determine whether it is appropriate to continue the psychotropic medication. If, as a result of the evaluation, the department seeks court authorization to continue the psychotropic medication, a motion for such continued authorization shall be filed at the same time as the dependency petition, within 21 days after the shelter hearing.

(c) Except as provided in paragraphs (b) and (e), the department must file a motion seeking the court's authorization to initially provide or continue to provide psychotropic medication to a child in its legal custody. The motion must be supported by a written report prepared by the department which describes the efforts made to enable the prescribing physician to obtain express and informed consent for providing the medication to the child and other treatments considered or recommended for the child. In addition, the motion must be supported by the prescribing physician's signed medical report providing:

1. The name of the child, the name and range of the dosage of the psychotropic medication, and that there is a need to prescribe psychotropic medication to the child based upon a diagnosed condition for which such medication is being prescribed.

2. A statement indicating that the physician has reviewed all medical information concerning the child which has been provided.

3. A statement indicating that the psychotropic medication, at its prescribed dosage, is appropriate for treating the child's diagnosed medical condition, as well as the behaviors and symptoms the medication, at its prescribed dosage, is expected to address.

4. An explanation of the nature and purpose of the treatment; the recognized side effects, risks, and contraindications of the medication; drug-interaction precautions; the possible effects of stopping the medication; and how the treatment will be monitored, followed by a statement indicating that this explanation was provided to the child if age appropriate and to the child's caregiver.

5. Documentation addressing whether the psychotropic medication will replace or supplement any other currently prescribed medications or treatments; the length of time the child is expected to be taking the medication; and any additional medical, mental health, behavioral, counseling, or other services that the prescribing physician recommends.

(d)1. The department must notify all parties of the proposed action taken under paragraph (c) in writing or by whatever other method best ensures that all parties receive notification of the proposed action within 48 hours after the motion is filed. If any party objects to the department's motion, that party shall file the objection within 2 working days after being notified of the department's motion. If any party files an objection to the authorization of the proposed psychotropic medication, the court shall hold a hearing as soon as possible before authorizing the department to initially provide or to continue providing psychotropic medication to a child in the legal custody of the department. At such hearing and notwithstanding s. 90.803, the medical report described in paragraph (c) is admissible in evidence. The prescribing physician need not attend the hearing or testify unless the court specifically orders such attendance or testimony, or a party subpoenas the physician to attend the hearing or provide testimony. If, after considering any testimony received, the court finds that the department's motion and the physician's medical report meet the requirements of this subsection and that it is in the child's best interests, the court may order that the department provide or continue to provide the psychotropic medication to the child without additional testimony or evidence. At any hearing held under this paragraph, the court shall further inquire of the department as to whether additional medical, mental health, behavioral, counseling, or other services are being provided to the child by the department which the prescribing physician considers to be necessary or beneficial in treating the child's medical condition and which the physician recommends or expects to provide to the child in concert with the medication. The court may order additional medical consultation, including consultation with the MedConsult line at the University of Florida, if available, or require the department to obtain a second opinion within a reasonable timeframe as established by the court, not to exceed 21 calendar days, after such order based upon consideration of the best interests of the child. The department must make a referral for an appointment for a second opinion with a physician within 1 working day. The court may not order the discontinuation of prescribed psychotropic medication if such order is contrary to the decision of the prescribing physician unless the court first obtains an opinion from a licensed psychiatrist, if available, or, if not available, a physician licensed under chapter 458 or chapter 459, stating that more likely than not, discontinuing the medication would not cause significant harm to the child. If, however, the prescribing psychiatrist specializes in mental health care for children and adolescents, the court may not order the discontinuation of prescribed psychotropic medication unless the required opinion is also from a psychiatrist who specializes in mental health care for children and adolescents. The court may also order the discontinuation of prescribed psychotropic medication if a child's treating physician, licensed under chapter 458 or chapter 459, states that continuing the prescribed psychotropic medication would cause significant harm to the child due to a diagnosed nonpsychiatric medical condition.

2. The burden of proof at any hearing held under this paragraph shall be by a preponderance of the evidence.

(e)1. If the child's prescribing physician certifies in the signed medical report required in paragraph (c) that delay in providing a prescribed psychotropic medication would more likely than not cause significant harm to the child, the medication may be provided in advance of the issuance of a court order. In such event, the medical report must provide the specific reasons why the child may experience significant harm and the nature and the extent of the potential harm. The department must submit a motion seeking continuation of the medication and the physician's medical report to the court, the child's guardian ad litem, and all other parties within 3 working days after the department commences providing the medication to the child. The department shall seek the order at the next regularly scheduled court hearing required under this chapter, or within 30 days after the date of the prescription, whichever occurs sooner. If any party objects to the department's motion, the court shall hold a hearing within 7 days.

2. Psychotropic medications may be administered in advance of a court order in hospitals, crisis stabilization units, and in statewide inpatient psychiatric programs. Within 3 working days after the medication is begun, the department must seek court authorization as described in paragraph (c).

(f)1. The department shall fully inform the court of the child's medical and behavioral status as part of the social services report prepared for each judicial review hearing held for a child for whom psychotropic medication has been prescribed or provided under this subsection. As a part of the information provided to the court, the department shall furnish copies of all pertinent medical records concerning the child which have been generated since the previous hearing. On its own motion or on good cause shown by any party, including any guardian ad litem, attorney, or attorney ad litem who has been appointed to represent the child or the child's interests, the court may review the status more frequently than required in this subsection.

2. The court may, in the best interests of the child, order the department to obtain a medical opinion addressing whether the continued use of the medication under the circumstances is safe and medically appropriate.

(g) The department shall adopt rules to ensure that children receive timely access to clinically appropriate psychotropic medications. These rules must include, but need not be limited to, the process for determining which adjunctive services are needed, the uniform process for facilitating the prescribing physician's ability to obtain the express and informed consent of a child's parent or guardian, the procedures for obtaining court authorization for the provision of a psychotropic medication, the frequency of medical monitoring and reporting on the status of the child to the court, how the child's parents will be involved in the treatment-planning process if their parental rights have not been terminated, and how caretakers are to be provided information contained in the physician's signed medical report. The rules must also include uniform forms to be used in requesting court authorization for the use of a psychotropic medication and provide for the integration of each child's treatment plan and case plan. The department must begin the formal rule-making process within 90 days after the effective date of this act.

(4)(a) A judge may order a child in an out-of-home placement to be examined by a licensed health care professional.

(b) The judge may also order such child to be evaluated by a psychiatrist or a psychologist or, if a developmental disability is suspected or alleged, by the developmental disability diagnostic and evaluation team of the department. If it is necessary to place a child in a residential facility for such evaluation, the criteria and procedure established in s. 394.463(2) or chapter 393 shall be used, whichever is applicable.

(c) The judge may also order such child to be evaluated by a district school board educational needs assessment team. The educational needs assessment provided by the district school board educational needs assessment team shall include, but not be limited to, reports of intelligence and achievement tests, screening for learning disabilities and other handicaps, and screening for the need for alternative education as defined in s. 1001.42.

(5) A judge may order a child in an out-of-home placement to be treated by a licensed health care professional based on evidence that the child should receive treatment. The judge may also order such child to receive mental health or developmental disabilities services from a psychiatrist, psychologist, or other appropriate service provider. Except as provided in subsection (6), if it is necessary to place the child in a residential facility for such services, the procedures and criteria established in s. 394.467 shall be used. A child may be provided mental health services in emergency situations, pursuant to the procedures and criteria contained in s. 394.463(1). Nothing in this section confers jurisdiction on the court with regard to determining eligibility or ordering services under chapter 393.

(6) Children who are in the legal custody of the department may be placed by the department, without prior approval of the court, in a residential treatment center licensed under s. 394.875 or a hospital licensed under chapter 395 for residential mental health treatment only pursuant to this section or may be placed by the court in accordance with an order of involuntary examination or involuntary placement entered pursuant to s. 394.463 or s. 394.467. All children placed in a residential treatment program under this subsection must have a guardian ad litem appointed.

(a) As used in this subsection, the term:

1. "Residential treatment" means placement for observation, diagnosis, or treatment of an emotional disturbance in a residential treatment center licensed under s. 394.875 or a hospital licensed under chapter 395.

2. "Least restrictive alternative" means the treatment and conditions of treatment that, separately and in combination, are no more intrusive or restrictive of freedom than reasonably necessary to achieve a substantial therapeutic benefit or to protect the child or adolescent or others from physical injury.

3. "Suitability for residential treatment" or "suitability" means a determination concerning a child or adolescent with an emotional disturbance as defined in s. 394.492(5) or a serious emotional disturbance as defined in s. 394.492(6) that each of the following criteria is met:

a. The child requires residential treatment.

b. The child is in need of a residential treatment program and is expected to benefit from mental health treatment.

c. An appropriate, less restrictive alternative to residential treatment is unavailable.

(b) Whenever the department believes that a child in its legal custody is emotionally disturbed and may need residential treatment, an examination and suitability assessment must be conducted by a qualified evaluator who is appointed by the Agency for Health Care Administration. This suitability assessment must be completed before the placement of the child in a residential treatment center for emotionally disturbed children and adolescents or a hospital. The qualified evaluator must be a psychiatrist or a psychologist licensed in Florida who has at least 3 years of experience in the diagnosis and treatment of serious emotional disturbances in children and adolescents and who has no actual or perceived conflict of interest with any inpatient facility or residential treatment center or program.

(c) Before a child is admitted under this subsection, the child shall be assessed for suitability for residential treatment by a qualified evaluator who has conducted a personal examination and assessment of the child and has made written findings that:

1. The child appears to have an emotional disturbance serious enough to require residential treatment and is reasonably likely to benefit from the treatment.

2. The child has been provided with a clinically appropriate explanation of the nature and purpose of the treatment.

3. All available modalities of treatment less restrictive than residential treatment have been considered, and a less restrictive alternative that would offer comparable benefits to the child is unavailable.

A copy of the written findings of the evaluation and suitability assessment must be provided to the department, to the guardian ad litem, and, if the child is a member of a Medicaid managed care plan, to the plan that is financially responsible for the child's care in residential treatment, all of whom must be provided with the opportunity to discuss the findings with the evaluator.

(d) Immediately upon placing a child in a residential treatment program under this section, the department must notify the guardian ad litem and the court having jurisdiction over the child and must provide the guardian ad litem and the court with a copy of the assessment by the qualified evaluator.

(e) Within 10 days after the admission of a child to a residential treatment program, the director of the residential treatment program or the director's designee must ensure that an individualized plan of treatment has been prepared by the program and has been explained to the child, to the department, and to the guardian ad litem, and submitted to the department. The child must be involved in the preparation of the plan to the maximum feasible extent consistent with his or her ability to understand and participate, and the guardian ad litem and the child's foster parents must be involved to the maximum extent consistent with the child's treatment needs. The plan must include a preliminary plan for residential treatment and aftercare upon completion of residential treatment. The plan must include specific behavioral and emotional goals against which the success of the residential treatment may be measured. A copy of the plan must be provided to the child, to the guardian ad litem, and to the department.

(f) Within 30 days after admission, the residential treatment program must review the appropriateness and suitability of the child's placement in the program. The residential treatment program must determine whether the child is receiving benefit toward the treatment goals and whether the child could be treated in a less restrictive treatment program. The residential treatment program shall prepare a written report of its findings and submit the report to the guardian ad litem and to the department. The department must submit the report to the court. The report must include a discharge plan for the child. The residential treatment program must continue to evaluate the child's treatment progress every 30 days thereafter and must include its findings in a written report submitted to the department. The department may not reimburse a facility until the facility has submitted every written report that is due.

(g)1. The department must submit, at the beginning of each month, to the court having jurisdiction over the child, a written report regarding the child's progress toward achieving the goals specified in the individualized plan of treatment.

2. The court must conduct a hearing to review the status of the child's residential treatment plan no later than 3 months after the child's admission to the residential treatment program. An independent review of the child's progress toward achieving the goals and objectives of the treatment plan must be completed by a qualified evaluator and submitted to the court before its 3-month review.

3. For any child in residential treatment at the time a judicial review is held pursuant to s. 39.701, the child's continued placement in residential treatment must be a subject of the judicial review.

4. If at any time the court determines that the child is not suitable for continued residential treatment, the court shall order the department to place the child in the least restrictive setting that is best suited to meet his or her needs.

(h) After the initial 3-month review, the court must conduct a review of the child's residential treatment plan every 90 days.

(i) The department must adopt rules for implementing timeframes for the completion of suitability assessments by qualified evaluators and a procedure that includes timeframes for completing the 3-month independent review by the qualified evaluators of the child's progress toward achieving the goals and objectives of the treatment plan which review must be submitted to the court. The Agency for Health Care Administration must adopt rules for the registration of qualified evaluators, the procedure for selecting the evaluators to conduct the reviews required under this section, and a reasonable, cost-efficient fee schedule for qualified evaluators.

(7) When a child is in an out-of-home placement, a licensed health care professional shall be immediately called if there are indications of physical injury or illness, or the child shall be taken to the nearest available hospital for emergency care.

(8) Except as otherwise provided herein, nothing in this section shall be deemed to eliminate the right of a parent, legal custodian, or the child to consent to examination or treatment for the child.

(9) Except as otherwise provided herein, nothing in this section shall be deemed to alter the provisions of s. 743.064.

(10) A court shall not be precluded from ordering services or treatment to be provided to the child by a duly accredited practitioner who relies solely on spiritual means for healing in accordance with the tenets and practices of a church or religious organization, when required by the child's health and when requested by the child.

(11) Nothing in this section shall be construed to authorize the permanent sterilization of the child unless

such sterilization is the result of or incidental to medically necessary treatment to protect or preserve the life of the child.

(12)   For the purpose of obtaining an evaluation or examination, or receiving treatment as authorized pursuant to this section, no child alleged to be or found to be dependent shall be placed in a detention home or other program used primarily for the care and custody of children alleged or found to have committed delinquent acts.

(13)   The parents or legal custodian of a child in an out-of-home placement remain financially responsible for the cost of medical treatment provided to the child even if either one or both of the parents or if the legal custodian did not consent to the medical treatment. After a hearing, the court may order the parents or legal custodian, if found able to do so, to reimburse the department or other provider of medical services for treatment provided.

(14)   Nothing in this section alters the authority of the department to consent to medical treatment for a dependent child when the child has been committed to the department and the department has become the legal custodian of the child.

(15)   At any time after the filing of a shelter petition or petition for dependency, when the mental or physical condition, including the blood group, of a parent, caregiver, legal custodian, or other person who has custody or is requesting custody of a child is in controversy, the court may order the person to submit to a physical or mental examination by a qualified professional. The order may be made only upon good cause shown and pursuant to notice and procedures as set forth by the Florida Rules of Juvenile Procedure.

(16)   At any time after a shelter petition or petition for dependency is filed, the court may order a person who has custody or is requesting custody of the child to submit to a substance abuse assessment or evaluation. The assessment or evaluation must be administered by a qualified professional, as defined in s. 397.311. The order may be made only upon good cause shown. This subsection does not authorize placement of a child with a person seeking custody, other than the parent or legal custodian, who requires substance abuse treatment.

HISTORY:

S. 20, ch. 78-414; s. 14, ch. 80-290; s. 2, ch. 84-226; s. 8, ch. 84-311; s. 74, ch. 86-220; s. 2, ch. 87-238; s. 230, ch. 95-147; s. 11, ch. 95-228; s. 59, ch. 98-403; s. 24, ch. 99-193; s. 1, ch. 2000-265; s. 151, ch. 2000-349; s. 3, ch. 2002-219; s. 885, ch. 2002-387; s. 2, ch. 2005-65; s. 3, ch. 2006-97, eff. June 7, 2006; s. 4, ch. 2006-227, eff. July 1, 2006; s. 3, ch. 2016-241, eff. July 1, 2016; s. 62, ch. 2016-241, eff. July 1, 2016.

§ 39.4075. Referral of a dependency case to mediation.

(1)   At any stage in a dependency proceeding, any party may request the court to refer the parties to mediation in accordance with chapter 44 and rules and procedures developed by the Supreme Court.

(2)   A court may refer the parties to mediation. When such services are available, the court must determine whether it is in the best interests of the child to refer the parties to mediation.

(3)   The department shall advise the parties that they are responsible for contributing to the cost of the dependency mediation.

(4)   This section applies only to courts in counties in which dependency mediation programs have been established and does not require the establishment of such programs in any county.

HISTORY:

S. 7, ch. 94-164; s. 60, ch. 98-403; s. 58, ch. 2003-402.

Editor's notes.
Former s. 39.4033.

§ 39.4085. Legislative findings and declaration of intent for goals for dependent children.

The Legislature finds and declares that the design and delivery of child welfare services should be directed by the principle that the health and safety of children should be of paramount concern and, therefore, establishes the following goals for children in shelter or foster care:

(1)   To receive a copy of this act and have it fully explained to them when they are placed in the custody of the department.

(2)   To enjoy individual dignity, liberty, pursuit of happiness, and the protection of their civil and legal rights as persons in the custody of the state.

(3)   To have their privacy protected, have their personal belongings secure and transported with them, and, unless otherwise ordered by the court, have uncensored communication, including receiving and sending unopened communications and having access to a telephone.

(4)   To have personnel providing services who are sufficiently qualified and experienced to assess the risk children face prior to removal from their homes and to meet the needs of the children once they are in the custody of the department.

(5)   To remain in the custody of their parents or legal custodians unless and until there has been a determination by a qualified person exercising competent professional judgment that removal is necessary to protect their physical, mental, or emotional health or safety.

(6)   To have a full risk, health, educational, medical and psychological screening and, if needed, assessment and testing upon adjudication into foster care; and to have their photograph and fingerprints included in their case management file.

(7)   To be referred to and receive services, including necessary medical, emotional, psychological, psychiatric, and educational evaluations and treat-

ment, as soon as practicable after identification of the need for such services by the screening and assessment process.

(8) To be placed in a home with no more than one other child, unless they are part of a sibling group.

(9) To be placed away from other children known to pose a threat of harm to them, either because of their own risk factors or those of the other child.

(10) To be placed in a home where the shelter or foster caregiver is aware of and understands the child's history, needs, and risk factors.

(11) To be the subject of a plan developed by the counselor and the shelter or foster caregiver to deal with identified behaviors that may present a risk to the child or others.

(12) To be involved and incorporated, where appropriate, in the development of the case plan, to have a case plan which will address their specific needs, and to object to any of the provisions of the case plan.

(13) To receive meaningful case management and planning that will quickly return the child to his or her family or move the child on to other forms of permanency.

(14) To receive regular communication with a caseworker, at least once a month, which shall include meeting with the child alone and conferring with the shelter or foster caregiver.

(15) To enjoy regular visitation, at least once a week, with their siblings unless the court orders otherwise.

(16) To enjoy regular visitation with their parents, at least once a month, unless the court orders otherwise.

(17) To receive a free and appropriate education; minimal disruption to their education and retention in their home school, if appropriate; referral to the child study team; all special educational services, including, where appropriate, the appointment of a parent surrogate; the sharing of all necessary information between the school board and the department, including information on attendance and educational progress.

(18) To be able to raise grievances with the department over the care they are receiving from their caregivers, caseworkers, or other service providers.

(19) To be heard by the court, if appropriate, at all review hearings.

(20) To have a guardian ad litem appointed to represent, within reason, their best interests and, where appropriate, an attorney ad litem appointed to represent their legal interests; the guardian ad litem and attorney ad litem shall have immediate and unlimited access to the children they represent.

(21) To have all their records available for review by their guardian ad litem and attorney ad litem if they deem such review necessary.

(22) To organize as a group for purposes of ensuring that they receive the services and living conditions to which they are entitled and to provide support for one another while in the custody of the department.

(23) To be afforded prompt access to all available state and federal programs, including, but not limited to: Early Periodic Screening, Diagnosis, and Testing (EPSDT) services, developmental services programs, Medicare and supplemental security income, Children's Medical Services, and programs for severely emotionally disturbed children.

The provisions of this section establish goals and not rights. Nothing in this section shall be interpreted as requiring the delivery of any particular service or level of service in excess of existing appropriations. No person shall have a cause of action against the state or any of its subdivisions, agencies, contractors, subcontractors, or agents, based upon the adoption of or failure to provide adequate funding for the achievement of these goals by the Legislature. Nothing herein shall require the expenditure of funds to meet the goals established herein except funds specifically appropriated for such purpose.

HISTORY:
S. 5, ch. 99-206.

§ 39.4086. Pilot program for attorneys ad litem for dependent children [Repealed.]

Repealed by s. 6, ch. 2010-5, effective June 29, 2010.

HISTORY:
S. 88, ch. 2000-139; s. 1, ch. 2001-370; s. 34, ch. 2010-102, eff. May 26, 2010.

§ 39.4091. Participation in childhood activities.

(1) FINDINGS AND INTENT.

(a) The Legislature finds that every day parents make important decisions about their child's participation in activities and that caregivers for children in out-of-home care are faced with making the same decisions for a child in their care.

(b) The Legislature also finds that when a caregiver makes decisions, he or she must consider applicable laws, rules, and regulations to safeguard the health and safety of a child in out-of-home care and that those rules and regulations have commonly been interpreted to prohibit children in out-of-home care from participating in extracurricular activities.

(c) The Legislature further finds that participation in these types of activities is important to the child's well-being, not only emotionally, but in developing valuable life-coping skills.

(d) It is the intent of the Legislature to recognize the importance of making every effort to normalize the lives of children in out-of-home care and to empower a caregiver to approve or disapprove a child's participation in activities based on the caregiver's own assessment using a reasonable and prudent parent standard, without prior approval of the department, the caseworker, or the court.

(2) DEFINITIONS. — When used in this section, the term:

(a) "Age-appropriate" means activities or items that are generally accepted as suitable for children of the same chronological age or level of maturity. Age appropriateness is based on the development of cognitive, emotional, physical, and behavioral capacity that is typical for an age or age group.

(b) "Caregiver" means a person with whom the child is placed in out-of-home care, or a designated official for group care facilities licensed by the Department of Children and Families pursuant to s. 409.175.

(c) "Reasonable and prudent parent standard" means the standard characterized by careful and sensible parental decisions that maintain the child's health, safety, and best interests while at the same time encouraging the child's emotional and developmental growth, that a caregiver shall use when determining whether to allow a child in out-of-home care to participate in extracurricular, enrichment, and social activities.

(3) REQUIREMENTS FOR DECISIONMAKING.

(a) Each child who comes into care under this chapter is entitled to participate in age-appropriate extracurricular, enrichment, and social activities.

(b) Caregivers must use a reasonable and prudent parent standard in determining whether to give permission for a child in out-of-home care to participate in extracurricular, enrichment, and social activities. When using the reasonable and prudent parent standard, the caregiver shall consider:

1. The child's age, maturity, and developmental level to maintain the overall health and safety of the child.

2. The potential risk factors and the appropriateness of the extracurricular, enrichment, and social activity.

3. The best interest of the child based on information known by the caregiver.

4. The importance of encouraging the child's emotional and developmental growth.

5. The importance of providing the child with the most family-like living experience possible.

6. The behavioral history of the child and the child's ability to safely participate in the proposed activity, as with any other child.

(c) The department and community-based care lead agencies are required to verify that private agencies providing out-of-home services to dependent children have policies consistent with this section and that those agencies promote and protect the ability of dependent children to participate in age-appropriate extracurricular, enrichment, and social activities.

(d) A caregiver as defined in this section is not liable for harm caused to a child in care who participates in an activity approved by the caregiver, provided that the caregiver has acted as a reasonable and prudent parent. This section does not remove or limit any existing liability protection afforded by statute.

(4) RULEMAKING. — The department shall adopt by rule procedures to administer this section.

HISTORY:
S. 2, ch. 2013-21, eff. July 1, 2013.

Editor's notes.
Section 1, ch. 2013-21, provides: "This act may be cited as the 'Quality Parenting for Children in Foster Care Act.' "

PART V.
PETITION, ARRAIGNMENT, ADJUDICATION, AND DISPOSITION.

§ 39.501. Petition for dependency.

(1) All proceedings seeking an adjudication that a child is dependent shall be initiated by the filing of a petition by an attorney for the department, or any other person who has knowledge of the facts alleged or is informed of them and believes that they are true.

(2) The purpose of a petition seeking the adjudication of a child as a dependent child is the protection of the child and not the punishment of the person creating the condition of dependency.

(3)(a) The petition shall be in writing, shall identify and list all parents, if known, and all current legal custodians of the child, and shall be signed by the petitioner under oath stating the petitioner's good faith in filing the petition. When the petition is filed by the department, it shall be signed by an attorney for the department.

(b) The form of the petition and its contents shall be determined by rules of juvenile procedure adopted by the Supreme Court.

(c) The petition must specifically set forth the acts or omissions upon which the petition is based and the identity of the person or persons alleged to have committed the acts or omissions, if known. The petition need not contain allegations of acts or omissions by both parents.

(d) The petitioner must state in the petition, if known, whether:

1. A parent or legal custodian named in the petition has previously unsuccessfully participated in voluntary services offered by the department;

2. A parent or legal custodian named in the petition has participated in mediation and whether a mediation agreement exists;

3. A parent or legal custodian has rejected the voluntary services offered by the department;

4. A parent or legal custodian named in the petition has not fully complied with a safety plan; or

5. The department has determined that voluntary services are not appropriate for the parent or legal custodian and the reasons for such determination.

If the department is the petitioner, it shall provide all safety plans as defined in s. 39.01 involving the parent or legal custodian to the court.

(4) When a child has been placed in shelter status by order of the court, a petition alleging dependency must be filed within 21 days after the shelter hearing, or within 7 days after any party files a demand for the early filing of a dependency petition, whichever comes first. In all other cases, the petition must be filed within a reasonable time after the date the child was referred to protective investigation. The child's parent or legal custodian must be served with a copy of the petition at least 72 hours before the arraignment hearing.

(5) A petition for termination of parental rights may be filed at any time.

HISTORY:
S. 20, ch. 78-414; s. 7, ch. 84-311; s. 1, ch. 85-338; s. 7, ch. 87-289; s. 14, ch. 88-337; s. 6, ch. 90-306; s. 5, ch. 92-170; s. 8, ch. 94-164; s. 62, ch. 98-403; s. 25, ch. 99-193; s. 13, ch. 2014-224, eff. July 1, 2014.

Editor's notes.
Former s. 39.404.

§ 39.502. Notice, process, and service.

(1) Unless parental rights have been terminated, all parents must be notified of all proceedings or hearings involving the child. Notice in cases involving shelter hearings and hearings resulting from medical emergencies must be that most likely to result in actual notice to the parents. In all other dependency proceedings, notice must be provided in accordance with subsections (4)-(9), except when a relative requests notification pursuant to s. 39.301(14)(b), in which case notice shall be provided pursuant to subsection (19).

(2) Personal appearance of any person in a hearing before the court obviates the necessity of serving process on that person.

(3) Upon the filing of a petition containing allegations of facts which, if true, would establish that the child is a dependent child, and upon the request of the petitioner, the clerk or deputy clerk shall issue a summons.

(4) The summons shall require the person on whom it is served to appear for a hearing at a time and place specified, not less than 72 hours after service of the summons. A copy of the petition shall be attached to the summons.

(5) The summons shall be directed to, and shall be served upon, all parties other than the petitioner.

(6) It is the duty of the petitioner or moving party to notify all participants and parties known to the petitioner or moving party of all hearings subsequent to the initial hearing unless notice is contained in prior court orders and these orders were provided to the participant or party. Proof of notice or provision of orders may be provided by certified mail with a signed return receipt.

(7) Service of the summons and service of pleadings, papers, and notices subsequent to the summons on persons outside this state must be made pursuant to s. 61.509.

(8) It is not necessary to the validity of a proceeding covered by this part that the parents be present if their identity or residence is unknown after a diligent search has been made, but in this event the petitioner shall file an affidavit of diligent search prepared by the person who made the search and inquiry, and the court may appoint a guardian ad litem for the child.

(9) When an affidavit of diligent search has been filed under subsection (8), the petitioner shall continue to search for and attempt to serve the person sought until excused from further search by the court. The petitioner shall report on the results of the search at each court hearing until the person is identified or located or further search is excused by the court.

(10) Service by publication shall not be required for dependency hearings and the failure to serve a party or give notice to a participant shall not affect the validity of an order of adjudication or disposition if the court finds that the petitioner has completed a diligent search for that party.

(11) Upon the application of a party or the petitioner, the clerk or deputy clerk shall issue, and the court on its own motion may issue, subpoenas requiring attendance and testimony of witnesses and production of records, documents, and other tangible objects at any hearing.

(12) All process and orders issued by the court shall be served or executed as other process and orders of the circuit court and, in addition, may be served or executed by authorized agents of the department or the guardian ad litem.

(13) Subpoenas may be served within the state by any person over 18 years of age who is not a party to the proceeding and, in addition, may be served by authorized agents of the department or the guardian ad litem.

(14) No fee shall be paid for service of any process or other papers by an agent of the department or the guardian ad litem. If any process, orders, or any other papers are served or executed by any sheriff, the sheriff's fees shall be paid by the county.

(15) A party who is identified as a person who has a mental illness or a developmental disability must be informed by the court of the availability of advocacy services through the department, the Arc of Florida, or other appropriate mental health or developmental disability advocacy groups and encouraged to seek such services.

(16) If the party to whom an order is directed is present or represented at the final hearing, service of the order is not required.

(17) The parent or legal custodian of the child, the attorney for the department, the guardian ad litem, the foster or preadoptive parents, and all other parties and participants shall be given reasonable notice of all proceedings and hearings provided for under this part. All foster or preadoptive parents must be provided with at least 72 hours' notice, verbally or in writing, of all proceedings or hearings relating to children in their care or children they are seeking to adopt to ensure the ability to provide input to the court.

(18) In all proceedings under this part, the court shall provide to the parent or legal custodian of the child, at the conclusion of any hearing, a written notice containing the date of the next scheduled hearing. The court shall also include the date of the next hearing in any order issued by the court.

(19) In all proceedings and hearings under this chapter, the attorney for the department shall notify, orally or in writing, a relative requesting notification pursuant to s. 39.301(14)(b) of the date, time, and location of such proceedings and hearings, and notify the relative that he or she has the right to attend all subsequent proceedings and hearings, to submit reports to the court, and to speak to the court regarding the child, if the relative so desires. The court has the discretion to release the attorney for the department from notifying a relative who requested notification pursuant to s. 39.301(14)(b) if the relative's involvement is determined to be impeding the dependency process or detrimental to the child's well-being.

HISTORY:

S. 20, ch. 78-414; s. 2, ch. 83-255; s. 6, ch. 92-170; s. 9, ch. 94-164; s. 4, ch. 97-276; s. 63, ch. 98-403; s. 26, ch. 99-193; s. 20, ch. 2000-139; s. 1, ch. 2002-65; s. 9, ch. 2008-245, eff. June 30, 2008; s. 8, ch. 2009-43, eff. July 1, 2009; s. 17, ch. 2012-178, eff. July 1, 2012; s. 1, ch. 2013-162, eff. July 1, 2013.

Editor's notes.

Section 1 of ch. 2009-43 provides: "This act may be cited as the 'Zahid Jones, Jr., Give Grandparents and Other Relatives a Voice Act.' "

Former s. 39.405.

§ 39.503. Identity or location of parent unknown; special procedures.

(1) If the identity or location of a parent is unknown and a petition for dependency or shelter is filed, the court shall conduct under oath the following inquiry of the parent or legal custodian who is available, or, if no parent or legal custodian is available, of any relative or custodian of the child who is present at the hearing and likely to have any of the following information:

(a) Whether the mother of the child was married at the probable time of conception of the child or at the time of birth of the child.

(b) Whether the mother was cohabiting with a male at the probable time of conception of the child.

(c) Whether the mother has received payments or promises of support with respect to the child or because of her pregnancy from a man who claims to be the father.

(d) Whether the mother has named any man as the father on the birth certificate of the child or in connection with applying for or receiving public assistance.

(e) Whether any man has acknowledged or claimed paternity of the child in a jurisdiction in which the mother resided at the time of or since conception of the child, or in which the child has resided or resides.

(f) Whether a man is named on the birth certificate of the child pursuant to s. 382.013(2).

(g) Whether a man has been determined by a court order to be the father of the child.

(h) Whether a man has been determined to be the father of the child by the Department of Revenue as provided in s. 409.256.

(2) The information required in subsection (1) may be supplied to the court or the department in the form of a sworn affidavit by a person having personal knowledge of the facts.

(3) If the inquiry under subsection (1) identifies any person as a parent or prospective parent, the court shall require notice of the hearing to be provided to that person.

(4) If the inquiry under subsection (1) fails to identify any person as a parent or prospective parent, the court shall so find and may proceed without further notice.

(5) If the inquiry under subsection (1) identifies a parent or prospective parent, and that person's location is unknown, the court shall direct the petitioner to conduct a diligent search for that person before scheduling a disposition hearing regarding the dependency of the child unless the court finds that the best interest of the child requires proceeding without notice to the person whose location is unknown.

(6) The diligent search required by subsection (5) must include, at a minimum, inquiries of all relatives of the parent or prospective parent made known to the petitioner, inquiries of all offices of program areas of the department likely to have information about the parent or prospective parent, inquiries of other state and federal agencies likely to have information about the parent or prospective parent, inquiries of appropriate utility and postal providers, a thorough search of at least one electronic database specifically designed for locating persons, a search of the Florida Putative Father Registry, and inquiries of appropriate law enforcement agencies. Pursuant to s. 453 of the Social Security Act, 42 U.S.C. s. 653(c)(4), the department, as the state agency administering Titles IV-B and IV-E of the act, shall be provided access to the federal and state parent locator service for diligent search activities.

(7) Any agency contacted by a petitioner with a request for information pursuant to subsection (6) shall

release the requested information to the petitioner without the necessity of a subpoena or court order.

(8) If the inquiry and diligent search identifies a prospective parent, that person must be given the opportunity to become a party to the proceedings by completing a sworn affidavit of parenthood and filing it with the court or the department. A prospective parent who files a sworn affidavit of parenthood while the child is a dependent child but no later than at the time of or before the adjudicatory hearing in any termination of parental rights proceeding for the child shall be considered a parent for all purposes under this section unless the other parent contests the determination of parenthood. If the known parent contests the recognition of the prospective parent as a parent, the prospective parent may not be recognized as a parent until proceedings to determine maternity or paternity under chapter 742 have been concluded. However, the prospective parent shall continue to receive notice of hearings as a participant pending results of the chapter 742 proceedings to determine maternity or paternity.

(9) If the diligent search under subsection (5) fails to identify and locate a parent or prospective parent, the court shall so find and may proceed without further notice.

HISTORY:

S. 10, ch. 94-164; s. 5, ch. 97-276; s. 64, ch. 98-403; s. 18, ch. 99-2; s. 27, ch. 99-193; s. 21, ch. 2000-139; s. 10, ch. 2008-245, eff. June 30, 2008; s. 8, ch. 2017-151, eff. July 1, 2017.

Editor's notes.

Former s. 39.4051.

§ 39.504. Injunction; penalty.

(1) At any time after a protective investigation has been initiated pursuant to part III of this chapter, the court, upon the request of the department, a law enforcement officer, the state attorney, or other responsible person, or upon its own motion, may, if there is reasonable cause, issue an injunction to prevent any act of child abuse. Reasonable cause for the issuance of an injunction exists if there is evidence of child abuse or if there is a reasonable likelihood of such abuse occurring based upon a recent overt act or failure to act. If there is a pending dependency proceeding regarding the child whom the injunction is sought to protect, the judge hearing the dependency proceeding must also hear the injunction proceeding regarding the child.

(2) The petitioner seeking the injunction shall file a verified petition, or a petition along with an affidavit, setting forth the specific actions by the alleged offender from which the child must be protected and all remedies sought. Upon filing the petition, the court shall set a hearing to be held at the earliest possible time. Pending the hearing, the court may issue a temporary ex parte injunction, with verified pleadings or affidavits as evidence. The temporary ex parte injunction pending a hearing is effective for up to 15 days and the

hearing must be held within that period unless continued for good cause shown, which may include obtaining service of process, in which case the temporary ex parte injunction shall be extended for the continuance period. The hearing may be held sooner if the alleged offender has received reasonable notice.

(3) Before the hearing, the alleged offender must be personally served with a copy of the petition, all other pleadings related to the petition, a notice of hearing, and, if one has been entered, the temporary injunction. If the petitioner cannot locate the alleged offender for service after a diligent search pursuant to the same requirements as in s. 39.503 and the filing of an affidavit of diligent search, the court may enter the injunction based on the sworn petition and any affidavits. At the hearing, the court may base its determination on a sworn petition, testimony, or an affidavit and may hear all relevant and material evidence, including oral and written reports, to the extent of its probative value even though it would not be competent evidence at an adjudicatory hearing. Following the hearing, the court may enter a final injunction. The court may grant a continuance of the hearing at any time for good cause shown by any party. If a temporary injunction has been entered, it shall be continued during the continuance.

(4) If an injunction is issued under this section, the primary purpose of the injunction must be to protect and promote the best interests of the child, taking the preservation of the child's immediate family into consideration.

(a) The injunction applies to the alleged or actual offender in a case of child abuse or acts of domestic violence. The conditions of the injunction shall be determined by the court, which may include ordering the alleged or actual offender to:

1. Refrain from further abuse or acts of domestic violence.

2. Participate in a specialized treatment program.

3. Limit contact or communication with the child victim, other children in the home, or any other child.

4. Refrain from contacting the child at home, school, work, or wherever the child may be found.

5. Have limited or supervised visitation with the child.

6. Vacate the home in which the child resides.

7. Comply with the terms of a safety plan implemented in the injunction pursuant to s. 39.301.

(b) Upon proper pleading, the court may award the following relief in a temporary ex parte or final injunction:

1. Exclusive use and possession of the dwelling to the caregiver or exclusion of the alleged or actual offender from the residence of the caregiver.

2. Temporary support for the child or other family members.

3. The costs of medical, psychiatric, and psychological treatment for the child incurred due to the abuse, and similar costs for other family members.

This paragraph does not preclude an adult victim of domestic violence from seeking protection for himself or herself under s. 741.30.

(c) The terms of the final injunction shall remain in effect until modified or dissolved by the court. The petitioner, respondent, or caregiver may move at any time to modify or dissolve the injunction. Notice of hearing on the motion to modify or dissolve the injunction must be provided to all parties, including the department. The injunction is valid and enforceable in all counties in the state.

(5) Service of process on the respondent shall be carried out pursuant to s. 741.30. The department shall deliver a copy of any injunction issued pursuant to this section to the protected party or to a parent, caregiver, or individual acting in the place of a parent who is not the respondent. Law enforcement officers may exercise their arrest powers as provided in s. 901.15(6) to enforce the terms of the injunction.

(6) Any person who fails to comply with an injunction issued pursuant to this section commits a misdemeanor of the first degree, punishable as provided in s. 775.082 or s. 775.083.

(7) The person against whom an injunction is entered under this section does not automatically become a party to a subsequent dependency action concerning the same child.

HISTORY:
S. 1, ch. 84-226; s. 1, ch. 91-224; s. 228, ch. 95-147; s. 10, ch. 95-228; s. 65, ch. 98-403; s. 28, ch. 99-193; s. 11, ch. 2008-245, eff. June 30, 2008; s. 9, ch. 2012-178, eff. July 1, 2012; s. 14, ch. 2014-224, eff. July 1, 2014; s. 9, ch. 2017-151, eff. July 1, 2017.

Editor's notes.
Former s. 39.4055.

§ 39.505. No answer required.

No answer to the petition or any other pleading need be filed by any child, parent, or legal custodian, but any matters which might be set forth in an answer or other pleading may be pleaded orally before the court or filed in writing as any such person may choose. Notwithstanding the filing of an answer or any pleading, the respondent shall, prior to an adjudicatory hearing, be advised by the court of the right to counsel and shall be given an opportunity to deny the allegations in the petition for dependency or to enter a plea to allegations in the petition before the court.

HISTORY:
S. 20, ch. 78-414; s. 229, ch. 95-147; s. 66, ch. 98-403.

Editor's notes.
Former s. 39.406.

§ 39.506. Arraignment hearings.

(1) When a child has been sheltered by order of the court, an arraignment hearing must be held no later than 28 days after the shelter hearing, or within 7 days after the date of filing of the dependency petition if a demand for early filing has been made by any party, for the parent or legal custodian to admit, deny, or consent to findings of dependency alleged in the petition. If the parent or legal custodian admits or consents to the findings in the petition, the court shall conduct a disposition hearing within 15 days after the arraignment hearing. However, if the parent or legal custodian denies any of the allegations of the petition, the court shall hold an adjudicatory hearing within 30 days after the date of the arraignment hearing unless a continuance is granted pursuant to this chapter.

(2) When a child is in the custody of the parent or legal custodian, upon the filing of a petition the clerk shall set a date for an arraignment hearing within a reasonable time after the date of the filing. If the parent or legal custodian admits or consents to an adjudication, the court shall conduct a disposition hearing within 15 days after the arraignment hearing. However, if the parent or legal custodian denies any of the allegations of dependency, the court shall hold an adjudicatory hearing within 30 days after the date of the arraignment hearing.

(3) Failure of a person served with notice to personally appear at the arraignment hearing constitutes the person's consent to a dependency adjudication. The document containing the notice to respond or appear must contain, in type at least as large as the balance of the document, the following or substantially similar language: "FAILURE TO PERSONALLY APPEAR AT THE ARRAIGNMENT HEARING CONSTITUTES CONSENT TO THE ADJUDICATION OF THIS CHILD (OR CHILDREN) AS A DEPENDENT CHILD (OR CHILDREN) AND MAY ULTIMATELY RESULT IN LOSS OF CUSTODY OF THIS CHILD (OR CHILDREN)." If a person appears for the arraignment hearing and the court orders that person to personally appear at the adjudicatory hearing for dependency, stating the date, time, and place of the adjudicatory hearing, then that person's failure to appear for the scheduled adjudicatory hearing constitutes consent to a dependency adjudication.

(4) At the arraignment hearing, each party shall provide to the court a permanent mailing address. The court shall advise each party that this address will be used by the court and the petitioner for notice purposes unless and until the party notifies the court and the petitioner in writing of a new mailing address.

(5) If at the arraignment hearing the parent or legal custodian consents or admits to the allegations in the petition, the court shall proceed to hold a disposition hearing no more than 15 days after the date of the arraignment hearing unless a continuance is necessary.

(6) At any arraignment hearing, if the child is in an out-of-home placement, the court shall order visitation rights absent a clear and convincing showing that visitation is not in the best interest of the child. Any order for visitation or other contact must conform to the provisions of s. 39.0139.

(7) The court shall review whether the department has made a reasonable effort to prevent or eliminate the need for removal or continued removal of the child from the home. If the court determines that the department has not made such an effort, the court shall order the department to provide appropriate and available services to assure the protection of the child in the home when such services are necessary for the child's physical, mental, or emotional health and safety.

(8) At the arraignment hearing, the court shall review the necessity for the child's continued placement in the shelter. The court shall also make a written determination regarding the child's continued placement in shelter within 24 hours after any violation of the time requirements for the filing of a petition or prior to the court's granting any continuance as specified in subsection (5).

(9) At the conclusion of the arraignment hearing, all parties and the relatives who are providing out-of-home care for the child shall be notified in writing by the court of the date, time, and location for the next scheduled hearing.

HISTORY:

S. 9, ch. 84-311; s. 12, ch. 94-164; s. 10, ch. 98-280; s. 67, ch. 98-403; s. 29, ch. 99-193; s. 3, ch. 2002-216; s. 3, ch. 2007-109, eff. July 1, 2007; s. 9, ch. 2009-43, eff. July 1, 2009.

Editor's notes.

Section 1 of ch. 2009-43 provides: "This act may be cited as the 'Zahid Jones, Jr., Give Grandparents and Other Relatives a Voice Act.' "

Former s. 39.408(1).

§ 39.507. Adjudicatory hearings; orders of adjudication.

(1)(a) The adjudicatory hearing shall be held as soon as practicable after the petition for dependency is filed and in accordance with the Florida Rules of Juvenile Procedure, but no later than 30 days after the arraignment.

(b) Adjudicatory hearings shall be conducted by the judge without a jury, applying the rules of evidence in use in civil cases and adjourning the hearings from time to time as necessary. In a hearing on a petition in which it is alleged that the child is dependent, a preponderance of evidence will be required to establish the state of dependency. Any evidence presented in the dependency hearing which was obtained as the result of an anonymous call must be independently corroborated. In no instance shall allegations made in an anonymous report of abuse, abandonment, or neglect be suffi-

cient to support an adjudication of dependency in the absence of corroborating evidence.

(2) All hearings, except as provided in this section, shall be open to the public, and a person may not be excluded except on special order of the judge, who may close any hearing to the public upon determining that the public interest or the welfare of the child is best served by so doing. The parents or legal custodians shall be allowed to obtain discovery pursuant to the Florida Rules of Juvenile Procedure, provided such discovery does not violate the provisions of s. 39.202. Hearings involving more than one child may be held simultaneously when the children involved are related to each other or were involved in the same case. The child and the parents, caregivers, or legal custodians of the child may be examined separately and apart from each other.

(3) Except as otherwise specifically provided, nothing in this section prohibits the publication of the proceedings in a hearing.

(4) If the court finds at the adjudicatory hearing that the child named in a petition is not dependent, it shall enter an order so finding and dismissing the case.

(5) If the court finds that the child named in the petition is dependent, but finds that no action other than supervision in the child's home is required, it may enter an order briefly stating the facts upon which its finding is based, but withholding an order of adjudication and placing the child's home under the supervision of the department. If the court later finds that the parents of the child have not complied with the conditions of supervision imposed, the court may, after a hearing to establish the noncompliance, but without further evidence of the state of dependency, enter an order of adjudication and shall thereafter have full authority under this chapter to provide for the child as adjudicated. If the child is to remain in an out-of-home placement by order of the court, the court must adjudicate the child dependent.

(6) If the court finds that the child named in a petition is dependent, but chooses not to withhold adjudication or is prohibited from withholding adjudication, it shall incorporate that finding in an order of adjudication entered in the case, briefly stating the facts upon which the finding is made, and the court shall thereafter have full authority under this chapter to provide for the child as adjudicated.

(7)(a) For as long as a court maintains jurisdiction over a dependency case, only one order adjudicating each child in the case dependent shall be entered. This order establishes the legal status of the child for purposes of proceedings under this chapter and may be based on the conduct of one parent, both parents, or a legal custodian.

(b) However, the court must determine whether each parent or legal custodian identified in the case abused, abandoned, or neglected the child or engaged in conduct that placed the child at substantial risk of imminent abuse, abandonment, or neglect. If a second parent is served and brought into the proceeding after the adjudication and if an evidentiary hearing for the second parent is conducted, the court shall supplement the adjudicatory order, disposition order, and the case plan, as necessary. The petitioner is not required to prove actual harm or actual abuse by the second parent in order for the court to make supplemental findings regarding the conduct of the second parent. The court is not required to conduct an evidentiary hearing for the second parent in order to supplement the adjudicatory order, the disposition order, and the case plan if the requirements of s. 39.506(3) or (5) are satisfied. With the exception of proceedings pursuant to s. 39.811, the child's dependency status may not be retried or readjudicated.

(c) If a court adjudicates a child dependent and the child is in out-of-home care, the court shall inquire of the parent or parents whether the parents have relatives who might be considered as a placement for the child. The court shall advise the parents that, if the parents fail to substantially comply with the case plan, their parental rights may be terminated and that the child's out-of-home placement may become permanent. The parent or parents shall provide to the court and all parties identification and location information of the relatives.

(8) At the conclusion of the adjudicatory hearing, if the child named in the petition is found dependent, the court shall schedule the disposition hearing within 30 days after the last day of the adjudicatory hearing. All parties shall be notified in writing at the conclusion of the adjudicatory hearing by the clerk of the court of the date, time, and location of the disposition hearing.

(9) An order of adjudication by a court that a child is dependent shall not be deemed a conviction, nor shall the child be deemed to have been found guilty or to be a criminal by reason of that adjudication, nor shall that adjudication operate to impose upon the child any of the civil disabilities ordinarily imposed by or resulting from conviction or disqualify or prejudice the child in any civil service application or appointment.

(10) After an adjudication of dependency, or a finding of dependency in which adjudication is withheld, the court may order a person who has custody or is requesting custody of the child to submit to a mental health or substance abuse disorder assessment or evaluation. The order may be made only upon good cause shown and pursuant to notice and procedural requirements provided under the Florida Rules of Juvenile Procedure. The assessment or evaluation must be administered by an appropriate qualified professional, as defined in s. 39.01 or s. 397.311. The court may also require such person to participate in and comply with treatment and services identified as necessary, including, when appropriate and available, participation in and compliance with a mental health

court program established under chapter 394 or a treatment-based drug court program established under s. 397.334. In addition to supervision by the department, the court, including the mental health court program or treatment-based drug court program, may oversee the progress and compliance with treatment by a person who has custody or is requesting custody of the child. The court may impose appropriate available sanctions for noncompliance upon a person who has custody or is requesting custody of the child or make a finding of noncompliance for consideration in determining whether an alternative placement of the child is in the child's best interests. Any order entered under this subsection may be made only upon good cause shown. This subsection does not authorize placement of a child with a person seeking custody, other than the parent or legal custodian, who requires mental health or substance abuse disorder treatment.

HISTORY:

S. 20, ch. 78-414; s. 9, ch. 84-311; s. 7, ch. 87-133; s. 12, ch. 94-164; s. 231, ch. 95-147; s. 12, ch. 95-228; s. 68, ch. 98-403; s. 30, ch. 99-193; s. 11, ch. 2006-86, eff. July 1, 2006; s. 4, ch. 2006-97, eff. June 7, 2006; s. 12, ch. 2008-245, eff. June 30, 2008; s. 2, ch. 2016-127, eff. July 1, 2016; s. 83, ch. 2016-241, eff. July 1, 2016; s. 10, ch. 2017-151, eff. July 1, 2017.

Editor's notes.

Former ss. 39.408(2), 39.409.

§ 39.5075. Citizenship or residency status for immigrant children who are dependents.

(1) As used in this section, the term:

(a) "Eligible for long-term foster care" means that reunification with a child's parent is not an appropriate option for permanency for the child.

(b) "May be eligible for special immigrant juvenile status under federal law" means:

1. The child has been found dependent based on allegations of abuse, neglect, or abandonment;

2. The child is eligible for long-term foster care;

3. It is in the best interest of the child to remain in the United States; and

4. The child remains under the jurisdiction of the juvenile court.

(2) Whenever a child is adjudicated dependent, the department or community-based care provider shall determine whether the child is a citizen of the United States. The department or community-based care provider shall report to the court in its first judicial review concerning the child whether the child is a citizen of the United States and, if not, the steps that have been taken to address the citizenship or residency status of the child. Services to children alleged to have been abused, neglected, or abandoned must be provided without regard to the citizenship of the child except where alienage or immigration status is explicitly set forth as a statutory condition of coverage or eligibility.

(3) If the child is not a citizen, the department or community-based care provider shall include in the

case plan developed for the child a recommendation as to whether the permanency plan for the child will include remaining in the United States. If the case plan calls for the child to remain in the United States, and the child is in need of documentation to effectuate this plan, the department or community-based care provider must evaluate the child's case to determine whether the child may be eligible for special immigrant juvenile status under federal law.

(4) If the child may be eligible for special immigrant juvenile status, the department or community-based care provider shall petition the court for an order finding that the child meets the criteria for special immigrant juvenile status. The ruling of the court on this petition must include findings as to the express wishes of the child, if the child is able to express such wishes, and any other circumstances that would affect whether the best interests of the child would be served by applying for special immigrant juvenile status.

(5) No later than 60 days after an order finding that the child is eligible for special immigrant juvenile status and that applying for this status is in the best interest of the child, the department or community-based care provider shall, directly or through volunteer or contracted legal services, file a petition for special immigrant juvenile status and the application for adjustment of status to the appropriate federal authorities on behalf of the child.

(6) If a petition and application have been filed and the petition and application have not been granted by the time the child reaches 18 years of age, the court may retain jurisdiction over the dependency case solely for the purpose of allowing the continued consideration of the petition and application by federal authorities. Review hearings for the child shall be set solely for the purpose of determining the status of the petition and application. The court's jurisdiction terminates upon the final decision of the federal authorities. Retention of jurisdiction in this instance does not affect the services available to a young adult under s. 409.1451. The court may not retain jurisdiction of the case after the immigrant child's 22nd birthday.

(7) In any judicial review report provided to the court for a child for whom the court has granted the order described in subsection (4), the court shall be advised of the status of the petition and application process concerning the child.

(8) The department shall adopt rules to administer this section.

HISTORY:
S. 1, ch. 2005-245.

§ 39.5085. Relative Caregiver Program.

(1) It is the intent of the Legislature in enacting this section to:

(a) Provide for the establishment of procedures and protocols that serve to advance the continued safety of children by acknowledging the valued re-source uniquely available through grandparents, relatives of children, and specified nonrelatives of children pursuant to subparagraph (2)(a)3.

(b) Recognize family relationships in which a grandparent or other relative is the head of a household that includes a child otherwise at risk of foster care placement.

(c) Enhance family preservation and stability by recognizing that most children in such placements with grandparents and other relatives do not need intensive supervision of the placement by the courts or by the department.

(d) Recognize that permanency in the best interests of the child can be achieved through a variety of permanency options, including permanent guardianship under s. 39.6221 if the guardian is a relative, by permanent placement with a fit and willing relative under s. 39.6231, by a relative, guardianship under chapter 744, or adoption, by providing additional placement options and incentives that will achieve permanency and stability for many children who are otherwise at risk of foster care placement because of abuse, abandonment, or neglect, but who may successfully be able to be placed by the dependency court in the care of such relatives.

(e) Reserve the limited casework and supervisory resources of the courts and the department for those cases in which children do not have the option for safe, stable care within the family.

(f) Recognize that a child may have a close relationship with a person who is not a blood relative or a relative by marriage and that such person should be eligible for financial assistance under this section if he or she is able and willing to care for the child and provide a safe, stable home environment.

(2)(a) The Department of Children and Families shall establish, operate, and implement the Relative Caregiver Program by rule of the department. The Relative Caregiver Program shall, within the limits of available funding, provide financial assistance to:

1. Relatives who are within the fifth degree by blood or marriage to the parent or stepparent of a child and who are caring full-time for that dependent child in the role of substitute parent as a result of a court's determination of child abuse, neglect, or abandonment and subsequent placement with the relative under this chapter.

2. Relatives who are within the fifth degree by blood or marriage to the parent or stepparent of a child and who are caring full-time for that dependent child, and a dependent half-brother or half-sister of that dependent child, in the role of substitute parent as a result of a court's determination of child abuse, neglect, or abandonment and subsequent placement with the relative under this chapter.

3. Nonrelatives who are willing to assume custody and care of a dependent child in the role

of substitute parent as a result of a court's determination of child abuse, neglect, or abandonment and subsequent placement with the nonrelative caregiver under this chapter. The court must find that a proposed placement under this subparagraph is in the best interest of the child.

4. A relative or nonrelative caregiver, but the relative or nonrelative caregiver may not receive a Relative Caregiver Program payment if the parent or stepparent of the child resides in the home. However, a relative or nonrelative may receive the Relative Caregiver Program payment for a minor parent who is in his or her care, as well as for the minor parent's child, if both children have been adjudicated dependent and meet all other eligibility requirements. If the caregiver is currently receiving the payment, the Relative Caregiver Program payment must be terminated no later than the first of the following month after the parent or stepparent moves into the home, allowing for 10-day notice of adverse action.

The placement may be court-ordered temporary legal custody to the relative or nonrelative under protective supervision of the department pursuant to s. 39.521(1)(c)3., or court-ordered placement in the home of a relative or nonrelative as a permanency option under s. 39.6221 or s. 39.6231 or under former s. 39.622 if the placement was made before July 1, 2006. The Relative Caregiver Program shall offer financial assistance to caregivers who would be unable to serve in that capacity without the caregiver payment because of financial burden, thus exposing the child to the trauma of placement in a shelter or in foster care.

(b) Caregivers who receive assistance under this section must be capable, as determined by a home study, of providing a physically safe environment and a stable, supportive home for the children under their care and must assure that the children's well-being is met, including, but not limited to, the provision of immunizations, education, and mental health services as needed.

(c) Relatives or nonrelatives who qualify for and participate in the Relative Caregiver Program are not required to meet foster care licensing requirements under s. 409.175.

(d) Relatives or nonrelatives who are caring for children placed with them by the court pursuant to this chapter shall receive a special monthly caregiver benefit established by rule of the department. The amount of the special benefit payment shall be based on the child's age within a payment schedule established by rule of the department and subject to availability of funding. The statewide average monthly rate for children judicially placed with relatives or nonrelatives who are not licensed as foster homes may not exceed 82 percent of the statewide average foster care rate, and the cost of providing the assistance described in this section to any caregiver may not exceed the cost of providing out-of-home care in emergency shelter or foster care.

(e) Children receiving cash benefits under this section are not eligible to simultaneously receive WAGES cash benefits under chapter 414.

(f) Within available funding, the Relative Caregiver Program shall provide caregivers with family support and preservation services, flexible funds in accordance with s. 409.165, school readiness, and other available services in order to support the child's safety, growth, and healthy development. Children living with caregivers who are receiving assistance under this section shall be eligible for Medicaid coverage.

(g) The department may use appropriate available state, federal, and private funds to operate the Relative Caregiver Program. The department may develop liaison functions to be available to relatives or nonrelatives who care for children pursuant to this chapter to ensure placement stability in extended family settings.

HISTORY:
S. 1, ch. 98-78; s. 70, ch. 98-403; s. 32, ch. 99-193; s. 24, ch. 2000-139; s. 1, ch. 2002-38; s. 12, ch. 2006-86, eff. July 1, 2006; s. 2, ch. 2007-5, eff. July 3, 2007; s. 10, ch. 2009-43, eff. July 1, 2009; s. 3, ch. 2010-210, eff. July 1, 2010; s. 20, ch. 2014-19, eff. July 1, 2014; s. 15, ch. 2014-224, eff. July 1, 2014; s. 11, ch. 2017-151, eff. July 1, 2017.

Editor's notes.
Section 1 of ch. 2009-43 provides: "This act may be cited as the 'Zahid Jones, Jr., Give Grandparents and Other Relatives a Voice Act.' "

§ 39.509. Grandparents rights.

Notwithstanding any other provision of law, a maternal or paternal grandparent as well as a stepgrandparent is entitled to reasonable visitation with his or her grandchild who has been adjudicated a dependent child and taken from the physical custody of the parent unless the court finds that such visitation is not in the best interest of the child or that such visitation would interfere with the goals of the case plan. Reasonable visitation may be unsupervised and, where appropriate and feasible, may be frequent and continuing. Any order for visitation or other contact must conform to the provisions of s. 39.0139.

(1) Grandparent visitation may take place in the home of the grandparent unless there is a compelling reason for denying such a visitation. The department's caseworker shall arrange the visitation to which a grandparent is entitled pursuant to this section. The state shall not charge a fee for any costs associated with arranging the visitation. However, the grandparent shall pay for the child's cost of transportation when the visitation is to take place in the grandparent's home. The caseworker shall docu-

ment the reasons for any decision to restrict a grandparent's visitation.

(2) A grandparent entitled to visitation pursuant to this section shall not be restricted from appropriate displays of affection to the child, such as appropriately hugging or kissing his or her grandchild. Gifts, cards, and letters from the grandparent and other family members shall not be denied to a child who has been adjudicated a dependent child.

(3) Any attempt by a grandparent to facilitate a meeting between the child who has been adjudicated a dependent child and the child's parent or legal custodian, or any other person in violation of a court order shall automatically terminate future visitation rights of the grandparent.

(4) When the child has been returned to the physical custody of his or her parent, the visitation rights granted pursuant to this section shall terminate.

(5) The termination of parental rights does not affect the rights of grandparents unless the court finds that such visitation is not in the best interest of the child or that such visitation would interfere with the goals of permanency planning for the child.

(6) In determining whether grandparental visitation is not in the child's best interest, consideration may be given to the following:

(a) The finding of guilt, regardless of adjudication, or entry or plea of guilty or nolo contendere to charges under the following statutes, or similar statutes of other jurisdictions: s. 787.04, relating to removing minors from the state or concealing minors contrary to court order; s. 794.011, relating to sexual battery; s. 798.02, relating to lewd and lascivious behavior; chapter 800, relating to lewdness and indecent exposure; s. 826.04, relating to incest; or chapter 827, relating to the abuse of children.

(b) The designation by a court as a sexual predator as defined in s. 775.21 or a substantially similar designation under laws of another jurisdiction.

(c) A report of abuse, abandonment, or neglect under ss. 415.101 - 415.113 or this chapter and the outcome of the investigation concerning such report.

HISTORY:
S. 9, ch. 90-273; s. 72, ch. 91-45; s. 7, ch. 93-156; s. 6, ch. 97-95; s. 71, ch. 98-403; s. 33, ch. 99-193; s. 4, ch. 2007-109, eff. July 1, 2007; s. 38, ch. 2016-24, eff. Oct. 1, 2016.

Editor's notes.
Former s. 39.4105.

§ 39.510. Appeal.

(1) Any party to the proceeding who is affected by an order of the court, or the department may appeal to the appropriate district court of appeal within the time and in the manner prescribed by the Florida Rules of Appellate Procedure. Appointed counsel shall be compensated as provided in this chapter.

(2) When the notice of appeal is filed in the circuit court by a party other than the department, an attorney for the department shall represent the state and the court upon appeal and shall be notified of the appeal by the clerk.

(3) The taking of an appeal shall not operate as a supersedeas in any case unless pursuant to an order of the court, except that a permanent order of commitment to a licensed child-placing agency or the department for subsequent adoption shall be suspended while the appeal is pending, but the child shall continue in custody under the order until the appeal is decided.

(4) The case on appeal shall be docketed, and any papers filed in the appellate court shall be entitled, with the initials but not the name of the child and the court case number, and the papers shall remain sealed in the office of the clerk of the appellate court when not in use by the appellate court and shall not be open to public inspection. The decision of the appellate court shall be likewise entitled and shall refer to the child only by initials and court case number.

(5) The original order of the appellate court, with all papers filed in the case on appeal, shall remain in the office of the clerk of the appellate court, sealed and not open to inspection except by order of the appellate court. The clerk of the appellate court shall return to the circuit court all papers transmitted to the appellate court from the circuit court, together with a certified copy of the order of the appellate court.

HISTORY:
S. 20, ch. 78-414; s. 11, ch. 84-311; s. 9, ch. 90-306; s. 8, ch. 92-170; s. 72, ch. 98-403; s. 34, ch. 99-193.

Editor's notes.
Former s. 39.413.

PART VI.
DISPOSITION; POSTDISPOSITION CHANGE OF CUSTODY.

§ 39.521. Disposition hearings; powers of disposition.

(1) A disposition hearing shall be conducted by the court, if the court finds that the facts alleged in the petition for dependency were proven in the adjudicatory hearing, or if the parents or legal custodians have consented to the finding of dependency or admitted the allegations in the petition, have failed to appear for the arraignment hearing after proper notice, or have not been located despite a diligent search having been conducted.

(a) A written case plan and a family functioning assessment prepared by an authorized agent of the department must be approved by the court. The department must file the case plan and the family functioning assessment with the court, serve a copy of the case plan on the parents of the child, and provide a copy of the case plan to the representative of the guardian ad litem program, if the program has been appointed, and a copy to all other parties:

1. Not less than 72 hours before the disposition hearing, if the disposition hearing occurs on or after the 60th day after the date the child was placed in out-of-home care. All such case plans must be approved by the court.

2. Not less than 72 hours before the case plan acceptance hearing, if the disposition hearing occurs before the 60th day after the date the child was placed in out-of-home care and a case plan has not been submitted pursuant to this paragraph, or if the court does not approve the case plan at the disposition hearing. The case plan acceptance hearing must occur within 30 days after the disposition hearing to review and approve the case plan.

(b) The court may grant an exception to the requirement for a family functioning assessment by separate order or within the judge's order of disposition upon finding that all the family and child information required by subsection (2) is available in other documents filed with the court.

(c) When any child is adjudicated by a court to be dependent, the court having jurisdiction of the child has the power by order to:

1. Require the parent and, when appropriate, the legal custodian and the child to participate in treatment and services identified as necessary. The court may require the person who has custody or who is requesting custody of the child to submit to a mental health or substance abuse disorder assessment or evaluation. The order may be made only upon good cause shown and pursuant to notice and procedural requirements provided under the Florida Rules of Juvenile Procedure. The mental health assessment or evaluation must be administered by a qualified professional as defined in s. 39.01, and the substance abuse assessment or evaluation must be administered by a qualified professional as defined in s. 397.311. The court may also require such person to participate in and comply with treatment and services identified as necessary, including, when appropriate and available, participation in and compliance with a mental health court program established under chapter 394 or a treatment-based drug court program established under s. 397.334. Adjudication of a child as dependent based upon evidence of harm as defined in s. 39.01(30)(g) demonstrates good cause, and the court shall require the parent whose actions caused the harm to submit to a substance abuse disorder assessment or evaluation and to participate and comply with treatment and services

identified in the assessment or evaluation as being necessary. In addition to supervision by the department, the court, including the mental health court program or the treatment-based drug court program, may oversee the progress and compliance with treatment by a person who has custody or is requesting custody of the child. The court may impose appropriate available sanctions for noncompliance upon a person who has custody or is requesting custody of the child or make a finding of noncompliance for consideration in determining whether an alternative placement of the child is in the child's best interests. Any order entered under this subparagraph may be made only upon good cause shown. This subparagraph does not authorize placement of a child with a person seeking custody of the child, other than the child's parent or legal custodian, who requires mental health or substance abuse disorder treatment.

2. Require, if the court deems necessary, the parties to participate in dependency mediation.

3. Require placement of the child either under the protective supervision of an authorized agent of the department in the home of one or both of the child's parents or in the home of a relative of the child or another adult approved by the court, or in the custody of the department. Protective supervision continues until the court terminates it or until the child reaches the age of 18, whichever date is first. Protective supervision shall be terminated by the court whenever the court determines that permanency has been achieved for the child, whether with a parent, another relative, or a legal custodian, and that protective supervision is no longer needed. The termination of supervision may be with or without retaining jurisdiction, at the court's discretion, and shall in either case be considered a permanency option for the child. The order terminating supervision by the department must set forth the powers of the custodian of the child and include the powers ordinarily granted to a guardian of the person of a minor unless otherwise specified. Upon the court's termination of supervision by the department, further judicial reviews are not required if permanency has been established for the child.

(d) At the conclusion of the disposition hearing, the court shall schedule the initial judicial review hearing which must be held no later than 90 days after the date of the disposition hearing or after the date of the hearing at which the court approves the case plan, whichever occurs earlier, but in no event shall the review hearing be held later than 6 months after the date of the child's removal from the home.

(e) The court shall, in its written order of disposition, include all of the following:

1. The placement or custody of the child.

2. Special conditions of placement and visitation.

3. Evaluation, counseling, treatment activities, and other actions to be taken by the parties, if ordered.

4. The persons or entities responsible for supervising or monitoring services to the child and parent.

5. Continuation or discharge of the guardian ad litem, as appropriate.

6. The date, time, and location of the next scheduled review hearing, which must occur within the earlier of:

a. Ninety days after the disposition hearing;

b. Ninety days after the court accepts the case plan;

c. Six months after the date of the last review hearing; or

d. Six months after the date of the child's removal from his or her home, if no review hearing has been held since the child's removal from the home.

7. If the child is in an out-of-home placement, child support to be paid by the parents, or the guardian of the child's estate if possessed of assets which under law may be disbursed for the care, support, and maintenance of the child. The court may exercise jurisdiction over all child support matters, shall adjudicate the financial obligation, including health insurance, of the child's parents or guardian, and shall enforce the financial obligation as provided in chapter 61. The state's child support enforcement agency shall enforce child support orders under this section in the same manner as child support orders under chapter 61. Placement of the child shall not be contingent upon issuance of a support order.

8.a. If the court does not commit the child to the temporary legal custody of an adult relative, legal custodian, or other adult approved by the court, the disposition order shall include the reasons for such a decision and shall include a determination as to whether diligent efforts were made by the department to locate an adult relative, legal custodian, or other adult willing to care for the child in order to present that placement option to the court instead of placement with the department.

b. If no suitable relative is found and the child is placed with the department or a legal custodian or other adult approved by the court, both the department and the court shall consider transferring temporary legal custody to an adult relative approved by the court at a later date, but neither the department nor the court is obligated to so place the child if it is in the child's best interest to remain in the current placement.

For the purposes of this section, "diligent efforts to locate an adult relative" means a search similar to the diligent search for a parent, but without the continuing obligation to search after an initial adequate search is completed.

9. Other requirements necessary to protect the health, safety, and well-being of the child, to preserve the stability of the child's educational placement, and to promote family preservation or reunification whenever possible.

(f) If the court finds that an in-home safety plan prepared or approved by the department will allow the child to remain safely at home or that conditions for return have been met and an in-home safety plan prepared or approved by the department will allow the child to be safely returned to the home, the court shall allow the child to remain in or return to the home after making a specific finding of fact that the child's safety, well-being, and physical, mental, and emotional health will not be endangered.

(g) If the court places the child in an out-of-home placement, the disposition order must include a written determination that the child cannot safely remain at home with an in-home safety plan and that removal of the child is necessary to protect the child. If the child is removed before the disposition hearing, the order must also include a written determination as to whether, after removal, the department made a reasonable effort to reunify the parent and child. Reasonable efforts to reunify are not required if the court finds that any of the acts listed in s. 39.806(1)(f)-(l) have occurred. The department has the burden of demonstrating that it made reasonable efforts.

1. For the purposes of this paragraph, the term "reasonable effort" means the exercise of reasonable diligence and care by the department to provide the services ordered by the court or delineated in the case plan.

2. In support of its determination as to whether reasonable efforts have been made, the court shall:

a. Enter written findings as to whether an in-home safety plan could have prevented removal.

b. If an in-home safety plan was indicated, include a brief written description of what appropriate and available safety management services were initiated.

c. Indicate in writing why further efforts could or could not have prevented or shortened the separation of the parent and child.

3. A court may find that the department made a reasonable effort to prevent or eliminate the need for removal if:

a. The first contact of the department with the family occurs during an emergency;

b. The department's assessment of the home situation indicates a substantial and immediate danger to the child's safety or physical, mental, or emotional health which cannot be mitigated by the provision of safety management services;

c. The child cannot safely remain at home, because there are no safety management services that can ensure the health and safety of the child or, even with appropriate and available services being provided, the health and safety of the child cannot be ensured; or

d. The parent is alleged to have committed any of the acts listed as grounds for expedited termination of parental rights under s. 39.806(1)(f)-(l).

4. A reasonable effort by the department for reunification has been made if the appraisal of the home situation by the department indicates that the severity of the conditions of dependency is such that reunification efforts are inappropriate. The department has the burden of demonstrating to the court that reunification efforts were inappropriate.

5. If the court finds that the provision of safety management services by the department would not have permitted the child to remain safely at home, the court may commit the child to the temporary legal custody of the department or take any other action authorized by this chapter.

(2) The family functioning assessment must provide the court with the following documented information:

(a) Evidence of maltreatment and the circumstances accompanying the maltreatment.

(b) Identification of all danger threats active in the home.

(c) An assessment of the adult functioning of the parents.

(d) An assessment of the parents' general parenting practices and the parents' disciplinary approach and behavior management methods.

(e) An assessment of the parents' behavioral, emotional, and cognitive protective capacities.

(f) An assessment of child functioning.

(g) A safety analysis describing the capacity for an in-home safety plan to control the conditions that result in the child being unsafe and the specific actions necessary to keep the child safe.

(h) Identification of the conditions for return which would allow the child to be placed safely back into the home with an in-home safety plan and any safety management services necessary to ensure the child's safety.

(i) The reasonable preference of the child, if the court deems the child to be of sufficient intelligence, understanding, and experience to express a preference.

(j) Child welfare history from the department's Statewide Automated Child Welfare Information System (SACWIS) and criminal records check for all caregivers, family members, and individuals residing within the household from which the child was removed.

(k) The complete report and recommendation of the child protection team of the Department of Health or, if no report exists, a statement reflecting that no report has been made.

(l) All opinions or recommendations from other professionals or agencies that provide evaluative, social, reunification, or other services to the parent and child.

(m) A listing of appropriate and available safety management services for the parent and child to prevent the removal of the child from the home or to reunify the child with the parent after removal, and an explanation of the following:

1. If the services were or were not provided.

2. If the services were provided, the outcome of the services.

3. If the services were not provided, why they were not provided.

4. If the services are currently being provided and if they need to be continued.

(n) If the child has been removed from the home and there is a parent who may be considered for custody pursuant to this section, a recommendation as to whether placement of the child with that parent would be detrimental to the child.

(o) If the child has been removed from the home and will be remaining with a relative, parent, or other adult approved by the court, a home study report concerning the proposed placement shall be provided to the court. Before recommending to the court any out-of-home placement for a child other than placement in a licensed shelter or foster home, the department shall conduct a study of the home of the proposed legal custodians, which must include, at a minimum:

1. An interview with the proposed legal custodians to assess their ongoing commitment and ability to care for the child.

2. Records checks through the State Automated Child Welfare Information System (SACWIS), and local and statewide criminal and juvenile records checks through the Department of Law Enforcement, on all household members 12 years of age or older. In addition, the fingerprints of any household members who are 18 years of age or older may be submitted to the Department of Law Enforcement for processing and forwarding to the Federal Bureau of Investigation for state and national criminal history information. The department has the discretion to request State Automated Child Welfare Information System (SACWIS) and local, statewide, and national criminal history checks and fingerprinting of any other visitor to the home who is made known to the department. Out-of-state criminal records checks must be initiated for any individual who has resided in a state other than Florida if that state's laws allow the release of these records. The

out-of-state criminal records must be filed with the court within 5 days after receipt by the department or its agent.

3. An assessment of the physical environment of the home.

4. A determination of the financial security of the proposed legal custodians.

5. A determination of suitable child care arrangements if the proposed legal custodians are employed outside of the home.

6. Documentation of counseling and information provided to the proposed legal custodians regarding the dependency process and possible outcomes.

7. Documentation that information regarding support services available in the community has been provided to the proposed legal custodians.

8. The reasonable preference of the child, if the court deems the child to be of sufficient intelligence, understanding, and experience to express a preference.

The department may not place the child or continue the placement of the child in a home under shelter or postdisposition placement if the results of the home study are unfavorable, unless the court finds that this placement is in the child's best interest.

(p) If the child has been removed from the home, a determination of the amount of child support each parent will be required to pay pursuant to s. 61.30.

Any other relevant and material evidence, including other written or oral reports, may be received by the court in its effort to determine the action to be taken with regard to the child and may be relied upon to the extent of its probative value, even though not competent in an adjudicatory hearing. Except as otherwise specifically provided, nothing in this section prohibits the publication of proceedings in a hearing.

(3) When any child is adjudicated by a court to be dependent, the court shall determine the appropriate placement for the child as follows:

(a) If the court determines that the child can safely remain in the home with the parent with whom the child was residing at the time the events or conditions arose that brought the child within the jurisdiction of the court and that remaining in this home is in the best interest of the child, then the court shall order conditions under which the child may remain or return to the home and that this placement be under the protective supervision of the department for not less than 6 months.

(b) If there is a parent with whom the child was not residing at the time the events or conditions arose that brought the child within the jurisdiction of the court who desires to assume custody of the child, the court shall place the child with that parent upon completion of a home study, unless the court finds that such placement would endanger the safety, well-being, or physical, mental, or emotional health of the child. Any party with knowledge of the facts may present to the court evidence regarding whether the placement will endanger the safety, well-being, or physical, mental, or emotional health of the child. If the court places the child with such parent, it may do either of the following:

1. Order that the parent assume sole custodial responsibilities for the child. The court may also provide for reasonable visitation by the noncustodial parent. The court may then terminate its jurisdiction over the child.

2. Order that the parent assume custody subject to the jurisdiction of the circuit court hearing dependency matters. The court may order that reunification services be provided to the parent from whom the child has been removed, that services be provided solely to the parent who is assuming physical custody in order to allow that parent to retain later custody without court jurisdiction, or that services be provided to both parents, in which case the court shall determine at every review hearing which parent, if either, shall have custody of the child. The standard for changing custody of the child from one parent to another or to a relative or another adult approved by the court shall be the best interest of the child.

(c) If no fit parent is willing or available to assume care and custody of the child, place the child in the temporary legal custody of an adult relative, the adoptive parent of the child's sibling, or another adult approved by the court who is willing to care for the child, under the protective supervision of the department. The department must supervise this placement until the child reaches permanency status in this home, and in no case for a period of less than 6 months. Permanency in a relative placement shall be by adoption, long-term custody, or guardianship.

(d) If the child cannot be safely placed in a nonlicensed placement, the court shall commit the child to the temporary legal custody of the department. Such commitment invests in the department all rights and responsibilities of a legal custodian. The department shall not return any child to the physical care and custody of the person from whom the child was removed, except for court-approved visitation periods, without the approval of the court. Any order for visitation or other contact must conform to the provisions of s. 39.0139. The term of such commitment continues until terminated by the court or until the child reaches the age of 18. After the child is committed to the temporary legal custody of the department, all further proceedings under this section are governed by this chapter.

Protective supervision continues until the court terminates it or until the child reaches the age of 18, whichever date is first. Protective supervision shall be terminated by the court whenever the court determines that permanency has been achieved for the child, whether with a parent, another relative, or a legal custodian, and that protective supervision is no longer needed. The termination of supervision may be with or without retaining jurisdiction, at the court's discretion, and shall in either case be considered a permanency option for the child. The order terminating supervision by the department shall set forth the powers of the custodian of the child and shall include the powers ordinarily granted to a guardian of the person of a minor unless otherwise specified. Upon the court's termination of supervision by the department, no further judicial reviews are required, so long as permanency has been established for the child.

(4) An agency granted legal custody shall have the right to determine where and with whom the child shall live, but an individual granted legal custody shall exercise all rights and duties personally unless otherwise ordered by the court.

(5) In carrying out the provisions of this chapter, the court may order the parents and legal custodians of a child who is found to be dependent to participate in family counseling and other professional counseling activities deemed necessary for the rehabilitation of the parent or child.

(6) With respect to a child who is the subject in proceedings under this chapter, the court may issue to the department an order to show cause why it should not return the child to the custody of the parents upon the presentation of evidence that the conditions for return of the child have been met.

(7) The court may enter an order ending its jurisdiction over a child when a child has been returned to the parents, provided the court shall not terminate its jurisdiction or the department's supervision over the child until 6 months after the child's return. The department shall supervise the placement of the child after reunification for at least 6 months with each parent or legal custodian from whom the child was removed. The court shall determine whether its jurisdiction should be continued or terminated in such a case based on a report of the department or agency or the child's guardian ad litem, and any other relevant factors; if its jurisdiction is to be terminated, the court shall enter an order to that effect.

HISTORY:
S. 20, ch. 78-414; s. 14, ch. 79-164; s. 2, ch. 80-102; s. 15, ch. 80-290; s. 11, ch. 83-217; ss. 9, 10, ch. 84-311; s. 6, ch. 85-80; s. 83, ch. 86-220; s. 8, ch. 87-289; s. 13, ch. 87-397; s. 30, ch. 88-337; s. 1, ch. 90-182; s. 2, ch. 90-211; ss. 7, 8, ch. 90-306; s. 71, ch. 91-45; s. 2, ch. 91-183; s. 5, ch. 92-158; s. 7, ch. 92-170; ss. 12, 13, ch. 94-164; s. 62, ch. 95-228; s. 4, ch. 97-96; s. 8, ch. 97-101; s. 9, ch. 97-276; s. 6, ch. 98-137; s. 11, ch. 98-280; s. 69, ch. 98-403; s. 31, ch. 99-193; s. 23, ch. 2000-139; s. 3, ch. 2001-68; s. 1, ch. 2002-219; s. 5, ch. 2005-239; s. 13, ch. 2006-86, eff. July 1, 2006; s. 5, ch. 2006-97, eff. June 7, 2006; s. 5, ch. 2007-109, eff. July 1, 2007; s. 13, ch. 2008-245, eff. June 30, 2008; s. 10, ch. 2012-178, eff. July 1, 2012; s. 3, ch. 2016-127, eff. July 1, 2016; s. 84, ch. 2016-241, eff. July 1, 2016; s. 12, ch. 2017-151, eff. July 1, 2017.

Editor's notes.
Former ss. 39.408(3), (4), 39.41; s. 39.508.

§ 39.522. Postdisposition change of custody.

The court may change the temporary legal custody or the conditions of protective supervision at a postdisposition hearing, without the necessity of another adjudicatory hearing.

(1) A child who has been placed in the child's own home under the protective supervision of an authorized agent of the department, in the home of a relative, in the home of a legal custodian, or in some other place may be brought before the court by the department or by any other interested person, upon the filing of a petition alleging a need for a change in the conditions of protective supervision or the placement. If the parents or other legal custodians deny the need for a change, the court shall hear all parties in person or by counsel, or both. Upon the admission of a need for a change or after such hearing, the court shall enter an order changing the placement, modifying the conditions of protective supervision, or continuing the conditions of protective supervision as ordered. The standard for changing custody of the child shall be the best interest of the child. When applying this standard, the court shall consider the continuity of the child's placement in the same out-of-home residence as a factor when determining the best interests of the child. If the child is not placed in foster care, then the new placement for the child must meet the home study criteria and court approval pursuant to this chapter.

(2) In cases where the issue before the court is whether a child should be reunited with a parent, the court shall review the conditions for return and determine whether the circumstances that caused the out-of-home placement and issues subsequently identified have been remedied to the extent that the return of the child to the home with an in-home safety plan prepared or approved by the department will not be detrimental to the child's safety, well-being, and physical, mental, and emotional health.

(3) In cases where the issue before the court is whether a child who is placed in the custody of a parent should be reunited with the other parent upon a finding that the circumstances that caused the out-of-home placement and issues subsequently identified have been remedied to the extent that the return of the child to the home of the other parent with an in-home safety plan prepared or approved by the department will not be detrimental to the child, the standard shall be that the safety, well-being, and physical, mental, and emotional health of the child would not be endangered by reunification and that reunification would be in the best interest of the child.

HISTORY:
S. 25, ch. 2000-139; s. 14, ch. 2006-86, eff. July 1, 2006; s. 3, ch. 2013-21, eff. July 1, 2013; s. 13, ch. 2017-151, eff. July 1, 2017.

Editor's notes.
Section 1, ch. 2013-21, provides: "This act may be cited as the 'Quality Parenting for Children in Foster Care Act.' "

§ 39.523. Placement in out-of-home care.

(1) LEGISLATIVE FINDINGS AND INTENT.

(a) The Legislature finds that it is a basic tenet of child welfare practice and the law that a child be placed in the least restrictive, most family-like setting available in close proximity to the home of his or her parents which meets the needs of the child, and that a child be placed in a permanent home in a timely manner.

(b) The Legislature also finds that there is an association between placements that do not meet the needs of the child and adverse outcomes for the child, that mismatching placements to children's needs has been identified as a factor that negatively impacts placement stability, and that identifying the right placement for each child requires effective assessment.

(c) It is the intent of the Legislature that whenever a child is unable to safely remain at home with a parent, the most appropriate available out-of-home placement shall be chosen after an assessment of the child's needs and the availability of caregivers qualified to meet the child's needs.

(2) ASSESSMENT AND PLACEMENT. When any child is removed from a home and placed into out-of-home care, a comprehensive placement assessment process shall be completed to determine the level of care needed by the child and match the child with the most appropriate placement.

(a) The community-based care lead agency or subcontracted agency with the responsibility for assessment and placement must coordinate a multidisciplinary team staffing with any available individual currently involved with the child including, but not limited to, a representative from the department and the case manager for the child; a therapist, attorney ad litem, guardian ad litem, teachers, coaches, Children's Medical Services; and other community providers of services to the child or stakeholders as applicable. The team may also include clergy, relatives, and fictive kin if appropriate. Team participants must gather data and information on the child which is known at the time including, but not limited to:

1. Mental, medical, behavioral health, and medication history;

2. Community ties and school placement;

3. Current placement decisions relating to any siblings;

4. Alleged type of abuse or neglect including sexual abuse and trafficking history; and

5. The child's age, maturity, strengths, hobbies or activities, and the child's preference for placement.

(b) The comprehensive placement assessment process may also include the use of an assessment instrument or tool that is best suited for the individual child.

(c) The most appropriate available out-of-home placement shall be chosen after consideration by all members of the multidisciplinary team of all of the information and data gathered, including the results and recommendations of any evaluations conducted.

(d) Placement decisions for each child in out-of-home placement shall be reviewed as often as necessary to ensure permanency for that child and address special issues related to this population of children.

(e) The department, a sheriff's office acting under s. 39.3065, a community-based care lead agency, or a case management organization must document all placement assessments and placement decisions in the Florida Safe Families Network.

(f) If it is determined during the comprehensive placement assessment process that residential treatment as defined in s. 39.407 would be suitable for the child, the procedures in that section must be followed.

(3) JUDICIAL REVIEW. At each judicial review, the court shall consider the results of the assessment, the placement decision made for the child, and services provided to the child as required under s. 39.701.

(4) DATA COLLECTION. The department shall collect the following information by community-based care lead agencies and post it on the Department of Children and Families' website. The information is to be updated on January 1 and July 1 of each year.

(a) The number of children placed with relatives and nonrelatives, in family foster homes, and in residential group care.

(b) An inventory of available services that are necessary to maintain children in the least restrictive setting that meets the needs of the child and a plan for filling any identified gap in those services.

(c) The number of children who were placed based upon the assessment.

(d) An inventory of existing placements for children by type and by community-based care lead agency.

(e) The strategies being used by community-based care lead agencies to recruit, train, and support an adequate number of families to provide home-based family care.

(5) RULEMAKING. The department may adopt rules to implement this section.

HISTORY:
S. 2, ch. 2002-219; s. 14, ch. 2017-151, eff. Jan. 1, 2018.

§ 39.524. Safe-harbor placement.—

(1) Except as provided in s. 39.407 or s. 985.801, a dependent child 6 years of age or older who is sus-

pected of being or has been found to be a victim of commercial sexual exploitation as defined in s. 409.016 must be assessed, and the department or a sheriff's office acting under s. 39.3065 must conduct a multidisciplinary staffing pursuant to s. 409.1754(2), to determine the child's need for services and his or her need for placement in a safe house or safe foster home as provided in s. 409.1678 using the initial screening and assessment instruments provided in s. 409.1754(1). If such placement is determined to be appropriate for the child as a result of this assessment, the child may be placed in a safe house or safe foster home, if one is available. However, the child may be placed in another setting, if the other setting is more appropriate to the child's needs or if a safe house or safe foster home is unavailable, as long as the child's behaviors are managed so as not to endanger other children served in that setting.

(2) The results of the assessment described in s. 409.1754(1), the multidisciplinary staffing described in s. 409.1754(2), and the actions taken as a result of the assessment must be included in the disposition hearing or next judicial review of the child. At each subsequent judicial review, the court must be advised in writing of the status of the child's placement, with special reference regarding the stability of the placement, any specialized services, and the permanency planning for the child.

(3)(a) By October 1 of each year, the department, with information from community-based care agencies and certain sheriff's offices acting under s. 39.3065, shall report to the Legislature on the prevalence of child commercial sexual exploitation; the specialized services provided and placement of such children; the local service capacity assessed pursuant to s. 409.1754; the placement of children in safe houses and safe foster homes during the year, including the criteria used to determine the placement of children; the number of children who were evaluated for placement; the number of children who were placed based upon the evaluation; the number of children who were not placed; and the department's response to the findings and recommendations made by the Office of Program Policy Analysis and Government Accountability in its annual study on commercial sexual exploitation of children, as required by s. 409.16791.

(b) The department shall maintain data specifying the number of children who were verified as victims of commercial sexual exploitation, who were referred to nonresidential services in the community, who were placed in a safe house or safe foster home, and who were referred to a safe house or safe foster home for whom placement was unavailable, and shall identify the counties in which such placement was unavailable. The department shall include this data in its report under this subsection so that the Legislature may consider this information in developing the General Appropriations Act.

HISTORY:
S. 5, ch. 2012-105, eff. Jan. 1, 2013; s. 3, ch. 2014-161, eff. July 1, 2014; s. 52, ch. 2014-224, eff. July 1, 2014; s. 7, ch. 2015-2, eff. June 30, 2015; s. 63, ch. 2016-241, eff. July 1, 2016; s. 38, ch. 2017-151, eff. July 1, 2017; s. 1, ch. 2017-23, eff. Oct. 1, 2017.

Editor's notes.
Section 1, ch. 2012-105, provides: "This act may be cited as the 'Florida Safe Harbor Act.' "

PART VII.
CASE PLANS.

§ 39.601. Case plan requirements [Repealed.]

Repealed by s. 35, ch. 2006-86, effective July 1, 2006.

HISTORY:
S. 9, ch. 87-289; ss. 5, 25, ch. 94-164; ss. 8, 16, ch. 95-228; s. 4, ch. 98-137; s. 74, ch. 98-403; s. 35, ch. 99-193; s. 26, ch. 2000-139.

§ 39.6011. Case plan development.

(1) The department shall prepare a draft of the case plan for each child receiving services under this chapter. A parent of a child may not be threatened or coerced with the loss of custody or parental rights for failing to admit in the case plan of abusing, neglecting, or abandoning a child. Participating in the development of a case plan is not an admission to any allegation of abuse, abandonment, or neglect, and it is not a consent to a finding of dependency or termination of parental rights. The case plan shall be developed subject to the following requirements:

(a) The case plan must be developed in a face-to-face conference with the parent of the child, any court-appointed guardian ad litem, and, if appropriate, the child and the temporary custodian of the child.

(b) Notwithstanding s. 39.202, the department may discuss confidential information during the case planning conference in the presence of individuals who participate in the conference. All individuals who participate in the conference shall maintain the confidentiality of all information shared during the case planning conference.

(c) The parent may receive assistance from any person or social service agency in preparing the case plan. The social service agency, the department, and the court, when applicable, shall inform the parent of the right to receive such assistance, including the right to assistance of counsel.

(d) If a parent is unwilling or unable to participate in developing a case plan, the department shall document that unwillingness or inability to participate. The documentation must be provided in writing to the parent when available for the court record, and the department shall prepare a case plan conforming as nearly as possible with the requirements set forth in this section. The unwillingness or inability of the parent to participate in developing a case plan does not preclude the filing of a petition for dependency or for termination of parental rights. The parent, if available, must be provided a copy of the case plan and be advised that he or she may, at any time before the filing of a petition for termination of parental rights, enter into a case plan and that he or she may request judicial review of any provision of the case plan with which he or she disagrees at any court hearing set for the child.

(2) The case plan must be written simply and clearly in English and, if English is not the principal language of the child's parent, to the extent possible in the parent's principal language. Each case plan must contain:

(a) A description of the identified problem being addressed, including the parent's behavior or acts resulting in risk to the child and the reason for the intervention by the department.

(b) The permanency goal.

(c) If concurrent planning is being used, a description of the permanency goal of reunification with the parent or legal custodian in addition to a description of one of the remaining permanency goals described in s. 39.01.

1. If a child has not been removed from a parent, but is found to be dependent, even if adjudication of dependency is withheld, the court may leave the child in the current placement with maintaining and strengthening the placement as a permanency option.

2. If a child has been removed from a parent and is placed with a parent from whom the child was not removed, the court may leave the child in the placement with the parent from whom the child was not removed with maintaining and strengthening the placement as a permanency option.

3. If a child has been removed from a parent and is subsequently reunified with that parent, the court may leave the child with that parent with maintaining and strengthening the placement as a permanency option.

(d) The date the compliance period expires. The case plan must be limited to as short a period as possible for accomplishing its provisions. The plan's compliance period expires no later than 12 months after the date the child was initially removed from the home, the child was adjudicated dependent, or the date the case plan was accepted by the court, whichever occurs first.

(e) A written notice to the parent that failure of the parent to substantially comply with the case plan may result in the termination of parental rights, and that a material breach of the case plan may result in the filing of a petition for termination of parental rights sooner than the compliance period set forth in the case plan.

(3) The case plan must be signed by all parties, except that the signature of a child may be waived if the child is not of an age or capacity to participate in the case-planning process. Signing the case plan constitutes an acknowledgment that the case plan has been developed by the parties and that they are in agreement as to the terms and conditions contained in the case plan. The refusal of a parent to sign the case plan does not prevent the court from accepting the case plan if the case plan is otherwise acceptable to the court. Signing the case plan does not constitute an admission to any allegation of abuse, abandonment, or neglect and does not constitute consent to a finding of dependency or termination of parental rights. Before signing the case plan, the department shall explain the provisions of the plan to all persons involved in its implementation, including, when appropriate, the child.

(4) The case plan must describe:

(a) The role of the foster parents or legal custodians when developing the services that are to be provided to the child, foster parents, or legal custodians;

(b) The responsibility of the case manager to forward a relative's request to receive notification of all proceedings and hearings submitted pursuant to s. 39.301(14)(b) to the attorney for the department;

(c) The minimum number of face-to-face meetings to be held each month between the parents and the department's family services counselors to review the progress of the plan, to eliminate barriers to progress, and to resolve conflicts or disagreements; and

(d) The parent's responsibility for financial support of the child, including, but not limited to, health insurance and child support. The case plan must list the costs associated with any services or treatment that the parent and child are expected to receive which are the financial responsibility of the parent. The determination of child support and other financial support shall be made independently of any determination of indigency under s. 39.013.

(5) When the permanency goal for a child is adoption, the case plan must include documentation of the steps the agency is taking to find an adoptive family or other permanent living arrangement for the child. At a minimum, the documentation shall include recruitment efforts that are specific to the child, such as the use of state, regional, and national adoption exchanges, including electronic exchange systems.

(6) After the case plan has been developed, the department shall adhere to the following procedural requirements:

(a) If the parent's substantial compliance with the case plan requires the department to provide services to the parents or the child and the parents agree to begin compliance with the case plan before the case plan's acceptance by the court, the department shall make the appropriate referrals for services that will allow the parents to begin the agreed-upon tasks and services immediately.

(b)   After the case plan has been agreed upon and signed by the parties, a copy of the plan must be given immediately to the parties, including the child if appropriate, and to other persons as directed by the court.

1.   A case plan must be prepared, but need not be submitted to the court, for a child who will be in care no longer than 30 days unless that child is placed in out-of-home care a second time within a 12-month period.

2.   In each case in which a child has been placed in out-of-home care, a case plan must be prepared within 60 days after the department removes the child from the home and shall be submitted to the court before the disposition hearing for the court to review and approve.

3.   After jurisdiction attaches, all case plans must be filed with the court, and a copy provided to all the parties whose whereabouts are known, not less than 3 business days before the disposition hearing. The department shall file with the court, and provide copies to the parties, all case plans prepared before jurisdiction of the court attached.

(7)   The case plan must be filed with the court and copies provided to all parties, including the child if appropriate, not less than 3 business days before the disposition hearing.

(8)   The case plan must describe a process for making available to all physical custodians and family services counselors the information required by s. 39.6012(2) and for ensuring that this information follows the child until permanency has been achieved.

HISTORY:

S. 15, ch. 2006-86, eff. July 1, 2006; s. 27, ch. 2008-245, eff. June 30, 2008; s. 11, ch. 2009-43, eff. July 1, 2009; s. 11, ch. 2012-178, eff. July 1, 2012; s. 15, ch. 2017-151, eff. July 1, 2017.

Editor's notes.

Section 1 of ch. 2009-43 provides: "This act may be cited as the 'Zahid Jones, Jr., Give Grandparents and Other Relatives a Voice Act.'"

§ 39.6012.   Case plan tasks; services.

(1)   The services to be provided to the parent and the tasks that must be completed are subject to the following:

(a)   The services described in the case plan must be designed to improve the conditions in the home and aid in maintaining the child in the home, facilitate the child's safe return to the home, ensure proper care of the child, or facilitate the child's permanent placement. The services offered must be the least intrusive possible into the life of the parent and child, must focus on clearly defined objectives, and must provide the most efficient path to quick reunification or permanent placement given the circumstances of the case and the child's need for safe and proper care.

(b)   The case plan must describe each of the tasks with which the parent must comply and the services to be provided to the parent, specifically addressing the identified problem, including:

1.   The type of services or treatment.

2.   The date the department will provide each service or referral for the service if the service is being provided by the department or its agent.

3.   The date by which the parent must complete each task.

4.   The frequency of services or treatment provided. The frequency of the delivery of services or treatment provided shall be determined by the professionals providing the services or treatment on a case-by-case basis and adjusted according to their best professional judgment.

5.   The location of the delivery of the services.

6.   The staff of the department or service provider accountable for the services or treatment.

7.   A description of the measurable objectives, including the timeframes specified for achieving the objectives of the case plan and addressing the identified problem.

(c)   If there is evidence of harm as defined in s. 39.01(30)(g), the case plan must include as a required task for the parent whose actions caused the harm that the parent submit to a substance abuse disorder assessment or evaluation and participate and comply with treatment and services identified in the assessment or evaluation as being necessary.

(2)   The case plan must include all available information that is relevant to the child's care including, at a minimum:

(a)   A description of the identified needs of the child while in care.

(b)   A description of the plan for ensuring that the child receives safe and proper care and that services are provided to the child in order to address the child's needs. To the extent available and accessible, the following health, mental health, and education information and records of the child must be attached to the case plan and updated throughout the judicial review process:

1.   The names and addresses of the child's health, mental health, and educational providers;

2.   The child's grade level performance;

3.   The child's school record;

4.   Assurances that the child's placement takes into account proximity to the school in which the child is enrolled at the time of placement;

5.   A record of the child's immunizations;

6.   The child's known medical history, including any known problems;

7.   The child's medications, if any; and

8.   Any other relevant health, mental health, and education information concerning the child.

(3)   In addition to any other requirement, if the child is in an out-of-home placement, the case plan must include:

(a) A description of the type of placement in which the child is to be living.

(b) A description of the parent's visitation rights and obligations and the plan for sibling visitation if the child has siblings and is separated from them.

(c) When appropriate, for a child who is 13 years of age or older, a written description of the programs and services that will help the child prepare for the transition from foster care to independent living.

(d) A discussion of the safety and the appropriateness of the child's placement, which placement is intended to be safe, and the least restrictive and the most family-like setting available consistent with the best interest and special needs of the child and in as close proximity as possible to the child's home.

HISTORY:
S. 16, ch. 2006-86, eff. July 1, 2006; s. 16, ch. 2017-151, eff. July 1, 2017.

§ 39.6013. Case plan amendments.

(1) After the case plan has been developed under s. 39.6011, the tasks and services agreed upon in the plan may not be changed or altered in any way except as provided in this section.

(2) The case plan may be amended at any time in order to change the goal of the plan, employ the use of concurrent planning, add or remove tasks the parent must complete to substantially comply with the plan, provide appropriate services for the child, and update the child's health, mental health, and education records required by s. 39.6012.

(3) The case plan may be amended upon approval of the court if all parties are in agreement regarding the amendments to the plan and the amended plan is signed by all parties and submitted to the court with a memorandum of explanation.

(4) The case plan may be amended by the court or upon motion of any party at any hearing to change the goal of the plan, employ the use of concurrent planning, or add or remove tasks the parent must complete in order to substantially comply with the plan if there is a preponderance of evidence demonstrating the need for the amendment. The need to amend the case plan may be based on information discovered or circumstances arising after the approval of the case plan for:

(a) A previously unaddressed condition that, without services, may prevent the child from safely returning to the home or may prevent the child from safely remaining in the home;

(b) The child's need for permanency, taking into consideration the child's age and developmental needs;

(c) The failure of a party to substantially comply with a task in the original case plan, including the ineffectiveness of a previously offered service; or

(d) An error or oversight in the case plan.

(5) The case plan may be amended by the court or upon motion of any party at any hearing to provide appropriate services to the child if there is competent evidence demonstrating the need for the amendment. The reason for amending the case plan may be based on information discovered or circumstances arising after the approval of the case plan regarding the provision of safe and proper care to the child.

(6) The case plan is deemed amended as to the child's health, mental health, and education records required by s. 39.6012 when the child's updated health and education records are filed by the department under s. 39.701(2)(a).

(7) Amendments must include service interventions that are the least intrusive into the life of the parent and child, must focus on clearly defined objectives, and must provide the most efficient path to quick reunification or permanent placement given the circumstances of the case and the child's need for safe and proper care. A copy of the amended plan must be immediately given to the persons identified in s. 39.6011(6)(b).

HISTORY:
S. 17, ch. 2006-86, eff. July 1, 2006; s. 3, ch. 2007-5, eff. July 3, 2007; s. 12, ch. 2009-43, eff. July 1, 2009; s. 3, ch. 2013-178, eff. Jan. 1, 2014.

Editor's notes.
Section 1 of ch. 2009-43 provides: "This act may be cited as the 'Zahid Jones, Jr., Give Grandparents and Other Relatives a Voice Act.' "

§ 39.602. Case planning when parents do not participate and the child is in out-of-home care.

(1) In the event the parents will not or cannot participate in preparation of a case plan, the department shall submit a full explanation of the circumstances and state the nature of its efforts to secure such persons' participation in the preparation of a case plan.

(2) In a case in which the physical, emotional, or mental condition or physical location of the parent is the basis for the parent's nonparticipation, it is the burden of the department to provide substantial evidence to the court that such condition or location has rendered the parent unable or unwilling to participate in the preparation of a case plan, either pro se or through counsel. The supporting documentation must be submitted to the court at the time the plan is filed.

(3) The plan must include, but need not be limited to, the specific services to be provided by the department, the goals and plans for the child, and the time for accomplishing the provisions of the plan and for accomplishing permanence for the child.

(4)(a) At least 72 hours prior to the hearing in which the court will consider approval of the case plan, all parties must be provided with a copy of the plan developed by the department. If the location of one or both parents is unknown, this must be documented in writing and included in the plan submitted to the court. After the filing of the plan, if the location of an absent parent becomes known, that parent must be served with a copy of the plan.

(b) Before the filing of the plan, the department shall advise each parent, both orally and in writing, that the failure of the parents to substantially comply with a plan may result in the termination of parental rights, but only after notice and hearing as provided in this chapter. If, after the plan has been submitted to the court, an absent parent is located, the department shall advise the parent, both orally and in writing, that the failure of the parents to substantially comply with a plan may result in termination of parental rights, but only after notice and hearing as provided in this chapter. Proof of written notification must be filed with the court.

HISTORY:
S. 9, ch. 87-289; s. 32, ch. 88-337; s. 26, ch. 94-164; s. 17, ch. 95-228; s. 12, ch. 98-280; s. 75, ch. 98-403; s. 36, ch. 99-193.

Editor's notes.
Former s. 39.452(1)-(4).

§ 39.603. Court approvals of case planning.

(1) All case plans and amendments to case plans must be approved by the court. At the hearing on the case plan, which shall occur in conjunction with the disposition hearing unless otherwise directed by the court, the court shall determine:

(a) All parties who were notified and are in attendance at the hearing, either in person or through a legal representative. The court may appoint a guardian ad litem under Rule 1.210, Florida Rules of Civil Procedure, to represent the interests of any parent, if the location of the parent is known but the parent is not present at the hearing and the development of the plan is based upon the physical, emotional, or mental condition or physical location of the parent.

(b) If the plan is consistent with previous orders of the court placing the child in care.

(c) If the plan is consistent with the requirements for the content of a plan as specified in this chapter.

(d) In involuntary placements, whether each parent was notified of the right to counsel at each stage of the dependency proceedings, in accordance with the Florida Rules of Juvenile Procedure.

(e) Whether each parent whose location was known was notified of the right to participate in the preparation of a case plan and of the right to receive assistance from any other person in the preparation of the case plan.

(f) Whether the plan is meaningful and designed to address facts and circumstances upon which the court based the finding of dependency in involuntary placements or the plan is meaningful and designed to address facts and circumstances upon which the child was placed in out-of-home care voluntarily.

(2) When the court determines that any of the elements considered at the hearing related to the plan

have not been met, the court shall require the parties to make necessary amendments to the plan under s. 39.6013. The amended plan must be submitted to the court for review and approval within 30 days after the hearing. A copy of the amended plan must also be provided to each party, if the location of the party is known, at least 3 business days before filing with the court.

(3) A parent who has not participated in the development of a case plan must be served with a copy of the plan developed by the department, if the parent can be located, at least 72 hours prior to the court hearing. Any parent is entitled to, and may seek, a court review of the plan prior to the initial judicial review and must be informed of this right by the department at the time the department serves the parent with a copy of the plan. If the location of an absent parent becomes known to the department, the department shall inform the parent of the right to a court review at the time the department serves the parent with a copy of the case plan.

HISTORY:
S. 9, ch. 87-289; s. 32, ch. 88-337; s. 26, ch. 94-164; s. 17, ch. 95-228; s. 76, ch. 98-403; s. 37, ch. 99-193; s. 27, ch. 2000-139; s. 18, ch. 2006-86, eff. July 1, 2006.

Editor's notes.
Former s. 39.452(5).

§ 39.6035. Transition plan.

(1) During the 180-day period after a child reaches 17 years of age, the department and the community-based care provider, in collaboration with the caregiver and any other individual whom the child would like to include, shall assist the child in developing a transition plan. The required transition plan is in addition to standard case management requirements. The transition plan must address specific options for the child to use in obtaining services, including housing, health insurance, education, a driver license, and workforce support and employment services. The plan must also consider establishing and maintaining naturally occurring mentoring relationships and other personal support services. The transition plan may be as detailed as the child chooses. In developing the transition plan, the department and the community-based provider shall:

(a) Provide the child with the documentation required pursuant to s. 39.701(3); and

(b) Coordinate the transition plan with the independent living provisions in the case plan and, for a child with disabilities, the Individuals with Disabilities Education Act transition plan.

(2) The department and the child shall schedule a time, date, and place for a meeting to assist the child in drafting the transition plan. The time, date, and place must be convenient for the child and any individual whom the child would like to include. This meeting shall be conducted in the child's primary language.

(3) The transition plan shall be reviewed periodically with the child, the department, and other individu-

als of the child's choice and updated when necessary before each judicial review so long as the child or young adult remains in care.

(4) The transition plan must be approved by the court before the child's 18th birthday and must be attached to the case plan and updated before each judicial review.

HISTORY:
S. 4, ch. 2013-178, eff. Jan. 1, 2014; s. 2, ch. 2017-8, eff. May 1, 2017; s. 17, ch. 2017-151, eff. July 1, 2017.

§ 39.604. Rilya Wilson Act; short title; legislative intent; requirements; attendance and reporting responsibilities.

(1) SHORT TITLE. — This section may be cited as the "Rilya Wilson Act."

(2) LEGISLATIVE INTENT. — The Legislature recognizes that children who are in the care of the state due to abuse, neglect, or abandonment are at increased risk of poor school performance and other behavioral and social problems. It is the intent of the Legislature that children who are currently in the care of the state be provided with an age-appropriate education program to help ameliorate the negative consequences of abuse, neglect, or abandonment.

(3) REQUIREMENTS. — A child from birth to the age of school entry, under court-ordered protective supervision or in the custody of the Family Safety Program Office of the Department of Children and Families or a community-based lead agency, and enrolled in a licensed early education or child care program must attend the program 5 days a week. Notwithstanding s. 39.202, the Department of Children and Families must notify operators of the licensed early education or child care program, subject to the reporting requirements of this act, of the enrollment of any child from birth to the age of school entry, under court-ordered protective supervision or in the custody of the Family Safety Program Office of the Department of Children and Families or a community-based lead agency. When a child is enrolled in an early education or child care program regulated by the department, the child's attendance in the program must be a required action in the safety plan or the case plan developed for the child pursuant to this chapter. An exemption to participating in the licensed early education or child care program 5 days a week may be granted by the court.

(4) ATTENDANCE AND REPORTING REQUIREMENTS.

(a) A child enrolled in a licensed early education or child care program who meets the requirements of subsection (3) may not be withdrawn from the program without the prior written approval of the Family Safety Program Office of the Department of Children and Families or the community-based lead agency.

(b)1. If a child covered by this section is absent from the program on a day when he or she is supposed to be present, the person with whom the child resides must report the absence to the program by the end of the business day. If the person with whom the child resides, whether the parent or caregiver, fails to timely report the absence, the absence is considered to be unexcused. The program shall report any unexcused absence or seven consecutive excused absences of a child who is enrolled in the program and covered by this act to the local designated staff of the Family Safety Program Office of the Department of Children and Families or the community-based lead agency by the end of the business day following the unexcused absence or seventh consecutive excused absence.

2. The department or community-based lead agency shall conduct a site visit to the residence of the child upon receiving a report of two consecutive unexcused absences or seven consecutive excused absences.

3. If the site visit results in a determination that the child is missing, the department or community-based lead agency shall report the child as missing to a law enforcement agency and proceed with the necessary actions to locate the child pursuant to procedures for locating missing children.

4. If the site visit results in a determination that the child is not missing, the parent or caregiver shall be notified that failure to ensure that the child attends the licensed early education or child care program is a violation of the safety plan or the case plan. If more than two site visits are conducted pursuant to this subsection, staff shall initiate action to notify the court of the parent or caregiver's noncompliance with the case plan.

HISTORY:
S. 1, ch. 2003-292; s. 21, ch. 2014-19, eff. July 1, 2014; s. 16, ch. 2014-224, eff. July 1, 2014.

PART VIII.
PERMANENCY.

§ 39.621. Permanency determination by the court.

(1) Time is of the essence for permanency of children in the dependency system. A permanency hearing must be held no later than 12 months after the date the child was removed from the home or within 30 days after a court determines that reasonable efforts to return a child to either parent are not required, whichever occurs first. The purpose of the permanency hearing is to determine when the child will achieve the permanency goal or whether modifying the current goal is in the best interest of the child. A permanency hearing must be held at least every 12 months for any child who continues to be supervised by the department or awaits adoption.

(2) The permanency goal of maintaining and strengthening the placement with a parent may be used in all of the following circumstances:

(a) If a child has not been removed from a parent, even if adjudication of dependency is withheld, the court may leave the child in the current placement with maintaining and strengthening the placement as a permanency option.

(b) If a child has been removed from a parent and is placed with the parent from whom the child was not removed, the court may leave the child in the placement with the parent from whom the child was not removed with maintaining and strengthening the placement as a permanency option.

(c) If a child has been removed from a parent and is subsequently reunified with that parent, the court may leave the child with that parent with maintaining and strengthening the placement as a permanency option.

(3) The permanency goals available under this chapter, listed in order of preference, are:

(a) Reunification;

(b) Adoption, if a petition for termination of parental rights has been or will be filed;

(c) Permanent guardianship of a dependent child under s. 39.6221;

(d) Permanent placement with a fit and willing relative under s. 39.6231; or

(e) Placement in another planned permanent living arrangement under s. 39.6241.

(4)(a) At least 3 business days before the permanency hearing, the department shall file its judicial review social services report with the court and serve copies of the report on all parties. The report must include a recommended permanency goal for the child, suggest changes to the case plan, if needed, and describe why the recommended goal is in the best interest of the child.

(b) Before the permanency hearing, the department shall advise the child and the individuals with whom the child will be placed about the availability of more permanent and legally secure placements and what type of financial assistance is associated with each placement.

(5) At the permanency hearing, the court shall determine:

(a) Whether the current permanency goal for the child is appropriate or should be changed;

(b) When the child will achieve one of the permanency goals; and

(c) Whether the department has made reasonable efforts to finalize the permanency plan currently in effect.

(6) The best interest of the child is the primary consideration in determining the permanency goal for the child. The court must also consider:

(a) The reasonable preference of the child if the court has found the child to be of sufficient intelli-

gence, understanding, and experience to express a preference; and

(b) Any recommendation of the guardian ad litem.

(7) If a child will not be reunited with a parent, adoption, under chapter 63, is the primary permanency option. If the child is placed with a relative or with a relative of the child's half-brother or half-sister as a permanency option, the court may recognize the permanency of this placement without requiring the relative to adopt the child. If the court approves a permanency goal of permanent guardianship of a dependent child, placement with a fit and willing relative, or another planned permanent living arrangement, the court shall make findings as to why this permanent placement is established without adoption of the child to follow. If the court approves a permanency goal of another planned permanent living arrangement, the court shall document the compelling reasons for choosing this goal.

(8) The findings of the court regarding reasonable efforts to finalize the permanency plan must be explicitly documented, made on a case-by-case basis, and stated in the court order.

(9) The case plan must list the tasks necessary to finalize the permanency placement and shall be updated at the permanency hearing if necessary. If a concurrent case plan is in place, the court may choose between the permanency goal options presented and shall approve the goal that is in the child's best interest.

(10) The permanency placement is intended to continue until the child reaches the age of majority and may not be disturbed absent a finding by the court that the circumstances of the permanency placement are no longer in the best interest of the child. If a parent who has not had his or her parental rights terminated makes a motion for reunification or increased contact with the child, the court shall hold a hearing to determine whether the dependency case should be reopened and whether there should be a modification of the order. At the hearing, the parent must demonstrate that the safety, well-being, and physical, mental, and emotional health of the child is not endangered by the modification.

(11) The court shall base its decision concerning any motion by a parent for reunification or increased contact with a child on the effect of the decision on the safety, well-being, and physical and emotional health of the child. Factors that must be considered and addressed in the findings of fact of the order on the motion must include:

(a) The compliance or noncompliance of the parent with the case plan;

(b) The circumstances which caused the child's dependency and whether those circumstances have been resolved;

(c) The stability and longevity of the child's placement;

(d) The preferences of the child, if the child is of sufficient age and understanding to express a preference;

(e) The recommendation of the current custodian; and

(f) The recommendation of the guardian ad litem, if one has been appointed.

(12) Placement of a child in a permanent guardianship, with a fit and willing relative, or in another planned permanent living arrangement does not terminate the parent-child relationship, including, but not limited to:

(a) The right of the child to inherit from his or her parents;

(b) The parents' right to consent to the child's adoption; or

(c) The parents' responsibility to provide financial, medical, and other support for the child as ordered by the court.

HISTORY:
S. 28, ch. 2000-139; s. 19, ch. 2006-86, eff. July 1, 2006; s. 12, ch. 2012-178, eff. July 1, 2012; s. 18, ch. 2017-151, eff. July 1, 2017.

§ 39.622. Long-term custody [Repealed.]

Repealed by s. 35, ch. 2006-86, effective July 1, 2006.

HISTORY:
S. 29, ch. 2000-139.

§ 39.6221. Permanent guardianship of a dependent child.

(1) If a court determines that reunification or adoption is not in the best interest of the child, the court may place the child in a permanent guardianship with a relative or other adult approved by the court if all of the following conditions are met:

(a) The child has been in the placement for not less than the preceding 6 months.

(b) The permanent guardian is suitable and able to provide a safe and permanent home for the child.

(c) The court determines that the child and the relative or other adult are not likely to need supervision or services of the department to ensure the stability of the permanent guardianship.

(d) The permanent guardian has made a commitment to provide for the child until the child reaches the age of majority and to prepare the child for adulthood and independence.

(e) The permanent guardian agrees to give notice of any change in his or her residential address or the residence of the child by filing a written document in the dependency file of the child with the clerk of the court.

(2) In its written order establishing a permanent guardianship, the court shall:

(a) List the circumstances or reasons why the child's parents are not fit to care for the child and why reunification is not possible by referring to specific findings of fact made in its order adjudicating the child dependent or by making separate findings of fact;

(b) State the reasons why a permanent guardianship is being established instead of adoption;

(c) Specify the frequency and nature of visitation or contact between the child and his or her parents;

(d) Specify the frequency and nature of visitation or contact between the child and his or her grandparents, under s. 39.509;

(e) Specify the frequency and nature of visitation or contact between the child and his or her siblings; and

(f) Require that the permanent guardian not return the child to the physical care and custody of the person from whom the child was removed without the approval of the court.

(3) The court shall give the permanent guardian a separate order establishing the authority of the permanent guardian to care for the child and providing any other information the court deems proper which can be provided to persons who are not parties to the proceeding as necessary, notwithstanding the confidentiality provisions of s. 39.202.

(4) A permanent guardianship of a dependent child established under this chapter is not a plenary guardianship and is not subject to the requirements of chapter 744.

(5) The court shall retain jurisdiction over the case and the child shall remain in the custody of the permanent guardian unless the order creating the permanent guardianship is modified by the court. The court shall discontinue regular review hearings and relieve the department of the responsibility for supervising the placement of the child. Not withstanding the retention of jurisdiction, the placement shall be considered permanency for the child.

(6) Placement of a child in a permanent guardianship does not terminate the parent-child relationship, including:

(a) The right of the child to inherit from his or her parents;

(b) The parents' right to consent to the child's adoption; and

(c) The parents' responsibility to provide financial, medical, and other support for the child as ordered by the court.

(7) The requirements of s. 61.13001 do not apply to permanent guardianships established under this section.

HISTORY:
S. 20, ch. 2006-86, eff. July 1, 2006; s. 4, ch. 2007-5, eff. July 3, 2007; s. 19, ch. 2017-151, eff. July 1, 2017.

§ 39.623. Long-term licensed custody [Repealed.]

Repealed by s. 35, ch. 2006-86, effective July 1, 2006.

HISTORY:
S. 30, ch. 2000-139.

§ 39.6231. Permanent placement with a fit and willing relative.

(1)   If a court finds that reunification or adoption are not in the best interests of a child, the court may place the child with a fit and willing relative as a permanency option if:

(a)   The child has been in the placement for at least the preceding 6 months;

(b)   The relative has made a commitment to provide for the child until the child reaches the age of majority and to prepare the child for adulthood and independence;

(c)   The relative is suitable and able to provide a safe and permanent home for the child; and

(d)   The relative agrees to give notice of any change in his or her residence or the residence of the child by filing a written document with the clerk of court.

(2)   The department and the guardian ad litem shall provide the court with a recommended list and description of services needed by the child and the family in order to ensure the permanency of the placement.

(3)   In its written order placing the child with a fit and willing relative, the court shall:

(a)   List the circumstances or reasons why reunification is not possible by referring to specific findings of fact made in its order adjudicating the child dependent or by making separate findings of fact;

(b)   State the reasons why permanent placement with a fit and willing relative is being established instead of adoption;

(c)   Specify the frequency and nature of visitation or contact between the child and his or her parents;

(d)   Specify the frequency and nature of visitation or contact between the child and his or her grandparents, under s. 39.509;

(e)   Specify the frequency and nature of visitation or contact between the child and his or her siblings; and

(f)   Require that the relative not return the child to the physical care and custody of the person from whom the child was removed without the approval of the court.

(4)   The court shall give the relative a separate order establishing his or her authority to care for the child and providing other information the court deems proper which can be provided to entities and individuals who are not parties to the proceeding as necessary, notwithstanding the confidentiality of s. 39.202.

(5)   The department shall continue to supervise the placement with the relative until further court order. The court shall continue to review the placement at least once every 6 months.

(6)   Each party to the proceeding must be advised by the department and the court that placement with a fit and willing relative does not preclude the possibility of the child returning to the custody of the parent.

(7)   The court shall continue to conduct permanency hearings in order to reevaluate the possibility of adoption or permanent guardianship of the child.

HISTORY:
S. 21, ch. 2006-86, eff. July 1, 2006.

§ 39.624. Independent living [Repealed.]

Repealed by s. 35, ch. 2006-86, effective July 1, 2006.

HISTORY:
S. 31, ch. 2000-139.

§ 39.6241. Another planned permanent living arrangement.

(1)   If a court finds that reunification is not in the best interests of a child, the court may approve placement of the child in another planned permanent living arrangement if:

(a)   The court finds a more permanent placement, such as adoption, permanent guardianship, or placement with a fit and willing relative, is not in the best interests of the child;

(b)   The department documents reasons why the placement will endure and how the proposed arrangement will be more stable and secure than ordinary foster care;

(c)   The court finds that the health, safety, and well-being of the child will not be jeopardized by such an arrangement; and

(d)   There are compelling reasons to show that placement in another planned permanent living arrangement is the most appropriate permanency goal. Compelling reasons for such placement may include, but are not limited to:

1.   The case of a parent and child who have a significant bond but the parent is unable to care for the child because of an emotional or physical disability, and the child's foster parents have committed to raising him or her to the age of majority and to facilitate visitation with the disabled parent;

2.   The case of a child for whom an Indian tribe has identified another planned permanent living arrangement for the child; or

3.   The case of a foster child who is 16 years of age or older who chooses to remain in foster care, and the child's foster parents are willing to care for the child until the child reaches 18 years of age.

(2)   The department and the guardian ad litem must provide the court with a recommended list and description of services needed by the child, such as independent living services and medical, dental, educational, or psychological referrals, and a recommended list and description of services needed by his or her caregiver.

(3)   The department shall continue to supervise the planned permanent living arrangement until the court

orders otherwise. The court shall continue to review the placement at least once every 6 months.

HISTORY:
S. 22, ch. 2006-86, eff July 1, 2006.

§ 39.6251. Continuing care for young adults.

(1) As used in this section, the term "child" means an individual who has not attained 21 years of age, and the term "young adult" means an individual who has attained 18 years of age but who has not attained 21 years of age.

(2) The primary goal for a child in care is permanency. A child who is living in licensed care on his or her 18th birthday and who has not achieved permanency under s. 39.621 is eligible to remain in licensed care under the jurisdiction of the court and in the care of the department. A child is eligible to remain in licensed care if he or she is:

(a) Completing secondary education or a program leading to an equivalent credential;

(b) Enrolled in an institution that provides postsecondary or vocational education;

(c) Participating in a program or activity designed to promote or eliminate barriers to employment;

(d) Employed for at least 80 hours per month; or

(e) Unable to participate in programs or activities listed in paragraphs (a)-(d) full time due to a physical, intellectual, emotional, or psychiatric condition that limits participation. Any such barrier to participation must be supported by documentation in the child's case file or school or medical records of a physical, intellectual, or psychiatric condition that impairs the child's ability to perform one or more life activities.

(3) The permanency goal for a young adult who chooses to remain in care is transition from licensed care to independent living.

(4)(a) The young adult must reside in a supervised living environment that is approved by the department or a community-based care lead agency. The young adult shall live independently, but in an environment in which he or she is provided supervision, case management, and supportive services by the department or lead agency. Such an environment must offer developmentally appropriate freedom and responsibility to prepare the young adult for adulthood. For the purposes of this subsection, a supervised living arrangement may include a licensed foster home, licensed group home, college dormitory, shared housing, apartment, or another housing arrangement if the arrangement is approved by the community-based care lead agency and is acceptable to the young adult, with first choice being a licensed foster home. A young adult may continue to reside with the same licensed foster family or group care provider with whom he or she was residing at the time he or she reached the age of 18 years.

(b) Before approving the residential setting in which the young adult will live, the department or community-based care lead agency must ensure that:

1. The young adult will be provided with a level of supervision consistent with his or her individual education, health care needs, permanency plan, and independent living goals as assessed by the department or lead agency with input from the young adult. Twenty-four hour onsite supervision is not required; however, 24-hour crisis intervention and support must be available.

2. The young adult will live in an independent living environment that offers, at a minimum, life skills instruction, counseling, educational support, employment preparation and placement, and development of support networks. The determination of the type and duration of services shall be based on the young adult's assessed needs, interests, and input and must be consistent with the goals set in the young adult's case plan.

(5) Eligibility for a young adult to remain in extended foster care ends on the earliest of the dates that the young adult:

(a) Reaches 21 years of age or, in the case of a young adult with a disability, reaches 22 years of age;

(b) Leaves care to live in a permanent home consistent with his or her permanency plan; or

(c) Knowingly and voluntarily withdraws his or her consent to participate in extended care. Withdrawal of consent to participate in extended care shall be verified by the court pursuant to s. 39.701, unless the young adult refuses to participate in any further court proceeding.

(6) A young adult who is between the ages of 18 and 21 and who has left care may return to care by applying to the community-based care lead agency for readmission. The community-based care lead agency shall readmit the young adult if he or she continues to meet the eligibility requirements in this section.

(a) The department shall develop a standard procedure and application packet for readmission to care to be used by all community-based care lead agencies.

(b) Within 30 days after the young adult has been readmitted to care, the community-based care lead agency shall assign a case manager to update the case plan and the transition plan and to arrange for the required services. Such activities shall be undertaken in consultation with the young adult. The department shall petition the court to reinstate jurisdiction over the young adult. Notwithstanding s. 39.013(2), the court shall resume jurisdiction over the young adult if the department establishes that he or she continues to meet the eligibility requirements in this section.

(7) During each period of time that a young adult is in care, the community-based lead agency shall pro-

vide regular case management reviews that must include at least monthly contact with the case manager. If a young adult lives outside the service area of his or her community-based care lead agency, monthly contact may occur by telephone.

(8)   During the time that a young adult is in care, the court shall maintain jurisdiction to ensure that the department and the lead agencies are providing services and coordinate with, and maintain oversight of, other agencies involved in implementing the young adult's case plan, individual education plan, and transition plan. The court shall review the status of the young adult at least every 6 months and hold a permanency review hearing at least annually. If the young adult is appointed a guardian under chapter 744 or a guardian advocate under s. 393.12, at the permanency review hearing the court shall review the necessity of continuing the guardianship and whether restoration of guardianship proceedings are needed when the young adult reaches 22 years of age. The court may appoint a guardian ad litem or continue the appointment of a guardian ad litem with the young adult's consent. The young adult or any other party to the dependency case may request an additional hearing or review.

(9)   The department shall establish a procedure by which a young adult may appeal a determination of eligibility to remain in care that was made by a community-based care lead agency. The procedure must be readily accessible to young adults, must provide for timely decisions, and must provide for an appeal to the department. The decision of the department constitutes final agency action and is reviewable by the court as provided in s. 120.68.

HISTORY:

S. 5, ch. 2013-178, eff. Jan. 1, 2014; s. 2, ch. 2015-112, eff. July 1, 2015.

Editor's Notes

Section 1, ch. 2015-112, provides: "This act may be cited as 'The Regis Little Act to Protect Children with Special Needs.' "

PART IX.
JUDICIAL REVIEWS.

§ 39.701.   Judicial review.

(1) GENERAL PROVISIONS.

(a)   The court shall have continuing jurisdiction in accordance with this section and shall review the status of the child at least every 6 months as required by this subsection or more frequently if the court deems it necessary or desirable.

(b)   The court shall retain jurisdiction over a child returned to his or her parents for a minimum period of 6 months following the reunification, but, at that time, based on a report of the social service agency and the guardian ad litem, if one has been appointed, and any other relevant factors, the court shall make a determination as to whether supervision by the department and the court's jurisdiction shall continue or be terminated.

(c)1.   The court shall review the status of the child and shall hold a hearing as provided in this part at least every 6 months until the child reaches permanency status. The court may dispense with the attendance of the child at the hearing, but may not dispense with the hearing or the presence of other parties to the review unless before the review a hearing is held before a citizen review panel.

2.   Citizen review panels may conduct hearings to review the status of a child. The court shall select the cases appropriate for referral to the citizen review panels and may order the attendance of the parties at the review panel hearings. However, any party may object to the referral of a case to a citizen review panel. Whenever such an objection has been filed with the court, the court shall review the substance of the objection and may conduct the review itself or refer the review to a citizen review panel. All parties retain the right to take exception to the findings or recommended orders of a citizen review panel in accordance with Rule 1.490(h), Florida Rules of Civil Procedure.

3.   Notice of a hearing by a citizen review panel must be provided as set forth in paragraph (f). At the conclusion of a citizen review panel hearing, each party may propose a recommended order to the chairperson of the panel. Thereafter, the citizen review panel shall submit its report, copies of the proposed recommended orders, and a copy of the panel's recommended order to the court. The citizen review panel's recommended order must be limited to the dispositional options available to the court in paragraph (2)(d). Each party may file exceptions to the report and recommended order of the citizen review panel in accordance with Rule 1.490, Florida Rules of Civil Procedure.

(d)1.   The initial judicial review hearing must be held no later than 90 days after the date of the disposition hearing or after the date of the hearing at which the court approves the case plan, whichever comes first, but in no event shall the review be held later than 6 months after the date the child was removed from the home. Citizen review panels may not conduct more than two consecutive reviews without the child and the parties coming before the court for a judicial review.

2.   If the citizen review panel recommends extending the goal of reunification for any case plan beyond 12 months from the date the child was removed from the home, the case plan was adopted, or the child was adjudicated dependent, whichever date came first, the court must schedule a judicial review hearing to be conducted by the court within 30 days after receiving the recommendation from the citizen review panel.

3. If the child is placed in the custody of the department or a licensed child-placing agency for the purpose of adoptive placement, judicial reviews must be held at least every 6 months until the adoption is finalized.

4. If the department and the court have established a formal agreement that includes specific authorization for particular cases, the department may conduct administrative reviews instead of the judicial reviews for children in out-of-home care. Notices of such administrative reviews must be provided to all parties. However, an administrative review may not be substituted for the first judicial review, and in every case the court must conduct a judicial review at least every 6 months. Any party dissatisfied with the results of an administrative review may petition for a judicial review.

5. The clerk of the circuit court shall schedule judicial review hearings in order to comply with the mandated times cited in this section.

6. In each case in which a child has been voluntarily placed with the licensed child-placing agency, the agency shall notify the clerk of the court in the circuit where the child resides of such placement within 5 working days. Notification of the court is not required for any child who will be in out-of-home care no longer than 30 days unless that child is placed in out-of-home care a second time within a 12-month period. If the child is returned to the custody of the parents before the scheduled review hearing or if the child is placed for adoption, the child-placing agency shall notify the court of the child's return or placement within 5 working days, and the clerk of the court shall cancel the review hearing.

(e) The court shall schedule the date, time, and location of the next judicial review during the judicial review hearing and shall list same in the judicial review order.

(f) Notice of a judicial review hearing or a citizen review panel hearing, and a copy of the motion for judicial review, if any, must be served by the clerk of the court upon all of the following persons, if available to be served, regardless of whether the person was present at the previous hearing at which the date, time, and location of the hearing was announced:

1. The social service agency charged with the supervision of care, custody, or guardianship of the child, if that agency is not the movant.

2. The foster parent or legal custodian in whose home the child resides.

3. The parents.

4. The guardian ad litem for the child, or the representative of the guardian ad litem program if the program has been appointed.

5. The attorney for the child.

6. The child, if the child is 13 years of age or older.

7. Any preadoptive parent.

8. Such other persons as the court may direct.

(g) The attorney for the department shall notify a relative who submits a request for notification of all proceedings and hearings pursuant to s. 39.301(14)(b). The notice shall include the date, time, and location of the next judicial review hearing.

(h) If a child is born into a family that is under the court's jurisdiction or a child moves into a home that is under the court's jurisdiction, the department shall assess the child's safety and provide notice to the court.

1. The department shall complete an assessment to determine how the addition of a child will impact family functioning. The assessment must be completed at least 30 days before a child is expected to be born or to move into a home, or within 72 hours after the department learns of the pregnancy or addition if the child is expected to be born or to move into the home in less than 30 days. The assessment shall be filed with the court.

2. Once a child is born into a family or a child moves into the home, the department shall complete a progress update and file it with the court.

3. The court has the discretion to hold a hearing on the progress update filed by the department.

(2) REVIEW HEARINGS FOR CHILDREN YOUNGER THAN 18 YEARS OF AGE.

(a) *SOCIAL STUDY REPORT FOR JUDICIAL REVIEW.* — Before every judicial review hearing or citizen review panel hearing, the social service agency shall make an investigation and social study concerning all pertinent details relating to the child and shall furnish to the court or citizen review panel a written report that includes, but is not limited to:

1. A description of the type of placement the child is in at the time of the hearing, including the safety of the child and the continuing necessity for and appropriateness of the placement.

2. Documentation of the diligent efforts made by all parties to the case plan to comply with each applicable provision of the plan.

3. The amount of fees assessed and collected during the period of time being reported.

4. The services provided to the foster family or legal custodian in an effort to address the needs of the child as indicated in the case plan.

5. A statement that either:

a. The parent, though able to do so, did not comply substantially with the case plan, and the agency recommendations;

b. The parent did substantially comply with the case plan; or

c. The parent has partially complied with the case plan, with a summary of additional progress needed and the agency recommendations.

6. A statement from the foster parent or legal custodian providing any material evidence con-

cerning the return of the child to the parent or parents.

7. A statement concerning the frequency, duration, and results of the parent-child visitation, if any, and the agency recommendations for an expansion or restriction of future visitation.

8. The number of times a child has been removed from his or her home and placed elsewhere, the number and types of placements that have occurred, and the reason for the changes in placement.

9. The number of times a child's educational placement has been changed, the number and types of educational placements which have occurred, and the reason for any change in placement.

10. If the child has reached 13 years of age but is not yet 18 years of age, a statement from the caregiver on the progress the child has made in acquiring independent living skills.

11. Copies of all medical, psychological, and educational records that support the terms of the case plan and that have been produced concerning the parents or any caregiver since the last judicial review hearing.

12. Copies of the child's current health, mental health, and education records as identified in s. 39.6012.

(b) *SUBMISSION AND DISTRIBUTION OF REPORTS.*

1. A copy of the social service agency's written report and the written report of the guardian ad litem must be served on all parties whose whereabouts are known; to the foster parents or legal custodians; and to the citizen review panel, at least 72 hours before the judicial review hearing or citizen review panel hearing. The requirement for providing parents with a copy of the written report does not apply to those parents who have voluntarily surrendered their child for adoption or who have had their parental rights to the child terminated.

2. In a case in which the child has been permanently placed with the social service agency, the agency shall furnish to the court a written report concerning the progress being made to place the child for adoption. If the child cannot be placed for adoption, a report on the progress made by the child towards alternative permanency goals or placements, including, but not limited to, guardianship, long-term custody, long-term licensed custody, or independent living, must be submitted to the court. The report must be submitted to the court at least 72 hours before each scheduled judicial review.

3. In addition to or in lieu of any written statement provided to the court, the foster parent or legal custodian, or any preadoptive parent, shall

be given the opportunity to address the court with any information relevant to the best interests of the child at any judicial review hearing.

(c) REVIEW DETERMINATIONS. — The court and any citizen review panel shall take into consideration the information contained in the social services study and investigation and all medical, psychological, and educational records that support the terms of the case plan; testimony by the social services agency, the parent, the foster parent or legal custodian, the guardian ad litem or surrogate parent for educational decisionmaking if one has been appointed for the child, and any other person deemed appropriate; and any relevant and material evidence submitted to the court, including written and oral reports to the extent of their probative value. These reports and evidence may be received by the court in its effort to determine the action to be taken with regard to the child and may be relied upon to the extent of their probative value, even though not competent in an adjudicatory hearing. In its deliberations, the court and any citizen review panel shall seek to determine:

1. If the parent was advised of the right to receive assistance from any person or social service agency in the preparation of the case plan.

2. If the parent has been advised of the right to have counsel present at the judicial review or citizen review hearings. If not so advised, the court or citizen review panel shall advise the parent of such right.

3. If a guardian ad litem needs to be appointed for the child in a case in which a guardian ad litem has not previously been appointed or if there is a need to continue a guardian ad litem in a case in which a guardian ad litem has been appointed.

4. Who holds the rights to make educational decisions for the child. If appropriate, the court may refer the child to the district school superintendent for appointment of a surrogate parent or may itself appoint a surrogate parent under the Individuals with Disabilities Education Act and s. 39.0016.

5. The compliance or lack of compliance of all parties with applicable items of the case plan, including the parents' compliance with child support orders.

6. The compliance or lack of compliance with a visitation contract between the parent and the social service agency for contact with the child, including the frequency, duration, and results of the parent-child visitation and the reason for any noncompliance.

7. The frequency, kind, and duration of contacts among siblings who have been separated during placement, as well as any efforts undertaken to reunite separated siblings if doing so is in the best interest of the child.

8. The compliance or lack of compliance of the parent in meeting specified financial obligations pertaining to the care of the child, including the reason for failure to comply, if applicable.

9. Whether the child is receiving safe and proper care according to s. 39.6012, including, but not limited to, the appropriateness of the child's current placement, including whether the child is in a setting that is as family-like and as close to the parent's home as possible, consistent with the child's best interests and special needs, and including maintaining stability in the child's educational placement, as documented by assurances from the community-based care provider that:

a. The placement of the child takes into account the appropriateness of the current educational setting and the proximity to the school in which the child is enrolled at the time of placement.

b. The community-based care agency has coordinated with appropriate local educational agencies to ensure that the child remains in the school in which the child is enrolled at the time of placement.

10. A projected date likely for the child's return home or other permanent placement.

11. When appropriate, the basis for the unwillingness or inability of the parent to become a party to a case plan. The court and the citizen review panel shall determine if the efforts of the social service agency to secure party participation in a case plan were sufficient.

12. For a child who has reached 13 years of age but is not yet 18 years of age, the adequacy of the child's preparation for adulthood and independent living. For a child who is 15 years of age or older, the court shall determine if appropriate steps are being taken for the child to obtain a driver license or learner's driver license.

13. If amendments to the case plan are required. Amendments to the case plan must be made under s. 39.6013.

(d) ORDERS.

1. Based upon the criteria set forth in paragraph (c) and the recommended order of the citizen review panel, if any, the court shall determine whether or not the social service agency shall initiate proceedings to have a child declared a dependent child, return the child to the parent, continue the child in out-of-home care for a specified period of time, or initiate termination of parental rights proceedings for subsequent placement in an adoptive home. Amendments to the case plan must be prepared as prescribed in s. 39.6013. If the court finds that the prevention or reunification efforts of the department will allow the child to remain safely at home or be safely returned to the home, the court shall allow the child to remain in or return to the home after making a specific finding of fact that the reasons for the creation of the case plan have been remedied to the extent that the child's safety, well-being, and physical, mental, and emotional health will not be endangered.

2. The court shall return the child to the custody of the parents at any time it determines that they have substantially complied with the case plan, if the court is satisfied that reunification will not be detrimental to the child's safety, well-being, and physical, mental, and emotional health.

3. If, in the opinion of the court, the social service agency has not complied with its obligations as specified in the written case plan, the court may find the social service agency in contempt, shall order the social service agency to submit its plans for compliance with the agreement, and shall require the social service agency to show why the child could not safely be returned to the home of the parents.

4. If, at any judicial review, the court finds that the parents have failed to substantially comply with the case plan to the degree that further reunification efforts are without merit and not in the best interest of the child, on its own motion, the court may order the filing of a petition for termination of parental rights, whether or not the time period as contained in the case plan for substantial compliance has expired.

5. Within 6 months after the date that the child was placed in shelter care, the court shall conduct a judicial review hearing to review the child's permanency goal as identified in the case plan. At the hearing the court shall make findings regarding the likelihood of the child's reunification with the parent or legal custodian within 12 months after the removal of the child from the home. If the court makes a written finding that it is not likely that the child will be reunified with the parent or legal custodian within 12 months after the child was removed from the home, the department must file with the court, and serve on all parties, a motion to amend the case plan under s. 39.6013 and declare that it will use concurrent planning for the case plan. The department must file the motion within 10 business days after receiving the written finding of the court. The department must attach the proposed amended case plan to the motion. If concurrent planning is already being used, the case plan must document the efforts the department is taking to complete the concurrent goal.

6. The court may issue a protective order in assistance, or as a condition, of any other order made under this part. In addition to the requirements included in the case plan, the protective order may set forth requirements relating to reasonable conditions of behavior to be observed for a specified period of time by a person or agency

who is before the court; and the order may require any person or agency to make periodic reports to the court containing such information as the court in its discretion may prescribe.

(3) REVIEW HEARINGS FOR CHILDREN 17 YEARS OF AGE.

(a) In addition to the review and report required under paragraphs (1)(a) and (2)(a), respectively, the court shall hold a judicial review hearing within 90 days after a child's 17th birthday. The court shall also issue an order, separate from the order on judicial review, that the disability of nonage of the child has been removed pursuant to ss. 743.044, 743.045, 743.046, and 743.047, and for any of these disabilities that the court finds is in the child's best interest to remove. The court shall continue to hold timely judicial review hearings. If necessary, the court may review the status of the child more frequently during the year before the child's 18th birthday. At each review hearing held under this subsection, in addition to any information or report provided to the court by the foster parent, legal custodian, or guardian ad litem, the child shall be given the opportunity to address the court with any information relevant to the child's best interest, particularly in relation to independent living transition services. The department shall include in the social study report for judicial review written verification that the child has:

1. A current Medicaid card and all necessary information concerning the Medicaid program sufficient to prepare the child to apply for coverage upon reaching the age of 18, if such application is appropriate.

2. A certified copy of the child's birth certificate and, if the child does not have a valid driver license, a Florida identification card issued under s. 322.051.

3. A social security card and information relating to social security insurance benefits if the child is eligible for those benefits. If the child has received such benefits and they are being held in trust for the child, a full accounting of these funds must be provided and the child must be informed as to how to access those funds.

4. All relevant information related to the Road-to-Independence Program, including, but not limited to, eligibility requirements, information on participation, and assistance in gaining admission to the program. If the child is eligible for the Road-to-Independence Program, he or she must be advised that he or she may continue to reside with the licensed family home or group care provider with whom the child was residing at the time the child attained his or her 18th birthday, in another licensed family home, or with a group care provider arranged by the department.

5. An open bank account or the identification necessary to open a bank account and to acquire essential banking and budgeting skills.

6. Information on public assistance and how to apply for public assistance.

7. A clear understanding of where he or she will be living on his or her 18th birthday, how living expenses will be paid, and the educational program or school in which he or she will be enrolled.

8. Information related to the ability of the child to remain in care until he or she reaches 21 years of age under s. 39.013.

9. A letter providing the dates that the child is under the jurisdiction of the court.

10. A letter stating that the child is in compliance with financial aid documentation requirements.

11. The child's educational records.

12. The child's entire health and mental health records.

13. The process for accessing his or her case file.

14. A statement encouraging the child to attend all judicial review hearings occurring after the child's 17th birthday.

15. Information on how to obtain a driver license or learner's driver license.

(b) At the first judicial review hearing held subsequent to the child's 17th birthday, the department shall provide the court with an updated case plan that includes specific information related to the independent living skills that the child has acquired since the child's 13th birthday, or since the date the child came into foster care, whichever came later.

1. For any child who may meet the requirements for appointment of a guardian pursuant to chapter 744, or a guardian advocate pursuant to s. 393.12, the updated case plan must be developed in a face-to-face conference with the child, if appropriate; the child's attorney; any court-appointed guardian ad litem; the temporary custodian of the child; and the parent, if the parent's rights have not been terminated.

2. At the judicial review hearing, if the court determines pursuant to chapter 744 that there is a good faith basis to believe that the child qualifies for appointment of a guardian advocate, limited guardian, or plenary guardian for the child and that no less restrictive decisionmaking assistance will meet the child's needs:

a. The department shall complete a multidisciplinary report which must include, but is not limited to, a psychosocial evaluation and educational report if such a report has not been completed within the previous 2 years.

b. The department shall identify one or more individuals who are willing to serve as the guardian advocate pursuant to s. 393.12 or as the plenary or limited guardian pursuant to chapter 744. Any other interested parties or participants may make efforts to identify such a guardian advocate, limited guardian, or plenary guardian. The child's biological or adoptive family members, including the child's parents if the parents' rights have not been terminated, may not be considered for service as the plenary or limited guardian unless the court enters a written order finding that such an appointment is in the child's best interests.

c. Proceedings may be initiated within 180 days after the child's 17th birthday for the appointment of a guardian advocate, plenary guardian, or limited guardian for the child in a separate proceeding in the court division with jurisdiction over guardianship matters and pursuant to chapter 744. The Legislature encourages the use of pro bono representation to initiate proceedings under this section.

3. In the event another interested party or participant initiates proceedings for the appointment of a guardian advocate, plenary guardian, or limited guardian for the child, the department shall provide all necessary documentation and information to the petitioner to complete a petition under s. 393.12 or chapter 744 within 45 days after the first judicial review hearing after the child's 17th birthday.

4. Any proceedings seeking appointment of a guardian advocate or a determination of incapacity and the appointment of a guardian must be conducted in a separate proceeding in the court division with jurisdiction over guardianship matters and pursuant to chapter 744.

(c) If the court finds at the judicial review hearing that the department has not met its obligations to the child as stated in this part, in the written case plan, or in the provision of independent living services, the court may issue an order directing the department to show cause as to why it has not done so. If the department cannot justify its noncompliance, the court may give the department 30 days within which to comply. If the department fails to comply within 30 days, the court may hold the department in contempt.

(d) At the last review hearing before the child reaches 18 years of age, and in addition to the requirements of subsection (2), the court shall:

1. Address whether the child plans to remain in foster care, and, if so, ensure that the child's transition plan includes a plan for meeting one or more of the criteria specified in s. 39.6251.

2. Ensure that the transition plan includes a supervised living arrangement under s. 39.6251.

3. Ensure the child has been informed of:

a. The right to continued support and services from the department and the community-based care lead agency.

b. The right to request termination of dependency jurisdiction and be discharged from foster care.

c. The opportunity to reenter foster care pursuant to s. 39.6251.

4. Ensure that the young adult, if he or she requests termination of dependency jurisdiction and discharge from foster care, has been informed of:

a. Services or benefits for which the young adult may be eligible based on his or her former placement in foster care;

b. Services or benefits that may be lost through termination of dependency jurisdiction; and

c. Other federal, state, local, or community-based services or supports available to him or her.

(4) REVIEW HEARINGS FOR YOUNG ADULTS IN FOSTER CARE. — During each period of time that a young adult remains in foster care, the court shall review the status of the young adult at least every 6 months and must hold a permanency review hearing at least annually.

(a) The department and community-based care lead agency shall prepare and submit to the court a report, developed in collaboration with the young adult, which addresses the young adult's progress in meeting the goals in the case plan. The report must include progress information related to the young adult's independent living plan and transition plan, if applicable, and shall propose modifications as necessary to further the young adult's goals.

(b) The court shall attempt to determine whether the department and any service provider under contract with the department are providing the appropriate services as provided in the case plan.

(c) If the court believes that the young adult is entitled under department policy or under a contract with a service provider to additional services to achieve the goals enumerated in the case plan, it may order the department to take action to ensure that the young adult receives the identified services.

(d) The young adult or any other party to the dependency case may request an additional hearing or judicial review.

(e) Notwithstanding the provisions of this subsection, if a young adult has chosen to remain in extended foster care after he or she has reached 18 years of age, the department may not close a case and the court may not terminate jurisdiction until the court finds, following a hearing, that the following criteria have been met:

1. Attendance of the young adult at the hearing; or

2. Findings by the court that:

a. The young adult has been informed by the department of his or her right to attend the hearing and has provided written consent to waive this right; and

b. The young adult has been informed of the potential negative effects of early termination of care, the option to reenter care before reaching 21 years of age, the procedure for, and limitations on, reentering care, and the availability of alternative services, and has signed a document attesting that he or she has been so informed and understands these provisions; or

c. The young adult has voluntarily left the program, has not signed the document in subsubparagraph b., and is unwilling to participate in any further court proceeding.

3. In all permanency hearings or hearings regarding the transition of the young adult from care to independent living, the court shall consult with the young adult regarding the proposed permanency plan, case plan, and individual education plan for the young adult and ensure that he or she has understood the conversation.

HISTORY:

S. 9, ch. 87-289; s. 11, ch. 90-306; s. 3, ch. 90-309; s. 3, ch. 91-183; s. 49, ch. 92-58; s. 6, ch. 92-158; s. 27, ch. 94-164; s. 78, ch. 98-403; s. 38, ch. 99-193; s. 32, ch. 2000-139; s. 2, ch. 2004-362; s. 7, ch. 2005-2; s. 2, ch. 2005-179; s. 23, ch. 2006-86, July 1, 2006; s. 8, ch. 2006-194, eff. July 1, 2006; s. 14, ch. 2008-245, eff. June 30, 2008; s. 4, ch. 2009-35, eff. July 1, 2009; s. 13, ch. 2009-43, eff. July 1, 2009; s. 13, ch. 2012-178, eff. July 1, 2012; s. 6, ch. 2013-178, eff. Jan. 1, 2014; s. 7, ch. 2014-17, eff. July 1, 2014; s. 1, ch. 2014-166, eff. July 1, 2014; s. 17, ch. 2014-224, eff. July 1, 2014; s. 3, ch. 2015-112, eff. July 1, 2015; s. 3, ch. 2016-10, eff. May 10, 2016; s. 3, ch. 2017-8, eff. May 1, 2017; s. 20, ch. 2017-151, eff. July 1, 2017.

Editor's Notes

The Individuals with Disabilities Education Act, referred to in this section, is codified as 20 U.S.C.S. § 1400 et seq.

Section 1 of ch. 2009-43 provides: "This act may be cited as the 'Zahid Jones, Jr., Give Grandparents and Other Relatives a Voice Act.' "

Former s. 39.453.

Section 1, ch. 2015-112, provides: "This act may be cited as 'The Regis Little Act to Protect Children with Special Needs.' "

Amendments.

The 2015 amendment added (3)(b)1. through (3)(b)3.; added "in this part" in the first sentence of (3)(c); and made a related change.

§ 39.702. Citizen review panels.

(1) Citizen review panels may be established in each judicial circuit and shall be authorized by an administrative order executed by the chief judge of each circuit. The court shall administer an oath of office to each citizen review panel member which shall authorize the panel member to participate in citizen review panels and make recommendations to the court pursuant to the provisions of this section.

(2) Citizen review panels shall be administered by an independent not-for-profit agency. For the purpose of this section, an organization that has filed for nonprofit status under the provisions of s. 501(c)(3) of the United States Internal Revenue Code is an independent not-for-profit agency for a period of 1 year after the date of filing. At the end of that 1-year period, in order to continue conducting citizen reviews, the organization must have qualified for nonprofit status under s. 501(c)(3) of the United States Internal Revenue Code and must submit to the chief judge of the circuit court a consumer's certificate of exemption that was issued to the organization by the Florida Department of Revenue and a report of the organization's progress. If the agency has not qualified for nonprofit status, the court must rescind its administrative order that authorizes the agency to conduct citizen reviews. All independent not-for-profit agencies conducting citizen reviews must submit citizen review annual reports to the court.

(3) For the purpose of this section, a citizen review panel shall be composed of five volunteer members and shall conform with the requirements of this chapter. The presence of three members at a panel hearing shall constitute a quorum. Panel members shall serve without compensation.

(4) Based on the information provided to each citizen review panel pursuant to s. 39.701, each citizen review panel shall provide the court with a report and recommendations regarding the placement and dispositional alternatives the court shall consider before issuing a judicial review order.

(5) The independent not-for-profit agency authorized to administer each citizen review panel shall:

(a) In collaboration with the department, develop policies to assure that citizen review panels comply with all applicable state and federal laws.

(b) Establish policies for the recruitment, selection, retention, and terms of volunteer panel members. Final selection of citizen review panel members shall, to the extent possible, reflect the multicultural composition of the community which they serve. A criminal background check and personal reference check shall be conducted on each citizen review panel member prior to the member serving on a citizen review panel.

(c) In collaboration with the department, develop, implement, and maintain a training program for citizen review volunteers and provide training for each panel member prior to that member serving on a review panel. Such training may include, but shall not be limited to, instruction on dependency laws, departmental policies, and judicial procedures.

(d) Ensure that all citizen review panel members have read, understood, and signed an oath of confidentiality relating to written or verbal information provided to the panel members for review hearings.

(e) Establish policies to avoid actual or perceived conflicts of interest by panel members during the review process and to ensure accurate, fair reviews of each child dependency case.

(f) Establish policies to ensure ongoing communication with the department and the court.

(g) Establish policies to ensure adequate communication with the parent, the foster parent or legal custodian, the guardian ad litem, and any other person deemed appropriate.

(h) Establish procedures that encourage attendance and participation of interested persons and parties, including the parents, foster parents, or legal custodian with whom the child is placed, at citizen review hearings.

(i) Coordinate with existing citizen review panels to ensure consistency of operating procedures, data collection, analysis, and report generation.

(j) Make recommendations as necessary to the court concerning attendance of essential persons at the review and other issues pertinent to an effective review process.

(k) Ensure consistent methods of identifying barriers to the permanent placement of the child and delineation of findings and recommendations to the court.

(6) The department and agents of the department shall submit information to the citizen review panel when requested and shall address questions asked by the citizen review panel to identify barriers to the permanent placement of each child.

HISTORY:
S. 12, ch. 90-306; s. 50, ch. 92-58; s. 79, ch. 98-403; s. 39, ch. 99-193.

Editor's notes.
Former s. 39.4531.
Section 501(c)(3) of the Internal Revenue Service, referred to in this section, is codified as 26 U.S.C.S. § 501(c)(3).

§ 39.703. Initiation of termination of parental rights proceedings; judicial review [Repealed.]
Repealed by s. 35, ch. 2006-86, effective July 1, 2006.

HISTORY:
S. 9, ch. 87-289; s. 28, ch. 94-164; s. 13, ch. 98-280; s. 80, ch. 98-403; s. 40, ch. 99-193; s. 1, ch. 2001-3.

§ 39.704. Exemptions from judicial review.
Judicial review does not apply to:

(1) Minors who have been placed in adoptive homes by a licensed child-placing agency; or

(2) Minors who are refugees or entrants to whom federal regulations apply and who are in the care of a social service agency.

HISTORY:
S. 9, ch. 87-289; s. 14, ch. 90-306; s. 81, ch. 98-403; s. 41, ch. 99-193.

Editor's notes.
Former s. 39.456.

PART X.
TERMINATION OF PARENTAL RIGHTS.

§ 39.801. Procedures and jurisdiction; notice; service of process.
(1) All procedures, including petitions, pleadings, subpoenas, summonses, and hearings, in termination of parental rights proceedings shall be according to the Florida Rules of Juvenile Procedure unless otherwise provided by law.

(2) The circuit court shall have exclusive original jurisdiction of a proceeding involving termination of parental rights.

(3) Before the court may terminate parental rights, in addition to the other requirements set forth in this part, the following requirements must be met:

(a) Notice of the date, time, and place of the advisory hearing for the petition to terminate parental rights and a copy of the petition must be personally served upon the following persons, specifically notifying them that a petition has been filed:

1. The parents of the child.

2. The legal custodians of the child.

3. If the parents who would be entitled to notice are dead or unknown, a living relative of the child, unless upon diligent search and inquiry no such relative can be found.

4. Any person who has physical custody of the child.

5. Any grandparent entitled to priority for adoption under s. 63.0425.

6. Any prospective parent who has been identified under s. 39.503 or s. 39.803, unless a court order has been entered pursuant to s. 39.503(4) or (9) or s. 39.803(4) or (9) which indicates no further notice is required. Except as otherwise provided in this section, if there is not a legal father, notice of the petition for termination of parental rights must be provided to any known prospective father who is identified under oath before the court or who is identified by a diligent search of the Florida Putative Father Registry. Service of the notice of the petition for termination of parental rights is not required if the prospective father executes an affidavit of nonpaternity or a consent to termination of his parental rights which is accepted by the court after notice and opportunity to be heard by all parties to address the best interests of the child in accepting such affidavit.

7. The guardian ad litem for the child or the representative of the guardian ad litem program, if the program has been appointed.

(b) If a party required to be served with notice as prescribed in paragraph (a) cannot be served, notice of hearings must be given as prescribed by the rules of civil procedure, and service of process must be made as specified by law or civil actions.

(c) Notice as prescribed by this section may be waived, in the discretion of the judge, with regard to any person to whom notice must be given under this subsection if the person executes, before two witnesses and a notary public or other officer authorized to take acknowledgments, a written surrender of the child to a licensed child-placing agency or the department.

(d) If the person served with notice under this section fails to personally appear at the advisory hearing, the failure to personally appear shall constitute consent for termination of parental rights by the person given notice. If a parent appears for the advisory hearing and the court orders that parent to personally appear at the adjudicatory hearing for the petition for termination of parental rights, stating the date, time, and location of said hearing, then failure of that parent to personally appear at the adjudicatory hearing shall constitute consent for termination of parental rights.

The document containing the notice to respond or appear must contain, in type at least as large as the type in the balance of the document, the following or substantially similar language: "FAILURE TO PERSONALLY APPEAR AT THIS ADVISORY HEARING CONSTITUTES CONSENT TO THE TERMINATION OF PARENTAL RIGHTS OF THIS CHILD (OR CHILDREN). IF YOU FAIL TO APPEAR ON THE DATE AND TIME SPECIFIED, YOU MAY LOSE ALL LEGAL RIGHTS AS A PARENT TO THE CHILD OR CHILDREN NAMED IN THE PETITION ATTACHED TO THIS NOTICE."

(4) Upon the application of any party, the clerk or deputy clerk shall issue, and the court on its own motion may issue, subpoenas requiring the attendance and testimony of witnesses and the production of records, documents, or other tangible objects at any hearing.

(5) All process and orders issued by the court must be served or executed as other process and orders of the circuit court and, in addition, may be served or executed by authorized agents of the department or the guardian ad litem.

(6) Subpoenas may be served within the state by any person over 18 years of age who is not a party to the proceeding and, in addition, may be served or executed by authorized agents of the department or of the guardian ad litem.

(7) A fee may not be paid for service of any process or other papers by an agent of the department or the guardian ad litem. If any process, orders, or other papers are served or executed by any sheriff, the sheriff's fees must be paid by the county.

HISTORY:

S. 9, ch. 87-289; s. 1, ch. 92-96; s. 32, ch. 94-164; ss. 6, 11, ch. 97-276; s. 83, ch. 98-403; s. 42, ch. 99-193; s. 21, ch. 2017-151, eff. July 1, 2017.

Editor's notes.

Former ss. 39.46, 39.462.

§ 39.802. Petition for termination of parental rights; filing; elements.

(1) All proceedings seeking an adjudication to terminate parental rights pursuant to this chapter must be initiated by the filing of an original petition by the department, the guardian ad litem, or any other person who has knowledge of the facts alleged or is informed of them and believes that they are true.

(2) The form of the petition is governed by the Florida Rules of Juvenile Procedure. The petition must be in writing and signed by the petitioner under oath stating the petitioner's good faith in filing the petition.

(3) When a petition for termination of parental rights has been filed, the clerk of the court shall set the case before the court for an advisory hearing.

(4) A petition for termination of parental rights filed under this chapter must contain facts supporting the following allegations:

(a) That at least one of the grounds listed in s. 39.806 has been met.

(b) That the parents of the child were informed of their right to counsel at all hearings that they attended and that a dispositional order adjudicating the child dependent was entered in any prior dependency proceeding relied upon in offering a parent a case plan as described in s. 39.806.

(c) That the manifest best interests of the child, in accordance with s. 39.810, would be served by the granting of the petition.

(d) That the parents of the child will be informed of the availability of private placement of the child with an adoption entity, as defined in s. 63.032.

(5) When a petition for termination of parental rights is filed under s. 39.806(1), a separate petition for dependency need not be filed and the department need not offer the parents a case plan with a goal of reunification, but may instead file with the court a case plan with a goal of termination of parental rights to allow continuation of services until the termination is granted or until further orders of the court are issued.

(6) The fact that a child has been previously adjudicated dependent as alleged in a petition for termination of parental rights may be proved by the introduction of a certified copy of the order of adjudication or the order of disposition of dependency.

(7) The fact that the parent of a child was informed of the right to counsel in any prior dependency proceeding as alleged in a petition for termination of parental rights may be proved by the introduction of a certified copy of the order of adjudication or the order of disposition of dependency containing a finding of fact that the parent was so advised.

(8) If the department has entered into a case plan with a parent with the goal of reunification, and a petition for termination of parental rights based on the same facts as are covered in the case plan is filed prior to the time agreed upon in the case plan for the performance of the case plan, then the petitioner must allege and prove by clear and convincing evidence that the parent has materially breached the provisions of the case plan.

HISTORY:

S. 9, ch. 87-289; s. 15, ch. 90-306; s. 14, ch. 92-170; ss. 29, 30, ch. 94-164; s. 13, ch. 97-276; s. 84, ch. 98-403; s. 43, ch. 99-193; s. 2, ch.

2001-3; s. 31, ch. 2006-86, eff. July 1, 2006; s. 1, ch. 2012-81, eff. July 1, 2012; s. 18, ch. 2014-224, eff. July 1, 2014.

Editor's notes.

Section 31, ch. 2006-86 reenacted (5) without change to incorporate amendments to statutory sections referenced therein.

Former ss. 39.461, 39.4611.

§ 39.803. Identity or location of parent unknown after filing of termination of parental rights petition; special procedures.

(1) If the identity or location of a parent is unknown and a petition for termination of parental rights is filed, the court shall conduct under oath the following inquiry of the parent who is available, or, if no parent is available, of any relative, caregiver, or legal custodian of the child who is present at the hearing and likely to have the information:

(a) Whether the mother of the child was married at the probable time of conception of the child or at the time of birth of the child.

(b) Whether the mother was cohabiting with a male at the probable time of conception of the child.

(c) Whether the mother has received payments or promises of support with respect to the child or because of her pregnancy from a man who claims to be the father.

(d) Whether the mother has named any man as the father on the birth certificate of the child or in connection with applying for or receiving public assistance.

(e) Whether any man has acknowledged or claimed paternity of the child in a jurisdiction in which the mother resided at the time of or since conception of the child, or in which the child has resided or resides.

(f) Whether a man is named on the birth certificate of the child pursuant to s. 382.013(2).

(g) Whether a man has been determined by a court order to be the father of the child.

(h) Whether a man has been determined to be the father of the child by the Department of Revenue as provided in s. 409.256.

(2) The information required in subsection (1) may be supplied to the court or the department in the form of a sworn affidavit by a person having personal knowledge of the facts.

(3) If the inquiry under subsection (1) identifies any person as a parent or prospective parent, the court shall require notice of the hearing to be provided to that person.

(4) If the inquiry under subsection (1) fails to identify any person as a parent or prospective parent, the court shall so find and may proceed without further notice.

(5) If the inquiry under subsection (1) identifies a parent or prospective parent, and that person's location is unknown, the court shall direct the petitioner to conduct a diligent search for that person before scheduling an adjudicatory hearing regarding the petition for termination of parental rights to the child unless the court finds that the best interest of the child requires proceeding without actual notice to the person whose location is unknown.

(6) The diligent search required by subsection (5) must include, at a minimum, inquiries of all known relatives of the parent or prospective parent, inquiries of all offices of program areas of the department likely to have information about the parent or prospective parent, inquiries of other state and federal agencies likely to have information about the parent or prospective parent, inquiries of appropriate utility and postal providers, a thorough search of at least one electronic database specifically designed for locating persons, a search of the Florida Putative Father Registry, and inquiries of appropriate law enforcement agencies. Pursuant to s. 453 of the Social Security Act, 42 U.S.C. s. 653(c)(4), the department, as the state agency administering Titles IV-B and IV-E of the act, shall be provided access to the federal and state parent locator service for diligent search activities.

(7) Any agency contacted by petitioner with a request for information pursuant to subsection (6) shall release the requested information to the petitioner without the necessity of a subpoena or court order.

(8) If the inquiry and diligent search identifies a prospective parent, that person must be given the opportunity to become a party to the proceedings by completing a sworn affidavit of parenthood and filing it with the court or the department. A prospective parent who files a sworn affidavit of parenthood while the child is a dependent child but no later than at the time of or before the adjudicatory hearing in the termination of parental rights proceeding for the child shall be considered a parent for all purposes under this section.

(9) If the diligent search under subsection (5) fails to identify and locate a prospective parent, the court shall so find and may proceed without further notice.

HISTORY:

S. 85, ch. 98-403; s. 33, ch. 2000-139; s. 22, ch. 2017-151, eff. July 1, 2017.

§ 39.804. Penalties for false statements of paternity.

Any male person or any mother of a dependent child who knowingly and willfully makes a false statement concerning the paternity of a child in conjunction with a petition to terminate parental rights under this chapter and causes such false statement of paternity to be filed with the court commits a misdemeanor of the first degree, punishable as provided in s. 775.082 or s. 775.083. A person who makes a statement claiming paternity in good faith is immune from criminal liability under this section.

HISTORY:

S. 34, ch. 94-164; s. 86, ch. 98-403; s. 34, ch. 2000-139.

Editor's notes.

Former s. 39.4627.

§ 39.805. No answer required.

No answer to the petition or any other pleading need be filed by any child or parent, but any matters which might be set forth in an answer or other pleading may be pleaded orally before the court or filed in writing as any such person may choose. Notwithstanding the filing of any answer or any pleading, the child or parent shall, prior to the adjudicatory hearing, be advised by the court of the right to counsel and shall be given an opportunity to deny the allegations in the petition for termination of parental rights or to enter a plea to allegations in the petition before the court.

HISTORY:
S. 9, ch. 87-289; s. 242, ch. 95-147; s. 87, ch. 98-403; s. 44, ch. 99-193.

Editor's notes.
Former s. 39.463.

§ 39.8055. Requirement to file a petition to terminate parental rights; exceptions.

(1)   The department shall file a petition to terminate parental rights within 60 days after any of the following if:

(a)   The child is not returned to the physical custody of the parents 12 months after the child was sheltered or adjudicated dependent, whichever occurs first;

(b)   A petition for termination of parental rights has not otherwise been filed, and the child has been in out-of-home care under the responsibility of the state for 12 of the most recent 22 months, calculated on a cumulative basis, but not including any trial home visits or time during which the child was a runaway;

(c)   A parent has been convicted of the murder, manslaughter, aiding or abetting the murder, or conspiracy or solicitation to murder the other parent or another child of the parent, or a felony battery that resulted in serious bodily injury to the child or to another child of the parent; or

(d)   A court determines that reasonable efforts to reunify the child and parent are not required.

(2)   Notwithstanding subsection (1), the department may choose not to file or join in a petition to terminate the parental rights of a parent if:

(a)   The child is being cared for by a relative under s. 39.6231; or

(b)   The department has documented in the report to the court a compelling reason for determining that filing such a petition is not in the best interests of the child. Compelling reasons for not filing or joining a petition to terminate parental rights may include, but are not limited to:

1.   Adoption is not the appropriate permanency goal for the child.

2.   No grounds to file a petition to terminate parental rights exist.

3.   The child is an unaccompanied refugee minor as defined in 45 C.F.R. s. 400.111.

4.   There are international legal obligations or compelling foreign-policy reasons that would preclude terminating parental rights.

5.   The department has not provided to the family, consistent with the time period in the case plan, services that the department deems necessary for the safe return of the child to the home.

(3)   Upon good cause shown by any party or on its own motion, the court may review the decision by the department that compelling reasons exist for not filing or joining a petition for termination of parental rights.

HISTORY:
S. 24, ch. 2006-86, eff. July 1, 2006; s. 15, ch. 2008-245, eff. June 30, 2008; s. 14, ch. 2012-178, eff. July 1, 2012.

§ 39.806.   Grounds for termination of parental rights.

(1)   Grounds for the termination of parental rights may be established under any of the following circumstances:

(a)   When the parent or parents have voluntarily executed a written surrender of the child and consented to the entry of an order giving custody of the child to the department for subsequent adoption and the department is willing to accept custody of the child.

1.   The surrender document must be executed before two witnesses and a notary public or other person authorized to take acknowledgments.

2.   The surrender and consent may be withdrawn after acceptance by the department only after a finding by the court that the surrender and consent were obtained by fraud or under duress.

(b)   Abandonment as defined in s. 39.01(1) or when the identity or location of the parent or parents is unknown and cannot be ascertained by diligent search within 60 days.

(c)   When the parent or parents engaged in conduct toward the child or toward other children that demonstrates that the continuing involvement of the parent or parents in the parent-child relationship threatens the life, safety, well-being, or physical, mental, or emotional health of the child irrespective of the provision of services. Provision of services may be evidenced by proof that services were provided through a previous plan or offered as a case plan from a child welfare agency.

(d)   When the parent of a child is incarcerated and either:

1.   The period of time for which the parent is expected to be incarcerated will constitute a significant portion of the child's minority. When determining whether the period of time is significant, the court shall consider the child's age and the child's need for a permanent and stable home. The period of time begins on the date that the parent enters into incarceration;

2. The incarcerated parent has been determined by the court to be a violent career criminal as defined in s. 775.084, a habitual violent felony offender as defined in s. 775.084, or a sexual predator as defined in s. 775.21; has been convicted of first degree or second degree murder in violation of s. 782.04 or a sexual battery that constitutes a capital, life, or first degree felony violation of s. 794.011; or has been convicted of an offense in another jurisdiction which is substantially similar to one of the offenses listed in this paragraph. As used in this section, the term "substantially similar offense" means any offense that is substantially similar in elements and penalties to one of those listed in this subparagraph, and that is in violation of a law of any other jurisdiction, whether that of another state, the District of Columbia, the United States or any possession or territory thereof, or any foreign jurisdiction; or

3. The court determines by clear and convincing evidence that continuing the parental relationship with the incarcerated parent would be harmful to the child and, for this reason, that termination of the parental rights of the incarcerated parent is in the best interest of the child. When determining harm, the court shall consider the following factors:

a. The age of the child.

b. The relationship between the child and the parent.

c. The nature of the parent's current and past provision for the child's developmental, cognitive, psychological, and physical needs.

d. The parent's history of criminal behavior, which may include the frequency of incarceration and the unavailability of the parent to the child due to incarceration.

e. Any other factor the court deems relevant.

(e) When a child has been adjudicated dependent, a case plan has been filed with the court, and:

1. The child continues to be abused, neglected, or abandoned by the parent or parents. The failure of the parent or parents to substantially comply with the case plan for a period of 12 months after an adjudication of the child as a dependent child or the child's placement into shelter care, whichever occurs first, constitutes evidence of continuing abuse, neglect, or abandonment unless the failure to substantially comply with the case plan was due to the parent's lack of financial resources or to the failure of the department to make reasonable efforts to reunify the parent and child. The 12-month period begins to run only after the child's placement into shelter care or the entry of a disposition order placing the custody of the child with the department or a person other than the parent and the court's approval of a case plan having the goal of reunification with the parent, whichever occurs first; or

2. The parent or parents have materially breached the case plan. Time is of the essence for permanency of children in the dependency system. In order to prove the parent or parents have materially breached the case plan, the court must find by clear and convincing evidence that the parent or parents are unlikely or unable to substantially comply with the case plan before time to comply with the case plan expires.

3. The child has been in care for any 12 of the last 22 months and the parents have not substantially complied with the case plan so as to permit reunification under s. 39.522(2) unless the failure to substantially comply with the case plan was due to the parent's lack of financial resources or to the failure of the department to make reasonable efforts to reunify the parent and child.

(f) The parent or parents engaged in egregious conduct or had the opportunity and capability to prevent and knowingly failed to prevent egregious conduct that threatens the life, safety, or physical, mental, or emotional health of the child or the child's sibling. Proof of a nexus between egregious conduct to a child and the potential harm to the child's sibling is not required.

1. As used in this subsection, the term "sibling" means another child who resides with or is cared for by the parent or parents regardless of whether the child is related legally or by consanguinity.

2. As used in this subsection, the term "egregious conduct" means abuse, abandonment, neglect, or any other conduct that is deplorable, flagrant, or outrageous by a normal standard of conduct. Egregious conduct may include an act or omission that occurred only once but was of such intensity, magnitude, or severity as to endanger the life of the child.

(g) The parent or parents have subjected the child or another child to aggravated child abuse as defined in s. 827.03, sexual battery or sexual abuse as defined in s. 39.01, or chronic abuse.

(h) The parent or parents have committed the murder, manslaughter, aiding or abetting the murder, or conspiracy or solicitation to murder the other parent or another child, or a felony battery that resulted in serious bodily injury to the child or to another child. Proof of a nexus between the murder, manslaughter, aiding or abetting the murder, or conspiracy or solicitation to murder the other parent or another child, or a felony battery to a child and the potential harm to a child or another child is not required.

(i) The parental rights of the parent to a sibling of the child have been terminated involuntarily.

(j) The parent or parents have a history of extensive, abusive, and chronic use of alcohol or a controlled substance which renders them incapable of caring for the child, and have refused or failed to complete available treatment for such use during the 3-year period immediately preceding the filing of the petition for termination of parental rights.

(k) A test administered at birth that indicated that the child's blood, urine, or meconium contained any amount of alcohol or a controlled substance or metabolites of such substances, the presence of which was not the result of medical treatment administered to the mother or the newborn infant, and the biological mother of the child is the biological mother of at least one other child who was adjudicated dependent after a finding of harm to the child's health or welfare due to exposure to a controlled substance or alcohol as defined in s. 39.01, after which the biological mother had the opportunity to participate in substance abuse treatment.

(*l*) On three or more occasions the child or another child of the parent or parents has been placed in out-of-home care pursuant to this chapter, and the conditions that led to the child's out-of-home placement were caused by the parent or parents.

(m) The court determines by clear and convincing evidence that the child was conceived as a result of an act of sexual battery made unlawful pursuant to s. 794.011, or pursuant to a similar law of another state, territory, possession, or Native American tribe where the offense occurred. It is presumed that termination of parental rights is in the best interest of the child if the child was conceived as a result of the unlawful sexual battery. A petition for termination of parental rights under this paragraph may be filed at any time. The court must accept a guilty plea or conviction of unlawful sexual battery pursuant to s. 794.011 as conclusive proof that the child was conceived by a violation of criminal law as set forth in this subsection.

(n) The parent is convicted of an offense that requires the parent to register as a sexual predator under s. 775.21.

(2) Reasonable efforts to preserve and reunify families are not required if a court of competent jurisdiction has determined that any of the events described in paragraphs (1)(b)-(d) or paragraphs (1)(f)-(m) have occurred.

(3) If a petition for termination of parental rights is filed under subsection (1), a separate petition for dependency need not be filed and the department need not offer the parents a case plan having a goal of reunification, but may instead file with the court a case plan having a goal of termination of parental rights to allow continuation of services until the termination is granted or until further orders of the court are issued.

(4) If an expedited termination of parental rights petition is filed, reasonable efforts shall be made to place the child in a timely manner in accordance with the permanency plan, and to complete whatever steps are necessary to finalize the permanent placement of the child.

HISTORY:
S. 9, ch. 87-289; s. 16, ch. 90-306; s. 4, ch. 90-309; s. 7, ch. 92-158; s. 35, ch. 94-164; s. 1, ch. 97-226; s. 12, ch. 97-276; s. 88, ch. 98-403; s. 2, ch. 98-417; s. 45, ch. 99-193; s. 35, ch. 2000-139; s. 3, ch. 2001-3; s. 12, ch. 2004-371; s. 25, ch. 2006-86, eff. July 1, 2006; s. 16, ch. 2008-245, eff. June 30, 2008; s. 2, ch. 2009-21, eff. July 7, 2009; s. 15, ch. 2012-178, eff. July 1, 2012; s. 1, ch. 2013-132, eff. July 1, 2013; s. 19, ch. 2014-224, eff. July 1, 2014; s. 16, ch. 2016-24, eff. Oct. 1, 2016; s. 16, ch. 2017-37, eff. Oct. 1, 2017; s. 23, ch. 2017-151, eff. July 1, 2017; s. 8, ch. 2017-107, eff. Oct. 1, 2017.

Editor's notes.
Section 12, ch. 2004-371 reenacted (1)(d) without change to incorporate amendments to statutory sections referenced therein.
Former s. 39.464.
Section 3, ch. 2013-132, provides: "This act shall take effect July 7, 2013, and applies to all unlawful acts of sexual battery occurring before, on, or after that date."

§ 39.807. Right to counsel; guardian ad litem.

(1)(a) At each stage of the proceeding under this part, the court shall advise the parent of the right to have counsel present. The court shall appoint counsel for indigent parents. The court shall ascertain whether the right to counsel is understood and, where appropriate, is knowingly and intelligently waived. The court shall enter its findings in writing with respect to the appointment or waiver of counsel for indigent parents.

(b) Once counsel has been retained or, in appropriate circumstances, appointed to represent the parent of the child, the attorney shall continue to represent the parent throughout the proceedings or until the court has approved discontinuing the attorney-client relationship. If the attorney-client relationship is discontinued, the court shall advise the parent of the right to have new counsel retained or appointed for the remainder of the proceedings.

(c)1. No waiver of counsel may be accepted if it appears that the parent is unable to make an intelligent and understanding choice because of mental condition, age, education, experience, the nature or complexity of the case, or other factors.

2. A waiver of counsel made in court must be of record. A waiver made out of court must be in writing with not less than two attesting witnesses and must be filed with the court. The witnesses shall attest to the voluntary execution of the waiver.

3. If a waiver of counsel is accepted at any stage of the proceedings, the offer of assistance of counsel must be renewed by the court at each subsequent stage of the proceedings at which the parent appears without counsel.

(d) This subsection does not apply to any parent who has voluntarily executed a written surrender of the child and consent to the entry of a court order therefor.

(2)(a) The court shall appoint a guardian ad litem to represent the best interest of the child in any termination of parental rights proceedings and shall ascertain at each stage of the proceedings whether a guardian ad litem has been appointed.

(b)   The guardian ad litem has the following responsibilities:

1.   To investigate the allegations of the petition and any subsequent matters arising in the case and, unless excused by the court, to file a written report. This report must include a statement of the wishes of the child and the recommendations of the guardian ad litem and must be provided to all parties and the court at least 72 hours before the disposition hearing.

2.   To be present at all court hearings unless excused by the court.

3.   To represent the best interests of the child until the jurisdiction of the court over the child terminates or until excused by the court.

(c)   A guardian ad litem is not required to post bond but shall file an acceptance of the office.

(d)   A guardian ad litem is entitled to receive service of pleadings and papers as provided by the Florida Rules of Juvenile Procedure.

(e)   This subsection does not apply to any voluntary relinquishment of parental rights proceeding.

HISTORY:
S. 9, ch. 87-289; s. 17, ch. 90-306; s. 36, ch. 94-164; s. 89, ch. 98-403; s. 46, ch. 99-193; s. 36, ch. 2000-139.

Editor's notes.
Former s. 39.465.

§ 39.808. Advisory hearing; pretrial status conference.

(1)   An advisory hearing on the petition to terminate parental rights must be held as soon as possible after all parties have been served with a copy of the petition and a notice of the date, time, and place of the advisory hearing for the petition.

(2)   At the hearing the court shall inform the parties of their rights under s. 39.807, shall appoint counsel for the parties in accordance with legal requirements, and shall appoint a guardian ad litem to represent the interests of the child if one has not already been appointed.

(3)   The court shall set a date for an adjudicatory hearing to be held within 45 days after the advisory hearing, unless all of the necessary parties agree to some other hearing date.

(4)   An advisory hearing is not required if a petition is filed seeking an adjudication for termination of parental rights based on a voluntary surrender of parental rights. Adjudicatory hearings for petitions for voluntary termination must be held within 21 days after the filing of the petition. Notice of the use of this subsection must be filed with the court at the same time as the filing of the petition to terminate parental rights.

(5)   Not less than 10 days before the adjudicatory hearing on a petition for involuntary termination of parental rights, the court shall conduct a pretrial status conference to determine the order in which each party may present witnesses or evidence, the order in which cross-examination and argument shall occur, and any other matters that may aid in the conduct of the adjudicatory hearing to prevent any undue delay in the conduct of the adjudicatory hearing.

HISTORY:
S. 9, ch. 87-289; s. 33, ch. 88-337; s. 18, ch. 90-306; s. 37, ch. 94-164; s. 90, ch. 98-403; s. 47, ch. 99-193.

Editor's notes.
Former s. 39.466.

§ 39.809. Adjudicatory hearing.

(1)   In a hearing on a petition for termination of parental rights, the court shall consider the elements required for termination. Each of these elements must be established by clear and convincing evidence before the petition is granted.

(2)   The adjudicatory hearing must be held within 45 days after the advisory hearing, but reasonable continuances for the purpose of investigation, discovery, or procuring counsel or witnesses may, when necessary, be granted.

(3)   The adjudicatory hearing must be conducted by the judge without a jury, applying the rules of evidence in use in civil cases and adjourning the case from time to time as necessary. For purposes of the adjudicatory hearing, to avoid unnecessary duplication of expense, the judge may consider in-court testimony previously given at any properly noticed hearing, without regard to the availability or unavailability of the witness at the time of the actual adjudicatory hearing, if the recorded testimony itself is made available to the judge. Consideration of such testimony does not preclude the witness being subpoenaed to answer supplemental questions.

(4)   All hearings involving termination of parental rights are confidential and closed to the public. Hearings involving more than one child may be held simultaneously when the children involved are related to each other or were involved in the same case. The child and the parents may be examined separately and apart from each other.

(5)   The judge shall enter a written order with the findings of fact and conclusions of law.

HISTORY:
S. 9, ch. 87-289; s. 19, ch. 90-306; ss. 8, 10, ch. 92-158; s. 38, ch. 94-164; s. 91, ch. 98-403.

Editor's notes.
Former s. 39.467.

§ 39.810. Manifest best interests of the child.

In a hearing on a petition for termination of parental rights, the court shall consider the manifest best interests of the child. This consideration shall not include a comparison between the attributes of the parents and those of any persons providing a present or potential placement for the child. For the purpose of determining the manifest best interests of the child, the court shall consider and evaluate all relevant factors, including, but not limited to:

(1) Any suitable permanent custody arrangement with a relative of the child. However, the availability of a nonadoptive placement with a relative may not receive greater consideration than any other factor weighing on the manifest best interest of the child and may not be considered as a factor weighing against termination of parental rights. If a child has been in a stable or preadoptive placement for not less than 6 months, the availability of a different placement, including a placement with a relative, may not be considered as a ground to deny the termination of parental rights.

(2) The ability and disposition of the parent or parents to provide the child with food, clothing, medical care or other remedial care recognized and permitted under state law instead of medical care, and other material needs of the child.

(3) The capacity of the parent or parents to care for the child to the extent that the child's safety, well-being, and physical, mental, and emotional health will not be endangered upon the child's return home.

(4) The present mental and physical health needs of the child and such future needs of the child to the extent that such future needs can be ascertained based on the present condition of the child.

(5) The love, affection, and other emotional ties existing between the child and the child's parent or parents, siblings, and other relatives, and the degree of harm to the child that would arise from the termination of parental rights and duties.

(6) The likelihood of an older child remaining in long-term foster care upon termination of parental rights, due to emotional or behavioral problems or any special needs of the child.

(7) The child's ability to form a significant relationship with a parental substitute and the likelihood that the child will enter into a more stable and permanent family relationship as a result of permanent termination of parental rights and duties.

(8) The length of time that the child has lived in a stable, satisfactory environment and the desirability of maintaining continuity.

(9) The depth of the relationship existing between the child and the present custodian.

(10) The reasonable preferences and wishes of the child, if the court deems the child to be of sufficient intelligence, understanding, and experience to express a preference.

(11) The recommendations for the child provided by the child's guardian ad litem or legal representative.

HISTORY:

S. 31, ch. 94-164; s. 18, ch. 95-228; s. 92, ch. 98-403; s. 26, ch. 2006-86, eff. July 1, 2006.

Editor's notes.

Former s. 39.4612.

§ 39.811. Powers of disposition; order of disposition.

(1) If the court finds that the grounds for termination of parental rights have not been established by clear and convincing evidence, the court shall:

(a) If grounds for dependency have been established, adjudicate or readjudicate the child dependent and:

1. Enter an order placing or continuing the child in out-of-home care under a case plan; or

2. Enter an order returning the child to the parent or parents. The court shall retain jurisdiction over a child returned to the parent or parents for a period of 6 months, but, at that time, based on a report of the social service agency and any other relevant factors, the court shall make a determination as to whether its jurisdiction shall continue or be terminated.

(b) If grounds for dependency have not been established, dismiss the petition.

(2) If the child is in the custody of the department and the court finds that the grounds for termination of parental rights have been established by clear and convincing evidence, the court shall, by order, place the child in the custody of the department for the purpose of adoption.

(3) If the child is in the custody of one parent and the court finds that the grounds for termination of parental rights have been established for the remaining parent by clear and convincing evidence, the court shall enter an order terminating the rights of the parent for whom the grounds have been established and placing the child in the custody of the remaining parent, granting that parent sole parental responsibility for the child.

(4) If the child is neither in the custody of the department nor in the custody of a parent and the court finds that the grounds for termination of parental rights have been established for either or both parents, the court shall enter an order terminating parental rights for the parent or parents for whom the grounds for termination have been established and placing the child with the department or an appropriate legal custodian. If the parental rights of both parents have been terminated, or if the parental rights of only one parent have been terminated and the court makes specific findings based on evidence presented that placement with the remaining parent is likely to be harmful to the child, the court may order that the child be placed with a legal custodian other than the department after hearing evidence of the suitability of the intended placement. Suitability of the intended placement includes the fitness and capabilities of the proposed legal custodian to function as the primary caregiver for a particular child; and the compatibility of the child with the home in which the

child is intended to be placed. If the court orders that a child be placed with a legal custodian under this subsection, the court shall appoint a legal custodian as the guardian for the child as provided in s. 744.3021 or s. 39.621. The court may modify the order placing the child in the custody of the legal custodian and revoke the guardianship established under s. 744.3021 or another relationship if the court subsequently finds the placement to be no longer in the best interest of the child.

(5) If the court terminates parental rights, the court shall enter a written order of disposition briefly stating the facts upon which its decision to terminate the parental rights is made. An order of termination of parental rights, whether based on parental consent or after notice served as prescribed in this part, permanently deprives the parents of any right to the child.

(6) The parental rights of one parent may be severed without severing the parental rights of the other parent only under the following circumstances:

(a) If the child has only one surviving parent;

(b) If the identity of a prospective parent has been established as unknown after sworn testimony;

(c) If the parent whose rights are being terminated became a parent through a single-parent adoption;

(d) If the protection of the child demands termination of the rights of a single parent; or

(e) If the parent whose rights are being terminated meets any of the criteria specified in s. 39.806(1)(c), (d), (f), (g), (h), (i), (j), (k), (l), (m), or (n).

(7)(a) The termination of parental rights does not affect the rights of grandparents unless the court finds that continued visitation is not in the best interests of the child or that such visitation would interfere with the permanency goals for the child.

(b) If the court terminates parental rights, it may, as appropriate, order that the parents, siblings, or relatives of the parent whose rights are terminated be allowed to maintain some communication or contact with the child pending adoption if the best interests of the child support this continued communication or contact, except as provided in paragraph (a). If the court orders such continued communication or contact, which may include, but is not limited to, visits, letters, and cards or telephone calls, the nature and frequency of the communication or contact must be set forth in written order and may be reviewed upon motion of any party, or, for purposes of this subsection, an identified prospective adoptive parent. If a child is placed for adoption, the nature and frequency of the communication or contact must be reviewed by the court at the time the child is placed for adoption.

(8) If the court terminates parental rights, it shall, in its order of disposition, provide for a hearing, to be scheduled no later than 30 days after the date of disposition, in which the department shall provide to the court an amended case plan that identifies the permanency goal for the child. Reasonable efforts must be made to place the child in a timely manner in accordance with the permanency plan and to complete whatever steps are necessary to finalize the permanent placement of the child. Thereafter, until the adoption of the child is finalized or the child reaches the age of 18 years, whichever occurs first, the court shall hold hearings at 6-month intervals to review the progress being made toward permanency for the child.

(9) After termination of parental rights, the court shall retain jurisdiction over any child for whom custody is given to a social service agency until the child is adopted. The court shall review the status of the child's placement and the progress being made toward permanent adoptive placement. As part of this continuing jurisdiction, for good cause shown by the guardian ad litem for the child, the court may review the appropriateness of the adoptive placement of the child.

HISTORY:
S. 9, ch. 87-289; s. 34, ch. 88-337; s. 21, ch. 90-306; s. 73, ch. 91-45; s. 39, ch. 94-164; s. 2, ch. 97-226; s. 1, ch. 98-50; s. 93, ch. 98-403; s. 48, ch. 99-193; s. 37, ch. 2000-139; s. 4, ch. 2001-3; s. 27, ch. 2006-86, eff. July 1, 2006; s. 28, ch. 2008-245, eff. June 30, 2008; s. 2, ch. 2013-132, eff. July 1, 2013; s. 24, ch. 2017-151, eff. July 1, 2017.

Editor's notes.
Former s. 39.469.
Section 3, ch. 2013-132, provides: "This act shall take effect July 7, 2013, and applies to all unlawful acts of sexual battery occurring before, on, or after that date."

§ 39.812. Postdisposition relief; petition for adoption.

(1) If the department is given custody of a child for subsequent adoption in accordance with this chapter, the department may place the child with an agency as defined in s. 63.032, with a child-caring agency registered under s. 409.176, or in a family home for prospective subsequent adoption. The department may thereafter become a party to any proceeding for the legal adoption of the child and appear in any court where the adoption proceeding is pending and consent to the adoption, and that consent alone shall in all cases be sufficient.

(2) In any subsequent adoption proceeding, the parents are not entitled to notice of the proceeding and are not entitled to knowledge at any time after the order terminating parental rights is entered of the whereabouts of the child or of the identity or location of any person having the custody of or having adopted the child, except as provided by order of the court pursuant to this chapter or chapter 63. In any habeas corpus or other proceeding involving the child brought by any parent of the child, an agent or contract provider of the department may not be compelled to divulge that information, but may be compelled to produce the child before a court of competent jurisdiction if the child is still subject to the guardianship of the department.

(3)   The entry of the custody order to the department does not entitle the department to guardianship of the estate or property of the child, but the department shall be the guardian of the person of the child.

(4)   The court shall retain jurisdiction over any child placed in the custody of the department until the child is adopted. After custody of a child for subsequent adoption has been given to the department, the court has jurisdiction for the purpose of reviewing the status of the child and the progress being made toward permanent adoptive placement. As part of this continuing jurisdiction, for good cause shown by the guardian ad litem for the child, the court may review the appropriateness of the adoptive placement of the child. When a licensed foster parent or court-ordered custodian has applied to adopt a child who has resided with the foster parent or custodian for at least 6 months and who has previously been permanently committed to the legal custody of the department and the department does not grant the application to adopt, the department may not, in the absence of a prior court order authorizing it to do so, remove the child from the foster home or custodian, except when:

(a)   There is probable cause to believe that the child is at imminent risk of abuse or neglect;

(b)   Thirty days have expired following written notice to the foster parent or custodian of the denial of the application to adopt, within which period no formal challenge of the department's decision has been filed; or

(c)   The foster parent or custodian agrees to the child's removal.

(5)   The petition for adoption must be filed in the division of the circuit court which entered the judgment terminating parental rights, unless a motion for change of venue is granted pursuant to s. 47.122. A copy of the consent executed by the department must be attached to the petition, unless waived pursuant to s. 63.062(7). The petition must be accompanied by a statement, signed by the prospective adoptive parents, acknowledging receipt of all information required to be disclosed under s. 63.085 and a form provided by the department which details the social and medical history of the child and each parent and includes the social security number and date of birth for each parent, if such information is available or readily obtainable. The prospective adoptive parents may not file a petition for adoption until the judgment terminating parental rights becomes final. An adoption proceeding under this subsection is governed by chapter 63.

(6)(a)   Once a child's adoption is finalized, the community-based care lead agency must make a reasonable effort to contact the adoptive family by telephone 1 year after the date of finalization of the adoption as a postadoption service. For purposes of this subsection, the term "reasonable effort" means the exercise of reasonable diligence and care by the community-based care lead agency to make contact with the adoptive family. At a minimum, the agency must document the following:

1.   The number of attempts made by the community-based care lead agency to contact the adoptive family and whether those attempts were successful;

2.   The types of postadoption services that were requested by the adoptive family and whether those services were provided by the community-based care lead agency; and

3.   Any feedback received by the community-based care lead agency from the adoptive family relating to the quality or effectiveness of the services provided.

(b)   The community-based care lead agency must report annually to the department on the outcomes achieved and recommendations for improvement under this subsection.

HISTORY:
S. 9, ch. 87-289; s. 41, ch. 94-164; s. 14, ch. 95-228; s. 94, ch. 98-403; s. 5, ch. 2001-3; s. 1, ch. 2004-389; s. 1, ch. 2008-151, eff. July 1, 2008; s. 4, ch. 2015-130, eff. July 1, 2015.

Editor's notes.
Former s. 39.47.

§ 39.813. Continuing jurisdiction.

The court which terminates the parental rights of a child who is the subject of termination proceedings pursuant to this chapter shall retain exclusive jurisdiction in all matters pertaining to the child's adoption pursuant to chapter 63.

HISTORY:
S. 95, ch. 98-403.

§ 39.814. Oaths, records, and confidential information.

(1)   The judge, clerks or deputy clerks, and authorized agents of the department shall each have the power to administer oaths and affirmations.

(2)   The court shall make and keep records of all cases brought before it pursuant to this part and shall preserve the records of proceedings under this part pursuant to the Florida Rules of Judicial Administration. Records of cases where orders were entered permanently depriving a parent of the custody of a child shall be preserved permanently.

(3)   The clerk shall keep all court records required by this part separate from other records of the circuit court. All court records required by this part shall not be open to inspection by the public. All records shall be inspected only upon order of the court by persons deemed by the court to have a proper interest therein, except that, custodians of the child and their attorneys, law enforcement agencies, and the department and its designees shall always have the right to inspect and copy any official record pertaining to the child. The court may permit authorized representatives of recog-

nized organizations compiling statistics for proper purposes to inspect and make abstracts from official records, under whatever conditions upon their use and disposition the court may deem proper, and may punish by contempt proceedings any violation of those conditions.

(4) All information obtained pursuant to this part in the discharge of official duty by any judge, employee of the court, authorized agent of the department, or law enforcement agent shall be confidential and exempt from the provisions of s. 119.07(1) and shall not be disclosed to anyone other than the authorized personnel of the court, the department and its designees, law enforcement agents, and others entitled under this part to receive that information, except upon order of the court.

(5) All orders of the court entered pursuant to this part shall be in writing and signed by the judge, except that the clerk or deputy clerk may sign a summons or notice to appear.

(6) No court record of proceedings under this part shall be admissible in evidence in any other civil or criminal proceeding, except that:

(a) Records of proceedings under this part forming a part of the record on appeal shall be used in the appellate court in the manner hereinafter provided.

(b) Records necessary therefor shall be admissible in evidence in any case in which a person is being tried upon a charge of having committed perjury.

(c) A final order entered pursuant to an adjudicatory hearing is admissible in evidence in any subsequent civil proceeding relating to placement of, access to, parental time with, adoption of, or parental rights and responsibilities for the same child or a sibling of that child.

(d) Evidence admitted in any proceeding under this part may be admissible in evidence when offered by any party in a subsequent civil proceeding relating to placement of, access to, parental time with, adoption of, or parental rights and responsibilities for the same child or a sibling of that child if:

1. Notice is given to the opposing party or opposing party's counsel of the intent to offer the evidence and a copy of such evidence is delivered to the opposing party or opposing party's counsel; and

2. The evidence is otherwise admissible in the subsequent civil proceeding.

(7) Final orders, records, and evidence in any proceeding under this part which are subsequently admitted in evidence pursuant to subsection (6) remain subject to subsections (3) and (4).

HISTORY:
S. 9, ch. 87-289; s. 14, ch. 90-360; s. 17, ch. 96-406; s. 3, ch. 97-226; s. 96, ch. 98-403; s. 49, ch. 99-193; s. 6, ch. 2005-239.

Editor's notes.
Former s. 39.471.

§ 39.815. Appeal.

(1) Any child, any parent or guardian ad litem of any child, any other party to the proceeding who is affected by an order of the court, or the department may appeal to the appropriate district court of appeal within the time and in the manner prescribed by the Florida Rules of Appellate Procedure. The district court of appeal shall give an appeal from an order terminating parental rights priority in docketing and shall render a decision on the appeal as expeditiously as possible. Appointed counsel shall be compensated as provided in s. 27.5304(6).

(2) An attorney for the department shall represent the state upon appeal. When a notice of appeal is filed in the circuit court, the clerk shall notify the attorney for the department, together with the attorney for the parent, the guardian ad litem, and any attorney for the child.

(3) The taking of an appeal does not operate as a supersedeas in any case unless the court so orders. However, a termination of parental rights order with placement of the child with a licensed child-placing agency or the department for subsequent adoption is suspended while the appeal is pending, but the child shall continue in an out-of-home placement under the order until the appeal is decided.

(4) The case on appeal must be docketed and any papers filed in the appellate court must be titled with the initials, but not the name, of the child and the court case number, and the papers must remain sealed in the office of the clerk of the appellate court when not in use by the appellate court and may not be open to public inspection. The decision of the appellate court must be likewise titled and may refer to the child only by initials and court case number.

(5) The original order of the appellate court, with all papers filed in the case on appeal, must remain in the office of the clerk of the appellate court, sealed and not open to inspection except by order of the appellate court. The clerk of the appellate court shall return to the circuit court all papers transmitted to the appellate court from the circuit court, together with a certified copy of the order of the appellate court.

HISTORY:
S. 9, ch. 87-289; s. 22, ch. 90-306; s. 1, ch. 90-309; s. 15, ch. 92-170; s. 42, ch. 94-164; s. 97, ch. 98-403; s. 50, ch. 99-193; s. 59, ch. 2003-402; s. 22, ch. 2007-62, eff. May 24, 2007.

Editor's notes.
Former s. 39.473.

§ 39.816. Authorization for pilot and demonstration projects [Repealed.]

Repealed by s. 38, ch. 2011-213, effective July 1, 2011.

HISTORY:
S. 98, ch. 98-403.

§ 39.817. Foster care privatization demonstration pilot project [Repealed.]

Repealed by s. 38, ch. 2011-213, effective July 1, 2011.

HISTORY:
  S. 99, ch. 98-403.

PART XI.
GUARDIANS AD LITEM AND GUARDIAN ADVOCATES.

§ 39.820. Definitions.

As used in this part, the term:

(1) "Guardian ad litem" as referred to in any civil or criminal proceeding includes the following: a certified guardian ad litem program, a duly certified volunteer, a staff attorney, contract attorney, or certified pro bono attorney working on behalf of a guardian ad litem or the program; staff members of a program office; a court-appointed attorney; or a responsible adult who is appointed by the court to represent the best interests of a child in a proceeding as provided for by law, including, but not limited to, this chapter, who is a party to any judicial proceeding as a representative of the child, and who serves until discharged by the court.

(2) "Guardian advocate" means a person appointed by the court to act on behalf of a drug dependent newborn pursuant to the provisions of this part.

HISTORY:
  S. 101, ch. 98-403.

§ 39.821. Qualifications of guardians ad litem.

(1) Because of the special trust or responsibility placed in a guardian ad litem, the Guardian Ad Litem Program may use any private funds collected by the program, or any state funds so designated, to conduct a security background investigation before certifying a volunteer to serve. A security background investigation must include, but need not be limited to, employment history checks, checks of references, local criminal history records checks through local law enforcement agencies, and statewide criminal history records checks through the Department of Law Enforcement. Upon request, an employer shall furnish a copy of the personnel record for the employee or former employee who is the subject of a security background investigation conducted under this section. The information contained in the personnel record may include, but need not be limited to, disciplinary matters and the reason why the employee was terminated from employment. An employer who releases a personnel record for purposes of a security background investigation is presumed to have acted in good faith and is not liable for information contained in the record without a showing that the employer maliciously falsified the record. A security background investigation conducted under this section must ensure that a person is not certified as a guardian ad litem if the person has an arrest awaiting final disposition for, been convicted of, regardless of adjudication, entered a plea of nolo contendere or guilty to, or been adjudicated delinquent and the record has not been sealed or expunged for, any offense prohibited under the provisions listed in s. 435.04. All applicants certified on or after July 1, 2010, must undergo a level 2 background screening pursuant to chapter 435 before being certified to serve as a guardian ad litem. In analyzing and evaluating the information obtained in the security background investigation, the program must give particular emphasis to past activities involving children, including, but not limited to, child-related criminal offenses or child abuse. The program has sole discretion in determining whether to certify a person based on his or her security background investigation. The information collected pursuant to the security background investigation is confidential and exempt from s. 119.07(1).

(2) This section does not apply to a certified guardian ad litem who was certified before October 1, 1995, an attorney who is a member in good standing of The Florida Bar, or a licensed professional who has undergone a comparable security background investigation as a condition of licensure within 5 years of applying for certification as a guardian ad litem.

(3) It is a misdemeanor of the first degree, punishable as provided in s. 775.082 or s. 775.083, for any person to willfully, knowingly, or intentionally fail, by false statement, misrepresentation, impersonation, or other fraudulent means, to disclose in any application for a volunteer position or for paid employment with the Guardian Ad Litem Program, any material fact used in making a determination as to the applicant's qualifications for such position.

HISTORY:
  S. 2, ch. 96-109; s. 102, ch. 98-403; s. 19, ch. 99-2; s. 35, ch. 2004-267; s. 25, ch. 2005-236; s. 2, ch. 2010-114, eff. Aug. 1, 2010; s. 20, ch. 2010-162, eff. July 1, 2010.

Editor's notes.
  Section 35, ch. 2004-267, reenacted (1) without change, effective July 1, 2004, to incorporate amendments to statutory sections referenced therein.
  Former s. 415.5077.
  Section 58, ch. 2010-114 provides: "The changes made by this act are intended to be prospective in nature. It is not intended that persons who are employed or licensed on the effective date of this act be rescreened until such time as they are otherwise required to be rescreened pursuant to law, at which time they must meet the requirements for screening as set forth in this act."

§ 39.822. Appointment of guardian ad litem for abused, abandoned, or neglected child.

(1) A guardian ad litem shall be appointed by the court at the earliest possible time to represent the child in any child abuse, abandonment, or neglect judicial

proceeding, whether civil or criminal. Any person participating in a civil or criminal judicial proceeding resulting from such appointment shall be presumed prima facie to be acting in good faith and in so doing shall be immune from any liability, civil or criminal, that otherwise might be incurred or imposed.

(2) In those cases in which the parents are financially able, the parent or parents of the child shall reimburse the court, in part or in whole, for the cost of provision of guardian ad litem services. Reimbursement to the individual providing guardian ad litem services shall not be contingent upon successful collection by the court from the parent or parents.

(3) Upon presentation by a guardian ad litem of a court order appointing the guardian ad litem:

(a) An agency, as defined in chapter 119, shall allow the guardian ad litem to inspect and copy records related to the best interests of the child who is the subject of the appointment, including, but not limited to, records made confidential or exempt from s. 119.07(1) or s. 24(a), Art. I of the State Constitution. The guardian ad litem shall maintain the confidential or exempt status of any records shared by an agency under this paragraph.

(b) A person or organization, other than an agency under paragraph (a), shall allow the guardian ad litem to inspect and copy any records related to the best interests of the child who is the subject of the appointment, including, but not limited to, confidential records.

For the purposes of this subsection, the term "records related to the best interests of the child" includes, but is not limited to, medical, mental health, substance abuse, child care, education, law enforcement, court, social services, and financial records.

(4) The guardian ad litem or the program representative shall review all disposition recommendations and changes in placements, and must be present at all critical stages of the dependency proceeding or submit a written report of recommendations to the court. Written reports must be filed with the court and served on all parties whose whereabouts are known at least 72 hours prior to the hearing.

HISTORY:
SS. 1, 2, 3, 4, 5, 6, ch. 63-24; s. 941, ch. 71-136; ss. 1, 1A, ch. 71-97; s. 32, ch. 73-334; s. 65, ch. 74-383; s. 1, ch. 75-101; s. 1, ch. 75-185; s. 4, ch. 76-237; s. 1, ch. 77-77; s. 3, ch. 77-429; ss. 1, 2, ch. 78-322; s. 3, ch. 78-326; s. 22, ch. 78-361; s. 1, ch. 78-379; s. 181, ch. 79-164; s. 1, ch. 79-203; s. 10, ch. 84-226; s. 3, ch. 90-211; s. 103, ch. 98-403; s. 51, ch. 99-193; s. 26, ch. 2005-236.

Editor's notes.
Former ss. 828.041, 827.07(16); s. 415.508.

§ 39.823. Guardian advocates for drug dependent newborns.

The Legislature finds that increasing numbers of drug dependent children are born in this state. Because of the parents' continued dependence upon

drugs, the parents may temporarily leave their child with a relative or other adult or may have agreed to voluntary family services under s. 39.301(14). The relative or other adult may be left with a child who is likely to require medical treatment but for whom they are unable to obtain medical treatment. The purpose of this section is to provide an expeditious method for such relatives or other responsible adults to obtain a court order which allows them to provide consent for medical treatment and otherwise advocate for the needs of the child and to provide court review of such authorization.

HISTORY:
S. 2, ch. 89-345; s. 104, ch. 98-403; s. 19, ch. 99-168; s. 5, ch. 2003-127; s. 14, ch. 2009-43, eff. July 1, 2009; s. 18, ch. 2012-178, eff. July 1, 2012.

Editor's notes.
Section 1 of ch. 2009-43 provides: "This act may be cited as the 'Zahid Jones, Jr., Give Grandparents and Other Relatives a Voice Act.' "
Former s. 415.5082.

§ 39.824. Jurisdiction.

The circuit court shall have exclusive original jurisdiction of a proceeding in which appointment of a guardian advocate is sought. The court shall retain jurisdiction over a child for whom a guardian advocate is appointed until specifically relinquished by court order.

HISTORY:
S. 2, ch. 89-345; s. 105, ch. 98-403; s. 21, ch. 2012-116, eff. July 1, 2012.

Editor's notes.
Former s. 415.5083.

§ 39.825. Petition for appointment of a guardian advocate.

A petition for appointment of a guardian advocate may be filed by the department, any relative of the child, any licensed health care professional, or any other interested person. The petition shall be in writing and shall be signed by the petitioner under oath stating his or her good faith in filing the petition. The form of the petition and its contents shall be determined by the Florida Rules of Juvenile Procedure.

HISTORY:
S. 2, ch. 89-345; s. 72, ch. 97-103; s. 106, ch. 98-403.

Editor's notes.
Former s. 415.5084.

§ 39.826. Process and service.

(1) Personal appearance of a person in a hearing before the court shall obviate the necessity of serving process upon that person.

(2) Upon the filing of a petition requesting the appointment of a guardian advocate, and upon request

of the petitioner, the clerk or deputy clerk shall issue a summons.

(3)　The summons shall require the person on whom it is served to appear for a hearing at a time and place specified. Except in cases of medical emergency, the time shall be not less than 24 hours after service of the summons. The summons shall be directed to and shall be served upon the parents. It shall not be necessary to the validity of a proceeding for the appointment of a guardian advocate that the parents be present if their identity or presence is unknown after a diligent search and inquiry have been made, if they have become residents of a state other than this state, or if they evade service or ignore a summons, but in this event the person who made the search and inquiry shall file a certificate of those facts.

(4)　Upon the application of a party, the clerk or deputy clerk shall issue, and the court on its own motion may issue, subpoenas requiring attendance and testimony of witnesses and production of records, documents, or other tangible objects at any hearing.

HISTORY:
S. 2, ch. 89-345; s. 107, ch. 98-403.

Editor's notes.
Former s. 415.5085.

§ 39.827. Hearing for appointment of a guardian advocate.

(1)　When a petition for appointment of a guardian advocate has been filed with the circuit court, the hearing shall be held within 14 days unless all parties agree to a continuance. If a child is in need of necessary medical treatment as defined in s. 39.01, s. 984.03, or s. 985.03, the court shall hold a hearing within 24 hours.

(2)　At the hearing, the parents have the right to be present, to present testimony, to call and cross-examine witnesses, to be represented by counsel at their own expense, and to object to the appointment of the guardian advocate.

(3)　The hearing shall be conducted by the judge without a jury, applying the rules of evidence in use in civil cases. In a hearing on a petition for appointment of a guardian advocate, the moving party shall prove all the elements in s. 39.828 by a preponderance of the evidence.

(4)　The hearing under this section shall remain confidential and closed to the public. The clerk shall keep all court records required by this part separate from other records of the circuit court. All court records required by this part shall be confidential and exempt from the provisions of s. 119.07(1). All records shall be inspected only upon order of the court by persons deemed by the court to have a proper interest therein, except that a child and the parents or custodians of the child and their attorneys and the department and its designees shall always have the right to inspect and copy any official record pertaining to the child. The court may permit authorized representatives of recognized organizations compiling statistics for proper purposes to inspect and make abstracts from official records, under whatever conditions upon their use and disposition the court may deem proper, and may punish by contempt proceedings any violation of those conditions. All information obtained pursuant to this part in the discharge of official duty by any judge, employee of the court, or authorized agent of the department shall be confidential and exempt from the provisions of s. 119.07(1) and shall not be disclosed to anyone other than the authorized personnel of the court or the department and its designees, except upon order of the court.

HISTORY:
S. 2, ch. 89-345; s. 19, ch. 91-71; s. 274, ch. 96-406; s. 44, ch. 98-280; s. 108, ch. 98-403.

Editor's notes.
Former s. 415.5086.

§ 39.828. Grounds for appointment of a guardian advocate.

(1)　The court shall appoint the person named in the petition as a guardian advocate with all the powers and duties specified in s. 39.829 for an initial term of 1 year upon a finding that:

(a)　The child named in the petition is or was a drug dependent newborn as described in s. 39.01;

(b)　The parent or parents of the child have voluntarily relinquished temporary custody of the child to a relative or other responsible adult;

(c)　The person named in the petition to be appointed the guardian advocate is capable of carrying out the duties as provided in s. 39.829; and

(d)　A petition to adjudicate the child dependent under this chapter has not been filed.

(2)　The appointment of a guardian advocate does not remove from the parents the right to consent to medical treatment for their child. The appointment of a guardian advocate does not prevent the filing of a subsequent petition under this chapter to have the child adjudicated dependent.

HISTORY:
S. 2, ch. 89-345; s. 62, ch. 94-164; s. 109, ch. 98-403; s. 32, ch. 2006-86, eff. July 1, 2006; s. 29, ch. 2008-245, eff. June 30, 2008; s. 19, ch. 2012-178, eff. July 1, 2012.

Editor's notes.
Former s. 415.5087.

§ 39.829. Powers and duties of guardian advocate.

It is the duty of the guardian advocate to oversee the care, health, and medical treatment of the child; to advise the court regarding any change in the status of the child; and to respond to any medical crisis of the child, including providing consent to any needed medical treatment. The guardian advocate shall report to the department if the natural parents abandon the child or if the natural parents reclaim custody of the child.

HISTORY:
S. 2, ch. 89-345; s. 110, ch. 98-403.

Editor's notes.
Former s. 415.5088.

§ 39.8295. Review and removal of guardian advocate.

(1) At the end of the initial 1-year appointment, the court shall review the status of the child's care, health, and medical condition for the purpose of determining whether to reauthorize the appointment of the guardian advocate. If the court finds that all of the elements of s. 39.828 are still met, the court shall reauthorize the guardian advocate for another year.

(2) At any time, the court may, upon its own motion, or upon the motion of the department, a family member, or other interested person remove a guardian advocate. A guardian advocate shall be removed if the court finds that the guardian advocate is not properly discharging his or her responsibilities or is acting in a manner inconsistent with his or her appointment, that the parents have assumed parental responsibility to provide for the child, or that the child has been adjudicated dependent pursuant to this chapter.

HISTORY:
S. 2, ch. 89-345; s. 111, ch. 98-403.

Editor's notes.
Former s. 415.5089.

§ 39.8296. Statewide Guardian Ad Litem Office; legislative findings and intent; creation; appointment of executive director; duties of office.

(1) LEGISLATIVE FINDINGS AND INTENT.

(a) The Legislature finds that for the past 20 years, the Guardian Ad Litem Program has been the only mechanism for best interest representation for children in Florida who are involved in dependency proceedings.

(b) The Legislature also finds that while the Guardian Ad Litem Program has been supervised by court administration within the circuit courts since the program's inception, there is a perceived conflict of interest created by the supervision of program staff by the judges before whom they appear.

(c) The Legislature further finds that the Governor's Blue Ribbon Task Force concluded that "if there is any program that costs the least and benefits the most, this one is it," and that the guardian ad litem volunteer is an "indispensable intermediary between the child and the court, between the child and DCF."

(d) It is therefore the intent of the Legislature to place the Guardian Ad Litem Program in an appro-

priate place and provide a statewide infrastructure to increase functioning and standardization among the local programs currently operating in the 20 judicial circuits.

(2) STATEWIDE GUARDIAN AD LITEM OFFICE. — There is created a Statewide Guardian Ad Litem Office within the Justice Administrative Commission. The Justice Administrative Commission shall provide administrative support and service to the office to the extent requested by the executive director within the available resources of the commission. The Statewide Guardian Ad Litem Office shall not be subject to control, supervision, or direction by the Justice Administrative Commission in the performance of its duties, but the employees of the office shall be governed by the classification plan and salary and benefits plan approved by the Justice Administrative Commission.

(a) The head of the Statewide Guardian Ad Litem Office is the executive director, who shall be appointed by the Governor from a list of a minimum of three eligible applicants submitted by a Guardian Ad Litem Qualifications Committee. The Guardian Ad Litem Qualifications Committee shall be composed of five persons, two persons appointed by the Governor, two persons appointed by the Chief Justice of the Supreme Court, and one person appointed by the Statewide Guardian Ad Litem Association. The committee shall provide for statewide advertisement and the receiving of applications for the position of executive director. The Governor shall appoint an executive director from among the recommendations, or the Governor may reject the nominations and request the submission of new nominees. The executive director must have knowledge in dependency law and knowledge of social service delivery systems available to meet the needs of children who are abused, neglected, or abandoned. The executive director shall serve on a full-time basis and shall personally, or through representatives of the office, carry out the purposes and functions of the Statewide Guardian Ad Litem Office in accordance with state and federal law. The executive director shall report to the Governor. The executive director shall serve a 3-year term, subject to removal for cause by the Governor. Any person appointed to serve as the executive director may be permitted to serve more than one term.

(b) The Statewide Guardian Ad Litem Office shall, within available resources, have oversight responsibilities for and provide technical assistance to all guardian ad litem and attorney ad litem programs located within the judicial circuits.

1. The office shall identify the resources required to implement methods of collecting, reporting, and tracking reliable and consistent case data.

2. The office shall review the current guardian ad litem programs in Florida and other states.

3. The office, in consultation with local guardian ad litem offices, shall develop statewide performance measures and standards.

4. The office shall develop a guardian ad litem training program. The office shall establish a curriculum committee to develop the training program specified in this subparagraph. The curriculum committee shall include, but not be limited to, dependency judges, directors of circuit guardian ad litem programs, active certified guardians ad litem, a mental health professional who specializes in the treatment of children, a member of a child advocacy group, a representative of the Florida Coalition Against Domestic Violence, and a social worker experienced in working with victims and perpetrators of child abuse.

5. The office shall review the various methods of funding guardian ad litem programs, shall maximize the use of those funding sources to the extent possible, and shall review the kinds of services being provided by circuit guardian ad litem programs.

6. The office shall determine the feasibility or desirability of new concepts of organization, administration, financing, or service delivery designed to preserve the civil and constitutional rights and fulfill other needs of dependent children.

7. In an effort to promote normalcy and establish trust between a court-appointed volunteer guardian ad litem and a child alleged to be abused, abandoned, or neglected under this chapter, a guardian ad litem may transport a child. However, a guardian ad litem volunteer may not be required or directed by the program or a court to transport a child.

8. The office shall submit to the Governor, the President of the Senate, the Speaker of the House of Representatives, and the Chief Justice of the Supreme Court an interim report describing the progress of the office in meeting the goals as described in this section. The office shall submit to the Governor, the President of the Senate, the Speaker of the House of Representatives, and the Chief Justice of the Supreme Court a proposed plan including alternatives for meeting the state's guardian ad litem and attorney ad litem needs. This plan may include recommendations for less than the entire state, may include a phase-in system, and shall include estimates of the cost of each of the alternatives. Each year the office shall provide a status report and provide further recommendations to address the need for guardian ad litem services and related issues.

HISTORY:
S. 1, ch. 2003-53; s. 91, ch. 2003-399; s. 1, ch. 2006-18, eff. July 1, 2006; s. 5, ch. 2012-123, eff. July 1, 2012.

§ 39.8297. County funding for guardian ad litem employees.

(1) A county and the executive director of the Statewide Guardian Ad Litem Office may enter into an agreement by which the county agrees to provide funds to the local guardian ad litem office in order to employ persons who will assist in the operation of the guardian ad litem program in the county.

(2) The agreement, at a minimum, must provide that:

(a) Funding for the persons who are employed will be provided on at least a fiscal-year basis.

(b) The persons who are employed will be hired, supervised, managed, and terminated by the executive director of the Statewide Guardian Ad Litem Office. The statewide office is responsible for compliance with all requirements of federal and state employment laws, and shall fully indemnify the county from any liability under such laws, as authorized by s. 768.28(19), to the extent such liability is the result of the acts or omissions of the Statewide Guardian Ad Litem Office or its agents or employees.

(c) The county is the employer for purposes of s. 440.10 and chapter 443.

(d) Employees funded by the county under this section and other county employees may be aggregated for purposes of a flexible benefits plan pursuant to s. 125 of the Internal Revenue Code of 1986.

(e) Persons employed under this section may be terminated after a substantial breach of the agreement or because funding to the program has expired.

(3) Persons employed under this section may not be counted in a formula or similar process used by the Statewide Guardian Ad Litem Office to measure personnel needs of a judicial circuit's guardian ad litem program.

(4) Agreements created pursuant to this section do not obligate the state to allocate funds to a county to employ persons in the guardian ad litem program.

HISTORY:
S. 6, ch. 2012-123, eff. July 1, 2012.

§ 39.8298. Guardian Ad Litem direct-support organization.

(1) AUTHORITY. — The Statewide Guardian Ad Litem Office created under s. 39.8296 is authorized to create a direct-support organization.

(a) The direct-support organization must be a Florida corporation not for profit, incorporated under the provisions of chapter 617. The direct-support organization shall be exempt from paying fees under s. 617.0122.

(b) The direct-support organization shall be organized and operated to conduct programs and activities; raise funds; request and receive grants, gifts, and bequests of moneys; acquire, receive, hold, invest, and administer, in its own name, securities, funds, objects of value, or other property, real or personal; and make expenditures to or for the direct or indirect benefit of the Statewide Guardian Ad Litem Office.

(c) If the executive director of the Statewide Guardian Ad Litem Office determines the direct-support organization is operating in a manner that is inconsistent with the goals and purposes of the Statewide Guardian Ad Litem Office or not acting in the best interest of the state, the executive director may terminate the contract and thereafter the organization may not use the name of the Statewide Guardian Ad Litem Office.

(2) CONTRACT. — The direct-support organization shall operate under a written contract with the Statewide Guardian Ad Litem Office. The written contract must, at a minimum, provide for:

(a) Approval of the articles of incorporation and bylaws of the direct-support organization by the executive director of the Statewide Guardian Ad Litem Office.

(b) Submission of an annual budget for the approval by the executive director of the Statewide Guardian Ad Litem Office.

(c) The reversion without penalty to the Statewide Guardian Ad Litem Office, or to the state if the Statewide Guardian Ad Litem Office ceases to exist, of all moneys and property held in trust by the direct-support organization for the Statewide Guardian Ad Litem Office if the direct-support organization ceases to exist or if the contract is terminated.

(d) The fiscal year of the direct-support organization, which must begin July 1 of each year and end June 30 of the following year.

(e) The disclosure of material provisions of the contract and the distinction between the Statewide Guardian Ad Litem Office and the direct-support organization to donors of gifts, contributions, or bequests, as well as on all promotional and fundraising publications.

(3) BOARD OF DIRECTORS. — The executive director of the Statewide Guardian Ad Litem Office shall appoint a board of directors for the direct-support organization. The executive director may designate employees of the Statewide Guardian Ad Litem Office to serve on the board of directors. Members of the board shall serve at the pleasure of the executive director.

(4) USE OF PROPERTY AND SERVICES. — The executive director of the Statewide Guardian Ad Litem Office:

(a) May authorize the use of facilities and property other than money that are owned by the Statewide Guardian Ad Litem Office to be used by the direct-support organization.

(b) May authorize the use of personal services provided by employees of the Statewide Guardian Ad Litem Office. For the purposes of this section, the term "personal services" includes full-time personnel and part-time personnel as well as payroll processing.

(c) May prescribe the conditions by which the direct-support organization may use property, facilities, or personal services of the office.

(d) Shall not authorize the use of property, facilities, or personal services of the direct-support organization if the organization does not provide equal employment opportunities to all persons, regardless of race, color, religion, sex, age, or national origin.

(5) MONEYS. — Moneys of the direct-support organization may be held in a separate depository account in the name of the direct-support organization and subject to the provisions of the contract with the Statewide Guardian Ad Litem Office.

(6) ANNUAL AUDIT. — The direct-support organization shall provide for an annual financial audit in accordance with s. 215.981.

(7) LIMITS ON DIRECT-SUPPORT ORGANIZATION. — The direct-support organization shall not exercise any power under s. 617.0302(12) or (16). No state employee shall receive compensation from the direct-support organization for service on the board of directors or for services rendered to the direct-support organization.

(8) REPEAL. — This section is repealed October 1, 2018, unless reviewed and saved from repeal by the Legislature.

HISTORY:
S. 1, ch. 2007-149, eff. July 1, 2007; s. 6, ch. 2014-96, eff. June 13, 2014.

PART XII.
DOMESTIC VIOLENCE.

§ 39.901. Domestic violence cases; treatment and rehabilitation of victims and perpetrators; legislative intent.

The Legislature recognizes that certain persons who assault, batter, or otherwise abuse their spouses and the persons subject to such domestic violence are in need of treatment and rehabilitation. It is the intent of the Legislature to assist in the development of domestic violence centers for the victims of domestic violence and to provide a place where the parties involved may be separated until they can be properly assisted.

HISTORY:
S. 1, ch. 78-281; s. 1, ch. 84-343; s. 113, ch. 98-403.

Editor's notes.
Former s. 409.601; s. 415.601.

§ 39.902. Definitions.

As used in this part, the term:

(1) "Coalition" means the Florida Coalition Against Domestic Violence.

(2) "Domestic violence" has the meaning set forth in s. 741.28.

(3) "Domestic violence center" means an agency that provides services to victims of domestic violence, as its primary mission.

(4) "Family or household member" has the meaning set forth in s. 741.28.

HISTORY:

S. 2, ch. 78-281; s. 2, ch. 79-402; s. 1, ch. 82-135; s. 71, ch. 83-218; s. 1, ch. 84-128; s. 2, ch. 84-343; s. 17, ch. 92-58; s. 19, ch. 93-200; s. 30, ch. 94-134; s. 30, ch. 94-135; s. 137, ch. 97-101; s. 114, ch. 98-403; s. 3, ch. 2002-55; s. 1, ch. 2012-147, eff. July 1, 2012.

Editor's notes.

Former s. 409.602; s. 415.602.

§ 39.903. Duties and functions of the department with respect to domestic violence.

The department shall:

(1) Operate the domestic violence program and, in collaboration with the coalition, shall coordinate and administer statewide activities related to the prevention of domestic violence.

(2) Receive and approve or reject applications for initial certification of domestic violence centers. The department shall annually renew the certification thereafter upon receipt of a favorable monitoring report by the coalition.

(3) Have the right to enter and inspect the premises of domestic violence centers that are applying for an initial certification or facing potential suspension or revocation of certification to effectively evaluate the state of compliance with minimum standards.

(4) Promote the involvement of certified domestic violence centers in the coordination, development, and planning of domestic violence programming in the circuits.

(5) Coordinate with state agencies that have health, education, or criminal justice responsibilities to raise awareness of domestic violence and promote consistent policy implementation.

(6) Cooperate with, assist in, and participate in, programs of other properly qualified state agencies, including any agency of the Federal Government, schools of medicine, hospitals, and clinics, in planning and conducting research on the prevention of domestic violence and the provision of services to clients.

(7) Contract with the coalition for the delivery and management of services for the state's domestic violence program. Services under this contract include, but are not limited to, the administration of contracts and grants.

(8) Consider applications from certified domestic violence centers for capital improvement grants and award those grants pursuant to s. 39.9055.

(9) Adopt by rule procedures to administer this section, including developing criteria for the approval, suspension, or rejection of certification of domestic violence centers and developing minimum standards for domestic violence centers to ensure the health and safety of the clients in the centers.

HISTORY:

S. 3, ch. 78-281; s. 3, ch. 79-402; ss. 2, 3, ch. 84-128; ss. 3, 5, ch. 84-343; s. 31, ch. 94-134; s. 31, ch. 94-135; s. 2, ch. 95-187; s. 55, ch. 96-418; s. 115, ch. 98-403; s. 4, ch. 2002-55; s. 1, ch. 2003-11; s. 2, ch. 2012-147, eff. July 1, 2012.

Editor's notes.

Former s. 409.603; s. 415.603.

§ 39.9035. Duties and functions of the coalition with respect to domestic violence.

As part of its delivery and management of the delivery of services for the state's domestic violence program, the coalition shall:

(1) Implement, administer, and evaluate all domestic violence services provided by the certified domestic violence centers.

(2) Receive and approve or reject applications for funding of certified domestic violence centers. When approving funding for a newly certified domestic violence center, the coalition shall make every effort to minimize any adverse economic impact on existing certified domestic violence centers or services provided within the same service area. In order to minimize duplication of services, the coalition shall make every effort to encourage subcontracting relationships with existing certified domestic violence centers within the same service area. In distributing funds allocated by the Legislature for certified domestic violence centers, the coalition shall use a formula approved by the department as specified in s. 39.905(7)(a).

(3) Evaluate certified domestic violence centers in order to determine compliance with minimum certification standards.

(4) Have the right to enter and inspect the premises of certified domestic violence centers for monitoring purposes.

HISTORY:

S. 3, ch. 2012-147, eff. July 1, 2012.

§ 39.904. Report to the Legislature on the status of domestic violence cases.

On or before January 1 of each year, the coalition shall furnish to the President of the Senate and the Speaker of the House of Representatives a report on the status of domestic violence in this state, which must include, but need not be limited to, the following:

(1) The incidence of domestic violence in this state.

(2) An identification of the areas of the state where domestic violence is of significant proportions, indicating the number of cases of domestic violence officially reported, as well as an assessment of the degree of unreported cases of domestic violence.

(3) An identification and description of the types of programs in the state which assist victims of domestic violence or persons who commit domestic violence, including information on funding for the programs.

(4) The number of persons who receive services from local certified domestic violence programs that receive funding through the coalition.

(5) The incidence of domestic violence homicides in the state, including information and data collected from state and local domestic violence fatality review teams.

HISTORY:
S. 4, ch. 84-343; s. 138, ch. 97-101; s. 116, ch. 98-403; s. 4, ch. 2012-147, eff. July 1, 2012.

Editor's notes.
Former s. 415.604.

§ 39.905. Domestic violence centers.

(1) Domestic violence centers certified under this part must:

(a) Provide a facility which will serve as a center to receive and house persons who are victims of domestic violence. For the purpose of this part, minor children and other dependents of a victim, when such dependents are partly or wholly dependent on the victim for support or services, may be sheltered with the victim in a domestic violence center.

(b) Receive the annual written endorsement of local law enforcement agencies.

(c) Provide minimum services that include, but are not limited to, information and referral services, counseling and case management services, temporary emergency shelter for more than 24 hours, a 24-hour hotline, training for law enforcement personnel, assessment and appropriate referral of resident children, and educational services for community awareness relative to the incidence of domestic violence, the prevention of such violence, and the services available for persons engaged in or subject to domestic violence. If a 24-hour hotline, professional training, or community education is already provided by a certified domestic violence center within its designated service area, the department may exempt such certification requirements for a new center serving the same service area in order to avoid duplication of services.

(d) Participate in the provision of orientation and training programs developed for law enforcement officers, social workers, and other professionals and paraprofessionals who work with domestic violence victims to better enable such persons to deal effectively with incidents of domestic violence.

(e) Establish and maintain a board of directors composed of at least three citizens, one of whom must be a member of a local, municipal, or county law enforcement agency.

(f) Comply with rules adopted pursuant to this part.

(g) File with the coalition a list of the names of the domestic violence advocates who are employed or who volunteer at the domestic violence center who may claim a privilege under s. 90.5036 to refuse to disclose a confidential communication between a victim of domestic violence and the advocate regarding the domestic violence inflicted upon the victim. The list must include the title of the position held by the advocate whose name is listed and a description of the duties of that position. A domestic violence center must file amendments to this list as necessary.

(h) Demonstrate local need and ability to sustain operations through a history of 18 consecutive months' operation as a domestic violence center, including 12 months' operation of an emergency shelter as provided in paragraph (c), and a business plan which addresses future operations and funding of future operations.

(i) If its center is a new center applying for certification, demonstrate that the services provided address a need identified in the most current statewide needs assessment approved by the department. If the center applying for initial certification proposes providing services in an area that has an existing certified domestic violence center, the center applying for initial certification must demonstrate the unmet need in that service area and describe its efforts to avoid duplication of services.

(2) If the department finds that there is failure by a center to comply with the requirements established under this part or with the rules adopted pursuant thereto, the department may deny, suspend, or revoke the certification of the center.

(3) The annual certificate automatically expires on June 30 of each state fiscal year unless the certification is temporarily extended to allow the center to implement a corrective action plan.

(4) The domestic violence centers shall establish procedures pursuant to which persons subject to domestic violence may seek services from these centers voluntarily.

(5) Domestic violence centers may be established throughout the state when private, local, state, or federal funds are available and a need is demonstrated.

(6) In order to receive state funds, a center must:

(a) Obtain certification pursuant to this part. However, the issuance of a certificate does not obligate the coalition to provide funding.

(b) Receive at least 25 percent of its funding from one or more local, municipal, or county sources, public or private. Contributions in kind, whether materials, commodities, transportation, office space, other types of facilities, or personal services, may be evaluated and counted as part of the required local funding.

(7)(a) All funds collected and appropriated to the domestic violence program for certified domestic violence centers shall be distributed annually according to an allocation formula approved by the department. In developing the formula, the factors of population, rural characteristics, geographical area, and the incidence of domestic violence shall be considered.

(b) A contract between the coalition and a certified domestic violence center shall contain provisions ensuring the availability and geographic accessibility of services throughout the service area. For this purpose, a center may distribute funds through subcontracts or to center satellites, if such arrangements and any subcontracts are approved by the coalition.

(8) If any of the required services are exempted from certification by the department under this section, the center may not receive funding from the coalition for those services.

HISTORY:
S. 5, ch. 78-281; s. 4, ch. 79-402; s. 2, ch. 82-135; s. 4, ch. 82-192; s. 3, ch. 84-128; s. 5, ch. 84-343; s. 32, ch. 94-134; s. 32, ch. 94-135; ss. 3, 8, ch. 95-187; s. 117, ch. 98-403; s. 2, ch. 2003-11; s. 5, ch. 2012-147, eff. July 1, 2012.

Editor's notes.
Former s. 409.605; s. 415.605.

§ 39.9055. Certified domestic violence centers; capital improvement grant program.

There is established a certified domestic violence center capital improvement grant program.

(1) A certified domestic violence center as defined in s. 39.905 may apply to the Department of Children and Families for a capital improvement grant. The grant application must provide information that includes:

(a) A statement specifying the capital improvement that the certified domestic violence center proposes to make with the grant funds.

(b) The proposed strategy for making the capital improvement.

(c) The organizational structure that will carry out the capital improvement.

(d) Evidence that the certified domestic violence center has difficulty in obtaining funding or that funds available for the proposed improvement are inadequate.

(e) Evidence that the funds will assist in meeting the needs of victims of domestic violence and their children in the certified domestic violence center service area.

(f) Evidence of a satisfactory recordkeeping system to account for fund expenditures.

(g) Evidence of ability to generate local match.

(2) Certified domestic violence centers as defined in s. 39.905 may receive funding subject to legislative appropriation, upon application to the Department of Children and Families, for projects to construct, acquire, repair, improve, or upgrade systems, facilities, or equipment, subject to availability of funds. An award of funds under this section must be made in accordance with a needs assessment developed by the Florida Coalition Against Domestic Violence and the Department of Children and Families. The department annually shall perform this needs assessment and shall rank in order of need those centers that are requesting funds for capital improvement.

(3) The Department of Children and Families shall, in collaboration with the Florida Coalition Against Domestic Violence, establish criteria for awarding the capital improvement funds that must be used exclusively for support and assistance with the capital improvement needs of the certified domestic violence centers, as defined in s. 39.905.

(4) The Department of Children and Families shall ensure that the funds awarded under this section are used solely for the purposes specified in this section. The department will also ensure that the grant process maintains the confidentiality of the location of the certified domestic violence centers, pursuant to s. 39.908. The total amount of grant moneys awarded under this section may not exceed the amount appropriated for this program.

HISTORY:
S. 2, ch. 2000-220; s. 22, ch. 2014-19, eff. July 1, 2014.

§ 39.906. Referral to centers and notice of rights.

Any law enforcement officer who investigates an alleged incident of domestic violence shall advise the victim of such violence that there is a domestic violence center from which the victim may receive services. The law enforcement officer shall give the victim immediate notice of the legal rights and remedies available in accordance with the provisions of s. 741.29.

HISTORY:
S. 7, ch. 78-281; s. 6, ch. 79-402; s. 6, ch. 84-343; s. 28, ch. 94-134; s. 28, ch. 94-135; s. 118, ch. 98-403.

Editor's notes.
Former s. 409.607; s. 415.606.

§ 39.908. Confidentiality of information received by department or domestic violence center.

(1) Information about clients received by the department or by authorized persons employed by or volunteering services to a domestic violence center, through files, reports, inspection, or otherwise, is confidential and exempt from the provisions of s. 119.07(1). Information about the location of domestic violence centers and facilities is confidential and exempt from the provisions of s. 119.07(1).

(2) Information about domestic violence center clients may not be disclosed without the written con-

sent of the client to whom the information or records pertain. For the purpose of state law regarding searches and seizures, domestic violence centers shall be treated as private dwelling places. Information about a client or the location of a domestic violence center may be given by center staff or volunteers to law enforcement, firefighting, medical, or other personnel in the following circumstances:

(a) To medical personnel in a medical emergency.

(b) Upon a court order based upon an application by a law enforcement officer for a criminal arrest warrant which alleges that the individual sought to be arrested is located at the domestic violence shelter.

(c) Upon a search warrant that specifies the individual or object of the search and alleges that the individual or object is located at the shelter.

(d) To firefighting personnel in a fire emergency.

(e) To any other person necessary to maintain the safety and health standards in the domestic violence shelter.

(f) Information solely about the location of the domestic violence shelter may be given to those with whom the agency has an established business relationship.

(3) The restriction on the disclosure or use of the information about domestic violence center clients does not apply to:

(a) Communications from domestic violence shelter staff or volunteers to law enforcement officers when the information is directly related to a client's commission of a crime or threat to commit a crime on the premises of a domestic violence shelter; or

(b) Reporting suspected abuse of a child or a vulnerable adult as required by law. However, when cooperating with protective investigation services staff, the domestic violence shelter staff and volunteers must protect the confidentiality of other clients at the domestic violence center.

HISTORY:

S. 6, ch. 78-281; s. 5, ch. 79-402; s. 7, ch. 84-343; s. 22, ch. 91-71; s. 33, ch. 94-134; s. 33, ch. 94-135; s. 277, ch. 96-406; s. 119, ch. 98-403.

Editor's notes.

Former s. 409.606; s. 415.608.

TITLE XLVII.

CRIMINAL PROCEDURE AND CORRECTIONS.

CHAPTER 984.
CHILDREN AND FAMILIES IN NEED OF SERVICES.

§ 984.01. Purposes and intent; personnel standards and screening.

(1) The purposes of this chapter are:

(a) To provide judicial and other procedures to assure due process through which children and other interested parties are assured fair hearings by a respectful and respected court or other tribunal and the recognition, protection, and enforcement of their constitutional and other legal rights, while ensuring that public safety interests and the authority and dignity of the courts are adequately protected.

(b) To provide for the care, safety, and protection of children in an environment that fosters healthy social, emotional, intellectual, and physical development; to ensure secure and safe custody; and to promote the health and well-being of all children under the state's care.

(c) To ensure the protection of society, by providing for a comprehensive standardized assessment of the child's needs so that the most appropriate control, discipline, punishment, and treatment can be administered consistent with the seriousness of the act committed, the community's long-term need for public safety, the prior record of the child, and the specific rehabilitation needs of the child, while also providing restitution, whenever possible, to the victim of the offense.

(d) To preserve and strengthen the child's family ties whenever possible, by providing for removal of the child from parental custody only when his or her welfare or the safety and protection of the public cannot be adequately safeguarded without such removal; and, when the child is removed from his or her own family, to secure custody, care, and discipline for the child as nearly as possible equivalent to that which should have been given by the parents; and to assure, in all cases in which a child must be permanently removed from parental custody, that the child be placed in an approved family home, adoptive home, independent living program, or other placement that provides the most stable and permanent living arrangement for the child, as determined by the court.

(e)1. To assure that the adjudication and disposition of a child alleged or found to have committed a violation of Florida law be exercised with appropriate discretion and in keeping with the serious-ness of the offense and the need for treatment services, and that all findings made under this chapter be based upon facts presented at a hearing that meets the constitutional standards of fundamental fairness and due process.

2. To assure that the sentencing and placement of a child tried as an adult be appropriate and in keeping with the seriousness of the offense and the child's need for rehabilitative services, and that the proceedings and procedures applicable to such sentencing and placement be applied within the full framework of constitutional standards of fundamental fairness and due process.

(f) To provide children committed to the Department of Juvenile Justice with training in life skills, including career education.

(2) The Department of Juvenile Justice or the Department of Children and Families, as appropriate, may contract with the Federal Government, other state departments and agencies, county and municipal governments and agencies, public and private agencies, and private individuals and corporations in carrying out the purposes of, and the responsibilities established in, this chapter.

(a) If the department contracts with a provider for any program for children, all personnel, including owners, operators, employees, and volunteers, in the facility must be of good moral character. Each contract entered into by either department for services delivered on an appointment or intermittent basis by a provider that does not have regular custodial responsibility for children and each contract with a school for before or aftercare services must ensure that the owners, operators, and all personnel who have direct contact with children are of good moral character. A volunteer who assists on an intermittent basis for less than 10 hours per month need not be screened if a person who meets the screening requirement of this section is always present and has the volunteer in his or her line of sight.

(b) The Department of Juvenile Justice and the Department of Children and Families shall require employment screening pursuant to chapter 435, using the level 2 standards set forth in that chapter for personnel in programs for children or youths.

(c) The Department of Juvenile Justice or the Department of Children and Families may grant exemptions from disqualification from working with children as provided in s. 435.07.

(3) It is the intent of the Legislature that this chapter be liberally interpreted and construed in conformity with its declared purposes.

HISTORY:
S. 87, ch. 97-238; s. 11, ch. 2001-125; s. 63, ch. 2004-267; s. 47, ch. 2010-114, eff. Aug. 1, 2010; s. 332, ch. 2014-19, eff. July 1, 2014.

Editor's notes.
Section 63, ch. 2004-267, reenacted paragraph (b) of subsection (2) without change to incorporate amendments to statutory sections referenced therein.

Section 58, ch. 2010-114 provides: "The changes made by this act are intended to be prospective in nature. It is not intended that persons who are employed or licensed on the effective date of this act be rescreened until such time as they are otherwise required to be rescreened pursuant to law, at which time they must meet the requirements for screening as set forth in this act."

§ 984.02. Legislative intent for the juvenile justice system.

(1) GENERAL PROTECTIONS FOR CHILDREN. — It is a purpose of the Legislature that the children of this state be provided with the following protections:

(a) Protection from abuse, neglect, and exploitation.

(b) A permanent and stable home.

(c) A safe and nurturing environment which will preserve a sense of personal dignity and integrity.

(d) Adequate nutrition, shelter, and clothing.

(e) Effective treatment to address physical, social, and emotional needs, regardless of geographical location.

(f) Equal opportunity and access to quality and effective education which will meet the individual needs of each child, and to recreation and other community resources to develop individual abilities.

(g) Access to preventive services.

(h) An independent, trained advocate when intervention is necessary and a skilled guardian or caretaker in a safe environment when alternative placement is necessary.

(2) SUBSTANCE ABUSE SERVICES. — The Legislature finds that children in the care of the state's dependency and delinquency systems need appropriate health care services, that the impact of substance abuse on health indicates the need for health care services to include substance abuse services where appropriate, and that it is in the state's best interest that such children be provided the services they need to enable them to become and remain independent of state care. In order to provide these services, the state's dependency and delinquency systems must have the ability to identify and provide appropriate intervention and treatment for children with personal or family-related substance abuse problems. It is therefore the purpose of the Legislature to provide authority for the state to contract with community substance abuse treatment providers for the development and operation of specialized support and overlay services for the dependency and delinquency systems, which will be fully implemented and utilized as resources permit.

(3) JUVENILE JUSTICE AND DELINQUENCY PREVENTION. — It is the policy of the state with respect to juvenile justice and delinquency prevention to first protect the public from acts of delinquency. In addition, it is the policy of the state to:

(a) Develop and implement effective methods of preventing and reducing acts of delinquency, with a focus on maintaining and strengthening the family as a whole so that children may remain in their homes or communities.

(b) Develop and implement effective programs to prevent delinquency, to divert children from the traditional juvenile justice system, to intervene at an early stage of delinquency, and to provide critically needed alternatives to institutionalization and deep-end commitment.

(c) Provide well-trained personnel, high-quality services, and cost-effective programs within the juvenile justice system.

(d) Increase the capacity of local governments and public and private agencies to conduct rehabilitative treatment programs and to provide research, evaluation, and training services in the field of juvenile delinquency prevention.

The Legislature intends that detention care, in addition to providing secure and safe custody, will promote the health and well-being of the children committed thereto and provide an environment that fosters their social, emotional, intellectual, and physical development.

(4) PARENTAL, CUSTODIAL, AND GUARDIAN RESPONSIBILITIES. — Parents, custodians, and guardians are deemed by the state to be responsible for providing their children with sufficient support, guidance, and supervision to deter their participation in delinquent acts. The state further recognizes that the ability of parents, custodians, and guardians to fulfill those responsibilities can be greatly impaired by economic, social, behavioral, emotional, and related problems. It is therefore the policy of the Legislature that it is the state's responsibility to ensure that factors impeding the ability of caretakers to fulfill their responsibilities are identified through the delinquency intake process and that appropriate recommendations to address those problems are considered in any judicial or nonjudicial proceeding.

HISTORY:
S. 88, ch. 97-238.

§ 984.03. Definitions.

When used in this chapter, the term:

(1) "Abandoned" means a situation in which the parent or legal custodian of a child or, in the absence of a parent or legal custodian, the person responsible for the child's welfare, while being able, makes no provision for the child's support and makes no effort to communicate with the child, which situation is sufficient to evince a willful rejection of parental obligations. If the efforts of such parent or legal custodian, or person primarily responsible for the

child's welfare to support and communicate with the child are, in the opinion of the court, only marginal efforts that do not evince a settled purpose to assume all parental duties, the court may declare the child to be abandoned. The term "abandoned" does not include a "child in need of services" as defined in subsection (9) or a "family in need of services" as defined in subsection (25). The incarceration of a parent, legal custodian, or person responsible for a child's welfare does not constitute a bar to a finding of abandonment.

(2) "Abuse" means any willful act that results in any physical, mental, or sexual injury that causes or is likely to cause the child's physical, mental, or emotional health to be significantly impaired. Corporal discipline of a child by a parent or guardian for disciplinary purposes does not in itself constitute abuse when it does not result in harm to the child as defined in s. 39.01.

(3) "Addictions receiving facility" means a substance abuse service provider as defined in chapter 397.

(4) "Adjudicatory hearing" means a hearing for the court to determine whether or not the facts support the allegations stated in the petition as is provided for under s. 984.20(2) in child-in-need-of-services cases.

(5) "Adult" means any natural person other than a child.

(6) "Authorized agent" or "designee" of the department means a person or agency assigned or designated by the Department of Juvenile Justice or the Department of Children and Families, as appropriate, to perform duties or exercise powers pursuant to this chapter and includes contract providers and their employees for purposes of providing services to and managing cases of children in need of services and families in need of services.

(7) "Caretaker/homemaker" means an authorized agent of the Department of Children and Families who shall remain in the child's home with the child until a parent, legal guardian, or relative of the child enters the home and is capable of assuming and agrees to assume charge of the child.

(8) "Child" or "juvenile" or "youth" means any unmarried person under the age of 18 who has not been emancipated by order of the court and who has been found or alleged to be dependent, in need of services, or from a family in need of services; or any married or unmarried person who is charged with a violation of law occurring prior to the time that person reached the age of 18 years.

(9) "Child in need of services" means a child for whom there is no pending investigation into an allegation or suspicion of abuse, neglect, or abandonment; no pending referral alleging the child is delinquent; or no current supervision by the Department of Juvenile Justice or the Department of Chil-

dren and Families for an adjudication of dependency or delinquency. The child must also, pursuant to this chapter, be found by the court:

(a) To have persistently run away from the child's parents or legal custodians despite reasonable efforts of the child, the parents or legal custodians, and appropriate agencies to remedy the conditions contributing to the behavior. Reasonable efforts shall include voluntary participation by the child's parents or legal custodians and the child in family mediation, services, and treatment offered by the Department of Juvenile Justice or the Department of Children and Families;

(b) To be habitually truant from school, while subject to compulsory school attendance, despite reasonable efforts to remedy the situation pursuant to ss. 1003.26 and 1003.27 and through voluntary participation by the child's parents or legal custodians and by the child in family mediation, services, and treatment offered by the Department of Juvenile Justice or the Department of Children and Families; or

(c) To have persistently disobeyed the reasonable and lawful demands of the child's parents or legal custodians, and to be beyond their control despite efforts by the child's parents or legal custodians and appropriate agencies to remedy the conditions contributing to the behavior. Reasonable efforts may include such things as good faith participation in family or individual counseling.

(10) "Child support" means a court-ordered obligation, enforced under chapter 61 and ss. 409.2551 - 409.2597, for monetary support for the care, maintenance, training, and education of a child.

(11) "Child who has been found to have committed a delinquent act" means a child who, pursuant to the provisions of chapter 985, is found by a court to have committed a violation of law or to be in direct or indirect contempt of court, except that this definition shall not include an act constituting contempt of court arising out of a dependency proceeding or a proceeding pursuant to this chapter.

(12) "Child who is found to be dependent" or "dependent child" means a child who, pursuant to this chapter, is found by the court:

(a) To have been abandoned, abused, or neglected by the child's parents or other custodians.

(b) To have been surrendered to the former Department of Health and Rehabilitative Services, the Department of Children and Families, or a licensed child-placing agency for purpose of adoption.

(c) To have been voluntarily placed with a licensed child-caring agency, a licensed child-placing agency, an adult relative, the former Department of Health and Rehabilitative Services, or the Department of Children and Families, after which placement, under the requirements of this chapter, a case plan has expired and the parent or parents have failed to substantially comply with the requirements of the plan.

(d) To have been voluntarily placed with a licensed child-placing agency for the purposes of subsequent adoption and a natural parent or parents signed a consent pursuant to the Florida Rules of Juvenile Procedure.

(e) To have no parent, legal custodian, or responsible adult relative to provide supervision and care.

(f) To be at substantial risk of imminent abuse or neglect by the parent or parents or the custodian.

(13) "Circuit" means any of the 20 judicial circuits as set forth in s. 26.021.

(14) "Comprehensive assessment" or "assessment" means the gathering of information for the evaluation of a juvenile offender's or a child's physical, psychological, educational, vocational, and social condition and family environment as they relate to the child's need for rehabilitative and treatment services, including substance abuse treatment services, mental health services, developmental services, literacy services, medical services, family services, and other specialized services, as appropriate.

(15) "Court," unless otherwise expressly stated, means the circuit court assigned to exercise jurisdiction under this chapter.

(16) "Delinquency program" means any intake, community control, or similar program; regional detention center or facility; or community-based program, whether owned and operated by or contracted by the Department of Juvenile Justice, or institution owned and operated by or contracted by the Department of Juvenile Justice, which provides intake, supervision, or custody and care of children who are alleged to be or who have been found to be delinquent pursuant to chapter 985.

(17) "Department" means the Department of Juvenile Justice.

(18) "Detention care" means the temporary care of a child in secure, nonsecure, or home detention, pending a court adjudication or disposition or execution of a court order. There are three types of detention care, as follows:

(a) "Secure detention" means temporary custody of the child while the child is under the physical restriction of a detention center or facility pending adjudication, disposition, or placement.

(b) "Nonsecure detention" means temporary custody of the child while the child is in a residential home in the community in a physically nonrestrictive environment under the supervision of the Department of Juvenile Justice pending adjudication, disposition, or placement.

(c) "Home detention" means temporary custody of the child while the child is released to the custody of the parent, guardian, or custodian in a physically nonrestrictive environment under the supervision of the Department of Juvenile Justice staff pending adjudication, disposition, or placement.

(19) "Detention center or facility" means a facility used pending court adjudication or disposition or execution of court order for the temporary care of a child alleged or found to have committed a violation of law. A detention center or facility may provide secure or nonsecure custody. A facility used for the commitment of adjudicated delinquents shall not be considered a detention center or facility.

(20) "Detention hearing" means a hearing for the court to determine if a child should be placed in temporary custody, as provided for under s. 39.402, in dependency cases.

(21) "Diligent efforts of social service agency" means reasonable efforts to provide social services or reunification services made by any social service agency as defined in this section that is a party to a case plan.

(22) "Diligent search" means the efforts of a social service agency to locate a parent or prospective parent whose identity or location is unknown, or a relative made known to the social services agency by the parent or custodian of a child. When the search is for a parent, prospective parent, or relative of a child in the custody of the department, this search must be initiated as soon as the agency is made aware of the existence of such parent, prospective parent, or relative. A diligent search shall include interviews with persons who are likely to have information about the identity or location of the person being sought, comprehensive database searches, and records searches, including searches of employment, residence, utilities, Armed Forces, vehicle registration, child support enforcement, law enforcement, and corrections records, and any other records likely to result in identifying and locating the person being sought. The initial diligent search must be completed within 90 days after a child is taken into custody. After the completion of the initial diligent search, the department, unless excused by the court, shall have a continuing duty to search for relatives with whom it may be appropriate to place the child, until such relatives are found or until the child is placed for adoption.

(23) "Disposition hearing" means a hearing in which the court determines the most appropriate dispositional services in the least restrictive available setting provided for under s. 984.20(3), in child-in-need-of-services cases.

(24) "Family" means a collective body of persons, consisting of a child and a parent, guardian, adult custodian, or adult relative, in which:

(a) The persons reside in the same house or living unit; or

(b) The parent, guardian, adult custodian, or adult relative has a legal responsibility by blood, marriage, or court order to support or care for the child.

(25) "Family in need of services" means a family that has a child who is running away; who is persistently disobeying reasonable and lawful demands of the parent or legal custodian and is beyond the control of the parent or legal custodian; or who is habitually truant from school or engaging in other serious behaviors that place the child at risk of future abuse, neglect, or abandonment or at risk of entering the juvenile justice system. The child must be referred to a law enforcement agency, the Department of Juvenile Justice, or an agency contracted to provide services to children in need of services. A family is not eligible to receive services if, at the time of the referral, there is an open investigation into an allegation of abuse, neglect, or abandonment or if the child is currently under supervision by the Department of Juvenile Justice or the Department of Children and Families due to an adjudication of dependency or delinquency.

(26) "Foster care" means care provided a child in a foster family or boarding home, group home, agency boarding home, child care institution, or any combination thereof.

(27) "Habitually truant" means that:

(a) The child has 15 unexcused absences within 90 calendar days with or without the knowledge or justifiable consent of the child's parent or legal guardian, is subject to compulsory school attendance under s. 1003.21(1) and (2)(a), and is not exempt under s. 1003.21(3), s. 1003.24, or any other exemptions specified by law or the rules of the State Board of Education.

(b) Activities to determine the cause, and to attempt the remediation, of the child's truant behavior under ss. 1003.26 and 1003.27(3), have been completed.

If a child who is subject to compulsory school attendance is responsive to the interventions described in ss. 1003.26 and 1003.27(3) and has completed the necessary requirements to pass the current grade as indicated in the district pupil progression plan, the child shall not be determined to be habitually truant and shall be passed. If a child within the compulsory school attendance age has 15 unexcused absences within 90 calendar days or fails to enroll in school, the State Attorney may, or the appropriate jurisdictional agency shall, file a child-in-need-of-services petition if recommended by the case staffing committee, unless it is determined that another alternative action is preferable. The failure or refusal of the parent or legal guardian or the child to participate, or make a good faith effort to participate, in the activities prescribed to remedy the truant behavior, or the failure or refusal of the child to return to school after participation in activities required by this subsection, or the failure of the child to stop the truant behavior after the school administration and the Department of Juvenile Justice have worked with the child as described in ss. 1003.26 and 1003.27(3) shall be handled as prescribed in s. 1003.27.

(28) "Intake" means the initial acceptance and screening by the Department of Juvenile Justice of a complaint or a law enforcement report or probable cause affidavit of delinquency, family in need of services, or child in need of services to determine the recommendation to be taken in the best interests of the child, the family, and the community. The emphasis of intake is on diversion and the least restrictive available services. Consequently, intake includes such alternatives as:

(a) The disposition of the complaint, report, or probable cause affidavit without court or public agency action or judicial handling when appropriate.

(b) The referral of the child to another public or private agency when appropriate.

(c) The recommendation by the juvenile probation officer of judicial handling when appropriate and warranted.

(29) "Judge" means the circuit judge exercising jurisdiction pursuant to this chapter.

(30) "Juvenile justice continuum" includes, but is not limited to, delinquency prevention programs and services designed for the purpose of preventing or reducing delinquent acts, including criminal activity by criminal gangs and juvenile arrests, as well as programs and services targeted at children who have committed delinquent acts, and children who have previously been committed to residential treatment programs for delinquents. The term includes children-in-need-of-services and families-in-need-of-services programs; conditional release; substance abuse and mental health programs; educational and vocational programs; recreational programs; community services programs; community service work programs; and alternative dispute resolution programs serving children at risk of delinquency and their families, whether offered or delivered by state or local governmental entities, public or private for-profit or not-for-profit organizations, or religious or charitable organizations.

(31) "Juvenile probation officer" means the authorized agent of the department who performs and directs intake, assessment, probation, or conditional release, and other related services.

(32) "Legal custody" means a legal status created by court order or letter of guardianship which vests in a custodian of the person or guardian, whether an agency or an individual, the right to have physical custody of the child and the right and duty to

protect, train, and discipline the child and to provide him or her with food, shelter, education, and ordinary medical, dental, psychiatric, and psychological care.

(33) "Licensed child-caring agency" means a person, society, association, or agency licensed by the Department of Children and Families to care for, receive, and board children.

(34) "Licensed health care professional" means a physician licensed under chapter 458, an osteopathic physician licensed under chapter 459, a nurse licensed under part I of chapter 464, a physician assistant licensed under chapter 458 or chapter 459, or a dentist licensed under chapter 466.

(35) "Mediation" means a process whereby a neutral third person called a mediator acts to encourage and facilitate the resolution of a dispute between two or more parties. It is an informal and nonadversarial process with the objective of helping the disputing parties reach a mutually acceptable and voluntary agreement. In mediation, decisionmaking authority rests with the parties. The role of the mediator includes, but is not limited to, assisting the parties in identifying issues, fostering joint problem solving, and exploring settlement alternatives.

(36) "Necessary medical treatment" means care that is necessary within a reasonable degree of medical certainty to prevent the deterioration of a child's condition or to alleviate immediate pain of a child.

(37) "Neglect" occurs when the parent or legal custodian of a child or, in the absence of a parent or legal custodian, the person primarily responsible for the child's welfare deprives a child of, or allows a child to be deprived of, necessary food, clothing, shelter, or medical treatment or permits a child to live in an environment when such deprivation or environment causes the child's physical, mental, or emotional health to be significantly impaired or to be in danger of being significantly impaired. The foregoing circumstances shall not be considered neglect if caused primarily by financial inability unless actual services for relief have been offered to and rejected by such person. A parent or guardian legitimately practicing religious beliefs in accordance with a recognized church or religious organization who thereby does not provide specific medical treatment for a child shall not, for that reason alone, be considered a negligent parent or guardian; however, such an exception does not preclude a court from ordering the following services to be provided, when the health of the child so requires:

(a) Medical services from a licensed physician, dentist, optometrist, podiatric physician, or other qualified health care provider; or

(b) Treatment by a duly accredited practitioner who relies solely on spiritual means for healing in accordance with the tenets and practices of a well-recognized church or religious organization.

(38) "Next of kin" means an adult relative of a child who is the child's brother, sister, grandparent, aunt, uncle, or first cousin.

(39) "Parent" means a woman who gives birth to a child and a man whose consent to the adoption of the child would be required under s. 63.062(1). If a child has been legally adopted, the term "parent" means the adoptive mother or father of the child. The term does not include an individual whose parental relationship to the child has been legally terminated, or an alleged or prospective parent, unless the parental status falls within the terms of either s. 39.503(1) or s. 63.062(1).

(40) "Participant," for purposes of a shelter proceeding, means any person who is not a party but who should receive notice of hearings involving the child, including foster parents, identified prospective parents, grandparents entitled to priority for adoption consideration under s. 63.0425, actual custodians of the child, and any other person whose participation may be in the best interest of the child. Participants may be granted leave by the court to be heard without the necessity of filing a motion to intervene.

(41) "Party," for purposes of a shelter proceeding, means the parent of the child, the petitioner, the department, the guardian ad litem when one has been appointed, and the child. The presence of the child may be excused by order of the court when presence would not be in the child's best interest. Notice to the child may be excused by order of the court when the age, capacity, or other condition of the child is such that the notice would be meaningless or detrimental to the child.

(42) "Preliminary screening" means the gathering of preliminary information to be used in determining a child's need for further evaluation or assessment or for referral for other substance abuse services through means such as psychosocial interviews; urine and breathalyzer screenings; and reviews of available educational, delinquency, and dependency records of the child.

(43) "Preventive services" means social services and other supportive and rehabilitative services provided to the parent of the child, the legal guardian of the child, or the custodian of the child and to the child for the purpose of averting the removal of the child from the home or disruption of a family which will or could result in an adjudication that orders the placement of a child into foster care or into the delinquency system or that will or could result in the child living on the street. Social services and other supportive and rehabilitative services may include the provision of assessment and screening services; individual, group, or family counseling; specialized educational and vocational services; temporary shelter for the child; outreach services for children living on the street; independent living services to assist adolescents in achieving a successful transition to adulthood; and other specialized services.

(44) "Protective supervision" means a legal status in child-in-need-of-services cases or family-in-need-of-services cases which permits the child to remain in his or her own home or other placement under the supervision of an agent of the Department of Juvenile Justice or the Department of Children and Families, subject to being returned to the court during the period of supervision.

(45) "Relative" means a grandparent, great-grandparent, sibling, first cousin, aunt, uncle, great-aunt, great-uncle, niece, or nephew, whether related by the whole or half blood, by affinity, or by adoption. The term does not include a stepparent.

(46) "Reunification services" means social services and other supportive and rehabilitative services provided to the parent of the child, the legal guardian of the child, or the custodian of the child, whichever is applicable; the child; and, where appropriate, the foster parents of the child for the purpose of enabling a child who has been placed in temporary shelter care to return to his or her family at the earliest possible time. Social services and other supportive and rehabilitative services shall be consistent with the child's need for a safe, continuous, and stable living environment and shall promote the strengthening of family life whenever possible.

(47) "Secure detention center or facility" means a physically restricting facility for the temporary care of children, pending adjudication, disposition, or placement.

(48) "Shelter" means a place for the temporary care of a child who is alleged to be or who has been found to be dependent, a child from a family in need of services, or a child in need of services, pending court disposition before or after adjudication or after execution of a court order. "Shelter" may include a facility which provides 24-hour continual supervision for the temporary care of a child who is placed pursuant to s. 984.14.

(49) "Shelter hearing" means a hearing provided for under s. 984.14 in family-in-need-of-services cases or child-in-need-of-services cases.

(50) "Staff-secure shelter" means a facility in which a child is supervised 24 hours a day by staff members who are awake while on duty. The facility is for the temporary care and assessment of a child who has been found to be dependent, who has violated a court order and been found in contempt of court, or whom the Department of Children and Families is unable to properly assess or place for assistance within the continuum of services provided for dependent children.

(51) "Substance abuse" means using, without medical reason, any psychoactive or mood-altering drug, including alcohol, in such a manner as to induce impairment resulting in dysfunctional social behavior.

(52) "Taken into custody" means the status of a child immediately when temporary physical control over the child is attained by a person authorized by law, pending the child's release, detention, placement, or other disposition as authorized by law.

(53) "Temporary legal custody" means the relationship that a juvenile court creates between a child and an adult relative of the child, adult nonrelative approved by the court, or other person until a more permanent arrangement is ordered. Temporary legal custody confers upon the custodian the right to have temporary physical custody of the child and the right and duty to protect, train, and discipline the child and to provide the child with food, shelter, and education, and ordinary medical, dental, psychiatric, and psychological care, unless these rights and duties are otherwise enlarged or limited by the court order establishing the temporary legal custody relationship.

(54) "Truancy petition" means a petition filed by the superintendent of schools alleging that a student subject to compulsory school attendance has had at least five unexcused absences, or absences for which the reasons are unknown, within a calendar month or 10 unexcused absences, or absences for which the reasons are unknown, within a 90-calendar-day period, or has had more than 15 unexcused absences in a 90-calendar-day period. A truancy petition is filed and processed under s. 984.151.

(55) "Violation of law" or "delinquent act" means a violation of any law of this state, the United States, or any other state which is a misdemeanor or a felony or a violation of a county or municipal ordinance which would be punishable by incarceration if the violation were committed by an adult.

HISTORY:

S. 4, ch. 97-234; s. 89, ch. 97-238; s. 1, ch. 97-276; s. 12, ch. 98-49; s. 235, ch. 98-166; s. 6, ch. 98-207; s. 64, ch. 98-280; s. 165, ch. 98-403; s. 126, ch. 99-3; s. 8, ch. 99-284; s. 74, ch. 99-398; s. 13, ch. 2000-135; s. 22, ch. 2000-235; s. 149, ch. 2000-318; s. 34, ch. 2001-3; s. 35, ch. 2001-64; s. 1046, ch. 2002-387; s. 123, ch. 2006-120, eff. Jan. 1, 2007; s. 29, ch. 2008-238, eff. Oct. 1, 2008; s. 89, ch. 2012-5, eff. May 8, 2012; s. 1, ch. 2012-56, eff. July 1, 2012; s. 333, ch. 2014-19, eff. July 1, 2014.

§ 984.04. Families in need of services and children in need of services; procedures and jurisdiction.

(1) It is the intent of the Legislature to address the problems of families in need of services by providing them with an array of services designed to preserve the unity and integrity of the family and to emphasize parental responsibility for the behavior of their children. Services to families in need of services and children in need of services shall be provided on a continuum of increasing intensity and participation by the parent and child. Judicial intervention to resolve the problems and conflicts that exist within a family shall be limited to situations in which a resolution to the problem or conflict has not been achieved through service, treatment, and family intervention after all available less

restrictive resources have been exhausted. In creating this chapter, the Legislature recognizes the need to distinguish the problems of truants, runaways, and children beyond the control of their parents, and the services provided to these children, from the problems and services designed to meet the needs of abandoned, abused, neglected, and delinquent children. In achieving this recognition, it shall be the policy of the state to develop short-term, temporary services and programs utilizing the least restrictive method for families in need of services and children in need of services.

(2) The Department of Juvenile Justice shall be responsible for all nonjudicial proceedings involving a family in need of services.

(3) All nonjudicial procedures in family-in-need-of-services cases shall be according to rules established by the Department of Juvenile Justice under chapter 120.

(4) The circuit court shall have exclusive original jurisdiction of judicial proceedings involving continued placement of a child from a family in need of services in shelter.

(5) The circuit court shall have exclusive original jurisdiction of proceedings in which a child is alleged to be a child in need of services. When the jurisdiction of any child who has been found to be a child in need of services or the parent, custodian, or legal guardian of such a child is obtained, the court shall retain jurisdiction, unless relinquished by its order or unless the department withdraws its petition because the child no longer meets the definition of a child in need of services as defined in s. 984.03, until the child reaches 18 years of age. This subsection shall not be construed to prevent the exercise of jurisdiction by any other court having jurisdiction of the child if the child commits a violation of law, is the subject of the dependency provisions under this chapter, or is the subject of a pending investigation into an allegation or suspicion of abuse, neglect, or abandonment.

(6) All procedures, including petitions, pleadings, subpoenas, summonses, and hearings, in family-in-need-of-services cases and child-in-need-of-services cases shall be according to the Florida Rules of Juvenile Procedure unless otherwise provided by law.

(7) The department may contract with a provider to provide services and programs for families in need of services and children in need of services.

HISTORY:
S. 8, ch. 87-133; s. 60, ch. 94-209; s. 19, ch. 96-398; s. 90, ch. 97-238; s. 65, ch. 98-280.

Editor's notes.
Former s. 39.42.

§ 984.05. Rules relating to habitual truants; adoption by State Board of Education and Department of Juvenile Justice. [Repealed]

Repealed by s. 117, ch. 2013-18, effective July 2, 2013.

HISTORY:
S. 18, ch. 84-311; s. 2, ch. 87-133; s. 3, ch. 87-289; s. 2, ch. 88-319; s. 16, ch. 94-209; s. 9, ch. 95-152; s. 17, ch. 97-234; s. 91, ch. 97-238; s. 66, ch. 98-280; s. 25, ch. 99-284; s. 14, ch. 2000-135; s. 1047, ch. 2002-387; s. 16, ch. 2005-263; s. 124, ch. 2006-120, eff. Jan. 1, 2007.

§ 984.06. Oaths, records, and confidential information.

(1) The judge, clerks or deputy clerks, or authorized agents of the department shall each have the power to administer oaths and affirmations.

(2) The court shall make and keep records of all cases brought before it pursuant to this chapter and shall preserve the records pertaining to a child in need of services until 10 years after the last entry was made or until the child is 18 years of age, whichever date is first reached, and may then destroy them. The court shall make official records, consisting of all petitions and orders filed in a case arising pursuant to this chapter and any other pleadings, certificates, proofs of publication, summonses, warrants, and other writs which are filed in the case.

(3) The clerk shall keep all court records required by this chapter separate from other records of the circuit court. Court records required by this chapter are not open to inspection by the public. All such records may be inspected only upon order of the court by a person deemed by the court to have a proper interest therein, except that, subject to the provisions of s. 63.162, a child and the parents or legal custodians of the child and their attorneys, law enforcement agencies, and the department and its designees may inspect and copy any official record pertaining to the child. The court may permit authorized representatives of recognized organizations compiling statistics for proper purposes to inspect and make abstracts from official records, under whatever conditions upon their use and disposition the court deems proper, and may punish by contempt proceedings any violation of those conditions.

(4) Except as provided in subsection (3), all information obtained pursuant to this chapter in the discharge of official duty by any judge, employee of the court, authorized agent of the department, or law enforcement agent is confidential and may not be disclosed to anyone other than the authorized personnel of the court, the department and its designees, law enforcement agencies, and others entitled under this chapter to receive that information, except upon order of the court.

(5) All orders of the court entered pursuant to this chapter must be in writing and signed by the judge, except that the clerk or a deputy clerk may sign a summons or notice to appear.

(6) A court record of proceedings under this chapter is not admissible in evidence in any other civil or criminal proceeding, except that:

(a) Records of proceedings under this chapter forming a part of the record on appeal shall be used in the appellate court.

(b) Records that are necessary in any case in which a person is being tried upon a charge of having committed perjury are admissible in evidence in that case.

HISTORY:
S. 8, ch. 87-133; s. 7, ch. 90-53; s. 241, ch. 95-147; s. 34, ch. 96-398; s. 92, ch. 97-238.

Editor's notes.
Former s. 39.443; s. 39.4451.

§ 984.07. Appointed counsel; compensation.

If counsel is entitled to receive compensation for representation pursuant to court appointment in a child-in-need-of-services proceeding, such compensation shall not exceed $1,000 at the trial level and $2,500 at the appellate level.

HISTORY:
S. 8, ch. 87-133; s. 93, ch. 97-238.

Editor's notes.
Former s. 39.447.
Section 1, ch. 92-37, provides: "Notwithstanding the provisions of chapter 39, Florida Statutes, to the contrary, the attorneys whose compensation was provided in the November 1989 Supplemental Appropriations Act and is continued in subsequent general appropriations acts shall provide legal representation in cases arising under sections 39.40 - 39.474, Florida Statutes." Provisions within ch. 39 were transferred to other locations by ch. 97-238, ch. 98-403, and ch. 2000-139. Some of the material within the cited range can be found at parts VI, VIII, and XI of ch. 39, as redesignated by ch. 98-403 and ch. 2000-139, and ch. 984, as redesignated by ch. 97-238.

§ 984.071. Resources and information.

(1) The Department of Juvenile Justice, in collaboration with the Department of Children and Families and the Department of Education, shall develop and publish an information packet that explains the current process under this chapter for obtaining assistance for a child in need of services or a family in need of services and the community services and resources available to parents of troubled or runaway children. In preparing the information packet, the Department of Juvenile Justice shall work with school district superintendents, juvenile court judges, county sheriffs, and other local law enforcement officials in order to ensure that the information packet lists services and resources that are currently available within the county in which the packet is distributed. Each information packet shall be annually updated. The school district shall distribute this information packet to parents of truant children and to other parents upon request or as deemed appropriate by the school district. In addition, the Department of Juvenile Justice shall distribute the information packet to state and local law enforcement agencies. Any law enforcement officer who has contact with the parent of a child who is locked out of the home or who runs away from home shall make the information available to the parent.

(2) The department, in collaboration with organizations that provide expertise, training, and advocacy in the areas of family and domestic violence, shall develop and maintain updated information and materials describing resources and services available to parents and legal custodians who are victims of domestic violence committed by children or who fear that they will become victims of such acts and to children who have committed acts of domestic violence or who demonstrate behaviors that may escalate into domestic violence. Such resources and services shall include, but are not limited to, those available under this chapter, domestic violence services available under chapter 39, and juvenile justice services available pursuant to chapter 985, including prevention, diversion, detention, and alternative placements. The materials shall describe how parents and legal custodians may access the resources and services in their local area. The department shall post this information on its website and make the materials available to certified domestic violence centers, other organizations serving victims of domestic violence, clerks of court, law enforcement agencies, and other appropriate organizations for distribution to the public.

HISTORY:
S. 17, ch. 97-281; s. 67, ch. 98-280; s. 334, ch. 2014-19, eff. July 1, 2014; s. 1, ch. 2017-123, eff. July 1, 2017.

§ 984.08. Attorney's fees.

The court may appoint an attorney to represent a parent or legal guardian under this chapter only upon a finding that the parent or legal guardian is indigent pursuant to s. 57.082. If an attorney is appointed, the parent or legal guardian shall be enrolled in a payment plan pursuant to s. 28.246.

HISTORY:
S. 1, ch. 94-329; s. 5, ch. 95-267; s. 94, ch. 97-238; s. 138, ch. 2003-402; s. 46, ch. 2008-111, eff. July 1, 2008.

Editor's notes.
Former s. 39.017.

§ 984.085. Sheltering unmarried minors; aiding unmarried minor runaways; violations.

(1)(a) A person who is not an authorized agent of the Department of Juvenile Justice or the Department of Children and Families may not knowingly shelter an unmarried minor for more than 24 hours without the consent of the minor's parent or guardian or without notifying a law enforcement officer of the minor's name and the fact that the minor is being provided shelter.

(b) A person may not knowingly provide aid to an unmarried minor who has run away from home without first contacting the minor's parent or guardian or notifying a law enforcement officer. The aid prohibited under this paragraph includes assisting the minor in obtaining shelter, such as hotel lodgings.

(2) A person who violates this section commits a misdemeanor of the first degree, punishable as provided in s. 775.082 or s. 775.083.

HISTORY:
S. 14, ch. 97-281; s. 335, ch. 2014-19, eff. July 1, 2014.

Editor's notes.
This section is also published at s. 985.731.

§ 984.086. Children locked out of the home; interagency cooperation.

The Department of Juvenile Justice and the Department of Children and Families shall encourage interagency cooperation within each circuit and shall develop comprehensive agreements between the staff and providers for each department in order to coordinate the services provided to children who are locked out of the home and the families of those children.

HISTORY:
S. 15, ch. 97-281; s. 15, ch. 2000-135; s. 336, ch. 2014-19, eff. July 1, 2014.

§ 984.09. Punishment for contempt of court; alternative sanctions.

(1) CONTEMPT OF COURT; LEGISLATIVE INTENT. — The court may punish any child for contempt for interfering with the court or with court administration, or for violating any provision of this chapter or order of the court relative thereto. It is the intent of the Legislature that the court restrict and limit the use of contempt powers with respect to commitment of a child to a secure facility. A child who commits direct contempt of court or indirect contempt of a valid court order may be taken into custody and ordered to serve an alternative sanction or placed in a secure facility, as authorized in this section, by order of the court.

(2) PLACEMENT IN A SECURE FACILITY. — A child may be placed in a secure facility for purposes of punishment for contempt of court if alternative sanctions are unavailable or inappropriate, or if the child has already been ordered to serve an alternative sanction but failed to comply with the sanction.

(a) A delinquent child who has been held in direct or indirect contempt may be placed in a secure detention facility for 5 days for a first offense or 15 days for a second or subsequent offense, or in a secure residential commitment facility.

(b) A child in need of services who has been held in direct contempt or indirect contempt may be placed, for 5 days for a first offense or 15 days for a second or subsequent offense, in a staff-secure shelter or a staff-secure residential facility solely for children in need of services if such placement is available, or, if such placement is not available, the child may be placed in an appropriate mental health facility or substance abuse facility for assessment. In addition to disposition under this paragraph, a child in need of services who is held in direct contempt or indirect contempt may be placed in a physically secure setting as provided under s. 984.226 if conditions of eligibility are met.

(3) ALTERNATIVE SANCTIONS. — Each judicial circuit shall have an alternative sanctions coordinator who shall serve under the chief administrative judge of the juvenile division of the circuit court, and who shall coordinate and maintain a spectrum of contempt sanction alternatives in conjunction with the circuit plan implemented in accordance with s. 790.22(4)(c). Upon determining that a child has committed direct contempt of court or indirect contempt of a valid court order, the court may immediately request the alternative sanctions coordinator to recommend the most appropriate available alternative sanction and shall order the child to perform up to 50 hours of community-service manual labor or a similar alternative sanction, unless an alternative sanction is unavailable or inappropriate, or unless the child has failed to comply with a prior alternative sanction. Alternative contempt sanctions may be provided by local industry or by any nonprofit organization or any public or private business or service entity that has entered into a contract with the Department of Juvenile Justice to act as an agent of the state to provide voluntary supervision of children on behalf of the state in exchange for the manual labor of children and limited immunity in accordance with s. 768.28(11).

(4) CONTEMPT OF COURT SANCTIONS; PROCEDURE AND DUE PROCESS.

(a) If a child is charged with direct contempt of court, including traffic court, the court may impose an authorized sanction immediately.

(b) If a child is charged with indirect contempt of court, the court must hold a hearing within 24 hours to determine whether the child committed indirect contempt of a valid court order. At the hearing, the following due process rights must be provided to the child:

1. Right to a copy of the order to show cause alleging facts supporting the contempt charge.

2. Right to an explanation of the nature and the consequences of the proceedings.

3. Right to legal counsel and the right to have legal counsel appointed by the court if the juvenile is indigent, pursuant to s. 985.033.

4. Right to confront witnesses.

5. Right to present witnesses.

6. Right to have a transcript or record of the proceeding.

7. Right to appeal to an appropriate court.

The child's parent or guardian may address the court regarding the due process rights of the child. The court shall review the placement of the child every 72 hours to determine whether it is appropriate for the child to remain in the facility.

(c) The court may not order that a child be placed in a secure facility for punishment for contempt unless the court determines that an alternative sanction is inappropriate or unavailable or that the child was initially ordered to an alternative sanction and did not comply with the alternative sanction. The court is encouraged to order a child to perform community service, up to the maximum number of hours, where appropriate before ordering that the child be placed in a secure facility as punishment for contempt of court.

(d) In addition to any other sanction imposed under this section, the court may direct the Department of Highway Safety and Motor Vehicles to withhold issuance of, or suspend, a child's driver license or driving privilege. The court may order that a child's driver license or driving privilege be withheld or suspended for up to 1 year for a first offense of contempt and up to 2 years for a second or subsequent offense. If the child's driver license or driving privilege is suspended or revoked for any reason at the time the sanction for contempt is imposed, the court shall extend the period of suspension or revocation by the additional period ordered under this paragraph. If the child's driver license is being withheld at the time the sanction for contempt is imposed, the period of suspension or revocation ordered under this paragraph shall begin on the date on which the child is otherwise eligible to drive. For a child in need of services whose driver license or driving privilege is suspended under this paragraph, the court may direct the Department of Highway Safety and Motor Vehicles to issue the child a license for driving privileges restricted to business or employment purposes only, as defined in s. 322.271, or for the purpose of completing court-ordered community service, if the child is otherwise qualified for a license. However, the department may not issue a restricted license unless specifically ordered to do so by the court.

(5) ALTERNATIVE SANCTIONS COORDINATOR. — There is created the position of alternative sanctions coordinator within each judicial circuit, pursuant to subsection (3). Each alternative sanctions coordinator shall serve under the direction of the chief administrative judge of the juvenile division as directed by the chief judge of the circuit. The alternative sanctions coordinator shall act as the liaison between the judiciary, local department officials, district school board employees, and local law enforcement agencies. The alternative sanctions coordinator shall coordinate within the circuit community-based alternative sanctions, including nonsecure detention programs, community service projects, and other juvenile sanctions, in conjunction with the circuit plan implemented in accordance with s. 790.22(4)(c).

HISTORY:
S. 95, ch. 97-238; s. 1, ch. 97-281; s. 2, ch. 2000-134; s. 16, ch. 2000-135; s. 125, ch. 2006-120, eff. January 1, 2007.

§ 984.10. Intake.

(1) Intake shall be performed by the department. A report or complaint alleging that a child is from a family in need of services shall be made to the intake office operating in the county in which the child is found or in which the case arose. Any person or agency, including, but not limited to, the parent or legal custodian, the local school district, a law enforcement agency, or the Department of Children and Families, having knowledge of the facts may make a report or complaint.

(2) A representative of the department shall make a preliminary determination as to whether the report or complaint is complete. The criteria for the completeness of a report or complaint with respect to a child alleged to be from a family in need of services while subject to compulsory school attendance shall be governed by s. 984.03(27). In any case in which the representative of the department finds that the report or complaint is incomplete, the representative of the department shall return the report or complaint without delay to the person or agency originating the report or complaint or having knowledge of the facts or to the appropriate law enforcement agency having investigative jurisdiction and request additional information in order to complete the report or complaint.

(3) If the representative of the department determines that in his or her judgment the interests of the family, the child, and the public will be best served by providing the family and child services and treatment voluntarily accepted by the child and the parents or legal custodians, the departmental representative may refer the family or child to an appropriate service and treatment provider. As part of the intake procedure, the departmental representative shall inform the parent or legal custodian, in writing, of the services and treatment available to the child and family by department providers or community agencies and the rights and responsibilities of the parent or legal guardian under this chapter.

(4) If the department has reasonable grounds to believe that the child has been abandoned, abused, or neglected, it shall proceed pursuant to the provisions of chapter 39.

HISTORY:
S. 8, ch. 87-133; s. 3, ch. 88-319; s. 234, ch. 95-147; s. 4, ch. 95-152; s. 8, ch. 95-280; s. 22, ch. 96-398; s. 168, ch. 97-101; s. 96, ch. 97-238; s. 5, ch. 97-281; s. 68, ch. 98-280; s. 166, ch. 98-403; s. 17, ch. 2000-135; s. 337, ch. 2014-19, eff. July 1, 2014.

Editor's notes.
Former s. 39.423.

§ 984.11. Services to families in need of services.

(1) Services and treatment to families in need of services shall be by voluntary agreement of the parent or legal guardian and the child or as directed by a court order pursuant to s. 984.22.

(2) These services may include, but need not be limited to:

(a) Homemaker or parent aide services.

(b) Intensive crisis counseling.

(c) Parent training.

(d) Individual, group, or family counseling.

(e) Community mental health services.

(f) Prevention and diversion services.

(g) Services provided by voluntary or community agencies.

(h) Runaway center services.

(i) Housekeeper services.

(j) Special educational, tutorial, or remedial services.

(k) Vocational, job training, or employment services.

(*l*) Recreational services.

(m) Assessment.

(3) The department shall advise the parents or legal guardian that they are responsible for contributing to the cost of the child or family services and treatment to the extent of their ability to pay. The department shall set and charge fees for services and treatment provided to clients. The department may employ a collection agency for the purpose of receiving, collecting, and managing the payment of unpaid and delinquent fees. The collection agency must be registered and in good standing under chapter 559. The department may pay to the collection agency a fee from the amount collected under the claim or may authorize the agency to deduct the fee from the amount collected.

(4) The department may file a petition with the circuit court to enforce the collection of fees for services and treatment rendered to the child or the parent and other legal custodians.

HISTORY:

S. 8, ch. 87-133; s. 4, ch. 90-53; s. 23, ch. 96-398; s. 97, ch. 97-238; s. 6, ch. 97-281.

Editor's notes.

Former s. 39.424.

§ 984.12. Case staffing; services and treatment to a family in need of services.

(1) The appropriate representative of the department shall request a meeting of the family and child with a case staffing committee to review the case of any family or child who the department determines is in need of services or treatment if:

(a) The family or child is not in agreement with the services or treatment offered;

(b) The family or child will not participate in the services or treatment selected; or

(c) The representative of the department needs assistance in developing an appropriate plan for services. The time and place selected for the meeting shall be convenient for the child and family.

(2) The composition of the case staffing committee shall be based on the needs of the family and child. It shall include a representative from the child's school district and a representative of the Department of Juvenile Justice, and may include a supervisor of the department's contracted provider; a representative from the area of health, mental health, substance abuse, social, or educational services; a representative of the state attorney; the alternative sanctions coordinator; and any person recommended by the child, family, or department.

(3) The case staffing committee shall reach a timely decision to provide the child or family with needed services and treatment through the development of a plan for services.

(4) The plan for services shall contain the following:

(a) Statement of the problems.

(b) Needs of the child.

(c) Needs of the parents, guardian, or legal custodian.

(d) Measurable objectives that address the identified problems and needs.

(e) Services and treatment to be provided, to include:

1. Type of services or treatment.

2. Frequency of services or treatment.

3. Location.

4. Accountable service providers or staff.

(f) Timeframes for achieving objectives.

(5) Upon receipt of the plan, the child and family shall acknowledge their position by accepting or rejecting the services and provisions in writing. If the plan is accepted, it shall be implemented as soon as is practicable.

(6) A case manager shall be designated by the case staffing committee to be responsible for implementing the plan. The case manager shall periodically review the progress towards achieving the objectives of the plan in order to:

(a) Advise the case staffing committee of the need to make adjustments to the plan; or

(b) Terminate the case as indicated by successful or substantial achievement of the objectives of the plan.

(7) The parent, guardian, or legal custodian may convene a meeting of the case staffing committee, and any other member of the committee may convene a meeting if the member finds that doing so is in the best interest of the family or child. A case staffing committee meeting requested by a parent, guardian, or legal custodian must be convened within 7 days, excluding weekends and legal holidays, after the date the department's representative receives the request in writing.

(8) Within 7 days after meeting, the case staffing committee shall provide the parent, guardian, or legal custodian with a written report that details the reasons for the committee's decision to recommend, or decline to recommend, that the department file a petition alleging that the child is a child in need of services.

HISTORY:

S. 8, ch. 87-133; s. 9, ch. 91-45; s. 19, ch. 95-267; s. 9, ch. 95-280; s. 4, ch. 96-369; s. 24, ch. 96-398; s. 98, ch. 97-238; s. 7, ch. 97-281.

Editor's notes.
Former s. 39.426.

§ 984.13. Taking into custody a child alleged to be from a family in need of services or to be a child in need of services.

(1) A child may be taken into custody:

(a) By a law enforcement officer when the officer has reasonable grounds to believe that the child has run away from his or her parents, guardian, or other legal custodian.

(b) By a law enforcement officer when the officer has reasonable grounds to believe that the child is absent from school without authorization or is suspended or expelled and is not in the presence of his or her parent or legal guardian, for the purpose of delivering the child without unreasonable delay to the appropriate school system site. For the purpose of this paragraph, "school system site" includes, but is not limited to, a center approved by the superintendent of schools for the purpose of counseling students and referring them back to the school system or an approved alternative to a suspension or expulsion program. If a student is suspended or expelled from school without assignment to an alternative school placement, the law enforcement officer shall deliver the child to the parent or legal guardian, to a location determined by the parent or guardian, or to a designated truancy interdiction site until the parent or guardian can be located.

(c) Pursuant to an order of the circuit court based upon sworn testimony before or after a petition is filed under s. 984.15.

(d) By a law enforcement officer when the child voluntarily agrees to or requests services pursuant to this chapter or placement in a shelter.

(2) The person taking the child into custody shall:

(a) Release the child to a parent, guardian, legal custodian, or responsible adult relative or to a department-approved family-in-need-of-services and child-in-need-of-services provider if the person taking the child into custody has reasonable grounds to believe the child has run away from a parent, guardian, or legal custodian; is truant; or is beyond the control of the parent, guardian, or legal custodian; following such release, the person taking the child into custody shall make a full written report to the intake office of the department within 3 days; or

(b) Deliver the child to the department, stating the facts by reason of which the child was taken into custody and sufficient information to establish probable cause that the child is from a family in need of services.

(3) If the child is taken into custody by, or is delivered to, the department, the appropriate representative of the department shall review the facts and make such further inquiry as necessary to determine whether the child shall remain in custody or be re-leased. Unless shelter is required as provided in s. 984.14(1), the department shall:

(a) Release the child to his or her parent, guardian, or legal custodian, to a responsible adult relative, to a responsible adult approved by the department, or to a department-approved family-in-need-of-services and child-in-need-of-services provider; or

(b) Authorize temporary services and treatment that would allow the child alleged to be from a family in need of services to remain at home.

HISTORY:
S. 8, ch. 87-133; s. 1, ch. 89-20; s. 232, ch. 95-147; s. 6, ch. 95-280; s. 20, ch. 96-398; s. 99, ch. 97-238; s. 23, ch. 2000-235.

Editor's notes.
Former s. 39.421.

§ 984.14. Shelter placement; hearing.

(1) Unless ordered by the court pursuant to the provisions of this chapter, or upon voluntary consent to placement by the child and the child's parent, legal guardian, or custodian, a child taken into custody shall not be placed in a shelter prior to a court hearing unless a determination has been made that the provision of appropriate and available services will not eliminate the need for placement and that such placement is required:

(a) To provide an opportunity for the child and family to agree upon conditions for the child's return home, when immediate placement in the home would result in a substantial likelihood that the child and family would not reach an agreement; or

(b) Because a parent, custodian, or guardian is unavailable to take immediate custody of the child.

(2) If the department determines that placement in a shelter is necessary according to the provisions of subsection (1), the departmental representative shall authorize placement of the child in a shelter provided by the community specifically for runaways and troubled youth who are children in need of services or members of families in need of services and shall immediately notify the parents or legal custodians that the child was taken into custody.

(3) A child who is involuntarily placed in a shelter shall be given a shelter hearing within 24 hours after being taken into custody to determine whether shelter placement is required. The shelter petition filed with the court shall address each condition required to be determined in subsection (1).

(4) A child may not be held involuntarily in a shelter longer than 24 hours unless an order so directing is made by the court after a shelter hearing finding that placement in a shelter is necessary based on the criteria in subsection (1) and that the department has made reasonable efforts to prevent or eliminate the need for removal of the child from the home.

(5) Except as provided under s. 984.225, a child in need of services or a child from a family in need of

services may not be placed in a shelter for longer than 35 days.

(6)   When any child is placed in a shelter pursuant to court order following a shelter hearing, the court shall order the natural or adoptive parents of such child, the natural father of such child born out of wedlock who has acknowledged his paternity in writing before the court, or the guardian of such child's estate, if possessed of assets which under law may be disbursed for the care, support, and maintenance of the child, to pay, to the department, fees as established by the department. When the order affects the guardianship estate, a certified copy of the order shall be delivered to the judge having jurisdiction of the guardianship estate.

(7)   A child who is adjudicated a child in need of services or alleged to be from a family in need of services or a child in need of services may not be placed in a secure detention facility or jail or any other commitment program for delinquent children under any circumstances.

(8)   The court may order the placement of a child in need of services into a staff-secure facility for no longer than 5 days for the purpose of evaluation and assessment.

HISTORY:
S. 8, ch. 87-133; s. 3, ch. 90-53; s. 6, ch. 90-208; s. 233, ch. 95-147; s. 7, ch. 95-280; s. 21, ch. 96-398; s. 100, ch. 97-238; s. 4, ch. 97-281.

Editor's notes.
Former s. 39.422.

§ 984.15. Petition for a child in need of services.

(1)   All proceedings seeking an adjudication that a child is a child in need of services shall be initiated by the filing of a petition by an attorney representing the department or by the child's parent, guardian, or legal custodian. If a child in need of services has been placed in a shelter pursuant to s. 984.14, the department shall file the petition immediately, including in the petition notice of arraignment pursuant to s. 984.20.

(2)(a)   The department shall file a petition for a child in need of services if the case manager or staffing committee requests that a petition be filed and:

1.   The family and child have in good faith, but unsuccessfully, used the services and process described in ss. 984.11 and 984.12; or

2.   The family or child have refused all services described in ss. 984.11 and 984.12 after reasonable efforts by the department to involve the family and child in services and treatment.

(b)   Once the requirements in paragraph (a) have been met, the department shall file a petition for a child in need of services within 45 days.

(c)   The petition shall be in writing, shall state the specific grounds under s. 984.03(9) by which the child is designated a child in need of services, and shall certify that the conditions prescribed in paragraph (a) have been met. The petition shall be signed by the petitioner under oath stating good faith in filing the petition and shall be signed by an attorney for the department.

(3)(a)   The parent, guardian, or legal custodian may file a petition alleging that a child is a child in need of services if:

1.   The department waives the requirement for a case staffing committee.

2.   The department fails to convene a meeting of the case staffing committee within 7 days, excluding weekends and legal holidays, after receiving a written request for such a meeting from the child's parent, guardian, or legal custodian.

3.   The parent, guardian, or legal custodian does not agree with the plan for services offered by the case staffing committee.

4.   The department fails to provide a written report within 7 days after the case staffing committee meets, as required under s. 984.12(8).

(b)   The parent, guardian, or legal custodian must give the department prior written notice of intent to file the petition. If, at the arraignment hearing, the court finds that such written notice of intent to file the petition was not provided to the department, the court shall dismiss the petition, postpone the hearing until such written notice is given, or, if the department agrees, proceed with the arraignment hearing. The petition must be served on the department's office of general counsel.

(c)   The petition must be in writing and must set forth specific facts alleging that the child is a child in need of services as defined in s. 984.03(9). The petition must also demonstrate that the parent, guardian, or legal custodian has in good faith, but unsuccessfully, participated in the services and processes described in ss. 984.11 and 984.12.

(d)   The petition must be signed by the petitioner under oath.

(e)   The court, on its own motion or the motion of any party or the department, shall determine the legal sufficiency of a petition filed under this subsection and may dismiss any petition that lacks sufficient grounds. In addition, the court shall verify that the child is not:

1.   The subject of a pending investigation into an allegation or suspicion of abuse, neglect, or abandonment;

2.   The subject of a pending referral alleging that the child is delinquent; or

3.   Under the current supervision of the department or the Department of Children and Families for an adjudication of delinquency or dependency.

(4)   The form of the petition and any additional contents shall be determined by rules of procedure adopted by the Supreme Court.

(5)   The department or the parent, guardian, or legal custodian may withdraw a petition at any time prior to the child being adjudicated a child in need of services.

HISTORY:
S. 8, ch. 87-133; s. 11, ch. 92-170; s. 235, ch. 95-147; s. 5, ch. 95-152; s. 26, ch. 96-398; s. 101, ch. 97-238; s. 8, ch. 97-281; s. 69, ch. 98-280; s. 167, ch. 98-403; s. 338, ch. 2014-19, eff. July 1, 2014.

Editor's notes.
Former s. 39.436.

§ 984.151. Truancy petition; prosecution; disposition.

(1) If the school determines that a student subject to compulsory school attendance has had at least five unexcused absences, or absences for which the reasons are unknown, within a calendar month or 10 unexcused absences, or absences for which the reasons are unknown, within a 90-calendar-day period pursuant to s. 1003.26(1)(b), or has had more than 15 unexcused absences in a 90-calendar-day period, the superintendent of schools or his or her designee may file a truancy petition.

(2) The petition shall be filed in the circuit in which the student is enrolled in school.

(3) Original jurisdiction to hear a truancy petition shall be in the circuit court; however, the circuit court may use a general or special master pursuant to Supreme Court rules. Upon the filing of the petition, the clerk shall issue a summons to the parent, guardian, or legal custodian of the student, directing that person and the student to appear for a hearing at a time and place specified.

(4) The petition must contain the following: the name, age, and address of the student; the name and address of the student's parent or guardian; the school where the student is enrolled; the efforts the school has made to get the student to attend school; the number of out-of-school contacts between the school system and student's parent or guardian; and the number of days and dates of days the student has missed school. The petition shall be sworn to by the superintendent or his or her designee.

(5) Once the petition is filed, the court shall hear the petition within 30 days.

(6) The student and the student's parent or guardian shall attend the hearing.

(7) If the court determines that the student did miss any of the alleged days, the court shall order the student to attend school and the parent to ensure that the student attends school, and may order any of the following: the student to participate in alternative sanctions to include mandatory attendance at alternative classes to be followed by mandatory community services hours for a period up to 6 months; the student and the student's parent or guardian to participate in homemaker or parent aide services; the student or the student's parent or guardian to participate in intensive crisis counseling; the student or the student's parent or guardian to participate in community mental health services if available and applicable; the student and the student's parent or guardian to participate in service provided by voluntary or community agencies as available; and the student or the student's parent or guardian to participate in vocational, job training, or employment services.

(8) If the student does not successfully complete the sanctions ordered in subsection (7), the case shall be referred to the case staffing committee under s. 984.12 with a recommendation to file a child-in-need-of-services petition under s. 984.15.

(9) The parent, guardian, or legal custodian and the student shall participate, as required by court order, in any sanctions or services required by the court under this section, and the court shall enforce such participation through its contempt power.

HISTORY:
S. 75, ch. 99-398; s. 24, ch. 2000-235; s. 1048, ch. 2002-387; s. 7, ch. 2014-39, eff. May 12, 2014.

§ 984.16. Process and service.

(1) Personal appearance of any person in a hearing before the court shall obviate the necessity of serving process on that person.

(2) Upon the filing of a petition containing allegations of facts which, if true, would constitute the child therein being named a child in need of services, and upon the request of the petitioner, the clerk or deputy clerk shall issue a summons.

(3) The summons shall require the person on whom it is served to appear for a hearing at a time and place specified. Except in cases of medical emergency, the time shall not be less than 24 hours after service of the summons. The summons may require the custodian to bring the child to court if the court determines that the child's presence is necessary. A copy of the petition shall be attached to the summons.

(4) The summons shall be directed to, and shall be served upon, the following persons:

    (a) The parents.

    (b) The legal custodian, actual custodian, and guardian ad litem.

    (c) The child.

(5) The jurisdiction of the court shall attach to the child and the parent, custodian, or legal guardian of the child and the case when the summons is served upon the child or a parent or legal or actual custodian of the child or when the child is taken into custody with or without service of summons and after filing of a petition for a child in need of services, and thereafter the court may control the child and case in accordance with this chapter.

(6) Upon the application of a party or the petitioner, the clerk or deputy clerk shall issue, and the court on its own motion may issue, subpoenas requiring attendance and testimony of witnesses and production of records, documents, or other tangible objects at any hearing.

(7) All process and orders issued by the court shall be served or executed as other process and orders of

the circuit court and, in addition, may be served or executed by authorized agents of the department.

(8)　Subpoenas may be served within the state by any person over 18 years of age who is not a party to the proceeding.

(9)　No fee shall be paid for service of any process or other papers by an agent of the department. If any process, orders, or other papers are served or executed by any sheriff, the sheriff's fees shall be paid by the county.

(10)　If the party to whom an order is directed is present or represented at the final hearing, service of such order shall not be required.

HISTORY:
S. 8, ch. 87-133; s. 12, ch. 92-170; s. 28, ch. 96-398; s. 102, ch. 97-238; s. 70, ch. 98-280.

Editor's notes.
Former s. 39.437.

§ 984.17. Response to petition and representation of parties.

(1)　At the time a petition is filed, the court may appoint a guardian ad litem for the child.

(2)　No answer to the petition or any other pleading need be filed by any child, parent, or legal custodian, but any matters which might be set forth in an answer or other pleading may be pleaded orally before the court or filed in writing as any such person may choose. Notwithstanding the filing of an answer or any pleading, the child or parent shall, prior to an adjudicatory hearing, be advised by the court of the right to counsel.

(3)　When a petition for a child in need of services has been filed and the parents, guardian, or legal custodian of the child and the child have advised the department that the truth of the allegations is acknowledged and that no contest is to be made of the adjudication, the attorney representing the department may set the case before the court for a disposition hearing. If there is a change in the plea at this hearing, the court shall continue the hearing to permit the attorney representing the department to prepare and present the case.

(4)　An attorney representing the department shall represent the state in any proceeding in which the petition alleges that a child is a child in need of services and in which a party denies the allegations of the petition and contests the adjudication.

HISTORY:
S. 8, ch. 87-133; s. 13, ch. 92-170; s. 236, ch. 95-147; s. 29, ch. 96-398; s. 103, ch. 97-238; s. 9, ch. 97-281.

Editor's notes.
Former s. 39.438.

§ 984.18. Referral of child-in-need-of-services cases to mediation.

(1)　At any stage in a child-in-need-of-services proceeding, the case staffing committee or any party may request the court to refer the parties to mediation in accordance with chapter 44 and rules and procedures developed by the Supreme Court.

(2)　A court may refer the parties to mediation.

(3)　The department shall advise the parties or legal guardians that they are responsible for contributing to the cost of the child-in-need-of-services mediation to the extent of their ability to pay.

(4)　This section applies only to courts in counties in which child-in-need-of-services mediation programs have been established and does not require the establishment of such programs in any county.

HISTORY:
S. 23, ch. 94-164; s. 27, ch. 96-398; s. 104, ch. 97-238.

Editor's notes.
Former s. 39.4365; s. 39.4431.

§ 984.19. Medical screening and treatment of child; examination of parent, guardian, or person requesting custody.

(1)　When any child is to be placed in shelter care, the department is authorized to have a medical screening performed on the child without authorization from the court and without consent from a parent or guardian. Such medical screening shall be performed by a licensed health care professional and shall be to examine the child for injury, illness, and communicable diseases. In no case does this subsection authorize the department to consent to medical treatment for such children.

(2)　When the department has performed the medical screening authorized by subsection (1) or when it is otherwise determined by a licensed health care professional that a child is in need of medical treatment, consent for medical treatment shall be obtained in the following manner:

(a)1.　Consent to medical treatment shall be obtained from a parent or guardian of the child; or

2.　A court order for such treatment shall be obtained.

(b)　If a parent or guardian of the child is unavailable and his or her whereabouts cannot be reasonably ascertained and it is after normal working hours so that a court order cannot reasonably be obtained, an authorized agent of the department or its provider has the authority to consent to necessary medical treatment for the child. The authority of the department to consent to medical treatment in this circumstance is limited to the time reasonably necessary to obtain court authorization.

(c)　If a parent or guardian of the child is available but refuses to consent to the necessary treatment, a court order is required, unless the situation meets the definition of an emergency in s. 743.064 or the treatment needed is related to suspected abuse or neglect of the child by the parent or guardian. In such case, the department has the authority to consent to necessary medical treatment. This authority is limited to the time reasonably necessary to obtain court authorization.

In no case may the department consent to sterilization, abortion, or termination of life support.

(3) A judge may order that a child alleged to be or adjudicated a child in need of services be examined by a licensed health care professional. The judge may also order such child to be evaluated by a psychiatrist or a psychologist, by a district school board educational needs assessment team, or, if a developmental disability is suspected or alleged, by the developmental disability diagnostic and evaluation team of the Department of Children and Families. The judge may order a family assessment if that assessment was not completed at an earlier time. If it is necessary to place a child in a residential facility for such evaluation, then the criteria and procedure established in s. 394.463(2) or chapter 393 shall be used, whichever is applicable. The educational needs assessment provided by the district school board educational needs assessment team shall include, but not be limited to, reports of intelligence and achievement tests, screening for learning disabilities and other handicaps, and screening for the need for alternative education pursuant to s. 1003.53.

(4) A judge may order that a child alleged to be or adjudicated a child in need of services be treated by a licensed health care professional. The judge may also order such child to receive mental health or intellectual disability services from a psychiatrist, psychologist, or other appropriate service provider. If it is necessary to place the child in a residential facility for such services, the procedures and criteria established in s. 394.467 or chapter 393 shall be used, as applicable. A child may be provided services in emergency situations pursuant to the procedures and criteria contained in s. 394.463(1) or chapter 393, as applicable.

(5) When there are indications of physical injury or illness, a licensed health care professional shall be immediately called or the child shall be taken to the nearest available hospital for emergency care.

(6) Except as otherwise provided herein, nothing in this section shall be deemed to eliminate the right of a parent, a guardian, or the child to consent to examination or treatment for the child.

(7) Except as otherwise provided herein, nothing in this section shall be deemed to alter the provisions of s. 743.064.

(8) A court shall not be precluded from ordering services or treatment to be provided to the child by a duly accredited practitioner who relies solely on spiritual means for healing in accordance with the tenets and practices of a church or religious organization, when required by the child's health and when requested by the child.

(9) Nothing in this section shall be construed to authorize the permanent sterilization of the child, unless such sterilization is the result of or incidental to medically necessary treatment to protect or preserve the life of the child.

(10) For the purpose of obtaining an evaluation or examination or receiving treatment as authorized pursuant to this section, no child alleged to be or found to be a child from a family in need of services or a child in need of services shall be placed in a detention facility or other program used primarily for the care and custody of children alleged or found to have committed delinquent acts.

(11) The parents or guardian of a child alleged to be or adjudicated a child in need of services remain financially responsible for the cost of medical treatment provided to the child even if one or both of the parents or if the guardian did not consent to the medical treatment. After a hearing, the court may order the parents or guardian, if found able to do so, to reimburse the department or other provider of medical services for treatment provided.

(12) Nothing in this section alters the authority of the department to consent to medical treatment for a child who has been committed to the department pursuant to s. 984.22(3) and of whom the department has become the legal custodian.

(13) At any time after the filing of a petition for a child in need of services, when the mental or physical condition, including the blood group, of a parent, guardian, or other person requesting custody of a child is in controversy, the court may order the person to submit to a physical or mental examination by a qualified professional. The order may be made only upon good cause shown and pursuant to notice and procedures as set forth by the Florida Rules of Juvenile Procedure.

HISTORY:

S. 8, ch. 87-133; s. 237, ch. 95-147; s. 30, ch. 96-398; s. 170, ch. 97-101; s. 105, ch. 97-238; s. 1049, ch. 2002-387; s. 164, ch. 2007-5, eff. July 3, 2007; s. 45, ch. 2013-162, eff. July 1, 2013; s. 339, ch. 2014-19, eff. July 1, 2014.

Editor's notes.

Former s. 39.439; s. 39.446.

§ 984.20. Hearings for child-in-need-of-services cases.

(1) ARRAIGNMENT HEARING.

(a) When a child has been taken into custody by order of the court, an arraignment hearing shall be held within 7 days after the date the child is taken into custody. The hearing shall be held for the child and the parent, guardian, or custodian to admit, deny, or consent to findings that a child is in need of services as alleged in the petition. If the child and the parent, guardian, or custodian admit or consent to the findings in the petition, the court shall proceed as set forth in the Florida Rules of Juvenile Procedure. However, if either the child or the parent, guardian, or custodian denies any of the allegations of the petition, the court shall hold an adjudicatory hearing within 7 days after the date of the arraignment hearing.

(b) When a child is in the custody of the parent, guardian, or custodian, upon the filing of a petition, the clerk shall set a date for an arraignment hearing within a reasonable time from the date of the filing of the petition. If the child and the parent, guardian, or custodian admit or consent to an adjudication, the court shall proceed as set forth in the Florida Rules of Juvenile Procedure. However, if either the child or the parent, guardian, or custodian denies any of the allegations of child in need of services, the court shall hold an adjudicatory hearing within a reasonable time from the date of the arraignment hearing.

(c) If at the arraignment hearing the child and the parent, guardian, or custodian consents or admits to the allegations in the petition and the court determines that the petition meets the requirements of s. 984.15(3)(e), the court shall proceed to hold a disposition hearing at the earliest practicable time that will allow for the completion of a predisposition study.

(2) ADJUDICATORY HEARING.

(a) The adjudicatory hearing shall be held as soon as practicable after the petition for a child in need of services is filed and in accordance with the Florida Rules of Juvenile Procedure, but reasonable delay for the purpose of investigation, discovery, or procuring counsel or witnesses shall, whenever practicable, be granted. If the child is in custody, the adjudicatory hearing shall be held within 14 days after the date the child was taken into custody.

(b) Adjudicatory hearings shall be conducted by the judge without a jury, applying the rules of evidence in use in civil cases and adjourning the hearings from time to time as necessary. In a hearing on a petition in which it is alleged that the child is a child in need of services, a preponderance of evidence shall be required to establish that the child is in need of services.

(c) All hearings, except as hereinafter provided, shall be open to the public, and no person shall be excluded therefrom except on special order of the judge who, in his or her discretion, may close any hearing to the public when the public interest or the welfare of the child, in his or her opinion, is best served by so doing. Hearings involving more than one child may be held simultaneously when the several children involved are related to each other or were involved in the same case. The child and the parent, guardian, or custodian of the child may be examined separately and apart from each other.

(3) DISPOSITION HEARING. — At the disposition hearing, if the court finds that the facts alleged in the petition of a child in need of services were proven in the adjudicatory hearing, the court shall receive and consider a predisposition study, which shall be in writing and be presented by an authorized agent of the department or its provider.

(a) The predisposition study shall cover:

1. All treatment and services that the parent, guardian, or custodian and child received.

2. The love, affection, and other emotional ties existing between the parents and the child.

3. The capacity and disposition of the parents to provide the child with food, clothing, medical care or other remedial care recognized and permitted under the laws of this state in lieu of medical care, and other material needs.

4. The length of time that the child has lived in a stable, satisfactory environment and the desirability of maintaining continuity.

5. The permanence, as a family unit, of the existing or proposed custodial home.

6. The moral fitness of the parents.

7. The mental and physical health of the family.

8. The home, school, and community record of the child.

9. The reasonable preference of the child, if the court deems the child to be of sufficient intelligence, understanding, and experience to express a preference.

10. Any other factor considered by the court to be relevant.

(b) The predisposition study also shall provide the court with documentation regarding:

1. The availability of appropriate prevention, services, and treatment for the parent, guardian, custodian, and child to prevent the removal of the child from the home or to reunify the child with the parent, guardian, or custodian after removal or to reconcile the problems between the parent, guardian, or custodian and the child;

2. The inappropriateness of other prevention, treatment, and services that were available;

3. The efforts by the department to prevent out-of-home placement of the child or, when applicable, to reunify the parent, guardian, or custodian if appropriate services were available;

4. Whether the services were provided;

5. If the services and treatment were provided, whether they were sufficient to meet the needs of the child and the family and to enable the child to remain at home or to be returned home;

6. If the services and treatment were not provided, the reasons for such lack of provision; and

7. The need for, or appropriateness of, continuing such treatment and services if the child remains in the custody of the parent, guardian, or custodian or if the child is placed outside the home.

(c) If placement of the child with anyone other than the child's parent, guardian, or custodian is being considered, the study shall include the designation of a specific length of time as to when custody by the parent, guardian, or custodian shall be reconsidered.

(d) A copy of this predisposition study shall be furnished to the person having custody of the child at the time such person is notified of the disposition hearing.

Any other relevant and material evidence, including other written or oral reports, may be received by the court in its effort to determine the action to be taken with regard to the child and may be relied upon to the extent of its probative value, even though not competent in an adjudicatory hearing. Except as provided in paragraph (2)(c), nothing in this section shall prohibit the publication of proceedings in a hearing.

(4) REVIEW HEARINGS.

(a) The court shall hold a review hearing 45 days after the disposition hearing. Additional review hearings may be held as necessary, but no less than 45 days after the date of the last review hearing.

(b) At the review hearings, the court shall close the case if the child has substantially complied with the case plans and court orders and no longer requires continued court supervision, subject to the case being reopened. If the child has significantly failed to comply with the case plan or court orders, the child shall continue to be a child in need of services reviewed by the court as needed, but no less than 45 days after the date of the last review hearing.

HISTORY:
S. 8, ch. 87-133; s. 238, ch. 95-147; s. 31, ch. 96-398; s. 106, ch. 97-238; s. 10, ch. 97-281; s. 71, ch. 98-280.

Editor's notes.
Former s. 39.44.

§ 984.21. Orders of adjudication.

(1) If the court finds that the child named in a petition is not a child in need of services, it shall enter an order so finding and dismissing the case.

(2) If the court finds that the child named in the petition is a child in need of services, but finds that no action other than supervision in the home is required, it may enter an order briefly stating the facts upon which its finding is based, but withholding an order of adjudication and placing the child and family under the supervision of the department. If the court later finds that the parent, guardian, or custodian of the child have not complied with the conditions of supervision imposed, the court may, after a hearing to establish the noncompliance, but without further evidence of the state of the child in need of services, enter an order of adjudication and shall thereafter have full authority under this chapter to provide for the child as adjudicated.

(3) If the court finds that the child named in a petition is a child in need of services, but elects not to proceed under subsection (2), it shall incorporate that finding in an order of adjudication entered in the case, briefly stating the facts upon which the finding is made,

and the court shall thereafter have full authority under this chapter to provide for the child as adjudicated.

(4) An order of adjudication by a court that a child is a child in need of services shall not be deemed a conviction, nor shall the child be deemed to have been found guilty or to be a criminal by reason of that adjudication, nor shall that adjudication operate to impose upon the child any of the civil disabilities ordinarily imposed by or resulting from conviction or disqualify or prejudice the child in any civil service application or appointment.

HISTORY:
S. 8, ch. 87-133; s. 239, ch. 95-147; s. 107, ch. 97-238; s. 72, ch. 98-280.

Editor's notes.
Former s. 39.441.

§ 984.22. Powers of disposition.

(1) If the court finds that services and treatment have not been provided or utilized by a child or family, the court having jurisdiction of the child shall have the power to direct the least intrusive and least restrictive disposition, as follows:

(a) Order the parent, guardian, or custodian and the child to participate in treatment, services, and any other alternative identified as necessary.

(b) Order the parent, guardian, or custodian to pay a fine or fee based on the recommendations of the department.

(2) When any child is adjudicated by the court to be a child in need of services, the court having jurisdiction of the child and parent, guardian, or custodian shall have the power, by order, to:

(a) Place the child under the supervision of the department's contracted provider of programs and services for children in need of services and families in need of services. "Supervision," for the purposes of this section, means services as defined by the contract between the department and the provider.

(b) Place the child in the temporary legal custody of an adult willing to care for the child.

(c) Commit the child to a licensed child-caring agency willing to receive the child and to provide services without compensation from the department.

(d) Order the child, and, if the court finds it appropriate, the parent, guardian, or custodian of the child, to render community service in a public service program.

(3) When any child is adjudicated by the court to be a child in need of services and temporary legal custody of the child has been placed with an adult willing to care for the child, a licensed child-caring agency, the Department of Juvenile Justice, or the Department of Children and Families, the court shall order the natural or adoptive parents of such child, including the natural father of such child born out of wedlock who has acknowledged his paternity in writing before the court,

or the guardian of such child's estate if possessed of assets which under law may be disbursed for the care, support, and maintenance of such child, to pay child support to the adult relative caring for the child, the licensed child-caring agency, the Department of Juvenile Justice, or the Department of Children and Families. When such order affects the guardianship estate, a certified copy of such order shall be delivered to the judge having jurisdiction of such guardianship estate. If the court determines that the parent is unable to pay support, placement of the child shall not be contingent upon issuance of a support order. The department may employ a collection agency for the purpose of receiving, collecting, and managing the payment of unpaid and delinquent fees. The collection agency must be registered and in good standing under chapter 559. The department may pay to the collection agency a fee from the amount collected under the claim or may authorize the agency to deduct the fee from the amount collected.

(4) All payments of fees made to the department under this chapter, or child support payments made to the department pursuant to subsection (3), shall be deposited in the General Revenue Fund.

(5) In carrying out the provisions of this chapter, the court shall order the child, family, parent, guardian, or custodian of a child who is found to be a child in need of services to participate in family counseling and other professional counseling activities or other alternatives deemed necessary for the rehabilitation of the child.

(6) The participation and cooperation of the family, parent, guardian, or custodian, and the child with court-ordered services, treatment, or community service are mandatory, not merely voluntary. The court may use its contempt powers to enforce its order.

HISTORY:

SS. 8, 12, ch. 87-133; s. 31, ch. 88-337; s. 18, ch. 93-120; s. 240, ch. 95-147; s. 32, ch. 96-398; s. 169, ch. 97-101; s. 108, ch. 97-238; s. 11, ch. 97-281; s. 73, ch. 98-280; s. 72, ch. 2006-227, eff. July 1, 2006; s. 340, ch. 2014-19, eff. July 1, 2014.

Editor's notes.

Former s. 39.442.

§ 984.225. Powers of disposition; placement in a staff-secure shelter.

(1) Subject to specific legislative appropriation, the court may order that a child adjudicated as a child in need of services be placed for up to 90 days in a staff-secure shelter if:

(a) The child's parent, guardian, or legal custodian refuses to provide food, clothing, shelter, and necessary parental support for the child and the refusal is a direct result of an established pattern of significant disruptive behavior of the child in the home of the parent, guardian, or legal custodian;

(b) The child refuses to remain under the reasonable care and custody of his or her parent, guardian,

or legal custodian, as evidenced by repeatedly running away and failing to comply with a court order; or

(c) The child has failed to successfully complete an alternative treatment program or to comply with a court-ordered sanction and the child has been placed in a residential program on at least one prior occasion pursuant to a court order under this chapter.

(2) This section applies after other alternative, less-restrictive remedies have been exhausted. The court may order that a child be placed in a staff-secure shelter. The department, or an authorized representative of the department, must verify to the court that a bed is available for the child. If the department or an authorized representative of the department verifies that a bed is not available, the department will place the child's name on a waiting list. The child who has been on the waiting list the longest will get the next available bed.

(3) The court shall order the parent, guardian, or legal custodian to cooperate with efforts to reunite the child with the family, participate in counseling, and pay all costs associated with the care and counseling provided to the child and family, in accordance with the family's ability to pay as determined by the court. Commitment of a child under this section is designed to provide residential care on a temporary basis. Such commitment does not abrogate the legal responsibilities of the parent, guardian, or legal custodian with respect to the child, except to the extent that those responsibilities are temporarily altered by court order.

(4) While a child is in a staff-secure shelter, the child shall receive education commensurate with his or her grade level and educational ability.

(5) If a child has not been reunited with his or her parent, guardian, or legal custodian at the expiration of the 90-day commitment period, the court may order that the child remain in the staff-secure shelter for an additional 30 days if the court finds that reunification could be achieved within that period.

(6) The department is deemed to have exhausted the reasonable remedies offered under this chapter if, at the end of the commitment period, the parent, guardian, or legal custodian continues to refuse to allow the child to remain at home or creates unreasonable conditions for the child's return. If, at the end of the commitment period, the child is not reunited with his or her parent, guardian, or custodian due solely to the continued refusal of the parent, guardian, or custodian to provide food, clothing, shelter, and parental support, the child is considered to be threatened with harm as a result of such acts or omissions, and the court shall direct that the child be handled in every respect as a dependent child. Jurisdiction shall be transferred to the Department of Children and Families, and the child's care shall be governed under the relevant provisions of chapter 39.

(7) The court shall review the child's commitment once every 45 days as provided in s. 984.20. The court

shall determine whether the parent, guardian, or custodian has reasonably participated in and financially contributed to the child's counseling and treatment program. The court shall also determine whether the department's efforts to reunite the family have been reasonable. If the court finds an inadequate level of support or participation by the parent, guardian, or custodian prior to the end of the commitment period, the court shall direct that the child be handled in every respect as a dependent child. Jurisdiction shall be transferred to the Department of Children and Families, and the child's care shall be governed under the relevant provisions of chapter 39.

(8) If the child requires residential mental health treatment or residential care for a developmental disability, the court shall refer the child to the Department of Children and Families for the provision of necessary services.

HISTORY:
S. 12, ch. 97-281; s. 74, ch. 98-280; s. 3, ch. 2000-134; s. 51, ch. 2010-117, eff. July 1, 2010; s. 341, ch. 2014-19, eff. July 1, 2014.

§ 984.226. Physically secure setting.

(1) Subject to specific legislative appropriation, the Department of Juvenile Justice shall establish physically secure settings designated exclusively for the placement of children in need of services who meet the criteria provided in this section.

(2) When a petition is filed alleging that a child is a child in need of services, the child must be represented by counsel at each court appearance unless the record in that proceeding affirmatively demonstrates by clear and convincing evidence that the child knowingly and intelligently waived the right to counsel after being fully advised by the court of the nature of the proceedings and the dispositional alternatives available to the court under this section. If the court decides to appoint counsel for the child and if the child is indigent, the court shall appoint an attorney to represent the child as provided under s. 985.033. Nothing precludes the court from requesting reimbursement of attorney's fees and costs from the nonindigent parent or legal guardian.

(3) When a child is adjudicated as a child in need of services by a court, the court may order the child to be placed in a physically secure setting authorized in this section if the child has:

(a) Failed to appear for placement in a staff-secure shelter under s. 984.225, or failed to comply with any other provision of a valid court order relating to such placement and, as a result of such failure, has been found to be in direct or indirect contempt of court; or

(b) Run away from a staff-secure shelter following placement under s. 984.225 or s. 984.09.

The department or an authorized representative of the department must verify to the court that a bed is available for the child. If a bed is not available, the court must stay the placement until a bed is available, and

the department must place the child's name on a waiting list. The child who has been on the waiting list the longest has first priority for placement in the physically secure setting.

(4) A child may be placed in a physically secure setting for up to 90 days. If a child has not been reunited with his or her parent, guardian, or legal custodian at the expiration of the placement in a physically secure setting, the court may order that the child remain in the physically secure setting for an additional 30 days if the court finds that reunification could be achieved within that period.

(5)(a) The court shall review the child's placement once every 45 days as provided in s. 984.20.

(b) At any time during the placement of a child in need of services in a physically secure setting, the department or an authorized representative of the department may submit to the court a report that recommends:

1. That the child has received all of the services available from the physically secure setting and is ready for reunification with a parent or guardian; or

2. That the child is unlikely to benefit from continued placement in the physically secure setting and is more likely to have his or her needs met in a different type of placement.

(c) The court shall determine if the parent, guardian, or custodian has reasonably participated in and has financially contributed to the child's counseling and treatment program.

(d) If the court finds an inadequate level of support or participation by the parent, guardian, or custodian before the end of the placement, the court shall direct that the child be handled as a dependent child, jurisdiction shall be transferred to the Department of Children and Families, and the child's care shall be governed by chapter 39.

(e) If the child requires residential mental health treatment or residential care for a developmental disability, the court shall refer the child to the Department of Children and Families for the provision of necessary services.

(6) Prior to being ordered to a physically secure setting, the child must be afforded all rights of due process required under s. 985.037. While in the physically secure setting, the child shall receive appropriate assessment, treatment, and educational services that are designed to eliminate or reduce the child's truant, ungovernable, or runaway behavior. The child and family shall be provided with family counseling and other support services necessary for reunification.

(7) The court shall order the parent, guardian, or legal custodian to cooperate with efforts to reunite the child with the family, participate in counseling, and pay all costs associated with the care and counseling provided to the child and family, in accordance with the family's ability to pay as determined by the court.

Placement of a child under this section is designed to provide residential care on a temporary basis. Such placement does not abrogate the legal responsibilities of the parent, guardian, or legal custodian with respect to the child, except to the extent that those responsibilities are temporarily altered by court order.

HISTORY:
S. 13, ch. 97-281; s. 75, ch. 98-280; s. 127, ch. 99-3; s. 4, ch. 2000-134; s. 1, ch. 2000-327; s. 126, ch. 2006-120, eff. January 1, 2007; s. 342, ch. 2014-19, eff. July 1, 2014.

§ 984.23. Court and witness fees.

In all proceedings under this chapter, no court fees shall be charged against, and no witness fees shall be allowed to, any party to a petition or any parent or legal custodian or child named in a summons. Other witnesses shall be paid the witness fees fixed by law.

HISTORY:
S. 8, ch. 87-133; s. 109, ch. 97-238; s. 76, ch. 98-280.

Editor's notes.
Former s. 39.4375.

§ 984.24. Appeal.

The state, any child, or the family, guardian ad litem, or legal custodian of any child who is affected by an order of the court pursuant to this chapter may appeal to the appropriate district court of appeal within the time and in the manner prescribed by the Florida Rules of Appellate Procedure.

HISTORY:
S. 8, ch. 87-133; s. 33, ch. 96-398; s. 110, ch. 97-238; s. 77, ch. 98-280; s. 168, ch. 98-403.

Editor's notes.
Former s. 39.445; s. 39.4441.

CHAPTER 985.
JUVENILE JUSTICE; INTERSTATE COMPACT ON JUVENILES.

PART I.
GENERAL PROVISIONS.

§ 985.01. Purposes and intent.
(1) The purposes of this chapter are:
(a) To increase public safety by reducing juvenile delinquency through effective prevention, intervention, and treatment services that strengthen and reform the lives of children.

(b) To provide judicial and other procedures to assure due process through which children, victims, and other interested parties are assured fair hearings by a respectful and respected court or other tribunal and the recognition, protection, and enforcement of their constitutional and other legal rights, while ensuring that public safety interests and the authority and dignity of the courts are adequately protected.

(c) To provide an environment that fosters healthy social, emotional, intellectual, educational, and physical development; to ensure secure and safe custody; and to promote the health and well-being of all children under the state's care.

(d) To ensure the protection of society, by providing for a comprehensive standardized assessment of the child's needs so that the most appropriate control, discipline, punishment, and treatment can be administered consistent with the seriousness of the act committed, the community's long-term need for public safety, the prior record of the child, and the specific rehabilitation needs of the child, while also providing, whenever possible, restitution to the victim of the offense.

(e) To preserve and strengthen the child's family ties whenever possible, by providing for removal of the child from the physical custody of a parent only when his or her welfare or the safety and protection of the public cannot be adequately safeguarded without such removal; and, when the child is removed from his or her own family, to secure custody, care, and discipline for the child as nearly as possible equivalent to that which should have been given by the parents.

(f)1. To assure that the adjudication and disposition of a child alleged or found to have committed a violation of Florida law be exercised with appropriate discretion and in keeping with the seriousness of the offense and the need for treatment services, and that all findings made under this chapter be based upon facts presented at a hearing that meets the constitutional standards of fundamental fairness and due process.

2. To assure that the sentencing and placement of a child tried as an adult be appropriate and in keeping with the seriousness of the offense and the child's need for rehabilitative services, and that the proceedings and procedures applicable to such sentencing and placement be applied within the full framework of constitutional standards of fundamental fairness and due process.

(g) To provide children committed to the department with training in life skills, including career and technical education, when appropriate.

(h) To care for children in the least restrictive and most appropriate service environments to ensure that children assessed as low and moderate risk to reoffend are not committed to residential programs, unless the court deems such placement appropriate.

(i) To allocate resources for the most effective programs, services, and treatments to ensure that children, their families, and their community support systems are connected with these programs at the points along the juvenile justice continuum where they will have the most impact.

(2) It is the intent of the Legislature that this chapter be liberally interpreted and construed in conformity with its declared purposes.

HISTORY:
S. 1, ch. 97-238; s. 12, ch. 2001-125; s. 64, ch. 2004-267; ss. 2, 87, ch. 2006-120, eff. January 1, 2007; s. 1, ch. 2014-162, eff. July 1, 2014.

§ 985.02. Legislative intent for the juvenile justice system.
(1) GENERAL PROTECTIONS FOR CHILDREN. — It is a purpose of the Legislature that the children of this state be provided with the following protections:
(a) Protection from abuse, neglect, and exploitation.

(b) A permanent and stable home.

(c) A safe and nurturing environment which will preserve a sense of personal dignity and integrity.

(d) Adequate nutrition, shelter, and clothing.

(e) Effective treatment to address physical, social, and emotional needs, regardless of geographical location.

(f)   Equal opportunity and access to quality and effective education, which will meet the individual needs of each child, and to recreation and other community resources to develop individual abilities.

(g)   Access to prevention programs and services.

(h)   Gender-specific programming and gender-specific program models and services that comprehensively address the needs of a targeted gender group.

(2)   SUBSTANCE ABUSE SERVICES. — The Legislature finds that children in the care of the state's delinquency system need appropriate health care services, that the impact of substance abuse on health indicates the need for health care services to include substance abuse services where appropriate, and that it is in the state's best interest that such children be provided the services they need to enable them to become and remain independent of state care. In order to provide these services, the state's delinquency system must have the ability to identify and provide appropriate intervention and treatment for children with personal or family-related substance abuse problems. It is therefore the purpose of the Legislature to provide authority for the state to contract with community substance abuse treatment providers for the development and operation of specialized support and overlay services for the delinquency system, which will be fully implemented and utilized as resources permit.

(3)   JUVENILE JUSTICE AND DELINQUENCY PREVENTION. — It is the policy of the state with respect to juvenile justice and delinquency prevention to first protect the public from acts of delinquency. In addition, it is the policy of the state to:

(a)   Develop and implement effective methods of preventing and reducing acts of delinquency, with a focus on maintaining and strengthening the family as a whole so that children may remain in their homes or communities.

(b)   Develop and implement effective programs to prevent delinquency, to divert children from the traditional juvenile justice system, to intervene at an early stage of delinquency, and to provide critically needed alternatives to institutionalization and deep-end commitment.

(c)   Provide well-trained personnel, high-quality services, and cost-effective programs within the juvenile justice system.

(d)   Increase the capacity of local governments and public and private agencies to conduct rehabilitative treatment programs and to provide research, evaluation, and training services in the field of juvenile delinquency prevention.

(4)   DETENTION.

(a)   The Legislature finds that there is a need for a secure placement for certain children alleged to have committed a delinquent act. The Legislature finds that detention should be used only when less restrictive interim placement alternatives prior to adjudication and disposition are not appropriate. The Legislature further finds that decisions to detain should be based in part on a prudent assessment of risk and be limited to situations where there is clear and convincing evidence that a child presents a risk of failing to appear or presents a substantial risk of inflicting bodily harm on others as evidenced by recent behavior; presents a history of committing a serious property offense prior to adjudication, disposition, or placement; has acted in direct or indirect contempt of court; or requests protection from imminent bodily harm.

(b)   The Legislature intends that a juvenile found to have committed a delinquent act understands the consequences and the serious nature of such behavior. Therefore, the Legislature finds that secure detention is appropriate to provide punishment for children who pose a threat to public safety. The Legislature also finds that certain juveniles have committed a sufficient number of criminal acts, including acts involving violence to persons, to represent sufficient danger to the community to warrant sentencing and placement within the adult system. It is the intent of the Legislature to establish clear criteria in order to identify these juveniles and remove them from the juvenile justice system.

(5)   SITING OF FACILITIES.

(a)   The Legislature finds that timely siting and development of needed residential facilities for juvenile offenders is critical to the public safety of the citizens of this state and to the effective rehabilitation of juvenile offenders.

(b)   It is the purpose of the Legislature to guarantee that such facilities are sited and developed within reasonable timeframes after they are legislatively authorized and appropriated.

(c)   The Legislature further finds that such facilities must be located in areas of the state close to the home communities of the children they house in order to ensure the most effective rehabilitation efforts, postrelease supervision, and case management. The placement of facilities close to the home communities of the children they house is also intended to facilitate family involvement in the treatment process. Residential facilities shall have no more than 90 beds each, including campus-style programs, unless those campus-style programs include more than one treatment program using different treatment protocols and have facilities that coexist separately in distinct locations on the same property.

(d)   It is the intent of the Legislature that all other departments and agencies of the state shall cooperate fully with the Department of Juvenile Justice to accomplish the siting of facilities for juvenile offenders.

The supervision, counseling, and rehabilitative treatment efforts of the juvenile justice system should avoid the inappropriate use of correctional programs and large institutions.

(6) PARENTAL, CUSTODIAL, AND GUARDIAN RESPONSIBILITIES. — Parents, custodians, and guardians are deemed by the state to be responsible for providing their children with sufficient support, guidance, and supervision to deter their participation in delinquent acts. The state further recognizes that the ability of parents, custodians, and guardians to fulfill those responsibilities can be greatly impaired by economic, social, behavioral, emotional, and related problems. It is therefore the policy of the Legislature that it is the state's responsibility to ensure that factors impeding the ability of caretakers to fulfill their responsibilities are identified through the delinquency intake process and that appropriate recommendations to address those problems are considered in any judicial or nonjudicial proceeding. Nonetheless, as it is also the intent of the Legislature to preserve and strengthen the child's family ties, it is the policy of the Legislature that the emotional, legal, and financial responsibilities of the caretaker with regard to the care, custody, and support of the child continue while the child is in the physical or legal custody of the department.

(7) GENDER-SPECIFIC PROGRAMMING.

(a) The Legislature finds that the needs of children served by the juvenile justice system are gender-specific. A gender-specific approach is one in which programs, services, and treatments comprehensively address the unique developmental needs of a targeted gender group under the care of the department. Young women and men have different pathways to delinquency, display different patterns of offending, and respond differently to interventions, treatment, and services.

(b) Gender-specific interventions focus on the differences between young females' and young males' social roles and responsibilities, access to and use of resources, history of trauma, and reasons for interaction with the juvenile justice system. Gender-specific programs increase the effectiveness of programs by making interventions more appropriate to the specific needs of young women and men and ensuring that these programs do not unknowingly create, maintain, or reinforce gender roles or relations that may be damaging.

(8) TRAUMA-INFORMED CARE. — The Legislature finds that the department should use trauma-informed care as an approach to treating children with histories of trauma. Trauma-informed care assists service providers in recognizing the symptoms of trauma and acknowledges the role trauma has played in the child's life. Services for children should be based on an understanding of the vulnerabilities and triggers of trauma survivors that traditional service delivery approaches may exacerbate, so that these services and programs can be more supportive and avoid retraumatization. The department should use trauma-specific interventions that are designed to address the consequences of trauma in the child and to facilitate healing.

(9) FAMILY AND COMMUNITY ENGAGEMENT. — The Legislature finds that families and community support systems are critical to the success of children and to ensure they are nondelinquent. Therefore, when appropriate, children who can safely be held accountable when served and treated in their homes and communities should be diverted from more restrictive placements within the juvenile justice system. There should be an emphasis on strengthening the family and immersing the family members in their community support system. The department should develop customized plans that acknowledge the importance of family and community support systems. The customized plans should recognize a child's individual needs, capitalize on their strengths, reduce their risks, and prepare them for a successful transition to, and unification with, their family and community support system. The child's family must be considered in the department's process of assessing the needs, services and treatment, and community connections of the children who are involved in the juvenile justice system or in danger of becoming involved in the system.

HISTORY:
S. 2, ch. 97-238; s. 13, ch. 2001-125; s. 1, ch. 2004-333; s. 3, ch. 2006-120, eff. January 1, 2007; s. 1, ch. 2008-65, eff. July 1, 2008; s. 167, ch. 2010-102, eff. May 26, 2010; s. 1, ch. 2011-70, eff. July 1, 2011; s. 2, ch. 2014-162, eff. July 1, 2014.

§ 985.03. Definitions.

As used in this chapter, the term:

(1) "Abscond" means to hide, conceal, or absent oneself from the jurisdiction of the court or supervision of the department to avoid prosecution or supervision.

(2) "Addictions receiving facility" means a substance abuse service provider as defined in chapter 397.

(3) "Adjudicatory hearing" means a hearing for the court to determine whether or not the facts support the allegations stated in the petition, as is provided for under s. 985.35 in delinquency cases.

(4) "Adult" means any natural person other than a child.

(5) "Arbitration" means a process whereby a neutral third person or panel, called an arbitrator or an arbitration panel, considers the facts and arguments presented by the parties and renders a decision which may be binding or nonbinding.

(6) "Authorized agent" or "designee" of the department means a person or agency assigned or designated by the department to perform duties or exercise powers under this chapter and includes contract providers and their employees.

(7) "Child" or "juvenile" or "youth" means any person under the age of 18 or any person who is alleged to have committed a violation of law occur-

ring prior to the time that person reached the age of 18 years.

(8) "Child in need of services" has the same meaning as provided in s. 984.03.

(9) "Child who has been found to have committed a delinquent act" means a child who, under this chapter, is found by a court to have committed a violation of law or to be in direct or indirect contempt of court, except that this definition does not include an act constituting contempt of court arising out of a dependency proceeding or a proceeding concerning a child or family in need of services.

(10) "Circuit" means any of the 20 judicial circuits as set forth in s. 26.021.

(11) "Comprehensive assessment" or "assessment" means the gathering of information for the evaluation of a juvenile offender's or a child's physical, psychological, educational, career and technical education, and social condition and family environment as they relate to the child's need for rehabilitative and treatment services, including substance abuse treatment services, mental health services, developmental services, literacy services, medical services, family services, and other specialized services, as appropriate.

(12) "Conditional release" means the care, treatment, help, supervision, and provision of transition-to-adulthood services provided to a juvenile released from a residential commitment program which is intended to promote rehabilitation and prevent recidivism. The purpose of conditional release is to protect the public, reduce recidivism, increase responsible productive behavior, and provide for a successful transition of the youth from the department to his or her family. Conditional release includes, but is not limited to, nonresidential community-based programs.

(13) "Court" means the circuit court assigned to exercise jurisdiction under this chapter, unless otherwise expressly stated.

(14) "Day treatment" means a nonresidential, community-based program designed to provide therapeutic intervention to youth who are served by the department, placed on probation or conditional release, or committed to the minimum-risk nonresidential level. A day treatment program may provide educational and career and technical education services and shall provide case management services; individual, group, and family counseling; training designed to address delinquency risk factors; and monitoring of a youth's compliance with, and facilitation of a youth's completion of, sanctions if ordered by the court. Program types may include, but are not limited to, career programs, marine programs, juvenile justice alternative schools, training and rehabilitation programs, and gender-specific programs.

(15)(a) "Delinquency program" means any intake, probation, or similar program; regional de-

tention center or facility; or community-based program, whether owned and operated by or contracted by the department, or institution owned and operated by or contracted by the department, which provides intake, supervision, or custody and care of children who are alleged to be or who have been found to be delinquent under this chapter.

(b) "Delinquency program staff" means supervisory and direct care staff of a delinquency program as well as support staff who have direct contact with children in a delinquency program.

(16) "Department" means the Department of Juvenile Justice.

(17) "Designated facility" or "designated treatment facility" means any facility designated by the department to provide treatment to juvenile offenders.

(18) "Detention care" means the temporary care of a child in secure or nonsecure detention, pending a court adjudication or disposition or execution of a court order. There are two types of detention care, as follows:

(a) "Secure detention" means temporary custody of the child while the child is under the physical restriction of a secure detention center or facility pending adjudication, disposition, or placement.

(b) "Nonsecure detention" means temporary, nonsecure custody of the child while the child is released to the custody of the parent, guardian, or custodian in a physically nonrestrictive environment under the supervision of the department staff pending adjudication, disposition, or placement. Forms of nonsecure detention include, but are not limited to, home detention, electronic monitoring, day reporting centers, evening reporting centers, and nonsecure shelters. Nonsecure detention may include other requirements imposed by the court.

(19) "Detention center or facility" means a facility used pending court adjudication or disposition or execution of court order for the temporary care of a child alleged or found to have committed a violation of law. A detention center or facility may provide secure custody. A facility used for the commitment of adjudicated delinquents shall not be considered a detention center or facility.

(20) "Detention hearing" means a hearing for the court to determine if a child should be placed in temporary custody, as provided for under part V in delinquency cases.

(21) "Disposition hearing" means a hearing in which the court determines the most appropriate dispositional services in the least restrictive available setting provided for under part VII, in delinquency cases.

(22) "Family" means a collective of persons, consisting of a child and a parent, guardian, adult custodian, or adult relative, in which:

(a) The persons reside in the same house or living unit; or

(b) The parent, guardian, adult custodian, or adult relative has a legal responsibility by blood, marriage, or court order to support or care for the child.

(23) "Family in need of services" has the same meaning as provided in s. 984.03.

(24) "Intake" means the initial acceptance and screening by the department or juvenile assessment center personnel of a complaint or a law enforcement report or probable cause affidavit of delinquency to determine the recommendation to be taken in the best interests of the child, the family, and the community. The emphasis of intake is on diversion and the least restrictive available services. Consequently, intake includes such alternatives as:

(a) The disposition of the complaint, report, or probable cause affidavit without court or public agency action or judicial handling when appropriate.

(b) The referral of the child to another public or private agency when appropriate.

(c) The recommendation by the department of judicial handling when appropriate and warranted.

(25) "Judge" means the circuit judge exercising jurisdiction pursuant to this chapter.

(26) "Juvenile justice continuum" includes, but is not limited to, prevention programs and services designed for the purpose of preventing or reducing delinquent acts, including criminal activity by criminal gangs, and juvenile arrests, as well as programs and services targeted at children who have committed delinquent acts, and children who have previously been committed to residential treatment programs for delinquents. The term includes children-in-need-of-services and families-in-need-of-services programs under chapter 984; conditional release; substance abuse and mental health programs; educational and career programs; recreational programs; community services programs; community service work programs; mother-infant programs; and alternative dispute resolution programs serving children at risk of delinquency and their families, whether offered or delivered by state or local governmental entities, public or private for-profit or not-for-profit organizations, or religious or charitable organizations.

(27) "Juvenile probation officer" means the authorized agent of the department who performs the intake, case management, or supervision functions.

(28) "Legal custody or guardian" means a legal status created by court order or letter of guardianship which vests in a custodian of the person or guardian, whether an agency or an individual, the right to have physical custody of the child and the right and duty to protect, train, and discipline the child and to provide him or her with food, shelter, education, and ordinary medical, dental, psychiatric, and psychological care.

(29) "Licensed child-caring agency" means a person, society, association, or agency licensed by the Department of Children and Families to care for, receive, and board children.

(30) "Licensed health care professional" means a physician licensed under chapter 458, an osteopathic physician licensed under chapter 459, a nurse licensed under part I of chapter 464, a physician assistant licensed under chapter 458 or chapter 459, or a dentist licensed under chapter 466.

(31) "Likely to injure oneself" means that, as evidenced by violent or other actively self-destructive behavior, it is more likely than not that within a 24-hour period the child will attempt to commit suicide or inflict serious bodily harm on himself or herself.

(32) "Likely to injure others" means that it is more likely than not that within a 24-hour period the child will inflict serious and unjustified bodily harm on another person.

(33) "Mediation" means a process whereby a neutral third person called a mediator acts to encourage and facilitate the resolution of a dispute between two or more parties. It is an informal and nonadversarial process with the objective of helping the disputing parties reach a mutually acceptable and voluntary agreement. In mediation, decisionmaking authority rests with the parties. The role of the mediator includes, but is not limited to, assisting the parties in identifying issues, fostering joint problem solving, and exploring settlement alternatives.

(34) "Mother-infant program" means a residential program designed to serve the needs of juvenile mothers or expectant juvenile mothers who are committed as delinquents, which is operated or contracted by the department. A mother-infant program facility must be licensed as a child care facility under s. 402.308 and must provide the services and support necessary to enable each juvenile mother committed to the facility to provide for the needs of her infants who, upon agreement of the mother, may accompany her in the program.

(35) "Necessary medical treatment" means care which is necessary within a reasonable degree of medical certainty to prevent the deterioration of a child's condition or to alleviate immediate pain of a child.

(36) "Next of kin" means an adult relative of a child who is the child's brother, sister, grandparent, aunt, uncle, or first cousin.

(37) "Ordinary medical care" means medical procedures that are administered or performed on a routine basis and include, but are not limited to, inoculations, physical examinations, remedial treatment for minor illnesses and injuries, preventive services, medication management, chronic disease

detection and treatment, and other medical procedures that are administered or performed on a routine basis and do not involve hospitalization, surgery, the use of general anesthesia, or the provision of psychotropic medications.

(38) "Parent" means a woman who gives birth to a child and a man whose consent to the adoption of the child would be required under s. 63.062(1). If a child has been legally adopted, the term "parent" means the adoptive mother or father of the child. The term does not include an individual whose parental relationship to the child has been legally terminated, or an alleged or prospective parent, unless the parental status falls within the terms of either s. 39.503(1) or s. 63.062(1).

(39) "Preliminary screening" means the gathering of preliminary information to be used in determining a child's need for further evaluation or assessment or for referral for other substance abuse services through means such as psychosocial interviews; urine and breathalyzer screenings; and reviews of available educational, delinquency, and dependency records of the child.

(40) "Prevention" means programs, strategies, initiatives, and networks designed to keep children from making initial or further contact with the juvenile justice system.

(41) "Probation" means the legal status of probation created by law and court order in cases involving a child who has been found to have committed a delinquent act. Probation is an individualized program in which the freedom of the child is limited and the child is restricted to noninstitutional quarters or restricted to the child's home in lieu of commitment to the custody of the department. Youth on probation may be assessed and classified for placement in day-treatment probation programs designed for youth who represent a minimum risk to themselves and public safety and do not require placement and services in a residential setting.

(42) "Relative" means a grandparent, great-grandparent, sibling, first cousin, aunt, uncle, great-aunt, great-uncle, niece, or nephew, whether related by the whole or half blood, by affinity, or by adoption. The term does not include a stepparent.

(43) "Respite" means a placement that is available for the care, custody, and placement of a youth charged with domestic violence as an alternative to secure detention or for placement of a youth when a shelter bed for a child in need of services or a family in need of services is unavailable.

(44) "Restrictiveness level" means the level of programming and security provided by programs that service the supervision, custody, care, and treatment needs of committed children. Sections 985.601(10) and 985.721 apply to children placed in programs at any residential commitment level. The restrictiveness levels of commitment are as follows:

(a) *MINIMUM-RISK NONRESIDENTIAL.* — Programs or program models at this commitment level work with youth who remain in the community and participate at least 5 days per week in a day treatment program. Youth assessed and classified for programs at this commitment level represent a minimum risk to themselves and public safety and do not require placement and services in residential settings. Youth in this level have full access to, and reside in, the community. Youth who have been found to have committed delinquent acts that involve firearms, that are sexual offenses, or that would be life felonies or first degree felonies if committed by an adult may not be committed to a program at this level.

(b) *NONSECURE RESIDENTIAL.* — Programs or program models at this commitment level are residential but may allow youth to have supervised access to the community. Facilities at this commitment level are either environmentally secure, staff secure, or are hardware-secure with walls, fencing, or locking doors. Residential facilities at this commitment level shall have no more than 90 beds each, including campus-style programs, unless those campus-style programs include more than one treatment program using different treatment protocols, and have facilities that coexist separately in distinct locations on the same property. Facilities at this commitment level shall provide 24-hour awake supervision, custody, care, and treatment of residents. Youth assessed and classified for placement in programs at this commitment level represent a low or moderate risk to public safety and require close supervision. The staff at a facility at this commitment level may seclude a child who is a physical threat to himself or herself or others. Mechanical restraint may also be used when necessary.

(c) *HIGH-RISK RESIDENTIAL.* — Programs or program models at this commitment level are residential and do not allow youth to have access to the community, except that temporary release providing community access for up to 72 continuous hours may be approved by a court for a youth who has made successful progress in his or her program in order for the youth to attend a family emergency or, during the final 60 days of his or her placement, to visit his or her home, enroll in school or a career and technical education program, complete a job interview, or participate in a community service project. High-risk residential facilities are hardware-secure with perimeter fencing and locking doors. Residential facilities at this commitment level shall have no more than 90 beds each, including campus-style programs, unless those campus-style programs include more than one treatment program using different treatment protocols, and have facilities that coexist separately in distinct locations on the same property. Facilities at this commitment level shall provide 24-hour awake supervision, custody, care, and treatment of residents. Youth assessed and classified for this level of placement require close supervision in a structured residential setting. Placement in programs at this level is prompted by a concern for public safety that outweighs placement in programs at lower commitment levels. The staff at a facility at this commitment level may seclude a child who is a physical threat to himself or herself or others. Mechanical restraint may also be used when necessary. The facility may provide for single cell occupancy, except that youth may be housed together during prerelease transition.

(d) *MAXIMUM-RISK RESIDENTIAL.* — Programs or program models at this commitment level include juvenile correctional facilities and juvenile prisons. The programs at this commitment level are long-term residential and do not allow youth to have access to the community. Facilities at this commitment level are maximum-custody, hardware-secure with perimeter security fencing and locking doors. Residential facilities at this commitment level shall have no more than 90 beds each, including campus-style programs, unless those campus-style programs include more than one treatment program using different treatment protocols, and have facilities that coexist separately in distinct locations on the same property. Facilities at this commitment level shall provide 24-hour awake supervision, custody, care, and treatment of residents. The staff at a facility at this commitment level may seclude a child who is a physical threat to himself or herself or others. Mechanical restraint may also be used when necessary. Facilities at this commitment level shall provide for single cell occupancy, except that youth may be housed together during prerelease transition. Youth assessed and classified for this level of placement require close supervision in a maximum security residential setting. Placement in a program at this level is prompted by a demonstrated need to protect the public.

(45) "Secure detention center or facility" means a physically restricting facility for the temporary care of children pending adjudication, disposition, or placement.

(46) "Shelter" means a place for the temporary care of a child who is alleged to be or who has been found to be delinquent.

(47) "Substance abuse" means using, without medical reason, any psychoactive or mood-altering drug, including alcohol, in such a manner as to induce impairment resulting in dysfunctional social behavior.

(48) "Taken into custody" means the status of a child immediately when temporary physical control over the child is attained by a person authorized by law, pending the child's release, detention, placement, or other disposition as authorized by law.

(49) "Temporary legal custody" means the relationship that a juvenile court creates between a child and an adult relative of the child, adult nonrelative approved by the court, or other person until a more permanent arrangement is ordered. Temporary legal custody confers upon the custodian the right to have temporary physical custody of the child and the right and duty to protect, train, and discipline the child and to provide the child with food, shelter, and education, and ordinary medical, dental, psychiatric, and psychological care, unless these rights and duties are otherwise enlarged or limited by the court order establishing the temporary legal custody relationship.

(50) "Temporary release" means the terms and conditions under which a child is temporarily released from a residential commitment facility or allowed home visits. If the temporary release is from a nonsecure residential facility, a high-risk residential facility, or a maximum-risk residential facility, the terms and conditions of the temporary release must be approved by the child, the court, and the facility.

(51) "Transition-to-adulthood services" means services that are provided for youth in the custody of the department or under the supervision of the department and that have the objective of instilling the knowledge, skills, and aptitudes essential to a socially integrated, self-supporting adult life. The services may include, but are not limited to:

(a) Assessment of the youth's ability and readiness for adult life.

(b) A plan for the youth to acquire the knowledge, information, and counseling necessary to make a successful transition to adulthood.

(c) Services that have proven effective toward achieving the transition to adulthood.

(52) "Trauma-informed care" means services that are provided to children with a history of trauma, recognizing the symptoms of trauma and acknowledging the role that trauma has played in the child's life. Trauma may include, but is not limited to, community and school violence, physical or sexual abuse, neglect, medical difficulties, and domestic violence.

(53) "Violation of law" or "delinquent act" means a violation of any law of this state, the United States, or any other state which is a misdemeanor or a felony or a violation of a county or municipal ordinance which would be punishable by incarceration if the violation were committed by an adult.

(54) "Waiver hearing" means a hearing provided for under s. 985.556(4).

HISTORY:

S. 4, ch. 97-234; s. 3, ch. 97-238; s. 1, ch. 97-276; s. 13, ch. 98-49; s. 7, ch. 98-207; s. 78, ch. 98-280; s. 169, ch. 98-403; s. 58, ch. 99-7;

s. 14, ch. 99-201; s. 9, ch. 99-284; s. 18, ch. 2000-135; s. 150, ch. 2000-318; s. 35, ch. 2001-3; s. 14, ch. 2001-125; s. 119, ch. 2002-1; s. 1050, ch. 2002-387; s. 67, ch. 2004-357; s. 1, ch. 2005-263; ss. 4, 56, 57, 59, ch. 2006-120; s. 2, ch. 2008-65, eff. July 1, 2008; s. 30, ch. 2008-238, eff. Oct. 1, 2008; s. 1, ch. 2010-123, eff. July 1, 2010; ss. 2, 3, ch. 2011-70, eff. July 1, 2011; s. 1, ch. 2011-236, eff. July 1, 2011; s. 2, ch. 2012-56, eff. July 1, 2012; s. 117, ch. 2013-15, eff. July 2, 2013; s. 343, ch. 2014-19, eff. July 1, 2014; s. 3, ch. 2014-162, eff. July 1, 2014.

§ 985.0301. Jurisdiction.

(1) The circuit court has exclusive original jurisdiction of proceedings in which a child is alleged to have committed:

(a) A delinquent act or violation of law.

(b) A noncriminal violation that has been assigned to juvenile court by law.

(2) The jurisdiction of the court shall attach to the child and the case when the summons is served upon the child and a parent or legal or actual custodian or guardian of the child, or when the child is taken into custody with or without service of summons and before or after the filing of a petition, whichever first occurs, and thereafter the court may control the child and the case in accordance with this chapter.

(3) During the prosecution of any violation of law against any person who has been presumed to be an adult, if it is shown that the person was a child at the time the offense was committed and that the person does not meet the criteria for prosecution and sentencing as an adult, the court shall immediately transfer the case, together with the physical custody of the person and all physical evidence, papers, documents, and testimony, original and duplicate, connected therewith, to the appropriate court for proceedings under this chapter. The circuit court is exclusively authorized to assume jurisdiction over any juvenile offender who is arrested and charged with violating a federal law or a law of the District of Columbia, who is found or is living or domiciled in a county in which the circuit court is established, and who is surrendered to the circuit court as provided in 18 U.S.C. s. 5001.

(4)(a) Petitions alleging delinquency shall be filed in the county where the delinquent act or violation of law occurred. The circuit court for that county may transfer the case to the circuit court of the circuit in which the child resides or will reside at the time of detention or placement for dispositional purposes. A child who has been detained may be transferred to the detention center or facility in the circuit in which the child resides or will reside at the time of detention.

(b) The jurisdiction to be exercised by the court when a child is taken into custody before the filing of a petition under subsection (2) shall be exercised by the circuit court for the county in which the child is taken into custody, which court shall have personal jurisdiction of the child and the child's parent or legal guardian. Upon the filing of a petition in the appropriate circuit court, the court that is exercising initial jurisdiction of the person of the child shall, if the child has been detained, immediately order the child to be transferred to the detention center or facility or other placement as ordered by the court having subject matter jurisdiction of the case.

(5)(a) Notwithstanding s. 743.07, and except as provided in paragraph (b), when the jurisdiction of any child who is alleged to have committed a delinquent act or violation of law is obtained, the court shall retain jurisdiction to dispose of a case, unless relinquished by its order, until the child reaches 19 years of age, with the same power over the child which the court had before the child became an adult.

(b) The court shall retain jurisdiction, unless relinquished by its own order:

1. Over a child on probation until the child reaches 19 years of age.

2. Over a child committed to the department until the child reaches 21 years of age, specifically for the purpose of allowing the child to complete the commitment program, including conditional release supervision.

(c) The court shall retain jurisdiction over a juvenile sexual offender, as defined in s. 985.475, who has been placed on community-based treatment alternative with supervision or who has been placed in a program or facility for juvenile sexual offenders, pursuant to s. 985.48, until the juvenile sexual offender reaches 21 years of age, specifically for the purpose of allowing the juvenile to complete the program.

(d) The court may retain jurisdiction over a child and the child's parent or legal guardian whom the court has ordered to pay restitution until the restitution order is satisfied. To retain jurisdiction, the court shall enter a restitution order, which is separate from any disposition or order of commitment, on or prior to the date that the court's jurisdiction would cease under this section. The contents of the restitution order shall be limited to the child's name and address, the name and address of the parent or legal guardian, the name and address of the payee, the case number, the date and amount of restitution ordered, any amount of restitution paid, the amount of restitution due and owing, and a notation that costs, interest, penalties, and attorney fees may also be due and owing. The terms of the restitution order are subject to s. 775.089(5).

(e) This subsection does not prevent the exercise of jurisdiction by any court having jurisdiction of the child if the child, after becoming an adult, commits a violation of law.

(6) The court may at any time enter an order ending its jurisdiction over any child.

HISTORY:

S. 5, ch. 90-208; s. 12, ch. 92-287; s. 2, ch. 93-37; ss. 19, 39, ch. 94-209; s. 21, ch. 94-342; s. 2, ch. 95-160; ss. 9, 27, ch. 97-238; s. 33, ch. 99-284; ss. 5, 11, ch. 2000-134; s. 36, ch. 2001-64; s. 65, ch. 2005-236; s. 19, ch. 2005-263; s. 5, ch. 2006-120, eff. Jan. 1, 2007; s. 2, ch. 2011-54, eff. July 1, 2011; s. 10, ch. 2011-70, eff. July 1, 2011; s. 3, ch. 2011-236, eff. July 1, 2011; s. 90, ch. 2012-5, eff. May 8, 2012; s. 6, ch. 2012-56, eff. July 1, 2012; s. 4, ch. 2014-162, eff. July 1, 2014; s. 104, ch. 2015-2, eff. June 30, 2015; s. 4, ch. 2015-133, eff. July 1, 2015.

Editor's notes.
Formerly s. 985.201 and s. 985.219(8): transferred by s. 5, ch. 2006-120, effective January 1, 2007; s. 39.022; s. 39.049.

§ 985.032. Legal representation for delinquency cases.

(1) For cases arising under this chapter, the state attorney shall represent the state.

(2) A juvenile who has been adjudicated delinquent or has adjudication of delinquency withheld shall be assessed costs of prosecution as provided in s. 938.27.

HISTORY:
S. 2, ch. 92-170; s. 13, ch. 94-209; s. 1334, ch. 95-147; s. 2, ch. 97-101; s. 10, ch. 97-238; s. 6, ch. 2006-120, eff. Jan. 1, 2007; s. 3, ch. 2013-112, eff. July 1, 2013.

Editor's notes.
Formerly s. 985.202: transferred by s. 6, ch. 2006-120, effective January 1, 2007; s. 39.014.

§ 985.033. Right to counsel.

(1) A child is entitled to representation by legal counsel at all stages of any delinquency court proceedings under this chapter. If the child and the parents or other legal guardian are indigent and unable to employ counsel for the child, the court shall appoint counsel under s. 27.52. Determination of indigence and costs of representation shall be as provided by ss. 27.52 and 938.29. Legal counsel representing a child who exercises the right to counsel shall be allowed to provide advice and counsel to the child at any time subsequent to the child's arrest, including prior to a detention hearing while in secure detention care. A child shall be represented by legal counsel at all stages of all court proceedings unless the right to counsel is freely, knowingly, and intelligently waived by the child. If the child appears without counsel, the court shall advise the child of his or her rights with respect to representation of court-appointed counsel.

(2) This section does not apply to transfer proceedings under s. 985.441(4), unless the court sets a hearing to review the transfer.

(3) If the parents or legal guardian of an indigent child are not indigent but refuse to employ counsel, the court shall appoint counsel pursuant to s. 27.52 to represent the child at the detention hearing and until counsel is provided. Costs of representation are hereby imposed as provided by ss. 27.52 and 938.29. Thereafter, the court shall not appoint counsel for an indigent child with nonindigent parents or legal guardian but shall order the parents or legal guardian to obtain private counsel. A parent or legal guardian of an indigent child who has been ordered to obtain private counsel for the child and who willfully fails to follow the court order shall be punished by the court in civil contempt proceedings.

(4) An indigent child with nonindigent parents or legal guardian may have counsel appointed pursuant to s. 27.52 if the parents or legal guardian have willfully refused to obey the court order to obtain counsel for the child and have been punished by civil contempt and then still have willfully refused to obey the court order. Costs of representation are hereby imposed as provided by ss. 27.52 and 938.29.

(5) Notwithstanding any provision of this section or any other law to the contrary, if a child is transferred for criminal prosecution pursuant to this chapter, a nonindigent or indigent-but-able-to-contribute parent or legal guardian of the child pursuant to s. 27.52 is liable for necessary legal fees and costs incident to the criminal prosecution of the child as an adult.

HISTORY:
S. 5, ch. 90-208; s. 220, ch. 95-147; s. 4, ch. 96-232; s. 11, ch. 97-238; s. 30, ch. 97-271; s. 129, ch. 99-3; s. 139, ch. 2003-402; s. 165, ch. 2004-5; s. 90, ch. 2004-265; s. 7, ch. 2006-120, eff. January 1, 2007; s. 3, ch. 2011-54, eff. July 1, 2011.

Editor's notes.
Formerly s. 985.203: transferred by s. 7, ch. 2006-120, effective January 1, 2007; s. 39.041.

§ 985.035. Opening hearings.

(1) All hearings, except as provided in this section, must be open to the public, and no person may be excluded except on special order of the court. The court, in its discretion, may close any hearing to the public when the public interest and the welfare of the child are best served by so doing. Hearings involving more than one child may be held simultaneously when the children were involved in the same transactions.

(2) Except as provided in subsection (1), nothing in this section shall prohibit the publication of proceedings in a hearing.

HISTORY:
S. 13, ch. 97-238; s. 8, ch. 2006-120, eff. January 1, 2007.

Editor's notes.
Formerly s. 985.205: transferred by s. 8, ch. 2006-120, effective January 1, 2007.

§ 985.036. Rights of victims; juvenile proceedings.

(1) Nothing in this chapter prohibits:

(a) The victim of the offense;

(b) The victim's parent or guardian if the victim is a minor;

(c) The lawful representative of the victim or of the victim's parent or guardian if the victim is a minor; or

(d) The next of kin if the victim is a homicide victim,

from the right to be informed of, to be present during, and to be heard when relevant at, all crucial stages of the proceedings involving the juvenile offender, to the extent that such rights do not interfere with the constitutional rights of the juvenile offender. A person enumerated in this section may not reveal to any outside party any confidential information obtained under this subsection regarding a case involving a juvenile offense, except as is reasonably necessary to pursue legal remedies.

(2) A law enforcement agency may release a copy of the juvenile offense report to the victim of the offense. However, information gained by the victim under this chapter, including the next of kin of a homicide victim, regarding any case handled in juvenile court must not be revealed to any outside party, except as is reasonably necessary in pursuit of legal remedies.

HISTORY:

S. 1, ch. 92-66; s. 14, ch. 97-238; s. 9, ch. 2006-120, eff. January 1, 2007.

Editor's notes.

Formerly s. 985.206: transferred by s. 9, ch. 2006-120, effective January 1, 2007; s. 39.0515.

§ 985.037. Punishment for contempt of court; alternative sanctions.

(1) CONTEMPT OF COURT; LEGISLATIVE INTENT. — The court may punish any child for contempt for interfering with the court or with court administration, or for violating any provision of this chapter or order of the court relative thereto. It is the intent of the Legislature that the court restrict and limit the use of contempt powers with respect to commitment of a child to a secure facility. A child who commits direct contempt of court or indirect contempt of a valid court order may be taken into custody and ordered to serve an alternative sanction or placed in a secure facility, as authorized in this section, by order of the court.

(2) PLACEMENT IN A SECURE DETENTION FACILITY. — A child may be placed in a secure detention facility for purposes of punishment for contempt of court if alternative sanctions are unavailable or inappropriate, or if the child has already been ordered to serve an alternative sanction but failed to comply with the sanction. A delinquent child who has been held in direct or indirect contempt may be placed in a secure detention facility not to exceed 5 days for a first offense and not to exceed 15 days for a second or subsequent offense.

(3) ALTERNATIVE SANCTIONS. — Each judicial circuit shall have an alternative sanctions coordinator who shall serve under the chief administrative judge of the juvenile division of the circuit court, and who shall coordinate and maintain a spectrum of contempt sanction alternatives in conjunction with the circuit plan implemented in accordance with s. 790.22(4)(c). Upon determining that a child has committed direct contempt

of court or indirect contempt of a valid court order, the court may immediately request the alternative sanctions coordinator to recommend the most appropriate available alternative sanction and shall order the child to perform up to 50 hours of community-service manual labor or a similar alternative sanction, unless an alternative sanction is unavailable or inappropriate, or unless the child has failed to comply with a prior alternative sanction. Alternative contempt sanctions may be provided by local industry or by any nonprofit organization or any public or private business or service entity that has entered into a contract with the Department of Juvenile Justice to act as an agent of the state to provide voluntary supervision of children on behalf of the state in exchange for the manual labor of children and limited immunity in accordance with s. 768.28(11).

(4) CONTEMPT OF COURT SANCTIONS; PROCEDURE AND DUE PROCESS.

(a) If a child is charged with direct contempt of court, including traffic court, the court may impose an authorized sanction immediately. The court must hold a hearing to determine if the child committed direct contempt. Due process must be afforded to the child during this hearing.

(b) If a child is charged with indirect contempt of court, the court must hold a hearing within 24 hours to determine whether the child committed indirect contempt of a valid court order. At the hearing, the following due process rights must be provided to the child:

1. Right to a copy of the order to show cause alleging facts supporting the contempt charge.

2. Right to an explanation of the nature and the consequences of the proceedings.

3. Right to legal counsel and the right to have legal counsel appointed by the court if the juvenile is indigent, under s. 985.033.

4. Right to confront witnesses.

5. Right to present witnesses.

6. Right to have a transcript or record of the proceeding.

7. Right to appeal to an appropriate court.

The child's parent or guardian may address the court regarding the due process rights of the child. Upon motion by the defense attorney or state attorney, the court shall review the placement of the child to determine whether it is appropriate for the child to remain in the facility.

(c) The court may not order that a child be placed in a secure detention facility for punishment for contempt unless the court determines that an alternative sanction is inappropriate or unavailable or that the child was initially ordered to an alternative sanction and did not comply with the alternative sanction. The court is encouraged to order a child to perform community service, up to the maximum number of hours, where appropriate before ordering that the child be placed in a secure detention facility as punishment for contempt of court.

(d)   In addition to any other sanction imposed under this section, the court may direct the Department of Highway Safety and Motor Vehicles to withhold issuance of, or suspend, a child's driver license or driving privilege. The court may order that a child's driver license or driving privilege be withheld or suspended for up to 1 year for a first offense of contempt and up to 2 years for a second or subsequent offense. If the child's driver license or driving privilege is suspended or revoked for any reason at the time the sanction for contempt is imposed, the court shall extend the period of suspension or revocation by the additional period ordered under this paragraph. If the child's driver license is being withheld at the time the sanction for contempt is imposed, the period of suspension or revocation ordered under this paragraph shall begin on the date on which the child is otherwise eligible to drive.

(5) ALTERNATIVE SANCTIONS COORDINATOR.
— There is created the position of alternative sanctions coordinator within each judicial circuit, pursuant to subsection (3). Each alternative sanctions coordinator shall serve under the direction of the chief administrative judge of the juvenile division as directed by the chief judge of the circuit. The alternative sanctions coordinator shall act as the liaison between the judiciary, local department officials, district school board employees, and local law enforcement agencies. The alternative sanctions coordinator shall coordinate within the circuit community-based alternative sanctions, including nonsecure detention programs, community service projects, and other juvenile sanctions, in conjunction with the circuit plan implemented in accordance with s. 790.22(4)(c).

HISTORY:
S. 14, ch. 94-209; s. 4, ch. 95-267; s. 24, ch. 97-238; s. 1, ch. 97-281; s. 15, ch. 98-207; s. 10, ch. 2000-134; s. 25, ch. 2000-135; s. 10, ch. 2006-120, eff. January 1, 2007; s. 5, ch. 2014-162, eff. July 1, 2014.

Editor's notes.
Formerly s. 985.216: transferred by s. 10, ch. 2006-120, effective January 1, 2007; s. 39.0145.

§ 985.039.   Cost of supervision; cost of care.

(1)   Except as provided in subsection (3) or subsection (4):

(a)   When any child is placed into nonsecure detention, probation, or other supervision status with the department, or is committed to the minimum-risk nonresidential restrictiveness level, the court shall order the parent of such child to pay to the department a fee for the cost of the supervision of such child in the amount of $1 per day for each day that the child is in such status.

(b)   When any child is placed into secure detention or placed on committed status and the temporary legal custody of such child is placed with the department, the court shall order the parent of such child to pay to the department a fee for the cost of the care of such child in the amount of $5 per day for each day that the child is in the temporary legal custody of the department.

(2)   The parent of any child who has been placed under the supervision or care of the department shall provide to the department his or her name, address, social security number, date of birth, driver license number or identification card number, and sufficient financial information so as to assist the court in determining the parent's ability to pay any fee associated with the cost of the child's supervision or care. If the parent refuses to provide the department with the information required by this subsection, the court shall order the parent to provide such information. The failure of the parent to comply with such order of the court constitutes contempt of court, and the court may punish the parent accordingly.

(3)   At the time of any detention or disposition hearing, the court shall receive the information described in subsection (2), as well as any other verbal or written information offered as to the ability of the parent of a child who is being placed under the supervision or care of the department to pay any fee imposed pursuant to this section and whether the payment of such fee will create a significant financial hardship. The court may apportion the obligation for the fee to each parent in a manner it deems appropriate; however, the total amount of the daily fee may not exceed the amounts specified in this section. Any finding made by the court as to the ability of the parent to pay such fee, including any finding of indigency or significant financial hardship, shall be in writing and shall contain a detailed description of the facts supporting such finding. If the court makes a finding of indigency and significant financial hardship, the court shall waive the fee or reduce it to an amount deemed appropriate.

(4)   Notwithstanding subsection (3), the court may reduce or waive the fee as to each parent if the court makes a finding on the record that the parent was the victim of the delinquent act or violation of law for which the child has been placed under the supervision or care of the department and that the parent is cooperating or has cooperated with the investigation of the offense.

(5)   The court shall order the payment of any fees required in this section as part of the detention or disposition order. Such order must include specific written findings as to what fees are ordered, reduced, or waived. If the court fails to enter an order as required by this section, the parent is deemed to have an obligation to pay to the department a fee in the amount of $1 per day for each day that the child is under the supervision of the department and $5 per day for each

day that the child remains in the care of the department.

(6) Notwithstanding subsection (1), with respect to a child who reaches the age of 18 prior to the detention or disposition hearing, the court may elect to direct an order required by this section to such child, rather than to the child's parent. With regard to a child who reaches 18 while under the supervision or care of the department, the court may, upon proper motion of any party, hold a hearing as to whether any party should be further obligated to pay any fee associated with cost of the supervision or care of such child. If the court does not enter an order under this subsection, it shall be presumed that the court intended for the parent to pay or to continue to pay the fees specified in this section. Any order entered pursuant to this subsection must include specific findings as to what fees are ordered, reduced, or waived as to the child.

(7) With respect to a child who has been placed under the supervision or care of the department and whose parent receives public assistance for any portion of such child's care, the department must seek a federal waiver to garnish or otherwise order the payment of a portion of the public assistance relating to such child, in an amount not to exceed the amount of the parent's obligation, in order to offset the costs to the department associated with providing supervision or care of such child.

(8) If any order entered pursuant to this section affects the guardianship of an estate, a certified copy of such order shall be delivered to the judge having jurisdiction over the guardianship of the estate.

(9) The department may employ a collection agency for the purpose of receiving, collecting, and managing the payment of any fees ordered pursuant to this section that have gone delinquent or unpaid for 90 days or more. The collection agency must be registered and in good standing under chapter 559. The department may pay for the services of the collection agency from available authorized funds or from funds generated by any collections under this subsection. Alternatively, the department may authorize the collection agency to withhold a specified amount of any fee collected as payment for its services.

(10) The department or the collection agency shall provide to the payor documentation of the payment of any fee paid pursuant to this section. Except as provided in subsection (9), all payments received by the department or the collection agency pursuant to this section shall be deposited in the department's Grants and Donations Trust Fund.

(11) Under no circumstance shall the court or the department extend the child's length of stay in the department's supervision or care solely for the purpose of collecting the fees specified in this section.

(12) No parent or child shall be liable for any fee provided in this section unless:

(a) The child is adjudicated delinquent, or has adjudication of delinquency withheld, for the offense that gave rise to the supervision or care; or

(b) The child is found to have violated an order of the court, including any order of supervision or care, and the costs are associated with the violation of such order.

If any funds are paid for the supervision or care of a child who is determined not to meet the criteria specified in paragraph (a) or paragraph (b), such funds shall be refunded to the payor forthwith.

(13) For purposes of this section, "parent" means any person who meets the definition of "parent" or "legal custody or guardian" in s. 985.03.

HISTORY:

S. 1, ch. 2004-241; s. 7, ch. 2005-263; s. 11, ch. 2006-120, eff. January 1, 2007; s. 6, ch. 2014-162, eff. July 1, 2014.

Editor's notes.

Formerly s. 985.2311: transferred by s. 11, ch. 2006-120, effective January 1, 2007.

§ 985.0395. Cost of supervision and care waiver; pilot program [Repealed.]

Repealed by s. 22, ch. 2010-4, effective June 29, 2010.

HISTORY:

S. 12, ch. 2006-62.

PART II.
RECORDS AND INFORMATION.

§ 985.04. Oaths; records; confidential information.

(1)(a) Except as provided in subsections (2), (3), (6), and (7) and s. 943.053, all information obtained under this chapter in the discharge of official duty by any judge, any employee of the court, any authorized agent of the department, the Florida Commission on Offender Review, the Department of Corrections, the juvenile justice circuit boards, any law enforcement agent, or any licensed professional or licensed community agency representative participating in the assessment or treatment of a juvenile is confidential and exempt from s. 119.07(1) and s. 24(a), Art. I of the State Constitution. This exemption applies to information obtained before, on, or after the effective date of this exemption.

(b) Such confidential and exempt information may be disclosed only to the authorized personnel of the court, the department and its designees, the Department of Corrections, the Florida Commission on Offender Review, law enforcement agents, school superintendents and their designees, any licensed professional or licensed community agency representative participating in the assessment or treatment of a juvenile, and others entitled under this chapter to receive that information, or upon order of the court.

(c) Within each county, the sheriff, the chiefs of police, the district school superintendent, and the department shall enter into an interagency agreement for the purpose of sharing information about juvenile offenders among all parties. The agreement must specify the conditions under which summary criminal history information is to be made available to appropriate school personnel, and the conditions under which school records are to be made available to appropriate department personnel. Such agreement shall require notification to any classroom teacher of assignment to the teacher's classroom of a juvenile who has been placed in a probation or commitment program for a felony offense. The agencies entering into such agreement must comply with s. 943.0525, and must maintain the confidentiality of information that is otherwise exempt from s. 119.07(1), as provided by law.

(2)(a)1. Notwithstanding any other provisions of this chapter, the name, photograph, address, and crime or arrest report of a child:

a. Taken into custody by a law enforcement officer for a violation of law which, if committed by an adult, would be a felony;

b. Charged with a violation of law which, if committed by an adult, would be a felony;

c. Found to have committed an offense which, if committed by an adult, would be a felony; or

d. Transferred to adult court pursuant to part X of this chapter,

are not considered confidential and exempt from s. 119.07(1) solely because of the child's age.

2. A public records custodian may choose not to electronically publish on the custodian's website the arrest or booking photographs of a child which are not confidential and exempt under this section or otherwise restricted from publication by law; however, this subparagraph does not restrict public access to records as provided by s. 119.07.

(b) This subsection is subject to the Open Government Sunset Review Act in accordance with s. 119.15 and shall stand repealed on October 2, 2021, unless reviewed and saved from repeal through reenactment by the Legislature.

(3) A law enforcement agency may release a copy of the juvenile offense report to the victim of the offense. However, information gained by the victim under this chapter, including the next of kin of a homicide victim, regarding any case handled in juvenile court, must not be revealed to any outside party, except as is reasonably necessary in pursuit of legal remedies.

(4)(a) Notwithstanding any other provision of this section, when a child of any age is taken into custody by a law enforcement officer for an offense that would have been a felony if committed by an adult, or a crime of violence, the law enforcement agency must notify the superintendent of schools that the child is alleged to have committed the delinquent act.

(b) Notwithstanding paragraph (a) or any other provision of this section, when a child of any age is formally charged by a state attorney with a felony or a delinquent act that would be a felony if committed by an adult, the state attorney shall notify the superintendent of the child's school that the child has been charged with such felony or delinquent act. The information obtained by the superintendent of schools under this section must be released within 48 hours after receipt to appropriate school personnel, including the principal of the school of the child and the director of transportation. The principal must immediately notify the child's immediate classroom teachers, the child's assigned bus driver, and any other school personnel whose duties include direct supervision of the child. Upon notification, the principal is authorized to begin disciplinary actions under s. 1006.09(1)-(4).

(c) The superintendent must notify the other school personnel whose duties include direct supervision of the child of the disposition of the charges against the child.

(d) The department shall disclose to the school superintendent the presence of any child in the care and custody or under the jurisdiction or supervision of the department who has a known history of criminal sexual behavior with other juveniles; is alleged to have committed juvenile sexual abuse as defined in s. 39.01; or has pled guilty or nolo contendere to, or has been found to have committed, a violation of chapter 794, chapter 796, chapter 800, s. 827.071, or s. 847.0133, regardless of adjudication. Any employee of a district school board who knowingly and willfully discloses such information to an unauthorized person commits a misdemeanor of the second degree, punishable as provided in s. 775.082 or s. 775.083.

(5) Authorized agents of the department may administer oaths and affirmations.

(6)(a) Records maintained by the department, including copies of records maintained by the court, which pertain to a child found to have committed a delinquent act which, if committed by an adult, would be a crime specified in s. 435.04 may not be destroyed under this section for 25 years after the youth's final referral to the department, except in cases of the death of the child. Such records, however, shall be sealed by the court for use only in meeting the screening requirements for personnel in s. 402.3055 and the other sections cited above, or under departmental rule; however, current criminal history information must be obtained from the Department of Law Enforcement in accordance with s. 943.053. The information shall be released to those persons specified in the above cited sections for the purposes of complying with those sections. The court may punish by contempt any person who releases or uses the records for any unauthorized purpose.

(b) Sexual offender and predator registration information as required in ss. 775.21, 943.0435, 944.606, 944.607, 985.481, and 985.4815 is a public record pursuant to s. 119.07(1) and as otherwise provided by law.

(7)(a) Records in the custody of the department regarding children are not open to inspection by the public. Such records may be inspected only upon order of the Secretary of Juvenile Justice or his or her authorized agent by persons who have sufficient reason and upon such conditions for their use and disposition as the secretary or his or her authorized agent deems proper. The information in such records may be disclosed only to other employees of the department who have a need therefor in order to perform their official duties; to other persons as authorized by rule of the department; and, upon request, to the Department of Corrections. The secretary or his or her authorized agent may permit properly qualified persons to inspect and make abstracts from records for statistical purposes under whatever conditions upon their use and disposition the secretary or his or her authorized agent deems proper, provided adequate assurances are given that children's names and other identifying information will not be disclosed by the applicant.

(b) The destruction of records pertaining to children committed to or supervised by the department pursuant to a court order, which records are retained until a child reaches the age of 24 years or until a serious or habitual delinquent child reaches the age of 26 years, shall be subject to chapter 943.

(8) Criminal history information made available to governmental agencies by the Department of Law Enforcement or other criminal justice agencies shall not be used for any purpose other than that specified in the provision authorizing the releases.

HISTORY:

S. 5, ch. 90-208; s. 14, ch. 91-57; s. 14, ch. 93-39; s. 2, ch. 93-196; s. 6, ch. 93-200; s. 23, ch. 93-230; s. 33, ch. 94-209; s. 1344, ch. 95-147; s. 117, ch. 95-418; s. 17, ch. 96-369; s. 18, ch. 96-388; s. 26, ch. 97-234; s. 4, ch. 97-238; s. 8, ch. 98-158; s. 128, ch. 99-3; s. 11, ch. 99-284; s. 19, ch. 2000-135; s. 15, ch. 2001-125; s. 120, ch. 2002-1; s. 1051, ch. 2002-387; s. 23, ch. 2004-267; s. 12, ch. 2006-120, eff, Jan. 1, 2007; s. 10, ch. 2007-209, eff. July 1, 2007; s. 55, ch. 2010-114, eff. Aug. 1, 2010; s. 1, ch. 2010-192, eff. July 1, 2010; s. 58, ch. 2014-191, eff. July 1, 2014; s. 42, ch. 2014-224, eff. July 1, 2014; s. 62, ch. 2016-24, eff. Oct. 1, 2016; s. 1, ch. 2016-78, eff. Mar. 24, 2016; s. 20, ch. 2016-104, eff. July 1, 2016.

Editor's notes

Section 23, ch. 2004-267, reenacted (2) without change to incorporate amendments to statutory sections referenced therein.

Former s. 39.045.

Section 58, ch. 2010-114 provides: "The changes made by this act are intended to be prospective in nature. It is not intended that persons who are employed or licensed on the effective date of this act be rescreened until such time as they are otherwise required to be rescreened pursuant to law, at which time they must meet the requirements for screening as set forth in this act."

§ 985.045. Court records.

(1) The clerk of the court shall make and keep records of all cases brought before it under this chapter. The court shall preserve the records pertaining to a child charged with committing a delinquent act or violation of law until the child reaches 24 years of age or reaches 26 years of age if he or she is a serious or habitual delinquent child, until 5 years after the last entry was made, or until 3 years after the death of the child, whichever is earlier, and may then destroy them, except that records made of traffic offenses in which there is no allegation of delinquency may be destroyed as soon as this can be reasonably accomplished. The court shall make official records of all petitions and orders filed in a case arising under this chapter and of any other pleadings, certificates, proofs of publication, summonses, warrants, and writs that are filed pursuant to the case.

(2) The clerk shall keep all official records required by this section separate from other records of the circuit court, except those records pertaining to motor vehicle violations, which shall be forwarded to the Department of Highway Safety and Motor Vehicles. Except as provided in ss. 943.053 and 985.04(6)(b) and (7), official records required by this chapter are not open to inspection by the public, but may be inspected only upon order of the court by persons deemed by the court to have a proper interest therein, except that a child and the parents, guardians, or legal custodians of the child and their attorneys, law enforcement agencies, the Department of Juvenile Justice and its designees, the Florida Commission on Offender Review, the Department of Corrections, and the Justice Administrative Commission shall always have the right to inspect and copy any official record pertaining to the child. Public defender offices shall have access to official records of juveniles on whose behalf they are expected to appear in detention or other hearings before an appointment of representation. The court may permit authorized representatives of recognized organizations compiling statistics for proper purposes to inspect, and make abstracts from, official records under whatever conditions upon the use and disposition of such records the court may deem proper and may punish by contempt proceedings any violation of those conditions.

(3) All orders of the court entered under this chapter must be in writing and signed by the judge, except that the clerk or deputy clerk may sign a summons or notice to appear.

(4) A court record of proceedings under this chapter is not admissible in evidence in any other civil or criminal proceeding, except that:

(a) Orders transferring a child for trial as an adult are admissible in evidence in the court in which he or she is tried, but create no presumption as to the guilt of the child; nor may such orders be read to, or commented upon in the presence of, the jury in any trial.

(b)   Orders binding an adult over for trial on a criminal charge, made by the committing trial court judge, are admissible in evidence in the court to which the adult is bound over.

(c)   Records of proceedings under this chapter forming a part of the record on appeal must be used in the appellate court in the manner provided in s. 985.534.

(d)   Records are admissible in evidence in any case in which a person is being tried upon a charge of having committed perjury, to the extent such records are necessary to prove the charge.

(e)   Records of proceedings under this chapter may be used to prove disqualification under ss. 110.1127, 393.0655, 394.457, 397.4073, 402.305, 402.313, 409.175, 409.176, and 985.644.

(5)   This chapter does not prohibit a circuit court from providing a restitution order containing the information prescribed in s. 985.0301(5)(d) to a collection court or a private collection agency for the sole purpose of collecting unpaid restitution ordered in a case in which the circuit court has retained jurisdiction over the child and the child's parent or legal guardian. The collection court or private collection agency shall maintain the confidential status of the information to the extent such confidentiality is provided by law.

HISTORY:
S. 5, ch. 97-238; s. 116, ch. 2000-349; s. 51, ch. 2004-11; s. 64, ch. 2005-236; s. 13, ch. 2006-120, eff. Jan. 1, 2007; s. 11, ch. 2007-209, eff. July 1, 2007; s. 7, ch. 2012-56, eff. July 1, 2012; s. 10, ch. 2013-109, eff. July 1, 2013; s. 7, ch. 2014-162, eff. July 1, 2014; s. 59, ch. 2014-191, eff. July 1, 2014; s. 12, ch. 2016-78, eff. Mar. 24, 2016; s. 34, ch. 2017-173, eff. July 1, 2017.

Editor's notes.
Formerly s. 985.05: transferred by s. 13, ch. 2006-120, effective January 1, 2007.

§ 985.046. Statewide information-sharing system; interagency workgroup.

(1)   The Department of Education, the Department of Juvenile Justice, and the Department of Law Enforcement shall create an information-sharing workgroup for the purpose of developing and implementing a workable statewide system of sharing information among school districts, state and local law enforcement agencies, providers, the Department of Juvenile Justice, and the Department of Education. The system shall build on processes previously authorized in statute and on any revisions to federal statutes on confidentiality. The information to be shared shall focus on youth who are involved in the juvenile justice system, youth who have been tried as adults and found guilty of felonies, and students who have been serious discipline problems in schools. The participating agencies shall implement improvements that maximize the sharing of information within applicable state and federal statutes and rules and that utilize statewide databases and data delivery systems to streamline access to the information needed to provide joint services to disruptive, violent, and delinquent youth.

(2)   The interagency workgroup shall be coordinated through the Department of Education and shall include representatives from the state agencies specified in subsection (1), school superintendents, school district information system directors, principals, teachers, juvenile court judges, police chiefs, county sheriffs, clerks of the circuit court, the Department of Children and Families, providers of juvenile services including a provider from a juvenile substance abuse program, and circuit juvenile justice managers.

(3)   The interagency workgroup shall, at a minimum, address the following:

(a)   The use of the Florida Information Resource Network and other statewide information access systems as means of delivering information to school personnel or providing an initial screening for purposes of determining whether further access to information is warranted.

(b)   A statewide information delivery system that will provide local access by participating agencies and schools.

(c)   The need for cooperative agreements among agencies which may access information.

(d)   Legal considerations and the need for legislative action necessary for accessing information by participating agencies.

(e)   Guidelines for how the information shall be accessed, used, and disseminated.

(f)   The organizational level at which information may be accessed and shared.

(g)   The specific information to be maintained and shared through the system.

(h)   The cost implications of an improved system.

(4)   The Department of Education, the Department of Juvenile Justice, and the Department of Law Enforcement shall implement improvements leading to the statewide information access and delivery system, to the extent feasible, and shall develop a cooperative agreement specifying their roles in such a system.

(5)   Members of the interagency workgroup shall serve without added compensation and each participating agency shall support the travel, per diem, and other expenses of its representatives.

HISTORY:
S. 61, ch. 95-267; s. 5, ch. 97-101; s. 6, ch. 97-238; s. 77, ch. 99-5; s. 20, ch. 2000-135; s. 14, ch. 2006-120, eff. January 1, 2007; s. 344, ch. 2014-19, eff. July 1, 2014.

Editor's notes.
Formerly s. 985.06: transferred by s. 14, ch. 2006-120, effective January 1, 2007; s. 39.0573.

§ 985.047. Information systems.

(1)(a)   For the purpose of assisting in law enforcement administration and decisionmaking, such as juvenile diversion from continued involvement with the law enforcement and judicial systems, the sheriff of the county in which juveniles are taken into custody is encouraged to maintain a central identification file on serious habitual juvenile offenders and on juveniles who are at risk of becoming serious habitual juvenile offenders by virtue of having an arrest record.

(b) The central identification file shall contain, but not be limited to, pertinent dependency record information maintained by the Department of Children and Families and delinquency record information maintained by the Department of Juvenile Justice; pertinent school records, including information on behavior, attendance, and achievement; pertinent information on delinquency and dependency maintained by law enforcement agencies and the state attorney; and pertinent information on delinquency and dependency maintained by those agencies charged with screening, assessment, planning, and treatment responsibilities. The information obtained shall be used to develop a multiagency information sheet on serious habitual juvenile offenders or juveniles who are at risk of becoming serious habitual juvenile offenders. The agencies and persons specified in this paragraph shall cooperate with the law enforcement agency or county in providing needed information and in developing the multiagency information sheet to the greatest extent possible.

(c) As used in this section, "a juvenile who is at risk of becoming a serious habitual juvenile offender" means a juvenile who has been adjudicated delinquent and who meets one or more of the following criteria:

1. Is arrested for a capital, life, or first degree felony offense or sexual battery.

2. Has five or more arrests, at least three of which are for felony offenses. Three of such arrests must have occurred within the preceding 12-month period.

3. Has 10 or more arrests, at least 2 of which are for felony offenses. Three of such arrests must have occurred within the preceding 12-month period.

4. Has four or more arrests, at least one of which is for a felony offense and occurred within the preceding 12-month period.

5. Has 10 or more arrests, at least 8 of which are for any of the following offenses:
   a. Petit theft;
   b. Misdemeanor assault;
   c. Possession of a controlled substance;
   d. Weapon or firearm violation; or
   e. Substance abuse.

Four of such arrests must have occurred within the preceding 12-month period.

6. Meets at least one of the criteria for criminal gang membership.

(2)(a) Notwithstanding any provision of law to the contrary, confidentiality of records information does not apply to juveniles who have been arrested for an offense that would be a crime if committed by an adult, regarding the sharing of the information on the juvenile with the law enforcement agency or county and any agency or person providing information for the development of the multiagency information sheet as well as the courts, the child, the parents or legal custodians of the child, their attorneys, or any other person authorized by the court to have access. A public or private educational agency shall provide pertinent records to and cooperate with the law enforcement agency or county in providing needed information and developing the multiagency information sheet to the greatest extent possible. Neither these records provided to the law enforcement agency or county nor the records developed from these records for serious habitual juvenile offenders nor the records provided or developed from records provided to the law enforcement agency or county on juveniles at risk of becoming serious habitual juvenile offenders shall be available for public disclosure and inspection under s. 119.07.

(b) The department shall notify the sheriffs of both the prior county of residence and the new county of residence immediately upon learning of the move or other relocation of a juvenile offender who has been adjudicated or had adjudication withheld for a violent misdemeanor or violent felony.

(3) A law enforcement agency or county that implements a juvenile offender information system must annually provide information gathered during the previous year to the delinquency and gang prevention council of the judicial circuit in which the county is located. This information must include the number, types, and patterns of delinquency tracked by the juvenile offender information system.

HISTORY:
S. 5, ch. 90-208; s. 5, ch. 92-287; s. 4, ch. 93-196; s. 4, ch. 93-230; s. 49, ch. 94-209; s. 17, ch. 95-267; s. 19, ch. 96-388; s. 166, ch. 97-101; s. 8, ch. 97-238; s. 14, ch. 2006-120, eff. Jan. 1, 2007; s. 31, ch. 2008-238, eff. Oct. 1, 2008; s. 168, ch. 2010-102, eff. May 26, 2010; s. 345, ch. 2014-19, eff. July 1, 2014.

Editor's notes.
Formerly s. 985.08: transferred by s. 14, ch. 2006-120, effective January 1, 2007; s. 39.0585.

PART III.
CUSTODY AND INTAKE; INTERVENTION AND DIVERSION.

§ 985.101. Taking a child into custody.

(1) A child may be taken into custody under the following circumstances:

(a) Pursuant to an order of the circuit court issued under this chapter, based upon sworn testimony, either before or after a petition is filed.

(b) For a delinquent act or violation of law, pursuant to Florida law pertaining to a lawful arrest. If such delinquent act or violation of law would be a felony if committed by an adult or involves a crime of violence, the arresting authority shall immediately notify the district school superintendent, or the superintendent's designee, of the school district with educational jurisdiction of the child. Such notification shall include other education providers such as the Florida School for the Deaf and the Blind, university developmental research schools, and private elementary and secondary schools. The information obtained by the superintendent of schools pursuant to this section must be released within 48 hours after receipt to appropriate school personnel, including the principal of the child's school, or as otherwise provided by law. The principal must immediately notify the child's immediate classroom teachers. Information provided by an arresting authority under this paragraph may not be placed in the student's permanent record and shall be removed from all school records no later than 9 months after the date of the arrest.

(c) By a law enforcement officer for failing to appear at a court hearing after being properly noticed.

(d) By a law enforcement officer who has probable cause to believe that the child is in violation of the conditions of the child's probation, nonsecure detention, postcommitment probation, or conditional release supervision; has absconded from nonresidential commitment; or has escaped from residential commitment.

Nothing in this subsection shall be construed to allow the detention of a child who does not meet the detention criteria in part V.

(2) Except in emergency situations, a child may not be placed into or transported in any police car or similar vehicle that at the same time contains an adult under arrest, unless the adult is alleged or believed to be involved in the same offense or transaction as the child.

(3) When a child is taken into custody as provided in this section, the person taking the child into custody shall attempt to notify the parent, guardian, or legal custodian of the child. The person taking the child into custody shall continue such attempt until the parent, guardian, or legal custodian of the child is notified or the child is delivered to the department under ss. 985.14 and 985.145, whichever occurs first. If the child is delivered to the department before the parent, guardian, or legal custodian is notified, the department shall continue the attempt to notify until the parent, guardian, or legal custodian of the child is notified. Following notification, the parent or guardian must provide identifying information, including name, address, date of birth, social security number, and driver license number or identification card number of the

parent or guardian to the person taking the child into custody or the department .

(4) Taking a child into custody is not an arrest except for the purpose of determining whether the taking into custody or the obtaining of any evidence in conjunction therewith is lawful.

HISTORY:
S. 5, ch. 90-208; s. 3, ch. 92-130; s. 7, ch. 92-287; ss. 26, 31, ch. 94-209; s. 1340, ch. 95-147; s. 7, ch. 95-267; ss. 15, 23, ch. 97-238; ss. 8, 13, ch. 98-207; s. 12, ch. 99-284; s. 6, ch. 2000-134; s. 22, ch. 2000-135; s. 16, ch. 2001-125; s. 2, ch. 2005-263; s. 15, ch. 2006-120, eff. January 1, 2007; s. 8, ch. 2014-162, eff. July 1, 2014.

Editor's notes.
Formerly ss. 985.207 and 985.215(3): transferred by s. 15, ch. 2006-120, effective January 1, 2007; s. 39.037.

§ 985.105. Youth custody officer. [Repealed]

HISTORY:
S. 58, ch. 2000-135; s. 16, ch. 2006-120, eff. January 1, 2007; repealed by s. 9, ch. 2014-162, effective July 1, 2014.

§ 985.11. Fingerprinting and photographing.

(1)(a) A child who is charged with or found to have committed an offense that would be a felony if committed by an adult shall be fingerprinted and the fingerprints must be submitted to the Department of Law Enforcement as provided in s. 943.051(3)(a).

(b) Unless the child is issued a civil citation or is participating in a similar diversion program pursuant to s. 985.12, a child who is charged with or found to have committed one of the following offenses shall be fingerprinted, and the fingerprints shall be submitted to the Department of Law Enforcement as provided in s. 943.051(3)(b):

1. Assault, as defined in s. 784.011.
2. Battery, as defined in s. 784.03.
3. Carrying a concealed weapon, as defined in s. 790.01(1).
4. Unlawful use of destructive devices or bombs, as defined in s. 790.1615(1).
5. Neglect of a child, as defined in s. 827.03(1)(e).
6. Assault on a law enforcement officer, a firefighter, or other specified officers, as defined in s. 784.07(2)(a).
7. Open carrying of a weapon, as defined in s. 790.053.
8. Exposure of sexual organs, as defined in s. 800.03.
9. Unlawful possession of a firearm, as defined in s. 790.22(5).
10. Petit theft, as defined in s. 812.014.
11. Cruelty to animals, as defined in s. 828.12(1).
12. Arson, resulting in bodily harm to a firefighter, as defined in s. 806.031(1).
13. Unlawful possession or discharge of a weapon or firearm at a school-sponsored event or on school property as defined in s. 790.115.

A law enforcement agency may fingerprint and photograph a child taken into custody upon probable cause that such child has committed any other violation of law, as the agency deems appropriate. Such fingerprint records and photographs shall be retained by the law enforcement agency in a separate file, and these records and all copies thereof must be marked "Juvenile Confidential." These records are not available for public disclosure and inspection under s. 119.07(1) except as provided in ss. 943.053 and 985.04(2), but shall be available to other law enforcement agencies, criminal justice agencies, state attorneys, the courts, the child, the parents or legal custodians of the child, their attorneys, and any other person authorized by the court to have access to such records. In addition, such records may be submitted to the Department of Law Enforcement for inclusion in the state criminal history records and used by criminal justice agencies for criminal justice purposes. These records may, in the discretion of the court, be open to inspection by anyone upon a showing of cause. The fingerprint and photograph records shall be produced in the court whenever directed by the court. Any photograph taken pursuant to this section may be shown by a law enforcement officer to any victim or witness of a crime for the purpose of identifying the person who committed such crime.

(c) The court shall be responsible for the fingerprinting of any child at the disposition hearing if the child has been adjudicated or had adjudication withheld for any felony in the case currently before the court.

(2) If the child is not referred to the court, or if the child is found not to have committed a violation of law, the court may, after notice to the law enforcement agency involved, order the originals and copies of the fingerprints and photographs destroyed. Unless otherwise ordered by the court, if the child is found to have committed an offense which would be a felony if it had been committed by an adult, then the law enforcement agency having custody of the fingerprint and photograph records shall retain the originals and immediately thereafter forward adequate duplicate copies to the court along with the written offense report relating to the matter for which the child was taken into custody. Except as otherwise provided by this subsection, the clerk of the court, after the disposition hearing on the case, shall forward duplicate copies of the fingerprints and photographs, together with the child's name, address, date of birth, age, and sex, to:

(a) The sheriff of the county in which the child was taken into custody, in order to maintain a central child identification file in that county.

(b) The law enforcement agency of each municipality having a population in excess of 50,000 persons and located in the county of arrest, if so requested specifically or by a general request by that agency.

(3) This section does not prohibit the fingerprinting or photographing of child traffic violators. All records of such traffic violations shall be kept in the full name of the violator and shall be open to inspection and publication in the same manner as adult traffic violations. This section does not apply to the photographing of children by the Department of Juvenile Justice or the Department of Children and Families.

HISTORY:

S. 5, ch. 90-208; s. 6, ch. 93-204; s. 28, ch. 94-209; s. 8, ch. 95-267; s. 2, ch. 96-293; s. 20, ch. 96-322; s. 17, ch. 96-388; s. 13, ch. 96-406; s. 162, ch. 97-101; s. 20, ch. 97-238; s. 14, ch. 99-284; s. 2, ch. 2002-51; s. 17, ch. 2006-120, eff. Jan. 1, 2007; s. 7, ch. 2007-112, eff. July 1, 2007; s. 64, ch. 2013-116, eff. July 1, 2013; s. 346, ch. 2014-19, eff. July 1, 2014; s. 10, ch. 2014-162, eff. July 1, 2014; s. 3, ch. 2015-46, eff. Oct. 1, 2015; s. 13, ch. 2016-78, eff. Mar. 24, 2016.

Editor's notes.

Formerly s. 985.212: transferred by s. 17, ch. 2006-120, effective January 1, 2007; s. 39.039.

Section 7, ch. 2007-112, reenacted (1)(b) without change to incorporate amendments to statutory sections referenced therein.

§ 985.115. Release or delivery from custody.

(1) A child taken into custody shall be released from custody as soon as is reasonably possible.

(2) Unless otherwise ordered by the court under s. 985.255 or s. 985.26, and unless there is a need to hold the child, a person taking a child into custody shall attempt to release the child as follows:

(a) To the child's parent, guardian, or legal custodian or, if the child's parent, guardian, or legal custodian is unavailable, unwilling, or unable to provide supervision for the child, to any responsible adult. Prior to releasing the child to a responsible adult, other than the parent, guardian, or legal custodian, the person taking the child into custody may conduct a criminal history background check of the person to whom the child is to be released. If the person has a prior felony conviction, or a conviction for child abuse, drug trafficking, or prostitution, that person is not a responsible adult for the purposes of this section. The person to whom the child is released shall agree to inform the department or the person releasing the child of the child's subsequent change of address and to produce the child in court at such time as the court may direct, and the child shall join in the agreement.

(b) Contingent upon specific appropriation, to a shelter approved by the department or to an authorized agent.

(c) If the child is believed to be suffering from a serious physical condition which requires either prompt diagnosis or prompt treatment, to a law enforcement officer who shall deliver the child to a hospital for necessary evaluation and treatment.

(d) If the child is believed to be mentally ill as defined in s. 394.463(1), to a law enforcement officer who shall take the child to a designated public receiving facility as defined in s. 394.455 for examination under s. 394.463.

(e) If the child appears to be intoxicated and has threatened, attempted, or inflicted physical harm on himself or herself or another, or is incapacitated by substance abuse, to a law enforcement officer who shall deliver the child to a hospital, addictions receiving facility, or treatment resource.

(f) If available, to a juvenile assessment center equipped and staffed to assume custody of the child for the purpose of assessing the needs of the child in custody. The center may then release or deliver the child under this section with a copy of the assessment.

(3) Upon taking a child into custody, a law enforcement officer may deliver the child, for temporary custody not to exceed 6 hours, to a secure booking area of a jail or other facility intended or used for the detention of adults, for the purpose of fingerprinting or photographing the child or awaiting appropriate transport to the department or as provided in s. 985.13(2), provided no regular sight and sound contact between the child and adult inmates or trustees is permitted and the receiving facility has adequate staff to supervise and monitor the child's activities at all times.

(4) Nothing in this section or s. 985.13 shall prohibit the proper use of law enforcement diversion programs. Law enforcement agencies may initiate and conduct diversion programs designed to divert a child from the need for department custody or judicial handling. Such programs may be cooperative projects with local community service agencies.

HISTORY:
S. 5, ch. 90-208; s. 9, ch. 92-287; s. 27, ch. 94-209; s. 1341, ch. 95-147; s. 19, ch. 97-238; s. 12, ch. 98-207; s. 7, ch. 2000-134; s. 18, ch. 2006-120, eff. Jan. 1, 2007; s. 9, ch. 2012-105, eff. Jan. 1, 2013; s. 6, ch. 2014-161, eff. July 1, 2014; s. 10, ch. 2017-164, eff. Oct. 1, 2017.

Editor's notes.
Former s. 985.211(1), (2), (5) and (7): transferred by s. 18, ch. 2006-120, effective January 1, 2007; s. 39.038.
Section 1, ch. 2013-105, provides: "This act may be cited as the 'Florida Safe Harbor Act.' "

§ 985.12. Civil citation.

(1) There is established a juvenile civil citation process for the purpose of providing an efficient and innovative alternative to custody by the Department of Juvenile Justice for children who commit nonserious delinquent acts and to ensure swift and appropriate consequences. The department shall encourage and assist in the implementation and improvement of civil citation programs or other similar diversion programs around the state. The civil citation or similar diversion program shall be established at the local level with the concurrence of the chief judge of the circuit, state attorney, public defender, and the head of each local law enforcement agency involved. The program may be operated by an entity such as a law enforcement agency, the department, a juvenile assessment center, the county or municipality, or another entity selected by the county or municipality. An entity operating the civil citation or similar diversion program must do so in consultation and agreement with the state attorney and local law enforcement agencies. Under such a juvenile civil citation or similar diversion program, a law enforcement officer, upon making contact with a juvenile who admits having committed a misdemeanor, may choose to issue a simple warning or inform the child's guardian or parent of the child's infraction, or may issue a civil citation or require participation in a similar diversion program, and assess up to 50 community service hours, and require participation in intervention services as indicated by an assessment of the needs of the juvenile, including family counseling, urinalysis monitoring, and substance abuse and mental health treatment services. A copy of each citation issued under this section shall be provided to the department, and the department shall enter appropriate information into the juvenile offender information system. Use of the civil citation or similar diversion program is not limited to first-time misdemeanors and may be used in up to two subsequent misdemeanors. If an arrest is made, a law enforcement officer must provide written documentation as to why an arrest was warranted. At the conclusion of a juvenile's civil citation program or similar diversion program, the agency operating the program shall report the outcome to the department. The issuance of a civil citation is not considered a referral to the department.

(2) The department shall develop guidelines for the civil citation program which include intervention services that are based upon proven civil citation or similar diversion programs within the state.

(3) Upon issuing such citation, the law enforcement officer shall send a copy to the county sheriff, state attorney, the appropriate intake office of the department, or the community service performance monitor designated by the department, the parent or guardian of the child, and the victim.

(4) The child shall report to the community service performance monitor within 7 working days after the date of issuance of the citation. The work assignment shall be accomplished at a rate of not less than 5 hours per week. The monitor shall advise the intake office immediately upon reporting by the child to the monitor, that the child has in fact reported and the expected date upon which completion of the work assignment will be accomplished.

(5) If the child fails to report timely for a work assignment, complete a work assignment, or comply with assigned intervention services within the prescribed time, or if the juvenile commits a subsequent misdemeanor, the law enforcement officer shall issue a report alleging the child has committed a delinquent act, at which point a juvenile probation officer shall process the original delinquent act as a referral to the

department and refer the report to the state attorney for review.

(6) At the time of issuance of the citation by the law enforcement officer, such officer shall advise the child that the child has the option to refuse the citation and to be referred to the intake office of the department. That option may be exercised at any time before completion of the work assignment.

HISTORY:

S. 5, ch. 90-208; s. 1, ch. 92-20; s. 23, ch. 94-209; s. 45, ch. 97-238; s. 19, ch. 98-207; s. 19, ch. 2006-120, eff. January 1, 2007; s. 1, ch. 2011-124, eff. July 1, 2011; s. 1, ch. 2015-46, eff. Oct. 1, 2015.

Editor's notes.

Formerly s. 985.301: transferred by s. 19, ch. 2006-120, effective January 1, 2007; s. 39.0255.

§ 985.125. Prearrest or postarrest diversion programs.

(1) A law enforcement agency or school district, in cooperation with the state attorney, may establish a prearrest or postarrest diversion program.

(2) As part of the prearrest or postarrest diversion program, a child who is alleged to have committed a delinquent act may be required to surrender his or her driver license, or refrain from applying for a driver license, for not more than 90 days. If the child fails to comply with the requirements of the program, the state attorney may notify the Department of Highway Safety and Motor Vehicles in writing to suspend the child's driver license for a period that may not exceed 90 days.

(3) The prearrest or postarrest diversion program may, upon agreement of the agencies that establish the program, provide for the expunction of the nonjudicial arrest record of a minor who successfully completes such a program pursuant to s. 943.0582.

HISTORY:

S. 1, ch. 99-267; s. 29, ch. 2001-125; s. 11, ch. 2001-127; s. 20, ch. 2006-120, eff. January 1, 2007; s. 4, ch. 2016-42, eff. July 1, 2016.

Editor's notes.

Formerly s. 985.3065: transferred by s. 20, ch. 2006-120, effective January 1, 2007.

§ 985.13. Probable cause affidavits.

(1) If the child is released, the person taking the child into custody shall make a written report or probable cause affidavit to the appropriate juvenile probation officer within 24 hours after such release, stating the facts and the reason for taking the child into custody. Such written report or probable cause affidavit shall:

(a) Identify the child, the parents, guardian, or legal custodian, and the person to whom the child was released.

(b) Contain sufficient information to establish the jurisdiction of the court and to make a prima facie showing that the child has committed a violation of law or a delinquent act.

(2) A person taking a child into custody who determines, under part V, that the child should be detained or released to a shelter designated by the department, shall make a reasonable effort to immediately notify the parent, guardian, or legal custodian of the child and shall, without unreasonable delay, deliver the child to the appropriate juvenile probation officer or, if the court has so ordered under s. 985.255 or s. 985.26, to a detention center or facility. Upon delivery of the child, the person taking the child into custody shall make a written report or probable cause affidavit to the appropriate juvenile probation officer. Such written report or probable cause affidavit must:

(a) Identify the child and, if known, the parents, guardian, or legal custodian.

(b) Establish that the child was legally taken into custody, with sufficient information to establish the jurisdiction of the court and to make a prima facie showing that the child has committed a violation of law.

(3)(a) A copy of the probable cause affidavit or written report made by the person taking the child into custody shall be filed, by the law enforcement agency which employs the person making such affidavit or written report, with the clerk of the circuit court for the county in which the child is taken into custody or in which the affidavit or report is made within 24 hours after the affidavit or report is made, excluding Saturdays, Sundays, and legal holidays. Such affidavit or report is a case for the purpose of assigning a uniform case number under this subsection.

(b) Upon the filing of a copy of a probable cause affidavit or written report by a law enforcement agency with the clerk of the circuit court, the clerk shall immediately assign a uniform case number to the affidavit or report, forward a copy to the state attorney, and forward a copy to the intake office of the department which serves the county in which the case arose.

(c) Each letter of recommendation, written notice, report, or other paper required by law pertaining to the case shall bear the uniform case number of the case, and a copy shall be filed with the clerk of the circuit court by the issuing agency. The issuing agency shall furnish copies to the juvenile probation officer and the state attorney.

(d) Upon the filing of a petition based on the allegations of a previously filed probable cause affidavit or written report, the agency filing the petition shall include the appropriate uniform case number on the petition.

HISTORY:

S. 5, ch. 90-208; s. 9, ch. 92-287; s. 27, ch. 94-209; s. 1341, ch. 95-147; s. 19, ch. 97-238; s. 12, ch. 98-207; s. 7, ch. 2000-134; s. 21, ch. 2006-120, eff. January 1, 2007; s. 11, ch. 2017-164, eff. Oct. 1, 2017.

Editor's notes.

Formerly subsections (3), (4), and (6) of s. 985.211: transferred by s. 21, ch. 2006-120, effective January 1, 2007; s. 39.038.

§ 985.135. Juvenile assessment centers.

(1)   As used in this section, "center" means a juvenile assessment center comprising community operated facilities and programs which provide collocated central intake and screening services for youth referred to the department.

(2)   The department shall work cooperatively with substance abuse programs, mental health providers, law enforcement agencies, schools, health service providers, state attorneys, public defenders, and other agencies serving youth to establish juvenile assessment centers. Each current and newly established center shall be developed and modified through the local initiative of community agencies and local governments and shall provide a broad array of youth-related services appropriate to the needs of the community where the center is located.

(3)   Each center shall be managed and governed by the participating agencies, consistent with respective statutory requirements of each agency, through an advisory committee and interagency agreements established with participating entities. The advisory committee shall guide the center's operation and ensure that appropriate and relevant agencies are collaboratively participating in and providing services at the center. Each participating state agency shall have operational oversight of only those individual service components located and provided at the center for which the state agency has statutory authority and responsibility.

(4)   Each center shall provide collocated central intake and screening services for youth referred to the department. The center shall provide sufficient services needed to facilitate the initial screening of and case processing for youth, including, at a minimum, delinquency intake; positive identification of the youth; detention admission screening; needs assessment; substance abuse screening and assessments; physical and mental health screening; and diagnostic testing as appropriate. The department shall provide sufficient staff and resources at a center to provide detention screening and intake services.

(5)   Each center is authorized and encouraged to establish truancy programs. A truancy program may serve as providing the central intake and screening of truant children for a specific geographic area based upon written agreements between the center, local law enforcement agencies, and local school boards. A center may work cooperatively with any truancy program operating in the area serving the center.

(6)   Each center must provide for the coordination and sharing of information among the participating agencies to facilitate the screening of and case processing for youth referred to the department.

(7)   The department may utilize juvenile assessment centers to the fullest extent possible for the purpose of conducting predisposition assessments and evaluations of youth. Assessments and evaluations may be conducted by juvenile assessment center staff on a youth while he or she is in a juvenile detention center awaiting placement in a residential commitment facility. If feasible, a youth may be transported from a juvenile detention center to a juvenile assessment center for the purpose of conducting an assessment or evaluation. Such assessments and evaluations may include, but are not limited to, needs assessment; substance abuse evaluations; physical and mental health evaluations; psychological evaluations; behavioral assessments; educational assessments; aptitude testing; and vocational testing. To the extent possible, the youth's parents or guardians and other family members should be involved in the assessment and evaluation process. All information, conclusions, treatment recommendations, and reports derived from any assessment and evaluation performed on a youth shall be included as a part of the youth's commitment packet and shall accompany the youth to the residential commitment facility in which the youth is placed.

HISTORY:

S. 36, ch. 94-209; s. 17, ch. 97-238; s. 10, ch. 98-207; s. 4, ch. 2000-327; s. 22, ch. 2006-120, eff. January 1, 2007.

Editor's notes.

Formerly s. 985.209; transferred by s. 22, ch. 2006-120, effective January 1, 2007; s. 39.0471.

§ 985.14.   Intake and case management system.

(1)   The department shall develop an intake and a case management system whereby a child brought into intake is assigned a juvenile probation officer if the child was not released, referred to a diversionary program, referred for community arbitration, or referred to some other program or agency for the purpose of nonofficial or nonjudicial handling, and shall make every reasonable effort to provide case management services for the child; provided, however, that case management for children committed to residential programs may be transferred as provided in s. 985.46.

(2)   The intake process shall be performed by the department or juvenile assessment center personnel through a case management system. The purpose of the intake process is to assess the child's needs and risks and to determine the most appropriate treatment plan and setting for the child's programmatic needs and risks. The intake process shall consist of a preliminary screening and may be followed by a comprehensive assessment. The comprehensive assessment may consist of a full mental health, cognitive impairment, substance abuse, or psychosexual evaluation. The intake process shall result in choosing the most appropriate services through a balancing of the interests and needs of the child with those of the family and the community . The department shall be responsible for making informed decisions and recommendations to other agencies, the state attorney, and the courts so that the child and family may receive the least intrusive

service alternative throughout the judicial process. The department shall establish uniform procedures for the department to provide a preliminary screening of the child and family for substance abuse and mental health services prior to the filing of a petition or as soon as possible thereafter and prior to a disposition hearing.

(3) The intake and case management system shall facilitate consistency in the recommended placement of each child, and in the assessment, classification, and placement process, with the following purposes:

(a) An individualized, multidisciplinary assessment process that identifies the priority needs of each child for rehabilitation and treatment and identifies any needs of the child's parents or guardians for services that would enhance their ability to provide adequate support, guidance, and supervision for the child. The process begins with the detention risk assessment instrument and decision, includes the intake preliminary screening and comprehensive assessment for substance abuse treatment services, mental health services, intellectual disability services, literacy services, and other educational and treatment services as components, additional assessment of the child's treatment needs, and classification regarding the child's risks to the community. The completed multidisciplinary assessment process must result in the predisposition report.

(b) A classification system that assigns a relative risk to the child and the community based upon assessments including the detention risk assessment results when available to classify the child's risk as it relates to placement and supervision alternatives.

(c) An admissions process that facilitates for each child the utilization of the treatment plan and setting most appropriate to meet the child's programmatic needs and provide the minimum program security needed to ensure public safety.

(4) The department shall annually advise the Legislature and the Executive Office of the Governor of the resources needed in order for the intake and case management system to maintain a staff-to-client ratio that is consistent with accepted standards and allows the necessary supervision and services for each child. The intake process and case management system shall provide a comprehensive approach to assessing the child's needs, relative risks, and most appropriate handling, and shall be based on an individualized treatment plan.

HISTORY:
S. 5, ch. 90-208; s. 8, ch. 92-287; s. 7, ch. 93-230; s. 35, ch. 94-209; s. 1346, ch. 95-147; s. 163, ch. 97-101; s. 18, ch. 97-238; s. 11, ch. 98-207; s. 23, ch. 2000-135; s. 23, ch. 2006-120, eff. Jan. 1, 2007; s. 91, ch. 2012-5, eff. May 8, 2012; s. 3, ch. 2012-56, eff. July 1, 2012; s. 46, ch. 2013-162, eff. July 1, 2013; s. 11, ch. 2014-162, eff. July 1, 2014.

Editor's notes.
Formerly 985.21(1) and (2): transferred by s. 23, ch. 2006-120, effective January 1, 2007; s. 39.047.

§ 985.145. Responsibilities of the department during intake; screenings and assessments.

(1) The department shall serve as the primary case manager for the purpose of managing, coordinating, and monitoring the services provided to the child. Each program administrator within the Department of Children and Families shall cooperate with the primary case manager in carrying out the duties and responsibilities described in this section. In addition to duties specified in other sections and through departmental rules, the department shall be responsible for the following:

(a) *REVIEWING PROBABLE CAUSE AFFIDAVIT.* — The department shall make a preliminary determination as to whether the report, affidavit, or complaint is complete, consulting with the state attorney as may be necessary. A report, affidavit, or complaint alleging that a child has committed a delinquent act or violation of law shall be made to the intake office operating in the county in which the child is found or in which the delinquent act or violation of law occurred. Any person or agency having knowledge of the facts may make such a written report, affidavit, or complaint and shall furnish to the intake office facts sufficient to establish the jurisdiction of the court and to support a finding by the court that the child has committed a delinquent act or violation of law.

(b) *NOTIFICATION CONCERNING APPARENT INSUFFICIENCIES IN PROBABLE CAUSE AFFIDAVIT.* — In any case where the department or the state attorney finds that the report, affidavit, or complaint is insufficient by the standards for a probable cause affidavit, the department or state attorney shall return the report, affidavit, or complaint, without delay, to the person or agency originating the report, affidavit, or complaint or having knowledge of the facts or to the appropriate law enforcement agency having investigative jurisdiction of the offense, and shall request, and the person or agency shall promptly furnish, additional information in order to comply with the standards for a probable cause affidavit.

(c) *SCREENING.* — During the intake process, the department shall screen each child or shall cause each child to be screened in order to determine:

1. Appropriateness for release; referral to a diversionary program, including, but not limited to, a teen court program; referral for community arbitration; or referral to some other program or agency for the purpose of nonofficial or nonjudicial handling.

2. The presence of medical, psychiatric, psychological, substance abuse, educational, or career and technical education problems, or other conditions that may have caused the child to come to the attention of law enforcement or the depart-

ment. The child shall also be screened to determine whether the child poses a danger to himself or herself or others in the community. The results of this screening shall be made available to the court and to court officers. In cases where such conditions are identified and a nonjudicial handling of the case is chosen, the department shall attempt to refer the child to a program or agency, together with all available and relevant assessment information concerning the child's precipitating condition.

(d) *COMPLETING RISK ASSESSMENT INSTRUMENT.* — The department shall ensure that a risk assessment instrument establishing the child's eligibility for detention has been accurately completed and that the appropriate recommendation was made to the court.

(e) *RIGHTS.* — The department shall inquire as to whether the child understands his or her rights to counsel and against self-incrimination.

(f) *MULTIDISCIPLINARY ASSESSMENT.* — The department shall coordinate the multidisciplinary assessment when required, which includes the classification and placement process that determines the child's priority needs, risk classification, and treatment plan. When sufficient evidence exists to warrant a comprehensive assessment and the child fails to voluntarily participate in the assessment efforts, the department shall inform the court of the need for the assessment and the refusal of the child to participate in such assessment. This assessment, classification, and placement process shall develop into the predisposition report.

(g) *COMPREHENSIVE ASSESSMENT.* — The department, pursuant to uniform procedures established by the department and upon determining that the report, affidavit, or complaint is complete, shall:

1. Perform the preliminary screening and make referrals for a comprehensive assessment regarding the child's need for substance abuse treatment services, mental health services, intellectual disability services, literacy services, or other educational or treatment services.

2. If indicated by the preliminary screening, provide for a comprehensive assessment of the child and family for substance abuse problems, using community-based licensed programs with clinical expertise and experience in the assessment of substance abuse problems.

3. If indicated by the preliminary screening, provide for a comprehensive assessment of the child and family for mental health problems, using community-based psychologists, psychiatrists, or other licensed mental health professionals who have clinical expertise and experience in the assessment of mental health problems.

(h) *REFERRALS FOR SERVICES.* — The department shall make recommendations for services and facilitate the delivery of those services to the child, including any mental health services, educational services, family counseling services, family assistance services, and substance abuse services.

(i) *RECOMMENDATION CONCERNING A PETITION.* — Upon determining that the report, affidavit, or complaint complies with the standards of a probable cause affidavit and that the interests of the child and the public will be best served, the department may recommend that a delinquency petition not be filed. If such a recommendation is made, the department shall advise in writing the person or agency making the report, affidavit, or complaint, the victim, if any, and the law enforcement agency having investigative jurisdiction over the offense of the recommendation; the reasons therefor; and that the person or agency may submit, within 10 days after the receipt of such notice, the report, affidavit, or complaint to the state attorney for special review. The state attorney, upon receiving a request for special review, shall consider the facts presented by the report, affidavit, or complaint, and by the department who made the recommendation that no petition be filed, before making a final decision as to whether a petition or information should or should not be filed.

(j) *COMPLETING INTAKE REPORT.* — Subject to the interagency agreement authorized under this paragraph, the department shall submit a written report to the state attorney for each case in which a child is alleged to have committed a violation of law or delinquent act and is not detained. The report shall be submitted within 20 days after the date the child is taken into custody and include the original police report, complaint, or affidavit, or a copy thereof, and a copy of the child's prior juvenile record. In cases in which the child is in detention, the intake office report must be submitted within 24 hours after the child is placed into detention. The intake office report may include a recommendation that a petition or information be filed or that no petition or information be filed and may set forth reasons for the recommendation. The state attorney and the department may, on a district-by-district basis, enter into interagency agreements denoting the cases that will require a recommendation and those for which a recommendation is unnecessary.

(2) Prior to requesting that a delinquency petition be filed or prior to filing a dependency petition, the department may request the parent or legal guardian of the child to attend a course of instruction in parenting skills, training in conflict resolution, and the practice of nonviolence; to accept counseling; or to receive other assistance from any agency in the community which notifies the clerk of the court of the availability of its services. Where appropriate, the department shall request both parents or guardians to receive such parental assistance. The department may, in determining whether to request that a delinquency petition be

filed, take into consideration the willingness of the parent or legal guardian to comply with such request. The parent or guardian must provide the department with identifying information, including the parent's or guardian's name, address, date of birth, social security number, and driver license number or identification card number in order to comply with s. 985.039.

(3)　When indicated by the comprehensive assessment, the department is authorized to contract within appropriated funds for services with a local nonprofit community mental health or substance abuse agency licensed or authorized under chapter 394 or chapter 397 or other authorized nonprofit social service agency providing related services. The determination of mental health or substance abuse services shall be conducted in coordination with existing programs providing mental health or substance abuse services in conjunction with the intake office.

(4)　Client information resulting from the screening and evaluation shall be documented under rules of the department and shall serve to assist the department in providing the most appropriate services and recommendations in the least intrusive manner. Such client information shall be used in the multidisciplinary assessment and classification of the child, but such information, and any information obtained directly or indirectly through the assessment process, is inadmissible in court prior to the disposition hearing, unless the child's written consent is obtained. At the disposition hearing, documented client information shall serve to assist the court in making the most appropriate custody, adjudicatory, and dispositional decision.

(5)　If the screening and assessment indicate that the interests of the child and the public will be best served, the department, with the approval of the state attorney, may refer the child for care, diagnostic, and evaluation services; substance abuse treatment services; mental health services; intellectual disability services; a diversionary, arbitration, or mediation program; community service work; or other programs or treatment services voluntarily accepted by the child and the child's parents or legal guardian. If a child volunteers to participate in any work program under this chapter or volunteers to work in a specified state, county, municipal, or community service organization supervised work program or to work for the victim, the child is considered an employee of the state for the purposes of liability. In determining the child's average weekly wage, unless otherwise determined by a specific funding program, all remuneration received from the employer is considered a gratuity, and the child is not entitled to any benefits otherwise payable under s. 440.15 regardless of whether the child may be receiving wages and remuneration from other employment with another employer and regardless of the child's future wage-earning capacity.

(6)　The victim, if any, and the law enforcement agency that investigated the offense shall be notified immediately by the state attorney of the action taken under subsection (5).

HISTORY:
S. 5, ch. 90-208; s. 16, ch. 93-39; s. 35, ch. 94-209; s. 12, ch. 95-267; s. 2, ch. 96-234; s. 18, ch. 97-238; s. 11, ch. 98-207; s. 2, ch. 99-257; s. 34, ch. 99-284; s. 17, ch. 2001-125; s. 2, ch. 2004-241; s. 24, ch. 2006-120, eff. Jan. 1, 2007; s. 47, ch. 2013-162, eff. July 1, 2013; s. 347, ch. 2014-19, eff. July 1, 2014; s. 12, ch. 2014-162, eff. July 1, 2014.

Editor's notes.
Formerly s. 985.21(3), (4) and (5): transferred by s. 24, ch. 2006-120, effective January 1, 2007; s. 39.047.

§ 985.15. Filing decisions.

(1)　The state attorney may in all cases take action independent of the action or lack of action of the juvenile probation officer and shall determine the action that is in the best interest of the public and the child. If the child meets the criteria requiring prosecution as an adult under s. 985.556, the state attorney shall request the court to transfer and certify the child for prosecution as an adult or shall provide written reasons to the court for not making such a request. In all other cases, the state attorney may:

(a)　File a petition for dependency;

(b)　File a petition under chapter 984;

(c)　File a petition for delinquency;

(d)　File a petition for delinquency with a motion to transfer and certify the child for prosecution as an adult;

(e)　File an information under s. 985.557;

(f)　Refer the case to a grand jury;

(g)　Refer the child to a diversionary, pretrial intervention, arbitration, or mediation program, or to some other treatment or care program if such program commitment is voluntarily accepted by the child or the child's parents or legal guardian; or

(h)　Decline to file.

(2)　In cases in which a delinquency report, affidavit, or complaint is filed by a law enforcement agency and the state attorney determines not to file a petition, the state attorney shall advise the clerk of the circuit court in writing that no petition will be filed thereon.

HISTORY:
S. 25, ch. 2006-120, eff. January 1, 2007.

§ 985.155. Neighborhood restorative justice.

(1) DEFINITIONS. — For purposes of this section, the term:

(a)　"Board" means a Restorative Justice Board established by the state attorney pursuant to subsection (3).

(b)　"Center" means a Neighborhood Restorative Justice Center established by the state attorney pursuant to subsection (2).

(c)　"First-time, nonviolent juvenile offender" means a minor who allegedly has committed a delinquent act or violation of law that would not be a crime of violence providing grounds for detention or incarceration and who does not have a previous record of being found to have committed a criminal or delinquent act or other violation of law.

(2) NEIGHBORHOOD RESTORATIVE JUSTICE CENTER.

(a) The state attorney may establish at least one Neighborhood Restorative Justice Center in designated geographical areas in the county for the purposes of operating a deferred prosecution program for first-time, nonviolent juvenile offenders.

(b) The state attorney may refer any first-time, nonviolent juvenile offender accused of committing a delinquent act to a Neighborhood Restorative Justice Center.

(3) RESTORATIVE JUSTICE BOARD.

(a) The state attorney may establish Restorative Justice Boards consisting of five volunteer members, of which: two are appointed by the state attorney; two are appointed by the public defender; and one is appointed by the chief judge of the circuit. The state attorney shall appoint a chair for each board.

(b) The board has jurisdiction to hear all matters involving first-time, nonviolent juvenile offenders who are alleged to have committed a delinquent act within the geographical area covered by the board.

(4) DEFERRED PROSECUTION PROGRAM; PROCEDURES.

(a) The participation by a juvenile in the deferred prosecution program through a Neighborhood Restorative Justice Center is voluntary. To participate in the deferred prosecution program, the juvenile who is referred to a Neighborhood Restorative Justice Center must take responsibility for the actions which led to the current accusation. The juvenile and the juvenile's parent or legal guardian must waive the juvenile's right to a speedy trial and the right to be represented by a public defender while in the Neighborhood Restorative Justice program. This waiver and acknowledgment of responsibility shall not be construed as an admission of guilt in future proceedings. The board or the board's representative must inform the juvenile and the parent or legal guardian of the juvenile's legal rights prior to the signing of the waiver.

(b) If the state attorney refers a juvenile matter to a Neighborhood Restorative Justice Center, the board shall convene a meeting within 15 days after receiving the referral.

(c) The board shall require the parent or legal guardian of the juvenile who is referred to a Neighborhood Restorative Justice Center to appear with the juvenile before the board at the time set by the board. In scheduling board meetings, the board shall be cognizant of a parent's or legal guardian's other obligations. The failure of a parent or legal guardian to appear at the scheduled board meeting with his or her child or ward may be considered by the juvenile

court as an act of child neglect as defined by s. 39.01, and the board may refer the matter to the Department of Children and Families for investigation under the provisions of chapter 39.

(d) The board shall serve notice of a board meeting on the juvenile referred to the Neighborhood Restorative Justice Center, the juvenile's parent or guardian, and the victim or family of the victim of the alleged offense. These persons and their representatives have the right to appear and participate in any meeting conducted by the board relative to the alleged offense in which they were the alleged juvenile offender or parent or guardian of the alleged juvenile offender, or victim or family of the victim of the alleged juvenile offender. The victim or a person representing the victim may vote with the board.

(5) SANCTIONS. — After holding a meeting pursuant to paragraph (4)(d), the board may impose any of the following sanctions alone or in any combination:

(a) Require the juvenile to make restitution to the victim.

(b) Require the juvenile to perform work for the victim.

(c) Require the juvenile to make restitution to the community.

(d) Require the juvenile to perform work for the community.

(e) Recommend that the juvenile participate in counseling, education, or treatment services that are coordinated by the state attorney.

(f) Require the juvenile to surrender the juvenile's driver license and forward a copy of the board's resolution to the Department of Highway Safety and Motor Vehicles. The department, upon receipt of the license, shall suspend the driving privileges of the juvenile, or the juvenile may be restricted to travel between the juvenile's home, school, and place of employment during specified periods of time according to the juvenile's school and employment schedule.

(g) Refer the matter to the state attorney for the filing of a petition with the juvenile court.

(h) Impose any other sanction except detention that the board determines is necessary to fully and fairly resolve the matter.

(6) WRITTEN CONTRACT.

(a) The board, on behalf of the community, and the juvenile, the juvenile's parent or guardian, and the victim or representative of the victim, shall sign a written contract in which the parties agree to the board's resolution of the matter and in which the juvenile's parent or guardian agrees to ensure that the juvenile complies with the contract. The contract may provide that the parent or guardian shall post a bond payable to this state to secure the performance of any sanction imposed upon the juvenile pursuant to subsection (5).

(b) A breach of the contract by any party may be sanctioned by the juvenile court as it deems appropriate upon motion by any party.

(c) If the juvenile disagrees with the resolution of the board, the juvenile may file a notice with the board within 3 working days after the board makes its resolution that the juvenile has rejected the board's resolution. After receiving notice of the juvenile's rejection, the state attorney shall file a petition in juvenile court.

(7) COMPLETION OF SANCTIONS.

(a) If the juvenile accepts the resolution of the board and successfully completes the sanctions imposed by the board, the state attorney shall not file a petition in juvenile court and the board's resolution shall not be used against the juvenile in any further proceeding and is not an adjudication of delinquency. The resolution of the board is not a conviction of a crime, does not impose any civil disabilities ordinarily resulting from a conviction, and does not disqualify the juvenile in any civil service application or appointment.

(b) If the juvenile accepts the resolution reached by the board but fails to successfully complete the sanctions imposed by it, the state attorney may file the matter with the juvenile court.

(c) Upon successful completion of the sanctions imposed by the board, the juvenile shall submit to the board proof of completion. The board shall determine the form and manner in which a juvenile presents proof of completion.

(8) CONSTRUCTION. — This section shall not be construed to diminish, impair, or otherwise affect any rights conferred on victims of crimes under chapter 960, relating to victim assistance, or any other provisions of law.

HISTORY:

S. 8, ch. 96-398; s. 24, ch. 97-96; s. 161, ch. 97-101; s. 47, ch. 97-238; s. 170, ch. 98-403; s. 2, ch. 2000-327; s. 26, ch. 2006-120, eff. January 1, 2007; s. 348, ch. 2014-19, eff. July 1, 2014.

Editor's notes.

Formerly s. 985.303: transferred by s. 26, ch. 2006-120, effective January 1, 2007; s. 39.0361.

§ 985.16. Community arbitration.

(1) PURPOSE. — The purpose of community arbitration is to provide a system by which children who commit delinquent acts may be dealt with in a speedy and informal manner at the community or neighborhood level, in an attempt to reduce the ever-increasing instances of delinquent acts and permit the judicial system to deal effectively with cases which are more serious in nature.

(2) PROGRAMS.

(a) Each county may establish community arbitration programs designed to complement the department's intake process provided in this chapter. Community arbitration programs shall provide one or more community arbitrators or community arbitration panels to hear informally cases which involve al-

leged commissions of certain delinquent acts by children.

(b) Cases which may be referred to a community arbitrator or community arbitration panel are limited to those which involve violations of local ordinances, those which involve misdemeanors, and those which involve third degree felonies, exclusive of third degree felonies involving personal violence, grand theft auto, or the use of a weapon.

(c) A child who has been the subject of at least one prior adjudication or adjudication withheld for any first or second degree felony offense, any third degree felony offense involving personal violence, grand theft auto, or the use of a weapon, or any other offense not eligible for arbitration, shall not be eligible for resolution of any current offense through community arbitration.

(d) Cases resolved through community arbitration shall be limited pursuant to this subsection.

1. For each child referred to community arbitration, the primary offense shall be assigned a point value.

a. Misdemeanor offenses shall be assigned two points for a misdemeanor of the second degree, four points for a nonviolent misdemeanor of the first degree, and six points for a misdemeanor of the first degree involving violence.

b. Eligible third degree felony offenses shall be assigned eight points.

2. There is not a restriction on the limit of separate incidents for which a law enforcement officer may refer a child to community arbitration, but a child who has accrued a point value of 12 or more points through community arbitration prior to the current offense shall no longer be eligible for community arbitration.

3. The point values provided in this paragraph shall also be assigned to a child's prior adjudications or adjudications withheld on eligible offenses for cases not referred to community arbitration.

(3) COMMUNITY ARBITRATORS. — The chief judge of each judicial circuit shall maintain a list of qualified persons who have agreed to serve as community arbitrators for the purpose of carrying out the provisions of this chapter. Community arbitrators shall meet the qualification and training requirements adopted in rule by the Supreme Court. Whenever possible, qualified volunteers shall be used as community arbitrators.

(a) Each community arbitrator or member of a community arbitration panel shall be selected by the chief judge of the circuit, the senior circuit court judge assigned to juvenile cases in the circuit, and the state attorney. A community arbitrator or, in the case of a panel, the chief arbitrator shall have such powers as are necessary to conduct the proceedings in a fair and expeditious manner.

(b) A community arbitrator or member of a community arbitration panel shall be trained or experienced in juvenile causes and shall be:

1. Either a graduate of an accredited law school or of an accredited school with a degree in behavioral social work or trained in conflict resolution techniques; and

2. A person of the temperament necessary to deal properly with cases involving children and with the family crises likely to be presented to him or her.

(4) PROCEDURE FOR INITIATING CASES FOR COMMUNITY ARBITRATION.

(a) Any law enforcement officer may issue a complaint, along with a recommendation for community arbitration, against any child who such officer has reason to believe has committed any offense that is eligible for community arbitration. The complaint shall specify the offense and the reasons why the law enforcement officer feels that the offense should be handled by community arbitration. Any juvenile probation officer or, at the request of the child's parent or legal custodian or guardian, the state attorney or the court having jurisdiction, with the concurrence of the state attorney, may refer a complaint to be handled by community arbitration when appropriate. A copy of the complaint shall be forwarded to the appropriate juvenile probation officer and the parent or legal custodian or guardian of the child within 48 hours after issuance of the complaint. In addition to the complaint, the child and the parent or legal custodian or guardian shall be informed of the objectives of the community arbitration process; the conditions, procedures, and timeframes under which it will be conducted; and the fact that it is not obligatory. The juvenile probation officer shall contact the child and the parent or legal custodian or guardian within 2 days after the date on which the complaint was received. At this time, the child or the parent or legal custodian or guardian shall inform the juvenile probation officer of the decision to approve or reject the handling of the complaint through community arbitration.

(b) The juvenile probation officer shall verify accurate identification of the child and determine whether or not the child has any prior adjudications or adjudications withheld for an offense eligible for community arbitration for consideration in the point value structure. If the child has at least one prior adjudication or adjudication withheld for an offense which is not eligible for community arbitration, or if the child has already surpassed the accepted level of points on prior community arbitration resolutions, the juvenile probation officer shall consult with the state attorney regarding the filing of formal juvenile proceedings.

(c) If the child or the parent or legal custodian or guardian rejects the handling of the complaint through community arbitration, the juvenile probation officer shall consult with the state attorney for the filing of formal juvenile proceedings.

(d) If the child or the parent or legal custodian or guardian accepts the handling of the complaint through community arbitration, the juvenile probation officer shall provide copies of the complaint to the arbitrator or panel within 24 hours.

(e) The community arbitrator or community arbitration panel shall, upon receipt of the complaint, set a time and date for a hearing within 7 days and shall inform the child's parent or legal custodian or guardian, the complaining witness, and any victims of the time, date, and place of the hearing.

(5) HEARINGS.

(a) The law enforcement officer who issued the complaint need not appear at the scheduled hearing. However, prior to the hearing, the officer shall file with the community arbitrator or the community arbitration panel a comprehensive report setting forth the facts and circumstances surrounding the allegation.

(b) Records and reports submitted by interested agencies and parties, including, but not limited to, complaining witnesses and victims, may be received in evidence before the community arbitrator or the community arbitration panel without the necessity of formal proof.

(c) The testimony of the complaining witness and any alleged victim may be received when available.

(d) Any statement or admission made by the child appearing before the community arbitrator or the community arbitration panel relating to the offense for which he or she was cited is privileged and may not be used as evidence against the child either in a subsequent juvenile proceeding or in any subsequent civil or criminal action.

(e) If a child fails to appear on the original hearing date, the matter shall be referred back to the juvenile probation officer who shall consult with the state attorney regarding the filing of formal juvenile proceedings.

(6) DISPOSITION OF CASES.

(a) Subsequent to any hearing held as provided in subsection (5), the community arbitrator or community arbitration panel may:

1. Recommend that the state attorney decline to prosecute the child.

2. Issue a warning to the child or the child's family and recommend that the state attorney decline to prosecute the child.

3. Refer the child for placement in a community-based nonresidential program.

4. Refer the child or the family to community counseling.

5. Refer the child to a safety and education program related to delinquent children.

6. Refer the child to a work program related to delinquent children and require up to 100 hours of work by the child.

7. Refer the child to a nonprofit organization for volunteer work in the community and require up to 100 hours of work by the child.

8. Order restitution in money or in kind in a case involving property damage; however, the amount of restitution shall not exceed the amount of actual damage to property.

9. Continue the case for further investigation.

10. Require the child to undergo urinalysis monitoring.

11. Impose any other restrictions or sanctions that are designed to encourage responsible and acceptable behavior and are agreed upon by the participants of the community arbitration proceedings.

The community arbitrator or community arbitration panel shall determine an appropriate timeframe in which the disposition must be completed. The community arbitrator or community arbitration panel shall report the disposition of the case to the juvenile probation officer.

(b) Any person or agency to whom a child is referred pursuant to this section shall periodically report the progress of the child to the referring community arbitrator or community arbitration panel in the manner prescribed by such arbitrator or panel.

(c) Any child who is referred by the community arbitrator or community arbitration panel to a work program related to delinquent children or to a nonprofit organization for volunteer work in the community, and who is also ordered to pay restitution to the victim, may be paid a reasonable hourly wage for work, to the extent that funds are specifically appropriated or authorized for this purpose; provided, however, that such payments shall not, in total, exceed the amount of restitution ordered and that such payments shall be turned over by the child to the victim.

(d) If a child consents to an informal resolution and, in the presence of the parent or legal custodian or guardian and the community arbitrator or community arbitration panel, agrees to comply with any disposition suggested or ordered by such arbitrator or panel and subsequently fails to abide by the terms of such agreement, the community arbitrator or community arbitration panel may, after a careful review of the circumstances, forward the case back to the juvenile probation officer, who shall consult with the state attorney regarding the filing of formal juvenile proceedings.

(7) REVIEW. — Any child or his or her parent or legal custodian or guardian who is dissatisfied with the disposition provided by the community arbitrator or the community arbitration panel may request a review of the disposition to the appropriate juvenile probation officer within 15 days after the community arbitration hearing. Upon receipt of the request for review, the juvenile probation officer shall consult with the state attorney who shall consider the request for review and may file formal juvenile proceedings or take such other action as may be warranted.

(8) FUNDING. — Funding for the provisions of community arbitration may be provided through appropriations from the state or from local governments, through federal or other public or private grants, through any appropriations as authorized by the county participating in the community arbitration program, and through donations.

HISTORY:

S. 5, ch. 90-208; s. 48, ch. 97-238; s. 20, ch. 98-207; s. 133, ch. 99-3; s. 27, ch. 2006-120, eff. January 1, 2007.

Editor's notes.

Formerly s. 985.304: transferred by s. 27, ch. 2006-120, effective January 1, 2007; s. 39.026.

§ 985.17. Prevention services.

(1) The Legislature finds that prevention services decrease recidivism by addressing the needs of at-risk youth and their families, preventing further involvement of such youth in the juvenile justice system, protecting the safety of the public, and facilitating successful reentry of at-risk youth into the community. To assist with decreasing recidivism, the department's prevention services shall strengthen protective factors and reduce risk factors using tested and effective approaches.

(2) A goal of the department's prevention services shall be to develop the capacity for local communities to serve their youth.

(a) The department shall engage faith and community-based organizations to provide a full range of voluntary programs and services to prevent and reduce juvenile delinquency, including, but not limited to, chaplaincy services, crisis intervention counseling, mentoring, and tutoring.

(b) The department shall establish volunteer coordinators in each circuit and encourage the recruitment of volunteers to serve as mentors for youth in department services.

(c) The department shall promote the sale of the Invest in Children license plate to help fund programs and services to prevent juvenile delinquency. The department shall allocate money for programs and services within each county based on that county's proportionate share of the license plate annual use fees collected by the county.

(3) The department's prevention services for youth at risk of becoming delinquent should:

(a) Focus on preventing initial or further involvement of such youth in the juvenile justice system by including services such as literacy services, gender-specific programming, recreational services, and after-school services, and should include targeted services to troubled, truant, ungovernable, abused, trafficked, or runaway youth. To decrease the likelihood that a youth will commit a delinquent act, the department should use mentoring and may provide specialized services addressing the strengthening of families, job training, and substance abuse.

(b) Address the multiple needs of such youth in order to decrease the prevalence of disproportionate minority representation in the juvenile justice system.

(4) The department shall expend funds related to the prevention services in a manner consistent with the policies expressed in ss. 984.02 and 985.01 and in a manner that maximizes accountability to the public and ensures the documentation of outcomes.

(a) As a condition of receipt of state funds, all entities that receive or use state moneys to fund prevention services through contracts with the department or grants from any entity dispersed by the department shall:

1. Design the programs providing such services to further one or more of the following strategies:

a. Encouraging youth to attend and succeed in school, which may include special assistance and tutoring to address deficiencies in academic performance and collecting outcome data to reveal the number of days youth attended school while participating in the program.

b. Engaging youth in productive and wholesome activities during nonschool hours that build positive character, instill positive values, and enhance educational experiences.

c. Encouraging youth to avoid the use of violence.

d. Assisting youth in acquiring the skills needed to find meaningful employment, which may include assisting the youth in finding a suitable employer.

2. Provide the department with demographic information, dates of services, and types of interventions received by each youth.

(b) The department shall monitor output and outcome measures for each program strategy in paragraph (a) and annually report the outputs and outcomes in the Comprehensive Accountability Report as provided in s. 985.632.

(c) The department shall monitor all state-funded programs that receive or use state moneys to fund the prevention services through contracts or grants with the department for compliance with all provisions in the contracts and grants.

HISTORY:
S. 13, ch. 2014-162, eff. July 1, 2014.

PART IV.
EXAMINATIONS AND EVALUATIONS.

§ 985.18. Medical, psychiatric, psychological, substance abuse, and educational examination and treatment.

(1) After a detention petition or a petition for delin-quency has been filed, the court may order the child named in the petition to be examined by a physician. The court may also order the child to be evaluated by a psychiatrist or a psychologist, by a district school board educational needs assessment team, or, if a developmental disability is suspected or alleged, by a developmental disabilities diagnostic and evaluation team with the Agency for Persons with Disabilities. If it is necessary to place a child in a residential facility for such evaluation, the criteria and procedures established in chapter 393, chapter 394, or chapter 397, whichever is applicable, shall be used.

(2) If a child has been found to have committed a delinquent act, or before such finding with the consent of any parent or legal custodian of the child, the court may order the child to be treated by a physician. The court may also order the child to receive mental health, substance abuse, or intellectual disability services from a psychiatrist, psychologist, or other appropriate service provider. If it is necessary to place the child in a residential facility for such services, the procedures and criteria established in chapter 393, chapter 394, or chapter 397, as applicable, must be used. After a child has been adjudicated delinquent, if an educational needs assessment by the district school board or the Department of Children and Families has been conducted, the court shall order the report included in the child's court record in lieu of a new assessment. For purposes of this section, an educational needs assessment includes, but is not limited to, reports of intelligence and achievement tests, screening for learning and other disabilities, and screening for the need for alternative education.

(3) When any child is detained pending a hearing, the person in charge of the detention center or facility or his or her designated representative may authorize a triage examination as a preliminary screening device to determine if the child is in need of medical care or isolation or provide or cause to be provided such medical or surgical services as may be deemed necessary by a physician.

(4) Whenever a child found to have committed a delinquent act is placed by order of the court within the care and custody or under the supervision of the Department of Juvenile Justice and it appears to the court that there is no parent, guardian, or person standing in loco parentis who is capable of authorizing or willing to authorize medical, surgical, dental, or other remedial care or treatment for the child, the court may, after due notice to the parent, guardian, or person standing in loco parentis, if any, order that a representative of the Department of Juvenile Justice may authorize such medical, surgical, dental, or other remedial care for the child by licensed practitioners as may from time to time appear necessary.

(5) Upon specific appropriation, the department may obtain comprehensive evaluations, including, but not limited to, medical, academic, psychological, be-

havioral, sociological, and vocational needs of a youth with multiple arrests for all level criminal acts or a youth committed to a minimum-risk or low-risk commitment program.

(6) A physician must be immediately notified by the person taking the child into custody or the person having custody if there are indications of physical injury or illness, or the child shall be taken to the nearest available hospital for emergency care. A child may be provided mental health, substance abuse, or intellectual disability services in emergency situations pursuant to chapter 393, chapter 394, or chapter 397, as applicable. After a hearing, the court may order the custodial parent or parents, guardian, or other custodian, if found able to do so, to reimburse the county or state for the expense involved in such emergency treatment or care.

(7) Nothing in this section shall be deemed to eliminate the right of the parents or the child to consent to examination or treatment for the child, except that consent of a parent shall not be required if the physician determines there is an injury or illness requiring immediate treatment and the child consents to such treatment or an ex parte court order is obtained authorizing treatment.

(8) Nothing in this section shall be construed to authorize the permanent sterilization of any child unless such sterilization is the result of or incidental to medically necessary treatment to protect or preserve the life of the child.

(9) Except as provided in this section, nothing in this section shall be deemed to preclude a court from ordering services or treatment to be provided to a child by a duly accredited practitioner who relies solely on spiritual means for healing in accordance with the tenets and practices of a church or religious organization, when requested by the child.

HISTORY:
S. 5, ch. 90-208; s. 15, ch. 93-39; s. 34, ch. 94-209; s. 1345, ch. 95-147; s. 42, ch. 95-267; s. 5, ch. 96-398; s. 3, ch. 97-101; ss. 23, 32, ch. 97-238; s. 13, ch. 98-207; s. 4, ch. 2005-263; s. 28, ch. 2006-120; s. 67, ch. 2006-227; s. 48, ch. 2013-162, eff. July 1, 2013; s. 349, ch. 2014-19, eff. July 1, 2014.

Editor's notes.
Formerly ss. 985.224 and 985.215(10)(e): transferred by s. 28, ch. 2006-120, effective January 1, 2007; s. 39.044; s. 39.046.

§ 985.185. Evaluations for disposition.

(1) A comprehensive evaluation for physical health, mental health, substance abuse, academic, educational, or vocational problems shall be ordered for any child for whom a residential commitment disposition is anticipated or recommended by an officer of the court or by the department.

(2) Prior to making a final disposition of the case, the court may order additional evaluations and studies to be performed by the department, by the county school system, or by any social, psychological, or psychiatric agencies of the state. The court shall order the educational needs assessment completed under s. 985.18(2) to be included in the assessment and predisposition report.

HISTORY:
S. 37, ch. 97-238; s. 29, ch. 2000-135; s. 29, ch. 2006-120, eff. January 1, 2007.

Editor's notes.
Formerly s. 985.229(1), (2): transferred by s. 29, ch. 2006-120, effective January 1, 2007.

§ 985.19. Incompetency in juvenile delinquency cases.

(1) If, at any time prior to or during a delinquency case, the court has reason to believe that the child named in the petition may be incompetent to proceed with the hearing, the court on its own motion may, or on the motion of the child's attorney or state attorney must, stay all proceedings and order an evaluation of the child's mental condition.

(a) Any motion questioning the child's competency to proceed must be served upon the child's attorney, the state attorney, the attorneys representing the Department of Juvenile Justice, and the attorneys representing the Department of Children and Families . Thereafter, any motion, notice of hearing, order, or other legal pleading relating to the child's competency to proceed with the hearing must be served upon the child's attorney, the state attorney, the attorneys representing the Department of Juvenile Justice, and the attorneys representing the Department of Children and Families .

(b) All determinations of competency shall be made at a hearing, with findings of fact based on an evaluation of the child's mental condition made by not less than two nor more than three experts appointed by the court. The basis for the determination of incompetency must be specifically stated in the evaluation. In addition, a recommendation as to whether residential or nonresidential treatment or training is required must be included in the evaluation. Experts appointed by the court to determine the mental condition of a child shall be allowed reasonable fees for services rendered. State employees may be paid expenses pursuant to s. 112.061. The fees shall be taxed as costs in the case.

(c) All court orders determining incompetency must include specific written findings by the court as to the nature of the incompetency and whether the child requires secure or nonsecure treatment or training environments.

(d) For incompetency evaluations related to mental illness, the Department of Children and Families shall maintain and annually provide the courts with a list of available mental health professionals who have completed a training program approved by the Department of Children and Families to perform the evaluations.

(e) For incompetency evaluations related to intellectual disability or autism, the court shall order the Agency for Persons with Disabilities to examine the child to determine if the child meets the definition of "intellectual disability" or "autism" in s. 393.063 and, if so, whether the child is competent to proceed with delinquency proceedings.

(f) A child is competent to proceed if the child has sufficient present ability to consult with counsel with a reasonable degree of rational understanding and the child has a rational and factual understanding of the present proceedings. The report must address the child's capacity to:

1. Appreciate the charges or allegations against the child.

2. Appreciate the range and nature of possible penalties that may be imposed in the proceedings against the child, if applicable.

3. Understand the adversarial nature of the legal process.

4. Disclose to counsel facts pertinent to the proceedings at issue.

5. Display appropriate courtroom behavior.

6. Testify relevantly.

(g) Immediately upon the filing of the court order finding a child incompetent to proceed, the clerk of the court shall notify the Department of Children and Families and the Agency for Persons with Disabilities and fax or hand deliver to the department and to the agency a referral packet that includes, at a minimum, the court order, the charging documents, the petition, and the court-appointed evaluator's reports.

(h) After placement of the child in the appropriate setting, the Department of Children and Families in consultation with the Agency for Persons with Disabilities, as appropriate, must, within 30 days after placement of the child, prepare and submit to the court a treatment or training plan for the child's restoration of competency. A copy of the plan must be served upon the child's attorney, the state attorney, and the attorneys representing the Department of Juvenile Justice.

(2) A child who is adjudicated incompetent to proceed, and who has committed a delinquent act or violation of law, either of which would be a felony if committed by an adult, must be committed to the Department of Children and Families for treatment or training. A child who has been adjudicated incompetent to proceed because of age or immaturity, or for any reason other than for mental illness, intellectual disability, or autism, must not be committed to the department or to the Department of Children and Families for restoration-of-competency treatment or training services. For purposes of this section, a child who has committed a delinquent act or violation of law, either of which would be a misdemeanor if committed by an adult, may not be committed to the department or to the Department of Children and Families for restoration-of-competency treatment or training services.

(3) If the court finds that a child has mental illness, intellectual disability, or autism and adjudicates the child incompetent to proceed, the court must also determine whether the child meets the criteria for secure placement. A child may be placed in a secure facility or program if the court makes a finding by clear and convincing evidence that:

(a) The child has mental illness, intellectual disability, or autism and because of the mental illness, intellectual disability, or autism:

1. The child is manifestly incapable of surviving with the help of willing and responsible family or friends, including available alternative services, and without treatment or training the child is likely to suffer from neglect or refuse to care for self, and such neglect or refusal poses a real and present threat of substantial harm to the child's well-being; or

2. There is a substantial likelihood that in the near future the child will inflict serious bodily harm on self or others, as evidenced by recent behavior causing, attempting, or threatening such harm; and

(b) All available less restrictive alternatives, including treatment or training in community residential facilities or community settings which would offer an opportunity for improvement of the child's condition, are inappropriate.

(4) A child who is determined to have mental illness, intellectual disability, or autism, who has been adjudicated incompetent to proceed, and who meets the criteria set forth in subsection (3), must be committed to the Department of Children and Families and receive treatment or training in a secure facility or program that is the least restrictive alternative consistent with public safety. Any placement of a child to a secure residential program must be separate from adult forensic programs. If the child attains competency, custody, case management, and supervision of the child shall be transferred to the department in order to continue delinquency proceedings; however, the court retains authority to order the Department of Children and Families to provide continued treatment or training to maintain competency.

(a) A child adjudicated incompetent due to intellectual disability or autism may be ordered into a secure program or facility designated by the Department of Children and Families for children who have intellectual disabilities or autism.

(b) A child adjudicated incompetent due to mental illness may be ordered into a secure program or facility designated by the Department of Children and Families for children having mental illnesses.

(c) If a child is placed in a secure residential facility, the department shall provide transportation to the secure residential facility for admission and from the secure residential facility upon discharge.

(d) The purpose of the treatment or training is the restoration of the child's competency to proceed.

(e) The service provider must file a written report with the court pursuant to the applicable Florida Rules of Juvenile Procedure within 6 months after the date of commitment, or at the end of any period of extended treatment or training, and at any time the Department of Children and Families, through its service provider, determines the child has attained competency or no longer meets the criteria for secure placement, or at such shorter intervals as ordered by the court. A copy of a written report evaluating the child's competency must be filed by the provider with the court and with the state attorney, the child's attorney, the department, and the Department of Children and Families .

(5)(a) If a child is determined to be incompetent to proceed, the court shall retain jurisdiction of the child for up to 2 years after the date of the order of incompetency, with reviews at least every 6 months to determine competency.

(b) Whenever the provider files a report with the court informing the court that the child will never become competent to proceed, the Department of Children and Families will develop a discharge plan for the child prior to any hearing determining whether the child will ever become competent to proceed and send the plan to the court, the state attorney, the child's attorney, and the attorneys representing the Department of Juvenile Justice. The provider will continue to provide services to the child until the court issues the order finding the child will never become competent to proceed.

(c) If the court determines at any time that the child will never become competent to proceed, the court may dismiss the delinquency petition. If, at the end of the 2-year period following the date of the order of incompetency, the child has not attained competency and there is no evidence that the child will attain competency within a year, the court must dismiss the delinquency petition. If appropriate, the court may order that proceedings under chapter 393 or chapter 394 be instituted. Such proceedings must be instituted not less than 60 days prior to the dismissal of the delinquency petition.

(6)(a) If a child is determined to have mental illness, intellectual disability, or autism and is found to be incompetent to proceed but does not meet the criteria set forth in subsection (3), the court shall commit the child to the Department of Children and Families and order the Department of Children and Families to provide appropriate treatment and training in the community. The purpose of the treatment or training is the restoration of the child's competency to proceed.

(b) All court-ordered treatment or training must be the least restrictive alternative that is consistent with public safety. Any placement by the Department of Children and Families to a residential program must be separate from adult forensic programs.

(c) If a child is ordered to receive competency restoration services, the services shall be provided by the Department of Children and Families . The department shall continue to provide case management services to the child and receive notice of the competency status of the child.

(d) The service provider must file a written report with the court pursuant to the applicable Florida Rules of Juvenile Procedure, not later than 6 months after the date of commitment, at the end of any period of extended treatment or training, and at any time the service provider determines the child has attained competency or will never attain competency, or at such shorter intervals as ordered by the court. A copy of a written report evaluating the child's competency must be filed by the provider with the court, the state attorney, the child's attorney, the Department of Children and Families, and the department.

(7) The provisions of this section shall be implemented only subject to specific appropriation.

HISTORY:
S. 4, ch. 96-398; s. 164, ch. 97-101; s. 31, ch. 97-238; s. 16, ch. 98-207; s. 72, ch. 2000-139; s. 30, ch. 2006-120, eff. Jan. 1, 2007; s. 24, ch. 2006-195, eff. June 12, 2006; s. 49, ch. 2013-162, eff. July 1, 2013; s. 350, ch. 2014-19, eff. July 1, 2014.

Editor's notes.
Formerly s. 985.223: transferred by s. 30, ch. 2006-120, effective January 1, 2007; s. 39.0517.

§ 985.195. Transfer to other treatment services.

Any child committed to the department may be transferred to intellectual disability, mental health, or substance abuse treatment facilities for diagnosis and evaluation pursuant to chapter 393, chapter 394, or chapter 397, as applicable, for up to 90 days.

HISTORY:
S. 5, ch. 90-208; s. 17, ch. 93-39; s. 78, ch. 97-238; s. 30, ch. 2006-120, eff. Jan. 1, 2007; s. 50, ch. 2013-162, eff. July 1, 2013.

Editor's notes.
Formerly s. 985.418: transferred by s. 30, ch. 2006-120, effective January 1, 2007; s. 3.063.

PART V.
DETENTION.

§ 985.24. Use of detention; prohibitions.

(1) All determinations and court orders regarding the use of detention care shall be based primarily upon findings that the child:

(a) Presents a substantial risk of not appearing at a subsequent hearing;

(b) Presents a substantial risk of inflicting bodily harm on others as evidenced by recent behavior, including the illegal possession of a firearm;

(c) Presents a history of committing a property offense prior to adjudication, disposition, or placement;

(d) Has committed contempt of court by:

1. Intentionally disrupting the administration of the court;

2. Intentionally disobeying a court order; or

3. Engaging in a punishable act or speech in the court's presence which shows disrespect for the authority and dignity of the court; or

(e) Requests protection from imminent bodily harm.

(2) A child alleged to have committed a delinquent act or violation of law may not be placed into secure or nonsecure detention care for any of the following reasons:

(a) To allow a parent to avoid his or her legal responsibility.

(b) To permit more convenient administrative access to the child.

(c) To facilitate further interrogation or investigation.

(d) Due to a lack of more appropriate facilities.

(3) A child alleged to be dependent under chapter 39 may not, under any circumstances, be placed into secure detention care.

(4) The department may, within its existing resources, develop nonsecure, nonresidential evening reporting centers as an alternative to placing a child in secure detention. Evening reporting centers may be collocated with a juvenile assessment center. If established, evening reporting centers shall serve children and families who are awaiting a child's court hearing and, at a minimum, operate during the afternoon and evening hours to provide a highly structured program of supervision. Evening reporting centers may also provide academic tutoring, counseling, family engagement programs, and other activities.

(5) The department shall continue to identify alternatives to secure detention care and shall develop such alternatives and annually submit them to the Legislature for authorization and appropriation.

HISTORY:

S. 5, ch. 90-208; s. 3, ch. 93-408; ss. 29, 30, ch. 94-209; ss. 21, 22, ch. 97-238; s. 80, ch. 98-280; s. 31, ch. 2006-120, eff. January 1, 2007; s. 14, ch. 2014-162, eff. July 1, 2014.

Editor's notes.

Formerly ss. 985.213(1) and (4) and 985.214(1) and (2): transferred by s. 31, ch. 2006-120, effective January 1, 2007; s. 39.042; s. 39.043.

§ 985.245. Risk assessment instrument.

(1) All determinations and court orders regarding placement of a child into detention care shall comply with all requirements and criteria provided in this part and shall be based on a risk assessment of the child, unless the child is placed into detention care as provided in s. 985.255(2).

(2)(a) The risk assessment instrument for detention care placement determinations and orders shall be developed by the department in agreement with representatives appointed by the following associations: the Conference of Circuit Judges of Florida, the Prosecuting Attorneys Association, the Public Defenders Association, the Florida Sheriffs Association, and the Florida Association of Chiefs of Police. Each association shall appoint two individuals, one representing an urban area and one representing a rural area. The parties involved shall evaluate and revise the risk assessment instrument as is considered necessary using the method for revision as agreed by the parties.

(b) The risk assessment instrument shall take into consideration, but need not be limited to, prior history of failure to appear, prior offenses, offenses committed pending adjudication, any unlawful possession of a firearm, theft of a motor vehicle or possession of a stolen motor vehicle, and probation status at the time the child is taken into custody. The risk assessment instrument shall also take into consideration appropriate aggravating and mitigating circumstances, and shall be designed to target a narrower population of children than s. 985.255. The risk assessment instrument shall also include any information concerning the child's history of abuse and neglect. The risk assessment shall indicate whether detention care is warranted, and, if detention care is warranted, whether the child should be placed into secure or nonsecure detention care.

(3) If, at the detention hearing, the court finds a material error in the scoring of the risk assessment instrument, the court may amend the score to reflect factual accuracy.

(4) For a child who is under the supervision of the department through probation, nonsecure detention, conditional release, postcommitment probation, or commitment and who is charged with committing a new offense, the risk assessment instrument may be completed and scored based on the underlying charge for which the child was placed under the supervision of the department and the new offense.

HISTORY:

S. 5, ch. 90-208; s. 7, ch. 92-287; s. 21, ch. 93-230; s. 3, ch. 93-408; s. 29, ch. 94-209; s. 9, ch. 95-267; s. 21, ch. 97-238; s. 79, ch. 98-280; s. 8, ch. 2000-134; s. 18, ch. 2001-125; s. 16, ch. 2002-55; s. 32, ch. 2006-120, eff. January 1, 2007; s. 15, ch. 2014-162, eff. July 1, 2014; s. 12, ch. 2017-164, eff. Oct. 1, 2017.

Editor's notes.

Formerly s. 985.213(2): transferred by s. 32, ch. 2006-120, effective January 1, 2007; s. 39.042.

§ 985.25. Detention intake.

(1) The department shall receive custody of a child who has been taken into custody from the law enforcement agency or court and shall review the facts in the law enforcement report or probable cause affidavit and

make such further inquiry as may be necessary to determine whether detention care is appropriate.

(a) During the period of time from the taking of the child into custody to the date of the detention hearing, the initial decision as to the child's placement into detention care shall be made by the department under ss. 985.24 and 985.245(1).

(b) The department shall base the decision whether to place the child into detention care on an assessment of risk in accordance with the risk assessment instrument and procedures developed by the department under s. 985.245, except that a child shall be placed in secure detention care until the child's detention hearing if the child meets the criteria specified in s. 985.255(1)(j), is charged with possessing or discharging a firearm on school property in violation of s. 790.115, or has been taken into custody on three or more separate occasions within a 60-day period.

(c) If the final score on the child's risk assessment instrument indicates detention care is appropriate, but the department otherwise determines the child should be released, the department shall contact the state attorney, who may authorize release.

(d) If the final score on the risk assessment instrument indicates detention is not appropriate, the child may be released by the department in accordance with ss. 985.115 and 985.13.

Under no circumstances shall the department or the state attorney or law enforcement officer authorize the detention of any child in a jail or other facility intended or used for the detention of adults, without an order of the court.

(2) The arresting law enforcement agency shall complete and present its investigation of an offense to the appropriate state attorney's office within 8 days after placement of the child in secure detention. The investigation shall include, but is not limited to, police reports and supplemental police reports, witness statements, and evidence collection documents. The failure of a law enforcement agency to complete and present its investigation within 8 days shall not entitle a juvenile to be released from secure detention or to a dismissal of any charges.

HISTORY:

S. 5, ch. 90-208; s. 31, ch. 94-209; s. 1343, ch. 95-147; s. 10, ch. 95-267; s. 23, ch. 97-238; s. 13, ch. 98-207; s. 4, ch. 99-284; s. 9, ch. 2000-134; s. 33, ch. 2006-120, eff. January 1, 2007; s. 16, ch. 2014-162, eff. July 1, 2014; s. 2, ch. 2017-164, eff. Oct. 1, 2017.

Editor's notes.

Formerly s. 985.215(1), (5)(b): transferred by s. 33, ch. 2006-120, effective January 1, 2007; s. 39.044.

§ 985.255. Detention criteria; detention hearing.

(1) Subject to s. 985.25(1), a child taken into custody and placed into detention care shall be given a hearing within 24 hours after being taken into custody.

At the hearing, the court may order continued detention if:

(a) The child is alleged to be an escapee from a residential commitment program; or an absconder from a nonresidential commitment program, a probation program, or conditional release supervision; or is alleged to have escaped while being lawfully transported to or from a residential commitment program.

(b) The child is wanted in another jurisdiction for an offense which, if committed by an adult, would be a felony.

(c) The child is charged with a delinquent act or violation of law and requests in writing through legal counsel to be detained for protection from an imminent physical threat to his or her personal safety.

(d) The child is charged with committing an offense of domestic violence as defined in s. 741.28 and is detained as provided in subsection (2).

(e) The child is charged with possession of or discharging a firearm on school property in violation of s. 790.115 or the illegal possession of a firearm.

(f) The child is charged with a capital felony, a life felony, a felony of the first degree, a felony of the second degree that does not involve a violation of chapter 893, or a felony of the third degree that is also a crime of violence, including any such offense involving the use or possession of a firearm.

(g) The child is charged with any second degree or third degree felony involving a violation of chapter 893 or any third degree felony that is not also a crime of violence, and the child:

1. Has a record of failure to appear at court hearings after being properly notified in accordance with the Rules of Juvenile Procedure;

2. Has a record of law violations prior to court hearings;

3. Has already been detained or has been released and is awaiting final disposition of the case;

4. Has a record of violent conduct resulting in physical injury to others; or

5. Is found to have been in possession of a firearm.

(h) The child is alleged to have violated the conditions of the child's probation or conditional release supervision. However, a child detained under this paragraph may be held only in a consequence unit as provided in s. 985.439. If a consequence unit is not available, the child shall be placed on nonsecure detention with electronic monitoring.

(i) The child is detained on a judicial order for failure to appear and has previously willfully failed to appear, after proper notice:

1. For an adjudicatory hearing on the same case regardless of the results of the risk assessment instrument; or

2. At two or more court hearings of any nature on the same case regardless of the results of the risk assessment instrument.

A child may be held in secure detention for up to 72 hours in advance of the next scheduled court hearing pursuant to this paragraph. The child's failure to keep the clerk of court and defense counsel informed of a current and valid mailing address where the child will receive notice to appear at court proceedings does not provide an adequate ground for excusal of the child's nonappearance at the hearings.

(j) The child is a prolific juvenile offender. A child is a prolific juvenile offender if the child:

1. Is charged with a delinquent act that would be a felony if committed by an adult;

2. Has been adjudicated or had adjudication withheld for a felony offense, or delinquent act that would be a felony if committed by an adult, before the charge under subparagraph 1.; and

3. In addition to meeting the requirements of subparagraphs 1. and 2., has 5 or more of any of the following, at least 3 of which must have been for felony offenses or delinquent acts that would have been felonies if committed by an adult:

a. An arrest event for which a disposition, as defined in s. 985.26, has not been entered;

b. An adjudication; or

c. An adjudication withheld.

As used in this subparagraph, the term "arrest event" means an arrest or referral for one or more criminal offenses or delinquent acts arising out of the same episode, act, or transaction.

(2) A child who is charged with committing an offense that is classified as an act of domestic violence as defined in s. 741.28 and whose risk assessment instrument indicates secure detention is not appropriate may be held in secure detention if the court makes specific written findings that:

(a) Respite care for the child is not available.

(b) It is necessary to place the child in secure detention in order to protect the victim from injury. The child may not be held in secure detention under this subsection for more than 48 hours unless ordered by the court. After 48 hours, the court shall hold a hearing if the state attorney or victim requests that secure detention be continued. The child may continue to be held in detention care if the court makes a specific, written finding that detention care is necessary to protect the victim from injury. However, the child may not be held in detention care beyond the time limits set forth in this section or s. 985.26.

(3)(a) The purpose of the detention hearing required under subsection (1) is to determine the existence of probable cause that the child has committed the delinquent act or violation of law that he or she is charged with and the need for continued detention. Unless a child is detained under paragraph (1)(d) or paragraph (1)(e), the court shall use the results of the risk assessment performed by the department and, based on the criteria in subsection (1), shall determine the need for continued deten-

tion. If the child is a prolific juvenile offender who is detained under s. 985.26(2)(c), the court shall use the results of the risk assessment performed by the department and the criteria in subsection (1) or subsection (2) only to determine whether the prolific juvenile offender should be held in secure detention.

(b) If the court orders a placement more restrictive than indicated by the results of the risk assessment instrument, the court shall state, in writing, clear and convincing reasons for such placement.

(c) Except as provided in s. 790.22(8) or s. 985.27, when a child is placed into detention care, or into a respite home or other placement pursuant to a court order following a hearing, the court order must include specific instructions that direct the release of the child from such placement no later than 5 p.m. on the last day of the detention period specified in s. 985.26 or s. 985.27, whichever is applicable, unless the requirements of such applicable provision have been met or an order of continuance has been granted under s. 985.26(4). If the court order does not include a release date, the release date shall be requested from the court on the same date that the child is placed in detention care. If a subsequent hearing is needed to provide additional information to the court for safety planning, the initial order placing the child in detention care shall reflect the next detention review hearing, which shall be held within 3 calendar days after the child's initial detention placement.

HISTORY:

S. 5, ch. 90-208; s. 4, ch. 92-79; s. 6, ch. 92-287; s. 31, ch. 94-209; s. 1343, ch. 95-147; s. 10, ch. 95-267; s. 5, ch. 96-398; s. 23, ch. 97-238; s. 13, ch. 98-207; s. 4, ch. 99-284; s. 9, ch. 2000-134; s. 24, ch. 2000-135; s. 37, ch. 2001-64; s. 19, ch. 2001-125; s. 17, ch. 2002-55; s. 4, ch. 2005-263; s. 34, ch. 2006-120, eff. January 1, 2007; s. 17, ch. 2014-162, eff. July 1, 2014; ss. 3, 13, ch. 2017-164, eff. Oct. 1, 2017.

Editor's notes.

Formerly s. 985.215(2): transferred by s. 34, ch. 2006-120, effective January 1, 2007; s. 39.044.

§ 985.26. Length of detention.

(1) A child may not be placed into or held in detention care for longer than 24 hours unless the court orders such detention care, and the order includes specific instructions that direct the release of the child from such detention care, in accordance with s. 985.255. The order shall be a final order, reviewable by appeal under s. 985.534 and the Florida Rules of Appellate Procedure. Appeals of such orders shall take precedence over other appeals and other pending matters.

(2)(a) Except as provided in paragraph (b) or paragraph (c), a child may not be held in detention care under a special detention order for more than 21 days unless an adjudicatory hearing for the case has been commenced in good faith by the court.

(b)   Upon good cause being shown that the nature of the charge requires additional time for the prosecution or defense of the case, the court may extend the length of detention for an additional 9 days if the child is charged with an offense that would be, if committed by an adult, a capital felony, a life felony, a felony of the first degree, or a felony of the second degree involving violence against any individual.

(c)   A prolific juvenile offender under s. 985.255(1)(j) shall be placed on nonsecure detention care with electronic monitoring or in secure detention care under a special detention order until disposition. If secure detention care is ordered by the court, it must be authorized under this part and may not exceed:

1.   Twenty-one days unless an adjudicatory hearing for the case has been commenced in good faith by the court or the period is extended by the court pursuant to paragraph (b); or

2.   Fifteen days after the entry of an order of adjudication.

As used in this paragraph, the term "disposition" means a declination to file under s. 985.15(1)(h), the entry of nolle prosequi for the charges, the filing of an indictment under s. 985.56 or an information under s. 985.557, a dismissal of the case, or an order of final disposition by the court.

(3)   Except as provided in subsection (2), a child may not be held in detention care for more than 15 days following the entry of an order of adjudication.

(4)(a)   The time limits in subsections (2) and (3) do not include periods of delay resulting from a continuance granted by the court for cause on motion of the child or his or her counsel or of the state. Upon the issuance of an order granting a continuance for cause on a motion by either the child, the child's counsel, or the state, the court shall conduct a hearing at the end of each 72-hour period, excluding Saturdays, Sundays, and legal holidays, to determine the need for continued detention of the child and the need for further continuance of proceedings for the child or the state.

(b)   The period for nonsecure detention care under this section is tolled on the date that the department or a law enforcement officer alleges that the child has violated a condition of the child's nonsecure detention care until the court enters a ruling on the violation. Notwithstanding the tolling of nonsecure detention care, the court retains jurisdiction over the child for a violation of a condition of nonsecure detention care during the tolling period. If the court finds that a child has violated his or her nonsecure detention care, the number of days that the child served in any type of detention care before commission of the violation shall be excluded from the time limits under subsections (2) and (3).

(5)   A child who was not in secure detention at the time of the adjudicatory hearing, but for whom residential commitment is anticipated or recommended, may be placed under a special detention order for a period not to exceed 72 hours, excluding weekends and legal holidays, for the purpose of conducting a comprehensive evaluation as provided in s. 985.185. Motions for the issuance of such special detention order may be made subsequent to a finding of delinquency. Upon said motion, the court shall conduct a hearing to determine the appropriateness of such special detention order and shall order the least restrictive level of detention necessary to complete the comprehensive evaluation process that is consistent with public safety. Such special detention order may be extended for an additional 72 hours upon further order of the court.

(6)   If a child is detained and a petition for delinquency is filed, the child shall be arraigned in accordance with the Florida Rules of Juvenile Procedure within 48 hours after the filing of the petition for delinquency.

HISTORY:

S. 5, ch. 90-208; s. 31, ch. 94-209; s. 1343, ch. 95-147; s. 5, ch. 96-398; s. 23, ch. 97-238; s. 13, ch. 98-207; s. 9, ch. 2000-134; s. 24, ch. 2000-135; s. 4, ch. 2005-263; s. 35, ch. 2006-120, eff. January 1, 2007; s. 18, ch. 2014-162, eff. July 1, 2014; s. 4, ch. 2017-164, eff. Oct. 1, 2017.

Editor's notes.

Formerly s. 985.215(5)(a), (c), (d), (e), (f), (g) and (7): transferred by s. 35, ch. 2006-120, effective January 1, 2007; s. 39.044.

§ 985.265.   Detention transfer and release; education; adult jails.

(1)   If a child is detained under this part, the department may transfer the child from nonsecure detention care to secure detention care only if significantly changed circumstances warrant such transfer.

(2)   If a child is on release status and not detained under this part, the child may be placed into detention care only pursuant to a court hearing in which the original risk assessment instrument and the newly discovered evidence or changed circumstances are introduced into evidence with a rescored risk assessment instrument.

(3)(a)   When a juvenile sexual offender is placed in detention, detention staff shall provide appropriate monitoring and supervision to ensure the safety of other children in the facility.

(b)   When a juvenile is released from secure detention or transferred to nonsecure detention, detention staff shall immediately notify the appropriate law enforcement agency, school personnel, and victim if the juvenile is charged with committing any of the following offenses or attempting to commit any of the following offenses:

1.   Murder, under s. 782.04;

2.   Sexual battery, under chapter 794;

3.   Stalking, under s. 784.048; or

4.   Domestic violence, as defined in s. 741.28.

(4)(a)　While a child who is currently enrolled in school is in nonsecure detention care, the child shall continue to attend school unless otherwise ordered by the court.

(b)　While a child is in secure detention care, the child shall receive education commensurate with his or her grade level and educational ability.

(5)　The court shall order the delivery of a child to a jail or other facility intended or used for the detention of adults:

(a)　When the child has been transferred or indicted for criminal prosecution as an adult under part X, except that the court may not order or allow a child alleged to have committed a misdemeanor who is being transferred for criminal prosecution pursuant to either s. 985.556 or s. 985.557 to be detained or held in a jail or other facility intended or used for the detention of adults; however, such child may be held temporarily in a detention facility; or

(b)　When a child taken into custody in this state is wanted by another jurisdiction for prosecution as an adult.

The child shall be housed separately from adult inmates to prohibit a child from having regular contact with incarcerated adults, including trusties. "Regular contact" means sight and sound contact. Separation of children from adults shall permit no more than haphazard or accidental contact. The receiving jail or other facility shall contain a separate section for children and shall have an adequate staff to supervise and monitor the child's activities at all times. Supervision and monitoring of children includes physical observation and documented checks by jail or receiving facility supervisory personnel at intervals not to exceed 10 minutes. This subsection does not prohibit placing two or more children in the same cell. Under no circumstances shall a child be placed in the same cell with an adult.

HISTORY:
S. 5, ch. 90-208; s. 3, ch. 93-408; ss. 29, 31, ch. 94-209; s. 1342, ch. 95-147; s. 2, ch. 95-266; s. 44, ch. 95-267; s. 5, ch. 96-398; ss. 21, 23, ch. 97-238; s. 13, ch. 98-207; s. 36, ch. 2006-120, eff. January 1, 2007; s. 19, ch. 2014-162, eff. July 1, 2014; s. 105, ch. 2015-2, eff. June 30, 2015; s. 23, ch. 2016-24, eff. Oct. 1, 2016; s. 31, ch. 2017-37, eff. Oct. 1, 2017; s. 16, ch. 2017-107, eff. Oct. 1, 2017; s. 5, ch. 2017-164, eff. Oct. 1, 2017.

Editor's notes.
Formerly s. 985.213(3) and 985.215(4), (8), (9) and (11): transferred by s. 36, ch. 2006-120, effective January 1, 2007; s. 39.042; s. 39.044.

§ 985.27.　Postdisposition detention while awaiting residential commitment placement.

The court must place all children who are adjudicated and awaiting placement in a nonsecure, high-risk, or maximum-risk residential commitment program in secure detention care until the placement or commitment is accomplished.

HISTORY:
S. 5, ch. 90-208; s. 31, ch. 94-209; s. 42, ch. 95-267; s. 5, ch.

96-398; s. 23, ch. 97-238; s. 13, ch. 98-207; s. 9, ch. 2000-134; s. 5, ch. 2000-327; s. 19, ch. 2001-125; s. 4, ch. 2005-263; s. 37, ch. 2006-120, eff. January 1, 2007; s. 20, ch. 2014-162, eff. July 1, 2014; s. 6, ch. 2017-164, eff. Oct. 1, 2017.

Editor's notes.
Formerly s. 985.215(10)(a)-(d), (f): transferred by s. 37, ch. 2006-120, effective January 1, 2007; s. 39.044.

§ 985.275.　Detention of escapee or absconder on authority of the department.

(1)　If an authorized agent of the department has reasonable grounds to believe that any delinquent child committed to the department has escaped from a residential commitment facility or from being lawfully transported thereto or therefrom, or has absconded from a nonresidential commitment facility, the agent shall notify law enforcement and, if the offense would require notification under chapter 960, notify the victim. The agent shall make every reasonable effort as permitted within existing resources provided to the department to locate the delinquent child, and the child may be returned to the facility or, if it is closer, to a detention center for return to the facility. However, a child may not be held in detention longer than 24 hours, excluding Saturdays, Sundays, and legal holidays, unless a special order so directing is made by the judge after a detention hearing resulting in a finding that detention is required based on the criteria in s. 985.255. The order shall state the reasons for such finding. The reasons shall be reviewable by appeal or in habeas corpus proceedings in the district court of appeal.

(2)　Any sheriff or other law enforcement officer, upon the request of the secretary of the department or duly authorized agent, shall take a child who has escaped from a residential commitment facility or from being lawfully transported thereto or therefrom, or has absconded from a nonresidential commitment facility, into custody and deliver the child to the appropriate juvenile probation officer.

HISTORY:
S. 5, ch. 90-208; s. 7, ch. 92-287; s. 54, ch. 94-209; s. 16, ch. 97-238; s. 9, ch. 98-207; s. 13, ch. 99-284; s. 3, ch. 2005-263; s. 38, ch. 2006-120, eff. January 1, 2007; s. 21, ch. 2014-162, eff. July 1, 2014; s. 14, ch. 2017-164, eff. Oct. 1, 2017.

Editor's notes.
Formerly s. 985.208: transferred by s. 38, ch. 2006-120, effective January 1, 2007; s. 39.064.

PART VI.
PETITION, ARRAIGNMENT, AND ADJUDICATION.

§ 985.318.　Petition.

(1)　All proceedings seeking a finding that a child has committed a delinquent act or violation of law shall be initiated by the state by the filing of a petition for delinquency by the state attorney.

(2) The petition shall be in writing and shall be signed by the state attorney under oath.

(3) The state attorney shall represent the state in all proceedings in which a petition alleges delinquency.

(4) When a petition has been filed and the child or his or her counsel has advised the state attorney that the truth of the allegations is admitted and that no contest is to be made of the allegations in the petition, the state attorney may request that the case be set for an adjudicatory hearing. If the child changes the plea at the adjudicatory hearing, the court shall continue the hearing to permit the state attorney to prepare and present the case for the state.

(5) The form of the petition and its contents shall be determined by rules of procedure adopted by the Supreme Court.

HISTORY:

S. 5, ch. 90-208; s. 14, ch. 93-230; s. 221, ch. 95-147; s. 26, ch. 97-238; s. 81, ch. 98-280; s. 36, ch. 99-284; s. 39, ch. 2006-120.

Editor's notes.

Formerly s. 985.218: transferred by s. 39, ch. 2006-120, effective January 1, 2007; s. 39.048.

§ 985.319. Process and service.

(1) Personal appearance of any person in a hearing before the court obviates the necessity of serving process on that person.

(2) Upon the filing of a petition containing allegations of facts which, if true, would establish that the child committed a delinquent act or violation of law, and upon the request of the petitioner, the clerk or deputy clerk shall issue a summons.

(3) The summons shall have a copy of the petition attached and shall require the person on whom it is served to appear for a hearing at a time and place specified. Except in cases of medical emergency, the time may not be less than 24 hours after service of the summons. If the child is not detained by an order of the court, the summons shall require the custodian of the child to produce the child at the said time and place.

(4) Law enforcement agencies shall act upon subpoenas received and serve process within 7 days after arraignment or as soon thereafter as is possible, except that no service shall be made on Sundays.

(5) The summons shall be directed to, and shall be served upon, the following persons:

(a) The child, in the same manner as an adult;

(b) The parents of the child; and

(c) Any legal custodians, actual custodians, guardians, and guardians ad litem of the child.

(6) If the petition alleges that the child has committed a delinquent act or violation of law and the judge deems it advisable to do so, under the criteria of s. 985.255, the judge may, by endorsement upon the summons and after the entry of an order in which valid reasons are specified, order the child to be taken into custody immediately, and in such case the person serving the summons shall immediately take the child into custody.

(7) If the identity or residence of the parents, custodians, or guardians of the child is unknown after a diligent search and inquiry, if the parents, custodians, or guardians are residents of a state other than Florida, or if the parents, custodians, or guardians evade service, the person who made the search and inquiry shall file in the case a certificate of those facts, and the court shall appoint a guardian ad litem for the child, if appropriate. If the parent, custodian, or guardian of the child fails to obey a summons, the court may, by endorsement upon the summons and after the entry of an order in which valid reasons are specified, order the parent, custodian, or guardian to be taken into custody immediately to show cause why the parent, guardian, or custodian should not be held in contempt for failing to obey the summons. The court may appoint a guardian ad litem for the child, if appropriate.

(8) Upon the application of the child or the state attorney, the clerk or deputy clerk shall issue, and the court on its own motion may issue, subpoenas requiring attendance and testimony of witnesses and production of records, documents, or other tangible objects at any hearing.

(9) All process and orders issued by the court shall be served or executed as other process and orders of the circuit court and, in addition, may be served or executed by authorized agents of the Department of Juvenile Justice at the department's discretion.

(10) Subpoenas may be served within the state by any person over 18 years of age who is not a party to the proceeding.

(11) No fee shall be paid for service of any process or other papers by an agent of the department. If any process, orders, or other papers are served or executed by any sheriff, the sheriff's fees shall be paid by the county.

HISTORY:

S. 5, ch. 90-208; s. 7, ch. 92-287; s. 39, ch. 94-209; s. 1347, ch. 95-147; s. 27, ch. 97-238; s. 11, ch. 2000-134; s. 40, ch. 2006-120; s. 15, ch. 2017-164, eff. Oct. 1, 2017.

Editor's notes.

Formerly s. 985.219(1)-(7), (9)-(12): transferred by s. 40, ch. 2006-120, effective January 1, 2007; s. 39.049.

§ 985.325. Threatening or dismissing an employee prohibited.

(1) An employer, or the employer's agent, may not dismiss from employment an employee who is summoned to appear before the court under s. 985.319 solely because of the nature of the summons or because the employee complies with the summons.

(2) If an employer, or the employer's agent, threatens an employee with dismissal, or dismisses an employee, who is summoned to appear under s. 985.319, the court may hold the employer in contempt.

HISTORY:

S. 40, ch. 94-209; s. 1348, ch. 95-147; s. 28, ch. 97-238; s. 41, ch. 2006-120.

Editor's notes.

Formerly s. 985.22: transferred by s. 41, ch. 2006-120, effective January 1, 2007; s. 39.0495.

§ 985.331. Court and witness fees.

In any proceeding under this chapter, court fees shall not be charged against, nor witness fees allowed to, any party to a delinquency petition or any parent or legal guardian or custodian or child named in a summons. Other witnesses shall be paid the witness fees fixed by law.

HISTORY:

S. 5, ch. 90-208; s. 29, ch. 97-238; s. 42, ch. 2006-120, eff. January 1, 2006.

Editor's notes.

Formerly s. 985.221: transferred by s. 42, ch. 2006-120, effective January 1, 2007; s. 39.073.

§ 985.335. No answer to petition required.

No answer to the petition alleging that a child has committed a delinquent act or violation of law need be filed by any child or his or her parent, legal custodian, or guardian. Any matters which might be set forth in an answer or other pleading may be pleaded orally before the court. An answer admitting the allegations of the petition may be filed by the child joined by a parent or the child's counsel. The answer must acknowledge that the child has been advised of the right to counsel, of the right to remain silent, and of the possible dispositions available to the court. It shall provide for a waiver of the adjudicatory hearing, a statement of consent to an order of adjudication, and an authorization for the court to proceed with a disposition hearing. Upon the filing of such an order, a disposition hearing shall be set at the earliest practicable time that will allow for the completion of the assessment and classification process resulting in the predisposition report.

HISTORY:

S. 5, ch. 90-208; s. 222, ch. 95-147; s. 30, ch. 97-238; s. 42, ch. 2006-120, eff. January 1, 2007.

Editor's notes.

Formerly s. 985.222: transferred by s. 42, ch. 2006-120, effective January 1, 2007; s. 39.051.

§ 985.345. Delinquency pretrial intervention programs.

(1)(a) Notwithstanding any other law, a child who is charged with a felony of the second or third degree for purchase or possession of a controlled substance under chapter 893; tampering with evidence; solicitation for purchase of a controlled substance; or obtaining a prescription by fraud, and who has not previously been adjudicated for a felony, is eligible for voluntary admission into a delinquency pretrial substance abuse education and treatment intervention program, including a treatment-based drug court program established pursuant to s. 397.334, approved by the chief judge or alternative sanctions coordinator of the circuit to the extent that funded programs are available, for a period based on the program requirements and the treatment services that are suitable for the offender, upon motion of either party or the court's own motion. However, if the state attorney believes that the facts and circumstances of the case suggest the child's involvement in the dealing and selling of controlled substances, the court shall hold a preadmission hearing. If the state attorney establishes by a preponderance of the evidence at such hearing that the child was involved in the dealing and selling of controlled substances, the court shall deny the child's admission into a delinquency pretrial intervention program.

(b) While enrolled in a delinquency pretrial intervention program authorized by this subsection, a child is subject to a coordinated strategy developed by a drug court team under s. 397.334(4). The coordinated strategy may include a protocol of sanctions that may be imposed upon the child for noncompliance with program rules. The protocol of sanctions may include, but is not limited to, placement in a substance abuse treatment program offered by a licensed service provider as defined in s. 397.311 or serving a period of secure detention under this chapter. The coordinated strategy must be provided in writing to the child before the child agrees to enter the pretrial treatment-based drug court program or other pretrial intervention program. A child whose charges are dismissed after successful completion of the treatment-based drug court program, if otherwise eligible, may have his or her arrest record and plea of nolo contendere to the dismissed charges expunged under s. 943.0585.

(c) At the end of the delinquency pretrial intervention period, the court shall consider the recommendation of the state attorney and the program administrator as to disposition of the pending charges. The court shall determine, by written finding, whether the child has successfully completed the delinquency pretrial intervention program. Notwithstanding the coordinated strategy developed by a drug court team pursuant to s. 397.334(4), if the court finds that the child has not successfully completed the delinquency pretrial intervention program, the court may order the child to continue in an education, treatment, or drug testing program if resources and funding are available or order that the charges revert to normal channels for prosecution. The court may dismiss the charges upon a finding that the child has successfully completed the delinquency pretrial intervention program.

(2)(a) Notwithstanding any other law, a child who has been identified as having a mental illness and who has not been previously adjudicated for a felony is eligible for voluntary admission into a delinquency pretrial mental health court intervention program, established pursuant to s. 394.47892, approved by the chief judge of the circuit, for a period to be determined by the court, based on the clinical needs of the child, upon motion of either party or the court's own motion if the child is charged with:

    1.   A misdemeanor;

    2.   A nonviolent felony, as defined in s. 948.01(8);

    3.   Resisting an officer with violence under s. 843.01, if the law enforcement officer and state attorney consent to the child's participation;

    4.   Battery on a law enforcement officer under s. 784.07, if the law enforcement officer and state attorney consent to the child's participation; or

    5.   Aggravated assault, if the victim and state attorney consent to the child's participation.

(b)   At the end of the delinquency pretrial mental health court intervention period, the court shall consider the recommendation of the state attorney and the program administrator as to disposition of the pending charges. The court shall determine, by written finding, whether the child has successfully completed the program. If the court finds that the child has not successfully completed the program, the court may order the child to continue in an education, treatment, or monitoring program if resources and funding are available or order that the charges revert to normal channels for prosecution. The court may dismiss the charges upon a finding that the child has successfully completed the program.

(c)   A child whose charges are dismissed after successful completion of the delinquency pretrial mental health court intervention program, if otherwise eligible, may have his or her criminal history record for such charges expunged under s. 943.0585.

(3)   Any entity, whether public or private, providing pretrial substance abuse education, treatment intervention, drug testing, or a mental health court program under this section must contract with the county or appropriate governmental entity, and the terms of the contract must include, but need not be limited to, the requirements established for private entities under s. 948.15(3). It is the intent of the Legislature that public or private entities providing substance abuse education and treatment intervention programs involve the active participation of parents, schools, churches, businesses, law enforcement agencies, and the department or its contract providers.

HISTORY:

S. 3, ch. 93-196; s. 37, ch. 94-209; s. 13, ch. 95-267; s. 50, ch. 97-238; s. 83, ch. 98-280; s. 10, ch. 2006-97, eff. June 7, 2006; s. 42, ch. 2006-120, eff. January 1, 2007; s. 8, ch. 2009-64, eff. July 1, 2009; s. 20, ch. 2016-127, eff. July 1, 2016.

Editor's notes.

Formerly s. 985.306: transferred by s. 42, ch. 2006-120, effective January 1, 2007; s. 39.0475.

§ 985.35. Adjudicatory hearings; withheld adjudications; orders of adjudication.

(1)(a)   Except as provided in paragraph (b), the adjudicatory hearing must be held as soon as practicable after the petition alleging that a child has committed a delinquent act or violation of law is filed and in accordance with the Florida Rules of Juvenile Procedure; but reasonable delay for the purpose of investigation, discovery, or procuring counsel or witnesses shall be granted. If the child is being detained, the time limitations in s. 985.26(2) and (3) apply.

(b)   If the child is a prolific juvenile offender under s. 985.255(1)(j), the adjudicatory hearing must be held within 45 days after the child is taken into custody unless a delay is requested by the child.

(2)   Adjudicatory hearings shall be conducted without a jury by the court, applying in delinquency cases the rules of evidence in use in criminal cases; adjourning the hearings from time to time as necessary; and conducting a fundamentally fair hearing in language understandable, to the fullest extent practicable, to the child before the court.

(a)   In a hearing on a petition alleging that a child has committed a delinquent act or violation of law, the evidence must establish the findings beyond a reasonable doubt.

(b)   The child is entitled to the opportunity to introduce evidence and otherwise be heard in the child's own behalf and to cross-examine witnesses.

(c)   A child charged with a delinquent act or violation of law must be afforded all rights against self-incrimination. Evidence illegally seized or obtained may not be received to establish the allegations against the child.

(3)   If the court finds that the child named in a petition has not committed a delinquent act or violation of law, it shall enter an order so finding and dismissing the case.

(4)   If the court finds that the child named in the petition has committed a delinquent act or violation of law, it may, in its discretion, enter an order stating the facts upon which its finding is based but withholding adjudication of delinquency.

(a)   Upon withholding adjudication of delinquency, the court may place the child in a probation program under the supervision of the department or under the supervision of any other person or agency specifically authorized and appointed by the court. The court may, as a condition of the program, impose as a penalty component restitution in money or in kind, community service, a curfew, urine monitoring, revocation or suspension of the driver license of the child, or other nonresidential punishment appropriate to the offense, and may impose as a rehabilitative component a requirement of participation in substance abuse treatment, or school or other educational program attendance.

(b)   If the child is attending public school and the court finds that the victim or a sibling of the victim in the case was assigned to attend or is eligible to attend the same school as the child, the court order shall include a finding pursuant to the proceedings described in s. 985.455, regardless of whether adjudication is withheld.

(c)   If the court later finds that the child has not complied with the rules, restrictions, or conditions of the community-based program, the court may, after a hearing to establish the lack of compliance, but without further evidence of the state of delinquency, enter an adjudication of delinquency and shall thereafter have full authority under this chapter to deal with the child as adjudicated.

(5)   If the court finds that the child named in a petition has committed a delinquent act or violation of law, but elects not to proceed under subsection (4), it shall incorporate that finding in an order of adjudication of delinquency entered in the case, briefly stating the facts upon which the finding is made, and the court shall thereafter have full authority under this chapter to deal with the child as adjudicated.

(6)   Except as the term "conviction" is used in chapter 322, and except for use in a subsequent proceeding under this chapter, an adjudication of delinquency by a court with respect to any child who has committed a delinquent act or violation of law shall not be deemed a conviction; nor shall the child be deemed to have been found guilty or to be a criminal by reason of that adjudication; nor shall that adjudication operate to impose upon the child any of the civil disabilities ordinarily imposed by or resulting from conviction or to disqualify or prejudice the child in any civil service application or appointment, with the exception of the use of records of proceedings under this chapter as provided in s. 985.045(4).

(7)   An adjudication of delinquency for an offense classified as a felony shall disqualify a person from lawfully possessing a firearm until such person reaches 24 years of age, unless the person's criminal history record for that offense has been expunged pursuant to s. 943.0515(1)(b).

HISTORY:
  S. 36, ch. 97-238; s. 38, ch. 99-284; s. 28, ch. 2000-135; s. 39, ch. 2001-64; s. 22, ch. 2001-125; s. 43, ch. 2006-120, eff. January 1, 2007; s. 7, ch. 2017-164, eff. Oct. 1, 2017.

Editor's notes.
  Formerly s. 985.228: transferred by s. 43, ch. 2006-120, effective January 1, 2007.

PART VII.
DISPOSITION; POSTDISPOSITION.

§ 985.43. Predisposition reports; other evaluations.

(1)   Upon a finding that the child has committed a delinquent act:

(a)   The court may order the department to prepare a predisposition report regarding the child's eligibility for disposition other than by adjudication and commitment to the department or for disposition of adjudication, commitment to the department, and, if appropriate, assignment of a residential commitment level. The predisposition report shall be the result of the multidisciplinary assessment, when such assessment is needed, and of the classification and placement process, and it shall indicate and report the child's priority needs, recommendations as to a classification of risk for the child in the context of his or her program and supervision needs, and a plan for treatment that recommends the most appropriate placement setting to meet the child's needs with the minimum program security that reasonably ensures public safety. A predisposition report shall be ordered for any child for whom a residential commitment disposition is anticipated or recommended by an officer of the court or by the department.

(b)   A comprehensive evaluation for physical health; mental health; substance abuse; or academic, educational, or vocational problems shall be ordered for any child for whom a residential commitment disposition is anticipated or recommended by an officer of the court or by the department. If a comprehensive evaluation is ordered, the predisposition report shall include a summary of the comprehensive evaluation.

(c)   A child who was not in secure detention at the time of the adjudicatory hearing, but for whom residential commitment is anticipated or recommended, may be placed under a special detention order, as provided in s. 985.26(5), for the purpose of conducting a comprehensive evaluation.

(2)   The court shall consider the child's entire assessment and predisposition report and shall review the records of earlier judicial proceedings prior to making a final disposition of the case. The court may, by order, require additional evaluations and studies to be performed by the department; the county school system; or any social, psychological, or psychiatric agency of the state. The court shall order the educational needs assessment completed under s. 985.18(2)

to be included in the assessment and predisposition report.

(3) The predisposition report, together with all other reports and evaluations used by the department in preparing the predisposition report, shall be made available to the child, the child's parents or legal guardian, the child's legal counsel, and the state attorney upon completion of the report and at a reasonable time prior to the disposition hearing. The predisposition report shall be submitted to the court upon completion of the report but no later than 48 hours prior to the disposition hearing. The predisposition report shall not be reviewed by the court without the consent of the child and his or her legal counsel until the child has been found to have committed a delinquent act.

HISTORY:
S. 37, ch. 97-238; s. 29, ch. 2000-135; s. 44, ch. 2006-120, eff. January 1, 2007.

Editor's notes.
Subsection (3) formerly s. 985.229(3): transferred by s. 44, ch. 2006-120, effective January 1, 2007.

§ 985.433. Disposition hearings in delinquency cases.

When a child has been found to have committed a delinquent act, the following procedures shall be applicable to the disposition of the case:

(1) The court shall notify any victim of the offense, if such person is known and within the jurisdiction of the court, of the hearing.

(2) The court shall notify and summon or subpoena, if necessary, the parents, legal custodians, or guardians of the child to attend the disposition hearing if they reside in the state.

(3) The court may receive and consider any other relevant and material evidence, including other written or oral reports or statements, in its effort to determine the appropriate disposition to be made with regard to the child. The court may rely upon such evidence to the extent of its probative value, even though such evidence may not be technically competent in an adjudicatory hearing.

(4) Before the court determines and announces the disposition to be imposed, it shall:

(a) State clearly, using common terminology, the purpose of the hearing and the right of persons present as parties to comment at the appropriate time on the issues before the court.

(b) Discuss with the child his or her compliance with any predisposition plan or other plan imposed since the date of the offense.

(c) Discuss with the child his or her feelings about the offense committed, the harm caused to the victim or others, and what penalty he or she should be required to pay for such transgression.

(d) Give all parties, as well as the victim or a representative of the victim, representatives of the school system, and the law enforcement officers involved in the case who are present at the hearing an opportunity to comment on the issue of disposition and any proposed rehabilitative plan. Parties to the case shall include the parents, legal custodians, or guardians of the child; the child's counsel; the state attorney; and representatives of the department.

(5) At the time of disposition, the court may make recommendations to the department as to specific treatment approaches to be employed.

(6) The first determination to be made by the court is a determination of the suitability or nonsuitability for adjudication and commitment of the child to the department. This determination shall include consideration of the recommendations of the department, which may include a predisposition report. The predisposition report shall include, whether as part of the child's multidisciplinary assessment, classification, and placement process components or separately, evaluation of the following criteria:

(a) The seriousness of the offense to the community. If the court determines under chapter 874 that the child was a member of a criminal gang at the time of the commission of the offense, the seriousness of the offense to the community shall be given great weight.

(b) Whether the protection of the community requires adjudication and commitment to the department.

(c) Whether the offense was committed in an aggressive, violent, premeditated, or willful manner.

(d) Whether the offense was against persons or against property, greater weight being given to offenses against persons, especially if personal injury resulted.

(e) The sophistication and maturity of the child.

(f) The record and previous criminal history of the child, including without limitations:

1. Previous contacts with the department, the former Department of Health and Rehabilitative Services, the Department of Children and Families, the Department of Corrections, other law enforcement agencies, and courts.

2. Prior periods of probation.

3. Prior adjudications of delinquency.

4. Prior commitments to institutions.

(g) The prospects for adequate protection of the public and the likelihood of reasonable rehabilitation of the child if committed to a community services program or facility.

(h) The child's educational status, including, but not limited to, the child's strengths, abilities, and unmet and special educational needs. The report shall identify appropriate educational and career goals for the child. Examples of appropriate goals include:

1. Attainment of a high school diploma or its equivalent.

2. Successful completion of literacy courses.

3. Successful completion of career and technical education courses.

4. Successful attendance and completion of the child's current grade or recovery of credits of classes the child previously failed, if enrolled in school.

5. Enrollment in an apprenticeship or a similar program.

It is the intent of the Legislature that the criteria set forth in this subsection are general guidelines to be followed at the discretion of the court and not mandatory requirements of procedure. It is not the intent of the Legislature to provide for the appeal of the disposition made under this section.

(7) If the court determines that the child should be adjudicated as having committed a delinquent act and should be committed to the department, such determination shall be in writing or on the record of the hearing. The determination shall include a specific finding of the reasons for the decision to adjudicate and to commit the child to the department, including any determination that the child was a member of a criminal gang.

(a) The department shall recommend to the court the most appropriate placement and treatment plan, specifically identifying the restrictiveness level most appropriate for the child if commitment is recommended. If the court has determined that the child was a member of a criminal gang, that determination shall be given great weight in identifying the most appropriate restrictiveness level for the child. The court shall consider the department's recommendation in making its commitment decision.

(b) The court shall commit the child to the department at the restrictiveness level identified or may order placement at a different restrictiveness level. The court shall state for the record the reasons that establish by a preponderance of the evidence why the court is disregarding the assessment of the child and the restrictiveness level recommended by the department. Any party may appeal the court's findings resulting in a modified level of restrictiveness under this paragraph.

(c) The court may also require that the child be placed in a probation program following the child's discharge from commitment. Community-based sanctions under subsection (8) may be imposed by the court at the disposition hearing or at any time prior to the child's release from commitment.

(8) If the court determines not to adjudicate and commit to the department, then the court shall determine what community-based sanctions it will impose in a probation program for the child. Community-based sanctions may include, but are not limited to, participation in substance abuse treatment, a day-treatment probation program, restitution in money or in kind, a curfew, revocation or suspension of the driver license of the child, community service, and appropriate educational programs as determined by the district school board.

(9) After appropriate sanctions for the offense are determined, the court shall develop, approve, and order a plan of probation that will contain rules, requirements, conditions, and rehabilitative programs, including the option of a day-treatment probation program, that are designed to encourage responsible and acceptable behavior and to promote both the rehabilitation of the child and the protection of the community.

(10) Any disposition order shall be in writing as prepared by the clerk of court and may thereafter be modified or set aside by the court.

HISTORY:

S. 38, ch. 97-238; s. 18, ch. 98-207; s. 131, ch. 99-3; s. 30, ch. 2000-135; s. 40, ch. 2001-64; s. 23, ch. 2001-125; s. 45, ch. 2006-120, eff. January 1, 2007; s. 32, ch. 2008-238, eff. Oct. 1, 2008; s. 351, ch. 2014-19, eff. July 1, 2014; s. 22, ch. 2014-162, eff. July 1, 2014.

Editor's notes.

Formerly s. 985.23: transferred by s. 45, ch. 2006-120, effective January 1, 2007.

§ 985.435. Probation and postcommitment probation; community service.

(1) The court that has jurisdiction over an adjudicated delinquent child may, by an order stating the facts upon which a determination of a sanction and rehabilitative program was made at the disposition hearing, place the child in a probation program or a postcommitment probation program. Such placement must be under the supervision of an authorized agent of the department or of any other person or agency specifically authorized and appointed by the court, whether in the child's own home, in the home of a relative of the child, or in some other suitable place under such reasonable conditions as the court may direct.

(2) A probation program for an adjudicated delinquent child must include a penalty component such as:

(a) Restitution in money or in kind;

(b) Community service;

(c) A curfew;

(d) Revocation or suspension of the driver license of the child; or

(e) Other nonresidential punishment appropriate to the offense.

(3) A probation program must also include a rehabilitative program component such as a requirement of participation in substance abuse treatment or in a school or career and technical education program. The nonconsent of the child to treatment in a substance abuse treatment program in no way precludes the court from ordering such treatment. Upon the recom-

mendation of the department at the time of disposition, or subsequent to disposition pursuant to the filing of a petition alleging a violation of the child's conditions of postcommitment probation, the court may order the child to submit to random testing for the purpose of detecting and monitoring the use of alcohol or controlled substances.

(4) A probation program may also include an alternative consequence component to address instances in which a child is noncompliant with technical conditions of his or her probation but has not committed any new violations of law. The alternative consequence component is designed to provide swift and appropriate consequences to any noncompliance with technical conditions of probation. If the probation program includes this component, specific consequences that apply to noncompliance with specific technical conditions of probation must be detailed in the disposition order.

(5) An identification of the child's risk of reoffending shall be provided by the department, taking into account the child's needs and risks relative to probation supervision requirements to reasonably ensure the public safety. Probation programs for children shall be supervised by the department or by any other person or agency specifically authorized by the court. These programs must include, but are not limited to, structured or restricted activities as described in this section and s. 985.439, and shall be designed to encourage the child toward acceptable and functional social behavior.

(6) If supervision or a program of community service is ordered by the court, the duration of such supervision or program must be consistent with any treatment and rehabilitation needs identified for the child and may not exceed the term for which sentence could be imposed if the child were committed for the offense, except that the duration of such supervision or program for an offense that is a misdemeanor of the second degree, or is equivalent to a misdemeanor of the second degree, may be for a period not to exceed 6 months.

(7) The court may conduct judicial review hearings for a child placed on probation for the purpose of fostering accountability to the judge and compliance with other requirements, such as restitution and community service. The court may allow early termination of probation for a child who has substantially complied with the terms and conditions of probation.

HISTORY:

S. 39, ch. 97-238; s. 1, ch. 98-55; s. 14, ch. 98-207; s. 82, ch. 98-280; s. 132, ch. 99-3; s. 15, ch. 99-284; s. 31, ch. 2000-135; s. 24, ch. 2001-125; s. 6, ch. 2005-263; s. 46, ch. 2006-120, eff. January 1, 2007; s. 23, ch. 2014-162, eff. July 1, 2014.

Editor's notes.

Formerly s. 985.231(1)(a): transferred by s. 46, ch. 2006-120, effective January 1, 2007.

§ 985.437. Restitution.

(1) The court that has jurisdiction over an adjudicated delinquent child may, by an order stating the facts upon which a determination of a sanction and rehabilitative program was made at the disposition hearing, order the child to make restitution in the manner provided in this section. This order shall be part of the probation program to be implemented by the department or, in the case of a committed child, as part of the community-based sanctions ordered by the court at the disposition hearing or before the child's release from commitment.

(2) The court may order the child to make restitution in money, through a promissory note cosigned by the child's parent or guardian, or in kind for any damage or loss caused by the child's offense in a reasonable amount or manner to be determined by the court. When restitution is ordered by the court, the amount of restitution may not exceed an amount the child and the parent or guardian could reasonably be expected to pay or make.

(3) The clerk of the circuit court shall be the receiving and dispensing agent. In such case, the court shall order the child or the child's parent or guardian to pay to the office of the clerk of the circuit court an amount not to exceed the actual cost incurred by the clerk as a result of receiving and dispensing restitution payments. The clerk shall notify the court if restitution is not made, and the court shall take any further action that is necessary against the child or the child's parent or guardian.

(4) A finding by the court, after a hearing, that the parent or guardian has made diligent and good faith efforts to prevent the child from engaging in delinquent acts absolves the parent or guardian of liability for restitution under this section.

(5) The court may retain jurisdiction over a child and the child's parent or legal guardian whom the court has ordered to pay restitution until the restitution order is satisfied or until the court orders otherwise, as provided in s. 985.0301.

HISTORY:

S. 47, ch. 2006-120, eff. January 1, 2007.

§ 985.439. Violation of probation or postcommitment probation.

(1)(a) This section is applicable when the court has jurisdiction over a child on probation or postcommitment probation, regardless of adjudication .

(b) If the conditions of the probation program or the postcommitment probation program are violated, the department or the state attorney may bring the child before the court on a petition alleging a violation of the program. A child who violates the conditions of probation or postcommitment probation must be brought before the court if sanctions are sought.

(2) A child taken into custody under s. 985.101 for violating the conditions of probation or postcommit-

ment probation shall be held in a consequence unit if such a unit is available. The child shall be afforded a hearing within 24 hours after being taken into custody to determine the existence of probable cause that the child violated the conditions of probation or postcommitment probation. A consequence unit is a secure facility specifically designated by the department for children who are taken into custody under s. 985.101 for violating probation or postcommitment probation, or who have been found by the court to have violated the conditions of probation or postcommitment probation. If the violation involves a new charge of delinquency, the child may be detained under part V in a facility other than a consequence unit. If the child is not eligible for detention for the new charge of delinquency, the child may be held in the consequence unit pending a hearing and is subject to the time limitations specified in part V.

(3) If the child denies violating the conditions of probation or postcommitment probation, the court shall, upon the child's request, appoint counsel to represent the child.

(4) Upon the child's admission, or if the court finds after a hearing that the child has violated the conditions of probation or postcommitment probation, the court shall enter an order revoking, modifying, or continuing probation or postcommitment probation. In each such case, the court shall enter a new disposition order and, in addition to the sanctions set forth in this section, may impose any sanction the court could have imposed at the original disposition hearing. If the child is found to have violated the conditions of probation or postcommitment probation, the court may:

(a) Place the child in a consequence unit in that judicial circuit, if available, for up to 5 days for a first violation and up to 15 days for a second or subsequent violation.

(b) Place the child in nonsecure detention with electronic monitoring. However, this sanction may be used only if a residential consequence unit is not available.

(c) If the violation of probation is technical in nature and not a new violation of law, place the child in an alternative consequence program designed to provide swift and appropriate consequences to any further violations of probation.

1. Alternative consequence programs shall be established, within existing resources, at the local level in coordination with law enforcement agencies, the chief judge of the circuit, the state attorney, and the public defender.

2. Alternative consequence programs may be operated by an entity such as a law enforcement agency, the department, a juvenile assessment center, a county or municipality, or another entity selected by the department.

3. Upon placing a child in an alternative consequence program, the court must approve specific consequences for specific violations of the conditions of probation.

(d) Modify or continue the child's probation program or postcommitment probation program.

(e) Revoke probation or postcommitment probation and commit the child to the department.

(5) Upon the recommendation of the department at the time of disposition, or subsequent to disposition pursuant to the filing of a petition alleging a violation of the child's conditions of postcommitment probation, the court may order the child to submit to random testing for the purpose of detecting and monitoring the use of alcohol or controlled substances.

HISTORY:

S. 48, ch. 2006-120, eff. January 1, 2007; s. 24, ch. 2014-162, eff. July 1, 2014.

§ 985.441. Commitment.

(1) The court that has jurisdiction of an adjudicated delinquent child may, by an order stating the facts upon which a determination of a sanction and rehabilitative program was made at the disposition hearing:

(a) Commit the child to a licensed child-caring agency willing to receive the child; however, the court may not commit the child to a jail or to a facility used primarily as a detention center or facility or shelter.

(b) Commit the child to the department at a restrictiveness level defined in s. 985.03. Such commitment must be for the purpose of exercising active control over the child, including, but not limited to, custody, care, training, monitoring for substance abuse, electronic monitoring, and treatment of the child and release of the child from residential commitment into the community in a postcommitment nonresidential conditional release program. If the child is not successful in the conditional release program, the department may use the transfer procedure under subsection (4).

(c) Commit the child to the department for placement in a program or facility for juvenile sexual offenders in accordance with s. 985.48, subject to specific appropriation for such a program or facility.

1. The child may only be committed for such placement pursuant to determination that the child is a juvenile sexual offender under the criteria specified in s. 985.475.

2. Any commitment of a juvenile sexual offender to a program or facility for juvenile sexual offenders must be for an indeterminate period of time, but the time may not exceed the maximum term of imprisonment that an adult may serve for the same offense.

(2) Notwithstanding subsection (1), the court having jurisdiction over an adjudicated delinquent child whose offense is a misdemeanor, or a child who is currently on probation for a misdemeanor, may not commit the child for any misdemeanor offense or any

probation violation that is technical in nature and not a new violation of law at a restrictiveness level other than minimum-risk nonresidential. However, the court may commit such child to a nonsecure residential placement if:

(a) The child has previously been adjudicated or had adjudication withheld for a felony offense;

(b) The child has previously been adjudicated or had adjudication withheld for three or more misdemeanor offenses within the previous 18 months;

(c) The child is before the court for disposition for a violation of s. 800.03, s. 806.031, or s. 828.12; or

(d) The court finds by a preponderance of the evidence that the protection of the public requires such placement or that the particular needs of the child would be best served by such placement. Such finding must be in writing.

(3) The nonconsent of the child to commitment or treatment in a substance abuse treatment program in no way precludes the court from ordering such commitment or treatment.

(4) The department may transfer a child, when necessary to appropriately administer the child's commitment, from one facility or program to another facility or program operated, contracted, subcontracted, or designated by the department, including a postcommitment nonresidential conditional release program, except that the department may not transfer any child adjudicated solely for a misdemeanor to a residential program except as provided in subsection (2). The department shall notify the court that committed the child to the department and any attorney of record for the child, in writing, of its intent to transfer the child from a commitment facility or program to another facility or program of a higher or lower restrictiveness level. The court that committed the child may agree to the transfer or may set a hearing to review the transfer. If the court does not respond within 10 days after receipt of the notice, the transfer of the child shall be deemed granted.

HISTORY:
S. 49, ch. 2006-120, eff. Jan. 1, 2007; s. 1, ch. 2011-54, eff. July 1, 2011; s. 92, ch. 2012-5, eff. May 8, 2012; s. 4, ch. 2012-56, eff. July 1, 2012; s. 25, ch. 2014-162, eff. July 1, 2014.

§ 985.442. Form of commitment; certified copy of charge attached.

(1) When any child is committed to the department, the commitment form to be used by the judge of the committing court shall be as prescribed by the department.

(2) The clerk of each court committing a child to the department shall prepare and attach to each commitment form a certified copy of the petition upon which the child is being committed to the department.

HISTORY:
S. 5, ch. 90-208; s. 40, ch. 97-238; s. 50, ch. 2006-120, eff. January 1, 2007.

Editor's notes.
Formerly s. 985.232: transferred by s. 50, ch. 2006-120, effective January 1, 2007; s. 39.078.

§ 985.445. Cases involving grand theft of a motor vehicle [Repealed.]

Repealed by s. 9, ch. 2011-70, effective July 1, 2011.

HISTORY:
S. 39, ch. 97-238; s. 3, ch. 97-281; s. 1, ch. 98-55; s. 14, ch. 98-207; s. 82, ch. 98-280; s. 132, ch. 99-3; s. 15, ch. 99-284; s. 12, ch. 2000-134; s. 31, ch. 2000-135; ss. 24, 25, ch. 2001-125; s. 1, ch. 2002-1; s. 141, ch. 2003-402; s. 4, ch. 2004-241; s. 6, ch. 2005-263; s. 4, ch. 2006-62, eff. July 1, 2006; s. 51, ch. 2006-120, eff. January 1, 2007; s. 18, ch. 2010-113, eff. July 1, 2010.

§ 985.45. Liability and remuneration for work.

(1) Whenever a child is required by the court to participate in any work program under this part or whenever a child volunteers to work in a specified state, county, municipal, or community service organization supervised work program or to work for the victim, either as an alternative to monetary restitution or as a part of the rehabilitative or probation program, the child is an employee of the state for the purposes of liability.

(2) In determining the child's average weekly wage unless otherwise determined by a specific funding program, all remuneration received from the employer is a gratuity, and the child is not entitled to any benefits otherwise payable under s. 440.15, regardless of whether the child may be receiving wages and remuneration from other employment with another employer and regardless of the child's future wage-earning capacity.

HISTORY:
S. 39, ch. 97-238; s. 3, ch. 97-281; s. 1, ch. 98-55; s. 14, ch. 98-207; s. 82, ch. 98-280; s. 132, ch. 99-3; s. 15, ch. 99-284; s. 12, ch. 2000-134; s. 31, ch. 2000-135; ss. 24, 25, ch. 2001-125; s. 121, ch. 2002-1; s. 141, ch. 2003-402; s. 4, ch. 2004-241; s. 6, ch. 2005-263; s. 4, ch. 2006-62, eff. July 1, 2006; s. 52, ch. 2006-120, eff. January 1, 2007.

Editor's notes.
Formerly s. 986.231(g): transferred by s. 52, ch. 2006-120, effective January 1, 2007.

§ 985.455. Other dispositional issues.

(1) The court that has jurisdiction over an adjudicated delinquent child may, by an order stating the facts upon which a determination of a sanction and rehabilitative program was made at the disposition hearing:

(a) Require the child and, if the court finds it appropriate, the child's parent or guardian, together with the child, to render community service in a public service program.

(b) Order the child and, if the court finds it appropriate, the child's parent or guardian, together with the child, to participate in a community work project, either as an alternative to monetary restitution or as part of the rehabilitative or probation program.

(c) Revoke or suspend the driver license of the child.

(d) Order the child, upon a determination of the child's inability to pay, to perform community service in lieu of all court costs assessed against the delinquent child, including costs of prosecution, public defender application fees, and costs of representation.

(2) If the child is attending or is eligible to attend public school and the court finds that the victim or a sibling of the victim in the case is attending or may attend the same school as the child, the court shall, on its own motion or upon the request of any party or any parent or legal guardian of the victim, determine whether it is appropriate to enter a no contact order in favor of the victim or a sibling of the victim. If appropriate and acceptable to the victim and the victim's parent or parents or legal guardian, the court may reflect in the written disposition order that the victim or the victim's parent or parents or legal guardian stated in writing or in open court that he or she did not object to the offender being permitted to attend the same school or ride on the same school bus as the victim or a sibling of the victim. If applicable, the court placement or commitment order shall include a finding under this subsection.

(3) Any commitment of a delinquent child to the department must be for an indeterminate period of time, which may include periods of temporary release; however, the period of time may not exceed the maximum term of imprisonment that an adult may serve for the same offense, except that the duration of a minimum-risk nonresidential commitment for an offense that is a misdemeanor of the second degree, or is equivalent to a misdemeanor of the second degree, may be for a period not to exceed 6 months. The duration of the child's placement in a commitment program of any restrictiveness level shall be based on objective performance-based treatment planning. The child's treatment plan progress and adjustment-related issues shall be reported to the court quarterly, unless the court requests monthly reports. The child's length of stay in a commitment program may be extended if the child fails to comply with or participate in treatment activities. The child's length of stay in the program shall not be extended for purposes of sanction or punishment. Any temporary release from such program must be approved by the court. Any child so committed may be discharged from institutional confinement or a program upon the direction of the department with the concurrence of the court. The child's treatment plan progress and adjustment-related issues must be communicated to the court at the time the department requests the court to consider releasing the child from the commitment program. The department shall give the court that committed the child to the department

reasonable notice, in writing, of its desire to discharge the child from a commitment facility. The court that committed the child may thereafter accept or reject the request. If the court does not respond within 10 days after receipt of the notice, the request of the department shall be deemed granted. This section does not limit the department's authority to revoke a child's temporary release status and return the child to a commitment facility for any violation of the terms and conditions of the temporary release.

(4) The court may, upon motion of the child or upon its own motion, within 60 days after imposition of a disposition of commitment, suspend the further execution of the disposition and place the child in a probation program upon such terms and conditions as the court may require. The department shall forward to the court all relevant material on the child's progress while in custody not later than 3 working days prior to the hearing on the motion to suspend the disposition.

HISTORY:
S. 39, ch. 97-238; s. 3, ch. 97-281; s. 1, ch. 98-55; s. 14, ch. 98-207; s. 82, ch. 98-280; s. 132, ch. 99-3; s. 15, ch. 99-284; s. 12, ch. 2000-134; s. 31, ch. 2000-135; ss. 24, 25, ch. 2001-125; s. 121, ch. 2002-1; s. 141, ch. 2003-402; s. 4, ch. 2004-241; s. 6, ch. 2005-263; s. 4, ch. 2006-62, eff. July 1, 2006; s. 53, ch. 2006-120, eff. Jan. 1, 2007; s. 4, ch. 2013-112, eff. July 1, 2013.

Editor's notes.
Formerly s. 985.231: transferred by s. 53, ch. 2006-120, effective January 1, 2007.

§ 985.46. Conditional release.

(1) The Legislature finds that:

(a) Conditional release is the care, treatment, help, supervision, and provision of transition-to-adulthood services to juveniles released from residential commitment programs to promote rehabilitation and prevent recidivism.

(b) Conditional release services can contribute significantly to a successful transition of a juvenile from a residential commitment to the juvenile's home, school, and community. Therefore, the best efforts should be made to provide for a successful transition.

(c) The purpose of conditional release is to protect safety; reduce recidivism; increase responsible productive behaviors; and provide for a successful transition of care and custody of the youth from the state to the family.

(d) Accordingly, conditional release should be included in the continuum of care.

(2) It is the intent of the Legislature that:

(a) Commitment programs include rehabilitative efforts on preparing committed juveniles for a successful release to the community.

(b) Conditional release transition planning begins as early in the commitment process as possible.

(c) Each juvenile committed to a residential commitment program be assessed to determine the need for conditional release services upon release from the commitment program.

(3) For juveniles referred or committed to the department, the function of the department may include, but shall not be limited to, assessing each juvenile placed in a residential commitment program to determine the need for conditional release services upon release from the program, supervising the juvenile when released into the community from a residential commitment facility of the department, providing such counseling and other services as may be necessary for the families and assisting their preparations for the return of the child. Subject to specific appropriation, the department shall provide for outpatient sexual offender counseling for any juvenile sexual offender released from a residential commitment program as a component of conditional release.

(4) A juvenile under nonresidential commitment placement continues on commitment status and is subject to transfer under s. 985.441(4).

(5) Participation in the educational program by students of compulsory school attendance age pursuant to s. 1003.21(1) and (2)(a) is mandatory for juvenile justice youth on conditional release or postcommitment probation status. A student of noncompulsory school-attendance age who has not received a high school diploma or its equivalent must participate in an educational program or career and technical education course. A youth who has received a high school diploma or its equivalent and is not employed must participate in workforce development or other career or technical education or attend a community college or a university while in the program, subject to available funding.

HISTORY:
S. 5, ch. 90-208; s. 55, ch. 94-209; s. 1354, ch. 95-147; s. 5, ch. 95-266; s. 47, ch. 95-267; s. 60, ch. 97-238; s. 17, ch. 99-284; s. 43, ch. 2000-135; s. 6, ch. 2000-137; s. 32, ch. 2001-125; s. 1052, ch. 2002-387; s. 8, ch. 2005-263; s. 54, ch. 2006-120, eff. January 1, 2007; s. 4, ch. 2011-54, eff. July 1, 2011; s. 26, ch. 2014-162, eff. July 1, 2014.

Editor's notes.
Formerly s. 985.316: transferred by s. 54, ch. 2006-120, effective January 1, 2007; s. 39.067.

§ 985.461. Transition to adulthood.

(1) The Legislature finds that youth are faced with the need to learn how to support themselves within legal means and overcome the stigma of being delinquent. In most cases, parents expedite this transition. It is the intent of the Legislature that the department provide youth in its custody or under its supervision with opportunities for participating in transition-to-adulthood services while in the department's commitment programs or in probation or conditional release programs in the community. These services should be reasonable and appropriate for the youths' respective ages or special needs and provide activities that build life skills and increase the ability to live independently and become self-sufficient.

(2) Youth served by the department who are in the custody of the Department of Children and Families and who entered juvenile justice placement from a foster care placement, if otherwise eligible, may receive independent living transition services pursuant to s. 409.1451. Court-ordered commitment or probation with the department is not a barrier to eligibility for the array of services available to a youth who is in the dependency foster care system only.

(3) For a dependent child in the foster care system, adjudication for delinquency does not, by itself, disqualify such child for eligibility in the Department of Children and Families' independent living program.

(4) As part of the child's treatment plan, the department may provide transition-to-adulthood services to children released from residential commitment. To support participation in transition-to-adulthood services and subject to appropriation, the department may:

(a) Assess the child's skills and abilities to live independently and become self-sufficient. The specific services to be provided shall be determined using an assessment of his or her readiness for adult life.

(b) Use community reentry teams to assist in the development of a list of age-appropriate activities and responsibilities to be incorporated in the child's written case plan for any youth who is under the custody or supervision of the department. Community reentry teams may include representatives from school districts, law enforcement, workforce development services, community-based service providers, and the youth's family. Such community reentry teams must be created within existing resources provided to the department. Activities may include, but are not limited to, life skills training, including training to develop banking and budgeting skills, interviewing and career planning skills, parenting skills, personal health management, and time management or organizational skills; educational support; employment training; and counseling.

(c) Provide information related to social security insurance benefits and public assistance.

(d) Request parental or guardian permission for the youth to participate in transition-to-adulthood services. Upon such consent, age-appropriate activities shall be incorporated into the youth's written case plan. This plan may include specific goals and objectives and shall be reviewed and updated at least quarterly. If the parent or guardian is cooperative, the plan may not interfere with the parent's or guardian's rights to nurture and train his or her child in ways that are otherwise in compliance with the law and court order.

(e) Contract for transition-to-adulthood services that include residential services and assistance and allow the child to live independently of the daily care and supervision of an adult in a setting that is not licensed under s. 409.175. A child under the care or supervision of the department is eligible for such services if he or she does not pose a danger to the public and is able to demonstrate minimally sufficient skills and aptitude for living under decreased adult supervision, as determined by the department, using established procedures and assessments.

(f) Assist the child in building a portfolio of educational and vocational accomplishments, necessary identification, resumes, and cover letters in an effort to enhance the child's employability.

(g) Collaborate with school district contacts to facilitate appropriate educational services based on the child's identified needs.

(5) For a child under the department's care or supervision, and without benefit of parents or legal guardians capable of assisting the child in the transition to adult life, the department may provide an assessment to determine the child's skills and abilities to live independently and become self-sufficient. Based on the assessment and within existing resources, services and training may be provided in order to develop the necessary skills and abilities.

(6) The provision of transition-to-adulthood services must be part of an overall plan leading to the total independence of the child from department supervision. The plan must include, but need not be limited to:

(a) A description of the child's skills and a plan for learning additional identified skills;

(b) The behavior that the child has exhibited which indicates an ability to be responsible and a plan for developing additional responsibilities, as appropriate;

(c) A plan for the provision of future educational, vocational, and training skills;

(d) Present financial and budgeting capabilities and a plan for improving resources and abilities;

(e) A description of the proposed residence;

(f) Documentation that the child understands the specific consequences of his or her conduct in such a program;

(g) Documentation of proposed services to be provided by the department and other agencies, including the type of services and the nature and frequency of contact; and

(h) A plan for maintaining or developing relationships with family, other adults, friends, and the community, as appropriate.

HISTORY:
S. 2, ch. 2011-236, eff. July 1, 2011; s. 352, ch. 2014-19, eff. July 1, 2014; s. 27, ch. 2014-162, eff. July 1, 2014.

§ 985.465. Juvenile correctional facilities or juvenile prison.

A juvenile correctional facility or juvenile prison is a physically secure residential commitment program with a designated length of stay from 18 months to 36 months, primarily serving children 13 years of age to 19 years of age or until the jurisdiction of the court expires. Each child committed to this level must meet one of the following criteria:

(1) The child is at least 13 years of age at the time of the disposition for the current offense and has been adjudicated on the current offense for:

(a) Arson;

(b) Sexual battery;

(c) Robbery;

(d) Kidnapping;

(e) Aggravated child abuse;

(f) Aggravated assault;

(g) Aggravated stalking;

(h) Murder;

(i) Manslaughter;

(j) Unlawful throwing, placing, or discharging of a destructive device or bomb;

(k) Armed burglary;

(l) Aggravated battery;

(m) Carjacking;

(n) Home-invasion robbery;

(o) Burglary with an assault or battery;

(p) Any lewd or lascivious offense committed upon or in the presence of a person less than 16 years of age; or

(q) Carrying, displaying, using, threatening to use, or attempting to use a weapon or firearm during the commission of a felony.

(2) The child is at least 13 years of age at the time of the disposition, the current offense is a felony, and the child has previously been committed three or more times to a delinquency commitment program.

(3) The child is at least 13 years of age and is currently committed for a felony offense and transferred from a moderate-risk or high-risk residential commitment placement.

(4) The child is at least 13 years of age at the time of the disposition for the current offense, the child is eligible for prosecution as an adult for the current offense, and the current offense is ranked at level 7 or higher on the Criminal Punishment Code offense severity ranking chart pursuant to s. 921.0022.

HISTORY:
S. 47, ch. 94-209; s. 15, ch. 95-267; s. 9, ch. 96-398; s. 10, ch. 97-194; s. 57, ch. 97-238; s. 16, ch. 99-201; s. 40, ch. 99-284; s. 55, ch. 2006-120, eff. January 1, 2007.

Editor's notes.
Formerly s. 985.313: transferred by s. 55, ch. 2006-120, effective January 1, 2007; s. 39.0581.

§ 985.47. Serious or habitual juvenile offender [Repealed.]

Repealed by s. 4, ch. 2011-70, effective July 1, 2011.

HISTORY:
S. 5, ch. 90-208; s. 2, ch. 92-287; s. 57, ch. 93-268; s. 223, ch.

95-147; s. 1, ch. 95-152; s. 1, ch. 95-256; s. 3, ch. 96-398; s. 14, ch. 96-406; s. 22, ch. 97-95; s. 54, ch. 97-238; s. 2, ch. 98-55; s. 22, ch. 98-207; s. 134, ch. 99-3; s. 27, ch. 99-284; s. 38, ch. 2000-135; s. 30, ch. 2001-125; s. 27, ch. 2004-335; s. 17, ch. 2005-263; s. 10, ch. 2006-62, eff. July 1, 2006; s. 56, ch. 2006-120, eff. January 1, 2007; s. 169, ch. 2010-102, eff. May 26, 2010; s. 19, ch. 2010-113, eff. July 1, 2010; s. 11, ch. 2011-70, eff. July 1, 2011.

§ 985.475. Juvenile sexual offenders.

(1) CRITERIA. — A "juvenile sexual offender" means:

(a) A juvenile who has been found by the court under s. 985.35 to have committed a violation of chapter 794, chapter 796, chapter 800, s. 827.071, or s. 847.0133;

(b) A juvenile found to have committed any felony violation of law or delinquent act involving juvenile sexual abuse. "Juvenile sexual abuse" means any sexual behavior that occurs without consent, without equality, or as a result of coercion. For purposes of this subsection, the following definitions apply:

1. "Coercion" means the exploitation of authority, use of bribes, threats of force, or intimidation to gain cooperation or compliance.

2. "Equality" means two participants operating with the same level of power in a relationship, neither being controlled nor coerced by the other.

3. "Consent" means an agreement including all of the following:

a. Understanding what is proposed based on age, maturity, developmental level, functioning, and experience.

b. Knowledge of societal standards for what is being proposed.

c. Awareness of potential consequences and alternatives.

d. Assumption that agreement or disagreement will be accepted equally.

e. Voluntary decision.

f. Mental competence.

Juvenile sexual offender behavior ranges from noncontact sexual behavior such as making obscene phone calls, exhibitionism, voyeurism, and the showing or taking of lewd photographs to varying degrees of direct sexual contact, such as frottage, fondling, digital penetration, rape, fellatio, sodomy, and various other sexually aggressive acts.

(2) Following a delinquency adjudicatory hearing under s. 985.35, the court may on its own or upon request by the state or the department and subject to specific appropriation, determine whether a juvenile sexual offender placement is required for the protection of the public and what would be the best approach to address the treatment needs of the juvenile sexual offender. When the court determines that a juvenile has no history of a recent comprehensive assessment focused on sexually deviant behavior, the court may, subject to specific appropriation, order the department to conduct or arrange for an examination to determine whether the juvenile sexual offender is amenable to community-based treatment.

(a) The report of the examination shall include, at a minimum, the following:

1. The juvenile sexual offender's account of the incident and the official report of the investigation.

2. The juvenile sexual offender's offense history.

3. A multidisciplinary assessment of the sexually deviant behaviors, including an assessment by a certified psychologist, therapist, or psychiatrist.

4. An assessment of the juvenile sexual offender's family, social, educational, and employment situation. The report shall set forth the sources of the evaluator's information.

(b) The report shall assess the juvenile sexual offender's amenability to treatment and relative risk to the victim and the community.

(c) The department shall provide a proposed plan to the court that shall include, at a minimum:

1. The frequency and type of contact between the offender and therapist.

2. The specific issues and behaviors to be addressed in the treatment and description of planned treatment methods.

3. Monitoring plans, including any requirements regarding living conditions, school attendance and participation, lifestyle, and monitoring by family members, legal guardians, or others.

4. Anticipated length of treatment.

5. Recommended crime-related prohibitions and curfew.

6. Reasonable restrictions on the contact between the juvenile sexual offender and either the victim or alleged victim.

(d) After receipt of the report on the proposed plan of treatment, the court shall consider whether the community and the offender will benefit from use of juvenile sexual offender community-based treatment alternative disposition and consider the opinion of the victim or the victim's family as to whether the offender should receive a community-based treatment alternative disposition under this subsection.

(e) If the court determines that this juvenile sexual offender community-based treatment alternative is appropriate, the court may place the offender on community supervision for up to 3 years. As a condition of community treatment and supervision, the court may order the offender to:

1. Undergo available outpatient juvenile sexual offender treatment for up to 3 years. A program or provider may not be used for such treatment unless it has an appropriate program designed for sexual offender treatment. The department shall not change the treatment provider without first notifying the state attorney's office.

2.   Remain within described geographical boundaries and notify the court or the department counselor prior to any change in the offender's address, educational program, or employment.

3.   Comply with all requirements of the treatment plan.

(f)   The juvenile sexual offender treatment provider shall submit quarterly reports on the respondent's progress in treatment to the court and the parties to the proceedings. The juvenile sexual offender reports shall reference the treatment plan and include, at a minimum, the following:

1.   Dates of attendance.

2.   The juvenile sexual offender's compliance with the requirements of treatment.

3.   A description of the treatment activities.

4.   The sexual offender's relative progress in treatment.

5.   The offender's family support of the treatment objectives.

6.   Any other material specified by the court at the time of the disposition.

(g)   At the disposition hearing, the court may set case review hearings as the court considers appropriate.

(h)   If the juvenile sexual offender violates any condition of the disposition or the court finds that the juvenile sexual offender is failing to make satisfactory progress in treatment, the court may revoke the community-based treatment alternative and order commitment to the department under s. 985.441.

(i)   If the court determines that the juvenile sexual offender is not amenable to community-based treatment, the court shall proceed with a juvenile sexual offender disposition hearing under s. 985.441.

HISTORY:
S. 39, ch. 97-238; s. 3, ch. 97-281; s. 1, ch. 98-55; s. 14, ch. 98-207; s. 82, ch. 98-280; s. 132, ch. 99-3; s. 15, ch. 99-284; s. 12, ch. 2000-134; s. 31, ch. 2000-135; ss. 24, 25, ch. 2001-125; s. 121, ch. 2002-1; s. 141, ch. 2003-402; s. 4, ch. 2004-241; s. 6, ch. 2005-263; s. 4, ch. 2006-62, eff. July 1, 2006; s. 57, ch. 2006-120, eff. January 1, 2007.

Editor's notes.
Formerly s. 985.231(3); transferred by s. 57, ch. 2006-120, effective January 1, 2007.

§ 985.48.   Juvenile sexual offender commitment programs; sexual abuse intervention networks.

(1)   In order to provide intensive treatment and psychological services to a juvenile sexual offender committed to the department, it is the intent of the Legislature to establish programs and strategies to effectively respond to juvenile sexual offenders. In designing programs for juvenile sexual offenders, it is the further intent of the Legislature to implement strategies that include:

(a)   Developing adequate commitment programs and facilities to ensure appropriate and effective treatment and ensure that decisions to release juvenile sexual offenders into the community are not made on the basis of inadequate space.

(b)   Providing an adequate number of well-trained staff to address the treatment needs of juvenile sexual offenders.

(c)   Providing intensive postcommitment supervision of juvenile sexual offenders who are released into the community with terms and conditions which may include electronic monitoring of a juvenile sexual offender for the purpose of enhancing public safety.

(d)   Providing notification to the school to which the juvenile sexual offender is returning, the parents or legal guardians of the victim, and law enforcement, when a juvenile sexual offender returns into the community.

(2)   Contingent upon a specific appropriation, the department shall implement and operate programs to provide intensive educational and psychological services and other treatment for juvenile sexual offenders.

(3)   Subject to specific appropriation, a child may be placed in a juvenile sexual offender program when committed to the department.

(4)   The program shall include educational components, life management training, substance abuse treatment, and intensive psychological treatment provided by appropriate mental health professionals. Juvenile sexual offenders shall be required to participate in all programs and treatment.

(5)   Based on assessed need for conditional release, the department shall provide an intensive conditional release component for monitoring and assisting the transition of a juvenile sexual offender into the community with terms and conditions that may include electronic monitoring of the juvenile sexual offender.

(6)   The department shall establish protocol and procedures to notify schools, the appropriate law enforcement agencies, and the court when a juvenile sexual offender returns to the community.

(7)   The department may contract with private organizations for the operation of a juvenile sexual offender program and conditional release.

(8)   The department shall conduct inspections of and quality assurance activities for each juvenile sexual offender program operated by or under contract with the department, based on standards specifically developed for these types of programs, to determine whether the program complies with department rules for continued operation of the program.

(9)   The department shall maintain records and other information necessary to evaluate the effectiveness of each juvenile sexual offender program and other outcome evaluation requirements.

(10)   A child protection team or the state attorney in any judicial circuit may establish a sexual abuse intervention network to assist in identifying, investigating, prosecuting, treating, and preventing sexual abuse

with special emphasis on juvenile sexual offenders and victims of sexual abuse.

(11) Membership of a sexual abuse intervention network shall include, but is not limited to, representatives from:

(a) Local law enforcement agencies;

(b) Local school boards;

(c) Child protective investigators;

(d) The office of the state attorney;

(e) The office of the public defender;

(f) The juvenile division of the circuit court;

(g) Professionals licensed under chapter 458, chapter 459, s. 490.0145, or s. 491.0144 providing treatment for juvenile sexual offenders or their victims;

(h) The guardian ad litem program;

(i) The Department of Juvenile Justice; and

(j) The Department of Children and Families .

(12) Each sexual abuse intervention network shall develop a cooperative working agreement describing the roles and responsibilities of all members towards the identification, investigation, prosecution, treatment, and reintegration of juvenile sexual offenders and the treatment of their victims.

(13) Subject to specific appropriation, availability of funds, or receipt of appropriate grant funds, the Office of the Attorney General, the Department of Children and Families, or the Department of Juvenile Justice shall award grants to sexual abuse intervention networks that apply for such grants. The grants may be used for training, treatment, conditional release, evaluation, public awareness, and other specified community needs that are identified by the network. A grant shall be awarded based on the applicant's level of local funding, level of collaboration, number of juvenile sexual offenders to be served, number of victims to be served, and level of unmet needs.

HISTORY:
S. 6, ch. 95-266; s. 48, ch. 95-267; s. 52, ch. 97-238; s. 9, ch. 98-158; s. 16, ch. 99-284; s. 36, ch. 2000-135; s. 58, ch. 2006-120, eff. Jan. 1, 2007; s. 14, ch. 2011-70, eff. July 1, 2011; s. 5, ch. 2013-118, eff. Oct. 1, 2013; s. 353, ch. 2014-19, eff. July 1, 2014.

Editor's notes.
Formerly s. 985.308; transferred by s. 58, ch. 2006-120, effective January 1, 2007; s. 29.0571.

§ 985.481. Sexual offenders adjudicated delinquent; notification upon release.

(1) As used in this section:

(a) "Convicted" has the same meaning as provided in s. 943.0435.

(b) "Electronic mail address" has the same meaning as provided in s. 668.602.

(c) "Internet identifier" has the same meaning as provided in s. 775.21.

(d) "Permanent residence," "temporary residence," and "transient residence" have the same meaning as provided in s. 775.21.

(e) "Professional license" has the same meaning as provided in s. 775.21.

(f) "Sexual offender" means a person who has been adjudicated delinquent as provided in s. 943.0435(1)(h) 1.d.

(g) "Vehicles owned" has the same meaning as provided in s. 775.21.

(2) The Legislature finds that certain juvenile sexual offenders pose a high risk of engaging in sexual offenses even after being released from commitment and that protection of the public from sexual offenders is a paramount governmental interest. Sexual offenders have a reduced expectation of privacy because of the public's interest in public safety and in the effective operation of government. Releasing sexual offender information to law enforcement agencies, to persons who request such information, and to the public by a law enforcement agency or public agency will further the governmental interests of public safety.

(3)(a) The department shall provide information regarding any sexual offender who is being released after serving a period of residential commitment under the department for any offense, as follows:

1. The department shall provide the sexual offender's name, any change in the offender's name by reason of marriage or other legal process, and any alias, if known; the correctional facility from which the sexual offender is released; the sexual offender's social security number, race, sex, date of birth, height, weight, and hair and eye color; tattoos or other identifying marks; the make, model, color, vehicle identification number (VIN), and license tag number of all vehicles owned; address of any planned permanent residence or temporary residence, within the state or out of state, including a rural route address and a post office box; if no permanent or temporary address, any transient residence within the state; address, location or description, and dates of any known future temporary residence within the state or out of state; date and county of disposition and each crime for which there was a disposition; a copy of the offender's fingerprints, palm prints, and a digitized photograph taken within 60 days before release; the date of release of the sexual offender; all home telephone numbers and cellular telephone numbers required to be provided pursuant to s. 943.0435(4)(e); all electronic mail addresses and Internet identifiers required to be provided pursuant to s. 943.0435(4)(e); information about any professional licenses the offender has, if known; and passport information, if he or she has a passport, and, if he or she is an alien, information about documents establishing his or her immigration status. The department shall notify the Department of Law Enforcement if the sexual offender escapes, absconds, or dies. If the sexual offender is in the custody of a private correctional

facility, the facility shall take the digitized photograph of the sexual offender within 60 days before the sexual offender's release and also place it in the sexual offender's file. If the sexual offender is in the custody of a local jail, the custodian of the local jail shall register the offender within 3 business days after intake of the offender for any reason and upon release, and shall notify the Department of Law Enforcement of the sexual offender's release and provide to the Department of Law Enforcement the information specified in this subparagraph and any information specified in subparagraph 2. which the Department of Law Enforcement requests.

2. The department may provide any other information considered necessary, including criminal and delinquency records, when available.

(b) The department must make the information described in subparagraph (a)1. available electronically to the Department of Law Enforcement in its database and in a format that is compatible with the requirements of the Florida Crime Information Center.

(c) Upon receiving information regarding a sexual offender from the department, the Department of Law Enforcement, the sheriff, or the chief of police shall provide the information described in subparagraph (a)1. to any individual who requests such information and may release the information to the public in any manner considered appropriate, unless the information so received is confidential or exempt from s. 119.07(1) and s. 24(a), Art. I of the State Constitution.

(4) This section authorizes the department or any law enforcement agency to notify the community and the public of a sexual offender's presence in the community. However, with respect to a sexual offender who has been found to be a sexual predator under chapter 775, the Department of Law Enforcement or any other law enforcement agency must inform the community and the public of the sexual predator's presence in the community as provided in chapter 775.

(5) An elected or appointed official, public employee, school administrator or employee, or agency, or any individual or entity acting at the request or upon the direction of any law enforcement agency, is immune from civil liability for damages resulting from the release of information under this section.

HISTORY:

S. 12, ch. 2007-209, eff. July 1, 2007; s. 6, ch. 2009-194, eff. July 1, 2009; s. 14, ch. 2010-92, eff. May 26, 2010; s. 10, ch. 2014-5, eff. Oct. 1, 2014; s. 28, ch. 2014-162, eff. July 1, 2014; s. 7, ch. 2016-104, eff. July 1, 2016; ss. 6, 10, ch. 2017-170, eff. June 26, 2017.

§ 985.4815. Notification to Department of Law Enforcement of information on juvenile sexual offenders.

(1) As used in this section, the term:

(a) "Change in status at an institution of higher education" has the same meaning as provided in s. 775.21.

(b) "Conviction" has the same meaning as provided in s. 943.0435.

(c) "Electronic mail address" has the same meaning as provided in s. 668.602.

(d) "Institution of higher education" has the same meaning as provided in s. 775.21.

(e) "Internet identifier" has the same meaning as provided in s. 775.21.

(f) "Permanent residence," "temporary residence," and "transient residence" have the same meaning as provided in s. 775.21.

(g) "Professional license" has the same meaning as provided in s. 775.21.

(h) "Sexual offender" means a person who is in the care or custody or under the jurisdiction or supervision of the department or is in the custody of a private correctional facility and who:

1. Has been adjudicated delinquent as provided in s. 943.0435(1)(h) 1.d.; or

2. Establishes or maintains a residence in this state and has not been designated as a sexual predator by a court of this state but has been designated as a sexual predator, as a sexually violent predator, or by another sexual offender designation in another state or jurisdiction and was, as a result of such designation, subjected to registration or community or public notification, or both, or would be if the person were a resident of that state or jurisdiction, without regard to whether the person otherwise meets the criteria for registration as a sexual offender.

(i) "Vehicles owned" has the same meaning as provided in s. 775.21.

(2) The clerk of the court that adjudicated and entered a disposition regarding the sexual offender for the offense or offenses for which he or she was convicted shall forward to the department and the Department of Law Enforcement a certified copy of any order entered by the court imposing any special condition or restriction on the sexual offender which restricts or prohibits access to the victim, if the victim is a minor, or to other minors. The Department of Law Enforcement may include on its Internet website such special conditions or restrictions.

(3) If a sexual offender is not sentenced to a term of residential commitment, the clerk of the court shall ensure that the sexual offender's fingerprints are taken and forwarded to the Department of Law Enforcement within 48 hours after the court sentences the offender. The fingerprints shall be clearly marked "Sexual Offender Registration."

(4) A sexual offender, as described in this section, who is under the supervision of the department but who is not committed shall register with the department within 3 business days after adjudication and disposi-

tion for a registrable offense and otherwise provide information as required by this subsection.

(a) The sexual offender shall provide his or her name; date of birth; social security number; race; sex; height; weight; hair and eye color; tattoos or other identifying marks; the make, model, color, vehicle identification number (VIN), and license tag number of all vehicles owned; permanent or legal residence and address of temporary residence within the state or out of state while the sexual offender is in the care or custody or under the jurisdiction or supervision of the department in this state, including any rural route address or post office box; if no permanent or temporary address, any transient residence; address, location or description, and dates of any current or known future temporary residence within the state or out of state; all home telephone numbers and cellular telephone numbers required to be provided pursuant to s. 943.0435(4)(e); all electronic mail addresses and Internet identifiers required to be provided pursuant to s. 943.0435(4)(e); and the name and address of each school attended. The sexual offender shall also produce his or her passport, if he or she has a passport, and, if he or she is an alien, shall produce or provide information about documents establishing his or her immigration status. The offender shall also provide information about any professional licenses he or she has. The department shall verify the address of each sexual offender and shall report to the Department of Law Enforcement any failure by a sexual offender to comply with registration requirements.

(b) If the sexual offender is enrolled or employed, whether for compensation or as a volunteer, at an institution of higher education in this state, the sexual offender shall provide the name, address, and county of each institution, including each campus attended, and the sexual offender's enrollment, volunteer, or employment status. Each change in status at an institution of higher education must be reported to the department within 48 hours after the change in status at an institution of higher education. The department shall promptly notify each institution of the sexual offender's presence and any change in the sexual offender's enrollment, volunteer, or employment status.

(c) A sexual offender shall report in person to the sheriff's office within 48 hours after any change in vehicles owned to report those vehicle information changes.

(5) In addition to notification and transmittal requirements imposed by any other provision of law, the department shall compile information on any sexual offender and provide the information to the Department of Law Enforcement. The department must make the information available electronically to the Department of Law Enforcement in its database in a format that is compatible with the requirements of the Florida Crime Information Center.

(6)(a) The information provided to the Department of Law Enforcement must include the following:

1. The information obtained from the sexual offender under subsection (4).

2. The sexual offender's most current address and place of permanent, temporary, or transient residence within the state or out of state, and address, location or description, and dates of any current or known future temporary residence within the state or out of state, while the sexual offender is in the care or custody or under the jurisdiction or supervision of the department in this state, including the name of the county or municipality in which the offender permanently or temporarily resides, or has a transient residence, and address, location or description, and dates of any current or known future temporary residence within the state or out of state; and, if known, the intended place of permanent, temporary, or transient residence, and address, location or description, and dates of any current or known future temporary residence within the state or out of state upon satisfaction of all sanctions.

3. The legal status of the sexual offender and the scheduled termination date of that legal status.

4. The location of, and local telephone number for, any department office that is responsible for supervising the sexual offender.

5. An indication of whether the victim of the offense that resulted in the offender's status as a sexual offender was a minor.

6. The offense or offenses at adjudication and disposition that resulted in the determination of the offender's status as a sex offender.

7. A digitized photograph of the sexual offender, which must have been taken within 60 days before the offender was released from the custody of the department or a private correctional facility by expiration of sentence under s. 944.275, or within 60 days after the onset of the department's supervision of any sexual offender who is on probation, postcommitment probation, residential commitment, nonresidential commitment, licensed child-caring commitment, community control, conditional release, parole, provisional release, or control release or who is supervised by the department under the Interstate Compact Agreement for Probationers and Parolees. If the sexual offender is in the custody of a private correctional facility, the facility shall take a digitized photograph of the sexual offender within the time period provided in this subparagraph and shall provide the photograph to the department.

(b) If any information provided by the department changes during the time the sexual offender is under the department's care, control, custody, or supervision, including any change in the offender's name by reason of marriage or other legal process, the department shall, in a timely manner, update the information and provide it to the Department of Law Enforcement in the manner prescribed in subsection (5).

(7) If the sexual offender is in the custody of a local jail, the custodian of the local jail shall register the offender within 3 business days after intake of the offender for any reason and upon release, and shall forward the information to the Department of Law Enforcement. The custodian of the local jail shall also take a digitized photograph of the sexual offender while the offender remains in custody and shall provide the digitized photograph to the Department of Law Enforcement.

(8) If the sexual offender is under federal supervision, the federal agency responsible for supervising the sexual offender may forward to the Department of Law Enforcement any information regarding the sexual offender which is consistent with the information provided by the department under this section and may indicate whether use of the information is restricted to law enforcement purposes only or may be used by the Department of Law Enforcement for purposes of public notification.

(9) A sexual offender, as described in this section, who is under the care, jurisdiction, or supervision of the department but who is not incarcerated shall, in addition to the registration requirements provided in subsection (4), register in the manner provided in s. 943.0435(3), (4), and (5), unless the sexual offender is a sexual predator, in which case he or she shall register as required under s. 775.21. A sexual offender who fails to comply with the requirements of s. 943.0435 is subject to the penalties provided in s. 943.0435(9).

(10)(a) The failure of a sexual offender to submit to the taking of a digitized photograph, or to otherwise comply with the requirements of this section, is a felony of the third degree, punishable as provided in s. 775.082, s. 775.083, or s. 775.084.

(b) A sexual offender who commits any act or omission in violation of this section may be prosecuted for the act or omission in the county in which the act or omission was committed, the county of the last registered address of the sexual offender, or the county in which the adjudication and disposition occurred for the offense or offenses that meet the criteria for designating a person as a sexual offender.

(c) An arrest on charges of failure to register when the offender has been provided and advised of his or her statutory obligations to register under s. 943.0435(2), the service of an information or a complaint for a violation of this section, or an arraignment on charges for a violation of this section constitutes actual notice of the duty to register. A sexual offender's failure to immediately register as required by this section following such arrest, service, or arraignment constitutes grounds for a subsequent charge of failure to register. A sexual offender charged with the crime of failure to register who asserts, or intends to assert, a lack of notice of the duty to register as a defense to a charge of failure to register shall immediately register as required by this section. A sexual offender who is charged with a subsequent failure to register may not assert the defense of a lack of notice of the duty to register.

(d) Registration following such arrest, service, or arraignment is not a defense and does not relieve the sexual offender of criminal liability for the failure to register.

(11) The department, the Department of Highway Safety and Motor Vehicles, the Department of Law Enforcement, the Department of Corrections, personnel of those departments, and any individual or entity acting at the request or upon the direction of those departments are immune from civil liability for damages for good faith compliance with this section and shall be presumed to have acted in good faith in compiling, recording, reporting, or providing information. The presumption of good faith is not overcome if technical or clerical errors are made by the department, the Department of Highway Safety and Motor Vehicles, the Department of Law Enforcement, the Department of Corrections, personnel of those departments, or any individual or entity acting at the request or upon the direction of those departments in compiling, recording, reporting, or providing information, or, if the information is incomplete or incorrect because the information has not been provided by a person or agency required to provide it, was not reported, or was falsely reported.

(12) Any person who has reason to believe that a sexual offender is not complying, or has not complied, with the requirements of this section and who, with the intent to assist the sexual offender in eluding a law enforcement agency that is seeking to find the sexual offender to question the sexual offender about, or to arrest the sexual offender for, his or her noncompliance with the requirements of this section:

(a) Withholds information from, or does not notify, the law enforcement agency about the sexual offender's noncompliance with the requirements of this section and, if known, the whereabouts of the sexual offender;

(b) Harbors, attempts to harbor, or assists another person in harboring or attempting to harbor the sexual offender;

(c) Conceals, attempts to conceal, or assists another person in concealing or attempting to conceal the sexual offender; or

(d) Provides information to the law enforcement agency regarding the sexual offender that the person knows to be false commits a felony of the third degree, punishable as provided in s. 775.082, s. 775.083, or s. 775.084. This subsection does not apply if the sexual offender is incarcerated in or is in the custody of a state correctional facility, a private correctional facility, a local jail, or a federal correctional facility.

(13)(a) A sexual offender must report in person each year during the month of the sexual offender's birthday and during every third month thereafter to the sheriff's office in the county in which he or she resides or is otherwise located to reregister.

(b) The sheriff's office may determine the appropriate times and days for reporting by the sexual offender, which must be consistent with the reporting requirements of this subsection. Reregistration must include any changes to the following information:

1. Name; social security number; age; race; sex; date of birth; height; weight; hair and eye color; tattoos or other identifying marks; fingerprints; palm prints; address of any permanent residence and address of any current temporary residence, within the state or out of state, including a rural route address and a post office box; if no permanent or temporary address, any transient residence; address, location or description, and dates of any current or known future temporary residence within the state or out of state; passport information, if he or she has a passport, and, if he or she is an alien, information about documents establishing his or her immigration status; all home telephone numbers and cellular telephone numbers required to be provided pursuant to s. 943.0435(4)(e); all electronic mail addresses and Internet identifiers required to be provided pursuant to s. 943.0435(4)(e); name and address of each school attended; employment information required to be provided pursuant to s. 943.0435(4)(e); the make, model, color, vehicle identification number (VIN), and license tag number of all vehicles owned; and photograph. A post office box may not be provided in lieu of a physical residential address. The offender shall also provide information about any professional licenses he or she has.

2. If the sexual offender is enrolled or employed, whether for compensation or as a volunteer, at an institution of higher education in this state, the sexual offender shall also provide to the department the name, address, and county of each institution, including each campus attended, and the sexual offender's enrollment, volunteer, or employment status.

3. If the sexual offender's place of residence is a motor vehicle, trailer, mobile home, or manufactured home, as defined in chapter 320, the sexual offender shall also provide the vehicle identification number; the license tag number; the registration number; and a description, including color

scheme, of the motor vehicle, trailer, mobile home, or manufactured home. If the sexual offender's place of residence is a vessel, live-aboard vessel, or houseboat, as defined in chapter 327, the sexual offender shall also provide the hull identification number; the manufacturer's serial number; the name of the vessel, live-aboard vessel, or houseboat; the registration number; and a description, including color scheme, of the vessel, live-aboard vessel, or houseboat.

4. Any sexual offender who fails to report in person as required at the sheriff's office, who fails to respond to any address verification correspondence from the department within 3 weeks after the date of the correspondence, or who knowingly provides false registration information by act or omission commits a felony of the third degree, punishable as provided in ss. 775.082, 775.083, and 775.084.

(c) The sheriff's office shall, within 2 working days, electronically submit and update all information provided by the sexual offender to the Department of Law Enforcement in a manner prescribed by that department.

HISTORY:

S. 13, ch. 2007-209, eff. July 1, 2007; s. 15, ch. 2010-92, eff. May 26, 2010; s. 66, ch. 2013-116, eff. July 1, 2013; s. 11, ch. 2014-5, eff. Oct. 1, 2014; s. 29, ch. 2014-162, eff. July 1, 2014; s. 63, ch. 2016-24, eff. Oct. 1, 2016; s. 8, ch. 2016-104, eff. July 1, 2016; ss. 7, 11, ch. 2017-170, eff. June 26, 2017.

§ 985.483. Intensive residential treatment program for offenders less than 13 years of age [Repealed.]

Repealed by s. 5, ch. 2011-70, effective July 1, 2011.

HISTORY:

S. 3, ch. 92-287; s. 58, ch. 93-268; s. 224, ch. 95-147; s. 2, ch. 95-152; s. 2, ch. 95-256; s. 10, ch. 96-398; s. 15, ch. 96-406; s. 23, ch. 97-95; ss. 3, 55, ch. 97-238; s. 2, ch. 98-55; s. 23, ch. 98-207; s. 135, ch. 99-3; s. 14, ch. 99-201; ss. 9, 28, ch. 99-284; ss. 18, 39, ch. 2000-135; s. 138, ch. 2001-266; ss. 1, 21, ch. 2005-263; s. 7, ch. 2006-62; s. 59, ch. 2006-120, eff. January 1, 2007; s. 165, ch. 2007-5, eff. July 3, 2007; s. 170, ch. 2010-102, eff. May 26; s. 20, ch. 2010-113, eff. July 1, 2010.

§ 985.486. Intensive residential treatment programs for offenders less than 13 years of age; prerequisite for commitment [Repealed.]

Repealed by s. 6, ch. 2011-70, effective July 1, 2011.

HISTORY:

S. 26, ch. 92-287; s. 3, ch. 95-152; s. 16, ch. 95-267; s. 11, ch. 96-398; s. 56, ch. 97-238; s. 29, ch. 99-284; s. 40, ch. 2000-135; s. 60, ch. 2006-120, eff. January 1, 2007; s. 52, ch. 2010-117, eff. July 1, 2010.

§ 985.4891. Sheriff's training and respect programs [Repealed.]

Repealed by s. 16, ch. 2010-113, effective July 1, 2010.

HISTORY:
S. 6, ch. 2006-62, eff. July 1, 2006.

§ 985.494. Commitment programs for juvenile felony offenders.

(1) Notwithstanding any other law and regardless of the child's age, a child who is adjudicated delinquent, or for whom adjudication is withheld, for an act that would be a felony if committed by an adult, shall be committed to a maximum-risk residential program if the child has completed two different high-risk residential commitment programs. The commitment of a child to a maximum-risk residential program must be for an indeterminate period, but may not exceed the maximum term of imprisonment that an adult may serve for the same offense.

(2) In committing a child to the appropriate program, the court may consider an equivalent program of similar intensity as being comparable to a program required under subsection (1).

HISTORY:
S. 48, ch. 94-209; s. 12, ch. 96-398; s. 58, ch. 97-238; s. 11, ch. 2006-62, eff. July 1, 2006; s. 62, ch. 2006-120, eff. January 1, 2007; s. 21, ch. 2010-113, eff. July 1, 2010; s. 8, ch. 2011-70, eff. July 1, 2011.

Editor's notes.
Formerly s. 985.314: transferred by s. 62, ch. 2006-120, effective January 1, 2007; s. 39.0584.

PART VIII.
AUTHORITY OF THE COURT OVER PARENTS OR GUARDIANS.

§ 985.511. Costs of representation.

The responsibilities of the parents or legal guardian of the child to pay costs associated with the representation of the child are prescribed under s. 985.033.

HISTORY:
S. 63, ch. 2006-120, eff. Jan. 1, 2007.

§ 985.512. Powers with respect to certain children.

In carrying out the provisions of this chapter, the court may order the parent or legal guardian of a child adjudicated dependent, a child in need of services, or a delinquent child to attend a course of instruction in parenting skills, to accept counseling, or to receive other assistance from any agency in the community which notifies the clerk of the court of the availability of its services. Where appropriate, the court shall order both parents or guardians to receive such parental assistance.

HISTORY:
S. 38, ch. 94-209; s. 12, ch. 97-238; s. 64, ch. 2006-120, eff. Jan. 1, 2007.

Editor's notes.
Formerly s. 985.204: transferred by s. 64, ch. 2006-120, effective January 1, 2007; s. 39.0476.

§ 985.513. Powers of the court over parent or guardian at disposition.

(1) The court that has jurisdiction over an adjudicated delinquent child may, by an order stating the facts upon which a determination of a sanction and rehabilitative program was made at the disposition hearing:

(a) Order the child's parent or guardian, together with the child, to render community service in a public service program or to participate in a community work project. In addition to the sanctions imposed on the child, the court may order the child's parent or guardian to perform community service if the court finds that the parent or guardian did not make a diligent and good faith effort to prevent the child from engaging in delinquent acts.

(b) Order the parent or guardian to make restitution in money or in kind for any damage or loss caused by the child's offense. The court may also require the child's parent or legal guardian to be responsible for any restitution ordered against the child, as provided under s. 985.437. The court shall determine a reasonable amount or manner of restitution, and payment shall be made to the clerk of the circuit court as provided in s. 985.437. The court may retain jurisdiction, as provided under s. 985.0301, over the child and the child's parent or legal guardian whom the court has ordered to pay restitution until the restitution order is satisfied or the court orders otherwise.

(2) Notwithstanding whether adjudication is imposed or withheld, the court may order the natural parents or legal custodian or guardian of a child who is found to have committed a delinquent act to participate in family counseling and other professional counseling activities deemed necessary for the rehabilitation of the child or to enhance their ability to provide the child with adequate support, guidance, and supervision. The court may also order that the parent, custodian, or guardian support the child and participate with the child in fulfilling a court-imposed sanction. In addition, the court may use its contempt powers to enforce a court-imposed sanction.

HISTORY:
S. 39, ch. 97-238; s. 3, ch. 97-281; s. 1, ch. 98-55; s. 14, ch. 98-207; s. 82, ch. 98-280; s. 132, ch. 99-3; s. 15, ch. 99-284; s. 12, ch. 2000-134; s. 31, ch. 2000-135; ss. 24, 25, ch. 2001-125; s. 121, ch. 2002-1; s. 141, ch. 2003-402; s. 4, ch. 2004-241; s. 6, ch. 2005-263; s. 4, ch. 2006-62, eff. July 1, 2006; s. 65, ch. 2006-120, eff. January 1, 2007.

Editor's notes.
Formerly s. 985.231(e): transferred by s. 65, ch. 2006-120, effective January 1, 2007.

§ 985.514. Responsibility for cost of care; fees.

(1) When any child is placed into detention care or into other placement for the purpose of being supervised by the department pursuant to a court order

following a detention hearing, the court shall order the child's parents to pay fees to the department as provided in s. 985.039.

(2) When any child is found by the court to have committed a delinquent act and is placed on probation, regardless of adjudication, under the supervision of or in the temporary legal custody of the department, the court shall order the child's parents to pay fees to the department as provided in s. 985.039.

(3) When the court under s. 985.565 orders any child prosecuted as an adult to be supervised by or committed to the department for treatment in any of the department's programs for children, the court shall order the child's parents to pay fees as provided in s. 985.039.

HISTORY:
S. 66, ch. 2006-120, eff. January 1, 2007; s. 30, ch. 2014-162, eff. July 1, 2014; s. 8, ch. 2017-164, eff. Oct. 1, 2017.

PART IX.
APPEAL.

§ 985.534. Appeal.
(1) An appeal from an order of the court affecting a party to a case involving a child under this chapter may be taken to the appropriate district court of appeal within the time and in the manner prescribed by s. 924.051 and the Florida Rules of Appellate Procedure by:

(a) Any child, and any parent or legal guardian or custodian of any child.

(b) The state, which may appeal from:

1. An order dismissing a petition or any section thereof;

2. An order granting a new adjudicatory hearing;

3. An order arresting judgment;

4. A ruling on a question of law when the child is adjudicated delinquent and appeals from the judgment;

5. The disposition, on the ground that it is illegal;

6. A judgment discharging a child on habeas corpus;

7. An order adjudicating a child insane under the Florida Rules of Juvenile Procedure; and

8. All other preadjudicatory hearings, except that the state may not take more than one appeal under this subsection in any case.

In the case of an appeal by the state, the notice of appeal shall be filed by the appropriate state attorney or his or her authorized assistant under s. 27.18. Such an appeal shall embody all assignments of error in each preadjudicatory hearing order that the state seeks to have reviewed. The state shall pay all costs of the appeal except for the child's attorney's fee.

(2) The Department of Legal Affairs shall represent the state upon appeal and shall be notified of the appeal by the clerk when the notice of appeal is filed in the circuit court.

(3) The taking of an appeal shall not operate as a supersedeas in any case unless pursuant to an order of the court.

(4) The case on appeal shall be docketed, and any papers filed in the appellate court shall be entitled, with the initials but not the name of the child and the court case number, and the papers shall remain sealed in the office of the clerk of the appellate court when not in use by the appellate court and shall not be open to public inspection. The decision of the appellate court shall be likewise entitled and shall refer to the child only by initials and court case number.

(5) The original order of the appellate court, with all papers filed in the case on appeal, shall remain in the office of the clerk of the court, sealed and not open to inspection except by order of the appellate court. The clerk of the appellate court shall return to the circuit court all papers transmitted to the appellate court from the circuit court, together with a certified copy of the order of the appellate court.

HISTORY:
S. 5, ch. 90-208; s. 225, ch. 95-147; s. 42, ch. 97-238; s. 31, ch. 99-284; s. 67, ch. 2006-120, eff. January 1, 2007.

Editor's notes.
Formerly s. 985.234: transferred by s. 67, ch. 2006-120, effective January 1, 2007; s. 39.069.

§ 985.535. Additional grounds for appeal by the state; time for taking.
(1) The state may appeal from a preadjudicatory hearing order dismissing a search warrant, suppressing evidence obtained by search and seizure, or suppressing a confession or admission made by a child. The appeal must be taken before the adjudicatory hearing.

(2) An appeal by the state from a preadjudicatory hearing order shall stay the case against a child upon whose application the order was made until the appeal is determined. If the court from which the appeal is taken determines that the evidence, confession, or admission that is the subject of the order would materially assist the state in proving its case against another child and that the prosecuting attorney intends to use it for that purpose, the court shall stay the case of that child until the appeal is determined. The trial court in its discretion may release a child whose case is stayed pending appeal. A child who is not released from custody pending appeal may petition the appellate court for expedited consideration of the appeal.

HISTORY:
S. 5, ch. 90-208; s. 43, ch. 97-238; s. 68, ch. 2006-120, eff. January 1, 2007.

Editor's notes.
Formerly s. 985.235: transferred by s. 68, ch. 2006-120, effective January 1, 2007; s. 39.0711.

§ 985.536. Order or decision when state appeals.

(1)　When the state appeals from an order dismissing a delinquency petition, or a count thereof, or an order granting a new adjudicatory hearing, and the order is affirmed, the appellate court shall direct the court from which the appeal was taken to implement the order. If an order dismissing a delinquency petition, or a count thereof, is reversed, the appellate court shall direct the court from which the appeal is taken to permit the child to be tried on the reinstated petition or count thereof. If an order granting a new trial is reversed, the appellate court shall direct that judgment of adjudication be entered against the child.

(2)　When the state appeals from a ruling on a question of law adverse to the state, the appellate court shall decide the question.

HISTORY:
S. 5, ch. 90-208; s. 44, ch. 97-238; s. 68, ch. 2006-120, eff. January 1, 2007.

Editor's notes.
Formerly s. 985.236: transferred by s. 68, ch. 2006-120, effective January 1, 2007; s. 39.072.

PART X.
TRANSFER TO ADULT COURT.

§ 985.556. Waiver of juvenile court jurisdiction; hearing.

(1)　VOLUNTARY WAIVER. —　The court shall transfer and certify a child's criminal case for trial as an adult if the child is alleged to have committed a violation of law and, prior to the commencement of an adjudicatory hearing, the child, joined by a parent or, in the absence of a parent, by the guardian or guardian ad litem, demands in writing to be tried as an adult. Once a child has been transferred for criminal prosecution pursuant to a voluntary waiver hearing and has been found to have committed the presenting offense or a lesser included offense, the child shall be handled thereafter in every respect as an adult for any subsequent violation of state law, unless the court imposes juvenile sanctions under s. 985.565(4)(b).

(2)　INVOLUNTARY DISCRETIONARY WAIVER. — Except as provided in subsection (3), the state attorney may file a motion requesting the court to transfer the child for criminal prosecution if the child was 14 years of age or older at the time the alleged delinquent act or violation of law was committed.

(3)　INVOLUNTARY MANDATORY WAIVER.

(a)　If the child was 14 years of age or older, and if the child has been previously adjudicated delinquent for an act classified as a felony, which adjudication was for the commission of, attempt to commit, or conspiracy to commit murder, sexual battery, armed or strong-armed robbery, carjacking, home-invasion robbery, aggravated battery, aggravated assault, or burglary with an assault or battery, and the child is currently charged with a second or subsequent violent crime against a person; or

(b)　If the child was 14 years of age or older at the time of commission of a fourth or subsequent alleged felony offense and the child was previously adjudicated delinquent or had adjudication withheld for or was found to have committed, or to have attempted or conspired to commit, three offenses that are felony offenses if committed by an adult, and one or more of such felony offenses involved the use or possession of a firearm or violence against a person; the state attorney shall request the court to transfer and certify the child for prosecution as an adult or shall provide written reasons to the court for not making such request, or proceed under s. 985.557(1). Upon the state attorney's request, the court shall either enter an order transferring the case and certifying the case for trial as if the child were an adult or provide written reasons for not issuing such an order.

(4)　WAIVER HEARING.

(a)　Within 7 days, excluding Saturdays, Sundays, and legal holidays, after the date a petition alleging that a child has committed a delinquent act or violation of law has been filed, or later with the approval of the court, but before an adjudicatory hearing and after considering the recommendation of the juvenile probation officer, the state attorney may file a motion requesting the court to transfer the child for criminal prosecution.

(b)　After the filing of the motion of the state attorney, summonses must be issued and served in conformity with s. 985.319. A copy of the motion and a copy of the delinquency petition, if not already served, must be attached to each summons.

(c)　The court shall conduct a hearing on all transfer request motions for the purpose of determining whether a child should be transferred. In making its determination, the court shall consider:

1.　The seriousness of the alleged offense to the community and whether the protection of the community is best served by transferring the child for adult sanctions.

2.　Whether the alleged offense was committed in an aggressive, violent, premeditated, or willful manner.

3.　Whether the alleged offense was against persons or against property, greater weight being given to offenses against persons, especially if personal injury resulted.

4.　The probable cause as found in the report, affidavit, or complaint.

5.　The desirability of trial and disposition of the entire offense in one court when the child's associates in the alleged crime are adults or children who are to be tried as adults.

6. The sophistication and maturity of the child.

7. The record and previous history of the child, including:

    a. Previous contacts with the department, the Department of Corrections, the former Department of Health and Rehabilitative Services, the Department of Children and Families, other law enforcement agencies, and courts;

    b. Prior periods of probation;

    c. Prior adjudications that the child committed a delinquent act or violation of law, greater weight being given if the child has previously been found by a court to have committed a delinquent act or violation of law involving an offense classified as a felony or has twice previously been found to have committed a delinquent act or violation of law involving an offense classified as a misdemeanor; and

    d. Prior commitments to institutions.

8. The prospects for adequate protection of the public and the likelihood of reasonable rehabilitation of the child, if the child is found to have committed the alleged offense, by the use of procedures, services, and facilities currently available to the court.

(d) Prior to a hearing on the transfer request motion by the state attorney, a study and report to the court relevant to the factors in paragraph (c) must be made in writing by an authorized agent of the department. The child and the child's parents or legal guardians and counsel and the state attorney shall have the right to examine these reports and to question the parties responsible for them at the hearing.

(e) Any decision to transfer a child for criminal prosecution must be in writing and include consideration of, and findings of fact with respect to, all criteria in paragraph (c). The court shall render an order including a specific finding of fact and the reasons for a decision to impose adult sanctions. The order shall be reviewable on appeal under s. 985.534 and the Florida Rules of Appellate Procedure.

(5) EFFECT OF ORDER WAIVING JURISDICTION.

(a) Once a child has been transferred for criminal prosecution pursuant to an involuntary waiver hearing and has been found to have committed the presenting offense or a lesser included offense, the child shall thereafter be handled in every respect as an adult for any subsequent violation of state law, unless the court imposes juvenile sanctions under s. 985.565.

(b) When a child is transferred for criminal prosecution as an adult, the court shall immediately transfer and certify to the adult circuit court all felony cases pertaining to the child, for prosecution of the child as an adult, which have not yet resulted in a plea of guilty or nolo contendere or in which a finding of guilt has not been made. If the child is acquitted of all charged offenses or lesser included offenses contained in the original case transferred to adult court, all felony cases that were transferred to adult court under this paragraph shall be subject to the same penalties such cases were subject to before being transferred to adult court.

HISTORY:
S. 34, ch. 97-238; s. 17, ch. 98-207; s. 37, ch. 99-284; s. 4, ch. 2000-119; s. 26, ch. 2000-135; s. 69, ch. 2006-120, eff. January 1, 2007; s. 354, ch. 2014-19, eff. July 1, 2014.

Editor's notes.
Formerly s. 985.226: transferred by s. 69, ch. 2006-120, effective January 1, 2007.

§ 985.557. Direct filing of an information; discretionary and mandatory criteria.

(1) DISCRETIONARY DIRECT FILE.

(a) With respect to any child who was 14 or 15 years of age at the time the alleged offense was committed, the state attorney may file an information when in the state attorney's judgment and discretion the public interest requires that adult sanctions be considered or imposed and when the offense charged is for the commission of, attempt to commit, or conspiracy to commit:

    1. Arson;

    2. Sexual battery;

    3. Robbery;

    4. Kidnapping;

    5. Aggravated child abuse;

    6. Aggravated assault;

    7. Aggravated stalking;

    8. Murder;

    9. Manslaughter;

    10. Unlawful throwing, placing, or discharging of a destructive device or bomb;

    11. Armed burglary in violation of s. 810.02(2)(b) or specified burglary of a dwelling or structure in violation of s. 810.02(2)(c), or burglary with an assault or battery in violation of s. 810.02(2)(a);

    12. Aggravated battery;

    13. Any lewd or lascivious offense committed upon or in the presence of a person less than 16 years of age;

    14. Carrying, displaying, using, threatening, or attempting to use a weapon or firearm during the commission of a felony;

    15. Grand theft in violation of s. 812.014(2)(a);

    16. Possessing or discharging any weapon or firearm on school property in violation of s. 790.115;

    17. Home invasion robbery;

    18. Carjacking; or

    19. Grand theft of a motor vehicle in violation of s. 812.014(2)(c) 6. or grand theft of a motor

vehicle valued at $20,000 or more in violation of s. 812.014(2)(b) if the child has a previous adjudication for grand theft of a motor vehicle in violation of s. 812.014(2)(c)6. or s. 812.014(2)(b).

(b) With respect to any child who was 16 or 17 years of age at the time the alleged offense was committed, the state attorney may file an information when in the state attorney's judgment and discretion the public interest requires that adult sanctions be considered or imposed. However, the state attorney may not file an information on a child charged with a misdemeanor, unless the child has had at least two previous adjudications or adjudications withheld for delinquent acts, one of which involved an offense classified as a felony under state law.

(2) MANDATORY DIRECT FILE.

(a) With respect to any child who was 16 or 17 years of age at the time the alleged offense was committed, the state attorney shall file an information if the child has been previously adjudicated delinquent for an act classified as a felony, which adjudication was for the commission of, attempt to commit, or conspiracy to commit murder, sexual battery, armed or strong-armed robbery, carjacking, home-invasion robbery, aggravated battery, or aggravated assault, and the child is currently charged with a second or subsequent violent crime against a person.

(b) With respect to any child 16 or 17 years of age at the time an offense classified as a forcible felony, as defined in s. 776.08, was committed, the state attorney shall file an information if the child has previously been adjudicated delinquent or had adjudication withheld for three acts classified as felonies each of which occurred at least 45 days apart from each other. This paragraph does not apply when the state attorney has good cause to believe that exceptional circumstances exist which preclude the just prosecution of the juvenile in adult court.

(c) The state attorney must file an information if a child, regardless of the child's age at the time the alleged offense was committed, is alleged to have committed an act that would be a violation of law if the child were an adult, that involves stealing a motor vehicle, including, but not limited to, a violation of s. 812.133, relating to carjacking, or s. 812.014(2)(c) 6., relating to grand theft of a motor vehicle, and while the child was in possession of the stolen motor vehicle the child caused serious bodily injury to or the death of a person who was not involved in the underlying offense. For purposes of this section, the driver and all willing passengers in the stolen motor vehicle at the time such serious bodily injury or death is inflicted shall also be subject to mandatory transfer to adult court. "Stolen motor vehicle," for the purposes of this section, means a motor vehicle that has been the subject of any criminal wrongful taking. For purposes of this section, "willing passengers" means all willing passengers who have participated in the underlying offense.

(d)1. With respect to any child who was 16 or 17 years of age at the time the alleged offense was committed, the state attorney shall file an information if the child has been charged with committing or attempting to commit an offense listed in s. 775.087(2)(a) 1.a.-p., and, during the commission of or attempt to commit the offense, the child:

a. Actually possessed a firearm or destructive device, as those terms are defined in s. 790.001.

b. Discharged a firearm or destructive device, as described in s. 775.087(2)(a)2.

c. Discharged a firearm or destructive device, as described in s. 775.087(2)(a)3., and, as a result of the discharge, death or great bodily harm was inflicted upon any person.

2. Upon transfer, any child who is:

a. Charged under sub-subparagraph 1.a. and who has been previously adjudicated or had adjudication withheld for a forcible felony offense or any offense involving a firearm, or who has been previously placed in a residential commitment program, shall be subject to sentencing under s. 775.087(2)(a), notwithstanding s. 985.565.

b. Charged under sub-subparagraph 1.b. or sub-subparagraph 1.c., shall be subject to sentencing under s. 775.087(2)(a), notwithstanding s. 985.565.

3. Upon transfer, any child who is charged under this paragraph, but who does not meet the requirements specified in subparagraph 2., shall be sentenced under s. 985.565; however, if the court imposes a juvenile sanction, the court must commit the child to a high-risk or maximum-risk juvenile facility.

4. This paragraph shall not apply if the state attorney has good cause to believe that exceptional circumstances exist that preclude the just prosecution of the child in adult court.

5. The Department of Corrections shall make every reasonable effort to ensure that any child 16 or 17 years of age who is convicted and sentenced under this paragraph be completely separated such that there is no physical contact with adult offenders in the facility, to the extent that it is consistent with chapter 958.

(3) EFFECT OF DIRECT FILE.

(a) Once a child has been transferred for criminal prosecution pursuant to an information and has been found to have committed the presenting offense or a lesser included offense, the child shall be handled thereafter in every respect as if an adult for any subsequent violation of state law, unless the court imposes juvenile sanctions under s. 985.565.

(b) When a child is transferred for criminal prosecution as an adult, the court shall immediately transfer and certify to the adult circuit court all felony cases pertaining to the child, for prosecution of the child as an adult, which have not yet resulted in a plea of guilty or nolo contendere or in which a finding of guilt has not been made. If a child is acquitted of all charged offenses or lesser included offenses contained in the original case transferred to adult court, all felony cases that were transferred to adult court as a result of this paragraph shall be subject to the same penalties to which such cases would have been subject before being transferred to adult court.

(c) When a child has been transferred for criminal prosecution as an adult and has been found to have committed a violation of state law, the disposition of the case may be made under s. 985.565 and may include the enforcement of any restitution ordered in any juvenile proceeding.

(4) An information filed pursuant to this section may include all charges that are based on the same act, criminal episode, or transaction as the primary offenses.

HISTORY:
S. 35, ch. 97-238; s. 130, ch. 99-3; s. 15, ch. 99-201; s. 1, ch. 99-257; s. 26, ch. 99-284; s. 2, ch. 2000-119; s. 27, ch. 2000-135; s. 1, ch. 2000-136; s. 21, ch. 2001-125; s. 4, ch. 2001-185; s. 5, ch. 2006-51, eff, July 1, 2006; s. 70, ch. 2006-120, eff. January 1, 2007; s. 5, ch. 2011-200, eff. July 1, 2011; s. 2, ch. 2016-7, eff. July 1, 2016.

Editor's notes.
Formerly s. 985.227: transferred by s. 70, ch. 2006-120, effective January 1, 2007.

§ 985.56. Indictment of a juvenile.

(1) A child of any age who is charged with a violation of state law punishable by death or by life imprisonment is subject to the jurisdiction of the court as set forth in s. 985.0301(2) unless and until an indictment on the charge is returned by the grand jury. When such indictment is returned, the petition for delinquency, if any, must be dismissed and the child must be tried and handled in every respect as an adult:

(a) On the offense punishable by death or by life imprisonment; and

(b) On all other felonies or misdemeanors charged in the indictment which are based on the same act or transaction as the offense punishable by death or by life imprisonment or on one or more acts or transactions connected with the offense punishable by death or by life imprisonment.

(2) An adjudicatory hearing may not be held until 21 days after the child is taken into custody and charged with having committed an offense punishable by death or by life imprisonment, unless the state attorney advises the court in writing that he or she does not intend to present the case to the grand jury, or has presented the case to the grand jury and the grand jury has not returned an indictment. If the court receives such a notice from the state attorney, or if the grand jury fails to act within the 21-day period, the court may proceed as otherwise authorized under this part.

(3) If the child is found to have committed the offense punishable by death or by life imprisonment, the child shall be sentenced as an adult. If the juvenile is not found to have committed the indictable offense but is found to have committed a lesser included offense or any other offense for which he or she was indicted as a part of the criminal episode, the court may sentence under s. 985.565.

(4)(a) Once a child has been indicted pursuant to this section and has been found to have committed any offense for which he or she was indicted as a part of the criminal episode, the child shall be handled thereafter in every respect as if an adult for any subsequent violation of state law, unless the court imposes juvenile sanctions under s. 985.565.

(b) When a child has been indicted pursuant to this section, the court shall immediately transfer and certify to the adult circuit court all felony cases pertaining to the child, for prosecution of the child as an adult, which have not yet resulted in a plea of guilty or nolo contendere or in which a finding of guilt has not been made. If the child is acquitted of all charged offenses or lesser included offenses contained in the indictment case, all felony cases that were transferred to adult court pursuant to this paragraph shall be subject to the same penalties such cases were subject to before being transferred to adult court.

HISTORY:
S. 33, ch. 97-238; s. 35, ch. 99-284; s. 38, ch. 2001-64; s. 71, ch. 2006-120, eff. January 1, 2007.

Editor's notes.
Formerly s. 985.225: transferred by s. 71, ch. 2006-120, effective January 1, 2007.

§ 985.565. Sentencing powers; procedures; alternatives for juveniles prosecuted as adults.

(1) POWERS OF DISPOSITION.

(a) A child who is found to have committed a violation of law may, as an alternative to adult dispositions, be committed to the department for treatment in an appropriate program for children outside the adult correctional system or be placed on juvenile probation.

(b) In determining whether to impose juvenile sanctions instead of adult sanctions, the court shall consider the following criteria:

1. The seriousness of the offense to the community and whether the community would best be protected by juvenile or adult sanctions.

2. Whether the offense was committed in an aggressive, violent, premeditated, or willful manner.

3. Whether the offense was against persons or against property, with greater weight being given

to offenses against persons, especially if personal injury resulted.

4. The sophistication and maturity of the offender.

5. The record and previous history of the offender, including:

    a. Previous contacts with the Department of Corrections, the Department of Juvenile Justice, the former Department of Health and Rehabilitative Services, the Department of Children and Families, law enforcement agencies, and the courts.

    b. Prior periods of probation.

    c. Prior adjudications that the offender committed a delinquent act or violation of law as a child.

    d. Prior commitments to the Department of Juvenile Justice, the former Department of Health and Rehabilitative Services, the Department of Children and Families, or other facilities or institutions.

6. The prospects for adequate protection of the public and the likelihood of deterrence and reasonable rehabilitation of the offender if assigned to services and facilities of the Department of Juvenile Justice.

7. Whether the Department of Juvenile Justice has appropriate programs, facilities, and services immediately available.

8. Whether adult sanctions would provide more appropriate punishment and deterrence to further violations of law than the imposition of juvenile sanctions.

(2) PRESENTENCE INVESTIGATION REPORT.

(a) Upon a plea of guilty, the court may refer the case to the department for investigation and recommendation as to the suitability of its programs for the child.

(b) Upon completion of the presentence investigation report, it must be made available to the child's counsel and the state attorney by the department prior to the sentencing hearing.

(3) SENTENCING HEARING.

(a) At the sentencing hearing the court shall receive and consider a presentence investigation report by the Department of Corrections regarding the suitability of the offender for disposition as an adult or as a juvenile. The presentence investigation report must include a comments section prepared by the Department of Juvenile Justice, with its recommendations as to disposition. This report requirement may be waived by the offender.

(b) After considering the presentence investigation report, the court shall give all parties present at the hearing an opportunity to comment on the issue of sentence and any proposed rehabilitative plan. Parties to the case include the parent, guardian, or legal custodian of the offender; the offender's coun-

sel; the state attorney; representatives of the Department of Corrections and the Department of Juvenile Justice; the victim or victim's representative; representatives of the school system; and the law enforcement officers involved in the case.

(c) The court may receive and consider any other relevant and material evidence, including other reports, written or oral, in its effort to determine the action to be taken with regard to the child, and may rely upon such evidence to the extent of its probative value even if the evidence would not be competent in an adjudicatory hearing.

(d) The court shall notify any victim of the offense of the hearing and shall notify, or subpoena if appropriate, the parents, guardians, or legal custodians of the child to attend the disposition hearing.

(4) SENTENCING ALTERNATIVES.

(a) *ADULT SANCTIONS*

1. CASES PROSECUTED ON INDICTMENT. — If the child is found to have committed the offense punishable by death or life imprisonment, the child shall be sentenced as an adult. If the juvenile is not found to have committed the indictable offense but is found to have committed a lesser included offense or any other offense for which he or she was indicted as a part of the criminal episode, the court may sentence as follows:

    a. As an adult;

    b. Under chapter 958; or

    c. As a juvenile under this section.

2. OTHER CASES. — If a child who has been transferred for criminal prosecution pursuant to information or waiver of juvenile court jurisdiction is found to have committed a violation of state law or a lesser included offense for which he or she was charged as a part of the criminal episode, the court may sentence as follows:

    a. As an adult;

    b. Under chapter 958; or

    c. As a juvenile under this section.

3. Notwithstanding any other provision to the contrary, if the state attorney is required to file a motion to transfer and certify the juvenile for prosecution as an adult under s. 985.556(3) and that motion is granted, or if the state attorney is required to file an information under s. 985.557(2)(a) or (b), the court must impose adult sanctions.

4. Any sentence imposing adult sanctions is presumed appropriate, and the court is not required to set forth specific findings or enumerate the criteria in this subsection as any basis for its decision to impose adult sanctions.

5. When a child has been transferred for criminal prosecution as an adult and has been found to have committed a violation of state law, the disposition of the case may include the en-

forcement of any restitution ordered in any juvenile proceeding.

(b) *JUVENILE SANCTIONS.* — For juveniles transferred to adult court but who do not qualify for such transfer under s. 985.556(3) or s. 985.557(2)(a) or (b), the court may impose juvenile sanctions under this paragraph. If juvenile sentences are imposed, the court shall, under this paragraph, adjudge the child to have committed a delinquent act. Adjudication of delinquency shall not be deemed a conviction, nor shall it operate to impose any of the civil disabilities ordinarily resulting from a conviction. The court shall impose an adult sanction or a juvenile sanction and may not sentence the child to a combination of adult and juvenile punishments. An adult sanction or a juvenile sanction may include enforcement of an order of restitution or probation previously ordered in any juvenile proceeding. However, if the court imposes a juvenile sanction and the department determines that the sanction is unsuitable for the child, the department shall return custody of the child to the sentencing court for further proceedings, including the imposition of adult sanctions. Upon adjudicating a child delinquent under subsection (1), the court may:

1. Place the child in a probation program under the supervision of the department for an indeterminate period of time until the child reaches the age of 19 years or sooner if discharged by order of the court.

2. Commit the child to the department for treatment in an appropriate program for children for an indeterminate period of time until the child is 21 or sooner if discharged by the department. The department shall notify the court of its intent to discharge no later than 14 days prior to discharge. Failure of the court to timely respond to the department's notice shall be considered approval for discharge.

3. Order disposition under ss. 985.435, 985.437, 985.439, 985.441, 985.45, and 985.455 as an alternative to youthful offender or adult sentencing if the court determines not to impose youthful offender or adult sanctions.

(c) *ADULT SANCTIONS UPON FAILURE OF JUVENILE SANCTIONS.* — If a child proves not to be suitable to a commitment program, juvenile probation program, or treatment program under paragraph (b), the department shall provide the sentencing court with a written report outlining the basis for its objections to the juvenile sanction and shall simultaneously provide a copy of the report to the state attorney and the defense counsel. The department shall schedule a hearing within 30 days. Upon hearing, the court may revoke the previous adjudication, impose an adjudication of guilt, and impose any sentence which it may lawfully impose, giving credit for all time spent by the child in the department. The court may also classify the child as a youthful offender under s. 958.04, if appropriate. For purposes of this paragraph, a child may be found not suitable to a commitment program, community control program, or treatment program under paragraph (b) if the child commits a new violation of law while under juvenile sanctions, if the child commits any other violation of the conditions of juvenile sanctions, or if the child's actions are otherwise determined by the court to demonstrate a failure of juvenile sanctions.

(d) *FURTHER PROCEEDINGS HEARD IN ADULT COURT.* — When a child is sentenced to juvenile sanctions, further proceedings involving those sanctions shall continue to be heard in the adult court.

(e) *SCHOOL ATTENDANCE.* — If the child is attending or is eligible to attend public school and the court finds that the victim or a sibling of the victim in the case is attending or may attend the same school as the child, the court placement order shall include a finding pursuant to the proceeding described in s. 985.455(2), regardless of whether adjudication is withheld.

It is the intent of the Legislature that the criteria and guidelines in this subsection are mandatory and that a determination of disposition under this subsection is subject to the right of the child to appellate review under s. 985.534.

HISTORY:

S. 1, ch. 97-69; s. 41, ch. 97-238; s. 3, ch. 2000-119; s. 13, ch. 2000-134; s. 32, ch. 2000-135; ss. 26, 27, ch. 2001-125; s. 142, ch. 2003-402; s. 5, ch. 2004-241; s. 20, ch. 2005-263; s. 72, ch. 2006-120, eff. January 1, 2007; s. 166, ch. 2007-5, eff. July 3, 2007; s. 12, ch. 2011-70, eff. July 1, 2011; s. 355, ch. 2014-19, eff. July 1, 2014.

Editor's notes.

Formerly s. 985.233: transferred by s. 103, ch. 2006-120, effective January 1, 2007.

§ 985.57. Transfer of children from the Department of Corrections to the Department of Juvenile Justice.

(1) When any child under the age of 18 years is sentenced by any court of competent jurisdiction to the Department of Corrections, the Secretary of Juvenile Justice may transfer such child to the department for the remainder of the sentence, or until his or her 21st birthday, whichever results in the shorter term. If, upon such person's attaining his or her 21st birthday, the sentence has not terminated, he or she shall be transferred to the Department of Corrections for placement in a youthful offender program, transferred to the supervision of the department, or be given any other transfer that may lawfully be made.

(2) If the child is under sentence for a term of years, after the department has supervised him or her for a sufficient length of time to ascertain that he or she has attained satisfactory rehabilitation, the department,

upon determination that such action is in the best interests of both the child and society, may relieve the child from making further reports.

(3)   When the child has, in the opinion of the department, so conducted himself or herself as to deserve a pardon, a commutation of sentence, or the remission in whole or in part of any fine, forfeiture, or penalty, the secretary may recommend that such clemency be extended to the child. In such case the secretary shall fully advise the Governor of the facts upon which such recommendation is based.

(4)   The department shall grant gain-time for good conduct, may grant extra good-time allowances, and may declare a forfeiture thereof. If any child who was sentenced pursuant to s. 921.18 is transferred to the department, the department may determine the exact sentence of the child, but the sentence may not be longer than the maximum sentence that was imposed by the court pursuant to s. 921.18. All time spent in the department shall count toward the expiration of sentence. Any child transferred to the department may, at the discretion of the secretary, be returned to the Department of Corrections.

(5)   Any child who has been convicted of a capital felony while under the age of 18 years may not be released on probation without the consent of the Governor and two members of the Cabinet.

HISTORY:

S. 5, ch. 90-208; s. 53, ch. 94-209; s. 1353, ch. 95-147; s. 77, ch. 97-238; s. 22, ch. 99-284; s. 54, ch. 2000-135; s. 35, ch. 2001-125; s. 20, ch. 2003-6; s. 73, ch. 2006-120, eff. January 1, 2007.

Editor's notes.

Formerly s. 985.417: transferred by s. 73, ch. 2006-120, effective January 1, 2007; s. 39.062.

PART XI.
DEPARTMENT OF JUVENILE JUSTICE.

§ 985.601.   Administering the juvenile justice continuum.

(1)   The Department of Juvenile Justice shall plan, develop, and coordinate comprehensive services and programs statewide for the prevention, early intervention, control, and rehabilitative treatment of delinquent behavior.

(2)   The department shall develop and implement an appropriate continuum of care that provides individualized, multidisciplinary assessments, objective evaluations of relative risks, and the matching of needs with placements for all children under its care, and that uses a system of case management to facilitate each child being appropriately assessed, provided with services, and placed in a program that meets the child's needs.

(3)(a)   The department shall develop or contract for diversified and innovative programs to provide reha-

bilitative treatment, including early intervention and prevention, diversion, comprehensive intake, case management, diagnostic and classification assessments, trauma-informed care, individual and family counseling, family engagement resources and programs, gender-specific programming, shelter care, diversified detention care emphasizing alternatives to secure detention, diversified probation, halfway houses, foster homes, community-based substance abuse treatment services, community-based mental health treatment services, community-based residential and nonresidential programs, mother-infant programs, and environmental programs. The department may pay expenses in support of innovative programs and activities that address identified needs and the well-being of children in the department's care or under its supervision, subject to the requirements of chapters 215, 216, and 287. Each program shall place particular emphasis on reintegration and conditional release for all children in the program.

(b)   The Legislature intends that, whenever possible and reasonable, the department make every effort to consider qualified faith-based organizations on an equal basis with other private organizations when selecting contract providers of services to juveniles.

(c)   The department may contract with faith-based organizations on the same basis as any other nongovernmental providers, without impairing the religious character of such organizations. Any faith-based organization may act as a contractor in the delivery of services under any program, on the same basis as any other nongovernmental provider, without impairing the religious character of such organization. A faith-based organization, which has entered into a contract with the department, shall retain its independence from state and local governments with regard to control over the definition, development, practice, and expression of its religious beliefs. The department shall not require a faith-based organization to alter its form of internal government or remove religious art, icons, scripture, or other symbols in order to be eligible to contract as a provider.

(d)   The department may include in any services contract a requirement that providers prepare plans describing their implementation of paragraphs (a) and (c). A failure to deliver such plans, if required, may be considered by the department as a breach of the contract that may result in cancellation of the contract.

(4)   The department shall maintain continuing cooperation with the Department of Education, the Department of Children and Families, the Department of Economic Opportunity, and the Department of Corrections for the purpose of participating in agreements with respect to dropout prevention and the reduction of suspensions, expulsions, and truancy; increased ac-

cess to and participation in high school equivalency diploma, vocational, and alternative education programs; and employment training and placement assistance. The cooperative agreements between the departments shall include an interdepartmental plan to cooperate in accomplishing the reduction of inappropriate transfers of children into the adult criminal justice and correctional systems.

(5) The department may provide consulting services and technical assistance to courts, law enforcement agencies, and other state agencies, local governments, and public and private organizations, and may develop or assist in developing community interest and action programs relating to intervention against, diversion from, and prevention and treatment of, delinquent behavior.

(6) In view of the importance of the basic values of work, responsibility, and self-reliance to a child's return to his or her community, the department may pay a child a reasonable sum of money for work performed while employed in any of the department's work programs. The work programs shall be designed so that the work benefits the department or the state, their properties, or the child's community. Funds for payments shall be provided specifically for salaries pursuant to this subsection, and payments shall be made pursuant to a plan approved or rules adopted by the department.

(7) The department shall administer programs and services for children in need of services and families in need of services and shall coordinate its efforts with those of the Federal Government, state agencies, county and municipal governments, private agencies, and child advocacy groups. The department shall establish standards for, providing technical assistance to, and exercising the requisite supervision of, services and programs for children in all state-supported facilities and programs.

(8) The department shall ensure that personnel responsible for the care, supervision, and individualized treatment of children are appropriately apprised of the requirements of this chapter and trained in the specialized areas required to comply with standards established by rule.

(9)(a) The department shall operate a statewide, regionally administered system of detention services for children, in accordance with a comprehensive plan for the regional administration of all detention services in the state. The plan must provide for the maintenance of adequate availability of detention services for all counties. The plan must cover all the department's operating circuits, with each operating circuit having access to a secure facility and nonsecure detention programs, and the plan may be altered or modified by the Department of Juvenile Justice as necessary.

(b) The department shall adopt rules prescribing standards and requirements with reference to:

1. The construction, equipping, maintenance, staffing, programming, and operation of detention facilities;

2. The treatment, training, and education of children confined in detention facilities;

3. The cleanliness and sanitation of detention facilities;

4. The number of children who may be housed in detention facilities per specified unit of floor space;

5. The quality, quantity, and supply of bedding furnished to children housed in detention facilities;

6. The quality, quantity, and diversity of food served in detention facilities and the manner in which it is served;

7. The furnishing of medical attention and health and comfort items in detention facilities; and

8. The disciplinary treatment administered in detention facilities.

(c) The rules must provide that the time spent by a child in a detention facility must be devoted to educational training and other types of self-motivation and development. The use of televisions, radios, and audio players shall be restricted to educational programming. However, the manager of a detention facility may allow noneducational programs to be used as a reward for good behavior. Exercise must be structured and calisthenic and aerobic in nature and may include weight lifting.

(d) Each programmatic, residential, and service contract or agreement entered into by the department must include a cooperation clause for purposes of complying with the department's quality assurance requirements, cost-accounting requirements, and the program outcome evaluation requirements.

(10) The department shall implement procedures to ensure that educational support activities are provided throughout the juvenile justice continuum. Such activities may include, but are not limited to, mentoring, tutoring, group discussions, homework assistance, library support, designated reading times, independent living, personal finance, and other appropriate educational activities.

(11) At the secretary's discretion, the department is authorized to pay up to $5,000 toward the basic funeral expenses for a youth who dies while in the custody of the department and whose parents or guardians are indigent and unable to pay such expenses and for which there is no other source of funding available.

HISTORY:

S. 5, ch. 90-208; s. 3, ch. 91-158; s. 18, ch. 94-209; s. 1335, ch. 95-147; s. 2, ch. 95-212; ss. 40, 43, ch. 96-398; s. 159, ch. 97-101; s. 64, ch. 97-238; s. 7, ch. 98-186; s. 25, ch. 98-207; s. 139, ch. 99-3; s. 18, ch. 99-284; s. 46, ch. 2000-135; ss. 33, 41, ch. 2001-125; s. 7, ch. 2001-185; s. 154, ch. 2005-2; s. 74, ch. 2006-120, eff. Jan. 1, 2007; s. 447, ch. 2011-142, eff. July 1, 2011; s. 5, ch. 2012-56, eff. July 1, 2012;

s. 356, ch. 2014-19, eff. July 1, 2014; s. 14, ch. 2014-20, eff. July 1, 2014; s. 31, ch. 2014-162, eff. July 1, 2014.

Editor's notes.
Formerly s. 985.404: transferred by s. 74, ch. 2006-120, effective January 1, 2007; s. 39.021.

§ 985.6015. Shared County/State Juvenile Detention Trust Fund.

(1) The Shared County/State Juvenile Detention Trust Fund is created within the department.

(2) The fund is established for use as a depository for funds to be used for the costs of juvenile detention. Moneys credited to the trust fund shall consist of funds from the counties' share of the costs for juvenile detention.

HISTORY:
S. 1, ch. 2005-114; s. 75, ch. 2006-120, eff. January 1, 2007; s. 2, ch. 2008-8, eff. July 1, 2008; s. 2, ch. 2016-152, eff. Mar. 29, 2016.

Editor's notes.
Formerly s. 985.4043: transferred by s. 75, ch. 2006-120, effective January 1, 2007.

§ 985.605. Prevention service program; monitoring; uniform performance measures. [Repealed]

HISTORY:
S. 33, ch. 2000-135; s. 2, ch. 2004-333; s. 76, ch. 2006-120, eff. January 1, 2007; repealed by s. 32, ch. 2014-162, effective July 1, 2014.

§ 985.606. Prevention services providers; performance data collection; reporting. [Repealed]

HISTORY:
S. 34, ch. 2000-135; s. 77, ch. 2006-120, eff. January 1, 2007; repealed by s. 32, ch. 2014-162, effective July 1, 2014.

§ 985.61. Early delinquency intervention program; criteria. [Repealed]

HISTORY:
S. 5, ch. 90-208; s. 21, ch. 93-200; s. 44, ch. 94-209; s. 4, ch. 97-101; s. 49, ch. 97-238; s. 35, ch. 2000-135; s. 28, ch. 2001-125; s. 78, ch. 2006-120; s. 171, ch. 2010-102, eff. May 26, 2010; s. 51, ch. 2013-162, eff. July 1, 2013; s. 357, ch. 2014-19, eff. July 1, 2014; repealed by s. 32, ch. 2014-162, effective July 1, 2014.

§ 985.614. Children locked out of the home; interagency cooperation.

The department and the Department of Children and Families shall encourage interagency cooperation within each circuit and shall develop comprehensive agreements between the staff and providers for each department in order to coordinate the services provided to children who are locked out of the home and the families of those children.

HISTORY:
S. 15, ch. 97-281; s. 21, ch. 2000-135; s. 79, ch. 2006-120, eff. January 1, 2007; s. 358, ch. 2014-19, eff. July 1, 2014.

Editor's notes.
Formerly s. 985.2066: transferred by s. 79, ch. 2006-120, effective January 1, 2007.

§ 985.618. Educational and career-related programs.

(1)(a) It is the finding of the Legislature that the educational and career-related programs of the Department of Juvenile Justice are uniquely different from other programs operated or conducted by other departments in that it is essential to the state that these programs provide juveniles with useful information and activities that can lead to meaningful employment after release in order to assist in reducing the return of juveniles to the system.

(b) It is further the finding of the Legislature that the mission of a juvenile educational and career-related program is, in order of priority:

1. To provide a joint effort between the department, the juvenile work programs, and educational and career training programs to reinforce relevant education, training, and postrelease job placement, and help reduce recommitment.

2. To serve the security goals of the state through the reduction of idleness of juveniles and the provision of an incentive for good behavior in residential commitment facilities.

3. To teach youth in juvenile justice programs relevant job skills and the fundamentals of a trade in order to prepare them for placement in the workforce.

(c) It is further the finding of the Legislature that a program which duplicates as closely as possible free-work production and service operations in order to aid juveniles in adjustment after release and to prepare juveniles for gainful employment is in the best interest of the state, juveniles, and the general public.

(2)(a) The department is strongly encouraged to require juveniles placed in a high-risk residential, a maximum-risk residential, or a serious/habitual offender program to participate in an educational or career-related program 5 hours per day, 5 days per week. All policies developed by the department relating to this requirement must be consistent with applicable federal, state, and local labor laws and standards, including all laws relating to child labor.

(b) Nothing in this subsection is intended to restore, in whole or in part, the civil rights of any juvenile. No juvenile compensated under this subsection shall be considered as an employee of the state or the department, nor shall such juvenile come within any other provision of the Workers' Compensation Law.

(3) In adopting or modifying master plans for juvenile work programs and educational and career training programs, and in the administration of the Department of Juvenile Justice, it shall be the objective of the department to develop:

(a) Attitudes favorable to work, the work situation, and a law-abiding life in each juvenile employed in the juvenile work program.

(b) Education and training opportunities that are reasonably broad, but which develop specific work skills.

(c) Programs that motivate juveniles to use their abilities.

(d) Education and training programs that will be of mutual benefit to all governmental jurisdictions of the state by reducing the costs of government to the taxpayers and which integrate all instructional programs into a unified curriculum suitable for all juveniles, but taking account of the different abilities of each juvenile.

(e) A logical sequence of educational or career training, employment by the juvenile work programs, and postrelease job placement for juveniles participating in juvenile work programs.

(4)(a) The Department of Juvenile Justice shall establish guidelines for the operation of juvenile educational and career-related programs, which shall include the following procedures:

1. Participation in the educational and career-related programs shall be on a 5-day-per-week, 5-hour-per-day basis.

2. The education, training, work experience, emotional and mental abilities, and physical capabilities of the juvenile and the duration of the term of placement imposed on the juvenile are to be analyzed before assignment of the juvenile into the various processes best suited for educational or career training.

3. When feasible, the department shall attempt to obtain education or training credit for a juvenile seeking apprenticeship status or a high school diploma or its equivalent.

4. The juvenile may begin in a general education and work skills program and progress to a specific work skills training program, depending upon the ability, desire, and education and work record of the juvenile.

5. Modernization and upgrading of equipment and facilities should include greater automation and improved production techniques to expose juveniles to the latest technological procedures to facilitate their adjustment to real work situations.

(b) Evaluations of juvenile educational and career-related programs shall be conducted according to the following guidelines:

1. Systematic evaluations and quality assurance monitoring shall be implemented, in accordance with s. 985.632(1), (2), and (5), to determine whether the programs are related to successful postrelease adjustments.

2. Operations and policies of the programs shall be reevaluated to determine if they are consistent with their primary objectives.

(c) The department shall seek the advice of private labor and management to:

1. Assist its work programs in the development of statewide policies aimed at innovation and organizational change.

2. Obtain technical and practical assistance, information, and guidance.

3. Encourage the cooperation and involvement of the private sector.

4. Assist in the placement of youth into meaningful jobs upon release from the residential program.

(d) The department and providers are strongly encouraged to work in partnership with local businesses and trade groups in the development and operation of educational and career programs.

(5)(a) The Department of Juvenile Justice may adopt and put into effect an agricultural and industrial production and marketing program to provide training facilities for persons placed in serious/habitual offender, high-risk residential, and maximum-risk residential programs and facilities under the control and supervision of the department. The emphasis of this program shall be to provide juveniles with useful work experience and appropriate job skills that will facilitate their reentry into society and provide an economic benefit to the public and the department through effective utilization of juveniles.

(b) The department is authorized to contract with the private sector for substantial involvement in a juvenile industry program which includes the operation of a direct private sector business within a juvenile facility and the hiring of juvenile workers. The purposes and objectives of this program shall be to:

1. Increase benefits to the general public by reimbursement to the state for a portion of the costs of juvenile residential care.

2. Provide purposeful work for juveniles as a means of reducing tensions caused by confinement.

3. Increase job skills.

4. Provide additional opportunities for rehabilitation of juveniles who are otherwise ineligible to work outside the facilities, such as maximum security juveniles.

5. Develop and establish new models for juvenile facility-based businesses which create jobs approximating conditions of private sector employment.

6. Draw upon the economic base of operations for disposition to the Crimes Compensation Trust Fund.

7. Substantially involve the private sector with its capital, management skills, and expertise in the design, development, and operation of businesses.

(c) Notwithstanding any other law to the contrary, including s. 440.15(8), private sector employers shall provide juveniles participating in juvenile work programs under paragraph (b) with workers' compensation coverage, and juveniles shall be entitled to the benefits of such coverage. Nothing in this subsection shall be construed to allow juveniles to participate in reemployment assistance benefits.

(6) The department, working with providers, shall inventory juvenile vocational and work training programs in use in commitment programs across the state. The inventory shall list the commitment program, the type of vocational or work program offered, the relevant job skills provided, and which programs work with the trades industry to place youth in jobs upon release.

HISTORY:

S. 35, ch. 96-398; s. 59, ch. 97-238; s. 29, ch. 98-207; s. 32, ch. 99-284; s. 42, ch. 2000-135; s. 90, ch. 2000-158; s. 5, ch. 2001-185; s. 122, ch. 2002-1; s. 39, ch. 2003-412; s. 68, ch. 2004-357; s. 80, ch. 2006-120, eff. Jan. 1, 2007; s. 86, ch. 2012-30, eff. July 1, 2012.

Editor's notes.

Formerly s. 985.315: transferred by s. 80, ch. 2006-120, effective January 1, 2007; s. 39.05841.

Section 93, ch. 2012-30, provides: "If any provision of this act or its application to any person or circumstance is held invalid, the invalidity does not affect other provisions or applications of the act which can be given effect without the invalid provision or application, and to this end the provisions of the act are severable."

§ 985.622. Multiagency plan for career and professional education (CAPE).

(1) The Department of Juvenile Justice and the Department of Education shall, in consultation with the statewide Workforce Development Youth Council, school districts, providers, and others, jointly develop a multiagency plan for career and professional education (CAPE) that establishes the curriculum, goals, and outcome measures for CAPE programs in juvenile justice education programs. The plan must be reviewed annually, revised as appropriate, and include:

(a) Provisions for maximizing appropriate state and federal funding sources, including funds under the Workforce Innovation and Opportunity Act and the Perkins Act.

(b) Provisions for eliminating barriers to increasing occupation-specific job training and high school equivalency examination preparation opportunities.

(c) The responsibilities of both departments and all other appropriate entities.

(d) A detailed implementation schedule.

(2) The plan must define CAPE programming that is appropriate based upon:

(a) The age and assessed educational abilities and goals of the student to be served; and

(b) The typical length of stay and custody characteristics at the juvenile justice education program to which each student is assigned.

(3) The plan must include a definition of CAPE programming that includes the following classifications of juvenile justice education programs that will offer CAPE programming by one of the following types:

(a) *TYPE 1.* — Programs that teach personal accountability skills and behaviors that are appropriate for students in all age groups and ability levels and that lead to work habits that help maintain employment and living standards.

(b) *TYPE 2.* — Programs that include Type 1 program content and an orientation to the broad scope of career choices, based upon personal abilities, aptitudes, and interests. Exploring and gaining knowledge of occupation options and the level of effort required to achieve them are essential prerequisites to skill training.

(c) *TYPE 3.* — Programs that include Type 1 program content and the competencies or the prerequisites needed for entry into a specific occupation.

(4) The plan must also address strategies to facilitate involvement of business and industry in the design, delivery, and evaluation of CAPE programming in juvenile justice education programs, including apprenticeship and work experience programs, mentoring and job shadowing, and other strategies that lead to postrelease employment. Incentives for business involvement, such as tax breaks, bonding, and liability limits should be investigated, implemented where appropriate, or recommended to the Legislature for consideration.

(5) The plan must also evaluate the effect of students' mobility between juvenile justice education programs and school districts on the students' educational outcomes and whether the continuity of the students' education can be better addressed through virtual education.

(6) The Department of Juvenile Justice and the Department of Education shall each align its respective agency policies, practices, technical manuals, contracts, quality-assurance standards, performance-based-budgeting measures, and outcome measures with the plan in juvenile justice education programs by July 31, 2015. Each agency shall provide a report on the implementation of this section to the Governor, the President of the Senate, and the Speaker of the House of Representatives by August 31, 2015.

(7) All provider contracts executed by the Department of Juvenile Justice or the school districts after January 1, 2015, must be aligned with the plan.

(8) The planning and execution of quality assurance reviews conducted by the Department of Education or the Department of Juvenile Justice after August 1, 2015, must be aligned with the plan.

(9) Outcome measures reported by the Department of Juvenile Justice and the Department of Education for students released on or after January 1, 2016, should include outcome measures that conform to the plan.

HISTORY:

S. 5, ch. 2000-137; s. 31, ch. 2001-125; s. 123, ch. 2002-1; s. 81, ch.

2006-120, eff. January 1, 2007; s. 172, ch. 2010-102, eff. May 26, 2010; s. 29, ch. 2014-184, eff. June 20, 2014; s. 45, ch. 2016-216, eff. July 1, 2016.

Editor's notes.
Formerly s. 985.3155: transferred by s. 81, ch. 2006-120, effective January 1, 2007.

§ 985.625. Literacy programs for juvenile offenders.

(1) INTENT. — It is the intent of the Legislature that mandatory literacy programs for juvenile offenders committed by the court and placed in residential commitment programs be established. Juvenile offenders shall have the opportunity to achieve reading and writing skills as a means to further their educational and vocational needs and to assist them in discontinuing a life of crime. The literacy programs shall be of high quality, targeted to the juvenile offender's assessed ability and needs, and use appropriate instructional technology and qualified educational instructors. The programs shall be offered in each residential commitment program operated by or under contract with the department and shall consist of standardized outcomes so that an offender who is transferred to another facility may be able to continue his or her literacy education with minimal disruption.

(2) JUVENILE OFFENDER LITERACY PROGRAMS. — The Department of Education, in consultation with the Department of Juvenile Justice, shall identify and, contingent upon specific appropriations, implement and administer juvenile offender literacy programs for each residential commitment program operated by or under contract with the department. These programs shall promote the reading and writing skills of juvenile offenders.

(a)1. An offender 16 years of age or younger who meets the criteria of this section shall be required to participate in a literacy program.

2. An offender 17 years of age or older who is admitted to a residential commitment program on or after July 1, 1998, shall be required to participate in a literacy program. An offender 17 years of age or older who was committed to a residential commitment program before July 1, 1998, may voluntarily participate in a program if the offender otherwise meets the requirements for eligibility.

(b) An offender is eligible to participate in a program if the offender is unable to read and write at a sixth-grade level and is not exempt under subsection (4).

(c) In addition to any other requirements determined by the department, a literacy program shall:

1. Provide for the participation of an offender who may not attain a sixth-grade or higher reading and writing level due to a medical, developmental, or learning disability but who can reasonably be expected to benefit from a literacy program.

2. Require an eligible offender to participate in a minimum of 240 hours of education per year unless the offender attains a sixth-grade or higher reading and writing level or is released from the commitment facility.

3. Require counseling for an offender who has not achieved a sixth-grade or higher reading and writing level after participation in a program. The counseling shall address the benefits of continuing in the program.

4. Include a system of incentives to encourage and reward the performance of an offender in a program.

5. Include a system of disincentives that may include disciplinary action if an offender refuses or intentionally fails to participate in good faith in a program.

6. Provide for reports to be maintained in the offender's records and forwarded to the appropriate educational facility upon the offender's release from the commitment facility.

(3) INITIAL ASSESSMENT. — When an offender is admitted to a residential commitment facility, the department or a provider under contract with the department shall immediately assess whether the offender has achieved a sixth-grade or higher reading and writing level. An assessment may be conducted at a juvenile assessment center as provided in s. 985.135 as a part of the intake process. If the department or a provider determines that an offender has not achieved a sixth-grade or higher reading and writing level, the offender shall participate in a program if the offender meets the criteria for participation.

(4) OFFENDERS EXEMPT FROM PARTICIPATION. — If an offender is not reasonably expected to benefit from a program as a result of a medical, developmental, or learning disability, the offender may not be required to participate in a program. The determination that an offender should be exempt from a program must be made by an appropriate psychologist, psychiatrist, or physician.

(5) EVALUATION AND REPORT. — The department, in consultation with the Department of Education, shall develop and implement an evaluation of the literacy program in order to determine the impact of the programs on recidivism. The department shall submit an annual report on the implementation and progress of the programs to the President of the Senate and the Speaker of the House of Representatives by January 1 of each year.

HISTORY:
S. 6, ch. 98-186; s. 137, ch. 99-3; s. 44, ch. 2000-135; s. 6, ch. 2001-185; s. 82, ch. 2006-120, eff. January 1, 2007.

Editor's notes.
Formerly s. 985.317: transferred by s. 82, ch. 2006-120, effective January 1, 2007.

§ 985.629. Contracts for the transfer of Florida children in federal custody.

To the extent that maintenance costs are borne entirely from federal funds, the department is empowered to contract with federal authorities for the return of Florida children who are in the custody of a federal court or a federal correctional institution for violation of federal law. Such children under contract are to be transferred to the exclusive custody and active control of the department, under the terms, agreements, and provisions of the contract.

HISTORY:

S. 5, ch. 90-208; s. 79, ch. 97-238; s. 83, ch. 2006-120, eff. January 1, 2007.

Editor's notes.

Formerly s. 985.419: transferred by s. 83, ch. 2006-120, effective January 1, 2007; s. 39.065.

§ 985.632. Quality improvement and cost-effectiveness; Comprehensive Accountability Report.

(1) INTENT. — It is the intent of the Legislature that the department establish a performance accountability system for each provider who contracts with the department for the delivery of services to children. The contract shall include both output measures, such as the number of children served, and outcome measures, including program completion and postcompletion recidivism. Each contractor shall report performance results to the department annually. The department's Bureau of Research and Planning shall summarize performance results from all contracts and report the information to the Legislature annually in the Comprehensive Accountability Report. The report shall:

(a) Ensure that information be provided to decisionmakers in a timely manner so that resources are allocated to programs that achieve desired performance levels.

(b) Provide information about the cost of such programs and their differential effectiveness so that the quality of such programs can be compared and improvements made continually.

(c) Provide information to aid in developing related policy issues and concerns.

(d) Provide information to the public about the effectiveness of such programs in meeting established goals and objectives.

(e) Provide a basis for a system of accountability so that each child is afforded the best programs to meet his or her needs.

(f) Improve service delivery to children through the use of technical assistance .

(g) Modify or eliminate activities or programs that are not effective.

(h) Collect and analyze available statistical data for the purpose of ongoing evaluation of all programs.

(2) DEFINITIONS. — As used in this section, the term:

(a) "Program" means any facility or service for youth that is operated by the department or by a provider under contract with the department.

(b) "Program component" means an aggregation of generally related objectives which, because of their special character, related workload, and inter-related output, can logically be considered an entity for purposes of organization, management, accounting, reporting, and budgeting.

(c) "Program group" means a collection of programs with sufficient similarity of functions, services, and youth to permit appropriate comparison amongst programs within the group.

(3) COMPREHENSIVE ACCOUNTABILITY REPORT. — The department, in consultation with contract service providers, shall develop and use a standard methodology for annually measuring, evaluating, and reporting program outputs and youth outcomes for each program and program group. The standard methodology must:

(a) Include common terminology and operational definitions for measuring the performance of system and program administration, program outputs, and program outcomes.

(b) Specify program outputs for each program and for each program group within the juvenile justice continuum.

(c) Specify desired child outcomes and methods by which to measure child outcomes for each program and program group.

(4) COST-EFFECTIVENESS MODEL. — The department, in consultation with the Office of Economic and Demographic Research and contract service providers, shall develop a cost-effectiveness model and apply the model to each commitment program.

(a) The cost-effectiveness model shall compare program costs to expected and actual child recidivism rates . It is the intent of the Legislature that continual development efforts take place to improve the validity and reliability of the cost-effectiveness model.

(b) The department shall rank commitment programs based on the cost-effectiveness model, performance measures, and adherence to quality improvement standards and shall report this data in the annual Comprehensive Accountability Report .

(c) Based on reports of the department on child outcomes and program outputs and on the department's most recent cost-effectiveness rankings, the department may terminate a program operated by the department or a provider if the program has failed to achieve a minimum standard of program effectiveness. This paragraph does not preclude the department from terminating a contract as provided under this section or as otherwise provided by law or contract, and does not limit the department's authority to enter into or terminate a contract.

(d) In collaboration with the Office of Economic and Demographic Research, and contract service providers, the department shall develop a work plan to refine the cost-effectiveness model so that the model is consistent with the performance-based program budgeting measures approved by the Legislature to the extent the department deems appropriate. The department shall notify the Office of Program Policy Analysis and Government Accountability of any meetings to refine the model.

(e) Contingent upon specific appropriation, the department, in consultation with the Office of Economic and Demographic Research, and contract service providers, shall:

1. Construct a profile of each commitment program that uses the results of the quality improvement data portion of the Comprehensive Accountability Report required by this section, the cost-effectiveness data portion of the Comprehensive Accountability Report required in this subsection, and other reports available to the department.

2. Target, for a more comprehensive evaluation, any commitment program that has achieved consistently high, low, or disparate ratings in the reports required under subparagraph 1. and target, for technical assistance, any commitment program that has achieved low or disparate ratings in the reports required under subparagraph 1.

3. Identify the essential factors that contribute to the high, low, or disparate program ratings.

4. Use the results of these evaluations in developing or refining juvenile justice programs or program models, child outcomes and program outputs, provider contracts, quality improvement standards, and the cost-effectiveness model.

(5) QUALITY IMPROVEMENT. — The department shall:

(a) Establish a comprehensive quality improvement system for each program operated by the department or operated by a provider under contract with the department. Each contract entered into by the department must provide for quality improvement .

(b) Provide operational definitions of and criteria for quality improvement for each specific program component.

(c) Establish quality improvement goals and objectives for each specific program component.

(d) Establish the information and specific data elements required for the quality improvement program.

(e) Develop a quality improvement manual of specific, standardized terminology and procedures to be followed by each program.

(f) Evaluate each program operated by the department or a provider under a contract with the department annually and establish minimum standards for each program component. If a provider fails to meet the established minimum standards, such failure shall cause the department to cancel the provider's contract unless the provider achieves compliance with minimum standards within 6 months

or unless there are documented extenuating circumstances. In addition, the department may not contract with the same provider for the canceled service for a period of 12 months. If a department-operated program fails to meet the established minimum standards, the department must take necessary and sufficient steps to ensure and document program changes to achieve compliance with the established minimum standards . If the department-operated program fails to achieve compliance with the established minimum standards within 6 months and if there are no documented extenuating circumstances, the department must notify the Executive Office of the Governor and the Legislature of the corrective action taken. Appropriate corrective action may include, but is not limited to:

1. Contracting out for the services provided in the program;

2. Initiating appropriate disciplinary action against all employees whose conduct or performance is deemed to have materially contributed to the program's failure to meet established minimum standards ;

3. Redesigning the program; or

4. Realigning the program.

(6) COMPREHENSIVE ACCOUNTABILITY REPORT SUBMISSION. — The department shall submit the Comprehensive Accountability Report to the President of the Senate, the Speaker of the House of Representatives, the Minority Leader of each house of the Legislature, the appropriate substantive and fiscal committees of each house of the Legislature, and the Governor, no later than February 1 of each year. The Comprehensive Accountability Report must contain, at a minimum, for each specific program component: a comprehensive description of the population served by the program; a specific description of the services provided by the program; cost; a comparison of expenditures to federal and state funding; immediate and long-range concerns; and recommendations to maintain, expand, improve, modify, or eliminate each program component so that changes in services lead to enhancement in program quality. The department shall ensure the reliability and validity of the information contained in the report.

(7) ONGOING EVALUATIONS; REPORTS. — The department shall collect and analyze available statistical data for the purpose of ongoing evaluation of all programs. The department shall provide the Legislature with necessary information and reports to enable the Legislature to make informed decisions regarding the effectiveness of, and any needed changes in, services, programs, policies, and laws.

HISTORY:
S. 72, ch. 97-238; s. 28, ch. 98-207; s. 34, ch. 2001-125; s. 1053, ch. 2002-387; s. 7, ch. 2004-333; s. 84, ch. 2006-120, eff. January 1, 2007; s. 173, ch. 2010-102, eff. May 26, 2010; s. 53, ch. 2010-117, eff. July 1, 2010; s. 33, ch. 2014-162, eff. July 1, 2014.

Editor's Notes
Formerly s. 985.412: transferred by s. 84, ch. 2006-120, effective January 1, 2007.
Section 32, ch. 2014-184, provides: "The reference in subsection (3) to s. 1003.52(19) should now be deemed to be to s. 1003.52(17)."

§ 985.636. Inspector general; inspectors [Repealed.]

Repealed by s. 7, ch. 2011-70, effective July 1, 2011.

HISTORY:
S. 37, ch. 2001-125; s. 85, ch. 2006-120, eff. January 1, 2007.

§ 985.64. Rulemaking.

(1) The department shall adopt rules pursuant to ss. 120.536(1) and 120.54 to implement the provisions of this chapter. Such rules may not conflict with the Florida Rules of Juvenile Procedure. All rules and policies must conform to accepted standards of care and treatment.

(2) The department shall adopt rules to ensure the effective provision of health services to youth in facilities or programs operated or contracted by the department. The rules shall address the delivery of the following:

    (a) Ordinary medical care.

    (b) Mental health services.

    (c) Substance abuse treatment services.

    (d) Services to youth with developmental disabilities.

The department shall coordinate its rulemaking with the Department of Children and Families and the Agency for Persons with Disabilities to ensure that the rules adopted under this section do not encroach upon the substantive jurisdiction of those agencies. The department shall include the above-mentioned entities in the rulemaking process, as appropriate. This subsection does not supersede the provisions governing consent to treatment and services found in ss. 39.407, 743.0645, and 985.18, or otherwise provided by law.

HISTORY:
S. 65, ch. 97-238; s. 230, ch. 98-200; s. 86, ch. 2006-120, eff. January 1, 2007; s. 2, ch. 2010-123, eff. July 1, 2010; s. 359, ch. 2014-19, eff. July 1, 2014.

Editor's notes.
Formerly s. 985.405: transferred by s. 86, ch. 2006-120, effective January 1, 2007.

§ 985.644. Departmental contracting powers; personnel standards and investigation.

(1) The department may contract with the Federal Government, other state departments and agencies, county and municipal governments and agencies, public and private agencies, and private individuals and corporations in carrying out the purposes of, and the responsibilities established in, this chapter.

    (a) Each contract entered into by the department for services delivered on an appointment or intermittent basis by a provider that does not have regular custodial responsibility for children and each contract with a school for services must ensure that all owners, operators, and personnel who have direct contact with children are subject to level 2 background screening pursuant to chapter 435.

    (b) A volunteer who assists the department or any program for children on an intermittent basis for less than 10 hours per month need not be screened if a person who meets the screening requirement of this section is always present and has the volunteer in his or her line of sight.

(2) The department shall adopt a rule establishing a procedure to provide notice of policy changes that affect contracted delinquency services and programs. A policy is defined as an operational requirement that applies to only the specified contracted delinquency service or program. The procedure must include:

    (a) Public notice of policy development.

    (b) Opportunity for public comment on the proposed policy.

    (c) Assessment for fiscal impact upon the department and providers.

    (d) The department's response to comments received.

(3)(a) All employees of the department and all personnel of contract providers for any program for children, including all owners, operators, employees, persons who have access to confidential juvenile records, and volunteers, must complete:

    1. A level 2 employment screening pursuant to chapter 435 before employment. The security background investigation conducted under this section must ensure that, in addition to the disqualifying offenses listed in s. 435.04, no person subject to the background screening provisions of this section has an arrest awaiting final disposition for, been found guilty of, regardless of adjudication, or entered a plea of nolo contendere or guilty to, or been adjudicated delinquent and the record has not been sealed or expunged for, any offense prohibited under the following provisions of state law or similar laws of another jurisdiction:

        a. Section 784.07, relating to assault or battery of law enforcement officers, firefighters, emergency medical care providers, public transit employees or agents, or other specified officers.

        b. Section 817.568, relating to criminal use of personal identification information.

    2. A national criminal records check by the Federal Bureau of Investigation every 5 years following the date of the person's employment.

    (b) Law enforcement, correctional, and correctional probation officers, certified pursuant to s. 943.13, are not required to submit to level 2 screenings as long as they are currently employed by a law enforcement agency or correctional facility. The department shall electronically submit to the Department of Law Enforcement:

1. Fingerprint information obtained during the employment screening required by subparagraph (a)1.

2. Fingerprint information for all persons employed by the department, or by a provider under contract with the department, in delinquency facilities, services, or programs if such fingerprint information has not previously been submitted pursuant to this section.

(c) All fingerprint information electronically submitted to the Department of Law Enforcement under paragraph (b) shall be retained by the Department of Law Enforcement and entered into the statewide automated biometric identification system authorized by s. 943.05(2)(b). Thereafter, such fingerprint information shall be available for all purposes and uses authorized for arrest fingerprint information entered into the statewide automated biometric identification system pursuant to s. 943.051 until the fingerprint information is removed pursuant to paragraph (e). The Department of Law Enforcement shall search all arrest fingerprint information received pursuant to s. 943.051 against the fingerprint information entered into the statewide automated biometric identification system pursuant to this subsection. Any arrest records identified as a result of the search shall be reported to the department in the manner and timeframe established by the Department of Law Enforcement by rule.

(d) The department shall pay an annual fee to the Department of Law Enforcement for its costs resulting from the fingerprint information retention services required by this subsection. The amount of the annual fee and procedures for the submission and retention of fingerprint information and for the dissemination of search results shall be established by the Department of Law Enforcement by a rule that is applicable to the department individually pursuant to this subsection or that is applicable to the department and other employing agencies pursuant to rulemaking authority otherwise provided by law.

(e) The department shall notify the Department of Law Enforcement when a person whose fingerprint information is retained by the Department of Law Enforcement under this subsection is no longer employed by the department, or by a provider under contract with the department, in a delinquency facility, service, or program. This notice shall be provided by the department to the Department of Law Enforcement within 6 months after the date of the change in the person's employment status. Fingerprint information for persons identified by the department in the notice shall be removed from the statewide automated biometric identification system.

(4) The department may grant exemptions from disqualification from working with children as provided in s. 435.07.

(5) The department may adopt rules to describe the procedure and requirements necessary to administer

the employment screening and fingerprint retention services for all employees of the department and all personnel of contract providers for any program for children, including all owners, operators, employees, and volunteers, including the collection of associated fees.

HISTORY:

S. 5, ch. 90-208; s. 3, ch. 91-93; s. 70, ch. 91-45; s. 15, ch. 91-57; s. 6, ch. 93-156; s. 15, ch. 94-134; s. 15, ch. 94-135; s. 9, ch. 95-158; s. 31, ch. 95-228; s. 118, ch. 95-418; s. 2, ch. 96-268; s. 1, ch. 97-238; s. 67, ch. 97-238; s. 12, ch. 2001-125; s. 1, ch. 2003-29; s. 33, ch. 2004-267; s. 64, ch. 2004-267; s. 13, ch. 2005-263; s. 87, ch. 2006-120, eff. Jan. 1, 2007; s. 48, ch. 2010-114, eff. Aug. 1, 2010; s. 65, ch. 2013-116, eff. July 1, 2013; s. 34, ch. 2014-162, eff. July 1, 2014.

Editor's notes.

Formerly ss. 985.01(2) and 985.407: transferred by s. 87, ch. 2006-120, effective January 1, 2007; s. 39.076.

Section 58, ch. 2010-114 provides: "The changes made by this act are intended to be prospective in nature. It is not intended that persons who are employed or licensed on the effective date of this act be rescreened until such time as they are otherwise required to be rescreened pursuant to law, at which time they must meet the requirements for screening as set forth in this act."

§ 985.6441. Health care services.

(1) As used in this section, the term:

(a) "Health care provider" has the same meaning as provided in s. 766.105.

(b) "Hospital" means a hospital licensed under chapter 395.

(2) When compensating health care providers, the department must comply with the following reimbursement limitations:

(a) Payments to a hospital or a health care provider may not exceed 110 percent of the Medicare allowable rate for any health care services provided if there is no contract between the department and the hospital or the health care provider providing services at a hospital.

(b)1. The department may continue to make payments for health care services at the contracted rates for contracts executed before July 1, 2014, through the current term of the contract if a contract has been executed between the department and a hospital or a health care provider providing services at a hospital.

2. Payments may not exceed 110 percent of the Medicare allowable rate after the current term of the contract expires or after the contract is renewed during the 2013-2014 fiscal year.

(c) Payments may not exceed 110 percent of the Medicare allowable rate under a contract executed on or after July 1, 2014, between the department and a hospital or a health care provider providing services at a hospital.

(d) Notwithstanding paragraphs (a)-(c), the department may pay up to 125 percent of the Medicare allowable rate for health care services at a hospital that reports, or has reported, a negative operating margin for the previous fiscal year to the Agency for Health Care Administration through hospital-audited financial data.

HISTORY:
S. 35, ch. 2014-162, eff. July 1, 2014.

§ 985.645. Protective action response.

(1) For purposes of this section, the term:

(a) "Direct care" means direct contact with youth for the purpose of providing care, supervision, custody, or control of youth in a detention facility, delinquency program, or commitment program within any restrictiveness level, which is operated by the department or by a provider under contract with the department.

(b) "Employee" means any person who exercises direct care. The term "employee" does not include a licensed medical professional, mental health counselor, substance abuse counselor, or social services counselor whose primary responsibilities are to provide treatment to youth in a detention facility, delinquency program, or commitment program within any restrictiveness level, which is operated by the department or by a provider under contract with the department.

(c) "Protective Action Response policy" means the policy governing the use of verbal and physical intervention techniques, mechanical restraints, aerosol and chemical agents, and Tasers by employees.

(d) "Taser" means any mechanism that is designed to emit or project an electronic, magnetic, or other type of charge or shock for the purpose of temporarily incapacitating a person.

(2) The department shall adopt rules under ss. 120.536(1) and 120.54 that:

(a) Establish a Protective Action Response policy that:

1. Defines the authorized level of response by an employee to each level of verbal or physical resistance by a youth.

2. Requires the use of verbal intervention techniques as the initial response by an employee to verbal or physical resistance by a youth, except where physical intervention techniques are necessary to prevent:

a. Physical harm to the youth, employee, or another person;

b. Property damage; or

c. The youth from escaping or absconding from lawful supervision.

3. Defines authorized physical intervention techniques and the situations under which employees may use these techniques for youth. Pain compliance techniques and use of less than lethal force shall be prohibited, except where necessary to prevent:

a. Physical harm to the youth, employee, or another person;

b. Property damage; or

c. The youth from escaping or absconding from lawful supervision. Lethal force shall be prohibited, except where necessary to protect the employee or another person from an imminent threat of great bodily harm or death. Prior authorization by an employee's supervisor for the use of physical intervention techniques shall be obtained when practical.

4. Defines authorized use of mechanical restraints and the situations under which employees may use such restraints on youth. Prohibited uses of mechanical restraints shall include the use of neck restraints and the securing of a youth to a fixed object. Supervision requirements for youth who are secured in mechanical restraints shall include constant and direct visual monitoring by an employee for purposes of ensuring youth safety and ascertaining indications by the youth that restraints are no longer necessary. Prior authorization by an employee's supervisor for the use of mechanical restraints shall be obtained when practical.

5. Prohibits the use of aerosol or chemical agents, including, but not limited to, oleoresin capsicum spray and ammonia capsules, on a youth unless required for medical treatment of the youth by a licensed medical professional.

6. Prohibits the use of a Taser on a youth.

(b) Establish training curricula for protective action response certification of employees and instructors. The training curriculum for employee certification shall, at a minimum, require the employee to:

1. Complete instruction on the Protective Action Response policy.

2. Obtain a passing score:

a. On a written examination that tests the employee's knowledge and understanding of the Protective Action Response policy.

b. During an evaluation by an instructor of the employee's physically demonstrated ability to implement the Protective Action Response policy.

(c) Require training curricula for protective action response certification of employees to be taught by instructors who have been certified under the training curriculum for protective action response certification of instructors.

(d) Require each employee who was not certified by the department in protective action response prior to July 1, 2006, to receive his or her protective action response certification by September 30, 2006, or within 90 calendar days following his or her date of hire, whichever date is later.

(e) Require any employee who exercises direct care prior to receiving his or her protective action response certification to be directly supervised by an employee who has received his or her protective action response certification.

HISTORY:
S. 8, ch. 2006-62, eff. July 1, 2006; s. 22, ch. 2010-113, eff. July 1, 2010.

Editor's notes.
Formerly s. 985.4055.

§ 985.648. Consultants.

The department may hire consultants to advise and confer with the judges of the circuit courts upon request of any such court and for the purpose of advising the department on programs, facilities, institutions, care, supervision, and all other services and treatment for children committed to the department's care under this chapter.

HISTORY:
S. 5, ch. 90-208; s. 68, ch. 97-238; s. 88, ch. 2006-120, eff. January 1, 2007.

Editor's notes.
Formerly s. 985.408: transferred by s. 88, ch. 2006-120, effective January 1, 2007; s. 39.075.

§ 985.652. Participation of certain programs in the State Risk Management Trust Fund.

Pursuant to s. 284.30, the Division of Risk Management of the Department of Financial Services is authorized to insure a private agency, individual, or corporation operating a state-owned training school under a contract to carry out the purposes and responsibilities of any program of the department. The coverage authorized herein shall be under the same general terms and conditions as the department is insured for its responsibilities under chapter 284.

HISTORY:
S. 69, ch. 97-238; s. 26, ch. 2000-122; s. 1941, ch. 2003-261; s. 89, ch. 2006-120, eff. January 1, 2007.

Editor's notes.
Formerly s. 985.409: transferred by s. 89, ch. 2006-120, effective January 1, 2007.

§ 985.66. Juvenile justice training; staff development and training; Juvenile Justice Training Trust Fund.

(1) LEGISLATIVE PURPOSE. — In order to enable the state to provide a systematic approach to staff development and training for judges, state attorneys, public defenders, law enforcement officers, school district personnel, and juvenile justice program staff that will meet the needs of such persons in their discharge of duties while at the same time meeting the requirements for the American Correction Association accreditation by the Commission on Accreditation for Corrections, it is the purpose of the Legislature to require the department to establish, maintain, and oversee the operation of juvenile justice training, programs, and courses in the state. The purpose of the Legislature in establishing staff development and training programs is to provide employees of the department, any private or public entity, or contract providers who provide services or care for children under the responsibility of the department with the knowledge and skills needed to appropriately interact with children and provide such care and services ; to positively impact the recidivism of children in the juvenile justice system; and to afford greater protection of the public through an improved level of services delivered by a professionally trained juvenile justice staff to children who are alleged to be or who have been found to be delinquent.

(2) STAFF DEVELOPMENT AND TRAINING. — The department shall:

(a) Designate the number and location of the training programs and courses; assess, design, develop, implement, evaluate, maintain, and update the curriculum to be used in the training of juvenile justice staff; establish timeframes for participation in and completion of training by juvenile justice staff; develop, implement, score, analyze, maintain, and update job-related examinations; develop, implement, analyze, and update the types and frequencies for evaluations of the training programs, courses, and instructors ; and manage the budget and contracts for all the training deliverables .

(b) Establish uniform minimum job-related preservice and inservice training courses and examinations for juvenile justice program staff.

(c) Consult and cooperate with the state or any political subdivision; any private entity or contractor; and with private and public universities, colleges, community colleges, and other educational institutions concerning the development of juvenile justice training and programs or courses of instruction, including, but not limited to, education and training in the areas of juvenile justice.

(d) Enter into contracts and agreements with other agencies, organizations, associations, corporations, individuals, or federal agencies as necessary in the execution of the powers of the department or the performance of its duties.

(3) JUVENILE JUSTICE TRAINING PROGRAM. — The department shall establish a certifiable program for juvenile justice training pursuant to this section, and all department program staff and providers who deliver direct care services pursuant to contract with the department shall be required to participate in and successfully complete the department-approved program of training pertinent to their areas of responsibility. Judges, state attorneys, and public defenders, law enforcement officers, school district personnel, and employees of contract providers who provide services or care for children under the responsibility of the department may participate in such training program. For the juvenile justice program staff, the department shall, based on a job-task analysis:

(a) Design, implement, maintain, evaluate, and revise a basic training program, including a competency-based examination, for the purpose of providing minimum employment training qualifications for all juvenile justice personnel. All program staff of the department and providers who deliver direct-care services who are hired after October 1, 1999, must meet the following minimum requirements:

1. Be at least 19 years of age.

2. Be a high school graduate or its equivalent as determined by the department.

3. Not have been convicted of any felony or a misdemeanor involving perjury or a false statement, or have received a dishonorable discharge from any of the Armed Forces of the United States. Any person who, after September 30, 1999, pleads guilty or nolo contendere to or is found guilty of any felony or a misdemeanor involving perjury or false statement is not eligible for employment, notwithstanding suspension of sentence or withholding of adjudication. Notwithstanding this subparagraph, any person who pled nolo contendere to a misdemeanor involving a false statement before October 1, 1999, and who has had such record of that plea sealed or expunged is not ineligible for employment for that reason.

4. Abide by all of s. 985.644(1) regarding fingerprinting and background investigations and other screening requirements for personnel.

5. Execute and submit to the department an affidavit-of-application form, adopted by the department, attesting to his or her compliance with subparagraphs 1.-4. The affidavit must be executed under oath and constitutes an official statement under s. 837.06. The affidavit must include conspicuous language that the intentional false execution of the affidavit constitutes a misdemeanor of the second degree. The employing agency shall retain the affidavit.

(b) Design, implement, maintain, evaluate, and revise an advanced training program, including a competency-based examination for each training course, which is intended to enhance knowledge, skills, and abilities related to job performance.

(c) Design, implement, maintain, evaluate, and revise a career development training program, including a competency-based examination for each training course. Career development courses are intended to prepare personnel for promotion.

(d) The department is encouraged to design, implement, maintain, evaluate, and revise juvenile justice training courses, or to enter into contracts for such training courses, that are intended to provide for the safety and well-being of both citizens and juvenile offenders.

(4) JUVENILE JUSTICE TRAINING TRUST FUND.

(a) There is created within the State Treasury a Juvenile Justice Training Trust Fund to be used by the department for the purpose of funding the development and updating of a job-task analysis of juvenile justice personnel; the development, implementation, and updating of job-related training courses and examinations; and the cost of juvenile justice training courses.

(b) One dollar from every noncriminal traffic infraction collected pursuant to ss. 318.14(10)(b) and 318.18 shall be deposited into the Juvenile Justice Training Trust Fund.

(c) In addition to the funds generated by paragraph (b), the trust fund may receive funds from any other public or private source.

(d) Funds that are not expended by the end of the budget cycle or through a supplemental budget approved by the department shall revert to the trust fund.

(5) ESTABLISHMENT OF JUVENILE JUSTICE TRAINING ACADEMIES. — The number, location, and establishment of juvenile justice training academies shall be determined by the department.

(6) SCHOLARSHIPS AND STIPENDS. — The department shall establish criteria to award scholarships or stipends to qualified juvenile justice personnel who are residents of the state who want to pursue a bachelor's or associate in arts degree in juvenile justice or a related field. The department shall handle the administration of the scholarship or stipend. The Department of Education shall handle the notes issued for the payment of the scholarships or stipends. All scholarship and stipend awards shall be paid from the Juvenile Justice Training Trust Fund upon vouchers approved by the Department of Education and properly certified by the Chief Financial Officer. Prior to the award of a scholarship or stipend, the juvenile justice employee must agree in writing to practice her or his profession in juvenile justice or a related field for 1 month for each month of grant or to repay the full amount of the scholarship or stipend together with interest at the rate of 5 percent per annum over a period not to exceed 10 years. Repayment shall be made payable to the state for deposit into the Juvenile Justice Training Trust Fund.

(7) PARTICIPATION OF CERTAIN PROGRAMS IN THE STATE RISK MANAGEMENT TRUST FUND. — Pursuant to s. 284.30, the Division of Risk Management of the Department of Financial Services is authorized to insure a private agency, individual, or corporation operating a state-owned training school under a contract to carry out the purposes and responsibilities of any program of the department. The coverage authorized herein shall be under the same general terms and conditions as the department is insured for its responsibilities under chapter 284.

HISTORY:

S. 5, ch. 90-208; s. 3, ch. 91-74; s. 21, ch. 91-201; s. 5, ch. 91-429; s. 21, ch. 94-209; s. 1336, ch. 95-147; s. 53, ch. 95-280; s. 1, ch. 97-215; s. 66, ch. 97-238; s. 26, ch. 98-207; s. 19, ch. 99-284; s. 25, ch. 2000-122; s. 48, ch. 2000-135; s. 1940, ch. 2003-261; s. 90, ch. 2006-120, eff. Jan. 1, 2007; s. 9, ch. 2006-296, eff. July 1, 2006; s. 13, ch. 2011-70, eff. July 1, 2011; s. 118, ch. 2013-18, eff. July 2, 2013; s. 36, ch. 2014-162, eff. July 1, 2014.

Editor's notes.
Formerly s. 985.406: transferred by s. 90, ch. 2006-120, effective January 1, 2007.

§ 985.664. Juvenile justice circuit advisory boards.

(1) There is authorized a juvenile justice circuit advisory board to be established in each of the 20 judicial circuits. Except in single-county circuits, each juvenile justice circuit advisory board shall have a county organization representing each of the counties in the circuit. The county organization shall report directly to the juvenile justice circuit advisory board on the juvenile justice needs of the county. The purpose of each juvenile justice circuit advisory board is to provide advice and direction to the department in the development and implementation of juvenile justice programs and to work collaboratively with the department in seeking program improvements and policy changes to address the emerging and changing needs of Florida's youth who are at risk of delinquency.

(2) The duties and responsibilities of a juvenile justice circuit advisory board include, but are not limited to:

(a) Developing a comprehensive plan for the circuit. The initial circuit plan shall be submitted to the department no later than December 31, 2014, and no later than June 30 every 3 years thereafter. The department shall prescribe a format and content requirements for the submission of the comprehensive plan.

(b) Participating in the facilitation of interagency cooperation and information sharing.

(c) Providing recommendations for public or private grants to be administered by one of the community partners that support one or more components of the comprehensive circuit plan.

(d) Providing recommendations to the department in the evaluation of prevention and early intervention grant programs, including the Community Juvenile Justice Partnership Grant program established in s. 985.676 and proceeds from the Invest in Children license plate annual use fees.

(e) Providing an annual report to the department describing the board's activities. The department shall prescribe a format and content requirements for submission of annual reports. The annual report must be submitted to the department no later than August 1 of each year.

(3) Each juvenile justice circuit advisory board shall have a minimum of 16 members. The membership of each board must reflect:

(a) The circuit's geography and population distribution.

(b) Diversity in the judicial circuit.

(4) Each member of the juvenile justice circuit advisory board must be approved by the Secretary of Juvenile Justice, except those members listed in paragraphs (a), (b), (c), (e), (f), (g), and (h). The juvenile justice circuit advisory boards established under subsection (1) must include as members:

(a) The state attorney or his or her designee.

(b) The public defender or his or her designee.

(c) The chief judge or his or her designee.

(d) A representative of the corresponding circuit or regional entity of the Department of Children and Families.

(e) The sheriff or the sheriff's designee from each county in the circuit.

(f) A police chief or his or her designee from each county in the circuit.

(g) A county commissioner or his or her designee from each county in the circuit.

(h) The superintendent of each school district in the circuit or his or her designee.

(i) A representative from the workforce organization of each county in the circuit.

(j) A representative of the business community.

(k) A youth representative who has had an experience with the juvenile justice system and is not older than 21 years of age.

(*l*) A representative of the faith community.

(m) A health services representative who specializes in mental health care, victim-service programs, or victims of crimes.

(n) A parent or family member of a youth who has been involved with the juvenile justice system.

(o) Up to five representatives from any of the following who are not otherwise represented in this subsection:

1. Community leaders.

2. Youth-serving coalitions.

(5) When a vacancy in the office of the chair occurs, the juvenile justice circuit advisory board shall appoint a new chair, who must meet the board membership requirements in subsection (4). The chair shall appoint members to vacant seats within 45 days after the vacancy and submit the appointments to the department for approval. The chair shall serve at the pleasure of the Secretary of Juvenile Justice.

(6) A member may not serve more than three consecutive 2-year terms, except those members listed in paragraphs (4)(a), (b), (c), (e), (f), (g), and (h). A former member who has not served on the juvenile justice circuit advisory board for 2 years is eligible to serve on the juvenile justice circuit advisory board again.

(7) At least half of the voting members of the juvenile justice circuit advisory board constitutes a quorum. A quorum must be present in order for the board to vote on a measure or position.

(8) In order for a juvenile justice circuit advisory board measure or position to pass, it must receive more than 50 percent of the vote.

(9) Each juvenile justice circuit advisory board must provide for the establishment of an executive committee of not more than 10 members. The duties and authority of the executive committee must be addressed in the bylaws.

(10) Each juvenile justice circuit advisory board shall have bylaws. The department shall prescribe a format and content requirements for the bylaws. All bylaws must be approved by the department. The bylaws shall address at least the following issues: election or appointment of officers; filling of vacant positions; meeting attendance requirements; and the establishment and duties of an executive committee.

(11) Members of juvenile justice circuit advisory boards are subject to part III of chapter 112.

HISTORY:

S. 50, ch. 2000-135; s. 12, ch. 2005-263; s. 91, ch. 2006-120, eff. Jan. 1, 2006; s. 1, ch. 2013-118, eff. Oct. 1, 2013; s. 37, ch. 2014-162, eff. July 1, 2014.

Editor's notes.

Formerly s. 985.4135: transferred by s. 91, ch. 2006-120, effective January 1, 2007.

§ 985.668. Innovation zones.

The department shall encourage each of the juvenile justice circuit boards to propose at least one innovation zone within the circuit for the purpose of implementing any experimental, pilot, or demonstration project that furthers the legislatively established goals of the department. An innovation zone is a defined geographic area such as a circuit, commitment region, county, municipality, service delivery area, school campus, or neighborhood providing a laboratory for the research, development, and testing of the applicability and efficacy of model programs, policy options, and new technologies for the department.

(1)(a) The juvenile justice circuit board shall submit a proposal for an innovation zone to the secretary. If the purpose of the proposed innovation zone is to demonstrate that specific statutory goals can be achieved more effectively by using procedures that require modification of existing rules, policies, or procedures, the proposal may request the secretary to waive such existing rules, policies, or procedures or to otherwise authorize use of alternative procedures or practices. Waivers of such existing rules, policies, or procedures must comply with applicable state or federal law.

(b) For innovation zone proposals that the secretary determines require changes to state law, the secretary may submit a request for a waiver from such laws, together with any proposed changes to state law, to the chairs of the appropriate legislative committees for consideration.

(c) For innovation zone proposals that the secretary determines require waiver of federal law, the secretary may submit a request for such waivers to the applicable federal agency.

(2) An innovation zone project may not have a duration of more than 2 years, but the secretary may grant an extension.

(3) Before implementing an innovation zone under this subsection, the secretary shall, in conjunction with the Office of Program Policy Analysis and Government Accountability, develop measurable and valid objectives for such zone within a negotiated reasonable period of time. Moneys designated for an innovation zone in one operating circuit may not be used to fund an innovation zone in another operating circuit.

(4) Program models for innovation zone projects include, but are not limited to:

(a) A forestry alternative work program that provides selected juvenile offenders an opportunity to serve in a forestry work program as an alternative to incarceration, in which offenders assist in wildland firefighting, enhancement of state land management, environmental enhancement, and land restoration.

(b) A collaborative public/private dropout prevention partnership that trains personnel from both the public and private sectors of a target community who are identified and brought into the school system as an additional resource for addressing problems which inhibit and retard learning, including abuse, neglect, financial instability, pregnancy, and substance abuse.

(c) A support services program that provides economically disadvantaged youth with support services, jobs, training, counseling, mentoring, and prepaid postsecondary tuition scholarships.

(d) A juvenile offender job training program that offers an opportunity for juvenile offenders to develop educational and job skills in a 12-month to 18-month nonresidential training program, teaching the offenders skills such as computer-aided design, modular panel construction, and heavy vehicle repair and maintenance which will readily transfer to the private sector, thereby promoting responsibility and productivity.

(e) An infant mortality prevention program that is designed to discourage unhealthy behaviors such as smoking and alcohol or drug consumption, reduce the incidence of babies born prematurely or with low birth weight, reduce health care cost by enabling babies to be safely discharged earlier from the hospital, reduce the incidence of child abuse and neglect, and improve parenting and problem-solving skills.

(f) A regional crime prevention and intervention program that serves as an umbrella agency to coordinate and replicate existing services to at-risk children, first-time juvenile offenders, youth crime victims, and school dropouts.

(g) An alternative education outreach school program that serves delinquent repeat offenders between 14 and 18 years of age who have demonstrated failure in school and who are referred by the juvenile court.

(h) A drug treatment and prevention program that provides early identification of children with alcohol or drug problems to facilitate treatment, comprehensive screening and assessment, family involvement, and placement options.

(i) A community resource mother or father program that emphasizes parental responsibility for the behavior of children, and requires the availability of counseling services for children at high risk for delinquent behavior.

HISTORY:
S. 76, ch. 97-238; s. 53, ch. 2000-135; s. 140, ch. 2001-266; s. 92, ch. 2006-120, eff. January 1, 2007.

Editor's notes.
Formerly s. 985.416: transferred by s. 92, ch. 2006-120, effective January 1, 2007.

§ 985.672. Direct-support organization; definition; use of property; board of directors; audit.

(1) DEFINITION. — As used in this section, the term "direct-support organization" means an organization whose sole purpose is to support the juvenile justice system and which is:

(a) A corporation not-for-profit incorporated under chapter 617 and which is approved by the Department of State;

(b) Organized and operated to conduct programs and activities; to raise funds; to request and receive grants, gifts, and bequests of moneys; to acquire, receive, hold, invest, and administer, in its own name, securities, funds, objects of value, or other property, real or personal; and to make expenditures to or for the direct or indirect benefit of the Department of Juvenile Justice or the juvenile justice system operated by a county commission or a circuit board;

(c) Determined by the Department of Juvenile Justice to be consistent with the goals of the juvenile justice system, in the best interest of the state, and in accordance with the adopted goals and mission of the Department of Juvenile Justice.

Expenditures of the organization shall be expressly used to prevent and ameliorate juvenile delinquency. The expenditures of the direct-support organization may not be used for the purpose of lobbying as defined in s. 11.045.

(2) CONTRACT. — The direct-support organization shall operate under written contract with the department. The contract must provide for:

(a) Approval of the articles of incorporation and bylaws of the direct-support organization by the department.

(b) Submission of an annual budget for the approval of the department.

(c) Certification by the department that the direct-support organization is complying with the terms of the contract and in a manner consistent with the goals and purposes of the department and in the best interest of the state. Such certification must be made annually and reported in the official minutes of a meeting of the direct-support organization.

(d) The reversion of moneys and property held in trust by the direct-support organization for the benefit of the juvenile justice system to the state if the department ceases to exist or to the department if the direct-support organization is no longer approved to operate for the department, a county commission, or a circuit board or if the direct-support organization ceases to exist;

(e) The fiscal year of the direct-support organization, which must begin July 1 of each year and end June 30 of the following year;

(f) The disclosure of material provisions of the contract, and the distinction between the department and the direct-support organization, to donors of gifts, contributions, or bequests, including such disclosure on all promotional and fundraising publications.

(3) BOARD OF DIRECTORS. — The Secretary of Juvenile Justice shall appoint a board of directors of the direct-support organization. Members of the organization must include representatives from businesses, representatives from each of the juvenile justice service districts, and one representative appointed at large.

(4) USE OF PROPERTY. — The department may permit, without charge, appropriate use of fixed property, facilities, and personnel services of the juvenile justice system by the direct-support organization, subject to this section. For the purposes of this subsection, the term "personnel services" includes full-time or part-time personnel, as well as payroll processing services.

(a) The department may prescribe any condition with which the direct-support organization must comply in order to use fixed property or facilities of the juvenile justice system.

(b) The department may not permit the use of any fixed property or facilities of the juvenile justice system by the direct-support organization if it does not provide equal membership and employment opportunities to all persons regardless of race, color, religion, sex, age, or national origin.

(c) The department shall adopt rules prescribing the procedures by which the direct-support organization is governed and any conditions with which a direct-support organization must comply to use property or facilities of the department.

(5) DEPOSIT OF FUNDS. — Any moneys may be held in a separate depository account in the name of the direct-support organization and subject to the provisions of the contract with the department.

(6) AUDIT. — The direct-support organization shall provide for an annual financial audit in accordance with s. 215.981.

(7) REPEAL. — This section is repealed October 1, 2018, unless reviewed and saved from repeal by the Legislature.

HISTORY:
S. 20, ch. 99-284; s. 51, ch. 2000-135; s. 139, ch. 2001-266; s. 92, ch. 2006-120, eff. January 1, 2007; s. 29, ch. 2014-96, eff. June 13, 2014; s. 38, ch. 2014-162, eff. July 1, 2014.

Editor's notes.
Formerly s. 985.4145: transferred by s. 92, ch. 2006-120, effective January 1, 2007.

§ 985.676. Community juvenile justice partnership grants.

(1) GRANTS; CRITERIA.

(a) In order to encourage the development of a circuit juvenile justice plan and the development and implementation of circuit interagency agreements under s. 985.664, the community juvenile justice partnership grant program is established and shall be administered by the department.

(b) In awarding these grants, the department shall consider applications that at a minimum provide for the following:

1. The participation of the agencies and programs needed to implement the project or program for which the applicant is applying;

2. The reduction of truancy and in-school and out-of-school suspensions and expulsions, the enhancement of school safety, and other delinquency early-intervention and diversion services;

3. The number of youths from 10 through 17 years of age within the geographic area to be served by the program, giving those geographic areas having the highest number of youths from 10 to 17 years of age priority for selection;

4. The extent to which the program targets high-juvenile-crime neighborhoods and those public schools serving juveniles from high-crime neighborhoods;

5. The validity and cost-effectiveness of the program; and

6. The degree to which the program is located in and managed by local leaders of the target neighborhoods and public schools serving the target neighborhoods.

(c) In addition, the department may consider the following criteria in awarding grants:

1. The circuit juvenile justice plan and any county juvenile justice plans that are referred to or incorporated into the circuit plan, including a list of individuals, groups, and public and private entities that participated in the development of the plan.

2. The diversity of community entities participating in the development of the circuit juvenile justice plan.

3. The number of community partners who will be actively involved in the operation of the grant program.

4. The number of students or youths to be served by the grant and the criteria by which they will be selected.

5. The criteria by which the grant program will be evaluated and, if deemed successful, the feasibility of implementation in other communities.

(2) GRANT APPLICATION PROCEDURES.

(a) Each entity wishing to apply for an annual community juvenile justice partnership grant, which may be renewed for a maximum of 2 additional years for the same provision of services, shall submit a grant proposal for funding or continued funding to the department. The department shall establish the grant application procedures. In order to be considered for funding, the grant proposal shall include the following assurances and information:

1. A letter from the chair of the juvenile justice circuit board confirming that the grant application has been reviewed and found to support one or more purposes or goals of the juvenile justice plan as developed by the board.

2. A rationale and description of the program and the services to be provided, including goals and objectives.

3. A method for identification of the juveniles most likely to be involved in the juvenile justice system who will be the focus of the program.

4. Provisions for the participation of parents and guardians in the program.

5. Coordination with other community-based and social service prevention efforts, including, but not limited to, drug and alcohol abuse prevention and dropout prevention programs, that serve the target population or neighborhood.

6. An evaluation component to measure the effectiveness of the program in accordance with s. 985.632.

7. A program budget, including the amount and sources of local cash and in-kind resources committed to the budget. The proposal must establish to the satisfaction of the department that the entity will make a cash or in-kind contribution to the program of a value that is at least equal to 20 percent of the amount of the grant.

8. The necessary program staff.

(b) The department shall consider the recommendations of the juvenile justice circuit advisory board as to the priority that should be given to proposals submitted by entities within a circuit in awarding such grants.

(c) The department shall make available, to anyone wishing to apply for such a grant, information on all of the criteria to be used in the selection of the proposals for funding pursuant to the provisions of this subsection.

(d) The department shall review all program proposals submitted. Entities submitting proposals shall be notified of approval not later than June 30 of each year.

(e) Each entity that is awarded a grant as provided for in this section shall submit an annual evaluation report to the department, the circuit juvenile justice manager, and the juvenile justice circuit advisory board, by a date subsequent to the end of the contract period established by the department, documenting the extent to which the program objectives have been met, the effect of the program on the juvenile arrest rate, and any other information required by the department. The department shall coordinate and incorporate all such annual evaluation reports with s. 985.632. Each entity is also subject to a financial audit and a performance audit.

(f) The department may establish rules and policy provisions necessary to implement this section.

(3) RESTRICTIONS. — This section does not prevent a program initiated under a community juvenile justice partnership grant established pursuant to this section from continuing to operate beyond the 3-year maximum funding period if it can find other funding sources. Likewise, this section does not restrict the number of programs an entity may apply for or operate.

HISTORY:
S. 75, ch. 97-238; s. 32, ch. 98-207; s. 21, ch. 99-284; s. 52, ch. 2000-135; s. 93, ch. 2006-120, eff. Jan. 1, 2007; s. 6, ch. 2013-118, eff. Oct. 1, 2013.

Editor's notes.
Formerly s. 985.415: transferred by s. 93, ch. 2006-120, effective January 1, 2007.

§ 985.682. Siting of facilities; criteria.

(1) When the department or a contracted provider proposes a site for a juvenile justice facility, the department or provider shall request that the local government having jurisdiction over such proposed site determine whether or not the proposed site is appropriate for public use under local government comprehensive plans, local land use ordinances, local zoning ordinances or regulations, and other local ordinances in effect at the time of such request. If no such determination is made within 90 days after the request, it shall be presumed that the proposed site is in compliance with such plans, ordinances, or regulations.

(2) If the local government determines within 90 days after the request that construction of a facility on the proposed site does not comply with any such plan, ordinance, or regulation, the department may request a modification of such plan, ordinance, or regulation without having an ownership interest in such property. For the purposes of this section, modification includes, but is not limited to, a variance, rezoning, special exception, or any other action of the local government having jurisdiction over the proposed site which would authorize siting of a facility.

(3) Upon receipt of a request for modification from the department, the local government may recommend and hold a public hearing on the request for modification in the same manner as for a rezoning as provided under the appropriate special or local law or ordinance, except that such proceeding shall be recorded by tape or by a certified court reporter and made available for transcription at the expense of any interested party.

(4) When the department requests such a modification and it is denied by the local government, the local government or the department shall initiate the dispute resolution process to reconcile differences on the siting of correctional facilities between the department, local governments, and private citizens. The department shall establish, by rule, procedures for dispute resolution. The dispute resolution process shall require the parties to commence meetings to reconcile their differences. If the parties fail to resolve their differences within 30 days after the denial, the parties shall engage in voluntary mediation or similar process. If the parties fail to resolve their differences by mediation within 60 days after the denial, or if no action is taken on the department's request within 90 days after the request, the department must appeal the decision of the local government on the requested modification of local plans, ordinances, or regulations to the Governor and Cabinet. Any dispute resolution process initiated under this section must conform to the time limitations set forth herein. However, upon agreement of all parties, the time limits may be extended, but in no event may the dispute resolution process extend over 180 days.

(5) The Governor and Cabinet shall consider the following when determining whether to grant the appeal from the decision of the local government on the requested modification:

(a) The record of the proceedings before the local government.

(b) Reports and studies by any other agency relating to matters within the jurisdiction of such agency which may be potentially affected by the proposed site.

(c) Existing studies, reports and information maintained by the department as the Governor and Cabinet may request addressing the feasibility and availability of alternative sites in the general area, and the need for a facility in the area based on the average number of petitions, commitments, and transfers into the criminal court from the county to state facilities for the most recent 3 calendar years.

(6) The Governor and Cabinet, upon determining that the local government has recommended no feasible alternative site and that the interests of the state in providing facilities outweigh the concerns of the local government, shall authorize construction and operation of a facility on the proposed site notwithstanding any local plan, ordinance, or regulation.

(7)   The Governor and Cabinet may adopt rules of procedure to govern these proceedings in accordance with the provisions of s. 120.54.

(8)   Actions taken by the department or the Governor and Cabinet pursuant to this section shall not be subject to the provisions of ss. 120.56, 120.569, and 120.57. The decision by the Governor and Cabinet shall be subject to judicial review pursuant to s. 120.68 in the District Court of Appeal, First District.

(9)   All other departments and agencies of the state shall cooperate fully with the department to accomplish the siting of facilities for juvenile offenders.

(10)   It is the intent of the Legislature to expedite the siting of, acquisition of land for, and construction by the Department of Juvenile Justice of state juvenile justice facilities operated by the department or a private vendor under contract with the department. Other agencies shall cooperate with the department and expeditiously fulfill their responsibilities to avoid unnecessary delay in the siting of, acquisition of land for, and construction of state juvenile justice facilities. This section and all other laws of the state shall be construed to accomplish this intent. This section shall take precedence over any other law to the contrary.

(11)(a)   The department shall acquire land and erect juvenile justice facilities necessary to accommodate children committed to the custody, care, or supervision of the department, and shall make additional alterations to facilities to accommodate any increase in the number of children. The department shall establish adequate accommodations for staff of the department who are required to reside continuously within the facilities.

(b)   Notwithstanding s. 255.25(1), the department may enter into lease-purchase agreements to provide juvenile justice facilities for housing committed youths, contingent upon available funds. The facilities provided through such agreements must meet the program plan and specifications of the department. The department may enter into such lease agreements with private corporations and other governmental entities. However, notwithstanding s. 255.25(3)(a), a lease agreement may not be entered into except upon advertisement for the receipt of competitive bids and award to the lowest and best bidder except if contracting with other governmental entities.

(c)   A lease-purchase agreement that is for a term extending beyond the end of a fiscal year is subject to the provisions of s. 216.311.

(12)(a)   Notwithstanding s. 253.025 or s. 287.057, when the department finds it necessary for timely site acquisition, it may contract, without using the competitive selection procedure, with an appraiser whose name is on the list of approved appraisers maintained by the Division of State Lands of the Department of Environmental Protection under s. 253.025(8). When the department directly contracts for appraisal services, it must contract with an approved appraiser who is not employed by the same appraisal firm for review services.

(b)   Notwithstanding s. 253.025(8), the department may negotiate and enter into an option contract before an appraisal is obtained. The option contract must state that the final purchase price may not exceed the maximum value allowed by law. The consideration for such an option contract may not exceed 10 percent of the estimate obtained by the department or 10 percent of the value of the parcel, whichever amount is greater.

(c)   This subsection applies only to a purchase or acquisition of land for juvenile justice facilities. This subsection does not modify the authority of the Board of Trustees of the Internal Improvement Trust Fund or the Division of State Lands of the Department of Environmental Protection to approve any contract for purchase of state lands as provided by law or to require policies and procedures to obtain clear legal title to parcels purchased for state purposes.

(13)   The department may sell, to the best possible advantage, any detached parcels of land belonging to the bodies of land purchased for the state juvenile justice facilities. The department may purchase any parcel of land contiguous with the lands purchased for state juvenile justice facilities.

(14)   The department may begin preliminary site preparation and obtain the appropriate permits for the construction of a juvenile justice facility after approval by the Board of Trustees of the Internal Improvement Trust Fund of the lease purchase agreement or option contract if, in the department's discretion, commencing construction is in the best interests of the state.

(15)   Insofar as the provisions of this section are inconsistent with the provisions of any other law, general, special, or local, the provisions of this section are controlling. Additionally, the criteria and procedures set forth in this section supersede and are in lieu of any review and approval required by s. 380.06.

HISTORY:
S. 5, ch. 90-208; s. 20, ch. 93-230; s. 56, ch. 94-209; s. 13, ch. 96-398; s. 5, ch. 96-410; s. 70, ch. 97-238; s. 27, ch. 98-207; s. 140, ch. 99-3; s. 94, ch. 2006-120, eff. Jan. 1, 2007; s. 57, ch. 2012-116, eff. July 1, 2012; s. 11, ch. 2013-152, eff. July 1, 2013; s. 39, ch. 2014-162, eff. July 1, 2014; s. 30, ch. 2015-30, eff. May 14, 2015; s. 47, ch. 2016-233, eff. July 1, 2016.

Editor's notes.
Formerly s. 985.41: transferred by s. 94, ch. 2006-120, effective January 1, 2007; s. 39.071.

§ 985.686.   Shared county and state responsibility for juvenile detention.

(1)   It is the policy of this state that the state and the counties have a joint obligation, as provided in this section, to contribute to the financial support of the detention care provided for juveniles.

(2) As used in this section, the term:

(a) "Detention care" means secure detention and respite beds for juveniles charged with a domestic violence crime.

(b) "Fiscally constrained county" means a county within a rural area of opportunity as designated by the Governor pursuant to s. 288.0656 or each county for which the value of a mill will raise no more than $5 million in revenue, based on the certified school taxable value certified pursuant to s. 1011.62(4)(a) 1.a., from the previous July 1.

(3) Each county shall pay the costs of providing detention care, exclusive of the costs of any preadjudicatory nonmedical educational or therapeutic services and $2.5 million provided for additional medical and mental health care at the detention centers, for juveniles for the period of time prior to final court disposition. The department shall develop an accounts payable system to allocate costs that are payable by the counties.

(4) Notwithstanding subsection (3), the state shall pay all costs of detention care for juveniles for which a fiscally constrained county would otherwise be billed.

(a) By October 1, 2004, the department shall develop a methodology for determining the amount of each fiscally constrained county's costs of detention care for juveniles, for the period of time prior to final court disposition, which must be paid by the state. At a minimum, this methodology must consider the difference between the amount appropriated to the department for offsetting the costs associated with the assignment of juvenile pretrial detention expenses to the fiscally constrained county and the total estimated costs to the fiscally constrained county, for the fiscal year, of detention care for juveniles for the period of time prior to final court disposition.

(b) Subject to legislative appropriation and based on the methodology developed under paragraph (a), the department shall provide funding to offset the costs to fiscally constrained counties of detention care for juveniles for the period of time prior to final court disposition. If county matching funds are required by the department to eliminate the difference calculated under paragraph (a) or the difference between the actual costs of the fiscally constrained counties and the amount appropriated in small county grants for use in mitigating such costs, that match amount must be allocated proportionately among all fiscally constrained counties.

(5) Each county shall incorporate into its annual county budget sufficient funds to pay its costs of detention care for juveniles who reside in that county for the period of time prior to final court disposition. This amount shall be based upon the prior use of secure detention for juveniles who are residents of that county, as calculated by the department. Each county shall pay the estimated costs at the beginning of each month. Any difference between the estimated costs and actual costs shall be reconciled at the end of the state fiscal year.

(6) Each county shall pay to the department for deposit into the Shared County/State Juvenile Detention Trust Fund its share of the county's total costs for juvenile detention, based upon calculations published by the department with input from the counties.

(7) The Department of Juvenile Justice shall determine each quarter whether the counties of this state are remitting to the department their share of the costs of detention as required by this section.

(8) The Department of Revenue and the counties shall provide technical assistance as necessary to the Department of Juvenile Justice in order to develop the most cost-effective means of collection.

(9) Funds received from counties pursuant to this section are not subject to the service charges provided in s. 215.20.

(10) This section does not apply to any county that provides detention care for preadjudicated juveniles or that contracts with another county to provide detention care for preadjudicated juveniles.

(11) The department may adopt rules to administer this section.

HISTORY:

S. 1, ch. 2004-263; ss. 1, 2, ch. 2004-473; s. 3, ch. 2006-62, eff. July 1, 2006; s. 95, ch. 2006-120, eff. Jan. 1, 2007; s. 11, ch. 2007-73, eff. July 1, 2007; s. 3, ch. 2008-8, eff. July 1, 2008; s. 54, ch. 2010-117, eff. July 1, 2010; s. 1, ch. 2011-53, eff. July 1, 2011; s. 1, ch. 2012-137, eff. Apr. 20, 2012; s. 42, ch. 2014-218, eff. July 1, 2014.

Editor's Notes

Formerly s. 985.2155: transferred by s. 95, ch. 2006-120, effective January 1, 2007.

Section 11, ch. 2007-73, amended (3) "[i]n order to implement Specific Appropriation 1169 of the 2007-2008 General Appropriations Act."

Section 56, ch. 2014-218, provides: "(1) The executive director of the Department of Economic Opportunity is authorized, and all conditions are deemed to be met, to adopt emergency rules pursuant to ss. 120.536(1) and 120.54(4), Florida Statutes, for the purpose of implementing this act.

"(2) Notwithstanding any other provision of law, the emergency rules adopted pursuant to subsection (1) remain in effect for 6 months after adoption and may be renewed during the pendency of procedures to adopt permanent rules addressing the subject of the emergency rules.

"(3) This section shall expire October 1, 2015."

§ 985.6865. Juvenile detention.

(1) The Legislature finds that various counties and the Department of Juvenile Justice have engaged in a multitude of legal proceedings regarding detention cost sharing for juveniles. Such litigation has largely focused on how the Department of Juvenile Justice calculates the detention costs that the counties are responsible for paying, leading to the overbilling of counties for a period of years. Additionally, litigation pending in 2016 is a financial burden on the taxpayers of this state.

(2) It is the intent of the Legislature that all counties that are not fiscally constrained counties and that have

pending administrative or judicial claims or challenges file a notice of voluntary dismissal with prejudice to dismiss all actions pending on or before February 1, 2016, against the state or any state agency related to juvenile detention cost sharing. Furthermore, all counties that are not fiscally constrained shall execute a release and waiver of any existing or future claims and actions arising from detention cost share prior to the 2016-2017 fiscal year. The department may not seek reimbursement from counties complying with this subsection for any underpayment for any cost-sharing requirements before the 2016-2017 fiscal year.

(3) As used in this section, the term:

(a) "Detention care" means secure detention and respite beds for juveniles charged with a domestic violence crime.

(b) "Fiscally constrained county" means a county within a rural area of opportunity as designated by the Governor pursuant to s. 288.0656 or each county for which the value of a mill will raise no more than $5 million in revenue, based on the certified school taxable value certified pursuant to s. 1011.62(4)(a)1.a., from the previous July 1.

(c) "Total shared detention costs" means the amount of funds expended by the department for the costs of detention care for the prior fiscal year. This amount includes the most recent actual certify forward amounts minus any funds it expends on detention care for juveniles residing in fiscally constrained counties or out of state.

(4)(a) Notwithstanding s. 985.686 and for the 2016-2017 state fiscal year, each county that is not a fiscally constrained county that has taken the action fulfilling the intent of this legislation as described in subsection (2) shall pay to the department its annual percentage share of $42.5 million. By June 1, 2016, the department shall calculate and provide to each county that is not a fiscally constrained county its annual percentage share by dividing the total number of detention days for juveniles residing in that county for the most recently completed 12-month period by the total number of detention days for juveniles in all counties that are not fiscally constrained counties during the same period. Beginning July 1, 2016, each such county shall pay to the department its annual percentage share of $42.5 million, which shall be paid in 12 equal payments due on the first day of each month. The state shall pay the remaining actual costs of detention care. This paragraph expires June 30, 2017.

(b) Notwithstanding s. 985.686, for the 2017-2018 fiscal year, and each fiscal year thereafter, each county that is not a fiscally constrained county and that has taken the action fulfilling the intent of this section as described in subsection (2) shall pay its annual percentage share of 50 percent of the total shared detention costs. By July 15, 2017, and each year thereafter, the department shall calculate and

provide to each county that is not a fiscally constrained county its annual percentage share by dividing the total number of detention days for juveniles residing in the county for the most recently completed 12-month period by the total number of detention days for juveniles in all counties that are not fiscally constrained counties during the same period. The annual percentage share of each county that is not a fiscally constrained county must be multiplied by 50 percent of the total shared detention costs to determine that county's share of detention costs. Beginning August 1, each such county shall pay to the department its share of detention costs, which shall be paid in 12 equal payments due on the first day of each month. The state shall pay the remaining actual costs of detention care.

(5) The state shall pay all costs of detention care for juveniles residing in a fiscally constrained county and for juveniles residing out of state. The state shall pay all costs of detention care for juveniles housed in state detention centers from counties that provide their own detention care for juveniles.

(6) Each county that is not a fiscally constrained county and that has taken the action fulfilling the intent of this section as described in subsection (2) shall incorporate into its annual county budget sufficient funds to pay its annual percentage share of the total shared detention costs required by subsection (4).

(7) Funds paid by the counties to the department pursuant to this section must be deposited into the Shared County/State Juvenile Detention Trust Fund.

(8) The department shall determine each quarter whether the counties are remitting funds as required by this section.

(9) Funds received from counties pursuant to this section are not subject to the service charges provided in s. 215.20.

(10) The department may adopt rules to administer this section.

HISTORY:
S. 1, ch. 2016-152, eff. Mar. 29, 2016.

§ 985.688. Administering county and municipal delinquency programs and facilities.

(1) A county or municipal government may plan, develop, and coordinate services and programs for the control and rehabilitative treatment of delinquent behavior.

(2) A county or municipal government may develop or contract for innovative programs that provide rehabilitative treatment with particular emphasis on reintegration and conditional release for all children in the program, including halfway houses and community-based substance abuse treatment services, mental health treatment services, residential and nonresidential programs, and environmental programs.

(3) A county or municipal government developing or contracting for a local program pursuant to this section

is responsible for all costs associated with the establishment, operation, and maintenance of the program.

(4) In accordance with rules adopted by the department, a county or municipal government may transfer a child, when necessary to appropriately administer the child's commitment, from one facility or program operated, contracted, or subcontracted by the county or municipal government to another such facility or program.

(5) In view of the importance of the basic value of work, responsibility, and self-reliance to a child's rehabilitation within his or her community, a county or municipal government may provide work programs for delinquent children and may pay a child a reasonable sum of money for work performed while employed in any such work program. The work involved in such work programs must be designed to benefit the county or municipal government, the local community, or the state.

(6) A county or municipal government developing or contracting for a local program pursuant to this section is responsible for following state law and department rules relating to children's delinquency services and for the coordination of its efforts with those of the Federal Government, state agencies, private agencies, and child advocacy groups providing such services.

(7) The department is required to conduct quarterly inspections and evaluations of each county or municipal government juvenile delinquency program to determine whether the program complies with department rules for continued operation of the program. The department shall charge, and the county or municipal government shall pay, a monitoring fee equal to 0.5 percent of the direct operating costs of the program. The operation of a program which fails to pass the department's quarterly inspection and evaluation, if the deficiency causing the failure is material, must be terminated if such deficiency is not corrected by the next quarterly inspection.

(8) A county or municipal government providing a local program pursuant to this section shall ensure that personnel responsible for the care, supervision, and treatment of children in the program are apprised of the requirements of this section and appropriately trained to comply with department rules.

(9) A county or municipal government may establish and operate a juvenile detention facility in compliance with this section, if such facility is certified by the department.

(a) The department shall evaluate the county or municipal government detention facility to determine whether the facility complies with the department's rules prescribing the standards and requirements for the operation of a juvenile detention facility. The rules for certification of secure juvenile detention facilities operated by county or municipal governments must be consistent with the rules for certification of secure juvenile detention facilities operated by the department.

(b) The department is required to conduct quarterly inspections and evaluations of each county or municipal government juvenile detention facility to determine whether the facility complies with the department's rules for continued operation. The department shall charge, and the county or municipal government shall pay, a monitoring fee equal to 0.5 percent of the direct operating costs of the program. The operation of a facility which fails to pass the department's quarterly inspection and evaluation, if the deficiency causing the failure is material, must be terminated if such deficiency is not corrected by the next quarterly inspection.

(c) A county or municipal government operating a local juvenile detention facility pursuant to this section is responsible for all costs associated with the establishment, operation, and maintenance of the facility.

(d) Only children who reside within the jurisdictional boundaries of the county or municipal government operating the juvenile detention facility and children who are detained for committing an offense within the jurisdictional boundaries of the county or municipal government operating the facility may be held in the facility.

(e) A child may be placed in a county or municipal government juvenile detention facility only when:

1. The department's regional juvenile detention facility is filled to capacity;

2. The safety of the child dictates; or

3. Otherwise ordered by a court.

(f) A child who is placed in a county or municipal government juvenile detention facility must meet the detention criteria as established in this chapter.

(10)(a) The department may institute injunctive proceedings in a court of competent jurisdiction against a county or municipality to:

1. Enforce the provisions of this chapter or a minimum standard, rule, regulation, or order issued or entered pursuant thereto; or

2. Terminate the operation of a facility operated pursuant to this section.

(b) The department may institute proceedings against a county or municipality to terminate the operation of a facility when any of the following conditions exist:

1. The facility fails to take preventive or corrective measures in accordance with any order of the department.

2. The facility fails to abide by any final order of the department once it has become effective and binding.

3. The facility commits any violation of this section constituting an emergency requiring immediate action as provided in this chapter.

4. The facility has willfully and knowingly refused to comply with the screening requirement for personnel under s. 985.644(1) or has refused to

dismiss personnel found to be in noncompliance with the requirements for good moral character.

(c) Injunctive relief may include temporary and permanent injunctions.

(11)(a) Notwithstanding the provisions of this section, a county is in compliance with this section if:

1. The county provides the full cost for detention for juveniles;

2. The county authorizes the county sheriff, any other county jail operator, or a contracted provider located inside or outside the county to provide detention care for juveniles;

3. The county sheriff or other county jail operator is accredited by the Florida Corrections Accreditation Commission or American Correctional Association; and

4. The facility is inspected annually and meets the Florida Model Jail Standards.

(b) A county or county sheriff may form regional detention facilities through an interlocal agreement in order to meet the requirements of this section.

(c) Each county sheriff or other county jail operator must follow the federal regulations that require sight and sound separation of juvenile inmates from adult inmates.

(d) A county or county sheriff that complies with this subsection is not subject to any additional training, procedures, or inspections required by this chapter.

HISTORY:
S. 27, ch. 92-287; s. 216, ch. 95-147; s. 71, ch. 97-238; s. 49, ch. 2000-135; s. 96, ch. 2006-120, eff. Jan. 1, 2007; s. 2, ch. 2011-53, eff. July 1, 2011; s. 8, ch. 2012-56, eff. July 1, 2012; s. 3, ch. 2016-152, eff. Mar. 29, 2016.

Editor's notes.
Formerly s. 985.411: transferred by s. 96, ch. 2006-120, effective January 1, 2007; s. 39.0215.

§ 985.69. Repair and maintenance funding for juvenile justice purposes.

Funds from juvenile justice appropriations may be used as funding for juvenile justice purposes that include, but are not limited to, remodeling or renovation of existing facilities, purchase of equipment and furniture, site development, and other necessary and reasonable costs associated with the repair and maintenance of facilities or programs.

HISTORY:
S. 16, ch. 96-398; ss. 24, 79, ch. 2002-402; s. 34, ch. 2003-399; s. 24, ch. 2005-3; s. 97, ch. 2006-120, eff. January 1, 2007; s. 40, ch. 2014-162, eff. July 1, 2014.

Editor's notes.
Formerly s. 985.4075: transferred by s. 97, ch. 2006-120, effective January 1, 2007.

§ 985.692. Juvenile Welfare Trust Fund.

(1) There is created in the Department of Juvenile Justice the Juvenile Welfare Trust Fund. The fund shall be credited with proceeds from the operation of canteens, vending machines, hobby shops, activity centers, farming projects, donations to a program, contracted telephone commissions, and other such facilities or programs designated as accruing to the Juvenile Welfare Trust Fund. The purpose of the trust fund shall be for the benefit and welfare of juveniles committed to or detained in facilities operated by the department or by private vendors contracting with the department.

(2) Notwithstanding the provisions of s. 216.301 and pursuant to s. 216.351, any balance in the trust fund at the end of any fiscal year shall remain in the trust fund at the end of the year and shall be available for carrying out the purposes of the trust fund.

HISTORY:
S. 1, ch. 99-327; s. 2, ch. 2002-120; s. 97, ch. 2006-120, eff. January 1, 2007.

Editor's notes.
Formerly s. 985.4041: transferred by s. 97, ch. 2006-120, effective January 1, 2007.

§ 985.694. Juvenile Care and Maintenance Trust Fund. [Repealed]

HISTORY:
S. 1, ch. 99-328; s. 2, ch. 2002-121; s. 97, ch. 2006-120, eff. January 1, 2007; repealed by s. 41, ch. 2014-162, effective July 1, 2014.

PART XII.
MISCELLANEOUS OFFENSES.

§ 985.701. Sexual misconduct prohibited; reporting required; penalties.

(1)(a)1. As used in this section, the term:

a. "Sexual misconduct" means fondling the genital area, groin, inner thighs, buttocks, or breasts of a person; the oral, anal, or vaginal penetration by or union with the sexual organ of another; or the anal or vaginal penetration of another by any other object. The term does not include an act done for a bona fide medical purpose or an internal search conducted in the lawful performance of duty by an employee of the department or an employee of a provider under contract with the department.

b. "Employee" includes paid staff members, volunteers, and interns who work in a department program or a program operated by a provider under a contract.

c. "Juvenile offender" means any person of any age who is detained or supervised by, or committed to the custody of, the department.

2. An employee who engages in sexual misconduct with a juvenile offender commits a felony of the second degree, punishable as provided in s. 775.082, s. 775.083, or s. 775.084. An employee

may be found guilty of violating this subsection without having committed the crime of sexual battery.

3. The consent of the juvenile offender to any act of sexual misconduct is not a defense to prosecution under this subsection.

4. This subsection does not apply to an employee of the department, or an employee of a provider under contract with the department, who:

a. Is legally married to a juvenile offender who is detained or supervised by, or committed to the custody of, the department.

b. Has no reason to believe that the person with whom the employee engaged in sexual misconduct is a juvenile offender.

(b) Notwithstanding prosecution, any violation of this subsection, as determined by the Public Employees Relations Commission, constitutes sufficient cause under s. 110.227 for dismissal from employment with the department, and such person may not again be employed in any capacity in connection with the juvenile justice system.

(2) An employee of the department, or an employee of a provider under contract with the department, who witnesses sexual misconduct committed against a juvenile offender, or who has reasonable cause to suspect that sexual misconduct has been committed against a juvenile offender, shall immediately report the incident to the department's incident hotline, and prepare, date, and sign an independent report that specifically describes the nature of the sexual misconduct, the location and time of the incident, and the persons involved. The employee shall deliver the report to the supervisor or program director, who is responsible for providing copies to the department's inspector general and the circuit juvenile justice manager. The inspector general shall immediately conduct an appropriate administrative investigation, and, if there is probable cause to believe that a violation of subsection (1) has occurred, the inspector general shall notify the state attorney in the circuit in which the incident occurred.

(3)(a) Any person who is required to prepare a report under this section and who knowingly or willfully fails to do so, or who knowingly or willfully prevents another person from doing so, commits a misdemeanor of the first degree, punishable as provided in s. 775.082 or s. 775.083.

(b) Any person who knowingly or willfully submits inaccurate, incomplete, or untruthful information with respect to a report required under this section commits a misdemeanor of the first degree, punishable as provided in s. 775.082 or s. 775.083.

(c) Any person who knowingly or willfully coerces or threatens any other person with the intent to alter testimony or a written report regarding an incident of sexual misconduct commits a felony of the third degree, punishable as provided in s. 775.082, s. 775.083, or s. 775.084.

HISTORY:

S. 2, ch. 97-215; s. 47, ch. 2000-135; s. 98, ch. 2006-120, eff. January 1, 2007; s. 42, ch. 2014-162, eff. July 1, 2014.

Editor's notes.

Formerly s. 985.4045: transferred by s. 98, ch. 2006-120, effective January 1, 2007.

§ 985.702. Willful and malicious neglect of a juvenile offender prohibited; reporting required; penalties.

(1) As used in this section, the term:

(a) "Employee" means a paid staff member, volunteer, or intern who works in a department program or a program operated by a provider under a contract with the department.

(b) "Juvenile offender" means any person of any age who is detained by, or committed to the custody of, the department.

(c) "Neglect" means:

1. An employee's failure or omission to provide a juvenile offender with the proper level of care, supervision, and services necessary to maintain the juvenile offender's physical and mental health, including, but not limited to, adequate food, nutrition, clothing, shelter, supervision, medicine, and medical services; or

2. An employee's failure to make a reasonable effort to protect a juvenile offender from abuse, neglect, or exploitation by another person.

(2)(a) An employee who willfully and maliciously neglects a juvenile offender without causing great bodily harm, permanent disability, or permanent disfigurement commits a felony of the third degree, punishable as provided in s. 775.082, s. 775.083, or s. 775.084.

(b) An employee who willfully and maliciously neglects a juvenile offender and in so doing causes great bodily harm, permanent disability, or permanent disfigurement commits a felony of the second degree, punishable as provided in s. 775.082, s. 775.083, or s. 775.084.

(c) Notwithstanding prosecution, any violation of paragraph (a) or paragraph (b), as determined by the Public Employees Relations Commission, constitutes sufficient cause under s. 110.227 for dismissal from employment with the department, and such person may not again be employed in any capacity in the juvenile justice system.

(3) An employee who witnesses the infliction of neglect upon a juvenile offender shall immediately report the incident to the department's incident hotline and prepare, date, and sign an independent report that specifically describes the nature of the incident, the location and time of the incident, and the persons involved in the incident. The employee shall deliver the report to the employee's supervisor or program director, who must provide copies to the department's inspector general and the circuit juvenile justice man-

ager. The inspector general shall immediately conduct an appropriate administrative investigation, and, if there is probable cause to believe that a violation of subsection (2) has occurred, the inspector general shall notify the state attorney in the circuit in which the incident occurred.

(4)(a) A person who is required to prepare a report under this section who knowingly or willfully fails to do so, or who knowingly or willfully prevents another person from doing so, commits a misdemeanor of the first degree, punishable as provided in s. 775.082 or s. 775.083.

(b) A person who knowingly or willfully submits inaccurate, incomplete, or untruthful information with respect to a report required under this section commits a misdemeanor of the first degree, punishable as provided in s. 775.082 or s. 775.083.

(c) A person who knowingly or willfully coerces or threatens any other person with the intent to alter testimony or a written report regarding an incident of neglect upon a juvenile offender commits a felony of the third degree, punishable as provided in s. 775.082, s. 775.083, or s. 775.084.

HISTORY:

S. 43, ch. 2014-162, eff. Oct. 1, 2014.

§ 985.711. Introduction, removal, or possession of certain articles unlawful; penalty.

(1)(a) Except as authorized through program policy or operating procedure or as authorized by the facility superintendent, program director, or manager, a person may not introduce into or upon the grounds of a juvenile detention facility or commitment program, or take or send, or attempt to take or send, from a juvenile detention facility or commitment program, any of the following articles, which are declared to be contraband under this section:

1. Any unauthorized article of food or clothing.

2. Any intoxicating beverage or any beverage that causes or may cause an intoxicating effect.

3. Any controlled substance, as defined in s. 893.02(4), or any prescription or nonprescription drug that has a hypnotic, stimulating, or depressing effect.

4. Any firearm or weapon of any kind or any explosive substance.

(b) A person may not transmit contraband to, cause contraband to be transmitted to or received by, attempt to transmit contraband to, or attempt to cause contraband to be transmitted to or received by, a juvenile offender into or upon the grounds of a juvenile detention facility or commitment program, except as authorized through program policy or operating procedures or as authorized by the facility superintendent, program director, or manager.

(c) A juvenile offender or any person, while upon the grounds of a juvenile detention facility or commitment program, may not be in actual or constructive possession of any article or thing declared to be contraband under this section, except as authorized through program policy or operating procedures or as authorized by the facility superintendent, program director, or manager.

(2) Any person who violates this section as it pertains to an article of contraband described in subparagraph (1)(a)1. commits a felony of the third degree, punishable as provided in s. 775.082, s. 775.083, or s. 775.084. In all other cases, a person who violates this section commits a felony of the second degree, punishable as provided in s. 775.082, s. 775.083, or s. 775.084.

HISTORY:

S. 3, ch. 97-215; s. 98, ch. 2006-120, eff. January 1, 2007; s. 33, ch. 2016-145, eff. July 1, 2016.

Editor's notes.

Formerly s. 985.4046: transferred by s. 98, ch. 2006-120, effective January 1, 2007.

§ 985.721. Escapes from secure detention or residential commitment facility.

An escape from:

(1) Any secure detention facility maintained for the temporary detention of children, pending adjudication, disposition, or placement;

(2) Any residential commitment facility described in s. 985.03(44), maintained for the custody, treatment, punishment, or rehabilitation of children found to have committed delinquent acts or violations of law; or

(3) Lawful transportation to or from any such secure detention facility or residential commitment facility,

constitutes escape within the intent and meaning of s. 944.40 and is a felony of the third degree, punishable as provided in s. 775.082, s. 775.083, or s. 775.084.

HISTORY:

S. 5, ch. 90-208; s. 13, ch. 92-287; s. 52, ch. 94-209; s. 12, ch. 95-152; s. 3, ch. 96-398; s. 113, ch. 97-238; s. 4, ch. 98-207; s. 59, ch. 98-280; s. 163, ch. 98-403; s. 136, ch. 99-3; s. 30, ch. 99-284; s. 41, ch. 2000-135; s. 41, ch. 2001-64; s. 18, ch. 2005-263; s. 99, ch. 2006-120, eff. Jan. 1, 2007; s. 3, ch. 2010-123, eff. July 1, 2010; s. 9, ch. 2012-56, eff. July 1, 2012; s. 44, ch. 2014-162, eff. July 1, 2014.

Editor's notes.

Formerly s. 985.3134: transferred by s. 99, ch. 2006-120, effective January 1, 2007; s. 39.061; s. 944.401.

§ 985.731. Sheltering unmarried minors; aiding unmarried minor runaways; violations.

(1)(a) A person who is not an authorized agent of the department or the Department of Children and Families may not knowingly shelter an unmarried minor for more than 24 hours without the consent of the minor's parent or guardian or without notifying a law enforcement officer of the minor's name and the fact that the minor is being provided shelter.

(b) A person may not knowingly provide aid to an unmarried minor who has run away from home without first contacting the minor's parent or guardian or notifying a law enforcement officer. The aid prohibited under this paragraph includes assisting the minor in obtaining shelter, such as hotel lodgings.

(2) A person who violates this section commits a misdemeanor of the first degree, punishable as provided in s. 775.082 or s. 775.083.

HISTORY:
S. 14, ch. 97-281; s. 100, ch. 2006-120, eff. January 1, 2007; s. 360, ch. 2014-19, eff. July 1, 2014.

Editor's notes.
Formerly s. 985.2065: transferred by s. 100, ch. 2006-120, effective January 1, 2007.
This section is also published at s. 984.085.

PART XIII.
INTERSTATE COMPACT ON JUVENILES.

§ 985.801. Interstate Compact on Juveniles; implementing legislation; legislative findings and policy.

(1) It is hereby found and declared:

(a) That juveniles who are not under proper supervision and control, or who have absconded, escaped or run away, are likely to endanger their own health, morals, and welfare, and the health, morals, and welfare of others;

(b) That the cooperation of this state with other states is necessary to provide for the welfare and protection of juveniles and of the people of this state.

(2) It shall therefore be the policy of this state, in adopting the Interstate Compact on Juveniles, to cooperate fully with other states:

(a) In returning juveniles to such other states whenever their return is sought; and

(b) In accepting the return of juveniles whenever a juvenile residing in this state is found or apprehended in another state and in taking all measures to initiate proceedings for the return of such juveniles.

HISTORY:
S. 1, ch. 57-298; s. 26, ch. 78-414; s. 80, ch. 97-238; s. 101, ch. 2006-120, eff. January 1, 2007.

Editor's notes.
Formerly s. 985.501: transferred by s. 101, ch. 2006-120, effective January 1, 2007; s. 39.25; s. 39.51.

§ 985.802. Execution of interstate compact for juveniles.

The Governor is authorized and directed to execute a compact on behalf of this state with any other state or states legally joining thereto in the form substantially as follows. This compact does not interfere with this state's authority to determine policy regarding juvenile offenders and nonoffenders within this state.

THE INTERSTATE COMPACT FOR JUVENILES
ARTICLE I

Purpose.

(1) The compacting states to this Interstate Compact recognize that each state is responsible for the proper supervision or return of juveniles, delinquents, and status offenders who are on probation or parole and who have absconded, escaped, or run away from supervision and control and in so doing have endangered their own safety and the safety of others. The compacting states also recognize that each state is responsible for the safe return of juveniles who have run away from home and in doing so have left their state of residence. The compacting states also recognize that Congress, by enacting the Crime Control Act, 4 U.S.C. s. 112 (1965), has authorized and encouraged compacts for cooperative efforts and mutual assistance in the prevention of crime.

(2) It is the purpose of this compact, through means of joint and cooperative action among the compacting states to: (A) ensure that the adjudicated juveniles and status offenders subject to this compact are provided adequate supervision and services in the receiving state as ordered by the adjudicating judge or parole authority in the sending state; (B) ensure that the public safety interests of the public, including the victims of juvenile offenders, in both the sending and receiving states are adequately protected; (C) return juveniles who have run away, absconded, or escaped from supervision or control or who have been accused of an offense to the state requesting their return; (D) make contracts for the cooperative institutionalization in public facilities in member states for delinquent youth needing special services; (E) provide for the effective tracking and supervision of juveniles; (F) equitably allocate the costs, benefits, and obligations of the compacting states; (G) establish procedures to manage the movement between states of juvenile offenders released to the community under the jurisdiction of courts, juvenile departments, or any other criminal or juvenile justice agency that has jurisdiction over juvenile offenders; (H) ensure immediate notice to jurisdictions where defined offenders are authorized to travel or to relocate across state lines; (I) establish procedures to resolve pending charges (detainers) against juvenile offenders prior to transfer or release to the community under the terms of this compact; (J) establish a system of uniform data collection of information pertaining to juveniles subject to this compact which allows access by authorized juvenile justice and criminal justice officials, and regular

reporting of activities under this compact to heads of state executive, judicial, and legislative branches and juvenile and criminal justice administrators; (K) monitor compliance with rules governing interstate movement of juveniles and initiate interventions to address and correct noncompliance; (L) coordinate training and education regarding the regulation of interstate movement of juveniles for officials involved in such activity; and (M) coordinate the implementation and operation of the compact with the Interstate Compact for the Placement of Children, the Interstate Compact for Adult Offender Supervision, and other compacts affecting juveniles, particularly in those cases where concurrent or overlapping supervision issues arise. It is the policy of the compacting states that the activities conducted by the Interstate Commission created in this compact are the formation of public policies and therefore are public business. Furthermore, the compacting states shall cooperate and observe their individual and collective duties and responsibilities for the prompt return and acceptance of juveniles subject to the provisions of the compact. The provisions of the compact shall be reasonably and liberally construed to accomplish the purposes and policies of the compact.

ARTICLE II

Definitions. —

(1) "Bylaws" means those bylaws established by the Interstate Commission for its governance or for directing or controlling its actions or conduct.

(2) "Compact administrator" means the individual in each compacting state, appointed pursuant to the terms of this compact, who is responsible for the administration and management of the state's supervision and transfer of juveniles subject to the terms of this compact, the rules adopted by the Interstate Commission, and the policies adopted by the state council under this compact.

(3) "Compacting state" means any state that has enacted the enabling legislation for this compact.

(4) "Commissioner" means the voting representative of each compacting state appointed pursuant to Article III of this compact.

(5) "Court" means any court having jurisdiction over delinquent, neglected, or dependent children.

(6) "Deputy compact administrator" means the individual, if any, in each compacting state appointed to act on behalf of a compact administrator pursuant to the terms of the compact who is responsible for the administration and management of the state's supervision and transfer of juveniles subject to the terms of this compact, the rules adopted by the Interstate Commission, and the policies adopted by the state council under this compact.

(7) "Interstate Commission" means the Interstate Commission for Juveniles created by Article III of this compact.

(8) "Juvenile" means any person defined as a juvenile in any member state or by the rules of the Interstate Commission, including:

(a) Accused delinquent — a person charged with an offense that, if committed by an adult, would be a criminal offense;

(b) Adjudicated delinquent — a person found to have committed an offense that, if committed by an adult, would be a criminal offense;

(c) Accused status offender — a person charged with an offense that would not be a criminal offense if committed by an adult;

(d) Adjudicated status offender — a person found to have committed an offense that would not be a criminal offense if committed by an adult; and

(e) Nonoffender — a person in need of supervision who has not been accused or adjudicated a status offender or delinquent.

(9) "Noncompacting state" means any state that has not enacted the enabling legislation for this compact.

(10) "Probation or parole" means any kind of supervision or conditional release of juveniles authorized under the laws of the compacting states.

(11) "Rule" means a written statement by the Interstate Commission adopted pursuant to Article VI of this compact which is of general applicability and implements, interprets, or prescribes a policy or provision of the compact, or an organizational, procedural, or practice requirement of the commission; has the force and effect of statutory law in a compacting state; and includes the amendment, repeal, or suspension of an existing rule.

(12) "State" means a state of the United States, the District of Columbia (or its designee), the Commonwealth of Puerto Rico, the United States Virgin Islands, Guam, American Samoa, and the Northern Mariana Islands.

ARTICLE III

Interstate Commission for Juveniles.

(1) The compacting states hereby create the "Interstate Commission for Juveniles." The Interstate Commission shall be a body corporate and joint agency of the compacting states. The Interstate Commission shall have all the responsibilities, powers, and duties set forth in this compact, and such additional powers as may be conferred upon it by subsequent action of the respective legislatures of the compacting states in accordance with the terms of this compact.

(2) The Interstate Commission shall consist of commissioners appointed by the appropriate appointing authority in each state pursuant to the rules and requirements of each compacting state and in consultation with the State Council for Interstate Juvenile Supervision created hereunder. The commissioner shall be the compact administrator, deputy

compact administrator, or designee from that state who shall serve on the Interstate Commission in such capacity under or pursuant to the applicable law of the compacting state.

(3) In addition to the commissioners who are the voting representatives of each state, the Interstate Commission shall include individuals who are not commissioners, but who are members of interested organizations. Such noncommissioner members must include a member of the national organization of governors, legislatures, state chief justices, attorneys general, Interstate Compact for Adult Offender Supervision, Interstate Compact for the Placement of Children, juvenile justice and juvenile corrections officials, and crime victims. All noncommissioner members of the Interstate Commission shall be ex officio, nonvoting members. The Interstate Commission may provide in its bylaws for such additional ex officio, nonvoting members, including members of other national organizations, in such numbers as shall be determined by the Interstate Commission.

(4) Each compacting state represented at any meeting of the Interstate Commission is entitled to one vote. A majority of the compacting states shall constitute a quorum for the transaction of business, unless a larger quorum is required by the bylaws of the Interstate Commission.

(5) The Interstate Commission shall establish an executive committee, which shall include commission officers, members, and others as determined by the bylaws. The executive committee shall have the power to act on behalf of the Interstate Commission during periods when the Interstate Commission is not in session, with the exception of rulemaking or amendment to the compact. The executive committee shall oversee the day-to-day activities of the administration of the compact, which shall be managed by an executive director and Interstate Commission staff. The executive committee shall administer enforcement and compliance with the provisions of the compact, its bylaws, and rules, and shall perform other duties as directed by the Interstate Commission or set forth in the bylaws.

(6) Each member of the Interstate Commission shall have the right and power to cast a vote to which that compacting state is entitled and to participate in the business and affairs of the Interstate Commission. A member shall vote in person and may not delegate a vote to another compacting state. However, a commissioner, in consultation with the state council, shall appoint another authorized representative, in the absence of the commissioner from that state, to cast a vote on behalf of the compacting state at a specified meeting. The bylaws may provide for members' participation in meetings by telephone or other means of telecommunication or electronic communication.

(7) The Interstate Commission shall collect standardized data concerning the interstate movement of juveniles as directed through its rules, which shall specify the data to be collected, the means of collection and data exchange, and reporting requirements. Such methods of data collection, exchange, and reporting shall, insofar as is reasonably possible, conform to up-to-date technology and coordinate its information functions with the appropriate repository of records.

ARTICLE IV

Powers and duties of the Interstate Commission. — The Interstate Commission shall have the following powers and duties:

(1) To provide for dispute resolution among compacting states.

(2) To adopt rules to effect the purposes and obligations as enumerated in this compact, and which shall have the force and effect of statutory law and shall be binding in the compacting states to the extent and in the manner provided in this compact.

(3) To oversee, supervise, and coordinate the interstate movement of juveniles subject to the terms of this compact and any bylaws and rules adopted by the Interstate Commission.

(4) To enforce compliance with the compact provisions, the rules adopted by the Interstate Commission, and the bylaws, using all necessary and proper means, including, but not limited to, the use of judicial process.

(5) To establish and maintain offices that are located within one or more of the compacting states.

(6) To purchase and maintain insurance and bonds.

(7) To borrow, accept, hire, or contract for services of personnel.

(8) To establish and appoint committees and hire staff that it deems necessary for carrying out its functions, including, but not limited to, an executive committee as required in Article III which shall have the power to act on behalf of the Interstate Commission in carrying out its powers and duties hereunder.

(9) To elect or appoint such officers, attorneys, employees, agents, or consultants; to fix their compensation, define their duties, and determine their qualifications; and to establish the Interstate Commission's personnel policies and programs relating to, inter alia, conflicts of interest, rates of compensation, and qualifications of personnel.

(10) To accept any and all donations and grants of money, equipment, supplies, materials, and services, and to receive, use, and dispose of such donations and grants.

(11) To lease, purchase, accept contributions or donations of, or otherwise to own, hold, improve, or use any property, real, personal, or mixed.

(12) To sell, convey, mortgage, pledge, lease, exchange, abandon, or otherwise dispose of any property, real, personal, or mixed.

(13) To establish a budget and make expenditures and levy dues as provided in Article VIII of this compact.

(14) To sue and to be sued.

(15) To adopt a seal and bylaws governing the management and operation of the Interstate Commission.

(16) To perform such functions as may be necessary or appropriate to achieve the purposes of this compact.

(17) To report annually to the legislatures, governors, judiciary, and state councils of the compacting states concerning the activities of the Interstate Commission during the preceding year. Such reports shall also include any recommendations that may have been adopted by the Interstate Commission.

(18) To coordinate education, training, and public awareness regarding the interstate movement of juveniles for officials involved in such activity.

(19) To establish uniform standards of the reporting, collecting, and exchanging of data.

(20) To maintain its corporate books and records in accordance with the bylaws.

ARTICLE V

Organization and operation of the Interstate Commission.

SECTION A. BYLAWS. — The Interstate Commission shall, by a majority of the members present and voting, within 12 months after the first Interstate Commission meeting, adopt bylaws to govern its conduct as may be necessary or appropriate to carry out the purposes of the compact, including, but not limited to:

(1) Establishing the fiscal year of the Interstate Commission;

(2) Establishing an executive committee and such other committees as may be necessary;

(3) Providing for the establishment of committees governing any general or specific delegation of any authority or function of the Interstate Commission;

(4) Providing reasonable procedures for calling and conducting meetings of the Interstate Commission and ensuring reasonable notice of each such meeting;

(5) Establishing the titles and responsibilities of the officers of the Interstate Commission;

(6) Providing a mechanism for concluding the operation of the Interstate Commission and the return of any surplus funds that may exist upon the termination of the compact after the payment or reserving all of its debts and obligations;

(7) Providing start-up rules for initial administration of the compact; and

(8) Establishing standards and procedures for compliance and technical assistance in carrying out the compact.

SECTION B. OFFICERS AND STAFF.

(1) The Interstate Commission shall, by a majority of the members, elect annually from among its members a chairperson and vice chairperson, each of whom shall have such authority and duties as may be specified in the bylaws. The chairperson or, in the chairperson's absence or disability, the vice chairperson shall preside at all meetings of the Interstate Commission. The officers so elected shall serve without compensation or remuneration from the Interstate Commission; provided that, subject to the availability of budgeted funds, the officers shall be reimbursed for any ordinary and necessary costs and expenses incurred by them in the performance of their duties and responsibilities as officers of the Interstate Commission.

(2) The Interstate Commission shall, through its executive committee, appoint or retain an executive director for such period, upon such terms and conditions, and for such compensation as the Interstate Commission deems appropriate. The executive director shall serve as secretary to the Interstate Commission, but may not be a member, and shall hire and supervise such other staff as may be authorized by the Interstate Commission.

SECTION C. QUALIFIED IMMUNITY, DEFENSE, AND INDEMNIFICATION.

(1) The Interstate Commission's executive director and employees shall be immune from suit and liability, either personally or in their official capacity, for any claim for damage to or loss of property or personal injury or other civil liability caused or arising out of or relating to any actual or alleged act, error, or omission that occurred, or that such person had a reasonable basis for believing occurred, within the scope of commission employment, duties, or responsibilities; provided that any such person is not protected from suit or liability for any damage, loss, injury, or liability caused by the intentional or willful and wanton misconduct of any such person.

(2) The liability of any commissioner, or the employee or agent of a commissioner, acting within the scope of such person's employment or duties for acts, errors, or omissions occurring within such person's state may not exceed the limits of liability set forth under the constitution and laws of that state for state officials, employees, and agents. Nothing in this subsection shall be construed to protect any such person from suit or liability for any damage, loss, injury, or liability caused by the intentional or willful and wanton misconduct of any such person.

(3) The Interstate Commission shall defend the executive director or the employees or representatives of the Interstate Commission and, subject to the approval of the Attorney General of the state

represented by any commissioner of a compacting state, shall defend such commissioner or the commissioner's representatives or employees in any civil action seeking to impose liability arising out of any actual or alleged act, error, or omission that occurred within the scope of Interstate Commission employment, duties, or responsibilities, or that the defendant had a reasonable basis for believing occurred within the scope of Interstate Commission employment, duties, or responsibilities; provided that the actual or alleged act, error, or omission did not result from intentional or willful and wanton misconduct on the part of such person.

(4) The Interstate Commission shall indemnify and hold the commissioner of a compacting state or the commissioner's representatives or employees, or the Interstate Commission's representatives or employees, harmless in the amount of any settlement or judgment obtained against such persons arising out of any actual or alleged act, error, or omission that occurred within the scope of Interstate Commission employment, duties, or responsibilities, or that such persons had a reasonable basis for believing occurred within the scope of Interstate Commission employment, duties, or responsibilities; provided that the actual or alleged act, error, or omission did not result from intentional or willful and wanton misconduct on the part of such persons.

ARTICLE VI

Rulemaking functions of the Interstate Commission.

(1) The Interstate Commission shall adopt and publish rules in order to effectively and efficiently achieve the purposes of the compact.

(2) Rulemaking shall occur pursuant to the criteria set forth in this article and the bylaws and rules adopted pursuant thereto. Such rulemaking shall substantially conform to the principles of the "Model State Administrative Procedures Act," 1981 Act, Uniform Laws Annotated, Vol. 15, p. 1 (2000), or such other administrative procedures act as the Interstate Commission deems appropriate consistent with due process requirements under the United States Constitution as now or hereafter interpreted by the United States Supreme Court. All rules and amendments shall become binding as of the date specified, as published with the final version of the rule as approved by the Interstate Commission.

(3) When adopting a rule, the Interstate Commission shall, at a minimum:

(a) Publish the proposed rule's entire text stating the reason for that proposed rule;

(b) Allow and invite any and all persons to submit written data, facts, opinions, and arguments, which information shall be added to the record and made publicly available;

(c) Provide an opportunity for an informal hearing if petitioned by 10 or more persons; and

(d) Adopt a final rule and its effective date, if appropriate, based on input from state or local officials or interested parties.

(4) Allow, not later than 60 days after a rule is adopted, any interested person to file a petition in the United States District Court for the District of Columbia, or in the Federal District Court where the Interstate Commission's principal office is located, for judicial review of such rule. If the court finds that the Interstate Commission's actions are not supported by the substantial evidence in the rulemaking record, the court shall hold the rule unlawful and set it aside. For purposes of this subsection, evidence is substantial if it would be considered substantial evidence under the Model State Administrative Procedures Act.

(5) If a majority of the legislatures of the compacting states rejects a rule, those states may, by enactment of a statute or resolution in the same manner used to adopt the compact, cause that such rule shall have no further force and effect in any compacting state.

(6) The existing rules governing the operation of the Interstate Compact on Juveniles superseded by this act shall be null and void 12 months after the first meeting of the Interstate Commission created hereunder.

(7) Upon determination by the Interstate Commission that a state of emergency exists, it may adopt an emergency rule that shall become effective immediately upon adoption; provided that the usual rulemaking procedures provided hereunder shall be retroactively applied to said rule as soon as reasonably possible, but no later than 90 days after the effective date of the emergency rule.

ARTICLE VII

Oversight, enforcement, and dispute resolution by the Interstate Commission.

SECTION A. OVERSIGHT.

(1) The Interstate Commission shall oversee the administration and operations of the interstate movement of juveniles subject to this compact in the compacting states and shall monitor such activities being administered in noncompacting states which may significantly affect compacting states.

(2) The courts and executive agencies in each compacting state shall enforce this compact and shall take all actions necessary and appropriate to effectuate the compact's purposes and intent. The provisions of this compact and the rules adopted hereunder shall be received by all the judges, public officers, commissions, and departments of the state government as evidence of the authorized statute and administrative rules. All courts shall take judicial notice of the compact and the rules. In any judicial or administrative proceeding in a compacting state pertaining to the subject matter of this compact

which may affect the powers, responsibilities, or actions of the Interstate Commission, the commission shall be entitled to receive all service of process in any such proceeding and shall have standing to intervene in the proceeding for all purposes.

SECTION B. DISPUTE RESOLUTION.

(1) The compacting states shall report to the Interstate Commission on all issues and activities necessary for the administration of the compact as well as issues and activities pertaining to compliance with the provisions of the compact and its bylaws and rules.

(2) The Interstate Commission shall attempt, upon the request of a compacting state, to resolve any disputes or other issues that are subject to the compact and that may arise among compacting states and between compacting and noncompacting states. The commission shall adopt a rule providing for both mediation and binding dispute resolution for disputes among the compacting states.

(3) The Interstate Commission, in the reasonable exercise of its discretion, shall enforce the provisions and rules of this compact using any or all means set forth in Article XI of this compact.

ARTICLE VIII

Finance.

(1) The Interstate Commission shall pay or provide for the payment of the reasonable expenses of its establishment, organization, and ongoing activities.

(2) The Interstate Commission shall levy on and collect an annual assessment from each compacting state to cover the cost of the internal operations and activities of the Interstate Commission and its staff which must be in a total amount sufficient to cover the Interstate Commission's annual budget as approved each year. The aggregate annual assessment amount shall be allocated based upon a formula to be determined by the Interstate Commission, taking into consideration the population of each compacting state and the volume of interstate movement of juveniles in each compacting state, and the Interstate Commission shall adopt a rule that is binding upon all compacting states governing the assessment.

(3) The Interstate Commission shall not incur any obligations of any kind prior to securing the funds adequate to meet the same, nor shall the Interstate Commission pledge the credit of any of the compacting states, except by and with the authority of the compacting state.

(4) The Interstate Commission shall keep accurate accounts of all receipts and disbursements. The receipts and disbursements of the Interstate Commission shall be subject to the audit and accounting procedures established under its bylaws. However, all receipts and disbursements of funds handled by the Interstate Commission shall be audited yearly by a certified or licensed public accountant, and the report of the audit shall be included in and become part of the annual report of the Interstate Commission.

ARTICLE IX

The State Council. —

Each member shall create a State Council for Interstate Juvenile Supervision. While each state may determine the membership of its own state council, its membership must include at least one representative from the legislative, judicial, and executive branches of government; at least one representative of victims groups; a parent of a youth who is not currently in the juvenile justice system; and the compact administrator, deputy compact administrator, or designee. Each compacting state retains the right to determine the qualifications of the compact administrator or deputy compact administrator. Each state council may advise and exercise oversight and advocacy concerning that state's participation in the activities of the Interstate Commission and other duties as may be determined by that state, including, but not limited to, development of policy concerning operations and procedures of the compact within that state.

ARTICLE X

Compacting states, effective date, and amendment.

(1) Any state, including the District of Columbia (or its designee), the Commonwealth of Puerto Rico, the United States Virgin Islands, Guam, American Samoa, and the Northern Mariana Islands, as defined in Article II of this compact, is eligible to become a compacting state.

(2) The compact shall become effective and binding upon legislative enactment of the compact into law by no less than 35 of the states. The initial effective date shall be the later of July 1, 2005, or upon enactment into law by the 35th jurisdiction. Thereafter, it shall become effective and binding as to any other compacting state upon enactment of the compact into law by that state. The governors of nonmember states or their designees shall be invited to participate in the activities of the Interstate Commission on a nonvoting basis prior to adoption of the compact by all states and territories of the United States.

(3) The Interstate Commission may propose amendments to the compact for enactment by the compacting states. No amendment shall become effective and binding upon the Interstate Commission and the compacting states unless and until it is enacted into law by unanimous consent of the compacting states.

ARTICLE XI

Withdrawal, default, termination, and judicial enforcement.

SECTION A. WITHDRAWAL.

(1) Once effective, the compact shall continue in force and remain binding upon each and every compacting state; provided that a compacting state may withdraw from the compact by specifically repealing the statute that enacted the compact into law.

(2) The effective date of withdrawal is the effective date of the repeal.

(3) The withdrawing state shall immediately notify the chairperson of the Interstate Commission in writing upon the introduction of legislation repealing this compact in the withdrawing state. The Interstate Commission shall notify the other compacting states of the withdrawing state's intent to withdraw within 60 days after its receipt thereof.

(4) The withdrawing state is responsible for all assessments, obligations, and liabilities incurred through the effective date of withdrawal, including any obligations the performance of which extends beyond the effective date of withdrawal.

(5) Reinstatement following withdrawal of any compacting state shall occur upon the withdrawing state's reenacting the compact or upon such later date as determined by the Interstate Commission.

SECTION B. TECHNICAL ASSISTANCE, FINES, SUSPENSION, TERMINATION, AND DEFAULT.

(1) If the Interstate Commission determines that any compacting state has at any time defaulted in the performance of any of its obligations or responsibilities under this compact, or the bylaws or duly adopted rules, the Interstate Commission may impose any or all of the following penalties:

(a) Remedial training and technical assistance as directed by the Interstate Commission;

(b) Alternative dispute resolution;

(c) Fines, fees, and costs in such amounts as are deemed to be reasonable as fixed by the Interstate Commission; or

(d) Suspension or termination of membership in the compact, which shall be imposed only after all other reasonable means of securing compliance under the bylaws and rules have been exhausted and the Interstate Commission has therefore determined that the offending state is in default. Immediate notice of suspension shall be given by the Interstate Commission to the Governor, the Chief Justice or the Chief Judicial Officer of the state, the majority and the minority leaders of the defaulting state's legislature, and the state council. The grounds for default include, but are not limited to, failure of a compacting state to perform such obligations or responsibilities imposed upon it by this compact, the bylaws, or duly adopted rules and any other ground designated in commission bylaws and rules. The Interstate Commission shall immediately notify the defaulting state in writing of the penalty imposed by the Interstate Commission and of the default pending a cure of the default. The commission shall stipulate the conditions and the time period within which the defaulting state must cure its default. If the defaulting state fails to cure the default within the period specified by the commission, the defaulting state shall be terminated from the compact upon an affirmative vote of a majority of the compacting states and all rights, privileges, and benefits conferred by this compact shall be terminated from the effective date of termination.

(2) Within 60 days after the effective date of termination of a defaulting state, the Interstate Commission shall notify the Governor, the Chief Justice or Chief Judicial Officer, the majority and minority leaders of the defaulting state's legislature, and the state council of such termination.

(3) The defaulting state is responsible for all assessments, obligations, and liabilities incurred through the effective date of termination, including any obligations the performance of which extends beyond the effective date of termination.

(4) The Interstate Commission shall not bear any costs relating to the defaulting state unless otherwise mutually agreed upon in writing between the Interstate Commission and the defaulting state.

(5) Reinstatement following termination of any compacting state requires both a reenactment of the compact by the defaulting state and the approval of the Interstate Commission pursuant to the rules.

SECTION C. JUDICIAL ENFORCEMENT. — The Interstate Commission may, by majority vote of the members, initiate legal action in the United States District Court for the District of Columbia or, at the discretion of the Interstate Commission, in the federal district where the Interstate Commission has its offices, to enforce compliance with the provisions of the compact and its duly adopted rules and bylaws against any compacting state in default. In the event judicial enforcement is necessary, the prevailing party shall be awarded all costs of such litigation, including reasonable attorney's fees.

SECTION D. DISSOLUTION OF COMPACT.

(1) The compact dissolves effective upon the date of the withdrawal or default of the compacting state which reduces membership in the compact to one compacting state.

(2) Upon the dissolution of the compact, the compact becomes null and void and shall be of no further force or effect, the business and affairs of the Interstate Commission shall be concluded, and any surplus funds shall be distributed in accordance with the bylaws.

ARTICLE XII

Severability and construction.

(1) The provisions of this compact are severable, and if any phrase, clause, sentence, or provision is deemed unenforceable, the remaining provisions of the compact shall be enforceable.

(2) The provisions of this compact shall be liberally construed to effectuate its purposes.

ARTICLE XIII

Binding effect of compact and other laws.
SECTION A. OTHER LAWS.

(1) Nothing herein prevents the enforcement of any other law of a compacting state which is not inconsistent with this compact.

(2) All compacting states' laws other than state constitutions and other interstate compacts conflicting with this compact are superseded to the extent of the conflict.
SECTION B. BINDING EFFECT OF THE COMPACT.

(1) All lawful actions of the Interstate Commission, including all rules and bylaws adopted by the Interstate Commission, are binding upon the compacting states.

(2) All agreements between the Interstate Commission and the compacting states are binding in accordance with their terms.

(3) Upon the request of a party to a conflict over meaning or interpretation of Interstate Commission actions, and upon a majority vote of the compacting states, the Interstate Commission may issue advisory opinions regarding such meaning or interpretation.

(4) In the event any provision of this compact exceeds the constitutional limits imposed on any compacting state, the obligations, duties, powers, or jurisdiction sought to be conferred by such provision upon the Interstate Commission shall be ineffective and such obligations, duties, powers, or jurisdiction shall remain in the compacting state and shall be exercised by the agency thereof to which such obligations, duties, powers, or jurisdiction are delegated by law in effect at the time this compact becomes effective.

HISTORY:

S. 1, 4, ch. 2005-80; s. 101, ch. 2006-120, eff. January 1, 2007; s. 1, ch. 2011-89, eff. May 31, 2011.

Editor's notes.

Formerly s. 985.502: transferred by s. 101, ch. 2006-120, effective January 1, 2007.

Section 5, ch. 2005-80 provides: "This act [which enacted this section] shall take effect July 1, 2005, or upon enactment of the compact into law by the 35th compacting state, whichever date occurs later." The 35th compacting state enacted the compact into law August, 2008.

Section 4, ch. 2005-80 provides: " Sections 985.502 [985.802] and 985.5025 [985.8025], Florida Statutes, shall stand repealed 2 years after the effective date of this act unless reviewed and saved from repeal through reenactment by the Legislature."

Pursuant to the introductory language of s. 1, ch. 2011-89, "notwithstanding the repeal of s. 985.802 by s. 4 of chapter 2005-80, effective two years after the effective date of s. 985.802," (which repeal took effect in August 2010), section 985.802 is revived and reenacted to read as set out.

§ 985.8025. State Council for Interstate Juvenile Offender Supervision.

(1) Pursuant to Article IX of the Interstate Compact for Juveniles in s. 985.802, the State Council for Interstate Juvenile Offender Supervision is created. The purpose of the council is to oversee state participation in the activities of the Interstate Commission for Juveniles.

(2) The council shall consist of seven members and the secretary of the Department of Juvenile Justice or his or her designee, who shall serve as the chair of the council and may vote only to break a tie. The compact administrator or his or her designee and the executive director of the Department of Law Enforcement or his or her designee shall serve as members of the council. The remaining members shall be appointed by the Governor for terms of 4 years; however, the Governor may, in writing and on an individual basis for each appointee, delegate the power of appointment to the Secretary of Juvenile Justice. Of the initial appointees, one shall be appointed for a term of 1 year, one shall be appointed for a term of 2 years, one shall be appointed for a term of 3 years, and two shall be appointed for terms of 4 years each.

(3) Appointees shall be selected from individuals with personal or professional experience in the juvenile justice system and may include a victim's advocate, employees of the Department of Children and Families, employees of the Department of Law Enforcement who work with missing and exploited children, and a parent who, at the time of appointment, does not have a child involved in the juvenile justice system.

(4) Council members shall serve without compensation, but they are entitled to reimbursement for per diem and travel expenses as provided in s. 112.061.

(5) The provisions of s. 24, Art. I of the State Constitution and of chapter 119 and s. 286.011 apply to proceedings and records of the council. Minutes, including a record of all votes cast, must be maintained for all meetings.

(6) If the council is abolished, its records must be appropriately stored, within 30 days after the effective date of its abolition, by the Department of Juvenile Justice or its successor agency. Any property assigned to the council must be reclaimed by the department or its successor agency. The council may not perform any activities after the effective date of its abolition.

HISTORY:

SS. 2, 4, ch. 2005-80; s. 102, ch. 2006-120, eff. January 1, 2007; s. 2, ch. 2011-89, eff. May 31, 2011; s. 361, ch. 2014-19, eff. July 1, 2014.

Editor's notes.

Formerly s. 985.5025: transferred by s. 102, ch. 2006-120, effective January 1, 2007.

Section 5, ch. 2005-80 provides: "This act [which enacted this section] will take effect July 1, 2005, or upon enactment of the compact into law by the 35th compacting state, whichever date occurs later." The 35th compacting state enacted the compact into law in August, 2008.

Section 4, ch. 2005-80 provides: " Sections 985.502 [985.802] and 985.5025 [985.8025], Florida Statutes, shall stand repealed 2 years after the effective date of this act unless reviewed and saved from repeal through reenactment by the Legislature."

Pursuant to the introductory language of s. 2, ch. 2011-89, "notwithstanding the repeal of s. 985.8025 by s. 4 of chapter 2005-80, effective two years after the effective date of s. 985.8025," (which repeal took effect in August 2010), section 985.8025 is revived and reenacted to read as set out.

§ 985.803. Juvenile compact administrator [Repealed.]

Repealed by s. 22, ch. 2009-20, effective July 1, 2009.

HISTORY:

S. 3, ch. 57-298; s. 26, ch. 78-414; s. 82, ch. 97-238; s. 3, ch. 2005-80; s. 101, ch. 2006-120.

§ 985.804. Supplementary agreements [Repealed.]

Repealed by s. 22, ch. 2009-20, effective July 1, 2009.

HISTORY:

S. 4, ch. 57-298; s. 26, ch. 78-414; s. 83, ch. 2005-80; s. 101, ch. 2006-120.

§ 985.805. Financial arrangements [Repealed.]

Repealed by s. 22, ch. 2009-20, effective July 1, 2009.

HISTORY:

S. 5, ch. 57-298; s. 26, ch. 78-414; s. 84, ch. 97-238; s. 3, ch. 2005-80; s. 101, ch. 2006-120.

§ 985.806. Responsibilities of state departments, agencies, and officers [Repealed.]

Repealed by s. 22, ch. 2009-20, effective July 1, 2009.

HISTORY:

S. 6, ch. 57-298; s. 26, ch. 78-414; s. 85, ch. 97-238; s. 3, ch. 2005-80; s. 101, ch. 2006-120.

§ 985.807. Additional procedures not precluded [Repealed.]

Repealed by s. 22, ch. 2009-20, effective July 1, 2009.

HISTORY:

S. 7, ch. 57-298; s. 26, ch. 78-414; s. 244, ch. 95-147; s. 86, ch. 97-238; s. 3, ch. 2005-80; s. 101, ch. 2006-120.

INDEX TO FLORIDA RULES OF JUVENILE PROCEDURE AND CHAPTERS 39, 984 AND 985, FLORIDA STATUTES (2017)

K

KEEPING CHILDREN SAFE ACT, 39.0139.

L

LAW ENFORCEMENT PERSONNEL.
Delinquency proceeding.
Depositions of, 8.060(d)(8).
Notice to appear, issuance by, 8.045(b).
Statements of, 8.060(d)(7).
Taking child into custody by, 985.101.
Dependency proceeding.
Protective investigation conducted by, 39.3065.
Referral of criminal case to, 39.301.
Taking child into custody by, 39.401.
Working agreements for criminal investigations, 39.306.
Families and children in need of services proceeding.
Taking child into custody by, 984.13.
Information systems, 985.047.
Interagency workgroup, 985.046.
Statewide information-sharing system, 985.046.

LEGAL CUSTODY.
Defined, 39.01(34).
Temporary legal custody.
Defined, 39.01(80).

LEGAL FATHER.
Defined, 39.01(35).

LEGISLATIVE INTENT.
Dependent children, 39.4085.
Detention, 985.02(4).
Domestic violence programs, 39.901.
Families and children in need of services proceeding, 984.02.
Juvenile justice system, 985.01, 985.02.
Medically complex children, services for, 39.001(4).
Mental health and substance abuse services, 39.001(6).
Prevention of abuse, abandonment, and neglect of children, 39.001(6).
Protections for children, 39.001(3).
Sexual exploitation services, 39.001(5).

LIKELY TO INJURE ONESELF.
Defined, 39.01(38).

LIKELY TO INJURE OTHERS.
Defined, 39.01(40).

M

MAILING ADDRESS, REQUIREMENT TO PROVIDE TO COURT, 8.224, 39.0131, 39.506(4).

MEDIATION.
Defined, 39.01(41), 984.03(35), 985.03.
Dependency proceeding, 8.290, 39.4075.
Families and children in need of services proceeding, 984.18.

MEDICAL DIRECTORS FOR CHILD PROTECTION.
District medical directors.
Qualifications, 39.303.
Training program, 39.303.
Statewide medical director for child protection.
Qualifications, 39.303.

MEDICAL NEGLECT.
Defined, 39.01(42).
Reports, 39.3068.

MENTAL INJURY.
Defined, 39.01(43).

MOTIONS.
Child in need of services proceeding.
Dismiss, to, 8.670(b), 8.685(e).
Generally, 8.670(a).
Sever, to, 8.670(c).
Delinquency proceeding.
Contempt proceeding, 8.150(c)(2).
Correct disposition or commitment error, to, 8.135(b).
Examination of child believed to be incompetent, 8.095(a)(1).
Juvenile sexual offender placement, form, 8.951.
Prehearing.
Dismiss, to.
Adjudicatory hearing, at, 8.110(k).
Generally, 8.085(a)(2).
Sworn, 8.085(a)(6).
Generally, 8.085(a)(1).
Sever, to, 8.085(a)(4).
Suppress, to, 8.085(a)(5).
Time for filing, 8.085(a)(6).
Waiver of jurisdiction, for, 8.105(b)(1), 8.105(b)(2).
Rehearing, for, 8.130.
Terminate or limit deposition, to, 8.060(k).
Testimony by closed-circuit television, for, 8.104(a)–(f).
Withdraw plea after drug court transfer, to, 8.075(g).